20⁰⁰
9
314341
D1032504

CUBA

Oakland Community College
Orchard Ridge Campus Library
27055 Orchard Lake Road
Farmington Hills, MI 48018

JL   Dominguez
1008   Cuba: order and revolution
.D65

DATE DUE			

8 10
9 1

Oakland Community College
Orchard Ridge Campus Library
27055 Orchard Lake Road
Farmington Hills, MI 48018

CUBA

ORDER AND REVOLUTION

Jorge I. Domínguez

THE BELKNAP PRESS
OF HARVARD UNIVERSITY PRESS
Cambridge, Massachusetts, and London, England • 1978

JL
1008
.D65

OR 10/82

Copyright © 1978 by Jorge I. Domínguez
All rights reserved
Printed in the United States of America

Second printing, 1979

Written under the auspices of the Center
for International Affairs, Harvard University

Library of Congress Cataloging in Publication Data

Domínguez, Jorge I., 1945–
    Cuba: order and revolution.

    Bibliography: p.
    Includes index.
    1. Cuba—Politics and government—1895–
2. Cuba—Economic conditions.   3. Cuba—Social
conditions.   I. Title.
JL1008.D65   320.9′7291′06   78-8288
ISBN 0-674-17925-0

To Mary and
to Lara and Leslie,
who helped in so many ways

CUBA

Gulf of Mexico

Colorados Archipelago

Havana

Varadero

SABANA ARCHIPELAGO

GUANIGUANICO

Artemisa

HAVANA

Matanzas

Cárdenas

MATANZAS

CORDILLERA DE PINAR DEL

Colón

RÍO

Pinar del Río

Santa Clara

ZAPATA PENINSULA

LAS VILLAS

CANARREOS

Playa Girón

Cienfuegos

SIERRA ESCAMBRAY

ISLE OF PINES

Nueva Gerona

ARCHIPELAGO

Bay of Pigs

FIRST EXILE LANDING, APRIL 17, 1961

Trinidad

(municipality)

Note: Provincial boundaries are those that
prevailed between 1902 and the early 60s.

0	100	200

miles

0	100	200

Km

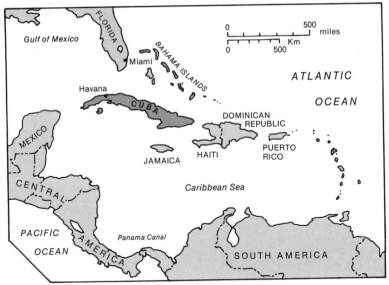

PREFACE

This book is about the politics and government of twentieth-century Cuba. Since all works of scholarship, even those that strive for impartiality, as this one does, are affected to some degree by the writers' own views, biases, and ideology, the reader of this book may find it helpful to know a few pertinent facts about my life. I was born in Cuba and left the country with my family in 1960, as a fifteen-year-old. I have not yet been able to return, although I have requested a visa from the Cuban government. I began to study Cuba as a senior in college and have kept abreast of social and political events there ever since. It was not until the summer of 1974, however, that I turned seriously to research on Cuba. By that time, almost half my life had been lived outside that country; a decade and a half had passed since the revolution; and I had been trying for several years to acquire the scholarly discipline necessary to approach the subject. Even so, the manuscript of this book was revised three times before the final copy was delivered to the publisher; in it I have tried consistently to resist the temptation to go beyond the conclusions merited by the evidence in my descriptions and explanations of events.

Awareness of my ideological framework may be important in judging the information offered here. There are broad areas where I agree with the policies of the current Cuban government and others where I disagree. In general, I agree more with its redistributive policies and less with its views on the organization of politics. Some of the government's actions, such as the virtual eradication of illiteracy, deserve vigorous applause; others, such as the lengthy imprisonment of numerous political dissidents, deserve equally vigorous condemnation. Thus I am a partisan neither of the Cuban government nor of its opposition; I have never belonged either to an organization seeking to overthrow the government or to one supporting it.

This is a long book, but it is intended to keep open research and writing on Cuba, not to close the subject. It builds on the work of other scholars, whose contributions are acknowledged throughout. My findings are often, necessarily, tentative—especially those that relate to recent events. At times I have taken issue with the work and views of others, including some who have served or are still serving in the Cuban government; they, in turn, may wish to take issue with me. My work will have succeeded as a contribution to scholarship if others take up where I have left off and update, reject, or modify what I have written.

I have acquired many personal and intellectual debts in my dozen years of work on Cuba. The first full draft of the book was written under a grant from the Antilles Research Program of Yale University, directed by Sidney W. Mintz and funded by the Ford Foundation. The updating and revision of the manuscript, as well as much of my other research and writing, have been made possible by the Center for International Affairs at Harvard University, directed at various times by Robert Bowie, Raymond Vernon, and Samuel P. Huntington. The center has been more than a source of financial support; it has also provided me with an intellectual home and has demonstrated that a community of scholars, in which the mind can flourish freely in an atmosphere of close criticism and generous enthusiasm, can be a reality. Throughout these years I have also received financial support, which I acknowledge gratefully, from the Woodrow Wilson Foundation, the Danforth Foundation, and the Society of Fellows at Harvard. The latter also allowed me to explore an intellectual world that has made this book possible.

Richard Morse, Karl Deutsch, and Samuel P. Huntington have guided my research at various stages. Edward Gonzalez provided very valuable comments on the manuscript of the book. The Institute of Cuban Studies, directed by María Cristina Herrera, has for many years been a forum for open and vigorous discussion of Cuban affairs and provided an opportunity for me to test some of my research. The works of Carmelo Mesa-Lago and Lourdes Casal are cited many times in this book, but their influence has been even greater than that fact implies. Mesa-Lago has become the dean of Cuban scholars, generously facilitating the work of others as he pursues his own. Casal has opened new ways of thinking about Cuba; even when we have not agreed, she has been a cheerful friend and a formidable scholar. Joel Migdal, Joseph S. Nye, Jr., and Raymond Vernon read parts of the manuscript and offered many useful suggestions. My students have forced me to revise, clarify, and even to change my arguments; one in particular, Michael F. Jimenez, suggested new perspectives on the Cuban peasantry.

I would like to thank Martha A. Achilles, Anne Carter, Beverly Davenport, Deborah Forrester, Kenje Gleason, Julia Lieberman, and Lisa Nekich for typing parts of the manuscript and David Mares and Janes Milner Mares for providing invaluable research assistance. Aida DiPace Donald's advice on the reorganization and revision of the book improved it greatly. Margaret Sevcenko rendered it more readable. And Barbara Gale turned this often clumsy manuscript into a finished book; her editing was accomplished with patience, intelligence, and good cheer throughout. I would also like to thank Marianne Perlak, who designed the book, and Robert Forget, who prepared the maps.

An early version of chapter 12 was presented in Atlanta at the 1976 meeting of the Latin American Studies Association; parts of chapters 2, 3, and 5, at the 1976 meeting of the American Political Science Association in Chicago. Other parts of the manuscript were presented at the Joint Seminar on Political Development of Harvard University and the Massachusetts Institute of Technology, at meetings of the American Association for the Advancement of Science and the Inter-University Seminar on Armed Forces and Society, and at several meetings sponsored by the Institute of Cuba Studies.

Parts of chapter 9 appeared as "The Civic Soldier in Cuba," in *Political-Military Systems: Comparative Perspectives,* edited by Catherine M. Kelleher, volume 4 of the Sage Research Progress Series on War, Revolution and Peacekeeping (Beverly Hills, Calif.: Sage Publications, 1974), pp. 209–238; as "Institutionalization and Civil-Military Relations in Cuba," *Cuban Studies* 6, no. 1 (January 1976): 39–65; and as "Racial and Ethnic Relations in the Cuban Armed Forces: A Non-Topic," *Armed Forces and Society* 2, no. 2 (Winter 1976): 273–290. Parts of chapter 10 appeared as "Sectoral Clashes in Cuban Politics and Development," *Latin American Research Review* 6, no. 3 (Fall 1971): 61–87. All are reprinted by permission.

CONTENTS

1   Introduction   1

PART ONE
Prerevolutionary Cuba

2   Governing through Pluralization, 1902–1933   11

    The Political Impact of Imperialism   12
    Imperialism and a Pluralized Economy   19
    Government Authority   28
    The Purposes of Government   33
    The Political Party System   38
    Cleavages outside the Party System   44

3   Governing through Regulation and Distribution,
    1933–1958   54

    The Retreat of Empire and the Rise of Hegemony   58
    Hegemony and the Economy   66
    Social Mobilization   71
    Economic Growth and Social Welfare   72
    Government Authority   76
    The Weight of Government   80
    The Purposes of Government   84
    Political Cleavages and Parties   95

4   The Breakdown of the Political System   110

    The Problem of Political Illegitimacy   110
    The Politics of Breakdown   123

PART TWO
Revolutionary Cuba: Governing through Centralization

5 International Influences, Society, and the Economy   137

  Hegemony and Revolutionary Politics 139
  Social Mobilization through Education 165
  The Economy and Social Welfare 173

6 Establishing a New Government   191

  Government Authority and the Centralization of Power 193
  Structuring Revolutionary Politics 206
  The Formation of the Communist Party 210
  Social Bases and Political Purposes 218
  Social Effects of Redistribution 221
  Bureaucratization and Social Change 233
  *The Constitution of 1976 and the Formalization of the
    State 243*
  The Law and the Courts 249

7 Mass Political Participation   260

  The Committees for the Defense of the Revolution 261
  The Cuban Women's Federation 267
  The Cuban Labor Confederation 271
  Youth Organizations 279
  *The Political Impact of Popular Participation in
    Government 281*
  Elections and Electoral Procedures 286
  Political Mobilization 298
  Measuring the Public Mood 303

8 The Communist Party   306

  The Ruling Elite 307
  Party Membership 315
  The Communist Youth Union 321
  Functions of the Communist Party 323
  Internal Party Structure 330
  Party Schools 336
  The Party's Claim to Rule 337

9 The Civic Soldier   341

  The Military Mission of the Armed Forces 345
  The Socioeconomic Mission of the Armed Forces 356
  The Political Mission of the Armed Forces 364

PART THREE
Political Processes and Change

10 Setting Public Policy   381

   Setting Economic Policy   383
   Setting Intellectual and Scientific Policy   391
   Policymaking and Social Institutions   408
   Legislation and Legislative Processes   415
   Planning for the Nation   417

11 Agrarian Conflict and Peasant Politics   423

   Agrarian Conflict before the Revolution   424
   Revolution, Revolutionary Rule, and Agrarian Conflict   435
   The National Association of Small Peasants   445

12 Political Culture   464

   Political Participation, Cooperation, and Individualism   465
   Explaining Continuity and Change after the Revolution   472
   Change among Students in the Early 1960s   474
   National Integration   478
   Forming the New Socialist Citizen   485
   Women and the Revolution   494
   Social Stress and Revolutionary Change   504

Appendixes

   A. The Impact of International Economic Factors on Internal Affairs:
      Three Perspectives   513
   B. Changes in the Height of Cubans   515
   C. Racial Inequality in Public Health   521
   D. Textual Changes in the Draft Constitution of 1976 and the
      Draft Family Code   527
   E. Members of the People's Socialist Party in the Communist Party's
      Central Committee   533
   F. Cooperation among Cuban Scientists   535

   Notes   541
   Bibliography   630
   Index   667

MAPS

Cuba   vi–vii
Distribution of the black population in Cuba, 1907   48
Principal focus of the black revolt in Oriente, 1912   48
Cuban provinces in 1969   245
Cuban provinces in 1976   246
Sites of the peasant revolution and counterrevolution in Cuba   439

TABLES

2.1   Direct United States private investment in Cuba, 1906–1927   21
2.2   Trade vulnerability (exports plus imports as a percentage of estimated national income), 1903–1929   24
2.3   Public-school enrollment in Cuba, 1902–1933   25
2.4   Estimated real national income per capita, 1903–1933   27
2.5   Index of daily wages, by province, 1909–1931   27
2.6   Congressional action on the national budget, 1902–1933   30
2.7   Government rule-making output, 1902–1933   31
2.8   Ratio of executive and presidential decrees to legislation passed by Congress, 1902–1933   31
2.9   Estimated government expenditures as a percentage of estimated national income, 1911–1933   32
2.10   Private foreign banking activity in Cuba, 1916–1931   33
2.11   Labor-related rule making by the Cuban government, 1902–1933   34
2.12   Reelection of members and changes of party affiliation in Congress, 1904–1933   43
2.13   Black social mobilization in Oriente province, 1907–1919   47
3.1   Direct United States private investment in Cuba, 1929–1958   67
3.2   Foreign and domestic ownership of Cuban sugar mills, 1927–1958   68

3.3	Cuban private banking activity, 1950–1959	68
3.4	Indexes of overall activity and foreign investments in industry and manufacturing in Cuba, 1946–1958	69
3.5	Trade vulnerability (exports plus imports as a percentage of estimated national income), 1928–1958	70
3.6	Illiteracy in 1953, by age cohorts	72
3.7	Estimated real national income, 1933–1940	73
3.8	Indicators of real economic growth, 1937–1958	74
3.9	Wages for all workers, 1945–1958	75
3.10	Government rule-making output, 1933–1958	81
3.11	Ratio of executive and presidential decrees to legislation passed by Congress, 1933–1958	82
3.12	Estimated government expenditures as a percentage of estimated national and domestic incomes, 1940–1957	83
3.13	Labor-related rule making by the Cuban government, 1933–1958	88
3.14	Reelection of members and changes of party affiliation in Congress, 1936–1954	105
3.15	Votes received by party coalitions, 1948	108
4.1	Indexes of commercial and industrial wages, 1958	122
5.1	Comparison of the Cuban work force and employable refugees	141
5.2	Cuban trade balances, 1960–1974	150
5.3	Cuban imports of fully completed factories, 1967–1974	152
5.4	Indexes of Cuba's terms of trade, 1968–1974	155
5.5	Rice production and imports, 1950–1974	161
5.6	Production of crude petroleum in Cuba, 1956–1974	163
5.7	Trade vulnerability (exports plus imports as a percentage of national income, gross national material product, and gross social product), 1962–1974	164
5.8	Enrollment in public universities and worker-peasant adult-education programs, 1958–1975	166
5.9	Enrollment in public secondary schools, 1958–1974	167
5.10	Enrollment in public primary schools, 1958–1974	168
5.11	Scholarships, 1963–1975	169
5.12	Educational skill level of Cuban workers	170
5.13	Product lines at peak and lowest production, 1959–1973	175
5.14	Agricultural production, 1951–1974	176
5.15	Aggregate per capita economic indicators, 1962–1974	177
5.16	Product lines showing increases and decreases in production, 1958–1973	178
5.17	Wages of state workers relative to aggregate economic indicators, 1962–1973	183
5.18	Mortality rates, 1953–1976	185

6.1	Percentage of Cuban production collectivized, 1961–1970	202
6.2	Expulsions from party membership in 1962	213
6.3	Admissions to party membership in 1962	213
6.4	Party membership as of March 12, 1963	214
6.5	Worker-peasant enrollment in party schools, 1962–1965	215
6.6	The social bases of revolutionary government: support in 1960	219
6.7	Organizational change in government enterprises, by sector, 1966–1971	238
6.8	Cabinet turnover, 1959–1977	241
7.1	Committees for the Defense of the Revolution, 1961–1976	262
7.2	Day care centers, 1962–1976	269
7.3	Representativeness of delegates to the thirteenth labor congress, 1973	294
7.4	Representativeness of delegates to the fourth peasant congress, 1971	297
8.1	Primary area of activity of Communist party Central Committee members in the Soviet Union and Cuba	312
8.2	Educational level of party leaders and members, 1971–1975	317
8.3	Party and Communist Youth Union members in work centers, 1968–1976	319
9.1	Military expenditures, 1940–1974	347
9.2	Military representation on Communist Central Committees in the People's Republic of China, Cuba, and the Soviet Union	375
10.1	Economic control of enterprises, 1964	386
10.2	Production of selected agricultural crops, 1950–1962	388
10.3	Cuban imports of selected categories of goods, 1955–1962	388
10.4	Salaries for personnel in scientific organizations, 1966–1972	398
10.5	Beer and malt production, 1967–1973	414
11.1	Profits and production of the West Indies Sugar Corporation, 1933–1959	426
11.2	Land tenure, 1946	432
11.3	Land tenure by province, 1946	435
11.4	Squatting, sugar farming, illiteracy, and unemployment in the Sierra Maestra	436
11.5	Squatting, sugar farming, illiteracy, and unemployment in southern Matanzas	442
11.6	Peasant cooperatives in the 1960s	449
11.7	Participation in peasant organizations, 1965 and 1967	450
11.8	Private agricultural production, 1967–1975	452
11.9	Participation in peasant organizations, 1969–1977	454
11.10	Peasant participation in production plans, 1971	455

12.1	Telephone calls, 1945–1974	479
12.2	Air passengers, 1958–1974	480
12.3	Mail, 1968–1974	481
12.4	Women in the paid work force, 1943–1975	499
12.5	Women in politics, selected institutions, 1946–1977	502
12.6	Mental illness, 1964–1974	505
12.7	Crime rates, 1959–1968	507
B.1	Height of male Cuban children and adolescents, 1919 and 1963	517
B.2	Height of young adult male Cubans	518
B.3	Height of white female Cuban children and adolescents, 1956 and 1963	520
F.1	Multiple authorship of scientific articles published in Cuban journals, 1960s and 1970s, by nationality	538

1

INTRODUCTION

Cuba's impact on our times has been far greater than one would expect from its small size. Its citizens brought about one of the very few radical national revolutions of the twentieth century. Some of its revolutionary heroes, such as Fidel Castro and Ernesto "Che" Guevara, became objects of admiration or fear abroad. The Cuban government's organizations and policies have become models for a number of developing countries. Cuba has launched efforts not unlike China's to change the nation's culture and to create a new citizen, although it has been less austere in its approach than China and more open to the rest of the world. Politics in Cuba has been an instrument for change in the economy, society, and culture as well as in individual experience. Yet success in transforming the country has thus far depended on a very high degree of political centralization and control by a relatively small and stable group of people.

Cuba has also directly affected international affairs. Occupied by United States troops twice in the early years of the twentieth century, it also provoked changes in United States policies toward Latin America in the 1930s. By the early 1960s, the revolutionary government was faced with major opposition from the colossus to the north. The United States sponsored the unsuccessful invasion by Cuban exiles at the Bay of Pigs in 1961 and confronted the Soviet Union in 1962 in a major crisis over missile emplacements in Cuba. The two superpowers came closer then to nuclear war than at any other time since 1945.

Cuba has not been a passive participant in recent world affairs. It cajoled the Soviet Union into supporting the establishment of the first Communist state in the Americas; in the 1960s, at great political and economic cost, it underwrote revolution in the western hemisphere and in other parts of the world as well.

Only three years ago, it sent thousands of troops to Angola to establish a Marxist-Leninist government, and it has developed mutual foreign-assistance programs with over two dozen countries the world over. What kind of nation is Cuba? Why should it matter so much to others? How can one begin to understand so many paradoxes and so much history? The story begins with power and its use and with the institutions created to serve it.

Cuba has lived under three different political systems in the twentieth century. The first was inaugurated on May 20, 1902, the day Cuba gained independence from the United States, and ended with the overthrow of President Gerardo Machado on August 12, 1933. The second period began sometime in 1934, after an interim year that helped to shape the second political system, and closed with the flight of Fulgencio Batista on December 31, 1958. The third political system began late in 1960, preceded also by an interlude. The distinguishing characteristic of each of these systems was the role played by government, that is, the government's response to other political organizations, to economic and social conditions and changes, and to the impact of international affairs on them.[1] The unusual but repetitive government reactions to these factors will be examined closely for each of the three twentieth-century political systems, and this political theme will be a major one in the book.

Decades ago, Harold Lasswell defined political science as an attempt to answer the questions who gets what, when, and how. Another way of posing the question might be to ask who governs, what for, and in what ways. The problem of legitimacy—the right claimed by the elite to rule the country, always a major issue in twentieth-century Cuban politics—is a persistent concern here. The relationships among politics, the economy, and society have varied since the beginning of the century. The power of government over society and its weight in the economy have increased from one political system to the next; the extent of government, assessed in terms of government expenditures, entrepreneurial activities, and regulation of social and economic relations, has also changed. All of these issues will be discussed as the three systems are examined.

In the first period one can identify a number of latent cleavages in Cuban economic and social life, but these had not yet become enduring bases for overt, collective political behavior. Under Cuba's first two modern political systems, the politics of incumbency and the politics of interest groups were somewhat independent from one another—sufficiently so to surprise me, since I had expected the opposite. It was not until the third political system that the division between the supporters and the opponents of the revolutionary government became severe enough to create, for the first time, a political structure that reflected divisions in the economy and the society. Because my principal concern has been with the workings of the political systems, the reasons for the breakdown of the first and second are only outlined. Similarly, although a fair amount of data is presented on international affairs, on local, regional, and provincial politics, and on Cuban economics, sociology, and anthropology, the test for their inclusion is their relevance to national politics.

The manifold factors that impinge upon government and shape its policies as well as the more general outcomes of government and politics are important scholarly concerns. The mechanisms of government and other organizations acting in politics have been of lesser interest. I think it is vital to look more closely at this governmental "black box," and so I will make an effort here to fill in some of the critical details of government, court, party, interest-group, and mass-organization structures and of certain of the major government policies they affected. I have learned that the long-term trend is one of increasing capabilities and concerns of the central government. I will try to explain why this was so.

Beyond the general questions already mentioned, certain issues will be examined carefully because they are historically important in Cuban life. Although Cuba long ago ceased to be a mostly rural society, for instance, agrarian issues still stand at the center of Cuban politics in the twentieth century. Sugar and the politics of sugar, rural peoples and agrarian protest have therefore had important roles in politics, especially under the second and third modern political systems.

Perhaps the most important task is to determine what difference the revolution has made in the lives of individual Cubans. The extent to which political values and attitudes have remained the same or have been changed by the revolutionary government is critical to any assessment of Cuban development. It is also one way of measuring the government's impact on the country's political future.

United States influence in Cuba up to 1930 brought about the multiplication of centers of political, economic, and social power and the consequent pluralization of the Cuban political system. Efforts by the United States in the 1930s to reduce its influence on Cuban affairs allowed the emergence of a reasonably capable, Cuban central government—one that could regulate economic and social affairs and redistribute the stakes of politics. The impact of the United States on the revolutionary political system, however, was in itself revolutionary and reversed its earlier effects. After 1960, the United States government attempted to overthrow the government of Cuba. To mount an effective resistance against the United States and to reduce its power, the Cuban government increased and centralized its own. At the same time, the Soviet influence in Cuba after 1960 contributed to the centralization of the revolution's political strength.

The pluralization of Cuban politics in the early years of the twentieth century was abetted by rapid modernization and reflected in the dramatic expan-

sion of the educational system. As more people became able to discern political developments and participated in politics, the task of ruling the masses
became more difficult. By the late 1930s, however, there was a slowdown in
the rate of modernization—an important event by itself but with an even more
significant result: a capable government emerged at last.

It can be shown that revolutionary rule completed the first phase in the
modernization of Cuban society when this process is measured by nearly universal literacy. At this educational level, widespread political participation in
mass and other organizations occurs, although in Cuba it is controlled by the
party and the government. The level was not high enough, however, to provide people with the psychological resources and intellectual skills to challenge the ruling elite on their own. As a result, the revolutionary political system has been made both possible and tolerable: possible because people can
participate and still be controlled; tolerable because relatively few people are
able or feel the need to challenge that control.

Cuba's performance in economic growth was strongly positive until the mid-
1920s, when it suffered a recession from which it did not recover until the
early 1940s. A good deal of the initial expansion was linked to the fortunes of
the sugar industry, but the economy of the later period of growth, and of the
mild and brief recession that began in the second half of the 1940s, was more
diversified. Although the Cuban economy apparently grew in 1959 and 1960,
just after Batista's fall, its performance in the decade that followed was dismal,
bracketed as it was by two severe recessions. It recovered in the early 1970s,
however, and may by now have returned to the prerevolutionary aggregate
level, despite a new, mild recession in 1976–77.

Each of Cuba's three modern political systems has depended for its legitimacy in part on economic performance: in all three cases, most people benefited. In the first, growth helped all classes; in the second, people profited from
a mixture of growth and redistributive, regulatory measures; in the third,
Cubans have enjoyed their fruits of redistribution and some recent economic
growth. Nationalism—combined with the welcome reduction of corruption,
an historic problem for the country—served for the first time to legitimate the
government. Charismatic legitimation was at least a possibility in each of
Cuba's political systems, but it only functioned after the revolution, when it
clearly became the major feature of the government's claim to the right to legitimate rule. Elections and legal and constitutional norms played some part
in legitimating the first two political systems, but their effectiveness remained
incomplete and tenuous. Under revolutionary rule, they became a part of the
claim to legitimacy only in the 1970s. Even then, it was plain that the revolution legitimated the elections, the law, the Constitution, and the courts and
not the other way around. Thus the principal claim to legitimate rule after
1960 has been that the revolution and its leaders rule because they are and

have always been right. Cuba's is not an elected revolution; right conduct and right policies are the decisive claims to legitimacy. Whether everyone agrees is, of course, another matter; that some do not is attested by several hundred thousand exiles, years of civil war, thousands of political prisoners, and the rigorous methods used to control the opposition that has remained.

The weight of government on society and the economy, slight in the early years of the century, had altered by mid-century. With one minor exception, the Cuban state under the first two political systems was not entrepreneurial; it left running the economy to private enterprise, though the second political system, unlike the first, sought to regulate a great many aspects of economic and social affairs. But government power became overwhelming under revolutionary rule, encroaching upon virtually every aspect of life.

Under the first political system, the potential cleavages in society and the economy were scarcely reflected in the country's politics; the politics of interest and the politics of incumbency were rather separate. The principal goal of interest groups was to keep government regulation of their activities at a minimal or nonexistent level. A fair number of incumbent politicians used public office for private gain. Under the second political system, the earlier two-track political system was modified; the politics of interest and the politics of incumbency remained separate, but interest groups took over the direct conduct of those areas of government of concern to them. Sugar-mill owners and sugar farmers made sugar policy; labor unions made labor policy; bankers made banking policy. The fragmentation of the government and of the interest-group structure meant that economically and socially powerful organizations were not accustomed to collaborating with each other for partisan purposes. When the basic premises of a capitalist economy were challenged after 1959, the major economic and social associations were incapable of cooperating with each other. Cuban politics was highly organized, but fragmented. It was not an absence of institutions that doomed the prerevolutionary system, but their very strength. They had been strong enough to exist independently from each other and consequently had no network of cooperation or alliance to build on in time of need. Prerevolutionary Cuba produced strong interest-group institutions but no strong social-class or national institutions. After 1960, these autonomous groups could no longer function, and the two-track political system was destroyed.

Some purposes of politics were often narrow. Under the first political system, many politicians used their office to get rich at public expense. While corruption remained an important purpose of politics for many incumbents under the second political system, the politics of regulation became the principal focus of a great deal of political activity, with considerable success. Corruption of a different sort appeared in the 1960s—the corruption of power to gain more power. It is difficult to estimate how widespread corruption is today, but there is evidently a good deal less than there was before the revolution. The purposes of politics have been transferred to large-scale social, economic, and political change, sometimes with resounding success; sometimes, abysmal failure. This book will document some of both.

The courts in Cuba responded to political events both before and after the revolution. At times, the domination of the courts by politics has been overwhelming. Before the revolution they appear to have had a great deal more autonomy than they have had since, but even in the postrevolutionary period they retain some small degree of autonomy; state prosecutors do not always win their cases. Thus the courts perform a limited role as defenders of individual rights in revolutionary Cuba, though only for those accused of crimes not regarded as political. Those accused of crimes against the state have few defenses before a colossally powerful government, but by the early 1970s their numbers were declining. Stable authoritarian rule does not require continual repression, and repressive acts are relatively rare in contemporary Cuba. When they do occur, they are viewed as a sign that the system has somehow failed.

The principal political weakness of the prerevolutionary systems of government was that neither the Presidents nor the Congresses had any clear electoral mandate. The Cuban Congress was less active during the 1940s—a decade claimed by some to have been a period of competitive politics—than it was under the first political system, while the activity of the executive branch increased substantially. Congressional control over the President consequently declined. The prerevolutionary political party system suffered from the same weak legitimacy, exacerbated by Batista's coup in 1952 and the subsequent fraudulent elections. Because prerevolutionary politics was fragmented, however, most of the major national offices and organizations had substantial autonomy.

After 1959, the ability of political and governmental organizations to operate without central direction, especially from Fidel Castro, declined drastically; in fact, a distinctive feature of Cuban politics today is the lack of autonomy for organizations, including government agencies. From another viewpoint, however, these organizations came to be valued by their members. They also became structurally more stable and complex, ideologically more coherent, and more readily adaptable to new tasks since the 1960s. Thus, except for the lack of organizational autonomy, the increase of political institutionalization—measured by these factors—has been rather substantial. Institutionalization was first noticeable in the armed forces, but it has since spread to other sectors. The period of radical politics somewhat retarded the institutionalization of government and other organizations, but the process accelerated again in the 1970s with certain major limitations. The centralization of power by the ruling elite within both party and government allowed it to control mass organizations and governmental institutions at both national and local levels. So tight were the control mechanisms that even the introduction of elections in the 1970s did not lead to more substantial political competition or popular control over the government. Through 1977, organized political participation under revolutionary rule continued to have only very limited effects on policymaking. Any impact it does have results mainly from an increase in citizens' contacts with public officials to secure help in solving individual and small-community problems.

By far the greatest degree of stability in the Cuban political system can be found among the upper-echelon officeholders. With very few exceptions, the people in power at the beginning of the 1960s remain in power in the 1970s. The Communist party suffered a devastating series of expulsions in the early 1960s and a more limited one in 1968. Very few of the members of the Central Committee established in 1965, however, had lost their jobs by 1977. Yet while the turnover of leaders within the Council of Ministers was regular and limited after 1960, the bureaucratic structures they devised were unstable in the radical period of the late 1960s and the early 1970s. The stability of incumbency made radical politics possible, but the instability of political and bureaucratic structures was the price paid for radicalism. By the mid-1970s, the stability of both personnel and organizations was increasing.

Politics in Cuba is organizationally based. The things that count in gaining power are proximity to Fidel Castro or to power in the Soviet Union, one's own position in organizations, and access to centers of power in other organizations. Fidel Castro remains at the center of all politics and is the decisive figure not only for the legitimation of the system but often even for affecting the minutiae of policy implementation.

The Cuban revolution has built on the Cuban past; political beliefs now shared by many Cubans show continuities with prerevolutionary themes. Some of these attitudes contribute to building the political system the revolutionary leadership wants. Cubans have long been predisposed toward political participation and cooperation, for instance, but they previously lacked participatory structures beyond the local level; now organizations have been provided to harness and control the masses' political energies. Cubans have also long been aware of the importance of government in their lives, and they have been able to calculate its costs and benefits to them.

Even before the revolution, Cuba had also been moving slowly but steadily toward the incorporation of women into the national life. At least nominally a Roman Catholic country, Cuba had become overwhelmingly secular in practice. The Cuban family, already buffeted by the revolution, now faces new threats from an exploding divorce rate, although attitudes toward the family remain essentially traditional. Ethnic differences, in Cuba's present as in its past, are neither admitted nor discussed. Every Cuban government has acknowledged the existence of racial discrimination under previous administrations, but not under its own, and the revolutionary government is no exception. Although there are substantial differences in chances for success between Cuban blacks and whites in the 1970s, organizations on behalf of blacks and limited to blacks are illegal. Cubans, including blacks themselves, tend to denigrate blackness and frown on evidence of overt, collective political action by blacks. Blacks gained from the revolution because they were disproportionately poor and the poor benefited disproportionately from the change of political systems, but the problem of ethnicity in contemporary Cuba remains a mixture of substantial equality of opportunity, substantial inequality of result, illegal organized black politics, and social inferiority based on color in everyday life.

For the individual, politics in Cuba has been permanently transformed. Many old concerns—fear of unemployment, for example—have disappeared. Some new ones, such as those related to the role of women, exhibit strong continuities with the past but have new dimensions as well. Rates of change in economic and social spheres clearly differ from community to community, and the degree of subcultural variation within Cuba may be increasing. The First Party Congress in December of 1975 and the Constitution of 1976 are likely to alter the situation only very moderately; in essence, they formalized politics as they already existed in Cuba.

The new National Assembly and other government bodies created by the Constitution are adapting to existing politics rather than altering the situation profoundly. These organizations, however, combined with Cuba's successful international intervention in Angola and the improved economy, also point to a new confidence and sense of accomplishment among the Cuban elite as it faces the next few years. Its principal accomplishment has been that it has survived at all.

As Batista climbed on the airplane that took him into exile on New Year's Eve, 1958, few could guess what even the broad outlines of Cuban politics would be in the next generation. Indeed, political life in twentieth-century Cuba has never been very predictable, but patterns since 1959 have proved to be the most unreliable of all. The future may shape itself in still more unforeseeable ways.

PART ONE

PREREVOLUTIONARY CUBA

2

GOVERNING THROUGH
PLURALIZATION, 1902–1933

Cuba's first twentieth-century political system operated under the shadow of the United States, which affected virtually every aspect of Cuban domestic life. From 1902 to 1933, the two nations were engaged in an imperial relationship, whose principal consequence for Cuba was the pluralization of its politics. ("Pluralization" is used here to mean the establishment of a multiplicity of sources, both groups and institutions, of authority and influence.) Because their development was so strongly shaped by external forces, the autonomy of many power centers within Cuba was sharply limited. Not only the fact but also the form of the United States–Cuban relationship contributed to pluralization; neither United States government agencies nor United States private enterprises (social, religious, and economic) acted in a sufficiently centralized and coordinated fashion to make unified politics in Cuba possible. Because the imperial penetration was diffuse, politics in Cuba were further fragmented.

The age of United States imperialism in Cuba was also characterized by substantial social modernization, especially as a result of an expansion of the educational system and of economic growth linked to sugar. Social and economic modernization, in turn, enabled more people to participate politically. The favorable performance of the economy during most of the period facilitated the qualified legitimation of the government, although the Cuban elite's claims to political legitimacy were not fully accepted during this period. Insurrections by groups in opposition to the ruling party punctuated Cuba's first three decades of qualified independence. The threat of requesting United States intervention or interference had been sufficiently successful to become the principal political resource for those out of power, thus keeping opposition politics alive, permitting political insurrections, and contributing to the multiplication

11

of centers of power. Although charismatic legitimation was not possible in this political system, electoral and legal-constitutional legitimation played a largely positive role in establishing some basis for the authority of the government. This basis for legitimacy was continuously suspect, however, because of pervasive electoral fraud and bureaucratic corruption.

The weight of the Cuban government on its society and economy was extremely limited, even by contemporary standards elsewhere in Latin America and in the United States (though it increased between 1925 and 1933). Government did so little, in fact, that many public officials were able to use their offices for personal enrichment. A two-track political system began to develop, with the politics of incumbency acquiring a certain autonomy from the politics of interest. Interest groups were primarily concerned with keeping the government's interference in social and economic areas to a minimum. Many latent cleavages can be identified in the Cuban society and economy during this period; none became overt political cleavages linked to collective action. The politics of incumbency was unconnected to these latent cleavages; it was characterized by low party loyalty. Party switching was common prior to election times. In fact, politicians switched not only to the probable victor but also to the probable loser and attempted to provoke United States interference by charges of election fraud. The loser of the election was not necessarily the loser of the presidency, since gaining that office required access to Washington as well as votes. Thus opposition parties required interference from the United States for their success. Competitive politics and dependence on the United States were two sides of the same coin.

Cuba's first political system ended when several negative factors converged. The pattern of economic growth took a sharp downturn; electoral and legal-constitutional legitimation broke down completely; incumbents altered the ordinary pattern of circulation of elites, freezing the pattern of office holding and making it impossible for new individuals to come to power; and new social forces emerged, partly as a result of preexisting trends of modernization, to claim a greater social, economic, and political role. Thus economic decline, rapid modernization, and institutional decay brought Cuba's first political system to an end.

The Political Impact of Imperialism

May 20, 1902, marked the beginning of two related experiments in political order. One was a change in the nature of the United States' expansion; the other, the birth of the Republic of Cuba. Up to this time, the United States had annexed territories acquired through war or purchase, subsequently incorporating most of them as states. Although the United States continued its annexations into the twentieth century, this form of expansion took second place to the indirect government of conditionally sovereign states—a system that I will call "imperialism." The techniques first employed with at least modest success in Cuba would later be used, with local variations, elsewhere in the American mediterranean during the first third of the twentieth century. Although my chief concern is with Cuba's internal government, the discussion will necessarily address the successes and failures of the more international of the twin experiments, that is, United States imperialism.

Cubans spent almost half of the years from 1868 to 1898 fighting for their independence from Spain. In 1898 the United States intervened militarily, swiftly defeated a weakened and weary Spain, and established a provisional government over Cuba. This First Occupation ended on May 20, 1902, when the first President of the Republic of Cuba, Tomás Estrada Palma, was sworn into office. The independence of the new republic was qualified, however, by an amendment to its constitution approved by the Cuban Constitutional Convention of 1901 at the insistence of the United States. The Platt Amendment had been drafted by United States Senator Orville Platt, approved by the United States Congress, and signed into law by President William McKinley. The crucial third article stated "that the government of Cuba consents that the United States may exercise the right to intervene for the preservation of Cuban independence, the maintenance of a government adequate for the protection of life, property and individual liberty, and for discharging the obligations with respect to Cuba imposed by the Treaty of Paris on the United States, now to be assumed and undertaken by the government of Cuba."[1] This clause remained in force until 1934, when it was revoked by agreement of the two countries. Thus Cuba began its career as a United States protectorate.

The practical effect of the Platt Amendment was to pluralize the Cuban political system. The United States government's intervention in the internal affairs of the republic prevented the early consolidation of a strong and capable central government in Cuba and fostered the rise and entrenchment of opposition groups by increasing political uncertainty. In addition, it multiplied the sources of political power so that no single group, not even the government, could impose its will on society or the economy for very long, and it prevented the development of a system of strong political cleavages that might have served as a foundation for an effective and stable party system. The spirit and practice of liberalism—competitive and unregulated political, economic, religious, and social life—overwhelmed a pluralized Cuba.

Evidence of the Platt Amendment's pluralizing effect can be seen in the response of the United States government to revolts in Cuba. This response, however, never took the form of a unified, deliberate action; the government itself was fragmented in its response to Cuban affairs, and its actions were contaminated by the needs of private interest groups. Graham Allison has argued persuasively that decision making in the United States government can be analyzed from several different perspectives. Rather than being a unitary actor, the United States government is a constellation of allied organizations—each with narrow goals—that respond quite differently to foreign affairs. Governmental leaders are more apt to choose a plan of action on which they can compromise than an optimal solution; thus decisions result from political bargaining among individual members of the government.[2] It was not only the United States government, of course, that affected Cuban politics. Once the United States government began to intervene or to interfere in Cuba, nongovernmental influences were felt as well. Businessmen probably did more to pluralize Cuban politics than bureaucrats.

In 1905, President Estrada Palma, head of the Conservative party (Partido Moderado), was reelected without opposition.[3] So much preelectoral coercion and fraud in voter registration were evident that the opposition Liberal party (Partido Liberal) abstained from running its candidates. After the election, the Liberals' leader, General José Miguel Gómez, who had been the party's presidential candidate before the decision to abstain, toured the United States arguing that it was the duty of the United States to right the wrongs done before the election by the Conservatives.

The Liberals revolted in August 1906. It was not until a week later that President Theodore Roosevelt became interested in the Cuban insurrection. During the months prior to the revolt, the strategic concerns of Roosevelt and of Secretary of State Elihu Root had been to reassure Latin Americans that the United States did not intend to turn them all into protectorates. The President's own response, therefore, was cautious and tended to limit military intervention. The interests of other individuals within the United States government, however, were at variance with those of President Roosevelt.

United States Consul General Frank Steinhart strongly favored intervention. Steinhart had been on the staff of General Leonard Wood, the military governor of Cuba, during the First Occupation and had since become a prominent member of the United States business community in Havana. In 1906, Consul Steinhart had begun the process, completed in 1907, of taking control of the Havana Electric Railway Company, and he was in no mood for political instability.[4] He first backed the Estrada Palma government against the rebels and then, with the consent and encouragement of the Cuban President, asked the United States to send warships to Cuba.

Although the United States Army assured President Roosevelt that it was prepared to do the job in Cuba if necessary, it painted military intervention in the bleakest terms: Cuba might prove a repetition of the Philippine experience, where they had been engaged in protracted counterguerrilla activities. Roosevelt's response to Steinhart and Estrada Palma's plea to intervene for the sake of order and property (the Liberal rebels were holding foreign property hostage)[5] was to send two warships to Cuba but to protect the United States

Army by doing no more. Because this intervention was not decisive, the effect of his decision was to prolong the war.

Commander William F. Fullam of the U.S.S. *Marietta* advocated the abolition of the Marine Corps and the use of sailors as landing parties; his command of the Cuban expedition was a golden chance to try out his theories. When he entered Cienfuegos harbor, United States sugar planters begged him to protect their mills; the rebels also welcomed the landings as a sign of the gradual collapse of the conservative government. When sailors from the U.S.S. *Denver* landed in Havana, a delegation from the Liberals' Central Revolutionary Committee, led by vice-presidential candidate Alfredo Zayas, offered immediate surrender to the ship's commander in an attempt at further eroding the authority of the Cuban government.

President Estrada Palma preferred to turn his government over to the United States rather than yield to the rebels. The Liberals thought intervention the most expeditious way to rid themselves of the government and expected to win free elections. Once the two United States warships were on their way, however, bureaucratic, business, and political interests came into play, gradually increasing United States involvement until Roosevelt's strategic preference for limited intervention was overcome and broad-scale intervention was ordered.

Both the fact and the method of United States intervention acted to pluralize Cuban politics and led to the collapse of the Estrada Palma government. Once the sailors had landed in Cienfuegos and Havana, the Cuban government and the rebels were even further polarized and more intransigent. If compromise between their positions had originally been difficult, it became impossible once each side perceived that it could gain by further United States involvement. Each side worked toward this end through the various centers of political power created by the gradual pattern of United States intervention, appealing to Consul Steinhart, to the naval commanders in Cienfuegos and Havana, and finally to Secretary of War William H. Taft.

Secretary Taft's last-minute mediation was aimed in part at allowing Estrada Palma to complete his second term as President. All senators and representatives elected in the fraudulent elections of 1905 (an overwhelmingly conservative group) would be forced to resign, however, along with all provincial and municipal officers. New laws, including a new electoral law, would be drafted and new elections held. Finally, the rebels would disarm and disband under a general amnesty. Estrada Palma and the conservatives rejected the plan outright, while the Liberals indicated cautious acquiescence. The political crisis ended with the resignation of Estrada Palma, the Vice President, and the entire cabinet and the refusal of the conservative-dominated Congress to meet. The routine of military intervention, in the meantime, was proceeding at full speed with more warships and landings. The Second Occupation, implicitly agreed upon by both Cuban factions as the second-best alternative, had begun.

The permanent effects of intervention were summarized aptly by Cuba's leading political thinker and future Conservative Vice President, Enrique José Varona: "The government of the United States . . . has sanctioned the complaints of the insurrectionists in Cuba . . . and has proposed them as the basis for an agreement to the government *de jure* of this republic. In a word, the government of the United States has exacted of the government of Cuba . . . that it abdicate before an armed insurrection."[6] The legitimacy granted to the opposition by the actions of United States naval commanders and mediators had the net result of lending greater solidity and standing to the opposition than ever before. The possibility of United States intervention was to become a crucial variable—and one that increased political uncertainty—in the years to come. In future political crises, each faction, especially that in opposition to the government, would seek United States support for its cause, thus weakening the central government of Cuba and strengthening the opposition even further. The protracted method of intervention, moreover, multiplied the centers of usable power, further pluralizing the political system.

The pluralizing effects of protracted intervention are also evident in the revolt of 1917.[7] Conservative President Mario García Menocal won reelection in a campaign that relied on widespread coercion and electoral fraud. The Liberal party rose in revolt in February 1917. President Wilson's attention was elsewhere; at the time the dominant strategic question for him was World War I rather than Cuba. In early February, the United States had broken diplomatic relations with Germany over unrestricted naval warfare against neutrals; thus the Cuban revolt was an unwelcome diversion. The President and Secretary of State Robert Lansing therefore instructed the United States minister to Cuba, William Gonzales, to give his public support to the government of President Menocal. Minister Gonzales repeatedly did so. Wilson also instructed the War Department to sell 10,000 rifles and 2 million rounds of ammunition to the Menocal government at the outset of the revolt, to be followed by more later.

The United States Navy, however, had a different set of interests, as did United States businesses in Cuba. Some of the largest U.S.-owned sugar plantations and mills were in Oriente, Cuba's easternmost province. The United States naval base at Guantánamo was also in Oriente, and the navy believed the area strategically important for the defense of the southern United States, the Caribbean, and the Panama Canal in case of war. Thus the same strategic concern—the world war—triggered different responses from President Wilson and the United States Navy. When the Liberal rebels attempted to close Santiago harbor by sinking two merchant ships at its mouth, the United States Navy instructed Commander Reginald Belknap to prevent Cuban government ships from entering Santiago in return for a promise from Liberal rebel Major Rigoberto Fernández not to obstruct the harbor. The United States sugar planters in Oriente supported the navy's actions because it permitted them to continue to export sugar and receive supplies. As a part of the Belknap-Fernández agreement, the navy agreed not to interfere with the Liberal rebel forces' administration of the city of Santiago.

In addition, United States Marines landed in both Santiago and Guantánamo in February and fanned out to protect United States property in Manzanillo, Cobre, Nuevitas, and Preston. On their own, the sugar interests in New York had appealed to the unofficial Liberal mission there, headed by Orestes Ferrara, for the protection of their property. Although the Liberal mission in New York was unable to secure President Wilson's support for the rebels, the Cuban government's requests for their arrest and extradition were ignored. Minister Gonzales's demands that Washington prevent the navy from doing as it pleased in Oriente also went unheeded.

On balance, President Wilson and the War Department's strong support for the Menocal government outweighed support for the Liberals from the navy and the sugar interests. Moreover, whereas Estrada Palma had had only about 3,000 troops in 1906, Menocal had 17,000 in 1917.[8] The revolt of 1917 is the only instance when the weight of United States intervention supported the government in Havana, that is, the only centralizing intervention. Yet even in 1917, United States response was not unified. The opposition was bolstered in Cuba's largest province and polarization of Cuban political groups was increased by foreign political and military interference. While the outcome of the 1917 intervention was to strengthen the Cuban government in the short run, the method employed did nothing to lessen the eagerness of Cuban political groups and parties for United States intervention.

These crises only illustrate the characteristics of intervention when the bases of political order were clearly at stake. When the Second Occupation ended with the election of Liberal rebel leader General José Miguel Gómez to the presidency, the United States began a policy of "preventive intervention," which I call "interference." A process of continuing interference in Cuban internal affairs was set in motion, in an attempt to avoid a third occupation. The United States interfered to discourage or prevent actions that were plainly corrupt and on a grand scale; at times, it also interfered to rescue innocent and not-so-innocent United States investors from deals that had gone sour. The United States stepped in to modify contracts for dredging ports and for draining the Zapata swamp under the Gómez government; it also forced President Menocal to veto a general amnesty bill. In these cases, diplomatic instruments sufficed, but more forceful measures were used at other times. In August 1917, United States Marines landed in Cuba for joint defense during World War I; they did not withdraw until January 1922. During this period, as many as 3,000 marines were stationed in the two sugar-rich easternmost provinces.[9]

The United States military governments in Cuba directly administered the presidential elections of 1901 and 1908; while the presidential election of 1912 was held without rebellion or foreign involvement, those of 1905 and 1916 led to the internal revolts and foreign interventions already discussed. The United States State Department, concerned that the events of 1916–17 would be repeated in the 1920 presidential elections, forced President Menocal to ask for a U.S. mission to take a new census and rewrite the election law; the opposition Liberals cheerfully joined in the request. The mission, headed by General Enoch Crowder, completed its work in 1919. The liberals wanted more, however; they asked for direct supervision of the elections and threatened abstention and revolt if it was not forthcoming. A compromise was struck when the incumbent government agreed to accept United States observers during the elections.

The elections were held and fraud again occurred, this time in the midst of financial crisis. Without asking or formally notifying President Menocal, President Wilson ordered General Crowder back to Cuba to rescue the country from economic collapse and electoral fraud. When Crowder sailed into Havana harbor on the U.S.S. *Minnesota*, the Liberals were jubilant; Menocal was incensed. New special elections were held in 1921 in those districts where fraud had been most rampant. Because these districts were few, the Liberals abstained, and their leaders appealed directly to Washington, for once without prior revolt. Washington upheld the Crowder-supervised election of the Menocal government's presidential candidate, Alfredo Zayas. General Crowder, however, stayed aboard the U.S.S. *Minnesota* in Havana harbor until the second half of 1922, dictating to President Zayas on economic, political, and social questions. The peak of his power came early in 1922 with the forced resignation of the Zayas cabinet and the appointment of what came to be known as the Honest Cabinet.[10]

Throughout the first quarter-century of Cuban government, therefore, the United States government regularly interfered in the internal affairs of the republic. Although the intervention or interference was regular and systematic, its political effects were variable. This uncertainty improved the chances of those out of power in Cuba and made opposition politics viable. The opposition's hopes of victory, however, depended on their precipitating a crisis of sufficiently large proportions to lead the United States to intervene. The method worked in 1906 and again in 1920–21, but the Liberals threw their chance away the second time by asking for more interference than the Harding administration was willing to give. It did not work in 1917, either, as the storms of World War I gathered. Thus the low but persistent level of organized political violence in Cuba can be directly linked to the opposition's need to provoke United States intervention as its best means to electoral success.

The elections themselves were not perceived as necessarily determining the country's next President but, rather, as regularly scheduled opportunities for a show of political strength and for bargaining—involving some controlled violence—among government and opposition forces, political organizations, and the United States. Electoral strength and access to United States support were the essential currencies for gaining power.

The Platt Amendment to Cuba's constitution had set up a two-layered executive: the lower layer comprised the Cuban President and his government; the upper layer, the United States President and his government. Appeals were often taken from the lower to the upper level. Gradual intervention, and the fragmentation characteristic of this upper level, however, increased pluralization. In 1906, both the actions of the President, the consul general in Havana, and the naval commanders in Havana and Cienfuegos and Secretary Taft's mediation multiplied the sources of power. In 1917 the United States had a separate policy at each end of the island. From 1919 to 1922, with brief interruptions, a third layer of executive authority—Proconsul Crowder—was added. At no time did political authority rest with a single set of institutions in Havana. Governing Cuba was a task shared by Havana and Washington; in times of crisis, the possibilities for further pluralization by the multiplication of power centers seemed endless.

Imperialism and a Pluralized Economy

Contrary to the three principal perspectives on the structural impact of international economic factors on the Cuban economy and political system (discussed in appendix A), external economic penetration brought about social, economic, and governmental pluralization in Cuba, in the short as well as in the long run. The power of the governing elites was weakened, and the power of opposition groups grew. Centers of political power multiplied as significant decision-making authority migrated away from Cuba and toward the United States, weakening not only the incumbent administration but the general authority of the state as well.

In general, the impact of foreign economic activity in any country depends on three factors: the prior level of social mobilization; the prior strength, capability, and autonomy of the host government; and the nature and degree of internal differentiation shown by the foreign economic activity itself. When, as in the Cuban case, the prior level of social mobilization is high, the prior capability and autonomy of the host government are low, and the foreign activity is highly decentralized both functionally and geographically, the result is a general increase in pluralization.[11] The operation of these factors in Cuba is worth examining in detail.

United States Economic Activity in Cuba

United States private investments in Cuba were worth about $50 million by 1894. By 1906 direct investment by United States enterprises amounted to nearly $160 million, with another $37 million in Cuban bonds. The inflow of foreign capital between 1898 and 1902 reached some $30 million, rising to $80 million between the two United States occupations. By 1911, two years after the end of the Second Occupation, direct investments totalled $175 million; bonds held in United States hands were worth $30 million. The most conservative estimate puts United States private investments in Cuba by 1927 at $1.14 billion, of which $100 million represented government bonds. (See table 2.1 for a breakdown of United States direct investments in Cuba.) The most striking development during the period from 1906 through 1927 was the twelvefold increase in investments in sugar, shown in table 2.1. Important increases took place in other areas, but several of them, such as railroads and utilities, were closely connected with the development of the sugar industry itself.

Sugar production requires cultivating and harvesting the cane, milling it to produce raw sugar, refining the raw sugar, and ultimately marketing the refined product. After the cane is harvested, it must be brought to the mill immediately or much of its sugar-producing value will be lost. Even with fairly advanced technology, transporting the bulky cane is cumbersome. Thus the sugar mills had to be in the countryside, close to the farms, and the cane could not be exported. These botanical and technological requirements led to the transformation of rural Cuba. Although the sugar industry was thus dispersed throughout the countryside, only raw sugar was processed in these mills; very little sugar was refined in Cuba.[12]

The absence of sugar refineries fragmented the industry economically and politically, preventing vertical integration, or self-sufficiency within the enterprise. (A vertically integrated industry controls production, processing, transportation, and marketing of a product—all phases, that is, from raw materials to the individual consumer.)[13] Two factors account for the relative absence of sugar refining in Cuba. First, traditional methods of sugar refining in the island were technologically backward and economically inefficient. With improvements in refining in the United States and Europe, the Cuban producers—most of whom were small and had little capital—went out of business. The second factor was the tariffs—high for refined sugar and low for raw sugar—imposed by the industrial countries, where agricultural subsidies were also often provided to cane and beet-sugar farmers. Farmers and industrial refiners in the United States and Europe were thus protected against possible Cuban competition.

The trend toward abandoning sugar refining in Cuba began in the 1880s and was reinforced by the industrial destruction of the War of Independence in

Table 2.1 Direct United States private investment in Cuba, 1906–1927 (in millions of dollars)

Economic sector	1906	1911	1927
Sugar	30	50	600
Railroads and shipping	25	30	120
Utilities	17.5	20	115
Mines	3	0	50
Trade and banking	4	30	30
Manufacturing (excluding sugar)	—	0	15
Agriculture (excluding sugar) and cattle raising	66	10	45
Real estate and mortgages	14	35	50
Hotels and entertainment	0	0	15
Total	159.5	175	1,040

Source: Leland Jenks, *Our Cuban Colony* (New York: Vanguard Press, 1928), pp. 161–165, 300.

1895–1898. The 1902 Reciprocity Treaty between Cuba and the United States set a duty on refined sugar that, in effect, was 8 percent higher than that on raw sugar. Although the United States reduced the real gap between tariffs for raw and refined sugar after 1913 so that the duties were no longer discriminatory, the structure developed by the industry since the 1880s was difficult to alter; Cuba continued to export raw sugar for refining in the United States. Cuban production of refined sugar was small; during several years it did not even meet domestic consumption requirements, and supplies had to be imported from the United States. In 1925 the Hershey Corporation established Cuba's first modern sugar refinery and thus began the first significant vertical integration of the industry.[14]

The structure of the sugar industry had important implications for the Cuban political system. Instead of a few vertically integrated companies that would control sugar production from the soil to the supermarket, reduce the effective number of social, economic, and political participants, and centralize power in a few enterprises, Cuba was faced with a fragmented sugar sector with many power centers. Nowhere was this pluralization clearer than when various interests sought to affect United States tariff policy in the late 1920s. Many sugar refining companies along the eastern seaboard of the United States—those without direct investments in Cuba—sought higher duties on refined sugar. A second lobby included the W. J. McCahan Refining Company, the National Sugar Refining Company, the Hershey Corporation, many other leading sugar companies in Cuba, and the Cuban association of mill owners; many of the United States refiners in this group had sugar mills in Cuba. Although they would have preferred to keep Hershey refined sugar out of the United States, these refiners did not want to offend the Cuban government. They lobbied strongly for low duties for raw Cuban sugar and were more hesitant on duties for refined sugar. A third lobby included Hershey (once again, because of its unique status) and the United States bottlers of carbonated beverages, who were interested in low duties on all sugar necessary in their industrial activities.[15]

The Cuban government itself had relatively little to say about such decisions. It lobbied diplomatically for lower tariffs on all Cuban products, but the centers of effective power were the United States President and Congressional committees and the organized lobbies in Washington. Such power was centralized neither in Havana nor in Washington but was diffused because of the existence of different and often competing interests within the sugar industry. Some United States refiners had no direct investment in Cuba but engaged in "pure" trade. Others had investments in mills producing raw sugar in Cuba; these enterprises achieved limited transnational vertical integration. Hershey, in a class by itself, was the only vertically integrated enterprise in Cuba. Two additional groups existed within the sugar industry—first, sugar mills owned primarily by Cubans and Spaniards, which engaged in virtually no refining and traded with United States refiners, and, second, those engaged in the agricultural phases of sugar production, which were relatively independent from the sugar mills.

In 1918–19, U.S.-owned sugar mills accounted for 51.4 percent of the harvest. By 1927, U.S.-owned mills accounted for 62.5 percent of sugar production, a proportion that rose to 68.1 percent in 1934.[16] While the migration of ownership to United States enterprises increased steadily during the first third of the twentieth century, an important residue of almost one-third of production remained in the hands of Cubans and "Cubanized" Spaniards. Because the U.S.-owned mills were the largest and most modern, they accounted for a larger proportion of the total output than their numbers would suggest. Thus at all times a higher percentage of sugar mills was under Cuban-Spanish control than would be expected from their share of production; this obstacle to vertical integration at the industrial level persisted throughout the period.

Up to the 1880s, there had been vertical integration between the sugar mill and the agricultural aspects of sugar production. The mill owner's slaves cultivated and harvested the sugar cane and worked in the mill. This link between agriculture and manufacturing was also broken in the 1880s, when abolition of slavery became essential to the restoration of political order in Cuba (blacks had fought on both sides in the Cuban wars of independence of the 1870s). A peaceful social revolution occured when the slaves became tenants and sharecroppers or, alternatively, members of the agricultural proletariat.[17] At about the same time, the increase in the world supply of beet and cane sugar in the second half of the nineteenth century also brought about a price collapse that drove inefficient mills into bankruptcy.

The bankruptcy of the aristocracy limited ownership of modern sugar factories to foreign enterprises or to Cubans closely linked to them. The denationalization of the Cuban upper class—the shift in the ownership of the means of production from national to foreign elites—occurred at the same time as the separation of agricultural and industrial sugar operations. Although the aristocracy controlled much of the sugar industry in the late colonial period, the twentieth century was faced with a diverse upper class composed of the noble former rich, the nonnoble new rich, and the owners and managers of the United States companies. The peasantry and the rural proletariat were less closely linked to the upper class than ever before.

Land owned and administered by sugar mills for cane planting and harvesting amounted to 30.3 percent of all the cane area in 1904–05; another 36.5 percent of the cane area was in the hands of tenants and sharecroppers on mill-owned land; the balance was owned by free farmers. By 1929, the free farmers still controlled 27.2 percent of the cane area; their position was eroded only by the depression.[18]

Sugar production doubled approximately once a decade in the early twentieth century. In 1903, Cuba produced about 1 million long Spanish tons of sugar. By 1912, it produced more than 1.9 million tons, and in the following year it reached 2.4 million. In 1919 Cuba produced more than 4 million tons for the first time; production reached 5 million tons in 1925. Sixty-three sugar mills were constructed between 1899 and 1927; twenty-three of them were constructed during the price rise of World War I, that is, between 1915 and 1918. Another eleven were built—with little foresight—in 1921–22. None was constructed in Cuba after 1927.[19]

If the sugar industry had been concentrated in the same geographic areas where sugar had always been produced, the pluralization might have been contained, but this was not the case. The eastern part of the island—the provinces of Oriente, Camagüey and the eastern part of Las Villas—produced only 35.7 percent of all sugar in 1902–03; by 1918–19, they accounted for 56.4 percent; and by 1929 their share was 69.5 percent.[20] The effect of this distribution was to decrease the importance of the island's former economic center around Havana and to integrate the eastern half of the island for the first time into economic production.

Cuba was sensitized to the outside world not only because of significant private, direct foreign investments but also because of trade. Virtually all of the sugar produced in Cuba was exported; sugar accounted for four-fifths of Cuba's exports on the average. Table 2.2 presents the ratio of trade (exports plus imports) to national income, one indicator of the sensitivity of the Cuban economy to the international system. The ratio is extraordinarily high in relation both to the experience of other countries during the same period and to a cross-section of countries in the mid-twentieth century.

Table 2.2　Trade vulnerability (exports plus imports as a percentage of estimated national income), 1903–1929

Year	Trade vulnerability	Year	Trade vulnerability
1903	72	1917	90
1904	62	1918	95
1905	77	1919	107
1906	81	1920	113
1907	83	1921	108
1908	75	1922	77
1909	72	1923	90
1910	73	1924	92
1911	80	1925	91
1912	74	1926	93
1913	80	1927	89
1914	73	1928	84
1915	72	1929	85
1916	83		

Sources: Computed from Julián Alienes Urosa, *Características fundamentales de la economía cubana* (Havana: Banco Nacional, 1950), p. 52; Foreign Policy Association, Commission on Cuban Affairs, *Problems of the New Cuba* (New York: Little and Ives, 1935), pp. 44, 49, 53 (hereafter cited as FPA, *Problems*). A cautionary footnote on the reliability of national-income estimates is found at table 2.4.

Social Mobilization and Political Participation

Social mobilization is the process by which major clusters of old social, economic, and psychological commitments are eroded or broken and people become available for new patterns of socialization and behavior. It involves a number of more specific processes, such as literacy, other kinds of educational advantages, urbanization, changes in occupational structure, and exposure to mass media. The chief determinant of social mobilization is education, which has an impact on a wide range of behavior. Social mobilization increases the number and size of politically relevant groups within the population, thus heightening pressures for the transformation of political practices and institutions, and changes the range of human needs that impinge on the political process. An increase in the level of social mobilization is likely to increase political participation.[21]

Contrary to the "black legend" of colonial government, Cuba had a respectable level of literaracy as Spanish rule drew to a close, judging by the standards of the age. In 1899, 43.2 percent of the population over ten years old was literate; this figure rose to 56.6 percent in 1907 (an increase of 1.68 percent each year, on the average). In 1919, the literate segment of the population represented 61.6 percent of the total (an increase of 0.42 percent each year), and by 1931 it had reached 71.7 percent (an average annual increase of 0.84 percent).[22]

An educational explosion occurred during the first United States occupation, raising enrollment to half of the school-age population and triggering an extremely rapid rate of social mobilization (see table 2.3). The political troubles of the early twentieth-century administrations and the fact that a sugar economy does not demand a high level of skill in its labor force are revealed in a sharp slowdown in the rate of social mobilization through the first World War and a drop in school enrollment to less than one-third of the school-age population. A new increase in enrollment occurred from an already high baseline during the second half of the 1920s. The government of President Gerardo Machado, who came to power in the spring of 1925, achieved the highest level of school enrollment ever in prerevolutionary Cuba. The 63 percent of the school-age population enrolled in 1926 included just under 30,000 students in private schools, too small a number to make much difference in terms of orders of magnitude. Not surprisingly, school enrollment declined during the depression; Cuba's level of literacy during the worst period of the depression, however, had not yet been surpassed in the 1950s by such countries as Colombia, Portugal, Venezuela, Mexico, Brazil, mainland China, Lebanon, and Peru. Its level of school enrollment at the peak of the Machado presidency was the highest in Latin America.[23]

Unfortunately, direct links between social mobilization and political participation are far more difficult to establish than literacy and school-enrollment

Table 2.3 Public-school enrollment in Cuba, 1902–1933

Year	Public-school enrollment	% of children aged 5–14 in school	% of total population in school
1902	172,273	50.9	10.9
1907	122,214	30.1	5.8
1919	234,038	28.7	8.1
1923	269,796	30.4	8.5
1925–26	433,200	63.0[a]	—
1931	426,708	—	10.7
1932–33	402,893	—	—
1933–34	366,854	—	—

Sources: Mercedes García Tudurí, "La enseñanza en Cuba en los primeros cincuenta años de independencia," in *Historia de la nación cubana*, ed. Ramiro Guerra y Sánchez, José M. Pérez Cabrera, Juan J. Remos, and Emeterio S. Santovenia (Havana: Editorial Historia de la Nación Cubana, 1952), 10:68; International Bank for Reconstruction and Development, *Report on Cuba* (Washington, D.C., 1951), pp. 410–412. All enrollment figures are for September of the calendar or academic year listed.

a. Includes children enrolled in both public and private schools.

figures. The rapid rate of social mobilization in the late 1920s coincided with a sharp economic slowdown. The 1930s witnessed an outbreak of political violence with strong revolutionary characteristics; profound changes were brought about in Cuba's political, social, and economic structure, and even more radical changes were threatened. Although the data at hand do not permit a direct test of the hypothesis, they suggest a textbook case of the revolutionary situation. Samuel Huntington has argued that as social mobilization outstrips economic development, social frustration develops; as social frustration meets blocked opportunities for mobility—an effect of the Cuban economic collapse—political participation increases. If political participation outruns political institutionalization, political instability is likely. Ted Robert Gurr and James C. Davies have also stressed the strong revolutionary potential of a decline in a system's social, political, and economic capabilities after a period during which they have been high or growing. These theoretical propositions are especially useful in explaining the revolutionary situation in Cuba during the 1930s.[24] The cessation of economic growth and the decay of political institutions will be discussed in later sections.

This situation came about when the baseline of political participation was already fairly high. The revolts of 1906 and 1917, described earlier in this chapter, and the years of fighting for independence during the last third of the nineteenth century had prepared Cubans for political participation. Voter turnouts in the contested 1908 presidential elections, administered by the United States during the Second Occupation, indicate a high level of politicization—32.8 percent of all adults (those aged twenty-one or over) voted. Because women were not allowed to vote, it is more accurate to say that 60.1 percent of the adult male population voted; since foreigners and certain others were also excluded, the number of voters rises to 71 percent of those registered. The percentage of adult males voting is quite respectable even by the standards of the middle of the twentieth century.[25]

Economic Growth

Substantial economic growth took place in Cuba under the first political system. Data on real national income per capita during the period, shown in table 2.4, are too tentative to do more than illustrate trends and orders of magnitude. Nevertheless, they suggest that the Cuban economy responded effectively to the foreign infusion and mobilization of capital and technology up to the mid-1920s and that the country recovered successfully and swiftly from the recessions of 1907–08 and 1921.

Wages showed a similar upward trend (table 2.5). The fact that the standard of living improved during this period helps to explain the maintenance of the political system, in spite of its weaknesses. Economic growth, while it lasted, served to legitimate an otherwise barely legitimate political system. In 1927–28, however, the international sugar market broke down. Until the end

Table 2.4 Estimated real national income per capita, 1903–1933 (in 1926 pesos)

Year	Estimated real national income per capita	Year	Estimated real national income per capita
1903	176	1919	214
1904	198	1920	257
1905	228	1921	195
1906	204	1922	214
1907	188	1923	232
1908	181	1924	239
1909	206	1925	199
1910	222	1926	172
1911	199	1927	188
1912	244	1928	164
1913	223	1929	159
1914	234	1930	155
1915	289	1931	136
1916	283	1932	108
1917	210	1933	109
1918	198		

Source: Alienes, *Características*, p. 52. Because there are not reliable data on Cuban national income until the 1940s, these statistics are extremely tentative and must be used cautiously. Reliable Cuban price-inflation data are not available for this period; because of the close economic ties between Cuba and the United States, Alienes justified his deflation of national-income estimates in current prices by the United States wholesale price index (1926 = 100), so that the statistics in the table are in 1926 prices. National income in current prices was estimated from data on government revenues, bank loans and deposits, and export trade; government revenue data, however, are not entirely reliable.

of the Machado presidency in 1933, estimated per capita real national income declined sharply. Wages plunged between 1921 and 1931.[26] It is little wonder that Cuba was rocked by revolution in the early 1930s. Income per capita fell as the level of social mobilization rose.

Table 2.5 Index of daily wages, by province, 1909–1931 (1923 = 100)

Year	Havana	Matanzas	Las Villas	Camagüey	Oriente
1909	75	91	90	75	73
1921–22	100	206	98	108	154
1931	71	86	85	112	102

Source: FPA, *Problems*, p. 86.

The collapse of the Cuban economy in the late 1920s was also directly related to the nature of its earlier growth, which took place in the absence of other structural economic, social, or political changes. The export-oriented economic growth did bring about a significant level of prosperity that trickled down through the social class structure, maintaining the political system. As the international economic environment for the sugar economy changed, however, prices fell, and the Cuban economy—which was not sufficiently diversified to withstand such unfavorable international circumstances—began its depression a few years ahead of the rest of the world, compounding the economic woes of the island.

Government Authority

Cuba's political and economic systems were highly pluralized; its society was strongly mobilized socially in 1902–1933. These structural characteristics, which resulted from the international context of the Cuban republic's early years, might have been contained or put to constructive political use if Cuba's central government had been capable and strongly institutionalized. An effective central government could have repressed rebellion, coordinated or suppressed the various economic and political elements within the country or impinging on it from outside, established a political party system based on real cleavages in social and economic structures, promoted economic development outside of the sugar industry, and sought social justice. None of these actions was possible to the new government, however, largely because it could not achieve legitimation either through the charismatic qualities of its leader or through legal or constitutional means.

All new nations face a crisis of legitimacy; those in power must claim the right to rule in a way that is believed in by the citizens. With the old order, the beliefs that justified its authority have disappeared. Charismatic authority, which depends on the extraordinary personal qualities of the ruler as perceived by the people, may serve to establish legitimacy in some new states. Because charisma is personal, however, this type of authority is extremely unstable; to succeed in the long run it must be institutionalized. The charismatic leader must strengthen the office of the chief executive and must either rise above party or develop an effective political cleavage between followers and opponents. He may develop a strong bureaucracy, a strong party system, or, preferably, both.[27]

The institutionalization of foreign intervention through the Platt Amendment created a severe crisis of legitimacy in Cuba in 1902. Historical accident made the situation even more difficult. Several Cuban politicians who might have been able to establish charismatic authority did not become President. José Martí, who planned and launched the last war of independence, was killed in battle. Calixto García, the chief Cuban general who cooperated with the United States in the war against Spain, died during the First Occupation. One of the two most important military heroes of the War of Independence, Antonio Maceo, was killed in battle; the other, Máximo Gómez, a Dominican by birth, refused to be nominated in spite of a special constitutional provision making him eligible for the presidency; he believed that the President should be a native-born Cuban. Gómez died in 1905.

With the first rank of national heroes eliminated, the presidency fell to Tomás Estrada Palma, a leader without the capacity to establish the authority of his government through his personal qualities. He had represented the Cuban rebels in Washington and had previously lived outside of Cuba for many years. Estrada Palma has been treated kindly by Cuban historians because he was perhaps the only President who failed to enrich himself while in office. It may be that he was incompetent even at being corrupt.[28] His nomination for the presidency, backed by the United States and the majority of prominent Cuban politicians, was challenged by the last President of the insurrectionist forces, Bartolomé Masó. Estrada Palma supported the Platt Amendment, while Masó opposed it. Masó eventually abstained from the elections because he thought they would be fraudulent. Although the Platt Amendment was a significant issue on the basis of which Estrada Palma might have become head of a party, he refused to affiliate with the parties that had nominated him. Thus he became President without promoting a partisan political cleavage, but without the benefit of party support in a noncompetitive election clouded by fraud and in a political system where the Platt Amendment institutionalized the limits of his power.

Estrada Palma was sixty-seven years old when he became President of a country in which he had not lived for years. He believed in balanced budgets and government austerity; his chief governmental program was the continuation of the educational growth policies of the First Occupation. As President, he failed dramatically to mobilize the Congress to approve the legislation necessary for the establishment of legitimate political order in the republic; in the absence of Congressional action, the laws of Spain continued to apply. The First Occupation had approved fifteen organic laws—those concerning the form of municipal, provincial, and national governments, executive, legislative, and judicial powers, and the civil service—and the Constitution of 1901 called for twenty-eight more. Only four of these were passed during Estrada Palma's presidency; another twelve were approved during the second United States occupation. The remainder were adopted very slowly in the subsequent years; Spanish colonial legislation continued in force in the meantime.

Estrada Palma eventually affiliated with the Conservative party in 1905 and established a precedent for mishandling the question of presidential succession. He presided over the use of military force and blatant fraud to reelect himself, removing local officials who would not go along with his plans. The Liberal party abstained and rebelled, appealing to Washington—in a pattern that would be repeated—to solve the question of succession in Cuba. Thus Estrada Palma contributed to the institutionalization of foreign intervention and to its pluralizing effects on Cuban politics. In the absence of charismatic legitimation, the search for other legitimating procedures began.

In addition to gaining authority through the leader's charismatic qualities, governments may achieve legal-rational legitimation. In this case, those in power are obeyed because the procedures under which they have reached office are widely accepted as appropriate. The legitimacy of the Cuban Constitution was tainted by the Platt Amendment. The Congress's failure to approve the laws organizing the government reinforced Estrada Palma's inability to generate acceptance of government authority. Congress also had a poor record in another crucial area, often failing to act on the budget (see table 2.6).

Table 2.6 Congressional action on the national budget, 1902–1933

Administration[a]	Budgets approved	Budgets not acted upon
Estrada Palma, 1902–1906	2	2
Gómez, 1909–1913	3	1
Menocal, 1913–1921	3	5
Zayas, 1921–1925	2	2
Machado, 1925–1933	9	0

Source: Computed from Germán Wolter del Río, "La hacienda de la república independiente," in *Historia*, ed. Guerra y Sánchez et al. 9:99–101.

a. There was no Congress during the Second Occupation, 1906–1909.

From 1902 through 1925, Congress acted on the budget only half the time. When no new budget was passed, the President extended the previous year's budget by executive decree, pending congressional action, which, of course, was not forthcoming. The Congress's frequent inaction reinforced the government's tendency toward presidential autocracy within the fairly narrow scope of issues that were the concern of the central government. Tables 2.7 and 2.8, which summarize rule-making activity under the first political system (all congressional laws, presidential and ministerial decrees, resolutions, statutes, and orders with the force of laws), indicate the increasing predominance of presidential over congressional rule making.

The data in table 2.7 support the general argument that Estrada Palma was reluctant to exercise his presidential authority; he issued decrees at a rate about half that for Gómez, the next lowest case. The Congress was modestly active by the standards of the first third of the twentieth century. Estrada Palma's cabinet, however, was unusually active in issuing decrees; it held the record for rule making until the Machado administration. Thus it appears that

Table 2.7   Government rule-making output, 1902–1933

Administration	Congressional laws/100 days	Presidential decrees/ 100 days	Cabinet decrees/ 100 days	Total rules/ 100 days
Estrada Palma, 1902–1906	6.5	11.1	6.4	24.0
Second Occupation, 1906–1909	0	28.5[a]	0.8	29.3
Gómez, 1909–1913	9.6	21.6	1.1	32.3
Menocal, 1913–1921	5.9	24.0	0.4	30.3
Zayas, 1921–1925	6.0	27.7	1.9	35.6
Machado, 1925–1933	10.6	45.4	12.7	68.7

Source: Compiled, coded, and computed from Milo A. Borges, *Compilación ordenada y completa de la legislación cubana de 1899 a 1950*, 2nd ed. (Havana: Editorial Lex, 1952), vol. 1. Because the length of administrations differed, the average number of laws passed or decrees issued every 100 days is indicated.

a. Decrees issued by the governor of Cuba, who was appointed by the President of the United States.

Estrada Palma, though personally an inactive President, allowed his cabinet a great deal of independent action. The total rule-making output of the Estrada Palma administration remains the lowest during the period, although the first government of a new nation might have been expected to make a great many rules by legislation or decree. The total level of rule making remained roughly constant from the second United States occupation through the Zayas administration. Executive rule-making power was monopolized by the President, with the cabinet sharply curtailed relative to the Estrada Palma administration. Under President Machado, total rule-making activity nearly doubled, and the Congress, the President, and the cabinet joined in expanding the powers of the central government.

Table 2.8   Ratio of executive and presidential decrees to legislation passed by Congress, 1902–1933

Administration	Executive decrees: laws[a]	Presidential decrees: laws
Estrada Palma, 1902–1906	2.7	1.7
Gómez, 1909–1913	2.4	2.3
Menocal, 1913–1921	4.2	4.1
Zayas, 1921–1925	4.9	4.6
Machado, 1925–1933	5.5	4.3

Source: Computed from Borges, *Compilación*, vol. 1.

a. Executive decrees include presidential and cabinet decrees.

Congressional rule-making activity through the Zayas presidency did not vary greatly from its level under Estrada Palma. What increased was presidential rule making. The ratios of presidential and overall executive decrees to legislation suggest a secular increase in executive, especially presidential, rule making throughout the entire period (see table 2.8). Under Machado, the edge of the executive over the Congress continued to grow, but the predominance of the President over Congress lessened. Data on rule making therefore suggest three distinct periods between 1902 and 1933: the Estrada Palma administration at the beginning of the era of independence, the Machado administration at the end, and the other presidencies in between. Throughout the period, government power through rule-making activity increased, but there was a two-decade-long plateau in the middle when no significant change took place. Growth came about primarily by the expansion of the executive; the Congress's pattern of activity remained essentially constant.

The level of government activity can also be judged from the percentage of national income represented by its expenditures (see table 2.9). If any trend is apparent, the economic burden of government may have been slightly higher in the early years; as the economy expanded during World War I, government

Table 2.9 Estimated government expenditures as a percentage of estimated national income, 1911–1933

Year	Government expenditures (% of national income)	Year	Government expenditures (% of national income)
1911	16	1923	13
1912	12	1924	13
1913	16	1925	20
1914	17	1926	24
1915	13	1927	22
1916	11	1928	24
1917	11	1929	26
1918	13	1930	30
1919	11	1931	29
1920	8	1932	34
1921	16	1933	26
1922	13		

Sources: Computed from Alienes, *Características*, p. 52; Cuban Economic Research Project, *A Study on Cuba* (Coral Gables, Fla.: University of Miami Press, 1965), pp. 220, 223. Government expenditures include those authorized in the national budget (whether passed by Congress or extended by presidential decree pending congressional action), those of municipal and provincial governments, expenditures for public works from a special fund established in 1925, and other payments authorized by the Congress or the President outside the national budget. Although many such extrabudgetary items are known, there is no guarantee that all have been discovered, a fact that suggests the tentativeness of these data.

grew more slowly than the economy as a whole and its weight in the economy fell. Once again the Machado presidency is distinct from earlier administrations. In its last years, government was actually contracting, but at a slower rate than the overall economy; until 1931, however, government expenditures were rising as the economy was falling. The Machado government, therefore, increased not only its rule-making activity but its weight on the economy.

The Purposes of Government

Government—particularly the presidency—had weight and was expanding. But, what for? The scope of issues and domain of persons affected by the Cuban government were surprisingly narrow in the face of governmental growth. The Cuban government had, for instance, no monetary power from 1902 to 1932. Except for some insignificant silver coinages in 1914 and 1920, neither the government nor an institution under its influence, such as a central bank, created money; because the United States dollar had free circulation in Cuba during this period, the government could not alter the exchange rate. It could not vary the money supply in response to internal economic conditions because the policy instruments were lacking, and an independent monetary policy was impossible. While the absence of a central bank was shared with other Latin American countries, the virtual absence of any banking legislation was peculiar to Cuba. At the time of the 1921 banking crash, no bank's books had ever been inspected by the government, and no penalties had ever been applied. There was no effective control over the establishment of new banks or over bank reserves.[29] When the Cuban banks collapsed in 1921, the government impassively witnessed the denationalization of banking in Cuba (see table 2.10). From 1921 on, the volume of the money supply in the republic was determined almost entirely by foreign banks and by the balance of payments.

Table 2.10 Private foreign banking activity in Cuba, 1916–1931

Year	% of loans in foreign banks	% of deposits in foreign banks
1916	27	21
1920	28	20
1921	81	69
1925	89	77
1929	85	74
1931	86	77

Source: Computed from Henry C. Wallich, *Monetary Problems of an Export Economy* (Cambridge, Mass.: Harvard University Press, 1950), p. 68.

Until 1933, Cuba also lacked any significant body of labor legislation. In 1919 Fernando Ortiz, then Cuba's leading social scientist, listed the labor legislation he felt the country needed. His catalogue included regulation of strikes, of syndicalization, and of the workday, minimum-wage legislation, health insurance, legislation on maternity leaves and social security, among other items.[30] Cuba was not unusual in this respect, by contemporary standards; however, even the relatively little government activity that took place did not address enough problems of labor. Of all the labor regulations approved by Congress or decreed by Presidents and cabinets, excluding social security, approximately 45 percent were concerned exclusively with the problems posed by port workers and their frequent strikes. Rule making concerned with salaries and wages was meager; general rule making was not very far-reaching. (See table 2.11 for a breakdown of labor rule making during these three decades.)

The most important piece of agrarian legislation to come before the Congress in the first three decades of the twentieth century was submitted in March 1903 by Liberal senator Manuel Sanguily and prohibited all contracts or agreements whereby Cuban land might pass to foreigners. Characteristically, the Congress failed to act on it. The two most important pieces of agrarian legislation approved were a 1909 law creating six agricultural schools (one in each province) and a 1922 law that made it possible for farmers to mortgage their land without mortgaging the property on the land; this

Table 2.11   Labor-related rule making by the Cuban government, 1902–1933[a]

Administration	General rules[b]	Rules regulating salaries and wages	Rules regulating port labor	Total labor-related rules	% of total rule making
Estrada Palma, 1902–1906	0	0	0	0	0
Second Occupation, 1906–1909	0	0	0	0	0
Gómez, 1909–1913	10	2	0	12	2.3
Menocal, 1913–1921	30	2	10	42	4.7
Zayas, 1921–1925	12	2	16	30	5.7
Machado, 1925–1933	30	0	47	77	3.7
Total	82	6	73	161	—
% of total labor-related rule making	51	4	45	100	—

Sources: Computed from Borges, *Compilación*, vol. 1; ibid., vol. 3: 709–750.

a. Rule making includes executive decrees and laws passed by Congress; all rule making dealing with social security is excluded.

b. All laws and decrees other than those dealing with salaries and wages, ports, and social security.

property—sugar, cane, tobacco, fruits and vegetables, buildings, machinery, and equipment—could be mortgaged separately.[31]

Cuban tariff policy was governed by the Reciprocity Treaty signed in 1903 with the United States. It provided that duties on Cuban imports into the United States—especially sugar—would always be 20 percent lower than those on similar imports from any other country; Cuban duties on imports from the United States were reduced by 20 to 40 percent. The United States made concessions on only a small number of products, since that was all Cuba was capable of exporting; Cuba, on the other hand, made concessions on a wide range of products. In terms of dollars, the reductions made by the United States averaged nearly twice as much as those made by Cuba.

Cuba's economic openness to United States imports destroyed all possibility of protecting its infant industries. The situation remained unaltered until President Machado decreed a new tariff schedule in 1927. Duties were increased on manufactured products and reduced on raw materials. It was the Cuban government's first effort—a modest one—to increase national production for the domestic market by protecting Cuban enterprises. In taking this step, Machado differed from previous Presidents, who were inactive in the area of tariff protectionism. A number of light industries increased production behind this tariff, and some United States enterprises, which had previously supplied the Cuban market through trade, responded to the tariff by investing directly in Cuba. Among others, Colgate-Palmolive-Peet first invested directly in Cuba in 1929, and Procter and Gamble did the same in 1931; both acquired and modernized Cuban soap and perfume firms, expanding their capacity. The 1927 tariff, however, was too limited and came too late to counteract the impact of the sugar depression.[32]

Neopatrimonial Politics

The purpose of government in Cuba, in practice, was to advance the interests of the individual officeholder. Cuba was not unique in this regard; nevertheless, the attitudes, beliefs, styles, and policies of the ruling elite exhibited patrimonial characteristics as these have been defined by Max Weber. In patrimonial political systems, access to government is sought primarily for the sake of private advantage and "all government authority and the corresponding economic rights tend to be treated as privately appropriated economic advantages."[33] Cuba was far more structurally differentiated, however, than the political systems Weber describes. Hence the term *neopatrimonial*, fashioned after Weber, will be used to describe the Cuban elite political culture—at least in terms of the actual uses of government and the public's perception of them. In highly differentiated systems such as Cuba's, neopatrimonial norms place the main opportunities for profit in the hands of politicians and bureaucrats. Cuban neopatrimonial politics did not ordinarily include programmatic considerations in addition to benefits to officeholders. In many instances of political corruption in other countries, services are performed and programs implemented benefiting large numbers of people; that such benefits occurred infrequently in early twentieth-century Cuba distinguishes Cuban neopatrimonial politics from other instances of political corruption.

The application of Weberian ideas to Cuba has some important limits. Because such a large part of the economy was in United States hands and the United States presence was ultimately protected by the willingness of its government to intervene, the propensity of neopatrimonial governments to be highly interventionist, on behalf of the ruler, in all major social, economic, and political spheres was sharply curtailed. Until such external constraints were removed in the 1930s, the Cuban government did not seek to regulate and control much of the economy, and incumbents were content to seek only their own gain. Because there was so little regulation of the economy, corporations typically did not need to go to the Cuban government for favors; only those who sought government contracts were involved in using the government for private gain. Thus, somewhat paradoxically, the Cuban government remained relatively independent of pressure from private groups, though it was subject to both the United States and to individual officeholder greed.

There is hardly a history of Cuba that is not replete with detailed descriptions of corruption in government, through every administration, although Estrada Palma is usually exempted personally.[34] Such lurid stories need not be repeated here. One institution, however, needs special mention: the lottery. Suppressed during the First and Second Occupations and vetoed by President Estrada Palma, the lottery was triumphantly resurrected by the Congress and President Gómez in 1909. Although the lottery was formally part of the Treasury Department for most of the period, it was, in fact, an autonomous entity, and its accounts were never audited; an effort to force an audit was vetoed by President Menocal. The President had direct authority over the lottery, but it was widely shared with public officials who controlled the collectorships established as intermediary agencies to distribute lottery tickets. The collectors performed no function and simply pocketed a profit. In the 1920s, each senator could expect to control about eight collectorships and each congressman, about three; between a third and half of all collectorships were reserved for the use of the director general of the lottery and the President.

The lottery system institutionalized the increase of income for public officials, awarding collectorships to members of all parties. The lottery bill of 1923, approved after President Zayas had rid himself of the puritan counsel of General Crowder and his moralizing mission, expanded the collectorship system; it passed the Senate unanimously and the House by 95 to 5. At that time only two senators and ten congressmen were known to have no collectorships.[35] Unlike other forms of governmental corruption, the lottery was legal, as was much of the income from it, but it was also the springboard for illegal gain (through overcharging for tickets, promoting bets on the drawings, and so on). The lottery, which provided money for public officials without their performing a service and depended on public officials for supervision, is perhaps the single best example of the institutionalization of public power for private purposes.

Government public-works contracts were also occasions for considerable corruption, and their cost increased astronomically as a result. Though President Menocal built fewer roads in eight years than President Gómez did in four, for example, Menocal's road building cost three times as much as that of Gómez.[36] The most impressive public-works projects, however, were initiated under President Machado, particularly the central highway linking one end of the island with the other. Although enormously costly, it has remained the chief artery for road communication—with very little improvement—into the 1970s.

The power of public officials was also evident in the presidential right to pardon and the congressional right to grant amnesty. Presidential pardons averaged about thirty per month under Gómez, Menocal, and Zayas; many of these pardons went to common criminals, and 120 of them, to convicted murderers. Presidential pardons were usually granted around election time, however, so monthly averages are deceptive. In the month before the 1916 presidential elections, Menocal pardoned 231 people; in the month before the 1920 presidential elections, he pardoned seventy-five (including nineteen convicted murderers). President Zayas pardoned sixty-three people before the 1922 congressional elections.[37]

Between 1902 and 1924, the Congress approved seventeen amnesty laws,[38] of which the beneficiaries varied considerably. A law passed in March 1909 emptied the jails of all prisoners not convicted of capital crimes. Amnesty for crimes committed during elections was granted in 1902, 1906, 1911, 1915, 1918, 1919, and 1924; the likelihood that amnesty would be approved encouraged the use of violence and fraud during elections. Indeed, this use of congressional power nicely complemented the willingness of the United States to intervene, so that it became personally costless to rebel.

Special cases required special bills; the 1915 amnesty law, for instance, covered only General Ernesto Asbert, the former governor of Havana province. While still governor, Asbert, a senator, and a congressman murdered the chief of the Havana police in broad daylight; the victim had been investigating Asbert's gambling establishments. The amnesty law of 1924 covered, among others, Congressman Joseph Cano, who had murdered another representative in 1922; the former mayor of Havana and the city council, giving them freedom from prosecution for corruption; the former provincial governors of Matanzas and Oriente, for corruption; and Alfredo Zayas, Jr., son of the President of the republic, for fraud and graft while he was assistant director general of the lottery (he was promoted to director general by his father after the indictment and with the trial pending).

Cuban legislation provided absolute immunity to the members of Congress, not only for acts committed and words uttered in the performance of duty but for all acts performed while in the Congress; the courts could try a member of Congress only if the house to which the member belonged removed immunity. From 1902 to 1923, 712 requests for removal of immunity were made to the House of Representatives, and only three were granted. About 100 requests were made to the Senate, only one of which was granted. It is not surprising, therefore, that 20 percent of the congressional candidates in the 1922 elections had criminal records. Congress was a safe place for a criminal, where he could vote himself amnesty.[39]

It is clear that the economic growth of the first quarter of the twentieth century in Cuba was not the result of a deliberate government policy so much as of a pluralized political, economic, and social structure that naturally induced such growth. On the one hand, the government was too weak to create serious obstacles to foreign economic penetration; on the other, its leaders were too concerned with their own private interests to worry about the economy. The President and the Congress were preoccupied with pensions, amnesties, public-works contracts, the lottery, and the politics of individual gain. They were not interested in the politics of regulation or the politics of growth. Patron-client relationships were emphasized within the government and within the party system; genuine social or economic cleavages were not reflected in the political sphere.

The Political Party System

José Antonio González Lanuza, president of the House of Representatives and leading Conservative party member under President Menocal, is said to have noted that there was "nothing more like a Conservative than a Liberal, and vice versa."[40] Although the Liberals were seen to some extent as the "party of the people," while the Conservatives were the "party of the aristocrats," there is little evidence that this difference amounted to more than rhetoric or that many people believed it to be genuine. In the 1924 presidential elections, for example, Conservative candidate Menocal's pictures showed him riding a horse; the Liberals countered with the slogan "On foot." Such were the great issues of the campaign.

Distinguishing Liberals from Conservatives was indeed difficult.[41] General José Miguel Gómez supported Tomás Estrada Palma's candidacy for the presidency in 1902, against the anti–Platt Amendment Liberal candidate Bartolomé Masó. In the 1904 congressional elections, Gómez appeared once again as a leading Conservative. Faced with Estrada Palma's reelection bid, however, Gómez switched to the Liberal party in time to capture their 1906 presidential nomination. As noted earlier, the previously anti-Platt Liberals revolted in 1906, openly asking for United States intervention under the terms of the Platt Amendment. In 1909 Gómez and Alfredo Zayas were elected President and Vice President, respectively.

In 1912, the Liberals nominated Zayas against Gómez's wishes. Gómez had toyed with renomination, but in the end he supported General Ernesto Asbert, Governor of Havana province. Asbert bolted the Liberal party, taking with him large Liberal factions in two other provinces, to form the Patriotic Coalition (Conjunción Patriótica). Thus the Gómez wing of the Liberal party and the Conservatives elected Conservative General Mario García Menocal to the presidency. Though Gómez denied later on that he had supported Menocal, in order to stay in the good graces of the Liberals, all available evidence points to the fact that he and his closest allies delivered the presidency to Menocal by using both their political machines and the rural guards wherever necessary.

In 1916, when Menocal sought reelection, the followers of Gómez and Zayas reunited within the Liberal party, nominating Zayas and Carlos Mendieta. Gómez got control of the Liberals in 1919, assuring himself of the Liberal nomination in 1920. The formerly orthodox Zayas then bolted and formed his own Popular party, which formed the National League with the Conservatives and brought Zayas to the presidency. Thus Gómez and Zayas were allied against Menocal in 1916; Gómez and Menocal joined together against Zayas in 1912; and Zayas and Menocal opposed Gómez in 1920. This is not the stuff of which party loyalty is made.

When the top leaders of the parties crossed the aisles with such ease, their subordinates, of course, did too. Cuba used a system of indirect elections, similar to that of the United States, under which the voters in each province chose a set of electors who cast the votes for President. Therefore, the votes were aggregated by provinces, not nationally, strengthening the hand of provincial politicians. The effective politician was the one who could help deliver an entire province by a party switch. When Gómez, then governor of Las Villas, left the Conservatives in 1905, he was subsequently able to deliver the province to the Liberals. When Asbert left the Liberal party in 1912, he was able to deliver the province of Havana to the Conservatives. In 1916, the Asbertist Liberals abandoned the Conservatives and returned to the Liberal party, once again delivering Havana to the provincial political machine's candidate. In 1920, Conservative politicians publicly admitted that they had failed to carry Havana province (the only one they did not carry in that election) because they could not make a deal with the machine. Even politicians who may have had programmatic goals changed their party affiliation. Dr. Eusebio Hernández, for example, has been described as the Liberal politician most interested in social programs of his time, one who may even have had an "inclination toward doctrinal socialism."[42] Hernández was the Liberal vice-presidential candidate in 1912; denied his party's nomination in 1916, he joined the Conservatives.

Changes in party affiliation are not phenomena unique to Cuba. Rather, they are typical of political systems in which party politics is weakly rooted in social cleavages and where the government and political parties are, as a consequence, relatively autonomous from group pressure.[43] In Cuba, unlike other countries, politicians were often willing to switch to the side that would probably lose the election. As already mentioned, Gómez switched from the President's party to the losing Liberals in time for the 1906 elections, and the Asbertist Liberals switched from the Menocal government, bent on reelection, to the losing Liberals in 1916. Conservative Vice President Emilio Núñez switched to the losing Liberals in 1920; Conservative politician Miguel Arango became the losing Liberal vice-presidential candidate in 1920.

Cuban politicians affiliated with the losing side for a variety of reasons. Some, like Conservative Vice President Enrique José Varona, who opposed Menocal's 1916 reelection bid, seem to have made the change on principle. The paradox of corrupt politics is that honest politicians must be prepared to change parties once their leader becomes corrupt, while run-of-the-mill politicians seek their own advantage. Jealousy and personal rivalry also play an obvious role. Thus former Liberal vice-presidential candidate Mendieta's support of Menocal's losing bid in 1924 can be partly explained by the fact that he had lost the Liberal presidential nomination. A third explanation for party changes is that the loser of the election was not necessarily perceived as the loser of the presidency. During this period, no incumbent President failed to elect his chosen candidate (often himself) to the presidency; this rate of success was sometimes embarrassing. In 1916, there were one million names on the voting lists, with 800,000 votes cast. The 1919 census, however, listed only 477,786 eligible voters. Although joining the President's opposition guaranteed electoral defeat, such changes of affiliation, accompanied by appropriate propaganda, were intended to show the incumbent's corruption and to lay the groundwork for the claim that the election was fraudulent. As noted earlier, they were an important factor in provoking United States intervention or interference to tip the presidency to the opposition. The Platt Amendment, therefore, had the joint effect of strengthening political polarization among factions in the short run and weakening the party system in the long run by encouraging changes in party affiliation.

Despite the weaknesses of the elections and the party system, they contributed to the legitimation of a political system that at least did not impede prosperity. Although the elections were not decisive at the presidential level (there were frequent appeals to Washington), they were generally decisive at all other levels. Even at the presidential level, the opposition needed popular support, in the form of votes, to bargain with Washington. Because the politics of incumbency were relatively independent of pressure from economic interest groups, elections served to legitimate the administration in power, while economic performance provided a broader underpinning for the entire social system. Thus the Cuban political system effectively claimed some qualified allegiance from its citizens. Its legitimacy was precarious, however, because elections could easily be manipulated and economic performance was at the mercy of the international economy.

All pretense of maintaining a multiparty system ended with the election of Gerardo Machado to the presidency on the Liberal ticket. The parties agreed to cooperate, bringing all effective opposition to an end. The Liberals, Populars, and Conservatives voted to suspend mandatory party reorganizations (the law had previously required the rotation of party leaders), thus ensuring the continuation of the incumbents in power. They proceeded to amend the Constitution to lengthen the terms of senators and congressmen and engineered the unopposed reelection of Machado for an extended term of six years. The cooperative party system explains the rise in congressional rule making under Machado (see table 2.7). Laws were approved with little or no opposition, many of them delegating vast powers to the executive, powers that were used, in turn, to increase the number of presidential and cabinet decrees.

The parties' cooperation, however, stripped the political system of its claims to legitimacy.[44] The Cuban government had always lacked autonomy, both because of the Platt Amendment and because of individual officeholders' neopatrimonial approach to government, but it had been somewhat independent of private interest groups. The cooperative party system eliminated the competition over access to government that had prevented any single set of persons from monopolizing power, maintaining a minimum of government autonomy; government was now totally controlled by machadistas. Because they were defined exclusively by their officeholding, the government's relative autonomy from social cleavages continued, although Machado's antilabor policies began to erode it. The merger of Cuban political parties, which had never been clearly defined in terms of programs and membership, diluted whatever minor differences had previously existed.

The loss of competition for access to power also sharply curtailed the need for political bargaining and compromise; while such bargaining had fostered neopatrimonial politics, or the use of public power for private ends, it also had given the government virtually unlimited flexibility, adaptability, and autonomy relative to private groups. In restricting access to power to incumbents, the new system eliminated none of the neopatrimonial problems; rather, it cut back drastically on executive adaptability while preserving an autonomy that became suicidal. It has already been shown that the power of government, its willingness to regulate, and its cost relative to national income increased during Machado's administration. While corruption continued, important legislation on tariffs and public works promoted economic growth. The

Cuban executive became more autonomous, powerful, and complex as it lost coherence and adaptability. While the amount of power in the political system increased and was concentrated in the presidency or central executive, political parties, Congress, the courts, and the military lost autonomy (as individual incumbents became more powerful), as well as organizational coherence and adaptability.

Institutionalized politics requires a degree of stability and predictability. Some stability of personnel is necessary to facilitate both the development of an organizational memory and of coherence and continuity of goals and the rise of expertise in the performance of complex tasks. Predictability is required so that politicians will understand the rules of the political game. In congressional politics, the proportion of members reelected is a useful indicator of both factors. A complete change of congressional membership with every election, so that all members were freshmen, would retard the development of expertise, prevent continuity and coherence of goals, and weaken organizational memories in the supervision of government activities. Thus institutionalization of the Congress required that a substantial proportion of its membership be reelected. Moreover, if the proportion of members reelected varied widely among elections, the political system would become unpredictable; if after years of a certain pattern of elite rotation, access was suddenly denied to aspiring politicians, a political crisis might well develop.

The Cuban House of Representatives reached a fairly high level of institutionalization, measured by the proportion of members reelected to at least a second term (table 2.12). [45] This level had been stable from 1910 to 1924, that is, during the years after the United States occupations and before Machado's presidency, with an average of 38 percent of the members reelected. Machado's reorganization of the party system, however, raised the average suddenly to 53 percent, a change that may have been seen by some politicians as further evidence that the incumbents had changed the rules of the political game in order to freeze others out of power indefinitely. In any case, the change in the rate of incumbent reelection became yet another destabilizing factor. In contrast to the proportion of congressmen reelected, the percentage of senators returning was quite small, not surprisingly, because of their eight-year terms. Many Senate seats, however, were filled by legislators who had gained experience in the House; their number rose quickly, remained high, and was not affected by the Machado presidency.

The data in table 2.12 also indicate the instability of the political party system in the early years of the republic. Between 1910 and 1922, an average of 21 percent of reelected House members changed parties; the rate in the Senate was more than twice that. After the first decade of independence, then, most Cuban politicians were loyal to their parties. At any one time, party changes characterized about a fifth. It was not always the same fifth of members who changed parties, however, so the proportion of politicians who switched parties at some time in their careers is substantially higher. For any single period, that fifth had considerable power, because it could mean the margin of victory. The cooperative party system established under Machado resulted in an unaccustomed level of party loyalty in both the Senate and the House, since it worked only when politicians were extremely loyal to the political machine. By changing the rules governing access to power and the pattern of rewards, Machado was able to inspire a degree of party stability that Cuba never experienced before or since.

Table 2.12 Reelection of members and changes of party affiliation in Congress, 1904–1933

	House of Representatives			Senate		
Year	House seats up for election	% of House members reelected [a]	% of reelected House members changing party [b]	Senate seats up for election	% of Senate members reelected or promoted [c]	% of reelected Senate members changing party [b]
1904	31	58	100	0	0	0
1905	32	25	100	12	58	100
1908	83	16	100	24	34	88
1910	41	46	22	0	0	0
1912	48	25	17	13	46	83
1914	48	42	35	0	0	0
1916	54	31	12	12	67	25
1918	60	43	19	0	0	0
1920	56	34	21	13	53	43
1922	56	43	21	0	0	0
1924	58	40	9	12	91	45
1926	70	51	3	0	0	0
1930	59	56	0	24	63	7
1932	69	51	0	0	0	0

Source: Computed from Mario Riera, *Cuba política, 1899–1955* (Havana: Impresora Modelo S.A., 1955).

a. Includes House members who served in the immediately preceding session as well as a few whose tenure had been interrupted.

b. The data on legislators changing their party affiliations are based only on the minority of congressmen who were reelected (or, in the Senate, who had served in the House), because it was only for this group that party identification could be established for two sessions.

c. Those reelected in the Senate include a few whose careers had been interrupted. Members promoted are those who had served previously in the House; 8 percent of the total Senate seats up for election in 1905 were captured by former congressmen, as were 13 percent in 1908, 23 percent in 1912, 50 percent in 1916, 38 percent in 1920, 83 percent in 1924, and 46 percent in 1930.

By the early 1930s, the economy was declining; social mobilization was increasing, along with the cost and rule-making activity of the government; changes in the rules of the political system and fraudulent elections favored incumbent party loyalists. It was clear that the political system could not last long, and former political leaders joined the opposition. Carlos Mendieta left the Liberal party and founded the Nationalist Union; former President Menocal, who—as head of the Conservatives—had sanctioned the cooperative system, now led many of his party members into the opposition. Political forces formerly outside of the party system emerged; labor and middle-class groups began to organize against the government. A socially mobilized people, in the midst of economic catastrophe, was faced with a decaying though more assertive government; Machado was overthrown in August 1933 through revolts, strikes, terrorism, and civil resistance.

The final collapse of the political system was not due only to these factors, however; the government's lack of autonomy, institutionalized through the Platt Amendment, contributed to its downfall. President Roosevelt appointed Sumner Welles ambassador to Cuba with instructions to mediate between the Machado government and the increasingly violent and powerful opposition. The United States was performing its old role, raising the hopes of the antigovernment forces and contributing to further polarization. In Cuba, the United States government's reluctance to intervene before 1933 had been widely interpreted as support for the government, making the cooperative party system possible. The Machado government's acceptance of the Welles mediation stripped it of its remaining legitimacy and increased the credibility of the opposition. Whatever the intentions of the United States (and Welles himself tilted steadily away from Machado), the scenario of previous interventions was reenacted, and the mediation gradually turned into open conflict between Machado and Welles. On August 12, 1933, Machado succumbed to Ambassador Welles's demand for his resignation—backed up by the desertion of the armed forces—and turned power over to General Alberto Herrera.[46]

Cleavages outside the Party System

During the first third of the twentieth century, Cuban political parties did not reflect any social or economic cleavages; they could not even reflect lasting political differences among individual leaders, because any politician was willing to ally himself with one day's enemy on the next. The relative autonomy of politics and government from pressure from private interest groups rested on the relative separation of politics from social cleavages. Deep cleavages existed in Cuban society, but they were not reflected in the major party system.

The Platt Amendment once seemed a likely issue to divide the parties. The Liberals opposed it at its adoption and through most of the Estrada Palma presidency. When they revolted in 1906 and 1917, however, they invoked the Platt Amendment, seeking United States intervention, and they welcomed the Crowder missions in 1919 and 1921 as means to wrest power from the Conservatives. In 1922, President Zayas launched a "nationalist" campaign to rid himself of General Crowder's interference, although he had sought intervention in 1906 and 1917. In short, although some politicians genuinely opposed the Platt Amendment, differences of opinion on this issue were not reflected in the party system. Louis Pérez has argued that the 1920 presidential elections may have been a struggle for control over the Cuban sugar industry, linking national and foreign interests, but one whose form made it impossible to organize Cuban politics around a nationalist-imperialist cleavage. The Cuban-American Sugar Company, and apparently General Crowder as well, favored Menocal and his candidate Zayas, who represented the Conservative-Popular alliance. The Cuba Cane Corporation and Undersecretary of State Norman H. Davis favored the Gómez-Arango Liberal candidacy. Both sides received political and financial support from abroad.[47]

Liberals and conservatives in Europe and in Latin America were often divided over the question of the proper relationship of an established church to the political system. In Cuba, the Roman Catholic church had been closely associated with the Spanish colonial government and fell into some disrepute under the republic. Much of the key legislation disestablishing the church was approved during the first United States occupation; civil marriage was introduced, and the church's quasi-monopoly over education was broken, mostly by the expansion of secular, public education. On balance, however, most Cuban politicians, regardless of party, would probably have gone further to limit the power of the church between 1898 and 1902; no striking differences in degree of anticlericalism appeared among parties. The antichurch feelings of Cuban politicians subsided after 1902, however. Although a divorce bill was signed into law by Conservative President Menocal, anticlerical sentiments were not pushed very far. Whenever strong anticlerical legislation was introduced in the Congress, it was typically quashed by up to two-thirds bipartisan majorities.[48]

Some leaders had sought unsuccessfully to create and sustain parties reflecting genuine political cleavages. The old hero of the wars of independence, General Máximo Gómez, attempted until his death in 1905 to group all those who had fought Spain in a Liberal party, leaving the Conservative party to those who had either supported Spain outright or sought autonomy under Spain. He did not get far, because the former hispanophiles mixed freely with the former rebels in the Conservative party. Indeed, the Conservative ticket of 1908 included General Menocal, an anti-Spanish rebel, and Rafael Montalvo, who had sought autonomy under Spain in the 1890s.[49]

Corruption became a political issue, but it was one that the parties themselves were not in a position to exploit. It was not until the 1924 elections that the party platforms included promises to "moralize" public administration. Corruption, however, was generally perceived to be bipartisan, and civic movements organized outside the party system to fight it. In the early 1920s Cuban intellectuals began to write about "Cuban decadence" and the "decay" of the republic and protested against some of the more flagrantly corrupt deals. The foundation of the University of Havana's students' federation was followed by a purge of nonworking professors; a group of veterans of the War of Independence included many civic figures, some of them disenchanted leaders from the major parties, who wanted to fight corruption in the Zayas government. This group included former Conservative Vice President Enrique José Varona; Zayas's former secretary of the treasury in the Crowder-inspired Honest Cabinet, Carlos Mendieta; the Liberal vice-presidential candidate in 1916, Enrique Hernández Cartaya, who also served as secretary of the treasury under Zayas; and many others. The movement died out when an attempted revolt, headed by Colonel Federico Laredo Brú (later President from 1936 to 1940), was easily defeated. Corruption, in short, began to create a profound cleavage in Cuban politics and society, but its eradication was not—and could not be—espoused by any of the major parties.[50]

Ethnicity

Ethnic cleavages were also deeply rooted in Cuban society.[51] In 1908, in the midst of the Second Occupation, the Independent Party of Color was organized;[52] its goals included a number of social programs not specifically ethnic, such as the eight-hour day, the distribution of land belonging to the state, and the abolition of the death penalty. Emphasis was placed on ending racial discrimination and on sharing bureaucratic jobs more equally between blacks and whites. There was considerable need for such programs. Legal discrimination against nonwhites had intensified during the two United States occupations; moreover, the Cuban Congress had refused to adopt a variety of bills prohibiting racial discrimination, many of them introduced by Senator Martín Morúa, himself a black. Until the formation of the Independent Party of Color, a crucial characteristic of the Cuban ethnic system had been that many of those who did not share in its benefits—in this case, the blacks—did not challenge its propriety. Morúa himself, as president of the Senate, introduced a bill that passed quickly, prohibiting any political parties or movements limited to members of any single ethnic category.

In 1912, the Independent Party of Color rebelled—partly to dramatize its grievances but more specifically to force the repeal of the Morúa Amendment to the election law. Although much of the party's national leadership was in Havana, the actual insurrection occurred mainly in southeastern Oriente province, with a secondary focus in Las Villas.[53]

The proportion of blacks was higher in the five municipalities in which the

Table 2.13 Black social mobilization in Oriente province, 1907–1919

Population group	Blacks as % of total population		% of population aged 10+ literate		% average increase in adult literacy, 1907–1919
	1907	1919	1907	1919	
Municipality					
Alto Songo	71.7	73.9	38.3	47.3	0.75
El Caney	53.0	53.2	53.9	63.3	0.78
Guantánamo	66.9	65.5	50.1	54.2	0.34
Santiago	55.4	52.8	80.3	80.4	0.01
San Luis	68.8	59.4	38.3	46.0	0.64
Cuba	29.7	27.2	56.6	61.6	0.42
All blacks	—	—	45.0	53.0	0.66
All native whites	—	—	58.6	62.6	0.33

Sources: Computed from *1907 Census*, pp. 273–274, 316–317, 463–464; *1919 Census*, pp. 406, 567–569.

revolt of 1912 was concentrated than in Cuba as a whole (see table 2.13); except for San Luis, the percentage of blacks in the population remained virtually constant from 1907 to 1919. Although the national literacy gap between blacks and whites in Cuba as a whole is significant, it is not overwhelming, and many blacks could read and write. No direct evidence is available on the proportion of adult blacks (including mulattoes) who were literate in these five municipalities; however, the rate of social mobilization in Cuba as a whole during this period was twice as rapid for blacks as for native whites. Thus much of the increase in adult literacy in these five municipalities probably reflected an increase in black adult literacy. The increases in the three most rural municipalities—Alto Songo, El Caney, and San Luis—are especially impressive. Between 1907 and 1919 there was no change in adult literacy in Santiago, the provincial capital, but its level was already quite high.

It is arguable, therefore, that the effects of social mobilization accounted for the events of 1912. The blacks of southeastern Oriente were geographically concentrated and changing their skills very quickly, at a rate that was high both in absolute and in relative terms. An increasing number could read the propaganda of the Independent Party of Color and its rebel leaders. The area appears to have been quite receptive to revolt during this period of change. Although the revolt might not have occurred without impetus from the party's national leaders, it might not have been so readily accepted if the attitudes and capabilities of blacks in southeastern Cuba had not been changing so rapidly. Furthermore, these municipalities, unlike the rest of Oriente, had not yet

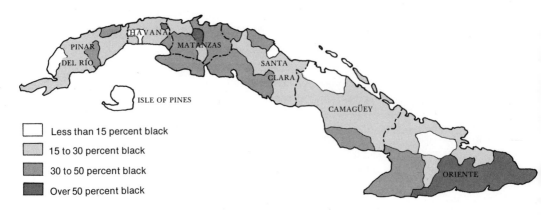

Less than 15 percent black

15 to 30 percent black

30 to 50 percent black

Over 50 percent black

PRINCIPAL FOCUS OF THE BLACK REVOLT IN ORIENTE, 1912

benefited from the sugar boom, which did not reach southeastern Oriente until after 1912. Thus in these municipalities a barely legitimate political system coexisted with rapid social mobilization and few economic rewards—a classic context for revolt.

When the revolt began, the United States government panicked; it landed four companies of marines in the Guantánamo area, site of both the heart of the revolt and the United States naval base, and sent warships to Havana, despite the fact that the Gómez government vigorously opposed intervention and was effectively defeating the revolt.[54] The black revolt was in fact crushed by Cubans alone, after the Conservative opposition rallied to the Gómez government and the President declared his willingness to defend civilization against barbarism. There were probably about 4,000 black rebels, mostly in Oriente, although some counts reached as high as 7,000; the government reportedly killed 3,000.

Although the revolt came to a bloody end, black Cubans profited from the economic expansion that began in Cuba at about this time. Some blacks continued in high government positions; Cuba's leading black politicians (Senators Martín Morúa and Juan Gualberto Gómez, Congressmen Agustín Cebreco and Generoso Campos Marquetti) had supported the Morúa Amendment to the electoral law and consequently opposed the revolt. Yet the presence of a few blacks did not mean a great deal. In the mid-1920s, depending on the method of racial classification used, there were between two and five blacks and mulattoes—out of 113 members whose photographs are available—in the Cuban House of Representatives; there were none in the Senate.[55] Blacks' representation in the House was not even a sixth of what would be expected from their share of the population.

At least some blacks—thousands of them—believed they had to organize outside the party system. When they revolted, the parties united against them; at other times, both parties sought their favor. Even though most of black members of Congress were Liberals[56] and though the Conservative party program explicitly favored white immigration, President Menocal courted one of the more important black secret societies in Cuba, Abakuá, to gain its support in the 1920 presidential election. In 1920, Senator Juan Gualberto Gómez, who had shifted with Zayas away from the Liberals and into the Popular party, provided black support for a coalition with the Conservatives. In 1924, Gómez broke with Zayas and the Popular and Liberal parties and supported Menocal's bid for reelection. The ethnic cleavage, therefore, while real and threatening, was not reflected in the party system, and the parties were alike in opposing black affirmations of identity as well as in courting their votes.[57]

Labor

Like their ethnic policies, the labor policies of the various administrations were virtually indistinguishable. It has already been shown that Cuba lacked any significant body of labor legislation; strikes had been common in Cuba since colonial times. In November 1902, Estrada Palma was faced with a strike that began among the tobacco workers and subsequently spread throughout the city of Havana, in which the workers demanded that native Cubans should not be discriminated against by the foreign owners and that salaries should be raised. This strike was repressed by the police, with many workers killed and wounded. When the mayor of Havana, supported by the minister of the interior, dismissed the chief of police for excessive brutality, Estrada Palma reinstated the chief and fired the mayor and the minister.[58] These early events set the tone for government response to labor and management issues for the next three decades.

None of the early twentieth-century administrations did much to improve the lot of workers. Liberal President Gómez vetoed a law providing accident insurance for workers. Chapman comments that "the nearest thing to a political policy that Gómez had was to give the country an administration that would be favorable to business."[59] Although labor may have had a slight tendency to vote Liberal, partly because of the efforts of such politicians as Liberal Senate President Morúa, the Menocal government also courted the labor vote, promoting a labor congress planned and controlled by the government under the direction of the minister of justice. Menocal had nevertheless to face a long series of strikes in the ports and in the sugar regions between 1917 and 1920; military repression was common, and foreign-born labor leaders were deported. The worst strikes under President Zayas occurred among railroad and sugar workers during the 1924–25 harvest; Zayas, too, would rely on the deportation of the foreign born and the use of troops to protect the sugar mills. Chapman approvingly notes that during strikes "Zayas pretty generally turned up on the side of the employer, even including the foreign capitalist, not hesitating at times to exile union leaders or in other ways use force."[60]

The pluralization characteristic of the Cuban economy made it difficult to coordinate the activities of the workers for politics and, to an even greater extent, to launch labor parties. A socialist party, made up of a few Havana workers and led by a poet, was organized briefly during the first United States occupation. Between 1904 and 1908, various socialist or labor parties were established, but none lived long except the Socialist party of Manzanillo (a city in Oriente province), which was able to elect city councilmen.[61] Made up primarily of tobacco workers, it continued to exist until the 1920s, when it merged with larger movements.

The development of a viable labor movement and labor parties awaited the growth of the large sugar mills, which concentrated sugar workers in particular regions; it also required the post–World War I repressions and the beginnings of the breakdown of the Cuban economy to produce enough incentives for labor to organize. When the Havana Labor Federation was formed in November 1920, the price of sugar had gone from 9⅛ cents per pound in mid-February 1920 to 22½ cents in mid-May; it would fall to 3¾ cents in December. The Cuban National Labor Confederation (CNOC), which quickly came under the control of the almost simultaneously founded Communist party, was organized in 1925 in response to the Zayas repressions.

Between 1925 and 1927, the Machado government launched a devastating attack against the CNOC and the Communists. Labor leaders were assassinated; Communist party leaders were tried in 1927; foreign-born leaders were deported. The Havana workers' federation was dissolved; the CNOC, suppressed; and the Communist party, banned. Machado formed his own docile labor unions, filled primarily by railroad, port, and maritime workers. Even with the labor movement under control, however, the economy was collapsing, wages were declining, and politicians were joining the opposition. Beginning with a general strike in Havana in 1930, the workers, most of them under Communist direction, waged constant war on the Machado government. During its last days, from the beginning of the last week of July 1933 until Machado resigned on August 12, Havana was virtually paralyzed.[62]

Just as there were no significant differences among the political parties in their attitudes and policies toward labor, the personal economic status of leading party politicians did not differ significantly. President Menocal had been the manager of the Cuban-American Sugar Company, organized by United States Congressman and subsequently Senator R. B. Hawley; Menocal had built and managed the huge Chaparra sugar mill and plantations. The Liberal vice-presidential candidate in 1920, former Conservative Miguel Arango, had been general manager of the other huge sugar company in Cuba, the Cuba Cane Corporation, and owned sugar mills himself. Liberal President Machado had managed the Cuban branch of the General Electric Company during the years immediately before he became President.[63]

The leaders of the parties were themselves relatively well off; their social and economic policies favored business while receiving labor support. Thus the underlying social cleavage between management and labor was not likely to be reflected in the major parties' programs. Both the Conservative Menocal and the Liberal Machado sought to promote captive labor movements; all the Presidents from Estrada Palma through Machado had a record of bloody repression against strikes. Socialist parties and large-scale labor movements developed only toward the end of the period, and even then they suffered unremitting repression. The power of the incumbents, then, rested on the parties, which were relatively independent of social cleavages; it also depended on their faithfulness to a capitalist system on a United States model, a system that the government defended. The government, however, was not interested in benefiting some capitalists at the expense of others; such differences among enterprises were not reflected systematically in party politics (although some temporary alliances were formed) and did not affect incumbency. Thus the government was autonomous from private groups, but not independent enough to challenge the basic legitimacy of the capitalist system. This limitation is one factor in the government's lack of autonomy relative to the United States.

In general, then, government remained problematic under the twentieth-century's first political system, when the republic was overwhelmed by its external protector. Cuba's political system was pluralized by the interaction of complex internal and international factors. Individual officeholders' approach to government was neopatrimonial; government authority in general was weak and barely legitimate. From 1902 through 1933, the Cuban political system had two claims to legitimacy. The first was that it did not impede, and may have facilitated, many years of economic prosperity; the second, that many officeholders were elected officials. Although elections, certainly at the presidential level, were not decisive, votes were one of the currencies of power and hence one of the means of systematic legitimation. Access to power was gained by the exercise of organizational power in elections and in bargaining with the United States; authority over Cuba was divided between Havana and Washington.

Because the Cuban government's impact on the society and the economy was modest, interest groups did not require considerable power over incumbents, who never challenged the basic legitimacy of the internal and international economic system. The purpose of politics was primarily the personal enrichment of officeholders, and the politics of incumbency was relatively autonomous from social and economic issues. Social cleavages that might have served as a basis for parties did not do so. Although party loyalty was strengthened after 1910, a substantial number of politicians switched sides at election time, delivering enough votes to ensure victory or to undermine the legitimacy of the electoral process sufficiently to provoke United States interference.

The political system came to an end under Machado, in many ways the most interesting President of the period. Machado sought to increase the government's involvement with society and the economy; he initiated the first serious program of economic development and curtailed the United States' previously unlimited access to the Cuban economy. He sought to increase party loyalty by changing the rules for access to power and expanded the educational system. At the same time that social mobilization was reaching an all-time high, however, the sugar economy collapsed. Machado's changes in the party system had excluded politicians who had expected access to office, and electoral fraud was common. The pluralized republic became involved in political and social bloodshed, under the watchful eye of the United States ambassador. The problem of government had not been solved in independent Cuba; it would have to be posed again.

Cuba's first political system owed much to the United States, particularly because it enabled opposition politics to operate effectively in Cuba. The United States economy provided direct and indirect stimuli for substantial economic growth, while United States occupations of the island promoted public health and educational measures. Indeed, the United States' very success in exercising influence over Cuba was the chief problem faced by Cuba's first independent political system. The opposition, which began to develop outside of the party system in the 1920s, felt that the republic was not Cuban enough. It could no longer accept the Platt Amendment; an economy and a society fully open to the United States, without regulation; or the need for United States participation in the selection of Cuban Presidents. These issues were the major ones to be faced by the Cuban political systems after Machado.

The Machado government, mildly and timidly, had begun the process of reducing United States influence and the openness of the Cuban economy, while curtailing political competition and increasing the government's weight in society and the economy. It would remain for the second and the third twentieth-century political systems to cut United States influence down further and eventually to root it out; in the meantime, they would reduce interest group autonomy and political competition well below the standards set in the first political system.

That Cuban economic and political openness were paradoxically closely tied to the forms of dependency on the United States became clear early in the twentieth century. Boundaries between the internal functioning of Cuban politics and its economy and international economic and political events were far from clear. One task remaining for future political systems was to clarify the boundary between the United States and Cuba; in the process, Cuban politics would be altered so extensively that the pattern of the early twentieth century would never be repeated.

3

GOVERNING THROUGH REGULATION AND DISTRIBUTION, 1933–1958

In 1933 and 1934, as in 1902, twin experiments in political order were launched: the further transformation of United States expansion, from imperialism to hegemony, and an increase in the Cuban government's independence from the United States. The changes, of course, were closely related. Under imperialism, the United States had been concerned with the details of internal rule—the identity of the incumbents, the procedures whereby they came to power, the relations between executive and legislative branches of the government, the mechanics of elections or military coups, and the probity or corruption of interal rule. Under hegemony, in Cuba as in other countries, its primary concern was the overall structure of the system. The identity of the incumbents mattered to the United States only when it affected the legitimacy and stability of the system as a whole. The United States would no longer mediate between rivals for power who accepted the basic rules of the game.

Under imperialism, policies had been imposed on the client, or dependent, state (in this case, Cuba); under hegemony, initiatives of the client state were resisted or reversed only when they were perceived as harmful. United States troops were engaged in temporary though frequent overseas occupations under imperialism; while such occupations are possible, in principle, under hegemony, they are rare—and none occurred in Cuba. The hegemonic system served the interests of both states; it had two basic advantages for the United States, one political and military and the other economic. The client state would be loyal to the hegemonic state in case of war and in normal diplomatic activity, and the flow of goods and capital between the hegemonic state and its client would be relatively unimpeded.

The shift to hegemony reduced the United States' effective authority over the client states of the American mediterranean but expanded it toward South

America. It grew gradually out of the United States' imperial experience over three decades, but particularly the events of 1933 and 1934 in Cuba. The change was neither insignificant nor cataclysmic. Cuba and other client governments also benefited because they became more autonomous, but only in a subsystem of the international system of states under the influence of the United States. In Cuba, the United States would interfere only when specific governmental policies threatened the structure of the hegemonic relationship and, in one isolated but fateful case, when the identity of the incumbent threatened the viability of the entire system. Hegemony limited the degree to which the United States government contributed to pluralization, since many of its actions now had a centralizing effect. Nothing in the hegemonic system prevented further pluralization of Cuban politics through a new infusion of United States enterprises, but the United States government no longer acted directly to pluralize Cuban politics, as it had under imperialism. Earlier, the United States government had been an agent of change; under hegemony, it became a pillar of order.

U.S.-owned enterprises also came to have less weight in Cuba's economy and politics. Important economic sectors, such as the sugar industry and the banks, gradually passed into Cuban hands. Private foreign investment mattered less by the 1940s than it had in Cuba's first political system. There was a fresh infusion of private foreign investment in the 1950s, but principally in manufacturing and mining, not banking and sugar. The only operation dominated by private foreign investment throughout the prerevolutionary period was public utilities; in fact, the state takeover of these enterprises was the Cuban left's only proposal for socialization until 1959.

Cuba's first political system had been characterized by vigorous and rapid rates of social mobilization and, until the late 1920s, of per capita economic growth. Under the second regime the level of social mobilization remained high but stationary. Political organizations thus had available a large pool of participants, but not many new people joined that pool between 1933 and 1958. The participation of the many and the exclusion of the few proved to be a durable problem difficult to overcome.

Until the end of World War II the Cuban economic situation was precarious. From the late 1940s until 1958, however, per capita economic growth resumed with a broader diversification than it had displayed in the past. Despite the period of stagnation, evidence indicates that the standard of living improved substantially under both prerevolutionary political systems and that people of all ages, races, and occupations and both sexes benefited. There is also evidence that gains were shared unequally, so that inequalities may in fact have widened, especially between whites and blacks.

Political legitimacy remained problematic under the second political system. As in the first three decades of the century, there was no charismatic legitimation of the government. What legitimation there was, was primarily legal-rational: the new political order could claim the right to rule because it brought prosperity and justice to many people. Thus legitimacy was linked to performance. By the late 1930s, some basis for government authority also derived from the approval of a new constitution and from reasonably competitive elections. Legitimacy remained elusive throughout the period from 1933 to 1958, however. Many constitutional provisions were never implemented, many institutions, such as the Congress, were not functioning properly, elections were not always honest, and the level of governmental corruption was already high and still rising. Batista's military coup on March 10, 1952, aggravated all these problems and added extensive, though inconsistent, repression to the list of political ills.

The government's weight in the society and the economy changed considerably under the second political system. The partial retreat of United States interests allowed the Cuban government to assert itself. Its regulatory activities increased markedly. Almost all this regulatory expansion was accounted for by the growth of the executive branch of the government. The Congress was less active from 1940 to 1958 than it had been from 1902 to 1933; for over a decade, it failed to approve the budget, thus granting unlimited discretion over spending and taxation to the presidency by default. Although the Cuban state was regulatory, however, it was not entrepreneurial. The ratio of government expenditures to national income remained essentially unchanged throughout the entire prerevolutionary period, during which the only enterprise taken over by the state was the western railroads.

Government regulation and distribution of economic and social goods were the keys to the stability of the second political system. Detailed and extensive regulation of the sugar industry contributed to economic order; after nearly a decade of class warfare, the effective regulation of organized labor by the late 1930s contributed to political order. Regulation and distribution were intended to ensure that every significant organized group had both a stake in economic and political order and access to power to guarantee that stake. Interest groups captured large portions of government bureaucracies and formulated national policy autonomously. The politics of interest was essentially separate from the politics of incumbency. Political cleavages linked to the economy and the society were reproduced within and among government bureaucracies, independent of elected officials; politicians and political parties, in turn, were fairly autonomous from interest-group pressure. Cuba had a two-track political system. The President's role was acting as a broker among competing bureaucracies captured by organized interest groups. Because access to government was both essential and constantly available to interest groups, they never openly opposed it.

Government regulation and distribution affected and benefited only organized interest groups, however, which helps to explain why the real wages of organized labor increased steadily under the second political system, even though the unemployment rate remained nearly constant; the persistence of substantial, especially seasonal, unemployment did not depress the general level of wages because organized labor secured both employment and rising wages. Thus, most Cubans who were politically organized benefited from government policies, while a large minority of Cubans, who were not organized, failed to benefit. The politics of regulation and distribution were virtually the only concern of Cuban governments until the late 1940s; economic growth policies and institutions were formulated and established only in the last decade of prerevolutionary rule.

The disjunction between political parties and interest groups prevented the development of nationwide political cooperation for pursuing class interests. Cuban politics was organized by groups, but not by class. The political party system developed its own rules, with a mixture of volatility and stability. Under the first political system, the independence of politics from social and economic cleavages, along with political uncertainty induced by the possibility of United States intervention, contributed to political volatility and partisan defections. When the social warfare of the early and mid-1930s ended, a "pure" political cleavage, cutting across social and economic lines, finally appeared: it was determined by whether one favored or opposed Fulgencio Batista.

From 1935 to 1944, when there was little political uncertainty, political support flowed to the government. When Batista announced that he would yield power in 1944, defections in both directions resumed. Because politics was not disciplined by responsiveness to social and economic cleavages, the politics of incumbency could be volatile; its only limitations were the declining importance and increasing isolation of the Communist party after 1947 and the appearance of corruption as a viable political issue. Groups appeared who were opposed to deals, compromise, and bargaining and who were thus questioning the basic mechanisms by which the second political system functioned.

Several factors contributed to political stability at the same time. The frequency of party changes guaranteed that no President's first administration ever lacked experienced personnel from the previous one. Electoral forces were relatively predictable during the period; Cuba's geographic regions were similar enough in ethnic and religious make-up that elections were won or lost nationally. Political parties and politicians cultivated programmatic vagueness and tailored services to particular individuals and groups. Still, Cuba's second twentieth-century political system had three major weaknesses: public doubts about its legitimacy, the frequency of political violence, and the exclusion of the politically unorganized from the benefits conferred by the government.

The Retreat of Empire and the Rise of Hegemony

The fall of President Gerardo Machado was linked to the policies and actions of the United States government, especially to those of Ambassador Sumner Welles, which were still based on the imperial relationship between the two countries. Welles justified his interference in Cuban internal affairs as a means of avoiding intervention, a policy developed by successive United States administrations since 1909. Machado tried to bypass Ambassador Welles by appealing directly to the White House, while the opposition tried to get rid of Machado by seeking United States support through the ambassador. Machado's formal, public acceptance of the Welles mediation was the beginning of the end for his administration, since it meant that his government gave up its claims to legitimacy. When he tried to reverse the process by calling on the forces of Cuban nationalism in late July and early August 1933, he failed.

In early August, Welles asked Machado to resign, threatening him with intervention, and on August 12 the armed forces deposed the President. There is no evidence that Ambassador Welles was behind the coup; rather, he worked consistently within the political process, which accorded the United States ambassador a paramount role. By negotiating publicly with the opposition and withdrawing visible support from the Machado government, the ambassador set the conditions for the President's removal. The revolution of 1933 was born in the United States Embassy.[1]

General Alberto Herrera, who took over when Machado resigned, turned over power to Carlos Manuel de Céspedes. Ambassador Welles's reports to Washington during the brief Céspedes administration still reflect classic imperial behavior. "I am now daily being requested for decisions on all matters affecting the Government of Cuba," he wrote. "These decisions range from questions of domestic policy and matters affecting the discipline of the Army to questions involving appointments in all branches of the government."[2]

On September 4, 1933, the Céspedes government was overthrown in a coup by noncommissioned officers and soldiers led by Sergeant-Stenographer Fulgencio Batista. A new government, headed by Ramón Grau, came to power with support from the new military leaders and from university students, but the United States government, on the ambassador's recommendation, refused to recognize it. Although Welles's request for a landing of United States troops was rejected by President Franklin Roosevelt, it was United States policy to replace the Grau government, and the island was encircled by thirty United States warships. Roosevelt's refusal to send in troops to depose Grau meant, however, that the process would be drawn out until power became either sufficiently concentrated in a few hands for Grau to be overthrown or sufficiently fragmented to cause the Grau administration to collapse. Actually both possibilities were realized. Virtually every center of power in Cuba split between September 1933 and January 1934. Division spread, from the armed forces to the university students, from the terrorist ABC to the conservative forces, fueled by the weapons that United States manufacturers such as Federal Laboratories sold to both the government and the opposition.[3] Finally, after then Colonel Batista had consolidated the armed forces once again, he gained enough power to overthrow Grau, who was replaced, in rapid succession, by Carlos Hevia, Manuel Márquez Sterling, and eventually Carlos Mendieta.

The making and unmaking of so many governments were linked to two factors: the pluralization of Cuban politics and the long-drawn-out, qualified United States intervention. This wrenching experience was superimposed on two other trends: the growing realization in the United States that imperialism was too burdensome a policy, and the growing Latin American opposition to intervention. At the Montevideo and Buenos Aires inter-American conferences, the Good Neighbor policy, the herald of hegemony, emerged from the ashes of imperialism in Cuba. The new inter-American policy led to the mutually advantageous treaty of June 1934, which abolished the Platt Amendment.

Plattism had not been mere formality in Cuba, but rather a deeply ingrained, adaptive response to the realities of the Cuban political system. Even with the Platt Amendment dead, Plattism lived on for a time. Shortly after the amendment was abolished, for example, President Mendieta, Secretary of State Cosme de la Torriente, and Ambassador Jefferson Caffery agreed that the time was not yet ripe for the removal of the naval squadron surrounding the island, despite the fact that the United States Navy had been pressuring its government for authority to leave since February 1934; the ships were not removed until September 1934.[4] Cuban politicians continued to seek United States government support. In 1935 the State Department had to issue a public disclaimer stating that the United States government neither favored nor opposed any political group in the coming elections.[5] In late 1936, when— at the insistence of Army Chief Batista—the Cuban Congress was in the process of impeaching President Miguel Mariano Gómez, members of the Gómez cabinet twice asked Ambassador Caffery for public support. Through the Cuban ambassador to the United States, Gómez himself asked for Roosevelt's support. The President chose not to interfere to stop the impeachment, nor did the State Department or the ambassador intervene. In true hegemonic fashion, however, Caffery sought and received a pledge from Batista that he would not overthrow the legitimate government of Cuba. The United States was willing only to insist that the dispute between Batista and Gómez be resolved through constitutional means.[6]

Cuban politicians did their best to involve the United States government and its ambassador in the selection of Cuba's President in the 1940 elections. The opposition sent Senator Ramón Zaydín of the Acción Republicana party to gain the support of Assistant Secretary of State Sumner Welles. Welles reacted by instructing the chargé at the United States embassy in Havana to tell Cuban politicians that the United States government "would under no conditions give any indication of whether it would or would not recognize a future government in Cuba."[7] His precautions were unavailing, however, for shortly thereafter Ambassador George S. Messersmith reported to Washington that

ex-President Menocal endeavored yesterday . . . to ascertain from me whether the Government of the United States would like him to join forces with Col. Batista or with Dr. Grau [the leader of the opposition]. General Menocal also expressed . . . his belief that Colonel Batista would resign his candidacy [for the Presidency] if he received an indication that this would be pleasing to the Government of the United States. Needless to say, I am taking no step which might indicate that the Government of the United States has any desire with reference to the group with which General Menocal may associate himself, or concerning Colonel Batista's candidacy.[8]

Similarly, in August 1942, Vice President Gustavo Cuervo Rubio asked Welles to give an opinion of his presidential candidacy. Welles refused to indicate "any preference, either by support or opposition to any Cuban citizen who might run for the Presidency of Cuba."[9] In spite of changes in United States policy, then, imperialism, as reflected in Cuban Plattism, died slowly.

Although the United States' hegemonic role did not include specifying the identity of the President of Cuba, the United States did require that the President's policies conform to the structure of open capitalist international and internal systems. Two documents formalized the new relationship between the nations. By the terms of the Reciprocity Treaty of 1934, the United States lowered tariffs for thirty-five Cuban products; the most important were the 20-percent reductions of import duties on Cuban sugar and tobacco. Cuba granted tariff reductions on 426 items. The United States Jones-Costigan Sugar Act of 1934 authorized the Secretary of Agriculture to determine the annual sugar requirements of the United States, to assign percentage quotas to the various sugar-producing areas, and to pay a premium over the prevailing world price to assure deliveries and protect producers in the United States, its dependencies, and Cuba. The act also limited the imports of Cuban refined sugar to 22 percent of the total. Thus the United States accepted domestic inflation through higher sugar prices, at least in part for the sake of long-term stability in Cuba. These two instruments institutionalized Cuba's economic openness to the United States and its dependent position.[10]

The United States government's consistent attempts to keep Cuban governments faithful to their country's role as client state can be seen in United States–Cuban relationships during the Grau administration of October 1944 through October 1948. Grau had been overthrown in January 1934, after heading Cuba's most revolutionary government up to that time, in part because of United States opposition. The second Grau administration was not strongly anticommunist until 1948, did not come to power with United States blessings, as did the administrations of the 1930s, and was a wartime ally of the United States only briefly. Grau made no special efforts to promote additional United States private foreign investment.

During this administration, the United States government strongly and repeatedly protested what it alleged were Cuban violations of the Reciprocity Treaty. Raw materials produced in Cuba were exempted from certain taxes by the Grau government in 1945. Taxes on the refining of crude petroleum extracted in Cuba were also removed, and gross sales taxes were reduced in 1946. All these actions sought to reduce imports. By the end of 1948, the United States had protested thirteen alleged trade treaty violations. There were other sources of conflict as well. In January 1947, the Grau administration required all United States cargo to be opened for inspection at the port of entry, rather than at the port of final destination; this decree created jobs for port workers, though it injured Seatrain Lines' development of containerized transportation. In December 1947 the Grau government prohibited the termination of agency contracts between United States and Cuban partners without prior authorization by the Cuban Labor Ministry. By the end of the Grau administration, United States private citizens' claims against the Cuban government amounted to 9.16 million pesos (the peso and the dollar had the same value). Some of the claims dated back to 1906. Of these claims, 14.6 percent had been adjudicated by Cuban courts but remained unpaid; another 56.4 percent had been acknowledged as legitimate by Cuban government agencies but also remained unpaid. The United States government protested against all of these actions, which they considered misdeeds of the Cuban government.[11]

The United States government had little success in settling these disputes during Grau's tenure, in part because it did not press very hard; it considered these matters to be troublesome, but not enough for vigorous action. Ambassador R. Henry Norweb put it this way in September 1946: "Relations between Cuba and the United States may only have been settling gradually to a basis different from that which existed prior to the abrogation of the Platt Amendment. As Cubans, generally, have become convinced that there is only a very remote possibility of the United States ever reverting to a frankly interventionist policy, they have had a tendency to flaunt their 'independence' in small ways."[12] An internal State Department memorandum on overall United States policy toward Cuba, written in July 1948, made it clear that the maintenance of economic and political stability was the United States' "fundamental objective in our relations with Cuba." A further reason for United States restraint, the writer noted, was that the "other American Republics continue to regard Cuban–United States relations as a barometer of the Good Neighbor policy and non-intervention."[13] The Cubans made good use of this strategic advantage.

In the spring of 1947, the State Department's Bureau of Inter-American Affairs initiated legislation that eventually became a section of the amended

Jones-Costigan Sugar Act. It authorized the Secretary of Agriculture to with-hold an increase in the sugar quota of any foreign country that denied fair treatment to United States citizens. Secretary of State George C. Marshall strongly supported the provision in order to obtain leverage in disputes con-cerning United States sugar mills in Cuba and general business conditions there, and in the other disputes already mentioned. Cuban ambassador Guil-lermo Belt protested what he considered "economic aggression" and took his case to the United States press and Congress, the Pan American Union, and other Latin American countries. Foreign ministers of Latin American govern-ments began to question United States ambassadors about the new policy, with the result that the State Department was compelled to deny that it in-tended to use the power to hold back increases except under grave circum-stances; the offending section was repealed by Congress shortly thereaf-ter.[14]

United States pressure on the Grau administration to settle these disputes consisted for the most part of acts of omission. State Department policy was not to support "any request which the Cuban government might make for United States credits so long as Cuba continues to ignore the various debts owed to United States citizens."[15] It was the policy of President Harry S. Truman, the department, and the embassy in Havana to do all they could, informally and behind the scenes, to resist and reverse Cuban policies considered prejudicial to United States economic interests. The thrust of United States pressure on the Grau government—including the ill-fated section of the Sugar Act—was to deny Cuba additional benefits and to link the granting of these benefits to the settlement of outstanding disputes.

Other issues affected the structure of the system more directly. The sugar-cane growers (colonos) linked to the U.S.-owned Tánamo sugar mill had a con-tract dispute with the mill owners in 1948. The Minister of Agriculture seized the mill under the "intervention" procedures of the Cuban government, which allowed a ministry (usually that of labor or agriculture) to take over an enterprise paralyzed by a contract dispute and administer it temporarily, at the owners' expense, until the dispute was settled. This procedure, the nor-mal effect of which was to coerce management to accept labor's terms, was used 101 times between 1934 and 1955, approximately thirty of them by the Grau government. As the United States Bureau of Foreign Commerce recog-nized, however, intervention occurred primarily as a result of labor disputes, and "nationality of ownership was of no particular significance."[16] The only important instance of government takeover of private enterprise before 1959 was the Batista government's purchase of Cuba's western railroads in 1953. Nevertheless, intervention—whenever it occurred—was apparently resisted with enormous vigor and reasonable success by the United States Embassy. After brief delays, for example, the ambassador reported to Washington that the executives of Tánamo Sugar Company were "highly pleased with the terms of the agreement" and had "expressed their warm appreciation of the Department's and the Embassy's efforts on behalf of the Company which they feel were responsible in large measure for the satisfactory solution which has been reached."[17]

The second threat to the structure of the system, as the Cold War opened, was the relative strength of Communism in Cuba. Ambassador Norweb attempted "on several occasions" to persuade President Grau to break with the Communist party; he knew of other, similar pressures on the President. But the embassy was also persuaded of the "probable ineffectiveness of any attempt to influence Communist developments in our direct relations with Cuba."[18] Consequently, in the absence of heavy pressure from the United States, Norweb was persuaded that Grau's decision to break with the Communists in 1947 did not arise from United States concern but from Grau's "personal disenchantment with the party on local issues."[19]

Finally, it is important to recognize the actions that the United States government refused to take in order to understand the difference between imperialism and hegemony. In 1947 the State Department strongly opposed the Department of Agriculture's efforts to promote anti-Cuban sugar legislation that would benefit domestic sugar producers. Though it was eager for Cuba to sign an economic treaty to settle disputed matters, the State Department rejected, in 1948, Ambassador Butler's proposal that Cuba be coerced into signing. The Assistant Secretary for Political Affairs, Norman Armour, did "not believe we should endeavor to force the Cuban government to accept the Treaty. The use of coercion might very well give rise to unfavorable repercussions in Cuba and the other American republics."[20]

Even before the Grau administration came to power in the 1940s, specific requests from United States business not merely to undo prejudicial policies but to impose affirmative ones were rejected. United States sugar mills enlisted Ambassador Caffery's support in 1937 and proposed that the United States government use coercion against Cuba if it implemented new legislation regulating the sugar crop. The State Department refused to interfere. Active lobbying could go on; coercion was taboo. The United States tried to keep Cuba faithful to bondholders and business interests not by imposing policies but by resisting Cuban "misbehavior." At times, the United States government perceived the integrity of the hegemonic system as requiring the sacrifice of short-term United States business interests in return for long-term stability. When the United States government refused to support the United States sugar-mill owners against the largely Cuban sugar farmers at the time the new regulations were approved in 1937, Undersecretary Welles said that if the Cuban sugar farmers were "to be kept as an inherently conservative and moderating influence in Cuban political and economic life . . . that point of view taken by certain Americans in Cuba to the effect that all advantages were to be obtained by the mill owners and none by the *colonos* was, in my judgment, as shortsighted as it was stupid."[21]

Only once under hegemony—toward the end of Batista's regime—did the United States perceive the continued incumbency of the President as a threat to the system's long-term stability.[22] As the political situation in Cuba deteriorated in the 1950s, the United States government was divided over the desirability of Batista's continuing in office. Early in 1958, the assistant secretary of state for inter-American affairs and the director of the Caribbean division came to believe that Batista might endanger the United States' relationship with Cuba; because they were not impressed with Fidel Castro, they made an effort to find a political solution that excluded both leaders. The views of these two officials were shared by the embassy's political and Central Intelligence Agency chiefs. Until late 1958, however, Ambassador Earl E. T. Smith believed that Batista and his government should receive United States support.

The most dramatic public break in United States confidence in Batista was the suspension of arms shipments, announced in Washington on March 14, 1958, because Batista was violating the terms of defense agreements restricting Cuba's use of the weapons to external defense. Ambassador Smith fought for months to reverse that decision and used every available means to persuade the State Department to cooperate with Batista. In late 1958, his pleas for support for Batista's chosen successor, Prime Minister Andrés Rivero Agüero, were flatly rejected. In Cuba, the suspension of United States weapons shipments was publicly recognized as a significant withdrawal of support from the Batista government and a blow to its legitimacy. This loss of confidence, coming just before the only formidable offensive launched against the rebels, was nearly fatal to the Cuban military, which had been trained by the United States and remained closely linked to it.

In June 1958, Raúl Castro kidnapped forty-eight United States and Canadian citizens in retaliation for the continuing shipment of supplies, purchased before the ban, to the Batista government through the Guantánamo base.[23] After two weeks of direct negotiation between United States Consul Parks Wollam and Raúl Castro, the hostages were released and the arms embargo against Batista tightened. This incident demonstrated that Batista could no longer protect foreigners in Oriente and further eroded the administration's power and legitimacy.

Attempts by the United States to maintain the stability of the hegemonic system were stymied, as so often in the past, by the inconsistent implementation of its policy. Ambassador Smith publicly and privately supported Batista at the same time that State Department policy undercut his legitimacy and weakened military morale. By mid-November 1958, Smith finally came to believe that the Batista government was collapsing. After the CIA reported in late 1958 for the first time ever that the United States should actively resist a

Castro victory, the foreign policy bureaucracy, finally unified, made a series of desperate efforts to force Batista to resign before Castro became too strong to be stopped. The State Department and the CIA sent William D. Pawley, a private businessman, former ambassador, and long-time friend of Batista, to Cuba on December 9, instructing him not to tell Batista he had been sent by the government; his efforts to persuade Batista to resign were unsuccessful. On December 17, Ambassador Smith, himself acting under orders from the State Department, tried in a two-and-a-half-hour meeting to convince Batista to resign. The message that the United States would no longer support Batista's government was given to Cuban Foreign Minister Gonzalo Güell. Word spread so quickly that the chairman of the Cuban Joint Chiefs of Staff, General Francisco Tabernilla Dolz, asked for an interview with the ambassador to discuss a possible military coup. It was too late for a "third force" solution, however. Batista fled on New Year's Eve, 1958, after all remaining props to his legitimacy had crumbled; even the conservatives and Ambassador Smith had abandoned him. The United States had been unable to maintain the structure of the political system in Cuba the one time it really mattered.

The shift from imperialism to hegemony also meant that, except in the extraordinary circumstances just described, the actions of the United States government did not always increase the level of pluralization of the political system. The effect, and often the intention, of many United States government policies was to support the flow of power to the political center. In the crucial year of 1934, for example, the United States government supported the Mendieta government, which it had done so much to create by contributing to the overthrow of Grau, abolishing the Platt Amendment, granting emergency loans, and establishing the economic treaties required for a short-term revival of the Cuban economy. In subsequent crises, the United States supported the Cuban government. In 1941, for example, the Army Chief of Staff, the Navy Chief of Staff, and the Chief of the national Police attempted a coup against President Batista because of his efforts to reduce exaggerated military influence over civilian affairs. United States Ambassador George S. Messersmith made it plain to the Cuban Secretary of Defense that the United States supported the constitutional government; the United States military attaché advised the Cuban commander of Camp Columbia in Havana (the single most important military regiment in Cuba) that the United States, on the threshold of a world war, did not favor the breakdown of stability in Cuba. The regiment remained loyal; Batista subdued the coup attempt from Camp Columbia.[24]

An unintended contribution to the increase of the President's power was the United States' pledge in early 1948, three months before the Cuban presidential elections, to purchase an additional million tons of sugar, outside of its regular sugar quota, for the United States Army in occupied areas. Up to this time, it had seemed that the 1948 Cuban sugar harvest would have a large unsold surplus. Grau was able to claim that his government had successfully placed the sugar outside the United States quota at a price both higher than that originally offered by the United States and higher than its price in the world sugar market.[25]

Thus, after the experience of three decades of intervention and interference in the details of internal Cuban politics, and after the painful affair of the removal of Presidents Machado and Grau, the United States established a new basis for Cuban relations that was consistent with the Good Neighbor policy. The shift toward hegemony was easier and swifter for the United States than for its Cuban clients, who were slow to believe that United States policy had really changed. The United States' restraint in Cuba was not entirely self-willed, however; the Cuban government learned to mobilize other Latin American governments for support in its periodic disputes with Washington. The United States government was also less directly involved with United States business on the island. At times maintaining hegemony required a defense of United States business against Cuban government encroachment; at others, the strengthening of the Cuban bourgeoisie at the expense of United States business. Further pluralization was of course possible, and some United States actions promoted it. Far more than previously, however, United States policy strengthened the incumbent government (at times to the chagrin and discomfort of the United States) and contributed to the flow of power to the presidency. The reduction of the United States influence in Cuba thus made a historic contribution to political centralization and political order, reducing externally induced political change.

Hegemony and the Economy

The behavior of United States private investment in Cuba between 1933 and 1958 is relatively consistent with a product-cycle model.[26] Two of its aspects are pertinent to a discussion of Cuban affairs. First, mature enterprises lost their initial advantage in technology, capital, and marketing of specific products over time as these were developed by the host country's own entrepreneurs. Cost advantages and economies of scale also disappeared. One typical response (though not the only one) is for the foreign company to divest itself of the operation. Second, decisions to invest abroad are often triggered by the companies' perception that their place in an established export market is threatened. A company that once traded with a country becomes an investor in it instead to prevent the loss of that market. Once one producer has made an investment, its competitors will do likewise to protect their market advantage. This process was exemplified in Cuba when Colgate-Palmolive-Peet was induced to invest in Cuba by the 1927 tariff and Procter and Gamble had to follow suit to meet the competition. Consequently new investments in some sectors can be accompanied by divestment in others; one product cycle ends and another begins.

Table 3.1 shows a sharp decline in the value of United States agricultural investments in Cuba after 1929. This had once been among the more mature of its investment sectors in Cuba, but by 1958 the absolute value of agricultural investments in current dollars was the same as it had been in 1936—and in real dollars obviously much less. There had previously been little foreign investment in petroleum and mining in Cuba; by the end of the Batista government, there were three foreign-owned petroleum refineries, although the country produced little crude oil. The exploitation of nickel and manganese resources had also risen considerably. Investments in manufacturing tripled between 1936 and 1958.[27] Thus two sectors where investment had been limited before 1929 became the growth sectors for foreign investment after 1929.[28]

Table 3.1   Direct United States private investment in Cuba, 1929–1958

Year	Total value (in millions of current U.S. dollars)	% old investments agriculture	% old investments utilities	% new investments manufacturing	% new investments petroleum and mining	% trade and other investments
1929	919	62.6	23.4	4.9	1.0	8.1
1936	666	39.7	47.3	4.1	0.9	8.0
1946	553	41.1	45.4	7.2	2.7	3.6
1953	686	38.6	43.3	8.5	3.5	6.1
1958	1,001	26.5	34.4	8.0	27.0	4.2

Sources: Computed from U.S., Department of Commerce, Bureau of Foreign Commerce, *Investment in Cuba* (Washington, D.C.: Government Printing Office, 1956), p. 10; Fulgencio Batista, *Piedras y leyes* (Mexico: Ediciones Botas, 1961), p. 415.

Most divestment occurred in the sugar industry, a mature enterprise. Almost two-thirds of its production was accounted for by U.S.-owned sugar mills in 1927, but by Cuban mills in 1958 (table 3.2). The nationalization of privately owned mills proceeded throughout the period. Similar trends can also be seen in banking, another mature enterprise (table 3.3). The Cuban banks' share of deposits and loans rose steadily during the 1950s, in contrast to the denationalization of banking in the 1916–1931 period (see table 2.10).

The original advantage of United States investments had been lost in these sectors. No new sugar mill had been built since the 1920s. Politics gave a helping hand to the product cycle in the sugar industry by encouraging foreigners to divest through strict regulation of all aspects of sugar production. At the same time Cuban governments, beginning around 1950 with the Prío presidency and continuing under Batista, encouraged direct private investment, domestic and foreign, in manufacturing, with incentives that included tax exemptions for new industries and tariff protection, particularly for fertilizers, tires, cement, and textiles. Some United States companies probably concluded that if they did not invest in Cuba they would lose that market to Cuban producers.[29]

Table 3.4 shows the patterns of competition. Foreign investment, especially

Table 3.2   Foreign and domestic ownership of Cuban sugar mills, 1927–1958

Nation of ownership	1927		1939	
	Number owned	% of total production	Number owned	% of total production
United States	89	62.5	66	55.1
Other foreign	29	—	52	22.5
Cuba	57	—	56	22.4
	1952		1958	
	Number owned	% of total production	Number owned	% of total production
United States	41	43.0	36	36.7
Other foreign	7	2.0	4	1.2
Cuba	113	55.0	121	62.1

Sources: Computed from Foreign Policy Association, Commission on Cuban Affairs, *Problems of the New Cuba* (New York: Little and Ives, 1935), pp. 226–227; U.S., Bureau of Foreign Commerce, *Investment*, p. 37; Cuban Economic Research Project, *A Study on Cuba* (Coral Gables, Fla.: University of Miami Press, 1965), p. 523 (hereafter cited as CERP, *Study*).

Table 3.3   Cuban private banking activity, 1950–1959

Year	% of loans in Cuban banks	% of deposits in Cuban banks
1950	53.0	49.5
1951	53.9	54.5
1954	56.5	56.7
1957	63.0	64.7
1958	63.1	61.1
1959[a]	62.7	64.4

Sources: Computed from Banco Nacional de Cuba, *Memoria, 1952–1953* (Havana: Editorial Lex, 1954), pp. 509, 527, 549, 567 (hereafter cited as *Memoria*); *Memoria, 1954–1955*, pp. 501, 521, 545, 563; *Memoria, 1957–1958*, pp. 383, 403, 425, 443; *Memoria, 1958–1959*, pp. 297, 313, 337. Percentages of loans and deposits given for each December.
   a. October.

Table 3.4 Indexes of overall activity and foreign investments in industry and manufacturing in Cuba, 1946–1958 (1946 = 100)[a]

Year	Overall industrial activity[b]	Foreign industrial investments[b]	Overall manufacturing activity	Foreign investments in manufacturing
1946	100	100	100	100
1950	108	113	105	135
1953	126	124	112	145
1954	130	126	114	138
1957	147	—	129	—
1958	—	227	—	200

Sources: Computed from Banco Nacional de Cuba, *La economía cubana en 1956–1957* (Havana: Editorial Lex, 1958), p. 57; U.S., Bureau of Foreign Commerce, *Investment*, p. 10; Batista, *Piedras*, p. 415.

a. Sugar processing in sugar mills and refineries excluded.

b. Includes manufacturing, construction, mining, and utilities. These data should be used with caution, as industrial activity cannot strictly be compared with investment patterns.

foreign manufacturing, grew faster overall than industrial and manufacturing activity in the Cuban economy; thus the foreign sector outpaced the domestic sector. Between 1950 and 1954, however, the foreign sector, particularly in manufacturing, lagged behind the Cuban economy as a whole. Cuban entrepreneurs were quick to take advantage of the new policies and institutions. This expansion of Cuban industrial entrepreneurship in nonsugar areas occurred in the face of a recession caused by problems with sugar production and prices. It is, therefore, reasonable to assume that the foreign sector led the domestic sector between 1954 and 1957–58 partly because it was protecting its share of the Cuban market from domestic entrepreneurs and partly because it could take advantage of favorable new legislation and credit institutions.

Prevailing scholarly interpretations of the post-1933 period continue to emphasize the strength of United States control and the absence of a Cuban national "bourgeoisie."[30] My own analysis dissents from the scholarly consensus; I believe the evidence suggests that after 1933 conditions changed substantially. The role of domestic Cuban entrepreneurs, modest before 1933, grew considerably since then. United States owners were expelled from the sugar industry and from banking after the thirties.[31] It was not until 1954 that the Prío and Batista administrations and Cuban enterpreneurs were able to induce U.S.-based multinational enterprises appreciably to increase their investments in Cuba again.

Cuba had been sensitized to the outside world not only by foreign investment but also by foreign trade. Between 1931 and 1944 the weight of foreign trade in Cuban national income (table 3.5) was reduced from its previous levels (see table 2.2). During that period foreign trade never accounted for more than 57 percent of national income, while from 1903 to 1930 it never accounted for less than 62 percent.

The years of retrenchment in foreign trade coincided with the years of retrenchment in direct private foreign investment and also with the years of sluggish and trendless shifts amounting to no real change in national income. Beginning in 1945, foreign trade again became a major factor in the Cuban national income, but the country's trade vulnerability to the outside world never again reached the heights of the period between World War I and the Great Depression. Cuban economic growth in the post–World War II period was fueled in part by a new increase in the weight of foreign trade in national income, as well as a resurgence in private foreign investment. Cuba partook of the recovery of the capitalist world. However, in investment as well as trade, the growth of the domestic Cuban economy was sufficiently strong that the pre-1931 trade-vulnerability levels were avoided.

Transnationalism in the middle third of the century differed considerably from the form it took in the preceding period. For two decades, the dominant thrust was divestment and decreased foreign trade in proportion to the economy. Divestment occurred alongside investment in new sectors of the economy only in the 1950s, and foreign trade expanded again. Transnationalism had contributed to the pluralization of the Cuban political system in the first thirty years of the century but contributed neither to growth nor to pluraliza-

Table 3.5 Trade vulnerability (exports plus imports as a percentage of estimated national income), 1928–1958

Year	Trade vulnerability	Year	Trade vulnerability	Year	Trade vulnerability
1928	84	1939	52	1949	68
1929	85	1940	54	1950	68
1930	64	1941	51	1951	72
1931	51	1942	46	1952	65
1932	47	1943	57	1953	63
1933	43	1944	53	1954	57
1934	50	1945	61	1955	63
1935	51	1946	62	1956	65
1936	51	1947	77	1957	69
1937	51	1948	77	1958	68
1938	53				

Sources: Computed from CERP, *Study*, pp. 400, 605; Julián Alienes Urosa, *Caracteristicas fundamentales de la economía cubana* (Havana: Banco Nacional, 1950), p. 52; *Memoria, 1954–1955*, p. 271; *Memoria, 1957–1958*, p. 133; *Memoria, 1958–1959*, p. 95.

tion between 1933 and the 1950s. The foreign component in the Cuban political system, public and private, was less dynamic until the fifties, when both were reactivated to pluralize Cuban politics. This retrenchment was matched by the emergence of Cuban enterprise, which would press demands on the government that it had not contended with before.

Social Mobilization

The acceleration of social mobilization in Cuba at the beginning of the century was aided by a prosperous period characterized by rapid economic growth and popular convictions about the value of universal education. This prosperity vanished in the late 1920s, however, not to reappear until after World War II. Under the precarious economic conditions that followed, the government ceased to be willing to commit large resources to education. Parents for whom the education of their children had been a marginal priority, to be undertaken only when good times permitted, preferred in harder times to make use of their children's labor. The result was educational stagnation, which persisted until the early forties when, partly as a result of national shock over the illiteracy figures revealed by the 1943 census, a new effort at mass education was launched. Its effects can be seen in the increasing literacy rates from 1943 to 1953. In 1943, 71.3 percent of the population aged ten or over was literate, an average annual decrease of 0.03 percent since 1931, when the literacy rate had been 71.7 percent. By 1953, 76.4 percent of the population aged ten or older could read and write; this figure represents an average annual increase of 0.51 percent in the literacy rate.[32] Adult literacy thus registered a modest advance. In the late 1940s school enrollment returned to the level of the late 1920s. In 1925–26, 63 percent of the population aged five through fourteen was in public or private school—a total of 462,800 children. By 1933–34, this number had declined to 366,854 (counting public-school students only, however). In 1949–50, the number of schoolchildren was 657,000, or 58.7 percent of the population aged five through thirteen. Based on the highest available estimates for enrollment in public primary schools, "superior" public primary schools, and private primary schools, the number of schoolchildren had reached 883,884 by 1958.[33]

The 1920s had been a period of remarkable educational achievement. The only three age cohorts to show an illiteracy rate of less than 20 percent in 1953 attended school either in the twenties or in the last years of the Machado regime in the early thirties (table 3.6); the figures for this period contrast dramatically with the poor showing of the late thirties and forties. Thus the expansion of political participation between 1933 and 1958 certainly cannot be explained by any improvement in public education. The level of social mobilization remained high throughout the period, however, when it was up to the political organizations to mobilize anyone available for political

Table 3.6 Illiteracy in 1953, by age cohorts[a]

Date of birth	% illiterate	Date of birth	% illiterate
1939–1943	31.8	1899–1903	22.0
1934–1938	22.5	1894–1898	23.9
1929–1933	20.1	1889–1893	28.0
1924–1928	18.0	1884–1888	35.8
1919–1923	18.9	1879–1883	41.2
1914–1918	19.1	1874–1878	44.3
1909–1913	20.4	1869–1873	50.0
1904–1908	21.5	1868 or earlier	60.1

Source: Adapted from 1953 Census, pp. 143–147.

a. Among the older cohorts some became literate as adults. Cuban adult education was not then, however, the massive program it would become in the 1960s.

action. At the same time, the degree of social mobilization did not increase, and a potential source of activity for political change remained untapped. The task achieved in mid-century was the political mobilization of those who had been mobilized socially before 1933; those who had not continued to be excluded from political activity.

The first third of the twentieth century had been a period of urbanization. This trend also changed in the 1940s and 1950s. People began to migrate from the towns and small cities to Havana; the size of that city increased enormously as a result, but without any acceleration in the rate of urbanization in the country generally.[34] Stagnation thus characterized two measures of social mobilization—education and general urbanization—in mid-century.

Economic Growth and Social Welfare

The substantial improvement in the standard of living that occurred in Cuba in the decades before the revolution is confirmed by a variety of indicators. The Cuban economy faced a decade and a half of trendless economic change up to 1948. After World War II, however, real economic growth began and continued until the revolution came to power (see tables 3.7 and 3.8), although growth was interrupted by a brief recession in 1953–1954. Real nonagricultural wages exhibited fairly steady growth, even during the period of overall economic stagnation, and continued at a high rate into the early 1950s. During the Batista period, from 1952 through 1958, however, real nonagricultural wages stagnated. Agricultural wages also increased after 1949; their rate of increase relative to nonagricultural wages was better in the 1950s than before. The wage share of national income rose until 1952, and fell thereafter (table 3.9).

Table 3.7 Estimated real national income, 1933–1940
(in 1926 pesos)

Year	Real national income (millions)	Real national income per capita
1933	446	109
1934	486	116
1935	544	128
1936	631	145
1937	711	161
1938	595	133
1939	633	139
1940	548	119

Source: Alienes, *Características*, p. 52. These statistics must be interpreted cautiously, since there are no reliable data on Cuban national income until the 1940s. As in table 2.4, national-income estimates based on government revenues, bank loans and deposits, and export trade were deflated by Alienes by the United States wholesale price index for 1926.

Overall, the Cuban economy (including wages) recovered successfully but slowly from the effects of the Great Depression. Real per capita income and all real wages increased faster annually under Prío in the late forties than under Batista; the Batista administration was the first to see real economic growth and a decline in nonagricultural workers' share of wages in real income.[35] The retrenchment of United States political imperialism and of direct private foreign investment, the decline in the contribution of foreign trade to national income, and the slowdown of social mobilization and of economic growth coincided until the post–World War II period. At that time, when the economic variables began to show growth again, direct private foreign investment was the last to grow. Patterns of political imperialism (except for 1958) and social mobilization did not change much in the 1950s compared to the two previous decades.

To say that standards of living improved in Cuba is not to say that all was well. The living conditions of those at the bottom of the social scale, particularly the agricultural workers, remained shockingly low. The statistics of their plight are well known. But even for them, time brought improvements. Real agricultural wages increased. The mean real cash income of the fifteen poorest agricultural-worker families in a 1934 survey rose at an annual rate of 5.4 percent until 1957; the mean real cash income of another twenty-five agricultural-worker families in 1934 rose at an annual rate of 0.5 percent until 1957.[36] Agricultural workers have income other than wages, especially in livestock and crops raised for household consumption, as well as income from payment in

Table 3.8 Indicators of real economic growth, 1937–1958 (in June 1937 prices)

Year	Real national income (in millions of pesos)	Real per capita income (in pesos)	Index of real per capita income (1946 = 100)	Real nonagricultural wages (pesos/month)	Index of real nonagricultural wages (1946 = 100)
1937	614	138	—	9.2	—
1938	466	103	—	9.5	—
1939	530	115	—	11.2	—
1940	472	100	—	11.8	—
1941	686	143	—	12.3	—
1942	526	107	—	11.5	—
1943	621	124	—	11.7	—
1944	693	137	—	13.1	—
1945	531	103	—	13.3	—
1946	601	115	100	14.5	100
1947	659	124	108	17.3	119
1948	580	108	94	15.8	109
1949	616	112	97	16.4	113
1950	750	135	117	18.6	128
1951	766	135	117	20.5	141
1952	773	135	117	24.2	167
1953	714	123	107	21.3	147
1954	761	129	112	21.2	146
1955	807	135	117	21.7	150
1956	883	146	127	23.7	163
1957	944	154	134	24.8	171
1958	884	142	123	23.5	162

Sources: Computed from *Memoria, 1950–1951*, pp. 225–226; *Memoria, 1954–1955*, pp. 271, 315, 318; *Memoria, 1957–1958*, pp. 133, 191, 194; *Memoria, 1958–1959*, p. 95. The National Bank revised its estimates periodically; in each case this table presents the most up-to-date statistics. These five measures have been deflated by the Cuban national retail food index in 1937 pesos as it stood every June. This is the only long-term price index available. It has the modest advantage of deflating income by a measure linked to the standards of living of poor people, for whom food absorbs a large share of income. Data for the years before 1950 have been estimated and therefore should be used cautiously.

kind, household industries, and so on.[37] Including this, the mean real total income of the thirty-four strictly defined agricultural-worker families rose at an average annual rate of 1.2 percent from 1934 to 1957. It is no vast improvement, but it is something. The levels reached in 1957 were not good, but they were still better than twenty-three years before.[38] These computations show that even those who were the most miserable as the revolution came to power were less miserable than they had been. Inequality was the rule in Cuba;

Table 3.9   Wages for all workers, 1945–1958

Year	Wages as % of domestic national income	Index of all real wages, unadjusted $(1950 = 100^a)$	Index of all real wages, adjusted $(1950 = 100^a)$
1945	55.3	—	—
1946	58.2	—	—
1947	54.9	—	—
1948	59.2	—	—
1949	61.4	86	—
1950	63.1	100	100
1951	62.9	104	101
1952	67.7	115	109
1953	66.9	102	99
1954	65.9	108	104
1955	64.5	113	108
1956	62.8	125	116
1957	61.1	129	121
1958	62.3	—	115

Sources: Computed from *Memoria, 1951–1952,* p. 217; *Memoria, 1954–1955,* p. 273; *Memoria, 1957–1958,* p. 134; *Memoria, 1958–1959,* pp. 95–96.

a. Wages have been deflated into June 1937 Cuban national retail food prices (in pesos); the difference between adjusted and unadjusted wages results from a periodic statistical adjustment made by the National Bank of Cuba in 1959. Both values are given so as not to rely exclusively on post-1959 statistics for the period before 1959.

some benefited from it; others did not. But even those at the bottom of the social structure had benefited from this period of relative prosperity to some extent.

That there was an improvement can be shown from physical anthropological surveys made of Cuban children, adolescents, and adults. Data from six of these surveys made between 1900 and 1964 concerning changes in the height of Cubans (appendix B) show the height of the average Cuban increasing considerably in the course of the twentieth century; this finding is attributed to an improved standard of living in the absence of perceptible changes in the composition of the population. The findings from the surveys appear to be consistent and reliable over time. Although the improvement in living standards benefited all three racial categories surveyed, both sexes, and all age groups tested, it was shared unequally; whites profited the most, and, as a result, the gap in life chances between whites and blacks widened considerably. The improvement in living standards occurred under both the first and the second twentieth-century political systems, although the beneficiaries may have differed in these two periods). The data do not yet show any appreciable difference attributable to the impact of the revolution.

Mortality rate is another yardstick for standard of living. The general-mortality rate in Cuba dropped from 15.18 per 1,000 inhabitants in 1906 to 12.24 in 1914 and 11.05 in 1932. It fell to 8.14 in 1946 and 6.38 in 1952. A possibly optimistic estimate put it at 4.93 in 1958. The infant-mortality rate fell from 58.5 infant deaths (before the age of one year) per 1,000 live births in 1926 to 51.5 in 1930, 40.5 in 1949, and 37.6 in 1953. A possibly optimistic estimate put it at 33.7 in 1958. Another source indicates that infant mortality may have risen to 76 during the 1930s but that it fell to the cited levels in the 1950s.[39] Over all, then, general- and infant-mortality rates declined substantially in prerevolutionary Cuba. There is perhaps no better measure for an improvement in the standard of living. These indicators lend greater credence, also, to the findings based on economic data that the conditions of living for the average Cuban had improved over time.

Government Authority

After the fall of President Machado and for the next decade and a half, the social and economic structures basic to the Cuban political system did not change a great deal. The level of social mobilization was high but stagnant. The United States retreated from empire building, a change to which Cuba's client politicians had a difficult time adapting. The retrenchment of foreign trade and investment contributed to economic stagnation. The old political system had been destroyed by Machado. The story of the period from 1933 to 1937 is one of virtually unremitting social and political warfare, but the opponents were fighting over a much shrunken store of goods. The levels of social, economic, and political pluralization were also high, and there were many participants and claims on the limited national resources. How could government establish its authority?

Governments succeeded each other upon the fall of President Machado in such rapid succession that no leader had time to consolidate his rule. Both General Alberto Herrera and Secretary of State Carlos Manuel de Céspedes, upon assuming presidential power, one for a day, the other for a few weeks, were weakened by being too closely associated with the *ancien régime* and the United States. The sixty-two-year-old Céspedes, like Estrada Palma, was almost a foreigner in his own country. Born in New York and educated in the United States and Europe, he had, as ambassador, also lived in the United States from 1914 to 1922, was subsequently Machado's minister to France, and then served as ambassador to Mexico until he resigned in protest. In August 1933, he was out of step with the mood of the revolution. On September 4, 1933, the sergeants and corporals of the armed forces, led by

Sergeant-Stenographer Fulgencio Batista, staged a military coup against the Céspedes government and their own military officers. After a brief attempt at collective rule, Ramón Grau was named President.

The new government, never recognized by the United States because it was too "radical," drew most of its support from the University of Havana's faculty and students and from the new military leadership. The Grau administration attempted to make significant alterations in portions of the Cuban social, economic, and political structure through legislation. In modified form, many of its legislative efforts shaped the second Cuban political system. The Grau government was buffeted by opposition from the left and the right, from Communists and from antirevolutionaries, and especially from the United States. The armed forces, led by a newly promoted Colonel Batista, ousted the Grau government in January 1934.

During the Grau period three men had emerged as potential leaders. Forty-six-year-old Grau himself, with his gentle and mild appearance, inspired loyalty and friendship. Although he seemed somewhat weak and indecisive, he could in fact be ruthless; he also had no clear political convictions and became increasingly opportunistic. He had been a well-known physician and university professor prior to becoming President. Grau could not compete in popularity with his minister of the interior, a twenty-seven-year-old named Antonio Guiteras. The more charismatic Guiteras was laconic, tough, idealistic, and incorruptible, fervently radical, and nationalistic; he stayed in power as Grau's deputy and competitor only until that government was overthrown in January of 1934. But he was removed from competition when he was killed in the spring of 1935, after just over a year in opposition. The third new leader was Sergeant-Stenographer Fulgencio Batista, whose popular appeal was not to develop until later. In the early fall of 1933, Batista concentrated on getting control over the armed forces and repressing insurrections against the new order.[40]

Aside from Guiteras's efforts at establishing authority based on popular appeal, the path chosen to establish legitimacy in the 1930s was legal and rational. The new order would seek to earn the right to rule because it worked, because it changed the structures of society to bring prosperity and justice to the people and dignity and honor to the country. Grau moved to consolidate his shaky rule in September 1933 by unilaterally declaring the Platt Amendment abolished (although United States consent was in fact required) and establishing the eight-hour day and compulsory organization of all professionals. On October 2, as the troops led by Batista were attacking their former officers, gathered in the National Hotel to resist and, they hoped, overthrow the new order, Grau established the Department of Labor. Victory over the officers was celebrated by granting legal and financial autonomy to the University of Havana—still Grau's main source of support. On November 7, 1933, one day before the terrorist ABC organization launched one of the most violent revolts against the government, Grau recognized labor's right to organize. On the very day of the revolt, Grau compelled all enterprises to employ no less than 50 percent Cubans and to devote no less than 50 percent of all salaries and wages to paying Cubans.[41] In early December, as United States Ambassador Welles made his last round of efforts to get Grau out of the presidency, Grau reduced the rates of the U.S.-owned electric company by 45 percent. In early January, as the university's student directorate shifted its support from Grau to Guiteras and Batista prepared to force Grau out of office, the President expropriated the land of former members of the Machado government as a first step toward land reform; he seized the Cuban Electric Company on January 14. On the following day, he was overthrown. Performance had not been enough to establish legitimacy in the absence of power, and power had flowed out of Grau's hands.

In January 1934, Carlos Hevia and Manuel Márquez Sterling served as President for only a few hours each. They were replaced by Carlos Mendieta, who was President for almost two years. A former Liberal vice-presidential candidate in 1916 and an unsuccessful contender for the Liberal presidential nomination in 1924, the sixty-one-year-old Mendieta had bolted the Liberal party as Machado's autocracy increased and had formed the Nationalist Union party. In 1931, along with former Conservative President Menocal, Mendieta landed in Cuba in an unsuccessful effort to overthrow Machado. Mendieta, too, tried to link legitimacy to performance. He began by proclaiming new constitutional statutes, restraining brutality against prisoners, granting political amnesty, and requiring a cooling-off period before strikes. Yet strikes almost engulfed his government during January and February of 1934, and he had to seek the support of an increasingly brutal military establishment. In March 1934 the Communist party called for a general strike; it was widely supported but was repressed violently under the National Defense Act. In June 1934, as terrorism increased, the Mendieta government issued a tough law of social defense and instituted other Draconian measures; the United States and Cuba agreed to abolish the Platt Amendment. Another general strike was called in March 1935 just a year after the first. Led primarily by the supporters of Grau and Guiteras, with uncertain and delayed Communist collaboration, again it was crushed when Mendieta declared a state of siege and unleashed the military without restraint.

The Mendieta government is judged by most Cuban historians as representing a return to conservatism and the end of reform.[42] It is difficult to make a case that Mendieta's government was revolutionary, although paradoxically, it was precisely that. The Mendieta government was perceived to be conservative; it received upper-class, military, and United States ambassadorial support precisely because of it. Yet the link between legitimacy and performance was not broken; Mendieta blessed with his conservative mantle those things that Grau and Guiteras had introduced under the banner of revolution. A great many of the goals and hopes of the fall of 1933 became accepted as law because the Mendieta government, on behalf of its supporters, legitimized them; they hoped, in return, that their rule would be legitimized by mass support. The Platt Amendment had been abolished; women were given the vote; procedures were written into law for "intervention," that is, taking over private enterprises in the course of a labor dispute to force what was usually a prolabor settlement; collective labor contracts were legislated, social security was expanded; minimum-wage and eight-hour-day laws were confirmed along with paid vacations; the dismissal of workers without cause was declared illegal.[43] The Mendieta government found legitimacy elusive, but its work was important in laying the foundations for the Cuban political system that gained in legitimacy by the late 1930s. The avalanche of legislation in 1934–35, institutionalizing many of the revolutionary aspirations of 1933, served the republic under subsequent Presidents to gain and keep the loyalty of those who so vigorously and bloodily battled Mendieta.

The problem of legitimacy in the 1930s was further complicated by the administration's reliance on military repression to remain in office. This dependence did not make the commander-in-chief of the army, Colonel Batista, any more popular than the President who called out the troops, but it made him indispensable. The result was the gradual reestablishment of two levels of power: before 1933, one source of power had been in Havana and the other in Washington; after 1933, both were in Havana, one in the Presidential palace, and the other in the military barracks, although both operated within the scope of United States hegemony. The duality of power was not resolved until Batista had been elected President in 1940 and had suppressed the attempted military coup in 1941.

The duality of power was illustrated most clearly by the impeachment of President Miguel Mariano Gómez in 1936. Gómez sought to reestablish civilian control over areas of government that had passed into military hands; at the same time Batista was becoming aware that repression by itself would never establish legitimate government in Cuba. The two met head on when, from the military barracks, Batista launched a program of rural education and public health, which he could not finance out of the ordinary military budget. He sought a nine-cent tax per bag of sugar to pay for the program, whereupon Gómez announced he would veto such a tax, if Congress approved it, because it would institutionalize military control over areas that should be civilian. A furious Batista, while pledging to United States ambassador Caffery that only constitutional procedures would be used, cajoled, bribed, and intimidated the members of Congress into approving his tax. The President vetoed it; he was then impeached by the House and convicted by the Senate for coercing the Congress through the exercise of a constitutional procedure. Vice President

Federico Laredo Brú became President; during the course of his presidency, the problems caused by dual power and weak authority came no closer to resolution.[44]

The Weight of Government

Government after the 1930s staked its fortunes on performance through legislation, and Cuba witnessed an explosion of government rule making from 1933 to 1958. In both of Cuba's two "unstable" periods (1933–1936 and 1952–1954), when a government was in power without the benefit of election and legitimation could come only through performance, the amount of rule-making activity was extraordinary. The record for rule making belongs to Cuba's least stable and most revolutionary administration—Grau's in the fall of 1933. During periods when Presidents came to power through constitutional, though occasionally dubious, means (as in 1954 when Batista was elected without opposition), the more normal patterns of rule-making activity returned, ranging from a low under Prío to a high under the first Batista administration. The overall differences are small, however, especially compared to the years before 1933; since that time government in Cuba has been two to three times more active than the Machado government and about five times more active, on the average, than the governments between 1902 and 1924. Grau's government intervened far more extensively than its predecessors. Although the fever pitch of activity of the 1933–1936 period was not sustained, the level remained very high (see table 3.10).

The rule making was also more differentiated, especially within the executive branch. Table 3.10 shows a nearly secular increase in cabinet rule making. Much of the legislation of the 1930s gave government departments extensive power requiring still more rule making by these departments, which led to differentiation of function within an increasingly complex executive branch. The peak of cabinet rule making was reached during the second Grau administration, when it exceeded presidential rule making (as it would in the last Batista administration as well. The cabinet therefore contributed to the increase in regulations made by the executive branch and to far greater complexity and internal differentiation of government.

The Cuban Congress had not been very active before 1933 (see tables 2.7 and 2.8), nor did it, unlike the executive, rise to the demands of the modernization of government (tables 3.10 and 3.11). The entire difference in the rule-making output of Cuban governments in the periods before and after 1933 resulted from an expansion of purely executive activity. The congressional low in lawmaking was reached between 1944 and 1948 under President Grau. In fact, from 1940 to 1958, Congress was *less* active than it had been between 1902 and 1933. It was active only briefly—from 1936 to 1940—in setting up the basic structures of the new post-1933 political system. The new Constitu-

Table 3.10 Government rule-making output, 1933–1958

Administration	Congressional laws/ 100 days	Presidential decrees/100 days	Cabinet decrees/ 100 days	Total rules/ 100 days
Unstable governments	2.0	151.5	35.1	188.6
Herrera-Céspedes-Pentarchy, 1933[a]	0	82.8	2.9	85.7
Grau, 1933–1934	0	230.2	10.8	241.0
Mendieta, 1934–1935	0	137.8	28.2	166.0
Barnet, 1935–1936	0	176.1	54.0	230.1
Gómez, 1936	11.5	139.3	61.4	212.2
Laredo Brú, 1936–1940	12.9	77.6	58.0	148.5
Batista, 1940–1944	2.9	96.9	73.9	173.7
Grau, 1944–1948	2.1	58.4	80.2	140.7
Prío, 1948–1952	5.0	65.0	63.5	133.5
Batista governments	2.7	110.4	77.1	190.2
Batista-Morales provisional, 1952–1954	0	162.8	73.3	236.1
Batista, 1954–1958	4.7	70.2	80.0	154.9

Sources: Compiled, coded, and computed from Milo A. Borges, *Compilación ordenada y completa de la legislación cubana de 1899 a 1950,* 2nd ed. (Havana: Editorial Lex, 1952), vols. 1 and 2; Mariano Sánchez Roca, *Compilación ordenada y completa de la legislación cubana de 1951 a 1958* (Havana: Editorial Lex, 1960), vol. 4.

a. The Pentarchy was a collective executive that replaced the presidency between September 4 and September 9, 1933.

tion, approved in 1940, called for a great deal of implementing legislation. Yet the burst of legislative activity responded to politics more than to law; Congress was active in the late 1930s because the unstable political conditions required activity, but it was relatively inactive after 1940 when only the Constitution required it. The executive branch stepped in with decrees that had the force of law, "pending Congressional action," which almost never came.

The inability of the Congress to adapt to the needs of modern government had several consequences. There was virtually no check on the exercise of executive power. The pre-1933 Congresses had a poor record of approving the budget law; from 1937 to 1949 they did not approve a single one. The 1937 budget law was simply extended by executive decree from year to year, with appropriate adjustments for raising additional revenue and incurring additional expenditures, "pending congressional action." President Prío successfully obtained congressional approval of the 1949–50 and 1951–52 budgets, but not that of 1950–51. The result was unsupervised executive activity, facilitating corruption and the abuse of power, activities in which individual Congressmen sometimes partook.[45] The rise in executive power over the

Table 3.11 Ratio of executive and presidential decrees to legislation passed by Congress, 1936–1958 (elected Presidents only)

Administration	Executive decrees: laws[a]	Presidential decrees: laws
Gómez, 1936	17.5	12.1
Laredo Brú, 1936–1940	10.5	6.0
Batista, 1940–1944	58.1	33.4
Grau, 1944–1948	65.3	27.8
Prío, 1948–1952	25.9	13.0
Batista, 1954–1958	32.0	14.9

Sources: Compiled, coded, and computed from Borges, *Compilación*, vols. 1 and 2; Sánchez Roca, *Compilación*, vol. 4.

a. Executive decrees include presidential and cabinet decrees.

Congress is clearly shown by the data in table 3.11; all ratios exceed those for the pre-1933 period, shown in table 2.8.

The inability of the Congress to fulfill its constitutional obligations weakened the legal-rational legitimacy of the political system, which was based upon results. The real standard of living in Cuba rose during this period, and the political system was working to the material advantage of its members. But, in the absence of legislation implementing the Constitution, a claimant to political power who argued that the system could be made to work even more effectively and justly would easily have been able to get a hearing. This cloud of constitutional quasi-legitimacy was never dispelled.

The inaction of Congress also made a mockery of legitimate political democracy. The political system was supposed to rest on democratic principles, but an unchecked executive, an unenforced Constitution, and a government without budgets did not inspire confidence in its belief in democracy. The differences among Cuba's governments during the period were blurred. It is usually claimed that the second Grau and the Prío administrations were the most democratic and that government under Batista and his "puppets" was less so. Yet Congress was most active under Batista's puppet Presidents, modestly active under Prío and during the second Batista administrations, and least active under Grau and during the first Batista administrations. Political democracy, however, depends on more than the actions of a congress. Civil liberties, for example, were more apt to be honored under Grau and Prío than under Batista; more people had a hand in policy making, political recruitment was more open, and political groups had greater autonomy under Grau and Prío.[46] But the formal procedures of democracy are also important for legitimation, and these were lacking.[47] This blurring of the differences among regimes further undermined their legitimacy, discredited political democracy, and facilitated the institutionalization of a more revolutionary brand of politics after 1959. Revolutionary leaders argued not only that the pre-Batista period of apparent democracy was no paradise but also that there had been no real difference among governments, whether democratic or dictatorial, before 1959.

In fact government had shown a slight tendency to increase its weight during these years (see table 3.12). But levels of government expenditure remained below those of the Machado government (see table 2.9) and about

Table 3.12   Estimated government expenditures as a percentage of estimated national and domestic incomes, 1940–1957

Year	Government expenditures (% of national income)	Government expenditures (% of domestic income)
1940	18	—
1941	11	—
1942	14	—
1943	12	—
1944	10	—
1945	13	—
1946	13	—
1947	12	—
1948	18	—
1949	15	10.2
1950	16	10.6
1951	16	10.3
1952	16	11.8
1953	16	13.3
1954	18	13.1
1955	17	12.3
1956	17	13.7
1957	16	12.4

Sources: Computed from CERP, *Study*, pp. 451, 455; *Memoria, 1957–1958*, p. 135. Because Cuba did not have a national budget for most of these years and because of extensive corruption, these statistics are at best reasonable approximations of the weight of government on the economy. Congress took no action to audit the final accounts for any fiscal year. The Tribunal de Cuentas, the auditing agency required by the Constitution, was not established until late 1950. There were also many extrabudgetary governmental activities, some connected with economic development and others, such as the lottery, with corruption. For a discussion of these problems, see Germán Wolter del Río, "La hacienda de la república independiente," in *Historia de la nación cubana*, ed. Ramiro Guerra y Sánchez, José M. Pérez Cabrera, Juan J. Remos, and Emeterio S. Santeovenia (Havana: Editorial Historia de la Nación Cubana, 1951), 9:116, 136, 139; Batista, *Piedras,* p. 397; International Bank for Reconstruction and Development, *Report on Cuba* (Washington, D.C., 1951), pp. 654–663.

equal to levels in the pre-Machado period. In the long run, no strong case can be made that the weight of the Cuban government in the economy increased significantly. Although government rule making increased, government expenditures did not increase as a proportion of the economy. Cuba acquired a regulative, not an entrepreneurial, state. Thus whatever increase there was in government power in the middle of the century took the form of an increase in government regulation, not an increase in its weight in the economy. It intervened in the economy through laws and decrees but did not become a part of it. Modern (post-1933) government in Cuba regulated private enterprise but did not replace it; they did not compete. Government supplied few services to the private sector; state takeover of economic enterprises was rare except on a temporary basis.

The Purposes of Government

Cuban politicians in the 1930s had to deal with class warfare in the form of virtually incessant strikes and repeated conflicts between sugar growers (*colonos*) and sugar-mill owners (*hacendados*). Earlier conflicts could be contained because economic growth had been steady. But when growth ceased, not to be resumed until the late 1940s, a political system had to be devised to manage conflict and to end violence. Pluralization and social mobilization had to stop; someone would have to lose, and the loser would also have to be controlled. It was up to Fulgencio Batista to devise such a system and make it work until the legitimating power of elections and economic growth was again available.

The essence of this new political system was governmental regulation, particularly of the sugar industry and organized labor—the former as the key to economic order and the latter to political order. Corruption had been common as an aid to establishing order in the government of both areas. From 1933 through the late 1940s, Cuban governments did not have policies that would encourage economic growth; government regulations were designed for a no-growth system. Difficult though the task of government was at that time, Batista succeeded. His political tragedy was that his actions destroyed his government in the 1950s, even with the advantage of far more auspicious economic conditions than those of the 1930s. He throve in difficult times, but not in prosperous ones.

Regulation of the Sugar Industry and of Organized Labor

Sugar was the basis of the Cuban economy and thus of the politics of regulation and distribution as well. Regulation of the sugar economy began under Machado in the late 1920s when international sugar prices fell and Cuban production yielded a surplus. Restrictions were placed on the planting, harvesting, and milling of sugar; these measures were not applied systematically, however, nor could they offset the effects of the worldwide depression. A fresh start was made in Washington in 1934 with the Jones-Costigan Sugar Act, which established sugar quotas in the United States market at prices that were normally kept higher and more stable than those in the international market. The short-term result rescued Cuba from economic catastrophe (see table 3.7). The Cuban extension of the quota system was decisive, beginning with the Sugar Stabilization Decree of January 1936. The crowning piece of legislation—and, consequently, the cornerstone of the Cuban political system until 1959—was the Sugar Coordination Act of 1937.[48]

The provisions of the Sugar Coordination Act depended on the continued legal restriction of sugar production, a fiction that was upheld by the Supreme Court even when harvests were not, in fact, restricted (as in 1942, 1944–1952, and 1957) in order to retain the protections of the act. The act had five principal features. First, it guaranteed to every colono registered as such in 1937 the right to sell 30,000 *arrobas* of sugar cane to a designated sugar mill (one arroba = 11.5 kilograms). In return, the farmer agreed to limit production to what the government allowed. This "grinding factor" could be willed to one's heirs but could not be renounced or sold; to make room for the small growers, the larger sugar plantations and the sugar mills that owned cane fields ("administration cane") were penalized. In addition, the act regulated minimum payments by the mill to the grower on the basis of the average sugar-cane yield. It did not establish a ceiling for these payments nor void any contract providing for higher payments, but it did provide a floor for the income of all growers in the island and raised the income of growers in the two easternmost provinces, who had been getting less than this minimum.[49] The act also extended the moratorium on repayment of debts granted to growers during the depression. Land rents for sugar lands were fixed at 5 percent of the mill's average sugar yield for the entire crop; rents would rise or fall as the price of sugar rose or fell, which happened frequently and significantly, or as the general average sugar yield rose or fell, which happened less frequently and with less effect.[50]

The act established the right of permanent occupancy. Every renter, subrenter, or sharecropper with a contract in 1937 to engage in sugar cultivation was guaranteed the right of permanent occupancy of the lands he worked so long as the grinding factor with the sugar mill was met (guaranteeing the mill a stable supply of cane) and rent was paid. If he complied, he could not be evicted. This right of permanent occupancy belonged to the farmer; it did not depend on the exclusive production of sugar. Instead, the act stipulated that it covered all land contracted for, including land devoted to other crops or buildings. Rents on land not devoted to sugar were to be fixed by private contract, however, and were not regulated by the act. A final provision of the act linked wages paid to labor to the current average price of sugar.

The regulation of the sugar industry by the formulae in the act had the unintended effect of institutionalizing economic inefficiency. Because payments to sugar growers were based on the mill's average yield for the entire crop, rather than on the yield of the sugar cane provided by each grower, there was no incentive for the grower to improve his cane yield. Indeed, the act provided that the percentage payment to the grower would decline as the cane yield increased. This provision was abandoned in the 1949–50 harvest and replaced by a uniform payment independent of yield.

The Sugar Stabilization Institute, established in 1931, was in charge of enforcing sugar regulations. It comprised five sugar-mill owners and two growers appointed by the President from lists submitted for his consideration. The Sugar Stabilization Decree of 1936 expanded its membership to twelve mill owners (six from U.S.-owned sugar mills), six growers, and one government delegate. After 1937, the government appointed three members (a grower, a mill owner, and the secretary-general of the Sugar Worker's Union). The institute was also charged with conducting the international relations of the sugar industry, severing them from official government agencies including the foreign ministry and foreign service; through that authority, it institutionalized access to political power for sugar-mill owners and growers that amounted to a legal and legitimate sugar cartel. A part of government had been put into private hands, and private interests actually conducted government policy in this area. This situation, better than any other, symbolized the marked change in the governance of Cuba. Private organizations came to control government agencies in charge of the country's domestic and international sugar policies.

The opening date for the harvest was set by decree. The institute allocated the crop to various markets, with the sugar output of each mill divided in the same proportion as the total crop. It also negotiated all international contracts; because most sugar was exported, this gave it effective marketing control. When the crop was restricted, the institute allocated production quotas for each mill and crop quotas for each grower (small growers were always guaranteed their minimum grinding factor).

Subsequent legislation, passed in response to rural conflicts, extended and intensified political regulation of the sugar economy. Conflicts occurred between mill owners and growers and between them and the workers. The President of the republic often had to intervene to defend the sugar workers against the mill owners and the growers, whose interests the Sugar Stabilization Institute usually represented. Cuban Presidents thus became brokers between a branch of the government controlled by management and the demands of workers. This role increased the President's discretionary power in sugar policy and restored to the government some of the autonomy that the Sugar Coordination Act had handed over to private enterprise.

The brokerage role was effectively exercised by all Cuban Presidents. When it became clear, for example, that the price of sugar for the 1948 harvest would fall, sugar wages were also scheduled to fall in accordance with the provisions of the Sugar Coordination Act. Because of economic recovery and the effects of World War II, however, they had been rising up to then, so President Grau simply froze sugar wages at the 1947 levels—the highest ever attained—effectively ending the flexible wage system established in the act.[51] Wages would not fall. At the end of 1955, sugar workers expected a small bonus according to the normal computations of sugar wages when prices rose. The Sugar Stabilization Institute, however, artificially depressed the price of sugar reserve stocks to save the mill owners and growers from having to pay the bonus. The sugar workers struck. Within four days, President Batista had intervened and granted all of labor's requests by decree.[52] In general, then, the Sugar Coordination Act did not protect the interests of labor, but through ad hoc measures, the President was able to counteract its antilabor effects, and, precisely because the measures were ad hoc, the President gained significant discretionary power. Although cartelization was most obvious in the sugar industry, it extended with local variations throughout the economy. Stabilization policies and institutions were established for all major commodities; regulation and controlled distribution became the basis for the relationship between the government and the economy.

Government regulation also affected labor, beginning with a marked increase after 1933 in legislation and decrees regulating labor (see tables 2.11 and 3.13). In less than two years in office, the Mendieta government produced more labor laws and decrees than all the pre-1933 administrations combined. Since Laredo Brú's accession to the presidency in late 1936, no administration failed to exceed the combined pre-1933 total. In addition, labor-related laws and decrees accounted for a larger proportion of the total number of regulations after 1933 than before—three to four times as much as the pre-1933 average. The relative stability of labor-related laws and decrees at about one-sixth of all rule making for the presidencies of Grau, Prío, and Batista suggests that this was standard for modern Cuban government.

All labor-related rule making increased, but the relative importance of ports legislation declined considerably compared with the earlier period (table 3.13). General labor laws and decrees continued to account for just over half of the total. The largest increase was in wage- and salary-related regulation. Under President Grau, in 1944–1948, laws and decrees pertaining to wages and salaries accounted for 9.5 percent of the total made by the President, the Congress, and the cabinet on all subjects—the highest proportion ever. General legislation controlled as well as benefited labor; wage and salary legislation worked to benefit it. Why, then, was there such a sharp rise in this category? There were several reasons.

First, labor challenged the very survival of the political system in the 1930s. All governments, beginning with Batista's puppet Presidents, had to control the militant labor force. The labor legislation was intended, in part, to ac-

Table 3.13 Labor-related rule making by the Cuban government, 1933–1958[a]

Administration	General rules[b]	Rules regulating salaries and wages	Rules regulating port labor	Total labor-related rules	% of total rule making
Unstable governments	265	53	39	357	15.3
Herrera-Céspedes-Pentarchy, 1933	0	0	0	0	0
Grau, 1933–1934	19	1	2	22	7.0
Mendieta, 1934–1935	141	29	25	195	16.8
Barnet, 1935–1936	52	14	7	73	19.9
Gómez, 1936	53	9	5	67	14.4
Laredo Brú, 1936–1940	114	48	36	198	9.6
Batista, 1940–1944	127	138	66	331	13.0
Grau, 1944–1948	114	196	69	379	18.4
Prío, 1948–1952	121	127	31	279	16.7
Batista governments	424	141	69	634	13.3
Batista-Morales provisional, 1952–1954	155	64	28	247	9.6
Batista, 1954–1958	269	77	41	387	17.7
Total	1,165	703	310	2,178	—
% of total rule making	54	32	14	100	—

Sources: Computed from Borges, *Compilación*, 3:709–750; Sánchez Roca, *Compilación*, 4:1262–1278, 1288.

a. Includes executive decrees and laws passed by Congress; all rule making dealing with social security is excluded.

b. Includes those dealing with work-related accidents, collective contracts, the length of the workday, strikes, protection of women at work, overtime work, vacations, dismissal of workers, and unionization and all other labor legislation except that which covered salaries and wages, ports, and social security. Special care has been taken to avoid counting the same item twice.

complish this goal. Second, article 61 of the Constitution of 1940 stipulated that minimum wages would be established by commissions made up of public and private members for each economic sector and region of the country. In 1941 President Batista decreed a universal wage increase of between 10 and 20 percent, except for sugar and government workers, the scale depending only on the worker's previous salary. No distinctions were made among economic sectors or regions. He also decreed increases of 15 to 25 percent in sugar workers' wages, without distinguishing among regions. Sugar workers received a further wage increase in 1942. In 1944, Batista declared another general salary increase, with a separate one for sugar workers.

In 1945 the Supreme Court declared unconstitutional all general wage and salary increases that did not conform to article 61 of the Constitution. President Grau accordingly revoked the Batista decrees that had been declared unconstitutional. At the same time, however, he froze wages at the level they had reached prior to the Supreme Court's decision but after the implementation of the Batista decrees.[53] Thus he complied in form but not in substance with the Court's ruling. Batista's wage increases were not rolled back, but the Court was successful in seeing that subsequent increases would be more closely tailored to specific economic sectors and regions.

By applying the Constitution literally, the Court introduced even greater particularism into Cuban politics. Presidents would bargain separately regarding wage increases with each separate sector's labor federation, and they could grant increases in one region but not in another. The possibilities for trading benefits for political support were multiplied many times by the Supreme Court decision, since the President could now benefit his allies without having at the same time to reward his enemies. Grau learned this lesson well, for he granted more salary increases than any other Cuban President. Particularism also extended to some general legislation. President Grau reduced the work day during the summer months in 1947. Batista, too, took advantage of it, issuing sixty separate decrees in 1956 (half of the 1956 total of labor-related rule making) regulating the summer work day for various economic sectors and municipalities.[54]

After the 1933 revolutions, Cuban governments sought to ensure job security for workers, but it took until 1938 for procedures for dismissal finally to be formulated. According to a 1938 decree, no employee or worker could be dismissed except on proof of proper cause duly established in administrative proceedings; the worker had the right of appeal to the courts. While the list of causes for dismissal was reasonable, in practice it became extremely difficult to dismiss a worker for any reason at all.[55] Throughout the 1940s, dismissal disputes that reached the Supreme Court were considerably more likely to be settled in favor of the worker. A count of cases cited in Supreme Court Justice Carlos M. Piedra's work on Supreme Court dismissals shows that workers won eighty-seven cases and management forty-nine from 1939 to 1945. A coding of similar Supreme Court cases cited in the work of Leopoldo Horrego Estuch on social legislation shows that workers won forty-two cases and management thirty from 1938 to 1948.[56] The findings for 1949 are similar.[57]

The situation changed dramatically in the 1950s, however, when, during the late Prío administration, the Court began to turn against workers by a ratio of two to one, and by an even greater ratio under Batista. The ratio was four to one against the workers in 1953, 1954, 1957, and 1958; it was three to one against them in 1952, and even higher in 1955. Only in 1956 was the ratio as low as that of the Prío administration.[58] The legislation had not changed, but interpretations of it had.

The main reason behind this change was a campaign launched in the early 1950s by all managerial organizations against the dismissal policy itself. Cuban and United States business argued strongly in favor of compensated dismissal, while the Cuban Labor Confederation (CTC), under Secretary-General Eusebio Mujal, fought just as strongly against any formal weakening of the law.[59] The result was a compromise. Formal protection for workers against dismissals did not change, but the courts were encouraged to make dismissals easier. Batista accepted management's argument that new investment—including new private foreign investment—was unlikely to come to Cuba unless the laws were implemented more flexibly. Compensated dismissal was made possible, and in practice it was frequently used.

Another policy favoring business under the Batista government was its virtual cessation of "interventions" in private enterprise in order to force management to settle disputes on labor's terms. In contrast, there had been eleven interventions between 1934 and 1944 and ninety under Grau and Prío, from 1945 to 1952. The Batista government's last major intervention—in the U.S.-owned Cuban Electric Company—was undertaken to settle a political dispute rather than to favor labor.[60]

Between 1933 and 1958, government did not take over any large segments of the economy, but it did increase its regulatory and distributive activity enormously. The regulatory system in the sugar industry extended from planting through international marketing. Because sugar was at the heart of the economy, this system ended up regulating much of Cuban economic life. As discussed earlier, sugar policy was captured by sugar-mill owners and sugar farmers through a government agency. Virtually all economic sectors were similarly regulated by private interest groups. Labor legislation served both to benefit and to control workers and enhanced the President's role as a broker mediating between management and labor. Protective legislation on job security decreased, along with the number of interventions, and labor's relative wage position deteriorated under Batista's second administration.

These trends go far to explain patterns in private foreign investment. Regulation accelerated the trend toward foreign-interest divestment, and it discouraged new investment. The policy of labor protection and high wages throughout the 1940s discouraged private foreign investment; when policies were less clearly prolabor and wages were rising less rapidly during Batista's second administration, it increased again, and consequently the economy in the late 1940s and the 1950s began again to grow. Labor's share fell, increasing profits, but without leading to a decline in labor's real wages. No one lost. It was not surprising, then, that Cuban labor on the whole supported Batista until the very end.

Economic Growth

For the most part, governments under the second twentieth-century political system in Cuba did not have policies for economic growth beyond regulation and distribution. Writing in 1950 about the sugar legislation, the prolabor regulation of wage scales and employment practices, and the moratoria on debt repayment, Henry Wallich observed that "the rationale of all of these actions had been distribution, not production."[61] The Sugar Coordination Act of 1937 institutionalized economic inefficiency. The 1950 World Bank Mission lamented that "taxes have been imposed with little or no regard to their economic or social effects, or to the posssibility of effective enforcement."[62] A study of the progressive individual income tax (first approved in 1931 but not even modestly enforced until after 1942) noted widespread and repeated tax evasion regardless of the administration in power; the tax law, too, was approved without regard to economic or financial impact and in addition operated throughout most of its history in the absence of a government budget.[63] Although sugar was the mainstay of the economic and political systems, Cuba relied almost entirely on other countries for the development of new varieties of sugar cane. Neither the government, nor the mill owners, nor the growers had established an effective agricultural-research program to adapt improved cane varieties to Cuban conditions. The Sugar Cane Experimental Station was grossly inadequate. Research on sugar cane by-products, though much discussed, had not progressed much through the 1940s except insofar as it concerned using cane in the production of alcohol.[64]

Labor strongly opposed mechanization, fearing it would result in unemployment. One of the more notable battles was over the bulk loading and shipping of sugar, which labor long resisted because it would eliminate jobs. The 1955 agreement provided that sugar must move in bags from the mill to the ship's hatch, where the bags would be opened and emptied. Enterprises could still save on labor outside Cuba, but not within it.[65] Labor's fear of unemployment was well justified.

Seasonal unemployment rates in Cuba remained steady for a decade and a half despite economic growth, which proved too capital-intensive to reduce unemployment substantially. Variations in unemployment rates occurred only from season to season within any given year; they were relatively constant from year to year for the same season. Census data from 1943 and 1953 and a 1956–57 employment survey show the following percentages of the labor force unemployed:

July–September 1943	21.1
August–October 1956	20.7
January–March 1953	8.4
February–April 1957	9.1

The overall annual rate of unemployment for 1956–57 was 16.4 percent. The 1953 census also found 12.9 percent "underemployed" from January through March 1953, and the survey found 13.8 underemployed in 1956–57. The 1943 census was taken in the "dead season," thus overestimating unemployment; the 1953 census was taken in mid-harvest, thus underestimating it. (The 1943 census is also flawed because over one-fifth of the respondents did not report their employment status.)[66] Both real national income and real per capita income were higher in 1956 than they had been in 1943, in spite of steady unemployment rates, and higher in 1957 than in 1953. Real wages were also higher, although labor's share of domestic national income had declined (see tables 3.8 and 3.9)—non-agricultural wages were twice as high in 1956 as in 1943.

Given these improvements one would expect a sharper decline in unemployment than actually occurred, especially since the general tendency of wages was upward even with seasonal variations in wage patterns; in other words, high unemployment and underemployment did not exercise a downward pressure on wages. Organized labor was strong enough to insulate the employed from the unemployed, which explains both the high premium on remaining employed and labor's commitment to a strong government policy against easy dismissals of workers. This fact also qualifies conclusions about an improvement in the real standard of living—although those improvements were not negated, they only benefited specific organized groups and did not significantly affect the misery of the impoverished core that still persisted in the late 1950s.[67]

Government policies were ineffective in increasing employment enough to make a real difference; this failure reinforced the attitudes among workers that inhibited the technical improvements essential to economic growth. In Lloyd Free's survey of urban Cuba in the spring of 1960, 23 percent of the respondents cited continued employment as their most important hope for their future, and 42 percent cited improvement in their standard of living; 22 percent cited unemployment as the most important fear and 19 percent, an inadequate standard of living. In a 1958 survey of rural workers—the group most vulnerable to seasonal employment variations—73 percent of the respondents said that the factor most crucial to their well-being was employment, and 69 percent looked to the government as the most likely source of relief.[68]

The government's indifference toward growth policies changed by the late 1940s, when the first period of noticeable growth since the 1920s began. Under President Prío, a budget law was finally approved by the Congress. The National Bank of Cuba, a general accounting office (Tribunal de Cuentas), and a government bank to increase lending for agricultural and industrial development were established. The Monetary Stabilization Fund was restructured in 1948. The institutionalization of economic growth continued under President Batista with the creation of a government export bank, a government institution to expand public works, another to stimulate private construction, and a bank for general economic and social development. Tax and tariff policies were also modified to stimulate economic growth, though Cuban tariff policy remained woefully inadequate until the end of the period. There had not really been any substantial change in the tariff policies devised to rescue Cuba, in the short run, from the depths of the depression of the 1930s. Industrialization occurred after the late 1940s despite this inadequate tariff policy, but it is certainly conceivable that a modernized tariff policy might have stimulated even further growth.

Research and development policies also changed in the 1950s. By 1958, Cuba was virtually self-sufficient in newsprint, which it made from cane bagasse, produced by Técnica Cubana in Cárdenas. Compañía Cubana Primadera in Camagüey had a large plant producing hard boards; Papelera Pulpa-Cuba in Las Villas produced bond paper. Productos Cubanos de Bagazo made hard boards for building houses, furniture, and acoustic insulation. Subproductos del Azúcar, at España sugar mill, produced dextran, a complex carbohydrate. Piensos Amazonas made mixed feed, and a plant at Central Jatibonico produced wax. Experimentation and marketing research on feeds, charcoal briquettes, detergents, and plastics, all using sugar-cane by-products were conducted, including making paper from bagasse, and yeast from cane juices. Sugar magnate Julio Lobo was pressing hard for agricultural and industrial modernization. The National Association of Sugar Mill Owners contributed money every year to support sugar research and development in Cuba and overseas. The West Indies Sugar Corporation and two other producers in Cuba had a cane-improvement project for testing, breeding, and selecting cane varieties. "Remarkable progress" in the development of new varieties with superior tonnage and cane yield was reported by 1956. This corporation began an extensive soil-research project in its own Cuban laboratories in 1948. The project continued in the 1950s, dealing with research on the use of fertilizers, soil conditioners, crop rotation, and cane-planting cycles.[69] Contrary to the impression often given that research on and development of sugar by-products did not begin until the 1960s, a considerable amount of it was being conducted in the 1950s, although not much before. This increase in research and development activity contributed to economic growth in the 1950s.

Corruption

Personal enrichment continued to be an important, if unstated, purpose of government in Cuba. Between 1934 and 1958, however, purposes other than the profit of the incumbents, many of whom were not corrupt, began to win out. As more groups participated actively in politics, government corruption reflected a broader spectrum of techniques.

Traditional cases of corruption need not be described here except to distinguish between outright theft of government funds and the use of government influence to get money out of private business.[70] Outright theft may have characterized Grau's government.[71] It apparently neither hindered nor helped economic growth. Influence peddling may have characterized Batista's administration; because it depended on an acceleration of economic activity for payoffs, its profitability is linked to economic growth. One could argue that Batista supported economic growth to increase his own income; whatever his motives, growth at least did result.[72]

Some corruption was institutionalized in the national lottery. President Batista perfected this use of the lottery, which had always served to enrich administrators and politicians. Batista's innovation was to use the lottery proceeds to buy political support. He did this by detaching the lottery from the general budget, so that none of its funds would enter the national treasury. Instead they were disbursed by the general director of the lottery and by the President. Batista gave a partial accounting of his use of these funds between 1952 and 1958. Since he wanted a favorable press, he gave newspapermen and their organizations at least $848,650. To labor unions he gave $1,347,000, excluding contributions to their social-security funds (an additional $3,670,472). He provided the Catholic church with $1,673,089 and allotted the remainder ($60,076,834) to semigovernmental social-assistance institutions. But the law could also be breached through the unrecorded disbursement of funds. Batista noted that "the deliveries in cash or in kind to specific individuals, or confidentially to individuals acting on behalf of their organizations, made by the President or Mrs. Batista, directly or through the Secretary to the Presidency, are omitted from this accounting." [73] Batista thus particularized politics further. Petitioners—individuals or organizations—could also contact him directly for payments. The result of his creativity in the corruption business was to spread the wealth beyond officeholders. The lottery itself and many of its uses were not corrupt; but it facilitated many corrupt acts by granting the President unsupervised discretion over the funds it generated and broadened his power base by increasing the domain of beneficiaries.

Sinecures were another accepted form of corruption, as were subsidies to private enterprises to finance featherbedding or to sustain a near-bankrupt company, a policy that was not corrupt according to prevailing norms and that was understandable in times of high unemployment. To provide government sinecures (called *botellas*), the Civil Service law was systematically ignored. The Ministry of Education, especially in the 1940s, was their chief source.[74] Virtually all cases of subsidies to enterprises or directly to workers represented a government effort to stem unemployment or to mitigate its effects. Thus workers laid off from bankrupt enterprises were able to collect subsidies indefinitely because they had been employed. These subsidies had to be bargained for separately because there was no comprehensive unemployment insurance, and workers often had to provide political support in order to get the money. Textile factories also received subsidies so long as they did not close down.[75] Like the use of the lottery, this type of corruption increased the weight of government by broadening the domain of its beneficiaries. These new forms of corruption had their influence on the character of government, as well. Whereas before 1933 officeholding was a prerequisite to getting rich through government, after 1933 it was necessary only if one wanted to get indecently rich. Personal benefit could be derived from government by individuals or by organized groups, at least on a modest scale, simply through particularistic contacts with public officials. It was no longer necessary to be one.

Political Cleavages and Parties

Because the fundamental characteristics of the political system had changed in the course of the century, so had the cleavages within it. Social and economic groups required access to political power, but they were relatively indifferent to the choice of incumbents; they sought access to government regardless of the administration. These groups had a stake in the system and wanted it preserved. They would engage in political disputes, in and out of government, but they would not normally use the political parties as channels to express their differences.

Sugar-mill owners and growers, for example, had ample opportunity to control the branch of government most relevant to them through the Sugar Stabilization Institute. Mill owners, including United States owners, and growers were members of the institute throughout the period, even though they were not always in sympathy with the incumbent President of Cuba. Sugar-mill owner José Manuel Casanova, for example, was president of the National Association of Sugar-Mill Owners in the revolutionary years of 1933 and 1934, and he continued to preside over this group at frequent intervals until his death; he also served several times as president of the Sugar Stabilization Institute.[76] Casanova and others retained access to the institute to regulate the sugar industry for their benefit and for what they believed to be the public interest. Access was institutionalized and stable. Disputes between mill owners and growers occurred within and outside government, but both wanted their access to government continued, and no President dared take it away. A similar pattern persisted in the stabilization schemes for other important commodities.

Institutionalized access was also provided through the National Bank of Cuba.[77] The government of Cuba was the majority shareholder in the bank, but private banks (both Cuban and U.S.-owned) were minority shareholders. The five-member board of directors of the National Bank included two representatives from business, one a Cuban and one a United States banker. When Batista overthrew President Prío in 1952, the three government representatives resigned; the representative of the Cuban banks, Joaquín Martínez Sáenz, became bank president as a public member; Carlos Núñez Gálvez, who had been an alternate private member before the coup, became a regular member. The representative of the United States bankers remained the same. The nine department heads before the coup remained in their posts; in fact, when the Batista government fell in 1958, six were still serving in the National Bank.

The National Bank had real independence, including the power to shut down banks that violated banking regulations; its staff of economists was competent and honorable. Even during Batista's presidency, the National Bank, under the leadership of Martínez Sáenz, kept its autonomy and its distance from the corruption of the period—although one of its satellites, the Bank for Social and Economic Development (BANDES), was an instrument for graft. Through the National Bank, bankers had direct and stable access to governmental institutions and, in turn, they helped to insulate this central economic institution from the winds of partisanship.

The Cuban Labor Confederation (CTC) is an example of a different sort. The confederation controlled no one agency because labor's interests were much broader than those of other groups. Labor required direct access to the presidency. The Cuban Confederation of Labor was legally established in 1939 as the result of a deal between Army Chief Batista and the Communist party. This collaboration was an important step toward the establishment of a viable political system. The politics of regulation, which Batista did so much to launch, required that every significant social force acquire a stake in the system. Labor had been the major obstacle to political stability, and consequently, labor was a major object of Batista's solicitude. The political basis of the policy was support for Batista from the Communists (who made him their presidential candidate in 1940) and support from Batista for Communist organization of and control over the Labor Confederation and many individual unions.

Labor gains required access to power. In 1944 the government coalition, to which the Communists belonged, lost the election to Ramón Grau. The Communist party and the Communist leadership of the Labor Confederation had accused the triumphant opposition of being fascists, reactionaries, and Trotskyites. Shortly after Grau's victory, but before he took office, the top echelon of the Labor Confederation made a deal with him: Grau would continue the prolabor policies of past governments and would retain the present labor leadership in return for their support. This agreement continued in force for almost three years.[78] Internal political pressures, including the government's desire to have its own leaders in charge of the confederation before the 1948 presidential elections, combined with pressures from the United States, to bring about the overthrow of the Communist leadership of the confederation. Minister of Labor Carlos Prío, who would become the government's presidential candidate in 1948, played the key role in replacing Communist Lázaro Peña as secretary-general with independent Angel Cofiño, and then with Auténtico Eusebio Mujal. In 1952, when Batista overthrew Prío, confederation secretary-general Mujal first called an unsuccessful general strike but then turned quickly to the same ploy used in 1944. A deal was struck whereby Batista would continue past prolabor policies and retain the present confederation leadership in return for their support. Mujal remained in power until Batista fell.[79]

The Cuban Labor Confederation never joined the opposition. This was, of course, a two-way relationship, since governments never wanted it to. Cuban labor leaders were not sufficiently autonomous from government, nor did they wield a powerful enough union base successfully to reject government efforts to take over their unions, as was the case in other Latin American countries.[80] Nor did Cuban labor leaders have any particular loyalties or convictions that would lead them to join the opposition when a government changed or when the relative position of the workers deteriorated, as in the 1950s. The Labor Confederation fought the government only within the context of the ruling coalition; labor in other countries would go into the opposition with far less provocation.

Access to power also depended upon maintaining continuity in the major labor posts. Of the twenty-two executive founders of the conferation in 1939, seven were still at their posts in 1945. Of its thirty executives in 1945, eight were still in office after the purge of the Communists in 1947; that is, eight of the thirteen non-Communists were unaffected by the shift. Of the thirty confederation executives in 1947, ten were still executives in 1956, despite Batista's coup in 1952.[81] Despite political changes during these three periods, between one-third and one-quarter of the labor executives remained at the helm. This continuing core ensured the stability and continuity of labor access to government independent of political party.

The divorce of the social from the political system before 1933 ended when direct access to government became essential for interest groups to stay in power. Access was maintained regardless of who was in office. Government became linked to political cleavages, which, in turn, were the consequences of social and economic cleavages. Thus social cleavages were reproduced within the government, not between the government and the opposition or between political parties. The Ministry of Labor, which was responsive to the Labor Confederation, might challenge the Sugar Stabilization Institute, which represented the sugar interests—but both were part of the government. The President's job was to mediate between these competing bureaucracies. This function enhanced his autonomy within his own government and gave him a bargaining position vis-à-vis the social groups with institutionalized access to government. But he could not threaten this access—and no President did— because it was essential to the politics of regulation on which the system depended. The positions of organized groups in government were not attacked by anyone. Cuban politics had changed considerably since 1933; the new goal was to prevent any one group from dislodging any other.

The Cuban experience supports Charles Anderson's generalization about the characteristics of change in Latin America.[82] Major new actors entered the Cuban political arena and gained access to power; the fundamental characteristics of the political system changed. After a brief period of adjustment, however, contenders for power did not seek to eliminate each other but accepted the rules of the game. Many politicians and political leaders prominent before 1933 remained active. The very purpose of the politics of regulation was to identify all significant social forces, give them a stake in the system, and then freeze the system insofar as possible, with only minor adjustments—and even these could be sources of conflict. The system was possible because the forces that had previously created multiple groups seeking power—United States interference, private foreign investment, social mobilization—were stagnant or in retreat. The system was necessary until the late 1940s because no sustained real growth took place. It legitimized politics because large numbers of Cubans participated in and benefited from its regulation and distribution. The requirement for participation was membership in an organized interest group. Organization virtually guaranteed access to power, because the system could not function or survive if major organized groups remained outside it. The unemployed, the squatters, and many of the poor did not have access to power, however, and did not benefit from the politics of regulation and distribution. To them, the Cuban dream was only a dream; for them, the system did not work.

So long as it did not challenge the basic structure of the system, competition for political office could be relatively free from political cleavages linked to social and economic interests. Politicians did not run on platforms to expel private groups from government bureaucracies but sought support from anywhere. At the same time, politicians were freed of the discipline that political cleavages might have imposed if social and economic groups had been linked to parties rather than to government and if groups had rotated in power. The lack of correlation between political parties and social and economic cleavages continued as before 1933. If large parts of government were no longer autonomous from social forces, political parties remained so. If much of government policy making was no longer independent of pressure from the groups affected by those policies, the electoral decision—the determination of who would hold office—was still quite autonomous from choices made by organized social or economic groups. Politicians retained broad discretion in "purely political" matters such as gaining office. Elections, in turn, provided additional evidence of performance that served to legitimate the political system, especially between 1940 and 1952.

The political party system retained its own rules, which were separate from those governing interest-group politics. It was more volatile than before, but these vacillations occurred along reasonably predictable lines. In the first thirty years of the twentieth century, the disjunction between politics and social and economic cleavages, along with uncertainty created by United

States intervention, facilitated defections both of opposition politicians to the government and of government politicians to the opposition. From 1933 to 1935, the new political system had not yet jelled. Bitter social and political conflict was still the norm; parties joined and left government in response to deeply felt events of a revolutionary age (as well as to personal feuds).

As a presidential election became more probable, a new system made its appearance. This new system was based on one basic political cleavage, independent of social and economic cleavages, which had emerged from the events of the revolutionary years—support for or opposition to Batista, for he was the irreducible core of government power. The most important, though not the only leader of the opposition was the deposed President Ramón Grau. The struggle between Batista and Grau was the one constant until 1958.

But from 1935 until the preparations for the 1944 elections, there was very little political uncertainty. It was assumed that the government would win, either at the polls or after the voting. Political defections flowed in only one direction: toward the government. The possibility that the United States would intervene had faded away after it shifted its course from empire to hegemony.

The five-times-postponed presidential elections were finally held in January 1936. A large share of the opposition, including Grau, the Communists, and the ABC, refused to participate, but there were still several opposition parties. The supporters of President Mendieta, primarily former Liberals, had called themselves Nationalists since the late 1920s; the former Liberal mayor of Havana, Miguel Mariano Gómez, had organized a party known as the Republicans; the former Conservative President Menocal had organized another called the National Democratic Union; a new liberal party had been reorganized by Ramón Vasconcelos; the deposed President Céspedes led a group called the Centrists. The Republicans first allied themselves with the Liberals, then broke with the Liberals and sided with the ruling Nationalists, supporting Gómez and Federico Laredo Brú, with Batista's blessing. The Liberals nominated Carlos Manuel de la Cruz; Menocal and Céspedes were also candidates. The provisional assemblies of the Liberal party, however, began to gravitate toward the government coalition and endorsed Gómez. When the Supreme Court ruled that it was unconstitutional for provincial assemblies to overrule the national party decision, Menocal and Céspedes threatened to withdraw.

United States ambassador Caffery, as a hegemonic guarantor of legitimacy, first supported an investigation and mediation by Princeton University president Harold W. Dodds, which made it possible for the Liberals to dump Cruz and endorse Gómez; he then played a role in Mendieta's resignation in early December, as a further gurantee of fair elections, so that Menocal would reenter the race and the electoral legitimacy of the system could be established. After the election, which Gómez and Laredo Brú won, it was discovered that the opposition had not elected a single senator, so the cabinet amended the Constitution retroactively to award two Senate seats per province to the party that ranked second in the voting. The legitimacy of a "democratic" system was at stake and would be preserved.[83] These elections revealed three crucial patterns that would last until 1958: the renewed political defections; the United States hegemonic role, preserving the system rather than imposing a candidate; and the opposition's political bargaining power.

The impeachment of President Gómez in 1936 was the next major partisan conflict. The issues have been discussed earlier, and the hegemonic role of the United States in preserving the system's constitutional legitimacy has also been noted. The roll-call votes on the President's impeachment were as follows:[84]

	House		Senate	
	For	Against	For	Against
Government				
Nationalists	22	8	7	2
Liberals	18	16	7	2
Republicans	5	20	1	3
Total government	45	44	15	7
Opposition				
Democrats	65	4	7	5
Unionists	1	1	—	—
Total opposition	66	5	7	5
Total votes	111	49	22	12

Only Gómez's own Republicans remained modestly loyal despite the preposterous charges against him. The Democratic opposition and the ruling Nationalists provided most of the proimpeachment votes. The ruling Liberals were divided. Some supporters of former President Menocal decided to make a statesmanlike stand against the farce in the Senate, but Gómez was abandoned by his coalition partners and by a fifth of his own party. Batista represented the power of government, and defections flowed to him.

The elections for the constitutional convention in 1939 provided another opportunity for a partisan clash and political defections. The government coalition included Liberals, Nationalists, Communists, Realists, and members of the Popular party and the National Democratic Union. The opposition was represented by Grau's Auténticos, Menocal's new party (the antiimpeachment Democrats), Gómez's unhappy Republicans, and the ABC. One can find parties theoretically of the left (Communists, Auténticos) and of the right (Nationalists, Menocal's Democrats) in both government and opposition. There was no ideological mantle with which either side could wrap itself. To general surprise, the opposition garnered forty-five delegates; the government, only thirty-six. Ramón Grau was elected convention president. Shortly after the convention opened, Menocal made a deal with Batista and the Democrats crossed the aisle to join the government, delivering him the leadership of the convention; Democrat Gustavo Cuervo Rubio eventually became Batista's running mate in the 1940 presidential elections. The Liberal party of Las Villas defected from the government to support Grau for local provincial reasons. In this new partisan clash, there was no uncertainty. Batista was elected President.[85]

Once Batista announced that he would abide by the provisions of the 1940 Constitution that barred his reelection in 1944, a measure of uncertainty returned to the political system. Did Batista plan to impose a successor or to hold free elections? Up to this time, Batista's power had rested on force, but his legitimacy depended on both government performance and observance of constitutional formalities. The return to uncertainty and the continued disjunction of socioeconomic cleavages and party politics allowed the return of two-way defections. This pattern was reinforced by the belief that Grau's Auténticos were the most popular party in Cuba and would come out ahead in a free election. The opposition had won in 1939, and the Auténticos received the most votes. If the elections were reasonably free, government machine pressure and opposition popularity would balance out, making the results close enough for individuals to influence by threatening defections in either direction. In the absence of U.S.-induced uncertainty, however, the relatively simple pre-1933 situation was not replicated.

The structure of party defections was based on three principles, of which the first facilitated flexibility, while the other two made certain alliances and defections less likely. First, interest groups—whether management or labor—always sought to retain direct and unimpeded access to power. Second, the Communist party was unlike the others in that its strength was linked to its control of labor. The Communists were willing to shift and unite with anybody, but when they were deprived of their labor power in 1947 and were strongly opposed by the United States as a threat to the system, no party was willing to be allied with them. With the party stripped of access to power, the Communist electoral strength quickly faded. When the Communist party was banned in 1952, no major new cleavage was created, since it had already been weakened and discredited by opportunism; relations among parties did become more rigid as a result, however. Third, the issue of political corruption, which surfaced in the mid-1940s as Cuba's first truly issue-oriented political cleavage, made coalitions between the Auténticos and the Ortodoxos very difficult. Although the issue of corruption was of principal concern to middle-class voters, it also cut across social and economic groups.

By the time of the 1944 elections, three government parties—the Nationalists, the Realists, and the Populars—had disbanded (the Realist and Popular parties had never received many votes), and most of their members had joined other government parties. The renegade Las Villas Liberals returned to their party and to the government. The opposition Republicans also disbanded;

some joined the ruling Liberals; others, Grau's Auténticos. The major defection occurred when the ruling Democrats divided and Vice President Cuervo Rubio organized a new, conservative Republican party allied to Grau, in opposition. Although Grau got only 42 percent of the votes in 1940, defections from the government could put him within reach of victory; the Republicans hoped to provide this margin. In the 1944 elections, the opposition won. In 1940 no truly conservative party had been allied with Grau in the opposition, but in 1944 the nonideological character of government and opposition coalitions was restored. Democrats and Communists joined hands to support the same government candidates; in the opposition, Auténticos joined hands with Republicans.[86]

Though the Communist-controlled Labor Confederation made a deal with President Grau shortly after these elections, the Communist party in Congress at first supported the defeated Batista coalition in the organization of Congress. That coalition had won control of both houses of Congress when Grau won the presidency. Communist isolation from power would not last long. In December 1945 the Communist party defected from the Batista coalition and joined the Grau government, giving it control of the Senate. Communists were elected first vice president in the Senate and in the House. In the 1946 municipal elections, Communists supported 126 candidates, of whom 103 were in the coalition. Of forty-five winners supported by the party in the first round, none was a Communist, thirty-four were Auténticos, and eleven belonged to the conservative Liberals, the Democrats, and the ABC. The Communist party was the only one in Cuba that claimed to be based on a real social cleavage; thus it could not afford to be as opportunistic as other parties. Nevertheless, having opposed Batista early in the 1930s, it supported him in 1938; having fought Grau since 1933, it supported him in 1944–45. The membership would not be willing to follow so many twists and turns indefinitely, for it was based on class. For example, of the 4,672 new members recruited between August and October 1942 (total membership in October 1942 was 22,001), 68 percent were workers, 17 percent were peasants, and 35 percent were blacks. Although the party sought broader support, even to the extent of dropping the word *Communist* from its name and becoming the People's Socialist Party (PSP), it did not succeed in finding it.

The Communist members of Congress were very active. Although they accounted for only 5.5 percent of the House membership, they submitted 15.5 percent of the bills (a total of thirty-five). Of these, ten pertained to labor and five to peasants; five others dealt with general economic matters. Only one of the thirty-five benefited an individual, in sharp contrast to the usual highly particularistic pattern of Cuban politics. Communist members of Congress astonished their colleagues by being disciplined, well organized, and well prepared. Their congressional delegation had a research advisory commission; the congressmen met in caucus and worked as a group on legislation. They voted together; each member's speeches were drafted in caucus. Communist congressmen were not supposed to enrich themselves in office. The party treasurer collected their salaries from the government and disbursed them to the congressmen. Communists were not, in fact, free of the corruptions of money, but they seem to have been freer than the other parties. Theirs was the only party with a persistent link to a social cleavage and to a social organization (in their case, labor). They were the only well-organized and well-disciplined party in Congress; talented and hard-working members of other parties in Congress had to act on their own. Communist defections were also disciplined and occurred en masse, as in 1938 and in 1945; they were consequently both more visible and more controversial. The opportunism was there for all to see. The party's dilemma was that it could not have it both ways: it could not both hold the allegiance of a single class and play opportunistic politics. It too often chose opportunism, and it lost its following.[87]

In 1948, a durable political cleavage emerged over corruption. A large number of the Auténticos defected to form the Cuban People's party (Ortodoxos), because the Auténtico administration had been weakened by the taint of corruption. The government coalition, elected with 55.3 percent of the vote, had lost so much ground that victory for the opposition was conceivable; Prío would eventually be elected with only 45.8 percent of the vote and only because the opposition was divided into three factions. In preparing for the elections, the opposition Ortodoxos, Liberals, and Democrats and a fraction of the followers of the still Auténtico Senator Miguel Suárez Fernández met to make various deals. The moralizing Ortodoxos found it difficult to bargain—as any party with a homogeneous constituency would—and they finally stood alone, supporting their leader, former Auténtico Senator Eduardo Chibás, for the presidency. The Liberals and Democrats supported Liberal Ricardo Núñez Portuondo. The Communists were spurned by everyone, though they were as willing to bargain as everyone else. Suárez Fernández supported his party's candidate, Carlos Prío, who won, again with Republican support.[88]

During the Prío presidency, most party defections were to the government. The Liberals and Democrats abandoned their opposition to the Auténticos and joined them. The Auténticos themselves divided for a time between supporters of Grau and Prío but reunited in anticipation of the 1952 elections, which were never held. As their scheduled date came nearer, two opposition candidates stood alone—Batista, standing for his own party, and Roberto Agramonte for the Ortodoxos. All other parties were with the government. When Batista took over the government on March 10, 1952, however, the Liberals and Democrats, once again, happily returned to his fold.[89]

The careers of some prominent politicians illustrate how defections worked. Gustavo Cuervo Rubio, a Democrat, was Batista's vice-presidential candidate in 1940 against Grau and the Auténticos. As Vice President, he defected to form the opposition Republican party, aligned with Grau's Auténticos. He switched again in time to rejoin the Democrats as their vice-presidential candidate, running with Liberal Núñez Portuondo against the Auténticos in 1948. Guillermo Alonso Pujol also went from the Democrats to the Republicans in 1944. He became Prío's vice-presidential candidate in 1948 in the Auténtico-Republican coalition. One of the ostensible reasons for founding the Republican party was Batista's collaboration with the Communists; anti-Communism was personified by Prío in 1948. Nevertheless, Republican Vice President Pujol joined with the Auténtico mayor of Havana, Nicolás Castellanos, to form the National Cuban party and, with support from the Communists and Batista, successfully reelected Castellanos over the regular Auténtico candidate, Antonio Prío, the President's brother. Ramón Zaydín was Speaker of the House as a Liberal under Machado. Although he opposed Batista over the impeachment of President Gómez and became a leading member of the Republicans, he returned to the Liberals and the Batista government in time to become prime minister. In 1944 he ran as the government's vice-presidential candidate against the Auténticos. In the late 1940s Zaydín led the Liberals into an alliance with Prío's Auténticos and joined his cabinet. Liberal Senator Eduardo Suárez Rivas, also a part of the early Batista coalition, became the coalition's president of the Senate after the 1944 elections. He was ousted by the Communist-Auténtico deal. Yet he, too, followed Zaydín into the Prío Cabinet in the late 1940s. After Batista's 1952 coup, Suárez Rivas joined the Auténticos, but with Grau's electoral wing (not Prío's insurrectionist wing). The shifts of the Communist party resulted in an ironic situation for Carlos Rafael Rodríguez: he is the only person to have served in both Batista's and Fidel Castro's cabinets.

Party leaders did not, of course, shift alone: they took with them large numbers of minor leaders and followers. These vacillations are typical of the politics of incumbency. Defections continued to occur within the established structure to both government and opposition. There was no ideological or class cohesion in either government or opposition, nor were social or economic cleavages reflected in party politics. Purely political cleavages, such as that between Batista and Grau or that resulting from reaction to corruption, cut across social and economic cleavages.

The proportion of Senate members who shifted parties when reelected or promoted from the House remained consistently high from 1936 to 1954; its low was a full one-third of the membership in 1948 (table 3.14). In the House, there was no sign of the stabilization of party loyalty that had occurred from 1910 to 1924. Instead, there were three party realignments in quick succession—one in 1936, one in anticipation of the 1944 elections, and one at the time of Batista's coup in 1952.

Between 1938 and 1950, the proportion of House members reelected was 47 percent, compared with 40 percent for the period from 1904 through 1932. This represents only a slightly higher level of institutionalization after 1938

Table 3.14 Reelection of members and changes of party affiliation in Congress, 1936–1954

Year	House of Representatives			Senate		
	House seats up for election	% of House members reelected[a]	% of reelected House members changing party[b]	Senate seats up for election	% of Senate members reelected or promoted[c]	% of promoted or reelected Senate members changing party[b]
1936	163	5	88	36	34	75
1938	80	45	22	0	0	0
1940	162	27	42	36	44	44
1942	57	61	54	0	0	0
1944	70	56	56	54	87	45
1946	66	48	25	0	0	0
1948	73	42	23	54	76	34
1950	66	48	44	0	0	0
1954	130	12	56	54	59	44

Source: Computed from Mario Riera, *Cuba política, 1899–1955* (Havana: Impresora Modelo S.A., 1955).

a. Includes House members who served in the immediately preceding session as well as a few whose tenure had been interrupted.

b. The data on legislators changing party affiliation are based only on the minority of congressmen who were reelected (or, in the Senate, who had served in the House) because it was only for this group that party identification could be established for two sessions.

c. Members promoted, that is, who had previously served in the House, made up 28 percent of elected Senators in 1936, 22 percent in 1940, 30 percent in 1944, 30 percent in 1948, and 37 percent in 1954.

than before. Indeed, a plausible case can be made that the level of institutionalization of the House of Representatives, measured by this indicator, remained unchanged for half a century. The same holds true for the Senate. There, however, the proportion of Senators reelected increased through House members' being promoted to the Senate after the 1930s.

The institutionalization of Congress, measured by the proportion of legislators reelected, correlates with the continuing low level of legislation for the half-century. The structural variables affecting the Congress changed little: the proportions of experienced legislators and newcomers were about the same; and the legislative output was about the same. This continuity remained even in the face of greater party volatility after the 1930s and the inability of the political system to stabilize party shifting as it had done between 1910 and the early 1930s.

A first clue to Batista's political problem in the 1950s appears in the data summarized in table 3.14. Only 12 percent of the representatives were experienced legislators, the second lowest rate since independence. Batista did not have the support of many of the traditional politicians, and he chose to place in the House many politicians who had limited political experience and were relatively unknown; they provided neither a challenge to his rule nor real political support for it. Batista's methods were different from Machado's, but both managed to alienate politicians. Machado coopted the incumbents and alienated the nonincumbents; Batista evicted the incumbents. Political crises occurred when the pattern of institutionalization was broken, either by impeding the normal circulation of elites, as under Machado, or by accelerating it, as under Batista. Institutionalization requires stability. The two Cuban Presidents who were overthrown by revolutions undermined their rule by weakening the Congress, although they did so in different ways.

The lack of political loyalty masked underlying elements of stability and continuity that helped to restrain the pulls of the party system and reassure the interest groups that the system was not threatened. One result of political disloyalty was that no elected President ever had to rely on a totally inexperienced cabinet. Miguel Mariano Gómez's secretary of state, José Manuel Cortina, had served Zayas; his secretary of communications, Rafael Santos Jiménez, had served Mendieta. His Vice President, Federico Laredo Brú, had served the President's father, the first President Gómez. Laredo Brú's first secretary of state, old General Rafael Montalvo, had served Estrada Palma and had run as Menocal's running mate in 1909. Batista's first cabinet included José Manuel Cortina as secretary of state, Andrés Domingo y Morales del Castillo, who had served Barnet, as secretary of the treasury, Juan Remos, who had served Laredo Brú, as secretary of education, and Carlos Saladrigas, who had served Céspedes and whose uncle was President Zayas, as Prime Minister. Grau's first cabinet included Batista's Vice President Cuervo Rubio in State and José Presno, who had served Céspedes, in Public Health. Grau, of course, had been President, and Vice President Raúl de Cárdenas had been Mendieta's Interior Secretary. Prío's first Cabinet included former President Carlos Hevia, also Grau's minister, and Edgardo Buttari, who had served Batista, in Labor. Batista's first cabinet after the coup included the faithful Domingo y Morales del Castillo as secretary of the presidency and Andrés Rivero Agüero in Education, both from his first administration. The pattern is, of course, even more pronounced in cabinets other than the first.[90] Shifts in party membership paradoxically contributed to continuity in administrative personnel and, consequently, served to reassure the interest groups with direct access to government that no fundamental change had occurred.

The careers of some individuals, such as the Liberal Rafael Guas Inclán, demonstrate the strong underlying stability of aspects of Cuban politics. Guas

Inclán was elected to the House of Representatives in 1924, when Machado was elected President; he became Speaker of the House shortly thereafter. Swept out of power by the 1933 revolution, he reappeared in the constitutional convention in 1939, was elected governor of Havana province in 1940, and was reelected in 1944, when his party's presidential ticket was defeated. He was elected to the Senate in 1948, although again his party's presidential candidate was defeated. In 1954, he became Batista's Vice President and, in 1958, was elected mayor of Havana—a post he could not assume because the revolutionary forces won. Unlike so many others, Guas Inclán was politically long-lived and loyal to his party.[91]

Another source of stability was the predictability of the electoral strength of the established parties. The oldest parties—that is, the Liberals and the Democrats (originally Conservatives)—showed persistent strength. In free elections, for example, they polled together 31.8 percent of the votes in the constitutional convention elections of 1939, when they were running against each other. In 1948, when they were running together in the opposition and their candidate finished second, they polled 30.4 percent. They remained consistently powerful parties, outranked normally only by the Auténticos. In 1952 their share of party registrations fell below their usual level, but registrations were never a good indicator of voter distribution.[92]

The Auténtico share of the vote was a fifth when they ran by themselves in 1939; their candidate Grau received 42 percent in 1940 and 55 percent in 1944. Their share fell back to 46 percent in 1948, when the party's candidate was Prío. The Auténticos' alliances shifted, as did their experience of government, but they remained the largest single party throughout the period. The strength of the party was a source of stability, since large coalitions typically had to be formed if the Auténticos were to be defeated. The Communist vote was also fairly stable; they received 97,944 votes in 1939, 81,200 in 1940, about 120,000 in 1944, and about 176,000 in 1946, their best showing; Communist votes fell to 143,033 in 1948. The Communists were never a major party, never outranking Liberals, Democrats, or Auténticos and falling behind the Ortodoxos almost as soon as that party had been organized. Although their power was insignificant compared with that of the Republicans, who outpolled them only slightly, they were a known quantity, in votes, orientation, and willingness to bargain to preserve their access to power.[93]

The two variable electoral forces in the 1940s were the Republicans (and their successors, the National Cuban party) and the Ortodoxos. The Republicans were almost completely a machine party, which never ran without coalition partners and sought to enlarge its power by swinging its votes from one side to the other. The Ortodoxos, though they received only 16.4 percent of the vote in 1948, their first elections, were a new, unknown, and dangerous electoral threat. In 1948, they had twice as many votes as party members, an unprecedented phenomenon, and their growth threatened other parties. They ranked only sixth in registrations for the 1952 presidential elections, but they were the real electoral force to contend with.

Electoral forces, therefore, like the social and economic forces of the period, were fairly stable, allowing politicians to make reasonable calculations about the probability of winning. The possibility of calculating electoral strength in itself provided a further element of stability for the system. What was lacking was party loyalty.

Stability also derived from the vagueness of ideological and programmatic pronouncements, except for those of the Communists. Appeals to the voter by non-Communist parties rarely addressed issues for fear of alienating voters. The 1948 presidential election, for example, dealt with two emotional subjects: one was corruption, and it was used to mobilize the opposition to reduce Prío's chances for a majority; the other was the accusation that Liberal-Democrat candidate Ricardo Núñez Portuondo and his followers were "machadistas" and would turn the clock back to the 1920s. It was used both to frighten voters away from the only candidate with a real chance to defeat Prío and to prevent an all-opposition coalition. Perhaps the most universally appealing slogan maker of all was President Ramón Grau. Examples from his store of mottoes are "Let there be candy for everyone" and "To govern is to distribute."[94]

Cuba's population was homogenous enough that campaigns were won or lost nationally. The party's provincial vote typically reflected the national proportions (table 3.15). The chief exceptions were Auténtico strength in Matanzas, Liberal-Democrat strength and Communist weakness in Pinal del Río, and the uneven Ortodoxo vote. The Ortodoxos, of course, were the "new and different party"; they were disproportionately strong in Havana and Oriente and weak elsewhere. On the whole, however, there was no pocket of the

Table 3.15 Votes received by party coalitions, 1948 (%)

Province	Auténticos/ Republicans	Liberals/ Democrats	Ortodoxos	Communists
Pinar del Río	48.4	41.6	8.1	1.9
La Habana	41.5	28.3	20.4	9.8
Matanzas	54.5	29.0	11.9	4.6
Las Villas	47.9	32.1	12.9	7.1
Camagüey	47.9	31.2	14.4	6.5
Oriente	44.8	27.4	20.3	7.5
Cuba (all provinces)	45.8	30.4	16.4	7.3

Source: Computed from William S. Stokes, "The 'Cuban Revolution' and the Presidential Elections of 1948," *Hispanic American Historical Review* 32, no. 1 (February 1951): 74.

country beholden to a particular party, no typical regional loyalties in which a party could seek refuge and, consequently, no special regional appeals that influenced campaigns. Religion was never really a political issue during the period. A minor dispute arose in the 1940s over Communist efforts to regulate the private schools more thoroughly and the Catholic church's successful resistance to the plan. It was not a serious issue, however, and it did not last long.[95]

From the early 1930s through the late 1950s the Cuban political system successfully separated the politics of government from the politics of incumbency. Interest-group access to government was direct and institutionalized. Competition for incumbency remained in a "pure" political arena. Cleavages linked to the society and economy were reflected directly in government, rather than through the political party system. Government bureaucracies were not autonomous, although individual officeholders—including the President—found autonomy in discretionary mediation allowed by competing interest groups and bureaucracies. Corruption continued to be the goal of some individuals in government, and it had the effect of increasing the power of those individuals and of government as a whole. Interest groups, while not seeking to stamp out corruption, did not allow the pursuit of personal enrichment to interfere with the basic stability of the politics of regulation. Political competition among individuals and parties was characterized both by distance from cleavages linked to society and the economy and by volatility. The volatility, however, occurred within certain rules and, paradoxically, rested on and contributed to a measure of underlying electoral and administrative stability.

The political system devised by Batista in the 1930's gave every significant, organized social, political, and economic force a stake in the government. Participation was broadened: new groups acquired access to power, and new parties were formed. All shared in access to power, and none—until the end—sought to eliminate the other. Interest-group politics provided stability; party politics provided flexibility. The political system had been legitimated by performance since the late 1930s and by elections between 1940 and 1952. The former method was decisive for the politics of interest groups, the latter for the politics of incumbency. Each required considerable autonomy and a restrained state. Politicians did not attack the autonomy of interest groups, and the interest groups left politics to the politicians. Civil liberties were fairly well maintained. During the 1940s, the combination of performance, elections, and autonomy appeared to have given the political system a large measure of legitimation, but legitimacy still remained a serious problem. The question is, why did it all break down?

4

THE BREAKDOWN OF THE
POLITICAL SYSTEM

The Cuban political system of the 1940s had several serious weaknesses: its legitimacy remained a serious issue, political violence was not contained, and the rural squatter problem persisted. The feeling that the system was somehow not legitimate was poorly articulated but nonetheless powerful: the Constitution was honored in the breach; Congress hardly worked; efforts by Congress and the Supreme Court to assert their authority were sidestepped by the President; and corruption was pervasive. Eventually it was the problem of corruption that first turned legitimacy into an issue of electoral significance, though the increasing use of violence was linked to it as well.

The problem of legitimacy increased far beyond its previous levels after Batista's coup in 1952, because elections were no longer a source of legitimacy. Eventually the use of violence by Batista's forces to repress the opposition became the most important of the issues that led to Batista's fall. Another was the decline of the economy. Contrary to prevailing views, I believe that economic interest, though still secondary, may have played a more important role than is usually assumed in building a vast coalition against Batista. A condition that was present throughout the period, the availability of ideologies of opposition, became more important as the Batista government degenerated. By the end of 1958, all the props that legitimated the system internally and internationally were gone.

The Problem of Political Illegitimacy

The erosion of formal legitimacy was linked to the undermining of two institutions established by the Constitution to maintain it:. the Congress and the Supreme Court. President Grau sabotaged Congress's authority. Because Grau did not at first control the Congress, he effectively paralyzed it by asking his supporters to absent themselves to prevent a quorum. The Congress had the right to force the President to remove ministers, according to the semiparliamentary system in effect. President Grau simply reassigned ministers to different cabinet posts and, when the Congress removed several ministers simultaneously, ruled through undersecretaries.[1]

The Supreme Court was part of the dominant political alliance.[2] Within these limitations, however, it did contribute something to the making of policy. But it did not challenge the system's dominant coalition, and it went down with it. It refused to review a case concerning the impeachment of President Gómez in 1936; it dismissed a challenge to the Batista coup of March 10, 1952; it implemented policy in accord with the wishes of the ruling coalition, as in upholding the dismissal of workers or the eviction of squatters. Its rulings were also at times undermined: President Grau's successful sidestepping of the Court's ruling against a general wage increase is one example. Another came when the Supreme Court declared unconstitutional a presidential decree on the sugar differential, which levied a new tax on sugar production, and the President formally accepted the ruling but never returned the money to the producers.

Many of the Court's rationalizations upholding the existing system at the same time undermined its prestige. While the Court's rulings on worker dismissals changed, some of its preposterous findings still lingered. The Court ruled that the state of emergency declared during World War II could remain in force until the peace treaties were signed, which permitted the President to rule by decree—Cuba was still at war with the Axis when Batista fell in 1958. As described earlier, the court ruled that the restriction of the sugar harvest was legal, even when the harvest was not in fact restricted, in order to preserve the politics of sugar regulation institutionalized through the Sugar Coordination Act of 1937. Thus the court was no more legitimate than the system as a whole, and it may have been less so.[3]

Violence had become endemic in Cuban politics since the revolution against Machado. There were two sources of political violence in Cuba up to the 1950s. One—especially important in the 1930s—was the honest belief of some that the 1933 revolution had been betrayed and that it could be fulfilled only through armed struggle against the reactionaries in power. The second was more instrumental. Because Cuban politics was both closely competitive and weakly legitimate, politicians used violence to advance their ends at election time or when nonviolent procedures were not effective. The manipulation of violent groups increased a politician's discretionary power because governments in the 1940s had not repressed these groups. Much of the violence was initiated by students from the University of Havana, where gang warfare was frequent. Gangs were predominantly nonideological, though most subscribed to some vague ideas of anti-imperialism, anarchism, and, with more immediate and concrete effects, anti-Communism.

The gangs reached their apogee under President Grau, when the largest ones were the Revolutionary Insurrectionist Union (UIR) and the Socialist Revolutionary Movement (MSR). Grau made Emilio Tró, head of UIR, director of the National Police Academy and Mario Salabarría, head of the Police Bureau of Investigations. On September 15, 1947, the police forces under their commands fought each other for hours and with considerable bloodshed at Orfilas in the city of Marianao, neighboring Havana, while the battle was broadcast over the radio to an astonished country. Gangs fought over control of patronage in the Ministry of Education; they trained to invade the Dominican Republic but were stopped by the United States. When Grau sought to gain control of the trade-union movement, gangs began to assassinate Communist labor leaders. There was no refuge from political violence, and the record of political assassination and other acts of terrorism in the 1940s is extensive.

Fidel Castro was a member of UIR and was accused of assassinating the president of the University Students' Federation, a charge that was never proved. One need not believe that Castro was engaged personally in crimes to agree with the perceptive generalization of Nelson Valdés and Rolando Bonachea that he grew up amid violence and learned early that violence could be used successfully to achieve one's ends in a barely legitimate political system. Political violence was possible even without a numerous following, as it could be undertaken by a small and disciplined group. Even when Castro joined the Ortodoxos and became a candidate for Congress, he organized the Ortodoxo Radical Action, a faction within the party that drew its membership largely from the gangs.[4]

Ideologies

The revolutionary ideology that emerged in the mid-1940s relied heavily on the accusation that the system was corrupt. Anticorruption polemics had appeared in Cuba from time to time since the early 1920s, but their appeal had been limited primarily to intellectuals. Party platforms had begun to include token anticorruption planks since the 1920s as well, but the issue had not caught political fire, as William Stokes points out so well.[5] Then the issue was picked up by one of Cuba's most effective orators: Auténtico Senator Eduardo Chibás, who, having defended President Grau against all his attackers but realizing that he himself would not be the Auténtico presidential candidate in 1948, bolted from the ruling party to form the Cuban People's party. Chibás left the Auténticos partly out of personal disappointment and partly out of moral indignation at the corruption of the Grau government. This new group came to be called the Ortodoxos because they claimed to be the "orthodox"—as distinct from the "authentic" (Auténtico)—interpreters of the people's ideals. Cuba did not necessarily have more corruption than other countries—

though it certainly had a great deal; the point is that corruption had finally become a viable, potent, and disruptive political issue by the 1940s.

Chibás had one plank—"stamp out corruption"; one slogan—"honor against money"; and one symbol—the new broom to sweep things clean. The time was ripe, for Grau's administration was generally thought to be particularly corrupt. Nonetheless, as the 1952 presidential elections neared, Chibás and the Ortodoxos were attacked for having no substantive program other than honesty in government. Chibás himself later admitted that in 1948 his party did not have a "thick and complex program" and that its "intransigence had had no other target than administrative corruption, political clientelism, and gangsterism in the presidential palace and in the streets." The party had drafted a platform in July 1947, but no one paid much attention to it.[6]

The corruption issue caught on quickly enough for Chibás to receive one-sixth of the vote after barely one year of organization (see table 3.15). The Ortodoxos, unlike other parties, had done well only in Havana and Oriente. Because Havana was the stronghold of the Cuban middle class, the strength of the Havana vote (40 percent of the Ortodoxo total) suggests that the Ortodoxo platform and hence the appeal of reformist moralizing was a peculiarly middle-class concern. Because the middle class belonged to the political elite and had access to the media, the issue of corruption became more important than was justified by popular concern.

A survey published in December 1951 indicates the distribution of support anticipated for the three presidential candidates in the aborted 1952 elections.[7]

	% of total surveyed	% of upper class	% of lower class
Hevia (Auténtico)	33.8	34.8	21.8
Agramonte (Ortodoxo)	30.0	19.7	14.6
Batista (United Action Party)	14.2	11.5	18.9
Undecided	23.0	34.0	44.7

It indicates a very close race between the government candidate, Hevia, and the Ortodoxo candidate, Agramonte, with Batista a distant third (a likely reason for his staging a military coup). The Ortodoxos drew less support from both the upper and lower classes than they did from the electorate as a whole. Thus their good general showing was entirely due to strong support from the middle class.

In Lloyd Free's survey, taken in the spring of 1960, respondents from the cities were asked to identify what they considered the best aspects of life in Cuba at that time. The second largest single item, following 26 percent who cited agrarian reform, was "honesty in government," specified by 19 percent; however, 31 percent of the population of Havana, 29 percent of the upper and upper-middle socioeconomic groups, and 26 percent of the oppositionists chose this response.[8] The responses of these three groups, which overlap heavily, indicate that the issue of honesty continued primarily to concern those who were relatively well off economically and had time to worry about such matters. These groups were also concentrated in Havana, just as the Ortodoxo vote had been in 1948.

Chibás hammered at the theme of corruption over the radio again and again. Eventually, however, he made an accusation he could not prove and dramatically committed suicide during a broadcast in 1951 (Agramonte then became the presidential candidate for 1952). Chibás's self-sacrifice in the name of righteousness provided further fuel for the campaign to stamp out corruption.

As Mauricio Solaún has perceptively pointed out, this "primitive radicalism" sought political, rather than social or economic, change and promoted rotation of power among the elites rather than class conflict.[9] The effect was to reduce the legitimacy of the entire political elite. Regardless of the honesty of particular individuals, the legitimacy of all government activity was questioned, weakening the entire system. Compromise and negotiation—the hallmarks of Cuban politics up to that time—became much less likely. Intransigence, said Chibás, was the shield of the righteous politician; it also destroyed the system.

Compared with the political appeal of the attack on corruption, the other ideologies available to the opposition paled in significance. These were nationalism, generationalism, and revolutionary betrayal. Nationalism had been an important and efficient ideology in the 1930s. The 1933 Grau government had decreed that no less than half of the employees and half of the payroll of every enterprise should be "native" Cuban. Nationalism had broad appeal across class lines because even professionals suspected that they were discriminated against when they sought employment in U.S.-owned enterprises. There was some basis for that belief: the documents of the Cuban Electricity Company (a subsidiary of American Foreign Power and Light, Inc.), which were seized by the Cuban government in 1960, show that eleven of the seventeen United States engineers employed in 1930 earned more than $330 a month and that no United States engineer earned less than $200 a month; ten of the twelve Cuban engineers earned less than $175 a month. Of course, the engineers' relative skill, which cannot be determined now, may have accounted for the discrepancy. But mere conviction that discrimination existed was powerful enough.[10]

Blatant United States interference, especially through Ambassadors Welles and Caffery, encouraged the buildup of nationalism as did the degree to which the United States dominated the Cuban economy. Cuban nationalism had its chauvinist side, as well: when in 1933 the Grau government ordered the deportation of Jamaicans and Haitians who had come to work in sugar plantations and had stayed illegally, Rogelio Pina, commissioned by the cabinet to study the matter, argued that previous policies had "Africanized" the country, lowered wages, and introduced a "low morality" (the Communist party, to its credit, opposed the deportations, because such demonstrations of chauvinism would divide the working class).[11] Cuban nationalism also displayed a streak of antisemitism in the late 1930s and of anti-Orientalism during World War II (all adult male Japanese, including several hundred on the Isle of Pines, were incarcerated for three years).[12] But in the 1930s it mainly stuck to the familiar anti-imperialist theme, protesting against United States economic and political control. President Grau's book on the Cuban revolution of 1933, published in 1936, placed the struggle against United States imperialism at the top of his program. As with many similar statements, however, though the diagnosis of the problem from a nationalist perspective was clear, the remedy remained elusive.[13]

By the 1940s and early 1950s, nationalism had declined in appeal as an ideology. Grau's government did little to advance it, even though nationalism was still in fashion elsewhere in Latin America—Perón purchased British properties and Venezuela's ruling party, Acción Democrática, increased the government's share of petroleum profits. The proportion of the national income accounted for by foreign trade increased during Grau's rule, but private foreign investment hit bottom (see tables 3.1 and 3.5). A defense of Grau against the charge of opportunism should never be attempted; yet, in this instance, the decline of nationalist commitment may be explained in part by his accurate appraisal of Cuba's condition: nationalization was in fact taking place. The United States government was no longer interfering in Cuba to the extent that it had in the past; private foreign investment was declining; by the early 1950s Cubans had control over the sugar industry and over banking (see tables 3.2 and 3.3).

Grau was not the only one to downplay nationalism; the Ortodoxos hardly dealt with it. Their 1947 programs did call for resolving the contradiction between political independence and economic dependence, but the measures to achieve this goal were almost entirely tied to internal economic development. There were only two "nationalistic" Ortodoxo planks; one called for a "calm and positive revision of the deficiencies which still persist" in the Reciprocity Treaty with the United States, hardly an earthshaking stand, and the other, for the state takeover of public utilities.[14] Public utilities was the only sector where the divestment stages of the product cycle had not taken their expected toll of private foreign investment, and their takeover remained the only "nationalistic" goal of the Cuban left until 1959.

The Communist party also downplayed nationalism. Aside from opposing the deportations of the Haitians and Jamaicans just mentioned, it had dropped its demands for wholesale state takeover of private foreign investments. Party general secretary Blas Roca proposed a plan for extensive new United States direct private foreign investment in Cuba in the spring of 1945. The only plank for state takeover confined itself to public utilities. In the climate of Soviet–United States alliance of World War II, Roca downplayed even that. The party supported this plank more actively thereafter but did not seek further state action. The Communist party's December 1958 program apologetically defended its continued support for the state takeover of public utilities, explicitly reassuring the public that the party did not propose the takeover of any other foreign enterprises.[15] The Cuban Communist party had been ironically trapped by the United States into a system of hegemony, except that the trap had been set by the United States Communist party. Earl Browder, general secretary of the United States Communist party (then temporarily dissolved) was twice as likely as Stalin to have his writings printed in *Fundamentos,* the official monthly journal of the Cuban Communist party, in 1941–1945. United States citizens outranked Russians two to one, as the following breakdown of the 53 foreign contributions to the journal shows.[16]

All United States authors	22
Earl Browder	11
All Soviet authors	12
Josef Stalin	5
Latin American authors	3
West European authors	12
East European authors	4

It would have been difficult for a Communist party with these ties to go in heavily for anti–United States nationalism.

The relative importance in the public eye of corruption and nationalism as issues can also be assessed by looking at Fidel Castro's writings. Castro's major statement to the people of Cuba was an edited version of his trial defense after his capture for attacking the Moncada military barracks in Santiago, Oriente, on July 26, 1953. *History Will Absolve Me* opens with an extensive discussion of the violations of legal procedure surrounding his trial and the torture and murder of many of his comrades. The main theme of the statement goes to the core of the problem of political legitimacy in the 1950s: the Batista government had come to power unconstitutionally by force; the constitutional organs had been either scuttled or ignored; corruption, torture, repression, and officially sanctioned murder had replaced the rule of law. Nationalism played a very limited role in Castro's defense. The five major laws that Castro said the revolution would proclaim were not specifically aimed at foreigners, and state takeover of public utilities is mentioned in a long list of other secondary measures to be implemented. The statement also included planks with social and economic content outside the discussion of legitimacy.[17] Fidel Castro's first "Manifesto to the People of Cuba," released on August 8, 1955, again stressed evidence of illegitimacy, including repression, corruption, and abuse of force. A fifteen-point program emphasized the need to root out moral evils and for social and economic change. Only one point in this program—the fifth—was clearly nationalistic; it reiterated the necessity for the state to take over foreign-owned utilities.[18]

By 1957–58, Fidel Castro's statements show two new concerns: stopping United States government shipments of weapons and munitions to the Batista government and preventing a United States intervention that might keep Castro from power. Castro succeeded in stopping the arms shipments; the intervention came too late to affect the outcome of the revolution. As the need to build a broad-based coalition arose, demands for the state to take over foreign-owned public utilities faded (along with "radical" proposals). In an article obviously appealing for United States support and published in the United States magazine *Coronet* in February 1958, Castro stated that he no longer had "plans for the expropriation or nationalization of foreign investment." He stated that he had changed his mind about taking over foreign-owned utilities and no longer favored it, concluding that "foreign investment will always be welcome and secure [in Cuba]." In the Caracas Pact, signed by most of the revolutionary organizations, weapons and interference are prohibited, but socialization is not mentioned.[19]

The November 1956 manifesto of the Twenty-sixth of July Movement (which is not attributed directly to Castro) raises the banner of nationalism once again. Its analysis of the Cuban condition follows nationalist canons. However, stress is placed on the perceived denationalization of Cuba after Batista's coming to power in March 1952. It also states that "it is improper in America to utilize the word 'imperialism,' " indeed, that the Twenty-sixth of July Movement seeks "constructive friendship" as a "loyal ally" of the United States. Similar moderate nationalist themes appear in the economic program of the Twenty-sixth of July Movement drafted by Regino Boti and Felipe Pazos. They, too, attribute the onset of denationalization to the Batista coup and government (not surprisingly, since Pazos had been the National Bank president before the coup). Neither statement calls for wholesale state takeover of private foreign investment, but both call for far more regulation of present and future investments and leave open the possibility that concessions obtained or granted fraudulently would be revoked.[20]

The reappearance of the nationalist theme, weaker in the statements made by Castro himself than in statements by prominent intellectuals, may have been as opportunistic as Grau's dropping of the theme in the 1940s, but it also accurately reflected a change in the facts. Table 3.1 shows a sharp acceleration of direct private foreign investment in Cuba under Batista, stimulated by a generous policy of tax exemptions and other concessions. The increasing importance of nationalism also led to opposition to Ambassador Earl Smith.

There was very little direct polling of the Cuban public on nationalist issues. The most interesting data come from two public-opinion polls, sponsored by business enterprises in 1950 and in 1956. Respondents were asked whether they had complaints about two Cuban and two U.S.-owned enterprises. A plurality of respondents in both polls had favorable attitudes toward all four; the U.S.-owned electric company drew the most complaints: 22 percent in the 1950 poll. The two Cuban-owned enterprises (a brewery and a rum distillery) were more popular than the foreign-owned electric company and petroleum refining and retailing company in both years. The popularity of the foreign-owned enterprises increased or stayed the same from 1950 to 1956, however, while the popularity of one of the Cuban-owned enterprises declined.

Respondents who had complaints were asked to state their reasons (data are available only for the electric company). Among the three principal complaints in both years were high cost and poor service; poor treatment of the public was also in the top three in 1956, while the company's status as a monopoly was in the top three in 1950. The fact that the enterprise was foreign owned was the fourth source of complaint in both years, but this complaint was voiced by only 6 percent of those with a complaint against the company in 1950 and by 7 percent in 1956. Thus nationalist responses were expressed by 1.3 percent of the Cuban urban population in 1950 and probably by a smaller percentage in 1956 because the number of complaints against the company had declined (a precise calculation cannot now be made).[21]

Thus the same nonnationalist pattern seen in other sources also appears among the public in the early 1950s. In these polls, working-class and poorly educated people were more likely to be favorable to the electric company. As mentioned earlier, the state takeover of the public utilities was the only such recommendation of the Cuban left; these data suggest that there was little public support even for that program. Given the prevailing climate, it is not surprising that in 1958 the Communist party was so apologetic about its support of any takeovers by the state and that Fidel Castro repudiated his earlier advocacy of the takeover of the electric utility the same year.

As late as the spring of 1960, the degree of nationalism among the urban public was still very low. When Lloyd Free and his associates asked 1,000 urban Cubans in the spring of 1960 to describe the best aspects of life in Cuba, only 6 percent mentioned national independence, the struggle for sovereignty, the inculcation of nationalism, or patriotism.[22] When people were asked about their aspirations for Cuba, only 9 percent mentioned either these things or similar ones such as economic self-sufficiency, an independent foreign policy, or freedom from external interference. Despite the fact that by that time substantial conflict had already occurred between Cuba and the United States, the frequency of nationalist responses is extraordinarily low. The Cuban public was hostile neither to U.S.-owned enterprises nor to the United States government before 1960. The resurgence of nationalism after

1960 must be traced to specific situations after that date. The low incidence of nationalist responses corresponds to the reduced presence of the United States in Cuba in the 1950s compared with the 1920s. There was no noticeable rise in nationalism in Cuba during the period, no burning and bursting demand for self-determination from the political soul of the country.

The swings in the importance of nationalism reflected reality accurately. Yet even in the writings with nationalist themes in the second half of the 1950s, the issues of legitimacy and corruption were paramount. Nationalist ideas often only entered as one aspect of corruption: the corruption of nationhood and the giving away of fraudulent concessions. The legitimacy and corruption themes far outweighed the nationalist theme in their contribution to the unmaking of Batista. Nationalism became an important factor in legitimating revolutionary rule after 1960; then it could be evoked to remind the people of perceived past injuries. But nationalism became a viable ideology in the 1960s only in response to events that occurred at that time. Nationalism was a useful theme in the Cuba of the 1930s and of the 1960s, but not in that of the two decades in between.

Generationalism is an ideology particularly suited to the politics of opposition and to the politics of regime consolidation if the group that seizes power is young, for its thrust is to demand that power be turned over to the new generation. Political analysis based on generational differences is a favorite tool of Cuban writers, who distinguish among the generation of the wars of independence, the generation of 1933, and the generation of 1953, currently in power.[23] This method has a limited ability to explain how power is seized. New people entered politics in large numbers at approximately the times mentioned by the generational analysts, but they were born at various times, had various experiences, and thus probably had various political attitudes.[24]

There are at least two problems with political analysis based on generational differences. First, it is difficult to decide where a generation begins and ends, indeed so difficult that trying to do so is often analytically useless.[25] Second, it is incorrect to attribute the overthrow of particular governments to specific generations, even when they can be identified with some precision, nor do the new entrants into politics at these times necessarily come from the same generation. Important entries into Cuban politics in the early 1930s were made not only by university students but also by workers. It was the workers who struck in August and, with the help of United States ambassador Sumner Welles, brought Machado down; who seized sugar mills in the summer and fall of 1933, establishing soviets and forcing the Grau government to radicalize its program; and who struck time and again in the mid-1930s until Batista agreed to a social compact.[26]

In the 1930s as in the 1950s, politicians who were no longer young took an active and important role in the struggle against incumbent government.

Mendieta and Menocal rose up in arms in 1931 against Machado; former President Prío and former education minister Aureliano Sánchez Arango financed, organized, or conducted a great many acts of violence against the Batista regime. When the presidential palace was attacked in March 1957, veterans of the Spanish Civil War, long-time members of the gangs of the 1940s, and university students fought together. The leader of the ill-fated *Corinthia* expedition in May 1957—a landing by Cuban exiles seeking to open a new military front in the war against Batista—was a World War II veteran. The professional military men who plotted against Batista with Colonel Ramón Barquín, the naval regiments that revolted in Cienfuegos in September 1957, and the members of the urban underground included people of all ages. The rebellion was not just a young people's movement, although the young in the Oriente and Las Villas mountains were admittedly the only ones in the field whom Batista was unable to crush. An accident, however, should not be turned into an analytical hypothesis.

In the 1950s, arguments that the previous generation had failed were used by the younger political leaders once they were in power to discredit their older political competitors. Generationalism is inherently divisive; to emphasize a "generation gap" is not a useful coalition builder on the road to power; consequently, it was at best a muted theme used by some groups opposing Batista (the most successful ones, as it turned out).[27] Because the successful groups were overwhelmingly young, however, it was easier for them to pull together to consolidate their rule; their common experiences in the struggle also simplified the spreading of increasingly more radical ideologies. After 1959, a generational argument was used against Fidel Castro's potential political competitors, but before 1959, it was not. It is an ideology for consolidating power, not for acquiring it.

The theme of a "revolution betrayed" plays a much larger role in revolutionary ideology than the theme of old versus young. It was used by the gangs of the 1940s, and it appears early in Fidel Castro's statements, though mainly in terms of the need to fulfill the revolutionary promises of the Constitution of 1940. It, too, would become a far more powerful ideology of consolidation after 1959, when the need to avoid another 1933–34 would be crucial.[28] Of the four ideologies of opposition available in Cuba in the 1950s, then, by far the most important, both because it struck at the core of the system and because it had wide appeal in the politically powerful middle classes, was the one that emphasized legitimacy and corruption versus honesty in government.

Interest

Perhaps no other hypothesis about the origins of the revolution has been held in such wide disrepute and treated with so much scorn as the possibility that economic conditions may have contributed to the fall of Batista. Leading scholars of the Cuban revolution, regardless of their views of the revolution, reject it.[29] Nonetheless there was a correlation between material conditions and the buildup of the anti-Batista coalition, though as a reason for the fall of Batista it was no doubt secondary. The overriding reason was that the legitimacy of the system was challenged at its very core, mobilizing key groups and eroding Bastista's bases of support. But the poor cannot eat legitimacy, nor even nationalism. Why, then, did they slowly turn toward the revolution?

The year 1957 was the Cuban economy's best ever (see tables 3.8 and 3.9), and organized labor partook of the benefits available. National commercial and industrial wages were even higher early in 1958 than they had been in early 1957 (see table 4.1); they fell in April, but there was no evidence at the beginning of the month that they would do so. Unemployment reached its lowest point in March 1958; the percentage of the work force unemployed in 1957 and 1958 was as follows:[30]

	1957	1958
January	12.6	8.9
February	11.1	7.9
March	9.1	7.0
April	10.3	9.6
May	11.1	10.5
June	13.5	12.5
July	14.2	12.3
August	15.1	13.2
September	14.6	13.4
October	—	13.4
November	13.1	16.8
December	11.8	18.0

When Fidel Castro and the Twenty-sixth of July Movement called a revolutionary general strike in early April 1958, the workers did not respond. The only part of the country where the call to strike was heeded was the province of Oriente, because the deterioration in real wages had begun sooner there than in the rest of the country (table 4.1). Oriente remained the one province where workers could be counted on to respond to revolutionary appeals. Except in August their real wages after March 1958 were consistently below those for 1957; in October and November, when the rebels captured virtually all of Oriente, wages were at recession levels. The better showing of wages in December 1958 could be attributed to the reestablishment of some order in those areas controlled by the rebels.

Organized industrial and commercial workers were concentrated in Havana. They remained loyal to Batista not only in April 1958 but also at other times when revolutionary strikes were called, in part because their real wages

Table 4.1 Indexes of commercial and industrial wages, 1958 (1957 = 100)

Month	Cuba	Oriente province	Havana province
January	101	100	101
February	104	124	101
March	102	95	103
April	95	80	104
May	98	87	107
June	95	80	109
July	98	89	106
August	100	100	106
September	97	85	106
October	94	68	108
November	81	62	93
December	89	88	98

Source: Computed from Banco Nacional de Cuba, Memoria, 1958–1959 (Havana: Editorial Lex, 1960), pp. 151–154. Wages in Oriente province and in Cuba as a whole have been deflated by the national retail food price index (1937 constant prices). Wages in the province of Havana have been deflated by the general wholesale price index for the city of Havana (1953 constant prices). In all cases, each month in 1957 was set at 100.

remained well above those of the banner year of 1957 until November 1958. Yet in early January 1959, just after Batista had fled, efforts were made by military men and conservative politicians, with United States encouragement, to organize a government representing a "third force," eliminating both Batista and Castro. In retaliation, Castro called a general strike, and the workers of Havana responded. One could argue that they could smell the winning side; one could also argue that their real wages had deteriorated in November and December of 1958 and that they were willing to support revolutionary change for country and pocketbook.[31]

The economic deterioration of 1958 became especially severe in its second six months. Middle- and upper-class Cubans, who worried about legitimacy and other political considerations, now had an additional reason to get rid of Batista in late 1958: he was no longer good for the economy. Organized labor also turned against him, even though he had always cultivated its support. His record in the 1950s included a decline in the relative economic position of labor, but a continuation of the increase in real wages. Batista had greater political support among the poor than among the rich, yet his link to organized labor was based on performance; labor affection and dissaffection corresponded closely to real economic trends. Castro found it easier to occupy Oriente province when the military collapsed because he had popular backing. But workers also responded to their changing situation. Castro was able to overcome his opponents in January 1959 because the *ancien régime* had no life left in it and because the workers of Havana were not faring so well. The social and economic distinctions between the ins and the outs—especially the gradual shift from "in" to "out"—can be specified with greater accuracy than is often thought.

The Politics of Breakdown

Batista's coup in March 1952 had shaken the foundations of the Cuban political system. After the initial realignment of politicians and political parties, the flexibility or adaptability of the Cuban political system—the rotation of political loyalties—came to a virtual halt. The coup became a purely political cleavage that politicians and parties would find difficult to bridge. The system of coalition and defection, which had been an integral feature of Cuban political life, was destroyed. The new puritan strains that arose in the 1940s, preaching intransigence and condemning bargaining and compromise, constricted politicians. Opponents indicted the Batista regime on three counts: it was born out of a military coup, fraudulent elections, and constitutional violations; it bred corruption; and it relied on repression, albeit sporadic, to stay in power.

The coup prevented the constitutional or electoral legitimation of the Cuban political system that might have been available after the new Constitution of 1940 had been approved. Instead the Constitution was honored in the breach, through not strictly observing many clauses and ignoring others entirely; consequently constitutional institutions performed poorly. Serious efforts to observe the Constitution did not even begin until the late 1940s. Elections had been reasonably honest and decisive since 1939, but the coup stopped constitutional and electoral legitimation dead in its tracks. To implement the Constitution it would be necessary to overthrow government. While Cuba had not been free of military influences in politics before 1952, the role of the military had declined since the 1930s, beginning during Batista's first presidency, when he adopted measures to demilitarize the administration and subdued a serious attempt at a coup. After 1952, however, the military emerged as the arbiter of political regimes; government and opposition expected that the survival of the Batista regime rested on military support. For the supporters of the overthrown Auténtico government and of the opposition Ortodoxos who wanted to clean out an illegitimate political system, the Batista coup was an outrage. These groups outnumbered Batista's supporters; they were also concentrated in the country's middle and upper classes.

The illegitimacy of the Batista regime remained a lively public issue thanks to the efforts not only of the opposition but also of the Batista government itself. Batista was not willing to legitimate his regime, as he had been in the 1930s, on the basis of performance alone. Although he tried hard to make a case for the legitimacy of his administration on grounds of national security and the need to fight communism, this effort was not credible because he had already given the Communist party power and prestige in his earlier regime and because Castro and the Communists were publicly at odds until the last months of the Batista regime. Batista insisted on legitimation through elections but was afraid of losing a free election. In 1954, former President Grau, suspicious of Batista's commitment to free elections, pulled out of the presidential election shortly before the balloting. Batista was then "elected" President without opposition. The turnout of registered voters dropped from 79.5 percent in 1948 to 52.6 percent in 1954.[32] This electoral farce, along with the higher rate of nonvoting, clouded the legitimacy of a regime that was based on force but did not wish to admit it. The presidential elections of 1958, a few months before Batista's fall, had two opposition candidates, but the elections were so obviously fraudulent that they served, once again, to undermine the government rather than to strengthen it.

The Batista government restricted freedom of the press, freedom of association and of political activity, and other features of the more open governments before 1952. Given the Batista government's problems with legitimacy, however, its best strategy would have been to choke off the opposition altogether. But the post-1964 Brazilian authoritarian solution had not yet been invented, and Batista's own experiences in the 1930s had taught him the difficulties of repression. What he failed to note was that in the 1930s he had created legitimacy, while in 1952 he had destroyed it.

Batista and the political elite had no firm convictions about efficient dictatorship—they even allowed the publication of twenty-five attacks against them by Fidel Castro in the Cuban press. The nine statements published—mostly in daily newspapers with wide circulation—either before Castro's attack on the Moncada military barracks in July 1953 or in 1955, after he had been released from prison and remained in Cuba thanks to Batista's political amnesty, do not pose so much of a question. But the Cuban press was also allowed to publish thirteen statements when Castro was already a political exile dedicated to the violent overthrow of the Batista regime, and two major revolutionary manifestoes, in 1957 and 1958, while Castro was in the mountains fighting Batista. Castro's interview with Herbert Matthews for the *New York Times* was also published in *Bohemia*, the leading Cuban news magazine, as were sixteen of Castro's twenty-five anti-Batista statements. Press censorship under Batista was distinctly inconsistent: a little oppression is a dangerous thing.[33]

Batista's rule was weakened by efforts on the part of civic groups to find a solution to the problem of legitimacy, whose only plausible outcome was Batista's resignation. He chose neither to suppress nor to ignore these groups; instead, he met with their leaders and ordered his lieutenants to meet publicly and privately with their representatives, effectively keeping the illegitimacy of his rule in the public eye. By recognizing the existence of those who would remove him from office, Batista weakened his own position. Because he had no intention of resigning, the failure of these mediations, of the "civic dialogue," further eroded his base of power. The most prominent of all of these groups was led in 1955–56 by Cosme de la Torriente, who had long been active in Cuban politics, and had a reputation for integrity (and for United States support), and by the Society of the Friends of the Republic, an ostensibly nonpartisan civic group heavily peopled with anti-Batista forces. Less long-lived was an effort at mediation by the Roman Catholic bishops of Cuba in February and March of 1958.[34]

A more persistent, equally unsuccessful, but more important effort was launched by the professional associations, led by the Havana Bar and National Medical Associations. They, too, sought a truce between Batista and Castro, followed by the termination of the Batista regime, but were not successful. Their failure led them gradually to support the insurrection, something the Catholic church and old Cosme de la Torriente could not bring themselves to do. The president of the Havana Bar Association, José Miró Cardona, had to seek diplomatic asylum; the National Medical Association began to protest the killing of defenseless civilians by repressive government forces. Eventually, as Batista was later bitterly to note, these professional associations supported the insurrection with personnel (especially underground resistance in Havana), funds, and public-relations work overseas. Rolando Bonachea and Marta San Martín argue that the actual fighters were helped primarily by the lower middle class and the workers, not by the rich. However, they also provide evidence of the active participation of individuals of upper-middle- and upper-class backgrounds in the insurrection, and they admit that the withdrawal of support for Batista by these people was an important element in the regime's downfall, even though only a small minority of them were active insurrectionists. Thus it is plausible that the upper-class organizations had an important political role to play in 1958, even if the social-class identity of the fighters may actually have been more varied.[35]

Another element in the breakdown of the system was repression, including the torture and murder of members of the opposition. Though the incidence of repression is significant, it is difficult to argue that Cuba witnessed more of it than other Latin American countries, or more than Cuba itself has suffered at other times in its history. But it was used inconsistently, and this uneven repression often encourages support for the opposition. Revelations about repression appeared in the press, whenever censorship was lifted, as part of the public rationale for the efforts of civic groups to find an end to the crisis of legitimacy. However subjectively repellent repression may be, it is arguable that Batista might have succeeded if he had simply applied it more consistently, which he refused to do. Batista and his cabinet ministers have acknowledged "excesses" under their rule, but they have justified them by attributing equal excesses to their opponents or rationalizing them as the "normal," if unfortunate, side effects of civil war.[36]

The erosion of the legitimacy of an already barely legitimate system not only drove more people into the opposition but also destroyed the morale of the armed forces. When Batista rose to power in 1952, one of his first acts was to raise the pay of soldiers and the police.[37] But Batista also recalled from retirement former military associates and relied heavily on politically inspired promotions within the officer ranks. These actions gave new strength to the wedge between professional and political officers that had always plagued the Cuban armed forces. Three major conspiracies against Batista, and many minor ones, were discovered within the military, quite apart from the events of the very end of the regime. The first was organized by Rafael García Bárcena, a former instructor at the Cuban War College, in April 1953; another far more important conspiracy led by Colonel Ramón Barquín and 220 other leading professional officers and troops was discovered in April 1956. In a third, on September 5, 1957, officers and sailors mutinied at the Cienfuegos naval base and fought unsuccessfully against the superior forces of the government.[38]

Batista's power had always relied on military support, although he did not rest his regime on this support alone. The rise of violent opposition to his rule within the military, therefore, was widely seen—both within the government and within the opposition—as fatal to his rule; it also had two additional effects that weakened Batista and strengthened Castro. Batista began to oppose the further professionalization of the military, including United States training, because he feared that professional officers would be apt to plot against him, and, to secure himself, he concentrated his forces in and around the city of Havana. Military deployments to fight the guerrillas in Oriente province were kept to 6,000 until mid-1958, when 12,000 troops (including 7,000 poorly trained conscripts) were finally sent there. The combination of military incompetence and low morale assured the failure of Batista's only serious military offensive against Castro in mid-1958. It was characterized by instances of military-unit disintegration, lack of support for units in combat, error (as when the Air Force dropped supplies in rebel-held areas), piecemeal and delayed attacks, desertion, and surrender.[39] The second half of 1958 witnessed the bribing of the military commander of Camagüey to let rebel columns pass and the theft of an armored train and of many supplies intended for the troops. Efforts to replace Batista, including contacts made by general Francisco Tabernilla Dolz, chairman of the Joint Chiefs of Staff, with the United States ambassador, mushroomed. When Batista left, general Eulogio Cantillo, who had been in contact with Castro, remained in command and tried briefly and unsuccessfully to rule independently. The degree to which there was or was not an understanding between Batista and Cantillo is not clear to this day.[40]

The violence of the 1940s spilled into the 1950s reinforced by moral righteousness. Terror and counterterror dominated urban Cuba, especially Havana, toward the end of the Batista regime.[41] The insurrectionist opposition to Batista gradually concentrated around the person of Fidel Castro through a mixture of competence, shrewdness, and luck. Castro's luck, in the form of the accidental elimination of any alternative leaders, was remarkable. The Prío-financed attack on the Goicuría military barracks in Matanzas in April 1956 failed; Barquín's plot in April 1956 failed; the university student attack on the presidential palace in March 1957 failed and ended with the death of the Havana student leader, a serious rival, José Antonio Echevarría; the Prío-financed landing of the *Corinthia* expedition in May 1957 failed; the Cienfuegos naval uprising failed; Frank País, leader of the Oriente provincial underground of the Twenty-sixth of July Movement, Castro's most serious rival within the organization, was killed in July 1957; the general strike of April 1958 failed, and led to the subordination of the urban and labor underground to the leadership in the mountains. Despite former President Prío's substantial financial backing of many groups besides his own (including Fidel Castro's), he had surprisingly little real political influence.[42]

Not all insurrectionary efforts independent of Castro failed, however. From the second half of 1957 onwards, guerrilla groups were operating in the mountains of central Cuba, among them the university students' Revolutionary Directorate, the splinter Escambray Second National Front, the Auténticos, and the Ortodoxos. Part of the reason for Castro's decision to send Ernesto "Che" Guevara and Camilo Cienfuegos from Oriente to invade central Cuba was to make sure that the fighting there would not be controlled by the independents. There were also a few forces in the Pinar del Río mountains. The urban underground, though less independent, was important to the end.

Fidel Castro was politically competent and shrewd as well as lucky. For a long time, survival was enough; his group flourished with squatter support in Cuba's only predominantly squatter area. Attacks on the armed forces sought less to defeat them than to stimulate their disintegration; a careful and successful effort was made to appeal to the honor of the military and the integrity of many officers to stop fighting for a regime that oppressed them as well. Political shrewdness also required a coalition—provided Castro would be leader—of the insurrectionists. Castro's was the longest surviving insurrectionary group, so no coalition was conceivable without him, and he allowed none to form that failed to recognize his supremacy. Efforts to form a coalition that did not acknowledge Castro's leadership explicitly were successfully sabotaged.

What, then, of the politics of interest? Interest groups continued to have their time-honored access to government under Batista, and he sought to expand it further by creating new institutions that would be susceptible to outside pressure—what he called "decentralization," of which he was very proud—and by strengthening the financial bases of the old interest groups. In 1955, for example, Batista ordered all workers to pay compulsory dues to the Cuban Confederation of Labor, immensely enriching its coffers. After the presidential palace was attacked in an attempt to assassinate Batista on March 13, 1957, representatives of Cuba's leading economic, social, political, and religious institutions paraded through the palace for several days wishing Batista well.[43] That year the Cuban economy reached new heights, so many had reason to thank the President.

Led by the professional associations, the interest groups began slowly to draw away from the Batista regime, in part because of increasing revulsion against the rising tide of corruption and repression, in part, especially in Oriente, because business could not survive being pro-Batista in rebel-held areas, and in part because many began to wonder whether the survival of those areas of the political system that were crucial to the interest groups was possible if Batista continued in power. The dissociation of the fate of the system from the fate of the incumbent was a long-standing characteristic of Cuban politics. There is nothing strange about its appearing again in the late Batista regime. The politics of regulation and distribution had been launched by Batista in the 1930s and had survived well enough without him. The independence of politicians and political forces from interest groups and social and economic forces also implied the reverse: the autonomy of the latter from the former. Not every group could do it. For example, General Secretary Eusebio Mujal and the other leaders of the Labor Confederation perceived probably correctly that they would sink or swim with Batista. But others could manage to swim without him.

A shift occurred when two events coincided. The first was the decline in the economy. When the only remaining legitimating prop for the Batista regime faltered, there was no further reason for the interest groups to sustain the regime. The second was the assurance that Castro's rise to power would not doom the system they had pledged their sacred interest to defend. By the end of 1958, the poor performance of the system was reason enough for the interest groups to support the removal of Batista. Raúl Cepero Bonilla has argued that the Sugar Stabilization Institute and the sugar-mill owners' and sugar farmers' associations had become Batista's puppets in the 1950s, that Batista had corrupted their leaders and intimidated their members by using threats of fiscal and other reprisals. While fear and corruption may have added to the loyalty of these groups to the Batista regime when the performance of the economy was improving, their decisive autonomy from Batista was tested in 1958. Sugar-mill owners and sugar farmers in Oriente and in Las Villas volunteered funds to the rebel armies in 1958; Batista had lost the support of these groups by the early fall. The plantations of the West Indies Sugar Corporation had come under rebel authority by July, when the corporation paid taxes to the insurrectionary forces and lent them its equipment. By the end of 1958, the associations of sugar-mill owners and sugar growers, through their officers and friendly cabinet members, confronted Batista with demands for his resignation. On the whole, there is impressive evidence that Cuban sugar-mill owners, sugar growers, cattlemen, bankers, and industrialists financed the rebellion to the tune of several million pesos.[44]

Were the politics of regulation and distribution threatened by Fidel Castro on the eve of revolutionary rule? From the perspective of those troubled times, the best that can be said is that the situation was ambiguous enough to make supporting Castro seem a rational act for the interest groups. Batista threatened prosperity; Castro could bring peace and prosperity again, and it was not really so obvious that he would destroy the system.

In *History Will Absolve Me*, Castro promised land reform, with "the State to compensate landowners on the basis of the average income they would have received from said land over a ten-year period."[45] Because many Cuban farmers enjoyed security from eviction and low and regulated rents under the Sugar Coordination Act, formal landownership was less decisive than it might have been in other countries. Compensated expropriation on the basis of average income (rather than a much more dangerous possible provision: declared value for tax purposes) was not very threatening. Another law would raise the minimum sugar-milling factor for small sugar growers and thus their income share in milled sugar. Both measures were marginal amendments to the Sugar Coordination Act intended to please the National Association of Sugar Growers, which supported the changes, at the expense of the mill owners. And a third law called for the workers to receive 30 percent of the profits of the enterprises for which they worked, which would have involved a significant transfer of income. There was also a heavy stress on stimulating industrialization, construction, and agricultural diversification and a pledge not to introduce new taxes because new programs could be paid for by eliminating corruption and cutting the military budget.

Castro's 1955 "Manifesto to the People of Cuba" was far less specific about land reform and profit sharing, though the ideas remained. The incentives for industrialization, construction, and agricultural diversification and the requirement that taxes due the government be paid without a net increase in the real tax rate were also mentioned.[46] The Twenty-sixth of July manifesto of 1956, however, was much less specific on these issues. Its social and economic planks emphasized social harmony rather than social conflict and showed a strong Roman Catholic influence in language and thought. The program looked to a "state of solidarity and harmony between [capital and labor] which will increase productivity considerably and will benefit everyone." Another plank spoke mystically about the "organic social order."[47] In Castro's July 1957 manifesto from the Sierra Maestra mountains, written together with Felipe Pazos and Raúl Chibás, the profit-sharing provision had vanished. Land reform remained vaguely defined, except that compensation would now occur "prior to" expropriation. Measures toward economic growth were still included, along with a pledge of a "healthy financial policy that safeguards the stability of our currency." Castro's article in the February 1958 issue of *Coronet* and an interview with Andrew St. George in *Look* magazine, another United States publication, in the same month continued to stress an increasingly moderate social and economic program. Only land reform with compensation and promises of economic growth remained. The Caracas Pact of all insurrectionary forces merely pledged to advance Cuba's "progress." The economic theses of the Twenty-sixth of July Movement stressed economic growth. [48]

Even at their most radical, Castro's proposals and those of the Twenty-sixth of July Movement had many points in common with the programs of the Ortodoxo party of the late 1940s and early 1950s and with intellectual Catholic proposals of the period. [49] The interest of Catholic intellectuals in land reform had led to the only thorough study of living conditions of agricultural workers in prerevolutionary Cuba. While many of these proposals were opposed by the major interest groups, they were not really radical in the context of the times, and many of them clearly appealed to sugar growers and to labor. The proposals appeared increasingly moderate with the passing of time and the need to broaden the insurrection's base of support. Thus by late 1958 only the sugar-mill owners had something to lose: formal ownership of their land. With an economic recession threatening Cuba, the sugar-mill owners voted to take their chances that, at last, the provisions of the Constitution of 1940 against latifundia—Castro promised to do no more than enforce them—would be implemented.

The main points of all of the documents were always political change, legitimacy, and purification of government. As the socioeconomic content of proposals declined, the stress on politics increased. Moderate nationalism reappeared, though with a change in emphasis from the expropriation of foreign property to the prevention of United States intervention. This modest nationalism helped to unify the broad coalition that was forming in response to the increase in private foreign investment under Batista and, consequently, under a cloud of suspicion, but it remained a secondary factor.

Over all, then, there was much for labor and sugar growers in Castro's program. Industrialists would probably come out ahead; United States enterprises had not been attacked deliberately, except for public utilities, where there had been a formal repudiation of an earlier plan to socialize them. Sugar-mill owners faced the likelihood of land reform that would compensate them as it took away land they had barely controlled since the Sugar Coordination Act of 1937. Batista had done much for these interest groups, but he had become a liability. The connections between the politics of regulation and distribution and the politics of incumbency were further weakened. Economic growth had stopped. Private foreign investment, which had contributed to growth in the

1950s, had not fundamentally altered the economic structure—as it had in the first thirty years of the century. Much of this newer investment had gone into mining in remote areas, isolated from the nerve centers of economics and politics and employing few; it contributed to growth and taxes but not to significant social and political change. No further pluralization had resulted from it, and it was now threatened by the possible danger of a new nationalism. But there was an ambiguity: had the earlier radical planks been dropped or camouflaged? It was a risk, but one that many interest groups judged worth taking for the sake of peace, liberty, and prosperity.

The last two props of the Batista regime—performance and United States support—remained with him into 1958. Labor west of Oriente stood by him against revolutionary strikes but left him gradually as the year drew to a close. The United States jolted him early in 1958 by suspending weapons shipments, thus impairing his military strength. A military trained by the United States was now spurned by that country. The warning in late November and early December that Batista had to go marked the resumption of a United States hegemonic role dormant since the 1930s. United States actions were the last in a long series of events that Batista had tolerated, or even induced, in order to provide legitimacy to his regime; by the very fact of questioning its legitimacy, however, he and the United States further undermined it.

Illegitimacy, violence, and private interest combined to topple the regime. Batista underestimated the importance of Castro's guerrillas, using that minor nuisance to strengthen his power. As matters worsened, he faced many threats—Castro's and other guerrillas, a military coup, the civilian underground in the cities, and the destruction of the economy through sabotage that would eliminate the last fragile reed of his legitimating performance. Batista chose to concentrate his strength on preventing a coup and on protecting property, especially the sugar harvest. Even in the midst of the one major military offensive in 1958, large numbers of troops were deployed to guard sugar mills and other property.[50] Batista understood that his legitimacy depended on economic performance; politics required that the government guarantee order. But the route toward effective order also required a military campaign, and the Batista regime never effectively undertook one.

Batista refused to acknowledge the basis of his power, and systematically undermined his regime by looking for an alternative legitimation that was not available to him. The corruption and repression of the regime increased the opposition and demoralized the military. The armed forces eventually stopped fighting and crossed over to the enemy. A once adaptable political system had become rigid, with a political cleavage that could not be bridged. The squatters became supporters of insurrection. The political violence of the 1940s was now concentrated on a single target. Economic growth, fueled by private foreign investment, prolonged Batista's rule but came too late fundamentally to alter the economic structure. Finally the performance failed. When private interest joined public righteousness, Batista's days were numbered. He fled on New Year's Eve, 1958.

Because the politics of regulation and distribution had remained dissociated from the politics of incumbency, many thought the system could continue as it had in the past even though the incumbent had fled. But there were still those earlier radical promises. The squatters were looking for land, perhaps suggesting to others in rural Cuba that there was something for them as well in the new order. The workers, at last injured by Batista's loss of prosperity, were clamoring for advantage, perhaps willing to listen to those who suggested that they had lost ground in six years. The fall of Batista was not the same as the coming of the revolution; it can be explained in political terms—the breakdown of the legitimacy of the system, the failure of the will to be a dictator. Though it was not so obvious that the political system, too, would change, the seeds had been sown in righteousness and in self-interest.

The Cuban revolution can be called inevitable only if a long string of assumptions is accepted. One has to assume that the socialization of the means of production was necessary, for that would have required—as it did—a break with the United States and with the old elites; it would also require substantial Soviet support. Without that assumption, changes could have been made in Cuba without the revolution, for it is plain that much had to change. A nonviolent solution to national problems did, however, become more difficult after Batista's coup of 1952. Up to that time, legitimation could plausibly have been achieved through performance and elections, and civil liberties could have been left intact. The policies of the Prío government, which was unique in modern Cuban history in emphasizing both distribution and growth, were a possible formula for a better future. It is also arguable that the probable victory of either Hevia or Agramonte in the elections of 1952, elections that were never held, might have begun to limit corruption in Cuban public life. Once Batista was in power, a political solution required his resignation; he chose not to resign, and his persistence made violent removal necessary. Even then, the defeat of the socially and economically less radical groups must be taken into account. As late as the early months of 1959, Fidel Castro still had many options available short of the one he chose. Many will argue that the coming of a radical revolution was good; if that is the case it is tautological to say that it was necessary. Short of that conviction, revolution was not a foregone conclusion in Cuba on March 9, 1952, nor even for much of the next several years.[51]

If the revolution did not have to happen, Cuba nevertheless exhibited conditions favorable to it. Economic decline set in in 1958; political institutionalization and electoral and constitutional legitimacy, always problematical, were dealt severe blows by Batista; Cuba's level of social mobilization, relatively stagnant since the 1930s, was high enough to support a revolution; a large number of Cubans had been sufficiently exposed to modern ways to coordinate their efforts for political purposes; interest groups were autonomous from political incumbents and thus relatively free to shift to the opposition. The hegemonic power was committed only to defending the structure of the system; Batista might have benefited from an imperial power committed to him personally. While the Cuban government was not entrepreneurial, it was highly regulative. There was a vast body of regulatory legislation available to the new revolutionary government, which permitted it to control economic and social behavior for a long time without having to break with traditional practice. Nationalism, which had declined in response to the decline in foreign investment in the 1940s, perked up with new foreign investment; in the 1950s the opposition charged that the government had made too many concessions in order to obtain investment. The politics of regulation and distribution emphasized the stable relationships of organized groups to the government and to each other and was vulnerable to political shock from any direction. The weakness of Congress and the Supreme Court, the disenfranchisement of the politically unorganized, such as the unemployed and the squatters, the presence of wide class, racial, and regional inequalities, the persistence of political violence and of corruption as an underminer of legitimacy and the perception that the Constitution remained unenforced all facilitated revolution. While the Cuban revolution did not have to happen, neither was it surprising that it did happen in a country such as Cuba. Modernization without modernity, weak political institutions and an economic depression in a context of political illegitimacy are the basic ingredients for the classic revolution.

PART TWO

REVOLUTIONARY CUBA: GOVERNING THROUGH CENTRALIZATION

5

INTERNATIONAL INFLUENCES, SOCIETY, AND THE ECONOMY

The coming to power of the new revolutionary elite opened another chapter in Cuba's twentieth-century history, although several basic features of its past remained to intrude on the revolutionary era. How Cuba is governed is shaped by international influences, by the level and rate of change of social mobilization, and by the performance of the national economy. Profound changes occurred in all three areas in the years that followed.

For the first time in twentieth-century Cuban history, international pressures on internal affairs allowed the unambiguous centralization of political power in very few hands, while an expanding government bureaucracy in Havana succeeded in claiming greater control over both society and the economy. The relations between the United States and the Cuban government contributed to this centralization in two quite different ways. First, Cuba exported its political opposition to the United States. The willingness of the United States to accept hundreds of thousands of Cuban exiles had the long-term effect of eliminating political dissent from their homeland, thereby facilitating the formation of a more politically pliable population. Second, the conflict between the United States and Cuba required the expansion of Cuban governmental capabilities to meet the foreign threat, including the socialization of most of the economy not only to eliminate United States enterprises on Cuban soil but also to prevent the Cuban private sector from collaborating with the United States. Military threats from the United States also required the buildup of Cuban military defenses and internal security. All these changes were unprecedented in Cuban history. Although they resulted from decisions of the Cuban elite, there were pressures from other segments of Cuban society as well. The resulting innovations required the breaking of many political promises that had been made on the road to power.

The centralization of power in Cuba was made possible by the gradual, though sustained, extension of Soviet hegemony in Cuba, even in the absence of geographic proximity or any prolonged or threatened military presence. No Red Army had liberated Cuba as a result of World War II; no Communist guerrillas had been struggling, as they had been in East Asia, against nationalists or colonialists for decades. The socialist state appeared without Soviet political and military intervention and far away from that first socialist stronghold. Aside from the few months surrounding the 1962 missile crisis, Soviet military forces have not been stationed in Cuba, and even then they apparently were not there to determine the internal character of the political system to any important extent.[1] Should the incumbents in Cuba have been seriously challenged, a "solution" such as that applied in Hungary and Czechoslovakia would have been logistically difficult and perhaps politically imprudent. Not unlike the United States in the 1930s, the Soviet Union for the first time had to learn how to maintain its hegemony effectively without recourse to the time-honored tools of imperial control. Although the Soviet Union began to extend its hegemony to Cuba in the summer of 1960, it was not fully in place until it had been accepted by the United States and Cuba two years later, in the aftermath of the Cuban missile crisis, and not complete until after 1968.

Soviet hegemony differs from the United States version in two important respects. First United States hegemony tends to encourage political pluralization; Soviet hegemony, with no private foreign investment or trade involved, tends to encourage political centralization. In myriad ways the Soviet Union has encouraged the construction of a powerful and centralized state in Cuba, one that could mediate between international influences, including the Soviet Union's, and Cuba's political, social, and economic systems. The Soviet Union's chosen instruments to assert its hegemony have been economic pressures and the promotion of factional bargaining within the top elite of the Cuban government and party. Not surprisingly, bureaucratization has been an integral tool for maintaining Soviet hegemony over Cuba in two ways, by increasing the state's capabilities, and by promoting competition among bureaucrats and bureaucracies.

The second important respect in which the two hegemonies differ is that the Soviet Union is concerned with the identity of incumbents and consequently involves itself in factional politics; however, it permits wide latitude in policy formulation, as indicated by its toleration of Cuban policy experimentation in the 1960s. The United States, on the other hand, was not concerned much with incumbent identity from the mid-1930s onwards. But Soviet hegemony is also similar to United States hegemony in one important respect. Both are less concerned with the details of government than the United States was under imperialism, and both are apt to defend the basic features of the hegemonic relationship when they are threatened.

Social mobilization has also influenced the character of government in Cuba. The revolutionary government completed the first phase of social mobilization—the achievement of almost universal literacy with a median educational level in the upper-primary-school range. Consequently, for the first time in the nation's history, the entire population was available for political mobilization by the newly powerful state. At the same time the general level and quality of social mobilization remained low enough that autonomous political participation, once the political opposition had been exported, was unlikely. In this way universal political participation and its control by government were made simultaneously possible.

The performance of the economy also played its part. Cuba's first two twentieth-century political systems had had creditable records of economic growth and of improvement in the welfare of the masses, but poorer records in terms of equity among individuals, groups, classes, and regions. The first decade of revolutionary rule reversed this pattern. Economic growth halted; the infant-mortality rate rose; housing construction slowed to a crawl, and the demand for housing far outstripped the supply, resulting in anguish for many people. Yet the capacity of the state to redistribute the proceeds from a stagnant and, at times, even deteriorating economy was impressive. Wages reached an all-time high in terms of percentage of the gross product in 1969; overt unemployment was ended; housing was redistributed from the rich exiles to the poor. Many social services were provided free of charge to the entire population, including education, health care, and recreational facilities. The Cuban revolution succeeded in redistribution but failed in growth during the first decade of its rule.

Economic growth resumed in the 1970s. Though strict comparisons are impossible, it is probable that the prerevolutionary levels of aggregate economic performance (taking into account price inflation and population growth but disregarding artificially low or high baselines) were finally surpassed by the mid-1970s. This growth was accompanied by a renewal of social inequalities, however, including a sharp decline in the wage share of the gross product, price inflation, and the reintroduction of cash payment for several previously free social services. Nevertheless, degrees of inequality in the late 1970s appear to remain substantially below what they were twenty years earlier.

Hegemony and Revolutionary Politics

The United States and Cuba

The net effect on Cuba of its relations with the United States after 1959 was to centralize its political system and to increase the internal autonomy of its political elite. When the revolutionary government came to power in January 1959, a few thousand people closely associated with the fallen Batista regime left the country; others were imprisoned or executed. Thus the first export of the opposition comprised at least a part of the leadership of the previous government. The second began in mid-1960 and continued until the fall of 1962, when it was interrupted by the missile crisis. During that period most of the rest of Cuba's political, economic, and social elites left the country. The net balance of immigration and emigration between 1961 and 1974 was negative—that is, Cuba lost more people than it gained. The net losses are shown in the following list:[2]

1960	62,379
1961	67,468
1962	66,264
1963	12,201
1964	12,791
1965	18,003
1966	53,409
1967	51,972
1968	56,755
1969	49,776
1970	56,404
1971	49,631
1972	16,856
1973	7,073
1974	3,893
Total	584,875

This exodus weakened the possibility of an internal challenge to the revolutionary political system. The exiles had left partly of their own will, partly induced by the government, partly enticed by the United States.[3] When they sought, unsuccessfully, to overthorw the revolutionary government at the Bay of Pigs in 1961, the Cuban government saw to it that the Cuban people believed the invaders acted as proxy for the United States and not that they represented a challenge by a legitimate Cuban group in opposition to the government.[4]

The third political emigration began in late 1965 and lasted until 1972. It resulted from an agreement between the United States and the Cuban government that permitted the departure of yet another group of Cubans, including numbers of skilled laborers in excess of their proportional share of the work force (table 5.1). This third political export not only further weakened the possibility of an internal challenge from an alternative elite, but it also helped homogenize the masses by exporting disaffected urban industrial workers. The unity of the political system was further consolidated.

None of these political exports would have been possible, however, without a willing importer. The strengthening of the regime that resulted from the willingness of the United States to import politically disaffected Cubans repre-

Table 5.1   Comparison of the Cuban work force and employable refugees[a]

Occupational category	1959–1962	1966[b]	1967[c]	1969	1970	1971
Professional, semi-professional, managerial, and executive	3.35	2.27	1.94	1.77	1.34	1.41
Clerical and sales	2.42	2.31	2.60	2.24	2.21	1.98
Domestic service, military, and police	0.85	1.09	1.03	1.05	1.09	1.07
Skilled, semiskilled, and unskilled labor	0.92	1.23	1.25	1.43	1.52	1.54
Agriculture and fishing	0.10	0.12	0.10	0.14	0.17	0.22

Sources: Computed from Richard R. Fagen, Richard A. Brody, and Thomas J. O'Leary, *Cubans in Exile: Disaffection and the Revolution* (Stanford: Stanford University Press, 1968), pp. 19, 115; Benigno Aguirre, "Differential Migration of Cuban Social Races," *Latin American Research Review* 11, no. 1 (1976):105.

a. The table shows the ratio of the percentage of employable emigrants in each occupational category to the percentage of the total Cuban work force in that occupation in 1953. Housewives, children, the retired, and the handicapped are excluded.

b. 12/1/65–12/31/66.

c. 1/1/67–12/1/67.

sents the inverse of the influence the United States had had on Cuban politics in previous periods.

The export of the elite opposition, however, seriously weakened Cuba's economy, though even this price had an important political benefit: it accelerated the circulation of elites. Counterrevolutionaries, nonrevolutionaries, and weak revolutionaries had all left and could be replaced by the politically committed, who could be given patronage employment to strengthen their loyalty and who would in turn ensure the political loyalty to the new government of the managers of economic enterprises.

Another external consequence of the revolutionary transformation in Cuba was the conflict with the United States. United States private investment in Cuba had been large, both in absolute terms and relative to the size of the Cuban economy (table 3.1). Its socialization transferred enormous power from United States businessmen in Cuba to the Cuban state. A state unaccustomed to exerting economic weight or to owning and administering economic enterprises found itself doing both. Private foreign investment had required and stimulated the pluralization of the economy; socialization destroyed the pluralized system and launched a new pattern of centralization. Most of this change occurred during the second half of 1960, when socialization was in large part accomplished; Cuban-owned private enterprises were also seized at this time. Thus the international radicalization and the internal socialization that characterized the Cuban revolution were intimately related, just as international and internal factors in Cuban politics had always been. This linkage served to concentrate power even further in the hands of the revolutionary elite.

The Cuban people were neither hostile to nor apprehensive of the United States in 1960, just prior to the great confrontation with it, despite periodic and increasing conflicts between the two governments since the revolutionary government had come to power. In April and May of 1960, one thousand urban Cubans (one half from Havana) were surveyed.[5] Asked to state their fears or worries for their country, only 6 percent cited invasion by, or aggression from, the United States, United States imperialism, or United States economic and other pressures as sources of apprehension. Threats, aggression, domination, or conquest by some other foreign power were cited by 6 percent, possibly linked to the 7 percent who mentioned fear of Communism, Communist infiltration or influence, or Communist government or dictatorship. Nationalist hopes or aspirations received very modest public support. Only 1 percent of the sample criticized Cuban government policy toward the United States; only 2 percent had pro–United States sentiments; only 5 percent had made anti–United States remarks in listing the worst apsects of life in Cuba. Among Cubans who made antirevolutionary remarks, only 3 percent criticized the Cuban government's policy toward the United States and only 6 percent expressed pro–United States sentiments. In sum, fears and aspirations linked to the United States did not loom large in Cuban public opinion.

There were, however, pressures from below that, though poorly articulated, nonetheless had a strategic impact upon Cuban relations with the United States. The year 1959 saw frequent strikes as workers sought to gain benefits from management out of the changed political conditions. Many of these strikes were directed against foreign-owned enterprises, and this raised the possibility of socialization. Royal Dutch Shell petroleum-refinery workers struck in early 1959, just as relations had become strained between the United Kingdom and the rebels prior to their coming to power. Because the United Kingdom had sold weapons to Batista, the rebels issued a revolutionary law that made all British property subject to socialization. Fidel Castro (not yet Prime Minister, but already head of the armed forces), in a remarkable speech to the Shell workers on February 6, 1959, stated that the law should not be applied to the partly British Shell because "we are not prepared . . . for a measure like that . . . because that would be a bad tactic at this time." Shell had made a triple offer: to remove the management personnel who had offended the revolutionary leadership, to donate $250,000 for housing and agrarian projects, and to raise salaries by 50 to 100 percent. Comandante Castro urged the petroleum workers to accept the offer and end the strike; called on all citizens to end a solidarity boycott on British products; and requested the revolutionary government to repeal the law.[6]

Other similar pressures from below accelerated and radicalized the implementation of the Agrarian Reform Act of 1959. This law—issued in May of 1959—was moderate in most respects, but it was strongly nationalist. The law subjected to socialization most farms of over 403 hectares and all farms of over 1,343 hectares. All farms of whatever size, however, were nationalized—that is, ownership was transferred from United States to Cuban public and private hands. Articles prohibited both foreign ownership of sugar lands, effective immediately, and future foreign ownership of all land except as otherwise provided by the government. The law affected all foreigners, not just the rich and the powerful. Throughout 1959 and early 1960, the application of the law discriminated against poor farmers and rural workers of Haitian or Jamaican origin. As in 1933, when many were deported, in 1959 many were denied land that would have been theirs had they been Cuban citizens—the Cuban revolutionaries were Cubans first and socialists second. Haitians and Jamaicans were, at least for the time being, outside the pale of benefits.

The strong nationalist orientation of the law meant that, when disputes arose on a farm between management and workers, the workers had far greater leverage if the owner was a foreigner. The National Institute for Agrarian Reform (INRA) was more willing to intervene, even to the extent of suspending the strict application of a moderate law, to take over foreign-owned land. Consequently local agrarian conflicts often had indirect repercussions on United States–Cuban relations (both governments were aware of this) and exerted pressure from below on the Cuban government to socialize.[7]

Pressures from below are not usually expressed with ideological elegance. Workers rarely demanded the socialization of foreign property explicitly. But worker-management disputes often struck a nationalist note, for the workers knew that the government would be more responsive to their plight if those themes were used. Although socialization of foreign property was not solely the result of pressure from below, it is incorrect to say that it occurred without such pressure, that it was simply the result of decisions by the revolutionary leadership, especially Fidel Castro. Most people were not interested in international affairs, nor were such issues the source of popular hopes or fears. There were few articulate demands for socialization from either urban or rural workers; but there were many instances of social conflict, and these had important international ramifications that helped to radicalize Cuban policy toward socialization.[8] Alternatives would have required a drastic moderation of Cuban government policy and probably the repression of at least some of the urban and rural strikes. That was a conceivable course—but not a revolutionary one.

It is the task of elites to formulate and articulate the babbled anxieties of their followers. But Castro and his colleagues did more than that, going far beyond the prevailing climate of opinion in Cuba in the conduct of their relations with the United States. Their decisions were made autonomously, in response to pressures from below and to the possibility that revolution might again occur in Cuba. In 1959, after a few weeks of relatively limited change in formal policy, the first two major changes in the policy of the revolutionary government were declared almost simultaneously. On April 9, Prime Minister Castro called off the elections, long promised as an integral part of his rebellion and of his challenge to Batista: "Revolution first, elections later." In addition, within the week he had announced, during a visit to the United States, that Cuba was no longer interested in United States aid. The significance of calling off the elections should be clear from the earlier discussion of constitutionalist themes in the rebellion of the 1950s. But did Cuba really not want United States aid? Would the United States have been willing to give it in any case?[9]

The economic theses of the Twenty-sixth of July Movement—written by Felipe Pazos and Regino Boti, who had become, in 1959, respectively president of the National Bank and minister of the economy—envisaged a more limited but still important role for new United States private investment, especially in joint ventures, and an extensive role for intergovernmental and United States government aid to Cuba to further its economic growth.[10] Castro reiterated the main lines of this policy on February 19, 1959, specifically welcoming United States private investment. On March 20, asked where the money for industrialization would come from, the Prime Minister confidently replied that "it could come from the United States, from England, from France, from Germany . . . It would seem that there is abundant capital in the world at this time because we have received many offers of loans and investments."[11] And on April 2, 1959, on the eve of his trip, the Prime Minister said: "We are going to initiate talks with all institutions concerned with credit and industrial development from all possible sources. In the trip to the United States I will be accompanied by Dr. Felipe Pazos, Regino Boti, the Minister of Economics, and the Minister of the Treasury, precisely in order that they should engage in as many talks as may be necessary to obtain money in the United States as well as Canada."[12]

A number of economic conditions with important conservative political consequences were placed on United States and International Monetary Fund (IMF) credits, to which Cuba would presumably have been subject had it accepted them.[13] Up to the beginning of April 1959, however, the Cuban leadership, including the Prime Minister, continued to be encouraged by their exploratory talks—so encouraged that Castro planned to take a top economic delegation with him to the United States and noted that he had "news from Dr. Pazos that there is an institution which is willing to give us money."[14] The response to preliminary offers of aid was so positive that they could not have had much effect on the subsequent change of attitude toward the United States. In those early days the Cuban leadership was willing to accept aid on the terms offered. One explanation put forth for the about-face that followed—

that the Cubans found no acceptable terms for aid—is probably without foundation.

An alternative explanation is that Castro's trip to the United States provoked a crisis within the revolutionary leadership. Very little is known about this conflict other than its results. The trip became a deadline for decision. Two basic decisions were made before the trip: there would be no elections and no United States aid would be accepted. The purpose of the visit was changed from getting aid for capitalist development to gaining time to prepare for far-reaching transformations, though not yet necessarily of a socialist character. These crucial decisions struck at the heart of twentieth-century Cuban politics and legitimacy, which had been based on elections and closely linked to the United States. But now neither elections nor the United States would legitimate the Cuban political system and its government. A new source of legitimacy had arisen: the revolution itself. No aid that the United States could have offered would have been compatible with the revolutionary transformation of Cuba as the leadership had begun to envisage it in the early spring of 1959. The decisive issue became, not United States aid or its conditions, but the nature of the revolution.

In December 1961, when Prime Minister Castro first proclaimed himself a Marxist-Leninist, he argued that, when the revolution came to power, it had a choice between retaining the existing social system or "moving forward."[15] While this speech included a number of statements that were politically useful but of questionable historical accuracy, this one is plausible and, unlike other themes in that particular speech, was subsequently repeated on other occasions. There is no evidence that these decisions were taken because of particular United States actions, nor that the United States "pushed" the revolutionary leadership into them. A small number of revolutionary leaders concluded well ahead of the rest of the population that it was impossible to conduct a revolution in Cuba without a major confrontation with the United States. A revolution certainly required not only extensive agrarian reforms but probably also major new state interventions in industry, at least in the sugar industry, in public utilities, and in mining. Since there was heavy United States private investment in all of these areas the leaders concluded that a confrontation must surely follow.

Though change may have been possible in Cuba without a major confrontation with the United States, it would not have amounted to a revolution. Ernesto "Che" Guevara had personally witnessed how United States support had overthrown the government of President Jacobo Arbenz in Guatemala. The protracted conflict between the United States and Mexico over comparatively minor issues was also familiar. The then-current example of the Bolivian revolution, which had maintained its ties to the United States, suggested that a significant retardation of change was apt to accompany efforts to preserve the

United States link.[16] The autonomous decisions of early April 1959 were so fundamental that they could only have been reached after a basic reassessment of what the revolution and Cuba's future were to be: there would be revolutionary change in Cuba legitimated by the revolution itself, and the United States would necessarily have to be expelled from its strategic place there.

Little time would elapse before these basic decisions were fully carried out. In May of 1959 the Agrarian Reform Act was approved. It was followed by the first major cabinet crisis and the departure of the moderate ministers from the government. In June, Guevara established official contact with the Soviet Union; and President Manuel Urrutia was forced out in July, leaving no doubt that the Prime Minister was the supreme officer of the revolutionary government. A variety of efforts to reconcile United States and Cuban points of view, including mediation by third parties, failed. Relations worsened through late 1959 and early 1960. Soviet Deputy Prime Minister Anastas Mikoyan arrived on February 4, 1960, to sign the first important Soviet-Cuban agreement. This agreement did not necessarily determine the shift to socialism—diplomatic relations were not restored until later—but it was a major economic and political turning point for the revolution.

At the same time, United States–Cuban relations took a further turn for the worse when the Belgian ship *La Coubre*, loaded with arms and ammunition for the Cuban government, exploded in Havana harbor in early March and Prime Minister Castro accused the United States government of sabotage. Publicly the United States government protested; privately, President Dwight D. Eisenhower would later write, "On March 17, 1960, . . . I ordered the CIA to begin to organize the training of Cuban exiles, mainly in Guatemala."[17] The two governments finally came to blows in late June, when the Cuban government requested foreign-owned petroleum refineries to process crude oil that the Cuban government had purchased from the Soviet Union. They refused, and Cuba socialized them between June 29 and July 1.

At the same time, a newly amended sugar act was making its way through the United States Congress, which included a clause authorizing the President to cut off Cuba's sugar quota; it received approval from House and Senate, both in committee and in the full houses, between June 27 and July 3. On July 5 the Cuban cabinet authorized the socialization of all United States property in Cuba. On July 6 President Eisenhower canceled Cuba's quota. On July 15 the Bank for Foreign Trade became Cuba's sole foreign-trade agency. On August 7 the large U.S.-owned industrial and agrarian enterprises actually were socialized, and on September 17, all United States banks. On October 19 the United States government prohibited exports to Cuba, except for nonsubsidized foodstuffs and medicines. On October 24 Cuba socialized all U.S.-owned wholesale and retail trade enterprises and the remaining smaller industrial and agrarian enterprises.

The Cuban government's confrontation with the United States, which led to the socialization of foreign-owned enterprises, need not have affected Cuban-owned business. Yet on October 13, 1960, 382 Cuban-owned businesses, including all the sugar refineries, banks, and large industries and the largest wholesale and retail enterprises, were socialized. Three days later the Urban Reform Act socialized all commercially owned real estate. These decisions are inexplicable if one tries to see the seizure of United States enterprises as being the result of short-term conflict between the two nations. In fact, the roots of that conflict are to be found in early 1959, not mid-1960: what occurred in 1960 was simply the implementation of what had been decided earlier. The socialization of large Cuban-owned enterprises was part of the tactics. Because Cuban entrepreneurs had close connections with the United States and because by this time they could certainly be presumed to oppose government policies, the survival of the revolutionary government required that the management of Cuban enterprises be passed to loyal revolutionaries, however bureaucratically incompetent. Inefficiency and full employment are politically preferable to sabotage and unemployment.

On another level, these actions also reflected a decision to socialize the means of production. Although the socialist character of the revolution would not be declared publicly until April 1961, these socialist policies were initiated beginning in the summer of 1960; they were justified in legislation on political and national-security grounds and also on the grounds that direct control of the means of production was required for economic planning. Economic centralization was viewed as a rational step toward growth.[18]

The conflict with the United States, leading to the socialization of United States private investment, had the indirect consequence of providing a context and a tactical reason for, and a general stimulation of, the socialization of all Cuban-owned enterprise except for very small businesses. Once again, internal and international factors were linked, and the revolutionary leadership acted autonomously; they were not compelled to socialize, although they responded to and articulated pressures from below. Rather, they fashioned the future of Cuba by anticipating probable consequences. Nationalization, but with enterprise left in private hands, had been possible in the spring of 1959; it was no longer politically or ideologically sufficient by the fall of 1960: political and economic power had to be concentrated in the hands of the revolutionary government. The United States, which earlier had served to pluralize Cuban politics by intruding itself into the Cuban social system, now served to centralize it by being expelled from that system. In both cases, its presence was a fundamental factor in shaping Cuban life in the twentieth century.

The continuation of the United States policy prohibiting trade and all other economic transactions with Cuba for the next two decades ensured Cuba's dependence on the Soviet Union. The United States embargo's economic effects were mixed. In the short term, the sugar purchases made by the United States to replace the lost Cuban supplies helped (along with the decline in

Cuban production) to drive up the world price of sugar.[19] More serious and longer-term effects arose from the difficulties Cuba faced in transferring its trading patterns to the socialist countries. Larger port facilities to handle long-haul trade were needed, as were Soviet shipping commitments to handle the trade and the adjustment of Cuban industry to new spare parts, new machinery, and new techniques. While this conversion was being carried out, the capacity of large segments of Cuban industry was underutilized for lack of spare parts and imported input.[20]

The most significant long-term political effect of the embargo was the need it created to place ever more power in the hands of the government. The fear of sabotage required political loyalty in the management of enterprise. The need to "cannibalize" some industries to supply spare parts for other required centralized management of entire sectors of the economy. The need to mobilize people to work where they were needed so that the country could become economically self-sufficient placed the entire economy and society on quasi-war status. Actual military attacks on Cuba, such as the Bay of Pigs invasion and countless exile raids, and the threat of attack, explicit at the time of the missile crisis and implicit thereafter until the United States turned its attention to Vietnam, also spurred the leadership toward greater political centralization. The need to defend the leadership against assassination plots—many, though not all, supported by the United States government—stimulated the rise of vast espionage networks.[21] The United States did not bring Cuba to its knees; it brought about political centralization in Cuba and alliance with the Soviet Union.

The international sugar market was favorable for the marketing of Cuban sugar in the 1970s. The International Sugar Organization computes a world average of daily price throughout the year for sugar in cents per pound, which is the arithmetical average of the New York Coffee and Sugar Exchange "spot" (daily) price and the London Exchange daily price. This price was 1.80 cents per pound in 1966; it rose to 1.92 cents in 1967, fell to 1.90 cents in 1968, and then rose steadily to 3.20 cents in 1969, 3.68 cents in 1970, 4.50 cents in 1971, 7.27 cents in 1972, 9.59 cents in 1973, and 29.60 cents in 1974.[22] It was about 10 cents in October 1976.[23]

The extraordinary increase in the world price of sugar became a powerful stimulant to the Cuban economy, dramatically improving its terms of trade—the amount of imports a country can buy with its exports (see table 5.4). Cuba launched the first sustained period of real growth in per capita income in revolutionary history. Capitalist sugar-price inflation at last rescued the Cuban economy in the early 1970s. The decline of the world price of sugar in 1975 ended the bonanza: Cuban annual economic-growth rates for the second half of the decade are expected to slow down by 40 percent, compared to the 1971–1975 period, under the 1976–1980 five-year plan.[24] But it is plain that the sustained increase of the world price of sugar from 1968 to 1974 had rescued the Cuban economy.

The Soviet Union and Cuba

Cuba's adoption of socialism should also be seen as a move to ensure that the Soviet Union would help the revolutionary government, and Soviet-Cuban relations have in fact strengthened it in its relations with society and the economy. They have also, as mentioned earlier, bureaucratized it. The Soviet Union, as a hegemonic power, has with equal success defended what it regards as the legitimate structure and boundaries of the international socialist subsystem—the subset of international relations among socialist states—as they pertain to Cuba.[25]

The socialist countries do not have any private investments in Cuba. The exchange of the United States for the Soviet Union as a hegemonic power eliminated that source of pluralization. Instead, the Soviet Union operates in three distinct areas in the Cuban social system: defense, trade, and economic aid.

Incorporated into the socialist international subsystem since 1960, Cuba has yet to sign a mutual defense pact with the Soviet Union and has yet to join the Warsaw Pact. Nevertheless, the closeness of relations between Cuba and the Soviet Union since the late 1960s suggests that the latter has extended its nuclear umbrella, which at first was not very sturdy. On July 9, 1960, Prime Minister Nikita Khrushchev declared that Soviet missiles would defend Cuba "in a figurative sense," and the agreement signed between Cuba, by Armed Forces Minister Raúl Castro, and the Soviet Union shortly thereafter did not mention nuclear weapons. The Soviet Union, however, pledged to "use all means at its disposal to prevent an armed United States intervention against Cuba,"[26] and its military commitment gradually increased through the missile crisis in the fall of 1962. The expectation of Soviet support in the case of nuclear war had become an integral part of Cuban military doctrine by the mid-sixties; the subordination of Cuban to Soviet foreign policy was acknowledged in the programmatic platform approved by the first congress of the Communist Party of Cuba in December of 1975.[27]

The second area of Soviet involvement is international trade. The agreement just mentioned with the Soviet Union, signed by Raúl Castro, also said that "the strength of the socialist countries . . . can fully take care of supplying Cuba . . . with all the necessary merchandise which is now denied to it by the United States and other capitalist countries."[28] In 1959 the United States accounted for 74 percent of Cuban export sales and supplied 65 percent of its imports; the socialist countries accounted for 2.2 percent of Cuban exports and 0.3 percent of its imports. By 1961, the socialist countries accounted for 74.0 percent of Cuban exports and 70.0 percent of its imports; the Soviet Union alone accounted respectively for 48.5 percent and 41.1 percent in 1961, and the United States accounted for 4.4 percent and 3.7 percent. In 1973, socialist countries accounted for 67.5 percent of Cuba's total trade (exports plus imports).

In the long run, the Soviet Union has supplied a larger proportion of Cuba's imports than it has taken from Cuba's exports. The Soviet share of Cuban trade, exclusive of trade with other socialist countries, has never matched the United States share before the revolution. The highest level of Cuban import dependence on the Soviet Union—60.9 percent—came in 1968; its greatest export dependence—51.9 percent—in 1967. A more normal Soviet share has been about 40 percent of exports, 50 percent of imports.[29] Because the socialist countries are politically heterogeneous, Cuba has acquired a somewhat higher level of trade diversification since the revolution. The crucial socialist help to Cuba in the form of trade came, of course, in 1960. The revolution might have collapsed had not the socialist countries bought Cuban sugar and supplied Cuba with critical imports.

The third area of Soviet support is provided directly as aid. One form of aid has been financing trade deficits that Cuba has incurred with its socialist partners, especially with the Soviet Union itself. From 1961 to 1974, Cuban

Table 5.2 Cuban trade balances, 1960–1974

Year	Total balance (in thousands of pesos)	Soviet/Cuban balance (in thousands of pesos)	Soviet share of deficit (%)	Cuban balance with other socialist countries (in thousands of pesos)[a]
1960	+ 28,415	+ 23,261	0	+ 18,006
1961	− 12,299	+ 41,120	0	− 24,242
1962	− 237,032	− 189,471	79.9	− 11,529
1963	− 322,185	− 297,059	92.2	− 40,062
1964	− 304,542	− 135,046	44.3	−133,935
1965	− 175,509	− 105,853	60.3	− 16,263
1966	− 327,727	− 247,266	75.4	− 9,384
1967	− 294,108	− 215,929	73.4	− 1,084
1968	− 451,116	− 382,151	84.7	− 9,132
1969	− 554,928	− 436,078	78.6	− 8,536
1970	− 261,491	− 161,930	61.9	+ 12,704
1971	− 526,322	− 427,149	81.2	+ 23,378
1972	− 418,945	− 490,292	117.0	+ 17,322
1973	− 314,005	− 334,263	106.5	+ 47,577
1974	− 3,731	− 214,549	5,750.4	+155,663
Total	−4,175,525	−3,572,655	85.6	+ 20,483

Sources: Computed from *Boletín 1971*, pp. 216–221; *Anuario 1972*, pp. 194–195; *Anuario 1973*, pp. 188–191; *Anuario 1974*, pp. 186–189. For estimates of 1975 and 1976 trade, see Central Intelligence Agency, *The Cuban Economy: A Statistical Review, 1968–1976* (Washington, D.C.: Library of Congress, 1976), p. 7.

a. Other socialist countries include eastern Europe (including Albania and Yugoslavia) and Mongolia only.

imports exceeded exports every year (table 5.2). The average Soviet share of the total deficit during the same period has been 85.6 percent. The Soviet willingness to finance these deficits has underwritten the revolution. Trade with eastern Europe in 1974 showed a surplus in Cuba's favor that eliminated the old debt. Soviet-Cuban bilateral trade, however, continued to show a large deficit.

A second form of aid has been to pay for Cuban sugar above the prevailing world market price and outside preferential international subsystem agreements (the Cuban deficit in its trade with the Soviet Union has occurred in spite of this premium). The Soviet Union has paid a cumulative sugar-price premium or subsidy amounting to $1,202.34 million from 1960 to 1971.[30] While the United States paid a similar premium on sugar before the revolution, there is one political difference. The sugar premium before the revolution was only partly captured by the state through taxation. It served, rather, to strengthen private business and to increase pluralization. But since the revolution it has been captured entirely by the Cuban state to consume or invest as it sees fit, and this factor adds further to centralization.

A third type of aid has been in the form of military equipment. On April 22, 1970, Prime Minister Castro indicated that Soviet military aid to Cuba through 1969 already amounted to $1.5 billion. Because Soviet-Cuban relations have become closer since 1969 and Cuban military capabilities and inventories modernized since the late 1960s, it is likely that the level of military aid has climbed. Most of this aid has been a gift; the Soviet Union has been providing weapons free of charge since 1962. Cuba, however, has repaid some of the cost of the weapons obtained from such other socialist countries as Czechoslovakia.[31]

A fourth form of aid has been direct credits for economic development. Often it has involved building a new factory, training Cuban personnel to operate it, and then turning it over to the Cubans. Between 1960 and 1964, excluding credits to finance trade deficits, the Soviet Union granted Cuba four credits worth $459 million, at interest rates varying between 2 and 2.5 percent, and amortization in ten to twelve years, for the development of metallurgy, electricity, petroleum, mining, chemical and fertilizer plants, and the sugar industry. In 1960 China granted a ten-year credit of $60 million at no interest, and Czechoslovakia, a ten-year credit of $40 million at 2.5 percent. Hungary granted a ten-year credit of $15 million at 2.5 percent in 1961; Poland, an eight-year credit of $12 million at 2.5 percent in 1960; Bulgaria, a ten-year credit of $5 million at 2.5 percent in 1961; and the German Democratic Republic, three ten-to-twelve-year credits worth a total of $60 million at 2.5 percent between 1960 and 1963. All these were for industrial projects and shipyards. Eight of the credits were given in 1960 and 1961, when the United States was turning out in full force against Cuba.

Although the economic impact of these early credits would not be felt for

several years, their political impact was immediate: Cuba could count on socialist support for revolutionary survival. Those who might have wavered in
their support for the revolutionary government in its hour of peril were now
reassured. Rumania also granted three ten-to-twelve-year credits worth $75
million, at 2.5 percent, $15 million of which was handed over in 1961 and the
rest in 1968–1969. While the first Rumanian credit was for industrial development, the last two were for the development of Cuban mining and petroleum.
These later credits also had considerable political significance.[32] Many development projects completed by the mid-1960s resulted from these credits from
socialist countries. Cuban reports on the opening of these new plants emphasized that they were "bought"—they were not gifts, but credits repayable
with interest.[33] See table 5.3 for a summary of the value of factories bought
from Cuba's three main socialist partners.[34]

Table 5.3 Cuban imports of fully completed factories, 1967–1974

| Year | Value (thousands of pesos) | Nation of export (% of total value) | | | % of total imports |
		USSR	Czecho-slovakia	East Germany	
1967	62,410	12.3	29.7	34.0	6.2
1968	51,302	47.4	9.2	17.5	4.7
1969	84,979	52.2	7.4	2.7	7.0
1970	48,087	52.0	15.7	9.7	3.7
1971	39,653	22.6	7.9	4.6	2.8
1972	29,793	44.6	7.3	1.5	2.5
1973	41,202	51.3	7.5	1.0	2.8
1974	86,394	45.1	7.0	0.6	3.9

Sources: Computed from *Boletín 1971*, pp. 218, 254–255; *Anuario 1972*, p. 227; *Anuario 1974*,
pp. 186–187, 220–221.

Between 1961 and 1971, aid from the Soviet Union and the other East European socialist countries, members of the Council for Mutual Economic Assistance, had been used to construct or modernize 200 important industrial
enterprises. The Soviet Union alone accounted for 160 of these projects, including the modernization of 114 sugar mills as a result of a Soviet-Cuban
agreement signed in 1965. The pace of Soviet economic-development aid accelerated in the early 1970s. By 1973 the Soviets had reportedly constructed
over a hundred "modern works" in Cuba; by the end of 1974 the enterprises
built or modernized by the Soviet Union accounted for 10 percent of the
Cuban gross industrial product. Linked to this Soviet economic aid was the
training of Cuban specialists in the Soviet Union; through 1971, about 4,500
Cubans were trained there; in 1974, over 800 were studying there. The

numbers of Soviet specialists in Cuba increased from one thousand in the early 1970s to "several thousands" by 1973 and possibly to six thousand by 1975.[35]

Cuba's relations with the Soviet Union and, more generally, with all the socialist countries, soured for a time in the middle and late 1960s over disagreements concerning internal and international policy.[36] Although the Soviet Union continued to finance Cuba's trade deficits and apparently to honor earlier credits granted for economic development, there were no new credits forthcoming, except those from Rumania. Moreover, there was no net aid from the East European socialist countries or Mongolia to finance Cuban trade deficits between 1970 and 1974 (table 5.2). The trade balance for those years was favorable to Cuba, and Cuba's excess exports were repaying earlier trade credits. These same countries had financed 22.6 percent of the total cumulative deficits between 1960 and 1964, worth 191.8 million pesos.

A fifth variety of aid has been more recent. It stems from the Soviet Union's recognition that Cuba would be unable to repay these credits within the original timetable, let alone with interest, and from a reconciliation between Cuba and the Soviet Union that began in the latter part of 1968, when Prime Minister Castro publicly endorsed the Soviet invasion of Czechoslovakia.[37] It came at a second crucial time in Cuba's revolutionary history: in 1970 the Cuban economy plunged to what was probably its lowest level since the revolution had come to power. The Soviet Union came to the rescue.

In December 1972 Cuba and the Soviet Union signed five agreements. The first postponed until January 1, 1986, repayments on credits granted to Cuba before January 1, 1973; its purpose was to equalize reciprocal trade balances and to provide technical and economic aid; repayment of interest on the debt according to previous agreements was also postponed until the credits are repaid in full. Repayments are scheduled to be completed in 2010. The second agreement granted credits free of interest charges for 1973, 1974, and 1975 to cover the unfavorable trade balance between the two countries. These new credits are scheduled for repayment beginning in 1986. The third agreement listed goods to be traded. The fourth provided Cuba with a credit worth 300 million rubles—a lot of money for a small economy—bearing an unspecified interest, for particular economic-development projects. The long hiatus in the series of Soviet credits for economic development was broken at last, and at a time when Cuba most desperately needed them. Prime Minister Castro emphasized that the Soviet Union had taken the initiative in selecting the projects for which this aid would be used, which suggests that Cuba had traded future economic growth for its own decision-making autonomy. The Soviet Union's hegemony was increased, even while the Cuban state was strengthened relative to its own society. The fifth agreement regulated trade prices. The 1972 agreements transformed many previous kinds of aid into at least partial gifts.[38] From a baseline somewhere between 1960 and 1964, the ten-to-twelve-year repayment period was extended to forty-seven to fifty-one years;

no interest would be charged during thirteen years of the repayment period (1973–1985), regardless of baseline.

A sixth type of aid is the provision of convertible currency to finance Cuban trade with the capitalist countries. This aid has proved difficult to quantify and even to document, but fragmentary evidence suggests that it is real and important. Cuba's balance of trade with nonsocialist countries was consistently negative from 1960 to 1971 (except for the year 1963, thanks to the high sugar prices).[39] Beginning in 1972, Cuba's trade with the nonsocialist countries began to show a surplus amounting to 74.1 million pesos in 1972, and 67.2 million pesos in 1974.[40] Cuba's trade deficit with the Soviet Union has become larger than the total Cuban trade deficit since 1972 (table 5.2). Thus Soviet credits to cover Cuba's trade debt with that country subsidized Cuban trade with nonsocialist countries, as well as with the Soviet Union's East European allies.

This Soviet subsidy made Cuba credit-worthy in convertible currency (dollars, yen, francs, pounds, etc.) in its trade with capitalist countries, and their financial institutions were able to float loans to Cuba.[41] Argentina opened the way in 1973 with $1.2 billion in credits to be used over a six-year period; in 1974, Canada granted $42 million in credits, and Spain gave a credit of $900 million. As a consequence of the extraordinarily high 1974 world sugar prices, France, Canada, the United Kingdom, and Japan extended credits in 1975 worth $1065.1 million. Cuba went directly into the Eurodollar capital markets to raise between $238 and $250 million.[42] Japan granted annual credits of $200 million, beginning in 1976.

Another achievement in 1975 was the improvement of economic relations with Mexico, although it is unclear how much this change will eventually yield.[43] Swedish aid to Cuba has increased as well, rising from 5 million pesos in 1972 to 12 million pesos in 1975, for a total of 33 million pesos from 1972 through 1975.[44] Cuba went into the Eurodollar market once again in 1976 to raise approximately $146 million, but it was forced to scale down its goal to approximately $83 million because the market could not absorb the higher sum. Apparently Cuba cannot raise funds in the capital markets unless lenders can assume that the full faith and credit of the Soviet Union stand behind Cuban borrowing. Prime Minister Castro has openly acknowledged this necessity.[45] In a very fundamental sense, then, the credits Cuba has received from capitalist countries should also be considered a form of Soviet aid to Cuba; they would probably not have been forthcoming had the Soviet Union not financed Cuban trade and borrowing in convertible currencies. It can be concluded as well that this new infusion of credit stimulated the Cuban economy in the mid-seventies.

An unidentified Cuban defector who used to work at the Cuban Central Planning Board has reported the cumulative Cuban debt to the Soviet Union in January 1971 to be $2.2 billion, exclusive of arms deliveries.[46] The cumulative aid extended to finance the trade deficit alone would have been $2.1 billion at that time. The debt includes additional sums for Soviet economic-development credits, the cost of Soviet technical advisers, and Soviet convertible-currency loans to finance trade deficits with other countries. Soviet aid to Cuba has been extensive and relatively generous. By 1974 the trade aid alone amounted to about $3.6 billion.

Other factors must be taken into account to assess the value of Soviet aid to Cuba. Cuban-Soviet net barter terms of trade have been estimated and compared to Cuba's overall terms of trade—which, of course, include the Soviet Union—in table 5.4.[47] "Terms of trade" is a measure of the amount of imports a country can buy with its exports. Most of Cuban-Soviet trade is barter trade; cash prices are imputed without cash changing hands. Cash is exchanged, however, in Cuban trade with capitalist countries. Cuba's terms of trade improved remarkably from the late 1960s to the mid-1970s, thanks to fairly stable import prices until 1974 and rapidly rising export prices. The rise in overall ex-

Table 5.4 Indexes of Cuba's terms of trade, 1968–1974 (1968 = 100)

Year	Import prices	Export prices	Terms of trade	Import prices paid to USSR	Export prices paid by USSR	Cuban-Soviet terms of trade	Sugar export prices	Sugar export prices paid by USSR
1968	100.0	100.0	100.0	100.0	100.0	100.0	100.0	100.0
1969	95.3	102.3	107.3	97.5	100.8	103.4	97.9	98.5
1970	93.0	119.1	128.1	98.3	117.0	119.0	109.3	98.5
1971	97.4	119.6	122.8	99.6	120.3	120.8	110.7	97.8
1972	96.9	132.6	136.8	106.4	122.8	115.4	127.7	98.1
1973	86.0	169.2	196.7	107.4	177.0	164.8	168.7	162.4
1974	133.9	296.8	221.7	130.3	261.1	200.4	330.6	264.7

Sources: Computed from *Anuario 1972*, pp. 198–233; *Anuario 1974*, pp. 190–227. Cuban-Soviet prices are available only after 1968. Information has been gathered for 20 export products and 114 import products, accounting for virtually the entire value of Cuban exports but only about 60 percent of the value of Cuban imports. Each of these products has been converted to its equivalent in 1968 prices; they are then summed to represent Cuban imports and exports in 1968 prices. The respective import and export amounts in current prices for subsequent years, multiplied by 100, were divided by the respective import and export amounts in 1968 constant prices, giving the Cuban import and export price indexes. The overall terms of trade were then estimated by dividing the price of Cuban exports multiplied by 100 by the price of Cuban imports. The same procedure was followed to estimate Cuban-Soviet net barter terms of trade. Information has been gathered for 10 Cuban products exported to the Soviet Union and for 38 products imported from the Soviet Union, accounting for virtually the entire value of Cuban exports to the Soviet Union but only about 60 percent of the value of Cuban imports from the Soviet Union—about the same as in the overall trade. For a different estimate of Cuba's terms of trade, see CIA, *The Cuban Economy*, p. 13; the CIA's statistics suggest terms even more favorable to Cuba.

port prices had been faster than the rise in sugar prices until 1974, although sugar exports account for three-quarters to four-fifths of the value of Cuban exports. Except for 1971 and 1973, prices paid by the Soviet Union for all Cuban goods rose more slowly than did Cuba's general export prices, a stability explained primarily by the unchanging Soviet prices for Cuban sugar through 1972; Soviet prices for other Cuban export products did go up. Through 1973 the prices Cuba paid for Soviet goods were higher than the prices it paid for imports generally.

During this seven-year period, prices in the capitalist markets were more favorable to Cuba than those in the Soviet market. This differential cannot be interpreted to mean, however, that Cuba would have been better off if it had done its trading elsewhere.[48] Differences in price behavior do not say enough about the long-term rationality of sacrificing short-term gains, and they say nothing about real product-by-product comparisons. They simply emphasize the favorable terms of non-Soviet trade with Cuba. Cuba's renewed prosperity in the early 1970s can be explained in part by the improvement of its terms of trade by 121.7 percent in these seven years. It would have been astonishing under these conditions if improvement had not been achieved given the favorable changes in its economic relations with other countries.

A more serious limitation on the value of Soviet aid to Cuba is suggested by a 1965 study undertaken by the National Bank of Cuba and quoted from an unidentified source by Goure and Weinkle. It found that the Soviet goods sold to Cuba had cost 50 percent more than what Cuba would have had to pay if it had been able to buy the same quality and types of goods from non-Communist countries. Edward Hewett has concluded, however, that the Council for Mutual Economic Assistance (CMEA) foreign trade prices for most goods are at about the same level as world market prices, with an appropriate time lag. The chief exception is that CMEA machinery and equipment prices are about 30 percent above the level suggested by capitalist market prices. The National Bank study may have been restricted to machinery and equipment, however, because the prices of those items are more easily ascertained by an organization with limited research facilities.[49]

To estimate whether Cuba might have been better off trading elsewhere (leaving aside the political fact that trade with capitalist countries would in any case have been either difficult or impossible in the early 1960s), the value of Cuban imports of machinery and equipment from the Soviet Union has first to be deflated by a constant equal to 1.5 to yield the capitalist market prices for these goods (1.5 reflects the 50-percent or 0.5 Soviet overcharge relative to world prices found in the National Bank study). The Cuban subsidy to the Soviet machinery and equipment industries is the difference between the value thus deflated and the actual price paid by Cuba to the Soviet Union. Similarly, the Soviet subsidy to Cuban sugar is the difference between the Soviet price and the prevailing capitalist market price for sugar in any given year.[50]

These two calculations clarify why the Cuban National Bank was concerned about its Soviet trade in 1965. In 1960, 1963, and 1964, Cuba was subsidizing the Soviet machinery and equipment industry at a higher rate than its sugar was being subsidized by the Soviet Union; Cuba came out ahead only in 1961 and 1962. For the period from 1960 through 1964, the value of Soviet sugar subsidies was 130.3 million pesos, while that of Cuban machinery and equipment subsidies was 102 million pesos. From 1965 through 1970, however, Cuba was winning the battle; premiums on sugar prices exceeded Cuban subsidies to Soviet machinery and equipment industries, by 1,015.3 million pesos versus 284.1 million pesos. The subsidies represented by these figures and the post-1968 shift in the terms of trade show the Soviet Union's willingness to underwrite the Cuban economy to a far greater extent than can be inferred from the formal agreements of the 1960s. Cuba's terms of trade improved vis-à-vis the Soviet Union, though less rapidly than Cuba's overall terms of trade, and Cuba received subsidies for its sugar industry substantially greater than any returned to the Soviet Union through premium prices for machinery and equipment.

Then from 1971 to 1975 the Soviets extended far less aid to Cuba than one might expect from the formal agreements. In 1971 sugar subsidies amounted to only 56.1 million pesos, compared with 68.3 million pesos in subsidies to the Soviet machinery and equipment industries. By late 1971 the world market price for sugar exceeded the Soviet price, and it remained higher for every month of 1972 except July and December, giving an average world price 13.4 percent higher than the average Soviet price for that year. In December 1972 the Soviet price rose to eleven cents a pound while the world price was just over nine cents. By the spring of 1973 the world price outstripped the stable Soviet price, and it remained higher throughout the year. Nevertheless, the average Soviet sugar price was 33.5 percent higher than the average world price in 1973 because of the premiums paid by the Soviets in early 1973. The average world price remained above the Soviet price, which remained unchanged, throughout 1974, for an annual excess of 51.5 percent. The Soviet price for Cuban sugar rose again in the late summer of 1974 to about twenty cents a pound, or half the then-prevailing world price. The new, higher Soviet price then overtook the declining world market price in the spring of 1975.

Because of sharp fluctuations in world sugar prices during 1975, a high and stable Soviet sugar price was an advantage, even though the Soviet price for sugar was lower than the prevailing world market price from late 1971 through 1975. The Soviet-Cuban agreement for 1976–1980 has set the Soviet price at thirty cents a pound, over twice the prevailing world market price in 1976. It has also set the Soviet nickel price for 1976–1980 50 percent higher than the prevailing world market price. It appears that Soviet subsidies for Cuba's main export products will once again be the norm through 1980.[51]

The Soviet price for petroleum through the early 1970s was still only about one-quarter of the price of Middle Eastern crude oil. The value of the Soviet oil subsidy to Cuba was about $175 million from 1972 to 1974. For 1976–1980 contracts, however, the price doubled. The new system of "mobile prices" permits price changes every year, instead of every five years, in order to keep the economies of members of the Council for Mutual Economic Assistance attuned to the world market. As Soviet oil is sold to Cuba at prices closer to world market prices, a sixfold increase in the price of imported oil over the late 1960s level will have occurred by 1980, compared with a sixfold increase in the world price of raw sugar from 1968 to 1976 and a fivefold increase in the Soviet sugar price from 1971 to 1976. In other words, given prevailing world market conditions and Soviet subsidies, the terms of Soviet-Cuban trade for sugar and oil in the late 1970s are about even.[52]

Although the value of Soviet aid to Cuba is considerable, the Soviet Union also derives some economic benefits from the relationship. It is a high-cost producer of beet sugar; capital and labor savings are incurred (or were, at least to 1972) if sugar is imported from Cuba rather than produced in the Soviet Union. This sugar supply also releases fertile Soviet lands for other crops in which the Soviet Union may have a comparative advantage in climate, soil, or cost of production. Sugar-cane supplies arrive in the Soviet Union during the first half of the year; since beet sugar is processed in the fall, the production cycle of Soviet sugar refineries is thus extended. In addition, the raw sugar purchased from Cuba is refined and then reexported to Finland, Iran, Iraq, Afghanistan, and other countries. In the future, of course, it may be a test of Soviet aid whether more refining is done in Cuba than in the Soviet Union. Cuba, unlike eastern Europe, buys the more expensive rather than the cheaper Soviet export products. Since a February 1966 agreement, the Soviet Union's Atlantic fishing fleet has also benefited from the use of Cuban ports, and Soviet satellite intelligence stations have been operating in Cuba since 1969.[53]

Cuba continues to receive military, technical, and economic aid. The terms of this aid, the renegotiated terms for the 1960s trade aid, and the price agreements for 1976–1980 are quite generous. Should the Soviet overcharges, however, spread beyond machinery and equipment, the generosity of this aid will be substantially reduced. There are other important political considerations affecting the value of Soviet aid to Cuba, however. An econometric study of the world sugar market indicates that Cuba could not have sold its sugar in the world market in 1960 if it had not entered into a preferential marketing system.[54] Cuba's choice at that time was thus either to capitulate to the United States or to sell to the Soviet Union. Until the early 1970s, when world demand for sugar began to outstrip supply, it was unrealistic to think that Cuba could have placed vast quantities of sugar in the world market at reasonable prices, and Cuba's trade balances would have been far worse than they were. Indeed, it is unlikely that the revolution would have survived.

The timing of Soviet aid has also been politically important. Military aid has been crucial for national security. Economic development credits were granted in the early 1960s and the early 1970s, both periods of political peril. The Soviet willingness to finance Cuba's trade deficits was equally beneficial. Cuba's alternative again would have been capitulation to the United States. The aid was granted when it was needed; the answer to what its economic cost will be lies in the future. But a revolutionary future would have been precluded without it. Even in the worst possible case, if the Soviet Union were to become Scrooge, one would still need to balance political survival against economic cost. Economic efficiency and low interest rates would be of no use to dead revolutionaries.

The final political consideration is equally important. The Soviet assistance strengthened the government relative to the rest of the social system: there were no Soviet private investment, no Soviet credits to the private sector, no Soviet financing of a pluralized political system. The Cuban government was free to dispose of this aid as it saw fit and thereby strengthened its hand. Through international political legitimation, economic assistance, and military aid, the Soviet Union gave the Cuban revolutionary government a decisive margin of survival. It remains to the diplomacy of the future to keep the economic costs of political survival low.

Soviet influence leading to the bureaucratization of the revolution and resulting in the establishment of increasingly larger and more complex administrative and political organizations has been no less important an effect of Cuban-Soviet relations. Soviet bureaucracies prefer to deal with other bureaucracies and not with individuals, however heroic their revolutionary past. Andrés Suárez has painstakingly traced the twists and turns of the Soviet-Cuban relationship in the first half of the 1960s and has concluded that Prime Minister Castro acquiesced in the formation and development of a revolutionary party, and eventually a Communist party, first as an effort to obtain further support from the Soviet Union, then as a condition of continued Soviet support. Whether or not the Cuban leaders took the initiative, the causal connection between bureaucratization and Soviet influence remains.[55]

Subsequent events further validated Suárez's analysis, when he extended it into the 1970s. As the disastrous year of 1970 came to an end, the Soviet Union once again rescued Cuba, but this time on condition that a major reorganization of the Cuban government, under Soviet guidance, be undertaken. The instrument for this reorganization was the Cuban-Soviet Commission for Economic, Scientific and Technical Collaboration, established in December 1970. The details of this agreement made evident how vast and decisive Soviet influence would become within the Cuban government, for they spelled out the means of coordinating the efforts of the Cuban Ministries of Foreign Trade, Merchant Marine and Ports, Basic Industries, and Mining and Metallurgy and of the Central Planning Board, the Agency for Agricultural Development (DAP), the Agricultural Mechanization Agency, the Institutes of Fishing and of Civil Aeronautics, and the Electric Power Enterprise. The commission itself would become a new agency and prod Cuba toward further bureaucratization and centralization of power. All the agencies it coordinated would have to establish systematic, formal bureaucratic procedures under the guidance of Soviet technicians (whose numbers in Cuba consequently increased vastly in the early 1970s) in order to make effective use of Soviet assistance. Moreover, the agencies and their individual leaders would not deal with issues on an ad hoc basis, as in the past, but through the intermediary of this new superagency. In the summer of 1972, Cuba finally joined the Council for Mutual Economic Assistance. As Boris Gorbachev has subtly indicated, this step both permitted and required international coordination of the Cuban economy and therefore very extensive planning.[56] The Cuban-Soviet commission has met frequently and regularly. These meetings have resulted, for the first time, in the full coordination of the Soviet and Cuban five-year plans for 1976–1980.

The Cuban bureaucracy had to increase if any meaningful integration with CMEA member countries was to be achieved.[57] The early 1970s witnessed a large-scale reorganization of Cuban government and party structure in other areas as well, also probably abetted by the Soviet Union, although the evidence for its involvement is less direct. A plausible supporting explanation is that the internal reasons for reorganization were plain to the Cuban leaders, though this is not to deny the direct and explicit link between the Soviet Union's policy preferences and the changes in Cuban politics exemplified by the Cuban-Soviet commission. The evidence from Cuban government defectors suggests that similar processes occurred in intelligence gathering and the provision of support for revolutions in Latin America. The Soviet Union helped to establish Cuba's bureaucracy in these areas in 1961. The return of Soviet influence at the end of the 1960s brought with it an increase in the internal differentiation and complexity of these organizations, accompanied by more moderate policies.[58]

Bureaucratization is often associated with infighting among factions over policy alternatives and the allocation of political power. There is a good deal of speculation about what Soviet preferences were as between this or that Cuban leader or faction. Without resorting to "Castrology," it is difficult to come to any definitive conclusions. Nevertheless, two important known cases of internationally induced bureaucratic disputes in Cuba suggest that this aspect of bureaucratization in Cuba was also linked to Soviet influence.

The promotion of bureaucratic infighting is the preferred method of the Communist states to influence other Communist states in less than major disputes (when various other methods including armed intervention may be used). Bureaucratic infighting in Cuba can be documented through direct evidence only in comparatively serious conflicts. Consequently it tends to appear at the same time as the use of economic pressures against Cuba and efforts by Communist states to influence Cuban politics.

The first example of this phenomenon is the Sino-Cuban dispute of 1966.[59] In the course of 1965 the Chinese government launched a major lobbying effort to win converts within the Cuban armed forces and thus to influence the Cuban government, despite private protests from President Osvaldo Dorticós and Prime Minister Castro. The dispute became public at the beginning of 1966, when the Tricontinental Conference was held in Havana to support revolutionary Communist movements in Africa, Asia, and Latin America. At that time, Castro revealed that China had refused to purchase as much sugar as Cuba wanted to sell and to sell as much rice as Cuba wanted to buy (rice is a staple in the Cuban diet). The Chinese first promoted bureaucratic infighting in Cuba. When that failed, they resorted to more vigorous measures to press their point of view. After Cuba's internal rice production collapsed in 1965 (table 5.5), the Chinese reduced their exports of rice to Cuba in 1966–1970.

Table 5.5 Rice production and imports (in thousands of tons), 1950–1974

Year	Production (milled rice)	Imports
1950	127	—
1956	287	—
1957	294	—
1958	229	—
1959	283	—
1960	307	—
1961	213	—
1962	206.9	—
1963	204.3	189.8
1964	123.5	285.5
1965	49.9	281.8
1966	68.4	145.9
1967	93.7	156.9
1968	94.9	177.2
1969	177.4	185.9
1970	290.9	199.0
1971	285.5	279.9
1972	239.1	255.8
1973	236.5	201.2
1974	309.2	276.3

Sources: *Boletín 1964*, p. 80; *Boletín 1970*, p. 198; *Boletín 1971*, p. 96; *Anuario 1972*, pp. 107, 201; *Anuario 1973*, p. 91; *Anuario 1974*, pp. 75, 193; United Nations, *Statistical Bulletin for Latin America* 3 (1966):22.

Then Chinese-Cuban relations again improved; this shift is also reflected in Cuba's imports of Chinese rice in the early seventies. But the Cuban participation alongside the Soviet Union in the Angolan civil war dealt another severe blow to Cuban-Chinese relations. On April 26, 1976, the Cuban government had substantially to reduce rice rations for the population, attributing this hardship in large part to the international situation.[60] It was part of the price the Cubans paid for their role in Angola. Cuban-Chinese relations, though less cordial than before, were not broken; both countries signed a five-year commercial agreement in June 1976, although without giving details of the treaty's contents.[61]

A second example is an even more significant one. A "microfaction" within the Cuban Communist party was holding discussions in 1967 and 1968 regarding Cuba's serious political and economic problems and their international repercussions. Aníbal Escalante, the discussion leader, had been removed as the party's organization secretary in March of 1962. He and the rest of the microfaction's membership had extensive ties with government and party officials in the Soviet Union, Czechoslovakia, and the German Democratic Republic, including access to the Central Committee of the Soviet Communist party. Their efforts to moderate the internal and international radicalism of the revolutionary government's policies and to prevent the further deterioration of Soviet-Cuban relations led ultimately in 1968, to the arrest of forty-three people, the expulsion from the party and imprisonment of nine people, the imprisonment of twenty-six others, and the resignations, under duress, of two members of the Cuban Central Committee who had headed, respectively, the Committees for the Defense of the Revolution (Cuba's principal mass organizations in 1968) and the Fruit Processing Enterprise.

The Soviet, Czech, and East German governments and parties encouraged this infighting as a means of indicating the limits of legitimate behavior that the Cubans were not expected to trespass,[62] and they proceeded to accomplish this in the following way. When Cuba protested about the international Communist support the microfaction was receiving, the Soviet Union slowed down the level of petroleum deliveries to Cuba in the face of Cuban requests for increased amounts. Then the Soviet press reported that production of petroleum and related products was so high that the Soviet Union would increase its exports of these products to Latin American countries, including Brazil and Chile, two nations with which Cuba had bitter disputes. This Soviet policy forced further fuel and gasoline rationing in Cuba.

In 1958 Cuba had produced only 1.8 percent of the crude oil it needed for domestic consumption; in 1967, when domestic crude-petroleum production reached a record high, it represented only 2.3 percent of consumption, a proportion that fell to 2.0 percent in 1971.[63] (Table 5.6 indicates Cuban crude-petroleum production.) Thus Cuba was at the mercy of the Soviets for oil. The Soviet Union granted 106.5 percent of Cuba's requests for gasoline for 1968

Table 5.6   Production of crude petroleum in Cuba (in thousands of tons), 1956–1974

Year	Production	Year	Production	Year	Production
1956	86	1963	30.8	1969	206.2
1957	63	1964	37.3	1970	159.1
1958	55	1965	57.4	1971	120.1
1959	27.6	1966	69.1	1972	112.2
1960	25.4	1967	113.6	1973	137.8
1961	28.1	1968	197.8	1974	168.0
1962	43.3				

Sources: United Nations, *Statistical Bulletin* 3 (1966):38; *Granma Weekly Review,* January 7, 1968, pp. 2–3; *Anuario 1974,* p. 128.

(that is, it sent more than requested), but only 64.2 percent of its requests for fuel oil and only 54.1 percent of its requests for gas oil.[64] As when facing the United States in 1960, Cuba had two choices: either to turn to other sources or to capitulate. Turning to the United States was impractical, if not unthinkable, at the time. During this difficult period, Cuba received new Rumanian aid for petroleum and mining development, which was of no more than symbolic significance. The Soviet share of Cuban petroleum imports remained essentially unchanged between 1967 and 1974, when it ranged from a high of 99.3 in 1967 to a low of 97.5 in 1971.[65] Cuba capitulated. The endorsement of the Soviet invasion of Czechoslovakia in August 1968 was the first evidence that a capitulation was coming.[66]

The Soviet government acted as a successful hegemonic power should; it was concerned with the structure of the international Communist subsystem and with Cuba's broad foreign and internal policies and structures. Because the Soviet Union was not an imperial power, however, it showed little interest in details but was greatly concerned with the identity of the incumbents. Although the power of the top leadership of the Cuban revolution was not threatened, the Soviet Union continued to be an active participant in Cuban factional politics. Its concern with personnel was, however, markedly different from that which had prevailed under United States hegemony and similar to that under United States imperialism. As the Cuban government became relatively less independent of the Soviet Union in the early 1970s, its autonomy relative to its own society increased.

Although no aggregate economic statistics available after 1960 are exactly comparable to those used in the preceding chapters, the discrepancies are not so great as to prevent a gross comparison; prior price deflation does not seriously affect indicators of trade vulnerability. A comparison of table 5.7 with tables 2.2 and 3.5 suggests that Cuban national income depended less heav-

Table 5.7   Trade vulnerability (exports plus imports as a percentage of national income, gross material product, and gross social product), 1962–1974[a]

Year	Trade/national income (%)[b]	Trade/GMP (%)[c]	Trade/GSP (%)[d]
1962	41.9	—	24.1
1963	35.1	—	20.7
1964	40.4	41.2	24.2
1965	41.1	37.6	23.6
1966	39.7	37.7	22.0
1967	—	41.7	23.6
1968	—	40.1	23.9
1969	—	45.3	26.1
1970	—	—	28.2
1971	—	—	25.1
1972	—	—	18.8
1973	—	—	22.0
1974	—	—	33.1

Sources: Computed from *Boletín 1970*, p. 30; *Anuario 1972*, pp. 30, 192; *Anuario 1973*, pp. 35, 186; United National Statistical Office, *Monthly Bulletin of Statistics* 22 (June 1968): 182.

a. The Cuban government defines gross social product (GSP) as the total value of all productive goods and services generated in the country. It is equal to the sum of the gross products of all productive sectors, calculated according to the complete cycle method and not according to enterprise output. Gross material product (GMP) is the total value of material production and services related to production, excluding the value of personal and other services not linked to material production; this method of calculation reduces the risk of counting the same production more than once. It differs from the more usual gross national product (GNP) in that it excludes most services, such as teaching, civil service, and entertainment.

b. Trade and national income previously deflated into 1965 constant prices.

c. Trade and GMP in current prices.

d. Trade and GSP previously deflated into 1965 constant prices for 1962–1966; in current prices thereafter.

ily on trade than at any other period in the twentieth century. Trade vulnerability had not been so low since the 1930s. The early 1960s were a period of considerable economic contraction in Cuba. While the standard of living probably remained well above that of the 1930s, the United States economic embargo reduced Cuban trade and spurred an effort toward economic self-sufficiency. Less trade and greater internal effort in the 1960s reduced Cuban dependence on trade by one-third from the level of the 1950s, at the same time that private foreign investment was ended. Nevertheless, Cuba has remained vulnerable to international trade pressure: it was as vulnerable in the mid-1970s as it had been fifteen years earlier and, as a result, was the target for economic coercion from the United States from 1960 to the present, from China in the late 1960s and again in the mid-1970s, and from the Soviet Union in 1968.

A number of international factors contributed to the centralization of political power in the hands of Prime Minister Castro and his colleagues. The export of the political opposition left behind a more homogeneous population, while the extrication of the United States from Cuban affairs removed private foreign investment as a source of political pluralization and created the need for a vast new Cuban bureaucracy. By not investing in the private sector and by channeling assistance through the government, the socialist countries also increase centralization. Their availability for trade, the Soviet nuclear umbrella, and aid from the Soviet Union were essential to the survival of the revolutionary government. The socialist link not only stimulated the creation of complex bureaucracies but also promoted intrabureaucratic disputes over policy and power. The socialist countries did not seek to weaken the Cuban government's power relative to its society, however; even when they sought influence in Cuba, they maintained the level of centralization by attempting to change government policies from within. As the new hegemonic power in Cuba, the Soviet Union has guaranteed internal Communist orthodoxy. The Cuban government, which has become increasingly loyal to the Soviet Union, has become legitimate at least in part because the hegemonic power has permitted it and has provided the substantial assistance required to advance the goals of the revolution and improve standards of living.

Social Mobilization through Education

The Cuban revolution accomplished the educational policies the United States had outlined under imperialism at the beginning of the twentieth century: Cuba became literate, but it did so in the 1960s entirely on its own. Educational change in Cuban twentieth-century history has been most pronounced at periods of crisis rather than of calm, presumably because the government hopes to improve the level of economic, social, and political performance.

The Cuban revolutionary government launched a literacy campaign in 1961. By the end of that year, the adult literacy rate was listed as 96.1 percent—the highest in Latin America and among the highest in the world. There is some doubt that the 1961 literacy campaign could have reduced the illiteracy levels so drastically, but the reduction of illiteracy was real, though perhaps less impressive, and it did represent a large-scale government effort to advance the level of education and break down the psychological barriers to participation by adults in efforts to educate them.[67] The literacy rate computed from the 1970 census has not been released, but informed scholars place

Table 5.8 Enrollment in public universities and worker-peasant adult-education programs, 1958–1975

Academic year	Universities	Worker-peasant adult schools	% of adults completing year
1958–59	25,514	—	—
1959–60	25,295	79,912	—
1960–61	19,162	66,577	—
1961–62	17,888	428,590	—
1962–63	17,259	468,456	—
1963–64	20,393	455,394	87.5
1964–65	26,271	817,998	65.5
1965–66	26,162	550,837	79.7
1966–67	28,243	430,078	81.3
1967–68	29,238	477,811	73.8
1968–69	32,327	349,217	84.9
1969–70	34,520	268,745	74.8
1970–71	35,137	278,087	78.7
1971–72	36,877	283,513	71.0
1972–73	48,735	278,707	83.3
1973–74	55,435	251,041	63.4
1974–75	—	208,636	—

Sources: Computed from Boletín 1971, pp. 270–273; Anuario 1973, p. 243; Anuario 1974, pp. 243, 244; Azucena Plasencia, "Montaña adentro: la batalla del sexto grado," Bohemia 67, no. 10 (March 7, 1975):35. Statistical series corrected by the Cuban government.

it between 95 and 96 percent.[68] The functional literacy rate, however, is unknown and probably much lower.

The dimensions of Cuba's educational revolution are indicated by tables 5.8 through 5.11. These tables present only public-school enrollment and therefore underestimate total educational enrollment in the early years. Some of the growth of the early 1960s simply reflects the socialization of erstwhile private schools. Adult-education programs on a large scale were promoted by the revolutionary government and showed healthy growth through the early seventies. The net effect of the revolution's educational policies can be seen in the number of students enrolled per 1,000 population at the beginning of several academic years and at four different educational levels:[69]

Academic year	Primary schools	General secondary schools	Technical secondary schools	Universities
1958–59	133	12	2.4	3.8
1964–65	176	18	5.9	3.5
1970–71	195	22	3.2	4.1
1973–74	210	29	6.3	6.1

Because the middle third of the twentieth century had witnessed educational stagnation in literacy and school enrollment, the quantitative educational achievements of the revolutionary government are truly impressive. In addition, the literacy campaign of 1961 was probably consolidated by the efforts in adult education during the remainder of the decade. Table 5.8 gives enrollment figures for only the most important adult-education programs. From 1962–63 through 1973–74, 528,518 adults completed the sixth grade in these programs.[70] The high drop-out rate for 1964–65 suggests that crash efforts to educate adults, such as the one made in that year, are not always successful (the same inefficiency can be seen in table 5.9 for enrollment in technical secondary schools in 1967–68, when another crash educational effort was vitiated by high dropout figures), further reason to doubt the efficacy of the literacy campaign in 1961 alone. Except for 1964–65, the proportion of participants remaining in the adult-education programs throughout the year is high and stable. The tapering off of the enrollment in the early 1970s can be taken as an indication of the long-term success of the program in ensuring a basic level of literacy in Cuban society. One effect of the government monopoly over the press, however, is that fewer daily newspapers are published in the absence of competition. Consequently, the rate of daily newspaper circulation

Table 5.9   Enrollment in public secondary schools, 1958–1974

Academic year	Initial enrollment in general schools	Initial enrollment in technical schools	% of initial general-school enrollees completing year	% of initial technical-school enrollees completing year
1958–59	63,526	15,698	—	—
1959–60	59,582	20,963	—	—
1960–61	89,754	25,632	—	—
1961–62	109,324	34,103	—	92.6
1962–63	123,118	35,966	84.2	87.6
1963–64	137,930	48,872	83.3	83.8
1964–65	136,726	48,531	82.8	77.2
1965–66	149,374	45,536	84.5	54.1
1966–67	171,421	51,477	78.7	45.0
1967–68	178,511	83,089	82.1	25.6
1968–69	187,575	55,860	71.2	53.4
1969–70	177,917	44,890	79.3	46.7
1970–71	186,667	27,566	88.4	64.1
1971–72	201,810	30,429	87.3	73.9
1972–73	222,481	41,940	92.0	81.0
1973–74	265,589	56,959	93.8	95.1

Sources: Computed from *Anuario, 1973,* pp. 236–237, 243; *Anuario 1974,* pp. 239–241. Statistical series corrected by the Cuban government.

Table 5.10 Enrollment in public primary schools, 1958–1974

Academic year	Initial enrollment	% of initial enrollment rural	% of initial enrollees completing year	% of initial rural enrollees completing year
1958–59	717,417	30.2	—	—
1959–60	1,050,119	43.6	—	—
1960–61	1,136,277	42.5	—	—
1961–62	1,166,888	44.5	—	—
1962–63	1,207,980	46.0	90.9	84.7
1963–64	1,315,959	43.1	93.5	95.0
1964–65	1,370,698	41.4	92.8	97.4
1965–66	1,332,088	43.0	93.8	95.2
1966–67	1,367,307	42.6	93.0	92.5
1967–68	1,397,711	41.9	94.7	95.3
1968–69	1,466,286	41.1	103.2	113.6
1969–70	1,558,145	40.1	96.3	96.7
1970–71	1,664,634	40.2	98.3	99.7
1971–72	1,759,167	40.1	98.3	98.4
1972–73	1,852,714	39.6	98.8	98.9
1973–74	1,899,266	39.4	98.4	97.9

Sources: Computed from *Anuario 1973*, pp. 234, 243; *Anuario 1974*, p. 238. Statistical series corrected by the Cuban government.

per 1,000 population fell from 129 (1952–1958 average) to 103 in 1973, just as the literacy rate was rising; only 14.8 percent of the daily newspaper circulation in 1973 was accounted for by newspapers not published in the city of Havana.[71]

The primary-school effort ended the prerevolutionary emphasis on education in urban areas from the first year of revolutionary rule. According to the 1953 census, 43 percent of the population lived in the rural areas; in 1970, 39.5 percent was rural. The distribution of school enrollment by 1970 (table 5.10) is what would be expected from the rural share of the population. The decline in the rural share of primary-school enrollment after the 1962–63 school year can be explained as the effect of rural migration to the cities. The proportion of students completing the year is virtually identical for urban and rural schools. The anomalous figures for the 1968–69 school year reflect some double counting as a result of a new program to send urban schoolchildren to the countryside. Even in the 1970s, however, the rural child still encounters inequality as he rises through the school system. In 1970 Havana province had 27.0 percent of the population; in 1973–74, it had only 23.7 percent of the primary-school teachers but 37.3 percent of the junior-high-school and 51.9 percent of the senior-high-school teachers.[72]

Class barriers to postprimary education weakened significantly during the 1960s and 1970s, when the total number of scholarships granted increased (table 5.11). The government's priorities were, first, to support technical secondary education and, second, to support the universities; other branches of education got what remained. The pressing need for trained personnel explains this pattern.

The degree of Cuban social mobilization reflects the virtual completion of the first stage of modernization, namely, almost universal literacy—represented by the completion of the first through sixth grades—in the urban and rural areas regardless of social class. By contrast, social mobilization had been high in the 1930s, 1940s, and 1950s, but it was concentrated in the urban areas and did not affect unskilled labor. The completion of this stage makes possible full national political participation for the first time in Cuban history. It has had the dual effect of allowing broad political participation and of increasing popular susceptibility to the political appeals from the government.

The quality and efficiency of Cuban social mobilization beyond this first stage is not very high. The development of university-trained personnel lagged until 1970. Despite massive scholarship funds for technical secondary education, violent fluctuations in enrollment have prevented schools from surpassing the levels of the late 1960s (see tables 5.8, 5.9, and 5.11). Enrollments for 1975–76, however, may have broken all previous records at the secondary-school level and initiated a new stage in the Cuban educational revolution;

Table 5.11   Scholarships, 1963–1975

	% of initial enrollment				
Academic year	Primary schools	General secondary schools	Technical secondary schools	Universities	Total scholarships, all levels
1963–64	1.9	12.6	38.2	32.4	86,384
1964–65	1.9	12.8	35.1	44.7	83,978
1965–66	2.1	13.4	67.8	53.2	102,165
1966–67	3.2	15.6	70.0	63.7	128,915
1967–68	3.5	16.4	87.5	64.2	168,754
1968–69	3.8	14.4	89.0	62.9	189,995
1969–70	3.9	24.3	91.1	55.2	197,247
1970–71	3.5	24.3	79.1	51.9	169,944
1971–72	2.8	21.2	62.4	44.6	152,687
1972–73	2.8	27.4	58.5	32.8	178,205
1973–74	2.5	36.3	64.1	31.0	227,253
1974–75	—	—	—	—	306,822

Sources: *Anuario 1972*, p. 247; *Anuario 1973*, pp. 234, 236–237, 243; *Anuario 1974*, p. 237; *Boletín 1971*, p. 280; *Granma*, January 16, 1976, p. 5.

Table 5.12   Educational skill level of Cuban workers

Skill level	1964		1974[a]	
	Number of workers	% of workers	Number of workers	% of workers
Literacy	584,487	53	—	—
Grade 3	309,821	28	734,204	40.8[b]
Grades 4 and 5	60,410	5	—	—
Grade 6+	147,435	13	1,065,796	59.2
All levels	1,102,153	99	1,800,000	100.0

Sources: María de los Angeles Periú, "Experiencias de la educación obrera y campesina en Cuba," *Cuba socialista* no. 42 (February 1965); *Granma Weekly Review*, March 9, 1975, p. 2.
a. Preliminary data.
b. For 1974, this category represents those with less than a sixth-grade education.

over 600,000 students are enrolled in the general program and over 100,000 in the technical and professional program. These totals reflect the impact of the high primary-school enrollments over many preceding years.[73] Data on the educational levels of the 1964 and 1974 labor censuses (table 5.12) show a striking improvement in the level of the work force from bare literacy to completion of the sixth grade. The scattered evidence suggests, however, that the number of those with more than a sixth-grade education is still very small.

The efficiency of the educational system beyond literacy is not very great either. In 1971–1972, 96.4 percent of children between the ages of six and twelve were enrolled in school; in 1974–75, this proportion rose to 99.5 percent, well above the highest prerevolutionary enrollment level in the 1920s. Enrollment was 99.8 percent for eight-year-olds in April 1972, falling only to 94.5 percent of the twelve-year-olds. However, the enrollment rate falls quickly for older children. In November 1974 only 77.3 percent of the fourteen-year-olds, 63.1 percent of the fifteen-year-olds, and 47.6 percent of the sixteen-year-olds were enrolled. The proportion of young people between thirteen and sixteen who were not studying remained "practically unchanged" from 1972 levels in April 1974.[74]

The educational system is not sufficiently effective to retain students beyond primary school and certainly not beyond junior high school; this pattern presents a problem not only of efficiency but also of socialization. The government expects students to be in school until age sixteen; thereafter, they can serve in the armed forces or find jobs. The many teenage dropouts, therefore, are idle, outside government and mass organization programs and contributing nothing to society. This minority of young teenagers does not receive training consistent with revolutionary norms; they are trained in idleness, not in revolutionary consciousness.

Internal inefficiency and low quality are also indicated by the drop-out rate from one grade to the next throughout the educational career of a given age cohort. Lowry Nelson has shown that the drop-out rate between the first and sixth grades was approximately 80 percent from 1959–60 to 1962–63. During those same years, the percentage failing to enroll in the second grade was somewhat above 50 percent. These were the years of large-scale educational expansion when a high drop-out rate was to be expected. The percentage failing to enroll in the second grade declined steadily to 30.9 percent by 1966–67, and to 6.6 percent in urban and 14.3 percent in rural areas in 1968–69.[75] The drop-out rate, though no longer so high by the second grade, has remained very high through the sixth grade. In 1965–66, 387,000 students registered in the first grade; only 82,300, or 21.3 percent, graduated from the sixth grade in six years. In 1969–70, 410,250 entered first grade; 46.0 percent finished sixth grade in six years. But completion of six grades of primary school, though not necessarily in six years, was becoming the norm in Cuba by the mid-1970s through adult-education programs; the government's goal was a sixth-grade education for everyone by 1980. Prime Minister Castro complained about the low promotion as well as the high drop-out rate and thereby politicized the issue. Promotion rates promptly increased, and by the fall of 1974 were getting higher from year to year. Since not enough evidence exists to track the drop-out rate for these age cohorts, it is not clear whether student performance has, in fact, improved, or whether teachers have simply been promoting unqualified students as a result of the politicization of the issue that resulted from the Prime Minister's complaints.[76]

Independent evaluations of the quality of teaching suggest that low promotion rates and high drop-out rates accurately reflect the low quality of teaching at least for the early 1960s. Louis Jones tested a sample of 5,572 students in urban and rural areas in March and June of 1962 for achievement in reading, arithmetic, spelling, and grammar with questions appropriate for each grade. In the first grade, the vast majority of the students had not learned the minimum standards in any of the tested areas. Performance was generally better in the fourth and sixth grades in the four tests, but many had dropped out by then, so a process of selection had taken place. Arithmetic, a necessary skill for competent performance in an economically modernized society, is a case study in point. Jones defined minimum acceptable achievement as 70 percent correct answers, a level reached by 43.1 percent of those tested in the first grade; 14.7 percent in the fourth grade; and 44.9 percent in the sixth grade. Repeated tests for the fourth and sixth graders made it possible to compare responses after a lapse of a few months. The most encouraging finding of the second test was that the urban-rural gap had narrowed but still favored the urban areas. Although the relative effectiveness of rural schools was higher, in absolute terms their level was, of course, still very low. The efficiency of rural schools was close to the national norm, by the measure in table 5.10. In general, Jones concludes that the level of academic achievement is "so low that it is alarming."[77] About 40 percent of the elementary-school teachers in 1976 had not graduated from any teacher-training school and were barely educated. The educational thesis of the 1975 First Party Congress recognized a catalogue of deficiencies in the educational system, including the low quality of instruction, the scarcity and lack of training of teachers, a very high pupil-teacher ratio, too much work for teachers that was not connected with the classroom, scarcities and irregular supplies of educational materials, and poor building maintenance.[78]

These criticisms of the quality and efficiency of the educational system since 1959 should not detract from the impressive educational achievements of the revolutionary government compared to the prerevolutionary period. Dropouts and low quality are not new, but a thorough evaluation of education—the most important indicator of social mobilization—requires assessments of these factors. The Cuban revolution's historic achievement in this area has been virtually universal literacy and completion of primary school. All children are at least exposed to education; all aspects of social life are thought to be suitable for study in school. Cubans have thereby become available for new kinds of organization and behavior on a national scale: every citizen can participate in the society, however modestly, and every citizen can absorb some minimal level of information from the revolutionary government. But the quality of education and the level of social mobilization are still low, more because citizens have found change too burdensome than because the government has failed to try.

Cubans are a primary-school–educated people. Even among the young, only between a fifth and a quarter reach the sixth grade in six years—that is, without repeating a grade—though most people complete the sixth grade eventually. Cuba has mass, near-universal social mobilization, however low its quality. Therefore it exhibits characteristics of both modernized and non-modernized societies.

Higher levels of educational training do not automatically produce a challenge to political authority: some countries with strong government control over their societies also have a high proportion of citizens with at least a secondary-school education. Education is a necessary, but not a sufficient, requirement for autonomous political participation. At the top of the political structure in the first half of the 1970s, this primary-school–educated people was led by junior-high-school graduates. Cuba's level and quality of social mobilization, therefore, are crucial in defining the current political system. Near-universal literacy permits near-universal political participation. The low quality of the social mobilization tends, in combination with the export of the opposition, to guarantee that there will be no significant political challenges to established authority. Political participation and a government control are simultaneously made possible.

In general, the first phase of modernization facilitates political mobilization and control without significant challenge to the central leadership. Citizens are capable of political activity under government direction, but few are sufficiently skilled and intellectually independent enough to act without it. A highly participative political system such as Cuba's would have been impossible without an increase in the level of social mobilization, but a high degree of government and party control over that participation would have been more difficult (though certainly still possible) if the quality of social mobilization had been much higher.

The Economy and Social Welfare

Revolutions are often disruptive of economic growth, but the economic cost of the civil war in the 1950s was comparatively small. The economy grew on a real per capita basis, though modestly, until 1957, stopping only in 1958. Partly because sufficient data have not been released and partly because the accounting system is different, no unbroken series of national accounts is available to show the annual performance of the Cuban economy after 1958. Much of the subsequent discussion must necessarily be tentative. [79]

Economic Growth

The consensus seems to be that the Cuban economy resumed its growth, interrupted briefly in 1958 by the civil war, in 1959 and 1960. Socialism did not come to Cuba until the summer of 1960; thus renewal of economic growth in 1959 and the first half of 1960 represented the last gasp of presocialist Cuba. The government then pursued a strongly redistributive policy, producing a shift in the structure of demand. The rich were less able to afford the mostly imported luxury and semiluxury goods; the poor were newly able to afford essential consumer goods, many of them produced in Cuba. Domestic manufacturing, burdened with an excess of installed industrial capacity, benefited from this shift in demand by increasing industrial production, while payments abroad for imported luxury and semiluxury goods declined. [80]

The peculiar way in which land-reform legislation was applied in 1959–1960 helped to increase agricultural production. Of all the land socialized in 1959 through 1961, 48.9 percent was taken as a result of laws aimed specifically at all United States landowners in Cuba; an additional 13.1 percent had been sold voluntarily, and another 13.1 percent, donated to the government. Only 3.7 percent of all the socialized land resulted from the February 1959 law socializing property belonging to officials of the Batista government, and only 27.2 percent from the land-reform act of May 1959. [81] Much of the land taken under the latter was used for cattle raising. Most land used for other purposes was unaffected by socialization until the second half of 1960, although its owners were well aware that they would one day be subject to the law. The act limited landownership to 402.6 hectares; farms with productivity 50 percent over the national average for that crop were limited to 1,342 hectares. Landowners were therefore stimulated to increase productivity in order to reduce the burden of socialization upon them. When it became evident that socialization was inescapable, agricultural workers demanded that farms be thoroughly exploited—so that they would not lose their jobs if production fell—or they would denounce the owner to the government for counterrevolutionary activities. The nonapplication of the land-reform act, coupled with strong political and social pressures from agricultural workers who wanted full employment, stimulated production.[82]

It is also agreed that the Cuban economy plunged in the early 1960s to a bottom reached in 1963, a delayed result of revolution. Its causes were various. As socialization threatened, private manufacturers reduced productive efforts. They did not want to invest in enterprises about to be lost. The new managers of state enterprises were often selected for their loyalty, not their competence. Workers' efforts were diverted to politics, not productivity. Managers and technicians left the country, a political gain for the government but at an economic cost. In the fall of 1962 the United States instituted first a sugar boycott, then a general economic embargo, and, briefly, a blockade.[83] The Cuban economy was reorganized in 1963 to emphasize sugar production, as it had in the prerevolutionary period, and to specialize in agriculture. Industry would serve agriculture and provide some essential consumer goods. The emphasis on sugar had become an obsession by the end of the 1960s; in 1970 an attempt was made to produce ten million tons of sugar—something which the Cuban economy has yet achieve. The economic recovery of the mid-1960s was interrupted at the end of the decade with a second economic plunge as severe as, if not worse than, the first.

Table 5.13 summarizes the best and the worst years for the production of 353 different items. A fifth of all industrial products had their worst year in 1963. That 1963 was a terrible year for the economy is also supported by table 5.14, which shows the worst statistics for post–World War II sugar production, total agricultural production, and agricultural production per capita. Per capita national income, gross material product, and gross social product (all in 1965 constant prices, to eliminate the impact of inflation) also fell (table 5.15). Because virtually all production data released by the Cuban government begin in 1963, they overstate the subsequent improvement in the Cuban economy. In fact, economic performance was dismal throughout the mid-sixties, even with the only available baseline dating from the depressed period. Cuba failed to grow economically per capita in constant prices between 1963 and 1966; the trend is slightly negative in two other indicators. Gross material product per capita (in current prices) had not yet recovered its 1964 level by 1969; it declined every year except one (1968) between 1964 and 1969—an average

Table 5.13   Product lines at peak and lowest production, 1959–1973[a]

Year	Industry[b] Number at peak production	Industry[b] Number at lowest production	Agriculture Number at peak production	Agriculture Number at lowest production	Cattle raising Number at peak production	Cattle raising Number at lowest production	Forestry Number at peak production	Forestry Number at lowest production	Fishing Number at peak production	Fishing Number at lowest production
1959	—	—	—	—	—	—	0	1	1	12
1960	—	—	—	—	—	—	5	0	1	1
1961	—	—	2	1	0	1	1	0	0	3
1962	20	54	4	5	0	2	4	2	0	2
1963	26	19	3	3	1	0	0	0	4	4
1964	14	25	2	2	0	0	0	0	1	5
1965	10	10	7	4	0	0	0	0	1	1
1966	22	15	1	2	0	0	0	0	1	1
1967	19	17	4	0	0	0	0	0	7	0
1968	12	30	2	4	0	2	0	0	4	6
1969	7	56	3	8	0	0	0	1	5	1
1970	27	21	0	5	0	0	0	5	6	1
1971	28	5	1	1	1	0	0	3	4	0
1972	74	7	1	1	1	1	1	0	2	2
1973	7	7	9	3	3	0	1	0	3	0

Sources: Computed from *Boletín 1971*, pp. 78, 96–104, 123, 142–143, 166–178; *Anuario 1972*, pp. 69, 72–73, 107–109, 132, 141–144, 154; *Anuario 1973*, pp. 52, 63–64, 66, 67–68, 70, 76–86, 124, 126, 128–132.

a. Measured by physical output.

b. Seven of the 259 industrial products are measured in terms of pesos, not output; two of these reached possibly price-inflated record levels in 1971, one in 1972, and two more in 1973.

annual decline of more than 2 percent in current prices. Gross social product per capita (in current prices) in 1969 was also still below its 1965 level. Total agricultural production recovered from 1963 to 1967; a less impressive improvement of per capita agricultural production also occurred, but it remained at prerevolutionary levels (table 5.14).

Table 5.14 Agricultural production, 1951–1974

Year	Raw sugar production (in thousands of metric tons)[a]		Index of total agricultural production (1952–56 = 100)[d]	Index of agricultural production per capita (1952–56 = 100)[d]
	Cuban government statistics[b]	Hagelberg statistics[c]		
1951	5,821	5,759	—	—
1952	7,298	7,225	—	—
1953	5,224	5,159	—	—
1954	4,959	4,890	—	—
1955	4,597	4,528	92	90
1956	4,807	4,740	94	90
1957	5,741	5,672	107	101
1958	5,863	5,784	107	98
1959	6,039	5,964	113	102
1960	5,943	5,862	115	101
1961	6,876	6,767	124	108
1962	4,883	4,815	102	87
1963	3,883	3,821	87	73
1964	4,475	4,590	95	77
1965	6,156	6,082	115	91
1966	4,537	4,867	97	75
1967	6,236	6,236	122	93
1968	5,165	5,315	111	82
1969	4,459	5,534	105	77
1970	8,538	7,559	155	111
1971	5,925	5,950	122	86
1972	4,325	4,688	—	—
1973	5,253	—	—	—
1974	5,925[e]	—	—	—

Sources: Anuario 1974, p. 124; Gerald B. Hagelberg, The Caribbean Sugar Industries: Constraints and Opportunities (New Haven: Yale University, Antilles Research Program, 1974), p. 112; CIA, The Cuban Economy, p. 3; Food and Agriculture Organization, Monthly Bulletin of Agricultural Economics and Statistics 21 (January 1972): 21, 23.

   a. Raw sugar production at 96 degrees polarity. One metric ton = 2204.6 pounds.
   b. 1951–1973 from Anuario 1974, p. 124.
   c. 1951–1972 from Hagelberg, Caribbean Sugar Industries.
   d. The average of the years 1952–1956 is used as the point of reference.
   e. From CIA, The Cuban Economy.

Table 5.15   Aggregate per capita economic indicators, 1962–1974 (in pesos)[a]

Year	National income (in 1965 prices)	GMP (in 1965 prices)	GMP (in current prices)	GSP (in 1965 prices)[b]	GSP (in current prices)[b]
1962	491	517	—	850	—
1963	485	511	—	823	—
1964	514	543	560	860	—
1965	504	536	536	878	878
1966	473	505	512	851	—
1967	—	—	507	—	895
1968	—	—	534	—	894
1969	—	—	501	—	868
1970	—	—	—	—	977
1971	—	—	—	—	1032
1972	—	—	—	—	1176
1973	—	—	—	—	1319
1974	—	—	—	—	1449

Sources: Computed from *Boletín 1970*, p. 30; *Anuario 1972*, pp. 18, 30; *Anuario 1973*, p. 32; *Anuario 1974*, pp. 22, 35, and erratum insert; United Nations, *Monthly Bulletin of Statistics* 22 (June 1968):182.

a. The Cuban government defines gross social product (GSP) as the total value of all productive goods and services generated in the country; it equals the sum of the gross products of all productive sectors, calculated according to the complete cycle method and not according to enterprise output. Gross material product (GMP) is the total value of material production and services related to production, excluding the value of personal and other services not linked to material production.

b. Except for 1974, where December data are used, counts are for June of each year.

The performance of the various sectors of the economy in the mid-sixties, shown in table 5.16, was fairly consistent. When 1964–1966 is compared with 1966–1968, the distribution of advances and declines is about the same in industry, agriculture, cattle raising, forestry, and fishing. The only differences are a few more advances in previously unreported sectors within industry, agriculture, and fishing in the second period. Neither the number of production peaks nor that of production lows is very high, especially in industry, a fact that supports the view that general consistency prevailed in the economy (see table 5.13); the precipitous fall of the early 1960s was halted by the middle of that decade. The more reliable aggregate per capita statistics in constant prices show a continuing negative though modest slide.

Cuba's achievement in sugar production in 1970 (see table 5.14) was matched by the terrible cost of that achievement in the rest of the economy (see tables 5.13 and 5.16).[84] In 1970, 21.6 percent of industrial products, 21.1 percent of agricultural products, and 41.7 percent of forestry products had

Table 5.16 Product lines showing increases and decreases in production, 1958–1973[a]

Years	Industry		Agriculture		Cattle raising		Forestry		Fishing	
	Rising	Falling	Rising	Falling	Rising	Falling	Rising	Falling	Rising	Falling
1958–64	—	—	—	—	—	—	7	0	18	4
1964–66	118	98	18	16	3	2	3	9	19	10
1966–68	124	98	23	15	3	2	3	9	21	10
1968–70	86	162	12	26	3	2	1	11	17	18
1970–71	188	62	21	17	4	1	8	4	19	18
1971–72	129	52	28	10	4	1	6	2	16	20
1972–73	124	49	26	12	4	1	5	1	9	7

Sources: Computed from *Boletín 1971*, pp. 78, 96–104, 123, 142–143, 166–178; *Anuario 1972*, pp. 69, 72–73, 107–109, 132, 141–144, 154; *Anuario 1973*, pp. 52, 63–64, 66, 67–68, 70, 76–86, 124, 126, 128–132.

a. Except for seven of the industrial products, which are measured in terms of total value in pesos, increases and decreases are measured in terms of physical output.

their worst production year. Between 1968 and 1970, declines outnumbered increases by almost two to one in industry and by over two to one in agriculture. All but one of the twelve product lines in forestry fell. The fishing industry, the darling of revolutionary performance, showed more declines than increases for the first time. The only aggregate economic statistic for 1970 is gross social product per capita (in current prices)—inflated by the size of the sugar crop and modest price increases. It masks the disastrous impact of that year on the economy. Because disaster struck after precipitous and then gradual economic decline, Cuba's overall economic performance was very poor as the first decade of socialism closed.

It is difficult to summarize Cuban economic performance in the early 1970s. At long last sustained economic growth may have gotten under way, but unfortunately the production data in the 1972, 1973, and 1974 statistical yearbooks are open to the charge of statistical manipulation, especially in the industrial sector.[85] Prime Minister Castro stated that the Cuban economy grew 5 percent in 1971, 9 percent in 1972, and 13 percent in 1973, but without noting which aggregate indicator he used. In 1974 Oneida Alvarez reported "more than 8 percent gross national product growth in 1971 and 1972." Carlos Rafael Rodríguez reported 10 percent for 1972 and estimated 14 percent for 1973.[86] Gross social product (GSP) grew 7.3 percent in 1971, 16.2 percent in 1972, 14.4 percent in 1973 and an estimated 10.3 percent in 1974. GSP per capita grew at an average annual rate of 9.2 percent between 1970 and 1974. President Dorticós reported a GSP growth of 11.5 percent in 1975.[87] All of these aggregate statistical series referring to different indicators are apparently stated in current prices.

There had, however, been price inflation in Cuba in the early 1970s. The government first "liberated" prices on alcoholic beverages, then on cigarettes and tobacco products, then gasoline, vacation plans, and a few other consumer goods; still others, production of which had been very small in the 1960s, were reintroduced at substantially higher prices. Cosmetics and perfumes were "liberated" in late 1973.

Day care centers began in 1977 to charge enrollment fees according to the family's ability to pay. The minimum fee—regardless of family income—was 3 pesos a month, rising to a maximum of 40 pesos a month. All these price increases were supposed to reduce the amount of money in circulation ("socialist inflation") and add to the value of the remaining currency. The higher prices for goods and services allowed the government to rely on material incentives to increase individual productivity.[88] Prices for everything except food, medicine, and essential clothing were decontrolled by the mid-seventies, a move that was made possible by increased production.

Because the statistics are apparently stated in current prices, some price deflation and adjustment for population growth are necessary before real growth can be determined—but there is little doubt that real growth did in fact occur.[89] Some of it was the result of the worldwide inflation of the price of sugar, the improvement in Cuba's terms of trade, and Soviet aid that allowed the import of consumer goods and helped rescue the Cuban economy. The delayed impact of worldwide inflation on most products and the decline in world sugar prices induced an economic recession in 1976. Cuba thus showed steady and real, if modest, per capita economic growth in the first half of the 1970s—for the first time since the revolutionary government came to power. The leading sector, construction, rose 169 percent in constant prices between 1970 and 1974. Industry increased by 35 percent in constant prices during the same period (see tables 5.13, 5.14, and 5.16).[90] Sugar production, however, declined from 1970 to 1972, contributing to the rise in world prices (table 5.14), but rose steadily thereafter to 1975. Agriculture was generally lagging, with no more than 4.6 percent total growth in constant prices from 1970 to 1974.[91]

On January 2, 1974, Armed Forces Minister Raúl Castro said that from 1958 through 1973 "the population of our country grew 32 percent . . . The growth obtained in material production goes beyond this figure."[92] This hardly represents an optimistic report on the economy. It may be stated in price-inflated current prices, and it uses 1958, characterized by both a civil war and a recession, as the baseline. The World Bank estimated that Cuba's annual growth rate of gross national product per capita from 1960 to 1970 was −0.6 percent, making an increase through 1973 barely sufficient to turn the rate of growth in gross product per capita to a plus sign relative to 1958, though perhaps still below the 1960 level.

Since 1970, there has been steady, economic improvement, led by the construction industry. Because industrial production reached an aggregate record only in 1973, however, and because of inflation, gross product per capita in constant prices in the mid-1970s may not be much larger than it was in the mid-1960s, and it may be below a good presocialist year (1960). A weak prerevolutionary year (1958) was finally surpassed only by 1973. But aside from unusually good or poor years, the mid-1970s probably surpassed the 1950s.[93]

Wages and Employment

The welfare of individuals cannot be inferred directly from aggregate economic performance, although the two are obviously connected. The Cuban government pursued strongly redistributive economic policies, and these must be examined before judgment on the welfare of the general population can be made.

A large proportion of income was transferred to nonagricultural workers in the first fifteen months of revolutionary rule, as shown by a comparison of their wages, in current prices, with the same month in 1958 (set at 100):[94]

	1959	1960
January	97	140
February	99	149
March	104	145
April	122	—
May	124	—
June	128	—
July	137	—
August	128	—
September	136	—
October	146	—
November	157	—
December	161	—

By March of 1959, wages were already above their 1958 levels, and they remained there. Although wages ordinarily decline seasonally by early summer and remain depressed until mid-fall, that did not really happen in 1959. In 1957, wages fell 17.7 percent between April and July, and in 1958, 24.1 percent from March to November. In 1959, however, they fell only 8.0 percent from a May high to an August low (December wages are excluded because they include a year-end bonus), and the autumn rise began earlier than usual.

The revolutionary government rapidly reduced unemployment from the high reached during the climax of the civil war in late 1958, but unemployment nonetheless remained a problem. The percentage of the work force that was unemployed in months for which information is available in 1959 and 1960 was as follows: [95]

	1959	1960
January	16.6	9.9
February	13.5	—
March	10.4	9.3
April	11.5	—
May	12.6	13.5
June	—	—
July	15.0	14.0
August	—	—
September	15.9	13.1
October	—	—
November	13.5	11.7
December	—	—

In January 1961, 9.5 percent of the work force was unemployed, as was 6.7 percent in March of that year. The period of presocialist revolutionary rule is similar to the prerevolutionary period in several respects. Gross product grew in 1959–1960, as it had been doing since the late 1940s. Employed workers, benefiting from union strength and government support, won substantial wage increases, as they had in the prerevolutionary period (except for the second Batista government in the 1950s). Unemployment persisted, both in the prerevolutionary period and in 1959 and 1960, and a high premium was placed on being employed. In the spring of 1960, 22 percent of the respondents in a survey were still citing unemployment as their greatest fear, and 23 percent cited employment as their greatest hope.[96] The Cuban political system was improving on those things that the prerevolutionary system had already done fairly well: economic growth and redistribution of income that favored organized labor. But it was not improving on what the prerevolutionary system had done badly: reduction of unemployment. Average annual unemployment in 1957 was 12.4 percent; it fell to 11.2 percent in 1958, rose to 13.6 percent in 1959, and fell to 11.8 percent in 1960—essentially no change.

The wage share of the economy was no lower in the 1960s than it had been at the end of the Batista regime, and it was probably higher (table 5.17). Many agricultural workers who were previously privately employed were added to the state payroll in the fall of 1963, a move called by the government the "second agrarian reform"; a large number of privately employed or self-employed retail workers were added in 1968 (the government called this the "revolutionary offensive"). Relatively few workers had been added to the state payroll during the intervening years (1963–1968), so there must have been a real upward trend during those years. From 1967 to 1970, average annual wages increased 4.1 percent, partly through the socialization of retail business and residual categories in industry and transportation, and partly through a real wage increase that led to large accumulations of money in private hands (much of which could not be spent because of rationing and the scarcity of consumer goods). Wages as a percentage of gross material or social product rose to an all-time high in 1969. Since then, however, the wage share of gross product has been declining. Wages increased 2.9 percent in 1971, 5.9 percent in 1972, and 9.7 percent in 1973. Civilian wages grew 24 percent less than gross product in 1974.[97] Compared to the reported increases in the gross product, wages have been lagging. Socialism in the 1960s redistributed income to wage earners, perhaps reaching an all-time high, although part of this monetary income could not be spent. The renewal of economic growth in the 1970s, not unlike the economic growth under Batista in the 1950s, has been associated with a decline in the wage share of gross product.

Socialism also brought about a decline of overt unemployment in the 1960s. Carmelo Mesa Lago estimates unemployment fell from 8.8 percent in 1962 to 4.5 percent in 1965 and 2.7 percent in 1968. It was 1.3 percent in 1970.[98] A shortage of labor then appeared. When that happened, the government resorted to largescale mobilization of unpaid and not always voluntary labor to

Table 5.17 Wages of state workers relative to aggregate economic indicators, 1962–1973 (in current prices)[a]

Year	Wages/ net material product (%)	Wages/GMP (%)	Wages/GSP (%)
1962	59.2	—	—
1963	59.4	—	—
1964	54.5	—	—
1965	59.5	—	—
1966	64.3	51.3	—
1967	—	59.2[b]	33.5
1968	—	61.6	36.8
1969	—	65.3	37.7
1970	—	—	34.1
1971	—	—	32.7
1972	—	—	29.8
1973	—	—	28.6

Sources: Computed from United Nations, *Monthly Bulletin of Statistics* 22 (June 1968):176, 182; *Anuario 1972*, pp. 30, 37, 39; *Anuario 1973*, p. 40; *Anuario 1974*, pp. 35, 41; *Boletin 1970*, p. 35.

a. The wages used to compute percentage of gross material product (GMP) have been revised by the Cuban government and are lower than those used to compute percentage of net material product. The data in this table are not strictly comparable to those in chapter 3, as they include only workers employed directly by the state. Although most workers were employed by the state (their proportion rose throughout the 1960s), substantial private employment remained, especially in agriculture, which would have to be added to these statistics before comparing them with prerevolutionary data. The national accounting system under the revolutionary government was also different from the prerevolutionary one, even though net material product is almost equivalent to national income and GMP is almost equivalent to GNP. The government has not published statistics consistently enough to fill the gaps.

b. Computation from yet further revised official wage statistics gives 67.9 percent. See *Granma Weekly Review*, November 25, 1973, p. 9.

face the shortage. Overt unemployment, however, was replaced by disguised unemployment, a solution reached at a cost to economic efficiency.

For the newly employed, nevertheless, steady job-holding and the security it represented was a new experience; both socially and psychologically, disguised unemployment is preferable to overt unemployment. By the early 1970s, the government was also making an effort to increase productivity and reduce disguised unemployment. Prime Minister Castro, at the Thirteenth Labor Congress in the fall of 1973, revealed the magnitude of disguised unemployment: jobs that had been done in prerevolutionary days by two hundred workers now required over seven hundred. Disguised unemployment was also found in the practice of guaranteeing jobs to seasonal workers year-round, especially in the sugar industry; these workers held jobs but did little work. The stabilization of work in seasonal jobs—a socially desirable result—led to the underutilization of labor and to a decline in productivity.[99]

Measures taken in late 1970 to remedy the problem of low productivity were in part successful, but only by leading to even more overt unemployment. At the Labor Congress, the Prime Minister noted "a greater demand for jobs"; "the time may come," he said, "when we will have a headache finding jobs for all those who want to work." The headache, in fact, had arrived some eighteen months earlier in two of the largest provinces, Las Villas and Oriente. President Dorticós noted the end of the labor shortage and the reappearance of regional unemployment there, while labor shortages were reported in Havana province and in the smaller Matanzas and Camagüey provinces. In February 1975 the secretary-general of the labor confederation reported "already a considerable number" of workers "without placement who were receiving a salary without working."[100]

Unemployment after the spring of 1971 was involuntary, for the government had approved an anti-"loafing" law making it a crime for any adult male between the ages of seventeen and sixty not to work if he was physically able to do so, even if he could afford not to. As a result of the law 101,019 persons signed up for work; half of them had never worked before.[101]

Health, Social Services, and Housing

The mortality rate remained virtually unchanged from the prerevolutionary period until 1970, when it at last declined below the prerevolutionary threshold (table 5.18). The exodus of medical personnel in the emigration of the early sixties is reflected in the rise of both total and infant-mortality rates to a peak in 1962. While the total mortality rate edged down thereafter, the infant-mortality rate shot up once again to peak in 1969. It declined again in the early seventies, to below the 1958 level. The infant-mortality rate faithfully reflects aggregate economic trends.[102] While the government's efforts to improve public health have begun to pay off in the 1970s, the effect of revolutionary rule was to interrupt the improvement in public health witnessed earlier in the twentieth century. Improvement began again only at the end of the first decade of revolutionary rule.

A powerful contribution to the improved welfare of the Cuban people had been made by the provision of important services free of charge. Electricity and telephone rates were reduced in 1959. High-quality education and medical care have been free of charge to every Cuban. As already noted, day care services were free until 1977. Prerevolutionary Cuba had provided some edu-

Table 5.18 Mortality rates, 1953–1976

Year	Deaths per 1,000 population	Deaths under age one per 1,000 live births
1953	6.3	35.0
1958	6.4	33.4
1959	6.5	34.7
1960	6.2	35.9
1961	6.5	37.6
1962	7.2	41.5
1963	6.8	37.1
1964	6.4	37.4
1965	6.5	37.8
1966	6.4	37.2
1967	6.3	36.4
1968	6.6	38.2
1969	6.7	46.7
1970	6.2	38.7
1971	6.0	37.4
1972	5.5	27.4
1973	5.7	28.9
1974	—	27.9
1976	—	22.8

Sources: Computed from *Anuario 1972*, pp. 18, 22; *Anuario 1973*, pp. 22, 26; *Anuario 1974*, p. 28; *Granma Weekly Review*, May 15, 1977, p. 11.

cation and medical care free of charge, but mostly in urban areas, and they were generally of lower quality than comparable private facilities. These services—now almost universally available free—are an outstanding achievement of revolutionary rule.

Sports events, many other recreational facilities, and public telephone service are also free of charge, although by the early 1970s these policies were apparently being reconsidered. Rates for electricity, water, long-distance transportation, and restaurant meals (including worker canteens) were increased.[103] As already mentioned, prices of consumer goods and services were also increased. Nevertheless, even with these changes, there has been a redistribution of income to favor the poor over the long run.

Rationing was introduced in Cuba during the 1962 economic collapse and has become an institutionalized procedure in Cuban life; its use declined somewhat in the early seventies, however, as increased production and induced price inflation "liberated" goods from the rationing system. Rationing was at the outset, and has always remained, indicative of the failure of the economy to grow. But rationing has also made it possible to guarantee a more adequate and fairer distribution of scarce goods, and in this sense the ration card summarizes the twin aspects of revolutionary economic performance: success in redistribution, failure in growth.

On March 10, 1959, the government cut rents by 50 percent up to $100 a month, 40 percent over $100 a month, and 30 percent over $200 a month. This and other housing laws of the first months of revolutionary rule were reformist, but none brought about socialization until the Urban Reform Act of October 14, 1960, when the state took over all rental housing units and proscribed private rental of immovables. The law set rents for tenants, the equivalent of no more than 10 percent of their income, to be paid to the state, and provided for a modest scale of compensation to the former owners, the most generous aspect of which was that it came in the form of a monthly rent for life rather than a lump sum.[104] Reform and socialization reduced the cost of housing, especially for the poor. While studies of the share of income paid for housing according to social class in prerevolutionary Cuba are in disagreement, 10 percent of income represents a reduction under any of them.[105]

Between 1946 and 1953, an average of 26,827 dwellings were constructed each year in all Cuba, 46.3 percent of them in Havana.[106] The number constructed between 1953 and 1958 is more difficult to determine, but most believe there was a construction boom, much of it in luxury and semiluxury housing in Havana. This hardly solved the housing problems of the middle class and the poor in Havana, not to mention the rest of the country. The National Bank estimated in 1958 that the acknowledged housing shortage was being reduced by only 7 percent per year.[107]

Maruja Acosta and Jorge Hardoy have estimated that Cuba needed approximately 28,000 housing units a year between 1953 and 1958, using a national average-occupancy rate of 4.8 people per unit. Given the average for 1946–1953 and a construction boom in 1953–1958, it is likely that the new aggregate demand for housing units was being met and even that some improvement was being made in the preexisting housing stock, as the National Bank indicated. Nevertheless, only 52.3 percent of urban construction in the 1953 census was judged to be of good quality, and the city of Havana had a large share of this housing. The quality of agricultural workers' housing was substandard, as was the quality of housing for the urban poor. Good housing was expensive.[108] The housing problems in prerevolutionary Cuba, therefore, were mainly qualitative and distributional.

After the emigration, many dwellings were available for governmental reallocation in the 1960s, especially in the city of Havana. Because of this, and perhaps because of government priorities, little new housing was built in the 1960s. Government estimates give an annual average of 17,089 housing units constructed between 1959 and 1963, a substantial reduction from the prerevolutionary average. The difference between this figure and the number of units actually required was partly made up by the housing made available by emigrants. The government has never published its estimate of housing needs. I assume the national urban occupancy rate of 4.2 people per unit in 1970 can be applied in the 1960s, because most of the exiles came from the urban upper and upper-middle classes and had an occupancy rate lower than the national average. Between 1960 and 1963 they made available an annual average of no more than 12,400 housing units,[109] for a total maximum increase in available housing equal to 29,289 units per year available to families of various sizes—the probable level of the 1950s.[110]

The rate of new housing construction continued to decline after 1963. The average number of housing units completed annually by the construction sector and local governments between 1964 and 1967 was 7,164. For those same years the average number of housing units made available annually by emigration (based on the 1970 urban occupancy rate of 4.2 people per unit) fell to no more than 8,106 for a total maximum increase in available housing equal to 15,270 units per year.[111] The quotas for the furniture industry in 1967 called for furnishing only 3,432 dwellings.[112] From 1968 to 1971, exiles made available no more than 12,653 housing units per year, while the annual average number of housing units completed by the construction sector and local governments was 5,073 (with a low of 4,004 in 1970). The combined annual increase in available housing amounted to 17,726.[113] Cuba needed to supply 37,500 housing units per year after 1970 in order to lodge the new inhabitants, and many more if the accumulated housing deficit was to be met.[114]

That the housing deficit worsened under revolutionary rule is suggested by the emphasis on housing construction in the 1970s. A small but carefully selected sample of sixty-nine divorced persons in 1970 showed that only 33 percent of the couples lived in their own housing units, independent of relatives and others, even though 96 percent would have preferred to live alone. Housing construction by the construction sector and local governments rose from a low of 4,004 in 1970 to 5,014 in 1971; 16,807 in 1972; and 20,710 in 1973; it fell to 18,563 in 1974. Exiles made available 11,817 units in 1971, but only 927 in 1974. On July 26, 1974, the Prime Minister noted that housing was being constructed at a rate between 25,000 and 30,000 units a year. However, the construction microbrigades mobilized to speed up housing construction in the early 1970s completed only 11,242 housing units in 1974 and started building only another 11,334. According to the Prime Minister, only 200,000 housing units were constructed between 1959 and 1975, for an annual average of 11,765; the emigration made available no more than 139,256 housing units from 1960 to 1974, or an annual average of 9,284.[115] If the estimate of Cuba's need for new housing at 37,500 units per year is correct, the housing deficit is still growing in the 1970s, despite these efforts. While the housing deficit, increased under revolutionary rule, is serious, improvement still lies in the future.

Nonetheless Cuba has made significant progress at least in the distribution of housing. Government allocation of housing left by the emigration and the lowering of rents have eliminated income discrimination in access to housing as well as making it cheaper overall. But, as with economic growth and improvements in infant mortality, lack of growth was a problem. Not enough new housing was built, and a serious housing shortage grew worse. In the 1950s, it had been easier to get housing, though what was obtained might be expensive or substandard. The revolutionary government built housing for the poor and reallocated the housing left by the rich. But population growth soon overcame the housing supply, at least until the early 1970s. Even the new efforts were still insufficient to meet the demand.

Generally speaking, the revolutionary social system proved rather more capable of addressing problems of distribution than problems of growth. The economy stagnated until the early seventies; public health shows a deterioration in the early and late 1960s and an improvement in the early 1970s, a net loss of a decade in improvement; housing deteriorated until the early 1970s, when it is possible, though unlikely, that the supply may actually have met annual demand. Revolutionary government and politics operated with a material scarcity unknown since the 1930s.

The distributional performance of the revolutionary government is a success story. Wages paid to labor reached an all-time high in 1969, though they declined thereafter relative to gross product. Unemployment, at last, was sharply reduced by the mid-sixties and has mostly remained very low ever since. The provision of social services free of charge is an outstanding achievement. Rationing, though indicative of economic failure, at least ensured a more just allocation of whatever resources there were. Although the regime retreated from egalitarianism in the early seventies, the commitment to the provision of many basic goods and services, free or very cheaply, remained. A substantial redistribution in the provision of health services to some extent made up for the "lost decade" in public health, though it is again a success of redistribution and not of net growth. The impressive redistribution of the housing stock benefited the rural areas disproportionately.

Unfortunately, most redistributed goods and services did not result from new growth, but from the reallocation of stable or shrinking resources. The performance of the Cuban revolutionary government in economics and welfare stressed, and was fundamentally successful in achieving, a redistribution that favored the poor. Scarcities were more equitably shared than they had been in the thirties. But that was the mark of the revolution; that was what made it radical. Its appeal for support has been based precisely on distributive social justice. What it failed to do was what prerevolutionary capitalist Cuba had done better—though not well enough—that is, to grow in aggregate economic measures and aggregate welfare. In the 1970s, the Cuban government proved more willing to sacrifice redistribution for the sake of growth, and this trend was further encouraged by favorable changes in international factors. Politics shifted from reallocating scarcities to sustaining growth. Ten years from now we can reassess whether socialist Cuba will have at long last outperformed presocialist Cuba in accomplishing both.

The governing of Cuba had been difficult before the revolution in part because United States hegemony did not sufficiently encourage the development of a capable and centralized government and, in the first third of the century, United States imperialism obstructed it. With the coming of the revolution, the net effect of outside influences on Cuban government altered dramatically. The conflict with the United States required a strong central government in Cuba if revolutionary rule was to persist; the United States absorption of a substantial part of the Cuban political opposition to the revolutionary government homogenized Cuban politics. Soviet hegemony bureaucratized Cuban government, first, by contributing to the development of capable and centralized bureaucracies, and, second, by promoting bureaucratic factionalism. Soviet hegemony depended on centralized and factionalized politics in Cuba in order to operate. As a competent hegemonial power, the Soviet Union defended the structure of Cuban politics whenever it was seriously threatened. Unlike United States hegemonial politics, Soviet hegemony accepts and promotes a powerful central government as an intermediary between outside influences and internal Cuban affairs, and it promotes factional conflict, but it does not penetrate the Cuban economy directly through private investment by its nationals.

Just as Soviet hegemony made centralized government possible when the United States was expelled from Cuba, so, too, social mobilization made possible the expansion of power by that central government. For the first time in Cuban history, virtually all adults were available for political participation promoted by a single and newly powerful central government. Yet the quality of social mobilization remained low enough that autonomous political participation was difficult, once the elite political opposition had been exported. Thus social mobilization made possible the expansion of government power over the entire citizenry by promoting controlled and closely monitored political participation.

Centralized government in Cuba operated in a context of material scarcity during the first decade of its rule. That scarcity resulted from both internal mismanagement and international hostility. These also persuaded the ruling elite that national security and economic rationality required even further centralization of power. Political centralization was necessary as well to ensure that the shrinking store of goods and services would be shared equitably. The revolutionary government found quick success in redistribution; growth eluded it for many years. A change in emphasis in the 1970s stressed the growth somewhat at the expense of the distribution. Yet the experience of the 1970s confirmed the wisdom of centralized politics to achieve economic goals. The centralization of economic power arose in a condition of material scarcity; the overcoming of that condition was attributed to the effective use of that central power. The structures within which Cuba was governed, internationally as well as internally, had been permanently changed. Factors external to the government of Cuba had contributed significantly to the establishment and maintenance of government through centralization for the first time in twentieth-century Cuban history.

6

ESTABLISHING
A NEW GOVERNMENT

A new political order emerged in Cuba in 1959, freed from the outset of the burden of a national legislature, an autonomous court system, political parties, and armed forces loyal to anyone but the revolutionary leadership. The separation of the politics of incumbency from the politics of interest, which had characterized prerevolutionary Cuban politics, had not prepared the interest groups for national political collaboration in self-defense when their interests clashed with those of the new revolutionary order. Shifts in international alliances left the Cuban middle and upper classes without political protection; old Cuba was politically weak.

The new order had four things in its favor as it set out to establish its claim to legitimate rule. The first and most important was Fidel Castro himself, particularly his extraordinary ability to generate enthusiastic and loyal support. The other three were the general conviction that the country had been brought safely through an ordeal and that anything associated with its past must be rejected, the reemergence of nationalism as a unifying force, and the immediately implemented redistribution of goods and services to the benefit of the lower-middle class and the poor, making the revolution, in the eyes of many, not only right but profitable.

With this broad initial popular support, the Cuban government was able rapidly to gain control over many aspects of the society and the economy; the weight of government rose to levels unprecedented in Cuban history when the revolutionary period entered its socialist phase. The degree of centralization became extraordinary, and the political opposition was crushed or disappeared.

Revolutionary politics and administration required considerable organizational innovation. The new organizations that resulted lacked autonomy. They were often inflexible and incapable of adaptation, but they were essential links between the revolutionary leadership and the transformation of politics and administration in Cuba. Revolutionary mobilization required mass and elite political organizations; revolutionary structural change required an elaborate bureaucracy. A full panoply of both appeared to meet the challenges of revolutionary rule.

This multiplication of organizations necessitated the formation of a single political organization to provide unity. While the resulting Communist party's early history was turbulent—it expelled about half its membership in 1962–63 over political and ideological disputes and personal animosities—the battle for its control would determine who would decide the revolution's future course. Its outcome was the centralization of power in the hands of the revolutionary leaders who had fought against Batista in the 1950s, especially in the hands of Fidel Castro.

As the revolution changed, so did the social bases of its political support. For the first time in Cuban history, social and economic cleavages were reflected in national politics. At first the urban working class and the peasantry supported the revolution to a far greater extent than the middle and upper classes did. Gradually, however, the extreme class lines of the early years of revolutionary rule became blurred; opposition spread, especially among the urban working class. To counteract this decline in political support and to achieve its goals of national transformation and social justice, the leadership implemented a variety of programs. One of its goals had been economic growth. Though the government tried, success in that quarter proved elusive; their failure was counteracted to some extent by impressive gains in redistribution. The most vigorous efforts toward redistribution were made in the early 1960s; the process then slowed, and it was halted and even partly reversed in the 1970s. Nevertheless, Cuba is a much more egalitarian society in the 1970s than it has ever been before.

The legitimation and institutionalization of political and administrative organizations began slowly during the 1960s, so slowly that many scholars prefer to place the date of their beginning in the next decade. Though the state's organizations had grown, considerable instability in their structure remained. Enterprises were established and dismantled with astonishing rapidity. The top administrative personnel was quite stable, but in the late 1960s, the relatively stable cabinet it composed presided over organizational chaos. Bureaucratic work was held in low repute; yet, despite antibureaucratic campaigns that included dismissals and salary reductions, the number of bureaucratic organizations had continued to grow every year. Corruption was sharply reduced in the forms that had become familiar to prerevolutionary Cuba; but new forms of corruption, principally abuse of power, arose to take their place.

As in the past, the courts remained part of the ruling political coalition, a role facilitated by a drastic overhaul of their personnel in the early years of revolutionary rule. The law was changed to allow the executive branch of the government almost unlimited discretion. Yet the power of the executive could at times be checked by the revolutionary court system when its exercise became arbitrary. The courts lost a great deal of their power and autonomy, but they continued to perform a moderating function between the newly omnipotent state and the citizen.

The one area where the state has continued to exercise its power is in requiring the lengthy incarceration of its political opponents. The law and the courts have tended to become deprofessionalized; procedures have been modified so that legal codes and the case method coexist in the court system. Much formerly innocent social behavior has now become a crime; for some petty crimes penalties have been made more severe, while for much criminal behavior penalties have been lightened. Decriminalization of penalties at the bottom has made arbitrary decisions at the top more tolerable.

Neither the law and the courts nor the bureaucracy served to legitimate the revolution. Rather, the revolution legitimated the law, the courts, and the bureaucracy, though only barely before 1970. The revolution also came to legitimate the new Constitution approved in 1976, which finally set down in writing the principal features of the revolutionary state—a state where power was centralized as never before in Cuba and used in more purposive fashion than the country had ever known. The identity of the wielders of power, the form of government, and its purposes all changed, altering the fundamental features of Cuban politics.[1]

Government Authority and the Centralization of Power

In January 1959 the armed forces of prerevolutionary Cuba had been destroyed; their leaders had fled or been jailed; many were to be executed. Soldiers were discharged, and in some cases they suffered the fate of their former leaders. The victorious rebel army became the Revolutionary Armed Forces under Commander-in-Chief Fidel Castro and his immediate and most trusted subordinates. By the fall of 1959, Raúl Castro, the Prime Minister's brother, would begin his long and distinguished tenure as armed forces minister.

Political organizations had fallen into disrepute, first after Batista's coup, and then gradually again during his rule. In 1959 the Congress was suspended indefinitely, the courts purged, and Batista's pocket political parties dissolved. The older, somewhat conservative political parties that had collaborated with him in the 1950s, the Liberals and the Democrats, two congeries of political machines that had successfully weathered the storms of the republic for a half-century, also disappeared. The suicide of Senator Eduardo Chibás in the early 1950s had weakened the Ortodoxo party, which was further divided during the 1950s by factional struggles and by disagreements over how best to oppose

Batista. The Auténticos had also divided between Prío's followers, who opposed Batista by violence, and Grau's, who opposed him through traditional nonviolent means. Little remained of the power of these parties by 1959, and the revolutionary government did nothing to reactivate them. In early 1959 former Ortodoxo leaders held many cabinet posts, but they lasted only a few months; they represented few but themselves. The only political group that renewed operations, especially toward the second half of 1959, was the old Communist party.

The prerevolutionary political system had successfully separated the politics of interest from the politics of incumbency. Interest groups had direct and institutionalized access to government. Competition for government office had remained in a purely political arena. Cleavages had been reflected directly in government, not through the party system. Government bureaucracies were not independent of interest groups: they were their agents. Individual officeholders, however, did have far greater discretionary authority. During the course of the struggle against Batista many people were not at all alarmed by the prospect of Batista's overthrow and, toward the end of his rule, even welcomed and contributed to his fall. The revolution seemed to operate primarily in the purely political sphere rather than affecting the interests of groups or individuals.

The lack of correlation between interest groups and political parties is one explanation for the relative ease with which the system was dismantled in 1959 and 1960. The Cuban social system had produced powerful institutions that reflected the interests of groups but not of whole classes. In fact, in defending their interests, these groups often ran up against those of others of the same class. They were unaccustomed both to cooperating with each other through political parties and to cooperating with the armed forces to affect the politics of incumbency. They had a narrow perspective on their political roles, competing with other interest groups readily but collaborating rarely. One could say that it was not the absence of institutions that doomed the prerevolutionary system but their very strength.[2] Cuban politics was trapped in an institutional structure that preserved a two-track system of interest groups and political parties. There was no interest-group cooperation through parties, and no more than a grudging cooperation outside them when a compromise was needed. The sugar growers and the sugar-mill owners, for example, cooperated in the regulation of the sugar industry while competing for advantage within the structure of government. Bourgeois class institutions and class cooperation were virtually nonexistent, while bourgeois group institutions were very strong. Without exaggerating the ability of interest groups in other countries to cooperate either through the armed forces or through political parties in order to link interest groups to the politics of incumbency, it is fair to say that Cuban groups had a comparatively limited capacity to aggregate their interests and a comparatively great capacity to articulate their own. An abyss of difference lay between the coordinated acts of the Chilean middle and upper classes through the political parties and the armed forces in 1972 and 1973, for instance, and the Cuban experience in 1959 and 1960. When the political track in the system collapsed, the inability of interest groups to work together proved suicidal.

The best study of the Cuban bourgeoisie, by Alfred Padula, Jr., shows that the long-standing pattern of conflict among the interest groups was exacerbated by revolutionary politics and that the narrow perspectives of interest groups and institutions encouraged competition. The Agrarian Reform Act of 1959, for example, was bitterly opposed by the cattle ranchers and the sugar-mill owners, while the sugar growers at first opposed it, then collaborated; thus split off, the growers were eventually overwhelmed. The act was fervently supported by industrialists, bankers, textile manufacturers, lawyers, private secondary-school administrators, and the hierarchy of the Catholic church—all of whom would eventually be crushed, and none of whom were capable of the coordinated activity needed to defend those who had been hit so hard and so soon. Even the leading organ of conservative economic and social opinion, *Diario de la Marina*, differed with the sugar-mill owners and with the cattle ranchers; it was to be the first major newspaper closed down by the revolutionary government.[3]

These conflicts were not new. Industrialists had long felt that they had little influence on government, because the sugar interests dominated; thus the sugar interests and the rest of the economy distrusted each other and found it difficult to cooperate. Sugar growers and sugar-mill owners had also competed for advantage, in an organized fashion, since the early 1930s; although they managed to cooperate on some issues, they were far apart on most. In August 1959 the sugar growers asked the government to intervene in forty-three of the 161 sugar mills: their own association had been unable to cooperate politically with the mill owners and reach some agreement to defend their joint interests.[4]

The *revolución del callo* (one in which people do not complain until their own corns, or *callos*, are stepped on) was underway, preparing for the socialist revolution yet to come. Let the Cuban government take over the plantations; it was not the industrialists' business to oppose it. Let the Cuban government intervene in the running of the U.S.-owned public utilities; it reduced rates and lowered overhead costs. Let the Cuban government challenge the United States; it gave more business to Cuban-owned private enterprises. Labor unions bedeviled business with strikes in 1959 and 1960; shortly thereafter, strikes—and union autonomy—would vanish in a socialized economy. No one joined to help anyone else. Interest groups sought solely to defend themselves—and found themselves alone.

Under the impact of revolutionary politics, moreover, the comparatively sturdy old interest-group institutions cracked from within. They fell not only through inability to cooperate but also because two kinds of often overlapping divisions fractured the unity and cohesion that had allowed them to function in the past. The associations of sugar-mill owners and sugar growers had long been controlled by their wealthiest members; they began to split according to the size of the sugar mill or plantation, and this division appeared to wreck the traditional politics of these associations. The cleavage partly coincided with, but was distinct from, the lines of purely political cleavage created by the revolution, which separated those who had supported the Batista government from those who had not. Because the owners of the largest mills and plantations were at the same time the leaders of these associations, they were also the most likely to have been in positions of power in the 1950s and hence to have collaborated with the Batista regime: the cattle ranchers were similarly divided by size and previous political affiliation. The industrialists were even more deeply divided. There was a split between the U.S.-owned businesses (whose executives were also divided among themselves according to what they produced) and the Cuban-owned enterprises, especially over the wisdom of certain aspects of industrial nationalism. Differences separated industrial sectors, some of which (especially those in light industry) benefited in the short run from the increase in demand for their products as a consequence of the rise in income among the poor (the result of revolutionary redistribution policies). There were also the differences common to all groups accruing from the size of the enterprise and from previous politics. The splits within the Catholic church depended almost exclusively on support of, or opposition to, revolutionary policies. Professional associations (of lawyers, physicians, pharmacists, architects, radio broadcasters, optometrists, and students, among others) split principally along political lines, but also partly from differences in their members' professional standing and income.[5]

By the second half of 1960, when the revolutionary government set out to challenge the bourgeois interest groups, many were already severely weakened, politically and financially, by isolated confrontations with the government. The government had also taken full control of several key interest groups in advance of that grand confrontation, and it had established, or was in the process of establishing, a full panoply of new organizations to mobilize its supporters for successful political combat. As matters worsened in 1960, remnants of political clientelism reappeared. In expecting that the United States would overthrow the revolutionary government, the Cuban rich lost their power waiting for Godot.

In January 1959, therefore, the old Cuban political system was fragile, while the resources legitimating revolutionary politics were vital, including the first, the best, the supreme political resource, then and thereafter, Fidel Castro himself. By talent, shrewdness, and luck, Castro had picked the right strategy to oppose Batista. He had even been lucky when his original swift attack on July 26, 1953, and the landing aboard the yacht *Granma* in December 1956 had failed. Time served to erode the legitimacy of prerevolutionary politics even further and to make their complete elimination even easier in 1959–60. The failure of Batista's other opponents had the effect of focusing attention on Castro and his group in the mountains and placing power in their hands far beyond what was justified by their military victories. The pattern of success and failure among the political opposition helped him as well.

Fidel Castro is energetic and he soon became a spellbinding orator as well. He would hold the attention of people for many hours, expounding on politics and his view of the future, asking for support, castigating his enemies. He preempted all television and radio programming whenever he wanted to address the country. The newspapers reproduced his speeches in full. And he talked and talked. In 1959, he made a public statement—typically a speech of considerable length—almost every other day. Between 1960 and 1962, he made a public statement two or three times every ten days. The frequency of his public addresses declined between 1966 and 1970 and stabilized at once every two weeks.[6]

The Central Committee, Political Bureau, and Secretariat of the Cuban Communist party were not formally established until the fall of 1965. Their foundation was the first indication of a shift to a slightly more collective style of public leadership that would rely less heavily on the person of the Prime Minister.[7] During the second half of the 1960s, however, political centralization continued to increase under Castro's leadership. It was only in the 1970s that both the public and the internal styles of government combined to form a slightly more collective kind of leadership.

Under the two previous twentieth-century political systems in Cuba no single leader had been available to act as the focal point of the legitimation—or relegitimation—of Cuban politics. Now, at long last, there was one. Castro had charisma, and charisma provides an authority that rests upon the extraordinary quality of the ruler as a person as it is perceived by the citizenry. Charisma depends on the leader's conviction that he is not dependent on election by his followers but has been "elected" by a supernatural authority, either God or some "historical force," and on the citizenry's sharing that conviction. Charismatic authority is very unstable and must be routinized if it is to remain successful. The routinization of charisma began very slowly during the 1960s as government legitimacy began to depend more on other people, institutions, and policies; it was not until the 1970s that the process appeared to be taking hold.

Fidel Castro's sense of mission is a theme of his many public statements. His first major manifesto, widely circulated in Cuba in 1959, was an edited version of his defense at his trial for attacking the Moncada barracks on July 26, 1953. It ended with these words addressed to the court: "Condemn me; it does not matter to me. History will absolve me."[8] History-as-god elects the revolutionary leader to act with and for his followers. On July 26, 1970, Prime

Minister Castro gave one of the more difficult speeches of his career in govern-ment, a report to the people on the recent economic collapse. Though he said in the middle of the speech that "the people can replace us whenever they wish—right now if you so desire!" he provided no suggestions as to how this could be done, for there was, in fact, no alternative. Indeed, the effect (proba-bly intended) of these remarks before a large crowd was to stimulate a general pro-Castro outcry. In the peroration, Castro reiterated the legitimacy of his claim to rule, as coming from history-as-god: "If we have an atom of value, that atom of value will be through our service to an idea, a cause, linked to the people."[9] The cause, the idea, history incarnate in the people elects the leader to serve, to implement, and hence to rule: the essence of charismatic legitima-tion.

No systematic study has been made to determine the extent of popular belief in Prime Minister Castro's charismatic qualities, especially in the crucial years when the regime's legitimacy was being established, but Lloyd Free's survey in the spring of 1960 provides some insight. Free found that 86 percent of the respondents supported the government and that 43 percent could be called "fervent" supporters. He noted that many of these fervent supporters mentioned the extraordinary qualities of, and their supreme faith in, Prime Minister Castro. He also noted that these statements had not really been required by the questionnaire; in order to be politically "safe," it would have been possible to fake support for the government without such expressions of enthusiasm.[10] This is not conclusive evidence, but it does show that many Cubans distinguished between the failures of the government, which they might be willing to criticize, and Fidel Castro himself, who is exempt from criticism.

Corroborating evidence is found in a survey of 1,070 Cuban students of both sexes and two age groups (sixteen to eighteen and nineteen to twenty-three), conducted in 1962 as a part of a UNESCO-sponsored study of youth values in six countries. Students in Cuba were asked to rank their preferences for the fol-lowing eight types of individual: social hero, wise man, saint, artist, business-man, politician, philosopher, and scientist. The social hero led the list for both Cuban age groups (39.4 percent and 38.1 percent), scoring well ahead of the second-ranked scientist (28.0 percent and 21.3 percent). Cubans were the only young people in six countries (the others were India, Malaya, Japan, France, and Canada) to place the hero first. Compared with other categories in Cuba, the social hero does very well, and for Cubans there is little doubt that the social hero *par excellence* is Fidel Castro.[11] The data from these two surveys are not conclusive, but they do strongly suggest his charismatic appeal to both the adult population and the young in the early 1960s; it had a power-ful grip on approximately 40 percent of the sampled urban populations. One has the impression that this proportion would be even higher in the rural areas. Although the power of, and reliance on, charismatic leadership as a source of legitimation has declined in Cuba, it is still a pillar of the new order.[12]

The political style of Fidel Castro had several important aspects.[13] He and his followers emphasized active engagement, as opposed to more mystical or theoretical pursuits, and the power of self-discipline, from the very launching of the armed struggle against Batista (while the old Communists were still waiting for objective conditions to ripen). The view was best summarized by a slogan that became popular in the late 1960s in the polemics against the timid Moscow-oriented Communist parties of Latin America, "The duty of every revolutionary is to make the revolution." There has been persistent reliance on will, and when that gave out, more will and still more will in the pursuit of victory. Individuals can overcome objective obstacles if they work hard enough and sacrifice themselves for the cause. Since Moncada in 1953 and the landing of the *Granma* in 1956, Fidel Castro has believed in the necessity of a revolutionary elite to lead the people and to awaken them to their responsibilities. Finally, only the maximum possible effort toward the optimal goal is worth pursuing; only the (apparently) unattainable goal is an acceptable one. The revolution was an unreachable goal, and yet it was achieved. Why not, then, 10 million tons of sugar in 1970? Why not, then, transforming the people of Cuba into revolutionary citizens? The persistent belief that an activist, determined vanguard should reach for nothing short of the impossible in the service of the revolution has been expounded by the leadership for many years.[14]

The Cuban revolution was legitimated not only by charisma but also by performance. The message repeated in speeches, in newspaper articles, in broadcasts, in virtually all significant appeals for popular support has been that the revolution delivered Cuba from a terroristic, corrupt, abusive and illegitimate political system. This message generated an immediate source of support. When in the spring of 1960 Lloyd Free asked people about their fears or worries for Cuba, the single most important response was "a return to the past," that is, a fear that Cuba would revert to tyranny, dictatorship, oppression, violence, or counterrevolution; it was mentioned by 30 percent of the respondents. The next largest set of responses came from the faithful (14 percent) who had no fears or worries for the country and felt that it was in capable hands.[15] This negative legitimacy—the concept that the present government is legitimate because it saved the country from the past—was prominent at the time of Free's survey and is still voiced in official political statements.

There has also been an appeal for revolutionary legitimacy from the very early years based on its subsequent achievements. Because economic performance has been poor, the provision of social services and, specifically, the redistributive efforts of the revolution have been stressed. On July 26, 1970, when the Prime Minister publicly acknowledged economic failure, his speech opened with a lengthy statistical presentation of the regime's achievements in redistribution. It was followed by this short peroration:

I don't believe there is a single Cuban who has the slightest doubt about the effort that has been made in connection with the health of the people, to remedy the tragic conditions in which millions of people in this country lived, where scores of thousands of families witnessed the death of their young ones . . . and I don't believe that anybody, much less any of those who have had an opportunity to travel in the interior of the country, has the slightest doubt as to the absolute necessity of the medical services provided by the Revolution . . . We don't believe there is a single Cuban who has any doubts about the essential and dramatic need of lifting this country out of the state of illiteracy and semi-illiteracy in which it finds itself . . . We don't know anybody who, when discussing education, has told us that we should have made less of an effort in education, granted fewer scholarships . . .[16]

Another equally early source of legitimacy was nationalism. Although nationalist ideologies played a minor though increasing role in the 1950s, they played a major role after January 1959. Nationalism affirmed the cultural, political, and historical integrity of the Cuban nation. It tended to emphasize the unity of the entire people rather than the legitimacy to be derived from any one segment of the population, such as the proletariat. Often *nation* is used to mean the working people of Cuba, or the worker-peasant alliance. But the stress is invariably on national unity; class enemies are also national enemies. Nationalism also gained strength—and added to the government's legitimacy—from the struggle against the revolution's enemies, in the form of either class interests within Cuba or the United States government and Cuban exiles in the United States. The revolution is legitimate at least in part because its enemies, both within and outside its borders, are so despicable. Class enemies are described as "worms"; foreign enemies, as "imperialists."

Examples of these themes abound. One version can be found in a speech given by the Primer Minister in the wake of a disastrous hurricane in the fall of 1963:

The entire nation absorbed the losses suffered by a part of the nation . . . No one can say "I lost"; the nation lost, over seven millions Cubans lost . . . Not a single citizen was left unprotected . . . Because the nation looks after everyone, the nation protects everyone, the nation insures everyone. The nation is no longer a conglomerate of individuals . . . It has come to be like a great family in which the strength and the resources of the nation reach everyone.[17]

A second dates from July 26, 1970:

I don't believe there is a single Cuban—we don't believe there is a single revolutionary—who thinks that this country should have folded its arms in the face of that most powerful imperialist enemy 90 miles from our shores, an enemy that did not hesitate to use all means and weapons to destroy our revolution.[18]

Charisma, political deliverance, distributional performance, and national-ism were four elements in the legitimation of revolutionary rule. In the ab-sence of elections and of organizational channels, they were the bases of the revolution's claim to the right to rule, supported through massive political demonstrations of hundreds of thousands of people who shouted their ap-proval of the government's, and specifically of Fidel Castro's course. But these enormous rallies were not the source of the legitimation, just as the elections that could have been held and won in 1959 would not have been the source of the legitimation. The revolution itself, its cause, and its leader were self-legit-imating. This legitimation, relying as it did on Castro's charisma, though not costless, was not unreasonable in those early years, for it clearly contributed to the revolution's survival and success. Mass assemblies ratified the govern-ment's legitimacy and provided support not only for its right to rule but also for its ability to do so. With the passing of time, mass participation, organiza-tion, and law assumed more important, though still subordinate, roles in polit-ical legitimation.

Government in the 1960s expanded its scope and domain beyond anything previously experienced in Cuba. Its expenditures, in proportion to net mate-rial product (a close equivalent of national income), dwarfed previous levels (see table 3.12). In the 1960s the Cuban government allocated two-thirds to four-fifths of its net material product through its expenditures; the following list shows government expenditures as a percentage of net material product (in current prices): [19]

1962	65.5
1963	64.1
1964	60.7
1965	67.9
1966	71.9

Because of the socialization of retail trade and of some industry, transpor-tation, and services, this proportion rose after 1966, reaching 79.0 percent by 1969.

State employment also increased as overt unemployment was virtually elim-inated; it made up the following percentages of total employment during the mid-1960s: [20]

1962	59.4
1963	66.9
1964	72.7
1965	74.1
1966	76.2

Some of the expansion of state employment reflected only disguised unemploy-ment, however. In the fall of 1963, the second Agrarian Reform Act made

Table 6.1 Percentage of Cuban production collectivized, 1961–1970

Economic sector	1961	1963	1965	1968	1970
Agriculture	37	70	61	70	70
Industry	85	95	96	100	100
Construction	80	98	98	100	100
Retail trade	52	75	89	100	100
Transportation	92	95	91	100	98
Wholesale and foreign trade	100	100	—	100	—
Banking	100	100	—	100	—
Education	100	100	—	100	—
Communications	—	—	100	—	100

Sources: Carmelo Mesa-Lago, "Economic Policies and Growth," in *Revolutionary Change in Cuba*, ed. Carmelo Mesa-Lago (Pittsburgh: University of Pittsburgh Press, 1971), p. 283; Anatolii Bekarevich, Vladimir N. Bondarchuk and N. M. Kukharev, *Cuba in Statistics* (Moscow: Academy of Sciences of the USSR, Institute of Latin America, 1972), p. 27. See also Osvaldo Dorticós, "La revolución cubana en su cuarto aniversario," *Cuba socialista* no. 17 (January 1963):2–3.

many agricultural workers employees of the state. The socialization of 1968 again increased the state's share of employment. The gradual collectivization of the means of production and of the educational system shows the very broad scope of government authority (table 6.1). By 1974, however, the central government also launched an experiment in Matanzas province that allowed private contracts between individuals for repair and minor construction services, such as painting, plumbing, electrical wiring, and the like, so long as the person providing the services was licensed and employed no subordinates; assistance of the provider's immediate family was permitted. This work had to be done outside regular work hours; no one could leave a job or an established work center to go into private business. The change meant that, if the water pipes broke or the stove did not work, a citizen did not have to rely on an incompetent and slow bureaucracy but, at long last, could hire someone to make the repairs. Similarly, many taxi drivers pay a tax plus a voluntary social-security tax for the right to work full time for themselves. The result has been the gradual desocialization of minor services.

The 1975 First Party Congress also approved sales through private channels by peasants to persons other than state agencies, provided the state agencies were unable to purchase the surplus and provided the sales were made under government license at official prices. This ruling relaxed the policies set in the late 1960s, which had banned private sales of any kind. The new procedures benefited both peasants (whose produce would not go to waste) and consumers (who could sidestep official buying policies legally).[21]

The launching of the revolution required a good deal of legislation to implement revolutionary reform, to repeal obstacles to revolutionary change, and to punish the revolution's enemies. All laws came from the cabinet, which combined executive and legislative powers until the approval of the Constitution of 1976. There was a legislative explosion in Cuba in 1959, when the total output was 190.1 laws every hundred days. The amount of rule making in that year was topped only by that of the revolutionary government of President Grau in the fall of 1933 (see table 3.10). Grau was in power only about four months, but the exceptional characteristics of initial revolutionary rule are nonetheless clear in his administration, as in 1959; the legislative explosion of 1959 was sustained for a period three times as long as that in 1933.

By 1960, however, the rate of law making had declined sharply to 62.3 laws every hundred days. It was not very different, though perhaps a bit on the low side, from the Cuban average for the late 1930s through the late 1950s. By 1961, law making had fallen to 18.8 per hundred days for January–October, a level just barely above that of Estrada Palma's time.[22] Unfortunately, the volume of departmental resolutions is not available, and the number of laws made from November 1961 to the present cannot be established with precision for each year. However, 7.4 laws per hundred days is a reasonably accurate figure in order of magnitude for lawmaking to the end of 1970. From early 1971 to January 2, 1975, the rate of lawmaking fell to about 3.8 per hundred days. From November 1961 to January 2, 1975, a rate of 6.3 laws per hundred days is reasonably accurate. In this respect, Cuba has become similar to the socialist countries of eastern Europe, whose legislatures have a very limited output; all socialist countries, once power is consolidated, differ in this respect from the rest of the world.[23]

The scope of the laws approved by the revolution was broad. They established the basic framework and left subsequent implementation to departmental resolutions. The low level of lawmaking also underlines the fundamental stability achieved by the government by the end of 1961. Relatively few laws were needed to alter a structure whose basic features were set quite early. The system's legal framework could change relatively little, by marginal increments very different from the drastic change of 1959, although there would be considerable change of policy and practice within that framework. The legal and institutional structure of the revolution was in place early in the 1960s; the stability of the structure would limit the possibility of subsequent changes and at the same time provide an order within which the many policy changes could occur.

The increase in the weight of government in Cuba was enormous, compared to prerevolutionary standards, in its ownership of the means of production, the size of its budget, and the number it employed. The prerevolutionary government had owned very little; it directly controlled only a small, if steady, proportion of national income, and it employed comparatively few people. It was a regulative and a distributive but not an entrepreneurial state. Prerevolutionary governments tended to legislate more and more frequently. In prerevolutionary Cuba, changes of government, by election or by coup, were numerous. Since 1960 there have been no comparable changes. Consequently the legal framework of the political system, now firmly established, is far more stable.

The weight of government also increased in an unquantifiable but no less important sense. The government assumed control of newspapers, magazines, journals, publishing houses, radio, and television. It exercised a monopoly over political socialization in the schools. All became organs of the government and of the Communist party. The ban on competitive political activity was enforced; by the end of 1960, all political opposition to the government and its policies had become illegal. In 1974 Fidel Castro could report with pleasure that "the opportunities to carry out opposition against the revolution are minimal." It has become impossible for the opposition to publish or associate, he noted, and it would remain so. The collective ownership of the means of production and the elimination of effective political criticism on a national scale clearly left enormous powers in the government's hands. The 1975 party congress considered the question of the intensification of the "ideological struggle" at length and approved measures to improve government control over public opinion, purifying it of "right or left deviations." This congress was more concerned with its authority over the flow of ideas than with its authority over the flow of beans and bananas; while controls over private peasant sales could be relaxed, controls over attitudes could not.[24]

The draft of the first socialist Constitution of the Republic of Cuba was approved in February 1976. Up to that time, the country had been governed by an amended version of the Constitution of 1940. Article 61 of the new Constitution states that none of the rights of citizens recognized in its other articles could be exercised against the Constitution and the laws, against the existence and the objectives of the state, or against the building of socialism and communism. Thus, for example, a public critique of the political system, even if the critic had done nothing to attack the government in any other way, would be in itself unconstitutional. Articles 52 through 57 of the Constitution, guaranteeing the rights of speech, press, association, religion, residence, and correspondence, explicitly reserve the power of the state to limit these rights and guarantees. The same is true of article 38d, guaranteeing the right of artistic creativity. Article 5 of the Constitution recognizes the role of the Communist party as the organization that directs the state and society and has authority over them. The party and the state, in the final analysis, determine the conditions for the exercise of constitutional rights. In contrast, article 37 of the prerevolutionary Constitution of 1940 did not deny the right to criticize the political system or the objectives of the state but only forbade the establishment of political organizations with principles contrary to those of representative democratic government. The individual rights guaranteed in articles 26 through 40 of the Constitution of 1940 are written in far stronger language and with fewer qualifications than articles 52 through 62 of the Constitution of 1976. Constitutional forms, of course, may vary from constitutional practice. On the whole, the liberal provisions, not the escape clauses, of the Constitution of 1940 prevailed until 1952, while the escape clauses, not the liberal provisions, prevailed in the 1950s and under revolutionary rule. These are not new restrictions on Cuban politics but rather the constitutional formalization of restrictions, imposed on Cuban politics in the early 1960s, that served to tighten those restrictions introduced by President Batista in the 1950s.[25]

Through the issuing of personal identification cards, the government began to acquire for the first time detailed computerized information on every citizen. The process began with the issuance of labor identification cards in April 1964. It was completed after the 1970 census, which asked for the name of the respondent and of family ascendants and descendants, age, sex, marital status, citizenship, residence, housing conditions, schooling, occupation, and military service. Identification cards, based on this information, were issued to the entire population. Since 1969 they have been linked to a labor file, showing a worker's employment history, including merits and demerits in all the jobs he or she has held in all places he or she has worked. Student identification cards provide similar information.[26] The introduction of rationing provided another tool for substantial control over individual patterns of expenditure. The need for a ration card and the close regulation of employment controlled and reduced short-term geographic mobility and long-term migration. The weight of the state over the individual was correspondingly increased.

In 1959 there was still political competition in Cuba, a good part of which was fought out within the ranks of the government. By the spring of 1960 the government had become much more homogeneous. The scope of politics was restricted when the critical discussion of many issues, including political incumbency, foreign policy, and nonsocialist economic organization, became illegitimate in late 1960. Discussion of these topics became impossible, except in private, because of the government's total monopoly over the mass media. The domain of politics was restricted when the opposition was barred from political activity. As the weight of government in society and the economy increased, this powerful government came to have no rivals in a restricted political system; effective national political competition and choice were no longer available.

Structuring Revolutionary Politics

Scholarship on the Cuban revolution has tended to focus on Prime Minister Castro, assigning to him a crucial role in legitimating initial revolutionary politics; much of the rest of this work will similarly emphasize his central position. But insufficient attention has been paid to how power—albeit often Castro's power—was organized, for one man alone cannot do everything. The politics of organization played a decisive role in the Cuban revolution from the very beginning.[27] Castro's style and substance are not antiorganizational but are strongly opposed to any organization that is autonomous and stable enough not to suit his activist style and maximalist goals. Fidel Castro has used and developed organizations that depend on him and the leadership and structures of which he can change. Consequently his methods, though not essentially antiorganizational, have obstructed any political, partisan, or administrative institutionalization requiring much autonomy and stability. The institutional compromise of the 1970s led to more stability under Soviet hegemony, but it continued to limit autonomy.

Political mobilization and political organization proceeded simultaneously in the early years of the revolution. It is impossible to understand the structure of revolutionary politics in Cuba without paying attention to its organization. To understand the efforts made in creating a new society and a new type of socialist citizen, one needs to focus both on the results of government efforts and on the mechanism used by the government to achieve those effects. Organizations, even if unstable in personnel and structures and lacking in autonomy, are the decisive link between the charismatic and the manipulative aspects of Cuban revolutionary rule, on the one hand, and political and social transformation and revolutionary survival, on the other.

In January 1959, the government's immediate task was the weakening or destruction of organizational autonomy; political activity was suspended, and many prerevolutionary organizations were disbanded. The revolutionary political movements, still fairly autonomous at the time, also played a role, although a very modest one. The old Communist party, the People's Socialist Party (PSP), had had a minor role in the struggle against Batista. As late as May 21, 1959, Prime Minister Castro still openly criticized the Communists, a "sin" he would confess in December 1961.[28]

The Twenty-sixth of July Movement entered a period of organizational decline, somewhat paradoxically, just as it had ostensibly won its victory. Its journal, *Cuba*, published by the Havana provincial branch, suspended publication after its first issue in 1959. The movement's national coordinator, Emilio Aragonés, had little power. The newspaper *Revolución*, which styled itself the movement's official organ, engaged in political and ideological battles with *Hoy*, the Communist party newspaper. However, *Revolución* soon came to reflect the opinions of the government more than of the movement. Two crucial political battles show that the revolutionary leaders, particularly Fidel Castro, were fully aware of the stakes of organizational politics and sought organizational power and control at the expense of organizational autonomy. They sought, in short, not to be antiorganizational but to harness the organizations for their own ends.

In the fall of 1959, two candidates stood for the presidency of the University Students' Federation (FEU): Pedro Boitel and Rolando Cubelas. Boitel was president of the engineering students' association and had been endorsed by the Twenty-sixth of July Movement's chapter at the University of Havana and by a number of other secondary- and university-student members. Cubelas was a medical student and a member of the Revolutionary Directorate. He claimed to be a "unity" candidate. On October 17, in a front-page letter to *Revolución,* Prime Minister Castro stated that the "revolutionary government and the Twenty-sixth of July Movement do not support any group in the struggle for the presidency of FEU." In a speech at the university, however, he argued for the election of Cubelas. Boitel withdrew, and Cubelas was elected on October 18.

At the fall 1959 congress of the Cuban Labor Confederation (CTC), the Twenty-sixth of July Movement's slate had a majority. The government pressed for "unity," but the labor congress delegates refused. When the Prime Minister addressed the congress, his words were interrupted by the chanting of "Twenty-six, Twenty-six." He then claimed the leadership of the movement while attacking those who would "unfurl the banner of the Twenty-sixth of July to stab the revolution to the heart." He stressed the need for "harmony" to "defend the revolution" and avoid "partisan quarrels." He asked and received authority from the congress to form a labor leadership "supported by all." The government at last got its unanimous vote.[29]

Prime Minister Castro and his colleagues intervened time and again to wrest power from those in the Twenty-sixth of July Movement who claimed an independent role for the organization. Organizational behavior autonomous from the Prime Minister was eliminated by the end of 1959. After the labor congress Castro claimed that he and the movement were identical. For if the movement were used to attack the "founder of this movement and the Prime Minister of the revolutionary government," then the "Twenty-sixth of July would cease to be the Twenty-sixth of July."[30] The seizure of power over the mass organizations was of decisive importance. The fall of 1959 marked the first obvious change in the political direction of revolutionary rule. The struggle for control of organizations required the destruction of their autonomy— reflecting not the neglect of, or opposition to, organizations but a recognition of their importance.

Organizational politics also required the creation of new mechanisms for concentrating and increasing the power of the revolutionary leadership for purposes of political mobilization and combat. The first political organization created under revolutionary rule was the militia, a volunteer civilian army formed in the fall of 1959 to defend the revolution against its enemies. While the University Students' Federation and the Labor Confederation had a stable and automatic membership, the militia could increase its membership—and hence its mobilizing power—without limit. The FEU and the CTC were specialized mass organizations with occupational prerequisites for membership; the militia could be made universal. Everyone with the desire could join. Joining it was a demonstration of support for the government; people voted with their feet and their time.

The takeover of the FEU and the CTC was indicative of the strength of the revolutionary leadership. By April of 1960 the militia claimed a membership of a hundred thousand; by the end of 1960, two hundred thousand; by 1961, up to three hundred thousand.[31] It provided a channel for popular support unavailable elsewhere and increased the government's coercive capacity because it could be used to mobilize people for any political or military purpose. The militia activated latent popular commitment to advance the revolutionary program and defeat its enemies. It was the first example of a link between the ability of the elite to mobilize and control and the transformation of the political system through the creation of organizations.

Forming a militia was an ad hoc response to the need for organized support at a critical time. This pattern was repeated during the socialization of the economy in the second half of 1960, a period that also saw a confrontation with the United States. The Cuban Women's Federation (FMC) was founded in August 1960, in response to an appeal by Prime Minister Castro to the women who supported the revolution to organize.[32] The Committees for the Defense of the Revolution were organized in September 1960, again as a reaction to a call from the Prime Minister to combat the revolution's internal enemies. The committees were an enlargement upon the idea of a militia. In 1959 conflict with the United States and internal enemies had just begun; in 1960 the revolution was fighting for its life against them. To defend itself, neither charismatic appeal nor police repression proved sufficient. Mobilizing a large part of the population was once more necessary to link revolutionary transformation, elite control, and political mobilization. The committees were set up on every city block and in every large building, factory, or work center to help the state security apparatus fight its enemies.

From the beginning, the committees' chief purpose was repression. Like the militia—and unlike the FEU, CTC, or FMC—the committees had no prerequisites, such as age, sex, or occupation, for membership; anyone could join. Like the militia and the FMC, the committees provided a way to organize and mobilize support and increase the government's powers of coercion. They activated revolutionary commitment; their tasks required no significant skills or specialization. But they had an advantage over the militia, which required a substantial commitment of time and effort; committee work required little more than reporting neighborhood gossip to the police, at least in the beginning. The militia required some minimal physical abilities, while committee work could be done by young and old, men and women, strong and weak. The militia required some physical stamina: going to training camps, drills, marches. Committee work was done at home or at work. In a society where men still ruled the home, male supporters of the revolution, who might have been reluctant to let their women join a paramilitary organization or a women's federation, were less likely to object to their joining a block committee. The committeees were a powerful weapon; César Escalante noted in 1961, "Today we can say that the security apparatus would not have been able by itself to thwart and control the criminal activity promoted by the counter-revolutionary and imperialist agents."[33]

The companion youth organization, Asociación de Jóvenes Rebeldes (AJR), was officially launched by the Prime Minister in a May 1960 television address, but it did not gather momentum until the fall and can thus be included among the responses to the crisis. Its first national plenary meeting was held in October 1960 to merge the AJR with the youth branches of the old Communist party and the Revolutionary Directorate. The new youth organization sought to mobilize and organize young people between the ages of fourteen and twenty-seven.[34]

The next two organizations created were planned in anticipation of changes to come rather than in response to the crisis at hand. The National Organization of Small Peasants (ANAP) was a response to the Prime Minister's directive in December 1960 that all small private farmers or peasants be organized, but the Bay of Pigs invasion delayed its foundation until May 17, 1961. Only farmers who owned sixty-seven hectares of land or less were supposed to join ANAP, even though the 1959 Agrarian Reform Act permitted ownership of far larger acreages (at least until those "rich farmers" lost their holdings through the second Agrarian Reform Act in the fall of 1963).[35]

By the summer of 1961 the revolutionary government had specialized organizations for young people, university students, women, and labor. It had more universal organizations such as the militia and the Committees for the Defense of the Revolution. The Twenty-sixth of July Movement continued to exist, at least on paper, as did the Revolutionary Directorate. No satisfactory way had yet been found to incorporate the old Communists into the revolution. This proliferation of mass organizations required coordination. The solution was yet another organization: the Integrated Revolutionary Organizations (ORI), founded in July 1961. This group formed the nucleus of what would eventually become the Communist party of Cuba, although it would not be formally designated as such for another four years. Between 1963 and 1965 it was known as the United Party of the Socialist Revolution.

Although there was no formally organized and active revolutionary party in the first thirty months of revolutionary rule, the mass organizations performed many of the functions of the party. Through their efforts their members were socialized into the norms of the new political system, and changes in the political culture were initiated. They acted as political recruiters, brought together the support of groups for the revolution, and articulated their joint concerns. They provided the symbolism of partisan struggle and performed social services for their members in the manner of a political machine. Although a party of the revolution did not exist, the importance of its absence should not be overly stressed. The existing organizations performed many of the functions—ranging from revolutionary mobilization to the provision of political favors—that would otherwise have been provided by a party. Political mobilization, social transformation and organizational acceleration were linked. Revolutionary organizations provided a means for the state to influence, shape, and control the society; prerevolutionary organizations had acted primarily to capture a chunk of the state. The crucial difference was that revolutionary organizations had little autonomy.

The Formation of the Communist Party

The Integrated Revolutionary Organizations began operation in an already restricted political system, where it had a monopoly over political incumbency and communications. There were several problems with this organization, which eventually became the official party, when it was launched in the summer of 1961. First, it was assumed that the old Communists would be easily integrated into it, under Castro's leadership, and this assumption proved mistaken. Second, it was assumed that there were organizations to be integrated, and this proved wrong as well. The Twenty-sixth of July Movement and the Revolutionary Directorate were phantom organizations: only the old Communists remained well organized, and thus most of the "integrated" power would fall to them. Third, the emphasis was on a pooling of old memberships, rather than on recruitment of new members who had not belonged to any of the three original organizations. Recruitment did not require mass participation. What new members there were, were appointed by the ORI leadership. The ORI's national directorate, announced in March 1962, was comprised of ten old Communists, thirteen from the Twenty-sixth of July Movement, and two from the Revolutionary Directorate. The most serious question remained whether the ORI would be autonomous or controlled by Prime Minister Castro.

Aníbal Escalante, an old communist, became the ORI organization secretary; he took his job seriously. The organization of party cells and the selection of party members had to be cleared through his office; the party became the controlling political organization, as it was supposed to be. The party cells, or nuclei, asserted their authority over administrators. Promotion and firing had to be cleared by the party and, if they involved high-ranking officials, by the organization secretary's office.

Political problems soon arose. Escalante gave preference to his old comrades in the prerevolutionary Communist party, partly to ensure his own position, partly to reward those faithful to him, and partly because these people were the only viable force by which to organize the party. But the rise of the ORI, and especially of Escalante's power, challenged the authority of the Prime Minister. By the end of March 1962, Castro had dismissed Escalante and sent him to Czechoslovakia for two years.[36]

The fall of Aníbal Escalante was the beginning of a massive restructuring of the Cuban party and of the decline of the old Communists. The new ORI organization secretary was Emilio Aragonés, the former national coordinator of the Twenty-sixth of July Movement. In the new six-man secretariat, only the fifth secretary was an old Communist. Both secretariat commissions (for labor and for party organization) were chaired by former Twenty-sixth of July members.[37] The main charges against Escalante had been that he was "ambitious" in trying to increase personal power, "sectarian" in favoring old Communists, and "in error" in organizing a party divorced from the masses and in appointing to the party people with questionable pasts. Four categories of members would now automatically be dismissed from the party or kept from joining it: those who either had been candidates or had voted in the elections of the fall of 1958, the last held under Batista; those who had occupied posts in the Batista government of the 1950s; those who had been expelled from revolutionary organizations and remained "unreformed"; and those "opportunists" who might use government or party positions to further private goals. The first category affected 17 percent of the ORI members from the province of Havana.[38] The last category gave unlimited discretion to those restructuring the party; anyone they disliked could be expelled as an "opportunist."

There were also four further tests for getting into the restructured party: acceptance of the two Declarations of Havana as the party's program; willingness to accept the discipline of the party cell and to pay dues; an "exemplary attitude" toward production, work, and socialist emulation; and willingness to participate in military exercises. The new method of party recruitment was based on the assumption that the masses should participate in the process. The ORI's organizational secretariat began to send party commissions to the various work centers, which then called assemblies, at which the people nominated men and women for election as "exemplary workers." Discussion and criticism of the nominees in the assembly included determining whether they passed all the requirements and tests for membership. The assembly then elected the most exemplary workers among them. The commission interviewed the exemplary workers to decide if they also had the personal and political qualities for party membership. Those selected by the commission were then presented to a new popular assembly for approval. The commission had full authority to select for the party all those who were "worthy" but who were not nominated by "temporarily sectarian majorities" and to exclude from the party all those who were "unworthy" but who had been nominated by "temporarily tolerant majorities."[39]

This method of party recruitment brought to general attention men and women who would make good party members and might otherwise have been overlooked. It avoided the practice of merely pooling the memberships of preexisting revolutionary organizations and provided new blood, a fresh stimulus for growth, and continuous political recruitment. The party became more than a conglomerate of old organizations; the new members were loyal only to the new party. The party leadership retained full control over access to party membership as it had in Escalante's time: all those favored by the elite were admitted; all those opposed were not. The party remained selective. Finally, the method involved many people, which broadened the base of political participation and added to the party's authority. The last two points give a new perspective on the process of legitimating revolutionary rule. The method of party organization is an example of the incipient routinization of Fidel Castro's charisma through the party. Ultimately legitimacy remained in the hands of the party as the agent of routinized charisma. Some legitimacy began to rest with the party, not just with Castro. The legitimacy of the party and its membership flowed mainly from the top—not from the election of exemplary workers; that made things easier, though it was also one important method of partisan legitimation. Thus an element of political participation began to enter both the process of legitimation, although the key source of legitimacy remained Castro himself, and the gradual routinization of charisma within the party.

What happened in 1962 and 1963? The numbers expelled from the party in the months after Escalante's fall varied considerably from province to province, from a high of 82.1 percent expelled in the mountains of Oriente to a low of 28.8 percent expelled in Camagüey. One-half of the Havana-province members were expelled. The party members who were eventually expelled and, by inference, the old Communist party, had had very limited prestige. No instance has been recorded when more than one-third of the old ORI members were elected by their fellow workers as "exemplary workers" (table 6.2).

Many old ORI members were saved only by the power of party commissions to appoint party members even if they had not been elected as exemplary workers by their fellows. Between one-sixth and one-third of all new ORI party members were appointed by the party commissions in this way. The proportion of old ORI members in the new ORI was still fairly high as a result either of election as exemplary workers or of direct appointment. The proportion of new members was smallest in Havana province and largest in

Table 6.2 Expulsions from party membership in 1962

Area	Preexpulsion membership	% expelled	% elected exemplary workers
Havana province	1,811	50.2	23.2
Oriente mountains	173	82.1	8.1
Oriente province	3,563	—	14.7
Las Villas province	4,589	—	23.8
Camagüey province (area 1)	386	28.8	30.6
Camagüey province (area 2)	175	—	8.5
Weighted average	a	49.0	20.4

Sources: Computed from Isidoro Malmierca, "La marcha de la construcción del partido en La Habana," *Cuba socialista* no. 14 (October 1962):109, 115; "El PURS en las montañas de Oriente," ibid., no. 24 (August 1963):117; Jorge Risquet, "La construcción del Partido en la provincia de Oriente," ibid., no. 15 (November 1962):118; "Las asambleas de selección de obreros ejemplares en la provincia de Las Villas," ibid., no. 13 (September 1962):132–133; José Fuertes Jiménez, "El trabajo organizativo en Camagüey," ibid., no. 15 (November 1962):122, 125 (figures given for two separate areas of the province).

a. The weighted average expelled was calculated from a total of 2,370; the weighted average elected exemplary workers, from a total of 10,697.

Table 6.3 Admissions to party membership in 1962[a]

Area	Postexpulsion membership	% new members	% appointed members
Havana province	1,480	38.9	32.6
Matanzas province	190	41.6	23.7
Oriente mountains	193	76.7	16.1
Camagüey province	452	39.2	34.7
Weighted average	2,311	42.3	30.9

Sources: Computed from Malmierca, "La marcha," p. 109; Raúl García Peláez, "La construcción del Partido en la provincia de Matanzas," *Cuba socialista* no. 16 (December 1962):122–123; "El PURS en las montañas," p. 117; Fuertes Jiménez, "El trabajo organizativo," p. 125.

a. Postexpulsion membership includes only members evaluated before the reports on which the table is based were published; among them are counted both new and old members elected exemplary workers and new and old members appointed to party membership. Both types of new member are counted in calculating the percentage of new members; both new and old appointed members are counted in calculating the percentage of appointed members. Because few new members were appointed, the overlap between these categories is probably small.

the mountains of Oriente. By any test, the expulsions from the party in 1962 were massive, extending far beyond the departure of Aníbal Escalante as organization secretary. They represented a major restructuring of the Cuban party (table 6.3).

Though the new method of party recruitment emphasized the exemplary-worker method, the proportion of workers was lower than published reports suggested (table 6.4). In the spring of 1963, 52 percent of the members were new; the rest had belonged to ORI before the expulsions. Thus only 8,321 could have become new party members exclusively through the exemplary-worker elections. On the basis of data in tables 6.3 and 6.4, only 69.1 percent of postexpulsion party members—that is, 11,057—were elected as exemplary workers, including both new members and old ORI members. Consequently, only 30.4 percent of the 36,334 elected exemplary workers (including preexpulsion and new members) were also selected to become party members. Exemplary-worker elections were far less significant than the Cuban party and government customarily suggest.

If approximately 48 percent of the members of the reconstituted party (7,681) were also members of the preexpulsion ORI, and if these in turn represented about 51 percent of those who belonged to the party prior to the expulsions, then the overall size of preexpulsion party membership was 15,061; but the new people were now fully loyal to the revolutionary elite. The party in Havana province took in fewer new members than the party elsewhere; only 24.3 percent of the Havana exemplary workers were elected to the new ORI; in the entire country outside Havana province, the figure rises to 34.4 percent.

Fifty percent of the members were of working-class origin, though that is not to say that they were themselves necessarily employed in blue collar jobs, for many of them were serving in administrative and managerial posts. Taking

Table 6.4 Party membership as of March 12, 1963

Province	Exemplary workers	Party branches	Party members	Probationers
Pinar del Río	4,406	394	3,343	669
Havana	11,279	549	4,059	680
Matanzas	2,122	132	807	204
Las Villas	6,703	406	2,307	146
Camagüey	5,217	355	3,313	282
Oriente	6,607	373	2,173	398
Total	36,334	2,209	16,002	2,024

Source: Hernán Barrera, "Building the United Party of the Socialist Revolution in Cuba," *World Marxist Review* 6, no. 12 (December 1963):56–58. Barrera reports that 50 percent of the party members were of working-class origin.

Table 6.5   Worker-peasant enrollment in party schools, 1962–1965

Date and school type[a]	Number of students	% industrial workers	% agricultural workers	% peasants
January–May 1962				
Provincial	855	16.7	8.8	4.9
Base	19,422	31.3	12.0	4.8
December 1962				
Provincial	1,611	24.1	9.8	3.4
Base	31,070	28.6	14.9	4.6
1963[b]				
Provincial	1,532	42.3	11.8	—
Base	25,524	34.3	16.1	—
1964				
All schools[c]	22,714	22.3	21.7	4.5
1965[d]				
Provincial	797	33.8	6.9	5.9
Base (boarding)	2,377	12.2	59.0	14.8
Base (night)	12,724	54.2[e]	—	—

Sources: Computed from the following articles by Lionel Soto: "Nuevo desarrollo de la instrucción revolucionaria," *Cuba socialista* no. 12 (August 1962):42; "Dos años de instrucción revolucionaria," ibid., no. 18 (February 1963):33–34; "Las escuelas de instrucción revolucionaria en una nueva fase," ibid., no. 30 (February 1964):76; "Las escuelas de instrucción revolucionaria en el ciclo político-técnico," ibid., no. 41 (January 1965):72; "El quinto aniversario de las EIR," ibid., no. 53 (January 1966):84–85.

a. The party had highly selective provincial schools, as well as base schools that most members could attend. Some of the base schools required students to board; most met only at night, so that students lived at home.

b. 73.8 percent of students at provincial schools and 24.0 percent of students at base schools were party members; the rest were not, though these were party schools.

c. Excludes an additional 15.1 percent of worker origin and 4.8 percent of peasant origin who were in administration; 27.5 percent of all students were party members; there is no guarantee that people of worker or peasant origin in administrative positions were excluded from the data in 1962 or 1963.

d. Excludes an additional 43.7 percent of worker origin employed in administration from the provincial schools, and 8.4 percent of worker origin employed in administration from the base boarding schools. More workers and peasants were found in party schools than in the party as a whole, because these lower-class members needed more training than their better-educated comrades. The schools provided basic skills and political education. Confidence in the representativeness of the data is increased by focusing on 1963 (where no distinction is made between origin and present employment): 54.1 percent of students in party provincial schools and 50.4 percent of those in party base schools were of working-class origin—in harmony with the aggregate 50 percent statistic for the party as a whole in 1963.

e. Includes industrial and agricultural workers.

class-composition data for enrollment in party schools as indicative of the party's class composition, probably a minority of the preexpulsion party was of working-class origin in 1962; presumably an even smaller proportion was actually employed in blue-collar occupations (table 6.5). The postexpulsion party, in contrast, had a much higher proportion of members of working-class origin; one purpose of the process of expulsion and admission initiated by Prime Minister Castro had been to increase the strength of the working class within the party. In this he succeeded, even though less than a third of those judged worthy by their fellow workers were in fact admitted. The large increases in the number of students of working-class origin in the school ranks in 1963, 1964 and 1965 presumably reflect an increase in their ranks in the party. People employed as workers made up 40.7 percent of the enrollment in provincial party schools (where most students were party members) in 1965; thus the proportion of party members in blue-collar occupations in 1965 was probably below this level. The party probably had a majority of members from working-class origins after 1963, but the fraction actually employed as workers was perhaps not much more than one-third.

But while the working class had a fairly large share of the party membership, the party had an insignificant share of the working class in its ranks. For different dates and geographic areas, the numbers and percentages of party members in work centers was as follows: [40]

	Number of workers	% of party members
Havana province, 1962	159,567	0.9
Matanzas province, 1962	18,864	1.0
Camagüey province, 1962	76,439	0.6
Ariguanabo Textile Factory (Havana), 1962	4,000	2.7
State Farm Mártires del Moncada (Las Villas), 1962	1,700	1.9
Oriente province mountains, 1963	1,175	16.4
Camagüey province, 1964	84,329	7.7

As for the national party, only 4.7 percent of 699,002 workers surveyed in February 1964 were party members. Over all, then, the proportion of party members in the working class was tiny in the early 1960s, but it was rising, especially in Camagüey between 1962 and 1964. These data reflect the selectivity of the party admissions process and the difficulty of relying for the legitimacy of the political system on the "elective" link between party and working class. The legitimation of the political system was aided by the exemplary-worker elections as a channel toward party admission, but the party share of the working class was so low that no generalized claim could rest on that. The legitimacy of the system and the party continued to come from above, not from below. The electoral mechanism made a contribution. Charisma would come to be in the behavior of party members: Fidel Castro's charisma would spread if they behaved in "exemplary" fashion. The political system would derive legitimacy from their conduct, since neither elections nor class representativeness was a reliable base of legitimacy.

Although the Cuban party has been shaken periodically by internal dissention (such as the microfaction struggle in 1968), no evidence exists of any further large-scale expulsions. Instead, the party has institutionalized the process of expulsion into a routine procedure. A study of the Havana provincial party's expulsions primarily though not exclusively after the removal of Escalante and his supporters shows that, from the fall of 1962 to the fall of 1963, the provincial party expelled 4.14 percent of its members and candidates for membership (354 out of a combined total of 8,552). About one-fifth of those expelled were both exemplary workers and members of the party; fully half were candidates who had been elected exemplary workers; and 30 percent were candidates not elected exemplary workers. Those in the last category were probably Escalante party members, put on probation during the party restructuring, who did not make the grade. These data are therefore not entirely free of the "Escalante taint," but for the most part they reflect an institutionalized process of party expulsion exclusive of Escalante's influence.

The Havana party found that 55 percent of the expulsions resulted from "errors" by the party's commissions in the admission of new members. An additional 20 percent was explained as "loss of quality" by members who had been admitted "correctly", that is, associations with friends, family, or church had led to a "loss of quality" (although what the specific loss was went unspecified). A further 8.5 percent said they had changed their minds and no longer wanted to belong to the party. The remaining category was miscellaneous and included "moral reasons, personal conflicts, and law-breaking." Though the categories are poorly defined, they reflect the problems that the party is ordinarily likely to find. The proportion of members and candidates expelled is small and does not threaten the long-term stability of the party membership. The existence of an institutionalized procedure for expulsion increases both party discipline and the calibre of the work carried out according to guidelines set by the leadership; it also reduces the willingness of party members to take risks. The statements of party leaders in the mid-1970s indicate that expulsions still regularly occur.[41]

Prime Minister Castro had been fully aware not only of the threat posed by Aníbal Escalante's possible rivalry but also of the more general implications of the party's restructuring. The expulsion was carried out by commissions from the regional party level, "composed of comrades personally selected by Comrade Fidel Castro in the Schools of Revolutionary Instruction" at the beginning of the process. Only after the process of restructuring had been going on for a while did Castro delegate responsibility for the selection of regional-commission members to the respective provincial party committees.[42]

The battle for the party was the battle for the control of the revolution and its future course. The chief source of legitimacy came to the routinization of Prime Minister Castro's charisma, supported by participatory and electoral features and even more by the superior conduct of party members. Although full political power remained in the hands of the revolutionary elite, the political reorganization of the party was linked to the political mobilization of hundreds of thousands of workers who had a say, albeit limited, in the party's organization.

Social Bases and Political Purposes

It is not possible to establish with precision the social bases of support for the Cuban revolutionary government. The government drew overwhelming support from all political and demographic categories, but at the core of this support were the least educated, the poor, and residents of towns outside Havana. While 86 percent of the respondents in one study supported the revolution, 90 to 93 percent of the least educated, of the poor, and of non-Havana residents were supporters. Forty-three percent of all sampled respondents were "fervent" supporters, compared with 48 to 49 percent of the least educated, of the poor, and of non-Havana residents. In contrast, while 30 percent of all the sampled respondents were critics of the revolutionary government, 47 to 56 percent of these were university educated, from the highest socioeconomic stratum, and Havana residents. Lloyd Free's survey, from which these figures are drawn, excluded the rural areas altogether (see table 6.6). But because the rural areas were typically even poorer and their inhabitants even less well educated, it can be assumed that they would be supporters of the revolutionary government as well.

Maurice Zeitlin conducted a survey of Cuban industrial workers in 1962. Although limited to one occupational category, Zeitlin's findings generally support the main conclusion just inferred from Free's data, namely, that the revolutionary government drew support from all categories, but that the core of its support came from what had previously been the most disadvantaged. Zeitlin found that 70.3 percent of the 202 industrial workers responding favored the revolution, 17.8 percent did not, and the balance was undecided; support for the revolution among the unemployed or underemployed prior to the revolution was 87.1 percent, compared with 61.6 percent among the regularly employed. Eighty percent of black industrial workers, and 67 percent of whites, were favorable to the revolution.[43]

The presence of these class and ethnic cleavages was in some important

Table 6.6   The social bases of revolutionary government: support in 1960 (%)

Social category	Supporters	Fervent supporters	Critics	Oppositionists
Primary-school education or none	90	49	23	6
Secondary-school education	83	35	35	13
University education	77	29	51	9
Upper and upper-middle class	71	34	47	18
Lower-middle class	87	39	33	9
Poor	90	48	21	4
Havana residents	72	34	56	19
Outside Havana	93	49	16	3
Total	86	43	30	8

Source: Lloyd A. Free, *Attitudes of the Cuban People Toward the Castro Regime* (Princeton: Institute for International Social Research, 1960), pp. 4, 5, 7, 14. "Supporters" are defined as those who indicated that Cuba was better off after the revolution than before; "fervent supporters" indicated that Cuba was very much better off (6 to 10 steps higher on a 10-point ladder); "critics" are those who said anything that could be construed as criticism of the revolutionary government (about two-thirds of the "critics" also appear in the "support" category); "oppositionists" indicated that Cuba was worse off after the revolution than before (they are also included in the "critic" category).

respects new to Cuban politics. Class politics existed in prerevolutionary Cuba. These data, however, indicate a direct link between class and group perceptions of political interest, on the one hand, and the politics of incumbency and support or opposition to government, on the other, that was new to Cuba. Revolutionary politics from 1959 through 1962 rested on Cuba's first cleavage that linked politics, economics, and society. This link is not unusual in comparative politics; it had simply not happened before in Cuba in quite that way.

Support for the government slipped over time. Although the surveys made in the late 1950s and early 1960s use different methods to estimate government support and although they are not strictly comparable, they do provide a consistent and coherent picture of the loss of government support and the slight attenuation of class cleavages in the urban areas. In mid-June 1959, the news magazine *Bohemia* reported that 90.3 percent of the population supported the government and only 1.3 percent opposed it.[44] By the spring of 1960, using different methods, Free estimated support for the government below that percentage, criticism much higher, and opposition somewhat higher. The proportion of those hostile to the government in Zeitlin's 1962 survey was far above anything previously recorded; Zeitlin's estimate of support for the government was also the lowest yet registered. The drop in support from Lloyd Free's lower-middle -class urban respondents to Maurice Zeitlin's regularly employed industrial workers—categories that seem to be roughly comparable—was from 87 percent to 62 percent, that is, 25 percentage points.

The pattern of emigration from Cuba (see table 5.1) suggests that through 1962 it was drawn almost entirely from the upper and middle classes, while industrial workers and peasants were underrepresented.[45] By the late 1960s, however, the distribution of exiles fairly accurately reflected the distribution of the urban work force. In 1966, it had acquired a distinctly lower-middle-class element; the overrepresentation of clerical and sales personnel—many from the metropolitan Havana area—was greater than the overrepresentation of professional and managerial personnel. By 1970 the overrepresentation of the urban working class overtook the overrepresentation of the professional and managerial personnel among emigrants from Cuba. These data suggest dissatisfaction with governmental policies among the lower-middle and working classes by the early 1970s and hence indicate a generalization of opposition to the regime throghout the urban sector. Working-class dissatisfaction with the revolutionary government may have reached an all-time high in 1970 and 1971. In contrast, many professional and managerial people remaining in Cuba had resumed their customary positions in charge of national affairs under revolutionary rule and were more content.

Unfortunately no other studies have been made to gauge patterns of support and opposition. At the beginning of revolutionary rule, membership in certain organizations was a clear indication of political loyalty; by now, however, membership has become almost universal. While this might mean that support for the government has also become almost universal, a more likely interpretation is that membership has become the condition for a tolerably useful and trouble-free life, although members may refuse to be very active without penalty. Many people not terribly enthusiastic about the revolution—but not counterrevolutionaries either—join routinely. It is part of civic life. Promotion, access to very scarce commodities and services, and other perquisites of the good life may depend on membership in these organizations. The two explanations have some things in common. Bitter opponents of the government are probably few in these organizations, although many members may be what Free called "critics" in 1960. Certainly no one would claim that all members were "fervent supporters." The only issue—and it cannot be settled satisfactorily—is the degree of commitment to the government implied by organizational membership.

There are at least two important differences between the political purposes that prevailed before the revolution and those that prevailed after it. First, the regulative and distributive purposes of prerevolutionary politics excluded those groups and strata that were not politically organized. The distributive purposes of revolutionary politics reached out to benefit those who had not benefited as much before: the rural people, the unemployed, the blacks, and many women. Second, the distributive priorities of revolutionary politics up to 1970 are comparable only to the priorities of the prerevolutionary political system from the late 1930s to the late 1940s. At these times, growth took a second place to distribution. The priority of growth over distribution, especially under Batista in the 1950s, may be compared to the situation in the 1970s, although the preference for growth has still not become absolute, and it has come in the wake of great strides toward an egalitarian society.

Social Effects of Redistribution

Public Health

Contrary to widespread belief, the performance of the Cuban health-care system was mixed throughout the 1960s and improved only in the 1970s. The number of cases per 100,000 population of the infectious diseases poliomyelitis, diphtheria, tuberculosis, tetanus, leprosy, measles, typhoid fever, syphilis, malaria and hepatitis declined from a peak toward the mid-1960s and began to show improvement. The prevalence of many of these diseases had actually increased during the early 1960s relative to the prerevolutionary period; leprosy, hepatitis, measles, and syphilis showed a higher rate per 100,000 population in the last reported year (late 1960s or early 1970s in each case) than in the 1950s. The rates of tuberculosis and typhoid fever in 1974 were just below those for 1958; both had become more common in the 1960s, and the situation had improved only after a substantial lag.[46]

The rates for brucellosis (an infection derived from contact with animals) increased steadily, and the last reported year shows the highest rates ever. From the mid-1960s to the early 1970s, the rates for dysentery, acute diarrhea, and diseases of the respiratory system increased (although the number of deaths from dysentery declined). The rates for chicken pox, parotitis (one form of which is mumps), and blennorrhagia (one form of which is gonorrhea) lessened from the 1960s onwards. Clear improvements over the prerevolutionary period had been achieved by 1974 in the prevention of poliomyelitis, tetanus, malaria, and diphtheria; in the case of poliomyelitis much of the difference can be explained by the availability of the Salk vaccine, which lent itself well to efficient distribution and was not, of course, available before the revolution.[47]

The most sensible explanation for the worsening performance of the national health-performance care system in the 1960s—usually not acknowledged by the Cuban government—is that it was simply one of the costs of revolutionary rule.[48] Large numbers of doctors and other health-care professionals left the country. Existing medical services and facilities were disrupted by political and military mobilizations. The inefficiencies in Cuban production of medicines (as in virtually all Cuban production) and the disruption of ties with the United States led to a shortage of medical supplies.[49] The crash training program for health-care personnel to replace the exiles may have resulted in less well trained people. Only by the early 1970s were these disruptions overcome and prerevolutionary levels of care generally surpassed.

The commitment of resources to the public-health system in several important areas has also decreased from prerevolutionary levels. The number of hospital beds per 1,000 population fell from 5.42 in 1958 to 5.31 budgeted beds (or 4.06 real beds) in 1974 (for 1958, private hospital beds are included). The number of physicians per 10,000 population fell from between 9.45 and 10.50 in 1958 to 7.46 in 1973; it rose again to 9.42 in 1974 and to a reported 11.1 in 1975. Some of the areas in which the health-care system has performed barely adequately, such as control of tuberculosis and leprosy, have not improved much, in part because of cutbacks in allocated funds. The number of real hospital beds allocated to treatment of leprosy in 1974 was below the 1964 level; for tuberculosis patients in 1974, the supply of beds had fallen to 23.5 of the 1964 level.[50]

The revolutionary government has not performed well in many areas, if one judges it by growth indicators, and health care is no exception.[51] Again it gets better grades for distribution than for growth. Medical services are now free. Although there were many free public hospitals before the revolution, the best medical care often required payment for private hospitals and health personnel. The chief effect of the revolution was not the introduction of free medicine but the elimination of limited access to quality medical care based on ability to pay. Class equality is more widespread within the constant volume of medical services. Urban-rural distribution has also shown substantial improvements, though much of it occurred in the early 1960s. Rural hospitals accounted for 0.3 percent of budgeted beds in general (urban and rural, nonspecialized) hospitals in 1958, 8.1 percent in 1962, and 9.7 percent in 1968, the peak year. This proportion then fell gradually to 5.4 percent in 1974. The proportion of real beds in rural hospitals fell steadily from 8.6 percent in 1964 to 5.7 percent in 1970, rising to 6.3 percent in 1974, still below the levels of the 1960s. The proportion of total outpatient visits to general hospitals and clinics made to rural hospitals and rural medical clinics remained basically unchanged between 1964 and 1974—34.8 percent and 35.2 percent, respectively—though the rural share had fallen as low as 26.1 percent in 1966 and risen as high as 37.6 percent in 1971. Public hospital beds per 1,000 population in Havana province fell from 1958 to 1969 but rose significantly, partly through socialization of private hospitals, in other provinces. From 1899 to 1943, the proportion of medical doctors in the province of Havana had been increasing. By 1955, 62.4 percent of all doctors practiced there. By 1968, this proportion had fallen to 55 percent, and by 1971, to 42 percent (its share of the population in the 1970 census was 27 percent). In 1965, there was one doctor for every 322 citizens of Havana; in the rural regional districts of Oriente province, such as Tunas-Puerto Padre and Bayamo-Jiguaní, there was one doctor per 8,065 and 6,131 people, respectively.[52] Thus, although the trend toward regional imbalances in health care had been reversed, significant inequalities remained into the 1970s.

The Cuban government rightly boasts that Cuban health standards are generally better than those of most other Latin American countries, although that has long been the case. By 1958 Cuba had already achieved a fairly "mature" status in terms of public health. For example, the ten principal causes of death in 1958 were by and large those characteristic of all advanced industrial societies, and they differ very little from the principal causes of death in 1972. The diseases of poverty—infections and hunger—had been conquered long ago in terms of their importance as major causes of death. In both 1958 and 1973 the six leading causes of death in Cuba were heart disease, malignant tumors, diseases of the central nervous system, early childhood diseases, influenza and pneumonia, and accidents, in that order. Birth defects were eighth in both years. Only three of the ten causes of death—all among the four least important—changed: in 1958, acute diarrheic diseases, hypertension (excluding the heart), and tuberculosis were seventh, ninth, and tenth; in 1973 suicides, respiratory diseases, and diabetes had replaced them.[53] The changes in these three categories bring Cuba closer to the typical health picture for an industrialized country in ways that were predictable from the long-term pattern of modernization in Cuban health indices. These data confirm once again the relative stability and good quality of health conditions in Cuba throughout the first dozen years of revolutionary rule. Because the pattern has been mixed, with some improvement along with some deterioration, the net effect has been positive but modest.

Although prerevolutionary Cuba had made significant strides in both public and privately supported health care, a great deal remained to be done. Because postrevolutionary publications at times misrepresent health conditions in prerevolutionary Cuba, some of the worst aspects of prerevolutionary health in Cuba will be reported using only prerevolutionary sources.

A survey of 23,691 persons in the city of Havana in 1937 showed that 69.1 percent had a positive reaction to a test for tuberculosis. A study of one thousand drinking-water samples, published in 1951, showed that 67.5 percent of the water in Cuba failed to meet the standards for purity decreed in 1941 and based on the criteria of the American Public Health Association.[54] A study of 253 children one year old or younger, who were taken to local public-health stations in the 1950s, showed that 54.5 percent of them had parasites. Havana province had the smallest proportion with parasites, 39.3 percent; the other five provinces ranged between 51 and 63 percent. However, the study was not a random sample, and rigorous testing was not uniformly used; other evidence suggested that the actual proportion of children with parasites was probably higher. A 1953 survey of 52,133 fecal samples from 295 rural neighborhoods in sixty-three municipalities (covering an area accounting for a third of the Cuban rural population) found evidence of parasites in 86.5 percent; a similar survey in 1954 of 8,122 fecal samples from three areas in Las Villas showed an incidence of parasites ranging from 66 percent in the town of Cabaiguán and the city of Santa Clara to 87 percent in rural Camajuaní. Dr. Arturo J. Aballí, one of Cuba's leading prerevolutionary pediatricians, reported that 92 percent of 160 children he examined at the children's hospital in Havana in 1950 suffered from "frankly deficient diets." By 1958, Dr. Aballí noted a general improvement in the quality of diets for children during the previous fifteen years, among rich and poor alike, but he also noted that the dietary deficiencies had disappeared altogether among the children whom he saw in his private practice, while they still remained among the children of poorer families whom he saw at the hospital.[55] Both public and private health care in Cuba was improving before the revolution; in some areas important successes had been achieved. Relative to the rest of Latin America, Cuba fared well, but there were still severe health problems, many of which remained an unhappy legacy for the revolutionary years.[56]

Though there has been a trend toward greater equality, the high concentration of medical care in urban areas—and especially in Havana—persists. The trend toward equality—except for the distribution of physicians—was more striking in the early 1960s. It has been halted and partially reversed in the allocation of hospital beds to the rural areas by the 1970s. But a new trend toward health improvement at last appeared in the decreasing mortality and disease rates of the early 1970s.

Race Relations

The record is also somewhat mixed as regards the treatment of blacks. There was little equality of result between blacks and whites in prerevolutionary Cuba, though there was probably more than in the United States and considerably more equality of opportunity. Blacks and mulattoes made up 25.3 percent of the population in 1943, 26.9 percent in 1953, and 26.0 percent in 1970. Among the population aged twenty or older in 1943, blacks accounted for 29.2 percent of the known illiterates. They accounted for 5.8 percent of the engineers, 9.5 percent of the physicians, and 11.9 percent of the lawyers and judges, on the one hand, but for 36.3 percent of unskilled workers and 55.7 percent of domestic servants, on the other. Among professionals and semiprofessionals 10.4 percent of the whites but 19.7 percent of the blacks earned less than thirty pesos a month in 1943; among unskilled workers, the comparable statistics are 37.3 percent of the whites and 50.9 percent of the blacks; among agricultural workers, 51.7 percent and 62.0 percent. Blacks scored lower in all income categories in 1943 in all occupations. Nevertheless, Benigno Aguirre has shown that there was a substantial improvement in the economic conditions of Cuban nonwhites between 1919 and 1943, including an increase in representation in elite occupations.[57]

Research conducted on the population of some Havana tenements (*solares*) in the late 1940s shows that black tenants were ordinarily in the majority; sometimes they accounted for over two-thirds of the tenement population. These buildings were in very poor condition. Blacks and whites both lived in tenements, but, although they belonged to the same income group, the white tenants usually had the best accommodations.[58] The darkness of the skin was also directly related to the likelihood of conviction and imprisonment for crimes. Whites were about one-third less likely to be convicted and imprisoned than one would expect from their share of the population, while blacks (excluding mulattoes) were two and a half times, and mulattoes between 22 and 47 percent, more likely to be convicted and imprisoned than their share of the population would predict.[59]

There was therefore a pervasive pattern of inequality of education, jobs, income, and life chances. There was also, however, a fair degree of mobility. Large numbers of blacks belonged to the professional class. Income gaps, while real, were not extreme. Blacks were not excluded from access to elite roles, as they were in the United States at the same time, nor was their income penalized so heavily.[60] They shared housing with whites, though unequally.

On March 22, 1959, the revolutionary government ended legal race discrimination in Cuba. Clubs and beaches were opened to all.[61] But legal race discrimination has been only part of the problem; only the tip of a hierarchical ethnic structure was backed by the laws. The government, however, has remained committed to full equality of opportunity regardless of color. Because blacks were disproprotionately represented among the poor, they are likely to benefit disproportionally from any improvement in the lot of the poor. Most Cuban blacks are probably better off than they used to be; Zeitlin's survey suggests strong black support for the revolutionary government in 1962.

The revolutionary government claims to have solved the race problem; it has therefore become subversive to speak or write about its existence. Black intellectuals who think that the revolutionary government still engages in race discrimination have gone into exile. Black-solidarity organizations have been banned. The intellectual, artistic, mutual-aid, and labor societies of and for blacks that existed in prerevolutionary Cuba have been forced to disband. Afro-Cuban writers, conscious of blackness as a distinctive characteristic of contemporary, not just historical, social life, have fallen into disfavor. Visitors to Cuba continue to be pleased by the greater ease of race relations compared with the United States, but they also continue to report persistent racism in public and private affairs, however subtle its manifestations. The government's failure to act to eliminate racism has contributed to its persistence. Standards of status and beauty in posters, newspapers, and contests remain white (the "Star" of the Havana carnival and most runners-up are usually white, as is the "Star" of the union of civilian workers in the armed forces).

Complaints about racial tokenism in revolutionary leadership and policies are perceived as illegitimate. At least two attempts made in the late 1960s to discuss race relations openly, as a legitimate political question, were sternly rebuffed by the government. Afro-Cuban religions are objects of solicitude as "folklore," but they do not enjoy the same respect and toleration accorded to Roman Catholicism, Protestantism (excluding Jehovah's Witnesses and some other sects), and Judaism.[62] At the local community level, the few studies that have been made are inconclusive concerning the degree of individual and collective sociopsychological change among Cuban blacks; these studies do agree, however, that the material conditions of blacks have improved considerably and that, to a large degree, they owe this to government policies.[63]

Only 9 percent of the hundred members appointed to the Central Committee of the Communist party of Cuba in 1965 were black or mulatto. In 1945, 9.3 percent of the Senate and 9.4 percent of the House of Representatives were black.[64] Then, as now, this is about one-third what would be expected from the number of blacks in the population; it suggests that the revolution has had little impact in increasing the black share of the elite. In the armed forces, scattered evidence suggests black overrepresentation at the troop level and underrepresentation at the officer level in the early 1970s. This discrepancy may have resulted from amendments to the selective-service legislation in 1973, which had the effect of freezing social stratification and institutionalizing the prevalent pattern of inequality because those with less education (disproportionately black) are the ones most frequently drafted into the military,[65] as opposed to the accepted forms of alternate service.

The revolutionary government has not released data that would permit a direct comparison between the life chances of black Cubans before and after the revolution. However, public-health studies permit some generalizations. Data from nineteen surveys conducted before 1959 and from twenty-three surveys conducted after that date bear on the inequality of result in vulnerability to disease seen in Cuban whites and nonwhites (they are summarized in appendix C). A four-part argument is consistent with most of the facts. First, blacks and mulattoes are more vulnerable to diseases than whites because they are disproportionately poorer, just as they were before the revolution. There was and continues to be inequality of result between blacks and whites in Cuba, though the differences are not and were not very large. Second, there is no published evidence on the immediate effects of the revolution on inequality in health between blacks and white—that is, for the period of the early to mid-1960s. By the early 1970s, however, public-health performance in Cuba was at last outstripping prerevolutionary performance, and presumably methods of gathering data in a more efficient health system are better. Thus the data for the early 1970s can be expected to reflect the ethnic structure more accurately than the data for the 1950s and earlier. Nevertheless, there is no apparent difference in nonwhite vulnerability to disease compared with whites—in this respect nonwhites were as disadvantaged in the early 1970s as they had been before the revolution.

Third, whites are sometimes disproprotionally represented in morbidity and mortality statistics covering diseases such as cancer and coronary attacks that are typical of wealthier people, whereas blacks are more often represented in the reports of diseases typical of poorer people; these include tuberculosis in particular, parasitic diseases, and accidents that occur more often among the poor. But blacks were also disproportionately represented in many studies concerning all types of diseases, because they were generally more vulnerable. Fourth, nonwhites had substantial access to medical care both in revolutionary and in prerevolutionary Cuba (otherwise these studies would have been impossible) but their greater poverty correlates with a greater vulnerability to disease and suggests that they needed more medical care than they received.

Although there has been a trend toward equality between black and white, especially in the job market and before the law, social and political inequality persists and can be traced, at least in part, to government policies. A close relationship between ethnicity and social class, measured by income, education, residence, and health, remains even in the 1970s. Much of the thrust toward equality came in the very early years of the revolution, with few new contributions since then, although antidiscriminatory policies, insofar as one can tell (the Cuban government asked questions about race in the 1970 census but has not released data that would allow comparison with prerevolutionary levels), have been applied consistently.

Income Distribution

Although data on prerevolutionary income distribution are inadequate, incomes since 1959 seem to have been better equalized. Wage scales set in the mid-1960s range from 64 to 844 pesos per month. From the 1960s to the 1970s the trend toward wage equalization continued. Average wages for state workers increased at an average annual rate of 0.9 percent from 1962 to 1966, but they declined at an average annual rate of 2.4 percent until 1971. They rose at an average annual rate of 3.9 percent between 1971 and 1973, but the 1973 level was still 5 percent below the 1966 level and 2 percent below the 1962 level. Because all of these wages are in current prices, inflation probably cut real wages further.[66] The wage share of gross product (table 5.17) rose until 1969 and declined thereafter. The change in economic policy in 1970–71 sought to increase the effectiveness of material incentives to labor to achieve that goal; average wages fell until 1971, so that smaller subsequent increases in wages and wage incentives for quality and higher productivity would be more apt to stimulate labor's contribution to production. The government had concluded that labor had surplus funds in the late 1960s because goods and services were rationed so that discretionary income could not be spent; wage incentives consequently had a limited influence on production. With the rise in prices and the relative decline in wages that occurred in the early 1970s, wage incentives began again to have a substantial impact on production.

The change in incentives policy that led to the decline in average wages halted the redistributiion of income; so much had already been accomplished, however, that Cuba remained a much more egalitarian country in 1973 than it had been years earlier. Agricultural wages were 61.7 percent of the national wage average in 1962, rising to a high of 94.0 percent in 1971; they were 93.4 percent in 1973. Industrial wages were 125.5 percent of the national average in 1962, rising to 128.9 percent in 1966 and falling to 104.0 percent in 1971; they were 105.7 percent in 1973.[67] Wages for agricultural workers, who have always been paid less than the national average, improved substantially during the 1960s, while industry held its own during the first half of that decade and then suffered during the second half (this shift explains in part the decline in industrial production shown in table 5.16). Between 1971 and 1973, however, average industrial wages rose about a third faster than average agricultural wages. The wage gap between the best-paid jobs (in civil aviation) and the worst-paid jobs (in forestry) for which data are available for both 1962 and 1972 narrowed from 2.7 to 1 to 1.9 to 1; the wage gap between the best- and the worst-paid jobs (electric power and nonsugar crops) in 1962 was 4.1 to 1; and in 1972, for civil aviation and day-care centers, 2.4 to 1. Policies more tolerant of inequalities halted and then reversed these trends, but Cuba had become, on balance, a far more egalitarian country—and would remain so without a sustained effort to reverse the trend, a policy change that seems unlikely to occur.

Regional equality of income also benefited somewhat from egalitarian policies over the long run. In 1953 the average cash income of a family in metropolitan Havana was 114.7 percent of the national average; outside Havana it was 89.4 percent. In 1972, these percentages were 113.2 percent and 94.0 percent.[68] The changes were modest and gradual and occurred over a period of two decades; they might have resulted simply from the economic development of Cuba's interior provinces. Nevertheless, only a commitment to that development on the part of the revolutionary government was likely to achieve such results, and the net effect of the trend has indeed been to equalize regional differences in family incomes.[69]

Some government policies were not aimed at benefiting the poor but simply at striking at the rich. In the second half of 1961, the government canceled Cuba's old currency and issued new currency. No one was allowed to exchange more than 10,000 pesos, and those who brought sums in excess of that amount lost it. Although pesos and dollars then had the same nominal value, the value of the peso in world money markets was only a small fraction of the value of the dollar, and it varied widely. Those who did not exchange their currency (in many cases because they were out of the country) lost all their money. The total amount of money in circulation in August 1961 was 1,187 million pesos; a total of 497.6 million pesos was confiscated. This policy was primarily political, not redistributive. Money in the bank, even in excess of 10,000 pesos, was not confiscated.[70] The rich who trusted socialist bankers were not affected by the confiscation; only the rich who had not trusted the revolutionary government's banks were. Nonetheless, the wealth of the old rich in Cuba was much reduced, but no redistribution was involved.

The Cuban revolution pursued an egalitarian policy both out of a regard for social justice and to gain political support linking legitimacy, government performance, and the social bases of rule. Impressive gains were made in equality of education and in spreading the wealth, both between social classes and between urban and rural areas. Impressive gains were made toward equality between classes in the provision of medical services, and less impressive gains toward equality between the city and the countryside. The condition of blacks has improved though they may have benefited because so many poor benefited, and blacks are often poor, rather than because they are blacks; blacks continue to be disadvantaged. Many of these egalitarian gains occurred in the first half decade of revolutionary rule; fewer of them later.

By the early 1970s, egalitarianism was losing out. It was denounced by Prime Minister Castro at the thirteenth labor congress in the fall of 1973; both wages and the wage share of gross product have declined. There was other evidence of increasing income inequality as well. Preferential access in the rationing system in the 1970s was used as a new individual material incentive to produce. In 1973, one hundred thousand television sets were given to vanguard workers through labor assemblies and party and union recommendations. Refrigerators and electrical appliances were also distributed in this fashion. Technicians, physicians, and labor-union leaders had preferential access to new cars imported from Argentina.[71] The rationing system, which had once been an instrument for equality, now became a method to benefit the elite with the goods provided by new trading partners. Peace was achieved at the cost of social justice.

The changes in the early 1970s were justified on the grounds that the Cuban economy needed to grow and that this goal required powerful material work incentives for individuals within the framework of socialism; despite them the distributional performance of the revolutionary government in the long run remains positive and even impressive in some respects. Since growth has also always been a crucial purpose of revolutionary politics, it remains to be seen whether distribution will be sacrificed to it.

Public Service and Private Privilege

Political office brings with it a variety of benefits to the incumbent that are not normally considered as corruption of power. In Cuba, however, the standards of conduct for public officials were raised in the 1960s to dizzying heights of commitment and probity, certainly unparalleled in the country's previous history; as a result a good deal of innocuous behavior on the part of public officials became problematic in the context of an economy of scarcity, where every "privilege" seemed damnable. The revolutionary public official was expected to be totally dedicated to public purpose. Perhaps the most extreme statement of this attitude was expressed in an official communiqué issued by President Dorticós and Prime Minister Castro in December 1964, after the minister of labor, Augusto Martínez Sánchez, attempted suicide. "According to fundamental revolutionary principles," the communiqué reads, "we think that this conduct is unjustifiable and improper for a revolutionary, and we believe that comrade Augusto Martínez Sánchez could not have been fully conscious when he engaged in such a deed, because every revolutionary knows that he does not have a right to deprive his cause of a life which does not belong to him, and which can only be legitimately sacrificed facing the enemy."[72] An equally extreme point of view, explicitly addressing the possible conflict between private and public interests is found in one of Che Guevara's more famous statements.

Our vanguard revolutionaries . . . cannot descend with small doses of daily affection to the terrain where ordinary men put their love into practice. The leaders of the revolution have children who do not learn to call their father with their first faltering words; they have wives who must be part of the general sacrifice of their lives to carry the revolution to its destination; their friends are strictly limited to their comrades in revolution. There is no life outside the revolution.[73]

Revolutionary public officials have not always lived up to these standards. It is not possible fully to evaluate the degree of deviation from them in the behavior of public officials because there is no legitimate and legal political opposition to ask embarrassing questions and no independent press to dig out and publish the details. All that is known on this subject is what the government chooses to tell. Nevertheless the government's credibility on the matter is high, for it has already punished miscreants even in high positions. The evidence of outright corruption is fairly rare, certainly rarer than in prerevolutionary Cuba.

In March 1966 the party's Political Bureau deprived Comandante Efigenio Ameijeiras of his military rank and privileges and fired him from his posts in the party and in the armed forces. He was deputy minister of the armed forces at the time and a member of the Central Committee of the Communist party. He had landed with Fidel Castro in the yacht *Granma* in December 1956. He was a legendary hero of the revolution, a powerful military man and bureaucrat, and a member of the party elite. Ameijeiras was accused of using his power for private purposes, including the protection of his friends. His conduct was "irresponsible"; the friends to whom he gave protection and access to power were "antisocial elements, vagabonds, and corrupt"; they were accused of drug addiction. The party and the government made it plain that Ameijeiras was not charged with treason. Unlike Rolando Cubelas, the "unity" president of the university students in 1959, who had been arrested and convicted for plotting to assassinate the Prime Minister shortly before Ameijeiras was disgraced, Ameijeiras was charged only with corruption. In addition, "several dozen persons" were arrested "in connection with the antisocial, illegal, and vicious activities of pseudo-revolutionary elements, that have used their offices, functions, responsibilities or connections to profit at the expense of the revolution." The Ameijeiras affair, like the Escalante affair in 1962, turned out to be only the beginning of a much more far-reaching "cleansing" of the revolutionary government and party. Revolutionary corruption differs in character from prerevolutionary corruption, but it is no less condemned.[74]

Corruption in revolutionary Cuba primarily, but not exclusively, takes the form of using power to obtain access to other things; it does not often involve money, not necessarily out of revolutionary virtue but because of structural change—money no longer mediates between power and the goals of corruption. In prerevolutionary Cuba, power was used to get money to get something more (often more money and more power). After the revolution, however, the role of money sharply declined in Cuba, partly because there was less for it to buy, and partly because the private sector was much smaller. Power itself became the currency of corruption. Power is corrupt when it is used to gain preferential access to scarce or rationed goods and services, access to illegal goods, such as drugs, or access to trips abroad, better housing, or protection in court against alleged misbehavior. Ameijeiras was charged with all these things: access to privileges, protection, material goods. He was not charged with theft or with taking commissions from virtually nonexistent private business. He was charged with a narrowly political crime, but in a social system where power had become the chief currency, that was serious enough. In 1962 Escalante had also been charged in part with political favoritism and with extensive use of patronage. But Escalante's main problem had been building up power through organizational control. Corruption of access, of course, made his fate even worse. Ameijeiras was not charged with setting up a political machine; his was a case of corruption through using power for private purposes.

Ameijeiras's case was not an example of corruption in its purest form. "Pure" corruption is the breaking of the law in the exercise of power to gain more power. In March 1966, Andrés Castellanos, general secretary of the Communist party in the municipality Jesús Menéndez, was found to have committed statistical fraud.[75] He had illegally and deceptively revised the records of the performance of sugar-cane cutters in his municipality to make them look better. If the fraud had not been discovered Castellanos might have risen through the party ranks. Curiously corruption of power for its own sake was not viewed as a crime as serious as Ameijeiras's. Castellanos was fired from his post, but he continued as a party member and was not brought to trial. This relative leniency is surprising because this variety of corruption hits at the very roots of a system that, at an accelerating pace in 1966, was trying to reduce the value of money. The corruption of politics would make the system unworkable. A similar case of "pure" corruption is that of the state pharmaceutical enterprise, which was found in mid-1964 to be purchasing goods on the black market in order to meet production targets and to be raising prices illegally in order to appear more cost effective. Once again there is no evidence of personal profit, nor of benefit to family or friends. Corruption was being used to improve the record of the administrators and ease their promotion up the ranks.[76]

Some cases of old-style corruption still crop up, however. Corruption through taking commissions from the private sector is apparently rare simply because the sector is small. But theft of public funds occurs. In early 1966 fourteen hotel employees in the city of Santa Clara stole merchandise from the hotel. Unlike statistical falsification for political advancement, old-fashioned corruption is punished severely: some of these workers received up to ten years in prison. In December 1974 the public prosecutor was outraged that a manager of an electronics plant had stolen 1,974 pesos. He stressed the need to "combat systematically and to punish with the greatest severity these . . . petty public thefts." The man was sentenced to ten years in prison. The administrator of an industrial-products retail unit, in charge of several stores, stole 23,000 pesos from the unit's sales and was required to return the stolen funds and sentenced to ten years in prison in February 1975.[77]

One of the nagging problems of rectitude for public officials is not corruption in the legal sense but contravening norms of exemplary socialist conduct (even if less exalted than in the passages quoted earlier). The problem is persistent because the behavior is not illegal and would even be considered normal in most countries of the world. But in an economy of scarcity, with a morality that stresses sacrifice, any privilege enjoyed by public officials skirts the boundaries of corruption. Privileges accrue to bureaucrats, technicians, foreign advisers, and the formerly rich. Their income can be spent in luxurious restaurants, to which they are admitted without having to wait in frequently long lines. Restaurants for bureaucrats serve better and unrationed food. The privileged, even in the 1960s, were given preference in the purchase of cars. Vacation resorts are more accessible to them; their housing is better, and they seem to be less affected by the housing shortage. They can go abroad, serve on diplomatic missions, be invited to diplomatic receptions.[78]

Public officials have at times been chided by Prime Minister Castro for using their power to take advantage of these privileges. The most drastic, though temporary, measures were taken in the Ministries of Foreign Trade and Foreign Relations in 1966, when many members of the Cuban diplomatic corps were fired, access to diplomatic receptions was limited and strictly regulated, and travel was sharply restricted. In 1970 Castro bitterly denounced those party members benefiting from "privilege, and even from corruption" and demanded their expulsion. In rural Matanzas in the late 1960s, some had been expelled from membership for partying with illegal food and liquor; but pulling strings for private benefit was felt to be legitimate by local party members.[79] The use of power to get more power was not frowned upon; the use of power to get more wealth was. The antiprivilege measures of the late 1960s were not enforced for very long. It is difficult to see how they could have been, for much of the privilege alleged was part of holding an elite position. By the early 1970s Castro publicly acknowledged and defended, as part of the office and as a necessary material incentive, many of these privileges. It was easier to do so then, because the Cuban economy was finally growing and the scarcities and privations seemed to be passing. The Prime Minister argued that the elite should have first what all would have eventually. Standard in most countries, this policy became standard in Cuba as well and was no longer the subject of public concern. The criteria for rectitude among public officials have been formally lowered.

Public purposes prevail in the Cuban government. This does not mean that Cuban public life is free of the pursuit of private interest, which continues to exist in both legal and illegal forms. Legal private interests in government are not substantially different from those in most countries. Illegal ones differ from corruption in other countries, and in prerevolutionary Cuba, only in that the intermediary function of money figures in it much less.

The Cuban revolution has rested much of its legitimacy on the routinization of Fidel Castro's charisma. This reliance requires conduct on the part of public officials that is thought to reflect his image—to be above reproach. Generally conduct has been good, and corruption is not a serious problem. Purposive government under the revolution became public regarding and redistributive. A powerful government, free of political competition, could and did implement its program of change. A key element of that program was vast redistribution of resources, linked to the building of both legitimacy and popular support.

Bureaucratization and Social Change

In the first months of revolutionary rule, most prerevolutionary governmental bureaucracies continued in operation. New ministries for social welfare, economics, the study of revolutionary legislation, and the recovery of misappropriated funds were added, but they did not last long. The Ministry for the Study of Revolutionary Laws was incorporated into the presidency when its minister, Osvaldo Dorticós, became President in July 1959. The Ministry for the Recovery of Misappropriated Funds became a branch of the Ministry of Finance in March 1960, and the minister transferred with it. The

Ministry of Social Welfare was dissolved in February 1960. A number of ministries had their names, but little else, changed. The most dramatic step was the suspension of tenure in the civil service. Some 50,000 of Cuba's 160,000 bureaucrats were replaced in the first three months of 1959.[80] In the early years, the revolutionary government successively created and eliminated central bureaucracies that failed to adapt to the rapidly changing political conditions. The inability of bureaucracies to adapt proved a major stumbling block to the early launching of bureaucratic institutionalization under revolutionary rule. Bureaucratic legitimation of the revolution would not soon be forthcoming.

Revolutionary change requires bureaucracies. Just as revolutionary political mobilization in the early years was linked to its organization, revolutionary structural change was linked to its bureaucratization. At each major structural turn, new government bureaucracies had to be created. In May 1959 the first Agrarian Reform Act was approved, and the National Institute for Agrarian Reform (INRA) was established to administer the law. In the summer and fall of 1960, the economy was socialized. The political crisis led to the creation of mass organizations; the structural crisis led to the creation of bureaucracies. On February 21, 1961, the Ministry of Industries was established to own, direct, and supervise Cuban industry and implement industrial policies. The Ministry of Internal Trade was established to take charge of wholesale and retail distribution. The Ministry of Foreign Trade was given a monopoly over external trade. The old Ministry of Commerce was abolished. All the formerly private banks became branches of the National Bank. The Central Planning Board (JUCEPLAN) was established to coordinate and plan the economy of the country.

The leadership was keenly aware, as President Dorticós said, that "the nationalizing decrees did not suffice by themselves to place us on the road to the development of socialism in our country . . . This goal required the immediate creation of institutions, of new state organizations that would emerge as a result of the structural changes in the economy."[81] The specific organizational pattern established at that time had problematic long-term consequences: first, the tremendous centralization of economic and political power in Guevara's Ministry of Industries—a vast monopoly; second, the failure to resolve jurisdictional conflicts and the creation of many new ones. The National Institute for Agrarian Reform, which absorbed the Ministry of Agriculture in 1961, was in charge of cane cultivation, while the Ministry of Industries was in charge of sugar processing; Internal Trade saw to internal distribution, and the Foreign Trade Ministry, to foreign trade. The process of coordination among all these new organizations, weak in technical talent because so much of it was exiled and politically pressured as well, proved difficult, and the Central Planning Board did not rise to the challenge. Third, the organizational overlaps soon resulted in political and personality conflicts. Fourth, only feeble attempts were made to coordinate the bureaucratic and the political organizations that had been established under revolutionary rule, and finally, there were drastic, though obviously necessary, personnel changes. All the chief administrators of the 161 sugar mills in 1959 had been replaced by 1961; 72 percent of the 966 most important positions at the sugar mills had changed hands as well.[82]

The economic collapse of the early 1960s led to vigorous debate over the organization and management of the economy and the role labor incentives should play in it. The resulting changes in policy were translated into organizational changes. The monopolistic Ministry of Industries was broken up between 1964 and 1967 after Guevara's departure. New ministries were established in its stead to oversee the sugar industry, the food industry, basic industry, light industry, and mining and metallurgy. At about the same time, the Ministries of Economics and Finance disappeared, and their functions passed to the Central Planning Board and the National Bank.

The next important shifts were made as a result of the 1970 collapse and were once again linked to organizational changes. The Ministry of Construction, which had performed poorly, was broken up into four new ministries, organized according to the various types of construction. The increasing presence of the Soviet Union was reflected in the establishment of the Ministry of Merchant Marine and Ports, which was supposed to improve the handling of Soviet ships and cargoes, and a commission to regulate Cuban-Soviet economic, technical, and scientific relations (directed by Carlos Rafael Rodríguez). The short-lived Ministry of Basic Industries was replaced by three new ministries in late 1974. The launching of Cuba's first five-year plan (1976–1980) led to the revival of a finance ministry and the appointment of ministerial-rank committees on prices and supplies.

The organizational growth of the early 1970s required additional coordination. Confusion resulted in the 1960s from a too rapid establishment of new enterprises combined with the too frequent dismantling of old ones. To prevent the chaos that might have resulted in the early 1970s from too speedy a renewal of growth, a ten-member executive committee of the cabinet, eight of whom held the rank of deputy prime minister, was formed in November 1972. Each of these deputy prime ministers was given responsibility for a cluster of ministries and subcabinet agencies: construction; transport and communications; basic industries; consumption; education, science, and culture; foreign relations; sugar; and financial management and labor (the last under the president). Raúl Castro continued as minister of the armed forces and First Deputy Prime Minister. Prime Minister Castro remained president of the National Institute for Agrarian Reform and continued to oversee a residual cluster including the armed forces, the interior ministry, all agriculture, public health, the Children's Institute, and the management of the cabinet itself.

This change improved coordination within sectors, and established the bureaucratic leadership that the Prime Minister alone had previously been unable to provide. At the same time, because the Prime Minister was left with responsibilities of particular interest to him, the management of most bureaucracies was shielded somewhat from his enthusiastic innovations and hence given some degree of stability.

A reorganization of all ministries was undertaken in November 1976 in order to remedy the disorganization remaining from earlier piecemeal reforms and to align Cuba's bureaucratic structure with its counterparts in the Soviet Union and other eastern European countries. Established at the top of the government hierarchy was the executive committee of the Council of Ministers, composed of the President of the republic (who also served as president of the Council of State, as required by the constitutional changes in 1976, and president of the Council of Ministers), the first vice president of the republic (also of the Council of State and the Council of Ministers), the eight vice-presidents of the Council of Ministers, and a secretary to the Council of Ministers—a total of eleven members. The President was authorized to take charge of any central organization at any time he deemed it necessary; he was to name all ministers and presidents of state committees; and he would decide when issues should be discussed by the executive committee rather than by the whole council. This new arrangement therefore centralized formal power in the President's office and in the executive committee. Fidel Castro became President, replacing Osvaldo Dorticós, a few days after this government reorganization went into effect. Raúl Castro assumed all the first vice-presidencies.

Organizations in the Council of Ministers were of two types. First, state committees, whose heads were called presidents, were in charge of functional areas cutting across many economic sectors. The nine state committees would oversee technical and material supply, science and technology, economic collaboration with other countries, construction, statistics, finance, standardization, prices, and labor and social security. The National Bank and the Central Planning Board also remained in the Council of Ministers. In addition, there were twenty-three ministries. Some, such as those for culture, education, higher education, justice, foreign affairs, and public health, dealt with services. Two dealt with the armed forces and internal security; the rest, with economic sectors: agriculture, foreign trade, domestic trade, communications, construction, the food industry, the sugar industry, the electric-power industry, light industry, the construction-materials industry, the fishing industry, the iron and steel and the machine industries, the chemical industry, mines and geology, and transportation. The reorganization entailed not so much the creation of entirely new agencies as the renaming of old ones and the downgrading or upgrading of many existing bureaucracies. The Council of Ministers was made up of these thirty-four agencies and the members of the executive committee.[83]

The long-term success of a revolution depends upon the creation of new political structures to concentrate, institutionalize, and increase power and to achieve whatever the goals of the revolution are to be. An institutionalized revolutionary government may not succeed, but the failure to institutionalize imperils it, forcing reliance on a single individual's charisma and on coercion for its continuation. Institutionalization is the process by which organizations and procedures acquire value and stability. Its level can be defined by the complexity and coherence of organizations and procedures as they lead to adaptability and autonomy. *Complexity* involves the multiplication of organizational subunits and their internal differentiation. *Coherence* involves a high degree of consensus on the functional boundaries of an organization and on conflict resolution within those boundaries. *Adaptability* is the capacity to respond to the challenges of time and changing environments; dropping old tasks, taking on new ones, and resolving problems of succession are its main components. *Autonomy* is the extent to which organizations and procedures are independent of other individual and social forces. Considerable attention will be paid to institutionalization in Cuba in subsequent sections; this one will focus primarily on valuation, stability, complexity, and adaptability.[84]

Organizational complexity under revolutionary rule is measured in part by the annual increase in the total number of enterprises as a result of their internal differentiation.[85] These government-owned enterprises, subordinate to ministries, actually carry out production. The rate of growth of these organizations accelerated around 1970. A less desirable result was the massive organizational confusion of 1971—possibly responsible for the economy's poor performance—brought about as new enterprises were established and almost a third of the old ones dismantled in 1970. Except for 1970, however, the proportion of enterprises dismantled was fairly stable between 1967 and 1971, with a high of 21.4 percent in 1968 and a low of 14.5 percent in 1971. This relatively high rate of political "bankruptcy" among socialist enterprises was detrimental to long-range planning and implementation of policies. The combined proportion of government enterprises either created or eliminated—the total turnover of organizational change—was also roughly constant from 1967 through 1971—between 40 and 50 percent—except for 1970, when total organizational change reached a high of 70.6 percent. In contrast, change in 1966 was lower, with only 7.1 percent of enterprises dismantled and a total change of 16 percent (see table 6.7).

These statistics suggest a fairly low level of institutionalization at the enterprise level. Instead of finding a way for existing enterprises to adapt to new conditions, the government simply dismantled them. To be sure, such a high rate of enterprise turnover permits swift responses to particular short-term problems, but it also results in confusion and fails to give sufficient time for organizational practices and procedures to take effect before new changes are introduced.

Patterns of institutionalization also varied considerably among economic

Table 6.7 Organizational change in government enterprises, by sector, 1966–1971[a]

Economic sector	% change	% ended	Number 12/31
		1966	
Agriculture (1/1/66: N = 114)	25.4	13.2	113
Industry (1/1/66: N = 42)	21.4	2.4	49
Construction (1/1/66: N = 24)	29.2	16.7	23
Transport and communications (1/1/66: N = 41)	24.4	7.3	45
Commerce (1/1/66: N = 57)	7.0	1.8	59
Service (1/1/66: N = 198)	8.6	5.1	195
Total (1/1/66: N = 476)	16.0	7.1	484
		1967	
Agriculture	85.8	25.7	152
Industry	28.6	12.2	51
Construction	17.4	8.7	23
Transport and communications	17.8	11.1	43
Commerce	30.5	20.3	53
Service	26.2	18.5	174
Total	39.7	18.6	496
		1968	
Agriculture	85.5	36.8	170
Industry	39.2	13.7	57
Construction	39.1	26.1	20
Transport and communications	20.9	14.0	40
Commerce	5.7	3.8	52
Service	24.1	16.7	158
Total	42.9	21.4	497
		1969	
Agriculture	107.6	45.9	197
Industry	15.8	7.0	58
Construction	45.0	25.0	19
Transport and communications	15.0	7.5	40
Commerce	48.1	11.5	65
Service	10.1	2.5	166
Total	49.9	20.1	545

Source: Computed from *Boletín 1971*, pp. 38–39.

Table 6.7—continued

Economic sector	% change	% ended	Number 12/31
		1970	
Agriculture	111.7	57.9	189
Industry	17.2	3.4	64
Construction	294.7	110.5	33
Transport and communications	40.0	30.0	32
Commerce	33.8	10.8	73
Service	36.7	6.0	207
Total	70.6	30.5	598
		1971	
Agriculture	58.7	17.5	234
Industry	37.5	14.1	70
Construction	78.8	0.0	59
Transport and communications	6.3	3.1	32
Commerce	132.9	52.1	94
Service	9.2	2.9	214
Total	46.7	14.5	703

a. "Percentage change" indicates the total number of enterprises created and enterprises dismantled during a year, multiplied by 100, divided by the total number of enterprises in existence at the end of the immediately preceding year. "Percentage ended" refers to the number of enterprises dismantled during a year, multiplied by 100, divided by the total number of enterprises at the end of the immediately preceding year. Agriculture includes cattle raising, forestry, and fishing.

sectors. The entire construction industry was reorganized in 1970. The Internal Trade Ministry was reorganized in 1971, so that its enterprises would correspond more closely to the political and administrative divisions of the country. An unsuccessful effort to produce ten million tons of sugar in 1970 also led to drastic changes in the organization of enterprises in the agricultural sector in 1969 and 1970. Following the industrial changes of 1966, the sectors including all services and all industry were more stable from year to year than the rest of the system, though they, too, were subject to many changes, especially in 1967, 1968, and 1970. Most changes were, not surprisingly, in enterprises that performed poorly. Changes were made in response to failures in agriculture, construction, transport, communications, and commerce. The organization of construction and commerce was totally revamped in 1970 and 1971, and that of agriculture underwent massive changes in 1969 and 1970.

Toward the end of 1964, Prime Minister Castro launched a campaign against "bureaucratism" as an evil in Cuban society; the campaign reached its peak about three years later. Its purpose was to shift people out of desk jobs into more productive ones or, if necessary, to send them back to school to learn useful skills. It was also used to weed out political dissidents from the bureaucracy. Some 31,500 bureaucrats were laid off by the end of 1967 from all sectors, and average wages fell by 8.0 percent from 1965 to 1966 in administration and finance.[86] The bureaucracy was in turmoil; the campaign had questioned the legitimacy of its work, undermined morale, and interrupted institutionalization. It set up yet another roadblock to the bureaucratic legitimation of the revolution; it also served, however, to reinvigorate its radical strain and was justified on the grounds of improving efficiency and performance and delivering the people from the habits of the past.

The impact of the antibureaucratic campaign was in the end modest. The rate at which enterprises were dismantled increased substantially from 1966 to 1967, but it was only in 1970, when the government was responding not to political preference but to economic calamity, that it reached its highest rate. The campaign did not halt the increase in the total number of enterprises—although the rate of growth during these years was much lower than it would subsequently become. A significant reduction in the number of enterprises in 1967 and 1968 was achieved only in the area of services (banks, cultural and educational activities, sports), where the 1966 level was nevertheless surpassed by 1970. Personnel in administration and finance fell by only 0.5 percent from 1965 to 1966.[87] In short, the lack of stability appears to be related to the economic performance of particular sectors rather than to a specific sociopolitical policy that affects all of them.

Another measure of bureaucratic stability is the amount of turnover among its personnel. Data on this subject are meager except at the cabinet level. By the end of 1959, over half of those who had been appointed to the cabinet at the beginning of the year had departed. This change of ministers resulted from the sharp radicalization of revolutionary rule: moderates and liberals left or were expelled. Since 1959 the rate of turnover has been remarkably low. About three ministers, on the average, have been replaced every year. Except for 1959 and 1962, the turnover in the cabinet has always been less than a fifth of its members (table 6.8). The percentage of ministers dismissed from 1966 to 1971 was consistently lower than that of enterprises dismantled during the same period. Thus the level of personnel stability, at least in the upper ranks, was greater than organizational stability in economic enterprises. At the top of the system, organizational upheaval appears to have gone on in the midst of personnel continuity, providing a degree of stability amid the confusion. It appears that while the revolutionary elite has not changed fundamentally, however, its members have yet to agree on what organizations are appropriate for managing its economy and society.

The mean tenure of cabinet ministers from 1960 through 1974 was approxi-

Table 6.8 Cabinet turnover, 1959–1977[a]

Year	Cabinet posts 1/1	Ministers dismissed	% dismissed
1959	21	12	57.1
1960	21	4	19.0
1961	19	3	15.8
1962	20	6	30.0
1963	20	1	5.0
1964	20	3	15.0
1965	20	2	10.0
1966	21	1	5.0
1967	21	3	14.3
1968	23	3	13.0
1969	23	2	8.7
1970	23	4	17.4
1971	27	1	3.7
1972	27	3	11.1
1973	34	4	11.8
1974	34	2	5.9
1975	37	0	0.0
1976	40	6	15.0
1977	45	—	—

a. The cabinet includes all the ministers, plus the President of the re-public, the Prime Minister, and, since 1959, the president of the National Bank. Since 1960 it has included the head of the National Institute for Agrarian Reform. Because Carlos Rafael Rodríguez remained in the cabinet, without portfolio, in 1965, he is not counted among those dismissed. In December 1972, when an executive committee of the cabinet was created, the table reflects only the net addition of new members. The total in 1975 was thirty ministers, ten members of the executive committee (including Prime Minister Fidel Castro and First Deputy Prime Minister Raúl Castro), and the President. The appointments of the three additional ministers listed in 1976 were announced at the December 1975 party congress, but their ministries were legally established only during the course of 1976. For 1977, the eleven members of the executive committee are added to the thirty-four ministers and presidents of state committees.

mately 4.38 years. Ministries controlling enterprises with severe economic problems were more likely to be unstable than the others. The following list shows the length of tenure in cabinet posts, by sector, during this period.[88]

National Bank	2.3	years
Mining/Metallurgy	2.7	
Sugar Industry	3.7	
Communications	3.75	

Transportation	3.75 years
Labor	3.75
Education	3.75
Basic Industry	4.0
Light Industry	4.0
Internal Trade	4.7
Food Industry	5.0
Agrarian Reform Institute	5.0
Interior	5.0
Foreign Trade	7.0
Cabinet Secretary	7.5
Justice	7.5
Foreign Relations	15.0
Armed Forces	15.0
Presidency	15.0
Prime Ministry	15.0

The National Bank, at the center of economic planning and control, has been most vulnerable, losing its presidents every two or three years. Mining production has fallen far short of hopes for exports and for petroleum-import substitution. The sugar industry was unable to achieve the goals set for the late 1960s and has performed disappointingly in the 1970s. Labor has created many problems for the government. Communications and transportation are unstable (see table 6.7). Turnover of ministers in these sectors has predictably been greater than in other areas of government. Education is exceptional because ministerial turnover has been rapid even though performance has been good.

From 1960 through 1976 the proportion of cabinet ministers dismissed ranged from about 5 to about 18 percent in all but four years (see table 6.8): 1960, when the effects of the radicalization of 1959 were still being felt; 1962, when the cabinet was feeling the effects of the dismissal of many party members; 1971, when a single minister was dismissed; and 1975, when no changes were made. The rate of turnover in the 1970s indicates both continuity and rotation. Because the proportion of enterprises dismantled was falling by 1971 and because the rate of organizational growth was very high, the period was above average in stability of personnel and organization—if the personnel trends observed in the cabinet are in fact reflected at the level of enterprise personnel. These data correlate well with the improvement of the country's economic performance and the influence of the Soviets in encouraging bureaucratization.

The obstacles to bureaucratic institutionalization up to the early 1970s included a pervasive sense that bureaucracies were bad and civil-service work somehow unworthy of revolutionaries and a commitment to dismantle existing bureaucracies that were not performing well and to rearrange things that were leading to instability. Organizational changes usually arise from the need to implement structural changes and, later, from the need to cope with economic failures; they rarely stem from policies aimed at the entire bureaucracy. An important element of stability in the midst of organizational change was provided by the continuity of membership within the cabinet and the low, if steady, rates of personnel turnover. During 1966–1971, the ranks of personnel were more stable than the organizations they administered. By the early 1970s, the rates of change in both organization and personnel had declined, auguring even greater stability. Eight of the thirteen members of the Political Bureau in 1977 had posts in the expanded cabinet or executive committee, and all but two had at some time served there. The stigma previously attached to bureaucratic service may at last be disappearing, but bureaucracies are still not much valued: in 1973, average wages in local administration were only 92.3 percent of the national average;[89] the comparable statistic for the metropolitan government of the city of Havana was even lower—81.7 percent of the national average wage. Of thirty-one specific subsectors in production and services throughout the economy for which average-wage data are available, the civil servants of metropolitan Havana ranked thirtieth.[90]

The Constitution of 1976 and the Formalization of the State

A constitutional commission was established within the Central Committee of the Communist party in the fall of 1965, but no constitution was forthcoming. On October 22, 1974, another commission was appointed, and this one submitted a draft constitution on February 24, 1975.[91] It was approved by the First Party Congress in December, after extensive public discussion, and by popular referendum in February of the next year. The new Constitution replaced the amended and largely ignored Constitution of 1940.[92] The chief change it provided in the organization of the revolutionary state was the establishment of a National Assembly (which met for the first time in December 1976) and of elected provincial and local governments throughout the country. From 1959 to 1976 formal legislative powers had been vested in the cabinet. The new Constitution shifted them to the National Assembly. The assembly elected a Council of State to function when the National Assembly was not in session. The president of the Council of State became also the President of the republic and of the cabinet; as already noted, Fidel Castro replaced Osvaldo Dorticós as President of the republic. The cabinet would no longer have formal legislative powers.

By the provisions of its Constitution, Cuba had broken with the practice found in other socialist countries of separating the head of state from the head of the government, a practice it, too, had followed from 1959 to 1976. The new Constitution reestablished a presidential system more consistent with Latin American practice. Although separate powers are specified for the president of the Council of State (the head of state) and the president of the Council of Ministers or cabinet (the head of government—formerly called the Prime Minister), the Constitution requires that the same person be president of both. The presidency under the new Constitution is a formalized version of the routinization of Fidel Castro's charisma: the head of state and of government are once again one. The cabinet is in charge of administration and is left with considerable power, including the power to draft legislation. The National Assembly decides on the constitutionality of legislation; the Supreme Court and the other courts are subordinate to the assembly and the Council of State.

The changes made in the constitutional draft between its initial publication and its final adoption are discussed in appendix D. With one exception, the net effect of the most important changes was to strengthen the power of the higher-ranking central elite and institutions at the expense of lower ranks and far beyond the already formidable powers envisaged in the original draft.

Another important change authorized by the First Party Congress was a new political and administrative division of national territory, which went into effect in the fall of 1976. Instead of the six provinces that had existed since the nineteenth century, there are now fourteen (the Isle of Pines was made a special municipality outside of this new system); the regions into which the provinces had been divided were abolished; and 169 municipalities were formed. While Pinar del Río and Matanzas remained essentially as they had been before the change, Havana province was divided into two (the city of Havana and the rest of the province); Las Villas, into three provinces (Cienfuegos, Villa Clara, and Sancti Spíritus); Camagüey, into two (Ciego de Ávila and Camagüey); and Oriente, into five (Las Tunas, Holguín, Granma, Santiago, and Guantánamo).[93]

It is, of course, still impossible to pass judgment on the National Assembly, since it has barely begun to function. However, some preliminary thoughts are possible. The formalization of the revolutionary state—the process of making explicit, through a constitution, codes of law and legislation, the rights and duties of citizens, and the procedures and organizations of the state—should not be confused with its institutionalization. Although formalization can contribute powerfully to the legal-rational legitimation and institutionalization of the state legitimation and institutionalization involve more than mere formalization. Thus whether or not the National Assembly has been institutionalized cannot be determined for some time. But certainly the formalization of the Cuban state has advanced considerably.

The people elect directly only the members of the municipal assemblies; these, in turn, elect the members of the provincial assemblies and the National Assembly. Deputies to the National Assembly serve part time, are not full-time professional legislators, and lack the autonomy that direct elections might have conferred. It is thus quite possible that their activities will remain

CUBAN PROVINCES IN 1969

PINAR DEL RÍO

Pinar del Río

HAVANA

Havana

Matanzas

MATANZAS

Santa Clara

LAS VILLAS

CAMAGÜEY

Camagüey

ORIENTE

Santiago de Cuba

ISLE OF PINES
(municipality)

150 miles

km

150

0

0

CUBAN PROVINCES IN 1976

mostly pro forma. The National Assembly may well end up behaving just as the elected local and provincial government assemblies and other socialist legislatures behave, but this remains to be seen. If it does happen, the National Assembly will have few real powers. The effect of the participation of deputies (and hence indirectly of citizens) will be very limited.

The National Assembly met for the first time in early December 1976, for a few days, to elect Fidel Castro as President and to ratify all his appointments. All the necessary votes were unanimous. The assembly also elected Blas Roca its president; he received 478 of the 479 votes cast. The National Assembly did not meet again until July 12, 1977; it adjourned two days later. Nine bills were submitted to the assembly by the government during this second session; all were approved unanimously. Debate, of course, had to be relatively brief and formal. For the most part the deputies listened; they were not expected to come up with significant, substantive policy recommendations. In the future, it may be expected that they will rarely, if ever, reject a bill. This unanimity is partly accounted for by the fact that 91.7 percent of the deputies were members of the Communist party and another 5 percent members of the Communist Youth Union. Only 28.5 percent have more than a secondary-school education; thus they may not be sufficiently skilled to take many legislative initiatives. About 44.5 percent of the deputies were not directly elected by the people to a municipal assembly; they are government and party officials constitutionally appointed as deputies by the municipal assemblies on the recommendation of a nominating commission chaired by a party member. The constitutional right of recall and the accountability specified as a duty may be used, as in local government, to keep wayward deputies in check.[94]

The National Assembly, however, has begun to make a number of contributions to policy making, and it will probably continue to do so. One contribution is likely to be service to constituencies on specific local issues. Citizens will have an avenue for complaint to national deputies as well as to local municipal-assembly delegates: the national deputies can defend their constituents' interests in the central bureaucracy. Participatory contacting of elected officials by citizens will be expanded and legitimated. Deputies had already raised many issues of this kind at the close of the July 1977 session of the National Assembly. The deputy from the municipality of Sagua la Grande, for instance, was concerned about problems in collection of rents for housing; the deputy from the municipality of Julio Antonio Mella wanted control over all housing in sugar-mill communities to pass from the sugar mill to local government officials; other requests were made on behalf of veterans of the rebel army of the 1950s, lawyers, and sugar-worker pensioners. By far the most interesting complaint was raised by five deputies from the city of Havana's Plaza de la Revolución municipality. They objected to the location of a new bus assembly plant in their district because it would contribute to the area's already severe pollution, and they wanted it located elsewhere. The problem received an immediate reply from President Castro, who said that it "could not be solved easily," although it is "good to look into these problems." The complaint was then referred to four of the twenty standing commissions of the National Assembly; all other complaints were also referred to commissions for study.[95]

Another contribution of the National Assembly may be the improvement of the technical quality of legislation. In past years, laws have been drafted by a few part-time legislators. Although most national deputies will not be full-time legislators, some will probably come to specialize in lawmaking and will have the time and inclination to attend to detail. Whether they will have a significant impact on content remains doubtful, however, judging from Cuban experiments in local government and from the first meetings of the National Assembly. Yet it is possible that some, although not much, subtle and restrained lobbying will now be possible through the National Assembly and its standing commissions: in the Soviet Union, Supreme Soviet committees make changes affecting only something like 1 percent of the budget.

In the July 1977 debates of the National Assembly, these points were well illustrated. National Assembly president Blas Roca's closing address summarized the spirit of the meeting: "All the deputies here unanimously agreed on the essence of our proposals. There were different opinions on details . . ."[96] One deputy proposed amending the charter for municipal government so that municipal delegates would have to render accounts to their constituents every four months, instead of every three months; after endorsement by Fidel Castro, the amendment was overwhelmingly approved. The Political Bureau of the party recommended an amendment to the law on the organization of the legal system to allow judges and prosecutors to be elected delegates and deputies to assemblies. The amendment was proposed to the committee on constitutional and legal affairs by Fidel Castro, the commission endorsed it, and the National Assembly approved it unanimously. Several commissions made technical modifications of draft bills on their own, which the National Assembly endorsed. Perhaps the tenor of the substantive discussion is best reflected by the newspaper Granma's comment that "the subject which produced the most discussion was the amount of time that should elapse between the application of a provisional disciplining measure against a worker by the administration of a work center and the decision of the Labor Council to approve or reject it."[97]

These actions of the National Assembly and its commissions improved the quality of legislation, and a few of the amendments had some substantive importance as well. Most of them involved details of modest or minor significance. Another feature of these sessions was Fidel Castro's almost continuous participation in the debates, often to seal the fate of the amendment at hand. There is no evidence that the passage of amendments in any way implied a defeat for him, or for the government, or for the party elite; on the contrary, all prevailed whenever they took a firm stand.

The National Assembly will also have the effect of strengthening the links among local leaders, as they gather from time to time in Havana to discuss affairs. Such a thing had not happened since the revolution came to power; local leaders stayed home, leaving national affairs to those already in Havana. Deputies will probably continue to have few real powers, but they will at least have some significant formal ones, with both local and national responsibilities. This fact, too, will have its effect and may contribute, however marginally, to better coordination between local needs and national policies. Finally, the National Assembly will symbolize the formalization of the revolution, the increase in reliance on legality, and the routinization of charisma.[98]

The Law and the Courts

The Cuban court system has always been a part of the ruling political coalition, whose function was to adapt legal doctrine to fit the changing times. This function continued after 1959, but the autonomy of the court system, never very great, was almost entirely eliminated in the early years of revolutionary rule.

The case that signaled the end of court autonomy was the trial of forty-five members of Batista's air force, who were charged with genocide, murder, and similar crimes stemming from air attacks on populated areas in Oriente during the last month of the insurrection. The government asked for the death penalty for forty of them and ten years in prison for the other five. The trial began on February 13, 1959. On March 2, the three-judge court (all former rebel army officers) acquitted all the defendants, ruling that the rebel forces were actually in the villages under attack and that this made them legitimate military targets. There was no evidence of intent to destroy racial, religious, or national groups, and the government had failed to prove premeditated murder or even to prove beyond doubt which of the defendants had in fact caused death or destruction. Despite protests from the bar association and others concerning double jeopardy, an angry Prime Minister Castro set up a review court on March 7. This court ruled that the prosecution had the right of appeal and then proceeded to convict forty-three of the forty-five defendants of genocide (which they defined for the purpose as the destruction of that part of the nation opposed to the Batista government). The death penalty was not imposed: twenty aviators got thirty years; the others drew lesser sentences.[99]

As a result, the courts, led by the Supreme Court, retreated, and the executive branch of the government assumed wide discretionary powers.[100] In 1960 the Supreme Court did not ordinarily find laws or executive decrees unconstitutional unless they invaded the prerogatives of the court system itself—that is, it usually opposed the government only on issues pertaining to its own organizational survival. On February 5 the Supreme Court found unconstitutional a presidential resolution declaring that a lower-court order could not be implemented. On March 7 it ruled unconstitutional a paragraph that prohibited appeals to the courts from decisions of the Labor Ministry. On April 12 the Supreme Court declared unconstitutional the rulings of the revolutionary tribunal of La Cabaña fortress for invading the ordinary jurisdiction of the courts. On May 9 the Supreme Court ruled that Ministry of Commerce resolutions were unconstitutional because they invaded the jurisdiction of the courts. The only Supreme Court ruling of unconstitutionality in 1960 aimed against executive laws or decrees that did not rest on defending the court organization was on a Treasury resolution. It rested on a Batista government law that had been declared unconstitutional; so it had itself to be declared unconstitutional on grounds of doctrinal consistency.[101]

At the same time the Supreme Court was upholding the constitutionality of dozens of revolutionary laws and decrees, though sometimes by less than unanimous decisions, and finding unconstitutional many prerevolutionary laws and decrees. In some instances it modified administrative decisions in ways that represented rulings against the governemnt. On September 26, 1960, for instance, the Supreme Court ordered the National Institute for Agrarian Reform to pay 19,000 pesos, instead of the 8,020 pesos it had given, in compensation to the owner of a socialized farm. More commonly, however, the Supreme Court annulled decisions of lower courts that refused to collaborate with the land-socialization program. The political function of the Supreme Court became one of facilitating land reform, though occasionally it ruled against the government regarding what was just compensation.[102]

By the end of 1960 the executive branch would no longer countenance Supreme Court restrictions on revolutionary acts of any sort. Between November 1960 and February 1961, twenty-one of the thirty-two justices of the Supreme Court resigned, often under duress, or were dismissed; six of the seven presidents of the appeals courts in the provinces and many lower-court judges also departed. The chief charge against the courts was that they had increased the cost of the land-reform programs by increasing the amount of indemnification for expropriation by more than 15 million pesos in 1960; the Supreme Court had rejected fifty-one government appeals and accepted nine, while it had accepted sixty-four appeals of landowners and rejected three. The executive branch would not countenance any restriction of administrative discretion by the courts; collaboration on substantive matters did not save the judiciary from the impact of the revolution on organizational autonomy.[103]

The Supreme Court had already reversed the trends of the earlier 1950s in rulings concerning worker dismissals. Between 1950 and 1958 management had won a majority of dismissal cases that reached the Supreme Court; in 1959 the workers won the majority. The executive soon took away the Court's jurisdiction over dismissal cases, so their performance in this area cannot be assessed for subsequent years.

From January 1959 to August 1961, the cabinet exercised its constitutional power to amend the fundamental law twenty-two times, or once every seven weeks. Whenever the executive deemed it necessary to take action forbidden by the fundamental law, a constitutional amendment was approved and enabling legislation based on the amendment was issued. According to the International Commission of Jurists, "all amendments to the Fundamental Law reveal a single purpose, namely, to concentrate arbitrary power in the hands of the ruling group."[104]

Changes in criminal legislation had the net effect of vastly increasing the executive's discretionary power, simplifying procedure by reducing protection to the accused, and strengthening its ability to punish. Criminal legislation was applied retroactively. The death penalty was imposed in the early years for political offenses and would be subsequently extended to cover serious nonpolitical crimes. Property of political offenders was confiscated fairly automatically, at times by administrative rulings without recourse to the courts. Those indicted for political offenses were deprived of habeas corpus. And those indicted for political offenses had no recourse on grounds of inconstitutionality. Many of these legal provisions are explained by the fact of the revolution; nevertheless they increased the government's discretionary and punitive powers enormously, especially because the government defined what was and was not a political offense. These broad powers remained in effect even after the conditions that gave rise to them subsided. By the 1970s, however, habeas corpus, modified by the unclear "loafing" law, was operative. But the government retained the right to appeal to higher courts, even in criminal cases, whenever the prosecution lost or whenever it deemed the punishment insufficient. Suspects were supposed to be arraigned before a judge within twenty-four hours. The International Commission of Jurists noted that the drafting of legislation itself increased the government's discretionary powers in the early 1960s. Although accurate definitions of offenses were often provided, there was almost invariably an escape clause, in the form of such phrases as "those of any nature whatsoever," "those performing any activity whatsoever considered as counterrevolutionary," and "those having counterrevolutionary aims." The government had full discretion to define what was "counterrevolutionary."[105]

Discretionary laws were not limited to the early years of the revolution. The 1976 Constitution reserves to the party and to the state full discretion to limit individual rights. According to article 8 of the 1971 law on loafing, for example, a worker "need commit no further act besides that which brought him into the precriminal state to be later adjudged to have violated article 8." A worker who does not change his behavior is liable for criminal punishment, double jeopardy notwithstanding. The law does not spell out the circumstances that amount to noncompliance. If a boss decides a worker is not working hard enough, the worker is liable for criminal punishment. Article 7 also required compliance with all measures, without spelling out what noncompliance was. An increase of executive discretion also results from the presence of mitigating circumstances, such as an unspecified "favorable labor and social record," or "any other social or human factor considered pertinent." Aggravating factors include a "negative labor and social record" and "any other moral or socially negative factors considered pertinent." The law also allows preventive detention.[106]

These changes have reduced the autonomy of the courts, eliminated the possibility of constitutional restraint, and reduced procedural obstacles, but they have also increased the government's discretionary power and concentrated legal power in executive hands. The government's powers to punish have also increased. Individuals accused of political crimes stand stripped of rights before a powerful state with full governmental discretion in defining the crime. The Ministry of the Interior, including regular and secret police, makes full use of this discretion. When these powers are added to the political, economic, and social powers discussed previously, it is clear that the powers of the revolutionary government are uncontestably vast by any previous Cuban standards.

The Supreme Court rulings in cases involving the government and a simple individual cannot be studied, but the following statistics may give some indication of a trend in the early years. Only cases where the winner and loser can be clearly ascertained are included. In September of 1962, of twenty-three social-security and retirement disputes, the government won twenty; in September–October 1962, the government won fourteen of fifteen criminal cases; in July–September 1963, the government won ten of twelve criminal cases; of five other cases in this period, the government won four.[107] Individuals can win against the government, at least often enough to keep them in litigation all the way to the Supreme Court. But individual victories are rare, though some have been important. They show that the revolutionary legal system, admittedly set up to favor the government, can still bring justice against arbitrary rulings. The International Commission of Jurists found "arbitrary" power in the earliest years, and no doubt there was much of it then, as there is today. Nevertheless, a focus on discretionary power may be more useful. Within the existing body of law, the government has wide discretion—but the courts do serve to check its arbitrary use. As the president of the Supreme Court said in September 1963, the courts should act so that revolutionary violence "should not exceed reasonable limits and become arbitrary"; "rationalized violence," he continued, had to be applied to progress toward communism but only "within just limits."[108] This check can be applied even in unexpected areas such as property law and rulings against military personnel.

The structural changes of the revolution left the private sector as a residual category. Law firms specializing in corporate and property law went out of business. The law firm of Salaya and Casteleiro, for instance, had twelve lawyers when the revolution came to power in January 1959; it still had eleven at the end of a year of marginal change. As the revolution became more radical, however, the number of lawyers fell: there were five by July of 1960 when the major socializations began. Two lawyers were left by the end of 1960; the firm closed in September 1961.[109] While that particular type of law firm did not have much of a future in revolutionary Cuba, property-law disputes continued to be fought against the government and won. In October 1962 the Supreme Court ruled against the city of Havana for raising rents for urban property and ordered the return of all excess rent paid to the government. In the same month it ruled that a soldier who had accidentally shot and killed a woman while he was on active duty was guilty and should be fined and sent to prison. On July 19, 1963, the Court ruled that a militiaman, on duty in an area full of armed counterrevolutionaries, who had shot and permanently disabled a person without observing all the procedures of identification, should be fined and sent to prison. Even possible counterrevolutionaries had the right to expect proper safeguards from military personnel on duty. There are many cases of soldiers or militiamen who commit violent crimes on or off duty and are sent to prison, often for as much as thirty years.[110] Though in no more than a small minority of the cases, the Supreme Court has at times acted to restrain arbitrary power, even though its general tendency has been to support discretionary power. The government's power is enormous but not quite absolute.

In other criminal matters, the Supreme Court has a less consistent record. For example, a married man, with children, took a teenage woman to a house of prostitution in July 1962; no deception or threats were involved prior to their having sexual relations; both were members of a Committee for the Defense of the Revolution. The man was acquitted of facilitating prostitution and of statutory-rape charges, because the woman "lacked honesty and virginity." The government appealed to the Supreme Court, which sustained the lower court. But the Supreme Court also upheld another lower-court ruling which had imposed a penalty on a man found guilty of a crime greater than the prosecution had asked for and criticized the prosecution for being "soft" on crime.[111]

Political Prisoners

The government's power has certainly been fully exercised when it comes to the incarceration of its critics. The number of political prisoners reached its highest point in 1961, in the wake of the failure of the Bay of Pigs invasion, when tens of thousands of people were arrested, though most of them were only held for brief periods. By 1965 the Cuban government admitted holding 20,000 political prisoners. Under President Batista in the 1950s, the prison on the Isle of Pines, where most political prisoners were kept, had only 1,558 inmates; even if one assumes that all were political prisoners and that there were others kept elsewhere, the highest estimates in the 1950s are several orders of magnitude below the admitted rate for the mid-1960s.[112] Cuba's rate of political imprisonment is well above that of other authoritarian Latin American governments. In 1974, after fifteen years of revolutionary rule, Cuba had no fewer than forty political prisoners for every 100,000 people in its population; in December 1975, barely two years after the start of military rule, Chile (according to opposition sources) had no more then forty-seven political prisoners per 100,000 population. This extremely conservative statistic in the Cuban case assumes no more than 4,000 political prisoners in 1974; Prime Minister Castro has been quoted as saying that there were 5,000 in 1975, of whom 3,000 were in rehabilitation camps and 2,000 in maximum-security prisons. In 1969 a former Spanish information officer in Havana reported 55,200 political prisoners; these numbers are closer to the estimates cited by Cuban exiles. In July, 1977, President Castro admitted to holding between 2,000 and 3,000 political prisoners, that is, between twenty-one and thirty-one per 100,000 population.[113]

The Cuban government has emphatically denied that it uses physical torture, though it readily admits to relying on "rehabilitation" to change the social and political behavior and opinions of all prisoners, including political ones. Even if no physical torture is involved, this "rehabilitation" is likely to lead to considerable psychological strain.[114] The Human Rights Commission of the Organization of American States has collected an extensive list of unanswered allegations that the treatment as well as the number of political prisoners may be considerably more serious than the Cuban government has admitted.[115] Amnesty International—a nonpartisan, private international organization monitoring political imprisonment around the world—has concluded that torture was probably used as a routine practice in Cuba in the early 1960s but by the 1970s found little or no evidence of physical torture, although there is still evidence of substantial psychological pressure. The increase in the Cuban economic-growth rate in the 1970s has apparently also helped to improve physical conditions in the prisons.[116] The Cuban government recognized that torture had been used in the early 1960s to the extent of court-martialing and convicting some military officers who had practiced it.[117] At the other end of the political spectrum, the complaints about prison conditions and treatment of political prisoners in Cuba, voiced by Cuban exiles who monitor them, have changed in character; the cases of ill-treatment described are much less serious in the mid-1970s than a decade earlier. Conditions in some Cuban prisons remain appalling, judging from the reports of many former prisoners, but torture is apparently no longer a routine administrative practice.[118]

Court Structure

The courts have also changed a great deal. The most striking innovation has been the introduction of popular tribunals. Planning for their establishment began in 1963; by October of 1966, there were thirty-one, of which twenty-two were in rural areas and five in semirural areas. The manual for their judges, published in November 1966, shows several changes in Cuban law and courts. The legislation to be applied by the popular tribunals comes primarily from the Social Defense Code of 1938. Lawyers wrote commentaries to the code and included many specific examples taken from the experiences of the previously existing popular tribunals. The manual does not include the actual legal text; therefore, the result has been a shift away from the tradition of relying on codes of law and toward a case method.[119] Collective legal memory is very limited. It includes only the previous decisions of a particular popular tribunal, the specific examples cited in the manual, and the intervention of the legal advisor to the court.

A partial explanation for this limited legal memory lies in another innovation: the judges of popular tribunals are not normally lawyers but elected lay judges. Until 1976, the party, the unions, and the Committees for the Defense of the Revolution nominated neighborhood judges through popular assemblies. The nominees took a three-week training course; the best were then picked by a committee that included the party municipal committee, a delegate from the Communist Youth Union, and a delegate from each mass organization. Since late 1976 the municipal assemblies have picked the judges under party direction. The elections have not normally been competitive, and the number of nominees ordinarily equals the number of posts. Little significance should be attached to the election procedure, because party and government officials effectively select the judges. The interesting innovation is that these are judges with virtually no legal training. The jurisdiction of these courts is limited to torts up to 1,000 pesos, misdemeanors, health violations, juvenile delinquency, and personal quarrels. Felonies, contract disputes, traffic violations, counterrevolutionary activities, and torts over 1,000 pesos fall to higher courts.[120]

The following penalties may be imposed by these popular tribunals: public admonition; compulsory education; fines up to 500 pesos; deprivation of rights (to go to a bar or to the movies, for instance); banishment (from a bar, a house, cock fights); house arrest, except to go to work; relocation to another neighborhood; deprivation of liberty up to six months with or without internment and with an obligation to work; confiscation of property; and payment of damages to the injured party. There are also practical remedies such as medical or psychological referrals, housing-agency referrals, partition of property, and arbitration. Through May 1966, at these experimental courts, 88 percent of all cases dealt with criminal rather than civil matters.[121]

The judges' manual does not include any rules of procedure, and there is no right of appeal based on procedural error. Fewer than 1 percent of all cases were appealed on substantive grounds through the fall of 1966; in all but one instance, the popular tribunal was sustained. Appeals of verdicts remained rare through the 1960s, but appeals regarding the severity of punishment were more common. The popular tribunals in each district share a legal adviser—a trained lawyer—who serves as court administrator and appellate judge. These advisers have the right to be present at the judges' deliberations though they do not always attend. The legal adviser therefore plays a key role in the establishment, supervision, and control of the courts. The party's role is limited to shaping the appointments of judges; after that the legal adviser runs the court.[122]

These structural features result in a very informal variety of court proceeding. The trials take place in the evenings and are public, except for cases involving a woman's honor, juvenile delinquency, or homosexuality. The people watch neighborhood judges dealing with local problems and often participate in the hearings, where they are brought by the Committees for the Defense of the Revolution. These sessions serve to educate the public on legal issues, to deter crime, to settle private disputes, and to administer justice quickly. But faced with a case method and limited legal memory, the popular tribunals also have wide discretion that is subject to abuse. Sentencing in cases of sexual offenses such as prostitution and rape, for example, can apparently be vindictive.[123] In 1972, the popular tribunals of Havana province judged 40,695 persons accused of some offense and found 72.3 percent of them guilty. A little over 40 percent of the sentences amounted, however, to no more than a public admonition.[124]

The government has been sufficiently satisfied with the operation of the popular tribunals to incorporate some of their aspects into the higher courts when the judicial system was reorganized in 1973. At that time the courts were placed firmly under the cabinet, eliminating any vestige of a separate branch of government. The regional tribunals received cases of sufficient importance to bypass the popular tribunals. The provincial tribunals heard appeals from regional tribunals and most of the cases involving serious crime, including counterrevolutionary activities. Military tribunals functioned within the armed forces. The Supreme Court heard appeals from all courts, including military cases, but divided up to hear cases of various types (criminal, civil, national-security, or military). The provincial courts had no military jurisdiction, and the regional courts had neither military nor internal-security jurisdiction. The popular tribunals had three nonprofessional judges; the regional tribunals, one professional and two nonprofessional judges; the provincial tribunals and the Supreme Court, three professional and two nonprofessional judges. These numbers refer to each chamber or *sala* of the court.

The increased use of nonprofessional judges apparently caused a sufficient number of difficulties by 1975 to warrant the inclusion of a new paragraph in the Constitution stating that the judicial work of the nonprofessional judges had priority over their other endeavors; competition had developed between the courts and the other enterprises that employed the nonprofessional judges regularly over who would get how much of their time. Until 1976, judges were appointed by party, government, and leaders of mass organization at each level except that of the popular tribunals. The national, provincial, and municipal assemblies have since acquired the formal right to elect judges at each appropriate level. At the national level, the Constitution empowered the Council of State to act on behalf of, and instead of, the National Assembly between sessions to supervise the court system; thus the cabinet lost the authority over the courts.

As in other areas, the initiative for nomination and hence the real appointment power rested with the Communist party. At the middle levels, nominations were handled by the party and mass-organization officials, with the advice of the local bar association. The government and party retained the right to dismiss any judge, listing a variety of reasons and ending with a discretionary clause, "whenever there is a serious cause which leads to a loss in public confidence."[125] The reorganization of the judicial system was followed, at long last, by the promulgation of new codes of law to replace those drafted before the revolution on criminal, civil, administrative, and labor procedure and of a new family code. These codes are used by courts other than popular tribunals, as socialist legality seeks to make the citizen more secure.

A few additional organizational changes were made in 1977. The number of provincial courts was increased from six to fourteen, to match the number of provinces. Because the Constitution of 1976 abolished regions, regional courts were abolished as well. The local popular tribunals were renamed municipal courts. The legal jurisdiction of labor councils in work centers was transferred to municipal courts; the provincial courts and the Supreme Court opened salas to hear appeals of labor disputes from lower courts. The Ministry of Justice, under party supervision, was empowered to make all nominations of judges for election by the respective assemblies.[126]

Revolutionary politics required that laws and legal institutions of the prerevolutionary order be overturned and changed to cope with the problems of a new society. Since revolutionary leaders depend more on commitment and action than on booklearning, there was some concern lest professional lawyers defuse the revolution and become an alternative elite. Instead the number of law students fell dramatically from 2,853 in 1958–59 to 135 in 1970–71 and rose only to 159 in 1971–72. Since the pool of lawyers had also been reduced through exile, there was a real shortage of lawyers by the end of 1974. Cuba is unique in Latin America in not having enough lawyers. Many of those they have are reportedly incompetent, and law students have often served as prosecutors. The decline in the number of lawyers and the prevalent political norms and forms of nonlegal legitimation have led to the deprofessionalization of legal institutions. Legitimacy has derived not from professional lawyers but from revolutionaries, not from continuity with the past but from breaking with it.

Revolutionary legislation has also redefined the role of lawyers. Although they are supposed to defend their clients, they are expected to "avoid making use of defense motions that prevent justice from fulfilling its social function." By 1973 only lawyers who belonged to state law firms could practice before a court, though within the law firm one could pick one's own lawyer. In civil cases lawyers are paid for their services in advance according to a schedule of fees set by government—while the fees are not very high, having to pay in advance discourages the use of lawyers. It has also had the effect of making it easier for the nonpoor in Cuba, as in other countries, to get legal advice. In criminal cases, the state pays for the defense lawyer. Lawyers are allowed to practice before popular (now municipal) tribunals but are assumed to be neither necessary nor welcome and appear rarely.[127]

Tensions continue to prevail within the Cuban legal system. Two legal procedures, the case method at the popular or municipal tribunal level and the code method at other levels, produce some of the tension; two types of judges, professional and nonprofessional add more, since only the municipal nonprofessional judges use the case method. Two legal tendencies are also evident, one toward a measure of popular participation under strictly controlled conditions at the level of the popular or municipal tribunals and another toward bureaucratic formalization at all levels. The diversity within the Cuban legal system facilitates experimentation and may enhance adaptability; paradoxically, it may also militate against the stability of legal organizations and procedures. Thus the peculiar Cuban form of legal and judicial formalization of diversity and tension may undermine long-term institutionalization of the law and the courts, even though it has contributed to the legal, rational, and bureaucratic legitimation of the state.

Revolutionary politics also led the government to categorize a wide variety of social behavior as criminal. Even private quarrels can end up in popular or municipal tribunals. Stealing from a government-owned factory can be a political crime and sentenced severely. Working insufficiently hard or repeated absenteeism have been made crimes. But revolutionary ideology has also placed considerable responsibility for the judicial disposition of purely local matters in lay hands. The result has been the decriminalization of the sentencing procedure (divorce proceedings have been similarly decriminalized in the Family Code);[128] thus many sentences amounted to no more than public admonitions. Even more severe sentences often involve neither fines nor imprisonment, the traditional tools of the courts; compulsory community service is the customary punishment. Decriminalization of sentencing is obviously limited to petty crimes, but it is no less important for that. It means that the wide discretionary powers of the government do not normally affect most ordinary citizens accused of misdemeanor. The full weight of government is reserved for more serious offenses. This safety valve at the bottom helps to legitimate the broad discretionary powers at the top.

The establishment of the new revolutionary political order in Cuba combined organizational growth and innovation with the preeminence of a charismatic political leader, to whom all of these organizations were subordinate. The organizational revolution of the 1960s lacked stability of both structure and personnel; the organizations formed had limited autonomy in policy decisions, and many were short-lived. Yet amid this organizational chaos, some institutionalizing trends appeared.

Internal military security had been achieved by the mid-1960s; continuity of leadership was quite remarkable after 1962. As organizations became more complex, some progress was made toward coordinating their functions. Very gradually, Fidel Castro began to share his authority, first with his most trusted subordinates, then with the top leaders of the party. The trend toward greater stability of the bureaucracy and the courts appeared in the early 1970s, capped by the introduction of a new Constitution, legal codes, and other legislation. The claims to legitimate revolutionary rule continued to depend upon Fidel Castro's charismatic talents, revolutionary symbols, and the successful redistribution of national wealth among the poor into the 1970s. But, beginning gradually in the 1960s, other factors contributed to legitimation, in particular the routinizing of Fidel Castro's charisma through the building of the Cuban Communist party and the establishment of more legal and rational sources of legitimation and governance.

The Soviet Union's successful reassertion of hegemony over Cuba contributed powerfully to the setting aside of the experiments of the late 1960s and to the building up of the central bureaucracies. The collapse of the Cuban economy at the end of the same decade was an indication to the leadership that it was time to change course. The radical policies adopted had proved politically unpopular, social bases of governmental support had been eroding, and disapproval was manifested in extensive labor absenteeism and the defeat of incumbents in local labor-union elections in 1970. The shift away from radical policies and from poorly institutionalized organizations was the regime's response to these signs of discontent. The new policies sought to improve the rate of economic growth and the welfare of the population, not merely to redistribute shrinking resources; they also sought to consolidate the revolution institutionally by stimulating and accelerating the programs that had barely surfaced in the 1960s.

7

MASS POLITICAL PARTICIPATION

The consolidation of revolutionary rule in Cuba required that the participation of the masses in politics be encouraged and that organizations be developed, both to harness and control mass political participation and to transform the society, the economy, the political system, and, ultimately, the culture. The governing of revolutionary Cuba has also gradually shifted from the mere destruction and re-creation of organizations, to processes of institutionalization.

Beginning in the early 1960s, new political structures were created to increase and concentrate power in order to achieve revolutionary goals. Institutionalization gradually occurred in government, in the party, and in the mass organizations. Organizations and procedures thus acquired value and stability, so that they no longer depended on a single individual or small group for their legitimacy and operations.

A lack of political autonomy from Fidel Castro and other top leaders has characterized organizations in revolutionary Cuba and has limited the processes of institutionalization; those at the top systematically prevail over time and across issue areas. Castro controls the central institutions of the Communist party, which in turn govern the subordinate levels; the party prevails over the administration and the mass organizations. Havana prevails over the rest of the country. In revolutionary Cuba, all levels of the mass organizations, the subordinate units of the party, and all elections lack important aspects of political autonomy and are subject to externally imposed constraints on the selection of leaders, election procedures, and policy making. Although the forms of dependence have changed somewhat over time, the fact of dependence remains constant.

The lack of political autonomy can, of course, be considered to be not a flaw but a revolutionary virtue. The revolution, or rather the revolutionary leadership in power, has laid claim to legitimate rule. This claim may or may not be valid, but it is central to politics in Cuba. The revolution and its leaders legitimate the Constitution, the courts, the administration, the party, the mass organizations, and the elections—and not vice versa. Elections are deliberately set up to be unrepresentative politically, in order to facilitate the routinization of Fidel Castro's charisma by bringing forth as candidates people who are said to resemble him in some way. The candidates are disproportionately drawn from the Communist party of Cuba.

The Committees for the Defense of the Revolution

Mass organizations were originally established to help protect the government from foreign and counterrevolutionary threats and attacks. With time their domain and scope expanded: more people and more different kinds of people began to join them. They undertook a wide variety of activities that no longer had any direct connection with the security of the revolution.

The most striking changes occurred within the Committees for the Defense of the Revolution (CDR). Data on membership in the committees reveal different types of commitment: the recycling of glass containers and the organization of blood donations, for example, both begun in the early 1960s. Since the late 1960s, the committees have run "exemplary parenthood" programs—to be an exemplary parent, one has to have a child with a 95 percent attendance record at school; one has to know school regulations and see to it that the child obeys them, studies, participates in rural education programs and in school activities, and passes all school courses; the parent also has to visit the school periodically and attend all school-related meetings.[1]

In the late 1960s, the committees sharply increased their activities, which were subsequently stabilized at a high level. Recycling efforts were probably encouraged by worsening shortages, but the exemplary-parenthood movement also grew. This increase in qualitative performance in the mid-1960s occurred, however, during the only period in the organization's history when membership actually declined and the number of committees was cut by one-third; performance leveled off in the early 1970s during a period of rapid organizational growth. It is possible that this pattern simply represents stresses on either membership growth or level of performance, but not both, perhaps because the size of the organization precludes doing both at the same time. Detailed data are available for the fall of 1963—a year when membership increased but quality declined (table 7.1). It turns out that either at a given time or over a period of time, the committees have been unable to achieve growth and quality simultaneously.[2]

Two events in the history of the organization, one in 1966 and one in 1968, shaped its character. The first was the dismissal in 1966 of the national coor-

Table 7.1 Committees for the Defense of the Revolution, 1961–1976

Year	Total membership	Number of committees (in thousands)	Glass containers recycled per member	Blood donations per 1,000 members [a]	Exemplary parents per 1,000 members
1961	798,703	107	—	—	—
1962	1,119,835	90	7.97	6.0	—
1963	1,656,195	103	7.04	2.3	—
1964	1,954,546	102	7.57	9.3	—
1965	2,011,476	102	3.31	5.0	—
1966	2,237,652	103	5.01	15.1	—
1967	1,704,689	72	19.72	21.6	—
1968	2,216,400	62	33.42	21.2	1.0
1969	3,222,147	63	15.76	32.9	—
1970	3,222,147	66	16.26	47.0	7.7
1971	3,500,125	68	15.93	36.5	9.0
1972	4,281,596	70	20.77	30.4	—
1973	4,751,963	72	19.84	31.1	16.7
1974	4,751,963	72	20.86	32.3	19.1
1975	4,800,000	—	14.88	32.3	226.3
1976	4,800,000	—	12.12	31.2	226.3

Sources: Computed from Mario Méndez, "Crecimiento," *Con la guardia en alto* 11, no. 9 (September 1972): 12; Aida Cárdenas, "La sangre ya no es mercancía," *Bohemia* 65, no. 18 (May 14, 1973): 6; *Granma*, February 8, 1974, p. 3; ibid., September 28, 1974, pp. 1, 4; Wilfredo Díaz, "Un país que no sea ahorrativo no avanza," *Con la guardia en alto* 10, no. 9 (September 1971): 30; ibid., 10, no. 10 (October 1971): 6. *Granma Weekly Review*, October 12, 1975, p. 8; *Granma*, February 6, 1976, p. 2; ibid., September 27, 1976, p. 3; Mario del Pino, "La donación de sangre en Cuba," *Cuadernos de historia de la salud pública* no. 43 (1969): 64–66; *Anuario 1973*, p. 18. Total membership figures for 1970, 1974, and 1975 and number of committees in 1974 are not altogether reliable; there may have been small increases.

a. Blood donations per 1,000 members reached a peak in 1970 because of a special drive to help the victims of an earthquake in Peru. Except for 1964 and 1965, the trend in CDR members' blood donations parallels the national trend. CDR blood-donation data are artificially inflated at least in 1962, 1963, 1967, and 1968; in those years some essential blood transfusions from one family member to another were included in the count as if they had been completely voluntary.

dinator of the committees, José Matar, a member of the prerevolutionary Communist party from his youth; two years later, he was implicated with Aníbal Escalante's microfaction among old Communists and was expelled from the party's Central Committee. Matar's dismissal in 1966 was also linked to new policies concerning organizational domain and scope. Since the early days, the committees had been organized both residentially in neighborhoods and functionally in factories, state farms, and bureaucracies. Under Matar the committees served as a bridge to the labor movement and as an alternative channel for worker activity. Under Matar's successor, Luis González Marturelos, the functional structure was dismantled. Organizational domain was restricted. The committees were no longer tied directly to the labor movement, though workers could belong to their neighborhood committees. The number of committees was cut by almost one-third, and overall membership declined by 23.8 percent from 1966 to 1967. Since over 800,000 new members were recruited from 1967 to 1968, this decline means that 16.9 percent of the membership had been expelled.[3] While most of this membership decline can be explained by the withdrawal from labor activities, these changes were also supposed to improve the quality of work of the committees and certify the revolutionary commitment of the members. Improvement in quality was combined with reduction of membership. It was three years before the 1966 membership level was surpassed.

The second major change was in organization. At the end of Matar's leadership, the tasks of the organization were stated as vigilance, local government, public health, and organizational growth. By early 1967, the order had been modified to read: organizational restructuring, local government, vigilance, and public health. Raúl Santana of the national organization office stressed the importance of the organizational restructuring and mentioned a broad variety of activities receiving priority in early 1967—conspicuously excluding revolutionary vigilance, the committees' original rationale. In March 1967 an agreement between the national headquarters of the committees and the Interior Ministry noted that vigilance "had been" the original rationale for this organization, mentioned its great achievements, and meekly indicated that "some aspects" must be continued. In mid-1967, Carol Miranda of the national organization office again listed many committee tasks, including "civil defense" but not "vigilance," in the miscellaneous category.[4] There was a clear decline in emphasis on internal-security affairs in favor of other activities.

The change in organizational scope proved unacceptable to the revolutionary elite. In September 1968 Prime Minister Castro indicated that the committees should give priority to revolutionary vigilance. Shortly thereafter the national office of the committees restored vigilance as the first task for the organization. Many resisted this reorientation; in fact the intervention of armed forces minister Raúl Castro was required in October 1968 and January 1969 to ensure that the new policies were implemented.[5]

Up to 1968 the Committees for the Defense of the Revolution were in the process of institutionalization. As the organization's original rationale faded in importance, its leaders, especially those at the local level, sought to change goals to adapt to the new social and political reality. They emphasized practical tasks and remedies for local problems through mass participation in policy implementation, though without implying local authority over setting the policy agenda or making policy. To increase the adaptability of the entire organization required some degree of autonomy for its local branches; they had to be capable of responding on their own to problems as they arose. This flexibility, of course, meant less direction from the national office and from the revolutionary elite. The committees' disengagement from labor unions, while it may have weakened the labor movement, also increased the autonomy of the CDRs nationally. The adoption of new tasks added to the organization's complexity in terms of scope at the same time that the elimination of labor cells restricted its domain. Both the restriction and the local and practical orientation increased the ideological coherence of the committees. They were less an instrument to enforce internal security than a method of dealing with local, practical problems.

The revolutionary elite was not yet ready in 1968, however, to divest itself of organizational control and give power to local bases. Goal setting remained a national prerogative. The committees' work in mobilization, was an important element of the country's political style. Cuba was then operating under a "mobilizational" system, a hierarchical system of authority in which the goals of the state, including modernization, become sacred. The postponement of immediate gratification is identified with social discipline and is required of individual consumers as members of the community. A mobilizational system stresses the urgency of action and the need for direct planning and drastic restratification of society; its atmosphere is one of crisis and attack; passivity is considered illegitimate; all social and economic life is politicized. In such a system, the government relies heavily on social and political coercion, and policies incompatible with the stated, preordained goals of the central authority are rejected.[6]

The Cuban system of mobilization was an extension of the political style of Fidel Castro; it could not allow a major civilian organization, once concerned with crisis and attack, to abandon the task of vigilance. To question the priority of vigilance or the hierarchy of goal setting was to question important characteristics of the system. Vigilance and goal setting were essential to mobilization: organizational autonomy and adaptability had to be sacrificed.

By 1973 the Committees for the Defense of the Revolution had dropped some of their earlier bars to membership and sought to encompass virtually the entire adult population (see table 7.1). In the fall of 1963, the committees included 33.1 percent of the adult population (33.7 percent of the adult rural population); membership had risen to 40 percent by 1964. By the fall of 1968, it still stood at 41.3 percent; within a year, however, it jumped to 57.3 percent, and within four, to 80 percent. When so many people belong to an organization, its character changes.[7] Even former members of the prerevolutionary upper class, still living in Cuba in mansions with domestic servants, have been reported to belong to a committee, because being a member makes life easier. It has become, in effect, a requirement for normal life in Cuba, whatever one's feelings toward revolutionary rule and policies. Nonmembership has become a more political act; those who are refused admission or refuse to join brand themselves clearly and publicly as nonsupporters of revolutionary rule. Fidel Castro said in 1975 that "if there are not more CDR members, it is because we want to protect the quality of CDR membership."[8] By the mid-1970s, then, revolutionary vigilance had to be concerned only with the minority of the population that lacked "quality," but at least that minority was more politically and ideologically homogeneous than before. Nonparticipants in Cuban political life stand vulnerably on the margins of a political system that does not thrive on noninvolvement or opposition.

By the mid-1970s, vigilance had been redirected to common, nonpolitical crime and ceased to have much of its former practical political connotation. Because such a great variety of people joined the committees, many more tasks could be undertaken by them.[9] Their traditional activities continued, but new and very effective mass public-health programs were added to them. From 1966 to 1972, one and a quarter million women were administered cytological tests; in 1974, 420,630 took them. In 1973 and 1974 over 1 million people received the polio vaccine through the committees' efforts. The committees had about 7,000 units promoting international solidarity, and about 500 units "watching the sea" for possible counterrevolutionary landings. About 66,000 members promoted school attendance. The committees have also been concerned about the increasing heterogeneity within the ranks and have promoted political study groups for adults to increase homogeneity. In 1973, 64.7 percent of the members were enrolled in such courses, as were 69.1 percent in 1974, but only 56.0 percent in 1975. The actual learning that goes on in these courses may be minimal. When Frances FitzGerald asked the woman head of a local committee outside the city of Havana in 1973 what subjects were discussed in their political study group, the woman could not remember a single one. But she spoke at length about her committee's role in neighborhood beautification, public health, and school attendance. The committees helped in the mass literacy campaign of 1961, they have helped to enforce housing regulations, and they have mobilized people for mass rallies. They helped to enforce the socialization of petty services and trade in 1968. They have supported local government activities and have acted as a forum for the discussions of draft legislation.[10]

The committees have also encouraged voluntary work—unpaid labor on one's own time. Through the 1960s, most volunteers worked in agriculture; in 1969, for example, its members contributed 16.7 million hours of volunteer time. By the early 1970s, the program shifted to construction; in 1972, 8.2 million hours were devoted to various construction tasks—a substantial decline compared to 1969, even though the membership had grown. In 1974 committees turned their attention to improving organizational controls. Only 57 percent of the membership had paid dues in 1973, but 83 percent paid up in 1974, as did 90 percent in 1975. The committees, like other mass organizations, had had severe problems of leadership instability in the late 1960s, but these had largely been overcome by 1974, when 65 percent of the leaders of the local committees and 62 percent of the leaders at the higher "zone" level were reelected.[11]

The membership of the national directorate of the Committees for the Defense of the Revolution became more stable in the early 1970s. While the leadership changed drastically from 1963 to 1969, when Matar was dismissed, approximately half of the national directorate still continued in office at the end of the years between 1969 and 1974, a roughly comparable period, even though coordinator González Marturelos was replaced by Jorge Lezcano. Changes in size and stability of membership in the committees' national directorate from 1963 through 1974 were as follows:[12]

	Original size	Remaining members
1963–1969	20	2
1969–1971	22	17
1969–1974	22	11
1971–1973	25	23
1973–1974	33	26

The national directorate became more complex; the number of leadership posts increased by 50 percent, from twenty to thirty-three, from 1969 to 1974; it increased only 10 percent, from twenty to twenty-two, from 1963 to 1969. This increase in size aided both stability and adaptability because experienced members could be retained while new ones were brought in to deal with expansion; more internal differentiation in members' functions became possible. Experience in the national directorate led to promotion. Of the eleven continuing members from 1969 to 1974, eight had been promoted to higher posts in the national bureau or secretariat of the national directorate or had been given more important provincial jobs (for example, from a post in Pinar del Río to one in Oriente). Efforts were also made to keep the lower-echelon professional leadership stable. Ninety-three percent of the 1974 professional cadres continued into 1975. The level of training also improved; 11 percent of approximately 2,500 professional cadres were studying politics in 1976.[13]

The changes in the functions performed by the committees were closely correlated to changes in national policy. The early 1960s required the rapid mobilization of the population. The late 1960s saw efforts both to increase individuals' commitment to the revolution by improving performance and to deal with organizational problems. To increase popular support in the early 1970s, efforts were made to add new members, and less stress was placed on individuals' superhuman voluntary sacrifice. The local committees, however, still lacked autonomy. The organization remained an instrument of the party, unable to set its own fundamental policies. Its statutes were elaborated in 1975 for approval at the organization's congress in 1977. Though the leadership had stabilized (a school to train them was set up in 1975), that the process of selection still underscored organizational dependence was evident in early 1974: "Jesús Montané, member of the Central Committee of the party, on behalf of the Central Committee's department in charge of mass organizations proposed—and the delegates enthusiastically accepted—the candidates for membership in the bureau, secretariat, and national leadership of the Committees for the Defense of the Revolution."[14] Instead of promoting María Teresa Malmierca, the deputy national coordinator since 1971 and national organization secretary before that, to the vacant post of national coordinator, the Central Committee of the party brought in Jorge Lezcano from outside. At that time Lezcano was secretary of organization of the Camagüey provincial party's executive committee; his career had emphasized his party ties. In 1974 as in 1968 the committees were not yet allowed to select their own leaders.

The Cuban Women's Federation

The Cuban Women's Federation (FMC) emphasized nonvigilance activities from its earliest days. It performed many of the functions usually performed by a lower class political party or machine, except that it did so within the context of a mobilization system. It, too, contributed to the 1961 literacy campaign. After 1960 it organized sewing classes, from which 94,796 women had graduated by 1970. It taught physical education and reading and set up courses to retrain former domestic servants and to train other women to join the labor force. Because so many women had no jobs for pay, the organization promoted volunteer labor; in 1970 women contributed 20.1 million hours of unpaid labor to the sugar harvest. Their total contribution of volunteer labor peaked in 1973 at 95.6 million hours; it fell back to 49.3 million hours in 1975. It set up "brigades" of women to assist in rural work in cooperation with the National Association of Small Peasants (ANAP). Twenty-five thousand women were enrolled in these activities in 1969, 54,451 in 1970, and about 110,000 in 1975. The federation also contributes to public health efforts; 35,000 of its members have obtained Red Cross first-aid certificates, and it sponsors courses on personal hygiene and pre- and postnatal care. It trains traffic policewomen, civil defense workers, promotes park beautification projects, and manages child-care centers.[15]

The women's federation grew very gradually until 1968, when a large-scale recruitment drive was launched to bring 51 percent of all adult women into the organization by 1970. In 1974, 74 percent had been enrolled; a 1975 computation showed 80 percent. Membership and number of local chapters in the organization from 1961 through 1977 were as follows:[16]

	Total membership	Number of branches
1961	17,000	—
1962	376,571	—
1963	417,514	—
1964	481,171	—
1965	584,797	10,694
1966	668,176	12,266
1967	783,295	13,620
1968	979,368	15,873
1969	1,210,815	24,470
1970	1,324,751	27,370
1971	1,401,348	30,217
1972	1,581,089	33,380
1973	—	—
1974	1,932,422	—
1975	2,051,906	46,425
1976	2,127,000	—
1977	2,182,953	49,146

The growth in membership is paralleled by a growth in organizational complexity. The FMC has always been more efficient at providing services directly to women than at persuading other organizations to provide them. By international standards, the Cuban Women's Federation has been conservative. Federation president Vilma Espín argued in 1969: "What one needs is to place five women where there were four men, . . . to let those men go to fill a place where they are needed more . . . Let women be employed even though a higher number may be required." She told a reporter for *Ms.* magazine, covering the federation's second congress in 1974, that the Cuban women's revolutionary movement is "feminine, not feminist." Attitudes that help "keep women in their place" are common. Minister of labor Jorge Risquet, who was subsequently promoted to the party secretariat, explained in 1970 why women would be exempt from the anti-loafing law: "Women have the job of reproducing as well as producing. They have to take care of the house, raise the children, and do other tasks along these lines, and this is not easy. From the political point of view, our people would not understand it if we were to treat women and men alike."[17]

A principal concern of the federation—the day-care-center program—presents a mixture of impressive performance and frustration (see table 7.2). Capacity, enrollment, and attendance have all increased, evidence of an important and successful commitment of resources to help families, especially women who wish to work for pay. Marvin Leiner's study of Cuban day care centers also indicates that their services are of high quality. Performance in growth, however, far exceeds performance in regional distribution; in 1968–69, 50.6 percent of the enrollment in day care centers was in Havana

Table 7.2 Day care centers, 1962–1976

Year	Number	Capacity	Registration	Mean attendance (December)
1962	109	10,470	6,369	4,458
1963	144	14,225	9,023	6,391
1964	157	15,265	11,994	8,757
1965	166	16,485	13,861	10,027
1966	194	18,426	19,361	13,782
1967	262	23,793	29,689	20,612
1968	332	31,235	38,702	26,268
1969	381	35,597	42,389	29,921
1970	433	40,348	42,731	30,317
1971	438	36,625	40,494	27,660
1972	451	35,374	41,478	28,823
1973	460	36,932	47,003	31,503
1974	645	—	50,524	—
1975	652	—	54,382	—
1976	674	—	63,993	—

Sources: *Boletín* 1971, pp. 300–301; *Anuario 1972*, p. 236; Comisión Nacional Cubana de la UNESCO, *Boletín* 11, no. 42 (November–December 1972): 35; *Granma*, November 26, 1974, p. 3; *Anuario 1973*, p. 232; *Granma Weekly Review*, January 4, 1976, p. 4; *Granma*, March 11, 1977, p. 3.

province (exclusive of the Isle of Pines), though only 41.8 percent of the country's working women lived there in 1969. Distribution along class lines is better; day care was free for families with mothers working for pay until 1977. Since then, all users pay at least 3 pesos a month, with the fees increasing to 40 pesos depending on income. Since 1966, the number of day care centers has proved insufficient to meet the demand; that is, registration, though not attendance, far exceeds capacity; day care centers' capacity has not been exceeded thanks to the children's erratic attendance. Prime Minister Castro acknowledged in 1974 that, despite present and planned construction of day care centers, capacity was not expected to meet the demand for the foreseeable future.[18] If the women's federation has pressed the government to build more day-care-center facilities, it has done so entirely behind the scenes, for there is nothing on the public record to suggest it, notwithstanding the efforts of the government and the federation to incorporate women into the work force.

In confrontations with other organizations, the women's federation has lost. The federation, like the Committees for the Defense of the Revolution, dismantled their factory and occupational branches in the late 1960s, leaving the field totally to the trade unions. The unions established a women's office in each union local. The Cuban Women's Federation opposed the move; it felt that the male-dominated trade unions would ignore women's concerns, and it proved right. The trade-union movement paid some attention to the needs and interests of women workers, but only after the 1969 campaign to incorporate women into the work force had failed, to the government's displeasure. The FMC by itself had little bargaining power.[19]

The Cuban Women's Federation has been headed by Vilma Espín, the wife of Raúl Castro, since its foundation, a fact that may account for the federation's excessive loyalty. The signs that the organization's lower ranks may wish to push the government a little harder are only indirect. They include apologies from the leadership about the inadequate day-care resources, a warning to the federation from the party national secretary, Antonio Pérez Herrero, that it "should fight ideological diversionism"; and the laughter that greeted the Prime Minister's defense of "proletarian socialist chivalry" (that is, traditional male courtesies such as opening doors and giving up bus seats) at the federation's second congress in 1974.[20]

Susan Kaufman Purcell has argued that "the impetus for the modernization of Cuban women comes from above." The Cuban government, she believes, has committed resources "to those aspects of the modernization of women which have been necessary for or supportive of the attainment of the regime's highest priority goals."[21] Chief among these was the incorporation of women into the paid work force, especially during the second half of the 1960s when prerevolutionary overt unemployment was transformed, through disguised unemployment and underemployment, into a labor shortage. (This topic will be discussed in the book's final chapter.)

An economic explanation for the degree of government commitment to women's liberation assumes that "those aspects of the modernization of women which have not been congruent with the higher priority goals of the revolution have been neglected or deemphasized by the regime."[22] This was true in the late 1960s but less so in the mid-1970s. The approval of the Family Code, proclaimed on International Woman's Day of the International Woman's Year after an extensive mass discussion intended for educational purposes (or as a nationwide "consciousness-raising" session, as one might say in the United States), is incomprehensible in terms of a strictly economic hypothesis. The Family Code addresses issues that are politically explosive, legally unenforceable, and far removed from the obvious economic priorities of the revolutionary government in the 1970s. Chapter 2, part 1, of the Family Code affirms the equality of the sexes in marriage; article 27 emphasizes that a working spouse is legally expected to help with household chores and the care of children as well, even if the other spouse is not working. Other aspects of the code emphasize equality between the sexes in ways that are new to Cuban culture. The thesis on women's equality was also extensively discussed in connection with the First Party Congress in 1975.[23]

Why did the government encourage this change in traditional sex-role patterns? Many prerevolutionary laws were on the books governing the family and relations between the sexes, many of them quite "advanced" in terms of equality for women. The code itself does not represent such a sharp break with the prerevolutionary constitutional and legal past, although the egalitarian language is stronger.[24] What was new was the breadth of the public discussion. The code would be law, and the law would be known. Government leaders and organizations had to report on what they were doing to foster equality between the sexes. In these things, far more than in legal terms, the Family Code was a break with the past, and a break not at all obviously related to the economic priorities of the revolutionary government. One must conclude that there was pressure from the women's federation to draft and approve the code and to discuss it so extensively. Although the Women's Federation lacks militancy, although many of its resources serve only to provide direct services for women, although it tends to lose many political battles, it must still have done some quiet, successful lobbying, perhaps coming from the lower ranks of the federation. In terms of its institutionalization, however, this particular success does not much affect its state of dependence on the government; the FMC was able to use its dependence successfully.

The women's federation is a large and complex organization that has maintained internal coherence by emphasizing direct services to women, education, and incorporation into the paid work force. It has been adaptable within this framework and has never faced a crisis of succession. About 99.3 percent of its 326,450 leaders are volunteers;[25] the remaining 0.7 percent are paid. Although many of its activities have contributed to the welfare of women in Cuba, especially economically, the organization has been careful to follow government wishes and not strike out on its own. Even though there is some evidence of rank-and-file unrest over the low priority recently assigned to providing services for women, the organization has not been openly critical and has been unsuccessful in advancing women's interests when they differ from those of men. But the federation has no doubt done some effective lobbying.

The Cuban Labor Confederation

Perhaps the most troubled mass organization under revolutionary rule has been the Cuban Labor Confederation (CTC). Unlike the committees and the women's federation, the confederation was never really voluntary: it included most workers regardless of their political leanings. It also had its problems of leadership. The national leadership in 1959 did not include anyone who had collaborated with Batista; it consequently represented the first complete break in continuity from the labor organization that had prevailed since the 1930s. Of the seventeen national leaders in 1959, five remained in the twelve-member leadership in 1961 after the eleventh labor congress. After the twelfth labor congress in 1966, only one member of the 1961 national committee remained. Of the twenty-five other heads of labor federations in 1961, only one remained in office in 1966. Miguel Martín, the secretary-general of the Communist Youth Union, was appointed secretary-general of the labor confederation. Martín was removed from that post two years later. Both actions were taken by the party's Political Bureau, not the CTC. The second secretary of the CTC became acting secretary-general under party and Labor Ministry supervision. After the thirteenth labor congress in 1973, only one of the eight members of the national committee elected in 1966 was returned to office, and only one of the fourteen heads of federations in 1966 was returned (Agapito Figueroa, who had managed to survive as head of the metallurgical workers' federation and later of the federation of workers in basic industry since 1961; he was made second secretary of the Cuban Labor Confederation in 1973). Lázaro Peña, the old labor leader from the 1930s and 1940s, was elected secretary-general of the confederation in 1973. After his death, instead of promoting Second Secretary Figueroa, the Political Bureau brought in Roberto Veiga as confederation secretary-general, from his post as head of the unions in Oriente province (where he had also been secretary of industry).[26] The national labor leadership was in complete turmoil ever few years after 1961, and subject to outside control by the party.

Instability characterized the entire labor organization whenever rank-and-file workers were allowed a relatively unhindered vote. In the elections for the twelfth labor congress in 1966, 74 percent of the delegates were newcomers. In the relatively free labor elections of the fall of 1970, 74.6 percent of the 22,289 labor leaders elected by mid-November were newcomwers; by the first week of December, 75.6 percent of the 117,625 leaders elected were newcomers.[27] The proportion of reelected labor leaders in relatively free elections tended not to surpass a quarter of the whole. Instability also resulted from the government's habit of rotating leaders. In 1975, 30 percent of the provincial labor leaders in the province of Camagüey had been in their posts only since 1970; in Las Villas, the corresponding statistic was 97 percent. This turnover was not exclusively a result of the election defeats of 1970; it also reflected a policy of transferring union leaders from job to job, especially in the late 1960s, the effect of which was to weaken the unions. This practice persisted even after the 1970 labor election. In a survey conducted during the second half of 1971, 24 percent of the labor leaders in 1,000 work centers in all provinces had been promoted or demoted by the government since the elections, a number that reveals just how dependent the unions were on government: the government removed the labor leaders it did not like.[28]

The high turnover in the labor leadership is probably related to the condition of labor under revolutionary rule. Workers who belonged to organized labor before the revolution were aware of the significant strides labor had made over those years. Partly in an effort to save production costs and partly for ideological reasons, the revolutionary leadership had begun to ask workers through the labor unions to give up many of those benefits. Although workers profited, as all citizens did, from the gains in social equity, many did not want to trade old benefits for new ones. Labor support for the revolutionary government was consequently eroded. By the eleventh labor congress in 1961, this erosion was apparent. The congress approved the eight-hour day, in effect adding work time since many already worked only seven hours. The congress also passed a regulation that the nine days of sick pay previously paid automatically would be paid only to those who could prove they had in fact been sick. Workers had previously received thirteen months' pay for twelve months' work, the last month's pay as an end-of-the-year bonus; the congress abolished that practice as well.

The congress also announced some new tasks for the unions: to increase production and productivity, to exceed the goals of the economic plan, to organize competition ("emulation") among workers to accomplish these aims and to reduce costs. Workers were to "rise above narrow and temporary interests" to tackle national issues constructively. The labor unions were restructured so that only one union could exist in each work place; old labor leaders accused of cooperating with the prerevolutionary leadership were removed.

The congress was notably free of discussions about defending the rights of workers against possible bureaucratic or managerial abuse or incompetence.[29] Elections took the form of approval of a single slate by acclamation. It was the job of labor leaders to enforce these policies; the leaders' unpopularity was linked to the unpopularity of the policies they enforced. Labor-union leaders were under enormous pressure from the rank and file, in the form of demands and criticism, and from the government and management, in the form of directives for increasing productivity. The union leaders not surprisingly sided with government and management—for it was to them, not to the rank and file that they actually owed their jobs.[30]

While economic considerations remained important, a new ideological vision of socialist man came to the fore. The most radical period of revolutionary rule in the 1960s saw a growing emphasis on moral over material incentives to stimulate work. Wage differentials were never abandoned, but many other forms of material incentives were abolished.[31] Fidel Castro reflected the tenor of the new radicalism as it took hold after late 1966 when he said, "Men are capable of responding to conscience, . . . of responding to moral incentives . . . And we have to promote these moral incentives among the people." A newspaper editorial echoed the same spirit when it wrote, "We must think of the construction of socialism and communism as a heroic feat. We must cultivate the spirit of heroism and the sense of social dignity that exists in our people."[32]

Cuba's heroic workers were paid according to their skills and the number of regular hours worked. They were no longer paid according to the quality of work, or the over- or underfulfillment of production goals. Revolutionary awareness, noted the labor minister, not higher pay, would increase productivity in a socialist society. Overtime pay was eliminated, though not, of course, overtime work. Unpaid overtime work was called "voluntary, unpaid labor."[33] In economic and political terms, the radical period was a disaster. Not all Cuban leaders went along with these policies, and some said so publicly. By August of 1969 President Dorticós spoke of the "abuse of overtime and the deceit of overtime." He told industrial managers they well knew that there was often overtime work because production was insufficient during the normal work day. Overtime work was little more than a method of covering up for management inefficiency at the expense of the workers.[34] Moral incentives were also used when Cuba tried to increase sugar production to 10 million tons in 1970—more than had ever been produced and about twice the average production of the mid-1960s—in the midst of a labor shortage. Some labor problems were the result of cruel trade-offs between equity and efficiency. In the 1950s seasonal workers had to work hard during the harvest in order to save for the rest of the year. The creation of new jobs to absorb the seasonally or permanently unemployed had two effects; it made hard work during the harvest no longer necessary for survival, and it directed workers (especially cane cutters) toward other occupations. The availability of many free services and the presence of rationing reduced the purchasing power of money and, along with it, the incentive to work harder. The effect of these otherwise praiseworthy changes created a labor shortage in the harvest season through a combination of occupational migration and productivity decline.[35]

Volunteer workers were required to replenish the depleted ranks of rural labor. To manage the transfer of labor from urban to rural areas, from factories to state farms, the revolutionary rulers gradually adopted military methods.[36] Policies of economic and political mobilization were gradually turned into policies of military mobilization for economic and political purposes. Political mobilization might have been salvaged if the workers had a chance to discuss it, and if volunteer work—undoubtedly truly voluntary in many cases—had been so in all. The collapse of the strength of labor unions and their leaders prevented this, and it had a disastrous effect on socialist economics, politics, and morality. By the fall of 1970, at last, national labor leaders were urging local leaders to curtail overtime by improving efficiency during the day. They criticized labor assemblies where fiery orations took the place instead of detailed analysis and worker participation. They also noted that after eighteen months of virtually uninterrupted work, labor deserved a paid vacation.[37]

Legal recourse for workers against abuses was also gradually shut off during the 1960s. In labor disputes, workers had the right of appeal outside the work place, but using 1967 as 100 percent, the rate of cases that went to the regional appeals commissions fell to 80 percent in 1968 and to 67 percent in 1969; the number of cases that went to the national appeals commission fell to 82 percent in 1968 and 50 percent in 1969.[38] Since worker discontent had clearly increased, this hardly represented a decline in labor disputes, but rather yet another example of the elimination of effective grievance procedures.[39]

Because one way of increasing production is to talk workers into doing more than is justified by wages, the labor unions established the Advanced Workers' Movement, a vanguard within the working class though not necessarily members of the Communist party. By May 1968, there were some 120,000 of these advanced workers; by February of 1969, there were 235,000, or about 18 percent of all organized workers. To become an advanced worker, one had to overfulfill the average daily production schedule while meeting all standards of quality, participate in voluntary work, belong to the militia (women and older men could fulfill this requirement by belonging to the women's federation or the committees), "maintain correct behavior," and have a positive attitude toward improving one's skills and increasing one's political involvement. The thirteenth labor congress in 1973 added to the list the saving of raw materials and energy resources and specified that workers had to take courses to improve their skills. They were elected in worker assemblies (these would at a later time be criticized by the leadership as fraudulent).[40] In September 1970 Prime Minister Castro noted that "in creating an organization which, we believe, is also important—the organization of the Advanced Workers' Movement—the workers' movement in general is being neglected" and added, "Unfortunately, for the last two years our workers' organizations have taken a back seat—not through the fault of either the workers' organizations or the workers themselves but through our fault, the party's fault, the fault of the country's political leadership . . . It happened somewhat unintentionally, spontaneously . . . as a result of a certain idealism."[41] Although it may have happened as a result of "idealism," it did not in fact happen unintentionally; and in the elections in the subsequent weeks, the workers did not agree to absolve the labor leadership—they turned the incumbents out wholesale.

The change in labor policies that began in the second half of 1970 was not spontaneous either. It was a reaction in part to the economic crisis and in part to the labor crisis. Cuban workers had had enough. Under the conditions of severe deprivation that had prevailed, by the Prime Minister's count, for two years, and with the blocking of channels for grievances in unions and courts, the workers staged a "strike." Strikes have been illegal in Cuba since the early days of the revolution, so the leadership described the 1970 event as "large-scale absenteeism." It was apparently uncoordinated, but it was large scale, and the leadership was plainly concerned. Prime Minister Castro noted that in August and September of 1970, 20 percent of the work force, around 400,000 workers, were absent on any given day. In Oriente, in August of 1970, 52 percent of the agricultural workers were absent from work; by January 1971, with the sugar harvest already under way, absenteeism among agricultural workers in Oriente province was still at 23 percent.[42] Oriente was the cradle of the revolution—the favorite social class in the favorite province—and there labor was indicating that they had had enough.

This protest is important because it shows that the power of the central leadership in Cuba had its limits. The government does not control absolutely; it cannot command indefinitely without some degree of compliance and support. The government cannot repress its own social base on too large a scale. Faced with this challenge, the government changed its policies. The changes that follow social catastrophes do not occur often, but when they do occur, they define the boundaries of power, as they did in Cuba in 1970.

There were two kinds of response. One was to encourage participation in elections and in assemblies of workers to discuss production, productivity, absenteeism, and other issues and to reorganize the trade unions. The other was to redefine the role of the unions. Minister of labor Jorge Risquet complained in August 1970 that when abuses or incompetence did occur, "the worker did not know where to go." Workers asked him about things that had already been legislated but that were not enforced because "there was no one to defend them." The minister then argued that while the improvement of production and productivity was still a task for the unions, they should first "look after the implementation of revolutionary legislation and of the rights established for the workers by revolutionary legislation." A year later he had modified his views. The workers' protest had receded, and he remarked, "As Fidel said on May Day, the main task of the workers' movement—now, tomorrow, always—is increasing labor productivity." Still he added that "the development of the constant contradiction that must necessarily turn up between the trade union organizations and the administration will strengthen the revolution every day . . . These contradictions are our best weapons against bureaucracy and inefficiency . . . These contradictions are not of an antagonistic nature because both parties are seeking the same objective and following the same political line." The welcoming of contradictions where the unions face up to management, however unantagonistically, though not new, was nonetheless markedly different from the experience of labor in the previous decade.[43]

Raúl Castro agreed that the unions had to watch out for the "specific interests" and the "particular achievements" of workers in each work center, but he said that this objective ranked fourth, behind implementing and promoting the goals of the government, of the party, and of the local administration.[44] By the time of the thirteenth labor congress in the fall of 1973, the role of the unions as a defender of the workers engaged in nonantagonistic contradictions with management was very qualified. Secretary-General-elect Lázaro Peña put it this way:

Criticism of various kinds was directed at certain aspects of administration in some fields . . . This workers' criticism, whose value will increase as time goes on, is indispensable and irreplaceable for the construction of a new society as long as it does not pry into things which are not any of its concern and as long as it is concrete and precise, contributing to solve problems . . . The criticism voiced in the assemblies cannot be viewed as the expression of any anti-administration trend because, if such were to develop, the CTC would be the first to oppose it, without cutting off concrete, precise criticism of any particular administration, criticism which is in line with the role which the trade union movement can and should play as a check and balance to the administration.[45]

Peña's speech represents at least a hint that criticism of the administration was not limited to details. The tension would continue between pressures from below and restraints from above. The unions were caught in conflict, for they were supposed simultaneously to stimulate criticism and to restrain it. Despite the injunction against abstract, imprecise criticism, many of the most important changes brought about by the workers' protest were very far reaching. The thirteenth congress recommended the revision of wage scales so that more and better work would be rewarded with more pay. It recommended limiting work to fifty-five hours a week, except for basic industries, sugar, construction, aviation, oil, and mining, where more work could be asked for. It recommended limiting double shifts to eight a month. While voluntary work would still continue, overtime work would be paid. The full reintroduction of material incentives was the result of changes in labor policy in the early 1970s. The First Party Congress in 1975 also approved the introduction of profit sharing at the enterprise level, to be implemented by 1980.

Fifteen months after the thirteenth congress, many of its resolutions had not yet been implemented. Overtime and double-shift pay was still not being given to workers in seven of the twenty-three sectors of the labor force in 1975; though compliance was much more extensive by 1976, instances of noncompliance remained. The link between rate of pay and the quality and quantity of work had been set for only 48 percent of the workers, probably because of resistance to these changes by party, government, or management officials since it would increase production costs or perhaps since they believe unswervingly in ideological incentives. Thus pressures on the government on labor matters came not only from below but also from these elite groups.

The thirteenth labor congress agreed that the workers should be compensated in cash for having worked through their vacations before 1973. In February 1976, twenty-seven months after the congress, the debt to the workers accumulated before 1973, amounting to 110 million pesos excluding interest, had not yet been paid because of the resistance of the financial bureaucracies. Although the thirteenth labor congress sought to facilitate job mobility for workers, the government refused to accept this recommendation wherever it interfered with its own economic priorities. Many instances of violations of labor legislation concerning occupational health and safety, working conditions, vacations, promotions, transfers, wages, and pension rights were also reported in 1976 and 1977. The nonfulfillment of the resolutions of the thirteenth labor congress shows the substantial limits to the influence of organized labor.[46]

Marifeli Pérez-Stable conducted a survey of fifty-seven workers in 1975; more than half were union leaders and four-fifths were advanced workers (twice their proportion in the labor movement). Responding to a question permitting a variety of answers, only ten of the fifty-seven said that one role of unions was to defend the interests of the workers. Most indicated that unions were supposed to improve production or educate their members. Labor leaders and elite workers had come to believe—or at least say—that unions should not independently defend working-class interests; five-sixths of the elite workers viewed the union as an arm of management. Some changes, however, have probably occurred. Asked where they would go if a problem arose in the work place, 72 percent of the fifty-seven said that they would turn to the union; it is unlikely that such a high proportion would have answered that way in the late 1960s. The "problems" referred to here, however, may have more to do with production than with defending their rights, in part because not many of the workers even know what their legal rights are. By 1975, although the workers had the right to recall union leaders, only 40 percent of the elite workers surveyed knew it; although management was legally obliged to respond to questions put by the workers, only 53 percent of the elite workers were aware of the fact. The changes in the actual role of the unions in the 1970s, therefore, have been modest at best.[47]

According to the Ministry of Labor in 1976, the labor council at the work center, not the labor union, is "authorized to settle disputes that may arise between the workers and the administration." Claims against management were to be filed before these labor councils. These councils had functioned as labor courts from 1964 to 1977. Matters pertaining to the violation of laws then passed to the regular courts; labor councils came to serve only as bodies for mediation and arbitration. The number of complaints against management regarding salaries, working conditions, and reassignments "increased considerably," according to the secretary-general of the labor confederation. The number of complaints appealed all the way to the national level fell in the 1960s, when the channels for protest were shut off, but they increased again in the 1970s (they fell from 1,469 in 1967 to 742 in 1969 and then rose every year in the 1970s to a high of 6,015 in 1975). The decline in appeals in the 1960s cannot be taken as an indication of a real decline in labor disputes but rather of a real decline in the opportunity to present grievances. The converse is also true: the increase in appeals in the 1970s cannot be taken as a net increase in real labor disputes, but must be viewed as a reflection of the availability and use of new grievance procedures.[48]

The process of selecting advanced workers also led to more protests in the 1970s. Consumer goods, including refrigerators and television sets, were often distributed through the labor unions only to advanced workers, who were also given preferential access to recreational facilities and resorts. Becoming an advanced worker entailed significant fringe benefits that explain the enthusiasm that went into acquiring that status. In 1973, 38 percent of the workers had become advanced workers. In 1975, the National Bank took over from the Cuban Labor Confederation the task of awarding credit to workers to purchase goods and services distributed through the unions. The bank charged 5 percent annual interest on loans to purchase refrigerators and 7.5 percent on loans to purchase television sets. A worker could also open a savings account on which the government paid 3 percent interest.[49]

Youth Organizations

There are four youth organizations in Cuba. The Communist Youth Union, a selective party organization, was originally a mass organization called the Association of Rebel Youth (AJR). The Cuban Pioneers' Union (UPC) is the Cuban version of the Boy Scouts. Besides serving recreational and educational purposes, its goal is to educate children into the norms of the new society. Up to 1966 the Pioneers were somewhat selective, but the decision was then made to turn the group into a mass youth organization. It had 342,351 members in August 1966 and reached 800,000 members by June 1967. In 1971 the organization became legally, though not practically, autonomous from the Communist Youth Union and was given its own administration; there were then 1.2 million Pioneers, approximately 90 percent of all primary-school students. At the end of 1975, 98.7 percent of the 1.9 million children in school were Pioneers. The Pioneers are, in fact, tutored and controlled by professional cadres—in 1975, 394 of these celebrated their tenth anniversary of uninterrupted service in the UPC. At this celebration Jesús Montané urged Pioneers on behalf of the Central Committee "to develop a sense of honor, modesty, courage, comradeship, love of both physical and intellectual work, respect for workers, and responsiblity in caring for social property . . . [and] a love for our Revolutionary Armed Forces and the Ministry of the Interior."[50]

The Federation of Secondary-School Students continues the tasks of socialization. It promotes school attendance, athletics, an honor code against cheating, and study groups. It, too, became legally, though not effectively, more independent in early 1971 when its first national congress was held. It held three annual congresses in a row and then, probably exhausted, decided at the third congress in late 1973 to hold congresses only every three years.[51]

The history of the University Students' Federation (FEU) has been more troubled. The entire Cuban university system was restructured in the early 1960s; university enrollment declined. Many rights that university students had enjoyed (and often abused) before the revolution were curtailed in the early 1960s. Both student discontent and government criticism of students increased in the mid-1960s. With the radicalization of the revolution in the late 1960s and the spread of military styles, the government imposed military discipline upon the university, including dress and hair codes. In December 1967 the federation was dissolved, and its duties were assumed by the Communist Youth Union. The official rationale was that 99 percent of the leaders of the federation were also members of the union and that the overlap was unnecessary and duplicated meetings and tasks; however, only 30 percent of the members of the federation were also members of the union. Because the union was a selective organization, this effectively cut off most university students from any organized political participation.[52]

The political demobilization of the university students in the late 1960s is the most important exception to the trends in the politics of the time, which, on the contrary, sought to expand organizational membership and control. At the beginning of 1971 the lapse was rectified, and the Federation of University Students was reestablished as a mass organization. The suspicion that the federation had been dismantled to eliminate a source of political trouble for the government is reinforced by the outpouring of remarks made by student leaders in early 1971 professing the loyalty of university students to the revolutionary government; similar sentiments appeared in the first proclamation of the new organization and in statements by university authorities.[53]

The effort to revitalize and reorganize the mass organizations in the 1970s included the calling of the fourth congress of the peasants' association (ANAP) in 1971, the thirteenth labor congress in 1973, and the second women's federation congress in 1974, all in preparation for the First Party Congress in 1975, followed by the congress of the Committees for the Defense of the Revolution in 1977. The trade unions were reorganized; membership grew in the voluntary organizations. All these actions were designed to repair organizations battered during the radical period in the late 1960s. But organizational revitalization and reorganization are not synonymous with institutionalization; at best, they are a beginning.

In the cases of the labor and youth organizations, obstacles to institutionalization still remain formidable. Only the Committees for the Defense of the Revolution and the Cuban Women's Federation have continued along an institutionalizing, though hardly independent, path. All organizations share a low level of autonomy from the central political authority. Only two—the committees and the students' federation—have tried to gain a measure of autonomy, with disastrous results. The women's federation and the committees score high on other indicators of institutionalization. By the mid-1970s they were extremely complex, stable in leadership, adaptable, and internally coherent. The youth organizations were least stable in leadership and structure. The labor movement may be able to adapt to the changing conditions ahead better than it has done in the past; it may develop a coherent ideology of ap-

propriate behavior, and it may stabilize its leadership. But all of these important organizations still showed a lack of autonomy relative to the party—that
still remained a key characteristic of Cuban politics in the late 1970s.[54]

The Political Impact of Popular Participation in Government

Politics in a mobilization system requires massive political participation to
support governmental goals.[55] Some citizens can participate in politics autonomously, deciding whether, when, and how to participate and whether to
support or to oppose. Others are pushed toward political action by parties or
government organizations; their participation is not autonomous. A subtype of
this sort of activation, political mobilization, is continuous, often nonelectoral,
participation, wherein massive social change is sought through political education under the direction of the party and the mass organizations. Political
mobilization in Cuba has sought to transform society, economics, politics, and
individual attitudes, to implement and articulate the innovations of the leadership, to routinize elite decisions and to standardize their implementation, to
resolve internal disputes, and to support the national leadership and its policies. Because there is no legal organized opposition in Cuba, all political
mobilization has been conducted by and for organizations loyal to the revolutionary government.

Since the early days of revolutionary rule, the Cuban government has encouraged attendance at the mass rallies it promotes and participation through
the mass organizations it sponsors. These provide reasonably accurate indications of political involvement. However, the impact of political participation
on decision making has been modest. In 1965 Prime Minister Castro was
asked to give an example of an occasion when Cuban leaders were in error and
the Cuban people had pointed it out to them. The Prime Minister replied that
some local problems had not yet been solved and that there were occasional
complaints about them. As for the broader question of error, he replied:
"Doubtless there must have been mistakes, but offhand I don't recall any,"
nor any occasion when the leadership had been "informed [of error] by the
people."[56] Apparently political participation served only to affect decisions
about local problems, and even in that area, there were severe constraints.
Local leaders could not respond to local demands from citizens without authority from the central leadership and institutions. Thus the effect of participation on local decision making was limited by the lack of local autonomy.

Throughout the early 1960s, each central organization had its own administrative scheme to divide the country into territories. Because the various agencies' divisions were all different, this arrangement resulted in chaos at the local
level. Local bodies called the Juntas de Coordinación, Ejecución e Inspección

(JUCEI) were established in 1961 to link the efforts of central agencies operating locally and to reduce the chaos. The juntas were appointed, not elected and their administration was highly centralized. Then, in 1967, elections were held in work centers and neighborhood assemblies throughout the country to launch a new system of local government that was supposed to respond to local needs and initiatives; the mass organizations brought over a million people to participate in the neighborhood assemblies. This policy was combined with the short-lived reorientation of the Committees for the Defense of the Revolution toward trying to solve local problems. But with the undercutting of the independence of the committees in late 1968 and the renewed demands for centralization in preparation for the 1970 sugar harvest, this experiment in local democracy was abandoned. By 1970 the executive officers of local districts were no longer elected directly by the people in mass assemblies organized by the mass organizations but rather by the local leaders of the party, the youth union, and the mass organizations.[57]

By the spring of 1974 the inefficiencies of extreme centralization had become more and more apparent. The national government launched an experiment in elected local government in the province of Matanzas; because it worked well enough, though not perfectly, it was extended to the entire country in the fall of 1976. Local governments in all the provinces now exercise the same powers, limited though they are, that were earlier granted to local governments in Matanzas. The new government, called "People's Power," has authority to "govern [and] administer economic institutions in the production and services fields, do construction and repair work, and, in general, carry out activities to meet the social, economic, cultural, educational, and recreational needs of the population."[58] In contrast to the broad sweep of this authority, however, the actual scope and domain of local government have remained sharply constrained.

Although all local production and service units were to be "turned over" by the central agencies to the local authorities, the latter, according to the Prime Minister, would not "be able to raise or lower prices and wages, change the school curriculum or introduce any books they want . . . All activities must follow norms and resemble each other all over the country." The Ministry of Education will still determine "methods, . . . programs, bibliographies, textbooks, evaluation of pupils and teachers, and so forth." Local government would simply make certain that these orders were followed; it would also have responsibility for the maintenance and repair of buildings and furniture. Grocery stores, butcher shops, and the like would follow distributional methods and prices set up by the Ministry of Internal Trade; local government would operate them from day to day. This division of responsibility probably means no more than that the previous operator would continue to run the business, but that local government acquired responsibility for maintenance and repair.

Movie theaters can only show the films selected by the National Film Institute, which also has responsibility for their equipment and its repair. Hospitals "will do exactly the same thing . . . with perfectly uniform procedures." Local government is responsible for hospital operation, "for seeing to it that it has sufficient personnel and for checking up on what kind of service it gives to the people." The central agency "will regulate the general organizational principles governing the internal operation of the unit . . . They will determine, modify, and channel proposals for setting or changing prices and rates." The central agency will determine all standards, methods, supplies, electricity use, equipment use, cost-accounting methods, auditing, and will provide "technical advice" and set policy for personnel training. The local government can propose personnel for technical courses, but the central agency will set the criteria. Technical personnel remain under the control of the central agency.[59]

At all times, according to First Deputy Prime Minister Raúl Castro, "the higher offices have the power to nullify an agreement or decision of the assemblies and executive committees at the lower levels when these contradict laws and regulations in force or affect the broader interests of other communities throughout the country." The escape clause provides the legal discretion to do anything, a characteristic of revolutionary legislation. These principles providing for government centralization are also laid down in several articles in the Constitution of 1976. Although appointment of administrative directors falls to local government officials, they must take into account "the opinion of the corresponding central agency"; in publich health and education, "selection will be made from a list presented by the corresponding central agency." The elected representatives of the people are urged to appoint, regulate, and supervise these administrators, but not to "interfere."[60] Among the examples cited of local government's "establishing norms and procedures on questions of local importance and activities subordinated to them" are scheduling cultural activities with local artists, "observing the overall guidelines established by the National Council of Culture," scheduling film showings by mobile units, and establishing hospital visiting rules.[61]

The scope of local authority is obviously extraordinarily restricted. Its principal job is to see to it that production and service plans and standards are fulfilled; its main function is repair and maintenance. The ability to pressure the bureaucracy and to control maintenance schedules, however, do at least allow a measure of response to many simple local needs. Evidence on actual challenges to bureaucrats is meager. The Matanzas provincial assembly approved all fourteen nominations made by the provincial bureaucracy for provincial administrative directors in December 1974 without any change; eleven of the directors had already been serving in these posts before the "transfer of power" from central to local government. On the other hand, only one of the eight proposals for administrative appointments at the municipal level on which the provincial assembly had to pass were approved, and other proposals from the municipalities were turned down.[62] Local government assemblies tend to accept proposals from the administration at their own level and tend to curtail the autonomy of subordinate units, as has always been the case. One exception was the dismissal of all regional restaurant managers of the Cárdenas region because of poor service.[63]

The new local government regulations, however, have had extraordinary impact on the lives of individual Cubans through the legitimation of citizen contact with public officials by the central authorities—what in the United States would be called "constituency service." The duties specified in the laws for elected officials add to the likelihood that these citizen contacts will affect local government decisions. Elected delegates to local government must report to their communities on their performance in open assemblies, must encourage the airing of local problems, and must either attempt to cajole, harass, and urge the administration into solving problems or explain to their constituents why they cannot be solved. Elected officials must make themselves available to citizens and to assemblies. Citizens can bring up problems either privately or in assemblies. It takes a good deal of initiative to speak out in either setting. Conflict results only with the bureaucracy, however, not with other citizens. A citizen does not campaign to change policy or form groups or organizations to challenge the government regardless of whether his cause is particular or general—although the government does encourage citizens to join organizations under its control.[64]

What are these complaints, and what are the solutions? For the first time in many years, they have been reported in the Cuban press. The following are some typical cases: In the western part of the city of Cárdenas, citizens reported that they had to wait as long as seven hours to see a doctor at the hospital and that the hospital administrator paid no attention to their complaints; in the same city, the local delegate reported that his efforts led to an increase in the running-water supply; as a result of citizen protest bicycles were being allowed in the main street again. In the Versalles section of the city of Matanzas, the neighbors complained of a water shortage, while the factories in the area were wasting water. In the Los Mangos district, the delegate noted that, for the first time, streets and sidewalks were being paved and built. In the western part of the city, working women complained that water was cut off on Sunday—the only day when they could do their laundry and wash the floors; the city was not providing garbage collection, and citizens were dumping refuse in the open. In response to the latter complaint the delegate said that he had already complained five times in three months, without success, but would try again. In the eastern part of the city, citizens complained that some barbershops charged people a peso for a haircut and others charged only eighty cents, ice cream parlors had only one flavor, and the ladies' room in the bus station had been closed for too long a time; the water problem was serious in that area, too. The delegate from this district reported that a grocery store had been repaired thanks to his intervention with the administration. In Varadero, there was no grocery store between Twenty-sixth and Forty-third Streets; because citizens had protested, one would be built. The people of Varadero also complained that intercity bus transportation to Cárdenas was deficient. In the Pueblo Nuevo–Playa district of Matanzas, mothers complained that milk was delivered too late for the children's breakfast, and everyone complained that the garbage truck did not come into the neighborhood. The delegate reported that, as a result of his intercession, the district was about to get a drug store and added that in his contacts with citizens "I think the most significant thing was that no personal problems were discussed. They were all problems concerning the community." The reporter added to that: "This has been true of all the rendering-of-accounts assemblies this reporter has attended. Nobody brought up personal problems, although this is not necessarily something to be frowned upon." Only approximately 50 percent of the population attends these assemblies, however, a result of ignorance, apathy, or boycott of revolutionary political institutions. If contacting public officials is to be the principal form of citizen participation independent of government control, it is important that it include more than faithful revolutionaries.[65]

The spread of this form of elected local government from Matanzas province to the rest of the country occurred in the fall of 1976, when the provisions of new Constitution were implemented. The new regulations for local government confirmed their high degree of subordination to the central government. The new responsibilities in the administration of local enterprises undertaken by local government "did not mean that a local enterprise could disregard national regulations concerning standards, procedures, methods, and so forth. A local enterprise that sells products to consumers cannot set prices different from those prevailing throughout the country, nor pay different wages for the same jobs, nor establish its own accounting system."[66] The scope and domain of local government authority remain extremely limited.

Yet citizens throughout Cuba have also received the benefits of participation through contacting public officials. Drinking-water wells in the town of Jatibonico, for example, had been polluted by a gasoline station for two years. Despite many complaints, nothing had been done until the new elected local government came to power, when remedial action was taken at last. The town of Regla was at last able to lobby effectively to get a second drug store for its 13,000 people. And citizens in many parts of metropolitan Havana complained repeatedly of infrequent garbage collections.[67]

The legitimation and spread of citizen contacting is one way the population affects government decisions. Local government in the mid- and late 1970s has developed a kind of public official whose job it has been to argue the little fellow's case before the bureaucracy. Even if complaints about "personal problems" are restricted, because they benefit individuals only rather than the larger group, the scope of community problems is quite large, ranging from garbage collection and water supply to ice cream flavors and different prices for haircuts. Dealing with these issues establishes a clear link between citizen participation and government performance. Even a revolutionary political system can learn something from machine politics and ward bosses.

Elections and Electoral Procedures

Political participation through elections is also restricted. The more important an election is, the less likely it is to be competitive, and the more likely the central government is to control it directly or through the party. Since no election before 1970 was either competitive or uncontrolled,[68] I shall concentrate here on the years since 1970 which saw some changes.

Between 1967 and 1974 local-government elections achieved some degree of competition and autonomy. In 1967 delegates to local government had to be members of some government-sponsored organization; because membership was still limited even for mass organizations, this was a severe restriction. Delegates were elected in work-center and neighborhood assemblies under the guidance of the party, other mass organizations, and the preexisting local administration. The voting was not by secret ballot but by a show of hands.[69] By 1974 local assemblies were being called to nominate candidates, although there was still no secret ballot. Running for office without having been nominated and elected at these assemblies was illegal. All Cuban citizens over age sixteen, including members of the armed forces but excluding certain political opponents of the regime, could participate in the nomination and election of delegates; certain political dissidents were also barred from voting. There were other disenfranchised groups as well. Approximately 3.1 percent of the 331,417 people old enough to vote in Matanzas province were disenfranchised for some reason. The nominees had to be willing to take an oath of loyalty to the country, the revolution, the working class, and the people, and promise "to respect in complete awareness and willingness the leading role of the Communist party of Cuba in our society."[70] The local assemblies nominated 11,019 candidates for local office in 1974; 57.2 percent of them were disqualified, and only 4,712 were left on the lists. This extraordinarily high rate of disqualification has not yet been explained, but it suggests the presence of sharp restrictions on local autonomy.[71]

Candidates who survived all those hurdles and were nominated could do nothing else to increase their chances of being elected. As the Prime Minister said "There were no campaigns, because a 'campaign' here is the record of the candidate's life." The government printed a biography of each candidate, showed films on the operations of local government, and handed out election materials for study and discussion. Neighborhood meetings were called to read, study, and watch. There were no debates among candidates, no public discussion of issues or differences, no programs or campaign promises, not even a printed statement of views accompanying the biography. The election itself was by secret ballot. When no candidate obtained a majority, a run-off election was held a week later. There were 4.4 candidates for each electoral post, even after over half of the original nominees had been disqualified.[72]

Compared with 1967, there were fewer formal restrictions in 1974 on who could be nominated. But political opponents of the government remained ineligible. Despite the high rate of political disqualification (57.2 percent of nominees in 1974), the electoral process was more open in 1974 than it had been in 1967. Although the number of candidates for each post in 1967 cannot be ascertained precisely, the choice was probably widened considerably by 1974. Secret ballots were used in 1974 at the election, but not the nomination, stage. But effective competition remained sharply restricted because there was no campaign—no public discussion of issues, disputes, problems, differences, or programs. Those who were most likely to be critical had been excluded in nominating assemblies, where there was no secret ballot, or disqualified after the assemblies. The government handled all publicity and printed all materials related to the election.

Are Cuban elections rigged? The outcome of fair and represenative elections should show some correspondence between the distribution of political affiliations among the electors and the same distribution among elected public officials; rules governing the election should not be biased so that members of certain organizations are much more likely to be elected than others. The mere fact that members of an organization are overrepresented among the elected elite could, of course, mean that the people recognize that they are the best qualified. Thus an unrepresentative election outcome can only be considered politically unrepresentative when the rules are demonstrably biased.

In 1974 the following percentages of local-government officials elected in Matanzas province were party members, members of the youth union, and women:[73]

	Number	Communist party	Communist Youth Union	Women
Municipality	1,014	46.1 percent	13.1 percent	3.0 percent
Region	151	60.3	14.4	6.9
Province	68	65.3	12.0	16.0

Although Communist party membership represents a tiny proportion of the adult population, the party and its youth organization accounted for 59.2 percent of all delegates elected at the municipal level in 1974. The rules governing these elections made the manipulation of the election by the Communist party easy. On the other hand, the Cuban Women's Federation could not campaign on behalf of women's candidates. Had that been allowed, the proportion of women elected might not have been so low as it was. In the far less autonomous local elections of 1967, in which the women's federation had been a more active participant, 12.3 percent of the local delegates elected in Matanzas province had been women. The proportion of women elected at the local level subsequently fell, even though the government's stated commitment to equality for women had risen. Matanzas seemed relatively "feminist" in 1967; its rate of election of women was above the 1967 national average of 10.9 percent.[74]

For the far more important regional and provincial assemblies, the delegates were selected from and elected by the municipal assemblies by secret ballot. There the level of competition fell sharply to 1.25 candidates per post. Autonomy was also significantly reduced. The party intervened in these elections to increase the number of women and of party members among those elected to the higher levels of government. Nominating committees operate at all levels except the municipal one; they are presided over and directed by the party at every level. Thus the increase in the weight of the party at the regional- and provincial-government levels is the direct result of the party's intervention in the nominating process.

The executive committees of the assemblies at the municipal, regional, and provincial levels are the effective rulers at each level. The members of the executive committees are nominated by committees presided over and directed by the party at all levels including the municipal. The chairman of the provincial nominating committee in Matanzas was the first secretary of the provincial party, Julián Rizo; at this level nine persons were nominated for seven places. All members of the provincial executive committee are Communist party members (although membership is not formally a requirement for office holding). Members of the executive committees at the regional and provincial levels in Matanzas in 1974 need not have been elected by the people at the municipal level. The nominating committees could recommend, and the assemblies appoint, anyone they found qualified for those posts. The majority of the regional executive-committee members in Cárdenas and Jovellanos, for instance, had not been popularly elected. This fact increased the autonomy of the higher organs of government relative to the population and weakened whatever popular control there was over government. The Constitution of 1976 requires, however, that all executive-committee members be elected to their respective assemblies.[75]

The municipal assemblies are expected to supervise the work of the local government delegates elected directly by the people. Recall provisions serve to deter improper behavior on the part of the elected delegates. Some of the 1,079 local delegates, for example, were judged by their municipal assemblies to have "failed to fulfill the duties of the delegates in their districts and in the respective municipal assemblies," and it was "unanimously" proposed that the delinquents be removed from office. In these cases, the citizens were faced with a recall election initiated by the assemblies and were asked to vote yes or no. The delegates were recalled, and a new election was held (elections were also held in other districts where seats had become vacant by migration or sickness; these were called substitution elections). While this may be a useful way to keep delegates honest, it also ensures the political homogeneity of local-government officials. By the end of 1975, eight delegates had been re- called, and nineteen others had been replaced with substitutes. The initiative again rests at the top, with popular compliance virtually assured. The removal of elected officials also occurred after the comparatively autonomous and com- petitive union elections in 1970.[76]

The implementation of the Constitution of 1976 required the extension of elected municipal assemblies from Matanzas to the entire country. Elections for these assemblies were held in October 1976. The delegates to the provin- cial and national assemblies were then elected by the delegates to the munici- pal assemblies. The new division of the country, also implemented in 1976, al- tered the number of provinces and of municipalities. The number of municipalities had risen from 126 in 1963 to 407 in 1973; it was fixed at 169 in 1976. The number of provinces was increased from six to fourteen. One change from the procedures followed in the Matanzas experiment was the elimination of the regional level—including assemblies and other offices—in the new Constitution.[77]

A new electoral law was issued in 1976 to govern the nationwide municipal elections held in October. This law was a decided improvement over the procedures that had been used in the Matanzas elections in 1974. The cat- egories of the disenfranchised have been reduced to include only the insane and convicted criminals; the political disqualifications that had removed about 3 percent of the adults from the voting rolls have been eliminated. In addition, the law requires that all candidates nominated in assemblies must appear on the ballot; the procedures that had disqualified 57.2 percent of the 1974 nom- inees have also been done away with. Electoral law and practice, however, re- tain other features that continue to limit severely the degree of autonomy and competition in the elections. Self-nomination remains impossible; one has to be nominated in an assembly by a show of hands. There is still no campaigning by the candidates and no discussion of the issues. Only the party, the govern- ment, and the mass organizations can distribute propaganda or organize meet- ings about the elections. Their individual members intervene frequently and vigorously at the nominating assemblies to ensure, in the words of María Teresa Malmierca of the National Electoral Commission, "that the comrades nominated as candidates be the best of revolutionaries." Though the most ob- vious anticompetitive provisions of the 1974 law were eliminated, the 1976 electoral law continued to make it impossible for critics of the government to exchange views and information or even to associate. Electoral practice also reduced the degree of competition that had prevailed in Matanzas in 1974 by reducing the average number of candidates for each post from 4.4 to 2.7 nationally, although this level of competition is in itself not inappropriate.[78]

The party's control of all campaign activities has been used to discourage opponents of the regime from remaining as candidates whenever they are nominated. The party and the government may include whatever they wish in a candidate's biography; the only way a candidate may be spared public attack and humiliation is by withdrawing from the race. Under these circumstances, an undetermined number of candidates withdrew in the 1976 elections.[79]

As in Matanzas in 1974, election to public office required a majority of the votes cast; if no candidate had a majority, a run-off election was held. Approximately 95.2 percent of the registered voters voted on October 10, 1976, and 94.9 percent voted in the run-off election a week later. Voter turnout was remarkably uniform throughout the country. Metropolitan Havana had the lowest turnout both times (93.0 percent and 92.8 percent); the provinces of Guantánamo and Sancti Spíritus topped the turnout both times, with 97.9 percent and 98.4 percent, respectively. About three-quarters of the delegates were elected in the first round.[80]

Although complete election statistics have not been published, fragmentary evidence suggests the extent of the party's control over the elections. Approximately 56 percent of all candidates nominated throughout the country were party members; 70.4 percent were members of either the party or the Communist Youth Union.[81] In six municipalities, or districts, of metropolitan Havana, the party's share of the municipal assemblies ranged from 65 percent in Boyeros to 80 percent in Plaza de la Revolución; the combined party and youth union share of these assemblies ranged from 78 percent in Marianao to 88 percent in Plaza de la Revolución.[82]

The 1976 electoral law reaffirmed the party's control over the far more important indirect elections for provincial and national assemblies. The list of nominees for the posts of provincial delegate and national deputy are prepared by commissions of the party, the Communist Youth Union, and the mass-organization leaders presided over by a party member. Among delegates elected in the fall of 1976, party members accounted for 71 percent of the provincial assembly of the city of Havana; together with youth union members, Communists made up 79 percent of its membership. For the province of Havana, excluding the city, the comparable statistics were 87 percent and 90 percent. Astonishingly, 91.7 percent of all the deputies to the National Assembly were party members; an additional 5.0 percent belonged to the Communist Youth Union, for a combined total of 96.7 percent Communists.[83]

Provincial delegates and national deputies need not have been elected by the people to the municipal assemblies; the nominating commisions may propose anyone they wish, whether or not they have ever faced the voters. In this way the degree of autonomy from popular control experienced by the provincial assemblies and the National Assembly is clearly established. Approximately 44.5 percent of those who became national deputies in 1976 had never been elected directly by the people.[84]

Recall provisions remain in the 1976 electoral law, but important members are protected from unruly municipal assemblies. The municipal assemblies cannot recall members of a provincial executive committee or of the national Council of State without the agreement of the respective provincial assembly or the National Assembly.[85] Notwithstanding some important improvements in the 1976 electoral law, autonomous electoral competition had not yet come to Cuba.

The 1976 elections also provided the first measure of how satisfied citizens were with their leaders, since municipal officials were elected in Matanzas province in 1974. Of the incumbent municipal delegates, 59.6 percent failed to win renomination. The reason for the high turnover is unclear. If it resulted from voter displeasure—as it did in the 1970 labor union elections—it could indicate some degree of electoral independence. But it could just as easily reflect party dissatisfaction with the delegates the people had chosen the last time. Although both the party and the government tried to give the impression that the experiment in Matanzas had been a success, the resolution concerning it approved at the First Party Congress was not so positive; rather, it criticized the performance of both party and elected local officials "in everything concerning the operation of these state institutions."[86] It is likely, in fact, that the high turnover can be explained by a combination of factors: the 1976 electoral law had some degree of independence and simultaneously permitted the party and the government to remove from office those elected officials not to their liking.

Local government in the mid-1970s set out to promote citizen contact that would affect decisions, but the autonomy, scope, and domain of local government and the autonomy and competitiveness of elections remained circumscribed. The party, government regulations stated, "must never meddle in the daily routine of the offices of the People's Power and its administrative apparatus." "The concrete administrative decisions" in management were to fall to local government, not to the party, along with "all state and administrative tasks that the party has had to take over until now." But the party retained supreme authority over local as well as national government, as the Constitution and the official oath made clear. The party's members controlled the local government elections; they had a majority in the assemblies and a virtual monopoly of the higher state offices. Thus the autonomy of local government remained minimal. The party had delivered itself from the daily administrative routines in order to control more, not less. Initiative in politics, even in the restructuring of political and administrative units, remained with the party. The new policy may in fact have simply increased the power of the more agile and more competent Communist party.[87]

The same trend applies to the labor unions. In the 1966 union elections, all those who had been labor leaders in prerevolutionary Cuba when Eusebio Mujal was secretary-general, all those who had been engaged in politics or military activities before the revolution, and all antisocial elements were officially barred from nomination. Candidates were chosen at assemblies of workers attended by the local members of the Communist party. The party did not put forth its own slate of nominees, however, and it was recommended that most delegates should not be party members. On the other hand, the nominations put forth by the workers themselves were not always honored. Municipal commissions of the party and the unions had the right to approve or reject the nominees, provided the average number of candidates per post did not sink below 1.25.[88] Thus the degree of autonomy and effective competition was sharply reduced, even if formal competition, especially at the municipal level, appeared to be at an acceptable level. The party and trade-union officials retained the right to exclude not only political opponents but anyone else as well.

Procedures were changed for the 1970 union elections. The regional office of the union presided over an assembly and provided the "necessary guidance." Anyone could be nominated. After the nominations, there was to be a debate about the qualities of the nominees, but the regulations stated that it was not intended to decide whether or not the nominee remained on the list of candidates; all the nominees would appear there. The recommended number of candidates per post was two or three, more than the 1.25 of 1966. Incumbents could be reelected, though most were not; voting was by secret ballot. The only legal restriction was a prohibition against campaigning.[89] The 1970 elections were held over a period of several weeks. The level of competition in the elections in the early weeks, when about one-seventh of all union posts were at stake, met the government's own standards for acceptable competition—2.1 candidates per post. Because there was more local electoral autonomy in 1970, the effective level of competition—about 1.8 candidates per office over all—was far higher than in 1966, when there had been 1.6 candidates for each local office, 2.1 for each municipal office, and 1.4 for each regional post. The level of competition fell, however, as the 1970 elections proceeded; through November 17, there were 2.1 candidates for each office, compared with 1.9 through December 2 and 1.6 thereafter.[90] The national labor-union authorities may have tried to rescue some of the incumbents from defeat by reducing the number of candidates per post toward the end of the electoral process.

The 1970 labor-union elections were autonomous and competitive, at least in the early stages, not only because they were required to be so but also because the 1966 restrictions had been abolished. The Prime Minister had pledged free elections: "Where we find that a work center elects a *mujalista* [i.e., union official under Eusebio Mujal], it should be a political red light signaling the backwardness, the confusion, and the poor political work found there; where we find that they elect a loafer . . . a demagogue, an agitator who may be making hay out of some justified complaint, it will serve to measure our political work in that center." The Minister of Labor claimed he welcomed the election of a "bad leader," because it served as a warning to the revolutionary leader. Later he was to remark that the "workers who were elected for some of the posts did not have sufficient merits"; but he argued that these were signals to the national leadership that should never be turned off.[91] Nonetheless many were turned off subsequently, as elected officials were removed by the party and the government.

The level of autonomy and competition in the early 1970 union elections has not been repeated; and the 1971 elections reached a new low in noncompetition, with an average of 1.6 candidates per post. Instead of holding the 1972 local union elections on schedule, the national confederation postponed them until the second half of 1973, to coincide with elections for the thirteenth labor congress. The procedures there also regressed to pre-1970 forms, although they perhaps were not so controlled as in 1966. Nominations were made in assemblies, but there was no requirement that the number of candidates should exceed the number of posts. The elections became entirely discretionary. If there was more than one nominee, voting was done by means of a show of hands or by acclamation. If there was only one, no election was held. The actual delegates to the labor congress were elected at conferences, at the regional and provincial levels, comprised of delegates who in turn were the result of poorly contested elections on the local level. At these conferences, the higher-ranking union authorities decided whether elections would be by acclamation or by secret ballot; subsequently the thirteenth congress voted to hold local elections only every two years.[92]

Only 47.8 percent of the delegates to the thirteenth labor congress were from the rank and file. The rest were delegates from the national and intermediate offices of the Cuban Labor Confederation who had not been elected by the workers and who appointed themselves as delegates. The same officials also decided how to apportion delegates to the congress. The embarrassment of the 1970 elections when union leaders were defeated in elections for delegates was avoided by this means. The apportionment of delegates to the thirteenth labor congress in 1973 among the unions was highly unequal. The workers worst represented at the congress were those from the most democratic unions—that is, those whose delegates were most likely to have faced a direct election—and also from the biggest unions; the workers best represented were those whose unions were dominated by labor bureaucrats who did not face direct local elections and from the smallest unions (table 7.3). The largest union, that of agricultural workers, had a delegation four-fifths of whose members were directly elected by the workers; it also had by far the lowest proportional representation at the congress. The smallest union, that of workers in civil aviation, had a delegation only one-third of whose members were

Table 7.3 Representativeness of delegates to the thirteenth labor congress, 1973

Trade union	Workers per delegate[a]	Workers per rank-and-file delegate[b]	% delegates rank-and-file	% of CTC membership
Agriculture	1,578	1,995	79.1	26.7
Construction	1,205	1,982	60.8	10.0
Education and science	1,158	2,007	57.7	10.2
Sugar industry	1,110	1,957	56.7	5.2
Light industry	1,010	1,928	52.4	4.1
Public health	975	2,004	48.6	5.2
Commerce	959	1,974	48.6	6.7
Transportation	907	1,971	46.0	5.0
Fishing	905	1,867	48.5	1.4
Basic industry	902	1,867	48.3	2.6
Mining	893	1,787	50.0	1.0
Tobacco	800	1,920	41.7	2.3
Public administration	792	1,904	41.6	4.3
Merchant marine and ports	784	1,778	44.1	1.3
Food industry	783	1,957	40.0	4.2
Hotels and restaurants	737	1,943	37.9	4.2
Civilian workers in armed forces	567	1,613	35.1	1.0
Petroleum	506	1,139	44.4	0.4
Journalism and publishing	487	1,190	40.9	0.5
Arts and entertainment	467	1,724	27.1	1.3
Forestry	410	1,727	23.7	1.2
Communications	407	1,765	23.1	1.0
Civil aviation	339	1,017	33.3	0.2
CTC total	926	1,936	47.8	100.0

Sources: Computed from Granma Weekly Review, November 4, 1973; Eduardo García Mouri, "Proceso de institucionalización en el sindicalismo cubano: papel de los sindicatos según el XIII Congreso CTC" (Paper presented at Seminar on Institutionalization in Cuba, Institute of Cuban Studies, Caracas, March 24–29, 1975), pp. 30–31.

a. Mean = 812; standard deviation = 295.

b. Mean = 1,783; standard deviation = 280. Rank-and-file delegates are those elected directly by the workers.

directly elected and by far the highest proportional representation at the congress. The inequalities are more pronounced in terms of the number of workers per delegate actually attending the congress than in terms of the ratio of workers to rank-and-file delegates. A major reason for the unequal apportionment of total delegates to the congress was to ensure the attendance of labor officials from the national, provincial, and regional levels of the small unions, those who would have had to face direct elections or be excluded altogether if strict proportional representation had been practiced.[93]

If the elections to the congress had been representative, then representation at the congress would have been equal to each union's share of the CTC membership, and the number of workers per delegate, the number of workers per rank-and-file delegate, and the percentage of delegates who were rank-and-file members would have been the same for all unions. In fact, the best explanation of the pattern of representation at the congress is the political decision made by national union and party officials to set the numbers of rank-and-file delegates at different levels and to guarantee the representation of labor bureaucrats who had not faced the electorate. These political decisions, of course, had to take into account the different sizes of the various unions, but their overall effect was to reduce to insignificance the direct impact of a union's share of CTC membership in the determination of its representation at the congress. Political decisions, therefore, mediated between the membership and representation at the congress and severely distorted the representation of the union membership in the process.

The unequal representation at the labor congress was merely part of the broader trend away from high competition, autonomy, and representativeness in electoral procedures that were instituted briefly in late 1970 in response to worker protests and gradually dismantled over the years. Many unions followed the CTC's lead in controlling elections more closely. For the nine posts in the national secretariat of the Food-Industry Workers' Union in March 1975, for example, there were only nine candidates. When they had been "elected," Agapito Figueroa, second secretary of the Cuban Labor Confederation, proposed that the food workers' congress "elect the remaining thirty-two comrades of the national committee of the Food-Industry Workers' Union, and this was approved by acclamation."[94]

Labor unions adopted new election procedures for their local elections in 1977, following the norms established for local-government elections in 1976. Local voting came to be by secret ballot only, but self-nomination remained impossible; one had to be nominated in an assembly before one could run for office. Nominations were discussed in the assembly, where the virtues as well as the defects of candidates were pointed out. These were substantial improvements over the procedures used at the time of the Labor Congress and immediately thereafter, but they still left ample room for the incumbent union officers and the party to shape the outcome of elections. Campaigning remained limited to the existing union organization and to the party.[95]

As in the case of local elections, union elections were controlled, uncompetitive and unrepresentative, even though the appearance of these elements improved in 1977. The unions could have defended workers' rights against administrative and managerial abuses and incompetence, but that power had eroded from 1970 to the labor congress in 1973, though it remained a legitimate activity. The political condition of workers grew worse during the 1970s, after a period of considerable improvement, but their economic and social condition improved significantly. The Cuban Labor Confederation may be becoming more institutionalized, but it is less apt to defend the interests of the workers and its elite is less controlled by the membership than it was in 1970. Cuban workers have received economic and social benefits in exchange for effective political participation within and through their unions. Compared with the late 1960s, however, Cuban workers were substantially better off not only economically but also politically in 1977. Political participation was so restricted in the late 1960s that the restrictions of the mid-1970s paled by comparison. A modest participatory legacy survives from the early 1970s.

The National Association of Small Peasants (ANAP) held elections in the fall of 1971 for delegates to the fourth congress of the association. In each association local, four people were to be elected: one of the heads of a women's brigade, one "advanced peasant," one of the heads of a mutual-aid brigade, and the president of the local chapter. All these became nominees for peasant association municipal elections to select candidates for delegates to the fourth congress from each of these four categories.

The fourth peasant congress was politically unrepresentative. (See table 7.4 for data for Cuba as a whole and for a single municipality.) The membership of the association at the time of the congress was about 202,000; most of the members of the women's brigade were not association members at all but rather wives of members. The insertion of women into the congress in this way, though they did not represent the association membership, was a decision that could perhaps be accepted as a gesture toward sexual equality. Other aspects of the lack of fair representation are far less defensible. Advanced peasants are those who volunteer to build schools and roads, produce well, and participate in mutual-aid brigades, government planning programs for private agriculture, and civil defense; they do not sell agricultural products in the free market. Not surprisingly, they are a minority of the peasants. Peasants in mutual-aid brigades make up only about a third of the total membership.

In contrast, the majority of the peasants who are not in the brigades and are not "advanced"—or, as in table 7.4, are not "exemplary"—are represented at most by local delegates who are presidents of the local association chapters. Because 25 percent of the delegates to the fourth congress were not elected locally but came from the intermediate and national offices of the association, the local chapter presidents made up only 18.8 percent of the delegates to the congress; they represented the entire chapter, not just the nonexemplary peasants. In addition, there were legal restrictions to the election of all association officials, including local ones. The 1967 charter of the ANAP prohibited the election of peasants who employed more than two agricultural workers; it also limited membership to those who owned less than sixty-seven hectares of

Table 7.4   Representativeness of delegates to the fourth peasant congress, 1971

Delegate category	ANAP members per rank-and-file delegate (Cuba)	ANAP members per rank-and-file delegate (Las Yaguas municipality)	% of ANAP membership
Advanced peasants	91	15	13
Women's brigade	152	54	—
Mutual-aid brigade	212	59	35
Nonexemplary peasants	400	—	65

Sources: Computed from "Diez años de trabajo," *ANAP* (April 1971): 8; "Convoca la ANAP al cuarto Congreso campesino," ibid. (September 1971): 29; Ramón Aymerich, "De la base al Congreso," ibid. (November 1971): 21; *Granma,* December 27, 1971, p. 5.

land and had committed no counterrevolutionary acts or "acts against the social interest." The amendments to the charter approved by the fourth congress prohibited the election of peasants employing any agricultural workers, except as authorized by the municipal association office.[96] It is likely, therefore, that the lack of political representativeness of the fourth congress has been underestimated in table 7.4. Because of legal restrictions and policy preferences, the local chapter presidents were probably more similar to the exemplary peasants than to the nonexemplary peasants. Nonexemplary peasants among the ANAP membership were thus severely underrepresented in terms of rank-and-file delegates (see table 7.4). The results of the fourth congress were politically radical, perhaps because most Cuban peasants were not effectively represented there. Delegates were apportioned by the national office of the ANAP according to "revolutionary quality," not by numbers alone, and certainly not by one-member–one-vote representation within the delegate ranks.

The second congress of the Cuban Women's Federation (FMC) was held in the fall of 1974. Both working women and party members were heavily overrepresented there. While only 34.7 percent of 1,932,422 federation members were working women, 77.7 percent of the 1,896 delegates for whom data are available were employed; each employed delegate thus represented 455 women; each unemployed delegate, 2,992. Communist party members made up 47.2 percent of the delegates but only 1.1 percent of the membership. Furthermore, relatively few delegates were directly elected by the rank and file— only 60.2 percent of the 1,916 delegates attending the congress.[97] The results of the second congress were the product of an assembly that was once again politically unrepresentative of the federation's membership and probably even more so of the distribution of opinions among all Cuban women.

The relative lack of electoral competition and of autonomy to elect whomever one wishes locally and the unrepresentative results were deliberate government policies that provide a clue to the basis for legitimate rule in Cuba in the mid-1970s. Revolutionary rule is not legitimated by voting; rather, an election is legitimated by revolutionary rule. The right to rule claimed by the revolutionary elite depends on the rightness of its conduct, individually and collectively—the institutionalization of Fidel Castro's charisma. It is on that "rightness," not on the vote, that the claim to legitimacy rests. Legitimate revolutionary rulers can "rightfully" exclude political opponents from electoral participation and can weight the scales so that those citizens who manifest "revolutionary qualities" to a higher degree are placed in office. Voting is a contributory, but not a decisive, mechanism for the legitimation of rule. Revolutionary leaders need not be troubled about the demonstrably unrepresentative elections for office in local government, labor unions, the peasants' federation, or the women's federation. The elections are meant to broaden the basis of rule and to expand popular participation—yet the revolution does not rule because it is elected, but because it is right. The party can be formed only by an elite, the vanguard of the people, the top revolutionaries. They rule because individually and collectively they reflect Fidel Castro's charisma. Legitimacy in Cuba continues to flow from the top.

Unrepresentative election results are therefore regarded as a virtue: they mean that the election has brought forth the best. The lack of competition is a strength, for it means that one can settle on the very best without dispute. The lack of autonomy is a necessary correlate, for those who rule rightfully must direct the masses toward proper revolutionary conduct. The risk of autocracy is one the political system willingly takes. Many Cubans have expressed their opposition to these claims both inside and outside the country. It is impossible to determine how widely the claim is believed. There is, however, no other plausible claim to legitimacy, given this analysis of political participation. Claims of the rightness or correctness of rule have, from the beginning, been based on deliverance from tyranny, distributional performance, nationalism, and the institutionalization of Fidel Castro's charismatic spell. Party members, by their correct conduct, become the bearers of his revolutionary zeal. They embody the revolutionary consciousness. These are the fundamental sources of the revolutionary elite's claim to legitimate rule.

Political Mobilization

Political participation in general and elections in particular do not legitimate the Cuban political system, but they contribute to it. An important element of the rightness of rule is contact with the masses. Thus one idea behind political mobilization is to force the leadership, especially in its intermediate ranks, to test its "rightness" by contact with the people. If public officials remained aloof it would be difficult to maintain a right to rule based on the personal and collective conduct of the elite. Mass political participation also has practical consequences. It brings out people and problems that might otherwise be overlooked. New ideas, especially ways of improving policy implementation, can be brought out through the consultative aspect of political mobilization. Political mobilization educates the masses about the goals and methods of revolutionary policies. It harnesses the masses to reorganize and transform values, roles, and social structures; it highlights the ever present need for revolutionary vigilance; it facilitates the implementation of policies that affect large numbers of people. Political mobilization is a large-scale political activity, educational, change-oriented, continuous, and often nonelectoral, under the hierarchical direction of the party and the mass organizations.

Rousseau wrote that "in a well-ordered city every man flies to the assemblies."[98] So, too, in a socialist state. From the early days of the revolutionary government, public demonstrations have been used extensively. Millions of members of mass organizations engage in activities ranging from physical labor to ideological study. Citizens also participate in the sort of assembly that Rousseau might have had in mind, that is, assemblies to discuss rules and legislation for the polity.

In 1968 Cuban workers discussed whether to give up overtime pay for overtime work, how to discourage absenteeism, and whether overfulfillment of work norms could be achieved in exchange for improvements in retirement and pension pay. By December 1968, 89 percent of the workers had talked about these issues. The 1971 law against loafing was discussed by 3,265,000 persons in 115,000 assemblies, which were not limited to employed workers. Reportedly, 76 percent of the assemblies approved the draft law unanimously and without changes, 24 percent proposed changes, but only 1 percent voted to make the law more lenient. During 1970 and 1971 meetings of workers were held in all sectors of the economy to discuss the problems that had arisen during the late 1960s; these led to the restructuring of many national labor unions.[99]

In preparation for the thirteenth labor congress, the Cuban Labor Confederation issued nine theses or propositions for discussion and approval; they dealt with the link between pay and the amount and quality of work, the repeal of the high pension and retirement-benefits law of 1968 because it was too costly, the link between the duties and the rights of labor, the role of unpaid voluntary work, the extent of labor participation in management and the state, the work of women and young people, socialist emulation, international solidarity, and the character of the CTC. There were 42,216 assemblies attended by 1,504,150 workers, or 88 percent of all those eligible, but only 72.8 percent of the total number of labor confederation members represented at the congress. Three theses were approved by 99.9 percent of the participants; four by 99.8 percent; and two by 99.5 percent. These last two dealt with the link between pay and work and with retirement benefits, the only theses directly affecting the material conditions of the workers and the only theses to draw more than a thousand negative votes (3,117 and 4,474 respectively).[100] That participation was closely controlled is plain from the following report to the Congress: "Voting was done by acclamation at all assemblies: that is, raising of hands to vote for or against, or to abstain, so the counting was based on estimates and is not an exact total, . . . although the number of votes against is exact because there were very few opposing votes . . . there was no attempt to demand the inclusion of things which were not within the normal framework of the theses."[101] It was risky to vote no, because one could be identified, and the discussion was confined to the things the workers were supposed to talk about.

Since the labor congress, assemblies have been held in each factory virtually every month to discuss production and other topics. The government broke down the 1974 and subsequent annual plans and the first five-year plan (for 1976–1980) so that they could be discussed more easily in these assemblies; about 61 percent of the labor-union members discussed the 1975 plan and about 65 percent discussed the 1976 plan. The performance of workers and managers agreed upon in so-called collective contracts is also evaluated.

The assemblies have a variety of purposes. One of them is to strengthen discipline; virtually the entire production assemblies are turned over to the plant manager to impress upon the workers the need for greater control of quality, greater productivity, and better discipline.[102] Another purpose is to discuss the implementation of details of the plan at the plant level and especially to indicate when some of the targets are too high. Approval of the plan at all levels of production rests, however, not with a particular enterprise or a specific plant but with the highest levels of the government and the party. Because they also initiate the plan, the impact of the workers' discussions is limited to the modification of details.[103] This is not necessarily a trivial impact; it is comparable to the procedures followed in the conduct of local government, where some feedback mechanisms permit improvement in the quality of government, the reception of criticism, and the legitimation of government decision making. These procedures have facilitated the development of tolerable, more popular, and more efficient revolutionary politics.

Cuban Labor Confederation secretary-general Roberto Veiga still complained in February 1975 that production assemblies were too formal, often little more than "a tiresome reading of cold statistics." Pedro Margolles of the party's Central Committee staff noted that through the mid-1970s worker participation in management was restricted to discussing the plans of a specific production or service unit. The theses of the thirteenth labor congress specified that the production assemblies could make recommendations to the administration, which retained "the right to reject those it found inconvenient, though it must report, at the next assembly . . . about its reasons." When

Marifeli Pérez-Stable investigated the degree of responsiveness perceived by fifty-seven elite workers under the new procedures, virtually all the respondents agreed that the workers had to be consulted, but only 58 percent agreed that what they said was influential. Presumably rank-and-file workers would have judged their influence as being even less. Only half of Pérez-Stable's elite workers thought that management should be required to answer workers' inquiries. These assemblies thus in no way hampered the exercise of power by the administration.[104]

Discussion is not limited to labor interests alone. The official number of participants in the constitutional discussions in 1975 was 6,216,000, though because of duplication the exact number is probably closer to 5,500,000—still an extraordinary number. About 88.5 percent of the official participants approved the draft Constitution without any changes; fewer than 2 percent voted against the draft, abstained, or objected in some other way. The rest approved the constitutional draft after suggesting some amendments; approximately 16,000 people (0.25 percent of the participants) made proposals for textual modifications and additions. Although the number of participants is impressive and the educational goals of the discussion may have been achieved, almost all participants did nothing but signify formal assent, usually by raising their hands in public assembly.[105]

In February 1976, 97.7 percent of the 5,602,973 who voted (95.7 percent of the 5,717,266 registered voters) favored the Constitution in a secret-ballot referendum; 98.0 percent of all registered voters voted; only 1 percent (54,070) cast a "no" vote. Havana province led in registered voters who failed to vote in favor of the Constitution with 5.0 percent; the two easternmost provinces, Camagüey and Oriente, had the fewest dissenters (about 3.3 percent).[106] Whatever their attitude toward the revolutionary government generally, Cubans no doubt felt that the new Constitution was likely to contribute at least marginally to a reduction of governmental arbitrariness and the protection of civil rights simply by codifying them. The high turnout and overwhelming approval can be considered a coincidence of interests between those who support revolutionary rule and those seeking to restrain it.

Approximately 2,195,537 people in 66,513 assemblies had discussed the draft of the Family Code by November 1974. When the discussion ended in February 1975, 98 percent of the participants approved the code. Much to the government's surprise, approximately 2.2 percent of the participants, though approving the draft code in general, had voted in favor of an amendment to Article 3 (which permitted marriage between boys as young as sixteen and girls as young as twelve), raising the minimum age of marriage for the girls; 48,042 people had taken it upon themselves to propose this amendment and vote for it. The government responded by raising the minimum age to fourteen—yet another example of government responsiveness to pressures from below, although this issue is politically trivial. This instance also shows that the government can choose to disregard the wishes of the majority, for the overwhelming number had voted not to amend article 3. Decisions result not from computing the will of the majority through voting; they are made by the government and party elite.

In preparation for the second congress of the women's federation in 1974, the draft statutes of the FMC were discussed by 79 percent of the members and the theses by 82 percent.[107] Their principal purpose was again to educate the public and gather support for policies.

Political mobilization in Cuba had two distinct aspects. One was participation in the implementation of production, health, educational, or other policies. Another was the directed discussion of important legislation; this aspect had minimal impact on decisions. Discussions served rather to educate the masses, to build political support, and to contribute to government legitimacy.

Political mobilization is also linked to elections not only in its educational effects but also by the government's efforts to keep the electoral turnout high, as it was with the constitutional referendum and the 1976 elections. The electoral turnout in the local elections in Matanzas shows how, faced with relatively low turnouts in the initial rounds, the party and government ensured a high rate of turnout in the final election; in several different elections, the percentage of eligible voters casting ballots was as follows:[108]

Local government elections, 1974	
Assemblies to elect chairmen	71.1
Assemblies for nominations	72.1
Elections, first round	93.6
Elections, run-offs	91.4
Local labor-union elections, 1970	75.9
Local labor-union elections, 1971	73.6
Constitutional referendum, 1976	98.0
Nationwide local-government elections, 1976	
Elections, first round	95.2
Elections, run-offs	94.9

The turnouts in local labor-union elections are low, considering the government's interest and the relative ease of mobilizing the employed population. The results suggest that when the ballot is secret a quarter of the workers stay away from the polls. Both absolute and relative labor electoral turnouts declined from 1970 to 1971, a reaction consistent with the workers' defeat of labor-union leaders in 1970, with the decline in effective participation thereafter, and with the long-term trends to be expected regarding the social bases of revolutionary support. Political mobilization is not a perfect tool, for it, too, can occasionally fail.

Measuring the Public Mood

Criticism is essential for any self-governing system. One characteristic of a political system that relies heavily on political mobilization is relatively little open criticism. One solution is a reliance on surveys, and these have been gaining in importance in recent years. The Institute for the Study of Internal Demand was established in 1971 as a part of the administration dealing with consumer goods and services. It was supposed to determine what the people's needs were so that relations between consumers, distributors, and producers could be rationalized and the consumer made happier. The institute established a network of a thousand observation posts in stores and schools to report problems and to observe changes in the prices of products no longer rationed. Its staff of about a hundred social scientists and assistants conducts extensive surveys, using stratified random-sampling techniques. It performs laboratory experiments with consumers, and it has developed programs for computer simulation. Its survey of the clothing needs of the population had a sample size of 20,000. In 1972, in collaboration with the central statistical office of the Central Planning Board, it conducted a survey of income. Since 1974 it has engaged in a large panel study (asking the same questions to the same people at three-month intervals) to determine the living standards of the population, including income and expenditures.[109]

Other organizations perform similar functions. One reason for strengthening the mass organizations in the early 1970s was to use them to gather information of this sort. In early 1975 the Natural Institute for Agrarian Reform and the National Association of Small Peasants undertook a study of land ownership and use. One result of the 1971 fourth congress of the ANAP was a resolution to undertake "the establishment of systematic data gathering on public opinion." These were to be "surveys, conducted every forty-five days using direct questions presented through a questionnaire."[110]

Earlier in 1971 an alternative and possibly more open methodology was adopted by the Committees for the Defense of the Revolution, which were supposed to find out what complaints people had about public services. Although they did not rely exclusively on surveys, their method was highly structured and strictly controlled the flow of complaints. Between January and June 1971, for example, 1,736 "opinions" were tabulated in the 1,104 committees of the city of Cárdenas, suggesting that the "sample" was confined to the local leader and sometimes one other person. Nevertheless, the people's willingness to express opinions was increasing. By the end of 1972, 15,700 meetings had been held to discuss public services, although they were more apt to involve telling people about the services than hearing their complaints. Early in 1973 Deputy Prime Minister Flavio Bravo complained that these assemblies "were prepared a bit mechanically in many places"—the usual formula for saying that the local authorities did a good deal of the talking and the audience most of the listening.[111] The leaders of the committees protested in 1976 that state organizations were slow in responding to complaints. Some even stopped holding meetings on the grounds that no remedies had been forthcoming from the state organizations, but meetings were begun again when the leaders were ordered to do so. Clearly, even when feedback was available, it was not much used; more seriously, there was little bureaucratic responsiveness to popular complaints.[112]

The difficulty in getting some sense of public mood without opening the entire system up to criticism may explain why so much stress is placed on participation through technical means like surveys. These methods gather information without threatening local officials and without risking any expression of coordinated opposition to national politics at the local level. Criticism of local government has grown, and it faces relatively few constraints. It is even reported in the national press. Observers report that discussions of local problems in mass organizations are also relatively uninhibited.[113] The constraints begin to appear only when discussion turns to regional, provincial, or national affairs. The net effect has been a substantial improvement in the flow of information to decision makers without any fundamental alteration in the characteristics of mass participation.

Participation, controlled in extent and limited in effect, rests on the peculiar characteristics of social mobilization in Cuba. The Cuban revolution has completed its first stage of social mobilization; virtually all citizens are literate, exposed to the modern world and a modern government, and open to influence from the press and other media. But the quality of social mobilization is low. Many Cubans have a primary-school education, but a substantial minority still do not, and education beyond the sixth grade is rare. The feeling that citizens are being effective, characteristic of the better educated, is missing in many cases, for education is a prerequisite of the more sophisticated forms of participation.[114] Cubans are socially mobilized enough to be politically mobilized by a competent government. They are not socially mobilized enough to have the psychological resources to participate politically on their own. The Cuban government need not coerce its people into silence—there is, of course, some coercion, but for the most part it is unnecessary.

Social mobilization made citizens available for the first stage of modern participation; the party, the mass organizations, and the government have transformed that possibility into fact. An improvement in the quality of social mobilization does not necessarily mean that citizens will rise up to amend the laws, vote against them, and propose alternatives. High-quality social mobilization is not sufficient to prevent strong political control. It is most unlikely that a successful challenge to the existing order can or will be made by the population, now that the opposition elite has been exported, or that the present pattern of political participation will change unless the structural characteristics of social mobilization are changed first. Social mobilization makes people available for politics, but it does not automatically make them political. Since the revolution, low-level, first-stage modernity has been joined to a political party and a government that promote political mobilization for ideological and practical reasons. It is the combination of organization and ideology with the maintenance of a minimal level of social mobilization that shapes the pattern of political participation in Cuba today.

In the first half of the 1970s, the nature of political participation in Cuba changed dramatically. First, a limited decision-making effect at the local level, exercised through contacting public officials, was made legitimate. Second, the amount of political participation was increased, as more people were incorporated into mass organizations and as more systematic discussion of major legislation was instituted. Third, discussion and criticism of specific local issues, in local government and mass-organization meetings, became more open and relatively unhindered. Fourth, procedures for assessing public opinion, including the use of surveys and the press and mass organizations, and a slightly greater emphasis on the consultative aspects of political mobilization, were established. Some potential changes, however, have not yet occurred. Political participation is neither autonomous nor competitive. Citizens cannot join any organization they may wish to form. Restraints on political criticism of nonlocal, non-"concrete" affairs remain. The government controls all mass media; the right to vote and to be a candidate for office is limited, although the legal limitations are less strict than the Communist party's control of nominations for provincial and national offices. The party and the government retain the authority to dismiss elected officials not to their liking, both in the unions and in local government. Many elections are not by secret ballot, and candidates have no right to campaign for political support and votes independent of the government and party.

Legitimation and decision making do not depend on votes; the bottom does not control the top, nor can it vote it out of office. Many government officials above the municipal level have never faced the voters directly. The results of elections are deliberately unrepresentative politically; elections are intended to bring out "the best revolutionaries," not to reflect the actual distribution of popular opinion. Thus the impact of mass participation on nonlocal, non-concrete policy matters is minimal. Most participation, in the form of political mobilization in the mass organizations, operates at the point of policy implementation; there is little impact on policymaking. The revolution claims to rule because it is right, because its leaders' personal and collective behavior is correct, and because of the high moral qualities of individual leaders and the appropriateness of their policies. The potential for unrestrained oligarchy is quite high.[115]

8

THE COMMUNIST PARTY

The Communist party of Cuba, though comparatively weak in the 1960s, has emerged in the 1970s as the governing institution. Its leadership comprises principally revolutionary fighters who became military officers in the 1960s and then assumed civilian responsibilities; these people have remained loyal to the Castro brothers. A second important group, smaller than the first, within the ranks of the party elite is made up of former members of the prerevolutionary Communist party then called the People's Socialist Party (PSP); some of these lost power in the late 1960s, during the revolutionary government's most radical period when its relations with the Soviet Union were strained, only to reemerge in the 1970s.

Party membership remains selective; only a tiny fraction of the population belongs to the party. Membership is now more independent of exemplary-worker status than it once was. Athough a majority of the party members may possibly come from working-class or peasant backgrounds, most are not employed as workers and are not even directly linked to production; they tend rather to be military people, party officials, and bureaucrats.

In the 1970s an effort was finally made to regularize relations among different organizations within the party and, in particular, to assign a function to the Central Committee. The committee had not met regularly for several years, and the party's internal organization was weak and disorganized. Dissatisfaction with its state led to the party's first congress in December 1975. Since then the primacy of the party has been firmly established; its relationship to the bureaucracy has been better defined, although it remains confusing and unsatisfactory. The party's authority over the mass organizations, in contrast, is clear. One reason for this apparent contradiction is the overlap in personnel—high between party and bureaucracy, low between party and everything else. By the 1970s party authority over mass organizations was also becoming institutionalized.

The Ruling Elite

Four key institutions govern the country. Two are within the Communist party—its Political Bureau and its Secretariat. A third is the executive committee of the Council of Ministers, of which all its members are also vice presidents. The fourth and most recent is the Council of State of the National Assembly. Cuba's ruling elite is characterized by overlapping membership in these key decision-making institutions. Eighteen people, who belong to two or more of them, are the country's most important decision makers.

Three people are members of all four bodies; they are ranked consistently as follows: Fidel Castro, president of the Council of State and the Council of Ministers, member of the Political Bureau, first secretary of the party, and commander-in-chief of the armed forces; Raúl Castro, first vice president of the Council of State and the Council of Ministers, member of the Political Bureau, second secretary of the party, and minister of the armed forces; and Carlos Rafael Rodríguez, vice president of the Council of State and the Council of Ministers, member of the Political Bureau, fourth secretary of the party, and head of the Foreign Relations Sector. Seven others are members of at least three of the four ruling bodies. Ramiro Valdés, head of the Construction Sector, and Guillermo García, Head of the Transportation and Communications Sector, are vice presidents of the Council of State and the Council of Ministers and members of the Political Bureau. Blas Roca is a vice president of the Council of State and also a member of the party's Political Bureau and Secretariat. Pedro Miret and Arnaldo Milián are members of the Council of State and of the party's Political Bureau and Secretariat. Osvaldo Dorticós (President of the republic from 1959 through 1976) is a vice president of the Council of Ministers and a member of both the Council of State and the party's Political Bureau; he is in charge of economic planning. José R. Machado is a member of the Council of State, the Political Bureau, and the Secretariat.

Eight others belong to two of the four ruling bodies. Juan Almeida is a vice president of the Council of State and a member of the Political Bureau. Joel Domenech, Flavio Bravo, Diocles Torralba, and Belarmino Castilla are vice presidents of the Council of Ministers and members of the Council of State. Osmany Cienfuegos is secretary to the executive committee of the Council of Ministers and a member of the Council of State. Armando Hart and Sergio del Valle are members of the Council of State and of the Political Bureau. All eighteen leading members of the ruling elite also belong to the Central Committee of the Communist party.

These people have reached the top in several ways. Fidel and Raúl Castro have always been there. Some others had been members of the prerevolutionary Communist party, who have always been civilians and tend to specialize in certain areas of politics or economics: they assumed important roles in the early 1960s, lost them in the late 1960s when revolutionary rule was at its most radical and relations with the Soviet Union were most strained, and assumed them again in the early 1970s when moderation and loyalty to the Soviet Union again reigned. Blas Roca had been the secretary-general of the prerevolutionary party for a quarter century. In the early 1960s, he became editor of the newspaper *Hoy;* when it was closed in the fall of 1965, Roca, a member of the Secretariat, became chairman of the Central Committee's commission on constitutional studies. It had little power, and did little, in the late 1960s, but by the early 1970s Roca was authorized to organize the redrafting of major legislation, reorganize the judicial system, and experiment in government organization. He joined the Political Bureau in 1975 and the Council of State in 1976. Carlos Rafael Rodríguez, who represented the prerevolutionary party in Batista's cabinet in the early 1940s, was the president of the National Institute for Agrarian Reform from 1962 to 1965, when he became a minister without portfolio and member of the Secretariat. He is now also at the top. After losing power in the late 1960s, he reemerged in 1970 in charge of foreign relations, including relations with the Soviet Union, and with extensive authority over the domestic economy. He joined the Political Bureau in 1975 and the Council of State in 1976.

Still others, the "civic soldiers," are veterans of the rebel army, having fought with Fidel and Raúl Castro in the 1950s. They rose through the ranks in the armed forces and were then sent out to govern civilian life. They are generalists, equally at home in military, bureaucratic, and party affairs. Guillermo García entered the Political Bureau in 1965 as chief of the Western Army. He has also served as the delegate of the Political Bureau to the provincial party in Oriente and is currently vice president of the Council of State and of the Council of Ministers in charge of the Transport and Communications Sector. Ramiro Valdés, long-time chief of internal security and member of the Political Bureau since 1965, was the head of the Construction Sector in the mid-1970s. A vice president of the Council of Ministers since 1972, he became vice president of the Council of State in 1976. Juan Almeida, the only black in the Political Bureau in 1965, has been chief of the Central Army, chairman of the Joint Chiefs of Staff, president of the provincial government of Las Villas, and head of the Construction Sector. He was the Political Bureau's delegate to Oriente in the mid-1970s and has served as one of the vice presidents of the Council of state.

Captain Osmany Cienfuegos was affiliated with the prerevolutionary Communist party for a time but then joined the Twenty-sixth of July Movement and rose to a position of leadership. He was named minister of public works (later renamed construction) in November 1959 and served until February 1966, when he became president of the commission on foreign relations of the party's Central Committee and secretary-general of the Organization for Solidarity with the Peoples of Africa, Asia, and Latin America. He thus assumed responsibility for an important aspect of Cuban support for guerrilla movements overseas. Cienfuegos joined the Central Committee in 1965 and the Council of State in 1976; he was appointed secretary both of the Council of Ministers and of its executive committee in 1976. Belarmino Castilla has been chairman of the Joint Chiefs and first deputy minister of the armed forces; he then became minister of education and, in the mid-1970s, was made head of the Education, Culture, and Science Sector, vice president of the Council of Ministers, and member of the Council of State.

Diocles Torralba was put in charge of the Sugar Sector, serving as vice president of the Council of Ministers. He had also been chief of antiaircraft defense and of the air force and Political Bureau delegate in the province of Pinar del Río. Torralba became a member of the Council of State in 1976. Unlike most of the others who, once exported to civil government, remained there, Pedro Miret alternated military and civilian roles for many years. He was minister of agriculture from June 1959 until 1961, when he returned to the armed forces to serve as chief of artillery, rising to deputy minister of the armed forces by the late 1960s. In 1969 he became minister of mining and metallurgy; he was promoted to be head of the Basic Industries Sector in December 1972, and he had joined the Secretariat by the fall of 1973, quitting his position in the cabinet in 1974. Miret entered the Political Bureau in 1975 and the Council of State in 1976. Sergio del Valle has stayed in the military, either within the armed forces or, since 1968, as interior minister. He has been a member of the Political Bureau since 1965 and of the Council of State since 1976.

A few others are former members of the old Communist party who have steadily been promoted or have at least become entrenched in office, without discernible periods of disfavor. Two began their revolutionary careers through the armed forces. Flavio Bravo combined his military role (chief of troops for the defense of Havana) with considerable economic experience; in 1969 he was the chief of the Camagüey province staff for the sugar harvest. He was made head of the Consumer Goods Industries and Domestic Trade Sector in the mid-1970s. Joel Domenech helped to expel prerevolutionary Communists who had been his former colleagues from the party in the early 1960s, when he served as secretary-general of the provincial party in Havana. Domenech was rewarded by being appointed to replace Ernesto Guevara as minister of industries. His ministry was pulverized by June 1967, after losing sugar industry, food industry, light industry, and mining and metallurgy as components; Domenech remained then as minister of basic industries. Although his power declined, he was not made so powerless as some of the others who had belonged to the Communist party before the revolution. He became head of the Basic Industries Sector in 1974 and a member of the Council of State in 1976. Arnaldo Milián was appointed secretary-general of the Las Villas party by Aníbal Escalante in 1961; he was still in office until the reorganization of the provinces in 1976, having weathered it all. He joined the Political Bureau in 1975 and the Secretariat and the Council of State in 1976.

Finally, the leadership includes civilian members of the Twenty-sixth of July Movement. Former President Dorticós had been a member of the Secretariat until the 1975 First Party Congress, when he was dropped (though retaining his other responsibilities as vice president of the Council of Ministers in charge of planning), probably because of ill health. He became a member of the Council of State in 1976. Although he belonged to the prerevolutionary Communist party, Dorticós joined the Twenty-sixth of July Movement in 1956 and became one of its leaders. Armando Hart was the very youthful minister of education in January 1959. In the fall of 1965, he entered the Political Bureau and became the party's secretary of organization. In 1971 he was sent to carry out unspecified tasks in Oriente, reemerging in early 1974 as secretary-general of the provincial party there. He was dropped from the Secretariat, but in 1976 he became a member of the Council of State and minister of culture. José Machado was minister of health from 1960 to 1969, when he became secretary-general of the Matanzas provincial party, then shifted to the same post in Havana in 1971. He joined the Political Bureau in 1975, the Council of State in 1976, and the party Secretariat in 1976.

Twelve of the eighteen top leaders held military posts at some point. Only two remained in them in the mid-1970s: the minister for the armed forces and the minister of the interior. None of the careers of these leaders was ever seriously interrupted; all either stayed at the top, were shifted to jobs of roughly comparable rank, or were promoted. All six without military experience were demoted at some point; three of these had been old, prerevolutionary Communists.[1]

The Political Bureau had had no old Communists from 1965 to 1975. When it was expanded to thirteen members by the First Party Congress no former member of the Political Bureau, all of whom were old comrades of Fidel and Raúl Castro, was dropped; instead, five members were added, three of whom were old Communists. The Political Bureau then had ten new and three old Communists; the Secretariat then had nine members, six new and three old Communists. One new Communist (Machado) and one old one (Milián) joined in 1976–1977. The inclusion of old Communists in the Political Bureau was the most important public signal of their renewed access to power; possibly in compensation, however, their share of the Central Committee membership was not increased.

The most consistently successful road to political power in Cuba has been close association with either Fidel or Raúl Castro, fighting with the rebel army in the 1950s, membership in the Twenty-sixth of July Movement, some military service during the 1960s, civilian employment at least by the early 1970s, some general skills, and resistance to the urge to engage in polemics. Membership in the prerevolutionary Communist party was not helpful between 1962 and 1970, though it became so again in the early 1970s, as the influence of the Soviet Union increased. A civilian career may become a more important avenue for leadership in the future, but it has yet to make its mark. Despite many government urgings that young Cubans specialize in a profession, that seems not to be the path to power. The next rung down in the power structure displays similar characteristics; a combined military-civilian pattern still seems the most likely route to power.

Of the twenty-five members of the national directorate of the party before the Escalante affair in 1962, ten were old Communists, one had belonged to the Revolutionary Directorate, and the rest were members of the Twenty-sixth of July Movement. Of the 100 members of the Central Committee in 1965, only twenty-three were old Communists. Thus their share fell from 40 percent to 23 percent. Three of the leading old Communists in 1962 have since been disgraced, but only one of the others. Before the First Party Congress, the old Communists claimed 22 percent of the remaining ninety members; after the congress, they represented 20.5 percent of the 112 full members and 18.5 percent of all 124 members, including alternate members of the party's Central Committee. (See appendix E for an analysis of old Communist membership in the Central Committee.) While 56 percent of the members of the national directorate in 1962 had military titles and 28 percent had military occupations, the comparable statistics for 1965 were 70 percent and 58 percent (table 8.1 gives other data on the military). At this more general level, the superiority of a civic-soldier career over an old Communist one as a path to power remains.

Old Communists who had lost their positions in the 1960s returned to middle-level power in the early 1970s, without displacing the former soldiers. Felipe Torres, for example, had been secretary-general of the Havana provincial party until July 1966 and a member of the Central Committee. Raúl Castro made it a point to mention that Torres had been replaced when his connection with the microfaction had been exposed in January 1968. He continued to serve as a Central Committee member, however, and reemerged in the early 1970s as ambassador to Bulgaria. Armando Acosta, long-time secretary-general of the Oriente provincial party in the 1960s, was also mentioned by name in Raúl Castro's speech as having been replaced. He returned to power, still as a member of the Central Committee, in the early 1970s.

The chief difference between Cuba and the Soviet Union had been the weight of the military within their respective Central Committees, though the trend in Cuba over the most recent ten-year period has been toward the Soviet pattern (see table 8.1). The proportion of members engaged primarily in party work has increased; the proportion in bureaucratic and other economic posts has remained steady. A possibly transient phenomenon is the rising number of Central Committee members in diplomatic posts. Some of these

Table 8.1 Primary area of activity of Communist party Central Committee members in the Soviet Union and Cuba (%)[a]

Area of activity	USSR 1961 (N = 175)	Cuba 1965 (N = 100)	Precongress Cuba 1975[b] (N = 90)	Full members postcongress Cuba 1975[b] (N = 112)	All members postcongress Cuba 1975[b] (N = 124)
Politics	37.7	10.0	23.4	28.6	26.6
Bureaucracy	24.0	17.0	21.1	17.9	17.7
Other economic activities	18.8	1.0	2.2	0.8	1.6
Military	8.2	58.0	38.9	32.1	32.3
Foreign relations	1.7	3.0	8.9	8.9	8.1
Other noneconomic activities	9.6	0	0	0	0
Mass organizations	0	7.0	2.2	6.3	8.1
Education and culture	0	4.0	3.3	5.4	5.6

Source: Soviet data adjusted from Zbigniew Brzezinski and Samuel P. Huntington, *Political Power USA/USSR* (New York: Viking Press, 1965), p. 153.

a. All Cuban members on active military duty are classified as military. All nonmilitary personnel who held posts in the Communist party or Communist Youth Union are classified under politics. All ministers and ministerial bureaucrats in Havana are classified as bureaucrats except for the ministers of the armed forces and the interior, the minister of education, and those working in other central educational bureaucracies, the foreign relations and foreign trade ministers, and members of the Foreign Relations Coordinating Commission of the Council of Ministers.

b. Data given before and after the First Party Congress held in December 1975. "All members" includes twelve alternates.

assignments may be graceful ways of getting some members out of jobs in which they are no longer doing well, but at least some must also reflect the importance of foreign relations to a dependent and vulnerable country with ambitions of international leadership. The decline in the size of the Central Committee from 1965 to 1975 resulted from deaths or expulsions.

The First Party Congress approved the distribution of activity that had prevailed among Central Committee members over the previous ten years. The new members are no different from the old in occupation and background. Most of them participated in the revolution of the 1950s, some are old Communists; very few are young. The new members of the Central Committee in 1975 were thus part of the "revolutionary family." The First Party Congress expanded the Central Committee to include more people, and it made other substantial changes. Of the ninety members before the congress, thirteen were dropped; thirty-five full and twelve alternate Central Committee members were added.

The civic-soldier pattern is also evident in the makeup of the committee. Twelve civic soldiers had already been exported in 1965 from military to civilian roles. Forty-four members of the 1965 Central Committee then on active military duty were reelected to the 1975 committee; during that ten-year interval seventeen shifted from military to civilian roles. Of the thirty-five full members elected to the Central Committee for the first time at the First Party Congress, sixteen had served in the armed forces after 1960, although only nine remained on active military duty in 1975. Thus, of the 112 full members of the 1975 Central Committee, thirty-six remained on active duty; thirty-five had been military officers at one time or another after 1960, but were principally engaged in civilian tasks by 1975. Members with past military experience accounted for 63 percent of the Central Committee total in 1975. The military share of the committee after the First Party Congress was only slightly below what it had been before. The number of military members on active duty increased by one, so the decline in the share simply resulted from the Central Committee expansion.

Because vacancies in the Central Committee remained unfilled pending the 1975 party congress, a divergence developed between the changing membership of the cabinet and that of the Central Committee. In the fall of 1965, all of the members of the cabinet, except the Minister of the Sugar Industry and the president of the National Bank, belonged to the Central Committee. By 1975 all ten members of the executive committee of the cabinet were members of the Central Committee, but only thirteen of the thirty ministers were Central Committee members. Two more ministers were elected full members of the Central Committee, and two more became alternates (all four had some military background). But this left thirteen people who had been ministers before the congress outside the committee. When the Council of Ministers was reorganized in December 1976, only half of its thirty-four ministers (but all its vice presidents and its president) were full or alternate Central Committee members. Thus a clear difference appeared between parts of the political and administrative elites. In contrast, all deputy ministers of the armed forces, who had not been members of the Central Committee before 1975, were elected as either full or alternate members.

Of the secretaries-general of the six provincial parties in existence until the 1976 provincial reorganization, only one who had been appointed by Aníbal Escalante before 1962 remained in office by 1976: Arnaldo Milián, the old Communist who has survived it all. Among those who were in office at the end of 1965, old Communists like Felipe Torres and Armando Acosta did not appear in public again until their rehabilitations in the early 1970s; Luis Méndez was also removed. José Naranjo, secretary-general of the Havana provincial party and formerly interior minister and mayor of Havana, became minister of the food industry in 1967. Naranjo has been in military, bureaucratic, and party positions. Provincial party secretary is a post fraught with peril because the person holding it is the chief Communist party executive officer "in the field," and the one who is blamed when things go wrong.

Two of the six provincial secretaries in 1976 made that post their career. One was Milán; the other, Julián Rizo, a former Captain, and the secretary-general of the Pinar del Río provincial party in late 1965, who shifted to the Camagüey provincial party in the late 1960s and to the Matanzas provincial party in the early 1970s, where he was in charge of the experiment in local government launched there in 1974. The four others, however, had more general skills. One was Armando Hart in Oriente, who became minister of culture in late 1976; another was José Machado in Havana. The secretary-general of the party in Pinar del Río province, Julio Camacho, is a civic soldier. After serving as minister of transportation between 1959 and 1961, he returned to the armed forces and rose to the position of chief of the Central Army. By the end of the 1960s, he had begun his long tenure in Pinar del Río. Raúl Curbelo is another example of the civic-soldier career. He fought in the 1950s and became minister of communications between 1960 and 1962, when he became chief of the air force, a post he held until 1965. Then Curbelo became vice president of the National Institute for Agrarian Reform and its effective head, since Prime Minister Castro, its president, was too busy. In 1973, he became secretary-general of the Camagüey provincial party.

Until 1976, no provincial secretary-general, except Milián, had been allowed to build up a territorial power base. The 1976 provincial reorganization promoted Milián to the party Secretariat to help oversee the changes but also deprived him at long last of direct control over Las Villas province. Rizo, Camacho, and Curbelo retained their posts after the reorganization (although Curbelo's Camagüey had become much smaller). Eleven additional secretaries-general were appointed to the provincial parties in 1976. Of the fourteen, ten were full members of the party's Central Committee, and one was an alternate. Provincial secretaries-general had owed their positions to their power within the national elite, not to a local territorial base. The procedure that had prevented the establishment of a territorial power base had also operated within the labor unions and the armed forces.[2] This practice was modified, however, in the 1976 appointments of new provincial secretaries-general. All but two of the eleven new ones had served in the region that became a province just prior to their appointments, although at least half of them had had other responsibilities in other parts of the country earlier in their careers. Thus local and national power were combined for the first time in the appointment of provincial party leaders by the Political Bureau (there was no pretense of election from below).

The importance of the party leadership is also evident in the Council of State and in the National Assembly. Every member of the party's Political Bureau is a member of the Council of State and of the National Assembly.

Every member of the party's Secretariat is a member of the National Assembly. Seventy of the 112 full members of the party's Central Committee belong to the National Assembly. All but one of the thirty-one members of the Council of State belong to the Central Committee. Six of the National Assembly's standing commissions are chaired by a Central Committee member; three others, by leading party officials just below the rank of Central Committee member; and none, by ordinary citizens with no other position of high responsibility. And 96.7 percent of all the National Assembly members are also party members or members of the Communist Youth Union.

Party Membership

The procedures for entering the party have changed in recent years. In particular, prerevolutionary background has become less important. Although election as an exemplary worker remains a path to party membership, as it was in the late 1960s, evidence suggests that it has been deemphasized in the mid-1970s. Instead the party cells take the initiative in identifying possible party members. Article 3 of the party's statutes, approved by the First Party Congress, requires that a prospective party member must receive not only the affirmative vote of two-thirds of the cell members but also the agreement of the party administration at the next highest level; control of the party elite over admissions has been retained. Prospective party members must also have been presented to a mass assembly for approval.[3] Fidel Castro told the First Party Congress that "the party reserves the right to select its members"; all that remained for the masses was "consultation." The autonomy of the party from the population has been increased, and the adaptability and responsiveness of the exemplary-worker method are lost.

In the early years of party formation, one could enter the party directly upon being found qualified. This was no longer the case by the mid-1970s. At that time apprenticeship took two often complementary forms. A candidate could start with membership in the Communist Youth Union; upon reaching the age of at least twenty-four and after belonging to the youth union for three years, that person could join the party. From 1972 to 1976, 64.6 percent of the members of the Communist Youth Union joined the party when they became old enough (the proportion had only been 50 percent in 1972); a third of the members, however, were turned down as lacking the qualifications for party membership. If the applicant has not been a member of the youth union, then there is a mandatory probationary period of one year for party aspirants or candidate-members. In early 1973 there were 30,000 candidate-members in Havana province alone. About 40 percent of those admitted to the party in 1975 and 54.9 percent in 1976 came from the youth union; the rest were new recruits. The new procedures were slow to spread through the country. Identification cards were not given to party candidate-members in the required formal ceremony in Santiago, Oriente (the provincial capital and the country's second largest city), or Tunas (also in Oriente province) until April 1975.[4]

The autonomy of the party elite was also maintained in the party statutes, which empowered the Central Committee, the Political Bureau, and the Secretariat to waive procedures for the admission of members for those who had served the revolution. One effect of deemphasizing the exemplary-worker route may be the broadening of the party's representation. By partially separating the selection of party members from work centers, membership through other channels becomes easier; it may serve to increase the representation in the party of women with young children, the retired, the handicapped, and others outside the work force. The statutes open the way to party membership for these people provided two party members who have belonged to the party for no less than two years are willing to vouch for their merits. They also mandate the establishment of party cells according to residence so as to allow nonworkers to be active in the party.[5] On the other hand, the procedures formalized in the statutes approved at the First Party Congress offset the benefits of this broadened base by strengthening oligarchical rule and reducing the possibility of popular influence over party membership.

Procedures for sanctions against party members, including expulsion from the ranks, also increase the autonomy of the party elite. Although a party cell can propose sanctions against one of its members higher up in the ranks, those sanctions cannot in fact be imposed unless the higher-ranking party organization concurs. All sanctions against all party members can be vetoed or revoked at any time by party officials above the level at which the sanctions were imposed.

Lack of education is no bar to party membership, but members with less than a sixth-grade education have to show that they are making efforts to learn and to commit themselves to a program of study that will bring them to the sixth-grade level. Part of the party's problem in managing the system is that it reflects Cuban demography all too well in its poorly educated leaders. In 1964, 77.8 percent of the Matanzas provincial party members had less than a sixth-grade education. In 1969, 79 percent of the entire national party membership was below that level, but only 27 percent of all party members were attending school in the spring of 1969.[6]

President Dorticós's report at the end of 1971 disclosed that the proportion of party members who did not have more than a sixth-grade education fell from 80 percent in 1970 to 79 percent in June 1971, 77 percent in September 1971, and 75 percent in late 1973. In September 1971, 32 percent did not have even a sixth-grade education. Data in table 8.2, however, suggest a substantial increase in the educational level of party members by 1975, but the level is still very low to be running a country. The proportion of party members in school fell from 27 percent in early 1969 to 25 percent at the end of the year but rose to 29 percent at the end of 1970 and 35 percent by the fall of 1971.[7]

Leadership in the party requires more than does mere membership, with one conspicuous exception. A university education is likely to reduce one's chances for becoming a leader unless one was a student long ago, in the rebellion of the 1950s (see table 8.2). University-educated people join the party, especially in Havana, but they are led by the high-school graduates who run the middle ranks of the party. Higher education seems to be a handicap to political leadership. Right conduct for a revolutionary requires an increase in skills, but without becoming an intellectual.

Table 8.2 Educational level of party leaders and members, 1971–1975 (%)

	Leaders	Members		
Educational level	1971	1971	1973	1975
Less than grade 6	8	32	—	20
Grade 6	58	45	75[a]	42
Junior high school	24	13	25[a]	25
Senior high school	9	7	—	9
University	1	3	—	4

Sources: Computed from "Primer activo nacional de educación interna del partido," *Ediciones COR* no. 16 (1971): 5; "Communist Party of Cuba," *World Marxist Review* 17, no. 3 (March 1974): 138; *Granma Weekly Review,* January 4, 1976, p. 9.

a. Data for 1973 classified as grade 6 or less and more than grade 6.

The low educational level of the population has many serious practical implications. A study of Camagüey provincial party members in 1971 showed that 50 percent had difficulties in understanding what they were told as well as what they read. The average skill level was not even the sixth grade claimed, but about the fourth. A substantial, though unspecified, number of party members told the pollsters that they could not learn any more because they were not bright enough; over half of the members under age twenty-five were not in school. One-fifth of the party members did not read any newspaper. The level of political information they had was low, though unspecified. Many party members did not know how the party was structured, and some did not even know the names of the party leaders in their own province, where the party was small.[8] The Communist party acts as a political elite, but its effectiveness is limited by incompetence. By the end of 1971, however, more education had become a requirement for promotion. Lack of education also became grounds for dismissal.[9]

Table 8.3 presents a varied, if inadequate, picture of the proportion of workers who are Communists. Most of the projects reported in the table appear there because the government chose to release the evidence; the proportion of workers who belong to the party and the Communist Youth Union, especially at the level of individual firms, may be overstated; managerial and white-collar personnel are indistinguishable from blue-collar workers. The Jaruco cement plant and the fertilizer construction site have a high proportion of members because Communists were selected for those projects, just as Communist maritime workers are sent to foreign ports. It is surprising that the Communist construction brigade alone had a high proportion of Communists in 1969; in 1972, just over a third of the members of the "Communist" brigade were Communists, and the proportion in the Panama Sugar Mill's advanced detachment is quite small.

The proportion of workers who are Communists at the sector level is tiny. Given the usual ratios of Communists to advanced workers, about half of those reported in the percentages for the national construction sector in 1971 are likely to be only advanced workers, not party members; the proportion of construction workers with party membership in 1971 may have been no more than 3 or 4 percent. The proportions are also small in electric power, in machine building, at the Venezuela Sugar Mill, and among high-productivity cane cutters in 1975. The percentage of Communists among journalists and scientists and among military officers and Interior Ministry personnel is very high. The surprising statistic is the small proportion of party members among labor-union leaders; this figure confirms that the table overstates blue-collar membership in the party, because the work centers or sectors for which data have not been released presumably have an even lower proportion of party members than does the labor leadership. The data released also serve as a guide to what is important in Cuba: control over the mass media, science, and the military is much more important than control over local labor unions. Fidel Castro complained to the First Party Congress that party representation among workers was weak in the sugar industry, basic industry, construction, transportation, education, and agriculture. By implication, the party was strong only in the armed forces, the Ministry of the Interior, and the bureaucracy. Forty percent of all party members in 1975 held administrative and political positions; of the delegates to the First Party Congress, 46 percent were in political and administrative jobs, 19 percent were in the armed forces and the Ministry of the Interior, and the remainder were spread out among all occupations in production, services, and education.[10]

A comparison of table 8.3 with similar figures for the early 1960s suggests that the proportion of workers in the party increased from the early 1960s, to the mid-1970s, even though it had probably fallen from the early to the late 1960s. Except in special projects, the proportions of Communist workers remain small, certainly at the sector level and often at the enterprise level as

Table 8.3 Party and Communist Youth Union members in work centers, 1968–1976

Year and work center or sector	% party	% CYU	Total % party and CYU	Number
1968				
New cement plant, Jaruco	66.5	—	—	227
1969				
Electric power enterprise	4.4	—	—	8,340
Farm machinery construction sector	2.9	3.2	6.1	12,743
Fertilizer sector	5.9	5.5	11.4	2,363
Fertilizer construction site	33.7	40.1	73.8	1,583
Automatic loading dock, Cienfuegos	16.7	5.0	21.7	240
Machine-building shop, Santa Clara	—	—	11.8	200
Venezuela Sugar Mill	4.9	4.5	9.4	1,500
Communist construction brigade	—	—	73–80	1,630
Advanced detachment, Panama Sugar Mill	15.8	6.8	22.6	444
1971				
Construction Sector	—	—	14–16[a]	160,000
Maritime and port workers	—	—	38.5	2,600
1972				
Communist construction brigade	17.2	20.2	37.4	1,756
Academy of Sciences	50.0	—	—	—
1968–1973				
Centennial Youth Column	—	—	18.2	110,000
1973				
Armed forces officers	—	—	85.0	—
1974				
Journalists	25.2	16.4	41.6	1,727
1975				
Cardboard enterprise	3.0	—	—	640
High-productivity cane cutters	11.9	3.8	15.7	4,639
Local labor-union leaders	5.3	7.8	13.1	174,712
Secretarial-school students	—	23.0	—	265
Ministry of the Interior	—	—	60.0	—
1976				
Ministry of the Interior	—	—	70.0	—

Sources: Computed from *Granma,* January 6, 1968, p. 1; ibid., June 8, 1974, p. 4; Gil Green, *Revolution, Cuban Style* (New York: International Publishers, 1970), p. 82; *Granma Weekly Review,* May 25, 1969, p. 3; ibid., August 10, 1969, pp. 8–9; ibid., January 11, 1970, p. 10; ibid., August 12, 1975, p. 1; ibid., June 20, 1971, p. 5; ibid., March 5, 1972, p. 4; ibid., July 7, 1974, p. 3; Ramiro Valdés, "Discurso pronunciado en la clausura de la II reunión nacional de las secretarías de construcción del partido," *Ediciones COR* no. 14 (1971): 5; "Los comunistas en Nuevitas," *Cuba internacional* 4, no. 36 (August 1972): 71; *Bohemia* 65, no. 31 (August 3, 1973): 28; Andrés Rodríguez, "Alta conciencia, alta productividad," ibid., 67, no. 4 (January 24, 1975): 56–57; José Abrantes, "La unidad monolítica en torno al partido y a Fidel," ibid., no. 25 (June 20, 1975): 59; Azucena Plasencia, "Cuadros administrativos," ibid., no. 26 (June 27, 1975): 36; Marifeli Pérez-Stable, "Los sindicatos en perspectiva" (Paper presented at Seminar on Institutionalization in Cuba, Institute of Cuban Studies, Caracas, March 24–29, 1975), p. 43; Marta Harnecker, *Cuba: ¿dictadura o democracia?* (Mexico: Siglo XXI, 1975), p. 65.

a. Includes advanced workers.

well. Even some so-called Communist brigades do not have Communist majorities.

In late 1972, 12 percent of party members were industrial workers and 28 percent were agricultural workers. A total of 55 percent held "jobs in various fields of material production" in late 1973. The proportion fell to 52 percent in the fall of 1975, including peasants. The difference between these statistics and the 1972 total of 40 percent is accounted for by managers and administrators who work in production. It is possible that the party had a majority of members of worker or peasant background in the mid-1970s but not of people employed as workers or peasants. Party rules for the election of delegates to party municipal assemblies in 1975 stipulated that 40 to 50 percent of those elected should be directly linked to production in their employment; however, only 31 percent of the members of municipal assembly executive committees were directly linked to production.[11] Although few workers are in the party, many party members are of worker or peasant background. Although the party remains exclusive, its membership reflects the demographic characteristics of the population, including its mainly proletarian background, but not its proletarian occupations.

The party elite is not very different from the rest of the Cuban elite. In a sample of 2,000 state farms studied in 1964, 40 percent of the administrators lacked a third-grade education. Of the 21,838 delegates elected to local governments in 1967, 61 percent had less than a sixth-grade education; 58 percent were of worker and 26 percent of peasant background. And of 1,014 local government delegates elected in Matanzas in 1974, 20 percent lacked a sixth-grade education.[12] Both the party and managerial elites have been improving their educational level, as has the country (tables 5.12 and 8.2). While obviously the party and the bureaucracy have a higher level of education than the labor force as a whole, it is certainly not very much higher. They remain insufficiently trained to handle complex and subtle tasks, but they are at least representative of the people whose strengths and failings they reflect. Despite this, electoral procedures preserve elite political attitudes that are often in sharp contrast to the distribution of opinion among the rest of the population.

Between 1962 and 1963 the party underwent the restructuring already described, followed by a year of rapid growth. Then growth ceased again until early 1969, that is, during the period of ideological radicalization and estrangement from the Soviet Union that also saw the deinstitutionalization of mass organizations and the appearance of sectarianism in the Communist Youth Union, the chief feeder organization for the party. From 1962 through 1975, the number of party members over all and for each 1,000 people in the general population was as follows:[13]

	Number	Number/1,000 population
1962 (March)	15,061	2.1
1963 (March)	16,002	2.2
1964 (March)	32,537	4.3
1965	50,000	6.5
1969 (early)	55,000	6.6
1969 (late)	70,000	8.4
1970	101,017	11.8
1971	134,211	15.4
1972 (late)	153,000	17.3
1973 (late)	170,000	18.8
1974 (end)	186,995	20.3
1975 (September)	202,807	21.5

The major emphasis on party growth in the late 1960s was in the central ministries. The party was formally established and organized in the Ministries of Communications, the Food Industry, Public Health, Transportation, and Foreign Relations between April 11 and April 19, 1967; in the Ministry of Construction the following month; and in the University of Havana beginning in April 1967 and ending in the fall of 1969.[14] Given the feverish party building in the central ministries, most of the slight increase between 1965 and early 1969 can be accounted for by bureaucrats and university-trained personnel, probably at the expense of working-class strength in the party. By 1975, the year of the First Party Congress, just over 2 percent of the population belonged to the party.

The Communist Youth Union

The Communist Youth Union is the successor to the earlier Association of Rebel Youth (AJR), which had been a mass organization. It then became selective and was renamed. Membership in the Communist Youth Union and its predecessor for the years for which data are available are shown in the following list:[15]

1961	80,000
1962 (early)	100,000
1962 (March–April, first congress)	80,000
1963 (December)	18,306
1964 (May)	29,528
1967 (January)	105,360
1972 (April, second congress)	130,968
1974 (April)	212,168
1975 (April)	262,000
1975 (October)	325,262
1977 (March)	390,000

Although the size of the organization at the time of its first Congress in the spring of 1962 is unclear, two facts are plain. First, the process of reducing the membership began before the first congress; second, membership expulsion after the first congress was the most extreme of any Cuban organization. By the most conservative estimates, 74.6 percent of those who were members at the first congress in 1962 had been expelled by the end of 1963. Although there are gaps in the available membership statistics, membership rose in the late 1960s, compared with 1967, and fell again by 1972.[16]

The Communist Youth Union has been Cuba's most exclusive and sectarian organization. At the beginning, it was controlled by the youth wing of the prerevolutionary Communist Party; in the late 1960s its high standards for entry concentrated its work upon the elite youth, ignoring the masses of young people. Outside of its own membership, the union concentrated its efforts on the Centennial Youth Column, which was established in 1968. Young people would go to Camagüey, the province where labor shortages were most severe, to work for three years in the fields as an alternative to military service. The youth column disappeared in the summer of 1973, when its functions were taken over by a restructured organization within the armed forces called the Army of Working Youth. A total of 110,000 young people belonged to the column at some point, and 20,000 of these belonged to the Communist Party or to the Communist Youth Union.[17]

The union's second congress in 1972 criticized its excessive elitism and its small membership, attributing them to "the application of mechanical and extremist concepts in conferring militancy." Measures were taken to triple the union's membership by the third congress in 1977; separate mass organizations for primary, secondary, and university students were established in 1971. Nevertheless, complaints of excessive elitism were still being voiced. Only 9.2 percent of those elected exemplary youths were admitted to membership in the union in 1972; the proportion was still only 15.7 percent in 1975. The union was also elitist because it had very few agricultural or industrial blue-collar workers among its membership; instead, its new recruitment program primarily sought out students, who accounted for approximately 13 percent of the membership in 1972, a figure that rose to about 31 percent in 1977. Thus the union's efforts to combat one kind of elitism—excessively high standards producing few members—led to another kind of elitism, namely, the predominance of students over workers in the recruitment efforts of the early 1970s. The bulk of the union's membership apparently came from professionals, scientists, schoolteachers, and white-collar workers generally.[18]

The other major problem of the union was lack of autonomy. The secretary-general of the union in 1964 complained of "excessive paternalism" by the party, which he said was underestimating the capabilities of the union's leadership; the party was making all union activities subject to its approval.[19] In 1974, armed forces minister Raúl Castro remarked: "The Communist Youth

Union has two main tasks. First, to work under the leadership of the party
. . . on the communist education of the new generation . . . Secondly, to
prepare its members and cadres for entry into the party."[20] The scope of the
union was defined entirely in terms of the party's interests. Structural features
of the youth union also underscored its dependence on the party. At the seventh national conference of the Communist Youth Union, held in April 1974,
only 35.3 percent of the 521 "youth leaders" were delegates from the Communist Youth Union; all others were party members. Even at the union's third
congress in 1977, party members accounted for one-third of all the delegates.[21] No clear organizational boundary separated the party and the union.
After the poor performance and unreliability of the early members of the
union in the 1960s, the political demobilization of university students, and the
net membership decline from the late 1960s to the early 1970s, the party
placed it more firmly under its own control. Training the future generation of
decision makers in dependence, however, may eventually present new problems.

Functions of the Communist Party

What do party members actually do? Aníbal Escalante, shortly before his
disgrace in 1962, said the party was linked to the masses through its cells; in
this way it conveyed the decisions of the revolutionary leadership, organized
and mobilized the masses, and gathered their thoughts and complaints. It
increased productivity; it politicized and educated. In sum, it duplicated the
activities of every other organization. Nothing was said about the limitations of
party power or about the residual powers to be left to the mass organizations,
managers, or bureaucrats.

After the Escalante affair in 1962, however, the party was given strict orders
not to interfere in administration, and the tide turned too far the other way.
The party's authority was crippled. Administrators at both the local and the
national level placed party members in administrative positions under their
own supervision, regardless of rank. They reassigned good workers who were
party members, without regard to political considerations. The party had
begun as the instrument through which a bureaucrat could gain power; now,
the bureaucracy became the instrument through which the party could reas-
sert authority.

In February 1963 new powers over the mass organizations and the bureaucracy were given to the national directorate of the United Party of the Socialist
Revolution (as the party was then called). The provincial parties were given
comparable powers on a provincial level except that they could not alter a national decision that was to be implemented through the provincial bureaucracy. The party was to be coordinator and supervisor and controller; it was to
mobilize for activities to be carried out under its command by other organiza-

tions. The party would also direct propaganda and political education, for which it also relied heavily on mass and bureaucratic organizations. At the local level it was supposed to represent the interests of the community to the next highest level of power. Political criteria were introduced for promotion: no party member or leader of a mass organization could be transferred by a manager or bureaucrat without the approval of his political supervisors, and no party member could be promoted on merit without prior approval by his political supervisors. [22]

The reforms of 1963 were intended to curtail what the Prime Minister perceived as the excessive autonomy of the mass organizations. [23] The party's control over them began to be asserted in 1963. Criteria for promotion were set by the party. For a member to become a leader of a Committee for the Defense of the Revolution, the party required active participation in vigilance, savings campaigns, public-health activities, and the like and prompt payment of rent. For a woman to become a leader of the Cuban Women's Federation, the party required voluntary labor and defense work. For labor leaders, the party required voluntary work, labor-dues payment, no prerevolutionary labor-union leadership record, no criminal record, and no prerevolutionary military record. Candidates had to have fulfilled production and productivity goals, participated in defense activities, and tried to improve their skills. [24] Political criteria were applied in promotion decisions in all groups and included participation in politics and in the party. Organizations could not develop their own separate merit standards apart from those of the Communist party.

A great many leaders of mass organizations are not party members. In the election of delegates for the twelfth labor congress in 1966, most delegates were not party members, by orders from above. Many of these new union leaders had not become party members a year later. Only 5.3 percent of the local union leaders in 1975 were party members (table 8.3); only 7 percent of these were women. The proportion of women in the party has been small but steady: 13.2 percent in 1963, 12 percent in late 1972, 13 percent in late 1973, 12.8 percent in late 1974, and not quite 15 percent in 1975. In 1965 only 5 percent of the members of the party's Central Committee were women, and only 5.3 percent of the 112 full members elected to the Central Committee in 1975 (although five of the twelve alternates were women). In 1974 only 6 percent of all party officials were women. This percentage was regarded as unacceptably low; Fidel Castro reported to the First Party Congress that 17 percent of all party-cell leaders and 13 percent of all members of provincial party executive committees were women. The party's tasks of supervision and control are performed more easily when there is relatively little membership overlap. Although by 1974 a substantial proportion of the leaders of the women's federation were party members and the proportion of working women was rising, there was still little overlap among women leaders, union leaders, and party leaders. In contrast to what had already taken place and would happen again, between the party and the bureaucracy, there was relatively little confusion about who was boss in the party's relations with mass organizations. The Central Committee's department for mass organizations had a decisive hand in selecting their leadership.[25]

When something needed to be changed, either the party intervened itself, or it had the national office of the organization intervene in the local chapters. For example, the Matanzas branch of the Cuban Women's Federation complained about revolutionary policies in 1963. The national office of the federation and the national and provincial branches of the party went "delegation by delegation—house by house" to determine what the political problems were in the area. Summarily cutting off the local chapter, they designated secretaries for the local, regional, and provincial chapters of the women's federation. When local leaders, on behalf of rank-and-file members, opposed this intervention, they were simply replaced. In January 1965 the party and the national office of the Committees for the Defense of the Revolution descended upon the provincial committee in Pinar del Río and fired its leaders for recruiting too large a part of the population into its ranks and not sufficiently stressing competition with other provinces.[26] Mass organizations were expected to subordinate their goals to the party's goals; the party was to direct their work at all levels. They were supposed to serve as "conveyer belts" between the party and the masses and to mobilize the population to "fulfill the goals and tasks set by the party."[27] By the mid-1970s their survey and public-opinion-gathering functions were also being stressed.

Central control by mass organizations over their branches continued in the mid-1970s. The Committees for the Defense of the Revolution were auditing all municipal branches of the organization; these "integral visits" concentrated on municipal committees that were thought to be in difficulty. The Cuban Labor Confederation also established a system of regular visits to its subordinate organizations; by 1975, they had made 1,316 of them. Said CTC secretary-general Roberto Veiga, "The mere announcement of these 'control-and-support visits' . . . had an extraordinary impact on our endeavors." Veiga also noted that the visits were backed and directed by the party, which also provided its "help."[28]

Determining the relationship between party and bureaucracy is more of a problem because of the overlap in official functions. Article 5 of the 1976 Constitution stipulates that the party has authority over state and society,[29] but since the same individuals are bureaucrats and party members this presents difficulties in practice. The Political Bureau cannot really exercise control over the executive committee of the Council of Ministers because six of its thirteen members belong to both. All the members of the executive committee are members of the party's Central Committee, as are half of the regular members of the cabinet. Leaders frequently rotate among party, bureaucracy, and military.

Nor are the roles themselves clearly defined. The problems of defining the role of the party relative to the bureaucracy is illustrated in a remark made by Armando Hart, the party's national organization secretary in the 1960s and thus the person responsible for defining the party's role. Addressing the graduates of the political science department at Havana University in the fall of 1969, Hart noted that "politics, in its new context, is no more than that: how to organize production and social life in general, ensuring an ever more enthusiastic and an ever more effective participation of the masses, of the people, in that production and in that social life." Two and a half years earlier, when Hart was discussing party-state relations in the central ministries, he could argue that "conditions have been created not to link the party with the central State apparatus but rather so that the Communists who work in the central State apparatus and those who work in intermediate and leading party organisms will be guided by the same spirit, by the same program." In order to drive home the point that bureaucratic and party roles were inextricably mixed, Hart set forth the party policy on bureaucratic promotion. After the reforms of 1963 no party member or mass-organization leader could be shifted or promoted without fulfilling political criteria; by 1967, the same applied to bureaucrats. Hart noted that if bureaucrats were passed over for party membership, "this does not imply that they should be relieved of any of their responsibilities." This generous (and practical) criterion apparently applied only to the lower ranks, however; "there cannot be dual leadership in a central State organization. The maximum authority of the party, in each branch of the State apparatus, will be that of the Minister or President of the organism, who works under the direction of the party Central Committee and Political Bureau. In case this should turn out to be impossible, we will have to consider the demotion of the executive." Because the fusion of partisan and bureaucratic roles was so extensive, the party cell in a central ministry was not distinct from the administration. Bureaucratic and managerial leaders helped define the work of the party cell in their organizations, and the work of the cells had to be related to the work of the bureaucracy.[30]

Bureaucrats welcomed a definition of the party's role that ended its interference with the authority of managers to make decisions. "The cell," wrote Joel Domenech, minister of industries, in the fall of 1966, "has no authority of its own to set in motion policies that affect the country's development." But it should alert the administration if something is going wrong. "The party cell cannot, and should not, turn itself into the administration, nor replace the tasks that are assigned to the latter." Finally, "the party, at various levels, does not have the authority to paralyze production in a factory." On the other hand, the minister thoroughly welcomed the party's support in administration: "The cell should be aware that its role lies not only in attending to political, social, and labor problems that may exist in a factory, but also that one of its essential goals, one of the basic reasons for its existence, is the achievement of the highest degree of efficiency in all aspects of a factory's production." The minister then gave a long list of things the party cell should know about in order to perform this task.[31]

The party organization secretary and the minister of industries agreed that the party should be concerned with production. The minister emphasized limits to the party's authority and gave it a subordinate role. The secretary emphasized that if roles were properly coordinated the problem of who was subordinate to whom would not become an issue. He accepted the subordination of the cell to a political manager. The secretary also stressed the fact that the criteria for promotion were normally political, not bureaucratic. The net effect was a shift by the party toward emphasis on productive, economic, and bureaucratic concerns. The party lost its identity.

The party was restructured during 1973, after the establishment of the executive committee of the cabinet in December 1972. New regulations were issued on the proper relationship between party and bureaucracy. The party sets general policy in all spheres. State organizations must work within those policies "and must not resolve any important matter without taking them into account." Personnel appointment, promotion, and training are under strict party control. The party controls and audits administrative work, although it refrains from interfering in matters of administrative detail. Party members must follow and apply party decisions, regardless of other roles they may be performing, and must seek to convince those who are not party members of "the rightness of these decisions and of the necessity of obeying them."[32] The party rules because the leaders of the party and the state are the same. Nothing in the new regulations weakens the role of the party—it is simply to be freed from detail so that it can rule more effectively. It continues to have vast powers over administration and the setting of policy.

According to Raúl Castro, "it is necessary to remove from its jurisdiction all state and administrative tasks which the party has had to take over until now . . . The party does not administer . . . it must never meddle in the routine work" of the administration. "In every instance, the concrete administrative decisions with regard to the management and use of personnel and material resources for a given task fall to the administration, not the party."[33] The party remains the supreme political and ideological, but not administrative, authority. Once a manager is in place, the party is expected to grant him substantial independence of action. Acting national organization secretary Jesús Montané laid the groundwork for these changes in 1971 when he said, "The role of the party is to provide political leadership and guidance. It must mobilize the masses to carry out the instructions of the revolutionary high command. The party . . . cannot subordinate its personality. Its guidance and control will be of a basically political nature . . . It must maintain its structural and organizational independence."[34]

The application of these norms has not been so simple. If party and administration appear to be distinct entities to theorists, they remain confused in practice. Consider the remarks of Ramiro Valdés, head of the Construction Sector of the executive committee of the cabinet and member of the Political Bureau, in 1971: "Administration means state, and party means vanguard . . . In fact, the head of a sector directs the administrative and political organizations in construction." He criticized the "deficiencies and deformations" of the past but added: "although the head of a branch or of an organization in the sector, national and provincial, has absolute authority and responsibility over administrative activities in their organization, and though the party cannot interfere nor undercut this authority, it is equally true that the administrative head also has political responsibilities." For example, the administrator must continue to develop "those political and moral actions and conduct that made possible his appointment as representative of the interests of the working class in that post." When Valdés went on to itemize the operational duties of the party, the list was led by combatting absenteeism, increasing productivity, ensuring full utilization of the work day, seeing to the maintenance of machinery and equipment, and conserving energy and raw materials. Political responsibilities, such as recruitment, education, and articulating complaints from workers under incompetent administrations are much further down the list.[35]

Despite extensive discussion about the respective roles of party and bureaucracy, considerable confusion remains. It is caused in part by the same people's holding dual roles. But it is caused to a larger degree by the fact that roles are confused. Although high-ranking party and government officials disagree occasionally over role definitions ("intersender role conflict"), it is generally agreed that the party is to be concerned with production. The modifications of the 1970s have not changed that. But what are the field officers supposed to do? Are they to monitor? If something goes wrong and monitors report it, are they to be praised for accurate reporting, punished for bringing bad news, or, most likely, reprimanded for not having foreseen trouble and done something about it? Party officers have often turned into administrators to avert disaster since they can reasonably assume that a failure in production will be blamed not only on the manager but also on themselves. The result has been tension not only between the party and the administration but also between the local levels of both and their superiors in the party and the bureaucracy. So long as party members can be held responsible for production in fact, no matter what the paper rules say, the lines between party and bureaucracy will continue to be blurred ("intrasender role conflict"). Change will also require the depoliticization of promotion policies, so that bureaucratic merit alone would lead to advancement. That, however, would open up an avenue to power outside of the party. Nothing in the Cuba of the mid-1970s suggests that is a likely development.

The First Party Congress sought once again to clarify the relationship between party and administration, but to no avail. The congress affirmed that administrative leadership positions should go to the person "who most completely fulfills the criteria for the post, regardless of party membership." However, it also decided that the first criterion to be applied in the evaluation of candidates for such positions was "political quality and reliability," followed by managerial skills and specific knowledge of the task at hand. The congress also ruled that certain key positions in the administration, the mass organizations, and the Communist Youth Union had to be reserved for party members. Raúl Castro went further a few months later in asserting the party's authority over managers: "Only the party . . . can decide on the most rational way to reassign cadres and resources." The principal responsibility for assignments to leadership posts fell to the party's provincial executive committees, rather than to other organizations. [36]

A very different, though no less important, type of monitoring is carried out by higher party ranks over their subordinates. Reports from 1964, well after the 1962 party restructuring, illustrate what the ordinary tasks of supervision include. The provincial party in Havana, for instance, intervened in the operations of the regional party branch at San José de las Lajas, covering eight municipalities (districts including towns and countryside) because their work concerning production was judged to be inadequate. The provincial party officers had discussions with each cell and prepared a work program for them. This step was followed by partisan assemblies at the municipal level where internal functioning as well as relations with the bureaucracy and the mass organizations were criticized. Local party leaders were dismissed from their posts when they were found irredeemably incompetent. Municipal party officials, in turn, intervened at the cell level. The municipal parties in Ceiba del Agua and in Punta Brava, both in Havana province, decided that the local cells were nominating candidates of poor caliber for admission to the party, and they intervened in 1964. [37] There is no doubt that the higher party officials have full authority to admit or deny admission to new members. An even more common instance of intervention is, of course, the removal of individuals from party posts, which has occurred regularly even at such high levels as that of provincial party secretary-general.

The full sweep of power from higher authorities, which may have made many local party leaders fearful of making a mistake, coupled with confusion between administrative and partisan tasks, led to the paralysis of party leadership. Organization secretary Armando Hart complained in January of 1970, "some municipal and regional party cadres have either lost their capacity for leadership or simply lack the necessary capacity to find correct executive solutions without hesitation or delay to the problems posed minute by minute by the harvest . . . Responsibility for leading the struggle for greater productivity in the cutting, loading, and hauling of cane and for constantly improving the attendance records in the canefields rests mainly on the regional and municipal party secretaries and on the heads of the various productive forces." [38]

Internal Party Structure

The Communist party is led by a Political Bureau, which had eight members in 1965 and was expanded to thirteen in 1975; a Secretariat; and a Central Committee appointed in 1965 by the national directorate of its organizational predecessor, the United Party of the Socialist Revolution.[39] Prime Minister and later President Castro has also headed the Political Bureau and the Secretariat. The Central Committee originally had 100 members; it was expanded to 112 full members at the First Party Congress in December of 1975, when twelve alternate members were also added. The reasons stated for expanding the size of the Political Bureau were to bring in individuals of merit (Fidel Castro singled out his old friend Pedro Miret), and to include the secretaries-general of the three principal provinces; the second provision explains why Arnaldo Milián, least praised by Fidel Castro, joined along with Machado; Hart was already there. The degree of control of the membership of the Central Committee by the top elite was stated plainly by Fidel Castro: "You do not run for a post in the Central Committee. That is principle number one. It must be up to the party to decide . . . No one proposes himself." In 1965, the party had no statutes and no written program. Civic soldiers dominated the Central Committee at the expense of old Communists. During the first decade and a half of the party's existence, its structure and leadership were not confirmed by any congress. Legitimation flowed from the institutionalization of Fidel Castro's charisma, the "correct" behavior of party members, and performance. The party congress, it is arguable, is legitimated by the party and by Fidel Castro, and not the other way around.

The national party Secretariat was reorganized in early 1973, when four new members were added to it; a fifth was added by the end of the year. The expanded Secretariat prepared for the thirteenth labor congress in 1973, for the second congress of the Cuban Women's Federation and the reorganization of the provincial parties in 1974, and for the First Party Congress in 1975, when its membership was reduced to nine after three members were removed.[40] A tenth member, Machado, was added in 1976, and an eleventh, Milián, in 1977.

The actual preparations for the First Party Congress were in the hands of the central preparatory commission, composed of all members of the Political Bureau and Secretariat at the time (except for Faure Chomón). The commission not only had the responsibility of guiding and supervising the preparations, but it also had veto power over all documents that would be submitted to the congress or presented for popular discussion. These preparations emphasized the autonomy of the party elite and drastically reduced the significance of the congress as a decision-making body. The congress had considerable symbolic importance; it formalized party procedures, enhanced the prestige of the party in the international Communist movement, and provided a deadline for making important decisions. But the most important decisions had already been made by the commission. Party statutes were drafted in 1974 and approved by the Political Bureau in early 1975, pending ratification by the congress, and were discussed by party members along with other documents ("theses") in preparation for the congress. The drafting commissions had received suggestions from all sources, but they retained the final decision regarding the text of all documents, subject to the approval of the central commission.

Preparations for the First Party Congress got under way in April 1975. Assemblies were held at all levels to evaluate party work and to elect, or reelect, leaders and delegates to the central party organizations. The electoral procedures for the First Party Congress were unrepresentative as usual. Municipal, sectional, and regional assemblies elected "pre-candidates" for delegate elections to the Congress by secret ballot. The same individual could be elected a precandidate from any number of places; Fidel and Raúl Castro apparently led the list, which also included nominees for Central Committee membership. The elections were mere formalities; it was the process of getting on the ballot, which the leadership controlled, that was crucial. In the Oriente provincial assembly, *Granma* reported, the "607 comrades proposed as delegates to the first congress all received 100 percent of the votes cast." However, the actual election of delegates rested with the six provincial party assemblies, the regional party assembly of the Isle of Pines, and the party conferences in the armed forces (including those under the Ministry of the Interior). Moreover, the preparatory commission identified important "selected work centers" that had the right to elect delegates directly to the congress. In Oriente, delegates elected directly at work centers accounted for only about 12 percent of that province's total delegation to the congress. [41] Members of local cells therefore could not elect whomever they wanted either to the congress or on a municipal or regional level. There was no assurance that the delegates to the congress would in any way reflect their constituents' views. The central party organizations controlled delegate selection, favored the elite, and had full power over the formulation of documents and whether and how they would be presented.

The congress itself was a happy affair, though uneventful since the important policy decisions had been made in advance. It took on the character of a reunion of the revolutionary family celebrating their long years in power; [42] 69 percent were veterans who fought in the 1950s against the Batista government. A third of the delegates were veterans of Playa Girón (the Bay of Pigs invasion). Although three-quarters of the party membership had belonged to the party for ten years or less, 44 percent of the delegates had belonged to the party for more than ten years. Although half of the party membership had belonged to the party for less than five years, only 10 percent of the delegates fell in that category. One out of every twelve had done their "internationalist duty," that is, had served overseas supporting a guerrilla movement or a friendly government. Forty-six percent were members of the upper-level political and administrative elite; 19 percent were military. The congress was as unrepresentative of the party rank and file as the congresses of the mass organizations, and for the same reason: rigged elections. Because any possible disagreement had been settled beforehand, Fidel Castro reported that "practically all the decisions were unanimously adopted, except that one word was misused, and a comrade correctly pointed out that it was misused. This was the democratic procedure used for discussing all the resolutions." Indeed. Among the documents receiving unanimous approval were Fidel Castro's so-called central report, the party's statutes and programmatic platform, the draft constitution, the proposed national administrative reorganization, and statements on science policy and on local government.[43]

The one instance where divisiveness may have cropped up in the congress had little to do with policy; it involved determining the membership of the Central Committee. But if there were disputes, they were probably limited to a few names. Fidel Castro could note the "practically unanimous way in which the leaders of the Central Committee have been elected," adding that "we are by no means criticizing those comrades who stated their opinions freely."[44]

In 1962 the national directorate of the United Party of the Socialist Revolution had a six-man secretariat, with three commissions, one each for organization, labor affairs, and the press. In 1965 the Central Committee of the Communist party had, in addition to the Political Bureau and Secretariat, standing commissions for the armed forces and internal security, the economy, education, foreign relations, and constitutional studies. A labor commission was added later. In the party restructuring of 1972 and 1973, still other commissions were formed. Replacing one economic department are departments for various industries, for agiculture, for construction, and for other economic enterprises; there are departments to supervise and control all mass organizations and the courts. The department for revolutionary orientation has similarly specialized and now includes a department for "scientific atheism"; there are departments for internal party affairs, including education, schools, publications, and organizations. All testify to the party's increasing internal differentiation. After 1973, the Secretariat began to meet every week, and the Political Bureau twice a month. Reporting procedures had been routinized by the mid-1970s, even before the convening of the congress.[45] One odd feature of party organization that was maintained was the posting of delegates from the Political Bureau to specific areas—Guillermo García and Juan Almeida, for instance, have both served as delegates in Oriente province, where they outrank the provincial party secretary-general. In the mid-1970s, Oriente had Almeida as delegate and another Political Bureau member, Armando Hart, as secretary-general. Comandante Luis Zayas was the Political Bureau's delegate to the Holguín region of Oriente in the early 1970s. When Miguel Martín was dismissed as head of the Labor Confederation in 1968, he was sent as delegate from the Political Bureau to the Ciego de Ávila-Jatibonico region in Camagüey, although this was admittedly not a promotion.

Boundaries within the party are somewhat fluid, so that low-ranking officials often are asked to participate in making decisions at higher levels. This lack of definition of organizational boundaries not only mitigates the problem of extreme organizational and personal dependence on the top but also introduces broader participation in making decisions. During the political and labor crisis after the 1970 harvest, meetings included members of the Political Bureau, the first secretaries and organization secretaries of the provincial parties, the national leaders of the mass organizations, the top officers of the armed forces and of the Ministry of the Interior, and a few others. When Prime Minister Castro returned from the Soviet Union in mid-1972, he reported at a three-day meeting of the Central Committee and then to another two-day meeting attended by 4,300 people from the central ministries, mass organizations, and armed forces and Interior Ministry, establishing a boundary between the two groups. After another trip to the Soviet Union, Angola, and other countries in 1977, he reported to a similarly constituted gathering of 4,790 people. At the end of 1973 meetings on the 1974 plan for the economy included the party's Political Bureau and Secretariat, the executive committee of the cabinet, ministers, heads of mass organizations, and the first secretaries of provincial organizations.[46]

These meetings represented the level just below the top eighteen. The Central Committee of the party alone does not actually constitute the elite; the elite is far more heterogeneous. Virtually all the Central Committee members attended the meetings, and almost all the people who attended the more selective meetings were Central Committee members, but it was not by virtue of their Central Committee membership that they sat there, but because of other titles they hold. The Central Committee itself has not been a very active organization; its functions are symbolic—to ratify what others have decided. Unlike the Political Bureau and the Secretariat before 1975, the Central Committee had not met regularly. It is independent neither from its superiors nor from its subordinates.

After the new Central Committee was elected in 1975, there were indications that it might meet more regularly. A meeting was held in connection with the congress; the committee has since met approximately once every six months. The committee has listened to reports by Fidel Castro on Angola and foreign affairs, to reports on party discipline and admissions and on the conduct of internal affairs in the preceding six months, and to reports on personnel changes and on implementing the new Constitution and reorganizing provinces and municipalities. Decisions are normally approved "unanimously." Before 1975, it had met almost exclusively to consider foreign relations and had discussed the implications of Che Guevara's death in Bolivia in 1967, Venezuelan charges against Cuba before the Organization of American

States in 1967, and the crisis in Cuban-Soviet relations in 1968. The Central Committee also formally conducted the expulsion of the microfaction from its own and the party's ranks in 1968. There is no evidence that it met at all between 1968 and 1972. Fidel Castro acknowledged as much in 1975 when he said that "for years the party's activities had been conducted by the Secretariat for organization. The Political Bureau functioned as the party's highest authority, but in practice the Central Committee did not exercise its functions." [47]

The party had been organized in provincial, regional, sectional, or municipal branches and in local cells; sectional branches existed for such national organizations as the armed forces in order to provide supervision of local cells comparable to that ordinarily provided by the municipal party branches. The party became more bureaucratically complicated as it was reorganized and as its membership grew in the early 1970s, especially at the lower levels. While the number of provincial party branches remained steady at six and the number of regional branches decreased only by one, from sixty to fifty-nine, between 1972 and 1973, municipal and sectional branches increased from 401 in 1972 to 416 in 1973; local cells, from 14,360 to 16,000. [48] After 1976, the party has conformed to a new administrative structure of provinces and municipalities that eliminates the regional level altogether.

Two long-standing features of party procedures concerning individual members have been identification cards and party dues. Members have carried identification cards since the fall of 1962; these register their complete party history, including their employment records in summary form. A schedule of party dues, linked to income, was established in August 1962. Members whose net earnings were less than 200 pesos a month contributed 1 percent of their net income; for those who earned over 500 pesos, it rose to 4 percent. The 1975 party statutes retained these requirements. [49]

The provincial party reorganization of 1974 revealed stability in party ranks coupled with a well-developed oligarchical structure. There was little competition in elections at the provincial level. The Oriente provincial party committee had sixty-one members and six alternates elected among seventy-seven candidates, or 1.1 candidates per post. Most of the incumbents were reelected, although how many cannot be identified precisely. The provincial assemblies, which elected leaders from such a limited group, included delegates from the municipal assemblies, the members of the regional committees, and delegates sent by the provincial party organizations in the armed forces and Ministry of the Interior. All elections at the cell level took place in assemblies by show of hands. At the municipal, regional, and provincial levels, elections were by secret ballot. At each level the immediately superior party organization had veto power over the list of nominees. From the very beginning the regional party ordinarily proposed the nominees for election for leadership at the sectional or municipal level; the provincial party ordinarily proposed the nominees for election at the regional level. Perhaps the most impressive feature of this system, as national secretary Pérez Herrero noted, was that in the process evaluations had been made of every party member.[50]

In anticipation of the congress, the 1975 party elections were an impressive mixture of continuity and change. In the cell elections, 35 percent of the officers were replaced; more than half of those elected to membership on municipal, regional, or provincial party committees had not previously been members.[51] Control and auditing committees have been established at the national and provincial levels and are responsible for party discipline, including dealing with ideological, political, social, and economic infractions. They can impose sanctions at all levels below their own; receive and judge appeals concerning sanctions imposed by lower-level party officers; and audit the organizational and financial work of the party as well.[52]

The party in the Ministries of the Armed Forces and of the Interior has a separate, more independent organization, directly under Fidel Castro and the Central Committee, though it may feed into party assemblies and administration. The organization of the party in the interior was dependent on the Havana provincial party, at least in the early stages. The party sent organizers from Havana into the interior, rather than using local talent. This guaranteed standardization, though at the cost of the excessive subservience to the center that would paralyze the party by the late 1960s.[53]

The dominance of the elite within the party, the control of elections, and interference in subordinate party units combine to emphasize the centralizing aspects of "democratic centralism." Widespread discussion is invariably followed by support of the government's views. The mass organizations are dependent on the party, lower units within any organization are dependent on their superiors, and the party in the provinces is subject to the Central Committee; everyone is subject to the party's Political Bureau and Secretariat, and they, finally, are subordinate to Fidel Castro. Control is so overwhelming that it is difficult to conceive how free discussion could possibly take place. Whatever free discussion there may once have been came to a halt after the microfaction was uncovered, expelled, and imprisoned in early 1968. The microfaction had not been charged with trying to overthrow the revolutionary system but simply with dissenting from within over specific leaders and policies. The scope of legitimate dissent within the party was so sharply restricted that very little took place until the failure of the 1970 harvest. Even in the mid-1970s, limits still prevail, although the chilling effect of the microfaction incident has waned. The "democratic" aspects of "democratic centralism" in Cuba may under clearly defined conditions allow limited criticism by an individual party member, but they do not allow factional organization and dissent as legitimate activities within the party, although factionalism no doubt exists. The revolutionary elite was at its most homogeneous shortly after the microfaction incident, when members of the Twenty-sixth of July Movement and, especially, civic soldiers predominated in the upper ranks of both party and government. The prohibition against factions within the party was made specific in the 1975 party statutes. Procedures to remove officials who have lost the confidence of their superiors were also approved by the First Party Congress.[54]

Party Schools

The growth of the Communist party was at first hindered by Prime Minister Castro's bias against professional cadres. An important element of the 1963 party reform had been "having the smallest number of professional leaders necessary for the work of the party and of the mass organizations."[55]

This bias, in the long run, had its most devastating effect on the Schools for Revolutionary Instruction. Set up in December 1960 to combat the purely practical orientation of much of the revolutionary leadership and to increase their skills, these schools gradually gained a good deal of autonomy both within the party and outside it. Up to June 1962 the schools had relatively little control over the assignment of their teaching and administrative personnel, and other party or state offices raided their staffs. After June 1962 the central office of the schools was given more authority, although this change did not ensure the schools against raids. Even in late 1964 other party and state offices were still taking over both the staff and the student body.[56]

The schools proved to be adaptable; their reaction to the Prime Minister's antitheoretical bias was to increase the economic, technical, and practical content of the curriculum. This compromise somewhat undermined their original purpose, which was to educate "Marxist-Leninists in a revolution going Marxist with neither a party to supply the cadres nor a rich indigenous Marxist tradition to draw on." This role was weakened as the schools turned vocational; when science and research seemed the way to the future, the schools began to sponsor them, but to no avail. The entire system was phased out in the fall of 1967. Booklearning was too sterile for the revolution; the books also came by and large from the Soviet Union at a time when Soviet ideological and political perspectives were in disfavor; finally, the staffing problems could not be solved.[57] The disappearance of the schools was very much in line with the general deinstitutionalization of the late 1960s: the party grew more slowly than it had before or since, its role remained confused, many of the mass organizations were crippled, and contact with the population was lost. All autonomous organizations suffered; the schools were totally wiped out.

The party schools were revived, however, in the 1970s. In the interim, the need to train a politically competent elite had become more obvious. In 1975 the "superior" track at the party's national school lasted for four and a half years (expanded from two and a half in 1974); the basic course lasted for a year and a half. The student body is composed of party officials from the national, provincial, and sometimes lower levels, members of the Communist Youth Union, and leaders of the mass organizations. They study philosophy, political economy, social psychology, and management. From 1960 to 1975, 1,537 students graduated from the national party school; another 3,294 were exposed to courses of at least one month's duration. Its enrollment in 1975 was 582 students. It also offers specialized courses and a program to train teachers of Marxism-Leninism.

Throughout 1974 the provincial schools taught basic educational skills, but they later switched to political and ideological training; the basic courses were eliminated altogether in 1976. Two educational tracks have been developed for specialization in economics or politics and ideology. Courses last a year and are attended by municipal leaders, along with leaders of the youth union and the mass organizations. Other schools teach party members down to the grass-roots level; courses last five or six months and are geared to various levels of specialization. Although Communist Youth Union and mass-organization leaders are eligible to attend party schools at all levels, they also have their own schools. No firm boundary exists between party and nonparty students; in 1975 there were thirty-seven party and mass-organization schools with a combined enrollment of 6,144 students.[58]

The Party's Claim to Rule

What is the basis of the party's claim to rule? Armando Hart answered eloquently for the mid-1970s. The party's authority, he writes,

is based on the party's own history; on the fact that it always marches at the vanguard; on its knowledge and interpretation, in the face of any situation, of the ideology and the interests of the proletariat; and on its accurate decisions in relation to diverse problems. It is also founded on the labor, political and historic prestige of party members. Party members have great authority not because they carry out this or that function but because of the example they set by their revolutionary conduct.[59]

Party members become like Castro. They rule not just because they perform a task well but because of their moral qualities. Correct behavior as a claim for legitimacy entails satisfactory performance combined with high moral quality or the emulation of the virtues of one man in delivering the country. The people are also expected to support the party because its members are not very different demographically from the ordinary Cuban, even though the party is selective, for only elitism in political recruitment can guarantee high quality of membership. The chief claims to legitimate rule in Cuba derive not from election but from the quality of the rulers and the way they rule.

The transfer of the right to rule from the charismatic leader to the potentially charismatic organization began in the aftermath of the 1962 party expulsion and expansion. It did not get very far during the 1960s, because the party did not grow, the roles of its members were ill defined, and the centralization of power was too great. By the mid-1970s, however, everyone—including Castro himself—was seeking to remedy these faults. Among the phrases used by the Prime Minister to characterize the role of the party before the First Party Congress were: "The party is the synthesis of everything . . . within it, our individual selves disappear, and we learn to think in terms of the collective; it is our educator, our teacher, our leader, and our vigilant conscience." "The party today is the soul of the Cuban revolution . . . Special emphasis [is to be placed] on exemplary behavior, moral and political quality, authority, and prestige before the masses of the men and women of its leading vanguard." "The purity of our party has been proved in the ideas and conduct of its members. And we want to combine these things: purity, honesty, a spirit of criticism, and freedom of opinion."[60] Although reality may fall short of these ideals, they are the basis of the government's claims to legitimate rule in the late 1970s.

A basic characteristic of the exercise of power in Cuba is the high degree of autonomy granted to top-ranking leaders and organizations, relative both to those below them and to economic and social pressures. Conversely, groups and organizations outside the government or in its lower echelons have little independence from political leaders. The result has been a high degree of political centralization and, for the first time in Cuban history, a single-track political system.

A number of political changes are evident in the Cuban government—and thus in the structure and functions of the party—as it enters the late 1970s. Perhaps most important, Fidel Castro has delegated considerable power to about eighteen leaders of the political elite, thus moving the government away from the absolute predominance of a single individual toward a more oligarchical rule. While Castro's primacy has not been questioned and he could probably still get his way in virtually any area—particularly because the Constitution of 1976 enshrined his political power—the political costs of doing so, both within Cuba and internationally, have increased considerably.

At the same time, the leading role of the Communist party, subordinate to the ruling leaders but with authority over the government, the society, and the economy, has been asserted with increasing emphasis and is backed up by the provisions of the new Constitution. Its leading role is perhaps clearest in its supervision of mass organizations. The lines of authority between party and bureaucracy, on the other hand, have always been blurred, even though the Cuban leadership attempted in the early 1970s to clarify these boundaries. Party structures—like those of the state, the courts, and the mass organizations—have been stabilized and formalized. Considerable tension continues to exist, however, between norms and actual practice; it arises principally between party and bureaucracy in the implementation of policy. This tension may prevent or undermine the evolution of stability in organizations and procedures.

While the party leadership has retained considerable autonomy from the rank and file, the members are still dependent on the leaders. "Centralism" clearly remains more important than "democracy" in the Cuban practice of democratic centralism. Similarly, the party continues to control the mass organizations. Whenever mass organizations or economic enterprises have sought to set goals, make policy, or undertake tasks on their own, their wings have been clipped. In the mid-1970s, nevertheless, these organizations began to engage in lobbying and, though not autonomous, were not without influence on government policy.

Increasingly, the party's role has been defined as governing, not as implementing specific policy. In the process, its autonomy from social and economic pressures has not declined but rather increased. Its membership, however, has been demographically representative of the population. In part because of its very representativeness, it has reflected a low educational level. Even though the party has not been significantly represented in most Cuban work centers, except for those in politically sensitive sectors, a substantial number of party members have from the beginning had working-class or peasant backgrounds. After selection as members, however, many workers are shifted to political or administrative posts, so the number of party members who are employed in production is much lower than the number of those of working-class origin.

Like mass and bureaucratic organizations, party structures have shown a far greater degree of internal differentiation and complexity in the mid-1970s than in the previous decade. For the most part, their stability has also increased, with the notable exception of the Communist Youth Union. The general adaptive capability of the political system has increased correspondingly. Mass organizations, above all the Committees for the Defense of the Revolution but also the Cuban Women's Federation, have reasonably stable procedures for shifting from old to new tasks; but the Communist Youth Union performed abysmally in the late 1960s: as a result it has been stripped of many of its responsibilities by the party and its extreme sectarianism led to a net decline in membership at that time.

During the 1970s the party's concern with ideological coherence has increased; this trend is evident in the continuing stress on education, including political education. The reappearance of the party schools, disbanded in the late 1960s, underscores the new ideological seriousness of the leaders. Their return to orthodoxy has defused the radicalism of the late 1960s, with its emphasis on moral incentives, its desire to build the new society almost overnight, and its love of grandiose projects.

Finally, legitimacy has come to rest not only on Castro's personal charisma, nationalism, and distributional performance—aided, at long last, by economic growth in the 1970s—but also in part on the legal system and elections. Charisma has been formalized, coming to rest in a collective leadership and more generally in the party as a whole. The Communist party has claimed the right to rule because its members behave correctly, because they are the most devoted revolutionaries among the citizens, and because their decisions have led to improved performance. Elections are perceived as a means of identifying the best revolutionaries, not of representing the people's opinions. The party and the elites in the political, mass, and bureaucratic organizations, however demographically representative, are manifestly unrepresentative politically.

Cuba entered the second half of the 1970s dependent on the Soviet Union but not pluralized by it. For the first time since the revolution it experienced economic growth and improved its terms of trade; as it retreated from the radicalism of the late 1960s, it became more pragmatic but also less attractive to those who had hoped the revolutionary elite would shoot for the stars in the late 1970s, just as they had done in the late 1950s. Authoritarian rule by an aging elite of white males was being institutionalized through the Communist party. The party decided; the bureaucracy implemented. Material prosperity was finally becoming available to many ordinary Cubans. Political autonomy continued to be rare; political competition remained quite limited, since opposition to prevailing policies and ideology was still impossible. But the government, led by the party, did govern. The future had finally arrived. It was dull red, but it worked.

9

THE CIVIC SOLDIER

Two major patterns of civilian control over the military can be identified. Samuel P. Huntington calls one "subjective" civilian control;[1] it ensures control over the military by increasing the authority of a governmental institution such as a parliament, of a social class such as the bourgeoisie, or of a political party such as the Communist party, over military institutions. The other, which Huntington calls "objective" civilian control, emphasizes a professional army, separate from politics, in command of military expertise and responsibility, and corporately autonomous.

Civilian control is far from being worldwide. Among economically underdeveloped countries, particularly new states with relatively weak political institutions, military control over civilian institutions is common. This control assumes two different forms.[2] One, the military acting as arbitrator, has no independent political organization or ideology; it is often content merely to supervise the leading civilian officials. When the army does take over directly, it often does so for a stated and limited period, handing the government back as soon as "acceptable" civilians are found to lead it. This variety of controlling military finds nothing wrong with the social and economic status quo and prefers a civilian government. The military acting as ruler, in contrast, has little confidence in civilian rule, rejects the existing social order, and expects to stay in power, to construct its own ideology, and perhaps develop a political organization to support its regime.

All these characterizations, and others like them,[3] are based on the assumption that there is always a firm distinction between civilians and military, that the two are at least potentially in conflict, that civilians are always capable of governing, and that military activity can be so strictly defined that taking over governments or performing normally civilian functions can readily be identified and analyzed as "unmilitary." Thus arise such terms as a "praetorian" polity, a "militarized" society, or a "politicized" army.

The facts in revolutionary Cuba contradict this dichotomy. Cuba has been ruled in large part by military men who govern large segments of both military and civilian life, who are held up as paragons to both soldiers and civilians, who are the bearers of the revolutionary tradition and ideology, who have politicized themselves by absorbing the norms and organization of the Communist party, and who have educated themselves to become professional in political, economic, managerial, engineering, and educational as well as military affairs. Their civilian and their military lives are fused. In this situation, at least until recently, one could not speak of either civilian control over the military or military control over civilians. But in the mid-1970s some new trends have appeared that may herald yet another change in the future.

The "civic soldier" has been a key political role in Cuba for a long time. Approximately two-thirds of the high-ranking officials have had civic-soldier careers; most of them learned this role during the uprising against Batista in the 1950s and the suppression of the anti-Communists in the early 1960s. Civil war, more than any other form of conflict, tends to integrate military and political roles. Civic soldiers head both military and civilian agencies in Cuba and, just as military agencies have had civilian tasks, civilian agencies have had military tasks and have used military forms of organization. The civic-soldier role includes not only former soldiers heading government organizations but also soldiers on active duty engaged in political, economic, or other nonmilitary activities.

Roles are defined in part by the expectations of others. When the characteristics of a role are defined by superiors and acknowledged by subordinates, the result is what some sociologists call the "sent role." The sent role of the civic soldier has included both military and civilian aspects. Thus a military commander's sent role includes nonmilitary duties, just as the sent roles of the minister of education or of a sugar-harvest administrator have included military duties. A renewal of specialization in the armed forces after 1973 reduced somewhat the fusion of civilian and military roles, but the armed forces have continued to perform at least some civilian functions.

This coexistence of military and civilian aspects of the civic-soldier role has implications for political conflict. There is relatively little evidence that any conflict that does occur takes place between civilians and military. When conflicts arise, civic soldiers are just as likely to split among themselves as the purely civilian minority. Nor have there been issues from which civic soldiers have stood aloof; they are involved in all public-policy issue areas. When the defense budget is debated, for example, civic soldiers are found on both sides of many issues; thus even on military subjects civic soldiers' opinions can divide, although no doubt pressures on their organizational loyalties are more difficult to reconcile than those felt by civilians.

Individuals whose roles have been defined by their superiors to include civilian and military aspects may experience objective role conflict, of which there are two kinds. "Intersender" conflict occurs when different superiors who share authority over a subordinate define the latter's role in different ways. Should the officer in charge of a motorized brigade, for example, emphasize training for combat or for a mechanized harvest? This officer is receiving different role definitions from the army and from sugar-harvest authorities. Another type of role conflict, called "intrasender" conflict, occurs when one superior defines different roles for the same subordinate. For example, the party prescribes that resources be committed both to defense and to industrial investments: how is a middle-ranking official to decide when to divert resources from one activity to the other?[4]

The leaders in the 1960s addressed themselves to the problem of conflicting expectations by trying to avoid extreme specialization within and between organizations and by relying on long-standing friendships from the guerrilla-warfare days. The Ministry of the Armed Forces demanded both economic and military performance but neglected to lay down rules for apportioning time. The problem led in 1973 to a reorganization of the armed forces that required greater specialization within the military. While the armed forces as a whole continued to perform both military and economic functions, specific units were assigned to one or the other. The military tasks of civilian agencies, however, increased in the early 1970s. The Ministry of Education and the Ministry of Light Industry still required their staffs to teach, produce, and prepare for war in schools and factories. Military specialization had different consequences for military personnel and civilians. Within the armed forces, specialization simplified the definitions of the roles of most military commanders and their subordinates. Superiors mandated either military or nonmilitary roles most of the time; because the same superior was no longer defining roles in quite different ways, intrasender role conflict declined. Within the civilian agencies, most plant managers, school principals, workers, and students continued to suffer from intrasender role conflict. These civilian agencies continued to receive role definitions from the party and government leadership that included both civilian and military aspects; subordinates had to perform many different, often conflicting tasks.

The increase in the military content of civilian organizations brought many more civilians under the partial authority of the Armed Forces Ministry, a change that also increased role conflicts. Individuals were faced more directly with conflict among different superiors—some emphasizing civilian and some military activities and together creating a serious intersender conflict. But the specialization of some military units exclusively on military tasks eliminated intersender role conflict for them, since no civilian agency defined a role for them in conflict with the armed forces ministry. The military units engaged in production still had to coordinate their work closely with civilian agencies, and thus intersender role conflict could still result. The 1973 reforms may have succeeded in reducing role conflicts only within the armed forces units specializing in military tasks.

Because the civilian and military aspects of the civic-soldier role are regarded as equally legitimate, organizations are flexible. The defense budget is not cut when threats to the state decline; rather, it is simply directed to the nondefense aspects of the civic-soldier role. Military elements were stressed again after the intervention in Angola. Since loyalty to the organization will often lead to changes in emphasis for the sake of its survival or growth, the legitimacy of the civic-soldier role has facilitated these shifts.[5]

Cuban civilian-military relations fall into three distinct periods. The first, from qualified independence in 1902 until the revolution that overthrew Machado in 1933, was one of subjective civilian control. The military often served as a presidential political machine, ensuring the victory of the President's party at the polls in return for participation in a system of widespread and institutionalized graft. The military also put down the insurrections that often followed elections; these uprisings were usually minor and designed to provoke United States interference to annul the election results. No military coups were attempted during this period.[6]

The armed forces acted as arbitrators from 1933 until the overthrow of Batista in 1958. There were two successful military coups, in September 1933 and March 1952, but no sustained military rule. Instead the military placed its chosen civilians in power, among them a thoroughly civilianized Senator Batista in 1952. In 1936 the military forced the Congress to impeach the President and replace him with the Vice President. From 1933 to 1940 effective political power was held by the commander-in-chief of the army, Colonel Fulgencio Batista, who often removed civilian Presidents. But a military officer on active duty never served as President of the republic. Military coups were attempted after 1940, but they all failed.

Batista relied on the existing political parties and borrowed their ideas both in 1933–1944 and in 1952–1958. Although he eventually developed a political organization, it was not a military one, but one of his own devising. As army chief in the 1930s, Batista toyed with corporatist political ideology but soon abandoned it. He expanded the role of the military into civilian areas, especially in education and public health, but he kept the military out of the economy. He emphasized a more effective distribution of such resources as education and public health that did not require directly taking from some to give to others. In early primary education and public health, the military supplanted civilians, but it brought to these tasks no skills that could not just as well have been provided by civilians. A technically or managerially competent military that stressed development was not the result, for the military was simply being used as "cheap labor."[7]

In the 1940s nonmilitary army activities were sharply restricted, as many educational and health functions were transferred to civilian agencies. When the Batista government sought in the 1950s to repress the opposition, they did not militarize the social system; the president chose to risk defeat rather than disrupt the economy. He deployed troops to protect private enterprises and to guarantee production, rather than to ensure the success of a military offensive. At the end of the Batista regime, therefore, the scope of military activities had been much restricted, the influence of the military on national life was limited, and attitudes toward the armed forces had become very negative.

During the third period, from 1959 until the present, the rule of Castro's government has fit none of the usual categories. While one can identify a ruling elite and some purely civilian leaders, it is not so easy to identify purely military ones. The vast majority of Cuba's ruling elite have held military rank, and no identifiable purely civilian elite has been available to take their place. There is little evidence of civilian-military conflict, not only because the purely civilian share of the elite is small, but also because the military's decisive political role is great, and the scope of its legitimate activity has never been clearly defined.

The Military Mission of the Armed Forces

The military mission of the Cuban armed forces was originally to provide for national defense and to suppress internal challenges to the authority of the government. More recently Cuba's participation in the Angolan civil war has added a third task—overseas combat. Since 1960 the Soviet nuclear shield has been one factor deterring a United States attack on Cuba, somewhat shakily in 1960 and more firmly after 1970. The Cuban armed forces, however, are responsible for their own subnuclear defense. Its major challenge thus far has been the Bay of Pigs invasion in April 1961. Since then, though with declining frequency, various exile groups have launched hit-and-run attacks on the island or have landed small parties, but they have all been quickly captured.

Cuba faced insurrections off and on, from December 1956 through 1965. Since then, episodes of internal resistance have been few and rapidly suppressed. From December 1956 to January 1959 Batista's government forces fought against Castro and his allies. During the second half of 1960 insurgents rose against Castro's government, particularly in the Escambray mountains of Las Villas province in central Cuba, an episode soon followed by the Bay of Pigs. In addition to that invasion, there were thirty-four infiltrations from abroad in 1960–1961. The Bay of Pigs and the abortive Escambray uprising discouraged insurrections briefly, but they resumed in 1962, when from March to September the number of bands in the Escambray rose from forty-two to seventy-nine. By July the government had created a special corps to fight the "bandits": the Lucha Contra Bandidos, or LCB. Although the LCB units undoubtedly fought some genuine bandits, their clear targets were counterrevolutionaries.[8]

From 1960 to 1965 counterrevolutionaries rose up against the Castro government in all six provinces. At one time the country had as many as 179 insurrectionary bands. The revolutionary government estimated the number of armed oppositionists killed or captured at 3,591; about 500 combat deaths in the LCB forces were reported, apart from deaths from other military actions and terrorism, along with losses of 1,000 million pesos from all three. Antigovernment forces numbered no more than a thousand at their peak strength. The total number of deaths in the 1960s was in the same range—roughly 2,000–2,500—as in the 1950s. The number of regular troops committed by the Cuban government to defending the regime against insurrection was ten times greater under Castro than it had been under Batista; the reserve forces under Castro were ten to fifteen times greater than under Batista; the amount of actual fighting was probably the same. The difference was that Batista's government lost and Castro's won. Revolutionary government in Cuba could not have survived without effective armed forces.[9]

Military expenditures were greatest in prerevolutionary Cuba through 1940, when the Batista forces were active outside of their strictly military responsibilities; such burdens reached their ebb just before Batista staged his coup in March 1952. Among the first measures after the takeover were pay raises for the military. Although the military budget grew during the Batista regime, its proportion of national income remained constant because the economy was growing as well. Even in 1958, when it was threatened with widespread insurrection, the Batista government was still committing only a small proportion of national income to arms; the share Castro has allocated to the military is at least two or three times larger (table 9.1). Castro has noted that at their peak in the early 1960s Cuban military expenditures totaled "close to" 500 million pesos. Thus the statistics in table 9.1 seriously underestimate actual military expenditures. All available data, however, point to a decline in the proportion of national income devoted to military expenditure after the early 1960s, as counterrevolutionary activity declined and the economy recovered from its near-collapse of 1962–63. This decline was interrupted in 1968; military expenditure then remained at a constant, high level as a result of the expansion of the military into the economic sphere. In addition to Cuba's own resources, the Soviet Union, according to Castro himself, supplied Cuba free of charge with weapons worth several thousand million pesos between 1960 and 1975.[10]

Size and Structure

Cuba's regular armed forces grew from 24,797 when Batista took over in 1952 to 29,270 on the day he fell from power in 1958. In addition, Batista had

Table 9.1 Military expenditures, 1940–1974

Year	Total expenditures (in millions of current pesos)	(in millions of current dollars)	Expenditures (computed from current prices) % of GNP[a]	% of GMP[b]
1940	19	—	4.5	—
1949–50	40	—	2.6	—
1951–52	42	—	2.2	—
1958	50	—	2.3	—
1961	—	175	7.6	—
1962	—	200	8.0	—
1963	213	213	5.6	—
1964	223	221	5.2	5.3
1965	214	213	4.4	5.1
1966	—	213	4.5	5.3
1967	—	250	4.8	6.1
1968	—	300	5.8	6.9
1969	—	250	4.5	6.0
1970	—	290	5.1	—
1971	—	290	5.2	—
1972	365	319	5.1	—
1974	400	—	—	—

Sources: Computed from Cuban Economic Research Project, *A Study on Cuba* (Coral Gables, Fla.: University of Miami Press, 1965), pp. 455, 461, 621; Dirección Central de Estadística, *Compendio estadístico de Cuba, 1966* (Havana: Junta Central de Planificación, 1966), p. 13; Carmelo Mesa-Lago, "Economic Policies and Growth," in *Revolutionary Change in Cuba,* ed. Carmelo Mesa-Lago (Pittsburgh: University of Pittsburgh Press, 1971), p. 319; *Granma Weekly Review,* August 6, 1972, p. 4; Frank Mankiewicz and Kirby Jones, *With Fidel* (Chicago: Playboy Press, 1975), pp. 118–119; U.S., Arms Control and Disarmament Agency, *World Military Expenditures, 1971* (Washington, D.C.: Government Printing Office, 1972), pp. 19, 27 (hereafter cited as *ACDA*); *ACDA, 1963–1973,* p. 28; *Boletín 1970,* p. 30.

a. National-income data, rather than gross national product, are used for 1940–1958. In constant prices, referring to national income, 6.5 percent in 1963, 5.6 percent in 1964, and 5.5 percent in 1965.

b. In constant prices, 8.2 percent in 1963; 7.1 percent in 1964; 6.6 percent in 1965; 6.6 percent in 1966.

army and navy reserves numbering 18,542 by December 1958.[11] According to Prime Minister Castro, the Revolutionary Armed Forces numbered about 300,000 at their peak in the early 1960s. By 1970 they had declined to 250,000, and by late 1974, to about 100,000. According to Raúl Castro, the Army of Working Youth had another 100,000. A large number of reserve forces were also available at various levels of readiness. The number of civilian workers under direct military command increased 23 percent between 1971 and 1975.

Foreign sources have estimated the size of the professional, regular Cuban armed forces at approximately 100,000 to 120,000 from the late 1960s on. The Institute for Strategic Studies estimated that Cuba's regular armed forces amounted to 117,000 in 1975 and that the ready reserves, which could be mobilized within a maximum of seventy-two hours, numbered about 90,000 (inactive reserves were not estimated). Therefore, the change in the Cuban armed forces from 1970 to 1974 represents a shift of personnel from semiprofessional, full-time soldiers to reserve status. The size of the truly professional forces has apparently remained constant.

In practice, Cuba's external defense rests with the navy, which is equipped to intercept landings and attacks by exiles and to prevent hit-and-run raids with its air and antiaircraft defense forces, and with the Frontier Corps, a unit under the Ministry of the Interior rather than a regular part of the armed forces, which serves as the first line of defense against landings while regular army units are being called up. Cuba's other military resources are not necessary for routine defense. Estimates of the number of naval personnel have varied from 6,000 to 7,500 between 1970 and 1975; the variation is explained by the practice of shifting officers and crew back and forth between the navy and the merchant marine. The size of the air force, including the antiaircraft defense forces, has risen from about 12,000 in 1970 to 20,000 in 1975. The size of the regular army has held steady for several years at no less than 90,000—not including the reserves and the Army of Working Youth. In addition, the Frontier Corps has about 3,000 troops, and internal-security units of the Ministry of the Interior, about 10,000.

Cuba also has an elite force under the jurisdiction of the Interior Ministry that is not part of the regular armed forces. This Special Forces Battalion of about 650 people was the group sent to Angola in the fall of 1975 to fight the South Africans, pending the arrival of reinforcements, while other Cuban units fought against the enemy Angolan units. Thus most of Cuba's professional forces are not engaged in routine defense, which is handled primarily by the navy, the Frontier Corps, and, to a lesser degree, the air force.[12] Altogether about 30,000 troops are concerned principally with external defense, although the air force is also available for overseas combat. An additional 10,000 are concerned solely with internal security; another 100,000 in the Army of Working Youth are mainly engaged in agricultural production, but have some nominal military training. Approximately 180,000 regular army and ready reserve troops are available either for internal security, external defense, or overseas combat, reinforced by the Special Forces Battalion; more than five hundred thousand reservists at various levels of readiness are available for combat in emergencies, and several tens of thousands of civilian workers provide logistical support under the direct commands of the ministry of the Armed Forces and the Interior Ministry. The total number of troops under the command of these two ministries, excluding the inactive reserves, and civilian workers under direct military command, was no fewer than 321,150 in the mid-1970's—the so-called order of battle. Within this number, however, there is substantial variation in the level of combat preparedness.

The force structure of the Cuban armed forces has remained stable since 1968, the pivotal date in Soviet-Cuban relations. Cuban-Soviet collaboration since that time, so important to the economy and internal stability, has produced only marginal changes in Cuba's force structure. By 1968, Cuba already had 300 heavy and medium-weight tanks; the introduction of lighter tanks increased the number to 600 by the mid-1970s and added flexibility to the corps. By 1968 the army had 200 armored personnel carriers, 100 assault guns, and 30 Frog-4 surface-to-surface missiles. The navy had between fifteen and eighteen submarine chasers and eighteen Komar patrol boats equipped with Styx surface-to-surface missiles. Five Osa patrol boats with Styx missiles, which have an effective radius of only fifteen miles, were added by the mid-1970s. The Samlet-missile coastal defense was also in place by 1968; since 1968 the navy has added only some helicopters. By 1968 the air force had twenty-four battalions, organized in 144 units, with about 600 surface-to-surface missiles. It was also equipped with a full complement of helicopters and transport planes; the number of training planes was increased from sixty to eighty-five.

From 1968 to 1974 the number of MiG-15s fell from sixty to fifteen and of MiG-17s from seventy-five to seventy; but at the same time the number of MiG-19s rose from twenty to forty, and of MiG-21s from forty-five to eighty. This shift represents both strengthening and modernization, since the MiG-15s are 1948 planes. The addition of the MiG-21s in 1965 made Cuba the first Latin American country with supersonic aircraft. The increase in their number and the introduction of thirty more modern MiG-21Fs were responses to the spread of supersonic aircraft in the rest of Latin America. The replacement of MiG-15 and MiG-17 planes by MiG-19s and MiG-21s also reflects a policy change: interceptors replaced fighter bombers. Because fighter bombers have a much wider range, they could easily have hit the United States or other American countries. Interceptors cannot. The fighter bombers, however old, are offensive weapons; the interceptors have a shorter flight radius. After the Angolan war in 1975, Cuba also added at least fifteen T-62 tanks, and several BM-21 multiple rocket launchers.[13]

Cuba's military doctrine was matured by 1967, once the survival of the revolution had been assured. It has remained essentially unchanged since, except for the air force's shift to defensive weapons, just mentioned. In the early 1960s, Cuba had a large standing force with limited competence; it could defeat an insurrection or withstand landings by exiles, but it would have had to rely on the Soviets in the event of a major attack. By the late 1960s and early 1970s, the desire for greater strategic autonomy reinforced the government's wish to reduce the personnel burden of the military on the Cuban economy; the result was a new emphasis on a modern, professional, "small" standing force combined with an easily mobilized reserve.[14] Policy emphasized that the national defense rested first with self-reliant Cuban forces. Soviet assistance would be used only to modernize weapons inventories, to assure a continued supply of munitions and spare parts, and to provide a nuclear-weapons shield.

The standing force was reduced by divesting the armed forces of its least professional units; total force size, as well as the size of the regular, professional units, remains the same. The funds spent on the military remain large and have even risen in the early 1970s as a result of this emphasis on professional forces and modern equipment (see table 9.1). The military share of the gross product is lower than it was in the counterrevolutionary period, but it is higher than it was in the mid-1960s.

With the new emphasis on reserves that can be mobilized efficiently, the militia disappeared altogether. Its political functions were taken over by the Committees for the Defense of the Revolution; its other functions passed to civil defense, which operates in every work center and trains citizens to cope with war and other disasters such as the frequent hurricanes. Its more militarized successor, the reserves, also replaced other nonprofessional units of the old armed forces.[15]

All men under fifty and all women under forty have a military-reserve classification according to age, skill, and prior military experience, which governs the length of time that an individual can be called up every year for military training. The shortest period is twelve days a year; the longest, three months. All civilian organizations must defer to the military when reserves are called up for training, and they must plan to do without the people involved, whether they are needed or not; still, being called up for two or three months at a time can seriously disrupt an individual's job, not to mention private life. The draft is run by a system of military registration that operates through work centers and schools and keeps records of the skills, rank, level of combat training, and political persuasion of every potential draftee. Once drafted, reservists participate in war games. For example, 70 percent of the personnel involved in the war games of the eastern army in Camagüey province in the fall of 1974 were reservists; the 3,940 reservists mobilized for from twenty to thirty days who participated in the Western Army's July 1975 war games made up more than half of the troops involved. Reservists accounted for 70 percent of the Cuban troops who fought in Angola in 1975–1976.[16]

Professionalizing the Military

The level of competence of the army has consequently improved by the mid-1970s. In 1971 only one of the units of the Western Army achieved a grade of better than 75 percent in marksmanship; other indicators among both officers and troops were equally low, resulting in an effort to "replace defects of instruction with enthusiasm." By the end of 1973 all the units of the Western Army were receiving grades above 75 percent.[17]

The professionalization of the armed forces can also be seen in changes in the military-school system. In 1959—60 the dropout rate in officers' school was 55 percent; by 1961–62, it had been reduced to 25 percent. The school for militia officers (the Ignacio Agramonte School in Matanzas) became the general officers' school in 1961; a school for political instructors in the armed forces (the Osvaldo Sánchez School) was established in May 1961 (both were closed in 1971 and their students transferred elsewhere). A nationwide system of cadet schools, including schools for navy, communications, infantry, artillery, tank corps, and air force personnel, was set up, and the Máximo Gómez War College for training for the top commands had been established by 1963. The first military junior and senior high schools for children between eleven and seventeen (the Camilo Cienfuegos Schools) were established in 1966. Graduates of the Camilo Cienfuegos senior high schools did not receive commissions immediately, but they had priority in admission to cadet schools. A technological institute was founded in 1966 to train military technicians and engineers. A school for administrators of military-equipment maintenance was set up in 1970. In 1969, 11.2 percent of the 214 students at the University of Havana's National Center for Scientific Research came from the armed forces or the Ministry of the Interior; 2.6 percent of the 307 papers presented in 1972 at the first national scientific conference of university students, and 2.6 percent of the 311 papers at the second, came from the military technological institute. The Naval Academy in Mariel, founded before the revolution, graduated 1,200 officers between 1959 and 1974; in 1974, it had 600 students and 170 faculty members and prepared officers for both the navy and the merchant marine.

In 1968 there were 10,000 military students enrolled in cadet schools in Cuba. A complete system of military schools included high schools; four basic-training cadet schools for the navy, artillery, air force, and other services (the Antonio Maceo Inter-Armas School, the Cuban equivalent of West Point, but with lower academic standards, had absorbed the training schools for infantry and communications and tank specialists); an advanced-training cadet school, the military technological institute, which included specialized research facilities; and a national war college. Continuing-education programs for alumni of the military technological institute were begun in 1975. This military-school system allowed admissions standards to be raised and programs of study to be lengthened. The 1,579 officers who graduated in 1970 had attended officers' school for between three and five years.

In 1976 the best-educated Cuban officers in the Angolan war were found among the military engineers and the air force. The engineers had completed senior high school and studied at the technical institute for five years. Air-force officers had been trained in the Soviet Union after a year of basic training in Cuba; they, too, needed a high-school diploma to qualify for admission. Artillery officers, naval officers, and other specialized army officers had to have completed the tenth grade before being admitted to the appropriate military school. Once admitted, artillery officers went through a three-year program; the others, a four-year program. All other officers with command responsibilities were trained at the Antonio Maceo Inter-Armas School, where a ninth-grade education qualified them for admission to a three-year course of study; thus most Cuban officers were only senior-high-school graduates. The school for administrators required only an eighth-grade education and a course of thirty months.

The improved military-school system contributed greatly to the ideological coherence of the armed forces, for the lower schools fed into the higher schools, eliminating the need to recruit untrained civilians who would require more extensive training. By 1971, 74 percent of the students admitted to the military technological institute were graduates of the Camilo Cienfuegos military high schools; by 1975, 63 percent of all graduating cadets from the naval academy, the artillery and general-officer schools, and the military technological institute had previously graduated from the military high schools. Although the fifty-eight comandantes (the highest rank at the time) and the 109 officers who received the title of military "vanguard" officer in 1973 were only twenty-nine years old on the average, they had served in the armed forces for an average of eleven years; 41 percent of the 151 "vanguard" officers had served for thirteen or fourteen years.[18]

At the end of 1973 and again at the end of 1976, military ranks and armed-forces hierarchy were reorganized to approximate the system most common in the rest of the world. Until 1973 the highest rank, comandante, had no clear equivalent elsewhere. Ranks within the armed forces were poorly differentiated. Since 1976 Fidel Castro remained as commander-in-chief; a rank below him was Raúl Castro as general of the army; the chiefs of the three main armies became division generals. Everyone along the line received a new rank corresponding to the universal system. Since 1973 former officers in civilian jobs have no longer been addressed by their military titles; inactive personnel are also discouraged from wearing uniforms and insignia.[19] The change is partly symbolic, but it also serves to draw a clear line between civilian and military roles and provides an incentive for officers attracted to the military life to stay in it and work for promotion there.

Clear definitions of rank led to a new consciousness within the officer corps that was soon reflected in a system of military clubs, which clearly separated commissioned officers from noncommissioned officers and troops. The clubs are intended to provide both recreation and cultural and political education. A military unit is entitled to a so-called Lenin-Martí salon; a battalion, to a club for noncommissioned officers and troops; a division, to an officers' club. A national officers' club was established in 1975. In practice, however, club facilities are not always so readily available. The major air force base at San Antonio de los Baños had six Lenin-Martí salons by the early spring of 1976, when the entire Army of Working Youth had only begun to start one. Since the air force was regarded as an elite branch of the service and the Army of Working Youth as a very plebian one, the availability of recreational facilities seemed contingent on rank and status.[20]

The professionalization of the armed forces and the stability of its doctrine and force structure are evidence of a high degree of military institutionalization; in fact, the process was well under way even during the 1960s. The long terms of service characteristic of the best officers, the integrated military-school system, and the autonomy of military organizations from civilian organizations for military recruitment have all since added to their stability and ideological coherence and have promoted officer loyalty to the armed forces. These factors would also have led to a military oligarchy had they been left unchecked by the Communist party. Professionalization has increased military autonomy because civilian technicians are less necessary, and it has added to the organizational complexity of the armed forces. The institutionalized armed forces, however, also need a larger share of the national budget. An added cost to civilians—and a gain for the military—was the expansion of military training and military control into the lives of many people. Another trend appeared in the mid-1960s, when the armed forces adopted social, economic, and political missions as well as purely military functions. From one point of view, civilians were militarized; from another, the military were civilianized. The result was the flourishing of the civic soldier at least through the mid-1970s.

The Angolan War

Although Cuba supported revolutionary movements in many countries since 1959, until recently that support had never been a part of the role and purpose of its armed forces. Cubans who had fought abroad had, at least officially, done so on their own, though not without open backing from their government. Che Guevara, for example, had resigned from all his positions in Cuba—under pressure to do so from Fidel Castro—before embarking on his career as an international revolutionary. Never before the Angolan war had the Cuban armed forces been committed to front-line overseas combat as part of their mission.

The Angolan war altered that pattern. Cuban military doctrine added a new mission for its armed forces; they would no longer be limited to the defense of the homeland but would also be ready to take the offensive overseas. The Cuban-Angolan agreement of 1976 committed Cuba to the unlimited defense of Angola against hostile neighbors, apparently including counterinsurgents within Angola itself. Although the treaty only requires Cuba to supply "military units and weapons necessary to support the People's Republic of Angola in case of aggression from outside," the Cuban government has chosen to categorize guerrillas opposed to the Luanda government as agents of outside forces.[21]

This change in doctrine was reflected in changes in war games, which began to include not only the defense of positions but long marches, the occupation of large areas, and the simultaneous deployment of large numbers and varieties of troops. The first of these new war games were held in July 1975, just as Angola prepared for independence. Motorized infantry maneuvers in Camagüey province in November emphasized techniques for seizing territory and for long marches. In early December, as the Angolan war reached its peak intensity, such exercises became even more complex—the largest and most complicated maneuvers ever held in Cuba.[22]

Cuba's victory in Angola proved the effectiveness of its military reforms. Approximately 20,000 Cuban troops were in Angola at any one time; the total number involved through troop rotation was probably much larger. The Angolan war also demonstrated the close military ties between the Soviet Union and Cuba: Cubans were carried over equipped only with light weapons; heavier weapons were supplied on the spot by the Soviets, so that Cuban weapons inventories were hardly touched by the war. Cuban civil air transports and merchant marine took Cuban troops to Angola. Apart from the Interior Ministry's Special Forces, Cuban troops included artillery, motorized, tank, rocketry, air force, and infantry units.[23]

The Angolan operation also indicated some of the organizational versatility of the Cuban armed forces. It showed, for instance, that troops could be mobilized by racial category. Half the Cuban troops in Angola were black, well above the black share of the armed forces and about double their representation in the general population. This disproportionate mobilization of blacks was meant to reduce the racial differences between the Cubans and their Angolan allies. Normally, however, racial distribution is carefully maintained in the divisions that constitute the Cuban army. Although the proportion of blacks in the population is twice as high in Eastern Cuba as it is in the rest of the country, for instance, there are no significant differences in the racial composition of Cuba's three main armies—Eastern, Central, and Western; troops are rotated throughout the country so that each reflects the makeup of the population as a whole. To increase the proportion of blacks among the Cuban units in Angola, then, special procedures had to be followed to select black troops from all three armies.[24]

Another organizational achievement was the joint operation of the army in Angola and in Cuba. Sometime between August 20 and September 5, 1975, the chairman of the Joint Chiefs of Staff, the chiefs of the three armies and of the air force, and other vice ministers of the Armed Forces Ministry were temporarily relieved of their posts. In October, as Cuba has acknowledged, military instructors began arriving in Angola; in fact, as many as 320 were there as early as May. In November the first regular troops arrived. By spring the war was over; by July 1976 the chiefs and vice ministers were back at their posts;[25] the commanders who had replaced them were reassigned overseas. The Cuban armed forces had managed to develop two sets of officers with experience in top command posts who could alternate responsibilities between the domestic and the overseas armed forces. The permanent chiefs have the rank of division general; the second-echelon chiefs, the rank of colonel or lieutenant colonel.

Wars, however, have a price in human lives, resources, and opportunity costs. The long-range cost of the Angolan war and the apparently endless Angolan-Cuban defense pact that followed cannot yet be assessed, but at least five kinds of obvious cost were incurred. First was the demand by the armed forces for more trained military personnel. The number of reservists trained doubled from 1974 to 1975. Second, there was evidence of civilian resistance to the war, at least among the elite. Managers did not want to part with skilled manpower; loopholes in the law allowed them to keep skilled personnel from being inducted by claiming that they were indispensable, leading Prime Minister Castro to remark that it was necessary "to combat the occasionally exaggerated criteria as to who cannot be dispensed with in production."[26] Civilian resistance to military exigency had not been seen in Cuba since the 1960s.

Third, there was apparently insubordination among some troops, although its extent cannot be determined and was probably limited; the military press discussed what disciplinary procedures should be employed to combat it. The first discussion of these appeared in late November 1975 as the Cuban intervention in Angola was rapidly escalating. Orders had to be obeyed, the government stressed, even if a formal complaint was in order, provided the command was not a breach of revolutionary constitutional and legal standards. A fourth cost of the war—widespread unhappiness among the Cuban people concerning compulsory military service—was equally obvious; up to this time, the revolutionary leadership had sought to give the impression that only religious fanatics opposed the draft. Now it became clear that even ordinary people found it disagreeable and thought it coercive. Finally, the regular procedures of political control by the Communist Youth Union broke down and the number of cadets joining it declined. A gap between military professionals and politicians was forming that was far wider than any experienced in the past, partly because of the very military professionalism required by the Angolan war.[27]

Notwithstanding these real costs, there is no reliable evidence of substantial opposition to the government's decision to send troops to Angola. Neither the general principle of committing troops for the sake of "internationalist solidarity" nor the specific decision to apply that principle to Angola can be seen to have been challenged in Cuba. Most Cubans probably supported the Angolan policy in 1975–1976. The war apparently exacerbated problems within the Cuban armed forces, however, and took its toll in popular acceptance of the military. Parents and spouses did not like to have their loved ones taken off to a distant war. The protracted nature of the 1977 war in Angola—where counterrevolutionary Angolan guerrillas have inflicted casualties on Cuban troops there—also appears to have presented new difficulties for the Cuban government.

The Angolan war in 1975–1976 demonstrated the improvements in Cuba's armed forces and military reserves, but it also caused a strain in civilian-military relations. If this tension continues in the years ahead, and if the demands for more military professionalization to cope with protracted war in Angola remain pressing, it will spell the demise of the civic soldier; the lines of conflict between civilian and military interests will then be too clearly drawn to permit continuing fusion of those roles.

The redefinition of the military mission of the Cuban armed forces in the mid-1970s was further evident in their active participation in Cuba's foreign-aid program. At the end of 1977, Cuba had about ten foreign military-assistance programs in Africa and the Middle East, of which the one in Angola was by far the largest. In addition, some Cuban military personnel performing civilian tasks were involved in other Cuban foreign-aid programs in another half dozen countries in Africa, Asia, and Latin America.[28]

The Socioeconomic Mission of the Armed Forces

In the years between the suppression of insurgency and the Angolan war in 1975 the military had to find something to do to justify their existence. They emphasized the nondefense objectives of the civic-soldier role to promote the growth of the military. One task they set for themselves was the supervision and rehabilitation of social deviants; another was the promotion of economic growth. These tasks had been anticipated for some time.

In 1963, when the law requiring compulsory military service was being discussed, Raúl Castro argued that a three-year tour of duty was justified because it would allow the military to perform missions other than those involving national defense and domestic order. "If we emphasize military training alone," he said, "if we only want an army, we can have [the draftees] for two years . . . [but] because we believe that the armed forces should help in the nation's economy . . . [we intend to make] the burden of military expenditures on our people a bit lighter; in other words, we must work as part of our service, especially in the sugar harvest."[29] In addition, the lazy, the corrupt, homosexuals, religious proselytizers, especially Jehovah's Witnesses, all classified as social deviants, would be drafted into special military units; they would be given no weapons but would instead be socially "rehabilitated" through national service. Although compulsory military service was claimed not to be primarily for these purposes, that was a not insubstantial side effect.[30]

In November 1965, the army's high command, with the Prime Minister's approval, formed groups called the Military Units to Aid Production (UMAP). These units would be filled by drafting social deviants, that is, everyone whose behavior was not strictly in accordance with the public definition of good citizenship. The first UMAP draftees were treated so brutally that some of their officers were court-martialed and convicted of torture, but the organization was soon brought under control by Ernesto Casillas, who headed the UMAP in its formative months.[31]

The UMAP functioned throughout the sugar harvests of 1965–66 and 1966–67, but it was not universally approved. When many intellectuals and university faculty were sent to the UMAP as alleged homosexuals, the Cuban National Union of Writers and Artists (UNEAC) protested to the Prime Minister. Although Castro had approved the establishment of the UMAP and at first spoke well of it, he agreed that treatment of UMAP draftees was scandalous; the UMAP was disbanded after the 1967 harvest. This decision was resisted by the army high command, whose journal ran articles in four different issues in the spring of 1967 defending the UMAP's record.[32] Castro's defeat of the military establishment in this case, even though he was himself a civic soldier, demonstrated his power and showed that there were limits to the potential expansion of the military. The military would still recruit and train "good revolutionaries," but its "rehabilitative" and truly repressive mission was thereafter sharply curtailed.

Production

The military was more successful in expanding its role into economic areas. Even from 1962 to 1964, when their strictly military mission was paramount, LCB units in the Escambray mountains were helping the peasants in the fields; this work fit in with their strategy in combatting insurgents who threatened that area and others.[33] But expansion of the military's economic activities came only after foreign and domestic military threats had declined.

Cutting sugar cane requires very limited skill. The principal use of the military in sugar harvests was to guarantee a cheap labor supply in times of labor scarcity. Batista had used the army similarly in the 1930s—though for distribution, not growth of the economy. In 1968, 51,000 soldiers were assigned to the sugar harvest (representing about 46 percent of the regular armed forces and about a fifth of all the armed forces); in 1969, 38,000 were assigned there (35 and 15 percent, respectively); in 1971, 43,000 (39 and 17 percent). In the extraordinary 1970 harvest, however, 70,000 troops were pressed into service, representing about 64 percent of the regular forces and 28 percent of all the armed forces generally.[34]

Unlike Batista's military in the 1930s, which contributed little in terms of technical and managerial skills to economic growth, the Revolutionary Armed Forces in the 1960s took on various nonmilitary technical and managerial jobs to encourage growth. In 1967, the air force operated sixty airplanes used in spraying and fertilizing fields, and the army formed a motorized brigade to run mechanized equipment for tilling new fields for sugar. By the spring of 1969 all farm machinery was under military supervision. Soldiers who had previously served in tank or motorized units were shifted to this new brigade. The Che Guevara Brigade, organized in the fall of 1968 into thirty-six subunits throughout the six provinces, operated entirely in agriculture. Its commander-in-chief, Raúl Guerra Bermejo, was also a member of the party's Central Committee. The brigade retained a strict military organization and chain of command; it took over all the machinery formerly administered by the state farms using civilian personnel.

In 1970 the military cut 20 percent of the giant sugar-cane harvest. They organized and operated the combines that mechanized cane cutting. They coordinated the cane loading at strategic locations and supervised the transportation of cane for the sugar mills in the eastern provinces; they operated all the tractors and cane lifters. They built roads, railroad tracks, and temporary housing. Members of the Luis Turcios Lima Brigade of the Eastern Army won the coveted title, National Heroes of Labor. The harvests in the late 1960s and in 1970 were directed from a national command post linked to the field through provincial, regional, and municipal outposts. The harvest took on all the aspects of a military campaign: it was a battle and a struggle no less essential to the survival of the revolution than the military engagements of earlier years.[35]

The growing economic role of the Cuban military served to blunt criticism that the armed forces were becoming an excessive burden on the Cuban economy, a complaint that was heard even in the early 1960s, when it was clear that the government depended on the armed forces for survival. Dissatisfaction grew in the mid-1960s, as insurrections were defeated. The old military objectives had been achieved; until new ones were found, the military organization needed a new objective for its survival. In 1966 the military agreed to cancel purchases of helicopters and military-transport aircraft and to purchase airplanes suitable for aerial crop spraying instead; they also agreed to transfer 250 pilots on active military service to these agricultural tasks. Both moves were justified on budgetary grounds.[36]

In mid-1967, these reallocations of money and manpower still did not satisfy all the critics. The military responded in two ways. First, they sharply increased their economic activities, and, second, they reasserted the priority of military expenditures in the national budget. Raúl Castro remarked on July 22, 1967, that the country had to "sacrifice even some aspects of its social development in construction work to earmark more of our resources for preparing the country for a war whose outbreak we cannot foresee." In January 1968, when the military had clearly become an active force in the economy, Fidel Castro acknowledged the priority of the military's needs in the allocation of scarce strategic resources such as petroleum.[37]

The armed forces won in the end. In 1968, the defense budget rose by 20 percent, its largest annual increase for the entire decade (see table 9.1). The proportion of gross national product made up by military expenditures rose to its highest level since 1962; the military budget was growing faster than the economy, even in a good year such as 1968. In return, one-fifth to one-half of military personnel cut sugar cane in 1968. Though the defense budget was retracted in 1969 to its 1967 level, it reached new heights again in 1972. Contrary to expectations, the military's expansion of its economic role continued and became more institutionalized with each subsequent harvest, until it is now routine for soldiers to engage in the annual "battle" of the sugar harvest. They have yet to prove that they are more successful than civilians in rescuing the Cuban economy, but their commitment to participating in it and the acceptance of it by the nation are no longer questioned.

However, the form of this participation has changed as a result of substantive changes in the internal organization of the Cuban armed forces. Because of objective role conflict in the performance of military units, the armed forces were reorganized in 1973 to combat the resulting decline in combat preparedness and the increase in costs. Field officers in units had been unable to cope with role conflict. For the first time in revolutionary history, the armed forces responded by creating new, highly specialized military units. The units within the armed forces that had engaged in production merged with the Centennial Youth Column, the voluntary agricultural work organization called the Followers of Camilo and Che, and the "minibrigades" for production, which had existed in the armed forces, to form the Army of Working Youth under the Ministry of the Armed Forces. This army specializes in production; when these tasks are completed, or if they are only seasonal, the members of the Army of Working Youth are expected to prepare for combat. Officers of the Army of Working Youth are military officers with their own training, ranks, and system of promotion. This organization allows the other military units to concentrate on their strictly military tasks.[38]

In practice, however, the Army of Working Youth has ended up working almost entirely in production, not in combat preparedness. They accounted for over a fifth of all cane cutters in the 1975, 1976, and 1977 harvests. The first secretary of the Oriente provincial party, Armando Hart, argued in 1975 that the Army of Working Youth had made an indispensable contribution to economic production in that province by providing a permanent agricultural work force stationed in the fields even between harvests, by covering work-force shortages in the least populated areas, and by providing a margin of safety in the number of workers available at peak harvest.[39] But its level of combat readiness remains extraordinarily low. While reservists apparently participate in war games, the Army of Working Youth seems not to do so and is consequently even less well trained than many reserve units. At the first conference of party members in the Army of Working Youth in the fall of 1975 it was noted that the army had sought to "strengthen its infrastructure to increase combat preparedness in the future," but evidently this has not yet occurred.[40] For one thing draftees into the Army of Working Youth are unruly. Reports concerning their performance in the 1976 harvest in Matanzas province— where half of the members were new to the work—suggest that the conscripts were not disciplined enough to be usefully assigned to any task, including farm labor. The officers in command were praised for their "tough, determined, and persistent attitude" in trying to overcome the "difficulties" encountered in shaping up their personnel,[41] but their efforts were apparently not entirely successful. The productivity of armed-forces personnel remains below the average of cutters generally and just a shade above that of student volunteers (in spite of the picture presented by the Cuban press, which lauds the efforts of the best military units a good part of the time). Compared with voluntary workers, their productivity is only half as much; since both groups are drawn disproportionately from the working class, class differences cannot explain this disparity. Neither group lives or works regularly in the countryside, and still the voluntary workers do twice as well as the draftees. For the first half of the 1973 harvest in Matanzas (until April 6), military cane cutters can be compared with other groups in terms of their productivity (the national average for all groups had been 176 arrobas per worker) and their representation in the harvest work force:

	Arrobas per cutter	% of provincial cane cutters
Regular workers	290	17
Volunteer workers	264	—
Peasant volunteers	226	41
Army of Working Youth	143	11
Havana student volunteers	128	—

National productivity for the entire harvest per cane cutter was 401 arrobas in 1974, 502 in 1975, 582 in 1976; in the Army of Working Youth, it was about 197 arrobas in 1974 and between 242 and 252 in 1975.[42]

Clearly the application of military conscription to the sugar-cane harvest is at best inefficient, if not grievously coercive as well. The problems of the Cuban economy are too complex for excessive reliance on the armed forces to solve them, and the political costs of maintaining an army for manual labor may well prove to be too high.

The civic-soldier pattern has spread overseas as Cuban military personnel began to operate in other countries. Some Cuban troops who went to Angola as soldiers shifted emphasis within the civic-soldier role to work in normally civilian activities. President Castro told Cubans working in construction in Angola in 1977 that they "must be workers and soldiers at the same time." That is part of the tradition begun by the Cuban health-care personnel, who arrived in Angola in October 1975 and who fought as soldiers in the war. In the 1970s Cuban civic soldiers have built roads and airports in Guinea, hospitals in Peru, and schools in Tanzania, while serving as military trainers and advisors.[43]

The armed forces have not abandoned either their economic or their military missions; they have reorganized to allow both to be pursued simultaneously. Fidel Castro noted that the organizational changes "made possible an increase in the armed forces' defensive power while at the same time maintaining their participation in economic tasks,"[44] further evidence of the institutionalization of a very adaptable military organization.

The development of the Army of Working Youth has perhaps paved the way for a much more drastic future step, namely, the devolution of all productive tasks back to civilians. The reasons for its establishment could also be taken as evidence of conflict within the armed forces. Some officers probably argued that the profession of arms was a full-time occupation and that military preparedness required undivided attention. Others may have argued that the armed forces should remain in production. This is only an inference; the net effect of the creation of the Army of Working Youth has in fact been to increase the power of the armed forces over production and to allow it to grow at the expense of civilian agencies. The consensus in the armed forces is that they ought to contribute directly to production, even if not all of its personnel should do so regularly.[45]

Military Training and Military Service

In the 1970s, the military expanded in two further directions. An experimental program of regular military training as an integral part of the senior-high-school and university curricula was inaugurated in 1975 and is being extended to all senior high schools. Courses are conducted in the eleventh and twelfth grades by armed forces officers. The minister of education, himself a former military man, stressed that these would be among the most important courses in senior high schools and universities, not only because of their contribution to the national security, but also because of their educational value, a comment that harks back to the original conception of the socioeconomic mission of the armed forces, which centered on the belief that military training would develop the "Communist personality" by instilling modesty, confidence, honesty, camaraderie, courage, affection and respect for other socialist countries, patriotism, and conscientious discipline. These programs are similar to the Reserve Officers' Training Corps (ROTC) programs in the United States, except that the Cuban program is still compulsory (though at present only for the students in the schools where it was inaugurated); the degree of military control over the educational program also seems to be greater in Cuba than it has been in the United States.[46] When the program becomes universal the government may be able to use it to require each citizen to have civilian and military roles fused into the civic-soldier pattern. The program, however, has potential problems. Students are faced with conflicting expectations from their superiors in the Ministries of Education and the Armed Forces; they must also decide how to allocate their own time. Thus this program has the potential for generating the same objective role conflicts that are typical of the civic-soldier experience.

Compulsory military service, instituted in 1963, and compulsory social service, instituted in 1973, have contributed to the preservation of Cuban social stratification, at least for the time being. Every young man must serve his country for three years at a place designated by the government; women may become soldiers if they choose to do so. One can enter the regular or the productive units of the armed forces or perform alternative civilian service. Only one-third of the young men of sixteen or seventeen entered the armed forces in 1972; the rest did other things. Since even the least skilled can cut cane, the social-service system includes everyone, but it does lead to the exemption of the best educated from military service in the strict sense. The protection of the well educated on the grounds that they serve the community is the conservative effect of the social-service system and one that benefits the elite, but the requirement that the best educated serve for a specified period where the government wants them to serve is rare among countries; it is the radical aspect of the law. The laws instituting compulsory service might have stipulated that some portion of secondary-school and university graduates must enter military service—or cut cane—but it did not, thus guaranteeing that educated Cubans would be exempted at least from the hardships of military or agricultural life.[47]

In the mid-1970s, even before the Angolan war, the importance of the armed forces was again being proclaimed. On November 22, 1974, Prime Minister Castro asserted that "our country will need . . . greater and greater defense capacity over an indefinite period," because "even if one day there should be economic and even diplomatic relations between [Cuba and the United States] that would not give us the right to weaken our defenses, for our defense can never depend on the good faith of imperialists." Seven months later Raúl Castro stressed the "essential need constantly to increase our military strength . . . despite the fact that the present balance of power favors the socialist camp and despite the positive advances made in international de-tente."[48] The need for military strength derived first from national security, then from its socioeconomic missions, and, finally, simply from the sense that the armed forces were "good in themselves" and that the survival of the revo-lution required nothing but the best.

While there is evidence that the military is valued as an institution by its of-ficers, some of the best of whom, though young, have already served in it for many years, there are also indications that military service is unpopular and ci-vilian service regarded as much preferable. This public perception has led to a variety of incentives to lure draftees into the regular forces. They pay more for overtime work and for high quality work, and good service is rewarded with gifts, foreign vacations, and early promotion, as well as with the usual array of banners, certificates, medals, flags, and insignia. Good soldiers are also re-warded with frequent furloughs and reduced terms of service. Punishments include suspension of leaves and extension of tours of duty, as well as demo-tion and imprisonment. At least some of these incentives would not be neces-sary if military service were more popular with draftees.[49]

One basis for dissatisfaction within the regular armed forces is poor pay. Prime Minister Castro reported to the First Party Congress that "so far it has not been possible to provide fair and just compensation" to the military—a particularly touchy point during the Angolan war. He added, however, that salaries for officers were being increased, that steps were being taken to build more military housing, and that new funds would soon improve the standard of living of military personnel more generally.

A much more serious problem was the low regard in which military service was held by the rest of the population. The Prime Minister told the First Party Congress that the "present concept as to who should be drafted" must be changed to eliminate "a situation in which military service, far from appearing and being presented as an honor, is regarded as something with which parents can threaten their sons who do not study, which teachers can use to intimidate their students, and which the agencies use as a threat and as a means to punish breaches of discipline." Although the armed forces were willing to undertake civilian tasks, civilians were not eager for military ones. The Prime Minister's admission that military service was generally unpopular was, rather surpris-ingly, made at the height of the Angolan war.[50]

The rest of the world has often put the military to peaceful uses, but rarely on the scale of the Cuban military's involvement in social and economic tasks.[51] Among the other Communist countries, the Soviet armed forces pro-vide the greatest contrast. They have stuck strictly to military concerns, argu-ing that modern technology requires that they give full attention to military pursuits. Even in the early years of the Soviet revolution, there was little of the kind of role expansion into nonmilitary employment practiced by the

Cuban armed forces,[52] either because of policy or because of military resistance to the idea. The Chinese come closer to Cuban practice. In the People's Republic of China the "Great Leap Forward" was probably comparable to Cuba's giant harvest of 1970; soldiers were involved in both. But officers in the Chinese army resisted using the military for social and economic tasks much more strongly than their Cuban counterparts have done, arguing along with their Soviet colleagues that the profession of arms is a full-time occupation.[53]

There is no comparable resistance within the Cuban military. On the contrary, soldiers seem to take on nondefense tasks with a great deal of enthusiasm. Although there may have been some resistance to work in the 1970 harvest, the military's participation was nonetheless extraordinary. Still the armed forces reverted quickly enough to their "normal" degree of participation, and there are indications that Fidel Castro wanted even more manpower than he got for the harvest.[54] The formation of the Army of Working Youth also suggested that some officers preferred specialization in military tasks and that they supported creating the Army of Working Youth to free themselves from production tasks. With these exceptions, however, the Cuban military seems willingly involved in social and economic tasks, partly because they have deliberately set about redesigning their mission so that it will appear useful to society in order to protect their budget, and partly to promote expansion of military organizations.

The Political Mission of the Armed Forces

The political mission of the Cuban military has four aspects. One is the absorption of the structure of the Communist party, so that the corporate autonomy of the military institutions is preserved and conflict between the party and the armed forces minimized. Another is the prevention of the cleavages that plagued the armed forces before the revolution, those between commissioned and noncommissioned officers and between professional and nonprofessional commissioned officers. A third is the political indoctrination of recruits and the weeding out of the unreliable. A final aspect is the development of cadres that can be exported to the civilian population, particularly to positions in the civilian elite. It is at this level that the civilian and military tasks of the soldier are fused by placing the civic soldier in the position of highest command in both the party and the military. The military commander is not merely a technician; he is also a political officer. A party leader is not only a politician; he is a technician and a manager competent in military as well as civilian tasks.

The Party in the Armed Forces

In 1961–1962 the party's crisis was a result of the confrontation between Fidel Castro and the prerevolutionary Communists, not of friction with the military. In those same years, however, the party sought to control the armed forces through political instructors who were first trained at the Osvaldo Sánchez School for the Revolutionary Armed Forces and then assigned to military units. Because they lacked military training and operational field experience and because they were imposed from outside to erode the chain of command, they were strongly opposed by the professional military commanders. These early political instructors were simply copying the experience of political commissars in the military in other Communist countries; one result of the massive expulsions from the party in 1962 was the abandonment of that system. Beginning in 1963, students at the Osvaldo Sánchez School were drawn directly from the military ranks and were usually already officers; the curriculum was revamped so that 40 percent of the program would be devoted to military topics, reviving the civic-soldier experience from guerrilla days, merging civilian and military responsibilities.[55]

By the end of 1963, party recruitment and party organization in the military had begun in earnest.[56] A trial run was made among the mountain corps (*compañías serranas*) in Oriente, followed by initial party organizations in the regular units of the Eastern Army. The members of each military unit were classified into eight ranks, from soldier to commanding officer. Each had an assembly, directed by a commission of political instructors appointed by the party's political bureau in the armed forces, to elect "exemplary combatants" (in addition to commissioned officers, all of whom were automatically named exemplary combatants). All exemplary combatants were interviewed individually and then met in rank groups with the commissions for criticism and self-criticism. The commission members selected the new Communist party members from these groups, after discussing the candidates both among themselves and with their ranking officers. The new members were presented to the rest of the unit and to the party cell, or *núcleo*, established within the unit; this cell included all party members regardless of military rank. Party officers were elected at the cell level in the unit and progressively upward in battalions and armies. Once a unit had a party cell, it could recruit on its own, without going through the procedure of electing exemplary combatants, but new recruits were still subject to final assembly approval.

Differences between military and civilian party-recruitment procedures were reduced in the 1970s when the party and the Communist Youth Union existed throughout the armed forces. From that time on, prospective members joined the youth union first and passed on into the party—whether a military or a civilian cell—at the appropriate age, provided political and ideological criteria were met.

In the beginning neither military orders nor officers' personal and political conduct could be criticized in the party cell. By the mid-1960s, this rule held only for the first year of party formation in a military unit. By the second year, although military orders and regulations still could not be questioned, the personal and political conduct of the officers could be discussed, regardless of the rank of either officer or critic. Both officers and particular orders could be criticized at all times by higher-ranking officers, however, and by political instructors assigned to higher-ranking military units.

Political work in the armed forces was directed by the national commission of the party in the armed forces, headed by Raúl Castro. Political instructors are not elected; they are appointed and assigned by the national commission upon completion of their training. Two political channels exist within the armed forces. One is the party, organized from the bottom up; the other is the political instructors, organized from the top down in political sections in the military units at all levels. The two channels are not wholly separate, however, but are coordinated in two ways. First, both the political instructors and all party members belong to the party's organization at each military level; second, they are all under the same command.

In contrast to the situation in the early 1960s and possibly in other Communist countries, "there is no separation of activity between military and party obligations."[57] Communist party organization parallels the military hierarchy. Criticism of one's superiors is difficult, but possible; innovation remains a prerogative of the top. Just as the party has penetrated the armed forces, so too the military has penetrated the party. The party within the armed forces is led by the military high command, not by civilian party cells or other agencies outside the military. The party in the armed forces is self-contained; nonmilitary party members have no authority over it. Party criticism within the military is criticism within the party, criticism of the military by the party, and criticism of the party by the military, all at the same time, because party and military are often fused.

The formation of the party in the military was complete by the end of 1966. It had moved geographically from the eastern to the western provinces and hierarchically from the bottom up. The last place to organize party cells was the national headquarters of the Army Chief of Staff. By the fall of 1970, 69.6 percent of all officers in the armed forces belonged to either the party or the Communist Youth Union. By the summer of 1973, the proportion rose to 85 percent; in 1976, it was still 86 percent. Since 1970 the fifteen-member advisory commission of party members of the armed forces to the Political Bureau has been composed entirely of commissioned officers, at least half of whom have the highest ranks in existence at the time in the Cuban military. In the fall of 1970, 69 percent of the members of the party in the military were commissioned officers. At the end of 1975, 48 percent of the entire western fleet (but 92 percent of its officers) belonged to the party or the youth union; 70 percent of the entire Interior Ministry belonged to the party or the youth union by mid-1976. Enlisted soldiers and draftees made up a large, though unspecified, proportion of the membership of the Communist Youth Union.[58] The high overlap between the officer corps and the party and youth union membership helps fuse political and military authority, though alone it is not sufficient for the task.

In the Soviet Union, by contrast, the proportion of military officers who belong to the party has grown over time: 32 percent in 1924, 65 percent in 1928, 86 percent in 1952, 90 percent in the early 1960s, 93 percent in 1966 (when 80 percent of all Soviet armed forces personnel were either in the party or in the Communist Youth Union, mostly the latter).[59] But this high representation has not prevented repeated conflicts between the party and the military throughout Soviet history.[60] In Cuba the militarization of the political instructors; the willing acceptance of political norms, roles, and structures by military officers; the unified leadership that has preserved a single military chain of command; the self-containment of the party within the military to preserve the institutional autonomy of the armed forces; and the presence of the civic soldiers at the core of the ruling elite in charge of civilian and military organizations have combined to prevent similar conflicts. In the Soviet Union, even when political commissars and military commanders agree on specific issues, the central organizations of the party have little contact with either.[61] In the absence of fusion at the top, conflict between Soviet central civilian and party organizations and military leaders will no doubt continue.

The chief problem in the relationship between party and military in Cuba has been the failure to fulfill political programs in military units. Military commanders tend to leave political matters to the political instructors. In the spring of 1968, according to the Army Chief of Staff, the result was not the concentration of power in the hands of the political instructors but the downgrading of political work. At that time, military commanders were urged to take more interest in the political education of their subordinates, even though the daily tasks were attended to by the instructors.[62] Thus there was no evidence of conflict between the party and military tasks at the level of the military unit. Apparently the military commanders ignored the request, because four years later, the quality of political work in the military was still low. Top party leaders complained that political issues were being handled merely as administrative matters within the party, that discussions were superficial, that too little time was allocated to political issues in the party in the armed forces, that issues concerning the internal affairs of the party were often ignored, that ordinary party members did not participate much in discussions and that, when they did, the officers or the political instructors interrupted to clarify or rebut the members' arguments.[63]

In the aftermath of the Angolan war, political problems have continued. The only criticism of the air force and antiaircraft defense units in 1976 dealt with the poor quality of their political work. The work of the Communist Youth Union was said to be particularly bad; "numerous" members of the youth union, who had reached the age of eligibility for party membership, were reported to be unacceptable because of poor political and ideological preparation. Futhermore, youth union procedures for monthly evaluation of its membership were not being enforced.[64]

A second problem of the party within the military was its lack of democracy. An absence of democratic procedures is not surprising in a military organization; given the ideological commitments of the party and the revolution, however, one would expect at least some degree of democracy in the party, even in its military branches. None exists in the military party, first because officers account for over two-thirds of its membership; military chiefs not only monopolize party debate but use their military rank to gain party rank. Although the chairmanship of party meetings is supposed to be elective, the military chief usually assumes the post automatically and uses it to curtail discussion. The second reason for nondemocratic procedures is that voting at the cell level is by acclamation; this method also makes it easy for officers to impose their views on cell members. At the higher levels, balloting is secret and direct, although all nominations for party office are made by the political sections. The election of delegates to the party conference, the governing body of the party in the military, is also by acclamation, and the amount of competition is once again low. In the 1972 elections for the party commission to supervise the work of the political sections, for instance, which were held at the party conference, the political sections nominated fifteen candidates for nine membership and four alternate posts; voting was by secret ballot. Although nominating twice as many people as posts (requiring twenty-six nominations in this case) is proposed now and again, it is rarely acted upon and the situation has not changed.[65]

A third problem of the party in the military is the military party's lack of autonomy from the nonparty military and vice versa, a fact that obscures both the political and the military chain of command. There is no clear boundary between party and technician. For example, a squadron engineer is not able to plan and implement a program for servicing airplanes without coordinating this work with the party cell's secretary and with the principal political officer, called the chief's substitute for political and partisan work. Similarly, the party secretary and the political officer cannot plan and implement their own political work; the squadron engineer also has the authority to tell party members what to do, even though the engineer may not be a party member. The Communist Youth Union in the armed forces is also not autonomous enough from the party; it has no control over the admission of new members. Those who are too young for party recruitment are simply sent to the youth union until they reach the age required to enter the party; the youth union in the military is little more than the party's annex.[66]

The proportion of soldiers and noncommissioned officers in the military party—almost one-third—is fairly high, much higher than in the Soviet military, where the proportion of soldiers and noncommissioned officers fell as low as 3 percent of all military party members in the 1940s.[67] The relatively high proportion of soldiers, corporals and sergeants among party members in Cuba can be explained by the revolution's commitment—qualified, as already noted—to democratic principles even within the armed forces, which is in part a reaction to the cleavage between commissioned and noncommissioned officers in the Cuban military before the revolution. Although this rivalry is at least latent in most military institutions, Cuba is particularly sensitive on the subject because army sergeants and corporals, led by Batista, overthrew the government and the officer corps in 1933. Many officers were arrested or killed. Cuban officers would not like to see another coup like Batista's.[68] The second major cleavage within the military before the revolution had formed between the professional officers, some trained in Cuba, some abroad, and those who owed their rank to their participation in military coups and shrewd politicking. In the 1950s about one-sixth of the officers were nonprofessionals.[69]

The revolutionary government tried to avoid these rivalries by instituting a new promotion policy. No less than three-quarters and more typically nine-tenths of all professional officers promoted and graduating cadets are members of either the Communist Party or the Communist Youth Union. Among commissioned officers promoted in 1968, party and youth union membership was as follows:[70]

	Number	Party and youth union members
First captains	35	94.3 percent
Captains	56	100.0
Lieutenants	1,757	78.1

For graduating cadets in the late 1960s and early 1970s the comparable figures are these:[71]

	Number	Party and youth union members
1969 (March)	414	97.0 percent
1969 (August)	731	89.0
1970	1,304	87.0
1973	—	95.0
1975	—	82.0

Among the officers promoted through the ranks, party membership is widespread; few belonged to the youth union. In 1968, none of the first captains and captains promoted and only 8.8 percent of the lieutenants promoted belonged to the youth union. Youth union membership, however, is more widespread among the graduating cadets; in March 1969, their numbers were equally divided between the party and the youth union. As the revolution becomes a matter of history, officers or cadets are now rarely promoted on account of their experience in the rebel army. Although all the first captains and captains promoted in 1968 had served in the rebel army, only a third of the lieutenants promoted had done so; only 1.2 percent of the cadets graduating in March 1969 had ever served in the rebel army. Party membership has become a prerequisite of promotion in the upper ranks and youth union membership of promotion from cadet status to the junior ranks. Even in the reserves, 74 percent of the 5,702 reserve officers promoted in 1975 and 80 percent of the five thousand promoted in 1976 belonged to either the party or the youth union.[72]

The conflict between party and military in the early 1960s had occurred in part because so few military men were party members. By the 1970s, promotion policies guaranteed almost total overlap of officers and party members. The political deficiencies within the armed forces, especially in the Communist Youth Union, may explain the decline in the proportion of graduating cadets belonging to the party or the youth union from 1973 to 1975; the decline may result in a sharper line's being drawn between military professionals and military politicians if the present pattern continues.

The new promotion policy provides a program of remedial training for officers with little formal military training. Although the Prime Minister had claimed that only officers professionally trained in military schools would be promoted, in fact officers with purely operational experience and no formal training were still going up the ranks in the late 1960s. Professionalizing the armed forces was easier said than done. The Ignacio Agramonte School for Officers in the city of Matanzas theoretically required a fifth-grade education for admission; this rule was frequently broken in the 1960s. It was not until 1967 that all entering students had achieved a sixth-grade education.[73] Nonetheless, the military's educational level was still better than that of the civilian political leadership; in 1969, 79 percent of all party members still did not have a sixth-grade education. Lack of education in the military, however, gradually became grounds for nonpromotion—in 1975 a number of military personnel in the Ministry of the Interior were not promoted because of too little schooling.[74]

A split appeared in 1975 concerning the value of schooling for military officers, notwithstanding its obvious link to promotion. Many officers, perhaps a majority, even in the units with the highest education levels, preferred to emphasize military practice and war games rather than classroom work, which remained the principal way to conduct political-education courses for officers. Although it remains the policy of the high command to insist on booklearning—including political education—a dispute about its value and its content broke out into the open for the first time.[75]

Through these promotion policies the revolutionary government sought to politicize the officer corps, especially the younger officers who had good professional training but little or no combat experience, but it also sought to professionalize and partly to politicize nonprofessional officers with a great deal of practical experience and very little formal training. The common grounds of professionalism and politics, the leaders believed, would reduce the rivalries that had weakened the Cuban military in the past. But resistance to the new policies had become evident by 1975, when fewer graduating cadets joined the party and the youth union and officers questioned the value of schooling.

The main task of the party in the armed forces is to support the authority of the military chain of command and enhance its prestige. Party members are expected to strengthen troop morale in and out of combat through propaganda, political education, and surveillance. They are active in the Angolan war, as they were against counterrevolutionaries in Cuba in the early 1960s. Party work in the military also has a useful byproduct: it yields a great deal of information about troops and officers alike, and this can be helpful in deciding about promotion or forced retirement in their careers. The practice of criticism and self-criticism in party cells has institutionalized the gathering of personal information and led to better discipline in the military; it has also generated support for the government, exposed opposition to it, and introduced political criteria for promotion.[76]

The military party's program is based on a system of *captación* or tutoring. Party and youth union members act as the tutors; each is given several nonparty members for supervision and is expected to find out about the anxieties and personal or family problems of their charges, educate them politically, and see to it that they attend political meetings and other party activities. The program is supposed to improve morale, discipline, and the level of education among the troops. Its byproducts, according to Raúl Castro, include the identification of homosexuals and of religious individuals for "rehabilitation." It is further intended to stimulate competition for promotion.

The party runs study groups for officers who are party members in proper ideology; there are less formal sessions with all military party members on all subjects, professional and personal as well; reports to headquarters by party members must describe all this activity as well as ordinary military work. The party tutors also work with members who are "lagging behind" most noticeably. Military party procedure requires an annual evaluation of each member's work, a special evaluation whenever a party member is charged with misbehavior, and another when any member is transferred. Whenever there are serious infractions there may be a court-martial, with a military tribunal made up exclusively of Communist party and Communist Youth Union members. In the fall of 1970, at the second national meeting of the military party, the two criticisms leveled against the party's work in the armed forces were, first, insufficient criticism and self-criticism among members and, second, failure to probe into members' personal affairs; these criticisms suggest that these programs had been rich lodes of information in the past.[77]

Systematic evaluation procedures were not established in the armed forces outside the party until 1966; before that time promotions depended entirely upon a superior officer's opinion of a candidate. The first general evaluation of all officers was completed in 1969, but the process did not become routine until 1975. All officers are now evaluated when they are first commissioned, when they shift assignments, when they complete four years in the same assignment, and when they retire. Although these procedures were modeled after party evaluations, they are less rigorous. At first undertaken by the commanding officer of the appropriate military unit, evaluations were made the responsibility of the immediately superior officer after 1975. The entire process, however, is supervised in each unit by a commission comprised of the chief's substitute for political work, the party's organization secretary, and the officer in charge of personnel; it consequently remained under close political scrutiny.[78]

Exporting Military Models

Up to now the discussion has focused on the political activities within the armed forces. But another, parallel development was the inverse of that endeavor—that is, the export of military models and personnel to the rest of the political system. Party organization in the armed forces by and large ended by 1966; in the civilian central administration, it began mostly in 1967. The party drew on that experience in building the civilian party, particularly the principle of unified command. Said Armando Hart: "There cannot be dual leadership in a central State organization. The maximum authority of the party, in each branch of the State apparatus, will be that of the minister or president of the organization, who works under the direction of the Party Central Committee and Political Bureau. If in any case this should turn out to be impossible, we will have to consider the demotion of the executive."[79]

In the military the party had made it a regular practice to hold assemblies for evaluating its work; they were held virtually every year in every unit at different levels. National meetings were held less regularly, but there was one in 1966 and another in 1970.[80] These, too, became models for the civilian party. Although there had been provincial assemblies in the civilian party since the early days,[81] the military version had a seriousness and regularity that were to be carried over into the civilian party.

The military had also developed cadres for assignment to specifically civilian duties, as the proportion of members of the Central Committee with military background indicates. This percentage has always been and still is very high, though it reached a peak in 1965. Since 1965, officers whose tasks within the leadership had been strictly military at that time have come to assume new responsibilities in civilian life. This civic-soldier career pattern predominates in all the leading institutions of party and government. Aside from the members of the top elite discussed earlier, there are many examples lower down on the ladder. Rogelio Acevedo, for instance, who headed the militia in 1960, has been a member of the Central Committee since 1965. From 1969 to 1972 he was the Political Bureau's delegate to Camagüey province; he has since returned to the armed forces as a deputy minister.

Navy Captain Rolando Díaz Astaraín, was minister for the recovery of misappropriated goods from November 1959 to March 1960, then minister of the treasury until June 1962. Back in the navy, he served as its commander-in-chief for four years then joined the merchant marine. Román Alvarez Rodríguez graduated from the naval academy as an officer in 1952, resigned his commission in 1955, and was subsequently imprisoned and exiled by the Batista government. In January 1959 he was made captain of one of Cuba's three frigates, the *Antonio Maceo.* He then switched to the industrialization department of the National Institute for Agrarian Reform and eventually to the merchant marine. At the beginning of 1964, he rejoined the navy as the second officer in command, in charge of combat preparedness. At the end of 1965, he returned to the merchant marine, again as a ship's captain. Some time in the late 1960s, in *Granma's* cautious phrasing, "the comrade also fulfilled his internationalist duties." He was back as navy second in command of the engineering council when he died in September 1974.

Jesús Reyes García was one of the original expedition that landed in Cuba with Fidel Castro aboard the yacht *Granma* in 1956. In 1960–1961, he was the chief of bodyguards in the Ministry of the Interior. He was in charge of the Havana bus lines in 1962, returning to the armed forces as a captain in 1963, attended military school in 1964, and subsequently became a naval machinist in the merchant marine. From the late 1960s until his death in 1974, he was director of an automobile-repair enterprise.[82] The careers of Díaz Astaraín, Alvarez Rodríguez, and Reyes García illustrate the frequent interchange of personnel between the navy and the merchant marine.

The 1973 reform of military ranks and titles included the provision that officers on the inactive list could no longer use their military titles. Although the change was primarily symbolic, it did help to distinguish between active and former officers in positions of power, and it may eventually serve to break down the civic-soldier model. When these civilianized officers rejoin the military, however, they immediately recover their titles, so the divorce between the two spheres is by no means complete. The practice of exporting cadres from military to civilian life, begun in the early 1960s, has also been continued. As leaders trained in the military ranks matured, their attention was shifted to civilian tasks. In the central ministries as well as at various levels of the civilian party ranks, one encounters inactive soldiers with great frequency.

The Cuban armed forces differ from the military that performs nonmilitary tasks in non-Communist countries in several ways: the party functions within the military, which is thoroughly politicized; the military performs not only managerial and technical but also menial tasks; and there have been no military coups in revolutionary Cuba, as there often have been in other countries where the military element within the government remains strong. The Cuban armed forces differ also from the Soviet armed forces in that they have a much broader perception of their role in society. Unlike the Soviets, they do not retreat behind strict military professionalism to avoid other tasks, and they exercise greater authority in the Central Committee. The Soviet pattern of military membership on the Central Committee—between 7 and 13 percent—was set by the late 1930s; before that time its share of the Central Committee was even smaller (table 9.2).[83]

The military in the People's Republic of China more closely resembles the Cuban,[84] but the armed forces' participation in central decision making is more stable and better institutionalized in Cuba than in China; moreover, there has been no purge of the Cuban military on the scale of the Lin Piao affair, nor any military coup attempt in Cuba comparable to Lin Piao's. If all Cuban Central Committee members with military titles at the time of their appointments are counted, then the Cuban military share of its party Central Committee easily exceeds that of the Chinese (table 9.2). If in the Chinese case members designated as military are in fact devoted strictly to military tasks, then the Chinese military representation on the committee has exceeded the Cuban share twice, in comparable situations (1949–1950 in China and 1962 in Cuba; the late 1960s in both countries). The Cuban military share exceeded that of the Chinese in the mid-1960s and mid-1970s. The trend in Cuba has been steady; in China it is more erratic.

Professional Chinese officers are known to have resisted becoming involved in nonmilitary tasks even during the Cultural Revolution. The injection of the armed forces into the Cultural Revolution was no military coup; rather, it was the consequence of a political decision made primarily by leaders outside the armed forces. The People's Liberation Army (PLA) did not set out to expand its role, as the Cuban armed forces had done between 1965 and 1968. Power simply gravitated to it, expanding its sphere of influence; the impetus had come from outside the military. During the Cultural Revolution, the rivalry between military professionals and military politicians simmered beneath the surface. Professional commanders who still opposed any large-scale political involvement were important in the anti–Lin Piao coalition. Cuban officers, in contrast, welcomed role expansion as the vehicle for organizational survival. It is possible that the establishment of the Army of Working Youth was a consequence of professional military resistance to nonmilitary tasks and that the new military specialization thus made possible effective fighting in Angola, but

Table 9.2 Military representation on Communist Central Committees in the People's Republic of China, Cuba, and the Soviet Union

Country and year	All members (includes alternates)		Full members (excludes alternates)	
	% military	Number	% military	Number
China				
1949–1950	38.1	168	—	—
1962	24.6	171	—	—
1969	—	—	51.2	170
1973	31.3	319	31.8	195
Cuba [a]				
1962				
Total military	—	—	56.0	25
Strictly military	—	—	28.0	25
1965				
Total military	—	—	70.0	100
Strictly military	—	—	58.0	100
1975				
Strictly military				
(before First Party Congress)	—	—	38.9	90
Strictly military				
(after First Party Congress)	32.3	124	32.1	112
Soviet Union				
1956	—	—	7.5	122
1966	—	—	8.2	195
1971	—	—	10.2	235

Sources: Donald W. Klein, "The 'Next Generation' of Chinese Communist Leaders," *China Quarterly* no. 12 (October–December 1962): 66; Ellis Joffe, "The Chinese Army after the Cultural Revolution: The Effects of Intervention," ibid., no. 55 (July–September 1973): 457; *China News Summary* no. 483 (September 6, 1973); Robert H. Donaldson, "The 1971 Soviet Central Committee: An Assessment of the New Elite," *World Politics* 24, no. 3 (April 1972): 382–409.

a. "Total military" members are those with military rank at the time of their appointment; "strictly military" members are those who were engaged primarily in military affairs, including political work within the military; this classification includes internal-security personnel in the Ministry of the Interior. Statistics for 1962, when the Central Committee had not yet been established, are for the national directorate of the United Party of the Socialist Revolution.

there is little real evidence to support the notion, which is inapplicable to the 1960s in any case. The effect of the reorganization in 1973 was not only to permit military specialization but also to increase military responsibilities over production by absorbing many of the civilian duties of the Communist Youth Union. While both the Cuban and the Chinese military have engaged in role expansion, Chinese officers have resisted it far longer and more strenuously than their Cuban counterparts. In China the impetus for role expansion came primarily from outside the armed forces, while in Cuba expansion has come about equally as a result of pressures from within and from outside.

In 1964 the Chinese were publicly called upon to "learn from the experience of the PLA in political education and ideological work." This appeal made the army a model for the rest of the system for at least a few months. During the Cultural Revolution, however, the export of political models to the rest of the political system was not emphasized; the PLA intervened primarily to restore order. It also exported middle- and low-level cadres to roles as regional or local political leaders through the Revolutionary Committees. In the years since the Cultural Revolution, however, civilian rule has been restored and the export of cadres from the military to the political system has been limited. Although some Maoists may have had a civic-soldier model in mind and although they may even have intended to diffuse this role, they did not in fact succeed to the degree that the leaders with a similar plan have succeeded in Cuba.

Revolutionary Cuba has been governed, in large part, by leaders whose civilian and military roles were fused during the insurgency against Batista and who have intentionally made the civic soldier the norm for all, even in purely civilian organizations. From the early 1960s to the mid 1970s, no alternative civilian elite capable of governing the country appeared in Cuba. There has also been little evidence of conflict between strictly civilian and strictly military leaders, because both types divide among themselves in disputes.

From 1965 to 1975, the survival and growth of the armed forces were achieved by reemphasizing the continuing legitimacy of old military objectives and expanding the roles of the military beyond defense. Military organizations did not fade away, but organizational boundaries became blurred. At the same time, national-defense strategy came to depend on civilian mobilization rather than on a standing armed force. With their strictly military functions fading in importance, the military took on social, economic, and political tasks.

Conflict between military and civilian agencies was reduced, at first, by the decrease in specialization within the military, so that both kinds of organizations undertook similar tasks in nonmilitary areas. The pressures of conflicting roles felt by civic soldiers serving in civilian agencies may also have diminished; they were no longer obliged to lobby for the reduction of their former comrades-in-arms' budgets since the military now performed nonmilitary tasks, diverting some military resources to assist civilians. Civilian party members learned from the military how to shape party structures; civilian party hierarchies filled vacant posts by drawing on civic soldiers.

These changes in the armed forces' definition of their role were generally welcomed by the elite because they reduced disputes within the leadership and made less acute the conflicts felt by civic soldiers administering civilian agencies and by low-ranking personnel in all agencies. However, the new role definitions created new role conflicts within the military. Civilian organizations began to compete with the armed forces for the time and resources of military units, thus creating intersender role conflict. Officers and soldiers also experienced role conflict in allocating their own time, exacerbating intrasender role conflict: should they emphasize military or other tasks? To cope with these new problems, the Army of Working Youth, which has devoted its energies almost entirely to production, was established in 1973. Military units once again became specialized. Some performed ordinarily civilian tasks in production and did little else; others performed almost exclusively military tasks. Role conflicts were reduced for personnel in units with military specialization, but not for the others, who have continued to experience them.

It has become fashionable to write about the militarization of the Cuban revolution, a concept that suggests the late 1960s were drastically different from other years. In fact, the behavior of the armed forces has remained essentially the same, although they did undertake more nondefense tasks in the late 1960s. I believe the concept of militarization is inappropriate to the Cuban situation because it fails to account for the special political quality of civic soldiers, who are important in many areas, from running the government to running farm equipment. These soldiers went to military school after they had fought and won the war against Batista, during which they acquired their extramilitary concerns for the first time. The Cuban civic soldiers have been different from the armed forces both in other Communist and in non-Communist countries because of their eagerness and conviction that military and political personnel and methods cannot be separate but must overlap if revolutionary goals are to be achieved.

Yet the civic soldiers remaining in the armed forces are soldiers still, and Cuba's reliance on them indicates important failures on the part of the revolutionary government. The need to employ the armed forces in the sugar harvests highlights the failure of economic production and the government's inability to handle problems of labor supply. The concept of the civic soldier evolved in Cuba in a context of the failure of economic growth. Nor has the performance of the military in economic production been any more successful than that of civilians. The years of least economic growth, that is, the late 1960s, were also those that saw the greatest degree of military responsibility for the economy and the highest level of political discontent in the civilian population. The use of military techniques in the 1970 harvest contributed to the workers' quasi-strike of that year. The more general adoption of military methods in politics stifled criticism from below and limited the adaptability of the political system.

What, then, is the future of the military in the political and economic life of Cuba? A number of developments in the mid-1970s suggest future trends that may prove to depart sharply from the domination of the civic soldier in the past. First, there is the possibility that military personnel exported to civilian life might at last become totally demilitarized and produce a civilian ruling elite for the first time since the fall of Aníbal Escalante in 1962. During the Angolan war there were already enough influential civilians around to object to the military's demands for personnel and resources. There was also popular dislike of compulsory military service; instances of insubordination occurred within the ranks; lack of discipline in the Army of Working Youth was a serious problem, and its level of combat preparedness was low; and the usefulness of formal military education—including political education—was being challenged. The military share of the Central Committee membership has declined, as has the proportion of graduating military cadets who belong either to the Communist Youth Union or to the Communist party. The time may have come to separate the military clearly from the civilian, so that the profession of arms in Cuba could be considered a full time occupation.[85]

On the other side, the expansion of the armed forces' role continues. The draft is used to force civilians to serve the state for three years, in military, productive, or other tasks designated by the government. Efforts to use military methods to educate Cuban young people have been accelerated. The importance of military skills has been reemphasized as a result of the Angolan war. The Army of Working Youth's very establishment is an example of military role expansion, because it absorbed the productive activities of the Communist Youth Union. The change in military doctrine relies on the mobilization of civilians in time of war and on improving the professional military competence of the very large reserve forces in preparation for war. The active reservists who serve as much as three months each year in the military typify the civic soldier, fusing civilian and military life year round. The militarization of the reserves and the growth of the Army of Working Youth have spread the civic-soldier role to the mass of the population. The military share of the Central Committee, while it may have declined from former days, is nonetheless still the highest in the Communist world, while the proportion of officers who belong to the party and the youth union exceeds four-fifths of the total. A civilian elite, though it now certainly exists, has not yet been well developed. Although pressures have arisen within the Cuban armed forces to put the civic soldier to rest, to stop using the military for civilian tasks, and to concentrate on military professionalism, they are not yet triumphant.

If the civilian organizations, already strengthened in the first half of the 1970s, can confront the military more effectively in coming years—if they can edge the armed forces out of productive work, find their own leaders, coordinate social services without relying on the draft, and resist military demands for a large share of the national income and the maintenance of a combat-ready reserve, then the day of the civic soldier in Cuba may indeed be near its end. The Angolan war may well have speeded that day.

PART THREE

POLITICAL
PROCESSES AND CHANGE

10

SETTING PUBLIC POLICY

No one person decides public policy in Cuba, and no one person ever has. Decisions are made by a process involving interlocking and hierarchical organizations, each with its own rules and center of authority. Two or more can share authority to decide specific issues; decisions in one issue area can have important implications for other issue areas. Almost invariably, however, decisions made at the top prevail when they come into conflict with decisions made lower down.

President Castro and, to a lesser degree, other members of the ruling elite, have the legal and practical authority to override decisions made at lower levels; they can dismiss officials as well, although the laws are less explicit on that point. They have exercised this power since the revolution, though with decreasing frequency in the 1970s, but even when they wielded it with greater frequency, there was a gap between the potential and the actual use of unrestricted authority. Some limited decision-making authority was always left to the lower ranks. Even though the legal authority to exercise absolute power has not been fully used, however, hierarchical decision making has left little autonomy for lower ranks when a mobilizational style has been used to exercise power.

The available resources for political action in 1959–1960 resembled those in nonrevolutionary countries, but there were significant differences. Because public opinion and private interest groups still wielded some power, the struggle for the control of the press and other forms of mass communication went on between the supporters and the opponents of the revolution. The issue at that point was not how to carry out the revolution but whether or not to do so. A good part of the battle went on within the government itself. Fidel Castro and his supporters had control of the Ministries of Labor and of Education; thus they possessed a tool by which to appeal for popular support. They also controlled the army, and, after the cabinet crises in the spring and fall of 1959, they finally also controlled the government.

At this point politics ceased to center on the question of "whether" and turned to the questions of "how." Public opinion became a secondary consideration. Political scope was restricted when the discussion of many issues (such as political incumbency, foreign policy, and nonsocialist economic organization) became illegitimate. Political domain was restricted because the opposition of the upper and middle classes and of those affiliated with previous Cuban governments could not manifest itself legally. As in any restricted political system, the main sources of power in Cuba today are organizational: closeness to Fidel Castro; position in one's own organization; ease of access to other organizations; and, at least at times, closeness to sources of power in the Soviet Union.[1] If the policy decision to be made is narrow in scope, it can be handled within one organization; if the policy is broad, then disputes ordinarily require Castro's intervention. Every dispute can be settled by him. Struggles over policy become entangled in bureaucratic maneuvering for power, since victory usually determines who will implement whose policies.

Proximity to the Soviet Union is the least dependable source of power and also the one most independent from Castro; its effectiveness fluctuates along with the state of relations with the Soviets at any given time. When relations are strained, as they were in the 1960s, the careers of the prerevolutionary Communists suffer; when they flourish, these careers blossom as well. In the 1970s the Soviet Union has provided limits to the exercise of Fidel Castro's power. Castro can probably still dismiss public officials close to the Soviet Union, but only at considerable political and economic cost.

The importance of these political resources and the degree of centralization vary depending on the subject at hand. Decisions on issues vital to the survival of the revolution—those determining economic policy, for example—are centralized and closely controlled; in such areas there is a reluctance even to accept information incompatible with elite goals. In less vital areas, much more organizational and individual competition is allowed; such issues include decisions in the arts, literature, science, and religion, responses to consumer demands or personal complaints from individual citizens and small organizations or the local branches of large organizations. Here some lobbying is allowed and is often successful; it depends for its success on the lobbyists' positions in their organizations and on the level of their contacts with other organizations, including the press. Lobbying also goes on within legislative and planning bodies, but the degree of mass popular influence on final decisions (as distinct from the detailed implementation of these decisions at the most local levels) remains slight.

Setting Economic Policy

Among the many subjects fought over within the revolutionary government, the economy has received the most attention. Cuba's first national economic choice—whether to concentrate on agriculture or on building up industry—took the form of a choice between the aims of the National Institute for Agrarian Reform (INRA) or of the Ministry of Industries, because both organizations were coextensive with these economic sectors, and, ultimately, between supporting Fidel Castro or supporting Ernesto "Che" Guevara. Because Guevara ruled his Ministry of Industries as an aggressive monopolist, the ensuing debate over centralization became a policy and power struggle that linked choices over degrees of centralization with the choice between agriculture and industry.

Cuba first chose industry. A policy of rapid industrialization in 1960–1962 was led by Guevara. "Cuba is a country of enormous wealth," he said, "it has everything it needs for industrialization . . . In a few years we will have developed from an agricultural into an industrial state." Guevara was against emphasizing sugar production, the processing of which he supervised. In March 1960, when asked about the problems arising from the loss of the sales guaranteed by the United States sugar quota, he replied: "I have not come just to speak about sugar. I wish that I did not have to speak about it. We would like sugar to be only one among many Cuban products."[2]

The commitment to rapid industrialization was not made by Guevara alone, of course. Regino Boti, minister of economics, promised, "In the next decade Cuba's economy will be the most developed in Latin America." As late as October 1962 Fidel Castro himself was still saying that in the four-year plan just inaugurated "the bases were established for an industry capable of manufacturing machinery and assuring the development of the Cuban economy." The government's economic planners also verified that the growth of the capital-goods industries had received high priority.[3]

Until about the middle of 1962 discussions showed little consideration of fundamental alternatives in policies and strategy, although circumstances did limit the range of possible choices. Once the decision was made to proceed with a policy of accelerated industrialization, other policies incompatible with this goal were not listened to. Sugar and agriculture in general would suffer. The elite and the bureaucracy created a climate of ideas and a style of decision making that precluded consideration of information suggesting that the policy might not be functioning effectively. A good example of this process was Prime Minister Castro's nationally televised scolding of his older brother Ramón, who had objected that the sugar industry was being allowed to decay.

There are two principal patterns of policy change. In one, the "incremental" style of decision making, the goals and implementation of policy are discussed continuously. Changes of policy are made gradually over time, with decision makers rarely scrapping the entire policy but focusing instead on marginal changes. A different style dominates in a "mobilizational" system, where hierarchical authority stifles criticism of the state's goals and policies. A sense of urgency and of planning in an atmosphere of crisis and attack is characteristic. Loyalty to proclaimed policies is crucial; a gradual and evolutionary approach to policy change is much more difficult to achieve than in the first system. Policy change often leads to scrapping an entire program rather than to a modification of only some of its aspects.[4]

Two setbacks in the economy highlighted the need for policy change in Cuba: the deterioration of the balance of payments and the sharp decline in sugar production in 1962 and 1963. Although the scope of the economic disaster soon became apparent, an increase in sugar production was actively considered only after the 1962 harvest; the economic managers—even those in agriculture—refused at first to consider this strategy for fear that it would disrupt the harmony and cohesion of the government. Even marginal changes, such as increasing sugar production while at the same time emphasizing industrialization and diversification, were rejected on the same grounds. Yet the crisis was so severe that some criticism broke through. The discussion of alternative remedies began cautiously. The Ministry of Foreign Trade argued that the industrialization program should concentrate entirely on developing domestic substitutes for imported products in order to solve the problem of the balance of payments.

Policy changed, however, only when Prime Minister Castro himself began to realize the magnitude of the 1963 harvest failure—it had been the worst harvest since World War II. When the change did come, it was rapid and total. The Prime Minister announced on June 4, 1963, that sugar and agriculture had become Cuba's chosen avenue for development.[5] Not coincidentally, the announcement came just after Castro's return from the Soviet Union. The Russians had pressured Cuba into shifting its economic strategy by providing the inducements of a guaranteed market and a high fixed price for sugar. The magnitude of the change and the sorry state of the economy led to a certain relaxation of the strictures on lower-echelon policymakers in 1963 and 1964.

The shift was interpreted as the result of a failure of a particular economic policy, not as a result of the process by which that policy was made. The policy was changed; the method of arriving at decisions was not. The result was again a fatal overemphasis, this time favoring agriculture, particularly sugar, over industry. By the late 1960s, no policy incompatible with earlier decisions favoring sugar and agriculture was considered. Castro's commitment to it has been unwavering. On June 27 of that year he declared that sugar had always been "the base of our economy and our development"; indeed, sugar exports had accounted for 85 percent of all Cuban exports and over a quarter of the country's national income in the decade before the revolution—facts that, however, had previously been neglected. The effect of bringing them up was thus all the more startling. On November 26 the Prime Minister went on to outline his new economic policy based on the subordination of industry to agriculture: "Industry will be born from agriculture. And what kind of industry? . . . Are we going to build cars and airplanes? Why should we build those things when other countries already produce them? . . . We need research into the chemistry of sugar . . . We are going to develop sugar derivatives . . . We shall develop an industry that starts from agriculture and can build upon an international division of labor."[6]

Guevara fought the new policy, but to save his industrial empire he made a small tactical concession: agriculture would be given a more important role, even if it was industry that guaranteed development. In March 1964 he declared: "Remember, comrades, that although in the years to come agriculture is Cuba's fundamental resource, there can be no vanguard country that has not developed its industry. Industry is the future." He continued to defend this view even after he had lost his position in the government. On February 26, 1965, at the second economic seminar of the Organization of Afro-Asian Solidarity, held in Algiers, he reiterated that "industrial development is what determines the growth of modern society."[7]

The other disputed aspect of the new economic policy, the extent of the centralization it required, took the form of a debate over budgetary policies. One side, favoring centralized budgetary control, argued that the part of the Cuban economy owned by the state was a single unit. Transfers from one place to another within the country did not involve buying and selling. Money, prices, and credits operated only in dealing with Cuban consumers or with foreign countries. Because enterprises lacked funds for investment, the system depended on administrative centralization for its operation. The other side argued that the part of the Cuban economy owned by the state was not a single economic unit but a variety of enterprises independently owned and controlled by the state. Transfers from one enterprise to another did involve buying and selling. Money and credits were needed to maintain control over production and to evaluate economic performance. Enterprises had to meet their own production costs. They had to be made responsible for maintenance and innovation. The system depended on a high level of economic autonomy for the component parts of the economy.[8]

Guevara and Luis Álvarez Rom, the minister of the treasury, defended centralization and budgetary-control methods. Alberto Mora, the minister of foreign trade, Marcelo Fernández, the president of the National Bank, and Carlos Rafael Rodríguez, the president of the National Institute for Agrarian Reform, took the other side. Because other debates were going on simultaneously among related interest groups, these men and their organizations were embroiled in controversies other than this one, though some of these conflicts could be resolved without affecting the others. The defeat of the old Communists—who happened to favor economic autonomy, material incentives, and curtailing the industrial effort—does not seem seriously to have affected the outcome of the economic conflict. But being on the losing side of too many issues could be troublesome. Regino Boti, the minister of economics, favored both industrialization and material incentives for labor; out of favor with Fidel Castro for the first reason and with Che Guevara for the second and for other reasons, he left the cabinet in 1964.[9]

Both systems of economic control were actually operating in Cuba in 1964, coordinated by the National Bank and by the Central Planning Board (JUCE-PLAN). The Ministry of Industries operated under the budgetary system (except for a mere 6.7 percent of its enterprises and 0.91 percent of its units); it accounted for 74 percent of the 221 state economic enterprises. The other state organizations (table 10.1) were all economically autonomous, but this system was not working as the theoretical model had predicted. Enterprises were rarely profitable, and they depended heavily on loans, frequently not repaid, from the National Bank.

Each side of the debate also marshaled its forces for concerted political action. Arguments favoring one or the other of these systems appeared in specialized journals and reflected the publications' ties. Ministries and their staffs supported their coalitions in various journals; a few dissenting articles were either reprints from rival publications or articles from the foreign press. The Ministry of Foreign Trade's *Comercio exterior* supported economic autonomy and was politically and economically consistent in its point of view, publishing eight articles supporting its position in 1963, eight in 1964, and no dissenting opinions in either year; in 1965, two articles supported budgetary controls; the other twelve on the subject argued for economic autonomy. The Ministry of Industries' *Nuestra industria* supported budgetary controls in a total of

Table 10.1   Economic control of enterprises, 1964

Government agency	Autonomous enterprises		Controlled-budget enterprises	
	Number	Number of units	Number	Number of units
National Institute for Agrarian Reform	25	1,124	0	0
Ministry of Industries	11	205	152	22,282
Ministry of Foreign Trade	14	—	0	0
Ministry of Internal Trade	9	135	0	0
Other state	10	28	0	0

Source: Salvador Vilaseca, "El Banco Nacional de Cuba y los sistemas de financiamiento," *Nuestra industria: revista económica* no. 1 (1965): 8.

twenty-two articles from 1963 through 1965, when only eight argued the case for economic autonomy for enterprises. It was ideologically consistent in 1963 and 1964 (publishing seven articles favoring budgetary controls and one favoring economic autonomy in 1963, ten and three in 1964); it was less so in 1965, however, when Guevara had lost control. In that year, *Nuestra industria* supported budgetary controls in only five articles and economic autonomy in four.

Guevara's aggressive empire-building had no doubt contributed to the formation of the coalition opposing him. He tried to get all activities connected with the processing of sugar, including many still under INRA's supervision, transferred to his ministry and argued that the functions of the National Bank should be as limited as would be consistent with the budgetary-control system. He insisted that his ministry have a measure of control over both domestic and foreign distribution of the goods that its units produced. The opposing coalition comprised those whose authority was threatened by his demands. Although the National Bank dealt with enterprises of both varieties, its role was more important in the autonomous system. When Guevara attacked the bank (precisely for these reasons), its president, Marcelo Fernández, promptly joined the opposition. The agricultural and trade organizations had little in common other than their reliance on the bank, but that reliance meant they had to defend the bank and maintain it as a channel for communication. Thus the ministers of the appropriate ministries joined the bank in opposition. Although no single minister could have unseated Guevara, the coalition could. Access to organizations other than one's own proved the key to the demise of the Ministry of Industries.

The effects of the highly centralizing economic policy favoring industralization were to discourage agriculture without helping industry. Before the revolution, the results of Batista's agricultural policy had been mixed. Agricultural production then increased from 1958 to 1960 (tables 5.14 and 10.2), a point that is important because land-reform measures, which encouraged small-property ownership and cooperatives, were introduced at the time. Production increased, and, although the increase cannot be attributed solely to the land reform because much of that reform was not implemented until after the 1960 harvest, the reform law's provisions protecting the most productive large farms probably stimulated private investment and contributed to the increase in production. Production declined from 1960 to 1962 (table 10.2) as the attempt was made to industrialize rapidly and the second land-reform act went into effect. Then a further disaster was inflicted by the government. It ordered the destruction of 134,200 hectares of sugar cane for the sake of agricultural diversification[10]—but the diversification did not materialize. Too many cattle were mistakenly slaughtered and their meat wasted, so that eventually the per capita beef consumption declined from between 65 and 70 pounds in 1959 to 39 pounds in 1962.[11] Nevertheless in 1962 the national budget specified that

Table 10.2 Production of selected agricultural crops, 1950–1962 (in thousands of tons)

Year	Rice	Maize	Potatoes	Sugar	Tobacco	Sweet potatoes
1950	125	278	90	5,528	42	295
1958	207	148	100	5,784	38	186
1960	307	214	109	5,862	52.2	272
1962	230	152	100	4,815	51.5	201

Sources: Economic Commission for Latin America, *Statistical Bulletin for Latin America* 3, no. 1 (1966): 22–24, 27, 31; ibid., 4, no. 2 (1967): 34, 37, 40, 42, 66; ibid., 6, no. 1 (1969): 36, 39, 42, 44, 68.

208 million pesos would be invested in industry and only 112 million in agriculture.[12] It took the disastrously reduced sugar harvest of 1963—only 3.8 million tons—to trigger the reversal of economic policy.

By 1962 the government's import policies reflected the bias against agriculture (table 10.3). Imports of agricultural machinery and equipment expanded until 1961 then were cut almost in half. Imports of industrial machinery and equipment declined in 1961 but only because socialization eliminated private industrial investment; they began to rise again in 1962. In 1961, the ratio of imports for industry to imports for agriculture was not quite 2:1; in 1962 it was 6.4:1. Consumers of nondurable goods and agriculture were subsidizing industrialization; the agricultural decline that set in as a result of government policy led to the food-supply crisis of 1963.

Erratic landownership policies may also have contributed to agricultural decline. Under the first land-reform law of 1959, 29 percent of the land went to the state and 12 percent to the sugar cooperatives. The second land-reform policy, instituted in 1960, socialized foreign and domestic property and ended the cooperatives. By December 1961 the state owned 41 percent of the land; members of the National Association of Small Peasants (ANAP) owned 39 percent; and bourgeois farmers (those owning over sixty-seven hectares of land),

Table 10.3 Cuban imports of selected categories of goods, 1955–1962 (in millions of current dollars)

Category	1955	1957	1960	1961	1962
Nondurable consumer goods	196.2	242.1	184.2	154.0	163.0
Agricultural machinery and equipment	10.9	16.2	23.6	32.1	18.0
Transportation machinery and equipment	16.7	24.3	26.7	71.0	75.1
Industrial machinery and equipment	66.8	127.8	57.8	59.3	115.7

Source: ECLA, *Statistical Bulletin* 3, no. 1 (1966): 101–109. Other import categories remained steady during this period.

20 percent. The third change in land-reform policy came with the second land-reform law, issued in 1963; it socialized the property of the bourgeois farmers and set a maximum of sixty-seven hectares for private landowning. This measure increased the state's share of agricultural land to 60 percent; in terms of total area, the state now controlled over 70 percent of the land.[13] Cuba had undergone three different landownership policies in four and a half years: production had risen after the first and the third were introduced and had fallen as a result of the second. Changes in production were not caused either by land-reform measures or by radicalism but rather by the other aspects of government policy already noted.[14]

The entire agricultural sector suffered, from the INRA managers to the peasants. The Ministry of Agriculture was dissolved in 1961, and its functions were transferred to INRA. Many former employees in the ministry lost their jobs. In early 1962 Antonio Núñez Jiménez, who had led INRA since the first land-reform act, and approximately four-fifths of the administrators of the state-owned people's farms were also dismissed. Industrial managers fared better. INRA's department of industrialization blossomed into the Ministry of Industries, headed by Guevara, in February 1961. Trade benefited from increased jobs and power when the Ministry of Trade was split into the Ministries for Internal Trade and for External Trade; unlike the old one, the new ministries had extensive control over all trade. The Ministries of Transport, of Communications, and of Construction, which could have been consolidated with some of the new ministries, if the government's goal had been the reduction of bureaucracy rather than the implementation of policy, were untouched. Bureaucratic restriction and growth varied by sector.[15]

Industry's performance during the early 1960s was disappointing. Compared with 1958 (which is set equal to 100), the index of production of selected industrial products in 1962 was as follows:[16]

Refined sugar	83.9
Beer	73.3
Textiles	86.5
Cigarettes	143.2
Refined petroleum	137.8
Cement	123.4
Electric power	154.4

Major investments had been made in cement and electric power just prior to the revolution, but both industries actually declined between 1961 and 1962.[17] With the exception of sugar, the pattern of industrial performance between 1958 and 1962 followed the directions set between 1957 and 1958 and for the same reasons: investments made or problems encountered in these areas before the revolution. The new government's policy of accelerated industrialization did not go far in practice; it was easily scrapped in 1963. Industrial workers had benefited little; unions had been crippled; and labor was defecting from the government and protesting its policies.[18]

The 1963 policy change at first brought about no significant difference in production (see table 5.16), although the tendency was still for industry to outpace agriculture between 1964 and 1966. There was also a slight increase in total agricultural production per capita (see table 5.14).[19] The emphasis on sugar, however, did not lead to large production increases. Although 6 million tons of sugar was produced in 1965 and 1967, less than 5 million was produced in 1964, 1966, and 1969 and barely more in 1968. The preeminence of the sugar sector did not necessarily lead to its economic growth.

To increase agricultural production, the government had to halt the flight of farm labor to the cities and towns. Given a labor policy that was still based on material incentives, agricultural wages had to be increased more rapidly than industrial wages. Between 1962 and 1966, wages in six different areas of agricultural work rose while none declined; there were increases in eight areas of industrial work and declines in three. Wage data also reflect differences in growth. From 1962 to 1966 annual median wages jumped from 954 to 1,059 pesos in agriculture and from 1,941 to 2,063 pesos in industry. Agricultural wages rose at an annual average rate of 2.8 percent, while industrial wages rose only 1.6 percent annually. Median industrial wages fell 24.1 percent (from 2,063 to 1,565 pesos per year) between 1966 and 1972, while median agricultural wages rose 22.9 percent (from 1,059 to 1,301) during the same period. Median agricultural wages rose 8.8 percent from 1972 to 1973, but median industrial wages rose by only 2.4 percent.[20]

Agricultural policy makers also found their jobs more stable than those in industry. In 1964 Guevara lost effective control over the Ministry of Industries (he stepped down formally the next year), and a Ministry of the Sugar Industry was established; in 1965 a Ministry of the Food Industry was organized; in 1967 what remained of the Ministry of Industries was split into three new ministries, one for basic industries, one for light industries, and one for mining and metallurgy. Guevara's empire had been divided into five parts in three years. The final split had been a result of an antibureaucratic campaign in which the ministries nearest the industrial sector were made to suffer the most. Three times as many people were dismissed from that ministry as from INRA.[21] Another supporter of industrialization, Regino Boti, minister of economics, was dismissed and his ministry absorbed by the office of the president of the republic. Guevara's ally in the battle for centralization, Luis Álvarez Rom, minister of the treasury, was dismissed in 1965 and his ministry was absorbed by the National Bank. Among those opposed to rapid industrialization and favoring decentralization, only Alberto Mora, minister of foreign trade, lost his job, and that was because of his alleged mishandling of import policy. The power of the National Bank was strengthened by the elimination of its competitors—the Ministries of Economics and the Treasury. Marcelo Fernández, the bank's president, received a vote of confidence from the leadership when he was shifted to the Foreign Trade Ministry to rescue the balance of payments. In 1965 Fidel Castro took over from Carlos Rafael Rodríguez as president of INRA. Agriculture's strength was now unmatched. Rodríguez remained as minister without portfolio and subsequently as party secretary and was assigned to crucial economic supervision, research, and ambassadorial tasks, but he had less influence than he had enjoyed before.

Despite all these debates and some variations sector by sector, there was in fact never much economic autonomy anywhere. By 1965 centralization prevailed even in those enterprises that had theoretically been autonomous;[22] it had been increased in the financial sector to benefit the National Bank, and it was holding its own in agriculture. Debate over centralization was simply an effective way of attacking Guevara's monopolistic Ministry of Industries; the goal was to decentralize that ministry, not the whole economy. The dissention was in fact not so much over industry versus agriculture or over what economic policy should be as over the swollen power of the Ministry of Industries. At the same time, the condition of industrial labor, both the union leadership and the rank and file, grew worse. The welfare of the peasants improved in the mid-1960s, but their political power had declined significantly by the late 1960s and early 1970s.

Decisions made regarding the economy in the early and mid-1960s emphasized not only the preeminence of Prime Minister Castro but also the importance of organizational resources. The mobilizational approach to decision making contributed to policy failures. Despite these constraints, however, there is evidence that disputes within bureaucracies and some incremental policy changes were allowed to continue. There was political autonomy, though to a very limited degree.

The mobilization system continued to function during the radical late 1960s. After the defeat of the microfaction in 1968, criticism was muted to a degree previously unknown. Any effort at introducing change prior to 1970 was greeted with hostility. The results were catastrophic; yet another abrupt and drastic shift of policy became necessary in the early 1970s, as the prerevolutionary Communists, with full Soviet support, regained their influence. Although the details of policy disputes in the early 1970s are still not clear, the mobilizational style was modified and a more pragmatic, incremental approach to the solving of economic problems could be discerned by the late 1970s.

Setting Intellectual and Scientific Policy

Public policy toward intellectuals is complicated by two characteristics that are less pervasive in other policy areas. Intellectuals, whether in the humanities, the social sciences, or the natural sciences, are a part of the educated elite and consequently tend to have autonomous psychological resources for political participation. If the generally low level of education in Cuba has made elite control over the mass of the population feasible, intellectuals' educational levels make control over them more difficult. In addition, although some intellectuals, especially natural scientists, work as teams, most of them work alone. This fact makes it more difficult to enforce policies designed to control them.

Literature and the Arts

Public policy toward intellectuals has been in general turmoil punctuated by particular crises from the beginning of revolutionary rule. Writers and artists, scholars and scientists have engaged in disputes with the government over policy. Some have had important positions in literary or scientific organizations created by the government; most have no base other than their own reputations.

The first government steps against some intellectuals, who had identified themselves politically with the revolution up to that point, were taken shortly after the economy was socialized.[23] A Cuban movie called P.M. was banned; the literary magazine *Lunes de revolución*, with a circulation of a quarter of a million, was closed down. Both reflected avant-garde intellectual trends in the United States and western Europe too closely. The Cuban National Union of Writers and Artists (UNEAC) was founded to enforce the new policies governing intellectual work, outlined by Prime Minister Castro in June of 1961: the government reserved discretionary powers of censorship, though it pledged not to censor artistic forms. A vague guideline for the content of intellectual production was provided by the dictum: "Within the revolution, everything; against the revolution, nothing." The applauding audience spent the next several years trying to decipher what that meant. At the same time, the government promised to support intellectual activities in schools, institutes, and publishing through subsidies in the form of salaries, scholarships, instruments, and other equipment.[24]

In late 1963 a vigorous and emotional public dispute broke out over the film industry. Almost all Cuban filmmakers signed a statement that "the formal categories of art have no class content," a position assailed by the old Marxist intellectuals, especially at the University of Havana. Another argument broke out between the prerevolutionary leader of the Communist party, Blas Roca, and the director of the film institute (ICAIC), Alfredo Guevara, over the censorship of specific films. With Prime Minister Castro's support, the Film Institute successfully resisted political supervision in the early and mid 1960s.[25]

Still another controversy broke out over the efforts of the government to extirpate homosexuality in Cuba, even using the armed forces to "rehabilitate" homosexuals and others they defined as social deviants through the Military Units to Aid Production (UMAP). The Cuban National Union of Writers and

Artists successfully enlisted Castro's support and forced the armed forces to disband these units two years after they were first established. But the government's panic about so-called social deviants was especially acute in its dealings with intellectuals and extended beyond the concerns of the military. In one notable instance, publication of the late José Lezama Lima's major novel, *Paradiso,* was delayed because of a section containing obvious homosexual references. It was eventually published because of Lezama's international reputation, not because he was backed by a strong organization. Some Cuban writers and some foreign writers visiting Cuba who were alleged to be homosexual were expelled from the country. The El Puente literary group was forced to disband because its members were also suspected of homosexuality.

In 1967–68, controversy raged in the literary magazine of the Communist Youth Union, *El caimán barbudo,* concerning the artistic merits of *La pasión de Urbino,* a novel by Lisandro Otero, a cultural official. The poet Heberto Padilla panned Otero's book while praising Guillermo Cabrera Infante's novel *Tres Tristes Tigres.* Shortly thereafter Cabrera Infante, already living abroad, broke publicly with the revolutionary government. Caught praising a defector's book, the editorial board of *El caimán barbudo* had to resign and Padilla's freedom to travel was limited. Another aspect of the controversy opened in 1968 when Padilla received the UNEAC prize for his poems, and Antón Arrufat the prize for his play *Siete contra Tebas,* which were then published with political disclaimers under the organization's auspices. The writers were attacked in the armed forces journal, *Verde olivo,*[26] in what quickly became a general polemic against the insufficient revolutionary content of Cuban literature. Three years later Padilla was placed under arrest for five weeks. In a rambling, incoherent, almost hysterical public confession of error, he subsequently accused other Cuban intellectuals of being insufficiently zealous, if not positively counterrevolutionary.[27]

Still another furor arose when some members of the old Communist party, led by Edith García Buchaca (later disgraced for prerevolutionary ties with the Batista government), sought to impose socialist realism on Cuban artistic and literary work in the early 1960s. While Castro declared that socialist realism should not monopolize art, especially films, the debate has continued, with those in favor of it stressing the need for revolutionary themes in literary and artistic work. The armed forces entered the fray in 1968. Government officials began to favor socialist realism more by 1971. Then Belarmino Castilla, the minister of education (promoted in 1973 to deputy prime minister for education, science, and culture), criticized "language deformations, distortions of history, and the introduction of ideas that are alien and opposed to our revolutionary conceptions through different artistic forms." The first national congress on education and culture noted in its declaration that "all trends are damnable and inadmissible that are based on apparent ideas of freedom as a disguise for the counterrevolutionary poison of works that conspire against the revolutionary ideology." Secretariat member Antonio Pérez Herrero called for "art expressions that will evaluate our socialist reality" and denounced "ultra-modern art concepts" from the West, but he also maintained that the "underestimation, scorn, and ignorance of art and culture, in general, of the socialist countries" was an example of "ideological diversionism."[28]

As in all spheres the role of Prime Minister Castro is decisive in settling these controvercies, but he does not often intervene. Disputes ordinarily go on without his interference both within intellectual associations and institutions and between them and the bureaucracies or the armed forces. Neither side consistently wins or loses. The armed forces, the writers' and artists' union, the film institute, and individual artists and writers have all had their occasional victories and defeats, and all continue to disagree. Disputes arise even over what type of music or of television program is "good" for Cuban radio and television.[29] Nor has the extraordinary sensitivity of the Cuban intellectual milieu to the political content of literary criticism faded. The apparent calm imposed over economic disputes by mobilizational styles has been absent in the more fragmented and modernized sphere of intellectual life.

Something of a double standard is used in judging Cuban intellectuals. The older ones, who acquired their reputations before the revolution and who have supported it since, can write more or less what they please, whether or not there is an iota of revolutionary content in their work. Alejo Carpentier and the late José Lezama Lima have been cases in point. Younger Cuban intellectuals, however, are expected to include contemporary revolutionary themes in their work and are criticized if they do not, although the government printing presses may still publish whatever they write. The 1976 Constitution guarantees stylistic freedom, but not freedom of content, and Fidel Castro reaffirmed this principle at the First Party Congress.[30] But the distinction between form and content is not always clear-cut. The government clearly prefers a muted Cuban version of socialist realism, but other styles are not forbidden. The establishment of a vice-presidency of the Council of State for education, science, and culture and of a Ministry of Culture in 1976 have made government policy toward literature and the arts more coherent. Much decision making remains fragmented among the various organizations grouping intellectuals; indeed each intellectual must make independent creative decisions by the nature of the work. Nonetheless these new government bodies have increased government centralization and control over all intellectual life in order to promote more effectively the kind of work that fits the government's preferences for "revolutionary" form and content in art and literature. The government believes that it is the duty of intellectuals, like other citizens, to make the revolution, even if that goal makes them appear somewhat parochial according to the intellectual standards of the outside world.

Science

Among natural scientists the situation is somewhat different. The early policies of the revolutionary government emphasizing political control made cooperation among scientists in Cuba more difficult. The government also increased centralization in science by claiming for itself the right to shape scientific research priorities rather than leaving these decisions to scientists themselves (see appendix F). From the mid-1960s to the early 1970s, with important exceptions, there were trends toward decentralization and increasing cooperation, although elements of centralization reappeared in the mid-1970s.

There are two reasons for the differences in government policy toward scientists and toward other intellectuals. First, as noted in the final declaration of the first national congress on education and culture and stated by Minister of Education Castilla, artists and writers can import foreign ideas that may contaminate the ideology of the revolution and of the population; these ideas may thus be used to propagate exactly what some Cuban government officials, led by Armed Forces Minister Raúl Castro, fear—"ideological diversionism."[31] The import of foreign scientific ideas, on the other hand, is not thought to pose the same problem. Second, the benefits of scientific research are tangible and therefore easier for bureaucrats to perceive than the benefits of art or literature. The government has consequently been willing to humor scientists because of the obvious benefits of their work to the public welfare, the economy, and national defense.

The university reform that went into effect on January 10, 1962, abolished tenure and limited faculty appointments to no more than ten years (they could be for as little as one year). Research was placed high on the list of the university's priorities, just below teaching and just above "moral, cultural, and political" education. The faculty was organized in departments that were expected to "conduct and coordinate research projects entrusted to them by competent authorities." Departments also had to provide technical advice to the government on request. The requirements were slow to produce the desired results, however. During 1963–64, no research was conducted at the school of arts and letters, the school of history, the school of law, or the school of political science at the University of Havana. The school of economics reported five research projects, which were little more than accounting and bookkeeping services for state enterprises. The dean of the faculty of humanities (later dissolved in a reorganization undertaken in 1976), which included all these schools, apologized to the Ministry of Education for the total lack of faculty research. Of the thirty professors charged with leadership duties in running the University of Havana in March 1961, about twenty held jobs in the revolutionary government, and more than half had posts in the militia or the regular armed forces.[32]

The January 1962 reforms also changed standards for admission and requirements for study at the universities. Each student was required to study three
semesters of dialectical and historical materialism, about 10 or 12 percent of
the total program. Academic freedom, like freedom in all intellectual endeavors, was limited: "against the revolution, nothing." Before the reforms,
many professors and students had left or had been expelled from the universities.[33] Enrollment had declined by a third, diminishing steadily every year
from 1958–59 to 1962–63 (see table 5.8). Political criteria were established for
admission. While no fewer than 50 percent of the law-school applicants who
were recommended by state and political organizations were admitted for the
1964–65 academic year, no more than 30 percent of those without such recommendations were accepted. But with or without, all had to be supporters of
the revolution.[34] Political criteria for admission to universities, senior high
schools, and selective vocational and technical schools have never been
dropped. On the contrary, they were tightened in 1977 at the secondary-
school level to give preference to government supporters in admissions to
selective schools, even if they are less well qualified academically than others
who may be lukewarm or opposed to the government. Even part-time students need to be recommended by their employers. All students in the University of Havana's school of political science must be also members either of
the Communist Youth Union or of the party.[35]

While the universities were still recovering from the political expulsions of
the early 1960s, the government issued a law on February 20, 1962, establishing the national commission of the Academy of Science of Cuba. The
academy was given authority over all scientific institutions with the aim of
"centralization of the available resources into a single institution" for the natural and social sciences. It could not only create but could also dismantle existing organizations, and it was backed by Prime Minister Castro himself. The
National Institute for Agrarian Reform and the academy struggled bitterly in
1964 for possession of the new sugar-cane research institute. Castro backed
the academy, and it won. It was also able, with his support, to wrest the national observatory from the navy and to establish the Institute of Meteorology
within its own orbit. The academy also acquired control of the marine
aquarium from the universities in 1964.[36]

Science policy in Cuba has been influenced by that in the Soviet Union and
the eastern European countries; many formal agreements have been signed
with the academies of science in other socialist countries.[37] At the time the
Cuban Academy of Science was established, Soviet scientific organizations
also emphasized centralization; the Central Committee of the Soviet Communist party criticized the duplication and fragmentation of scientific efforts and
the parallel research efforts in the Soviet Academy and in the academies of the
various Soviet republics. The Soviet party was even more concerned, however, over the delays between discovery and application, and this worry led to

a policy change in 1968. Duplication of effort was now to be encouraged as leading to a healthy state of competition. Research projects would be assigned to several organizations simultaneously in order to achieve results more quickly and efficiently. Competition was also expected to help prevent "monopolies" in science and technology.[38] In the 1950s and early 1960s, concern with costs had led the Soviet Union to give a scientific monopoly to the Soviet Academy; now concern over quality and a determination to increase the speed and efficiency of innovation led them to stimulate competition and to break up the monopoly even at the price of duplication. Cuban science followed a similar path, at least until the mid-1970s, when the trend turned again toward centralization.

The Cuban Academy of Science continued to absorb or to create scientific organizations throughout the 1960s. The Institute of Oceanology was inaugurated in January 1965; the Institute of Biology, in July; the Institute of Meteorology, in October; the Institute of Tropical Research, in the fall of 1966; the Food Chemistry Institute and the Institute of Geology, in 1967; and the Institute of Atomic Physics, in January 1969. Many of these organizations were formed by a kind of institutional bifurcation; the Institute of Geography and Geology, for instance, established in 1962, had split in two by 1967.[39] Some sections of the academy changed dramatically over short periods of time. In 1969 the biology section, for example, included an Institute of Biology and a department of botany and forest ecology; by 1972 it had institutes for zoology and botany and a department of forest ecology; by 1975 it had institutes for botany, for ecological studies, and for brain research. The atmospheric sciences section of 1969 disappeared into two institutes within the geosciences section by 1972 and then was reunited as the Institute of Meteorology in 1975. The agricultural section went from six institutes in 1969 to five in 1972 (losing a rice-research institute), fell again to three in 1975 (losing food chemistry and plant improvement), and wound up with sugar-cane research, soils, and tropical research. The number of institutes in the academy dropped from thirty in 1972 to twenty-two in 1975; it also had thirty-two research centers, five departments, and five working groups in 1975.[40] In short, the Cuban Academy of Sciences grew and became increasingly centralized through the 1960s, then contracted and spun off research organizations performing different activities in the early 1970s. The result was a mushrooming of scientific groups and the breakup of the academy's monopoly on scientific research—trends parallel with Soviet practice in the same period.

The chief threat to the monopoly of the Academy of Science has been the University of Havana, especially its National Center for Scientific Research (CNIC), founded in 1965. The center emphasized biological and medical research through 1969, but industrial and agricultural research were added in the next few years. It was reorganized in December 1974 to give more attention to agricultural research and to research on animal husbandry, and it sponsored scientific seminars every two years after 1967; the number of papers rose from 30 in 1967 to 418 in 1973. In December 1973, biomedical research accounted for 40.7 percent of all the papers; chemistry and technology, for 34.0 percent; and agriculture, for 21.8 percent. The center had four branches in 1975: its biomedical section conducted research on brain dysfunction, drugs, medicinal plants, diseases, and immunology; its agricultural section investigated using yeast as feed for cattle; its bioengineering section researched aspects of food, fermentation, and environmental pollution; and its chemical section investigated industrial and mining problems. Only 22 percent of the center's personnel were university graduates.[41] There was thus a division of labor between it and the academy in the 1960s; the center worked on biological and medical research; the academy on other topics. As the center undertook the same kinds of research as the academy, competition replaced the division of labor by the early 1970s. The academy also developed educational activities, graduating a thousand specialists in eleven fields of science in 1974.[42] In Cuba, as in the Soviet Union, concern with high-quality research had overcome concern with cutting costs, even though in Cuba this goal entailed both greater sacrifices and greater faith in science because of its more limited national resources.

Although no complete budgetary data exist, figures are available on total salaries paid by the government in scientific institutions. The budget for salaries of CNIC did not change from 1966 through 1968, while the academy's budget for salaries increased by 89 percent (table 10.4). These data reflect the general changes in Cuban science policy, which mirror those in the Soviet Union. From 1968 through 1971 the academy's budget for salaries remained unchanged; it rose again in 1972, while the university center's budget for salaries increased 117 percent from 1968 through 1971 and kept on rising.

Table 10.4 Salaries for personnel in scientific organizations, 1966–1972

	Academy of Science		National Center for Scientific Research		Institute for Research on Animal Husbandry	
Year	Total salaries (in millions of current pesos)	Index (1966 = 100)	Total salaries (in millions of current pesos)	Index (1966 = 100)	Total salaries (in millions of current pesos)	Index (1966 = 100)
1966	3.6	100	0.6	100	0.4	100
1967	5.5	153	0.6	100	0.6	150
1968	6.8	189	0.6	100	0.8	200
1969	6.5	181	0.9	150	1.0	250
1970	6.6	183	1.1	183	1.1	275
1971	6.7	186	1.3	217	1.1	275
1972	7.5	208	1.4	233	1.0	250

Sources: Computed from *Boletín 1971*, pp. 52–53; *Anuario 1972*, pp. 38–39.

The revolutionary government was principally interested in supporting sugar research. The short-term effect of its coming to power was the disruption of scientific work, although some have suggested that the low scientific output in Cuba in the early 1960s merely reflected a continuation of prerevolutionary conditions. However, the World Bank's comments on Cuba's limited research-and-development activities related to sugar apply only to the 1940s, and the report had had its impact long before the revolution. Research and development and the incorporation of new findings into production advanced substantially in the 1950s. The rate of industrial innovation in both large and small sugar mills also accelerated.[43] The Cuban Sugar Technicians' Association (ATAC), founded in 1927, had long issued a bulletin, but it became a regular monthly publication in 1952. Publication was suspended in late 1962 but resumed in January 1966. The sugar technicians gathered every year in a professional conference without fail from 1927 to 1961 but ceased to meet between 1962 and 1964. Founded by fifteen people in 1927, the ATAC grew to 1,789 members in 1952, but it had shrunk to only 430 members by 1967.[44] In 1968 it was revived once again, and association conferences have since been held regularly every two years; the bulletin and other sugar-science publications appear at regular intervals as well. The association's membership had again passed the thousand mark by the end of the 1960s. Sugar-cane research and development and application of the results to practice increased in the decade preceding the revolution; the new government interrupted this process in its early years.

The quality of scientific work is hard to judge in the best of circumstances. It is even more difficult to judge in Cuba, either before or since the revolution, because of the paucity of information. My impression, however, is that the quality of scientific research related to sugar in the 1970s is at least as good as and probably better than it had been before the revolution; this level should be credited, of course, simply to the cumulative growth of science and its research techniques. There is more direct evidence, however, on the sheer volume of work of Cuban scientists. Scientific productivity in sugar research also surpassed the prerevolutionary period. Thirty-three papers were presented at the association conference in 1965; this number rose to 52 in 1967, 88 in 1968, 134 in 1970, and 273 in 1972. The average number of scientific papers presented at association meetings each year was 33.1 from 1927 to 1961; it rose to 47.5 between 1962 and 1972—a 44-percent increase. Between 11 and 15 percent of these papers have been given by foreigners.[45] Research activity in the field of sugar science in Cuba had clearly recovered by the early 1970s.

The Cuban Institute for Research on Sugar-Cane Derivatives was founded in its current form in 1963 (research on these subjects had been carried out by the private sector before the revolution); it was affiliated first with the Ministry of Industries and later with its successor, the Ministry for the Sugar Industry.

The institute thus constituted a major exception to the monopoly of research institutes held by the Academy of Science at that time. Che Guevara's power was still sufficient in 1963 to keep the institute out of its hands. In 1964, however, the Prime Minister authorized the academy to set up its own Institute for Sugar-Cane Research; it did not become very active until 1967.[46] The Institute for Research on Sugar-Cane Derivatives had a staff of 350 in 1973, of whom only 75, or 21.4 percent, were university graduates. It did research on fermentation, cellulose, and chemical hydrolysis conducted in twenty-seven laboratories and four field stations.

A third research institution, also affiliated with the Sugar Ministry, was the Sugar Research Institute, which was in charge of the experimental sugar mill, named for Pablo Noriega, in Havana province. Although it was supposed to combine production and research activities there, it concentrated on production from 1967 to 1972, doing very little in the way of research. A research emphasis reappeared in 1973. In 1975 the institute was conducting experiments with methods for burning and harvesting sugar cane and eliminating the impurities introduced by cutting it with mechanized combines. It had a staff of 598 persons in 1975, of whom 45, or 7.5 percent, were university graduates.[47]

Research plans for 1976 through 1980 call for the development of a large scientific complex, the Center for Integrated Cane Development, at the Pablo Noriega sugar mill, housing the Sugar Research Institute, the Institute for Sugar-Cane Research and the Sugar-Cane Derivatives Institute. Some of the research activities of the Iron and Steel and Machine Ministry and of the Ministry of Agriculture (which replaced the National Institute for Agrarian Reform in 1976) will also be transferred there. Total investments are budgeted until 1980 at around 27.4 million pesos, of which half has been financed by foreign grants (15.7 percent of it from the United Nations Development Program). The total number of people to be employed in the compound by 1980 is estimated at 1,749, of whom 15 percent will be university graduates and 26 percent secondary-school graduates with training as technicians. Useful though it is, the combined facility can only add to the centralization of sugar research.[48]

Until now sugar research has been surprisingly diversified.[49] Although the institutes of the ministry, the academy, and the University of Havana have done most of it competitively, smaller organizations have also made their contribution. It is perhaps the clearest example of the breakdown of the academy's research monopoly that its researchers conducted only 37.9 percent of the 1,168 projects in agricultural research in the entire country in 1971.[50] While there was neither a monopoly nor a division of labor among existing research organizations in the agricultural sciences up to the mid-1970s, some research organizations were clearly stronger than others in some areas (the University of Havana's center was particularly strong in biomedical research, for example). Cuba was following a strategy of fostering competition among scientific organizations even at the cost of duplication.

What was the attitude of government toward scientific research? Did they know what they were doing? President Dorticós outlined its policy at the first national scientific forum of university students in December of 1972. He described it as "a process of centralized allocation of human and material resources to continue the research effort"; in other words, there would be no privately supported science. He added, however, that "no one agency in a country should have a monopoly over research."[51] The Cuban government's concentration on applied research contrasts with emphases in the Soviet Union and eastern Europe. Györy Rozsa has pointed out that the Cuban academy does not engage in basic or theoretical research and that, indeed, all Cuban research organizations concentrate on applied research and development. The only basic research found by Marcel Roche in 1969 was in biochemistry and ultrastructure (a branch of biophysics) at the University of Havana's center, and even there it only amounted to 5 percent of the center's activities.[52]

In 1972 President Dorticós boasted that "a connection between the various scientific branches and the practical problems of our society" had appeared in the majority of scientific papers presented at the students' forum and that the conference had "not constituted an attempt at intellectual exhibitionism without practical value"; he went on to warn scientists against the perils of establishing "a caste of aristocratic-minded researchers" divorced from the country's practical problems. Tirso Sáenz, interim president of the academy in 1972, denounced "research for research's sake" and pledged to support only research linked to production. Cuba, however, resembles the Soviet Union in that each central ministry had acquired a research-and-development department by the mid-1970s. These ministerial research institutes work only on practical projects that are very close to the production line; their participation in national scientific conferences, where basic and applied research are emphasized, has been extremely modest.[53]

The proportion of gross national product allocated to research and development fell from 1.2 percent (91.7 million pesos) in 1969 to 1 percent in 1974; the research-and-development budget had fallen to 75 million pesos by 1975. In 1969, there were 1,850 scientists and engineers and 2,453 technicians (in full-time equivalents) in research and development. In 1974, development took over 70 percent of the funds and what was called basic research well under 10 percent, with applied research getting the rest.[54] The profile of resource allocation to science in Cuba is closer to that in industrialized capitalist countries than it is to either less developed or socialist countries. Some less developed countries greatly emphasize basic research, while allocating well under 1 percent of their gross national product to science. The Soviet Union allocates more resources to research and development than Cuba does, but it, too, emphasizes basic research.[55] Cuba differs from industrialized capitalist countries only because its allocation of resources to basic research is extraordinarily low, probably amounting to only about 2 to 3 percent of the country's scientific resources.

Although Cuba's science organizations prospered for a while after the initial years of revolutionary rule, new crises surfaced in the mid-1970s. The National Council on Science and Technology was established in June 1974 and launched a new, more centralized pattern for Cuban science; supervision and control were the new priorities. Although some Cuban officials argued that this was simply a logical step in the development of Cuban science, which required organization and "centralized direction" as it matured, it in fact represented a more fundamental move away from competition and toward "rationalization." Deputy Prime Minister for Education, Science, and Technology Belarmino Castilla explained that "duplication of research, an irrational use of material and human resources, and a lack of sufficient integration" among research efforts must be eliminated, a view that reflects the accountant's approach to research and development that prevailed in the Soviet Union in the 1950s and early 1960s. New "problems" were discovered in the Cuban Institute for Research on Sugar-Cane Derivatives, for example; researchers found it difficult to divide their work into stages, calculate the time each would require, and account for costs. These so-called problems, however, were created only by the government's wish to know what every scientist was doing at all times; except for cost accounting, these problems would not have existed had a more decentralized procedure existed for organizing Cuban science.

The University of Havana became the first institution to have a scientific council; it was set up in March 1975 with fifty professors and no students. Other universities followed suit. The new scientific councils are intended to delineate approaches and identify major problems to be investigated; scientists then work on topics within this centrally determined framework. Belarmino Castilla boasted in 1977 that research was "going ahead in a much more organized and controlled way" that corresponded to "the needs of the country." Working scientists advise the councils, and the decision makers are often active or retired scientists; enforcement of these safeguards, however, is entirely at the discretion of the councils. Funding of research topics outside the framework set at the top is permitted for "flexibility"; but these "unplanned" projects are examined "rigorously" before funding is approved and never constitute a large part of the research effort. Individual initiative in choosing areas for scientific work has apparently been drastically curtailed since 1974.

An example of the operation of the new system can be drawn from medical science. A scientific council for medical research was established within the

Ministry of Public Health in February 1974 to plan, direct, and audit medical research; another of its tasks was to be "participation in the approval of research programs and projects." Its executive committee included representatives of the medical faculties of the universities, the academy, the University of Havana's National Center for Scientific Research, and the medical services of the armed forces. Its assembly included these groups and, in addition, the thirty-nine specialized professional scientific associations and the six provincial science councils (fourteen since 1977). The scientific council for medical research is subordinate to the National Council on Science and Technology. Its decisions are implemented by other research councils within its own subordinate organizations. Within the Ministry of Public Health itself—that is, independent of the academy and the universities—eleven research-and-development institutes have been established between 1966 and 1977. These were placed under the control of the ministry's research department in March 1974 so it could implement the policies set by the scientific council for medical research within the ministry. These ministerial research and development institutes emphasize development but allow some applied research.

One institute within the Ministry of Public Health engages in research on endocrinology. Founded in 1967, it teaches specialists in postgraduate courses that stress the official view of "how to work as a team in scientific research." The subjects of its principal research projects are diabetes, the endocrinology of reproduction, and thyroid problems. Its researchers are "guided and supported" by the Ministry of Public Health's national bureau of research; its policies are set by the national scientific council for medical research, which approves and controls all research proposals. This council is, in turn, subordinate to the National Council on Science and Technology.

Bureaucratic control has been established over scientists and science policy in all disciplines at the national, sectoral, ministerial, and academic levels and in both basic research and applied research and development. The reasons given for centralization and "rationalization" of research activities are the elimination of duplication and competition and the conservation of economic and human resources. The effect is concentration of power over science in government bureaucracies, curtailing individual scientific initiative and the autonomy of research organizations and ensuring that no one research organization can acquire a monopoly over research in any field.[56]

Centralization is also the aim behind the foundation of the new Ministry of Higher Education. The Ministry of Education had enough work to do tending to elementary and secondary education. Established in 1976, the Higher Education Ministry supervises research and teaching in the universities and allied institutions. It is responsible for the universities of Havana, Las Villas, Camagüey, and Oriente, the university centers of Pinar del Río, Matanzas, Holguín (and presumably the Isle of Pines), the two Agrarian Science Institutes (in Havana and Bayamo), the Engineering Sciences Institute, and the Institute of Mining and Metallurgy in Moa. The principal research institutions remain attached to centers located in the city of Havana, including the university, the Agrarian Science Institute and the Engineering Institute.[57]

The themes of control and planning in science are obviously consistent with general trends in Cuba in the 1970s, but they can well end up hindering basic research. Scientists build upon what others have done. There is little real waste or duplication of effort in basic science other than that inherent in a speculative and unpredictable activity, which is difficult to plan in detail. Basic and applied science and development are parts of a continuum. To sacrifice one end for short-term gains at the other is shortsighted. Cuba can import its basic science and technology, but that alternative is also not without its costs, increasing as it does both political and economic dependence on foreign powers. It has important foreign exchange costs. It can also frustrate whatever local talent there might be, leading to low morale and possibly to a "brain drain." It imperils the quality of graduate education in Cuba, just as it is getting started.[58]

Science has long been centralized in Havana, and relationships between Havana and institutes in the provinces have long been notably weak, perhaps accounting for the fact that only 13 percent of the graduates of all universities were in any way engaged in research in 1975. Centralized facilities are a rational way of conserving scarce resources and expensive equipment and of using them efficiently, but this goal is achieved at the cost of the quality of education elsewhere. The academy's geologists all moved to the University of Oriente in 1965 to establish a school of geology there, for example, but they were back in Havana to stay only two years later. Of the 214 students enrolled in advanced courses at the University of Havana's center through September of 1969, 45.8 percent came from that university, only 6.5 percent from the University of Las Villas, and 1.4 percent from the University of Oriente; the latter two both lacked equivalent courses. The other students came from the bureaucracy. The universities at Oriente and Las Villas do not have research centers; their faculties have little research support. Members from the University of Havana presented ten times as many papers at the 1970 sugar-science conference as those from the University of Oriente, even though the latter is located in the country's leading sugar-producing province. Since the sugar enterprises engage in little research and development, leaving even the most detailed aspects of innovation to the academy, the universities, and the ministry's central research institutes, this discrepancy is all the more striking. To counteract the concentration of research in Havana, the Academy of Science established branches in Oriente province and the Isle of Pines by 1972 and in Pinar del Río, Las Villas, and Camagüey by the beginning of 1975. In 1975 the Camagüey higher-education center was raised to the status of a university—Cuba's fourth—and was named for Ignacio Agramonte. It had twelve professional programs and 3,200 students; higher-education centers were also set up in Holguín, Pinar del Río, Matanzas, and the Isle of Pines.[59]

In addition to the current control of the scientific community, limitations on academic freedom have long been provided for in the university statutes of 1962. By 1972, moreover, a majority of the members of the academy were party members and thus subject to party discipline. Interim academy president Tirso Sáenz argued that "no Academy of Science . . . nor research institute will be without a thorough politicization of all its workers, of all its leaders, of all its researchers." Party secretary Antonio Pérez Herrero said that "knowledge of Marxist-Leninist science was indispensable" for Cuban scientists. But political restraints have always affected Cuban science; there is little evidence that in practice this factor alone has posed a problem.[60]

Sporadic political interference with science on particular occasions has caused more difficulties. When the 1962 university reform made the departments subordinate to higher authorities, their actual supervisor became the rector of the university. The rector at Havana, for example, appoints all the faculty deans and school directors and the councils that are supposed to advise these officials. Marcel Roche remarked in 1969 that he had "heard several investigators mention that their projects had been suggested directly by the rector."[61] This variety of political interference apparently knows no limits.

The most spectacular case of political interference with science was the clash between the director of the Institute for Research on Animal Husbandry and the Prime Minister in 1969. Castro had decided that crossbreeding imported Holstein bulls with native Zebu cows would result in a milch cow that could give more milk on pasture feeding. After he had started his program two Englishmen, Dr. Thomas Preston and Dr. Malcolm Willis, became director and deputy director, respectively, of the Institute for Research on Animal Husbandry. Preston and Willis believed that genetic crossbreeding was a slow and inefficient way of improving milk production and concentrated instead on research into the effects of changing environment and of a diet that emphasized grain and molasses.

At the institute's first congress, held in May 1969, Preston, Willis, and J. Clark, an English engineer, presented a paper showing that the Prime Minister's cherished hybrid Holstein-Zebu was an inefficient milk producer. Preston also reported that sugar was not essential to the human diet, that it had unhealthy side effects, and that its main future use should be as animal feed. The Prime Minister denounced Preston and Willis's work in a major address to the congress, saying that he had given broad freedom of research to the institute at the outset but that he felt it necessary to intervene when its directors began pursuing a line of research with which he disagreed: "By requesting and insisting, we have now succeeded in having some research done on pasturage." Castro, however, did not stop any particular research projects, suppress publications, nor prevent foreign researchers from saying he was wrong. At the congress he simply criticized the idea of using sugar to feed animals rather than humans, the emphasis on research into grain feeds, and the downgrading of genetic crossbreeding as a means of improving milk production.[62]

Eventually the antagonists reached a compromise. Although the institute had proved that sorghum from Israel was a superior feed, it agreed that the expense of importing it would be too great to implement its use in Cuba; work on sorghum was stopped, and the possibility that further research could eventually make its use economically feasible was ignored. The institute stuck to its guns regarding the inefficiency of the crossbreeding program, however, and continued research on the use of molasses for cattle feed. In 1970 its investigators had found a way to substitute molasses entirely for grain, with some supplementary use of pasturage. Its budget actually grew from 1969 to 1970, declining only in 1972 (see table 10.4). One result of the 1969 congress was that the institute lost its independence and was merged with the University of Havana, under a vice-rector appointed by the rector of the university. From 1965 to 1969, the institute had been autonomous from all other research organizations—even from the universities, the academy, and the ministries; it had depended directly on Fidel Castro. In 1976 it became one of the four sections of the Institute for Agrarian Sciences attached directly to the new Ministry of Higher Education. Although Preston lost the autonomy of his institute to the scientific bureaucracy, he remained working, writing, and publishing papers in Cuba through the early 1970s. He was too valuable for the Cuban government to lose his services entirely.[63]

Political pressures impair good research; an atmosphere of rigid controls and disciplinary restriction is not conducive to creative experimentation.[64] Although the amount of research being done continued to increase, it remained subject to intervention by the rector of the University of Havana and by the Prime Minister at virtually every turn, until by the mid-1970s a whole series of detailed procedures had been installed to control scientific activities. Decision making in science, has not, however, suffered from the mobilizational style typical of decisions over the economy, except for the government-induced stress on applied research to the virtual exclusion of basic science. There is no comparison, however, between the government's tight control over economic policies and the leeway given to an organization such as the Institute for Research on Animal Husbandry—even when the Prime Minister disagreed with its priorities. The Academy of Science, like the Ministry of Industries, lost the monopoly it had built in the early 1960s, but, unlike the ministry, it has never been dismantled. Still, the trend toward bureaucratic centralization is unmistakable, even in sugar science, and has consequences that are not yet wholly clear.

Closeness to Castro was the key political resource. The academy owed its early success to its close links to Castro; the fate of the Institute for Research on Animal Husbandry is also tied closely to his approval or disapproval. Nonetheless the process of organizational growth and differentiation still depends to some extent on the scientific organizations themselves. The academy had to use its skills in bringing its case before the Prime Minister and challenging its competitors; the University of Havana had to prove that it, too, could do valuable research and therefore had a claim on the budget.

As already noted, trends in science policy in Cuba parallel trends in the Soviet Union. Extensive agreements governing science and technology have been signed between Cuba and other socialist countries; many scientists from those countries have come to work in Cuba, producing extensive Soviet influence on Cuban science. Debates in science share some characteristics with those in other intellectual disciplines. Individual scientists, like other intellectuals, have held their ground even when they have been challenged by government authorities. Although few party and government officials claim to know about science—at least in comparison with the numbers who claim knowledge in the fields of literature and the arts—the political authorities still stress that science ought to have a "revolutionary theme," that is, a direct contribution to the economy, an aspect of the "populism" that dominates all Cuban intellectual life: painters paint posters, novelists exalt revolutionary heroes, music harmonizes struggle, and scientists promote prosperity. The decisive role of Fidel Castro is common to all decision-making areas, although the existence of some organizational resources independent of him has also been somewhat important in the making of science policy. The scientific world has been freer of conflict than the general intellectual world. A double standard is not needed in judging scientific work, and the distinction between form and content is not applicable. Direct Soviet influence may also be consistently greater in science than in other aspects of intellectual life.

Political restrictions in the intellectual world reached a peak in the early 1970s; in the scientific world they were only foreshadowed in the mid-1970s. Some degree of political control and intervention has always been around, nor is it likely to disappear, but it has encountered more resistance among scientists and intellectuals than in other areas of public policy. The most obvious difference between the intellectual world and the rest of the social system is the capacity of its members to think and act autonomously. There are no "established dissenters" in Cuban science[65] and no organized intellectual or scientific opposition to government policies. Cuban intellectuals, including scientists, are no different in this respect from their fellow citizens. There is, however, some modest evidence that intellectuals, scientists included, chafe under the detailed planning and accounting rules that bureaucrats choose to impose; even whole institutes may at times refuse to cave in; and writers and artists do resist intellectual populism.

Policymaking and Social Institutions

The Role of the Press and of Citizen Complaints

The individual contacting of public officials allowed by new procedures regulating local government was a significant change in the mid-1970s. Along with it, letters to the editor reappeared in the press, as did a modest amount of investigative reporting. News publicizing successful pressures on the bureaucracy has had its effects on decision making, albeit only when the decisions are relatively unimportant to national policy. There is no mobilizational style in this type of decision making; on the contrary, these proecedures seek to open up channels of access to government. These initiatives require that citizens have the capacity to participate politically on their own, independent of government, party, and mass organizations. There is ordinarily little coordination of efforts among citizens; those with complaints usually act alone. Their chief resource is to exploit the publication of letters of complaint; indeed, their only political resource is access to organizations, because proximity to Fidel Castro or to the Soviet Union and organizational position are irrelevant to this kind of decision making. Some citizen complaints have been described in an earlier chapter. Others lament the poor quality of services in government agencies, the shortage of housing, crooked taxi drivers, the poor maintenance of public gardens, delays in awarding pensions to retired workers, environmental pollution, slow mail and telegraph services, erratic water supply, and the lack or poor quality of medical services.[66]

Complaints against the bureaucracy have sometimes been striking, especially those regarding the incompetence of officials in the Ministry of Education. Complaints from graduates of the Hermanos Gómez Technical Institute are a case in point. The institute was established in 1970 as a night school for workers; four classes had graduated by 1976, but bureaucratic procedures within the Ministry of Education still prevented the issuance of certificates proving the students had completed their programs. The ministry finally promised in 1976 to do something by September—six years after the institute had opened. A similar, though less extreme, case of ministerial delay involved teaching certificates for six primary-school teachers who graduated in 1975–76; at least they had to wait only eight months. The Ministry of Education's fondness for red tape was also criticized by a woman who was sent to seven different offices when she made a simple inquiry about how to apply for a scholarship to a technical school. Even outside the Ministry of Education, things are often not much better. The government-run wristwatch-repair business normally takes sixty days to repair a watch; at least one customer, however, had to part with his for twenty-eight months. The government finally gave him a new one.[67]

Investigative reporting keeps the complaints of citizens in the public eye; when they go unanswered, the unresponsiveness of bureaucratic organizations comes in for some intensive scrutiny. In 1975 *Granma* published complaints about the poor quality of bread in state bakeries in Havana; the flour industry promised remedial action, but two months later the bread had not improved. Journalists seized this opportunity to engage in a variety of populist rhetoric against a branch of government, the likes of which the Cuban public had not seen in fifteen years. *Granma* published similar complaints about ice cream with a similar follow-up; *Bohemia* launched a campaign against inferior restaurants, complete with letters from disgruntled customers, visits to particularly bad restaurants, and interviews with embarrassed bureaucrats.[68]

Some complaints are not so well received, although they, too, are published. Cuba's National Rifle Association complained that they had been requesting new rifles for three years to no avail; they also protested the bans on certain weapons, on hunting on certain days, and on hunting certain animals. The national hunting commissioner criticized the hunters for refusing to accept his previous explanations, reiterating that the new rifles were on their way and that the prohibitions were there for good reasons. A high-school student who complained that Cuba had no mountain-climbing program was told by the sports institute that there were higher priorities than mountain climbing. Mothers protesting the busing of their preschoolers to schools in Santa Clara received no answer at all. Residents of villages and small towns complaining of the lack of electric services, even when there were power lines nearby, were told that electrifying their areas had low priority in the national plan.

The success of even some citizens, however, apparently produced an avalanche of letters. By mid-1975, letter writers were being told to go through "proper channels" rather than appealing to the press. People who wanted rural electrification of their areas were told to deal only with the provincial electricity officials. A Santa Clara worker's complaint that he had been denied social-security benefits was answered by a Labor Ministry investigation and by an admonition to use proper channels in the future. In Matanzas province, a woman from Perico asking for more electricity and a man from the city of Matanzas asking for an amusement park were both told by the staff of *Bohemia* not to write to them but rather to bring the problems up in local-government assemblies.

Several of these protests showed some signs of coordinated action. The complaints about bread, ice cream, and school busing were the results of letter-writing campaigns and included signed petitions. The complaints of the Loma de la Candela Committee for the Defense of the Revolution (in Güines, Havana province) about improper electricity billings and of the National Rifle Association demonstrate that even government-sponsored small or local organizations may be used as autonomous lobbies to advance group interests against government bureaucracies.[69] Although the party and government formally control virtually all organizations in Cuba, they do not prevent lobbying about specific issues so long as they do not affect national policy. There is, however, no evidence of a major national organization publicly challenging government policy.

Protests are not new to Cuba. The Havana newspaper *Hoy*, the organ of the prerevolutionary Communist party, noted on April 3, 1964, that it constantly received letters from readers asking for its intercession with government officials. Some letters dealt only with personal problems; others, with larger issues. In either case *Hoy* simply passed them along to the authorities without follow-up. The protests in the spring of 1968 over rationing and severe shortages of consumer goods were counteracted by Castro when he launched the revolutionary offensive, the revolution's most radical period of mobilization.[70] Protests had to go through official channels, which often scorned or repressed them. Newspapers did little critical or investigative reporting. One suspects that when *Hoy* told its readers their complaints were being referred to the very authorities they were complaining about, this response was hardly the one the letter writers had hoped for. The mid-1970s differed from the past not in the existence of protest but in its being directly acknowledged and answered to some degree.

The longest lasting instance of a successful citizen initiative so far was the prolonged existence of the *jardines infantiles* (literally, kindergartens), established by Haydée Salas and Lela Sánchez in 1964 and patterned after Finnish day nurseries. Their establishment was at first supported by Prime Minister Castro and a number of national bureaucracies. They were seen, however, as a political and philosophical challenge to the more numerous *círculos infantiles* operated by the Cuban Women's Federation, and their appearance consequently created some competition among nurseries and day care centers. The círculos emphasized cleanliness, structured learning, and fixed schedules; the jardines emphasized free play, exploration, and spontaneity; had a more flexible schedule; and involved the family in a way that the círculos did not. The jardines stressed autonomy and creativity; the círculos, conformity and achievement. The jardines were absorbed into the círculos in 1971, and Salas and Sánchez were removed from their posts. Political centralization and the FMC's círculo philosophy had won in the end. Still, the jardín initiative had lasted seven years and had gained some powerful support. As their number grew from 20 in 1966 to 178 in 1971, however, the competition became too much for the system.[71] Centralization and the need to instill the virtues of discipline and authority took over child-care politics.

The Role of the Churches

The churches are the only institutions not directly under government control. They confronted the revolutionary government with the full fury of antagonistic sacred and ideological warfare in the early 1960s.[72] The government's attack upon the Catholic church was far more effective than the most systematic attack in the rest of Latin America, that by Mexico in the 1920s and 1930s, when the number of priests fell by 14 percent and the number of inhabitants per priest rose from 3,443 to 5,088. In Cuba, the number of priests dropped by 77.7 percent between 1959 and 1970, and the number of inhabitants per priest rose from 6,601 in 1959 to 37,180 in 1970 and to 48,675 in 1976.[73] After many years of hostility, however, a rapprochement has been achieved in the 1970s between the leaders of the churches and the revolution. Although Protestants and Jews led the way in the late 1960s, the shift in official Catholic attitude was politically far more important.

A pastoral letter from the Catholic Bishops—the first in eight years—was read in all the Cuban Catholic churches on April 20, 1968. The bishops argued that "morality demands today from each man the duty to fulfill his vocation toward development"; this principle applied to a Cuban Catholic "immersed in such a reality as ours, where the basic motivation he faces is the problem of development"—that is to say, work is good, and it is good to work. The bishops also denounced the United States policies that were isolating Cuba. In a second pastoral letter on September 3, 1969, taking their cue from Pope John XXIII's encyclical *Pacem in terris*, the bishops distinguished between an ideology and the person who believes it. They called on Catholics to respect the "honesty" of Communists; "nor should we avoid collaboration in the practical order of our terrestrial realizations." Catholics should collaborate in "the undertaking of development" with "all people of good will, be they atheists or believers." Catholic priests should "orient with fidelity the insertion of our Christians in that new pluralistic world." Catholics should also "admit with serene objectivity the healthy elements in the criticism of religion." In both letters, the only comment that could possibly be construed as a criticism of the Cuban revolutionary government was this: "There are internal difficulties due to the fact that these problems are new and involve complex technical demands, although they are also a product of the deficiencies and the sins of men." In mid-June 1974, the bishops again asked their people to be a part of the present society, "not as elements of harmful division" but rather contributing to national harmony. In November 1976, the Catholic bishops condemned terrorist attacks carried out by Cuban exiles against Cuban civilian aircraft. They had broken with their allies of the early 1960s—the United States and the exiles.[74]

Roman Catholic organizational activity, however, remains circumscribed. Because all church schools were taken over by the government early in its rule, religious instruction is limited to Sunday schools within the church building itself. Religious processions are forbidden. Catholic lay organizations, called Christian communities, exist in a number of parishes but are far weaker than Catholic lay organizations in other countries. Nevertheless, although some individual Protestant groups get along with the government better than the Catholic church, the Catholic bishops seem to have far more cordial working relations with the government than the leaders of any other major church organizations.[75]

Some Protestants, notably Sergio Arce Martínez, president of the Evangelical Theological Seminary in Matanzas, argued that the churches must first tend to their own sins, past and present, before railing against the sins of the revolutionary government, and the major Cuban churches seem to be following this advice. They no longer criticize the revolutionary government and they encourage their congregations to take part in government-directed development. There is, however, some discord among the churches. The Evangelical Theological Seminary in Matanzas, though formally sponsored jointly by the Presbyterian, Episcopal, and Methodist churches, is actively supported only by the Presbyterians, whose president is also the school's president. The others seem to believe that the school is too political.[76]

Four other, smaller Protestant seminaries also exist, as well as a functioning Cuban Council of Churches comprising fifteen Protestant denominations. The council's Center for Ecumenical Studies, headed by Arce, was founded in 1968; the Catholic Center for Christian Studies was set up in 1969—both seek links between the churches and the government. The Protestant Christian Student Movement is probably the most active religious organization of Cuban laity that openly supports the revolutionary government. Protestant churches seem to rely more on the religious work of individual church members to spread their point of view, while the Catholic church relies more on its clergy. The activity of all the churches is, in fact, partly supported by the government, which makes paper and a printing press available to them for their periodical publications. Although the churches and the government once clashed violently, religious toleration, within sharp limits, came to prevail in the 1970s. Since the mid-1960s political activity critical of the government on the part of the churches has been very rare. Perhaps the last such criticism occurred when the Protestant Cuban Council of Churches joined the Cuban National Union of Writers and Artists and other groups in protesting against the Military Units to Aid Production (UMAP).[77]

Some denominations, however, still dissent from both the government and the emerging religious consensus. A steady battle continues between the government and some sects, notably the Jehovah's Witnesses. Some Afro-Cuban sects have also been subject to persecution. These sects do not distinguish between the sacred and the secular, a view incompatible with the revolution, and have suffered because of it. The declaration of the first national congress on education and culture reaffirmed the government's long-standing antisectarian policy.[78]

The difference seen between the Roman Catholic church and other religious sects is made obvious in article 54 of the 1976 Constitution, which guarantees freedom of religious belief but provides for punishment of anyone who, on religious grounds, challenges the state on matters of education, employment, compulsory military service, honoring the flag (and other national symbols), or performing any patriotic or revolutionary duty. The Roman Catholic bishops have publicly accepted this article. But its prohibitions are obviously at the heart of disputes between government and other sects.[79] Religious organizations that continue to criticize the government also continue to suffer repression. The major denominations, however, have suspended their criticism of the government and are careful to restrict their formal organizational autonomy to spiritual concerns. The churches of Cuba criticize the government less than the government criticizes itself or allows individual citizens to criticize it. Apparent ecclesiastical autonomy may be a symptom of government flexibility, but it has no practical political significance.

The First Party Congress clarified the government's attitude toward religion. It reaffirmed freedom of religious belief, within the restrictions just described and excluding any belief that would conflict with public-health regulations (such as those of Christian Scientists, for example). The congress decided that the "struggle for a scientific concept free of prejudice and superstition is subordinated to the struggle for the construction of the new society . . . Believers, nonbelievers, members of religious orders, and atheists have participated, continue to participate, and must necessarily participate" in the building of the new society. The party's theoretical commitment to atheism would not be vigorously pursued in practice, but active believers continue to be excluded from party membership and important posts and are not allowed to teach at the Institute of Pedagogy of Havana University.[80]

Consumer Pressures

The severe economic problems of the 1960s, which necessitated rationing and sacrifices as a part of the new ideology, prevented marketing pressures from affecting the allocation of goods with any consistency, although such pressures have operated to some degree throughout the revolutionary period. By 1968 full socialization of all trade and services had been achieved. But months after the takeover, demands for the goods that many small businesses used to provide, especially snack foods, were being heard. The state organizations were slow to respond; despite their considerable reluctance, however, they had eventually to increase production of snack foods.[81]

The closing of state-owned and private bars (drinking in private was still allowed) and the halving of beer production in 1967 and 1968, at the same time as production of nonalcoholic malt beverages was doubled (table 10.5), caused similar discontent. The government had converted part of brewery production from beer to malt in an attempt to alter consumer tastes, but it had to abandon the effort by 1970. The breweries were reconverted to beer production, since

Table 10.5 Beer and malt production, 1967–1973 (in thousands of hectoliters)

Year	Beer	Malt
1967	1359.6	245.2
1968	784.1	496.3
1969	658.8	656.8
1970	1001.5	524.2
1971	1308.6	558.4
1972	1665.5	584.1
1973	1851.3	495.3

Sources: *Boletín 1971*, pp. 174–175; *Anuario 1973*, p. 131.

beer-drinking consumers had successfully resisted efforts to change their tastes. In the fall of 1973 the Prime Minister told the thirteenth labor congress, "If you want some good news, the comrades in the service sector have suggested a slight drop in the price of alcoholic beverages." *Granma* discreetly reported the response of the assembly as "[Applause]."[82]

Little information is available regarding preferences in the arts and literature, but Lisandro Otero, vice president of the National Council of Culture, noted that it took a long time before the products of "high culture" had a large audience. The government was trying to move public taste toward high culture, but to little avail.[83] When it came to popular entertainment, politically suitable films had a hard time as well. Between forty-three and fifty-seven Soviet films were shown every year in Cuba from 1961 through 1964, accounting for a fifth to a quarter of all films shown. When relations between the two countries cooled, the number fell to fifteen in 1967 and fourteen in 1968, a mere eighth of the offerings. By 1972 Cuban-Soviet relations were much improved, but the twenty-eight Soviet films were back up only to a fifth of the offerings;[84] clearly the didactic Soviet style was not very popular. In the meantime, visitors report a continuing high demand for Hollywood films, as well as for programs on television featuring 1950s rock-and-roll and popular music—ideological criticisms from on high notwithstanding.[85]

In the 1970s the government began to rely heavily on surveys to determine marketing demands as well as to help maintain more effective government control. No consumer movement could emerge independent of the party and the government. Although survey results are not generally made public, the decision to increase housing construction in the early 1970s may have been determined by these findings. For example, a small 1970 survey of divorced couples in Havana found that the housing shortage may have been a major cause of divorce; although virtually all couples had wanted to live by themselves during their marriages, two-thirds of them had to live with their relatives because they could not find housing.[86]

Legislation and Legislative Processes

Little is known about what legislative processes were functioning in Cuba in the 1960s. The cabinet had both legislative and executive authority; laws were formulated in the bureaucracy and presented to the cabinet for approval. Some aspects of the legislative process leading to major laws or legal codes began to be formulated in 1969 with the establishment of the Law Study Commission and in 1970 with the establishment of its secretariat, which drafted major legislation, and submitted it to the commission for discussion. Draft legislation was then submitted to ministries and other state agencies, attorneys in state law firms, judges, and other authorities. Evidence suggests that there was considerable lobbying by members of the elite to change laws at this point. The secretariat then prepared second drafts reflecting the comments it had received. These second drafts were submitted for discussion by the people through their mass organizations with the requirement that all opinions expressed had to be in a written record. These procedures were followed only for legislation that the government declared to be of major importance.[87]

What difference does popular participation make? It is impossible to know whether differences between the draft and the final document are attributable to popular reactions, to further refinements within the Law Study Commission, or to the influence of others in positions of power. What changes were made in particular cases, however, can be assessed (see appendix D). The few nontrivial changes made in the Family Code, for instance, cannot be readily attributed to the impact of popular participation; they are better explained as the results of technical or legal refinements by lawyers, family counselors, social workers, and the relevant bureaucracies.

The statement announcing the promulgation of the Family Code noted that the Law Study Commission, "accepted and included in the draft text all suggestions it considered rational and useful, independent of the number who voted for them."[88] The participation of the people was entirely consultative and for the benefit of their "political education." The commission and ultimately the cabinet retained full discretion. This government control can also be seen with reference to the change in the minimum age for marriage for girls in article 3 of the Family Code. Blas Roca, the official mainly responsible for the entire process, admitted that the age limit was changed in response to popular pressure,[89] but proposals to amend article 3 were supported by only 2.2 percent of the 2,195,537 members participating in the Committee for the Defense of the Revolution assemblies, only 2.1 percent of the 1,003,282 Labor Confederation members participating, and 2.0 percent of the 103,152 participating members of the peasants' association (the only detailed and virtually complete count available).[90] Therefore, the votes of no less than 97 percent of the participating persons who did not vote for the proposed changes were set aside. Public officials were evidently so surprised that as many as 2 percent of the people would oppose the government's draft on any point, however minor, that they had to assume—probably correctly—that a great many more people felt similarly but were reluctant to express their views. In terms of democratic majorities, however, the people have no effect on legislation; all decisions are made by the elite; even on a disputed matter such as the marriage age in the Family Code, the apparently overwhelming majority was disregarded on the grounds that a tiny minority was in reality reflecting the popular will.

The discussion of the draft Constitution in 1975 shows a similar phenomenon. The text of the draft Constitution was prepared by a special commission established on October 22, 1974, which included leaders of the party, the government, and the mass organizations. It was formally presented to Prime Minister Castro on February 24, 1975, was discussed for somewhat less than forty hours in joint sessions of the Political Bureau and Secretariat of the party Central Committee. A great many changes were introduced in the text, a third of which were made by Prime Minister Castro himself. The amended text was then approved for popular discussion; suggestions would be reviewed by a constitutional commission empowered with full authority to accept or reject all suggestions and to pass on the draft to the First Party Congress. The congress approved it and a popular referendum ratified it in 1976.[91]

The Cuban press reported only two items in the draft Constitution that underwent any substantial public discussion. One was whether to insert an amendment declaring Spanish to be the official language, as the Constitution of 1940 had done. The other was whether to change the country's name from the Republic of Cuba to the Socialist Republic of Cuba, even though the draft already stated, "the Republic of Cuba is a socialist state." Both amendments received considerable popular support, although the press also published some dissenting views. Nationalist university students, in particular, objected to the name change.[92] The government allowed free discussion, since neither question affected substantive policy in any way. In the end neither amendment was accepted.

In late May of 1975 Blas Roca, the guiding hand behind the ratification procedure, remarked on the extensive discussion of the official name and language for the nation and went on to report another proposal, this time to insert a clause into the Constitution providing for compulsory education through secondary school. Such an amendment would have required extensive rearrangement of government priorities, and Roca opposed it precisely on those grounds. But what is significant is that the Cuban press had not mentioned the proposal at all. Presumably government representatives had opposed these amendments at the local level and had lost, but then the directive had been sent down from the leadership in clearer terms to limit the debate: henceforth suggestions "not in accord with the fundamental principles" of the government would be rejected.[93]

Although the actual changes made in the draft Constitution are not obviously related to popular reactions, they can be attributed to lobbying by the groups that would benefit from them. Most of the substantive changes benefited those in office by increasing their discretionary powers and their authority over their subordinates. Most of the other changes were merely symbolic, enshrining in the Constitution the state's obligation to support various activities and organizations; these pledges of government support, however, were clearly thought important enough for their beneficiaries to extract them from the government. As was not the case in the discussions of the Family Code, the text of the Constitution, a much more important and complex document, inspired lobbying activities that were often successful, though again only on minor but nontrivial issues.

At no point did the people elect a constitutional assembly or a congress to prepare the draft; rather, the authorities controlled the entire process. When significant amendments were suggested, they were quickly stopped by government leaders. The new Constitution requires certain changes in legislative procedures (described in chapter 6). Nevertheless, the basic feature of the legislative process remained complete elite control, allowing participation to enhance legitimacy and to permit individual legislators to serve their constituencies by initiating legislative drafts and monitoring bureaucratic performance. The National Assembly's committees also worked to improve the technical quality of the laws. The 1976 Constitution guarantees that the higher offices of the state can override any legal challenge from below.

Planning for the Nation

The center of the formal planning apparatus for the nation is the Central Planning Board (JUCEPLAN).[94] The first long-range plan, prepared in the 1960s and covering 1962–1965, was so unrealistic that it was abandoned shortly after it was made. State budgets with charges and payments between the units of the state were abandoned by the second quarter of 1967. Interest on loans was also no longer collected; farmers were no longer required to pay taxes; and the connection between salaries and sales was severed at the firm level. The government discouraged students from preparing for careers in economic planning. University programs in political economy and public accounting were abolished in 1967. Enrollment at the Institute of Economics at Havana University fell by 72.2 percent from 1964–65 to 1969–70.[95] For the first decade and a half of socialism, Cuba proceeded on the basis of annual plans, which were then further modified and often contradicted by "miniplans" made for each farm or factory separately; the practice led to virtually continual bottlenecks in the economy. Special or extra plans were constantly being promulgated either to replace those set by the Central Planning Board and considered unrealistic or to encourage some particular sector. The economy was centralized through the formal planning systems; although mini-, special, and extra plans seemed to introduce some degree of decentralization, in fact they were introduced directly from Havana, often by the Prime Minister himself, and had the effect of recentralizing from a bureaucracy to a single individual—at the cost of general bureaucratic anarchy. These violations of bureaucratic planning had virtually none of the advantages of decentralization and all the disadvantages of centralization. Personal whim replaced rational allocation.

Political modifications were made at the local or sectoral level to get around the limitations and obstacles of the planning system. Ministries, enterprises, plants, and special plan managers in the 1960s "had to compete savagely for the necessary inputs" because the planning system was unable to allocate "inputs" in the face of so many modifications.[96] Black markets developed as a result, as a means for individuals and for government enterprises to secure what they would not get through allocation. The black market has continued to operate in the 1970s. *Sociolismo* (the "buddy system") replaced *socialismo* (socialism) in aspects of ministerial, enterprise, plant, and special-plan management and among party and government officials at the local level.[97] Labor planning also had to be gotten around. Work norms, on which salaries were based in the first half of the 1960s and again in the 1970s, were juggled to attract skilled workers away from other jobs at a wage closer to their scarcity price. State-enterprise managers raided the universities in the 1960s for skilled personnel and put them under contract. Students "were being offered high wages to lure them into a specific job, and a real competition was developing between agencies for them," complained Castro. The government prohibited placing university students under contract and developed a system whereby students could instead combine work and study.[98]

Bureaucratism also took its toll. Meetings, decision delays, and other measures to avoid taking responsibility and thus possible reprisals became a means of survival. At the same time, the spoils system was in obvious effect. Appointees with literally no administrative or managerial training or experience were chosen to head whole factories because they were politically loyal. President Dorticós mentioned the prevalence of political appointments as one of the chief deficiencies of the Cuban administration as the country prepared for its giant effort in 1970. Political patronage was probably necessary in the beginning to discourage counterrevolutionary efforts, but it was not justifiable after that.[99]

Under Soviet pressure, a long-range planning group was established in 1969 to coordinate the preparation for the Cuban-Soviet economic agreement that was to go into effect at the end of 1970. The Central Planning Board abandoned its administrative tasks to concentrate on planning. Enterprises that had effectively been run as bureaucratic offices were at last being required to account for their productive and financial performance. Workers were encouraged to participate in the details of implementating plans.[100]

The new planning system in the 1970s retains a high degree of centralized discretion, but it at least relies on regular bureaucratic procedures. At the top the party's Political Bureau sets national goals, decides the principal strategies for development, and approves the plan in the final instance. At the second level the Central Planning Board carries out the mandates of the Political Bureau; it formulates "preliminary accounts" that become the basis for exchanging information within the board itself and with the ministries. JUCE-PLAN also coordinates all aspects of the formulation of plans. The executive committee of the Council of Ministers, which reflects the Cabinet's organization into sectors, coordinates the formulation and implementation of the plan within each sector; the executive committee, however, never directly implements the plan. The central ministries also participate in plan formulation at the stage of the preliminary accounts; they may include the ministerial offices throughout the country in these discussions as well. This stage is concluded when the Central Planning Board, after further consultation with top party and government officials, publishes the revised document, now called the "control accounts," which specifies in more detail the plan's operations.

The state enterprises, each of which may group several factories, farms, shops, or other production units, help to formulate those aspects of the plan that affect implementation. All production units discuss the control accounts that pertain to their own work; workers and managers suggest changes relative to how the plan will apply to them and how it will operate in their unit. It is only at this level that any degree of popular participation occurs.[101] The Central Planning Board and the top party and government officials retain full power to accept or reject suggestions from lower ranks. The planning stage is concluded when the Central Planning Board issues its final "directive accounts," which become the annual plan. The plan's fulfillment is then obligatory for all bureaucracies, enterprises, and production units. The third stage is thus the one for implementation. The central ministries are the highest-ranking structures concerned with the direct implementation of the annual plan. The state enterprises and, of course, the individual production units implement the plan within their own spheres of authority.

The First Party Congress added some more organizations and procedures to the planning process. It also approved the country's first five-year plan (for 1976–1980), which was this time fully integrated with member countries of the Council for Mutual Economic Assistance, and approved proposals for reestablishing both a state budget and a system of charges and payments between units of government beginning in 1977. The earlier practice of concentrating only on physical production targets was replaced by a new emphasis on costs, including depreciation, and on prices. New state committees on prices, technical and material supply, finance, statistics, and standardization have been set up to carry out these decisions.

Each enterprise now has its own budget, and there are charges and payments among enterprises. Beginning in 1978 an experimental group of enterprises drawn from various sectors will be allowed to operate almost independently; they can modify, though not suspend, the plan. They can never set prices or wages different from those that prevail elsewhere. Each will be required to show a profit and to account for this profitability; they must use the accounting system set in Havana. Credits, interest on loans, and state taxes will be charged directly to them for the first time in a decade. They will be able to use their own funds for investment and may rent out their idle equipment. Profitability after taxes and interest paid will be used to measure costs, evaluate investments, and determine level of performance.

Profit sharing was also approved by the First Party Congress for introduction on an experimental basis. Each enterprise will retain a part of its profits to distribute among the manager and the best workers. The government remains committed to the maintenance of enterprises, even if they are unprofitable, however, so long as they contribute to the "satisfaction of the people's material and spiritual requirements."[102] If this plan is actually carried out, it will represent the first move toward economic decentralization since 1960. The main beneficiaries will be the managers, who will gain new decision-making authority and a bonus from profits.

Decision making in Cuba has always been a complex process involving many participants. One, Fidel Castro, has been decisive for most issue areas; closeness to the Prime Minister has often been a crucial political resource. Those who have had the support of the Soviet Union have been politically most autonomous from Castro but have seen their fortunes rise and fall along with Soviet influence in Cuba. Closeness to the Soviet Union is probably most important for major decisions on national policy but is also important at lower levels. Thus attitudes toward Soviet socialist-realist literature could be used to identify intellectuals' ideological diversionism, and Soviet influence on science policy in Cuba has been considerable. Even the frequency with which Soviet films are screened has varied to some extent according to politics. The two major factions within the Cuban ruling elite have been those close to Castro since the early 1950s and those who belonged to the prerevolutionary Communist party and thus have ties to the Soviets. Although Castro has had to yield to Soviet views in important areas of national politics in the 1970s, he has remained in clear control of decisions on many issues and policies.

A grasp of factional politics is indispensable for understanding power relationships within the Cuban elite and with the Soviet Union, while organizational politics is the key to understanding other aspects of decision making in Cuba. Factions are groups of individuals with shared worldviews in different organizations. The economic debate of the early 1960s was influenced by factional politics, but the main coalitions were defined primarily by organizational stakes, loyalties, and resources. The politics of intellectual and scientific life in Cuba, though affected by factional struggles, also has strong organizational aspects. Even the exertion of pressure in the early and mid-1970s by individual citizens or small groups has required access to the mass media, local government, or government-sponsored organizations.

Mobilizational styles of decision making prevail more often in matters of national importance than in purely local or less important matters. As the significance of issues to the government decreases, it becomes easier for individuals to break through and criticize existing policies. At the same time, decision making becomes less centralized; more individuals or groups affect policy in these matters. At the top of government, only two main factions and a few organizations or coalitions compete over policy; lower down, even individuals or small organizations acting alone, occasionally in opposition to the Prime Minister and without Soviet backing, can have an impact on policy. The characteristics necessary to make the attempt to influence decisions—psychological independence and a sense that the individual can influence policy—are found most often among intellectuals, including scientists, but are present also among ordinary citizens who have complaints to make.

Like other aspects of Cuban politics, decision making is strongly hierarchical. Restrictions on political autonomy were increased for scientists and other intellectuals in the early and mid-1970s; individual citizens were given somewhat greater leeway at about the same time. That autonomy is limited at all levels, however, does not mean there is none. Within existing constraints, organizations and individuals can act independently and lobby on particular issues; it is precisely this fact that has made political conflict possible in Cuba. The only nationwide organizations in Cuba that were—at least formally—fully autonomous from the government in the mid-1970s were the churches; except for a few sects, however, all religious groups have chosen to limit their independence to purely religious matters and not to criticize government or party. Like any other organization, though, they can be expected to act to defend their own interests if necessary.

Some new procedures for legislation and planning were instituted in the early and mid-1970s, and more are scheduled for the late 1970s. Because of the national importance of these matters, they have been tightly controlled by the government, decision making has been centralized, and popular participation has been limited. The masses—and even lower-echelon officials—are typically consulted only about the details of implementation at the local level; the impact of popular opinion on major legislation has been slight. Experiments planned to begin in 1978, however, may bring about more decentralization of the planning process; if these changes occur, managers will benefit more than the public at large.

No consistent winners or losers are readily apparent on the political scene in revolutionary Cuba, at least among those fundamentally loyal to the political system. Even Prime Minister Castro has had his defeats. So have the armed forces and that most powerful ally, the Soviet Union. Such disparate organizations as the Cuban National Union of Writers and Artists, the Academy of Science, the Cuban Women's Federation, the Institute for Research on Animal Husbandry, and the National Rifle Association have taken issue with government policy and even occasionally won. Those closest to power in foreign-policy, security, and economic matters are obviously the most apt to win in these issue areas; toward the bottom of the pyramid of power, the victories become more and more minor. Substantive national policymaking is clearly still the business of the ruling elite, and in the third decade of the revolution it will no doubt remain the prerogative of those at the top.

11

AGRARIAN CONFLICT
AND PEASANT POLITICS

Agrarian conflict has persisted throughout twentieth-century Cuban history, but its features were altered by the revolution. Before 1960 conflicts were waged between the large agricultural enterprises and farmers and agricultural workers, among the large enterprises themselves, between one type of farmer and another, and between landowner and squatter. After 1960 the battles were fought between worker and peasant. The policies adopted by the new government in the rural areas exacerbated these peasant-worker conflicts, although it contained them when they occurred without attempting to resolve their causes. Government power over the countryside increased; the rural standard of living improved.

Rural wealth, organization, power, and tenure before 1960 took many forms. About half the farmers either owned their land outright or cultivated sugar, which gave them secure land tenure by the terms of the Sugar Coordination Act of 1937. Sugar farmers were also the best organized politically and had the highest standard of living, though the wealth was very unequally shared. The large minority who did not cultivate sugar had legal protection, but this often led to endless litigation over evictions and other grievances.

Less than a tenth of the peasants were without any legal claim to the land they tilled. These squatters accounted for some of prerevolutionary Cuba's agrarian conflicts, principally in Oriente, the province where most of them were concentrated. It was there also that Fidel Castro and his guerrillas landed after the first plans to overthrow Batista had failed. This more or less accidental event brought the leaders of the revolution into contact with what was essentially an atypical rural dweller. The revolutionary government's policies in 1959 and thereafter were influenced by this experience, a fact that explains why so much of their early legislation was devoted to solving the

423

problems of Cuba's few squatters, while the many more peasants who were not squatters and the even more numerous agricultural workers received less government attention. The early experiences of the revolutionary leadership distorted the new government's agrarian policies for several years, and were one reason for the striking differences between the rural revolution in the 1950s and the rural counterrevolution in the 1960s.

Cuba's prerevolutionary peasants were politically contentious and psychologically and economically modern. The revolutionary government sought to bring political order and social equality to the countryside by abolishing their many competitive rural political organizations and replacing them with the single National Association of Small Peasants (ANAP), in which political and ideological merit rather than wealth or social status would determine political leadership and access to power. This association, unlike the other mass organizations in the early 1960s, looked after the interests of its members, lobbying vigorously on their behalf among the other offices of the state. The expansion of the power of the state into the countryside in subsequent years curtailed ANAP's autonomy and adaptability, turning it into an extension of a government whose policies a majority of the peasantry continued to resist even into the 1970s. In particular, most peasants stubbornly opposed government programs that required them to surrender the right to decide how their land would be used, a resistance that remains to the present day.[1]

Agrarian Conflict before the Revolution

Fulgencio Batista's new approach to politics in the late 1930s consisted of organizing policies of regulation and distribution. Not surprisingly, sugar, the core of the economy, was regulated and organized most extensively, but this did not prevent hostility between the association of sugar-mill owners (*hacendados*) and that of the sugar farmers (*colonos*). The sugar farmers were a group conscious of their shared interests. Their opposition to the mill owners had an anti-imperialist element, since most of the mill owners were foreigners. The sugar farmers' association proved to be one of the lasting organizational contributions of the revolution of 1933. Established by law, with compulsory membership and dues for all sugar farmers including tenants and sharecroppers, the association was supposed to protect them from the sugar-mill owners. But the sugar farmers were also in conflict with the agricultural sugar workers, whom they regarded as sources of political and social instability, and were divided among themselves, principally along lines that resulted from inequities of income and landownership. The lack of harmony among the sugar farmers contributed to their relative political ineffectiveness at the outset of revolutionary rule.[2]

One quarrel in the prerevolutionary sugar industry centered on the division of profits: the farmers sought a larger share; they wanted the mills to pay more for the cane they sold, while the mill owners complained that costs were rising. When the Technical Sugar Commission made a study of sugar-mill costs in the 1951 harvest, it found significant economies of scale, with the larger and more modern mills enjoying lower unit costs; it also found that each mill's profit margin was very low.[3] The profits of the companies up to 1951 had been higher, however, especially those of the large, modern enterprises, most of which were owned by United States businesses.

The West Indies Sugar Corporation, Cuba's seventh largest landowner in the 1950s, owned four sugar mills, one recently modernized, accounting for 3.4 percent of Cuban sugar production in 1953 and 1958; it had owned three mills from 1933 to 1946, with two-digit profits every year but one from 1939 through 1952 (table 11.1). Scattered data suggest that this prosperity was not unique. Even in the worst years of the 1930s, another giant, the Cuban-American Sugar Corporation, which produced between 5.5 and 6.0 percent of Cuban sugar, had net profits relative to sales of 6.3 percent in 1936 and 5.9 percent in 1937; it recorded only a small loss, 1.5 percent, in 1938.[4] It is difficult to estimate United Fruit Company profits in Cuba. Although the company's share of Cuban production declined from 6.9 percent in 1919 to 5.1 percent in 1929 and 3.8 percent in 1942, and although it claimed to have lost several million dollars in Cuba in the early and mid-1930s, it nevertheless launched a vast program of investments in its two sugar mills, as well as in schools, public-health facilities, new colonies, and other activities, an unlikely move for a company that was losing money.[5]

The profitable operations in Cuba in the 1940s and early 1950s may not have depended directly on sugar-mill operations, narrowly defined, but rather on "administration" cane (cane raised on the sugar mill's own land by agricultural workers), rents on land, transportation, marketing, refining, and related activities; profits may also have resulted from bookkeeping practices that shifted costs and profits. The sugar companies, however, stoutly resisted suggestions that they were getting rich. The Cuban-American Sugar Company told its stockholders in 1938 that the Sugar Coordination Act had "substantially increased the *colonos'* portion of the sugar production"; costs rose as a result of labor, colono, and other social laws.[6] Disregarding its increased profits for 1937, the West Indies Sugar Corporation reported to its stockholders that "the cost of producing a pound of sugar on the estates of your Corporation in Cuba has increased about 40 percent" because of the costs arising from social legislation. The corporation complained about the cost of complying with old and new social legislation in its 1944, 1945, 1948, 1949, 1951, and 1954 reports.[7] Nonetheless, these were among the most profitable years in the company's history.

The sugar farmers set about changing the structure of payments in the sugar industry. The Sugar Coordination Act linked sugar-mill payments for the farmer's cane to the price of sugar and to the sugar yield; it also tied land rents to sugar prices. The sugar farmers had no complaints about rents for sugar land, which were regulated by law, but only about rents for nonsugar land, which were not. But they failed in the attempt to have nonsugar land rents reduced and regulated as well. Blackstrap molasses had been the exclusive

Table 11.1 Profits and production of the West Indies Sugar Corporation, 1933–1959[a]

Year	Net profit or loss (in thousands of current dollars)	Net profit or loss (% of total sales)	Production in short tons (1946 = 100)
1933	−700.8	−16.7	32
1934	77.7	1.3	47
1935	−253.6	−3.6	46
1936	202.5	2.8	41
1937	909.7	9.8	52
1938	186.8	2.3	51
1939	1,304.4	14.8	47
1940	1,647.0	16.5	49
1941	140.4	1.8	40
1942	3,970.5	22.2	71
1943	2,516.3	17.3	49
1944	4,126.6	20.1	83
1945	3,868.9	19.5	62
1946	5,894.2	20.0	100
1947	10,280.6	23.0	125
1948	7,819.1	17.8	132
1949	3,689.1	10.0	119
1950	6,897.2	16.4	123
1951	12,193.1	22.1	123
1952	5,598.3	12.1	140
1953	1,271.4	3.6	101
1954	−930.4	−3.0	95
1955	1,450.0	4.9	89
1956	1,936.0	6.5	94
1957	5,929.1	17.7	158
1958	126.6	0.7	113
1959	294.7	1.6	118

Source: Computed from West Indies Sugar Corporation, *Annual Report,* 1933–1959; the year closed on September 30.

a. Data on profits and sales are for the corporation as a whole, including its operations in the Dominican Republic; data on production are for Cuba alone. The sale of the Dominican operations in 1957 suggests that the corporation was doing better in Cuba.

property of the sugar mill until 1945, when President Ramón Grau granted the sugar farmers a share of the price of molasses. The mill owners prevented the implementation of this decree for two years, challenging it in the courts and Congress, but the sugar farmers won in the end. The average price per gallon of blackstrap molasses for the West Indies Sugar Corporation was 13 cents in 1947, of which the corporation retained 8.43 cents and the balance went to the sugar farmers.[8]

President Carlos Prío decreed an increase in the price to be paid by the mill for cane for the 1949–50 harvest. The sugar farmers would get 48 percent of the value of the cane independent of yield, instead of a share that ranged from 46 to 48 percent. President Batista increased this share in 1953 to between 49 and 50 percent. The progress of the farmers in this area was steady through three different administrations. The Sugar Coordination Act had guaranteed the right of each sugar farmer to the sale of up to 30,000 *arrobas* of cane to a designated mill—the so called grinding factor (1 arroba = 25 pounds or 11.5 kilograms). This regulation prevented the sugar mill from favoring its own administration cane or that of friends and thus cushioned the effect of a depressed market on the small farmer. In a depression the sugar mill could only cut its purchases from the big producers. The grinding factor was increased by Batista in 1953 to a maximum of 40,000 arrobas. Sugar farmers who produced less than 30,000 arrobas made up 68.5 percent of the total in 1951 and 66.7 percent in 1959; an additional 7.5 percent produced between 30,000 and 40,000 arrobas in 1959. Those producing between 30,000 and 50,000 arrobas made up 11.8 percent of sugar farmers in 1951 and 12.5 percent in 1959.

In spite of these measures to protect the small farmer, inequities remained. In the 1951 harvest, 3.9 percent of the sugar farmers produced 56.1 percent of all the cane not produced by the sugar mills themselves, while 68.5 percent of the sugar farmers grinding less than 30,000 arrobas accounted for only 11.1 percent of production. There was little variation from harvest to harvest. Evidence for the 1960s suggests that the gap has narrowed considerably, but substantial inequality remains. The conflicts between mill owners and farmers never ceased either. As late as 1959, the sugar farmers were calling upon the revolutionary government to take over operations temporarily ("intervene") at forty-three sugar mills, about one-fourth of the total, because they were unduly slow in paying for cane.[9]

Warfare was not unremitting, however. The sugar farmers and mill owners also found areas of cooperation, resulting in a complex pattern of interest-group conflicts and collaboration. The political system permitted, indeed depended upon, this kind of regulated conflict. The associations jointly ran the Sugar Stabilization Institute. In 1954, at the time the West Indies Sugar Corporation was protesting legislation to benefit the sugar farmers, it was also reaching an agreement with the farmers supplying its Central Palma facility to modernize the mill. The farmers agreed to pay 40 percent of the cost during the first five years; the mill and the farmers then lobbied together successfully for exemption from tariffs on the machinery and equipment required.[10] Mill owners and farmers joined to oppose several presidential decrees raising agricultural workers' wages. They also collaborated to oppose President Grau's establishment of the "sugar differential"—a bonus payment to workers—in 1946. The sugar price differential, on which the bonus was based, was somewhat artificially derived from sugar sales to various countries throughout the year and in fact represented an income-transfer tax collected by the government from mill owners and farmers and distributed to workers. Although the Supreme Court ruled in favor of the mill owners and farmers, the President managed to get around the Court's decision.[11]

Sugar farmers were also fighting agricultural workers on a number of other grounds. The farmers thought of themselves as businessmen, as entrepreneurs. They tended therefore to collaborate with mill owners rather than with the agricultural workers if they possibly could.[12] Their relations with workers perhaps reached an all-time low in the mid-1940s, when the semiofficial journal of the sugar farmers' association spoke of the "desperate" conditions in the countryside, with "illegal strikes, sabotage and abuses . . . and acts totally in defiance of management authority" in the eastern provinces and went on to argue against wage increases for farm workers. Senator Aurelio Álvarez, president of the sugar farmers' association, denounced these disturbances as the result of Communist agitation among the agricultural workers and reported the closing down of many farms. He offered to form an alliance with the mill owners, if they would agree to the farmers' receiving a share of the price for molasses. The Communist party, in its turn, denounced Álvarez and the rest of the association's leaders as reactionaries, pledged to support an increase in the workers' wages, and offered the farmers support in their struggle against the mill owners over molasses price sharing. But the Communists devoted most of their attention to the squatters, few of whom were sugar farmers.

Communist rural organization was still extremely weak in 1945, apart from the agricultural workers. Its peasant associations had been dissolved altogether, so that Communists would join other existing organizations. Because there were few Communists in the countryside, even among agricultural workers, the party had little leverage. The party and the sugar farmers' association continued to do battle, however, until the party eventually disappeared altogether.[13]

Farmers were also divided among themselves according to the commodities they produced. Gains made by one farmers' group did not necessarily benefit another. The Sugar Coordination Act of 1937 was good for sugar farmers, but coffee farmers wanted similar advantages and complained—to no avail—that they had been excluded. The sugar association's quasi-official journal rejoined that the coffee farmers were led not by farmers but by processors, as was the

Coffee Stabilization Institute.[14] The difference in treatment lay, of course, in sugar's strategic role in the Cuban economy. The state closely regulated all aspects of sugar production through the Sugar Coordination Act. Its interest in other aspects of agriculture was less intense. The nonsugar farmers had not yet developed sufficient clout to obtain protection from the government, while the sugar farmers could and did both require and increase beneficial regulation. There was no unified peasant class, just as there was no sustained agreement between farmers and mill owners. Group, not class, conciousness, prevailed.

Squatters and Tenure Security

The Sugar Coordination Act guaranteed land tenure—the "right of permanent occupancy"—to the sugar farmers so long as they met their rent and cane-delivery commitments to the sugar mill. It provided effective tenure security to all of them, whether tenants, subtenants, or sharecroppers. Since the subject of tenure does not even come up in the records of the sugar farmers' association in the 1940s, it can be assumed that their guarantees were working; tenure problems could be found, but only among those producing other commodities.[15] Outside of sugar, however, the problem of eviction was serious, especially during the Grau and Prío presidencies from 1944 through 1952, a period of economic expansion with a brief contraction in 1948 (see table 3.8). Enterprises needed more land for sugar; the government resorted to evictions to get it. The total number of rural eviction cases before the Supreme Court for 1945, 1948, 1950, and 1952 was 116; in the four years between 1955 and 1958, there were probably 89 more. The Batista government frequently battled with the peasants, but at least in this respect he did better by them: the rate of evictions decreased during his administration.

From 1940 to 1959, landowners won about three-quarters of their eviction cases, though the ratio of their victories over the peasants fell slightly from 3.5 to 1 between 1945 and 1952 to 3.3 to 1 between 1955 and 1958. While the Supreme Court's promanagement bias in job-dismissal cases increased during Batista's rule compared to previous years, its prolandowner bias declined slightly in land-eviction cases during the same period. Landowners, of course, still won most often. Very few of the eviction cases involved sugar farmers at any time, however, suggesting that the tenure security provisions of the Sugar Coordination Act were working well.[16] The rare cases involving a sugar farmer were typically based on nonpayment of rent.

The effects of the evictions brought to the Court were greater than comparative figures show, because some evictions involved many families. A single decision in 1948 evicted ten families near Holguín in Oriente; a case in Pinar del Río the same year resulted in the eviction of nine families near Consolación del Norte; another in Oriente in 1950 ended in evicting twenty families near Mayarí. In addition, many cases never reached the Supreme Court, since Supreme Court decisions became precedents for the rest of the court system.[17]

Both the frequency and significance of rural land-eviction cases had declined by the 1950s, with the help of legislation designed to stop them. The Constitution of 1940 suspended for two years all court cases against rural squatters on farms occupied by no fewer than twenty-five families and all cases involving the eviction of tenants and sharecroppers from farms of five *caballerías* or less (1 caballería = 13.4 hectares or 33.1 acres). In April 1942, Batista suspended evictions from farms smaller than two caballerías for the duration of the war, provided the rent was paid; his decree was declared unconstitutional by the Supreme Court, however. In January 1945, Grau decreed the suspension of all pending rural eviction cases until legislation could be passed to protect the more than 2,000 peasants in Las Villas province threatened with eviction. Like Batista, Grau excluded evictions based on nonpayment of rent, as he affirmed in a new decree issued in July. The constitutionality of both decrees was upheld by the Supreme Court.[18]

The Congress's major contribution to prerevolutionary agrarian legislation was a November 1948 law that sought to regulate relations between landowners and tenants in rural Cuba not already covered by the provisions of the Sugar Coordination Act. It set land rents at 6 percent of the total value of sales declared to the government for tax purposes in any given year. Unlike the Sugar Coordination Act, however, it did not guarantee tenure. Instead, it stipulated six-year contracts, with the possibility of eviction when the contract expired, when the tenant died or became physically disabled, or when the terms of the sharecropping or tenancy contract were not fulfilled, a category that included nonpayment of rent. This law superseded Grau's decree restricting grounds for eviction to nonpayment of rent. Eviction for a variety of reasons again became legal, and this opened the way for still more serious agrarian disputes.[19]

In May 1950 President Prío suspended the provisions of the 1948 law allowing for eviction at the expiration of contract, pending congressional legislation; eviction could still proceed on other grounds. The Supreme Court found this decree unconstitutional in October 1952. A decree issued by Prío in November 1950 again suspended all rural eviction cases pending in court, except those based on nonpayment of rent, until legislation modifying this law could be passed. A further decree, in July of the next year, provided for government rent loans to squatters, at 2-percent interest repayable in ten years, if the Ministry of Justice determined that rent arrears did not exceed two years' worth, or 250 pesos; it also provided that the government could force the landowner to sell up to two caballerías of disputed land, which the government would then sell to the squatter at 2-percent interest repayable in twenty-five years. Evictions while forced-sale cases were pending in court were prohibited by decree in December 1951.[20]

In May 1952, two months after seizing power, Batista suspended all rural evictions pending further legislation; in July, however, he reopened the possibility that nonpayment of rent could be grounds for rural eviction but also extended the right of permanent occupancy of rural land to tenants and subtenants in farms smaller than 5 caballerías and reduced rents from 6 percent of the value of sales in 1948 (as stipulated by the 1948 law) to 5 percent of the value of sales in 1948—ignoring the increase in the value of sales since 1948. The protection extended by this decree did not invalidate existing agreements with sugar and tobacco farmers; it did not cover sharecropping contracts, which remained under the 1948 law; it did not apply to agricultural workers; and it did not apply to farms near towns, where evictions for suburban development remained legal. Despite these limitations, the extension of the right of permanent occupancy to many farmers working in farms smaller than 5 caballerías meant that contracts could not be terminated nor tenants evicted so long as they tilled the soil and paid the rent.[21]

The disputes remained unsettled, and the constitutionality of the Batista decree was challenged. But the legislation worked to protect land tenure. There is clear evidence in INRA documents dating from 1959–1960 that both this decree, which had the force of law, and other legislation were enforced by the Batista government. A decree extending the right of permanent occupany to those who had become sugar farmers after 1937 and had not been protected under the Sugar Coordination Act passed that year was declared unconstitutional by the Supreme Court. Batista continued to side with the sugar farmers' association on this question, issuing decrees in January and February 1953, and May 1954, all to the same effect: the extension of land tenure guarantees to those who became sugar farmers after 1937.[22] Patently unconstitutional decrees violated the sanctity of contract provisions of the Constitution and usurped congressional power to legislate these matters. Yet they were issued from time to time as an effective legal means to suspend evictions by at least temporarily sidestepping earlier Supreme Court rulings.

The squatters remained outside the law. Squatters are defined strictly as farmers who paid no rent and who had no legal title (not even tenancy or sharecropping) to the land they tilled. The Supreme Court ruled that anyone found to be a squatter was automatically subject to eviction,[23] and neither the President nor the Congress ever contested that view. The principle of guaranteed land tenure—the right of permanent occupancy—never violated that basic tenet of agrarian capitalism: tenure might be protected and rents could be low and controlled, but rent had to be paid.

Three categories of farmers could be found, then, in prerevolutionary Cuba. Sugar farmers working the land before 1937, and their heirs, were legally and politically protected. Nonsugar farmers, while acquiring considerable political clout and some important legal protections, had a much shakier hold on their land, but legal and political moves had still much reduced the probability of

Table 11.2   Land tenure, 1946

Type of tenure[a]	Number of farms	% of total	Average size of farm (in hectares)	% farms under 1 hectare
Ownership	48,792	30.5	60.6	0.8
Administration	9,342	5.8	248.4	0.4
Tenancy	46,048	28.8	58.9	1.0
Subtenancy	6,987	4.4	30.8	1.1
Sharecropping	33,064	20.7	16.7	0.8
Squatting	13,718	8.6	17.8	11.3
Other	2,007	1.2	35.9	12.2
Total (all types)	159,958	100.0	56.7	1.9

Source: Computed from *1946 Census*, pp. 387, 401, definitions on pp. 87–88. Only one pre-revolutionary agricultural census was made; caution must be exercised in extrapolating its results across time.

a. "Other" tenure arrangements are mainly farms whose owners did not report tenancy type to the census; because the average size of these other farms is twice as great as the average size of squatter farms, although the proportion of minifundia (farms under one hectare) is the same, it is probably incorrect to assume that the other farms belong mainly to squatters; they may have belonged to people from all tenancy categories who feared that the census could be used to raise their taxes and refused to cooperate as a result. Administration land belonged to the sugar mill, which exploited it through an administrator and agricultural workers. Tenants rented the land for cash; subtenants rented the land for cash from tenants; sharecroppers rented the land and paid in kind; squatters had no title whatsoever and paid nothing.

eviction. Those who had no title to or contract for the land and paid no rent were defined as squatters, who had no legal or political protection.

The number of squatters was small; they accounted for 8.6 percent of all farms but for 51.3 percent of all farms smaller than one hectare (table 11.2). Many peasants denied that they were squatters. In the Supreme Court land-eviction cases, a majority of the defendants claimed they were not squatters; disputes in the Court tended to involve contested boundaries, conflicting or lost titles, expiration of contracts, neglect of land, and delays in rent payments. Thus many squatters were not counted as such in the 1946 agricultural census, which consequently understated the extent of squatting and tenure insecurity.

Rural farmers who enjoyed secure land tenure in 1946 included the 26.6 percent of all farms cultivating sugar. Although the census did not measure the relationship of types of land tenure to crops cultivated, other sources make it clear that approximately 53.7 percent of the sugar farmers in 1950 did not own the land they tilled.[24] Assuming the same proportion held in 1946, 22,849 sugar farmers who did not own their land, representing 22.4 percent of the 101,824 nonowners and 14.3 percent of all farms, were entitled to permanent land tenure. Therefore 50.6 percent of the farms had no tenure-security problems, because 36.3 percent belonged to farm owners or to the sugar mills (administration land), and another 14.3 percent were in the hands of nonowners protected by the Sugar Coordination Act. Leaving aside the 8.6 percent of the farmers who were unprotected squatters and the 1.2 percent in other, miscellaneous categories, approximately 39.6 percent of the farmers were in an intermediate state. Their tenure was shakier than that of farmers with protection, but they were certainly in a stronger position than the squatters; they had considerable political clout and some legal benefits.

Lists of large corporate landholdings in prerevolutionary Cuba have customarily been included in works on prerevolutionary agriculture, but they are misleading, if not meaningless, without some indication of the nature of the tenure arrangements that governed the land. If a corporation owned land rented to tenants and sharecroppers growing sugar cane, its actual control over the land was extraordinarily restricted; evictions were virtually impossible, and rents were both low and controlled. Land rented for other purposes was equally regulated; eviction took years of litigation and also had clear political costs. Not surprisingly, the number of land evictions was declining by the 1950s.

Agrarian Reform

If "agrarian reform" means no more than the transfer of titles of ownership from private hands to the state, to poor farmers, to tenants and sharecroppers, or to any combination of these, then prerevolutionary Cuba did not have much reforming to its credit. Of the 109,141 caballerías of state land that the 1937 Sugar Coordination Act made subject to distribution to peasants, only 0.2 percent was actually ever distributed (to 1,815 peasants between 1937 and 1952).[25] If, however, "agrarian reform" means changing tenure and use, cultivation, credit, and marketing practices, and social and political conditions in the countryside generally, then by this definition Cuba was much reformed; the Sugar Coordination Act was the linchpin in these changes.

On March 27, 1938, the first steps toward agrarian reform were taken when each of 250 farmers in the province of Pinar del Río received title to 50 acres of state land, but *Tierra libre* (the quasi-official journal of the sugar farmers' association) complained in 1940 that the agrarian-reform commission had done nothing further. The program was then reactivated in late 1941 and 1942 to the extent of giving land to 543 farmers in the Cienfuegos region of Las Villas, and the Sierra Maestra region of Oriente and to another 192 farmers in the Sagua de Tánamo region of Oriente in 1944, but corruption charges were soon made against these projects as well.[26] None of these grants required the purchase or confiscation of private land; the state parceled out some of its own.

In 1951 the Prío government created an Agrarian Development Fund of 5 million pesos. With it the government acquired farm areas such as Ventas de Casanova in Oriente province—long the scene of conflict over tenure in the 1930s and 1940s—and Limpios de Taguasco in Las Villas province, and par-

celed them out in farms of two caballerías each, which they sold to the peasants with twenty-year mortgages at 2-percent interest. The recently established Industrial and Agricultural Development Bank administered the
fund. The government also established procedures for the forced sale of disputed private land. Although this program could have been the beginning of a
broader effort at agrarian reform, it was soon criticized for its economic inefficiencies by the World Bank. President Batista later claimed that he had continued a program of land-title redistribution in the 1950s, but he apparently
canceled the Prío government's program, and there is no reliable evidence of
the existence of any other.[27] In any event, all the programs to transfer landownership titles in prerevolutionary Cuba were modest in scale.

All governments publicly acknowledged the need for land redistribution
and title transfers but did little about it. This combination could only exacerbate the conflict and frustration bred over decades. Although the opposition
criticized the government for not implementing reforms, its own plans did not
go far beyond what the government contemplated. For example the most radical formulation of Fidel Castro's agrarian ideas, found in the pamphlet *History
Will Absolve Me*, would have granted titles of ownership to tenants, sharecroppers, and squatters on farms up to five caballerías in size, with the state
compensating the landowners over a ten-year period. This proposal was consistent with the socioeconomic platform, admittedly de-emphasized, of the
Ortodoxo party. Castro differed from the Prío government in saying that the
state would compensate the old owners without clarifying whether the new
owners would have to pay anything to the state, but otherwise both agreed
that expropriation was needed and that the state should be a buffer between
the peasants and the previous owners.

The Batista government granted permanent occupancy, while Castro advocated granting ownership titles; unlike Batista's, Castro's program covered
sharecroppers and squatters; both agreed that farmers working less than five
caballerías of land, rather than large landowners, were entitled to protection
and that tenants should be protected by law. Castro's program differed from
the Prío and Grau decrees suspending evictions and regulating rents in that it
would have granted titles of ownership and abolished rents altogether. Grau
and Prío, however, protected all insecure farms, not just the small ones. But
all three agreed that tenants and sharecroppers should be given secure rights
to their land. Castro said sugar farmers should receive 55 percent of the value
of the sugar cane they grew and called for a grinding factor of 36,000 arrobas.
But the 55-percent figure was taken from the sugar growers' association and
had been proposed by the Communist party in 1948; the increase in the grinding factor had been under discussion since the Sugar Coordination Act was
passed in 1937, and Batista had increased it to 40,000 arrobas months earlier—
Castro's proposed increase would actually have meant a smaller grinding factor.[28] In general outline, then, Castro's agrarian program was scarcely more

radical than the measures already being carried out by the governments of the time and no more radical than what other opposition groups proposed. Castro simply took a position slightly to the left of the national consensus; he did not go beyond those limits.

Revolution, Revolutionary Rule, and Agrarian Conflict

When the original plans for a swift overthrow of the Batista government after the landing of the *Granma* in December 1956 had failed, Fidel Castro and a handful of comrades went into hiding in the Sierra Maestra mountains of southern Oriente province and began a decade of civil war in the countryside. Their presence did not at first imply insurgency by the rural population, but eventually the peasants there came to side with the revolutionaries in their midst because the revolutionaries appeared to understand their grievances.

Oriente province, where Castro led the rural insurrection against Batista and where it was contained until the later months of 1958, differed from the rest of rural Cuba in that more than four-fifths of Cuba's squatters lived there and over half of the minifundia, far more than its share of the farm population, were concentrated in the area (table 11.3). (Minifundia are farms one caballería or less that are too small for efficient production, on which farm operators subsist by using primitive agricultural methods.) Oriente was also a major sugar-producing area. Although only a tenth of Cuba's sugar-cane farms were there, they were among the largest and were cultivated primarily by agricultural workers. Aside from these enormous plantations, there were many small farms and squatters, but so few of them raised sugar that little protection was available for them from the Sugar Coordination Act. Although Oriente had the largest number of land-eviction cases before the Supreme Court of any province, its share of cases was still below its share of the rural population. Land-

Table 11.3 Land tenure by province, 1946

Province	% of farmers	% of Supreme Court eviction cases[a]	% of squatters	% of sugar farmers	% of farms under 1 hectare
Pinar del Río	14.4	18.8	2.9	3.1	6.1
Havana	8.9	19.3	1.8	14.4	4.4
Matanzas	7.8	7.2	0.6	21.1	1.6
Las Villas	25.1	17.9	4.6	39.8	24.3
Camagüey	11.6	11.6	6.7	11.2	10.8
Oriente	32.2	25.2	83.4	10.4	52.8

Source: Computed from *1946 Census*, pp. 317, 402–408, 1018–20

a. For 1940, 1945, 1948, 1950, 1952, 1955, 1956, 1957, 1958 (5 months), and 1959.

owners, however, were more likely to win court cases against the peasants in Oriente than in any other province.[29] Oriente also originated about half the "major peasant struggle" cases between 1902 and 1958.[30] The two western-most provinces had many land eviction cases before the Supreme Court because suburban and urban development there had been explicitly exempted by Batista from the legal protection of the 1952 decree.

The Sierra Maestra area clearly had serious problems with squatting. Squatters accounted for 22.3 percent of the farmers in Oriente, but the four municipalities (a division somewhat similar to a county in the United States) of the Sierra Maestra exceeded even those levels—Niquero by almost fourfold (table 11.4). Because these municipalities, or districts, were much less urbanized than the country as a whole, the problem of squatting was widespread. The range of holding was enormous: 40.5 percent of the farms in the four districts had less than five hectares of land; 65.1 percent reportedly produced less than 500 pesos in any given year; 0.4 percent of the farms were larger than a thousand hectares; and seven huge plantations were larger than five thousand. The adult illiteracy rate was two to three times the national average. On the other hand, except in Niquero, the unemployment rate was low, and farms averaged 5.1 workers per farm.[31] But most of the population was made up of farmers, not agricultural workers. The problem was one of land insecurity, not of unemployment.

When Fidel Castro's insurrection came, it had settled in the only part of Cuba where latifundia and land-tenure insecurity were still issues, and where prerevolutionary agrarian legislation had had little protective effect. Its survival in the Sierra Maestra would have been unlikely without peasant support; providentially for Castro, this was the only area of Cuba where he could have found insecure peasants facing hostile landowners and government. The Sierra Maestra squatters had for some time been organized in bands to protect themselves against landlords who tried to evict them. The social bandit, a mix-

Table 11.4 Squatting, sugar farming, illiteracy, and unemployment in the Sierra Maestra

Municipality	% rural (1953)	% squatters in farm population (1946)	% sugar farmers (1946)	% illiterates age 10+ (1953)	% labor force unemployed (1953)
Campechuela	73.6	56.4	12.8	61.7	3.3
Cobre	83.1	27.5	0.9	48.9	8.3
Manzanillo	48.0	59.0	16.4	56.9	8.0
Niquero	83.1	81.9	9.2	62.1	15.8

Sources: Computed from *1946 Census*, pp. 418–419, 1066–70; *1953 Census*, pp. 66, 151–152, 167–168.

ture of outlaw and protester, was the form that peasant social and political organization had taken. When Castro's band appeared in the area, it was almost immediately joined by these peasant bands, who no doubt recognized the guerrillas as allies.[32]

It has been argued that "an agrarian revolution implies a peasant party, a peasant leadership, and a peasant ideology."[33] By this definition Cuba did not have an agrarian revolution. The majority of Cuban peasants did not revolt, because most of them had adequate legitimate means for coping with their grievances. But the absence of violence does not necessarily imply an absence of grievance, but simply that most of it, except in Oriente, was contained within a nonviolent political system. The Cuban revolution had some peasant leaders and organization; it was responsive to some peasant grievances, and it occurred in the countryside. In these respects, it was not all that different from other major revolutions in the modern world.[34]

Peasant support for Fidel Castro's group was conditional upon his helping them keep their land. The guerrillas would honor the land occupied by squatters, treat the squatters well, and help fight evictions. One of the laws issued by Fidel Castro in the Sierra Maestra in the fall of 1958 guaranteed two caballerías of land free of charge to every peasant then cultivating them. Peasants could force owners to sell them up to five caballerías of land.[35] But the law dealt only with squatters; it did nothing for the hundreds of thousands of agricultural workers who were the rural majority, about breaking up the latifundia, or about foreign ownership.

The guerrillas also gained support in the Sierra Maestra when Batista tried to evacuate the area as a counterinsurgency measure. The plan was never carried out in full, but enough steps were taken, including killing a number of peasants, to alienate the mountain people and push them into the arms of the guerrillas. Many landowners also diverted the military from antiguerrilla to antisquatting campaigns.[36] The net effect was to merge the political and the social disaffection in the Sierra Maestra.

The guerrillas, in the meantime, pursued two other policies that strengthened their power and prestige among the mountain peasants. They attacked the many bandits in the mountains who preyed on the peasants and executed their leaders; in the process, they eliminated political competition and prevented any use of these bands by Batista's armed forces. Some of these conquered bandits actually joined the guerrilla forces. Second, they were careful to pay for the supplies they requisitioned from the peasants.[37] The most systematic effort to mobilize support, however, was made by Raúl Castro in the Sierra Cristal and Guantánamo mountains in northern and northeastern Oriente. In late 1958 he organized peasant associations to support the guerrilla forces and to carry out a land reform that included the establishment of peasant cooperatives and established peasant committees to run the small towns and villages. Raúl Castro also called a peasant congress that was held in the fall of 1958, with several hundred delegates attending; several thousand peasants had participated in its preparation. The guerrillas pledged their support for agrarian reforms in exchange for help from the peasants; an agrarian bureau was founded by the revolutionary group to deal with peasant issues.[38]

The Agrarian Reform Laws of the New Government

The revolutionary leaders had learned their rural politics in an atypical countryside, and this determined the nature of their first Agrarian Reform Law, promulgated in May 1959. The law set a maximum size of thirty *caballerías* for farms, except for range land and farms that were 50 percent more productive than the national average; these could be as large as one hundred caballerías. Foreign and sugar-mill ownership of land was prohibited, as were tenancy, sharecropping, and similar arrangements. Former tenants, share-croppers, and squatters would get two caballerías of the land they had tilled free; the owners could then be compelled to sell them three more caballerías, for a total of five. The remaining land would be given, in order, to peasants who had been evicted in years past, peasants who had less than two caballerías of land, agricultural workers from the region, peasants being resettled, and agricultural workers being resettled. Veterans of the revolutionary army had priority within each category. Compensation for expropriated land, to be paid in bonds over twenty years at 4.5-percent interest, was never paid. The law established the National Institute for Agrarian Reform (INRA) to promote cooperatives, especially in the big plantations that had been cultivated by agricultural workers.[39]

The 1959 law was almost irrelevant for the almost half a million agricultural workers in Cuba. After land was given to the squatters, tenant farmers, and sharecroppers, little was left over for the agricultural workers, once the commitment had been made not to break up the large holdings. For the nonsquatter peasant there were some modest benefits. The 1959 law abolished rents for sugar farmers who did not own the land, although rent was never an issue in the first place, and gave them title to the land they worked. This change was no more than symbolic since this type of farmer could not have been evicted in any case. Nonsugar farmers who did not own land received the same benefits. In their case, a title had some concrete advantage, however, since their tenure had been much less secure.

The distinction between agricultural worker and peasant has been made by Sidney Mintz, who defines workers as landless, propertyless, wage-earning, store-buying, and corporately employed and peasants as tied to land, which they own, rent, or squat upon, as producing most of their crops for family consumption, and as self-employed. Some agricultural workers or rural proletarians may share some peasant characteristics because they tend ultimately to come from peasant families and to be part of the same rural society; they may

SITES OF THE PEASANT REVOLUTION
AND COUNTERREVOLUTION IN CUBA

SOUTHERN ORIENTE

Manzanillo
Campechuela
CAMPECHUELA
MANZANILLO
Bayamo
Palma Soriano
El Cobre
EL COBRE
Santiago de Cuba
Niquero
NIQUERO
SIERRA
MAESTRA

0   50
          miles
0   50
          Km

MATANZAS

ORIENTE

SOUTHERN MATANZAS

UNIÓN DE REYES

JOVELLANOS

SAN JOSÉ
DE LOS RAMOS

PERICO

LOS ARABOS

PEDRO BETANCOURT

AGRAMONTE

COLÓN

ALACRANES

BOLONDRÓN

JAGÜEY
GRANDE

MANGUITO

0   25
          miles
0   25
          Km

even oscillate between the two categories.[40] One effect of the 1959 Agrarian Reform Act was to accelerate this oscillation. Cuban workers wanted work or land to improve their lot. Because the only way to get benefits from the 1959 law was to claim that they were peasants, many rural proletarians accentuated their peasant roots. This process served to increase competition between workers and peasants for government benefits and finally led to conflict between them. Some have argued that Cuban rural proletarians were not interested in land but only in income, steady work, and fringe benefits. Juan Martínez Alier's research with the documents of INRA's legal department, however, has destroyed that notion. The discontent of agricultural workers caused them to put pressure on the government for more radical measures in the hope of getting benefits.[41]

That some agricultural workers tried to become peasants is supported by Brian Pollitt's survey of 1,061 rural households, made up of 3,535 people, in eleven areas in 1966, where occupational data were collected for both 1957 and 1966. Of these 1,580 were agricultural workers in 1957, but only 1,250 in 1966; 881 were farmers in 1957, as were 952 in 1966. While 4.5 percent of the 1957 farmers had become agricultural workers, 9.7 percent of the 1957 agricultural workers had become farmers by 1966. Of the 133 who could have been classified in either group in 1957, 8.2 percent permanently became agricultural workers, but 16.5 percent became farmers; only 2.2 percent of the farmers had become workers. This survey suggests that the claim that there is a sharp division between peasant and agricultural worker, or that rural people are bound by tradition to a particular economic role that rarely changes and are unable to calculate the advantages of change, is invalid.[42]

Even before the Agrarian Reform Law, rural conflict was evident. Within six weeks of the revolution's coming to power peasants invaded new lands or stopped rent payments on the land they tilled. The government issued a law on February 20, 1959, banning the unauthorized appropriation of land; those who took land illegally would automatically forfeit future benefits. But even then the land invasions did not stop. With the help of old Communist party leaders, seizures continued in Oriente province, leading to some of the sharpest conflicts between Prime Minister Castro and the old Communists in 1959. They continued even after the Agrarian Reform Law was issued in May, perhaps because it neglected to deal with agricultural workers' demands.[43] While peasant land invasions seem to have been brought under control by the summer of 1959, the government could do nothing about the nonpayment of rents. The National Institute for Agrarian Reform insisted throughout 1959 that rents on unexpropriated land had to be paid, but local peasant organizations, supported by local branches of the Twenty-sixth of July Movement, decided that they did not. The institute did not authorize the suspension of rent payments until July 1960, but it did not try to enforce rent payments, in contrast to its harsher measures against land invasions.[44] The latter threatened public order, as nonpayment of rents did not.

Although the sugar farmers' association cooperated with the revolutionary government throughout most of 1959, the old conflict between its members and agricultural workers was reawakened by the new measures. The sugar farmers opposed the abolition of all tenancy and sharecropping contracts and the severe restrictions placed on their autonomy as farmers: their land could not be sold or mortgaged and its cultivation was to be controlled more closely by government regulation. They also objected to being given the land without having to pay for it; they would have preferred government loans to enable them to purchase the land. They opposed the wage increases decreed for agricultural workers, and the rise in compulsory accident-insurance rates. On January 30, 1961, the government dissolved their association for opposing its policies.[45]

The Peasant Counterrevolution

Since the revolution Cuban leaders have customarily attributed any insurgencies against the regime to reactionary counterrevolutionary activity supported by the United States. In only one instance—in rural southern Matanzas province in 1962–1963—did they admit that a counterrevolutionary insurrection had taken place that was justified at least in part by a purely indigenous situation.

Matanzas was a province of prosperous farmers. It had the lowest proportion of squatters and of minifundia among the Cuban provinces, well below its share of the farm population. Its proportion of sugar-cane farmers was second of the provinces and about three times greater than would be expected from its share of the farm population (see table 11.3).[46] It was, in short, the antithesis of Oriente province. Matanzas farmers had done well before the revolution, but they received only modest benefits from the Agrarian Reform Act. Many of them were no doubt grateful for the abolition of rents, for the acquisition of title to their land, and for benefits in education, health, and income, but here especially title to the land had only symbolic value, for there had been few problems of tenure security, and rents were, as elsewhere, both low and regulated. Landowners were least likely to win land-eviction cases arising in Matanzas in the Supreme Court, and there were fewer such cases than the province's share of the farm population would predict. Matanzas had the lowest proportion of cases before the Court of any province in Cuba (see table 11.3); after 1957 only two were ever put on the Court's docket.

According to the 1946 agricultural census, only 11.5 percent of the farms in the twelve southern districts in the province were smaller than five hectares. Only 0.3 percent of the farms were larger than a thousand hectares, and none was larger than five thousand. Only 27.1 percent of the farms in these twelve districts had a 1945 production value of less than 500 pesos a year. There were on the average six permanent agricultural workers per farm, a level 17.6 percent higher than that in the Sierra Maestra; the average number of part-time workers per farm was 26 percent more than in the Sierra Maestra.[47] But in 1953 unemployment in southern Matanzas was nonetheless also higher than in the Sierra Maestra. Illiteracy, however, was well below the level in the Sierra Maestra and only slightly above the national average. There were very few squatters and a high rate of sugar cultivation, both in contrast to the Sierra Maestra (table 11.5).

Even in the light of the need for caution in using 1946 and 1953 census data to discuss events in the early 1960s, the differences between the two areas in many crucial respects are striking. The Sierra Maestra, but not southern Matanzas, had a serious problem of land insecurity. The Sierra Maestra, with a few wealthy, large landowners and many poor small farmers, had been ripe for a fight between squatters, on the one hand, and the government and the large landowners, on the other, when the revolution came. Southern Matanzas, with no latifundia, had many prosperous farmers, but it also had many more agricultural workers than the Sierra Maestra; these workers were unemployed, either permanently or seasonally, and were also able to read and write about the region's social ills. This area was ripe for a class struggle between the

Table 11.5 Squatting, sugar farming, illiteracy, and unemployment in southern Matanzas

Municipality	% rural (1953)	% squatters in farm population (1946)	% sugar farmers (1946)	% illiterates age 10+ (1953)	% labor force unemployed (1953)
Agramonte	58.7	0.3	75.4	33.3	18.5
Alacranes	46.6	0.3	59.6	31.4	8.9
Bolondrón	59.4	0.2	46.0	35.5	11.8
Colón	41.1	1.3	70.1	30.1	12.9
Jagüey Grande	48.6	0.5	73.4	29.6	5.6
Jovellanos	34.9	0.0	78.9	27.8	12.6
Los Arabos	63.7	0.0	68.7	31.1	11.2
Manguito	59.6	0.1	81.0	41.7	26.1
Pedro Betancourt	51.8	2.5	76.3	32.1	14.2
Perico	40.2	1.4	81.9	26.0	16.2
San José de los Ramos	63.2	1.1	67.8	19.7	9.8
Unión de Reyes	19.3	0.0	95.1	25.8	10.7

Sources: Computed from *1946 Census*, pp. 397–398, 413–414, 1038–46; *1953 Census*, pp. 64, 151–152, 167–168.

agricultural workers and their peasant employers, neither of whom had benefited much from the 1959 agrarian-reform legislation. The Sierra Maestra
peasants had supported the revolution in the 1950s because it supported
them. When the revolutionary government favored the southern Matanzas agricultural workers in the early 1960s, the peasants in that area joined the counterrevolution. The social bases of revolution and counterrevolution in the
countryside were thus very different. The revolutionary government added to
its troubles by failing to recognize fully that the peasantry that had supported
it in its early days was a very different group from the peasantry that opposed
it in the 1960s.

Neither revolutionary nor counterrevolutionary peasants, however, rebelled on the basis of their own psychological resources or grievances alone;
nonpeasant leadership was present in both cases. In both instances, peasants
revolted against what they perceived as an intrusion of arbitrary outside power
that threatened the security of their land and of their way of life. In both cases,
the protest was focused on national and local government; they were not
reckless or wild protests against unknown forces.[48]

Government policies in Matanzas province suffered from a series of what
Carlos Rafael Rodríguez labeled "serious mistakes." When problems arose in
the early 1960s, government and party officials called either assemblies of agricultural workers or assemblies where workers at least had a majority, to decide
what was to be done about the recalcitrant peasants. The workers pressed for
the socialization of the peasants' land. The conflict between the two groups
exploded chiefly because the government sided with the workers. The National Institute for Agrarian Reform had already assumed a more radical stance
in Matanzas than it had in the country as a whole. Of the eleven INRA decrees
issued to regulate agrarian affairs in that province of which the content could
be classified clearly, nine were clearly more radical than those governing the
rest of the nation.[49]

The Communist party was both small and incompetent in Matanzas in the
early 1960s. By the end of 1962 it was concentrating on worker recruitment to
the total exclusion of peasants. In March 1963 there were only 807 party
members in the entire province, well below the province's proportional share
of the population. The secretary-general of the provincial party in 1962,
Leónides Calderío (the brother of Blas Roca, a pseudonym for Francisco Calderío) was, in Castro's words, in "deplorable physical condition"; the post had
been regarded as a suitable sinecure for a sick man.[50]

The conflict in southern Matanzas grew after 1961 and finally erupted at the
beginning of 1963.[51] The peasants feared that the socialization of their land
was imminent. When the land of some peasants actually engaged in, or collaborating with, the counterrevolution was socialized, it was done without explanation. In some cases there was no reason—not even counterrevolutionary
collaboration—for seizing peasant land, other than the arbitrary decision of the

workers and the local government. Peasants selling their products in nearby towns were arrested and charged with black-market activities; others were arrested for no evident reason. Finally the Prime Minister denounced the "despotism" of lower officials in Matanzas, and the ensuing peasant revolt became the government's one admitted case of authentic rebellion. Sugar was burned, officials assassinated, property sacked, and agriculture sabotaged. Peasants revolted against the arbitrary power of government that, in alliance with the peasants' traditional enemies, the agricultural workers, was threatening their land and their way of life. This danger far outweighed any benefits that the peasants had received from the revolution.

Although military and security measures were immediately taken, the government recognized from the beginning that the problem was too complex to be solved by those measures alone. Officials were dismissed for breaking laws and other procedures; local government was reorganized; mass and political organizations were restructured; and the land was returned by the state to the peasantry. The government was certainly aware of where the problem lay, and it redressed many of the injustices that it had committed.

The Communist party then went to work to reestablish face-to-face contact. Officials made two thousand visits to families in southern Matanzas. These visits were soon institutionalized into a regular practice in which four hundred two-person teams (one male party member and one member of the Cuban Women's Federation) regularly visited peasant families. Each pair was responsible for ten to fifteen peasant families; although at first they came from outside the region, the system eventually used members of the restructured local party. The government also launched various programs to benefit the peasants directly, no longer relying on the faulty assumption that all peasants had automatically benefited from the 1959 land-reform act. Marketing facilities were improved and stores, schools, roads, and cultural, sports, and recreational facilities were built for their benefit.

Assemblies were organized that were restricted to peasants. At first attendance was low, but it soon increased. The local chapter of the National Association of Small Peasants (ANAP) lost its autonomy; it was limited to farmers who owned less than five caballerías of land. Before the revolution relations among peasants had been harmonious enough (mostly because they fought the agricultural workers far more than they fought each other) for the local chapters of the peasants' association in southern Matanzas to admit landowners who owned more than five caballerías of land, even though they were not legally entitled to membership. In the municipality or district of Perico, for example, 411 farmers owned less than five caballerías, and 64 owned more; 32.3 percent of the smaller landowners, but 75 percent of the larger ones, had belonged to the local ANAP chapter. The larger landowners had comprised 26.5 percent of the local association membership but only 13.3 percent of the farmer population. Some of them had had substantial influence. Now they were expelled under the new policy. The local chapter was placed under strict party control, and what was once a focal point of resistance became an arm of government. The government's local policies had changed, but the peasants had lost their autonomous political organization—the only tool they had to hold government to its promises.

The cordial relations between the small farmers and larger landowners that had remained from prerevolutionary times were expressed in southern Matanzas in the comparative harmony that marked relations among sugar-mill owners, sugar farmers, and, at times, agricultural workers. When the owner of a sugar mill was a native Cuban living in the community, he might provide his inferiors with political support and economic benefits, often including higher-than-average wages for his workers, as well as serving as godfather to their children.[52] Through a variety of procedures, including the family-visitation program, the restructuring of the peasants' association, and the second Agrarian Reform Act, the government set out to end these patron-client ties. The leaders of the peasants' association were often the bosses of the prerevolutionary period; they appeared in new revolutionary guise but with the same tendencies toward nepotism and *sociolismo* (the "buddy system") that helped to shield individuals from the full force of the government by solving problems outside formal bureaucratic channels.

The pacification of southern Matanzas and other areas ended with the second agrarian reform law in the fall of 1963. The state took all of a single owner's land beyond five caballerías unless it was exceptionally productive, in which case it was cultivated privately but in cooperation with the state. In contrast to its implementation of the 1959 act, the state compensated landowners for these expropriations, under the terms of the new law, up to 250 pesos a month for ten years.[53]

The National Association of Small Peasants

The National Association of Small Peasants (ANAP) was founded in May 1961 to unite all peasants in one organization for the first time in Cuban history, in effect establishing an official peasant class.[54] It replaced earlier autonomous organizations of rural producers, which the government had taken over or abolished in 1960–1961. All Cuban mass organizations were founded at times when the revolutionary government was threatened. The peasant association, no exception, was founded shortly after the Bay of Pigs invasion, when the United States government was still very hostile toward Cuba. It was supposed to reinforce political support for the government, receive its instructions, and act as a channel to convey peasant grievances to the bureaucracy. It was the only one of the mass organizations of the early 1960s that did make known the concerns of its members fairly effectively; and it did defend their interests with some success, at least in the beginning, although occasionally with doubtful consequences for the nation as a whole.

In the early 1960s, for example, the state wholesale-purchasing organizations set prices for commodities along with the producers and the leaders of the ANAP. Requests from the latter for higher prices for agricultural raw materials to be processed were rarely granted, however, since the Ministry of Industries and its affiliates objected. Instead, because there was no consumer association (theoretically, of course, consumers were represented by the state), the government organizations tried to satisfy the peasants by increasing the prices of nonprocessed foodstuffs sold directly to consumers. The effect on the supply structure was disastrous, as peasants shifted from industrial to consumer crops.[55] The peasants' association had effectively defended the interests of its members, but clearly at the expense of the economy as a whole, in part because of the imbalance in the relative power of the interest groups concerned.

As in other cases of decision making, the key political resources were organizational; those who were unorganized—in this instance, the consumers—lost the most. Yet this case also shows the modern traits of Cuban peasants, such as their ability to coordinate pressures, to shift from crop to crop, and to calculate costs and benefits for their own advantage. This modern approach to political bargaining was not tempered by any socialist "spirit of sacrifice." The problem resulted not from lack of modernization or the inability to cooperate but from an imbalance of power among organizations and interests.

The association was also responsible for administering agricultural loans from May 1961 to May 1963, when the National Bank took over. During those two years only 41.2 percent of the loans granted were recovered; 11.2 percent of them were in default; the balance was classified as "uncollected." During the first two years of Bank administration, 98.3 percent were recovered, although more credits were granted under Bank than under ANAP administration.[56] The association's loans had often in effect been grants; the bank maintained that these were loans repayable with interest. The association's credit policies, like its price policies, were intended to benefit members; the bank was trying to safeguard the national interest.

Throughout the early 1960s, there were fixed national prices for all crops, but because soil and other conditions differ from region to region, these served to distort regional economies. A survey of the Holguín-Gibara peasants in 1966 showed that black beans yielded a loss of 21 pesos per year on the average (at a rate of 7.5 pounds per hectare) while plantains yielded a loss of 30 pesos. In contrast, papayas yielded a gain of 547 pesos. The peasants of this region soon shifted from their traditional crops, black beans and plantains, which were essential to the Cuban diet, to papaya, which was not. In the private sector in Oriente from 1963 to 1966, bean production, adjusted for the effects of the second agrarian reform law, fell 62.5 percent and papaya production rose 264.7 percent until regional price policies were adopted in 1965. Another survey showed a labor shortage in Neiva in the Cabaiguán region of Las Villas in 1965. To ensure a stable labor supply the peasants there reestablished sharecropping, even though it was illegal; local government officials went along with it. Agricultural workers were given a piece of land to cultivate in return for their work in the owner's fields.[57] Both surveys indicate that Cuban peasants were rational and modern enough to calculate their costs and change their farming techniques to others that would benefit them more. The revolutionary virtue of personal sacrifice had not taken hold; instead peasants made use of changes in national policy to better their own lot.

Government officials responded to these peasant reactions to the realities of the marketplace with repressive measures. Neither the problems nor the repressions were limited to southern Matanzas, but they were most severe there. When peasants sought to sell products directly or through private retailers at higher prices, rather than to state agencies at lower prices, INRA officials, in cooperation with local government and military authorities, illegally coerced the peasants into selling to the state by arbitrarily confiscating their produce. Some peasants were forced by the government to harvest prematurely to ease the scarcity in Havana; their losses were insufficiently compensated by price increases. The results led the peasants, in the words of Carlos Rafael Rodríguez, to "collaborate" with the enemy "out of fear or lack of faith in the future." There were revolts in every one of Cuba's six provinces. Only the peasants of the Sierra Maestra remained loyal to the revolution; they were still benefiting from the change of governments.[58]

By mid-1963 the peasants' association had lost its responsibilities for price and credit policy to the vice ministry for private and cooperative production of the National Institute for Agrarian Reform and to the National Bank. Although the association could still audit the actions of these state organizations toward the peasantry, it no longer handled any policies of importance. The government sought to change the character of the ANAP. It increased the association's ability to mobilize and control the peasants but restricted its ability to represent them and to lobby on their behalf. The government also increased control over marketing and opposed peasant sales to buyers other than state enterprises. In August 1965 the ANAP lost its right to authorize the slaughtering of livestock, an authority that had typically led to private marketing locally. Control passed to the state beef enterprise in Havana. Similar measures were directed against rice farmers in 1966.[59]

Cooperative Farms, 1959–1967

The 1959 Agrarian Reform Act had not broken up the large cattle ranches and sugar plantations. These had instead been designated as cooperatives owned collectively by the agricultural workers, though in practice they were hardly true cooperatives. Their administrators were controlled by the National Institute for Agrarian Reform and did not even have to consult the councils elected by the cooperative or to report to the cooperative members. The state held only 29.2 percent of the land in the spring of 1961; it controlled an additional 11.8 percent as cooperatives; and the remaining 59.0 percent remained in private hands. The Institute for National Agrarian Reform began the formal fusion of state farms and cooperatives in the first half of 1962. By the time the National Congress of Sugar-Cane Cooperatives voted 1,381 to 3 to turn the cooperatives into state farms in August 1962, it was already a *fait accompli*.[60]

This change instilled suspicions among peasants that full socialization was next. Peasants began to resist joining cooperatives, perhaps beause they did not want to cooperate, but more likely because they did not want to give up their land to a socialist state. The erosion of the terms of the 1959 agrarian law added to the atmosphere of suspicion: peasants ceased to have any faith in the promises of government, and the demoralization led to the catastrophic decline in agricultural production.

The National Association of Small Peasants then initiated two new types of cooperatives designed to create a resurgence of trust among the peasants while retaining state control. One was the credit-and-service cooperative, which was supposed to negotiate loans, purchase supplies and equipment that could be owned in common, repair fences and roads, organize mutual aid, and market the harvest. All those joining this kind of cooperative remained the sole owners of their own land and equipment. They farmed individually. The other new type of cooperative was the agrarian society. Its members turned ownership of land, livestock, and equipment over to the cooperative and received in return regular employment and wages and a dividend at the end of year. They owned the land and farmed it collectively. In the period after the most severe conflicts between peasants and the government, credit-and-service cooperatives expanded appreciably in number, area, and membership, but the agrarian societies reached their peak in mid-1964 and declined thereafter (table 11.6). In May 1965, 32.4 percent of the membership of the ANAP were members of cooperatives, as were 37.0 percent in December 1967. Only 34.5 percent of all peasants had joined cooperatives of any kind by the end of 1967; the agrarian societies comprised a tiny fraction even of these. Only forty-one agrarian societies remained by 1975, and forty-three by 1977.[61]

No substantial differences can be found in size of landholding per member between credit-and-service cooperatives and agrarian societies in 1963. Government officials had argued that the small landowners were more likely to join the agrarian societies and the larger landowners more likely to join the credit-and-service cooperatives, but this apparently proved not to be the case (table 11.6). The government favored the agrarian societies until the third peasant congress in May 1967 by handing over state lands to these private co-

Table 11.6   Peasant cooperatives in the 1960s

Date	Number	Total size (in hectares)[a]	Members	Hectares/ member	Members/ cooperative
		Credit-and-service cooperatives			
January 1963	527	432,472	46,133	9.37	87.5
Mid-1964	899	—	55,826	—	62.1
Late 1965	—	499,994	56,000	8.93	—
May 1967	1,119	695,728	77,933	8.93	69.7
Late 1967	1,301	1,067,900	79,067	13.51	60.8
		Agrarian societies			
January 1963	328	37,131	3,884	9.56	11.8
Mid-1964	265	—	4,174	—	15.8
Late 1965	—	30,003	2,600	11.54	—
May 1967	136	20,515	1,707	12.02	12.6
Late 1967	126	19,685	1,511	13.03	12.0

Sources: Computed from Antero Regalado, "El camino de la cooperación agraria en Cuba," *Cuba socialista* no. 22 (June 1963): 49, 54; idem, "Las funciones de la ANAP," ibid., no. 35 (July 1964):15; Carlos Rafael Rodríguez, "La revolución cubana y el campesinado," ibid., no. 53 (January 1966):49; Antero Regalado, "Proclamamos que a ocho años de revolución nuestra clase obrera tiene un magnífico aliado en nuestro campesinado," *ANAP* 7, nos. 5–6 (May–June 1967): 7; José Acosta, "La revolución agraria en Cuba y el desarrollo económico," *Economía y desarrollo* no. 17 (May–June 1973): 155.

a. 1 caballería = 13.4 hectares = 33.1 acres.

operative farmers as a form of subsidy and encouragement.[62] This policy explains the increase in number of hectares of land held per member in agrarian societies between 1963 and 1967. This government preference for the agrarian societies had created a distinction in size of landholding per member between credit-and-service cooperatives and the agrarian societies by 1965. The gap was narrowed once again as a result of the decision by the third peasant congress to increase government control over peasant production by stimulating all forms of cooperation; one result was a 53-percent increase in the land held by credit-and-service cooperatives within six months of the congress. A persistent difference between the two types of cooperative remained the number of members; credit-and-service cooperatives were always big, while agrarian societies remained small.

In 1965 members of the peasants' association who did not belong to cooperatives were likely to own more land than ANAP members who did belong to cooperatives (table 11.7). As a result of the government campaign to increase the proportion of peasants and land in cooperatives, however, this difference had diminished considerably by the end of 1967. Contrary to the official record, in fact, the larger landowners were more likely in 1967 to belong to

Table 11.7 Participation in peasant organizations, 1965 and 1967

	May 1965			December 1967		
Membership	Number	Total hectares	Hectares/ peasant	Number	Total hectares	Hectares/ peasant
Cooperative, ANAP	58,269	540,194	9.27	80,578	1,087,584	13.50
Noncooperative, ANAP	121,833	1,594,037	13.08	137,154	1,752,278	12.78
Noncooperative, non-ANAP	—	—	—	15,947	113,846	7.14

Source: Computed from Acosta, "La revolución," pp. 155–156.

both the peasants' association and a cooperative than were small landowning peasants. Peasant resistance to collaboration with the government remained most persistent among the poor, probably because the larger landowners were more likely to have run commercial farms and to have had past experience with government bureaucracies and with mechanisms such as credit-and-service cooperatives than the smaller landowners, many of whom were subsistence farmers. The larger landowners followed the guidelines of the revolutionary government; the subsistence farmers resisted them, just as they had always resisted government in the past. Still, government regulations benefited the small landowners more than they did the larger ones, and this fact tended to reduce the gap between them to some extent.

The government also adopted credit policies that would favor the cooperative movement, particularly the agrarian societies. If a farmer not affiliated with any cooperative borrowed more than 5,000 pesos, the interest rate was 6 percent; for less than 5,000 pesos, 4 percent. Regardless of amount, however, interest was only 3.5 percent for a credit-and-service-cooperative and 3.0 percent for an agrarian-society.[63] All credit applicants were screened by the ANAP for political loyalty before they were screened for credit rating.[64] Given this weapon for ensuring allegiance, not to mention the inducements of land and credit, it is all the more striking that a majority of peasants continued to refrain from joining any cooperative and that still fewer joined the agrarian societies (and even this small number declined over the years). Whatever the benefits, the peasants probably continued to regard the cooperative movement as just one step further toward full socialization.

Peasant Participation and Government Control, 1967–1977

From the government's point of view, the organizational structure of the National Association of Small Peasants was unsatisfactory. Although the government tried to identify a peasant class in 1961 by making it coextensive with association membership, division by crop specialty persisted. Sugar farmers were grouped in sugar-cane delegations within the association and obtained credits directly from the sugar mills, just as they had always done. Consequently, unless they produced other crops in addition to sugar cane, this group saw no need for joining a cooperative in addition to their delegation.[65] Up to the time the second Agrarian Reform Act was passed in the fall of 1963, many farmers who owned more than five caballerías of land and were thus legally ineligible for membership in the peasants' association belonged to it anyway, not only in hostile southern Matanzas but also in loyal areas such as Baracoa in northern Oriente.[66] Even after most of the land in farms larger than five caballerías was taken over, difficulties remained. Many ANAP members still followed traditional practice. Whereas the prerevolutionary patron may have had more property and greater access to power, the patron now held a position as leader in the local association and still lorded it over the peasant clients. Some local associations continued to operate through the mid-1960s as little fiefdoms, with no communication among themselves or between them and national headquarters. They paid scant attention to revolutionary political propaganda or education programs.[67] Some credit-and-service cooperatives even marketed their products collectively and privately at higher prices, rather than selling to the government.[68]

This was the political setting for the third peasant congress, which gathered in May 1967. The government increased benefits for peasants. In return the peasants were supposed to submit to government policy and give up their political autonomy. The National Bank's loans to peasants would henceforth be interest free, although the principal had to be repaid. All property taxes and all taxes on private peasant production were abolished, although income tax remained in force.[69] Prime Minister Castro reiterated his pledge that there would be no socialization. "We have never," he said, "made any attempt to establish socialist production among the small farmers. [Applause.] We especially recommended not fostering cooperatives. Why? Because you begin to form cooperatives and those rumors gain force . . . [spreading] the lie that we want to socialize the farmer's land." Although Castro restated his belief in the beneficial effects of economies of scale, he guaranteed stable private farm ownership and production. He also announced that the National Institute for Agrarian Reform had increased prices, though only temporarily, above economically justifiable levels for crops raised by private farmers.[70]

In return for these benefits the third peasant congress condemned all sales to buyers other than state enterprises. Estimates of private sales had varied between 24.0 percent and 73.4 percent of private peasant production—that is, production not from state farms. The private buyers were not just individuals but state organizations such as the armed forces, the Tourism Institute, the Ministry of Construction, the Hydraulic Resources Institute, and the state-farm cafeterias. The presidents of the local peasants' associations were just as likely as other peasants to sell privately. No law prohibited these sales, and the peasants had no economic incentive to stop them.[71] The resolution passed by the third peasant congress was in essence a concession to the government. The government also obtained a pledge from the congress that peasants would discontinue the illegal practice of sharecropping.[72] The statutes of the ANAP, approved at the third congress, emphasized increases in production and productivity, sales to the government, national defense, promotion of cooperation, and ideological awareness as goals. No provision specified that the association was to represent its constituent interests to other organizations.[73]

Finally, having lost interest in the cooperative movement, the government sought instead to gain direct control over private production. Its most immediate reason was the 10-million-ton sugar harvest planned for 1970, but control was not limited to sugar-cane farmers. This was the fourth major change in agrarian policy—the others having taken place in 1959, 1961, and 1963. As a consequence of 1963 Agrarian Reform Act, the government owned 70 percent of the national land, but only 57 percent of the arable land and only 40 percent of the high-yield acreage.[74] Peasants still controlled a large, though declining share of production outside of sugar cane (table 11.8). It was therefore impossible to plan centrally unless greater political and economic control was achieved over peasant production.

Some of the most productive farms were still owned by relatively large landowners with more than five caballerías of land, as allowed by the loopholes in

Table 11.8 Private agricultural production, 1967–1975 (% of total)

Product	1967	1973	1975
Tomatoes	96	—	—
Tobacco	92	82	81
Beets, carrots, radishes	84	—	—
Coffee	83	74	58
Papayas	80	—	—
Other fruit	68	—	—
All fruit	—	47	—
Starchy vegetables	46	41	46[a]
Other vegetables	71	31	—
Cattle ownership	42	43	26
Sugar cane	—	21	18

Sources: *Granma Weekly Review*, June 18, 1967, p. 12; "Transformación de la familia campesina," *ANAP* (December 1973): 5; *Bohemia* 67, no. 13 (March 28, 1975): 58.

a. All vegetables.

the agrarian laws. The 1967 cattle census showed that there were at least 3,131 ranches over five caballerías holding 255,052 head of cattle. About one-third of these were in province of Camagüey. The relationship between the size of the ranch and number of cattle shows a pattern familiar the world over: in 1967, 61.5 percent of the farmers owned only 28.7 percent of the cattle, while 16.7 percent of the farmers owned 46.3 percent. Farms larger than five caballerías made up 1.6 percent of the total and controlled 8.8 percent of the cattle. Inequality remained even during the government's most radical period, though it was much less severe than before the revolution. [75]

To control the highly productive private sector better, to reduce agrarian inequality, to limit the ANAP's autonomy and that of individual peasants, and to improve centralized agrarian planning, the government launched new policies. In April 1966, a year before the third peasant congress, new procedures were introduced that facilitated state purchase of peasant land if the owners wanted to sell voluntarily and were old, sick, or endowed with a suitably high order of revolutionary consciousness. By January 1967, 1,700 farms had been bought by the state. [76] The third peasant congress then approved the launching of "specialized" plans, incorporating private peasant farms into a single production plan along with some state-owned farms. The state now plans and directs this production; peasants are paid according to the amount delivered. Peasants lose the autonomy to decide about production in exchange for credit, fertilizer, technical assistance, and an assured labor supply (including military or volunteer labor). They retain private ownership but must work according to an official, planned design. The congress also approved the initiation of "integrated" plans, in which peasants can turn their land over to the state and move to the city or to another area designated by the state. If they do, the state guarantees that they will retain a small plot for family consumption, with the state paying rent for the use of the land. Peasants are urged to become agricultural workers on the land they have turned over, and elderly peasants can surrender their land to the state in exchange for a lifelong pension. These schemes—according to which political autonomy is exchanged for material benefit—were refined and reaffirmed at the fourth peasant congress in December 1971. [77]

The number of peasants in specialized plans rose from 26,028 in 1971 to 37,311 in 1973; in integrated plans, there were 24,528 in 1971 and 28,857 in 1973 (table 11.9). At the end of 1973, the total peasant family population was 1,943,000. As these numbers show, the incorporation of peasants into production plans had hardly taken hold, except in the provinces of Havana and Matanzas, by the fourth peasant congress in 1971 (table 11.10). The high proportion of peasants incorporated into production plans in Matanzas is a legacy of the earlier thorough party work there, which also paved the way for the 1974 experiments in local government. The low proportion of peasant incorporation in Oriente probably does not reflect political disloyalty but a characteristic indifference there to any government policies that involved the local people in the world outside. In Havana and Matanzas, where peasant incorporation was the norm, the largest landowners were likely to be unincorporated; elsewhere the difference in size of landholding between incorporated and unincorporated peasants was negligible (table 11.10).

The government's effort to control peasant production through these plans was no more successful than the cooperative movement had been in the 1960s. Only 24.9 percent of the peasants in 1971 and 26.3 percent in 1973 belonged to these plans, and only the less radical specialized plans were growing with any rapidity (table 11.9). Peasant resistance continued from the 1960s to the 1970s, with no consistent pattern over time between size of peasant holding and probability of cooperation with the government. Ideological documents suggesting that the peasants with smallest landholdings are the most revolutionary and the bulwarks of the "worker-peasant alliance" continued to be incorrect: larger landowners were more likely to cooperate with government policies in the agrarian societies, in joining cooperatives, and in joining the ANAP. Only two of the six provinces in 1971 showed any sign that small

Table 11.9 Participation in peasant organizations, 1969–1977

Date	ANAP members	In specialized or integrated production plans	Advanced peasants		Mutual-aid brigades	
			Men	Women	Men	Women
October 1969	—	—	—	—	62,739	32,204
Early 1971	—	—	29,974	—	70,000	50,000
December 1971	202,776	50,556	43,272[b]	—	—	—
Late 1972	220,000	[a]	54,990	15,932	86,361[b]	—
Late 1973	251,154	66,168	—	—	107,247[b]	—
Early 1975	—	—	81,255	34,970	—	—
Late 1975	232,358	—	—	—	110,000[b]	—
May 1977	209,617	30,000	84,409	34,238	—	—

Sources: Alfredo Reyes Trejo, "El campesino cubano marcha con su revolución," *Verde olivo* 16, no. 20 (May 19, 1974): 37; "Transformación de la familia campesina," pp. 5, 7; "Diez años de trabajo," *ANAP* (April 1971): 8; "Balance del 72," *ANAP* (February 1973): 24; *Bohemia* 67, no. 13 (March 28, 1975): 58; F. Petrenko, "Avangard Kubinskovo Naroda," *Partiinaia Zhizn* no. 8 (April 1973): 78; Acosta, "La revolución," pp. 152–153; *Granma Weekly Review*, January 4, 1976, p. 6; Margaret Randall, "La mujer cubana en 1974," *Casa de las Américas* 15, no. 89 (March–April 1975): 67; *Granma*, May 16, 1977, pp. 4, 6. See also Raúl Castro, "El congreso campesino en armas," *ANAP* (October 1973): 10.

a. Raúl Castro reported that 136,000 peasants belonged to specialized production plans at the end of 1972, a total he claimed represented 75 percent of the peasantry. While this figure is inconsistent with other evidence, it may serve to indicate how swift and drastic agrarian-policy shifts were between 1971 and 1973.

b. Includes women.

Table 11.10   Peasant participation in production plans, 1971

Province	Specialized plan		Integrated plan		No plan	
	% of ANAP members	% of land	% of ANAP members	% of land	% of ANAP members	% of land
Pinar del Río	4.3	2.3	6.8	8.8	88.9	88.9
Havana	59.0	39.4	38.5	45.4	2.5	15.2
Matanzas	80.5	54.4	9.7	19.7	9.8	25.9
Las Villas	4.3	4.0	33.2	33.8	62.5	62.2
Camagüey	1.2	1.5	4.2	4.9	94.6	93.6
Oriente	8.4	1.9	0.5	0.5	91.1	97.2
All provinces	12.8	8.8	12.1	15.6	75.1	75.6

Source: Computed from Acosta, "La revolución," p. 158.

peasants were becoming any more likely to cooperate with the government than they had been in the past.

The fourth peasant congress had ratified a formal renewal of land-eviction policies, and these were put into effect in the late 1960s. While the congress reiterated that peasants would not ordinarily be forced to sell their land to the state, exceptions included any evictions that were thought to improve productivity, establish industries, or build dams and roads. Small plots in the midst of a state farm could also be taken by forced sale. Prime Minister Castro, in a remarkable political faux pas, justified these evictions on the grounds that they were consistent with prerevolutionary law and practice. The policy on evictions was reaffirmed by the fifth congress in 1977. Evictions and voluntary sales to the government had reduced the peasant share of arable land from 43 percent in 1965 to 32 percent in 1971, 30 percent in 1975, and 21 percent in 1977.[78] These evictions differed from those of the prerevolutionary period in that all peasants were compensated and relocated. Eminent domain exists in most countries, and it can be exercised in rational ways in keeping with the public interest; safeguards can be maintained to cushion the impact on individuals through compensation and relocation. Nevertheless, they are evictions, and they do result in individual suffering; in this revolutionary Cuba was no exception.

The private market for peasant crops continued to thrive. Because the exhortations of the third peasant congress proved insufficient to discourage private sales, among other reasons, the government launched the "revolutionary offensive" in the spring of 1968 that socialized all small private businesses. Government studies found that 20 percent of the merchandise involved in these businesses was obtained legally through allocations from the Ministry of Internal Trade, 18 percent was obtained illegally, and the rest was bought directly from the peasants through private channels. Nonstate grocery stores sold 77 million pesos, or 31 percent, of Cuba's groceries. By the fourth peasant congress, private sales had become illegal. ANAP members were supposed to cooperate with the repressive measures that were introduced, though a loophole allowed them to transport up to twenty-five pounds of produce to give to distant relatives. The measures were largely unavailing; substantial quantities of agricultural production continued to be sold through private channels directly to consumers.[79]

The fourth congress approved sanctions against peasants who did not cultivate their land efficiently; they could be expelled from the association and, in extreme cases, evicted. The congress also faced up to a new problem: not all peasants who turned over their land to an integrated plan had done so out of revolutionary fervor; some had in fact received so much money from the state for it that they no longer had to work at all. The congress approved the application of sanctions against nonworking peasants in integrated plans, beginning with the suspension of state rent payments and followed by the enforcement of criminal penalties under the loafing law. The congress also approved a reduction in rents below the amount judged essential to cover necessities, in order to provide an incentive not only to turn the land over to the state but also to continue working.[80]

In the late 1960s, the government organized the Advanced Peasants' Movement as a rural parallel to the Advanced Workers' Movement. Its procedures, refined by the fourth congress, included assemblies to be held every six months. Before each assembly, the leadership of the local association was supposed to make a "prior evaluation" of the political acceptability of the candidates for advanced-peasant status. Nine qualities were required of male candidates through the mid-1970s: an advanced peasant must exploit the land according to local production plans, must be available to participate in civil defense and mutual-aid brigades, must not sell through private chanels, and must be active in the association. These are the essential criteria. In addition, an advanced peasant should participate in political-education activities, should be educated to the sixth-grade level, should not oppose the employment of women for pay, and should contribute to the education of the young and encourage their participation in the Cuban Pioneers' Union. Women as well as men could become advanced peasants. They had to belong to the Cuban Women's Federation and to a mutual-aid brigade, actively contribute to their children's education, participate in civil defense or health brigades, and oppose private sales.[81]

The Advanced Peasants' Movement was intended to stimulate political mobilization among the peasantry and marked a complete shift from the association's lobbying activities of the early 1960s. The ANAP's new role, added to its statutes by the fourth congress, was now to oppose sales through private channels, encourage the resocialization of prisoners on parole, and develop the mutual-aid brigades. Lobbying was not included, although the congress had voiced a complaint that matters affecting the peasantry were handled by too many organizations and that its membership wasted too much time in the bureaucratic shuffle—a far cry from the association's central role in avoiding precisely those pitfalls for its members a decade earlier.[82]

The development of mutual-aid brigades also illustrates a shift in the association's role. The mutual-aid brigades were set up in 1969 to facilitate cooperation among peasants for specific tasks and to encourage peasant work on state farms. The mutual-aid brigades for peasant women had similar purposes. In January 1973 peasant "columns" were organized so that some peasants could become agricultural workers for brief periods at peak harvest time. The cooperative-farm movement had allowed peasants an autonomy in decision making that had no part in the mutual-aid brigade movement; the cooperatives had benefited the peasants directly, while the brigades responded to party and government needs and initiatives. The government came to emphasize the more ambitious Advanced Peasants' Movement over the mutual-aid brigades by 1975.[83]

Despite all these efforts and stronger government control, disputes between peasants, especially the more prosperous ones, and agricultural workers continued. One source of conflict was the difference in income. The average annual income of private farmers in the mid-1960s was 2,450 pesos, with some ranging as high as 20,000 pesos; the average annual income of agricultural workers in state farms at that time was about 800 pesos. After the second peasant congress in 1963, ANAP statutes had forbidden any peasant who regularly employed more than two agricultural workers from holding association office; the third congress reaffirmed that stand.[84] The fourth congress, however, showed that the problem still remained. Tapes of meetings called by the local chapters of ANAP and the agricultural workers' union recorded verbal disputes between agricultural workers and poor peasants of the Escambray region; these were played at that congress: Prime Minister Castro then denounced them as "incredible" because of the "serious accusations" made by the workers against the peasants. The peasant-association statutes were then amended to forbid any peasant who employed even one agricultural worker from holding association office, except as authorized by the municipal, or district, committees,[85] in an effort at preventing conflicts at least between peasant leaders and agricultural workers. The peasant association protested that nothing had been said in the "theses" or basic programmatic documents for the thirteenth labor congress scheduled for the fall of 1973 about the "worker-peasant alliance." Cuban Labor Confederation secretary-general Lázaro Peña claimed that this was an oversight,[86] but it is more likely to have been a reflection of the continuing conflict between peasants and agricultural workers that no amount of official propaganda could brush aside.

Although there were fewer local bosses in the ANAP than there had been earlier, the association's national president, José Ramírez, was still complaining about their influence in 1967 (when many were finally dismissed) and, even as late as 1971, about how stubbornly people were sticking to the old ways of doing things. The ANAP made surveys of its membership every forty-five days in an attempt to improve the leadership's information about the members. It also tried to include peasants in adult political-education classes, where they studied Castro's speeches,[87] and to mobilize them politically. A measure of its success was that only three of the 6,164 local peasant associations failed to approve the party thesis prepared on the agrarian question for the First Party Congress (all three were in Havana province) and that 91.2 percent of the membership approved it, although many of those who opposed it simply stayed home. But of those who voted, only 0.4 percent voted against this thesis.[88]

The fourth congress in 1971 concluded that the association leadership was unstable. The national president had been at the helm since the organization was founded, but below him only six of the twenty-seven members of the 1967 national executive committee had been reelected in 1971. New training schools were established after the fourth congress and a new policy mandating training of cadres was approved at the congress in an effort to remedy this situation.[89]

The peasants' association was probably at its most adaptable and autonomous in the early 1960s; ten years later it was a complex bureaucracy with a domain that grew larger with its membership. Thus it had lost ground on some of the measures of institutionalization but gained it on others. There were 1,500 local organizations at the beginning; this number had risen to 2,611 by the second congress in 1963 then fell slightly to 2,590 by the third congress in 1967; five years later it was back up to 6,108 and grew to 6,164 by mid-1975. By the mid-1970s, there were also 322 district, or municipal, organizations. The national organization had offices for organization, production, ideology, education, and international relations, a structure that, except for international relations, was reproduced at the lower levels.[90] Political life was tightly controlled at the national center and by the party monitoring it from outside. The association president was the only peasant member of the party's Central Committee.

The First Party Congress's resolution on the agrarian question had said: "It is necessary, in the coming years, to advance gradually toward higher forms of production on the land of the peasant sector until it is totally transformed and incorporated within the socialist sector of our economy." The congress reiterated its "respect for the working peasant's free will" and acknowledged "his right to work his plot individually, [the government] providing him with material and technical assistance . . . as long as he remains a private producer." Although the congress proclaimed as a goal the "elimination of every form of private ownership of the means of production," its guidelines for the peasants' association were ambiguous, though no more so after than before the congress. The association should continue to press for control over peasant production and land, but the limits of that pressure remained vague—peasant "free will" was to be respected. At the national plenary meeting of the ANAP in March 1975 President Ramírez congratulated the National Institute for Agrarian Reform on its "efforts . . . to overcome its many deficiencies," a sarcastic remark that showed that the battle between the peasants' association and the state organizations, as old as the revolution, was still lively. The "deficiencies" continued.[91]

The First Party Congress also set new financial policies for the peasantry, in line with the new general economic policies, that canceled several agreements of the 1967 third peasant congress and included new taxes in addition to the graduated income tax. Profits from peasant cooperatives would be subject to a new corporate tax, and all peasants and peasant cooperatives employing agricultural workers or voluntary labor supplied by the state would be taxed heavily so that the gains of this labor would accrue to the state and not to any individual. All loans by the National Bank would henceforth bear interest. The peasants were, however, given one benefit—the legalization of private sales, provided the state did not need or could not collect the produce. These sales had to be made at official prices and be approved by the local government.[92] In 1967 the peasants had given up their relative autonomy in exchange for freedom from taxes and interest-free loans; in 1975 these benefits were removed but government control remained.

At long last, however, the government had to admit that the agrarian policies of the previous decade had not worked. The fifth peasant congress, which gathered in May 1977, marked the end of the government's emphasis on inducing peasants to join specialized or integrated plans. Fidel Castro admitted that neglecting private cooperatives while emphasizing the build up of state farms had been a mistake. The number of peasants in specialized or integrated plans went down by half from 1973 to 1977 (see table 11.9), as it became evident to peasants that pressures to join those plans had been relaxed. The government also began to pay attention to the ordinary ANAP member, rather than focusing only on advanced peasants; the number of advanced peasants, both men and women, remained virtually unchanged from 1975 to 1977. The new policies called for creating cooperatives wherever private farms predominated; peasants would be urged to join integrated or specialized plans only if their farms were isolated from other private farms and close to a state farm or if their farms required extensive capital investment for production. President Castro also announced, to the cheers of the peasant congress, that the land of a small state farm "surrounded by peasant land" would be "incorporated into the [private] cooperative. The world is not going to come to an end." The owners will thus have three choices; to join a private cooperative, to join a state farm through an integrated or specialized plan, or to remain independent producers.[93]

New economic policies were also put into effect. The Ministry of Agriculture, which replaced INRA in 1976, increased tractor allocations to private cooperatives from 80 to 500. Most prices paid by the state for agricultural products had remained fixed at the 1965 levels; costs, of course, had risen. It is no wonder that private sales had thrived. Fixed national prices were at last abolished in 1977. Henceforth prices would vary by region, as well as by supply and demand; prices for tobacco had already begun to increase in 1976 in anticipation of these changes.[94]

If much changed, much remained the same. Although cooperatives were to be promoted, government control over them had to be maintained. Permission to set up a cooperative, according to President Castro, had to come from the "provincial committee of ANAP—controlled by the national executive" and from the Ministry of Agriculture's provincial office. Castro noted that "controls are necessary, because tomorrow we might well have a strong and uncontrolled cooperative movement on our hands"—something the government could not allow. Financial controls over the peasantry also remained in place. The National Bank recovered 97.3 percent of the loans issued between 1971 and 1976.[95]

ANAP continued to be a highly centralized, and somewhat arbitrary, mass organization. Although the statutes called for the fifth congress to be held in December 1975, the ANAP leadership chose to postpone it twice. When the fifth congress was held, all key resolutions were approved "unanimously." The ANAP was also unwilling to allow its members a free vote on policies toward the peasantry before the congress. Two kinds of assemblies were called ahead of time; at the first, discussion was open but no votes were taken. The ANAP's president explained that special commissions of ANAP cadres were sent to visit families after the first assembly to gather suggestions and to build support for the proposed policy changes. Thus the second assembly, where votes were taken, was held only after this detailed political work had been done. Although virtually all peasants participated actively in these meetings, there were only 116 suggestions for policy change. If leadership instability had been a problem at the fourth congress, the rise of an oligarchy was the problem at the fifth. The membership of the ANAP's national executive committee was reduced from twenty-seven to twelve, of whom nine continued from the previous committee; 97 percent of all ANAP leadership cadres had been at their posts for over a year in May 1977.[96] ANAP, party, and government were thus willing to relax many economic policies but not to ease their own centralized political control over the peasantry.

Cuba faces the late 1970s with several problems relating to its peasants still unresolved. The National Association of Small Peasants is deliberately unrepresentative and has served too much to implement government policies that a majority of the peasantry has not supported. Conflicts between peasants and agricultural workers continue. Many peasants are not inclined to sacrifice themselves and their families in the public interest. Although many are willing to cooperate with their neighbors, they are less willing to cooperate with those they do not know. Conflicts between government and peasants, partly fueled by the incompetence of the agrarian bureaucracy, have not been resolved.

Overall, however, different groups have reacted differently to government policies. Sierra Maestra peasants remained loyal to the revolution, although they were less enthusiastic about the cooperative movement. Matanzas peasants, responding to extensive government efforts to contain their rebellion, were fully incorporated into government production plans by 1971. Most peasants, as individual rural citizens, probably respond warmly to the improvement in their standard of living brought about by revolutionary educational and public-health policies. Despite this good will and the strong political loyalty most peasants feel to the revolution, however, they have resisted many of the government's agricultural policies.

The revolution did not invent the problems of the countryside, of course. It has solved as well as created problems, but conflict has still not disappeared. Improvement in the future therefore depends on the government's ability to use its assets in the countryside more effectively to obtain a majority of peasant support for policies that have so far been unpopular. To begin with, the government would have to grant more political autonomy to the peasants' association, to recognize lobbying to defend peasant interests as a legitimate role for the organization, and to modify electoral procedures within the association so that the leadership reflects the concerns of the rank and file more accurately. More political and economic authority should devolve from the Ministry of Agriculture to the peasants, both collectively and individually.

These policies would be in line with moves toward economic decentralization that have been instituted in the industrial sector; they have yet to be approved for the private agricultural sector. Such decentralization would probably end the pressures to eliminate private peasant farms and would allow the peasants a great deal more autonomy in making decisions about what to grow and how to dispose of their produce. Legalization of private sales, beyond the modest 1975 reform, would put the black market out of business. On the whole, these policies would eventually result in rural Cubans' being empowered to act on their own. This goal was proclaimed by Fidel Castro in 1953, but the government has moved steadily away from it in the 1960s and 1970s.

Agrarian political conflict in Cuba has been uninterrupted by the revolution, although its characteristics have changed. Before the revolution, conflict arose among giant agricultural enterprises, farmers, and agricultural workers and among different types of farmers, all of whom wished to maximize their private power and access to government; landowners also battled against squatters. The immediate effects of the revolution were to do away with the autonomy of the largest agricultural enterprises by socializing them; to increase the autonomy of the state in agrarian politics; to contain, but not to end, conflict among different groups of peasants; to exacerbate conflict between peasants and agricultural workers; and to put an end to evictions. In the long run, the political autonomy of worker and peasant organizations has been curtailed—a trend consistent with those in other areas of Cuban politics. Conflict between peasants and workers has continued, in less explosive form, although measures have repeatedly been taken to promote an "alliance" between them. Evictions by eminent domain were reinstituted on a modest scale in the late 1960s. Throughout the period, the state's control over the peasants has increased.

The presence of conflict in prerevolutionary Cuba does not mean that landlords always won land-eviction cases or that a few companies effectively controlled vast tracts of land. Instead, the degree of wealth, organization, power, and tenure security among peasants varied depending on what they grew. In general, sugar farmers were the best organized, had the easiest access to government, were comparatively wealthy, and were most secure in their tenure, even if they did not own land, by the provisions of the Sugar Coordination Act of 1937. Farmers who owned their land had few tenure problems. At the other end of the scale were squatters, who were poor, relatively unorganized, with virtually no access to power, and quite insecure; yet they were able to disrupt the fragile calm of the political atmosphere. The most active among them benefited from the modest land-reform programs. Between these extremes were nonsugar farmers who were protected by extensive, though controversial, legislation governing all aspects of rural economic and social relations. Much of this legislation reduced land evictions and improved tenure security and the standard of living.

By a historical accident, the insurrection led by Fidel Castro was based in the one area where squatting was a severe problem. Their experience with the peasants in the Sierra Maestra gave the revolutionaries a distorted view of rural Cuba, which their early legislation reflected: it helped the squatters but did little for sugar farmers or agricultural workers. Unlike those of other socialist states, Cuba's was a relatively urbanized society when the revolution came to power. Even in the countryside, there were more agricultural workers than peasants, although the distinctions between these two rural types are often blurred both in theory and in practice. The agricultural workers' many individual actions were felt as collective pressure to radicalize the revolution by the new government. Of the many counterrevolutionary efforts of the early 1960s, the only one not blamed exclusively on outsiders occurred in southern Matanzas, an area nearly opposite in social characteristics to the Sierra Maestra. The southern Matanzas insurrection was eventually defeated not only by military repression but also by shrewd policies, which included the return of illegally seized land to the peasants.

Neither the peasants nor the agricultural workers gained much, as organized groups, in the early 1960s; government economic-growth policies were punishing the countryside as a side effect of its unsuccessful attempt at industrialization. Yet they benefited considerably as individual citizens from other government policies; rural educational opportunities improved remarkably; rural public health, more modestly. Rural income also rose faster than urban income during the period. In exchange for relinquishing their political autonomy, the peasants did gain important material advantages, at least until 1975, when new taxes and interest policies cancelled out many of the benefits peasants had enjoyed earlier.

Theoreticians often suggest that peasants owning small farms are more likely than others to collaborate with the government, but this pattern is only rarely demonstrable. In Cuba, larger commercial landowners were the most familiar with government organizations and were more likely to collaborate with them. The government, however, was more likely to favor the small, often subsistence farmer. In the early and mid-1960s, furthermore, many larger landowners were illegally admitted to local peasants' association chapters, and many association leaders were in fact local bosses who maintained traditional patron-client relationships with smaller landowners.

The relations between the revolutionary government and the National Association of Small Peasants were troubled in the 1960s and 1970s. The ANAP began as a relatively autonomous and readily adaptable political organization in the early 1960s, effectively representing the peasants' viewpoint to government organizations. But the government did not long tolerate this behavior and soon clipped the association's wings. Its role shifted as a result from that of a lobbyist defending its members' interests to that of an agent of the party and the government stimulating controlled mass participation through political mobilization. Through the ANAP, the government launched a long campaign to establish full control over the peasants, first through cooperatives and then through incorporating them into government production plans. Only about a third of the peasantry has collaborated in these endeavors, however.

Both before and after the revolution Cuban peasants have had the capacity for political participation and organization. They have been "subjectively competent," that is, aware of and oriented toward the national government and modern enough to manipulate the bureaucracy for their own purposes. They have been able to maximize their profits rationally by shifting from crop to crop, for instance, and did so in response to various policies of the revolutionary government. Thus their behavior has been modified but not fundamentally altered by the revolution and its policies.

12

POLITICAL CULTURE

Political studies often consider a country's political culture: its citizens' beliefs about politics, its symbols and values, and citizens' own convictions and attitudes about government and political organizations. Such an examination is revealing because the political culture of every country is the product of its history as expressed in both public events and private experiences. It embodies a society's central political values and should be understood not only as states of mind but also as patterns of action.[1] Recognizing this fact, many states try to effect changes in their political culture by controlling these events and experiences—the most obvious modern examples being the Communist countries, where political culture is not just the environment in which the political process takes place but also the chief result of that process.[2]

The outstanding work on how this attempt has worked in socialist Cuba is Richard Fagen's *Transformation of Political Culture in Cuba*. Fagen argues that the transformation of the Cuban people into socialist citizens has been one of the chief goals of the revolution; it is to be accomplished through full participation by all citizens in mass organizations and other directed activities that aim to inculcate the standard socialist virtues (many of which are shared by those who are not socialists) of cooperation, egalitarianism, self-sacrifice, service, hard work, self-improvement, obedience, and incorruptibility, to which list the absence of economic motivations and atheism might be added. The First Party Congress endorsed these as the core values that must replace individualism, laziness, selfishness, and lack of discipline. Fagen, however, has said little about the impact of history on the present—that is, whether the Cuban past was helping or hindering the acquisition of socialist values and in what ways. In addition, although he tells us a good deal about the hopes and plans of the elite and about the organizations that are contributing to the cultural changes the elite desires to effect, Fagen presents little empirical data about the attitudes and beliefs of ordinary citizens.[3]

Socialism found fertile soil in Cuba. Participation, cooperation, approval of government intervention, and political awareness are none of them new to Cuba. While not all socialist values were equally consistent with prerevolutionary attitudes and while opposition and resistance to change did occur, many socialist goals found their echo in Cuban traditions. Much of the prerevolutionary political culture continued into the revolutionary era, quite in harmony with the aims of the new government.

The persistence of the past and the changes that occurred independent of any policy decisions made by the ruling elite suggest that individuals retained a more substantial degree of autonomy in belief and behavior than would have been allowed in a genuinely totalitarian state. The Cuban revolutionary government has extraordinary powers; it curtails the freedom of action of organizations and of individuals to a far greater extent than any of its predecessors had ever attempted. Yet, in part through deliberate policy and in part through the resilience of citizens, not everything has changed that the government wanted changed, and some things have changed in spite of opposition from the government. The processes that account for change in Cuba are primarily related to modernization but have also resulted quite generally from the experience of the revolution itself, at times changing stuctures unexpectedly; these processes often began outside government policy and are likely to remain independent of it.

Although the past has not faded entirely and has helped to shape the present, the extent of the change is substantial, most of it in the direction of modern socialist values. There is more variation within the political culture than had existed before the revolution; Cuban citizens may now hold rather sharply differentiated political values. This cultural heterogeneity may become a new source of tension between government and society in the decades ahead.

If the coming of a socialist revolution to Cuba was not inevitable, the spread of socialist values, though also not inevitable, is less surprising. Government intervention was already extensive before the revolution and prepared the way for the state that burgeoned after it. Political participation, an essential part of Cuban revolutionary politics, is not new to Cuba either, although it has taken novel revolutionary forms.

Political Participation, Cooperation, and Individualism

Prerevolutionary Cuba boasted high levels of electoral participation. In the 1944 presidential elections, 80.7 percent of those eligible voted; in the 1948 presidential elections, 79.5 percent. These elections were reasonably free, orderly, and competitive. When they were not, the voters stayed away. In the presidential elections of 1954 when Batista was the only candidate, the percentage of eligible voters that voted dropped to 52.6 percent, still a high proportion. That the public abstained from voting in such large numbers, even when the government tried to get people to the polls, suggests a political sophistication greater than would be expected if Cuba had been a traditional society. It indicates an electorate that was fairly well informed and capable of coordinated political action. Other data confirm this impression. In a 1951 poll, 93 percent could express what they thought of the government. In 1949, 93 percent knew that Senator Eduardo Chibás had been temporarily imprisoned. In 1950 as many as 47 percent were aware that the national government had embarked on a new economic policy.[4] By the standards of public-opinion research, these statistics are very high.

Even in rural areas political participation and cooperation were clearly valued. In a survey of 1,675 families in rural areas of the province of Las Villas in 1958, 80.5 percent of the respondents answered that they "believed unified action by the whole neighborhood could solve some local problems." Those aged fifteen to thirty-nine were more likely to believe in the efficacy of cooperative effort than older people. Almost two-thirds of the men and a majority of the women participated in social activities. The same research team surveyed 677 rural schools in the province and found that almost 79 percent of them had organized parent-teacher associations mandated by law. In 40 percent of all the rural schools, four or more meetings had been held during the school year, and 51 percent of the schools with associations had met four times or more. Almost all of them had raised funds themselves; 16 percent of the rural schools and 21 percent of the rural schools with associations had raised 26 pesos or more, a substantial sum in those days, and 37.7 percent of the books came from sources outside the education ministry, amounting to 22,184 volumes from private sources.[5]

At the beginning of 1957, the Catholic Students' Association of the University of Havana surveyed a thousand agricultural workers throughout the country. When asked what institution could help solve their problems, 68.7 percent named the government, followed by management (16.7 percent), and the union (6.8 percent). Clearly those at the bottom of the social structure believed in government's ability to deal with problems if it wanted to.[6]

There are many instances of this cooperative and participatory tradition, many of them unconnected with political parties or government organizations. One is the Abakuá, the secret society that emerged in the first half of the nineteenth century from an Afro-Cuban religion, which originated among the Yoruba in Africa, to build up solidarity among its several thousand members, not all of whom were blacks, for social, economic, and political action. The Abakuá was hierarchically organized. The early brutality of its initiation rites had been discarded by the 1950s, and, despite persecution by various Cuban governments, it survived and flourished. It included the poor as well as white-collar employees, teachers, soldiers, politicians (including members of Congress and of the cabinet), and other professionals. Essentially a mutual-aid society and strong in the cities of Havana, Matanzas, and Cárdenas, especially in the port-workers' unions in the 1940s and 1950s, it unsuccessfully resisted the new government's takeover of all unions in 1960–61.[7] The Abakuá's existence, therefore, is evidence of cooperative activity in prerevolutionary Cuba; since the revolution it has been replaced by the activities of mass organizations.

Additional evidence of cooperative themes can be found in Afro-Cuban culture. Much of Afro-Cuban religious dance, especially the ring and the procession, is group activity. John DuMoulin has argued that group activities reflect "deeply rooted characteristics of Cuban popular culture." He has noted that "there is profoundly integrated in Cuban culture a feeling of participation in the social activity of those persons with whom one has face to face contact. This emphasis is evident in many aspects of social life—its new political expression has helped to give the Cuban revolution a special character." Cooperative themes are at least as frequent as individualistic themes in Afro-Cuban aphorisms that originated among Yoruba slaves imported from Africa, suggesting the coexistence of these two tendencies in Afro-Cuban folklore.[8] Neither group folk dance or aphorisms calling for cooperation are, of course, unique to Cuba; they can be found in many cultures. Yet they can be found in Cuba, too; contrary to the impression given by some scholars and by the revolutionary government, prerevolutionary Cuba was not marked only by individualism but also by cooperation in social activities. Much of its cooperative tradition was rooted in Afro-Cuban religion. The Cuban revolution was able to build upon that tradition and to use it for new secular purposes. What was once only social cooperation eventually became the basis for political participation.

The upper end of the social scale was equally cooperative. Indeed, organizations were more apt to be constructed around group or regional than around class interests. Long before Spain had anything like them, for instance, Spanish immigrants in Cuba had organized into thirteen charitable societies in the city of Havana alone, each representing different regions or provinces of Spain. The two biggest were the Centro Gallego, founded by Spanish Galicians, and the Centro Asturiano, set up by Asturians. Established in 1879, the Centro Gallego provided an employment bureau, a night school, and a social center; its 95,000 members paid 3 pesos a month for comprehensive medical programs, including preventive care, for themselves and their families. The Centro Asturiano, with 90,000 members, performed similar functions. The next largest centers were those for immigrants from the Canary Islands and from Castille; they also provided full medical coverage. The Casino Español was an upper-class social club; the Spanish Republican Circle had left-wing members; and the two Basque and the two Catalan associations drew their membership according to politics. Spanish immigrants, their children, and their grandchildren belonged to these centers. Although a few members of non-Spanish background were admitted, blacks and Orientals were excluded. The Centro Asturiano had 109 delegations in the interior of the country, but, generally speaking, the provincial Spanish associations were much less active than those in Havana. Spurred by necessity, Spanish immigrants in Cuba acted cooperatively and for civic purposes to a far greater extent than their progenitors had done in the mother country.[9] These organizations and especially their health-care systems paved the way for the new socialist system by creating a tradition of corporate rather than individual responsibility for the sick and the needy.[10]

In a more rural setting, George M. Stabler studied Bejucal, eighteen miles south of metropolitan Havana, in 1954 and found a behavior pattern mixing cooperative and individualistic themes. Some town doctors there had organized a prepaid medical-insurance plan open to everyone for 3.50 pesos a person per month. Some people in the countryside were beginning to join, but even that price was too high for most of them. A farmers' cooperative association was also established shortly after World War II, though it, too, failed for lack of funds and because it did not sufficiently replace the ready credit, security in case of crop failure, dependable urban support, and personal relations of the *bodeguero* (literally, "grocery-store owner") upon whom the people had traditionally relied. These failures were both quite clearly the result of impoverishment, however, and not of any absence of cooperative zeal. The rural population also tended to be more suspicious of political parties and of the elected officials of the national government and were more electorally passive than the people in the cities.[11]

On the other hand, the government did assist in some local programs, such as improving local roadways, provided the residents raised one-third of the funds. The Bejucal farmers had collected enough money for three roads by 1954. Stabler reports that they believed the primary responsibility of adults was to protect their families from a hostile world. Protection included educating one's children, working hard, and maintaining ties of mutual aid, such as the emergency organizations in the neighborhood during hurricane season. But it also included lending money to others in times of need, joining clubs, and exchanging presents, as if to ensure help from others whenever it was called for. Such traditional common endeavors as barn raisings, lending equipment, and labor sharing at harvest time flourished in Bejucal.[12]

Stabler also took a nonrandom sample of Bejucal farmers, using procedures that were carefully spelled out and cautious. He studied twenty-two matched pairs of farmers who differed according to the agricultural technology they used. Although his sample is small, it is sufficient to generalize about the small Bejucal rural community. Thirty-nine percent of the forty-four farmers belonged to organized farm groups; there were no differences according to the level of agricultural technology. These farmers believed in government involvement so long as it could be kept separate from elections and political parties. When asked whether they thought they needed "a strong governmental program" to provide credit and other facilities, 93 percent of Stabler's forty-four respondents said yes. Stabler found that the more technologically advanced farmers were significantly more likely to believe that they had influence in government. The government agricultural inspector posted in rural Bejucal, a trained agronomist hired by the Ministry of Agriculture, was also highly respected by the farmers. When farmers were asked about the best source of information on good agricultural practice, the inspector led the list for both types of farmers. In practice, he clearly took a back seat to relatives and friends in influencing the farmers' daily activities.[13]

In spite of considerable evidence of cooperative behavior, however, Cubans have a poorly demonstrated reputation for being ferociously individualistic. Three different theories have been developed to account for Cubans' alleged individualism. One of Cuba's leading prerevolutionary intellectuals, Jorge Mañach, had a theory about Cuban individualism that centered on *choteo,* an ironic response to most aspects of life that was widespread in Cuba; he argued that it was the "enemy of order." Order implies authority, and choteo mocked all authority. It arose from a lack of social cohesion. "The Cuban is generally happy if he is not bothered . . . He remains aloof from, and even acquiescent to, the arrogance and the excessive rigors of authority so long as he does not suffer personal injury himself." The structural base of the choteo was the low level of legitimacy of economic and political institutions; it had three effects: it cushioned adversity, providing an escape from disaster; it hindered discipline and precluded achieving any long-term goal requiring perseverance and authority; and it was a leveler, chipping away at the distinctions, privileges, and rights of the old, the rich, the powerful, and the traditionally sacred.[14]

After the 1961 Bay of Pigs invasion failed, a number of the prisoners were interviewed on Cuban television. The transcripts of these interviews became the basis for yet another theory about Cubans' individualistic tendencies. According to this theory, the bourgeoisie emphasized individualism at the expense of group solidarity or social responsibility; each of the prisoners had dissociated himself from the real or alleged crimes of the rest, an attitude that was found even among those who had belonged to the Batista government. Prisoners who had held positions of responsibility under Batista claimed that they had performed a useful social service in office and had not taken graft. Those who had been rich before the revolution claimed that they bore no responsibility for prerevolutionary politics. Catholic beliefs seemed to reinforce this tendency to distinguish between behavior and moral stance; a Catholic chaplain among the invading force saw his involvement as a spiritual mission, not as part of a political conspiracy.[15] Another more plausible explanation for these careful distinctions is, of course, that the prisoners were trying to save their own skins by dissociating themselves from the conspiracy or from Batista.

A third theory claims that individualism in Cuba resulted not from a national psychology or from the characteristics of the bourgeoisie and Roman Catholicism but from the specific nature of the Cuban economy. For example, anthropological studies in the municipalities or districts of Santa Isabel de las Lajas and San Juan de las Yeras in Las Villas province show that the vast size and hierarchical structure of the modern sugar plantation hindered the development of worker organizations and fragmented the labor union movement when it was finally established.[16]

A more accurate view of Cuban values before the revolution may be that both themes, individualism and cooperation, coexisted in the country's political culture, albeit with some tension. In prerevolutionary times, all Cubans did not mock illegitimate authority and dissociate themselves from those who corrupted national life; from the 1940s onwards many middle-class Cubans sought, first through the Ortodoxo party and then through the revolution, to purify national life. These actions, above all the revolution, required political cooperation to overthrow the old government and establish a new one; if Cubans had been entirely individualistic, there could have been no revolution. A revolution also requires a willingness to submit to a new authority.

Prerevolutionary Cubans preferred to associate in groups that were not openly partisan. Farmers, in Bejucal or Las Villas, favored cooperative activities to work on local problems. Agricultural workers knew that the state had considerable influence on the economy; they were convinced that government could solve problems if it would only try. Few of them expected solutions from union action because the unions were so fragmented. Despite their dislike of partisan politics, Cubans did vote in high numbers and were informed enough to discriminate between honest and fraudulent elections. By the 1950s they were repelled by the charade of national electoral politics, but they persisted in believing both in government action as a solution to social and economic problems and in the importance of personal involvement with local issues. Thus they distinguished among levels of government as well as among kinds of government action, some of which they supported and others of which they opposed. Consequently when the revolution came to power, government intervention in the social system was expected and accepted as desirable. Many citizens joined together to pursue the collective goals of the revolution through the new national and local organizations.

The Cuban revolution changed the characteristics of participation. All of it became politicized, nationalized, and centralized. The government discouraged political indifference and began to harness political participation to transform society and to increase its own power and control. Preexisting participatory organizations gradually became less diversified, less competitive, and less autonomous. Finally, since politics was too important a subject to leave to the people, new revolutionary organizations were established to stimulate the cooperative action latent in Cuban political culture and to make it difficult to pursue a life in isolation.

Religion

A word should be said about the importance of religious beliefs in Cuba. The Havana University Catholic Students' Association national survey of 4,000 people in all six provinces in 1954 found that 96.5 percent of the respondents said they believed in God, although 19 percent claimed to belong to no organized religion. Ninety-one percent of all Cuban children were baptized as Catholics, but only 50 percent of these received first communion; 72.5 percent of all respondents, but only 52 percent of the rural respondents, said they were Catholics. Only 24 percent of the Catholics and only 17 percent of all those with a religious affiliation attended services regularly, and only 16 percent of all marriages were formalized in church. Of the people who said they were Catholics, twenty-seven percent said that they had literally never seen a priest.[17]

In the 1958 survey of rural Las Villas, only 13 percent of the men and 11.3 percent of the women responding professed no religion. When asked whether they had attended church during the past month, however, only 4.5 percent of the Catholic males and 6.1 percent of the Catholic females had done so. Virtually all the Protestants and members of others sects had attended services, but they accounted for only 3.7 percent of the male and 3.9 percent of the female respondents in this survey, while Catholics comprised 83.3 percent of the males and 84.8 percent of the females. The 1957 survey of agricultural workers throughout the country found that 41.4 percent professed no religion and that 52.1 percent were Catholics; but 27.3 of the Catholics had never seen a parish priest, and an additional 58.3 percent had only a passing acquaintance with one; of the Catholic heads of household, 88.8 percent had not attended mass during the past year. Only 16.0 percent of the married Catholics had been married by the church. Fewer than 10 percent of the rural people of Bejucal attended mass regularly in 1954; there was not even a church building there although there was a small shrine dedicated to Santa Barbara, a saint who was also significant in the Afro-Cuban religion. Thus institutional religions, especially the Roman Catholic church, had an extremely weak hold on the population in prerevolutionary Cuba. Despite some symbolic identification with the Catholic church, the beliefs and behavior of the Cubans were secular and thus did not come into conflict with socialist values. A study of Roman Catholicism in Latin America in the mid-1950s found that Catholicism was weaker in Cuba than in the majority of these countries.[18]

Nevertheless, the secularism of Cubans should not be exaggerated. If institutional religion was weak, religious beliefs were stronger, especially those associated with the Afro-Cuban sects. The Catholic Students' Association's 1954 survey found that 25 percent of the respondents had consulted spiritualists, almost all of them linked to Afro-Cuban sects. Most of this group had not gone beyond primary school; 33 percent of them came from the lower class and an additional 57 percent from the lower middle class. The importance of spiritualism was very high in some areas of Cuba. In the city of Bayamo in the province of Oriente, 60 percent of the respondents had consulted spiritualists. Apart from spiritualism, 12 percent of the national sample had consulted Afro-Cuban religious authorities, and as many as 28 percent consulted astrologers regularly.[19] Moreover, 14, or 4.3 percent, of 328 severe cases of phobia registered in the psychiatric department of the Havana Children's Hospital were diagnosed as having an exclusively religious cause. These were instances of trauma that had no other explanation; in addition there were other cases where religious beliefs contributed to emotional disturbances.[20]

Secularism prevailed, but nevertheless, one-quarter of the population was active in spiritualist religious activities, one-sixth in organized or institutional religious activities, and no less than a tenth in Afro-Cuban religious sects. The importance of religious belief and affiliation varied from region to region. Afro-Cuban sects tended to be of greater importance in Oriente, for instance, and the Catholic church tended to be of greater importance in metropolitan Havana.

Explaining Continuity and Change after the Revolution

How does one explain the occurrence and the nature of change? A variety of approaches can be distinguished from each other primarily by whether they emphasize the persistence of the past or the encroachment of the future; those stressing the future differ about the source, rate, and scope of the changes that occur. Five alternative hypotheses have been put forward to explain the extent of change in Cuban political beliefs from the prerevolutionary period to the present. The "null" hypothesis claims that no significant change has occurred in the fundamental political beliefs held by most Cubans. Despite the panoply of organizations and the intentions of the government, Cubans think about things today in the same ways they always have, whatever those ways may be. A closely related hypothesis states that changes, if they have occurred, have resulted from totalitarian "brainwashing" on an individual or selective scale. The implication is that change will not take place unless it is coerced. A third hypothesis argues for significant change but maintains that it is the continuation of the processes of modernization that had already begun in prerevolutionary Cuba and that the impact of the revolution has consequently been marginal; change would have continued in the same direction even without the change of governments. These changes coincided also with the goals of the revolutionary elite. The past was actually useful to the spread of revolutionary values since some of its traditions were compatible with socialism, as were some patterns of changing beliefs; nonetheless, the changes neither required socialism to occur nor were caused or accelerated by it.

Some argue that revolutionary Cuba has reversed the popular social-science tenet that behavior follows belief—in other words, the "revolutionary model" argues that participation in revolutionary organizations and activities will lead to changes in individual beliefs and political culture. New behavior will change old beliefs. This notion and its opposite are not necessarily mutually exclusive, however, since both admit feedback between belief and behavior; only the emphasis is different. The revolutionary model has two inherent hypotheses. One—the fourth hypothesis—says that structural and behavioral changes alter attitudes; people see changes and behave accordingly, but the basic set of values has not changed much. New beliefs do not change structures on their own. The beliefs that change deal only with empirical facts; beliefs about more abstract values remain intact, and a certain ideological incoherence can result. The other—the final hypothesis—states that the structural and resulting behavioral changes lead to new basic values and orientations more compatible with the socialist ethos. These new values then result in further behavioral and structural changes. This explanation tends to circle back to the standard social-science model of beliefs governing change. I shall refer to this view as the "new citizen" hypothesis and to the fourth view as the "structural" hypothesis. Both stem from the expectation that behavioral changes will precede and induce changes in beliefs. Consequently both result in interpretations that differ only in terms of the extent and coherence of the new beliefs and of their ability independently to change structures.

Unqualified support for the revolution and its policies is not required by the new-citizen hypothesis. The new citizen is expected to make "constructive and concrete criticism." However, all new citizens must be revolutionaries, or, in other words, must exhibit exemplary socialist behavior, though not all supporters of the revolution need necessarily be proper socialist citizens. One can support revolutionary policies because one has gained from them or be active in a revolutionary organization because it is personally profitable (for example, one may work hard in a factory in order to win a promotion, a prize, a vacation, or a television set). These individualistic motives are not incompatible with support for the revolutionary government, though they may be inconsistent with the socialist values of selfless behavior and concern for the collective good.

Consequently, although behavioral change may precede and induce a change in values, the observation of the former is itself an insufficient basis for inferring the latter change.

As a specific example, a worker may be observed to be laboring happily. It is possible to conclude that the worker is happy because he has always been so; that the worker is merely pretending to be happy in order to stay out of trouble; that the worker has been "modernized" (this is especially likely in the case of women who have joined the paid labor force); that he is happy to be employed at all, having previously experienced unemployment; or that he is happy because he is cooperatively and selflessly working for the common good. Simply by looking at the worker, it is not possible to determine which of these explanations, if any, is correct. On the other hand, if the worker exhibits "negative" behavior, such as refusing to do "voluntary" work, one can at least infer that the last explanation—that he is a selfless new citizen—can be crossed off the list, though it is not necessarily true that this is a crack in the to-talitarian veil, unless the unhappy worker risks telling us the reasons for, and the duration of, that unhappiness.

Some scholars, especially those who adhere to the "null" or to the totalitarian hypotheses, will object to the reliance on survey data as evidence in analyzing revolutionary Cuba. Most surveys, however, try not to ask obviously political questions that may frighten those who oppose, or are skeptical about, the revolutionary government. Even assuming that Cubans under revolutionary rule cannot give an interviewer a straight answer on overtly political issues, it is still likely that they will answer questions that are less loaded politically. There is still reason to doubt the surveys' validity and reliability, however; so many Cuban exiles, including workers and peasants, have admitted lying to interviewers, especially to foreigners, that one must exercise great caution in using these surveys.[21]

Change among Students in the Early 1960s

Louis Jones and his associates conducted a survey of 1,805 young teenage junior high school students in 44 schools in Havana province between April and June 1960; the same questions were repeated with 239 students in the same kinds of schools in June 1965.[22] When asked whether their parents were trying to influence their vocational choices, 92 percent of the students surveyed said that they were. When asked whether they wanted to become economically independent of their parents, 56 percent of the students in 1960 and 71 percent of the students in 1965 said that they did. Only 5 percent in 1960 and 4 percent in 1965 said that they disliked their studies, but 92 percent in both 1960 and 1965 said that they believed their studies would not be useful later in life. These answers suggest that parental behavior toward children had not changed between the two surveys, that children's desire for autonomy was marginally greater in 1965 but was high in both years, and that, on both occasions, students liked their studies but did not think they were useful, even though this attitude ran counter to the official line. The willingness of the students to express that opinion is therefore an important finding that increases confidence in the reliability of the survey, although it may also mean that major changes in the Cuban schools were not made until after 1965.

In response to a question about whether they would like to study for a profession but believed they lacked the opportunity, 54 percent of the 1960 sample but only 8 percent of the 1965 sample said yes; only 12 percent claimed a similar lack of opportunity for learning a craft in 1965, compared with 49 percent in 1960. When students were asked whether they believed they had opportunities to learn the skills necessary for a job they would like, positive replies increased from 70 percent to 95 percent. Those worried about getting a job fell from 81 percent to 45 percent; those worried about finding a job after they finished their studies fell from 71 percent to 35 percent. These figures suggest that junior-high-school students were aware that important structural changes had occurred in Cuba in the early 1960s to remove obstacles to their social mobility. The proportion of students who believed they lacked economic resources to continue their studies fell from 93 percent to 58 percent. Students were also asked whether they thought they needed to earn a lot of money to pay for their studies; the proportion answering yes fell from 61 percent to 32 percent. Belief that money was necessary to pursue an education had also fallen substantially.

Only three other questions that bear exclusively on the new-citizen hypothesis were included in the Jones group's survey. The proportion of students who said earning a good salary was the only consideration when they looked for a job fell from 34 to 7 percent. The proportion that said yes when asked whether they wanted to have a lot of money fell from 64 percent to 29 percent. When asked whether they would pursue the career they wished without regard for economic advantage 55 percent in 1960 and 77 percent in 1965 said yes. These are answers consistent with the new-citizen argument, although admittedly at the junior-high-school level the reality behind the questions is remote.

However, two-thirds of the junior-high-school students in 1960 were already agreeing that a good salary was not the only thing they would look for in a job; it is impossible to guess, of course, whether the other gratifications they would look for were consistent with exemplary socialist citizenship, either in 1960 or in 1965. The students' answers may simply show that they had realized that money was not very useful in an economy of scarcity (they were not asked whether they were interested in acquiring power). Over half the students surveyed in 1960 were prepared to disregard money in their search for a job; that the proportion increased still further in 1965 can be regarded either as a reaction to objective changes or as a sign of further inroads made by the new ideology. These answers, then, could be explained by the structural argument alone, without reference to the new-citizen hypothesis, by assuming that beliefs about money changed not because of a new selflessness but because students accurately perceived that money was less necessary to get ahead in Cuba in 1965.

No evidence of changes in beliefs about the family and schools appears in this study, and this lack of change is consistent with the "null" hypothesis. There is evidence, however, that attitudes toward money that were compatible with socialist values already existed in 1960; this finding is consistent with the modernization hypothesis. The survey provides evidence of a new faith in social mobility, consistent with the structural argument. Finally, students were more likely to give answers consistent with the new, socialist-citizen norms; caution is necessary in interpreting these answers, however, because they can also be explained by a structural argument alone. It is not possible to test the totalitarian explanation of change in Cuba with these data, but objections to the validity and reliability of the survey on the grounds that questions could not be answered honestly are not persuasive. The process of change in Cuba has been complex; as is so often the case, no single, simple hypothesis will suffice to explain it.

The changes discussed here all occurred prior to the "radical" period of the late 1960s, that is, before a concerted effort was made to mold the population along socialist lines. The fact of the revolution itself—even apart from the policies of its leaders—changed individual beliefs profoundly. Some scholars have argued that beliefs were changed in the late 1960s as a direct result of the leaders' policies; the data presented here suggest instead that important changes preceded the decisions of the ruling elite, which, in turn, served to support what was already happening, at least among young students.

Gustavo Torroella conducted a survey in the spring of 1962 as part of a six-nation study of young people's values sponsored by UNESCO.[23] According to his results, 89.6 percent of the respondents believed that the family was an "indispensable institution" in society and 97.2 percent wished to have families themselves. In comparison with the five other countries surveyed, Cuba topped the list whenever answers giving high value to the family were tabulated. A high value was also placed on professional and white-collar occupations; 65 percent of the respondents wanted to be professionals and an additional 12.1 percent wanted to be administrators and managers. Agricultural and other manual work trailed well behind in popularity.[24] Torroella's survey confirmed Jones's finding of the high value of the family among Cuban young people, well above that in the other countries studied. The appearance of the same kinds of answer in two surveys on the same subject increases our confidence in the validity of these surveys—what is called survey cross-validation. Cubans' beliefs about the worth of occupations remained traditional; their lack of interest in agricultural and manual work was contrary to government policy. The students' willingness to report views opposed to the official line also increases confidence in the surveys' validity.

The most surprising answer in the survey was given in response to the question whether it was sometimes necessary to destroy in order to build a better world: 60.1 percent said no. In 1962 the tearing down of the old order must have been too immediate for these young people, the youngest of whom were thirteen years old when the revolution came to power in 1959. At least until that memory faded, a large majority of Cuba's young people would have reservations about the necessity of the methods actually used in Cuba to achieve a better world. Responses of "partly," "at times," or "it depends" were classified as favoring destruction; thus the negative responses were all unambiguous.[25]

Cuban young people in 1962 did accent some socialist values: 66.8 percent said that they preferred to work in teams and only 18.2 that they preferred to work alone. Since Cuba ranked behind France and India on that question, however, it is not apparent that the enthusiasm for teamwork necessarily derives from socialism. Only 20.7 percent of the young Cubans said they would like to earn a lot of money, and they stood at the bottom of the list of nations surveyed in that respect. But again, though this response pattern is consistent with socialist values, it may also simply reflect the decline in the importance of money to get ahead in Cuba.

In contrast, and in clear contradiction to socialist values, 55.1 percent of the Cubans, ranking behind only Japan and Malaya, said they would like to enjoy a great many pleasures. In addition, 68.5 percent of the young Cubans preferred guaranteed security; only 21.5 percent said they liked to take risks. This orientation suggests that they may make competent and conformist bureaucrats, although, despite their desire for job security (possibly a hangover from the days of widespread unemployment), approximately two-thirds of the young people said they liked to "struggle," compete, and try new things, but within an ordered environment. On this point the Canadians outranked the Cubans, and the Indians were tied with them.[26]

When asked to state which virtues they cherished the most out of a list of thirteen, 39.3 percent placed justice first; Cubans were the only group to do so; four of the six countries did not even list it in the top three. Four-fifths of the young Cubans believed that they had more reason to feel hope than fear or doubt about the future. Nine-tenths said they believed humanity was getting better, not worse—a far more vigorous faith in progress than in any other country surveyed. Although their feelings about the importance of work were not tested directly, 93 percent of the young Cubans wanted to be and feel useful in later life, ranking third on this point in the international survey. When asked to state in an open-ended question what mattered most to them, 22.3 percent of the Cubans specified a high standard of living; 16.7 percent mentioned family. National and political considerations both followed, with 14.1 and 9.9 percent of the responses, respectively. When students were asked about their principal worries, concerns about the building of socialism ranked at the top, though it was mentioned by only 20.6 percent, followed by concerns with their studies, noted by 20.1 percent.[27]

No clear pattern is evident in these results. Some beliefs, such as a preference for teamwork or a liking for competition and work, are consistent with socialism but not peculiar to it and not altogether consistent with each other.

Cubans were more optimistic and more concerned about justice than young people in other countries. Their limited interest in making money, coupled with a strong desire for pleasure and a better standard of living, reflects both the comparative uselessness of money in revolutionary Cuba—in accord with a structural but not with a new-citizen argument—and a hedonism inconsistent with socialist ideology. Their interest in job security suggests a conservative view that is bolstered by their disapproval of the notion that it is necessary to destroy in order to build a better world.

It is not surprising that socialist ideology had not really taken hold among Cuban young people by the spring of 1962, when the socialist phase was only about a year old. If one interprets Torroella's survey as reflecting the last gasp of prerevolutionary beliefs, it supports the view that the revolution had little impact on popular attitudes. Young Cubans already tended to be cooperative and claimed to like novelty and challenge. The survey probably simply catches a culture in transition, exhibiting a mixture of continuity, modernization, structural changes, and a hint of the socialism to come. The low regard for money coupled with the high regard for pleasure is precisely what would be predicted by the accurate perception of a fact coupled with a basic continuity of belief.

These surveys show strong elements of continuity between the prerevolutionary period and the early 1960s, some of the ongoing attitudes being consistent with new socialist ideology, and some not. The most important shifts in beliefs grew from structural changes of which the students were aware, combined with hints of socialism by 1965. Important changes occurred simultaneously with structural changes and preceded government policies designed to change beliefs. The "null" hypothesis has therefore to be rejected: elements of socialism tending toward the creation of a new citizen had appeared by 1965, but through the first half of the 1960s the changes were more consistent with the modernization and structural hypotheses.

National Integration

National integration is the process of molding a people, often culturally and socially distinct in ethnic, religious, and linguistic groups, into a single territorial unit and a single national identity; it involves changes in the feelings individuals have toward the nation and toward each other as members of the community. These attitudes in turn depend upon communication among citizens.[28]

The extent of national and international communication and changes in its pattern can be measured roughly by data on telephone calls made, letters sent, and air travel. Air travel is taken to indicate the amount of communication among the upper socioeconomic groups, while telephone calls and mail are indications of communications among the middle class. These measures, of course, exclude the quarter of the people in the 1950s who did not know how to write, as well as those too poor to own a telephone. Evidence will be introduced later in the chapter to assess the degree of national integration among these groups. As long as international telephone communications were difficult, intranational communication remained high (table 12.1). As international communications improved, international telephone calls increased more rapidly than interurban calls within the country through 1958, and the ratio of domestic interurban to international telephone calls declined. That ratio is an index of Cubans' increasing awareness of and contact with the rest of the world in relation to their awareness of and contact with others in their own society.

Table 12.1   Telephone calls, 1945–1974

Year	Domestic interurban: international calls	Index of domestic interurban calls (1958 = 100)	Index of international calls (1958 = 100)
1945	35.8	29	9
1952	15.6	73	53
1953	16.5	79	54
1954	16.9	86	58
1955	14.8	90	69
1956	13.2	95	81
1957	11.8	99	95
1958	11.3	100	100
1962	20.0	181	103
1963	30.7	199	73
1964	40.1	223	63
1965	38.3	242	71
1966	40.3	252	71
1967	60.4	282	53
1968	61.5	309	56
1969	67.0	335	57
1970	73.0	330	51
1971	68.3	329	54
1972	72.3	370	58
1973	68.4	384	64
1974	67.9	407	68

Sources: Computed from *Anuario 1957*, p. 248; C. Paul Roberts and Mukhtar Hamour, eds., *Cuba, 1968: Supplement to the Statistical Abstract of Latin America* (Los Angeles: University of California, Latin American Center, 1970), pp. 122–123; *Boletin 1971*, p. 201; *Anuario 1972*, p. 181; *1974*, p. 171.

While both domestic and international telephone communications increased in prerevolutionary Cuba, there was a relatively faster increase in international communications.

After the revolution, instead of growing, international telephone calls declined, as did international air travel (table 12.2), after 1958. Both trends resulted from the U.S.-led isolation of Cuba. Except for the disorganized years of 1959–1962, however, both telephone and air-travel data show an impressive increase in domestic communications from 1962 until the end of the decade. The ratio of national to international communication shows a striking increase of domestic concerns at the expense of international concerns. Cubans were not only communicating more with each other, but they were also communicating less with foreigners. Cuban isolationism in telephones and air travel reached its peak in 1970, judging by national-to-international message ratios, while the same measures show an increase of international communications after 1970. Cubans were less likely to send letters abroad after 1970, however, perhaps because ties between them and the exiles weak-

Table 12.2   Air passengers, 1958–1974[a]

Year	Domestic: international passengers	Index of domestic passengers (1958 = 100)	Index of international passengers (1958 = 100)
1958	1.1	100	100
1959	0.9	78	96
1960	0.7	54	85
1961	2.9	52	19
1962	7.0	48	7
1963	11.6	102	9
1964	16.4	170	11
1965	16.5	170	11
1966	20.3	187	10
1967	19.2	209	12
1968	20.1	211	11
1969	20.7	274	14
1970	27.2	354	14
1971	26.9	398	16
1972	23.3	375	17
1973	17.9	323	19
1974	12.1	272	24

Sources: Computed from Roberts and Hamour, *Cuba: 1968*, pp. 112–113; *Anuario 1972*, p. 170; *Anuario 1974*, p. 155.

a. International passengers are Cubans traveling overseas only.

Table 12.3   Mail, 1968–1974[a]

Year	Domestic mail: letters sent outside Cuba	Index of domestic mail sent (1968 = 100)	Index of letters sent outside Cuba (1968 = 100)
1968	584	100	100
1969	443	71	94
1970	409	61	88
1971	469	68	84
1972	639	64	58
1973	819	61	43
1974	1070	64	35

Sources: Computed from *Anuario 1972*, p. 181; *Anuario 1974*, p. 171.
a. Domestic mail excludes certified mail.

ened (table 12.3). Domestic telephone communication continued to grow after 1970, but air travel and mail stabilized and even showed modest declines.

These measures of communication show consistent trends: a long-term increase in domestic communications (except for mail from 1968 to 1970), an increase of international communications before the revolution, a sharp decline in the 1960s, and a modest recovery (except for mail) in the early 1970s, which well reflects the effectiveness of the hostile policies of the United States against Cuba. The decline in international communications in the 1960s was clearly involuntary, but it did encourage trends toward national integration. A shift in the balance of communication in the 1950s toward relatively more international contact, which can also be seen as an increase in cosmopolitanism, was followed by a sharp reversal indicative of the growth of domestic communications networks at the expense of international communications after 1960.

Aggregate data on communications cannot, of course, prove that national integration occurs; they can, however, indicate whether people are dealing with fellow citizens or with people abroad, that is, whether individuals are oriented toward national or extranational concerns either from preference or because the opportunities for outside contact have been curtailed. These data suggest that the process of building up a national community in revolutionary Cuba was helped by the involuntary decline in foreign contacts.

Cuba's prerevolutionary level of national integration was high by other measures of communications, such as reading the national press or traveling within the country. In the 1958 survey of rural Las Villas, 9.4 percent of the sampled respondents received the Havana newspaper *Prensa libre;* 12.7 percent received the Havana newspaper *El país;* and 41.5 percent received the

Havana news magazine *Bohemia*. During the month preceding the rural Las Villas survey, each man and woman had made an average of one trip outside the neighborhood. Most had gone as far as the nearest town; one-fifth of the men and one-sixth of the women had gone to the provincial capital, and one-fifth and one-sixth had gone to places other than the nearest town, Havana or the provincial capital; 3 to 4 percent had gone to Havana. A quarter of the respondents had lived where they then resided for ten years or less, while a fifth had plans to move—two-thirds of them to migrate to a city or town.[29] In Bejucal 30 percent of the forty-four farmers surveyed by Stabler in 1954 read agricultural magazines, and half reported receiving information about agricultural practices from the press or radio; half visited the town of Bejucal three or more times a week.[30] For rural Cubans, though not the poorest, such access to the national press and such mobility are striking. Subsistence farmers in other countries might not even have gone to the local town market, much less elsewhere. Rural Cubans in these surveys were not parochial people.

Religion, as shown by evidence described earlier, was not a serious matter for disputes. Even at the time of the most serious religious disputes in 1962, only 28.2 percent of the student respondents in Torroella's survey said they would not marry people with different religious beliefs. Ideological differences were clearly a greater barrier to marriage than religious ones: 39.7 percent said they would not marry people with political convictions different from their own.[31] Their view was officially sanctioned by government marriage counselors, who argued that ideological and political differences were far more serious impediments to marriage than religious ones.[32] In practice, however, "religious differences" usually meant those between Catholics and atheists.

While religious concerns were not very important for Torroella's students in 1962, neither had they disappeared entirely. The questions asked in his survey suggested a level of religious identification existed among at least a few that had remained unaffected by the government's campaign against organized religion in the early 1960s. When asked to rank values or motivations, 7.3 percent of the students selected religious values over others such as knowledge, social service, power, wealth, or creativity. When they were asked in an open-ended question whom in history they would like to resemble, most said that they were happy as they were and wished to resemble no one else. Others mentioned many people. Jesus came fourth with 3.5 percent, not too far behind Lenin (who led the list, though mentioned by less than a tenth), Castro, and Martí, ranked in that order, and ahead of Marx, who was named by 2.4 percent. In response to a question described in an earlier chapter, 11.2 percent of the sample ranked saints highest among several social roles, even over social heroes and scientists; over all, saints ranked fourth out of eight possible choices. Finally, 11.0 percent of the students said they believed they were subject to supernatural forces (7.3 percent) or occult forces (3.7 percent).[33]

Religious sects continued to be important in a few localities through the 1960s; for example, in 1969, 42 percent of all 238 people in Santa Rosa, in the Bayamo region of Oriente, belonged to religious sects—an admission obviously contrary to government preferences. Leaders in Afro-Cuban sects, especially women, were apt also to be leaders in the Cuban Women's Federation. The revolution was generally quite tolerant of the Afro-Cuban religions.[34]

Official Roman Catholic statistics show that the proportion of baptized Catholics declined from 90.4 percent in 1961 to 50.3 percent in 1976, indicating a sharp drop in the number of people at least nominally affiliated with the church. However, there had been a large gap in prerevolutionary Cuba between citizens practicing this superficial Catholicism and those with a more serious commitment indicated by attendance at church services. The number of the latter no doubt declined as well, though by how much is unclear. In 1967, only 0.54 percent of the population of Camagüey province attended Catholic services regularly. This is not very different from the immediate prerevolutionary church-attendance statistics, but it represents a substantial drop from the attendance figures in the 1954 national survey conducted by the Catholic university students, described earlier, possibly because it overrepresented the city of Havana. If that is the case, the 1967 Camagüey survey probably shows no more than the continually very low level of regular church attendance outside of Havana. Religious beliefs, as opposed to attendance, have remained at about the same level, albeit a fairly low one; 7 percent of senior-high-school and university students ranked religious above other values even in the midst of a campaign against religion, and 19 percent ranked religious values at least third in a list of seven.[35]

The high ranking of saints may not reflect the influence of Catholicism so much as the influence of the Afro-Cuban religions, which have a somewhat more tenacious hold upon the population. Belief in supernatural or occult forces was less common in 1962 than belief in spiritualism was in 1954, but the 1954 survey by the Catholic Students' Association found spiritualism connected with a low educational level, while senior-high-school and university students held similar convictions in 1962. The total number of believers in supernatural forces is therefore probably no lower than it was before the revolution. The government's antireligious policies in the early 1960s made only a modest difference—it reduced the number of nominal Catholics, but not of those few who were practicing Catholics. Cuba had already become, and still remains, a largely secular society.

While there was little race discrimination in practice in Cuba either before or after the revolution, a modest amount of overt racism nevertheless continued to crop up. When Torroella asked Cuban students in 1962 whether they believed that there were inferior and superior races, only 4.1 percent said yes; but when he asked if they would marry someone of another race, 57.9 percent said yes (quite a large proportion of positive responses) and 27.3 percent said no, with the rest not answering or expressing doubts.[36] Self-denigration among black Cubans was still pervasive in the 1940s; its many forms included imitation of whites in dress, denial of the African past, efforts by light-skinned mulattoes to pass as white, and the breaking of kinship ties with darker-skinned relatives.[37] Verena Martínez Alier's superb book on race and sex in nineteenth-century Cuba documents the prevalance of these practices at that time. She not only found opposition by white parents to their children's marriage with people of color but also observed mulatto parents protecting their offspring from "marrying down" and seeking to "advance" their children's color. There were no similar objections from darker parents to lighter marriage partners.[38]

The Cuban social system had achieved a consensus on what a proper ethnic hierarchy was and on how to sustain it. Nonwhites devalued blackness as whites did. In a study of Cuban workers in exile in the 1960s, Geoffrey E. Fox found that many blacks and mulattoes accepted the definition of themselves as members of an inferior race. They wanted others to ignore the problem of race discrimination and were "embarrassed" that the revolutionary government made an issue of it.[39] Problems related to race rarely had the blatantly pathological consequences evident from excessive religious feelings: in the 1950s only one of the first two hundred psychiatric cases treated at Havana's children's hospital was diagnosed as having resulted from racial attitudes.[40]

Lourdes Casal studied a random sample of thirty Cuban novels published between 1950 and 1967 and found a serious underrepresentation of blacks as characters in all of them, although blacks have been significantly less underrepresented in novels written since the revolution.[41] Blacks appeared just as infrequently as major characters in novels written both before and after the revolution. They have usually been portrayed as lazy, stupid, smelly, dirty, musical and responsive to rhythm, loudmouthed, cowardly, and endowed with extraordinary sexual powers. Most blacks in the sample novels are also aware that their race is an obstacle to mobility. Mulattoes, especially women, want lighter-skinned descendants and take offense if they are called "black." Interracial marriages are unacceptable at all social levels, and these include the marriage of mulattoes to darker-skinned people.

While there is relatively little overt racism at least among the young, a strong and persistent pattern of prejudice nonetheless continues, or at least is still reflected in Cuban literature. This could be in part because all the novels studied were written by people who grew up before the revolution, while the young people surveyed in 1962 had begun to absorb revolutionary urgings against racism and provide a more accurate picture of what postrevolutionary attitudes were going to be. Given the deliberate politicization of the race question in the early 1960s, however, students might also have felt it necessary to be cautious about what they said. In addition, both white and black Cubans have always tended to deny that racism in Cuba even existed. The novels might in fact be closer to reality, unencumbered as they are by these delusions of equality. On balance, there was probably an increase in national integration in Cuba and a reduction in, though not the total elimination of, discrimination against blacks.

Forming the New Socialist Citizen

A government policy designed to develop a "new," socialist, citizen was launched in the mid-1960s, to some degree stimulated by Guevara's essay, "Man and Socialism in Cuba."[42] It was in part aimed at motivating citizens to work harder in a precarious economy with declining material incentives. It was soon followed by Cuba's most radical period, the "revolutionary offensive" launched in the spring of 1968. Although by 1966 policy had already taken a radical turn that would continue through 1970, the campaign to establish new citizenship reached a fever pitch in 1968 that has not since been repeated.

Ostensibly inspired by this campaign, many young men and women volunteered for the Centennial Youth Column, performing hard agricultural labor in the province of Camagüey while participating in its study programs. While they were there the magazine *Cuba* interviewed thirty-five of them, asking them about their reasons for joining the youth columns. Only seventeen of the thirty-five gave "revolutionary" responses, and fourteen of those said membership in the column would help them in their studies (studying is one of the virtues of a new citizen, but thirteen of these responses stressed personal benefits rather than benefits to the country; only the fourteenth's reason was properly "revolutionary").[43] Five of the twenty-four men said they had volunteered at least in part to avoid military service (the column was a legal alternative to the draft); seven of both sexes cited economic advantages, a response that suggests the volunteers came from poor families; and thirteen simply wanted to get away from whatever uncomfortable situations they had been in. Other responses that appeared three times or less included a search for novelty, desire to be with a lover, a wish to live in the countryside, and family or peer pressure to volunteer; two of the eleven women gave feminist reasons.

Proper revolutionary responses were statistically independent of sex, level of education, and whether one was employed or not but were strongly related to work experience, organizational membership, and age.[44] The average age of the respondents was 20.2; the respondents labeled revolutionary were four years older than the nonrevolutionary respondents, on the average. Since the average age of the revolutionary respondents was about fifteen at the time of the Bay of Pigs invasion, personal experience of the formative struggles of socialism in Cuba may have increased their revolutionary zeal. The average level of schooling in the survey was between fifth and sixth grade. That education was unrelated to responses runs counter to the expectations of the government, which regarded the schools as effective molders of young people and adults alike in new-citizen values. In general, while schooling can affect political participation and attitudes, however, it is not always easy to predict the direction that influence will take. Participation in organizations, years of employment, and experience in the revolutionary struggles prove to be much more critical, a point of crucial significance for the Cuban regime.[45] As Richard Fagen has argued, the revolutionary organizations and the activities they sponsor have been a far more effective tool for change in Cuba than the schools.

Economic motives for joining the column were found significantly only among males (no women gave that reason) but are independent of all other background variables as well as of revolutionary responses. Revolutionary respondents and members of revolutionary organizations were just as likely as others to give that reason. Evading military service was a reason tested among men only; it was related to age and occupation but statistically independent of schooling, organizational membership, and revolutionary responses—that is, revolutionary respondents and members of revolutionary organizations were as likely to be looking for ways of evading military service as anyone else. Young unemployed males most vulnerable to the draft, regardless of political persuasion, were most apt to give that response. The desire to study was independent of sex, schooling, organizational membership, or revolutionary beliefs, but it was significantly related to whether one was employed, work experience, and age.[46] Those who wanted to study were younger than others and either were unemployed or had worked very little.

The desire to get away was independent of schooling but significantly related to sex, work, age, revolutionary beliefs, and organizational membership.[47] The escapists were generally younger, unemployed women who did not belong to revolutionary organizations and did not give revolutionary responses. In short, schooling had no influence on motivation, and age had the most. Older youths were more likely to give revolutionary responses; younger ones, to want to study, escape from home, or avoid military service. Revolutionaries were just as likely as the others to want to study, get more money, or avoid military service, but the revolutionaries were not apt to be escapist; although their responses were related to the length of time they had worked, if they had been employed, whether or not they were employed had no bearing on revolutionary responses.

Revolutionary responses, work, and study did not cohere ideologically into a new citizen. Revolutionary responses and study are unrelated; study and work are related in ways contrary to government wishes—those who work do not want to study. Revolutionary responses are thus formalistic; they are related to participatory experiences but have no relevance for most socialist-citizen themes. Participation in organized revolutionary life increased revolutionary responses, but in itself that may not have influenced the behavior of the young in very significant ways, especially since this survey was strongly biased. The thirty-five respondents were chosen by *Cuba,* the magazine that made the survey, as representing the new citizens among that minority of Cuban young people who volunteered for agricultural work. If even the cream of the revolutionary crop gave answers other than those expected from new citizens, as at least half of them apparently did, then the new-citizen norms had probably not taken a very strong hold on the rest of the population.

Cooperative values and behavior consistent with the new-citizen hypothesis may appear more often among the revolutionary vanguard and in those areas of the social system where they already existed, among Cuban scientists, for instance (see appendix F). An analysis of thirty scientific journals published in Cuba from the 1940s through the 1970s shows that cooperative behavior among Cuban scientists—as measured, roughly, by coauthorship of articles—was generally low both before and after the revolution; Cuban scientists tend to cooperate somewhat more often with foreign scientists than with fellow Cubans. Cuban medical science—always the one with the stronger cooperative traits—is the only science to have shown any very substantial increase in cooperative patterns from the prerevolutionary to the revolutionary period. Although the Cuban government has promoted cooperation among scientists since the 1960s, these findings indicate that its extent cannot be explained simply as a response to government policies.

The principal explanation for patterns of scientific cooperation seems to be that Cuban scientists are more apt to behave according to the practices of their specific disciplines the world over than according to norms found generally in Cuban culture or those promulgated in government policies. The exception to this otherwise stable long-term trend was the early years of revolutionary rule, when established patterns of scientific cooperation were briefly disrupted by the revolution itself. These patterns support either the hypothesis that there has been no fundamental change in Cuban values, when one considers sciences such as zoology and botany, which show no change in cooperative work from the prerevolutionary to the revolutionary period, or the hypothesis that changes in Cuba result from world wide processes of modernization that are not altered by the specific government in power, when one considers the medical sciences.

Other evidence suggests that values have changed slowly if at all. In 1962 Maurice Zeitlin collected data on the attitudes of 202 industrial workers in some of the largest and most modern factories in Cuba. He asked them what they thought of their work: whether they liked it, what their reasons were for feeling the way they did, whether they had felt differently before industrial socialization, and, if so, why. Zeitlin then categorized the attitudes of the 147 of the 202 workers whose responses could be clearly classified as either positive or negative toward work and the work place, both before and after socialization. Zeitlin identified himself to the workers as having permission from the Ministry of Industries, the administrator, and the union delegate to make the survey, so it is surprising that 53 percent of the workers described no change in their attitudes toward work: 36 percent had what Zeitlin labeled positive and 17 percent had negative attitudes both before and after the revolution. Their attitudes were the same under the former "exploiters" as under the new "liberators." Three percent had changed their attitudes from positive to negative; a more substantial minority had changed from negative to positive work attitudes.[48] Although this finding is consistent with a structural explanation of cultural change—that is, that beliefs change after the structure changes—the fact of the matter is that there was no change in beliefs whatsoever among a majority of the workers.

There is little evidence available by which to measure new-citizen selflessness and discipline. A survey among workers attending work assemblies made by the Ministry of the Food Industry in early 1971 showed that the workers' personal requirements were still at the top of the list of their concerns about their jobs: 76 percent mentioned the need for more and better tools; 75 percent mentioned occupational health and safety problems; and 69 percent mentioned on-the-job protection. The quality of production was mentioned as a problem by 61 percent, and absenteeism, by 57 percent.[49] These assemblies were held at a time when the government was trying to reduce absenteeism and improve the quality of production, so the fact that 40 percent of the workers failed to mention these problems may be more suggestive—indicating a lack of interest in at least the official campaign—than the proportion who did bring them up.

In a speech before the thirteenth labor congress in November 1973, Prime Minister Castro admitted that Cuba was "not yet prepared to live in Communism" and that it was necessary to "correct the idealistic mistakes" already made. He gave as an example an experiment in the Alamar district of Havana, where some familes were given ninety quarts of water a day free of charge but had to pay for anything over that allotment; in other buildings of the district, all water was free but water meters were installed to measure use. The people whose water was all free were using four to five times as much as those who had to pay for the excess; the families in the latter group in fact never surpassed the ninety-quart quota. The government decided to charge for water. Electricity rates were also raised to force conservation.[50] The results of official government surveys clearly provided ample arguments for the abandonment of reliance on the self-discipline of the new socialist citizen.

Although appropriate beliefs about civil liberties are not specified in government formulations of new citizenship, the issue is of obvious importance in defining the political culture. When Zeitlin asked the 142 industrial workers who supported the revolution what they thought should be done about public criticism of the government or the revolution, only 27 percent said that it should not be tolerated. As the workers' level of formal education and of interest in politics increased, the probability of their expressing a respect for civil liberties also rose; the increase was dramatic in the case of formal education, from 30 percent among those with no formal education to 82 percent among those with more than a primary-school education. The respondent's father's occupation, intensity of support for the revolution, and prerevolutionary attitudes toward Communists were unrelated to that response.[51]

Gustavo Torroella, in his 1962 UNESCO study, asked his Cuban students more complex questions about civil liberties. He found that 59 percent of his 1,070 respondents thought it unjust to censure an individual for an act committed in good faith; 54.1 percent thought evil intentions should be punished even if they resulted in no harmful actions, and 48.3 percent thought that an individual should be punished for faults committed by the group to which he belonged, even if the individual was personally blameless. In contrast, only 17.2 percent of the young Malayans and 18.9 percent of the French young people thought that guilt by association was an acceptable notion.[52]

Generally Cubans were reasonably tolerant toward racial differences, unconcerned about religious disputes, respectful of women's rights (though maintaining a double standard in sexual matters), tolerant of individual criticism of the government, but students were rather antilibertarian when it came to determining guilt and punishment. The relation between educational level and civil-libertarian attitudes in 1962 was unclear, because Zeitlin's and Torroella's surveys disagree. Punitive attitudes might have resulted from residual attitudes toward the prerevolutionary upper class and the exiles or from the general politically combative spirit of 1962.

Lourdes Casal's survey of contemporary novels included a test for the frequency of twelve values.[53] These were ranked according to a measure of positive to negative references. The values of egalitarianism and social change always ranked high; they came to rank slightly higher after the revolution. Individuality always ranked low but came to rank slightly lower after the revolution. The ranking of these values, as well as the direction of the changes, is consistent with new-citizen themes. Cooperation always ranked low; it ranked slightly higher after the revolution; pleasure and a comfortable life always ranked high but came to rank slightly lower after the revolution. The ranking of these values is incompatible with new-citizen themes, but the direction of the changes is consistent with them. Yet all of the changes from the years before the revolution were so slight that the principal conclusion is that Cuba's basic value structure, as manifest in these novels, did not change in any major way.[54] The imagery of postrevolutionary novels also shows a statistically significant increase in the need for individual achievement, consistent with socialist values.[55] Although postrevolutionary novels often reflect prerevolutionary society, they may also be setting norms for the new one. The trends in fiction favorable to social change, cooperation, egalitarianism, and achievement may mirror changes in postrevolutionary society and serve as guidelines for new socialist citizens.

A few fairly complete anthropological reports have been written on value changes. Alberto Díaz found that the Haitian-Cubans of Guanamaca, in the municipality of Esmeralda, Camagüey province, had a "passive attitude" in 1962.[56] People showed very limited interest, if any, in cooperative endeavors and believed that changes would come only from outside—from the national government in general and from Fidel Castro in particular, a conviction that was used to justify the lack of community action. Rosalía García Herrera studied the community of La Guinea in the municipality of Santa Isabel de Las Lajas, Las Villas province, probably in the late 1960s or early 1970s. Santa Isabel had long had an active cultural life, with its own press; it had been relatively isolated from the outside world. Its population, including the young, was conservative, and provincialism in attitude prevailed, though mostly among the old, both before and after the revolution. La Guinea was almost entirely black and heavily influenced by two major Afro-Cuban sects, the Yoruba or Lucumí *santería* and the Bantu or Congo *regla de palo*. Its population had had a high rate of illiteracy, strong familial, kinship, and religious ties, and a tradition of mutual aid in the form of loans, child care, communal enforcement of "right conduct," and help in emergencies. Keeping the streets of the community clean was a nongovernment, collective responsibility that predated the revolution. The Bantu religion had begun to decline in La Guinea in the 1930s; the Yoruba religion by 1959, with the death of its spiritual leader; both were on the wane long before any revolutionary antireligious campaign as a result of modern secular trends and historical accident. Cooperation and secularism in La Guinea were consistent with socialist values but were clearly not in any way caused by them.[57]

In the Escambray region, the mountainous area at the core of Las Villas province, in 1971 and 1972 the revolutionary government encouraged the migration of many peasants to a dairy farm located near a new town that had been built for the dairy industry. Although the peasants had the option of staying where they were, the government tried to persuade them to move in every way possible; it sent a theater group to perform educational plays, dispatched university students to discuss the advantages of the move, and set up local branches of mass organizations to change the beliefs of the peasants. The sources of resistance to the move proved to be a profound attachment to the land the people had dwelt on and cultivated and a strong preference for laboring alone. The peasants were willing to participate in state plans only so long as they could continue to work their plots on their own. Another source of resistance was religion; the many Jehovah's Witnesses in the region were not inclined to cooperate with the government. Because the government invested so many economic and political resources in the Escambray region, the peasants did finally move, but these were hardly new citizens; without the government's massive effort they probably would have continued to live as they had always lived.[58]

Lise Rochon studied the Jesús Feliú agrarian society near Cacocum, between Holguín and Bayamo, in Oriente, in the summer of 1966 and reported that communitarian ideology and behavior had been weak before the revolution, but I believe she undervalued the evidence of cooperation. Mutual aid, including home building and food sharing, had been common, not only for relatives but also for neighbors; a local union of agricultural workers and other associations had also existed, although Rochon says they were very weak. The Afro-Cuban religion, as in other parts of the Bayamo area, was strong. Agrarian societies show the highest form of cooperation among peasants in the revolutionary period—well above what had existed before the revolution, especially if Rochon was correct. Thus the initiative for establishing the community must have come from outside. The results of its formation were crop diversification, cooperative labor, and community ownership of the means of production, all characteristic of such communities. Rochon found two sources of conflict in the community: collective labor itself and the tendency to form cliques in familial, mass, and political organizations, though these groups also helped to resolve conflicts at times. Factors enhancing integration included the lack of social stratification, pride in the community, the schools, and attendance at Afro-Cuban religious activities, since participation in the latter two was independent of community cleavages.[59]

Guanamaca had been changed very little by 1962, and La Guinea remained unchanged into the late 1960s or early 1970s. Life in Guanamaca was altered only by externally induced structural change; beliefs in La Guinea were relatively unresponsive to externally induced change. The substantial changes in Escambray were all externally induced. The people of Jesús Feliú, on the other hand, had responded more creatively to structural change coming from outside the area and appeared more willing to merge new beliefs and behaviors with the traditional ones. New structures, such as the school, and old ones, such as the Afro-Cuban religion, aided cooperation; old structures, such as the family, and new ones, such as political organizations, lent themselves both to conflict and to the resolution of conflict. Although changes came from the outside, and although structural changes preceded changes in individual beliefs, both were taking place. The changes in Guanamaca, Escambray and Jesús Feliú are consistent with a structural explanation of revolutionary change but not yet with a new-citizen explanation; the experience of La Guinea is consistent in part with the hypothesis based on no change and in part with the modernization hypothesis.

Change in urban communities has also fallen far short of new-citizen aims. Douglas Butterworth studied the four hundred people in the community of Buena Ventura, on the southern edge of the city of Havana, who had been resettled there by the revolutionary government; they had previously lived in Las Yaguas, one of Havana's worst prerevolutionary slums. Clearly, then, structural change had affected the lives of these people profoundly. The government had established a local branch of the Committees for the Defense of the Revolution in Buena Ventura, which worked well so long as strong support for it came from outside Buena Ventura. By the mid-1960s, however, the committee began to decay; not a single task was still being performed by 1970. In Butterworth's words, "all guard duty had stopped; health, recuperation of raw materials, and other campaigns had long ceased to be undertaken; block meetings were no longer held." The committee's president was a small-time black marketeer; its organization secretary was a leading practitioner of Afro-Cuban religion who combined religious with political power to abuse her neighbors; prostitution, drug traffic, gambling, and other illegal activities were rampant. Butterworth concluded that the efforts to build socialist citizens among the former slum dwellers failed because these people had "no history of organization . . . beyond the family." Apart from the actions undertaken by the government, then, Buena Ventura is an example of the absence of change in individual beliefs and behavior.[60]

Social class proved not to be significant in the explanation of changes in beliefs and behavior in the 1960s. A survey of the eighty-one students at the school of geology of the University of Havana in the first semester of the 1964–65 academic year revealed that scholarship students and students who worked received somewhat higher grades (though not significantly higher) than students who were dependent on their parents.[61] A survey conducted during the 1968–69 school year among 136 first-year chemistry students and 161 first-year electrical-engineering students found that dropping out or remaining in school was significantly related to level of academic achievement in the previous school year and IQ. There was no significant relationship in either sample between the drop-out rate and sex, the holding of a scholarship, or either parent's level of education.[62] In short, these and the works cited earlier show that social class became unrelated to beliefs and to important measures of intellectual performance in a more egalitarian setting of the late 1960s.

Marifeli Pérez-Stable surveyed fifty-seven workers from work places throughout the country, half of whom were trade-union leaders and four-fifths, vanguard workers. New-citizen themes were very frequently cited by all of them. National and economic development, cooperation, and equality were mentioned by three-quarters, but only half mentioned socialism, and less than a third mentioned obedience and sacrifice. People over thirty-five were more likely than younger ones to mention the new-citizen themes and interpret them in ways similar to the revolutionary leadership. These findings accord with those reported earlier concerning the Centennial Youth Column, that is, that the older people who had participated directly in the revolutionary struggles were more likely to support new-citizen themes than the younger ones were. Pérez-Stable also found that education was a crucial variable in determining the amount of information and the political attitudes an individual displayed. The better educated the group the more likely it was to express a right to recall trade-union leaders, to consider that the defense of the workers' interests, and not just production, was a principal and proper concern for the unions, to view voluntary labor as necessary both for economic development and for the development of the new-citizen conscience, and to support the incorporation of women into the paid work force not only for economic development but also because it thought women would benefit.[63]

Social class, especially as indicated by educational level, may once again have become an important determinant of belief and behavior in Cuba in the mid-1970s. Its influence in the 1960s was confounded by both the emigration of a great many educated Cubans and by the educational revolution; as the emigration slowed down and as processes of educational change stabilized, its importance in shaping political attitudes may have reappeared. If this finding is replicated in other studies, the revolutionary transformation in the 1960s may have come to an end; the structure of political attitudes in Cuba may again be shaped by variables similar to those found important in studies in other countries.

Finally, participation in revolutionary organizations has not always led to optimal results from the government's viewpoint. In the survey of the geology students, the ten students who had no affiliation with any mass or political organization had the highest average grades, followed first by members of the Communist party and of the Communist Youth Union and then by leaders of the University Students' Federation. Membership in mass organizations, exclusive of the youth union and the party, was associated with lower grades. The most encouraging finding for the government is that students who also had jobs had somewhat higher average grades than students who did not. More troublesome for the leadership is the finding that work and organizational membership, especially youth union and party membership, did not lead to the highest academic achievement.[64]

Important changes have occurred on the individual level since the revolution and have affected Cubans' beliefs and behavior, but the pattern is not simple and the changes have not always been related directly to government policies. Experience as a worker and participation in mass or political organizations make revolutionary beliefs more likely, at least among certain young volunteers, but the ideological correctness of these young people's responses does not necessarily carry over into their other values or their behavior. Many small communities, though not all, show changes in attitudes as a result of structural changes but prerevolutionary traditions and ideas often prevail, and new beliefs are accepted mostly when they can be fused with the old. The same continuity between prerevolutionary and postrevolutionary patterns is apparent in Cuban fiction and science; it is also evident in the relationship re-established in the 1970s between educational level and beliefs, a tie that was broken or weakened in the previous decade. Most Cubans apparently do not exemplify or even profess the new citizen's values. Although the ideology from which these values are derived is not in principle incoherent, it has become so in practice. As a result, it cannot be relied on alone to create the virtues the government would like citizens to possess. If the leadership wants cooperation among peasants or among scientists, it will have to focus on the interests of specific groups; if it wants to stimulate work and study, it will have to address these matters directly rather than trying to induce them through persuading citizens to adopt the new-citizen ideology wholesale.

Women and the Revolution

The Cuban Women's Federation was strong, though nonmilitant and orga-nizationally dependent, and had begun to lobby with some effectiveness in the early 1970s. The leaders of the revolution have been somewhat ambivalent about the role of women in society. Che Guevara, the revolution's most radical theorist, wrote in 1965:

Our vanguard revolutionaries must idealize their love for the people . . . They cannot descend with doses of daily affection to the terrain where ordinary men put their love into practice. The leaders of the revolution have children who do not learn to call their father with their first faltering words; they have wives who must be part of the general sacrifice of their lives to carry the revolution to its destination; their friends are strictly limited to their comrades in revolution. There is no life outside the revolution.[65]

Shortly after Guevara wrote these words joining masculinity with revolution, labor shortages began to appear and the revolutionary leadership had to in-crease female participation in the paid work force. Prime Minister Castro called upon women to make a "revolution within the revolution."[66]

The revolutionary government's lag in promoting the active participation of women in society notwithstanding, some important changes had begun prior to the change in government policy. In the paired student surveys in 1960 and 1965, five answers showed differences between men and women of 10 percent or more in 1965, representing an increase from differences in 1960. Students were asked whether they lacked opportunities to learn a craft; the proportion of men who said they did fell from 52 percent to 18 percent, but the propor-tion of women fell from 48 percent to 8 percent. The proportion of men wor-ried about unemployment fell from 80 percent to 37 percent and the compara-ble proportion of women, from 82 percent to 51 percent. When asked whether they would pursue the career of their choice even if it would not be economically advantageous to do so, the proportion of men who said yes rose from 54 percent to 68 percent but the proportion of women answering yes rose from 56 percent to 83 percent. The proportion of men who said they wanted to make a lot of money fell from 72 percent to 43 percent; among women, it fell from 58 percent to 19 percent. In response to a question about whether they wanted to become more independent from their parents, yes answers by men rose from 55 to 65 percent; yes answers by women, from 56 to 75 percent; this may reflect the fact that Cuban women had long been more dependent on their families. Men and women agreed in their answers to other questions.[67] These answers indicate that women felt much more than men did that they had opportunities for study; women were less motivated by economic gain than men were; and women wished more strongly to become independent from their parents than men did. Women also saw themselves, accurately, as having fewer job opportunities than men. A majority of Cuban women were concerned about inadequate occupational opportunities when the government sought to accelerate their incorporation into the work force.

Evidence that beliefs about the role of women in society, consistent with, but not limited to, socialist values, had appeared in Cuba even before government support comes from Torroella's survey in 1962. When asked whether men and women should have equal rights in work, public life, education, and recreation, between 89.9 and 95.3 percent of the 1,070 students said yes to all four questions. However, when asked whether men and women should have equal freedom, especially sexual freedom, 54.7 percent said no and only 39.2 percent said yes.[68] This was an important difference in beliefs concerning the rights of women in public and in private. Nevertheless, support for women's rights before the government fully committed itself on that issue was high.

A survey of 202 persons, asking their opinions about local problems, was conducted in May 1967 in the small town of Santa Fe on the Isle of Pines. Seventy percent of the sample were old residents of the island and 30 percent were recent immigrants. When asked to identify local problems, 36 percent mentioned the lack of recreational facilities; 35 percent mentioned inadequate housing; 32 percent, the need for increased production, including production for local consumption; 25 percent, the need for services to free women from housework; 24 percent, inadequate transportation; 21 percent, the poor water supply. Other responses amounted to no more than 8 percent of the sample.[69]

The mention of the five problems unrelated to women was statistically independent of age, length of residence, date of immigration to the Isle of Pines, level of schooling, or school attendance since the revolution came to power. Listening to the news on the radio was significantly related only to awareness of production problems; readership of the daily newspaper *Granma* was significantly related only to awareness of housing and recreational problems. Organizational membership was related only to awareness of the lack of recreation facilities. Men were more aware of production and housing problems. The only variable that systematically separated the population into clear groups was whether one worked or not: those who worked were significantly more aware of local problems in production, housing, transportation, and recreation. The only strong relationships were those between awareness of production problems and work experience and between awareness of recreational problems and organizational membership.[70] There were few significant or predictable divisions in the town on these local issues. Social class as measured by schooling was unrelated to beliefs, as it was in other studies in the 1960s. Organizational membership did not explain belief patterns well.

The one issue clearly dividing the two groups of citizens was the role of women in society. The three dependent variables were approval of paid work outside the house for married women with families, mention of the need to provide supporting services so that women could work outside the home, and, among housewives not working outside the home, the desire to work if given the opportunity. The decisive independent variable, significantly and strongly related to all these answers, was organizational membership: those who belonged to mass organizations were much more likely to approve of women's working outside the home, mention the need for supporting services to permit it, and, if the respondents were housewives, to want to work themselves. No other independent variable explained these attitudes as well as organizational membership.

Schooling, sex, and work were statistically independent of these responses. The surprising fact that sex and work experience were unrelated to beliefs about the role of women suggests that there has been a considerable impact on the thinking of men in general and of housewives, probably through organizational membership. Whether citizens listened to the news, how old they were, and whether those under thirty-five had attended school since the revolution were significantly related to mention of the need for supporting services for working women. This is the only published survey of the late 1960s reported here in which any variable connected with schooling was significantly related to any belief. Being a regular reader of *Granma* and length of residence were modestly but significantly related to approval of women's work and the mention of the need for services. The only variable that was significantly related to housewives' wanting to work outside the home was organizational membership.[71]

The impact of membership in organizations can be clarified further, looking only at long-time residents on the Isle of Pines. Among those old residents who did not belong to organizations, no differences were found between the twenty-four men and the thirty-seven women. Among organizational members who were long-time residents, there were strong and significant differences between men and women. Although only 16 percent of the thirty-eight old-resident male organization members coupled their approval of women's work outside the home with mention of the need for services for women, 45 percent of the forty-four old-resident, member women did so; while 45 percent of the old-resident organized men did not approve of women's work, only 7 percent of the old-resident organized women did not approve.[72] The effect of organizational membership among old-resident women was to increase their awareness of the needs of working women. The degree of activity within an organization did not, however, affect beliefs about the role of women.[73]

The fact that this survey was conducted on the Isle of Pines in 1967 may show an awareness of women's issues that was far above the usual, because other evidence suggests that its population was far to the left of the national norm. The daily Havana newspaper *Granma* interviewed ten young people who had gone to the Isle of Pines in 1967 to work for two years and who had been selected by *Granma* because of their revolutionary commitment. When asked what qualities they desired in a spouse, one man and one woman mentioned only revolutionary qualities; another woman and two men mentioned revolutionary and personal reasons (love, for example), and the other four women and one man mentioned only personal reasons. Valery Volkov has reported that "to call someone a 'family man' almost amounted to an insult" on the Isle of Pines.[74] General revolutionary consciousness, which tends to be linked to approval of roles for women outside the home, may have been higher there than in the rest of Cuba.

It is also important not to overestimate the amount of change since the revolution. The continuing importance of the family as indicated in student surveys has already been stressed; a sexual double standard still prevails, as well. A 1975 survey in the town of Batabanó, Havana province, about which no details are known, asked people to name the most important inventions of the century. The most frequent answers were antibiotics, the radio, and the miniskirt. The thesis or central document on women's equality discussed at the 1975 First Party Congress noted that many entertainment programs continued to portray women as sex objects or as passive and ornamental creatures suitable only for housework and marriage. The emphasis is particularly pronounced in the beauty contests for the carnival, which still persist in revolutionary Cuba. The party congress, however, did not call for their abolition but only for further "study," noting the popularity of this kind of entertainment.[75]

In 1970, a survey was conducted among twenty-six divorced men and forty-three divorced women in metropolitan Havana; though the sample is small, the sampling procedures were very thorough. When asked who should have the authority in marriage (the man, the woman, or both), 61.5 percent of the men and 60.5 percent of the women chose the man. The beliefs even of divorced men and women about the husband's authority in marriage were extraordinarily traditional. Women were significantly more likely than men to believe that women should work for pay outside the home, though 26 percent of the sixty-nine respondents believed an increase in divorce was attributable to women's liberation, while 17 percent said that women ought to work for pay "to help the country's development."[76] This survey suggests that basic beliefs about the family and authority in marriage are very traditional, but that there are important differences between men and women in beliefs about women's work; at the same time, beliefs reflecting the philosophy of women's liberation and beliefs consistent with the revolutionary government's ideology concerning work appeared among a sixth of the respondents.

Among the fifty-seven upper-echelon workers interviewed by Marifeli Pérez-Stable, support for the incorporation of women into the paid work force was nearly total. That survey was conducted just after the extensive discussions on the Family Code and on the role of women in society; its findings suggest that these workers had been influenced by those discussions. However, a majority of the workers said that women should work only because the country needed them to, not because it was good for women. Only one worker, a woman, gave what Pérez-Stable classified as a purely feminist response.[77]

Naturally, behavior was not revolutionary even among all women. A survey of the mothers of 1,225 children between one and three years old, conducted in Havana by the Ministry of Public Health with the cooperation of the University of Havana, the Children's Institute, and the Cuban Women's Federation, found that their chief preoccupation regarding their children was a traditional one: concern with how much they ate, and tricking them into eating when the children did not want to.[78] At the other end of traditional female behavior, optimistic reports notwithstanding, prostitution remained in Cuba during the height of radicalism in the late 1960s and into the early 1970s. Apparently streetwalking has been eliminated, but other forms of prostitution have not.[79]

The Cuban government has also tried to harness traditional female stereotypes for new purposes, leaving the stereotype itself to persist. For example, there were symbolic weddings in 1973 between female members of the Committees for the Defense of the Revolution and male members of the Centennial Youth Column, just prior to the absorption of the column into the Army of Working Youth. A marriage contract was read at the ceremony whereby the woman agreed to wash, sew, iron, sweep, and beautify the environment and to participate in cultural and ideological activities, while the Centennial Youth Column members worked. Male CDR members in symbolic weddings with female youth column members simply pledged to help with the cutting, gathering, and moving of cane.[80]

A modernization hypothesis is sufficient to explain the trends in the incorporation of Cuban women into the paid work force; indeed, it is difficult to perceive any effects of the advent of the revolution on women's employment, since the rate of incorporation is fairly steady (table 12.4). The development of spot unemployment—that occurring only in some regions for a period of time—and the easing of the labor shortage in the early 1970s were associated with a declining proportion of women in the work force. The improvement in the economy later in the 1970s, as the price of sugar rose, may have brought them back in. The modernization hypothesis is also supported by a comparison of the proportion of Cuban women of working age (fifteen to sixty-four) actually employed in 1972 in Cuba (22.7 percent, up from 15.5 percent in 1956–57) and among exiles in the United States (54 percent).[81] The experience of personal change through international migration and the generally

Table 12.4 Women in the paid work force, 1943–1975

Year	% women in economically active population	% women in labor force
1943	10.2	—
1953	13.7	17.2
1956–57	14.2	—
1968	15.6	—
1969	17.7	22.9
1970	—	23.8
1971	—	22.9
1972	—	21.8
1974	—	25.3[a]
1975	—	28.0

Sources: Computed from *1943 Census* p. 780; *1953 Census*, pp. 167–168; Gustavo Gutiérrez, *El empleo, el subempleo y el desempleo en Cuba* (Havana: Consejo Nacional de Economía, 1958), tables 2, 5; José A. Moreno, "From Traditional to Modern Values," in *Revolutionary Change in Cuba*, ed. Carmelo Mesa-Lago (Pittsburgh: University of Pittsburgh Press, 1971), pp. 479–480; *Anuario 1972*, pp. 21, 34; *Verde olivo* 16, no. 42 (October 20, 1974): 26; *Granma Weekly Review*, December 8, 1974, p. 2; ibid., January 4, 1976, p. 5. The economically active population is made up of respondents whose principal activity during the year before the census was working; the labor force is the number of people who were working during the week before the census. Because the 1953 census was taken at sugar-harvest time, the labor-force statistic for that year is higher. Data for 1969–1974 refer only to nonmilitary employees of the state. Data for 1975 include all employment.

a. All employment: 24.0 percent

higher levels of education among exiles were far more powerful than the revolutionary experience in Cuba in bringing women into the work force.

In 1969 the revolutionary government and the Cuban Women's Federation appealed to nonworking women to go to work. The federation visited 400,000 women and talked 144,253 of them into working; 29,501 worked only briefly and then quit, however. Because so many women working in 1969 quit their jobs, the net increase in the number of women working was only 25,477 in 1969. In the six years between 1969 and 1974, 713,924 women joined the work force but so many others left it that the net increase was only 196,903. Because the total female population increased by about 425,000 during those same years, much of the increase of women in the work force results simply from population growth. The proportion of women in the work force actually changed very little between 1970 and 1974. Considering that many women would have tried working in those years simply as a result of modern trends and thus even in the absence of federation visits, it is plain that the government, party, and federation have made little headway in increasing the employment of women. In 1969, 68.5 percent of the 181,625 women between seventeen and thirty-four who had no physical handicaps, no children, and no job refused to work. This finding not only throws further doubt on the pervasiveness of new-citizen beliefs in a large part of the young-adult population, but it also suggests that the regime cannot be called totalitarian. Young women, even during the government's most radical period, remained free not to work for pay. They were not forced to take jobs, even when the government needed them.[82]

The general increase in the rate at which women joined the paid work force was probably interrupted in the early 1960s as an unintended side effect of policies that sought to help women. The increase in the purchasing power of the poor attenuated the financial incentive for women to work; the reduction in the incidence of domestic service eliminated what had been an important source of employment for women before the revolution; and the inclusion of women in educational programs gave them an alternative occupation.[83]

The impact of the revolution on women's employment in later years may be seen more clearly in the jobs women now hold or may hold in the future. Women accounted for 46 percent of the enrollment in Cuban medical schools in 1971–72, for half the enrollment in the natural sciences, and for 42 percent of the enrollment in economics; women continued to be overrepresented in elementary and secondary-school teaching and in the humanities and underrepresented in agronomy and in engineering, but a shift had clearly occurred.[84]

Another traditional view of women's work that continued from the past but assumed a new form can be seen in the transmutation of domestic servants into child-care workers. These women continued to care for children, though certainly in more prestigious circumstances, and also continued to be poorly paid. Many prerevolutionary domestic servants were trained in the early years of revolutionary rule to staff the day care centers. In 1973, day-care workers, who were overwhelmingly female, were the lowerst paid of all occupational sectors in Cuba; their wages were equal only to 77 percent of the average national wage.[85]

Notwithstanding its efforts to incorporate women into salaried work, the revolutionary government has prohibited the employment of women in nearly three hundred occupations. Although even Cuban scholars had expected that women would become eligible for all jobs, as a result of the approval of the Family Code and other moderately feminist ideological statements, so long as they met the pertinent qualifications, the government's list was reaffirmed and even extended in June of 1976, with the concurrence of the Cuban Women's Federation and of the Cuban Labor Confederation. Women employed at the time in any of the prohibited occupations had to be transferred to other jobs, and henceforth no women could be hired to fill them. The reasons given continued to be based on concern for women's health and safety, but the choice of occupations was itself baffling. Many of the jobs neither posed any obvious danger to health nor required any particular physical strength. Among them were the positions of assistant railway conductor, cemetery worker (all kinds, not just grave digger), deep-sea diver, and house painter (if it required work five meters or more above the ground).[86]

In a society where women have long been subordinate to men, the divorce rate may indicate the degree of choice available to women. The Cuban Women's Federation has in part perceived divorce as a way out of excessively authoritarian marriages that curtail women's personal development; it has thus facilitated streamlining divorce proceedings, while using the courts to enforce alimony payments more thoroughly and providing day-care services. In any event, extraordinary changes have occurred. In 1958 the rate was 8.3 divorces per 100 marriages. It rose to 9.7 in 1962, doubling to 18.0 by 1968, and it doubled again to 36.1 by 1973. One out of every three Cuban marriages was breaking up in the early 1970s.[87]

No significant change occurred in the role of women in politics over three decades before and after the revolution. Women have always been less likely to be elected than to be appointed to public office. Batista appointed more women to the Consultative Council after his coup in 1952 than were elected to the House of Representatives in the 1940s and 1950s; four times as many women appeared in local-government roles in Matanzas province in the uncompetitive and controlled election of 1967 than in the more competitive and autonomous election of 1974. The proportion of women among delegates elected in the first round of the nationwide 1976 local elections was 6.6 percent. Government and party then intervened more actively a week later, so that the porportion of women among delegates elected in the second round was 11.8 percent, for a combined total of 8.0 percent (table 12.5).[88]

Table 12.5 Women in politics, selected institutions, 1946–1977

Institution	Year	% women	Total number
House of Representatives	1946	3.4	136
	1948	4.4	136
	1954	2.3	130
Consultative Council	1952	7.5	80
Integrated Revolutionary Organizations			
National directorate	1962	4.0	25
Communist party Central Committee			
Members	1965	5.0	100
	1975	5.4	112
Alternates	1975	41.7	12
United Party of the Socialist Revolution			
Members	1963	13.2	16,002
Communist party			
Members	1974	12.8	186,995
Before First Party Congress	1975	13.2	—
After First Party Congress	1975	15.0	202,807
National officials	1974	6.0	—
	1975	5.5	—
Provincial leaders			
Before party elections	1975	6.3	—
After party elections	1975	13.0	—
Cell leaders	1975	17.0	—
Matanzas local government			
Delegates	1967	12.3	1,783
	1974	3.0	1,014
	1976	10.9	844
Regional officials	1974	6.9	151
Provincial officials	1974	16.0	68
Committees for the Defense of the Revolution			
Professional national staff	1976	9.0	—
Regional leaders	1975	7.0	—
	1976	26.0	—
Local leaders	1976	36.0	—

Sources: Computed from Mario Riera, *Un presidente constructivo* (Miami: 1966), pp. 105–107; idem, *Cuba política, 1899–1955* (Havana: Impresora Modelo, 1955), pp. 550–559, 568–575, 607–620; Hernán Barrera, "Building the United Party of the Socialist Revolution in Cuba," *World Marxist Review* 6, no. 12 (December 1963): 56–58; *Granma Weekly Review*, October 8, 1967, p. 3; ibid., August 4, 1974, p. 3; ibid., December 8, 1974, p. 12; ibid., January 4, 1976, p. 9; ibid., December 5, 1976, p. 1; ibid., December 12, 1976, p. 5; *Granma* February 6, 1976, p. 2; ibid., October 19, 1976, p. 1; ibid., December 3, 1976, p. 4; ibid., July 13, 1977, p. 2; Comité Central del Partido Comunista de Cuba, Departamento de Orientación Revolucionaria, *Sobre el pleno ejercicio de la igualdad de la mujer* (Havana: Imprenta Federico Engels, 1976), p. 30.

Table 12.5—continued

Institution	Year	% women	Total number
National Assembly			
Council of State			
Members	1976	12.9	31
Committee heads	1976	25.0	20
Committee secretaries	1976	40.0	20
Deputies	1976	22.2	481
Elite			
Party Political Bureau members	1977	0.0	13
Party Secretariat members	1977	0.0	10
Executive committee of the cabinet	1977	0.0	12
Provincial party secretaries-general	1977	0.0	14
Ministers	1977	5.9	34

In 1977, no women were members of the key institutions of the party and the government—the party's Political Bureau and Secretariat or the executive committee of the Council of Ministers—or serving as provincial party secretaries-general. The differences between the proportion of women in the House of Representatives and in the Consultative Council, on the one hand, and in the party's National Directorate or Central Committee or among party, regional, or local-government officers, on the other hand, are trivial. The proportion of women in the national party and in local delegate roles in Matanzas province declined from the 1960s to the early 1970s, increasing only slightly thereafter in the party.

The only thing to cheer a feminist is the evidence of government commitment to expanding the role of women in politics. The government and the party intervened, as already noted, to see that more women were elected in 1976. In general, the degree of government and party control over all elections increases with the importance of the election. The fact that the proportion of women officeholders was higher in provincial than in regional and local posts in Matanzas in 1974 suggests a conscious government effort to increase women's share of those offices. Similarly, the proportion of women deputies to the National Assembly is two and a half times the proportion of women elected to municipal assemblies in 1976. The National Assembly has yet to show that it is one of the country's key institutions; if it were to become so, then a substantial number of women might come to have important influence. Yet even within the National Assembly as it is now, women are disproportionately well represented among committee secretaries and disproportionately poorly represented in the Council of State. Thus the party's and the government's efforts to increase the participation of women in political life seem to be limited to the middle ranks of provincial officials and National Assembly deputies. The proportion of women declines sharply again as one gets closer to real influence over the levers of power in the Political Bureau, among ministers, and even in the Council of State.

There are several explanations for the low representation of women in positions of leadership. After the 1974 local-government elections in Matanzas led to the election of few women, 635 registered voters, including 333 women, were interviewed to find out why. When women voters were asked if they would have been willing to serve as elected officials had they been elected, 54.3 percent said no. A majority claimed they were too busy at home with husband and children, even though local-government posts were only part-time (workers employed for pay had to retain their regular jobs) and could be performed in the evenings and on weekends. When all respondents were asked to list the criteria for election, only 20 percent said that men had to be "moral, serious, and decent," but 45 percent required those traits of women before they would vote for them.[89] Two reasons for the few women in the leadership were that people set much higher standards for them than for men and that a majority of women did not want to serve to begin with. The women's refusal, of course, described real obstacles to running for office, including the lack of enough child care facilities and probable hostility from husbands and other men.

Evidence of discimination against women emerged from a nationwide survey of 5,168 workers from 211 work centers in 1974. Thirty-eight percent reported that their work centers did not promote women; 22.8 percent reported that the administration believed that women's home and family responsibilities would interfere with their performance of the duties of upper-level positions.[90] Altogether no less than a fifth of all laborers reported discrimination against women that reduced their opportunties for promotion.

There has been considerable change in the condition of women in Cuba: divorce has become easier, child-care facilities have grown strikingly, although they are still insufficient, and birth-control devices are easily available. Visitors report considerably less change in relations between men and women in their private lives, and other evidence supports that impression.[91] Attitudes toward the family have changed little. Nonetheless many dramatic changes in the role of women in society would probably not have occurred without the revolution. Changes in the incorporation of women into the paid work force, however, have continued to occur at the same rate as before the revolution, while the role of women in politics has hardly changed at all.

Social Stress and Revolutionary Change

The discussion of the revolutionary years in this book began with the emigration of hundreds of thousands of Cubans from their native land. Although their departure broke up families, friendships, and professional and political associations, some of those who remained behind also faced personal difficulties, though in many cases not until the revolutionary offensive of 1968 ushered in the most radical period and pressure to become new citizens became severe. Many radical policies were carried on into 1969, but the ideological stress was shifted to the effort to bring forth the giant 1970 sugar harvest; emotional pressure was thus lessened considerably.

The rate of outpatient psychiatric consultations increased fourfold in 1968 (table 12.6). For Cubans whose attitudes were diametrically opposed to the revolution and for those in total agreement the psychic stress may not have been so great as it was on the third group in between—those supporting the new government politically but unhappy about some of the changes in lifestyle it required. These people may well have been the ones who took their problems to the psychiatrist in such large numbers. Available estimates of the number of psychologically distressed people are conservative; there may well have been many more.

The increase in psychiatric consultations, however, might well simply reflect the availability of free medical service in revolutionary Cuba and the gradual increase in public awareness of both the problem of mental illness and the possible therapies. This hypothesis—which assumes forces of modernization interacting with structural change—is well supported by the strong association between the rate of psychiatric hospital admissions and gross social product per capita from 1964 through 1974 (see table 5.15). The rate of psychiatric outpatient consultations, however, is statistically unrelated to either the rate

Table 12.6 Mental illness, 1964–1974

Year	Psychiatric admissions	Admissions/ 10,000 population	Outpatient psychiatric consultations	Consultations/ 10,000 population
1964	5,972	8.0	12,660	16.9
1965	5,705	7.4	7,054	9.1
1966	5,680	7.2	9,618	12.2
1967	7,664	9.5	11,219	13.9
1968	8,042	9.8	53,250	64.9
1969	10,428	12.5	15,929	19.1
1970	9,365	11.0	21,716	25.4
1971	9,145	10.5	25,784	29.7
1972	10,165	11.5	32,484	36.7
1973	11,848	13.1	23,339	25.8
1974	13,245	14.3	11,996	12.9

Sources: *Boletín 1971*, pp. 296–297; *Anuario 1972*, pp. 18, 259; *Anuario 1973*, pp. 22, 259; *Anuario 1974*, pp. 22, 263.

of psychiatric hospital admissions or to gross social product per capita over the same period.[92] Thus the rate of outpatient psychiatric consultations is independent of both economic-growth trends and severe mental illness. This alternative hypothesis thus cannot by itself explain either the sharp increase in 1968 or the subsequent decline; the fact that the hospital-admission rate did not change much in 1968 further supports the view that the problem was temporary. The weak relationship between consultation and admissions, however, supports the modernization explanation; it implies that more people who were not seriously mentally ill were consulting psychiatrists. The stress of accepting radical policies is, nevertheless, the likely explanation for the one-time increase in minor mental-health complaints in 1968.

Supporting evidence for the view that 1968 may have been a difficult year even for many revolutionaries comes from a survey of 559 third-year medical students at the University of Havana. It found that 78.5 percent of the students used drugs, for the most part relatively mild ones; 35.2 percent used the tranquilizer meprobamate, 31.7 percent used amphetamines, and 6.0 percent used barbiturates. Medical students are typically subject to a highly charged atmosphere of academic tension and have relatively easy access to drugs. Drug use in Cuba in 1968 may, of course, be a part of the worldwide increase about that time. Yet even mild drug use was officially disapproved in Cuba, not only as a crime but also as evidence of ideological deviation.[93] Thus drug use by these students may have reflected the higher-than-normal tension felt by most Cubans in 1968, as well as international fads, but it also added to tensions between users and the government. The problem of severe tension has not disappeared: suicide became the seventh most frequent cause of death in Cuba in 1972 and again in 1973—the first times suicides had ranked in the top ten—despite official condemnation of it as unrevolutionary (self-sacrifice was only condoned when fighting the enemy).[94]

An important aspect of the 1968 revolutionary offensive was the socialization of the remaining small trade and service businesses. Government surveys show that 36.6 percent of all these businesses had been established after 1960; 10.2 percent had been established in 1967–68 in the interior of the province of Havana. In metropolitan Havana, 51.7 percent had been established since 1960. Although comparable national statistics were not published, the problem was national. Havana province's share of the businesses socialized in 1968 was approximately in line with its share of the population, as was the case in all but two of the other provinces.[95] One-fifth of the businesses had a gross daily income of over 100 pesos, and an additional 35.5 percent had a gross daily income between 50 and 99 pesos. The government has released very few data on these businesses, but those available suggest that it is unlikely these businesses sold less than a combined total of five million items a day; they may have sold at the rate of an item per day per Cuban.[96] A substantial proportion of these businesses acquired part of their merchandise from peasants through the black market. Given their national distribution, they came close to doing business with every single citizen. Private entrepreneurship flourished in revolutionary Cuba during the 1960s wherever it had not been banned. Anticapitalist ideologies had clearly failed to take hold among tens of thousands; most Cubans were evidently not much troubled by the thought that they were supporting a petty bourgeoisie.

While very few of those who disagree with the revolution or with socialist values have been treated as criminals, all criminals are automatically regarded as enemies of the state and of socialism. Apparently this attitude has had some practical effect, for the general crime rate and the homicide rate declined after 1959 (table 12.7). Crimes against property also declined drastically in 1963–1964, apparently as a result of the passage of a draconian law instituting the death penalty for armed robbery and related crimes—a law still on the books and enforced at times; but they increased steadily again after 1964 with the coming of hard times. Crimes against persons continued to decline during 1968, the year of the revolutionary offensive, but crimes against property continued to increase.

Cuba had had a relatively homogeneous culture before the revolution.

Table 12.7   Crime rates, 1959–1968 (per 100,000 population)

Year	All crimes	All crimes against property	Homicide and murder
1959	2,905	543.1	38.2
1960[a]	2,855	482.7	36.7
1961	2,440	461.6	37.2
1962	2,304	489.4	35.0
1963	2,415	232.6	13.7
1964	2,033	133.2	8.0
1965	1,529	272.2	8.4
1966	1,638	317.0	7.6
1967[b]	1,270	335.2	6.8
1968	1,179	341.4	6.1

Sources: Computed from *Granma Weekly Review*, April 6, 1969, pp. 7–9; *Anuario 1972*, p. 18.

a. Additional statistics for 1960: 373.1 cases of theft; 104.2 of armed robbery; 3.3 of murder; 9.8 of rape (all per 100,000 population).

b. Additional statistics for 1967: 225.2 cases of theft; 89.3 of armed robbery; 1.1 of murder; 5.0 of rape (all per 100,000 population).

Change has occurred quite unevenly, however, in the past two decades, so that there may be now much greater cultural heterogeneity. Subcultures may be arising that could fragment the society in the future. Thus, for example, the practice of science has become more different among the disciplines than had been the case before the revolution. Guanamaca, La Guinea, and Jesús Feliú were probably much closer to each other before than since the revolution, and it is unlikely that feminism would have divided the people of Santa Fe so strongly in earlier years. In 1961 nominal Roman Catholicism was almost equally distributed throughout the country; the range of adherence to Catholicism varied only between a low of 83.3 percent and a high of 98.0 percent among the six dioceses. The revolution's secularism was carried much further in some regions than in others; the range of adherence to Catholicism in 1976 in the six dioceses varied between 75.1 percent and 31.6 percent. The willingness of the population to elect women to positions in local government also became more sharply differentiated by region in the 1976 elections than in the 1967 elections; metropolitan Havana was 2.6 times more likely than Camagüey province to elect women to local-government posts in 1967 but 4.8 times more likely than Ciego de Ávila province in 1976.[97] The pace of change, then, has been so disparate that Cubans may now share certain fundamental values to a lesser extent than they did in the past. I believe this fact will make the implementation of national policies much more difficult in the years ahead and may lead to new sources of tension between government and society.

If the revolutionary government is successful in its aims, profound changes in individuals' political and social beliefs will be the most important and the longest lasting effects of the revolution. It inherited from prerevolutionary Cuba a secular society, a citizenry that expected government intervention, was highly politicized, and was willing to pursue collective goals, especially through nonpartisan mutual-aid organizations. Political participation and cooperation at the local level was extensive, but national political parties were generally perceived as weak and often illegitimate. Citizens liked their country, made use of local government, and believed in the efficacy of their own political involvement in local affairs. At the same time they reacted to the national government with pessimism and distrust. These tendencies reflect the paradoxical coexistence of individualism and cooperation in prerevolutionary Cuba. The revolutionary government increased citizens' interest in politics, channeled it into centralized, national organizations, and reduced the autonomy of local organizations in order to remake Cuban society. It owes much of the success it has had to Cubans' predisposition toward social change, already in evidence before 1959 and perhaps the most crucial factor in guaranteeing that success.

From this cultural baseline, however, considerable change has occurred. Those who argue the opposite are only correct when they discuss a few specific areas: some aspects of women's role, family values, and scientific work habits, for instance, remain much as they were. Neither does it seem to be true that all the change in Cuba derives from the impact of a totalitarian state, although political prisoners and dissidents have certainly felt the force of the government's nearly absolute authority.

In fact, postrevolutionary Cuba not only demonstrates continuities with the past but has built upon it in many ways. Processes of modernization were already at work before the revolutionary leaders took over, although the results have been largely compatible with their desires. Before the revolution, national integration had already reached a high level; since the revolution, religious and racial disputes have been either minor or brief. Domestic communication among those who have access to communications networks—not by any means the entire population—has increased, often at the expense of international communications; this phenomenon was aided by U.S.-induced isolation of Cuba in the early 1960s. Cubans of both sexes held reasonably modern attitudes toward the role of women in society even before the Cuban government committed itself to moderate feminism; this issue, however, divides the population more sharply than others. The incorporation of women into the paid work force has clearly depended more on ongoing modernization than on government efforts, while the poor representation of women in politics and the strength of traditional family values are the most important examples of the absence of change in areas government policy has attempted to alter.

Not all change in Cuba results from modernization. The revolution itself unleashed processes of change that were not directly controlled by its leaders. Radical policies aimed at transforming the country's culture were adopted only in the mid-1960s, yet important changes in beliefs had occurred well before that. Some new beliefs resulted from accurate perceptions of the nature of structural change, such as the reduced importance of money in an economy of scarcity. Others can be interpreted as structurally induced shifts toward the evolution of a new citizen with socialist values. These two types of change contradict the "water faucet" theory of change in Cuba, a variant of the totalitarian hypothesis. According to this view, changes in belief and behavior occurred in the late 1960s, but the turn away from moral incentives and other radical policies in the 1970s will eventually shut off any further alteration of individual values. Not much evidence is yet available on the effect of recent policy changes on beliefs. But I believe the existence of changes—before the government mandated them and independent of government action—suggests strongly that changes will continue, though perhaps less dramatically, regardless of shifts in policy. In short, modernizing and revolutionary structural processes are operating in Cuba to change individuals' lives; they were independent of government policy at the start and are likely to remain so.

Certain new attitudes may be regarded as the results of the promulgation of the new-citizen ideology, but it is difficult to argue that this explanation is both necessary and sufficient to account for them. New beliefs are not strong or widespread enough to modify behavior further. In practice, the new citizen ideology is incoherent and may appear in only some of an individual's attitudes. The evidence that citizens are any more selfless than before is weak; on civil liberties, it is ambiguous and troublesome. Some new beliefs, often fused with the old, rather than replacing them, have strengthened stereotypes, such as those limiting women's roles.

Certain patterns of change in postrevolutionary Cuba are important for comparative social research. First, social class, as measured primarily by educational level, cannot be shown to be a significant and unambiguous determinant of patterns of belief in the mid- and late 1960s; class gradually began to affect beliefs again in the 1970s. This fact suggests that the short-term impact of revolutionary rule may be to suspend the relationship, usually present, between social class and beliefs. As revolutionary rule is consolidated and institutionalized, power and privilege are again being joined in a new ruling class, albeit quite different from the prerevolutionary one. I believe this process may lead to a new link between social class and political opinion. Second, membership in mass organizations, unlike social class, has always affected beliefs strongly, as does work experience, though less so; this relationship is consistent with the view that active participation in revolutionary work and organizations is the chief instrument for individual change. The new citizen ideology that has resulted, however, has been so incoherent that it is not likely to assist further efforts at government-induced change very much. Finally, some evidence indicates that considerable psychological strain has resulted for individuals from the process of revolutionary change.

The ideological pronouncements of the Cuban government and the Communist party do not challenge the view that the past continues to have a substantial impact upon the present; they simply argue that its impact is a bad thing. The First Party Congress complained that changes in the ideological superstructure were lagging behind changes in the economic structure; old ideas, perceptions, habits, and rules of conduct persisted. The defeated classes and the imperialists added to the problem by introducing vices, prejudices, and reactionary attitudes through their propaganda in order to weaken the moral fiber of the revolution. These attitudes include "bourgeois and petty bourgeois nationalism" and revisionist, pseudo-Marxist ideas. This persistence of the past is used to explain inefficiency, lack of discipline, absenteeism, low productivity, low output, poor quality, selfishness, too much devotion to family and friends rather than to the public interest, a desire for luxury, and the continuation of bureaucratism.

The burden of the argument and the evidence presented here challenge some of the First Party Congress's assertions but support others. I believe the

Cuban revolution could not have been possible without contributions from the country's past. Some of these have made for a better society; others have not. The party provides an analysis that may relieve those in office from responsibility, but it ignores many of the sources of Cuban political culture and its characteristic patterns of change. In the future, it may be more difficult for party and government officials to gloss over these problems if they wish to construct policies that will effect genuine cultural change. [98]

Change in Cuba is a result of modernizing and of revolutionary structural processes; neither new-citizen ideologies nor totalitarian repression have been effectively applied. Whatever its explanations, the change is real and impressive. [99]

For the time being, changes in individual beliefs are likely to continue remaking the old Cuban into a different type of citizen, but one whose revolutionary characteristics do not preclude ties to prerevolutionary values. Although the change is far short of the government's new-citizen goals and is shaped by both past and present, it has permanently altered political life in Cuba.

Appendix A

THE IMPACT OF INTERNATIONAL ECONOMIC FACTORS ON INTERNAL AFFAIRS: THREE PERSPECTIVES

There are three principal perspectives from which to reflect upon the structural impact of international economic factors on a nation's internal affairs.[1] The first may be called the "orthodox dependency perspective." Its core political propositions may be summarized in the following way. First, there is a very low degree of client autonomy. Second, external economic penetration is not internally differentiated to any significant political extent, that is, its form does not matter politically. Third, some client elites fully collaborate with external penetration, providing access, maintaining the system of penetration, and being in turn strengthened by it. Fourth, capitalism is the motive force behind dependency. Fifth, the dependent economy is kept from being developed by the dominant external economy. Sixth, there is a rational, coherent, continuous pattern of intended domination. External economic penetration therefore limits the sovereignty of the underdeveloped state, turning it into a client, while it strengthens the local, "host" government. Because economic development is restricted, little structural differentiation occurs; consequently, there is also little political differentiation.

The second approach may be called the "unorthodox dependency perspective"; its basic propositions are not drastically different from those of the orthodox perspective. They differ, however, in the following respects. First, a much more substantial degree of autonomy is afforded to the client state by competition among major foreign powers in international affairs, by the limitations and incompetence of imperial powers, and by the client's shrewdness in using resources. Autonomy is explicitly created by political action; it is what a Marxist might call a "subjective condition" that can repeatedly overcome the "objective condition" of dependency. Second, external economic penetration is politically differentiated, by the type of imperial power, by the type of client state, and by the form of penetration. Third, the role of client elites is viewed the same way as in the orthodox perspective. Fourth, the creation of client states is not peculiar to capitalist states but may occur in any situation where power is asymmetrical. Fifth, only certain sorts of development, not all, are prevented in the client state; what F. H. Cardoso has called "associated-dependent development" may occur. This is not the optimal pattern for development, but it is development nonetheless. Sixth, there is no necessary assumption of rationality, coherence, or unified imperial policy.

From a different perspective, which can be called the "transnational," Samuel Huntington has argued that the growth of transnational organizations, that is, organizations that operate across and often in disregard of national boundaries, increases the demands for access to the territories of nation-states. The national governments that control this valuable access will be strengthened. Consequently the growth of transnational operations does not challenge the nation-state but rather reinforces it. By the same token, conflict is most likely to occur between transnational organizations and government when the government is weak. Weak governments resort to nationalization as a way of mobilizing popular nationalist sentiment. Thus if strong transnational organizations strengthen governments, strong governments are more likely to provide a politically secure environment for transnational organizations. Second, Huntington introduces a time factor into the politics of transnational operations. While he agrees with the thrust of dependency theory that the short-term effect of transnational operations on a society is conservative, he argues that the longer-term impact may be quite different and significantly transformative.

These perspectives therefore argue that the government of the ruling local or host elite is strengthened in the short run. Huntington, however, argues that transformation may occur in the long run as a result of the influx of capital and technology, including new skills. Both orthodox dependency and transnational perspectives so far seem to pay little attention to internal differentiation within the external activity. Huntington, for instance, is especially concerned with pointing out similarities among transnational organizations, whether economic or political, public or private, civil or military, religious or secular. Both orthodox dependency theorists and Huntington pay limited attention to the preexisting characteristics of the host society and government; the crucial variable is external, not internal.

Appendix B

CHANGES IN THE
HEIGHT OF CUBANS

The height of Cubans of both sexes, three racial categories, and all ages increased substantially during the twentieth century. Because the composition of the population did not alter drastically during the same period, the principal explanation for the increase in height is the improvement in the standard of living. Data on changes in body weight yield similar conclusions. Although every age, sex, and racial category benefited, whites gained the most. This difference suggests an increase in the inequality of life chances, especially from 1919 to 1963–64, so that those who had a better initial standard of living gained disproportionately. Increases in height occurred under both the first and second political systems. No evidence about trends in the 1960s and the 1970s, which might suggest what effects the revolution has had, is yet available.

The first measurement was taken at Harvard University, where Cuban teachers had been brought for training, in August 1900. Of 494 women, 71 percent were of Cuban parentage, apparently white, as were 74 percent of the 479 men. Only 4 percent of the women and 2 percent of the men were reported to be of "mixed" parentage; 3 percent of the women and 7 percent of the men were of Spanish parentage; and the remainder had one Cuban parent, probably white, and one Spanish parent. The median ages were twenty-seven for men and twenty-four for women; the age ranges were sixteen to sixty-four years for men and thirteen to fifty-nine years for women. Median heights were 163.32 cm for men and 153.16 cm for women.[1]

The second recorded measurement of adult Cubans was made by Israel Castellanos among 13,007 Cuban-born prisoners from all provinces who were jailed between 1909 and 1925. Among 5,678 white male prisoners, the median age was twenty-six; the age range was sixteen to sixty-four; and the median height was 166 cm. Castellanos had excluded sick, injured, or physically deformed prisoners because he wanted to approximate a physically normal population. Although socioeconomic data are not available, the teachers sent to Harvard for training were probably from a higher social class than the convicts. The age distribution is the same. It is striking to find a substantial increase over the first (1.64 percent) appearing in the second of these two studies, notwithstanding the fact that the second group probably came from a lower social class. Had two samples been drawn from the same class, the increase might have been even higher. Moreover, the median height of 3,118 male mulatto prisoners was 167 cm, and that of 3,914 male black prisoners was 169 cm. Their age distribution was comparable to the white prisoner population. Thus if the Cuban teacher survey is compared to the entire Cuban prison population, the median height can be seen to have increased even further. In the Castellanos survey, the mean heights for males were 165, 166 and 167 cm, for whites, mulattoes, and blacks, respectively; the mean heights of women prisoners were 156 cm among 85 whites, 157 cm among 98 mulattoes, and 160 cm among 114 blacks.[2]

A third, less reliable survey was conducted by Frederick Hulse in the early 1930s. This survey is less reliable because the sample was not scientifically random and because subjects were not stratified by age group. They were young adult males of two types: either students at the University of Havana or men in Havana and Las Villas provinces whose parents had been born between 1870 and 1885. Thus his was a relatively young adult sample, with a substantial upper- and middle-class component because of the apparently high, though unspecified, representation of university students at a time when access to higher education was substantially class-bound. The mean height of Hulse's 154 young white male adults was 169.42 cm. Hulse's 35 mulattoes measured 167.49 cm and his 22 blacks, 168 cm; because there were very few blacks and mulattoes in the university sample, their social class was probably comparable to the prison population measured by Castellanos, and their height reflects that similarity.[3] If Hulse's white male adults are compared with the white males in the Harvard study, with whom they probably share a class identity in large part, then the height increase was 3.73 percent, or approximately 6 cm, in three decades, that is, during the course of Cuba's first political system.

The best studies of the height (and weight) of Cubans were two large random samples of Havana schoolchildren stratified by age, sex, and race. One was the research of Georges Rouma in 1919, awarded a prize by the Paris Anthropological Society;[4] the other, the collaborative research project conducted in 1963–64 by East European and Cuban scholars and officials.[5] Rouma had surveyed 790 male children, approximately 100 of each age from 6 to 14; the 1963 collaborative team surveyed 452 male children from ages 6.5 to 13.5, or about 56 of each age (table B.1 summarizes a small portion of the data from

Table B.1 Height of male Cuban children and adolescents, 1919 and 1963 (in millimeters)

Age[a]	Whites		Mulattoes		Blacks	
	1919	1963	1919	1963	1919	1963
6.5	1119	1158	1137	1167	1121	1201
10.5	1298	1365	1326	1357	1350	1380
13.5	1425	1522	1444	1531	1460	1534

Sources: Georges Rouma, "Le développement physique de l'écolier cubain: blanc, nègre et mulâtre," *Bulletin de la Société d'Anthropologie de Bruxelles* 35 (1920): 390, 393, 396; Teresa Laska-Mierzejewska, "Morphological and Developmental Difference Between Negro and White Cuban Youths," *Human Biology* 42, no. 4 (December 1970): 586.

a. In the 1919 survey, 6.5–7, 10.5–11, and 13.5–14. The 1963 survey may include all children between 6 and 7, 10 and 11, and 13 and 14; if so, data for 1963 would include smaller children for each age group than in 1919, and the height increase would consequently be larger.

these studies). The most striking result of comparing these and other surveys is that the height of Cubans increased, regardless of age, race, or sex. A second finding pertains to the different growth trends for the racial categories. Both surveys found that blacks were taller than whites; mulattoes were typically, though not always, in an intermediate position. These trends are consistent with the prison studies conducted by Castellanos, but not with Hulse's smaller study. The 1919 and 1963 surveys show that height gains were largest among whites in all age groups except 6-year-olds and 11-year-olds.[6]

Because Cuban blacks were poorer than Cuban whites, the fact that they were consistently taller must be attributed to genetic, not environmental, factors.[7] The fact that surveys decades apart have reached similar findings reinforces their credibility. Moreover, the composition of the Cuban population did not change from 1919 to 1963. Immigration virtually ended with the Great Depression, the laws nationalizing labor, and the deportation of Haitians and Jamaicans in the early 1930s. The proportion of the population that was foreign born fell from 11.7 percent in 1919 to 11.0 percent in 1931, 5.2 percent in 1943, and 2.6 percent in 1953. Up to 1930, immigration came, as in the past, from Spain; the new immigration came from Jamaica and Haiti. Approximately 243,651 Haitians and Jamaicans entered Cuba as seasonal workers between 1908 and 1933, 37 percent of them before 1919. The 1931 census counted 120,309, and estimates ranged up to 180,000 before the deportation of thousands of these workers.[8] It is reasonable, therefore, to assume that most immigrants entered Cuba before 1919, when over a third of the Haitians and Jamaicans arrived; many of them were subsequently expelled. In 1939, 6.3

percent of Cuban blacks were found to have the genetic sickle-cell trait in blood tests, as did 6.5 percent in 1960 and 6.2 percent in 1974.[9] By this measure, there seem not to have been any significant genetic changes in the Cuban black population over three decades. It is also unlikely that there were any significant genetic changes in the Cuban population as a whole.

The relative stability of the population means that the increase in the height of Cubans between 1919 and 1963 must have resulted from a substantial improvement in standard of living—a finding consistent with other data available for the period. While differences among racial categories were not great for women, however, the faster rate of increase for white boys than for black boys suggests that inequality of living conditions widened. The white boys, whose living standards were already better, grew faster, presumably because their standard of living improved more quickly. The increase of the standard of living in prerevolutionary Cuba is akin to a variable positive-sum game: all gain, but some gain far more than others. Similar conclusions, for all racial categories and ages and both sexes, can be reached with body-weight data.

A comparison of the pertinent age groups of the male prison population measured by Israel Castellanos with the 1963–64 study shows an increase in height for all racial categories and all ages (table B.2); there were too few women prisoners in the pertinent age groups for a comparison. Whites also show a greater increase than blacks at ages 16, 17, 18, and 19 but not at age 20.

Table B.2   Height of young adult male Cubans (in centimeters)

Age	Whites		Blacks	
	Prison	1963	Prison	1963
16	160	166	164	167
18	163	169	167	171
20	165	168	168	172

Sources: Israel Castellanos, "La talla de los delincuentes en Cuba," *Revista de técnica policial y penitenciaria* 6, nos. 1–6 (January–June 1937): 116, 118; M. F. Pospisil, "El peso y la talla de los escolares de la ciudad de La Habana," *Serie ciencias biológicas* no. 3 (May 1969): 69. The prison survey was conducted between 1909 and 1925. The age 16 for the prison survey covers 16 to 17; age 18, 18 to 19; and 20, 20 to 21. Age 16 in the 1963 survey covers 15.5 to 16.5; 18, 17.5 to 18.5; and 20, 19.5 to 20.5. Thus the 1963 data include younger males for each age group than those in the prison study, and the height increase is consequently larger.

Although the Castellanos study spanned a long period, it helps to establish that not all of the gain can be attributed to the first political system; a substantial proportion must probably also be attributed to the second political system. The Castellanos study included 1,124 male young adults, about 225 per age group; the 1963–64 study included 267 male young adults, about 53 per age group.

If Hulse's data are believed and are compared with Castellanos's prison survey and the 1963–64 collaborative survey, the entire increase in the height of Cuban mulattoes and blacks occurred after the early 1930s, while all of the increase in the height of whites occurred before the early 1930s. Because Hulse's is the weakest survey, however, this hypothesis cannot be fully tested. Nevertheless, it is consistent with other data presented in chapters 2 and 3. The condition of Cuban blacks was more precarious during the first political system, as symbolized by the race war of 1912. From the 1930s onwards, the standard of living for the organized working class, where blacks were disproportionately represented, improved substantially. It is thus possible that inequalities between whites and blacks widened during the first political system and narrowed during the second. This issue cannot be settled. It remains true that, whatever the pattern may have been, the net result in the early 1960s was that whites had benefited far more than blacks since 1919, though all had benefited substantially.

A remaining question is whether the 1963–64 results are already showing the impact of four or five years of revolutionary rule or whether they simply record longer trends. Changes in height and weight occur very slowly; it is unlikely that much change occurs in such a short period of time. The available evidence suggests that no change took place between 1956 and 1963. The 1956 survey was made by Manuel Rivero de la Calle among white females in church-affiliated and other private schools in the city of Santa Clara; the number of subjects is not known. The size of the sample of white women in Havana in 1963 was 987, about 66 per year. The Santa Clara women were more likely to be upper- or middle-class, while the Havana women were more representative of the city's population; however, general living conditions in Havana have long been the best in Cuba. To the extent that the height and weight data in these surveys suggest a trend, it is that Santa Clara children below age 10 were somewhat taller and heavier than Havana children of comparable age; the reverse was the case, though it was less pronounced, among children 11 years old and older. The findings from both surveys suggest that standards of living were more favorable toward those born in the 1940s than toward those born in the 1950s. However, the principal conclusion remains that there is no apparent sustained difference between two surveys made just before and just after the revolution.

This finding is reinforced by the conclusion that there were no statistically significant geographic variations in height in the only study providing break-

Table B.3 Height of white female Cuban children and adolescents, 1956 and 1963 (in centimeters)

Age	1956 (Santa Clara)	1963 (Havana)
6	115.9	113.7
10	135.4	133.6
14	154.2	154.6
18	155.3	156.9

Source: Pospisil, "El peso y la talla," p. 71. Pospisil reports on both the 1963 survey, in which he participated, and the 1956 survey made by Manuel Rivero de la Calle; the latter is not more directly available.

downs by province. Castellanos' prison study showed that the mean heights for white females were 156 cm in Havana province and 155 cm in Las Villas.[10] There is, therefore, no reason to believe that there should have been preexisting regional differences between the 1956 and 1963 surveys.

Appendix C

RACIAL INEQUALITY
IN PUBLIC HEALTH

Data from nineteen surveys conducted before and twenty-three surveys conducted after 1959 can be used to measure inequalities in vulnerability to disease between Cuban whites and nonwhites. All relevant studies are described here, even though the number of cases is small in some. The nonwhite representation in each study must be assessed in terms of the ethnic distribution in the province where the study was conducted. In 1953, the proportion of blacks and mulattoes in the population was 20.3 percent in Pinar del Río, 22.4 percent in Havana, 22.2 percent in Matanzas, 17.4 percent in Las Villas, 21.5 percent in Camagüey, 40.8 percent in Oriente, and 26.0 percent in the country as a whole.[1]

Diseases of Poverty

Silvio Ruiz Miranda and his colleagues have shown that the incidence of severe burns among Cuban children correlates with socioeconomic factors. From September 1969 to September 1973, 1,647 children were admitted to the city children's hospital in Santa Clara for treatment of severe burns. The investigators found that 84.9 percent of them had fathers with less than a sixth-grade education, an educational level well below the probable level for the population as a whole in the early 1970s; this was approximately the educational level of the labor force according to the 1964 census but lower than that of the labor force in 1975. The conditions of 56.1 percent of 833 homes surveyed among the burned children ranged from "poor" to "terrible" (the lowest three judgments on a five-point scale); 53.4 percent of the children came from rural homes, although the rural share of the population around the hospital was a slightly lower 50.4 percent. This survey did not record ethnicity; however, it establishes a relationship between this type of accident and poverty. Guillermo Hernández Amador and his colleagues asked only questions about ethnicity in a study of 3,301 burned children treated between 1962 and 1972 in a Havana children's hospital; blacks and mulattoes accounted for 36 percent of the cases. Taken together, the two surveys demonstrate clear relationships among poverty, blackness, and severe burns in children in the late 1960s and early 1970s.[2]

A study of 4,477 deaths caused by intestinal parasites during the period 1934–1949 (exlcuding 1941–1942) shows that 32.1 percent of the dead of all ages were blacks or mulattoes; among 2,541 children up to age five, the nonwhite share rose to 36.0 percent. A study of 1,000 children in two Havana slums, made at an unspecified date before the revolution, found that 46.5 percent of the children were blacks or mulattoes. Parasites were found in 94.5 percent of the white children in these areas, 94.5 percent of the mulatto children, and 92.2 percent of the black children. Race did not account for the likelihood of parasitic disease among the poor, but because the poor were disproportionately black, blacks suffered from it most often. A 1937 survey of 23,691 adults and children in the city of Havana found that 16,361 had tuberculosis, 35.2 percent of whom were nonwhite; in the same year, 40.7 percent of 21,000 patients under age fifteen at the tuberculosis clinic were nonwhite. A study of 318 deaths from tuberculosis among patients of all ages in two Havana hospitals for the periods 1938–1952 and 1943–1952 shows that blacks and mulattoes accounted for 44 percent, well above their share of the provincial population. T. Valledor and his coworkers found that 44 percent of 25 children, primarily from Havana, who responded positively to a tuberculin skin test in the 1940s and 1950s were blacks or mulattoes. José Mir del Junco and his colleagues studied 245 cases of tuberculosis successfully treated in Havana's Angel Aballí Children's Hospital between January 1, 1965, and June 30, 1971. They found that blacks and mulattoes accounted for 57.6 percent of the cases. A study of 200 patients with leprosy in the early 1970s in Havana showed that 35.5 percent were nonwhite.[3]

Four studies of premature infants in the Havana hospital for women workers were published in the 1950s. A survey of 200 deaths among premature infants found that 46 percent of those who died were black or mulatto; a second study, of 226 premature births, found 37 percent black or mulatto; a third, of 110 premature births in 1955, found 36.4 percent black or mulatto; and a fourth, of 395 premature infants with circulatory-system difficulties born in 1956–1958, found 39.5 percent black or mulatto. The nonwhite rates of premature births and of death and disease among premature infants were consistently 1.5 to 2 times the black and mulatto share of the provincial population of Havana.[4]

Two studies were concerned with the 1952–53 poliomyelitis epidemic, both in hospitals in Havana. One examined 514 cases of the disease and found

21.1 percent blacks and mulattoes among the patients (about their share of the population); the other, surveying 306 patients, found only 13.4 percent blacks and mulattoes. A study of 200 cases of sepsis over a three-year period in the Havana municipal center for premature infants found that 29 percent of the infants affected were blacks or mulattoes; a study of 35 cases of acute diarrhea among premature infants in the same center over a three-and-a-half-year period found only 14 percent blacks and mulattoes; a 1958 study of 200 children up to age two with cases of acute diarrhea in the Havana children's hospital found that 32.5 percent were black or mulatto. The only study available for the early 1960s shows an epidemic of 250 reported cases of aseptic meningitis among children in Havana in 1960; a small study of 50 of these patients found that 82 percent were white.[5]

Diseases of Affluence

Among 65 lung cancers diagnosed at the Havana University hospital in 1947, 33.8 percent afflicted nonwhites. Between October 1969 and September 1971, there were 70 patients with cancer of the colon and rectum at Havana's Tenth of October Hospital; of the 46 for whom data were available, 85 percent were white. A study of breast cancer among 136 women for whom data were available, made between June 1961 and December 1973 in a Havana hospital, found that 75 percent were white. A study of all 63 cases of cancer of the lip treated at the Santiago hospital between 1963 and 1970 found that 90.4 percent of the patients were white—an extraordinary statistic, half again more than the white share of the population in that province. A study of metastatic cancer of the cervix, including the 183 cases found in the National Cancer Registry and in the Santiago hospital registry, found that only 68.8 percent of the patients were white. Unfortunately, national data were mixed with data from Oriente. By the standards of that province, whites are disproportionately represented in this cancer study, as in the others, but not by national standards.[6]

In a 1958 study of cases of interventricular communication (a congenital defect in which the chambers of the heart are incompletely separated), made in two hospitals in the city of Havana, 77.8 percent of the 90 patients who could be coded were white. Of the first hundred patients treated in a special coronary-care unit in the Matanzas provincial hospital after November 1971, 86.2 percent were white. Among 200 heart-attack patients treated at the Camagüey provincial hospital from 1966 through 1972, 77.5 percent were white. Cancer and heart disease are common among relatively rich, industrialized populations; whites are often disproportionately represented among patients with these disorders. Because blacks tend to be poorer and to show a greater vulnerability to diseases of all kinds, however, they are occasionally disproportionately represented even in studies of diseases usually associated with prosperity. In a study of 200 hypertensive patients under age fifty-five treated in the Camagüey provincial hospital between 1962 and 1971, for instance, the black and mulatto share was 37.5 percent, well above their share of the provincial population. In a national study of 6,635 people, hypertension was found in 12 percent of white males and 14 percent of white females, but in 16 percent of black and mulatto males, 22 percent of mulatto females, and 28 percent of black females. Of 75 women treated for varicose veins in the Pinar del Río provincial hospital in 1969 and 1970, 17.3 percent were black or mulatto, just under their share of the population in that province; but among 400 patients of both sexes who were treated for varicose veins at Havana's Calixto García Hospital, blacks and mulattoes accounted for 31 percent of the cases.[7]

A 1954 study of 32 diabetics of known ethnicity on the verge of death at Calixto García Hospital shows 47 percent to have been nonwhite. In the 1970 census of consumers of drugs for the control of diabetes, whites accounted for 76.7 percent. However, Oriente province accounted for a smaller percentage of such purchases than would be expected from its share of the national population; the researchers indicated that the poorer quality of services in that province was the probable reason for this disproportionately low representation (although Oriente had 35.1 percent of the population in the 1970 census, it had only 17 percent of the consumers of antidiabetic drugs; Havana province, with 27 percent of the population, had 48.9 percent). A national study would probably have shown disproportionate numbers of black patients with this disease as well. A small study of 30 cases of diabetic gangrene selected at random between 1965 and 1969 shows a black and mulatto share of 30 percent.[8] Because diabetic gangrene, as opposed to diabetes alone, would certainly be more likely among poor people, it is not surprising that the nonwhite share increases.

Finally, an assortment of diseases surveyed only once or twice shows an ethnic pattern similar to that for diseases of the circulatory system. White appear disproportionately often among patients in some very small surveys; although there is always a possibility of statistical error, the findings are plausible because the diseases surveyed are typical of prosperous populations. Yet even among patients with these disorders, blacks are often surprisingly common. In a national study of 645 surgical cases, blacks and mulattoes accounted for 28.9 percent; probably because Oriente province, where nonwhites are concentrated, lacks sufficient medical-care personnel and facilities, it accounted for only 7.5 percent of the 645 cases, about a quarter of its actual share of the national population. Thus nonwhites were also disproportionately represented in this study. Thirty-four percent of 38 rheumatic patients who developed infections at Havana's Las Ánimas Hospital between 1945 and 1951 were black or mulatto. Of 29 patients who underwent special treatment for portal hypertension (a complication of cirrhosis of the liver) at Calixto García Hospital in Havana between February 1961 and October 1972, 89.7 percent were white. And 87 percent of 23 patients treated for obstructive anuria at Havana's Nephrology Institute were white. However, blacks and mulattoes made up 31.2 percent of 32 kidney-transplant patients undergoing a special diagnostic procedure at this institute between February 7, 1970, and March 15, 1972. Of the 240 patients who began psychiatric treatment in the central region of the city of Havana during the second half of 1972, 38.3 percent were blacks and mulattoes. Of 200 people operated on for thyroid problems at the Havana military hospital between February 1964 and December 1971, blacks and mulattoes made up 37 percent.[9] In this last instance, disproportionate representation of blacks and mulattoes may reflect their disproportionate presence in the Cuban military.

Evidence is available concerning only one type of accident among adults for the early 1970s—foreign matter in the esophagus. No plausible correlation can be found between choking and socioeconomic conditions, and, in fact, blacks and mulattoes account for 19 percent of 53 cases treated at the Camagüey provincial hospital, just below what would be expected from their share of the population in that province.[10]

General Trends

Both before and after the revolution, Cuban blacks have shown a higher vulnerability to diseases of all sorts than whites. For the most part, whites are disproportionately represented only in some surveys specifically examining diseases that are typical of relatively wealthy populations with relatively long life expectancies, such as cancer, heart disease, and circulatory disorders. Even among patients suffering from these diseases, there is in many cases a strongly disproportionate representation of blacks. In contrast, whites appear disproportionately often as patients in studies of diseases not characteristic of prosperous populations considerably less frequently: in two small surveys of patients with parasitic diseases, one taken before the revolution and one in 1960 and both probably unrepresentative, and in one of two prerevolutionary surveys of patients with poliomyelitis. Blacks predominate among patients with parasitic diseases, those with tuberculosis and leprosy, and those who suffer accidents tied to poverty, such as severe burns; their children are also more likely to be ill at birth. Nonwhites are affected by these conditions far more often than would be expected from their share of the population.

The available evidence also ties the higher vulnerability of blacks not to genetic disorders (as in sickle-cell anemia) but to social and economic factors, especially greater poverty. Thus blacks have been more vulnerable to disease because they have been disproportionately poor, both before and after the revolution. In addition, a study of the consumption of antidiabetic medications, the only one that bears directly on the problem of unequal access to the health-care system since the revolution, strongly suggests that blacks, who are concentrated in Oriente province, have much more restricted access to medical services and disease-control products than whites. These surveys may therefore still understate the frequency of disease among Cuban blacks, because blacks have had less contact with the health-care system. It is arguable that if blacks had received the same amount of care as whites, disease statistics reported for them in the 1970s would be even higher. Still, their access to health care has been substantial in recent decades, even before the revolution, or these studies could not have been conducted in the first place.

There is no evidence suggesting an increase in black vulnerability to disease because of the revolution; nor is there evidence bearing directly on the early 1960s, except for one small survey of aseptic meningitis. Most of the evidence dates either from the late 1960s and early 1970s or from the prerevolutionary period. Because standards of public-health care in Cuba in the 1970s finally surpassed those of the 1950s, the high incidence of disease among blacks may reflect an improvement in health coverage and statistical accounting. Nevertheless, the clear relationship between ethnicity and social class (noted elsewhere in matters of income, education, and place of residence) remains marked in health as well. Cuban blacks and mulattoes are demonstrably poorer; because they are poorer, they are more likely than whites to become sick. This was true before the revolution, and it is still true in the 1970s.

Appendix D

TEXTUAL CHANGES IN THE DRAFT CONSTITUTION OF 1976 AND THE DRAFT FAMILY CODE

The revolutionary government customarily submits the texts of important legislative drafts for general discussion. Although it is virtually impossible to attribute changes to specific purposes or individuals, the changes themselves are easily identified, and inferences can at least be made about the net effect of the policy debates that produced them.

The Constitution of 1976

A draft Constitution was published for general discussion in *Granma;* the final draft was approved by the First Party Congress in December 1975, published in final form in the *Gaceta Oficial,* and submitted for approval in a referendum; its adoption was proclaimed on February 24, 1976.[1] Between the first published draft and the final text changes were made to the preamble and to sixty of the 141 articles; in addition, the order of several of the articles and of paragraphs within articles was changed. Altogether 113 changes were made, of which sixty-six can be categorized as minor shifts in grammar, syntax, or style. Twenty-seven substantive changes affected ideological principles in the Constitution and twenty changes affected the organization of the state.

Textual Changes

Thirteen of the twenty-seven changes of constitutional principles were minor and noncontroversial. For example, in a long list of duties of the Communist Youth Union (article 6), which already included educational and scientific duties, the obligation to promote cultural activities was added; article 35 was modified to read that persons needed legal standing before they could be formally married. All but three of the fourteen more important changes of constitutional principles were also noncontroversial. For example, the preamble now mentions the struggle of the Cuban Indians; article 10 includes a much more detailed definition of sovereignty mentioning inland waterways, subsoil resources, and the like; and article 73 formally empowers the National Assembly to submit legislation to the people for discussion. Six of the twenty changes in the organization of the state are also minor and noncontroversial. For example, article 72 (formerly article 69) reduces the number of members in the Council of State from thirty-one to thirty; article 110 provides more detail on the form of local organizations.

Three changes of constitutional principle may have elicited controversy. Article 7 of the final draft indicates that the working class is the "fundamental class" of Cuban society; that phrase was not in the original draft. Nothing was inserted about the worker-peasant alliance, an alternative formulation of the ideological preeminence of the working class that avoids minimizing the role of the peasantry. Article 38c mentions the contribution of military preparedness to the development of proper citizens; that phrase was not included in the original draft. An alternative formulation might have emphasized patriotic activities without specifying military training. Finally, article 53 in the original draft guaranteed the rights of association to the "intellectual and manual workers, from city and countryside"; the final text guarantees this right to the "intellectual and manual workers, peasants, women, students, and other sectors of the working people." Apparently the peasantry, the women, and the students did not want to be left out.

Eleven changes in the organization of the state may have elicited controversy. Their net effect was to ensure a greater centralization of power in the hands of the elite and central institutions than had been envisioned in the original draft. Article 69 mandates that the deputies of the National Assembly be elected by the municipal assemblies; the original article (formerly 73) left the matter open, but articles 135 and 139 of the draft implied that its framers expected to mandate the direct election of deputies to the National Assembly. Article 135 in the final draft was also modified in the same direction.

New article 91h may strengthen the authority of the President of the Republic relative to the Council of State. This new paragraph states that the President must sign all acts approved by the Council of State; although the phrase "presidential veto" is never mentioned, the paragraph is open to the interpretation that the President may stop the actions of the Council of State by refusing to sign its decree-laws and resolutions.

The powers of the Council of State relative to the National Assembly in the area of foreign affairs were strengthened in the final draft. Article 96d of the original stipulated that the ratification of treaties was a prerogative of the National Assembly; new article 96ch transfers that prerogative to the Council of State. Article 88m makes it plain that the council has the authority to ratify or give notice of the termination of treaties. In the original draft, article 70*i* recognized the assembly's right to ratify or terminate treaties; that paragraph has been dropped from the final text. The National Assembly retains the power to overrule the decisions of the Council of State (article 73*c, ch,* and *r*); however, it is evident that the final framers of the Constitution preferred to handle international affairs within the confines of the smaller Council of State.

The independence of the judiciary is curtailed further in the final text than had been envisaged in the original draft. Article 122 of the original draft mandated the subordination of the courts only to the National Assembly. As indicated in chapter 6, the National Assembly meets infrequently, affording a degree of formal independence to the courts between its sessions. The final text subordinates the courts to the Council of State.

The authority of the executive committee of the Council of Ministers over this council was strengthened by a new paragraph in Article 95 that authorizes the executive committee to decide on all urgent matters over which the Council of Ministers ordinarily has jurisdiction.

At the local level, article 116*ch* authorizes the executive committee of the provincial government to annul the decisions of the executive committee of the municipal government when the municipal assemblies are not in session; in the original draft, the power to discipline the municipal executive committee belonged exclusively to the municipal assembly and was subject only to the general authority of higher-ranking assemblies to annul all acts of lower-ranking assemblies—a power that is retained in the final draft. The change in this article expedites discipline from above. New article 116*h* further empowers executive committees at all levels to suspend and replace enterprise managers and government administrators, pending subsequent ratification by the pertinent assemblies; once again, the apparent purpose is to centralize power and make it more efficient.

A new paragraph in article 127 requires nonprofessional judges to emphasize their judicial duties, not their other responsibilities; these changes are probably meant to give the court system greater authority over the employers of nonprofessional judges, especially at the local level.

Only one of the possibly controversial changes in the organization of the state did not increase the power of central high-ranking leaders and institutions. In the original draft, article 115 permitted the provincial assemblies to elect people outside the assembly to positions in the provincial executive committee; they would become members of the provincial assembly upon appointment. That paragraph was dropped in the final text. Article 115 now mandates that all members of executive committees at all levels must have been duly elected deputies to the assemblies. All executives are now subject to election, either directly by the people or by the municipal assemblies; it is no longer possible for the provincial assemblies to elect executives not subject to election by lower-ranking bodies or by the people.

The net effect of ten of the eleven controversial changes in the constitutional draft was to strengthen the power of the high-ranking elites and institutions far beyond the already formidable power specified in the original draft: President over Council of State, council over National Assembly and courts, executive committee of the Council of Ministers over cabinet, provincial over municipal government, provincial and municipal executives over their assemblies, and courts over the nonjudicial employers of nonprofessional judges. Direct election of National Assembly deputies became indirect, making it far easier to manipulate and screen candidates. Although no one change was very significant, cumulatively they all point in the same centralizing direction.

The Beneficiaries of the Changes

One way of analyzing the constitutional changes is to consider the people or organizations that could have benefited from them. It can be argued that at least twenty-eight of the forty-seven substantive changes have identifiable beneficiaries. Many of them have already been identified.

Seventeen of the changes that can be regarded as beneficial to someone are noncontroversial ones. Of these, ten are minor; eight of these involve only constitutional principles. Two specified the duties and responsibilities of the state to support cultural and literary activities (articles 6 and 13); one took note of the sensibilities of residents of the Isle of Pines by referring to "the citizens of the republic" and not merely to those of the island of Cuba (article 29*a*). The specific activities of state workers (article 38*c*), of health educators (article 49), of workers in day schools and adult education (article 50), and of the film industry (article 52) were singled out as being praiseworthy and deserving of encouragement and support by the state. Two minor changes empowered local-government executive committees to replace managers and administrators (article 116*f*) and specifically ordered the state's prosecutor to be zealous in defending the property of mass organizations (article 123*ch*).

Of the seven more significant noncontroversial changes benefiting identifiable groups, two may facilitate the work of the Ministries of Foreign Relations and Foreign Trade by extending property guarantees to all people, not just to citizens, and by recognizing the duty to compensate all persons injured by the state or its agents, regardless of citizenship (articles 22 and 26). New paragraph *b* of article 29 specifically guarantees citizenship to the children of Cuban personnel working overseas. A change in the preamble specifically mentions the honored dead of the armed forces. A new paragraph in article 44 praising voluntary labor is of interest especially to the Cuban Women's Federation and the Committees for the Defense of the Revolution. A change in article 86*d* takes away the right of legislative initiative from any organ of the Cuban Labor Confederation and lodges it in its national directorate. Finally, Articles 88*q* and 98*d* are escape clauses, common in Cuban legislation, which had been missing from the original constitutional draft. They give broad, unenumerated powers to the Council of State and the Council of Ministers.

The net effect of the changes in the constitutional text has been twofold. The first and most important has been centralization of power well beyond the already formidable authority granted the central government in the original draft. Second, symbolic and some practical textual changes have responded to the concerns of a variety of organizations that wanted some specific wording of importance to them inserted or changed in the draft constitution. These changes have given a wide range of citizens and organizations a feeling of participation that has contributed to the constitutional legitimation of the revolution.

The Family Code of 1975

The Family Code was extensively discussed in 1974 and promulgated in 1975 (see chapter 7).[2] There were 167 articles in the published draft; the people made suggestions to modify 121 of these, but only seventy-nine articles in the end showed any change whatsoever; forty-seven revealed no more than very minor changes of syntax. Because one article was dropped in the final code, another seven articles had changes only in reference numbers. All but seven changes amounted to no more than minor clarifications of language.

The seven substantive changes from the draft to the law were the following: the minimum age at which a woman could marry was raised from twelve to fourteen years (article 3); a court could declare a missing person legally dead without any delay, allowing a spouse to remarry without waiting the customary three years (article 4); a court could deny visiting rights to a divorced parent, either temporarily or indefinitely (article 90, draft 91); older siblings, not just grandparents and uncles, could legally claim guardianship over younger siblings (article 108, draft 109); someone in need would have first claim on parents or grandparents rather than on children or grandchildren (article 124, draft 125); a court could designate as guardian of a handicapped adult someone other than a relative (article 148, draft 149); and the death of a baby could be registered by the parents and did not require court action (draft article 71).

The only one of these provisions that was widely discussed and received a reasonable amount of popular support was the raising of the legal marriage age for women to fourteen. The other changes are not trivial, but they deal with technical points not likely to be of general interest. It is very likely that legal experts, family counselors, social workers, and the relevant bureaucracies, including the Law Study Commission itself, came up with these changes on their own. No changes were made between draft and final bill to articles 24 through 28, which defined the rights and duties of men and women in marriage and were of great interest to Cuban feminists. No alterations other than minor changes in syntax were made in the articles dealing with divorce. In short no changes were made in those articles of the draft Family Code where popular discussion might have made a difference.

Appendix E

MEMBERS OF THE PEOPLE'S SOCIALIST PARTY IN THE COMMUNIST PARTY'S CENTRAL COMMITTEE

Various people have provided lists of former members of the People's Socialist party (PSP), the prerevolutionary Communist party, who became members of the Central Committee of the Cuban Communist party. The following is my best judgment of the PSP share of the Central Committee in 1965. Armando Acosta, Severo Aquirre, Flavio Bravo, Joel Domenech, Elena Gil, Fabio Grobart, Secundino Guerra, Manuel Luzardo, Isidoro Malmierca, Juan Marinello, Miguel Martín, Arnaldo Milián, José Ramírez, Blas Roca, Carlos Rafael Rodríguez, Ursinio Rojas, Clementina Serra, Leonel Soto, Julio Tarrau, and Felipe Torres were members from 1965 to 1975. Lázaro Peña died in 1974 before completing his term of office. Two others, Ramón Calcines and José Matar, became members in 1965 but were expelled in 1968. This accounts for the total of twenty-three prerevolutionary Communists in the Central Committee (out of a hundred members) in 1965; it was reduced to twenty by 1975, on the eve of the First Party Congress (22 percent of the ninety members remaining).

One reason for the differences among lists has been the various treatments of the three men who were members of both the prerevolutionary Communist party or its youth section and of the Twenty-sixth of July Movement: Raúl Castro, Osvaldo Dorticós, and Osmany Cienfuegos. It seems sensible not to categorize them as prerevolutionary Communists when analyzing factional disputes within the Cuban elite. Raúl Castro has long been associated with his brother; former President Dorticós remained faithful and at his posts during the bitter disputes with the Soviet Union and with the prerevolutionary Communists; Cienfuegos has long been associated with Cuban support for revolutionary groups around the world, especially with attacks on orthodox Communist party members in other countries in the late 1960s. Including them in the count of prerevolutionary Communists has the interesting statistical effect of giving the old Communists a majority of thirteen of the twenty-five-member national directorate of the Integrated Revolutionary Organizations in 1962, before the fall of Aníbal Escalante, and a 50-percent share thereafter. It increases their Central Committee share to twenty-six in 1965, to twenty-three on the eve of the First Party Congress, and to twenty-five after the congress.

At the First Party Congress, the following old Communists joined the Central Committee: José Felipe Carneado, Rafael Francia, Ladislao González Carvajal, Nicolás Guillén, Zoilo Marinello, Alfredo Menéndez Cruz, and Raúl Valdés Vivó. Luzardo, Martín, Serra, and Tarrau were dropped. Therefore the old Communist share of the 112-member Central Committee was 20.5 percent in 1975, a slight drop from its previous share (its proportion of the entire Central Committee, including an additional twelve alternates, dropped to 18.5 percent).[1]

Appendix F

COOPERATION AMONG
CUBAN SCIENTISTS

Scientists are a part of the Cuban elite. Since the early 1960s they have been encouraged by the Cuban government to work cooperatively. Consequently the degree of cooperation that exists among them can serve as a gauge of the success or failure of at least that particular government policy. For lack of other evidence, one indicator has been singled out: whether scientific articles published in Cuban journals are signed by one or several authors. The publication of research results is at the heart of the scientific enterprise; authorship patterns identify, at least in a gross way, the manner in which research is conducted. While members of a research team working cooperatively may publish their results individually, those who publish their work jointly are likely to have cooperated at earlier stages of the research. Authorship patterns therefore do not show the total amount of scientific cooperation; however, they do indicate the minimal amount of scientific cooperation that is taking place. Scientific cooperation, moreover, does not necessarily lead to "good" science; some of the most significant scientific work may be performed by scientists working alone. Yet the absence of cooperation among these leading members of Cuban society might suggest that efforts to promote cooperation among ordinary citizens are not likely to succeed: this, then, is a study of cooperation among scientists, not a study of how to do science well.

Scientific fields differ in their traditions of cooperation, including single or joint authorship. The Cuban government's goal has been to increase cooperation across fields over time. Yet changes in the degree of scientific cooperation may result not only from government policy but also from changes in scientific practice over time in a particular country, from the increasing influence of foreign scientists, or from worldwide changes in a discipline over time. My analysis of authorship patterns will attempt to distinguish among the effects of these possible explanations.

Medical science has long been practiced in Cuba. The percentages of medical research articles published in various Cuban journals that were signed by more than one author are as follows: [1]

	%	Total number
Revista cubana de laboratorio clínico		
1948–1958	56.6	122
1959–1961	56.2	32
Revista cubana de cardiología		
1951–1958	74.8	107
1959–1960	60.7	28
Archivos del Hospital Universitario General Calixto García		
1951–1958	51.7	294
1959–1960	23.3	30
Revista cubana de pediatría		
1954–1958	55.6	216
1959–1962	55.0	131
1972–1975	81.0	100
Tropical medicine journals		
1948–1958	56.2	176
1959–1960	42.9	21
1971–1974	79.3	29
Revista cubana de medicina		
1962–1963	33.3	72
1972–1975	78.7	155
Revista cubana de cirugía		
1962–1963	30.0	60
1972–1975	76.4	165

Judging from the almost identical results in authorship patterns in medical journals, subfields of medical science have had similar traditions of cooperation. The majority of articles in prerevolutionary medical journals resulted from cooperative research, a fact that reflects the character of the discipline rather than the influence of socialism; cooperation was most common in cardiology. As measured by authorship patterns, the degree of cooperation either remained the same or declined from the prerevolutionary to the early revolutionary period. The short-term effect of the revolution was to disrupt personal and professional relations among medical scientists somewhat and to reduce their numbers through emigration. Cooperation increased dramatically, however, from the 1960s to the 1970s, surpassing prerevolutionary levels. This result is consistent with government policy, though not necessarily caused by it.

The case of medical science suggests one possible explanation for patterns of scientific cooperation. It could be argued that independent research is more frequent in the formative years of a science, while cooperation becomes more likely when the field matures, in part because personal relations develop within the discipline in any given country. Cooperation did increase as medical science matured in Cuba. However, zoology and botany are also well-established sciences in Cuba. Zoologists and botanists have published their work in Cuba's natural-history journal and in *Poeyana;* molecular biologists have published in *Serie biológica*. Considering scientific articles signed only by Cuban authors, no significant difference appears in the likelihood of multiple authorship from the 1940s through the 1970s (table F.1). Zoologists and botanists remain as individualistic as ever.

An alternative explanation, however, may account for these differences among Cuba's older scientific disciplines. Objective differences exist among the sciences. Those requiring large, complex, and expensive equipment are forced into cooperative efforts; scientists in disciplines where such equipment is not necessary are more likely to do independent research. This may be one reason why zoologists and botanists do not cooperate much, while medical scientists cooperated a good deal in the 1970s. It may also explain why medical scientists cooperated more in the 1970s, when they had more sophisticated equipment, than they did before the revolution. But it does not explain why the level of cooperation among medical scientists was already so high before the revolution, when they did not have such expensive equipment. The level of cooperation in medical research before the revolution was higher than in any other field of science included in table F.1, as measured by a comparison of multiple-authorship patterns among articles with only Cuban authors. This explanation also does not distinguish among degrees of cooperation in sciences using complicated equipment. Cuban scientists engaged in research on fishing (including marine biology, aspects of meteorology, some studies of navigation, and other applied sciences) also used large, complex, and expensive equipment, yet they were among the least likely to coauthor articles.

The Cuban government's efforts to increase cooperation among scientists is a third possible explanation of authorship patterns. The increase in multiple authorship among medical scientists from the prerevolutionary to the revolutionary period supports the view that government policies may have worked to this end. The lack of an increasing cooperative trend among zoologists and botanists, however, casts doubt on this explanation; similarly, the absence of multiple authorship of articles signed only by Cubans in geology and in fishing research suggests that government policy has not had much impact in these fields. Except in medical research, a majority of all articles signed only by Cubans bear the name of a single author.

Science in Cuba has been strongly influenced by the work of foreign scientists both before and during the revolutionary period (medicine had been the

Table F.1 Multiple authorship of scientific articles published in Cuban journals, 1960s and 1970s, by nationality.[a]

Journal or institution	All articles		Articles with Cuban authors		Articles with Cuban authors only		Articles with foreign authors[b]		Articles with foreign authors only[b]	
	% multiple authors	Total number	% multiple authors	Total number	% multiple authors	Total number	% multiple authors	Total number	% multiple authors	Total number
Institute for Research on Animal Husbandry	77	101	86	79	35	17	86	84	45	22
Fishing Research Center	43	61	70	30	0	9	50	52	16	31
Oceanography journals	66	44	74	34	44	16	78	27	40	10
Geology journals	60	55	72	43	0	12	77	43	17	12
Serie biológica	83	29	90	21	50	4	68	25	62	8
Poeyana, 1964–1969	45	69	51	51	13	31	65	34	29	17
Poeyana, 1970–1974	30	67	31	56	11	44	62	16	25	8
Natural-history journal	20	81	21	76	15	71	—	—	—	—

Sources: Coded and computed from Instituto de Investigaciones Científicas de la Economía Pesquera Marina y de la Oceanografía de Toda la Unión and Centro de Investigaciones Pesqueras de Cuba, *Investigaciones pesqueras soviético-cubanas* (Moscow: Editorial Pischevaja Promyshlennost, 1965–1971), vols. 1–3; Instituto de Ciencia Animal, *Instituto de Ciencia Animal* (Havana: Universidad de La Habana, 1970); *Estudios* 1–2 (1966–1967); *Serie oceanológica*, nos. 1–18 (1968–1973); *Ciencias: investigaciones marinas* (ser. 8), nos. 1–13 (October 1972–November 1974); *Revista de geología* 1, no. 1 (1967); *Serie geológica*, nos. 2–4 (1968–1969); ibid., nos. 6–13 (1972–1973); *Serie Oriente*, nos. 4, 7–10, 12 (1970–1973); *Actas*, nos. 1, 2 (1972); *Serie biológica*, nos. 1–28 (1967–1970); *Poeyana* (ser. A), nos. 1–134 (1964–1974); *Poeyana* (ser. B), nos. 1 and 2; *Memorias de la Sociedad Cubana de Historia Natural* 19–25 (1947–1961).

a. Total publications are not known; books are not included, and a few additional articles may exist. Three oceanography journals are treated as one, as are four geology journals.

b. With one exception, all foreigners engaged in research on fishing and oceanography were from the Soviet Union; all foreigners engaged in research on molecular biology were from East European countries, mostly from Czechoslovakia; all but three of the articles on research in animal husbandry signed by foreigners presented research by scientists from the United Kingdom or the United States. Soviet and East European scientists published in the geology journals and in *Poeyana*; however, all non-Cuban scholars appearing in these journals wrote alone, with fellow nationals, or with Cubans, not with foreigners of another nationality (the single exception was an article by a Rumanian, a Bulgarian, and a Cuban published in *Poeyana*).

most autonomous field of Cuban science). Thus a fourth explanation of patterns of cooperation in science is that they were shaped by foreign scientists. One measure of this impact on cooperative behavior is the proportion of foreign scientists who coauthored articles with their Cuban colleagues. Among articles that included foreign scientists as authors, multiple authorship prevailed in all fields (see table F.1). At first blush, this finding might seem to suggest that foreign scientists have brought cooperative habits with them to Cuba. Yet this is not quite the case. Among scientific articles in Cuban journals with only foreign authors, multiple authorship prevails only among the molecular biologists. Foreign scientists are thus not inherently inclined toward multiple authorship; rather, they appear more cooperative in Cuba because they came there to work with Cuban scientists.[2]

It might still be argued that the more cooperative foreign scientists communicate their work habits to their Cuban colleagues. To assess this argument, two variables in table F.1 can be compared: the percentage of articles that include Cuban authors (working with foreigners, with other Cubans, or alone) and the percentage of articles including foreigners (working with Cubans, with fellow nationals, or alone).[3] These measure the direct foreign impact on Cuban scientists. Cubans are somewhat more likely than non-Cubans to sign articles jointly in two of the fields and less likely in four; there is no difference in one. There is a moderate relationship between those fields in which foreigners cooperate more often and those in which Cubans do so. Both Cubans and foreigners are more likely to cooperate in research on animal husbandry in the 1970s, for example, and less likely to cooperate in research in zoology and botany. Given the small number of cases, however, this relationship is not strong enough to warrant confidence. Direct, face-to-face foreign influence on Cuban science, therefore, does not seem to explain variations in cooperation among scientific subfields well enough.

A fifth explanation for variations in cooperation from science to science is that attitudes are shaped by worldwide norms in different disciplines, each of which becomes a scientific subculture. The pattern of cooperation ought to be comparable for each field of science regardless of national origin and in the absence of any direct contact between Cubans and foreigners. This factor can be measured by the proportion of articles signed only by Cubans compared with the same statistics for foreigners.[4] Non-Cubans are more likely to cooperate with their fellow nationals than Cubans with other Cubans in six of the seven areas included in table F.1 (oceanography is the exception). There is a strong and nearly perfect relationship between those fields in which foreign scientists cooperate the most among themselves and those in which Cubans do the same; molecular biologists are at the top, that is, are most likely to cooperate in this way, while geologists and fishing researchers are at the bottom.

The single most important and consistent explanation for variation in cooperation among scientific disciplines, therefore, is that worldwide norms for each discipline shape the behavior of scientists in Cuba as in other countries. Cooperation proceeds according to the norms of each discipline; it is independent of the objective differences that exist among sciences, the length of time the science has been practiced in Cuba, the direct influence of foreign scientists, and even Cuban government policy. The norms for each scientific discipline thus nurture different scientific subcultures that may include widely different attitudes toward cooperation as well as toward other patterns of behavior. Scientists respond to the norms of their own discipline—a transnational scientific subculture—more readily than they do to cues from the national culture or to government policies. The generally low level of cooperation among Cuban scientists without direct foreign influence suggests that new-citizen norms about cooperation have not taken hold. Medical scientists have always cooperated in Cuba; their present higher proportion of cooperative enterprise reflects both custom and changing norms in worldwide medical research rather than Cuban government policy or changes in Cuban culture.

NOTES

In the notes, census and other Cuban statistical publications are referred to by abbreviated titles. More information about these materials may be found in the section of the bibliography listing statistical publications of the Cuban government.

1. INTRODUCTION

1. Studies of comparative politics during the past quarter century have been governed by three principal schools of thought. One concentrates on the impact of changes in society and the economy on government and politics. Studies emphasizing economic and social modernization have downplayed the study of government and political organizations when describing the internal social and economic preconditions, obstacles, opportunities, and patterns of change within which government and politics operate. A second way of approaching comparative politics is to assess the impact of international affairs on the domestic economy, society, and polity. The older literature on imperialism and the more recent literature on dependency are both examples of that school. These studies also de-emphasize the importance of governmental and political organizations and describe the international preconditions, obstacles, opportunities, and patterns of change within which the domestic affairs of countries operate. A third approach concentrates on governmental and political organizations, such as political parties and bureaucracies, their patterns of institutionalization and decay, and their relations with the society and the economy. These studies sometimes accept the domestic analyses of the first approach and the international analyses of the second and sometimes ignore them both.

2. GOVERNING THROUGH PLURALIZATION, 1902–1933

1. Quoted in Leonel-Antonio de la Cuesta, ed., *Constituciones cubanas* (Miami: Ediciones Exilio, 1974), p. 158; see also the extended discussion in Russell H. Fitzgib-

bon, *Cuba and the United States, 1900–1935* (Menasha, Wis.: Banta, 1935), pp. 67–93, 272–273.

2. Graham Allison, *The Essence of Decision* (Boston: Little, Brown, 1971), pp. 32–35, 78–96, 162–181.

3. The description of the events of 1906 is largely based on those of Allan Reed Miller, *The Politics of Intervention: The Military Occupation of Cuba, 1906–1909* (Columbus: Ohio State University Press, 1968), pp. 51–53, 59–102; Dana G. Munro, *Intervention and Dollar Diplomacy in the Caribbean, 1900–1921* (Princeton: Princeton University Press, 1964), pp. 125–133.

4. Leland H. Jenks, *Our Cuban Colony* (New York: Vanguard Press, 1928), pp. 170–172.

5. A number of rebel commanders not only asked explicitly for United States intervention, but also provoked it by attacking United States property. See Jorge Ibarra, "Agosto de 1906: una intervención amañada," *Revista de la Biblioteca Nacional José Martí,* 3rd period, vol. 15, no. 1 (January–April 1973):172–173.

6. Quoted in Charles E. Chapman, *A History of the Cuban Republic* (1927; reprint ed., New York: Octagon Books, 1969), p. 216.

7. This description of events is based largely on Munro, *Intervention,* pp. 489–498; Jenks, *Cuban Colony,* pp. 186–191; and Fitzgibbon, *Cuba and the United States,* pp. 157–159.

8. Carlos M. Trelles, *El progreso (1902 a 1905) y el retroceso (1906 a 1922) de la República de Cuba* (Havana: Imprenta El Score, 1923), p. 13.

9. Munro, *Intervention,* pp. 469–476, 480–489, 498–503.

10. Ibid., pp. 503–529; Chapman, *A History,* pp. 398, 401–403, 406–411, 420–424, 443–449; and Dana G. Munro, *The United States and the Caribbean Republics, 1921–1933* (Princeton: Princeton University Press, 1974), pp. 16–43.

11. In the case of Venezuela, the same variables operated differently and led to a contrasting outcome. In early twentieth-century Venezuela, the existing level of social mobilization was low; the capability and autonomy of the government were high; and foreign economic activity was highly concentrated both functionally and geographically. There the effect was to strengthen and concentrate further power in the government after the coming of foreign petroleum investments during the first third of the twentieth century. The petroleum industry was vertically integrated and highly concentrated geographically. The Gómez government, already powerful, became even more so. In the long run, Venezuelan society was pluralized, but its government has remained unusually powerful and capable.

12. Albert Hirschman has hypothesized about output utilization or forward linkages in economic development. All other things being equal, "every activity that does not by its nature cater exclusively to final demands will induce attempts to utilize its outputs as inputs in some new activities." Political factors, however, distorted the operation of the forward linkage mechanism with regard to turning raw into refined sugar in Cuba; thus this argument did not apply there. See Albert Hirschman, *The Strategy of Economic Development* (New Haven: Yale University Press, 1958), p. 100.

13. The petroleum industry is the archetype of the vertically integrated enterprise, since it controls the production of crude oil, its refinement, its transportation to the major markets, and its sale to retail consumers. See Raymond Vernon, *Sovereignty at Bay: The Multinational Spread of U.S. Enterprises* (New York: Basic Books, 1971), chap. 2.

14. Cuban Economic Research Project, *A Study on Cuba* (Coral Gables, Fla.: University of Miami Press, 1965), pp. 94, 251–253 (hereafter cited as CERP, *Study*).

15. Robert F. Smith, *The United States and Cuba* (New Haven: College and University Press, 1960), pp. 53–54.

16. CERP, *Study*, p. 238; Foreign Policy Association, Commission on Cuban Affairs, *Problems of the New Cuba* (New York: Little and Ives, 1935), p. 227 (hereafter cited as FPA, *Problems*).

17. But see Hugh Thomas, *Cuba: The Pursuit of Freedom* (New York: Harper & Row, 1971), chap. 23.

18. FPA, *Problems*, pp. 270–271.

19. CERP, *Study*, pp. 235, 237.

20. Julián Alienes Urosa, *Características fundamentales de la economía cubana* (Havana: Banco Nacional, 1950), p. 44.

21. Karl W. Deutsch, "Social Mobilization and Political Development," *American Political Science Review* 55, no. 3 (September 1961); Alex Inkeles, "Participant Citizenship in Six Developing Countries," *American Political Science Review* 63, no. 4 (December 1969); Norman H. Nie, G. Bingham Powell, Jr., and Kenneth Prewitt, "Social Structure and Political Participation: Developmental Relationships," *American Political Science Review* 63, no. 2 (June 1969) and no. 3 (September 1969); and Samuel P. Huntington and Jorge I. Domínguez, "Political Development," in *The Handbook of Political Science*, ed. Fred Greenstein and Nelson Polsby (Reading, Mass.: Addison-Wesley, 1975), vol. 3.

22. *1899 Census*, p. 361; *1907 Census*, p. 273; *1919 Census*, p. 366; *1943 Census*, p. 777; *1953 Census*, p. xxxix. The average annual increase has been computed from the literacy-level figures.

23. Comparative data may be found in Bruce M. Russett, Hayward R. Alker, Jr., Karl W. Deutsch, and Harold D. Lasswell, *World Handbook of Political and Social Indicators* (New Haven: Yale University Press, 1964), pp. 221–226; International Bank for Reconstruction and Development, *Report on Cuba* (Washington, D.C., 1951), pp. 408, 413–414 (hereafter cited as IBRD, *Report*).

24. Samuel P. Huntington, *Political Order in Changing Societies* (New Haven: Yale University Press, 1968), pp. 53–56; Ted Robert Gurr, *Why Men Rebel* (Princeton: Princeton University Press, 1970), pp. 24–58; James C. Davies, "The J-Curve of Rising and Declining Satisfactions as a Cause of Some Great Revolutions and a Contained Rebellion," in *Violence in America*, ed. Hugh Davis Graham and Ted Robert Gurr, 2 vols. (Washington, D.C.: Government Printing Office, 1969), 2:547–576.

25. Computed from Fitzgibbon, *Cuba and the United States*, pp. 140–141; *1907 Census*, p. 232. See also Russett et al., *World Handbook*, pp. 82–87, for comparative data.

26. The decline in wages and employment can also be documented at the level of individual enterprises. Research on documents "captured" in 1960 from the Cuban Electricity Company (a subsidiary of American Foreign Power and Light Company) when it was taken over by the government shows a significant decline both in wages and in the number of workers employed in the early 1930s. In 1930, 974 workers were paid less than $80.00 a month; 844 earned $85.00–150.00; 219 earned $155.00–300.00; and 48 earned more than $300.00 a month. A total of 2,085 workers were employed. In 1933, however, the number of workers paid less than $80.00 a month had increased to 1,102, while the number earning between $85.00 and $150.00 had declined to 535; the

number earning between $155.00 and $300.00, to 139; and the number earning more than $300.00 a month, to 10. The total number of workers employed was 1,786. This is the universe of wages and employment. When these figures are taken as a sample, the difference between the years is statistically significant (chi-square statistic is 97.57, significant at 0.001 for three degrees of freedom). Computed from María de los Angeles Ayón, "El movimiento obrero en el monopolio eléctrico," in *Monopolios norteamericanos en Cuba: contribución al estudio de la penetración imperialista* (Havana: Instituto Cubano del Libro, 1973), p. 179.

27. H. H. Gerth and C. Wright Mills, *From Max Weber* (New York: Galaxy Books, 1958), pp. 196, 295–301; Seymour Martin Lipset, *The First New Nation* (Garden City, N.Y.: Anchor Books, 1967), pp. 18–26.

28. Chapman, *A History*, pp. 143–146, 152–154, 161–162, 174, 183–185, 188, 518.

29. Henry C. Wallich, *Monetary Problems of an Export Economy* (Cambridge, Mass.: Harvard University Press, 1950), pp. 35, 40, 42, 50. The volume of money in circulation was determined entirely by private bank credit and by the balance of payments. Wallich calls it an "outstanding example of a purely automatic (monetary) system."

30. Fernando Ortiz, *La crisis política cubana* (Havana: Imprenta y Papelería La Universal, 1919), pp. 14–15; José Enrique Sandoval, "Ordenamiento social," in *Historia de la nación cubana*, ed. Ramiro Guerra y Sánchez, José M. Pérez Cabrera, Juan J. Remos, and Emeterio S. Santovenia, 10 vols. (Havana: Editorial Historia de la Nación Cubana, 1952), 9:401–406.

31. Manuel Sanguily, *Defensa de Cuba*, ed. Emilio Roig de Leuchsenring (Havana: Oficina del Historiador de la Ciudad de La Habana, 1948), p. 110; Alberto Arredondo, *Cuba: tierra indefensa* (Havana: Editorial Lex, 1945), pp. 184–185, 276–277; Alberto Blanco, "El movimiento jurídico en los primeros cincuenta años de independencia," in *Historia*, ed. Guerra y Sánchez et al., 8:375–376.

32. Munro, *Intervention*, pp. 29–33; CERP, *A Study*, pp. 218–222; Jesús Chía, "El monopolio en la industria del jabón y del perfume," in *Monopolios norteamericanos en Cuba: contribución al estudio de la penetración imperialista* (Havana: Instituto Cubano del Libro, 1973), pp. 23, 25, 28, 33–34.

33. Max Weber, *The Theory of Social and Economic Organization*, trans. A. M. Henderson and Talcott Parsons (New York: Free Press, 1965), pp. 347, 351–352, 355.

34. See, for instance, Emeterio S. Santovenia and Raúl M. Shelton, *Cuba y su historia*, 2nd ed. (Miami: Rema Press, 1966), 3:28–31, 34, 42, 44, 51, 53. Because this history was published by and for Cuban exiles who were not eager to besmirch the reputation of prerevolutionary Cuba, the discussion of corruption is, in fact, limited; but there is just too much evidence for the authors to ignore.

35. Chapman, *A History*, pp. 331, 547–559.

36. Trelles, *El progreso*, pp. 18–19.

37. Fernando Ortiz, *La decadencia cubana* (Havana: Imprenta y Papelería La Universal, 1924), pp. 15–16.

38. Chapman, *A History*, pp. 526–537.

39. Ortiz, *La decadencia*, p. 16.

40. Attributed to González Lanuza by Santovenia and Shelton, *Cuba y su historia*, p. 217.

41. Among the many interesting treatments of this subject are J. R. Portocarrero, *El problema político-financiero-social de Cuba* (Havana, 1921), pp. 66, 68–70, 75, 79; F. Lozano Casado, *La personalidad del General José Miguel Gómez* (Havana: Imprenta y Papelería de Rambla, Bouza, 1913), pp. 12, 14, 18, 55–79; Francisco Ichaso, "Ideas y aspiraciones de la primera generación republicana," in *Historia*, ed. Guerra y Sánchez et al., 8:342; Chapman, *A History*, pp. 145–146, 169–170, 173–174, 313–315, 347–351, 354–356, 398–401, 484–487.

42. Miguel Angel Carbonell, "Las generaciones libertadoras: veinticinco años de independencia," in *Historia*, ed. Guerra y Sánchez, et al., 8:269, 296–300.

43. The Philippine political system, for example, was also characterized by frequent party switching. In the Philippines, however, changes of affiliation were almost exclusively to the party of the presidential candidate who was expected to win or of the newly elected President. See Jean Grossholts, *Politics in the Philippines* (Boston: Little, Brown, 1964), pp. 136–156.

44. For a general discussion of this question, see Huntington, *Political Order*, pp. 12–24.

45. The level of political institutionalization, measured by reelection of members, is just short of that in the United States House of Representatives during the first century of its existence. In the Cuban House, a majority of the members were serving their first terms, while in the United States House at that time (and certainly in the twentieth century) a majority are not first-term representatives. Nelson W. Polsby, "The Institutionalization of the U.S. House of Representatives," *American Political Science Review*, 62, no. 1 (March 1968):146.

46. The outstanding work on Machado's fall is Luis E. Aguilar's *Cuba 1933: Prologue to Revolution* (Ithaca: Cornell University Press, 1972); see especially pp. 49–151. See also Munro, *The United States*, pp. 342–370; Jules R. Benjamin, "The Machadato and Cuban Nationalism," *Hispanic American Historical Review* 55 (February 1975).

47. Ricardo Dolz, *El proceso electoral de 1916* (Havana: Imprenta y Papelería La Universal, 1917), pp. 8–9; Louis A. Pérez, Jr., "Capital, Bureaucrats and Policy: The Economic Contours of United States–Cuban Relations, 1916–1921," *Inter-American Economic Affairs* 29, no. 1 (Summer 1975):76, 79.

48. Ismael Testé, *Historia eclesiástica de Cuba* (Burgos: Tipografía de la Editorial El Monte Carmelo, 1969), 1:275–276, 279, 284, 399–403; Fitzgibbon, *Cuba and the United States*, pp. 35–37, 45; Miller, *The Politics of Intervention*, pp. 25–26, 49, 194; Leopoldo Horrego Estuch, *Martín Morúa Delgado: vida y mensaje* (Havana: Editorial Sánchez, 1957), pp. 161, 209, 211.

49. *Cuadernos de historia habanera* no. 7 (1936):168–169, 174, 178, 180–182.

50. Ortiz, *La decadencia*, pp. 14–16; Trelles, *El progreso*, pp. 9–10, 16–19, 24–25; Chapman, *A History*, pp. 466–479, 487; Emilio Roig de Leuchsenring, *La colonia superviva* (Havana: Imprenta El Siglo XX, 1925), p. 7 (the author hails the "marked improvement" in controlling corruption upon Machado's election); Julio Le Riverend, *La república: dependencia y revolución* (Havana: Instituto del Libro, 1969), pp. 199–214.

51. Huntington and Domínguez, "Political Development"; for a discussion of the devaluation of "blackness" by blacks, see the excellent study by Verena Martínez Alier, *Marriage, Class and Color in Nineteenth-Century Cuba: A Study of Racial Attitudes*

and Sexual Values in a Slave Society (London: Cambridge University Press, 1974), pp. 91–99. The system of ethnic stratification in Cuba and in the rest of Latin America differed significantly from similar systems elsewhere. Cuba's was based on an agglomerative political culture and a vertical or hierarchical system of ethnicity. An agglomerative political culture is one that emphasizes superordinate and subordinate relations but at the same time affirms the basic humanity of all people; even the lowliest have certain rights guaranteed by cultural norms. Vertical or hierarchical ethnic stratification results from conquest (including the conquest of blacks through the slave trade). The "rightness" of the hierarchy is widely accepted; those at the bottom agree that it is proper to give more honor to those at the top. For those at the bottom of the ethnic structure, mobility consists not in affirming their own separate identity but in blending themselves into the dominant patterns through "whitening," in the case of white-black relations. White is valued; black is devalued. Organizations limited to one ethnic group are frowned upon, especially in the subordinate group; only individual mobility is legitimate. Hierarchical ethnic stratification is socially quite stable; the probability of violence is less than in ethnic systems where the major groups look down on each other and none is accepted as dominant. When a vertical ethnic structure cracks, however, considerable violence may result. Breakdowns tend to occur either when the legitimacy of the political system is in serious question or when social mobilization increases simultaneously with a contraction of the economy.

52. Sources for this account of the Independent Party of Color are Rafael Fermoselle, *Política y color en Cuba: la guerrita de 1912* (Montevideo: Ediciones Geminis, 1974); Emilio Roig de Leuchsenring, *Males y vicios de Cuba republicana* (Havana: Oficina del Historiador de la Ciudad de La Habana, 1959); Horrego Estuch, *Martín Morúa*, pp. 195–197, 207–208, 218, 243, 247–254; Le Riverend, *La república*, pp. 123–126; Rafael Conte and José Capmany, *Guerra de razas: negros contra blancos en Cuba* (Havana: Imprenta Militar de Antonio Pérez, 1912); Thomas, *Cuba: Pursuit of Freedom*, pp. 514–524, 1141; CERP, *Study*, p. 237. For an example of Cuban white-supremacist literature, see Gustavo Mustelier, *La extinción del negro* (Havana: Imprenta de Rambla, Bouza, 1912).

53. Black revolts also occurred in central Las Villas, especially the municipalities of Las Cruces and Santa Isabel de las Lajas. As in the municipalities in southeastern Oriente, the concentration of blacks and mulattoes in the population in these municipalities was higher than the national or provincial averages; however, Las Cruces and Santa Isabel were only about one-third black and mulatto, well under the figures for southeastern Oriente. Although the level of literacy in Santa Isabel was approximately that of the black national average in 1907 and 1919, with an average annual increase of 0.55 percent, literacy in Las Cruces rose an average of 0.92 percent each year and reached 65.8 percent in 1919. Thus the Las Villas municipalities experienced a pattern of social mobilization similar to that in southeastern Oriente. The municipalities in Oriente may have been better able to launch a large-scale revolt because of their higher concentration of blacks and their less favorable economic situation. Computed from *1907 Census*, pp. 318–319, 464; *1919 Census*, pp. 406–407, 566.

54. Munro, *Intervention*, pp. 476–480.

55. Computed from Luisa Margarita de la Cotera O'Bourke, *¿Quién es quién en Cuba?* (Havana: Julián Martín, 1925), pp. 58–84.

56. Eduardo Suárez Rivas, *Un pueblo crucificado* (Miami: Service Offset Printers, 1964), p. 177.

57. Partido Conservador Nacional, *Programa* (Havana: Imprenta La Prueba, 1919), p. 16; Chapman, *A History*, pp. 405, 487; Lydia Cabrera, *La sociedad secreta Abakuá* (Havana: Ediciones C. R., 1958), pp. 9–22, 59–60.

58. Horrego Estuch, *Martín Morúa*, pp. 199–201.

59. Chapman, *A History*, p. 274.

60. Ibid., p. 504. See also Lozano Casado, *Gómez*, p. 33; Horrego Estuch, *Martín Morúa*, pp. 200, 213–215; Le Riverend, *La república*, pp. 130–136, 215–219.

61. José Rivero Muñiz, *El primer partido socialista cubano* (Havana: Imprenta Nacional, 1962), pp. 52–55, 69–70, 82–84, 89, 95–104, 117–120; Jorge García Montes and Antonio Alonso Ávila, *Historia del partido comunista de Cuba* (Miami: Rema Press, 1970), pp. 15–19, 31–34; Fabio Grobart, "El movimiento obrero cubano de 1925 a 1933," *Cuba socialista* 6, no. 60 (August 1966): 91.

62. Grobart, "El movimiento obrero," pp. 91–112; Le Riverend, *La república*, pp. 220–221, 246–247, 262, 266–268, 287–288; García Montes and Alonso Ávila, *Historia del partido comunista*, 57–58, 65, 71–77, 106–108, 112–113, 121–125; FPA, *Problems*, pp. 187–188; Aguilar, *Cuba 1933*, pp. 80–86, 121–124, 144–151; Mirta Rosell, *Luchas obreras contra Machado* (Havana: Instituto Cubano del Libro, 1973).

63. Jenks, *Cuban Colony*, pp. 179, 185, 269; Raúl Miranda, *Siluetas de candidatos* (Matanzas: Imprenta y Librería La Pluma de Oro, 1910), pp. 35–37.

3. GOVERNING THROUGH REGULATION AND DISTRIBUTION, 1933–1958

1. The events of the 1933 revolution have been well narrated elsewhere; this chapter discusses only those incidents that are pertinent to an understanding of the governing of Cuba. For a general contemporary work on the revolution of 1933, see Luis Aguilar, *Cuba 1933: Prologue to Revolution* (Ithaca: Cornell University Press, 1972); for works written in the 1930s from different perspectives, see Carleton Beals, *The Crime of Cuba* (Philadelphia: Lippincott, 1933), and Alberto Lamar Schweyer, *Cómo cayó el presidente Machado*, 2nd ed. (Havana: M. Cárdenas, 1938); for contemporary works emphasizing United States–Cuban relations, see Bryce Wood, *The Making of the Good Neighbor Policy* (New York: Columbia University Press, 1961), chaps. 2 and 3; Irwin F. Gellman, *Roosevelt and Batista: Good Neighbor Diplomacy in Cuba, 1933–1945* (Albuquerque: University of New Mexico Press, 1973), pp. 15–82.

2. Quoted in *Foreign Relations of the United States, 1933* (Washington, D.C.: Government Printing Office, 1952), 5:368 (hereafter cited as *FRUS*).

3. Gellman, *Roosevelt and Batista*, pp. 117–118.

4. Ibid., pp. 109–110.

5. *FRUS, 1935*, 4:476.

6. Gellman, *Roosevelt and Batista*, pp. 147–151.

7. *FRUS, 1940*, 5:741.

8. *FRUS, 1940*, 5:742.

9. Quoted in Gellman, *Roosevelt and Batista*, p. 208.

10. Robert F. Smith, *The United States and Cuba: Business and Diplomacy, 1917–1960* (New Haven: College and University Press, 1960), pp. 157–164.

11. *FRUS, 1946,* 11:740; *FRUS, 1948,* 9:553–554, 568–569.

12. *FRUS, 1946,* 11:749.

13. *FRUS, 1948,* 9:562.

14. *FRUS, 1947,* 8:609, 616–617, 622–624; *FRUS, 1948,* 9:563.

15. *FRUS, 1948,* 9:563–564, 570–577.

16. U.S., Department of Commerce, Bureau of Foreign Commerce, *Investment in Cuba* (Washington, D.C.: Government Printing Office, 1956), p. 19.

17. *FRUS, 1948,* 9:552, 554–557.

18. *FRUS, 1946,* 11:722.

19. *FRUS, 1947,* 8:621.

20. *FRUS, 1947,* 8:614–615; *FRUS, 1948,* 9:557–560.

21. Gellman, *Roosevelt and Batista,* pp. 143–144, 162–163. Gellman's otherwise excellent book is marred by occasional misjudgments of interpretation. He argues, for example, that "by 1945 the U.S. exercised even greater control over the Cuban economy than it had before 1933" (p. 6). Yet there was change in both degree and kind of control, from imperialism to hegemony, including complex processes of divestment and new investment.

22. This discussion is based on U.S., Congress, Senate, Committee on the Judiciary, Subcommittee to Investigate the Administration of the Internal Security Act and Other Internal Security Laws, *Hearings,* 86th Cong., 2nd sess., pt. 10, 2 and 8 September 1960, pp. 712, 738–739; ibid., pt. 9, 27 and 30 August 1960, pp. 687–691, 694, 697, 706, 709; idem, *Hearings,* 87th Cong., 1st sess., pt. 5, 9 January, 8 February 1961, 2 February 1962, pp. 554–556, 658–659; Earl E. T. Smith, *The Fourth Floor* (New York: Random House, 1962), pp. 108, 113, 150, 160–176, 181; Ramón Bonachea and Marta San Martín, *The Cuban Insurrection, 1952–1959* (New Brunswick, N.J.: Transaction Books, 1974), pp. 244–245; Cole Blasier, "The Elimination of United States Influence," in *Revolutionary Change in Cuba,* ed. Carmelo Mesa-Lago (Pittsburgh: University of Pittsburgh Press, 1971), pp. 44–49. On the demoralization of Batista's armed forces as a result of the United States arms embargo, see Ramón Barquín, *Las luchas guerrilleras en Cuba: de la colonia a la Sierra Maestra* (Madrid: Editorial Playor, 1975), 1:529.

23. These shipments included corrections of errors on deliveries prior to March 4, 1958, and the delivery of weapons ordered before then.

24. Edmund Chester, *A Sergeant Named Batista* (New York: Holt, 1954), pp. 180–191; Louis A. Pérez, Jr., *Army Politics in Cuba, 1898–1958* (Pittsburgh: University of Pittsburgh Press, 1976), pp. 118–121.

25. *FRUS, 1948,* 9:545–551.

26. For a fuller discussion, see Raymond Vernon, *Sovereignty at Bay* (New York: Basic Books, 1971), pp. 65–77. The data needed to test this hypothesis fully are not available, but the pattern is credible enough to use until disproved.

27. The older United States manufacturing enterprises also invested new capital in their older establishments and introduced new products. Along with newer investors, for example, Procter and Gamble began producing synthetic detergents in Cuba in 1950; Colgate-Palmolive followed in 1951. The technology for the production of synthetic detergents was new in Cuba; the factories were also new and represented substantial capital investment. See Jesús Chía, "El monopolio en la industria del jabón y del perfume," in *Monopolios norteamericanos en Cuba: contribución al estudio de la*

penetración imperialista (Havana: Instituto Cubano del Libro, 1973), pp. 35–37. The value of investments in public utilities had risen in current dollars from 1936 to 1958 (the decline in its share during the 1950s was due to the Batista government's purchase of the United Railways of Havana in 1953). Thus the mature utilities sector was the only one that failed to behave as the product-cycle model predicts.

28. In 1972, the U.S. Foreign Claims Settlement Commission reported that the value of property owned in Cuba by United States corporations and native and naturalized citizens that had been socialized by the revolutionary government was $1,799.5 million, exclusive of interest. The commission apparently included in its total the claims of former Cuban citizens who had become United States citizens and the revaluation of property that some owners had not valued accurately enough in the commission's opinion. Although it excluded almost half the claims filed with it as exaggerated, the commission's purpose was to make a diplomatic case. In fact, for purposes of judging the political effect of direct United States investment in Cuba, the statistics published and accepted as accurate in the late 1950s are more significant than those published in 1972. The earlier, lower estimates are therefore used here. See Sidney Freidberg, "The Measure of Damages in Claims Against Cuba," *Inter-American Economic Affairs* 23, no. 1 (Summer 1969):67–86; Lynn Darrell Bender, "U.S. Claims against the Cuban Government: An Obstacle to Rapprochement," *Inter-American Economic Affairs* 27, no. 1 (Summer 1973):9.

29. Emeterio S. Santovenia and Raúl M. Shelton, *Cuba y su historia*, 2nd ed. (Miami: Rema Press, 1966), 3:166–168, 192–195; Banco Nacional de Cuba, *Economic Development Program, Progress Report*, no. 1 (1956).

30. The following authors disagree on many points, but all stress continuation of dependence using the same evidence: Dennis Wood, "The Long Revolution: Class Relations and Political Conflict in Cuba, 1868–1968," *Science and Society* 34, no. 1 (Spring 1970):12–15, 22; Nelson P. Valdés, "La diplomacia del azúcar," *Aportes* no. 18 (October 1970):103–106; Edward Gonzalez, *Cuba Under Castro: The Limits of Charisma* (Boston: Houghton Mifflin, 1974), pp. 54–65.

31. Cattle raising and beef processing had been predominantly Cuban owned. Cubans had also taken over the insurance business and, in 1957, partial ownership of the Cuban Telephone Company, through the issuance of new stock. The Cubanization of the sugar industry in 1959 took place first privately and only later through state takeover. Alfred L. Padula, Jr., "The Fall of the Bourgeoisie: Cuba, 1959–1961" (Ph. D. diss., University of New Mexico, 1974), pp. 55–56, 125, 213–217, 382.

32. *1943 Census*, pp. 777, 926, 930–931; *1953 Census*, p. xxxix.

33. Mercedes García Tudurí, "La enseñanza en Cuba en los primeros cincuenta años de independencia," in *Historia de la nación cubana*, ed. Ramiro Guerra y Sánchez et al. (Havana: Editorial Historia de la Nación Cubana, 1952), 10:68; International Bank for Reconstruction and Development, *Report on Cuba* (Washington, D.C., 1951), pp. 410–412 (hereafter cited as IBRD, *Report*); Mercedes García Tudurí, "Resumen de la historia de la educación en Cuba," *Exilio* 3, nos. 3–4, and 4, no. 1 (Winter 1969–Spring 1970): 115–116.

34. Donald R. Dyer, "Urbanism in Cuba," *Geographical Review* 57, no. 2 (April 1957):226–228.

35. If one excludes the unusually good year of 1952 and the civil-war year of 1958, the conclusions do not change very much. From 1948 through 1951, the average annual

real nonagricultural wage increase outpaced the average annual increase in real per capita income by 9.8 percent to 8.2 percent. From 1953 through 1957, the average annual increase in real nonagricultural wages lagged behind the average annual increase in real per capita income by 4.1 percent to 6.3 percent.

36. Surveys of agricultural workers are inadequate for rigorous tests. It is possible to infer general trends by comparing a small survey ($N = 41$) conducted by the research team of the Foreign Policy Association in 1934 and a much larger one ($N = 1,000$) conducted by the Havana University Catholic Students' Association in 1957. The 1934 survey overrepresented Oriente province, typically more backward, while the 1957 survey underrepresented it. The 1957 survey's figures on mean cash income are deflated into 1937 national retail food prices (the closest approximation available to 1934 prices).

37. In 1934, approximately 40 percent of the mean real income of poor and middle-income families was in kind. A comparable proportion is assumed for 1957 and deflated into 1937 Cuban national retail food prices, the only long-term price index available. In addition, seven of the forty-one families in the 1934 survey probably would not have qualified for inclusion in the 1957 survey, because they either lived in urban areas or had no cash income. Thus only thirty-four families from the 1934 survey are used for the second test.

38. Computed from Foreign Policy Association, Commission on Cuban Affairs, *Problems of the New Cuba* (New York: Little and Ives, 1935), pp. 81–90 (hereafter cited as FPA, *Problems*); Oscar Echevarría Salvat, *La agricultura cubana, 1934–1966* (Miami: Ediciones Universal, 1971), pp. 7, 55–58, 69. To deflate the 1957 survey, the national retail food index (1937 prices) was used as it stood in June 1957; see Banco Nacional de Cuba, *Memoria, 1957–1958* (Havana: Editiorial Lex, 1959) p. 194 (hereafter cited as *Memoria*). For a valuable critique of the 1957 survey, see Brian H. Pollitt, "Estudios acerca del nivel de vida rural en la Cuba pre-revolucionaria: un análisis crítico," *Teoría y práctica* nos. 42–43 (November–December 1967):48–49. For a different conclusion, see Nelson P. Valdés, "Health and Revolution in Cuba," *Science and Society* 35, no. 3 (Fall 1971): 313–315. However, Valdés seems to have compared the 1957 median cash income with the 1934 mean real income, without adequate price deflation. For another set of economic indexes, see Jorge Pérez-López, "An Index of Cuban Industrial Output, 1930–1958" (Ph.D. diss., State University of New York–Albany, 1974).

39. Roberto Hernández, "La atencíon médica en Cuba hasta 1958," *Journal of Inter-American Studies* 11, no. 4 (October 1969):543–544; Valdés, "Health and Revolution," p. 331.

40. Compare the biographical descriptions in Aguilar, *Cuba 1933*, pp. 170–173; Gellman, *Roosevelt and Batista*, pp. 36–37, 56–57; and Hugh Thomas, *Cuba: The Pursuit of Freedom* (New York: Harper & Row, 1971), p. 650.

41. For a discussion of the lasting impact of these decrees, see Leopoldo Horrego Estuch, *Legislación social de Cuba* (Havana: Editorial Librería Selecta, 1948–1949) 1:147; 2:103, 254–255.

42. Santovenia and Shelton, *Cuba y su Historia*, pp. 118, 124.

43. Horrego Estuch, *Legislación*, 1:37–38, 343, 1077–78.

44. Fulgencio Batista, *Revolución social o política reformista* (Havana: Prensa Indoamericana, 1944); Consejo Corporativo de Educación, Sanidad y Beneficencia, *Militarismo, anti-militarismo y seudo-militarismo* (Ceiba del Agua: Talleres del Instituto Cívico-Militar [1939?]); Pérez, *Army Politics in Cuba*, pp. 101–115.

45. Germán Wolter del Río, "La hacienda de la república independiente," in *Historia*, ed. Guerra y Sánchez et al., 9:99–101.

46. For a full-fledged effort, see Enrique A. Baloyra, "Political Leadership in the Cuban Republic, 1944–1958" (Ph.D. diss., University of Florida–Gainesville, 1971), especially pp. 304–315.

47. Information on congressional output exists for twenty-seven countries from all continents in the 1960s, but not for earlier years. The Cuban congressional output in the 1940s and 1950s lagged behind that of all other non-Communist countries in this group. Only three Communist countries' parliaments were less active. See Jean Blondel, *Comparative Legislatures* (Englewood Cliffs, N.J.: Prentice-Hall, 1973), pp. 156–157.

48. The material in this section is based on Eduardo Varona Martínez and Rafael González Labrada, *El colono* (Havana: Impresores Úcar, García, 1958), pp. 11–30; IBRD, *Report*, pp. 804–805, 812–819; Cuban Economic Research Project, *A Study on Cuba* (Coral Cables, Fla.: University of Miami Press, 1965), pp. 335–336, 339–346 (hereafter cited as CERP, *Study*); *Anuario azucarero de Cuba* 22 (1958):109, 181–183.

49. Every 100 arrobas of sugar cane yielded an average of 12.5 arrobas of sugar. The act guaranteed that every grower would get a 48-percent share (*arrobaje*) of the average sugar yield of the mill for the entire crop, so long as it did not exceed 12 percent of the cane. If the average yield was between 12 and 13 percent, the arrobaje fell to 47 percent; if it rose above 13 percent, the arrobaje fell to 46 percent.

50. The applicable average arrobaje was 47 percent. Growers who owned their land received an additional 5 percent. This left 48 percent for the sugar mill. Alternatively, when the growers did not own their land, the sugar mill received 53 percent for its share of production and rent.

51. Horrego Estuch, *Legislación*, 1:415.

52. Jorge García Montes and Antonio Alonso Ávila, *Historia del partido comunista de Cuba* (Miami: Rema Press, 1970), pp. 476–477.

53. Isidro A. Vilches González, *Derecho cubano del trabajo* (Havana: Jesús Montero, 1948), pp. 531–542; José Enrique Sandoval, "Ordenamiento social," in *Historia*, ed. Guerra y Sánchez et al., 9:430–432, 449–451; Horrego Estuch, *Legislación*, 1:353–355, 360–362, 371, 374, 378, 386, 387, 397, 415.

54. Computed from Mariano Sánchez Roca, *Compilación ordenada y completa de la legislación cubana de 1951 a 1958* (Havana: Editorial Lex, 1960), 4:1262–78, 1288.

55. Horrego Estuch, *Legislación*, 1:229–242.

56. Compiled from Carlos M. Piedra, *La inamovilidad de los trabajadores* (Havana: Cultural, 1945), pp. 46ff.; Horrego Estuch, *Legislación*, 1:230–240.

57. Some of these decisions in the 1940s were outrageous; rulings in the following cases were all against dismissal. "Although it has been proven that the employee fought with a fellow worker in the work place, it cannot be established with the evidence available that there was a disruption of order in the work place" (Supreme Court, ruling no. 871, 25 September 1945). "It has only been proven that [the worker, P.] created a public scandal in his work place by provoking a fight with A. A.Z., also a worker, who was in charge of allocating tasks among workers in the work place . . . and that P. fought violently, for he was charged with having attacked and injured Z. [However] of the thirteen witnesses who testified, one was Z. and of the twelve others only two testified that P. attacked Z. . . . [In addition] Z. is not P.'s boss but simply . . . another

worker charged by the boss with allocating tasks among the workers" (Supreme Court, ruling no. 28, 20 January 1944). "Although it is established that the worker was absent from the work place from August 26, without notifying his employer, until October 1, 1939, it is also established that he was absent because he was sick, and had been sick even before he stopped going to work . . . and although the worker should have notified his employer immediately of the cause of his absence, the omission of such a detail is not sufficient to justify dismissal" (Supreme Court, ruling no. 638, 28 June 1944). "Loss of trust is never a just cause for dismissal" (Supreme Court, ruling no. 379, 19 April 1945). See Piedra, *Inamovilidad*, pp. 74, 85–86, 98–99, 110–111; IBRD, *Report*, pp. 148–152, 363–364.

58. The pattern of Supreme Court decisions in cases of worker or employee dismissals from 1949 through 1959 was as follows:

	Cases won by worker	Cases won by management	Total cases
1949	21	13	34
1950	26	43	69
1951	26	64	80
1952	33	90	123
1953	22	86	108
1954	31	125	156
1955	38	124	162
1956	50	104	154
1957	29	117	146
1958	11	40	51
1959	41	40	81

Coded and computed from cases in the index of *Reportorio judicial: contencioso-administrativo* 26 (1950):9, 10, 14; *Repertorio judicial: materia social* 27 (1951):9, 10, 15; ibid., 28 (1952):11–12; ibid., 29 (1953):12–14; ibid., 30 (1954):11–13; ibid., 31 (1955):11–14; ibid., 32 (1956):12–14; ibid., 33 (1957):15–18; ibid., 34 (1958):15–17; ibid., 35 (1959):16–18. Only cases where the identity of the winners and losers could be clearly established are included in this count. Only a small fraction of cases were appealed from administrative proceedings all the way up to the Supreme Court, but only the records of that Court are available. The Supreme Court, of course, set the pattern for the lower courts.

59. Efrén Córdova Cordovés, "Problemas actuales de la intervención del Estado en la economía laboral cubana," *Anuario de la Facultad de Ciencias Sociales y Derecho Público* (1955–1956):269–275; Ruby Hart Phillips, *Cuba: Island of Paradox* (New York: McDowell, Obolensky, 1959), p. 261. Praise for the efforts of the Cuban Labor Confederation under Mujal can be found even in unlikely quarters; see Julio Le Riverend, *La república: dependencia y revolución* (Havana: Instituto del Libro, 1969), p. 358.

60. On compensated dismissals and interventions, see U.S., Bureau of Foreign Commerce, *Investment*, pp. 19, 21–22, 25. For a discussion of the cozy relationship between some Cuban labor unions and private foreign investors, whose business partners they became, see Philip C. Newman, *Cuba before Castro: An Economic Appraisal* (New Delhi: Prentice-Hall of India, 1965), pp. 13–15, 120–123.

61. Henry C. Wallich, *Monetary Problems of an Export Economy* (Cambridge, Mass.: Harvard University Press, 1950), p. 24.

62. IBRD, *Report*, p. 666.

63. José Pérez Cubillas, "El impuesto sobre la renta personal y el cincuentenario de la República," *Anuario de la Facultad de Ciencias Sociales y Derecho Público*, (1952):51–55.

64. IBRD, *Report*, pp. 798–803.

65. U.S., Bureau of Foreign Commerce, *Investment*, pp. 24–25; Julio Chacón y Reyes, "Antecedentes del azúcar a granel en Cuba," *Cuba azúcar* (July–August 1966):16–23.

66. Unemployment and underemployment data from the 1956–57 employment survey are reasonably similar to data from the 1943 and 1953 censuses. For unemployment, see Gustavo Gutiérrez, *El empleo, el subempleo y el desempleo en Cuba* (Havana: Consejo Nacional de Economía, 1958), tables 2, 6; *1953 Census*, pp. 167–168; *1943 Census*, pp. 1042–57. For underemployment, Carmelo Mesa-Lago, "The Labor Force, Employment, Unemployment and Underemployment in Cuba: 1899–1970," *Sage Professional Papers in International Studies* 1, no. 9 (1972):15–34. Mesa-Lago's work provides an indispensable discussion of the variable quality of these statistics, as well as a more extensive discussion of their meaning.

67. The underemployment rate may have declined in the 1950s. The underemployment statistics for the 1953 census and the 1956–57 survey are almost the same. Because unemployment in 1956–57 was twice as high as in 1953, underemployment should have been at about one-quarter of the population in the 1956–57 survey instead of 13.8 percent. One possible explanation is the weakening of the antidismissal policy. As dismissals became easier, an underemployed status was more precarious; workers had either to secure permanent employment or join the unemployed.

68. Lloyd A. Free, *Attitudes of the Cuban People toward the Castro Regime* (Princeton: Institute for International Social Research, 1960), pp. 22–23; Francisco Dorta Duque, *Justificando una reforma agraria* (Madrid: Raycar, 1960), p. 46.

69. Santovenia and Shelton, *Cuba y su historia*, pp. 160–163, 166–168, 190–192; Wolter del Río, "Hacienda," pp. 154, 254–258; CERP, *Study*, pp. 458–459, 462–466. For a discussion of research and development in the 1950s, see Salustiano García Díaz, "Las industrias de subproductos y derivados de la caña y del azúcar," *Anuario azucarero de Cuba* 22 (1958):45–48; Julio Lobo, "Necesaria la modernización agrícola e industrial," ibid., 51; Henry Hass, "El año: en la defensa e investigación del azúcar," ibid., 54–55. See also West Indies Sugar Corporation, *Annual Report* (1955): 5–6; ibid. (1956):6.

70. Eduardo Suárez Rivas, *Un pueblo crucificado* (Miami: Service Offset Printers, 1964), pp. 270–276; José Suárez Núñez, *El gran culpable* (Caracas, 1963), pp. 20–25; Phillips, *Cuba: Island of Paradox*, pp. 249–254; Baloyra, "Political Leadership," pp. 93–96; Thomas, *Cuba: Pursuit of Freedom*, pp. 738–740, 746–747, 764–765, 768. For an admission of corrupt practices and a justification of them because "everybody did it" by Batista's cabinet ministers, see Fulgencio Batista, *Piedras y leyes* (Mexico: Ediciones Botas, 1961), p. 430; Padula, "Fall of the Bourgeoisie," pp. 63–70.

71. President Grau was charged with the theft of 174 million pesos; on July 4, 1950, gunmen invaded the court where the case against Grau was lodged and stole all

the documents; the case never went to trial, no one was arrested, and the documents were never found.

72. For a general discussion, see James C. Scott, *Comparative Political Corruption* (Englewood Cliffs, N.J.: Prentice-Hall, 1972); Joseph S. Nye, Jr., "Corruption and Political Development: A Cost-Benefit Analysis," *American Political Science Review* 61, no. 2 (June 1967):417–427.

73. Tribunal de Cuentas, *Recopilación y análisis de los ingresos presupuestales de Cuba* (Havana, 1953), pp. 203–212; *Leyes y decretos* 50 (1923):466; *La jurisprudencia al día* (1954):582, 1586–1587; Batista, *Piedras*, pp. 153–160, 397.

74. Antonio Lancís y Sánchez, "Elecciones y administración en la República," *Anuario de la Facultad de Ciencias Sociales y Derecho Público* (1952):103; Pérez Cubillas, "Impuesto," p. 56; Wolter del Río, "Hacienda," pp. 130–131.

75. Horrego Estuch, *Legislación*, 2 (1949):192–194, 239, 874–875; IBRD, *Report*, pp. 173–174, 185–186.

76. Fermín Peraza, *Diccionario biográfico cubano* (Havana: Ediciones Anuario Bibliográfico Cubano, 1951), pp. 67–68.

77. *Memoria, 1950–1951; Memoria, 1951–1952; Memoria, 1957–1958.* For a general study, see Charles P. Leon, "The National Bank of Cuba: A Study in Institutional Change" (Ph.D. diss., New York University, 1964); Padula, "Fall of the Bourgeoisie," pp. 336, 338.

78. See Blas Roca, "Algunos problemas de nuestro trabajo electoral," *Fundamentos* 3, nos. 27–28 (November–December 1943):191, 199, 201; "Editorial: ante las elecciones," *Fundamentos* 4, no. 33 (May 1944):3; Blas Roca, "Significación y alcance de la entrevista Grau-CTC," *Fundamentos* 4, no. 37 (September 1944); García Montes and Alonso Ávila, *Historia del partido comunista*, pp. 200–202, 331–333.

79. García Montes and Alonso Ávila, *Historia del partido comunista*, pp. 382–383; Phillips, *Cuba: Island of Paradox*, p. 262; Ralph Lee Woodward, "Urban Labor and Communism in Cuba," *Caribbean Studies* 3, no. 3 (October 1963):23–24; Woodward plays down Prío's role.

80. In the rest of Latin America, labor confederations have followed the parties and leaders that supported them in government into the opposition after electoral defeats or military coups. The links between organized labor and the peronistas in Argentina, the communists and socialists in Chile, the APRA (Alianza Popular Revolucionaria Americana) in Peru, or Acción Democrática in Venezuela, not only in times of crisis but also in normal times, are well documented. See, for example, John D. Powell, *Political Mobilization of the Venezuelan Peasant* (Cambridge, Mass.: Harvard University Press, 1971), pp. 86–95; François Bourricaud, *Power and Society in Contemporary Peru* (New York: Praeger, 1967), pp. 315–316; James Petras, *Politics and Social Forces in Chilean Development* (Berkeley and Los Angeles: University of California Press, 1970), pp. 162–164, 168–174; Samuel Baily, *Labor, Nationalism and Politics in Argentina* (New Brunswick, N.J.: Rutgers University Press, 1967), pp. 163–184.

81. Computed from Mario Riera Hernández, *Historial obrero cubano* (Miami: Rema Press, 1965), pp. 292, 294, 295, 298–301. For quantitative data on numbers of unions, nonpaying unionists, and unionists paying dues to the confederation at the end of the first Batista regime, see Secretaría de Finanzas, Confederación de Trabajadores de Cuba, *Balance general, 1943–1944* (Havana: Editorial Cenit, [1944?]), pp. 152, 160, 162, 169. For later data on numbers of unions and unionized workers, see Sandoval, "Ordenamiento social," pp. 437–438.

82. Charles W. Anderson, "Toward a Theory of Latin American Politics," in *Government and Politics in Latin America*, ed. Peter G. Snow (New York: Holt, Rinehart and Winston, 1967).

83. Russell H. Fitzgibbon and H. Max Healey, "The Cuban Elections of 1936," *American Political Science Review* 30, no. 4 (August 1936):724–735.

84. Computed from Mario Riera Hernández, *Cuba libre, 1895–1958* (Miami: Colonial Press, 1968), pp. 157–160.

85. Gustavo Gutiérrez, "La convención constituyente y la Constitución de 1940," in *Historia*, ed. Guerra y Sánchez et al., 8:130–134.

86. Carlos Márquez Sterling, *Historia de Cuba* (New York: Las Americas, 1969), pp. 504–505, 508–510, 514–515; 1940 election data computed from Gellman, *Roosevelt and Batista*, p. 182.

87. See Fabio Grobart, "Una emulación de tipo especial," *Fundamentos* 2, no. 16 (November 1942):575–577 for data on class composition; "Las candidaturas senatoriales de la Coalición Socialista Democrática y la Unión Revolucionaria Comunista," *Fundamentos* 4, no. 29 (January 1944):6–8; "Carta a los afiliados del Partido Socialista Popular," *Fundamentos* 4, no. 31 (March 1944):241; "Una carta del Partido Socialista Popular a Batista," *Fundamentos* 4, no. 38 (October 1944):375–376, which includes this statement: "Today, as you [Batista] leave the Presidency, our Party wants to state that it is satisfied about the collaboration we have had and about the support we have given to your government performance . . . We want to reiterate that you can count on our affection and on our respect and appreciation toward your principles as a democratic and progressive ruler"; "Carta del Partido Socialista Popular al Dr. Grau San Martín," ibid., pp. 377–378; Fabio Grobart, "*La II Asamblea Nacional del Partido Socialista Popular*," ibid., pp. 331–332; idem, "Como se cumplen las resoluciones de la II Asamblea Nacional," ibid., no. 40 (December 1944):500–501. The computations are based on congressional data coded from Aníbal Escalante and Juan Marinello, "El trabajo de los socialistas en la última legislatura," *Fundamentos* 5, no. 41 (January 1945):8, 10–12, 15–16; "Como aprecian los socialistas el IV Congreso de la CTC," ibid., p. 48; Blas Roca, "El camino hacia la unidad nacional," ibid., no. 43 (March 1945):175–176, 183, 196–197 (here Blas Roca, the general secretary, acknowledges opposition within the party against the deal with Grau); see idem, "Fortalezcamos la vigilancia revolucionaria en nuestras filas," ibid., 3, no. 19 (March 1943) on corruption in the Party; see idem, *El triunfo popular en las elecciones* (Havana, 1946), pp. 8, 12–16, 20–21 on the 1946 elections; see also García Montes and Alonso Ávila, *Historia del partido comunista*, pp. 289–290. See also sources in n. 78.

88. William S. Stokes, "The 'Cuban Revolution' and the Presidential Elections of 1948," *Hispanic American Historical Review* 32, no. 1 (February 1951):37–79; 1944 election data computed from Gellman, *Roosevelt and Batista*, p. 213.

89. Márquez Sterling, *Historia de Cuba*, pp. 550–556.

90. Extracted from Riera, *Cuba libre*, pp. 48, 53, 59, 70, 86, 91, 94, 104, 105, 133, 137, 141–142, 150, 155–156, 160, 170, 172–174, 183, 213–214, 216; idem, *Un presidente constructivo* (Miami, 1966), p. 95; Phillips, *Cuba: Island of Paradox*, pp. 165, 181.

91. Riera, *Presidente constructivo*, p. 212.

92. Computed from Gutiérrez, "Convención," pp. 130, 134; Stokes, " 'Cuban Revolution' and Presidential Elections," p. 74; and Thomas, *Cuba: Pursuit of Freedom*, p. 774.

93. The 1939 votes are from Gutiérrez, "Convención," pp. 130, 134; 1940 votes from Roca, *Triunfo popular*, p. 13; 1944 and 1946 votes from Boris Goldenberg, "The Rise and Fall of a Party: The Cuban Communist Party (1925–1959)," *Problems of Communism* 19, no. 4 (July–August 1970):75–76; 1948 votes from Stokes, " 'Cuban Revolution' and Presidential Elections," p. 74.

94. Stokes, " 'Cuban Revolution' and Presidential Elections"; Suárez Rivas, *Crucificado*, pp. 183, 184.

95. Gustavo Amigó, "La iglesia católica en Cuba," *Revista javeriana* 28, no. 138 (September 1947); ibid., no. 140 (November 1947):170, 328; Roca, "Camino hacia la unidad nacional," p. 189.

4. THE BREAKDOWN OF THE POLITICAL SYSTEM

1. William S. Stokes, "The Cuban Parliamentary System in Action, 1940–1947," *Journal of Politics* 11, no. 2 (May 1949):356–360; Eduardo Suárez Rivas, *Un pueblo crucificado* (Miami: Service Offset Printers, 1964), pp. 209–211.

2. This argument is similar to one put forth about the United States Supreme Court by Robert Dahl in "Decision Making in a Democracy: The Role of the Supreme Court as a National Policy Maker," in *Readings in American Political Behavior*, ed. Raymond E. Wolfinger (Englewood Cliffs, N.J.: Prentice-Hall, 1966), pp. 165–181. Jonathan Casper has recently brought up to date and criticized Dahl's work in "The Supreme Court and National Policy Making," *American Political Science Review* 70, no. 1 (March 1976); this critique is based in part on aspects peculiar to the United States political system, not applicable to a study of Cuba; other features of his critique modify Dahl's judgment. Casper suggests a broader scope for Supreme Court activity within the dominant political alliance. That is, in fact, the view that seems to fit the Cuban case.

3. Carlos Márquez Sterling, *Historia de Cuba* (New York: Las Americas, 1969), pp. 478, 543–544, 567, 573; Suárez Rivas, *Pueblo crucificado*, p. 207. For a general study, see Carl Moses, "Judicial Control of the Constitutionality of Legislation in Cuba" (Ph.D. diss., University of North Carolina, 1958).

4. Nelson P. Valdés and Rolando Bonachea, "Fidel Castro y la política estudiantil de 1947 a 1952," *Aportes* no. 22 (October 1971):23–40; Luis Ortega, "Las raíces del Castrismo," in *Diez años de revolución cubana* (Río Piedras: Editorial San Juan, 1970); William S. Stokes, "National and Local Violence in Cuban Politics," *Southwestern Social Science Quarterly* 34, no. 2 (September 1953):57–64.

5. William S. Stokes, "The 'Cuban Revolution' and the Presidential Elections of 1948," *Hispanic American Historical Review* 32, no. 1 (February 1951):49–50, 52–54.

6. Grupos de Propaganda Doctrinal Ortodoxa, *Doctrina del Partido Ortodoxo* (Havana: Fernández, 1951), especially pp. 3–4.

7. Boris Goldenberg, *The Cuban Revoluton and Latin America* (New York: Praeger, 1965), p. 111. In this survey, "upper class" was defined to include large landowners, senior officials, and top professional people; "lower class," to include unskilled workers, domestic servants, and the unemployed. No data for other groups were reported.

8. Lloyd A. Free, *Attitudes of the Cuban People toward the Castro Regime* (Princeton: Institute for International Social Research, 1960), pp. 10–11.

9. Mauricio Solaún, "El fracaso de la democracia en Cuba," *Aportes* no. 13 (July 1969):59–60.

10. María de los Angeles Ayón, "El movimiento obrero en el monopolio eléctrico," in *Monopolios norteamericanos en Cuba: contribución al estudio de la penetración imperialista* (Havana: Instituto Cubano del Libro, 1973), p. 175.

11. Foreign Policy Association, Commission on Cuban Affairs, *Problems of the New Cuba* (New York: Little and Ives, 1935), pp. 212–216 (hereafter cited as FPA, *Problems*).

12. Fernando Ortiz, "Defensa cubana contra el racismo antisemita," *Revista bimestre cubana* 70 (1955); the original was published in 1939. See also Ruby Hart Phillips, *Cuba: Island of Paradox* (New York: McDowell, Obolensky, 1959), p. 192; Dennison Nash and Louis C. Schaw, "Personality and Adaptation in an Overseas Enclave," *Human Organization* 21, no. 4 (Winter 1962–63): 253–255; Dennison Nash and Louis C. Schaw, "Achievement and Acculturation: A Japanese Example," in *Context and Meaning in Cultural Anthropology*, ed. Melford E. Spiro (New York: Free Press, 1965).

13. Ramón Grau San Martín, *La revolución cubana ante América* (Mexico: Imprenta Manuel León Sánchez, 1936), pp. 25–26, 82–84, 101, 105–106.

14. Grupos de Propaganda Doctrinal Ortodoxa, *Doctrina*, especially pp. 13, 45.

15. Blas Roca, "Algunos problemas de las relaciones cubano-americanas en la postguerra," *Fundamentos* 5, no. 44 (April 1945): 263, 269–273; idem, "Dos cartas," ibid., pp. 357–358. See also Samuel Farber, "Revolution and Social Structure in Cuba, 1933–1959" (Ph.D. diss., University of California–Berkeley, 1969), p. 302.

16. Computed from all issues of *Fundamentos* from 1941 through 1945. Three separate reprints of parts of Earl Browder's book are included in his count; a four-part article by Palmiro Togliatti is counted as four separate contributions, and a three-part article by Tito, as three.

17. All references to Fidel Castro's writings before he came to power are from the superb collection assembled by Rolando Bonachea and Nelson P. Valdés, eds., *Revolutionary Struggle, 1947–1958: The Selected Works of Fidel Castro* (Cambridge, Mass.: M.I.T. Press, 1972). For this first major statement, see pp. 164–221.

18. Ibid., especially p. 269.

19. Ibid., pp. 346, 354–355, 366, 388.

20. Regino Boti and Felipe Pazos, "Algunos aspectos del desarrollo económico de Cuba," *Revista bimestre cubana* 75 (July–December 1958): 257–258, 265–268; the manifesto is reprinted in Rolando Bonachea and Nelson P. Valdés, eds. *Cuba in Revolution* (Garden City, N.Y.: Anchor Books, 1972); see especially pp. 117–131, 138–139.

21. The 1950 poll randomly sampled 2,099 people aged eighteen and over in towns with populations of more than 5,000; the 1956 poll sampled 2,149 people eighteen and over, through quota sampling according to sex and age, in thirty cities in all six provinces. The data are available from the seized documents of the Cuban Electric Company, at that time a subsidiary of American Foreign Power and Light, Inc.; they have been analyzed by East German scholars. Horst Handke and Elli Mohrmann in "Relaciones públicas de un monopolio estadounidense en América Latina," included in *Monopolios norteamericanos en Cuba: contribución al estudio de la penetración imperialista* (Havana: Instituto Cubano del Libro, 1973), pp. 223–226, 248.

22. Free, *Attitudes of the Cuban People*, pp. i, 10, 24–25.

23. For examples of generational analysis, see Miguel Angel Carbonell, "Las generaciones libertadoras: veinticinco años de independencia"; and Francisco Ichaso, "Ideas y aspiraciones de la primera generación republicana," in *Historia de la nación cubana*, ed. Ramiro Guerra y Sánchez, José M. Pérez Cabrera, Juan J. Remos, and Emeterio S. Santovenia, 10 vols. (Havana: Editorial Historia de la Nación Cubana, 1952).

24. Maurice Zeitlin, *Revolutionary Politics and the Cuban Working Class* (New York: Harper Torchbooks, 1970), chap. 9.

25. For the problems posed by generationalist interpretations, see the introduction to Bonachea and Valdés, *Revolutionary Struggle*, pp. 2 (n. 2), 9–10, 69–70 (where a vote by the Ortodoxo National Congress is oddly interpreted as a "youthful" act), 94, 99 (where Fidel Castro's generational membership is questioned).

26. For the views of the Foreign Policy Association in 1935, see FPA, *Problems*, pp. 161–216.

27. For the main example I have found of modest use in the 1950s, see the Twenty-sixth of July Movement's 1956 manifesto in Bonachea and Valdés, *Cuba in Revolution*, pp. 120–121, 127.

28. For an argument that places far more weight on nationalism, generational political analysis, and generationalism, see Edward Gonzalez, *Cuba under Castro: The Limits of Charisma* (Boston, Houghton Mifflin, 1974), pp. 19–78.

29. Andrés Suárez, *Cuba: Castroism and Communism, 1959–1966* (Cambridge, Mass.: M.I.T. Press, 1967), p. xiii; Theodore Draper, *Castro's Revolution: Myths and Realities* (New York: Praeger, 1962), pp. 3–59; James O'Connor, *The Origins of Socialism in Cuba* (Ithaca: Cornell University Press, 1970), p. 41.

30. International Labor Office, *Yearbook of Labor Statistics* (Geneva, 1959), p. 186.

31. For legislation against political strikes, see Acuerdo-Ley, no. 2, April 2, 1958, in Mariano Sánchez Roca, *Compilación ordenada y completa de la legislación cubana de 1951 a 1958* (Havana: Editorial Lex, 1960), 4:962; for a description of the strikes referred to in the text, see Ralph Lee Woodward, "Urban Labor and Communism in Cuba," *Caribbean Studies* 3, no. 3 (October 1963):30; Zeitlin, *Revolutionary Politics*, pp. 226–227; Hugh Thomas, *Cuba: The Pursuit of Freedom* (New York: Harper & Row, 1971), pp. 959, 988–990, 1030.

32. For a discussion of Castro's relations with the Communists by anti-Communist authors who tend to emphasize the pervasiveness of the Communists but nevertheless note Castro's distance from them prior to 1958, see Jorge García Montes and Antonio Alonso Ávila, *Historia del partido comunista de Cuba* (Miami: Rema Press, 1970), pp. 454–455, 478, 492, 503–504, 510, 520–521, 525–526; for voting data, see Enrique A. Baloyra, "Political Leadership in the Cuban Republic, 1944–1958" (Ph.D. diss., University of Florida–Gainesville, 1971), p. 152. Adam Przeworski found, in studying European elections, that the electoral demobilization of groups—such as occurred in Cuba in the 1950s—has a very sharp destabilizing effect on politics that constitutes a serious threat to political institutions. See his "Institutionalization of Voting Patterns, or Is Mobilization the Source of Decay?," *American Political Science Review* 69, no. 1 (March 1975), especially pp. 64–67.

33. Computed from Bonachea and Valdés, *Revolutionary Struggle*. Ted Gurr has hypothesized that a regime's coercive control varies curvilinearly with the size and

resources of its military and internal security forces and with the severity of its sanctions, control being least when size, resources, and severity are at intermediate levels. Ted Robert Gurr, *Why Men Rebel* (Princeton: Princeton University Press, 1970), pp. 239–240.

34. Thomas, *Cuba: Pursuit of Freedom*, pp. 870–875, 982–983; Márquez Sterling, *Historia de Cuba*, pp. 584–586, 625–631; Ramón Barquín, *Las luchas guerrilleras en Cuba: de la colonia a la Sierra Maestra* (Madrid: Editorial Playor, 1975), 1:154–161, and 2:500–503.

35. For a general discussion of the middle class in Cuba, see Juan F. Carvajal, "Observaciones sobre la clase media en Cuba"; Lowry Nelson, "The Social Class Structure in Cuba"; Carlos M. Raggi, "Contribución al estudio de las clases medias en Cuba," all three in *Materiales para el estudio de la clase media en América Latina: la clase media en México y Cuba*, ed. Theo R. Crevenna (Washington, D.C.: Unión Panamericana, 1950), vol. 2; Jorge Martí, "Class Attitudes in Cuban Society on the Eve of the Revolution, 1952–1958," *Specialia Interamericana* no. 3 (August 1971):28–35. For a discussion of Batista's bitterness, see Fulgencio Batista, *Respuesta* (Mexico: Imprenta Manuel León Sánchez, 1960), p. 168. See also Ramón Bonachea and Marta San Martín, *The Cuban Insurrection, 1952–1959* (New Brunswick, N.J.: Transaction Books, 1974), pp. 84–85, 103–105, 207, 263.

36. Fulgencio Batista, *Piedras y leyes* (Mexico: Ediciones Botas, 1961), pp. 406–407, 431.

37. *La jurisprudencia al día: sección de legislación* (1952):218, 222.

38. Louis A. Pérez, Jr., *Army Politics in Cuba, 1898–1958* (Pittsburgh: University of Pittsburgh Press, 1976), pp. 137–138, 145–151; Barquín, *Luchas guerrilleras*, 1:165–186; ibid., 2:468–482 (the best record of the minor conspiracies appears in 2:789–801).

39. Harold R. Aaron, "Why Batista Lost," *Army* 15, no. 14 (September 1965):64–71; Barquín, *Luchas guerrilleras*, 2:569–622.

40. For a thorough discussion of military elements of the civil war, see Barquín, *Luchas guerrilleras*, 1:291–370, 383–397, 407–431, 440–455; ibid., 2:463–467, 484–499, 509–524, 550–780, 841–870. See also Bonachea and San Martín, *Cuban Insurrection*, pp. 229–236, 240–262; Pérez, *Army Politics in Cuba*, pp. 139–143, 153–158; for a discussion of corruption within the military, see José Suárez Núñez, *El gran culpable* (Caracas, 1963), pp. 64–67, 112, 120–122, 160.

41. For a full presentation, see Bonachea and San Martín, *Cuban Insurrection*.

42. On Prío's use of money for political purposes, see ibid., pp. 66, 69, 75, 79, 124, 129, 134, 162, 186, 240, 279.

43. Batista, *Piedras*, pp. 381, 391, 441–447.

44. Raúl Cepero Bonilla, "Política azucarera, 1952–1958," in his *Obras históricas* (Havana: Instituto de Historia, 1963), pp. 310–319. See also Alfred L. Padula, Jr., "The Fall of the Bourgeoisie: Cuba, 1959–1961" (Ph.D. diss., University of New Mexico, 1974), pp. 74–109; Carlos Rafael Rodríguez, "The Cuban Revolution and the Peasantry," *World Marxist Review* 8, no. 10 (October 1965): p. 64; West Indies Sugar Corporation, *Annual Report* (1958):1; ibid. (1959):3–4; Batista, *Respuesta*, p. 168; Suárez Núñez, *Gran culpable*, p. 113.

45. Quoted in Bonachea and Valdés, *Revolutionary Struggle*, p. 185.

46. Documents from ibid., pp. 186, 190–191, 270–271.

47. Bonachea and Valdés, *Cuba in Revolution*, especially p. 132.

48. Bonachea and Valdés, *Revolutionary Struggle*, pp. 346–347, 364–371, 387–388.

49. See Loree Wilkerson, *Fidel Castro's Political Programs from Reformism to Marxism-Leninism* (Gainesville: University of Florida Press, 1965); also Grupos de Propaganda Doctrinal Ortodoxa, *Doctrina*.

50. Suárez Núñez, *Gran culpable*, pp. 94–96. See also the letters of General Francisco Tabernilla Dolz, chairman of the Joint Chiefs of Staff, accusing Batista when both were in exile, in ibid., pp. 156ff.; Pérez, *Army Politics in Cuba*, pp. 272–273; Bonachea and San Martín, *Cuban Insurrection*, p. 230.

51. From a different perspective, some Soviet scholars have reached a similar conclusion. Kiva Maidanik and Mijail Poliakov have argued that "if the Cuban revolution was not accidental, it was not inevitable either." See "El triunfo del pueblo cubano y el proceso revolucionario mundial," *America Latina* no. 1 (1974):86.

5. INTERNATIONAL INFLUENCES, SOCIETY, AND THE ECONOMY

1. For a useful statement on Cuban-Soviet military relations, see the testimony of Paul F. Wallner (Western Area Analyst, Defense Intelligence Agency), in U.S., Congress, House, Committee on Foreign Affairs, Subcommittee on Inter-American Affairs, "Soviet Activities in Cuba," *Hearings*, 92nd Cong., 2nd sess., pt. 3 (Washington, D.C.: Government Printing Office, 1972).

2. *Anuario 1972*, p. 22; *Anuario 1973*, p. 26; *Anuario 1974*, p. 26.

3. The export of the opposition depended on the willingness of the United States to accept them. The United States imported them partly for humanitarian reasons, partly because it was thought they could overthrow the revolution from abroad, partly to embarrass the Cuban government internationally, and partly because many of the exiles were easily assimilated because they had been linked by profession, business, education, and culture to the United States.

4. The Cuban government mounted an impressive political campaign to this effect through the media and mass political organizations; it even included televised interviews with many invaders. See the four volumes of *Playa Girón: derrota del imperialismo* (Havana: Ediciones R, 1962). These themes, of course, have been developed even further since that time.

5. Lloyd A. Free, *Attitudes of the Cuban People toward the Castro Regime* (Princeton: Institute for International Social Research, 1960), pp. 18, 24, 25.

6. Fidel Castro, *Discursos para la historia* (Havana: Imp. Emilio Gall, 1959), 1:50–52, 75–81.

7. See Juan and Verena Martínez Alier, *Cuba: economía y sociedad* (Paris: Ruedo Ibérico, 1972), chap. 5, especially pp. 199–200, on the Haitian-Jamaican problem; for United States protests on agrarian matters, see, for example, U.S., Department of State, *American Foreign Policy: Current Documents, 1959* (Washington, D.C.: Government Printing Office, 1963), pt. 3, pp. 342–343; and U.S., Department of State, *Bulletin, 1960* (Washington, D.C.: Government Printing Office, 1960), p. 158.

8. For evidence of labor militancy, including strikes, in 1959–1960, see Alfred L. Padula, Jr., "The Fall of the Bourgeoisie: Cuba, 1959–1961" (Ph.D. diss., University of

New Mexico, 1974), pp. 120–121, 129–130, 147–148, 194, 200–202, 206, 270–272, 347, 349, 351–352, 395.

9. For an excellent and succinct description of United States–Cuban relations at this time, see Cole Blasier, "The Elimination of United States Influence," in *Revolutionary Change in Cuba*, ed. Carmelo Mesa-Lago (Pittsburgh: University of Pittsburgh Press, 1971); see also Ambassador Philip W. Bonsal's *Cuba, Castro and the United States* (Pittsburgh: University of Pittsburgh Press, 1971); Herbert Dinerstein, *The Making of a Missile Crisis: October 1962* (Baltimore: Johns Hopkins University Press, 1976).

10. The official standing of these economic theses was underscored by their republication in the government's newspaper, *Revolución*, January 22, 1959, p. 2; ibid., January 23, 1959, p. 2.

11. F. Castro, *Discursos*, pp. 125–126; *Revolución*, March 21, 1959, p. 2.

12. Quoted in *Revolución*, April 3, 1959, p. 1.

13. William Appleman Williams, *The United States, Cuba and Castro* (New York: Monthly Review Press, 1962), pp. 91–109; others have made the same observation.

14. Quoted in *Revolución*, April 3, 1959, p. 1.

15. Fidel Castro, *El partido marxista-leninista* (Buenos Aires: Ediciones La Rosa Blindada, 1965), p. 114.

16. See, for example, Howard F. Cline, *The United States and Mexico* (New York: Atheneum, 1965); Richard W. Patch, "Bolivia: U.S. Assistance in a Revolutionary Setting," in *Social Change in Latin America Today*, ed. Richard Adams et al. (New York: Vintage Books, 1960).

17. Dwight D. Eisenhower, *Waging Peace* (Garden City, N.Y.: Doubleday, 1965), p. 524; for Guevara's first contacts with the Soviet Union on behalf of the Cuban government, see *Revolución*, June 30, 1959, p. 10; ibid., September 8, 1959, p. 18.

18. See O'Connor's perceptive comments in *The Origins of Socialism in Cuba* (Ithaca: Cornell University Press, 1970), p. 166.

19. See also Maryanna Craig Boynton, "Effects of Embargo and Boycott: The Cuban Case" (Ph.D. diss., University of California–Riverside, 1972), pp. 123–124, 149–150.

20. For some Cuban statistical studies on these issues, see Raul León, "La planificación del comercio exterior," *Cuba socialista* no. 28 (December 1963), especially p. 3; Juan M. Castiñeiras, "La industria ligera en la etapa actual," *Cuba socialista* no. 34 (June 1964), especially p. 4; Ramón Guillén, "Plan de automatización de la industria azucarera de Cuba," *Cuba azúcar* (April–June 1969), especially pp. 7–9. See also Edward Boorstein, *The Economic Transformation of Cuba* (New York: Monthly Review Press, 1968), pp. 54–61, 64.

21. U.S., Congress, Senate, Select Committee to Study Governmental Operations with Respect to Intelligence Activities, *Alleged Assassination Plots Involving Foreign Leaders: An Interim Report*, 94th Cong., 1st sess. (Washington, D.C.: Government Printing Office, 1975), pp. 71–90.

22. In December of 1972, it stood at 9.15 cents per pound (when the Soviet-Cuban agreement to pay about 11 was signed). In the second week of February 1974, the price in the New York Exchange was 18.5 cents. It rose to a high of about 65 cents per pound in late November 1974, but it then fell quickly again to a level of about 40 cents per pound by the end of 1974 (or twice the revised Soviet price of late summer

1974). International Sugar Organization, *Sugar Yearbook, 1972* (The Hague: N.J. Drukkerij's-Gravenhage, 1972), pp. 364–365 (hereafter cited as *Sugar*); *New York Times*, February 11, 1974, pp. 53, 55; ibid., November 29, 1974, p. 64; ibid., December 17, 1974, p. 59.

23. *Sugar 1972*, pp. 364–365; *New York Times*, October 8, 1976, p. 8; and Omer Mont'Alegre, "Das alternativas de 1974 as perspectivas de 1975," *Brasil açucareiro* 85, no. 3 (March 1975):30.

24. *Granma Weekly Review*, December 28, 1975, pp. 5, 8.

25. For somewhat contrasting interpretations, see George J. Boughton, "Soviet-Cuban Relations, 1956–1960," *Journal of Inter-American Studies and World Affairs* 16, no. 4 (November 1974):436–453; Edward Gonzalez, "Castro's Revolution, Cuban Communist Appeals and the Soviet Response," *World Politics* 21, no. 1 (October 1968):39–68.

26. *Revolución*, July 21, 1960, p. 1.

27. Raúl Castro, "Graduación del III curso de la escuela básica superior 'General Máximo Gómez,' " *Ediciones al orientador revolucionario* no. 17 (1967): 21; *Granma Weekly Review*, January 4, 1976, pp. 10–11.

28. Quoted in *Revolución*, July 21, 1960, p. 1.

29. For 1959, Cuban Economic Research Project, *A Study on Cuba* (Coral Gables, Fla.: University of Miami Press, 1965), p. 708 (hereafter cited as CERP, *Study*); for 1961–1971, *Boletín 1971*, pp. 216–221; for 1972, *Anuario 1972*, pp. 194–197; for 1973, *Granma Weekly Review*, January 6, 1974, p. 2.

30. The main source for these computations is Leon Goure and Julian Weinkle, "Soviet-Cuban Relations: The Growing Integration," in *Castro, Cuba and Revolution*, ed. Jaime Suchlicki (Coral Gables, Fla.: University of Miami Press, 1972), p. 170, for volume of sugar imported by the Soviet Union until 1970, Soviet price for sugar, and world price until 1965 (which Goure and Weinkle take from *Sugar 1969*); world prices for 1966 and thereafter are taken from *Sugar 1972*, p. 364; 1971 sugar-volume data from Gerald B. Hagelberg, *The Caribbean Sugar Industries: Constraints and Opportunities* (New Haven: Yale University, Antilles Research Program, 1974), p. 116. There is consensus even among scholars with differing ideologies on the size of the subsidy for 1960–1967, the period for which comparable data are available. Anatolii Bekarevich estimates the Soviet sugar subsidy for those years at $730.1 million; Goure and Weinkle estimate it at $736.0 million, a difference of less than one percent. See Anatolii Bekarevich, *Cuba* (Moscow: Nauka, 1970), p. 213; Goure and Weinkle, "Soviet-Cuban Relations," p. 170.

31. Fidel Castro, "¡Un pueblo así es un pueblo invencible!" *Cuba socialista* no. 16 (December 1962); *Granma Weekly Review*, August 25, 1968, pp. 2–3; ibid., May 3, 1970, p. 3; ibid., August 6, 1972, p. 4.

32. Eric N. Baklanoff has summarized most of the available information on aid in the form of credits to the end of the 1960s. See "International Economic Relations," in *Revolutionary Change in Cuba*, ed. Carmelo Mesa-Lago, p. 268.

33. For example, by the mid-1960s, the German Democratic Republic sold textile, cement, and thermoelectric plants. Czechoslovakia sold four factories to produce screws, nuts, and washers, a motor and diesel compressor factory, and cement and shoe factories. Poland sold an electric-arch steel factory. Bulgaria sold a feldspar processing plant. A Yugoslav credit for $10 million had not yet been used by the fall of 1965 (and

hence was not included in this list). The Soviet Union sold a repair-piece factory for sugar mills and mining enterprises, a fishing port with a floating dock, two electric plants, a car-repair plant, a ship-repair plant, and a fertilizer plant; it also sold equipment to enlarge Cuba's largest steel mill. In addition, the Soviet Union donated a hospital, a prefabricated-housing plant, a plant for repairing communications equipment, and a quartz-crystal processing plant, as well as automation and electronics equipment. Most Soviet aid, however, was in credits, not donations. For the East European countries, see *Cuban Economic News* 1, no. 1 (July 1965):3, 5; ibid., nos. 2–3 (August–September 1965):3–4, 6; ibid., no. 4 (October 1965):5; ibid., no. 5 (November 1965):2, 4; ibid., no. 9 (March 1966); ibid., no. 11 (May 1966):5; ibid., no. 12 (June 1966):5; for the Soviet Union, *Cuban Economic News* 1, no. 5 (November 1965):10; ibid., no. 6 (December 1965):3, 9; ibid., 2, no. 16 (October 1966):1.

34. In 1971, for the first time, the capitalist countries (the United Kingdom, Spain, and Japan, in particular) began to rely on this method of exporting to Cuba.

35. Yuri Gavrikov, "América Latina y los paises del CAME: algunos problemas de la colaboración," *Panorama latinoamericano* (Novosti) no. 150 (July 1, 1972):5–6; idem, "URSS-Cuba: colaboración y solidaridad," ibid., no. 163 (February 15, 1973):3–5; Boris Gorbachev, "Cuba: algunas cuestiones de su integración económica con los paises del socialismo," ibid., no. 171 (August 1, 1973):3; Boris Gvozdariov, "URSS-Cuba: unidad de criterios y posiciones," ibid., no. 184 (April 1, 1974):6; O. Darusenkov, "Cuba Builds Socialism," *International Affairs* no. 11 (November 1975):21; "Science and Education in Cuba," *International Affairs* no. 1 (January 1976):154; *Los Angeles Times*, May 21, 1975, p. 15.

36. See D. Bruce Jackson, *Castro, the Kremlin, and Communism in Latin America* (Baltimore: Johns Hopkins University Press, 1969).

37. For an earlier assessment, see Jorge I. Domínguez, "Taming the Cuban Shrew," *Foreign Policy* no. 10 (Spring 1973):94–116.

38. *Granma Weekly Review*, January 14, 1973, p. 2.

39. Cuban foreign-trade statistics do not provide complete coverage of every country, making it difficult to establish dimensions clearly; thus aggregates often differ. The CIA's estimates of the Cuban trade surplus with non-Communist countries (converted into pesos) are 74.4 million for 1972 and 20.7 million for 1973; Cuba, in fact, had a deficit with these countries in 1973. Computed from Central Intelligence Agency, *Cuba: Foreign Trade* (Washington, D.C., 1975), p. 5 (hereafter cited as CIA, *Cuba*).

40. Computed from *Anuario 1973*, pp. 188–191, *Anuario 1974*, pp. 186–189.

41. Before these new lines of credit opened up, the principal sources of non-Communist foreign aid to Cuba were the international intergovernmental organizations and the Scandinavian countries. In 1972 the United Nations Development Program (UNDP) approved the establishment of a center for research into the industrial uses of bagasse in Cuba, with the UNDP contributing $3 million; the Food and Agriculture Organization approved a grant of $1 million in 1972–1974 for fishing research and development in Cuba; the United Nations Children's Fund (UNICEF) signed an agreement with Cuba for the construction of central kitchens in day-care centers, financed by Finland in an undetermined amount; and Sweden began a foreign-aid program to Cuba in 1972, starting with $5 million. See *Cuba Economic News* 8, no. 56 (1972):1; Raúl Lazo, "El centro de investigaciones pesqueras," *Bohemia* 67, no. 4 (October 3, 1975):37; *Granma Weekly Review*, December 22, 1975, p. 5; ibid., July 6, 1975, p. 3.

42. Compiled from U.S., Department of Commerce, "United States Commercial Relations with Cuba: A Survey," in U.S., Congress, House, Committee on International Relations, Subcommittees on International Trade and Commerce and International Organizations, "U.S. Trade Embargo of Cuba," *Hearings*, 94th Cong., 2nd sess. (Washington, D.C.: Government Printing Office, 1976), p. 602 (hereafter cited as U.S., Department of Commerce, "Commercial Relations with Cuba"); and CIA, *Cuba*, p. 16. On the Eurodollar market, see Clyde H. Farnsworth, "The Communists' Soaring Debt," *New York Times*, June 6, 1976, sec. 3, p. 5.

43. *Bohemia* 68, no. 11 (March 12, 1976):49; *Granma Weekly Review*, August 31, 1975, p. 4.

44. *Granma Weekly Review*, July 6, 1975, p. 3.

45. Farnsworth, "The Communists' Debt," p. 5; Frank Mankiewicz and Kirby Jones, *With Fidel* (Chicago: Playboy Press, 1975), p. 204.

46. Goure and Weinkle, "Soviet-Cuban Relations," p. 166.

47. Computations for table 5.4 are based on 98.4 to 98.7 percent of exports (17 to 20 products) and 59.0 to 63.2 percent of imports (109 to 114 products) for each year; over 90 percent of exports to the Soviet Union (7 to 10 products) and 54.7 to 62.7 percent of Soviet imports (36 to 38 products) are included.

48. Far more specific data would be needed to compare products similar in quality and equally available to Cuba from the Soviet and the capitalist markets. Far longer time series for each of many products are also necessary to assess the long-term utility to Cuba of the Soviet trade in comparison with other feasible marketing strategies.

49. A time lag is necessary because CMEA prices are set for a period of years relying on capitalist market prices; thus CMEA prices in year x must be compared to capitalist market prices in year $y - x$, where y may be as many as five years earlier than x. Differences in transportation costs can well account for the statistical difference in reports by Hewett for CMEA and by the Cuban National Bank. Edward A. Hewett, *Foreign Trade Prices in the Council for Mutual Economic Assistance* (London: Cambridge University Press, 1974), pp. 43–45, 58, 178–179.

50. Soviet sugar-volume imports, 1960–1970, Soviet sugar prices and world prices until 1965, computed from Goure and Weinkle, "Soviet-Cuban Relations," pp. 166, 170; world prices, 1966–1971, from *Sugar 1972*, p. 364; 1971 sugar-volume data from Hagelberg, *Caribbean Sugar Industries*, p. 116 (1 metric ton = 2204.6 pounds). For information tending to corroborate the study cited but unidentified by Goure and Weinkle, see *Cuban Economic News* 2, no. 11 (May 1966):7; Economist Intelligence Unit, *Quarterly Economic Review: Cuba, Dominican Republic, Haiti and Puerto Rico* no. 1 (1966):6.

51. For world and Soviet sugar prices, see *Sugar 1972*, pp. 364–365; *New York Times*, daily reports on sugar prices; see also *Latin America* 8, no. 35 (September 6, 1974):279; U.S., Department of Commerce, "Commercial Relations with Cuba," p. 628. For the 1976–1980 Soviet-Cuban agreements, see Carlos Rafael Rodríguez, "Los logros de la economía cubana," *Economía y desarrollo* no. 25 (September–October 1974):160; *Granma Weekly Review*, March 14, 1976, p. 5.

52. On petroleum prices, see *Newsweek*, January 6, 1975, p. 9; U.S., Department of Commerce, "Commercial Relations with Cuba," p. 597; *New York Times*, January, 26, 1975, sec. 3, p. 57; ibid., March 2, 1975, sec. 3, p. 25; *Granma*, September 30,

1974, p. 2; "CMEA and Raw Materials Prices," *World Marxist Review* 18, no. 5 (May 1975):139.

53. On Soviet economic benefits from its Cuban ties, see Gorbachev, "Cuba: algunas cuestiones," pp. 10–11; Anatolii Bekarevich, "Principios de colaboración entre Cuba y la URSS," *Panorama latinoamericano* (Novosti) no. 98 (May 25, 1970):3, 6, 8; Ivan Petushko, "Desarrollo integral de la industria azucarera de Cuba," *América Latina* no. 1 (1975):44.

54. Boynton, "Effects of Embargo," p. 123.

55. Andrés Suárez, *Cuba: Castroism and Communism, 1959–1966* (Cambridge, Mass.: M.I.T. Press, 1967), pp. 137–142, 178–185, 196–197, 225–226.

56. Boris Gorbachev, "Cuba: la revolución y la economía," *Panorama latinoamericano* (Novosti) no. 185 (April 15, 1974):6.

57. *Granma Weekly Review*, September 12, 1971, p. 7; ibid., September 19, 1971, p. 3; ibid., July 23, 1972, p. 10; Carlos Rafael Rodríguez, "The Advantages of Socialism Are the Basis of Our Achievements," *New Times* no. 1 (January 1974):13. For Suárez's work, see "Soviet Influence and Cuban Factions," in *Soviet and Chinese Influence in the Third World*, ed. Alvin Z. Rubinstein (New York: Praeger, 1975); "How the Cuban Regime Works" (Paper delivered at South East Conference on Latin American Studies, Chapel Hill, N.C., April 1972); "The Politics of Cuba under Castro: How Socialist Is Cuba?" (Paper delivered at annual meeting, American Political Science Association, New Orleans, La., September 1973); "La construcción del socialismo en Cuba: el papel del partido" (Paper presented at Seminar on Institutionalization in Cuba, Institute of Cuban Studies, Caracas, March 24–29, 1975).

58. Brian Crozier, "Soviet Pressures in the Caribbean: The Satellisation of Cuba," *Conflict Studies* no. 35 (May 1973), summarizes evidence from the defectors from Cuban intelligence agencies.

59. The most succinct presentation of the Cuban view, with considerable evidence, is "Respuesta del comandante Fidel Castro, primer secretario del Partido Comunista de Cuba y primer ministro del Gobierno Revolucionario, a las declaraciones del Gobierno chino," *Política internacional* 4, no. 13 (First Quarter 1966).

60. Although the Cuban government partly blamed high international rice prices for the rice-ration reductions, those prices had actually fallen by 36 percent during the twelve months preceding new rationing measures. The average international rice price in the first quarter of 1976 (FOB Bangkok; white 5 percent brokens) was less than half the 1974 average. I am grateful to Linda A. Bernstein (Foreign Demand and Competition Division, Economic Research Service, United States Department of Agriculture) for the information on international rice prices.

61. *Granma Weekly Review*, March 14, 1971, p. 1; ibid., January 4, 1976, p. 11; *Granma*, January 27, 1976, p. 1; ibid., January 30, 1976; p. 1; ibid., April 26, 1976, p. 6; ibid., June 11, 1976, p. 1.

62. For the important documents on the microfaction, see "Informe del comandante Raúl Castro al Comité Central del Partido Comunista de Cuba," *Verde olivo* 9, no. 5 (February 4, 1968), supplement; and its conclusion in ibid., 9, no. 6 (February 11, 1968); in the latter issue, see also "Intervención del compañero Carlos Rafael Rodríguez en la reunión del Comité Central" and "Informe del Fiscal en el juicio seguido a Aníbal Escalante y 36 acusados más."

63. *Granma Weekly Review*, January 7, 1968, pp. 2–3; Osvaldo Dorticós, "Análisis y perspectivas del desarrollo de la economía cubana," *Economía y desarrollo* no. 12 (July–August 1972):51.

64. *Current Digest of the Soviet Press* 19, no. 50:15–16; ibid., 20, no. 5:18; *Granma Weekly Review*, January 7, 1968, pp. 2–3.

65. *Boletín 1971*, pp. 250–251; *Anuario 1972*, pp. 222–223; *Anuario 1974*, pp. 216–217.

66. Many other foreign-policy shifts occurred, but none relevant to my subject. In a detailed chronology of events of the Cuban revolution and of Cuban-Soviet relations by leading Soviet scholars of Cuba from 1960 through 1972, there are several entries for each year, except for 1968 which is omitted completely. Anatolii D. Bekarevich and N. M. Kukharev, *The Soviet Union and Cuba* (Moscow: Nauka, 1973), p. 286.

67. For discussions of the literacy campaign in 1961, see Richard Jolly, "Education: The Pre-Revolutionary Background," in *Cuba: The Economic and Social Revolution*, ed. Dudley Seers (Chapel Hill: University of North Carolina Press, 1964); and Richard R. Fagen, *The Transformation of Political Culture in Cuba* (Stanford: Stanford University Press, 1969).

68. Michel Huteau and Jacques Lautrey, *L'éducation à Cuba* (Paris: Maspero, 1973), p. 27.

69. This count is based on the highest possible enrollments in primary and general secondary schools, both public and private, for the prerevolutionary period. It controls for the effects of both population growth and socialization of the primary and general secondary schools. Figures for the technical secondary and university levels include only public schools. Sources for the computations are *Anuario 1973*, p. 22, for population data as of June 30 preceding the opening of classes in September; tables 5.8, 5.9, and 5.10 for initial enrollment data for 1964–65 and 1970–71 in all categories and for 1958–59 in technical schools and universities; Mercedes García Tudurí, "Resumen de la historia de la educación en Cuba," *Exilio* 3, nos. 3–4, and 4, no. 1 (Winter 1969–Spring 1970):115–116, for primary-school enrollment in 1958. I have followed a suggestion in Carmelo Mesa-Lago, "Availability and Reliability of Statistics in Socialist Cuba," *Latin American Research Review* 4, no. 2 (Spring 1969):72, in adding 30 percent to the general secondary-school enrollment figures for 1958–59, taken from table 5.9. For a discussion of the impact of the pattern of Cuban population growth on school enrollments, see Lisandro Pérez, "The Demographic Dimensions of the Educational Problem in Socialist Cuba," *Cuban Studies* 7, no. 1 (January 1977):33–57.

70. On sixth-grade adult-education graduates, see Azucena Plasencia, "Montaña adentro: la batalla del sexto grado," *Bohemia* 67, no. 10 (March 7, 1975):35.

71. Nelson Amaro, *La revolución cubana . . . ¿por qué?* (Guatemala City: Talleres Gráficos Rosales, 1967), p. 66; computed from "Communist Party of Cuba," *World Marxist Review* 17, no. 3 (March 1974), p. 139.

72. Computed from Donald R. Dyer, "Urbanism in Cuba," *Geographical Review* 47, no. 2 (April 1957):224–233; "Cuba económica," *Economía y desarrollo* no. 25 (September–October, 1974):211; *1970 Census*, pp. 12, 15.

73. *Granma Weekly Review*, September 14, 1975, p. 3.

74. Ibid., April 17, 1972, p. 5; ibid., April 14, 1974, p. 3; ibid., December 15, 1974, p. 2.

75. Lowry Nelson, *Cuba: The Measure of a Revolution* (Minneapolis: University of Minnesota Press, 1972), p. 141; Samuel Bowles, "Cuban Education and the Revolutionary Ideology," *Harvard Educational Review* 41, no. 4 (November 1971):495.

76. *Granma Weekly Review*, April 16, 1972, p. 5; ibid., December 15, 1974, p. 2; ibid., September 14, 1975, p. 2; "Perfeccionamiento del sistema nacional de educación," *Bohemia* 67, no. 5 (January 31, 1975): 31; *Granma*, February 6, 1975, p. 3; Comité Central del Partido Comunista de Cuba, Departamento de Orientación Revolucionaria, *Política educacional* (Havana: Instituto Cubano del Libro, 1976), pp. 17–18.

77. Louis Jones, "Investigación del aprovechamiento escolar en la educación primaria en el curso de 1961–62," *Psicología y educación* 1, no. 1 (January–May 1964):10, 13–15, 19–20.

78. Departamento de Orientación Revolucionaria, *Política educacional*, pp. 18–19; *Granma*, September 3, 1976, p. 2.

79. For two good discussions, see Carmelo Mesa-Lago, "Economic Policies and Growth," in *Revolutionary Change in Cuba*, ed. Carmelo Mesa-Lago; and Archibald R. M. Ritter, *The Economic Development of Revolutionary Cuba: Strategy and Performance* (New York: Praeger, 1974).

80. Felipe Pazos, "Comentarios a dos artículos sobre la revolución cubana," *El trimestre económico* 29, no. 113 (January–March 1962):3–11.

81. Data from Jorge Rodríguez Beruff, "La reforma agraria cubana (1959–1964): el cambio institucional," *Revista de ciencias sociales* 14, no. 2 (June 1970):218; on voluntary sales and donations under land reform, see Padula, "Fall of the Bourgeoisie," pp. 144–145.

82. Pazos, "Comentarios," pp. 8–9, and Martínez-Alier, *Cuba*.

83. For a sympathetic account by a participant, see Boorstein, *Economic Transformation*.

84. For a discussion of the 1970 sugar harvest and its effects, see Sergio Roca, "Cuban Economic Policy and Ideology: The Ten Million Ton Sugar Harvest," *Sage Professional Papers in International Studies* 4, no. 02-044 (1976):5–70.

85. Although the variation in the availability of industrial data in Cuban statistical yearbooks through 1971 was minor and trivial (under 7 percent for any given year), the same is not true, for example, for the 1972 and 1973 yearbooks. The number of products for which data are unavailable is 15 for 1964–1966, 9 for 1966–1968, 7 for 1968–1970, 7 for 1970–71, and 103 for 1971–1972. The steady improvement in statistical coverage and quality for industrial statistics evident in the 1971 yearbook was reversed in the 1972 publication, which omitted data on 78 previously reported industrial products, and the 1973 publication, which left out information for 86 industrial products (respectively 30 percent and 33 percent of the known and existing lines in industry). Therefore the number of products that declined in 1972 and 1973 (in table 5.16) and the number of worst-production items for 1972 and 1973 (table 5.13) may be far larger than recorded.

86. *Granma Weekly Review*, November 25, 1973, p. 9; Oneida Alvarez, "Revolutionary Cuba's Economic Development," *World Marxist Review* 17, no. 11 (November 1974):97; Rodríguez, "Los logros de la economía cubana," p. 156.

87. *Granma*, May 1, 1976, p. 2.

88. Eugenio Rodríguez Balari, "Trabajo y desarrollo del Instituto de la Demanda Interna," *Economía y desarrollo* no. 21 (January–February, 1974):158, 161; *Granma*, July 21, 1977, p. 4.

89. Estimates of the Cuban gross national product by the U.S. Arms Control and Disarmament Agency, whose methodology for the computations on Cuba is vague, appear to be inaccurate. The trends for the 1960s are incompatible with those reported in table 5.15, and the data in that table must be preferred to unexplained estimates; they are the Cuban government's unflattering best estimates. If the agency is probably wrong for the 1960s, then it is also probably wrong for the early 1970s, when it records an 8.4-percent decline in gross national product in constant prices for 1970–1972. Cuba's real gross product probably grew far less than the statistics quoted in the text suggest at first blush, but it is unlikely that the rate in per capita constant prices was negative. See U.S., Arms Control and Disarmament Agency, *World Military Expenditures and Arms Trade, 1963–1973* (Washington, D.C.: Government Printing Office, 1974), pp. 7, 10, 28.

90. At the end of 1971, production for light industry, apparently in current prices, was just above the level of 1967, its best year for the late 1960s. Basic industrial production at the end of 1971 was 11 percent over 1967, also its best year for the late 1960s. Light and basic industrial production grew again in 1972 and 1973. The food industry also grew every year from 1970 to 1974 (in current prices), but its annual rate of increase fell from 7 percent in 1970–1972 to 4 percent in 1974. These records can be compared only with the second half of the 1960s, when the respective ministries were created. Basic industry, with the largest growth rates, accounted for the smaller share of the industrial structure. Some of its achievement prior to 1973, however, is brought into question, for it was only then that the government reported that aggregate physical production reached a new record in basic industry, while the record value of the production had already been reported in 1971. The Ministry of Mining and Metallurgy reported little growth in 1971 and 1973. In sum, Cuban industrial production, apparently in current prices, recovered in 1971. Because of price inflation, a record aggregate physical-production level may have been reached only in 1973. The rate of increase of industrial production fell from 12 percent in 1973 to 8 percent in 1974. *Granma Weekly Review*, January 30, 1972, pp. 8, 10; ibid., January 21, 1973, pp. 7–8; ibid., April 8, 1973, p. 9; ibid., January 6, 1974; "Cuba económica," *Economía y desarrollo* no. 10 (March–April 1972):177; ibid., no. 22 (March–April, 1974):191, 197–198; Dorticós, "Análisis," pp. 28–61; *Granma*, January 25, 1975, p. 5; "Cuba económica," *Economía y desarrollo* no. 34 (March–April 1976):183 (hereafter cited as "Cuba economica 1976").

91. Computed from "Evolución del producto social global," *Economía y desarrollo* no. 32 (November–December 1975):193; for an announcement of the recession by Fidel Castro, see *Granma*, September 30, 1976, p. 2.

92. *Granma Weekly Review*, January 13, 1974, p. 2.

93. *Finance and Development* 10, no. 1 (March 1973):26–27; for a comparison of 1973 with 1957, see Central Intelligence Agency, *The Cuban Economy: A Statistical Review* (Washington, D.C.: Library of Congress, 1976), p. 2.

94. Computed from Cuban Economic Research Project, *Labor Conditions in Communist Cuba* (Coral Gables, Fla.: University of Miami Press, 1963), p. 71.

95. International Labor Office, *Yearbook of Labor Statistics, 1959* (Geneva, 1959), p. 186; computed from O'Connor, *Socialism in Cuba*, p. 333.

96. Free, *Attitudes of the Cuban People*, pp. 22–23.

97. Computed from *Anuario 1972*, p. 39; *Anuario 1973*, p. 40; *Anuario 1974*, p. 40; "Cuba económica 1976," p. 179.

98. Computed from Carmelo Mesa-Lago, "The Labor Force, Employment, Unemployment and Underemployment in Cuba: 1899–1970," *Sage Professional Papers in International Studies* 1, no. 9 (1972):40. See also José Gutiérrez Muñiz, "Conferencia mundial de población: opiniones de Cuba," *Economía y desarrollo* no. 29 (May–June 1975):178.

99. *Granma Weekly Review*, November 25, 1973, p. 8.

100. Ibid., p. 9; Dorticós, "Análisis," p. 52; *Granma*, February 6, 1975, p. 2. In 1970, 13 percent of a labor force of 721 persons in Valle del Perú in the San José de las Lajas region of Havana province was unemployed. The labor force is defined to include both employed and unemployed workers but excludes housewives and others working at home, students, the physically handicapped, people under age seventeen, men over sixty, and women over fifty-five, except for those who have chosen to enter the labor force. Computed from Oscar Mazorra and Mario Montero, "Estudio demografico de 'Valle del Perú,' " *Economía y desarrollo* no. 6 (April–June 1971):136.

101. *Granma Weekly Review*, March 28, 1971, p. 1; ibid., May 16, 1971, p. 2.

102. For fifty countries in the late 1950s, the Pearson product-moment correlation between gross national product per capita in constant prices and the infant-mortality rate was $r = -.76$, which explains 58 percent of the variance. See Bruce Russett, Hayward R. Alker, Jr., Karl W. Deutsch, and Harold D. Lasswell, *World Handbook of Political and Social Indicators* (New Haven: Yale University Press, 1964), p. 277.

103. Carmelo Mesa-Lago, *Cuba in the 1970s* (Albuquerque: University of New Mexico Press, 1974), pp. 38–42.

104. Maruja Acosta and Jorge Hardoy, *Urban Reform in Revolutionary Cuba* (New Haven: Yale University, Antilles Research Program, 1973), pp. 55, 61–66.

105. CERP, *Study*, p. 434.

106. Computed from ibid., p. 433.

107. In the early 1960s, Cuban government officials estimated that only 10,020 dwellings, on the average, were constructed annually between 1945 and 1958. Carmelo Mesa-Lago has shown that their estimates of housing construction in 1959–60 are in gross error; the accuracy of their estimates for the prerevolutionary period is thus in doubt as well. See Mesa-Lago, "Availability of Statistics," pp. 69–72.

108. Sources are CERP, *Study*, pp. 432–436; Acosta and Hardoy, *Urban Reform*, pp. 46–47; Mesa-Lago, "Availability of Statistics," pp. 69–72. For agricultural workers' housing, see Francisco Dorta Duque, *Justificando una reforma agraria* (Madrid: Raycar, S. A., 1960), p. 40.

109. This is a maximum estimate. Because many of these buildings were turned to uses other than housing the population, the number of housing units made available by the emigration was probably lower.

110. Acosta and Hardoy, *Urban Reform*, p. 60; *1970 Census*, pp. 1, 12; *Anuario 1972*, p. 22; *Anuario 1973*, p. 26; *Anuario 1974*, p. 26.

111. *Anuario 1972*, pp. 22, 160; *Anuario 1974*, p. 26.

112. *Granma Weekly Review,* May 28, 1967, p. 9.

113. *Anuario 1972,* pp. 22, 160; *Anuario 1974,* p. 26. The housing shortage was just as severe in the rural as in the urban areas in the late 1960s. See Michael A. Pettitt, "Social and Economic Change in the Community around a Sugar Mill in Cuba" (Ph.D. diss., University of California–Berkeley, 1973), pp. 307–308.

114. Acosta and Hardoy estimate housing demand at 40,000, using the 1953 national-average occupancy rate of 4.8, whereas the national-average occupancy rate was 4.5 in 1970. Thus the new demand was closer to 37,500. See Acosta and Hardoy, *Urban Reform,* p. 51; *1970 Census,* pp. 1, 12. The Acosta-Hardoy estimate of the annual production of housing units in the late 1960s is also too high. For a description of the physical deterioration of the city of Havana, including its housing stock, see Jean-Pierre Garner, *Une ville, une révolution: La Havane* (Paris: Editions Anthropos, 1973), pp. 123, 290. For a discussion of the relationship between policies to control internal migrations and housing policies, see Jean Marieu, "Quelques données récentes sur la population cubaine," *Cahiers d'outre-mer* 27, no. 106 (April–June 1974):165.

115. Computed from Jorge Hernández et al., "Estudio sobre el divorcio," *Humanidades,* ser. 1 (Ciencias Sociales), no. 3 (January 1973):42; *Anuario 1972,* p. 160; *Anuario 1973,* p. 50; *Anuario 1974,* pp. 26, 148; *Granma Weekly Review,* August 4, 1974, p. 5; ibid., December 28, 1975, p. 6; Comisión Nacional Cubana de la UNESCO, *Boletín* 12, no. 46 (July–August, 1973):35; *Granma,* February 25, 1975, p. 1; ibid., April 26, 1975, p. 1.

6. ESTABLISHING A NEW GOVERNMENT

1. For discussions of the changes in Cuban politics during the first three years of revolutionary rule, see Andrés Suárez, *Cuba: Castroism and Communism, 1959–1966* (Cambridge, Mass.: M.I.T. Press, 1967); James O'Connor, *The Origins of Socialism in Cuba* (Ithaca: Cornell University Press, 1970); Alfred L. Padula, Jr., "The Fall of the Bourgeoisie: Cuba, 1959–1961" (Ph.D. diss., University of New Mexico, 1974); Hugh Thomas, *Cuba: The Pursuit of Freedom* (New York: Harper & Row, 1971), book 11; Maurice Halperin, *The Rise and Decline of Fidel Castro* (Berkeley and Los Angeles: University of California Press, 1972); Wyatt MacGaffey and Clifford Barnett, *Twentieth-Century Cuba* (Garden City, N.Y.: Anchor Books, 1965), pp. 294–401; and Theodore Draper's two books, *Castro's Revolution: Myths and Realities* (New York: Praeger, 1962), and *Castroism: Theory and Practice* (New York: Praeger, 1965).

2. For a different view, see Robin Blackburn, "Prologue to the Cuban Revolution," *New Left Review* (London), October 1963; Dennis B. Wood, "The Long Revolution: Class Relations and Political Conflict in Cuba, 1868–1968," *Science and Society* 34, no. 1 (Spring 1970):1–41.

3. Padula, "Fall of the Bourgeoisie," pp. 132–137, 143, 196–199, 227–229, 244–245, 251, 281.

4. Ibid., pp. 148, 155, 199, 209, 251–253.

5. Ibid., pp. 50, 52, 116, 179–180, 183–190, 193, 211–212, 237–239, 243–244, 254, 265, 286, 310–311, 446–454, 457–460, 517–520, 524–525, 527–528.

6. Computed from Rolando Bonachea, "A Briefly Annotated Bibliography of Fidel Castro's Works: 1959–1970," *Cuban Studies Newsletter* 3, no. 2 (June 1973):2–58.

7. For a discussion of this turning point by Castro himself, see Lee Lockwood, *Castro's Cuba, Cuba's Fidel* (New York: Vintage Books, 1969), p. 183.

8. See the full text in Rolando Bonachea and Nelson P. Valdés, eds., *Revolutionary Struggle, 1947–1958: The Selected Works of Fidel Castro* (Cambridge, Mass.: M.I.T. Press, 1972), vol. 1.

9. *Granma Weekly Review,* August 2, 1970, pp. 4, 6; for a general study, see Mary B. Gallagher, "The Public Address of Fidel Castro Ruz: Charismatic Leader of a Modern Revolution" (Ph.D. diss., University of Pittsburgh, 1970).

10. Lloyd A. Free, *Attitudes of the Cuban People toward the Castro Regime* (Princeton: Institute for International Social Research, 1960).

11. Gustavo Torroella, *Estudio de la juventud cubana* (Havana: Comisión Nacional Cubana de la UNESCO, 1963), foldout between pp. 130–131; André Berge, "Young People in the Orient and Occident: General Report on the Survey," *International Journal of Adult and Youth Education* 16, no. 2 (1964):67 (I am grateful to Lourdes Casal for the bibliographic reference). The survey was stratified to include students from the cities of Havana, Santa Clara, and Santiago in approximately equal numbers; it included 581 students aged sixteen to eighteen and 489 aged nineteen to twenty-three. Within each school and each age and sex category, random sampling was used; the questionnaires were administered by teachers. Choices for ordering in the other countries were limited to heroes, saints, men of science or learning, and artists.

12. For a perceptive discussion of these themes, from which I have benefited, see Richard R. Fagen, "Charismatic Authority and the Leadership of Fidel Castro," *Western Political Quarterly* 18, no. 2, pt. 1 (June 1965):275–284.

13. For a related discussion that comes to similar conclusions, see the excellent analysis in Edward Gonzalez, *Cuba under Castro: The Limits of Charisma* (Boston: Houghton Mifflin, 1974), p. 83.

14. For perhaps the most sensitive and useful interview in which Fidel Castro discusses these issues, see Lockwood, *Castro's Cuba,* chap. 4.

15. Free, *Attitudes of the Cuban People,* p. 25.

16. Quoted in *Granma Weekly Review,* August 2, 1970, p. 3.

17. *Obra revolucionaria* no. 27 (1963):17.

18. *Granma Weekly Review,* August 2, 1970, p. 3.

19. Computed from *Boletín 1970,* p. 30; United Nations Statistical Office, *Monthly Bulletin of Statistics* 22 (June 1968):176. Detailed budget statistics for the late 1960s have not been published. The 1969 estimate is from Boris Gorbachev and Arnold Kalinin, "Algunos aspectos socio-económicos y políticos de la experencia de la revolución cubana," *Panorama latinoamericano* (Novosti) no. 96 (May 4, 1970):13.

20. Computed from *Boletín 1970,* p. 30.

21. *Granma,* December 25, 1974, p. 3; *Bohemia* 67, no. 9 (February 28, 1975):82; *Granma,* March 17, 1975, p. 5; Comité Central del Partido Comunista de Cuba, Departamento de Orientación Revolucionaria, *Sobre la cuestión agraria y las relaciones con el campesinado* (Havana: Instituto Cubano del Libro, 1976), pp. 61–62.

22. Computed from *Proclamas y leyes del govierno provisional de la revolución, 1959* (Havana: Editorial Lex), 1:108–111, 3:263–270, 5:311–318, 6:311–318, 7:219–222, 8:275–283, 10:305–312, 11:301–307, 12:557–561, 13:443–448, 14:197–200, 15:401–406; ibid., *1960,* 16:261–264, 17:337–341, 18:369–371, 19:255–258, 20:303–306, 21:295–298, 22:281–282, 23:399–401, 24:329, 331, 25:273, 26:257,

27:395–398; ibid., *1961,* 28:305–306, 29:227–228, 30:167, 31:5, 32:5, 33:313–314, 34:313, 35:241–243, 36:243–245, 37:124. These figures are not strictly comparable to those in table 3.10, which included laws, and presidential and cabinet department decrees; these figures include laws only and exclude constitutional amendments, proclamations, resolutions, and presidential and all cabinet department decrees. Many of the post-1959 laws, however, would have been pre-1959 presidential decrees; thus the closest comparison would be with the combined total of laws and presidential decrees per one hundred days of table 3.10.

23. Although the laws of the revolution are normally issued in sequence, the sequence sometimes skipped a number, or a law was issued with a title but no number. Precise estimates are consequently impossible for the period after 1961. The numbers computed have not been verified against the detailed record and are based on the assumption of continuous numbering. Law number 1287 was issued on January 2, 1975 (*Granma,* January 27, 1975, p. 5). For international comparisons, see Jean Blondel, *Comparative Legislatures* (Englewood Cliffs, N.J.: Prentice-Hall, 1973), pp. 63, 156–157.

24. Frank Mankiewicz and Kirby Jones, *With Fidel* (Chicago: Playboy Press, 1975), pp. 94–97. See also Comité Central del Partido Comunista de Cuba, Departamento de Orientación Revolucionaria, *Sobre la lucha ideológica* (Havana: Instituto Cubano del Libro, 1976).

25. For the 1976 Constitution, see *Granma,* January 15, 1976, pp. 4–5. For the text of the 1940 Constitution and subsequent amendments, see Leonel Antonio de la Cuesta, *Constituciones cubanas* (New York: Ediciones Exilio, 1974).

26. *Trimestre* no. 10 (April–June 1964):67, 69; *Granma Weekly Review,* August 1. 1971, p. 3; *Granma,* September 4, 1970, p. 3; ibid., March 21, 1975, p. 3. For Fidel Castro's comments on the relative absence of geographic mobility, see Mankiewicz and Jones, *With Fidel,* pp. 106, 108.

27. Here I part company with some distinguished scholars. See Suárez, *Cuba: Castroism and Communism,* especially its foreword by Ernst Halperin; Draper, *Castro's Revolution* and *Castroism;* and Gonzalez, *Cuba under Castro.* Gonzalez is somewhat ambivalent on this point; the antiorganizational theme appears on pp. 83 and 147, but it is modified on pp. 163–167, 179, and 220–221.

28. *Revolución,* May 22, 1959; ibid., December 2, 1961.

29. *Revolución,* October 14, 1959, p. 1; ibid., October 17, 1959, p. 1; ibid., October 19, 1959, p. 2; ibid., November 23, 1959, p. 4.

30. *Revolución,* November 23, 1959, p. 4.

31. MacGaffey and Barnett, *Twentieth-Century Cuba,* chap. 15; Peter S. H. Tang and Joan Maloney, *The Chinese Communist Impact on Cuba* (Chestnut Hill, Mass.: Research Institute on the Sino-Soviet Bloc, 1962).

32. *Revolución,* January 14, 1963, p. 4; ibid., August 24, 1964, p. 5.

33. César Escalante, "Los Comités de Defensa de la Revolución," *Cuba socialista* no. 1 (September 1961).

34. Adolfo Rivero, "La Unión de Jóvenes Comunistas de Cuba," *Cuba socialista* no. 12 (August 1962).

35. Antero Regalado, "Cinco años de la vida de la ANAP," *Cuba socialista,* no. 57 (May 1966).

36. For ORI's birth, see *Revolución,* July 27, 1961. For its organization under

Escalante, see "El núcleo de revolucionarios activos y algunos aspectos de su funcionamiento," *Cuba socialista* no. 7 (March 1962); "Organización y funcionamiento de un núcleo por departamentos," ibid., no. 8 (April 1962). For Prime Minister Castro's criticism of Escalante and the party's operation up to that time, Fidel Castro, *El partido marxista-leninista* (Buenos Aires: Ediciones La Rosa Blindada, 1965), speeches of March 16 and March 26; see also Fidel Castro, "Discurso del Primer Ministro en el Comité Provincial de Matanzas," *Cuba socialista* no. 9 (May 1962).

37. "Integración del Secretariado y de Comisiones de la Dirección Nacional de las ORI," *Cuba socialista* no. 7 (March 1962); "Vida de la organización revolucionaria," ibid., no. 8 (April 1962):136–137.

38. Joel Domenech, "Experiencias del trabajo de reestructuración y depuración de las ORI en La Habana," *Cuba socialista* no. 10 (June 1962):32–33, 38.

39. Ibid.; Isidoro Malmierca, "La marcha de la construcción del Partido en La Habana," *Cuba socialista* no. 14 (October 1962):116–118; see also "La selección del trabajador ejemplar," ibid., no. 9 (May 1962); and "Changes in the Work of Party Branches in Cuba," *World Marxist Review* 5, no. 8 (August 1962):70–71. For discussions at the party-cell level, see "Dos experiencias de la reestructuración de los Núcleos Revolucionarios Activos en Marianao," *Cuba socialista* no. 12 (August 1962). For a visiting anthropologist's transcript of field tapes concerning the selection of exemplary workers in rural Matanzas, see Michael A. Pettitt, "Social and Economic Change in the Community around a Sugar Mill in Cuba" (Ph.D. diss., University of California–Berkeley, 1973), pp. 139–143.

40. These scattered data come from work centers for which public reports on workers' assemblies for exemplary-worker elections are available. All provincial party members are included, even those not elected exemplary workers. The percentage would be lower if the entire working class were used. Computed from Malmierca, "La marcha," p. 109; Raúl García Peláez, "La construcción del Partido en la provincia de Matanzas," *Cuba socialista* no. 16 (December 1962):122–123; José Fuertes Jiménez, "El trabajo organizativo en Camagüey," ibid., no. 15 (November 1962):125; "Vida de la organización revolucionaria," ibid., no. 10 (June 1962):123, 125; "El PURS en las montañas de Oriente," ibid., no. 24 (August 1963):117; José Fuertes Jiménez, "Hacia un partido más vigoroso en Camagüey," ibid., no. 34 (June 1964):132; "Balance de la construcción del PURS," ibid., no. 32 (April 1964):133.

41. Isidoro Malmierca, "La lucha por la fuerza de las filas del Partido en La Habana," *Cuba socialista* no. 26 (October 1963); *Granma Weekly Review*, December 22, 1974, p. 4.

42. Malmierca, "La marcha," p. 113; see also Lionel Soto, "Las escuelas de instrucción revolucionaria en el ciclo político-técnico," *Cuba socialista* no. 41 (January 1965):77.

43. Maurice Zeitlin, *Revolutionary Politics and the Cuban Working Class* (New York: Harper Torchbooks, 1970), pp. 44, 65, 77.

44. *Revolución*, June 20, 1959, p. 18.

45. Data on emigration (see table 5.1) have a conservative bias, since only Cubans registered with the Refugee Emergency Center are counted. Many wealthier Cubans did not need public assistance and therefore did not register. If all exiles were included, one would expect to find a larger proportion of upper-class Cubans. In addition, the pattern of the mid-1960s may result from the earlier departures that had

reduced the numbers in the upper and middle classes. Because these groups also had resources that made emigration easier (money, knowledge of English, transferable skills), the pattern of exile versus continued residence may be a consequence as much of the social structure as of the distribution of political opinions.

46. Because tuberculosis can become dormant and remain undetected, improved techniques in screening can reveal preexisting cases; the increased prevalence of tuberculosis therefore need not mean new cases but, on the contrary, may indicate improved public-health services.

47. *Boletín 1971*, pp. 304–305; *Anuario 1972*, p. 263; *Anuario 1973*, p. 263; *Anuario 1974*, pp. 266–267. Carmelo Mesa-Lago, "Availability and Reliability of Statistics in Socialist Cuba," *Latin American Research Review* 4, no. 2 (Spring 1969):70.

48. Some of the apparent worsening of public-health performance in the 1960s may in fact reflect better reporting of diseases in the rural areas. However, it is generally recognized—even by Cuban government officials—that statistical reporting in Cuba was in a very poor state in the early 1960s, so any improved reporting in the rural areas was probably canceled out by worse reporting in the urban areas. Statistical reporting improved in Cuba only in the early 1970s—and it showed declining rates. Confidence in the validity of the morbidity statistics is reinforced by the mortality statistics in table 5.18. Both infant- and general-mortality figures show increases that peaked in 1962. The overall mortality rate then declined a bit, but it remained above the prerevolutionary level for the entire decade (except for 1967). Improvement in the treatment of some diseases was canceled out by the neglect of others. The infant-mortality rate continued to rise in the 1960s. Because the morbidity and mortality trends are related, statistical error does not adequately explain the changes. Peter Orris has challenged the validity of the infant-mortality rate, furthermore, because coverage was expanded in 1963 to include some deaths previously unreported. However, the increase in infant mortality from 1960 through 1962 cannot be explained by a change in procedure, since the same procedures were used. The new procedures introduced in the mid-1960s remained unchanged until 1971; infant mortality rose again until 1969, probably because of the general disorganization that hit Cuba as the economy collapsed. Procedures were changed again in 1972. Thus the rapid decline from 1971 to 1972 could be the result of a change in reporting, but the increases that peaked in 1962 and 1969 could not. See Mesa-Lago, "Availability of Statistics"; Eduardo Dorticós Mauri, "Problemas de la estadística en el sector agropecuario," *Cuba socialista* no. 35 (July 1964); *Anuario 1974*, p. 28; Peter Orris, "The Role of the Consumer in the Cuban National Health System" (M.P.H. thesis, Yale University, 1970), p. 39 (I am grateful to Diane Dakin for bringing the last source to my attention).

49. For a discussion of these problems, see Ross Danielson, "Cuban Health Care in Process: Models and Morality in the Early Revolution," in *Topias and Utopias in Health* (The Hague: Mouton, 1975), pp. 322–323, 327.

50. Computed from *Boletín 1971*, pp. 295–297; *Anuario 1972*, pp. 18, 25; *Anuario 1973*, pp. 256, 257, 259; *Anuario 1974*, pp. 260–261, 263; supplemented by Roberto Hernández, "La atención médica en Cuba," *Journal of Inter-American Studies* 11, no. 4 (October 1969):553; Vicente Navarro, "Health Services in Cuba," *New England Journal of Medicine* 287, no. 10 (November 9, 1972):957–958 (I am grateful to Dr. Jaime Arias for bringing the last source to my attention). See also Ricardo Leyva,

"Health and Revolution in Cuba," in *Cuba in Revolution*, ed. Rolando Bonachea and Nelson P. Valdés (Garden City, N.Y.: Anchor Books, 1972), with the caution that the statistics on pp. 480–481 are higher than official government statistics; Nelson Valdés, "Health and Revolution in Cuba," *Science and Society* 35, no. 3 (Fall 1971). See also *Granma*, June 12, 1975, p. 4; "Cuba económica," *Economía y desarrollo* no. 34 (March–April 1976):189.

51. The total volume of outpatient consultations in public medical facilities rose from 11.3 million in 1964 to 23.9 million in 1974. Several factors influenced this increase. Since 1964 medical-school graduates have pledged not to be involved in the private practice of medicine; even though some private practitioners graduated before that time, they have gradually been shifting to government service. Thus a substantial part of the increase in public outpatient consultation from 1964 to 1973 can be accounted for by the gradual socialization of formerly private practice. Second, half the population of the city of Havana and 400,000 people elsewhere in Cuba belonged to prepaid medical plans (*mutualismo*) in 1966. Many, though apparently not all, of these plans were included in the Ministry of Public Health's budget beginning in the early 1960s. Their takeover by the state—including the phasing out of all prepaid plans included in the state budget—was accelerated in the late 1960s and completed by 1970. The increase in public outpatient consultations from 13.7 million in 1966 to 21.8 million in 1969 may therefore reflect in part the absorption of these plans by the state. Third, the population grew. Some of the increase in services simply kept up with this growth. See *Boletín 1971*, pp. 296–297; *Anuario 1973*, pp. 256–259; *Anuario 1974*, p. 263; Sally Guttmacher and Lourdes García, "Social Science and Health in Cuba: Ideology, Planning and Health," in *Topias and Utopias*, ed. Ingman and Thomas, p. 512; and Danielson, "Cuban Health Care," pp. 326, 331.

52. *Boletín 1968*, pp. 44–45; *1970 Census*, pp. 12, 15; *Boletín 1971*, pp. 295–297; *Anuario 1972*, pp. 257–259; *Anuario 1974*, pp. 261, 263; *1953 Census*, pp. 49–50; Navarro, "Health Services in Cuba," p. 956; Hernández, "La atención," pp. 550–551; Facultad de Ciencias Médicas, Universidad de la Habana, *Docencia de las ciencias médicas en Cuba* (Havana: Ministerio de Salud Pública, 1966), p. 5. For a single specialty, see Jorge McCook Martínez, "Angiología social: experiencia en Cuba," *Revista cubana de cirugía* 11, nos. 5–6 (September–December 1972):483–484.

53. *Boletín 1968*, p. 306; *Anuario 1973*, p. 263; *Anuario 1974*, p. 267.

54. Because 60.4 percent of the samples came from Havana province, the study probably underrepresents severe drinking-water impurity. The study covered water from wells, aqueducts, and springs, as well as from bottled soda. Only 4.3 percent of the bottled soda included unacceptable water, but between 53 percent and 83 percent of the other three categories of water contained impurities.

55. Pedro Domingo, "La vacunación BCG y su aplicación en Cuba," *Revista cubana de tuberculosis* 17, no. 3 (July–September 1953):175; Teodoro Drake Galinena, with Guillermina Tenorio and Olga Martínez Cobiella, "Consideraciones bacteriológicas de exámenes de agua de consumo: estudio de mil casos," *Revista cubana de laboratorio clínico* 5, no. 5 (January–March 1951):199–201; Rafael Calvó Fonseca, "La incidencia del parasitismo intestinal en niños menores de un año," *Revista cubana de pediatría* 30, no. 9 (September 1958):479–480, 483; idem, "Estudio del parasitismo en nuestro medio, visto principalmente como causa de mortalidad," *Revista Kuba de*

medicina tropical y parasitología 11, nos. 7–12 (1955):57–58; Arturo J. Aballí, "Distrofias infantiles en nuestro medio," *Revista cubana de pediatría* 30, no. 9 (September 1958):491, 502.

56. For a sympathetic discussion of the organization and achievements of the Cuban public-health system in the 1960s, see Orris, "Role of the Consumer"; Michael Liebowitz, "The Cuban Health Care System: A Study in the Evaluation of Health Care Systems" (M.D. diss., Yale University, 1969). I am grateful to Diane Dakin for bringing these sources to my attention.

57. Computed from *1943 Census,* pp. 930–931, 1112–14, 1203–05; see also Benigno Aguirre, "Differential Migration of Cuban Social Races," *Latin American Research Review* 11, no. 1 (1976):106–110.

58. David Arnes, "Negro Family Types in a Cuban *Solar,*" *Phylon* 11, no. 2 (1950):159–163.

59. The following tabulation shows the ratio of the proportion of those convicted and imprisoned, by racial category, to the proportion of each racial group in the population; a ratio of 1.00 would indicate that the proportion of those arrested belonging to any group and its share of the population were the same.

	1932:1931	1943
Whites	0.71	0.67
Mulattoes	1.22	1.47
Blacks	2.54	2.73

Computed from *1943 Census,* p. 335; *1953 Census,* pp. 49–50.

60. Herbert S. Klein, *Slavery in the Americas* (Chicago: Quadrangle Books, 1967), pp. 260–264.

61. For a statement of government policy, see José Felipe Carneado, "La discriminación racial en Cuba no volverá jamás," *Cuba socialista* no. 5 (January 1962).

62. Carlos Moore, "Cuba: The Untold Story," *Présence africaine,* Eng. ed., no. 24 (1964); Carneado, "La discriminación," p. 65; Elizabeth Sutherland, *The Youngest Revolution: A Personal Report on Cuba* (New York: Dial Press, 1969), pp. 138–168; Barry Reckford, *Does Fidel Eat More than Your Father?* (London: Andre Deutsch, 1971), pp. 127–128; John Clytus, with Jane Rieker, *Black Man in Red Cuba* (Coral Gables, Fla.: University of Miami Press, 1970). For a defense of the government, see René Depestre, "Letter from Cuba," *Présence Africaine* no. 28, Eng. ed. (1965); for a statement by a visiting Indian that there is no race discrimination, see V. R. Krishna Iyer, *Cuban Panorama* (Trivandrum: Prabatham, 1967):12; for expression of deeply felt racism by a poor white, briefly a member of the Communist Youth Union, see Oscar Lewis, Ruth M. Lewis, and Susan M. Rigdon, *Four Men* (Urbana; University of Illinois Press, 1977), pp. 451–528; for evidence that the government does accord respect and toleration to Afro-Cuban religions, especially when linked to Roman Catholic rituals, see Alberto P. Díaz, "La semana santa haitiano-cubana," *Etnología y folklore* no. 4 (July–December 1967). See also David Booth, "Cuba, Color and the Revolution," *Science and Society* 40, no. 2 (Summer 1976):171–172, on political discussion and its problems; Booth's article describes race relations very well before and after the revolution. See photographs in *Verde olivo* 13, no. 27 (July 4, 1971):10–12; ibid., no. 28 (July 11, 1971):56–57; *Granma Weekly Review,* July 1, 1973, p. 3.

63. Alberto P. Díaz, "Guanamaca: una comunidad haitiana," *Etnología y folklore* no. 1 (1966):28; Lise Rochon, "La sociedad agropecuaria 'Jesús Feliú': un caso de cambio en el medio rural bajo un régimen socialista de transición," *Etnología y folklore* no. 4 (July–December 1967):35.

64. Computed from Lowry Nelson, *Rural Cuba* (Minneapolis: University of Minnesota Press, 1950), p. 157; Comisión de Orientación Revolucionaria, *Mil fotos: Cuba* (Havana: Ediciones COR, 1966).

65. See Jorge I. Domínguez, "Racial and Ethnic Relations in the Cuban Armed Forces: A Non-Topic," *Armed Forces and Society* 2, no. 2 (Winter 1976), for a more detailed study of ethnicity in Cuban civilian and military life before and after the revolution.

66. The statistical computations in this and the following paragraph are based on *Boletín 1970*, p. 36; *Anuario 1973*, p. 41; *Anuario 1974*, p. 41.

67. These statistics should be taken as indicative of trends and orders of magnitude and not as a precise interval scale; reclassification of workers and work sectors may have affected the statistics. Nevertheless, these data are in accord with other known trends for the period.

68. Fernando González, "Población y desarrollo: consideraciones generales," *Economía y desarrollo* no. 27 (January–February 1975):154.

69. For Fidel Castro's commitment to developing Oriente province, see Mankiewicz and Jones, *With Fidel*, p. 107; for an excellent study of trends in urban-rural inequality, with findings parallel to those presented here, see Sergio Roca, "Distributional Effects of the Cuban Revolution: Urban versus Rural Allocations" (Paper presented at 88th annual meeting, American Economic Association, Dallas, Texas, December 1975).

70. Raúl Cepero Bonilla, "El canje de billetes: un golpe a la contrarrevolución," *Cuba socialista* no. 2 (October 1961).

71. *Granma Weekly Review*, August 5, 1973, pp. 2, 5; ibid., September 2, 1973, pp. 8–9; ibid., November 25, 1973, pp. 7, 10–11.

72. *Revolución*, December 9, 1964, p. 1.

73. Ernesto Guevara, "Man and Socialism in Cuba," in *Man and Socialism in Cuba*, ed. Bertram Silverman (New York: Atheneum, 1971), p. 352.

74. *Granma*, March 9, 1966, pp. 5, 7, 8; ibid., March 11, 1966, p. 3; ibid., March 14, 1966, p. 4; ibid., March 17, 1966, p. 1; ibid., March 21, 1966, p. 1; *New York Times*, August 28, 1966, p. 27.

75. *Granma*, March 30, 1966, p. 3.

76. Ministerio de Industrias, Dirección Económica, "Proposición de un sistema de precios utilizando los costos planificados como precios de entrega dentro del sector estatal," *Nuestra industria: revista económica* nos. 22–23 (June 1967):91–92.

77. *Granma*, February 25, 1966, p. 3; ibid., February 22, 1975, p. 5; *Granma Weekly Review*, December 20, 1974, p. 4.

78. Roberto Hernández and Carmelo Mesa-Lago, "Labor Organization and Wages," in *Revolutionary Change in Cuba*, ed. Carmelo Mesa-Lago (Pittsburgh: University of Pittsburgh Press, 1971), pp. 229–231; Sutherland, *Youngest Revolution*, pp. 16–20; Zeitlin, *Revolutionary Politics*, pp. xix–xxii; Reckford, *Does Fidel Eat More?*, p. 26; K. S. Karol, *Guerrillas in Power* (New York: Hill and Wang, 1970), pp. 429–434; and Archibald Ritter, *The Economic Development of Revolutionary Cuba: Strategy and*

Performance (New York: Praeger, 1974), p. 291. For discussions of corruption witnessed and described by individuals in 1969–1970, including instances of abuse of power by party members and government officials, see "The Exchange," in Oscar Lewis, Ruth M. Lewis, and Susan M. Rigdon, *Neighbors* (Urbana: University of Illinois Press, 1978); idem, *Four Women* (Urbana: University of Illinois Press, 1977), pp. 382–386; for the breakdown of some local Committees for the Defense of the Revolution because of the corruption of its local leadership, see Lewis et al., *Four Men*, pp. 391–407, and Douglas Butterworth, "Grass Roots Political Organization in Cuba: A Case of the Committees for the Defense of the Revolution," in *Latin American Urban Research*, ed. Wayne Cornelius and Felicity Trueblood (Beverly Hills, Calif.: Sage Publications, 1974), pp. 194, 196–197.

79. *Granma*, March 14, 1966, p. 6; "Discurso del Comandante Fidel Castro en la plenaria provincial de la CTC," *Pensamiento Crítico* no. 45 (October 1970):94. Pettitt, "Social and Economic Change," p. 349.

80. Padula, "Fall of the Bourgeoisie," p. 529.

81. Osvaldo Dorticós, "Los cambios institucionales y políticos de la revolución socialista cubana," *Cuba socialista* no. 1 (September 1961).

82. Padula, "Fall of the Bourgeoisie," p. 532. For an anthropologist's observations on the priority of political over economic criteria in the selection of party members, but of economic and technical over political criteria in the selection of managers, see Pettitt, "Social and Economic Change," pp. 157, 321–323.

83. *Granma Weekly Review*, December 3, 1972, p. 2; ibid., December 12, 1976, p. 5; *Granma*, November 24, 1976, pp. 3–6.

84. For a discussion of these terms and some instances of their application, see Samuel P. Huntington, *Political Order in Changing Societies* (New Haven: Yale University Press, 1968), pp. 12–24; Ted Robert Gurr, *Why Men Rebel* (Princeton: Princeton University Press, 1971), pp. 282, 310; and Jorge I. Domínguez and Christopher Mitchell, "The Roads Not Taken: Institutionalization and Political Parties in Cuba and Bolivia," *Comparative Politics* 9, no. 2 (January 1977).

85. The data must be used with caution because the word *enterprise* can include many things. In 1971, for example, the Ministry of the Sugar Industry was subdivided into eleven enterprises while the National Institute for Agrarian Reform had 199. Enterprises are normally subdivided down to the factory or shop level. The value and volume of their output vary considerably. Nevertheless, enterprise statistics do give us a gross picture of the stability or instability of centralized management in Cuba.

86. *Revolución*, September 29, 1964, p. 4; *Granma Weekly Review*, October 8, 1967, p. 4; *Boletín 1970*, p. 30; see also Carmelo Mesa-Lago, "The Labor Force, Employment, Unemployment and Underemployment in Cuba: 1899–1970," *Sage Professional Papers in International Studies* 1, no. 9 (1972):58, 60.

87. Computed from *Boletín 1970*, p. 34.

88. The computation excludes 1959, an exceptional year; it includes ministries created before 1970 and still in existence at the end of 1974.

89. In 1974 the national government made some important changes in the local government of Matanzas province (one of the six) on an experimental basis. The new procedures were extended to the whole country in the 1976 Constitution. It is far too early to tell whether the formalization of local government in Cuba has yet to amount to institutionalization, in the sense that the term is used here.

90. Computed from *Anuario 1974*, p. 41.

91. *Granma Weekly Review*, October 20, 1974, p. 4; ibid., November 3, 1974, p. 1; ibid., March 2, 1975, p. 5; *Bohemia* 67, no. 9 (February 28, 1975):50.

92. *Granma*, January 15, 1976, pp. 4–7.

93. Ibid., July 9, •976, p. 4.

94. *Granma*, December 3, 1976, pp. 1, 4; *Granma Weekly Review*, December 12, 1976, p. 5; ibid., July 24, 1977, pp. 1, 9.

95. *Granma*, July 15, 1977, p. 3.

96. *Granma Weekly Review*, July 24, 1977, p. 1.

97. Ibid., p. 9; *Granma*, July 13, 1977, p. 3.

98. For a comparison of the Cuban legislature with that of the Soviet Union, see David Lane, *Politics and Society in the USSR* (New York: Random House, 1970), pp. 142–165, 243–251; for a comparison with Communist legislatures in general, see Blondel, *Comparative Legislatures*, pp. 52, 57, 60, 91, 102, 107, 113, 115, 120, 126, 137.

99. Francisco José Moreno, "Justice and Law in Latin America: A Cuban Example," *Journal of Inter-American Studies and World Affairs* 12, no. 3 (July 1970):368–369, 372–373.

100. The following paragraphs concerning 1960 are based on an examination of all Supreme Court decisions published in *La jurisprudencia al día* (1960).

101. Ibid., sentence 5, February 5, 1960 (January 20), pp. 6–8; sentence 10, March 7, 1960 (February 20), pp. 24–28; sentence 26, April 12, 1960 (April 20), pp. 65–69; sentence 38, March 9, 1960 (May 10), pp. 90–91; and sentence 64, September 26, 1960 (September 20), pp. 148–149.

102. Ibid.; see especially the cases in sentence 687, September 26, 1960 (September 20), pp. 461–462; sentence 942, November 22, 1960 (November 20), pp. 560–562; for findings in the opposite direction, see sentence 936, November 18, 1960 (November 20), pp. 558–559; sentence 656, September 13, 1960 (September 20), pp. 442–443; sentence 676, September 21, 1960 (September 20), pp. 541–543. For a general discussion, see Padula, "Fall of the Bourgeoisie," pp. 165–166.

103. International Commission of Jurists, *Cuba and the Rule of Law* (Geneva: H. Studer, 1962), pp. 64–65.

104. Ibid., p. 112.

105. Ibid., pp. 112, 114, 130–131; Ted Morgan, "Cuba," *New York Times Magazine*, December 1, 1974, p. 116; Comité Central del Partido Comunista de Cuba, Comisión de Estudios Jurídicos, *Órganos del sistema judicial* (Havana: Empresa de Medios de Propaganda, 1975), p. 25 (hereafter cited as *Órganos*); *Granma*, May 7, 1975, p. 4.

106. Ian McColl Kennedy, "Cuba's *Ley contra la vagancia*—The Law on Loafing," *UCLA Law Review* 20, no. 6 (August 1973):1203, 1207, 1211–12, 1214, 1216, 1219.

107. Computed from *Revista cubana de jurisprudencia* 1, no. 11 (November 1962):41–50, 69–102; ibid., 2, no. 8 (September–October 1963): 41–43, 59–64, 67–94.

108. Enrique Hart, "Discurso de apertura ante los tribunales," *Revista cubana de jurisprudencia* 2, no. 8 (September–October 1963):5–6.

109. Agustín Cruz, "It Took Only Three Years: The Destruction of a Law Firm," *American Bar Association Journal* 50, no. 1 (January 1964):63–66.

110. *Revista cubana de jurisprudencia* 1, no. 11 (November 1962):64–65, 93–94; ibid., 2, no. 8 (September–October 1963):67–68; see also pp. 73–75, 79–91, 82–85, 85–89 for sentences dealing with military or militia personnel.

111. Ibid., 2, no. 8 (September–October 1963): 75–76; ibid., 1, no. 11 (November

1962):90. For a criticism of judges who oppose preventive detention in traffic accidents, see Santiago Cuba, "La lucha contra la criminalidad," ibid., 2, no. 8 (September–October 1963):29.

112. Lockwood, *Castro's Cuba*, pp. 230, 247; Delfín Rodríguez et al., "Latifundismo y especulación: notas para la historia agraria de la Isla de Pinos, 1900–1958," *Serie Isla de Pinos* no 23, p. 10.

113. For a comparative study of worldwide political imprisonment, see Jorge I. Domínguez, "An Assessment of Human Rights Conditions," in Jorge I. Domínguez et al., *Human Rights and International Relations* (New York: McGraw-Hill, 1978); for other data on Cuba, see the excellent long article by Frank Greve and Miguel Perez, "Castro's Jails: Still Bulging 17 Years Later," *Miami Herald*, May 23, 1976, p. 16-A; Morgan, "Cuba," p. 117; Mankiewicz and Jones, *With Fidel*, p. 100. For 1977 data, see *Granma Weekly Review*, July 17, 1977, p. 4; population extrapolated from *Anuario 1974*, p. 22.

114. *Granma Weekly Review*, June 13, 1971, p. 3; ibid., June 10, 1973, p. 11; Nicolás León Cotayo, "Un recorrido por el sistema penal cubano," *Cuba internacional* 5 (May 1973).

115. Among others, see Organization of American States, Inter-American Commission on Human Rights, *Report Regarding the Situation of Human Rights in Cuba*, OEA/Ser. L/V/II.17, Doc. 4 rev., June 13, 1967; idem, *Second Report on the Situation of Political Prisoners in Cuba*, OEA/Ser. L/V/II.23, Doc. 6, rev. 1, November 17, 1970; and idem, *Fifth Report on the Status of Human Rights in Cuba*, OEA/Ser.G./ CP/INF.872/76, June 1, 1976.

116. Amnesty International, *Report on Torture* (London: Gerald Duckworth, 1973), p. 191. See also an excellent report by Theodore Jacquenay, "The Yellow Uniforms of Cuba," *Worldview* 20, nos. 1–2 (January–February 1977):4–10.

117. *Granma*, April 14, 1966, p. 8.

118. Greve and Perez, "Castro's Jails"; see idem, "Heavy Political Tones Dominate Style of Justice under Castro," and " 'Boniato Massacre': What Really Happened?" *Miami Herald*, May 24, 1976.

119. Dirección Nacional de los Tribunales Populares, *Manual de los Tribunales Populares* (Havana: Ministerio de Justicia, 1966), especially pp. xi–xii (hereafter cited as *Manual*); Santiago Cuba, "Acerca de los Tribunales Populares," *Cuba socialista* no. 24 (August 1963); idem, "Los Tribunales Populares," *Verde olivo* 7, no. 41 (October 16, 1966):26.

120. Jesse Berman, "The Cuban Popular Tribunals," *Columbia Law Review* 69, no. 8 (December 1969):1321–22, 1355–56; Frank Agüero, "Nuevo sistema judicial," *Verde olivo* 13, no. 14 (April 14, 1971):37; *Ley de organización del sistema judicial* (Havana: Ministerio de Justicia, 1973), article 83 (hereafter cited as *Ley judicial*); and *Órganos*, p. 23.

121. *Manual*, pp. 12–18; Cuba, "Los Tribunales," p. 27; Berman, "Popular Tribunals," p. 1332.

122. *Manual*, p. iii; Cuba, "Los Tribunales," p. 27; Berman, "Popular Tribunals," pp. 1337–45.

123. Berman, "Popular Tribunals," pp. 1350–54.

124. *Granma*, February 26, 1973, p. 4.

125. *Granma Weekly Review*, September 5, 1971, p. 8; Agüero, "Nuevo sistema

judicial," pp. 35–37; *Granma*, April 10, 1975, pp. 4–5; ibid., January 15, 1976, p. 16; *Organos*, pp. 19, 23; *Ley judicial*, articles 26, 28, 30, 31, 77–82, 92–93, 99–100.

126. *Granma*, July 14, 1977, p. 2.

127. *Boletín 1971*, p. 277; *Granma Weekly Review*, October 2, 1974, p. 5; *Granma*, January 21, 1975, p. 3; ibid., January 23, 1975, p. 3; ibid., June 9, 1975, p. 2; *Ley judicial*, article 171 and interim resolutions 10 and 11.

128. José Suárez Moreno, "El código de familia," *Verde olivo* 16, no. 24 (June 16, 1974):13.

7. MASS POLITICAL PARTICIPATION

1. Jorge López and Roberto Gill, "¿Cumple Ud. con el deber de educar y formar a sus hijos?" *Con la guardia en alto* 11, nos. 1–2 (January–February 1972): 63.

2. In a competition among the provincial organizations, the national coordinator's office awarded "emulation" points in recognition of good performance. The Pearson product-moment correlation between a province's emulation-point total and that province's percentage of the population enrolled in the committees is r = −.848. A linear-regression equation where Y is the total of a province's emulation points and X is the percentage of the population enrolled in the committees in that province is: $Y = 170.67 - 2.545X$. Thus a 1-percent increase in membership in 1963 cost a province about three emulation points. Computed from data in José Matar, "Tres años de lucha y experiencia," *Guía para la acción* no. 4 (October 1963): 82–88; ibid., no. 5 (December 1963): 9–10. Not all local committees performed better as a result of the changes in the mid-1960s. For the history of a local committee that decayed in activities and organization after 1965, its best year, see Douglas Butterworth, "Grass Roots Political Organization in Cuba: A Case of the Committees for the Defense of the Revolution," in *Latin American Urban Research*, ed. Wayne Cornelius and Felicity Trueblood (Beverly Hills, Calif.: Sage Publications, 1974), 4:183–202.

3. "Estos siete años han sido años de lucha, de sacrificios y victorias," *Con la guardia en alto* 6, no. 10 (October 1967): 32–33; Mario Méndez, "Crecimiento," ibid., 11, no. 9 (September 1972): 12.

4. Marta Vignier, "Una entrevista de Prensa Latina," ibid., 6, no. 2 (February 1967): 4; "Reunión nacional de chequeo de la emulación," ibid., p. 45; Alberto Masó, "Tareas fundamentales," ibid., no. 5 (May 1967): 24–25; "Comunicado conjunto en la lucha contra la delincuencia," ibid., no. 2 (March 1967): 55; "Emulación: tareas y metas de los CDR," ibid., no. 6 (June 1967): 8–9.

5. "Síntesis de acuerdos tomados por la Dirección Nacional de los CDR en su última reunión," ibid., 7, no. 11 (November 1968): 16; "Tarea no. 1 de los CDR: vigilancia revolucionaria," ibid., no. 12 (December 1968): 9; *Verde olivo* 9, no. 40 (October 6, 1968): 60; *Granma Weekly Review*, May 11, 1969, p. 8.

6. David Apter, in *The Politics of Modernization* (Chicago: University of Chicago Press, 1965), pp. 359–360.

7. Cándido Jústiz and Lucas Martínez, "Los CDR en las zonas campesinas," *Guía para la acción* no. 4 (October 1963): 94; José Matar, "Sigue impetuoso el desarrollo de los CDR," *Con la guardia en alto* 3, no. 1 (September 1964): 12; "1969," ibid., 8, no. 9 (September 1969): 12; *Granma*, February 8, 1974, p. 3; ibid., September 28, 1974, p. 1.

8. Quoted in Ted Morgan, "Cuba," *New York Times Magazine*, December 1, 1974, p. 10; *Granma Weekly Review*, October 12, 1975, p. 3.

9. For an excellent discussion of these trends in the early history of the committees, see Richard Fagen, *The Transformation of Political Culture in Cuba* (Stanford: Stanford University Press, 1969), chap. 4; for the definitive shift away from priority on political vigilance, see Marta Harnecker, *Cuba: ¿dictadura o democracia?* (Mexico: Siglo XXI, 1975), p. 114.

10. *Granma Weekly Review*, October 2, 1966, p. 2; ibid., January 22, 1967, p. 6; ibid., March 31, 1968, p. 2; ibid., April 7, 1968, p. 3; *Granma*, February 6, 1976, p. 2; Luis Báez, "Hacia una mayor calidad, organización y conciencia," *Bohemia* 67, no. 8 (February 21, 1975): 53; Frances FitzGerald, "A Reporter at Large: Slightly Exaggerated Enthusiasms," in *The New Cuba: Paradoxes and Potentials*, ed. Ronald Radosh (New York: Morrow, 1976), pp. 154–155.

11. *Granma Weekly Review*, October 1, 1972, p. 4; ibid., September 24, 1972, pp. 4–5; *Granma*, September 28, 1974, p. 4; "Reunión nacional de septiembre," *Con la guardia en alto* 8, no. 10 (October 1969): 22; Jorge Lezcano, "Informe central presentado al pleno," ibid., 14, no. 4 (April 1975): 11–12.

12. Computed from "Conclusiones del IV chequeo de la emulación nacional y planes de los frentes de los CDR para 1964," *Guía para la acción* no. 5 (December 1963); *Con la guardia en alto* 8, no. 10 (October 1969): 13; ibid., 10, no. 12 (December 1971): 12; ibid., 12, no. 1 (January 1973); *Granma*, February 11, 1974, p. 3.

13. Computed from *Granma*, February 6, 1976, p. 2; ibid., July 16, 1976, p. 3.

14. Quoted from *Granma Weekly Review*, February 17, 1974, p. 3; see also *Granma*, February 22, 1975, p. 5.

15. Sara González and Carmen Gómez, "La FMC y la educación: diez años de trabajo," *Mujeres* 10, no. 8 (1970): 20–22; José M. Otero and Gladys Castaño, "La mujer en la producción," ibid., pp. 62–63; *Bohemia*, (September 1, 1967): 60–64; *Granma Weekly Review*, January 6, 1976, p. 6; Margaret Randall, "La mujer cubana en 1974," *Casa de las Américas* 15, no. 89 (March–April 1975): 67; *Granma*, March 10, 1976, p. 3.

16. "Lograr una base organizativa sólida," *Mujeres* 10, no. 8 (1970): 88; *Granma Weekly Review*, August 1, 1971, p. 2; *Verde olivo* 14, no. 36 (September 3, 1972): 6; *Granma Weekly Review*, December 8, 1974, p. 6; ibid., April 27, 1975, p. 6; ibid., August 31, 1975, p. 6; ibid., January 4, 1976, p. 6; *Granma*, March 3, 1977, p. 2.

17. Espín quoted in Ana Ramos, "La mujer y la revolución en Cuba," *Casa de las Américas* 11, nos. 65–66 (March–June 1971): 67; Heidi Steffens, "Notes from Abroad: Cuba—The Day Women Took Over Havana," *Ms.* 3, no. 10 (April 1975): 28–37 (I am grateful to Susan Bancroft for this reference); Risquet quoted in *Granma*, September 9, 1970, p. 5.

18. Marvin Leiner, with Robert Ubell, *Children Are the Revolution: Day Care in Cuba* (New York: Viking Press, 1974), pp. 5–6, 56, 61, 188–189; *Anuario 1972*, p. 34; *Granma Weekly Review*, August 4, 1974, p. 5; *Granma*, July 21, 1977, p. 4.

19. *Granma*, November 26, 1974, p. 4.

20. *Granma Weekly Review*, December 30, 1973, p. 4; ibid., December 8, 1974. For a sensitive discussion of the problem of the political autonomy of the Cuban Women's Federation, see Max Azicri, "Women's Development through Revolutionary Mobilization: A Study of the Federation of Cuban Women" (Paper presented at annual

meeting, International Studies Association, St. Louis, Mo., March 16–20, 1977), pp. 5–6, 9, 11.

21. Susan Kaufman Purcell, "Modernizing Women for a Modern Society: The Cuban Case," in *Female and Male in Latin America*, ed. Ann Pescatello (Pittsburgh: University of Pittsburgh Press, 1973), pp. 258–259.

22. Purcell, "Modernizing Women," p. 259.

23. For the text of the Family Code," see *Granma*, March 3, 1975, pp. 3–5; for a discussion of prerevolutionary culture on this point, see Geoffrey E. Fox, "Honor, Shame and Women's Liberation in Cuba: Views of Working Class Emigré Men," in *Female and Male in Latin America*, ed. Ann Pescatello; Mirta de la Torre Mulhare, "Sexual Ideology in Pre-Castro Cuba: A Cultural Analysis" (Ph.D., diss., University of Pittsburgh, 1969). See also *Granma Weekly Review*, September 14, 1975, p. 7.

24. Compare, for example, with articles 20, 43–46, of the Constitution of 1940, in Leonel Antonio de la Cuesta, ed., *Constituciones Cubanas* (New York: Ediciones Exilio, 1974), pp. 246, 251–252; compare also with the extensive legal references in *Granma*, March 3, 1975, pp. 3–5.

25. *Granma Weekly Review*, August 31, 1975, p. 6.

26. Computed from Mario Riera, *Historial obrero cubano* (Miami: Rema Press, 1965), pp. 300–301; *Granma Weekly Review*, November 25, 1973, p. 12; Eduardo García Mouri, "Proceso de institucionalización en el sindicalismo cubano: papel de los sindicatos según el XIII Congreso CTC" (Paper presented at Seminar on Institutionalization in Cuba, Institute of Cuban Studies, Caracas, March 24–29, 1975), pp. 19–20, 30–31.

27. Miguel Martín, "Informe al Congreso," *Cuba socialista* no. 62 (October 1966): 108; *Granma*, November 19, 1970, p. 1; ibid., December 3, 1970, p. 1.

28. Marifeli Pérez-Stable, "Los sindicatos en perspectiva" (Paper presented at Seminar on Institutionalization in Cuba, Institute of Cuba Studies, Caracas, March 24–29, 1975), p. 39; *Granma*, April 4, 1975, p. 5; García Mouri, "Proceso," p. 22.

29. Carlos Fernández, "El XI Congreso Nacional de la CTC-R," *Cuba socialista* no. 6, (February 1962): 50–53.

30. Adolfo Gilly, *Inside the Cuban Revolution*, trans. Félix Gutiérrez (New York: Monthly Review Press, 1964), pp. 13, 16–18.

31. See especially Robert M. Bernardo, *The Theory of Moral Incentives in Cuba* (University, Ala.: University of Alabama Press, 1971); Bette Evans, "The Moral versus Material Incentives Controversy in Cuba" (Ph.D. diss., University of Pittsburgh, 1972); Fagen, *Transformation of Political Culture*, chap. 6; Joseph Kahl, "The Moral Economy of a Revolutionary Society," in *Cuban Communism*, ed. Irving L. Horowitz (New Brunswick, N.J.: Transaction Books, 1970), pp. 95–115; Roberto Hernández and Carmelo Mesa-Lago, "Labor Organization and Wages," in *Revolutionary Change in Cuba*, ed. Carmelo Mesa-Lago (Pittsburgh: University of Pittsburgh Press, 1971), pp. 209–249; two essays by Carmelo Mesa-Lago, "Economic Significance of Unpaid Labor in Socialist Cuba," *Industrial and Labor Relations Review* 22, no. 3 (April 1969): 339–357, and "Cuba: teoría y práctica de los incentivos," Latin American Studies Series, occasional paper no. 7 (Pittsburgh: University of Pittsburgh, 1971).

32. *Granma*, September 29, 1966, p. 5; *Granma Weekly Review*, January 22, 1967, p. 6.

33. *Granma Weekly Review*, July 16, 1967, p. 3; ibid., September 8, 1968, p. 2; ibid., October 27, 1968, p. 4.

34. "Discurso del Presidente de la República, Dr. Osvaldo Dorticós, en la escuela de cuadros de mando del Ministerio de la Industria Ligera," *Pensamiento crítico* no. 45 (October 1970): 148.

35. Brian H. Pollitt, "Employment Plans, Performance and Future Prospects in Cuba," in *Third World Employment*, ed. Richard Jolly et al. (London: Penguin Books, 1973), pp. 255–258, 261–262.

36. K. S. Karol, *Guerrillas in Power*, trans. Arnold Pomerans (New York: Hill and Wang, 1970); René Dumont, *Cuba: ¿es socialista?* trans. Mariela Álvarez (Caracas: Editorial Tiempo Nuevo, 1970).

37. "Comunicado de la CTC," *Pensamiento crítico* no. 48 (October 1970): 176–177.

38. *Granma Weekly Review*, August 17, 1969, p. 2.

39. Nelson P. Valdés, *Cuba: ¿socialismo democrático o burocratismo colectivista?* (Bogotá: Ediciones Tercer Mundo, 1973), pp. 57–58.

40. *Granma Weekly Review*, March 2, 1969, p. 4; ibid., March 16, 1969, p. 10; *Granma*, January 20, 1975, p. 1.

41. *Granma Weekly Review*, October 4, 1970, p. 2.

42. *Granma*, September 8, 1970, p. 5; "La microemulación oriental del deber y el honor," *Bohemia* 65, no. 26 (June 29, 1973): 91–92.

43. *Granma*, August 1, 1970, pp. 5–6; *Granma Weekly Review*, October 24, 1971, p. 5.

44. *Verde olivo* 13, no. 39 (September 26, 1971): 10–11.

45. *Granma Weekly Review*, November 18, 1973, p. 4. In 1964 Adolfo Gilly, wrote: "One leader who enjoys the unanimous opposition of the Cuban workers . . . [is] the Secretary-General of the CTC, Lázaro Peña. This is not a secret or gossip among the initiated. It is an opinion current in the streets of Havana and all over Cuba, and it blossoms into the open a few minutes after you start talking about the union situation" (*Inside the Cuban Revolution*, p. 13).

46. *Granma*, February 6, 1975, pp. 1, 3, 4; ibid., May 27, 1975, p. 3; ibid., July 23, 1975, p. 4; ibid., February 17, 1976, p. 5; ibid., February 19, 1976, p. 1; ibid., March 1, 1976, p. 3; ibid., March 19, 1977, pp. 2–4; *Granma Weekly Review*, January 4, 1976, p. 2.

47. Marifeli Pérez-Stable, "Cuba's Workers 1975: A Preliminary Analysis" (Paper presented at meeting of the Latin American Studies Association, Atlanta, March 1976), pp. 4, 5, 8, 11.

48. *Granma*, February 6, 1975, p. 3; ibid., February 8, 1975, p. 4; ibid., February 19, 1976, p. 4; ibid., August 11, 1976, p. 3; ibid., August 12, 1977, p. 3; *Granma Weekly Review*, August 17, 1969, p. 2.

49. *Granma Weekly Review*, November 18, 1973, pp. 4–5; *Granma*, February 6, 1975, p. 4; ibid., April 11, 1975, p. 5; Pérez-Stable, "Los sindicatos," pp. 31–32.

50. *Granma Weekly Review*, January 15, 1967, p. 4; ibid., February 19, 1967, p. 2; ibid., June 25, 1967, p. 3; ibid., November 6, 1966, p. 10; ibid., February 28, 1971, p. 2; ibid., January 4, 1976, p. 7; *Granma*, April 3, 1975, p. 4.

51. *Revolución*, January 7, 1965, p. 2; *Granma*, February 7, 1971, p. 9; "III Congreso de la FEEM," *Verde olivo* 16, no. 1 (January 6, 1974): 55, 57.

52. On limitations of student rights, see "La reforma de la enseñanza superior en Cuba," *Universidad de La Habana* no. 154 (January–February 1962): 31–79. On student discontent and government criticism of them, see *Política internacional* no. 16 (1966): 297–308. On the dissolution of the federation, see *Granma Weekly Review*, December 17, 1967, p. 10; *New York Times*, November 26, 1967, p. 20. On the general topic, see Jaime Suchlicki, *University Students and Revolution in Cuba, 1920–1968* (Coral Gables, Fla.: University of Miami Press, 1969), chaps. 5–6.

53. *Granma Weekly Review*, March 21, 1971, pp. 1, 7; ibid., May 30, 1971, pp. 3–4; ibid., August 1, 1971, p. 2.

54. For a fascinating discussion of government strategies to mobilize the population through mass organizations in the 1960s, see Max Azicri, "The Governing Strategies of Mass Mobilization: The Foundations of Cuban Revolutionary Politics," *Latin American Monograph Series* no. 2 (Erie, Pa.: Northwestern Pennsylvania Institute for Latin American Studies, 1977); see also Azicri's "Study of the Structure of Exercising Power in Cuba: Mobilization and Governing Strategies (1959–1968)" (Ph.D. diss., University of Southern California, 1975). Azicri shows a government policy that is complex and highly differentiated in its appeals to the population; however, he may have overestimated the degree of autonomy experienced by the mass organizations engaging in political mobilization in the 1960s. While he demonstrates organizational complexity and subtlety, he does not quite demonstrate organizational independence.

55. For comparative data, see James R. Townsend, *Political Participation in Communist China* (Berkeley and Los Angeles: University of California Press, 1969); James H. Oliver, "Citizen Demands and the Soviet Political System," in *Communist Systems in Comparative Perspective*, ed. Leonard Cohen and Jane Shapiro (Garden City, N.Y.: Anchor Books, 1974).

56. Lee Lockwood, *Castro's Cuba, Cuba's Fidel* (New York: Vintage Books, 1969), p. 150.

57. René Saladrigas, "Criterios para una reestructuración político-administrativa de Cuba," *Cuba socialista* no. 17 (January 1963): 44–45; Arnaldo Milián, "Experiencias de las JUCEI en Las Villas," *Cuba socialista* no. 3 (November 1961): 42–51; "¿Qué es el Poder Local?," *Bohemia* 59, no. 36 (September 8, 1967): 71; ibid., no. 38 (September 22, 1967): 68; Jorge López and Wilfredo Díaz, "¿Qué es un distrito?" *Con la guardia en alto* 10, no. 2 (February 1971): 6.

58. *Granma Weekly Review*, May 19, 1974, p. 1; *La constitución de los órganos de poder popular* (Havana: Imprenta Federico Engels, 1974), p. 36 (hereafter cited as *Constitución OPP*); I am grateful to Lourdes Casal for a copy of this document.

59. *Granma Weekly Review*, August 4, 1974, p. 4; *Constitución OPP*, pp. 36–37.

60. Quoted in *Granma Weekly Review*, September 8, 1974, p. 4; *Granma*, January 15, 1976, pp. 5–6.

61. *Granma Weekly Review*, December 22, 1974, p. 8.

62. *Granma*, December 24, 1974, p. 1.

63. Harnecker, *Cuba: dictadura?* p. 168.

64. *Constitución OPP*, pp. 32–33. For a theoretical discussion of modes of participation, see Sidney Verba and Norman Nie, *Participation in America: Political Democracy and Social Equality* (New York: Harper & Row, 1972), pp. 44–55. Some complaint was permitted in 1967 when the elected local governments were established, but it must have been a short-lived experiment, because references to complaints by indi-

viduals are rare in the literature of the late 1960s and early 1970s; see Michael A. Pettitt, "Social and Economic Change in the Community around a Sugar Mill in Cuba" (Ph.D. diss., University of California–Berkeley, 1973), p. 312.

65. *Granma*, December 13, 1974, p. 1; ibid., December 14, 1974, p. 4; ibid., December 16, 1974, p. 1; ibid., December 17, 1974, p. 5; ibid., December 18, 1974, p. 3; ibid., April 7, 1975, p. 3; *Granma Weekly Review*, December 29, 1974, p. 5; "Rendición de cuentas," *Bohemia* 67, no. 3 (March 28, 1975): 62–63; José Arañaburu, "El trabajo de los CDR a la luz de la creación de los poderes populares se fortalece, se profundiza, se hace mucho más necesario," *Con la guardia en alto* 14, no. 5 (May 1975): 13. For further evidence of the government's perception that contacting public officials for the benefit of a single individual is improper, see Harnecker, *Cuba: dictadura?* pp. 180, 201; see also her extensive interviews providing examples of citizen contacting of government and consequent solutions to local problems on pp. 168–169, 172–175, 179–181, 184–190, 196–201, 203–207, 212, 221–231. Contacting the government to achieve collective goals tends to be more frequent than contacting it on private problems, not only in Cuba but in other countries as well. Only about 3 percent of the contacts made by low-income urban residents who had migrated to Mexico City with government officials dealt with personal or family needs in the early 1970s. In the United States, only about one-third of the individual appeals to government officials in the late 1960s dealt with personal problems. See Wayne Cornelius, "Urbanization and Political Demand Making: Political Participation among the Migrant Poor in Latin American Cities," *American Political Science Review* 68, no. 3 (September 1974): 1135; Verba and Nie, *Participation in America*, 67.

66. *Granma*, January 12, 1977, p. 2.

67. Ibid., April 9, 1977, p. 4; ibid., June 14, 1977, p. 4.

68. See, for example, *Granma Weekly Review*, October 4, 1970, p. 2.

69. *Bohemia* 59, no. 36 (September 8, 1967): 28–33, 62–63, 71; ibid., no. 37 (September 15, 1967): 54–55, 71, 81–82.

70. *Granma Weekly Review*, June 2, 1974, p. 4; ibid., June 9, 1974, p. 6; ibid., July 21, 1974, p. 1; *Constitución OPP*, p. 30; Harnecker, *Cuba: dictadura:* p. 143. Those ineligible to vote included candidates in the last prerevolutionary election (November 3, 1958); anyone deprived of political rights by a court; anyone who had ever asked to leave the country; and the mentally incompetent and anyone under arrest or on parole. The following could not be nominated: anyone who had been a prerevolutionary labor-union leader; anyone serving in the Batista government or armed forces; pacifists.

71. Pedro Margolles, "Building up a System of Representative Bodies," *World Marxist Review* 18, no. 2 (February 1975): 64.

72. *Granma Weekly Review*, August 4, 1974, p. 3; ibid., September 8, 1974, p. 3.

73. Ibid.; *Constitución OPP*, p. 31; Harnecker, *Cuba: dictadura?* p. 155. Data are only available for 1,014 of the 1,079 municipal delegates.

74. Computed from *Granma Weekly Review*, October 8, 1967, p. 3.

75. Harnecker, *Cuba: dictadura?* pp. 152, 155; *Granma*, April 10, 1975, p. 5; ibid., January 15, 1976, p. 6.

76. *Granma Weekly Review*, July 21, 1974, p. 3; ibid., August 4, 1974, p. 7; *Constitución OPP*, pp. 26–29; *Granma*, January 27, 1975, p. 1; ibid., January 15, 1976, p. 6; Harnecker, *Cuba: dictadura?* p. 192.

77. *Granma Weekly Review*, January 4, 1976, p. 5; *Granma*, January 15, 1976, p. 6.

78. *Granma*, July 21, 1976, p. 4; ibid., July 22, 1976, pp. 2–3; ibid., September 2, 1976, p. 1; *Granma Weekly Review*, August 22, 1976, p. 4.

79. See Fidel Castro's description in *Granma*, September 30, 1976, p. 2; see also William J. Bowe, "Cuba Notes" (Chicago, 1976), pp. 44, 63.

80. Computed from *Granma*, October 12, 1976, p. 1; ibid., October 19, 1976, p. 1.

81. Ibid., September 29, 1976, p. 2; ibid., September 30, 1976, p. 2.

82. Computed from ibid., November 1, 1976, p. 3.

83. Ibid., July 22, 1976, pp. 2–3; ibid., November 8, 1976, p. 3; ibid., December 3, 1976, p. 4.

84. Ibid., July 22, 1976, pp. 2–3; ibid., December 3, 1976, p. 4.

85. Ibid., July 22, 1976, pp. 2–3. For a general discussion of the point of view of the Cuban government on these elections, see Blas Roca, "Specific Features of Socialist Democracy in Cuba," *World Marxist Review* 20, no. 2 (February 1977): 15–17.

86. *Granma*, September 1, 1976, p. 1; Comité Central del Partido Comunista de Cuba, Departamento de Orientación Revolucionaria, *Sobre los órganos del poder popular* (Havana: Imprenta Federico Engels, 1976), p. 9.

87. *Granma Weekly Review*, September 8, 1974, p. 5; *Constitución OPP*, pp. 17–18, 22; *Granma*, April 8, 1975, p. 4.

88. Martín, "Informe," pp. 108–109; *Granma*, June 17, 1966, p. 4.

89. *Granma*, October 30, 1972, p. 2.

90. Computed from Martín, "Informe" p. 108; *Granma*, November 19, 1970, p. 1; ibid., December 3, 1970, p. 1; *Granma Weekly Review*, August 1, 1971, p. 2; ibid., May 7, 1972, p. 2.

91. "Discurso del Cmdte. Fidel Castro en la plenaria provincial de la CTC," *Pensamiento crítico* no. 45 (October 1970): 108; *Granma*, August 1, 1970, p. 6; *Granma Weekly Review*, October 24, 1971, p. 4.

92. *Granma*, February 24, 1973, p. 1; *Granma Weekly Review*, November 4, 1973, p. 5; *Verde olivo* 17, no. 1 (January 1975): 12.

93. There is a very weak direct relationship between each union's share of the Confederation membership (X_4) and its actual representation at the Congress (X_1), after one controls for the effect of the intervening political variable (X_3). Although the zero-order correlation between membership share and actual representation is very high, it is in fact channeled through the impact of the intervening political variable (the path through an intervening X_3 is far stronger than the path through an intervening X_2). To explain representation at the labor congress of 1973 one therefore needs to know both the share of the membership and the outcome of elite political decisions; the impact of the former variable is felt, for the most part, only through the intervention of the latter.

Intercorrelations among the four variables, computed from table 7.3, are as follows:

X_1 and X_2	.69
X_1 and X_3	.94
X_1 and X_4	.81
X_2 and X_3	.41

$$X_2 \text{ and } X_4 \qquad .46$$
$$X_3 \text{ and } X_4 \qquad .79$$

Or, in figure form:

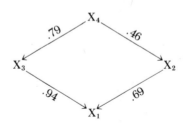

Predictions:	actual	versus	expected
$r_{23} = r_{34}r_{24}$	.41		$.36 = (.79)\,(.46)$
$r_{14} = r_{13}r_{34}$	.81		$.74 = (.94)\,(.79)$

Workers per delegate (X_1), the dependent variable, is the actual pattern of representation at the congress. Workers per rank-and-file delegate (X_2) refers to the minority of the delegates actually elected by the workers directly at the base. The percentage of rank-and-file delegates (X_3) is the key independent political variable; it tells us what decisions were made by the leaders of the confederation and of each federation in the process of apportioning union delegates between labor bureaucrats and rank-and-file delegates. The percentage of the confederation membership (X_4) is the key demographic variable. If representation at the congress were a perfect reflection of the distribution of union membership, then X_1, X_2, and X_4 would be constants. For the methodology used here, see Herbert Blalock, *Causal Inferences in Nonexperimental Research* (Chapel Hill: University of North Carolina Press, 1964), chap. 3.

94. *Granma*, March 4, 1975, p. 2.

95. Ibid., May 23, 1977, p. 1.

96. "Reglamento general de la ANAP," *ANAP* 7, nos. 5–6 (May–June 1967): 22; "Convoca la ANAP al cuarto Congreso campesinó," ibid. (September 1971): 29; "Dictamen de la comisión de organización al IV Congreso nacional campesino," ibid., (December 1971–January 1972): 32.

97. Computed from *Granma Weekly Review*, December 8, 1974, pp. 2, 5; *Verde olivo* 16, no. 42 (October 20, 1974): 26; G. Zafesov, "Cuba: Signs of Momentous Changes," *International Affairs* (Moscow) no. 9 (September 1974): 116; *Granma*, November 26, 1974, p. 1. These calculations are based on the conservative assumption that every employed woman and every woman member of the Communist party was a member of the FMC; while the assumption is plausible, it cannot be proved. If fewer employed women and women party members belonged to the FMC, then the over-representation of women in these groups who did belong to the FMC was even greater than the text suggests.

98. J. J. Rousseau, *The Social Contract and Discourses*, trans. G. D. H. Cole (New York: Dutton, 1950), p. 93.

99. *Granma Weekly Review*, October 6, 1968, p. 28; ibid., December 29, 1968, p. 1; ibid., October 4, 1970; ibid., August 7, 1971, p. 2; ibid., March 14, 1971, p. 1.

100. Computed from ibid., November 4, 1973, p. 4; García Mouri, "Proceso," p. 31.

101. *Granma Weekly Review,* November 4, 1973, p. 4.

102. Harnecker, *Cuba: dictadura?* pp. 43–53; computations from *Granma Weekly Review,* January 4, 1976, p. 6.

103. Armando López Coll and Armando Santiago, "Notas sobre el proceso de planificación en Cuba," *Economía y desarrollo* no. 29 (May–June 1975): 17, 21, 22.

104. Ibid., no. 25 (September–October 1974): 209; *Granma,* February 6, 1975, p. 4; Pérez-Stable, "Cuba's Workers 1975," p. 8. For a view that stresses more autonomous rank-and-file participation, see Pérez-Stable, "Los sindicatos," pp. 20–23. See also Margolles, "Building up a System," p. 62; *Bohemia* 65, no. 34 (August 24, 1973): 36.

105. Computed from *Granma Weekly Review,* January 4, 1976, p. 5; *Granma,* January 15, 1976, p. 3; ibid., January 26, 1976, p. 5.

106. Computed from *Granma Weekly Review,* February 19, 1976, p. 3.

107. Computed from ibid., November 29, 1974, p. 2; *Granma,* November 26, 1974, p. 5; ibid., March 2, 1975, p. 5.

108. *Granma Weekly Review,* August 4, 1974, p. 3; computed from *Anuario 1972,* p. 35; *Granma,* October 11, 1971, p. 1; ibid., February 17, 1976, p. 4; *Granma Weekly Review,* May 7, 1972, p. 2; *Bohemia* 67, no. 18 (May 2, 1975): 59; *Granma,* October 12, 1976, p. 1; ibid., October 19, 1976, p. 1. These estimates for labor-union elections are conservative. In 1970, 1,282,675 workers voted; in 1971, 1,244,688. The number of administrative and managerial posts was subtracted from the total of the 1970 and 1971 labor forces to yield the blue-collar worker subtotal; in addition, 10 percent of this subtotal was subtracted on the assumption that not all workers were labor-union members in 1970–71; the resulting probable confederation memberships are 1,690,284 for 1970 and 1,690,318 for 1971. These are low statistics because it is known that there were 2,065,505 members in 1973; the actual turnout in 1970–71 is thus probably overestimated. At the beginning of 1975, 90 percent of all workers belonged to labor unions, a figure that rose to 93 percent at the end of that year.

109. Eugenio Rodríguez Balari, "Trabajo y desarrollo del Instituto de la Demanda Interna," *Economía y desarrollo* no. 21 (January–February 1974): 153–155, 161–162; ibid., no. 25 (September–October 1974): 213; Louis Wolf Goodman, "The Social Sciences in Cuba," *Items* 30, no. 4 (December 1976): 54–61.

110. "Dictamen de la comisión ideológica al IV Congreso nacional campesino," *ANAP* (December 1971–January 1972): 43.

111. Roberto Gil, "Cada día más: ojos y oídos de la revolución," *Con la guardia en alto* 10, no. 8 (August 1971): 6–8; ibid., 11, no. 10 (October 1972): 21; Flavio Bravo, "Recabamos una vez más la ayuda de esta poderosa organización de masas," ibid., 12, nos. 3–4 (March–April 1973): 33.

112. *Granma,* February 6, 1976, p. 2; Harnecker, *Cuba: dictadura?* p. 132.

113. Conversations with Lourdes Casal, February 28, 1975, and March 24–28, 1975, and with Marifeli Pérez-Stable, March 24–28, 1975; Harnecker, *Cuba: dictadura?* 118–131.

114. Gabriel Almond and Sidney Verba, *The Civic Culture* (Boston: Little, Brown, 1965), pp. 315–324; Alex Inkeles, "Participant Citizenship in Six Developing Countries," *American Political Science Review* 63 (1969): 1122–23, 1139–46.

115. For a theoretical statement, based on comparative data, bearing on the issues raised here, see Robert Dahl, *Polyarchy: Participation and Opposition* (New Haven: Yale University Press, 1971), Chap. 1, especially p. 3.

8. THE COMMUNIST PARTY

1. Faure Chomón was the only person in the top leadership in the early 1970s who was subsequently dropped. Unlike the others, he had belonged neither to the Twenty-sixth of July Movement nor to the prerevolutionary Communist party. He was the first revolutionary ambassador to the Soviet Union and returned in March 1962, just as the Escalante scandal was breaking, to become minister of communications. He then served as minister of transportation for eight years. Chomón was a virulent critic of the old Communists, accusing several of them of crimes against the revolution in a 1964 trial. He was appointed to the Secretariat in 1965. When the old Communists and the Soviet Union regained favor, Chomón was demoted. He moved to Oriente province in 1971 and was elected to the executive bureau of the provincial party in 1974. At the First Party Congress in 1975, Chomón was dropped from the Secretariat; he remained a member of the Central Committee and was appointed secretary-general of the new Tunas provincial party in 1976.

2. See especially the Central Intelligence Agency's *Directory of Personalities of the Cuban Government, Official Organizations, and Mass Organizations* (Washington, D.C., 1974).

3. Comité Central del Partido Comunista de Cuba, Departamento de Orientación Revolucionaria, *Estatutos del partido comunista de Cuba* (Havana: Imprenta Federico Engels, 1976), pp. 10–11 (hereafter cited as *Estatutos del partido*).

4. F. Petrenko, "Avangard Kubinskovo Naroda," *Partinaia Zhizn* no. 8 (April 1973): 76; *Granma Weekly Review*, April 14, 1972, p. 2; ibid., June 18, 1967, p. 4; ibid., January 4, 1976, pp. 8–9; *Granma*, April 12, 1975, p. 3; ibid., April 22, 1975, p. 2; ibid., January 8, 1976, p. 2; ibid., April 2, 1977, p. 4; *Estatutos del partido*, pp. 10–11; "Communist Party of Cuba," *World Marxist Review* 17, no. 3 (March 1974): 139; *Juventud rebelde*, July 10, 1975, p. 6. For interviews with party factory workers about how they select members, see Marta Harnecker, *Cuba: ¿dictadura o democracia?* (Mexico: Siglo XXI, 1975), pp. 59–70. Fidel Castro told Frank Mankiewicz and Kirby Jones in 1974 that "The party . . . is made up of exemplary members . . . elected by the masses; to be a member of the party you have to be nominated at your place of employment." He neglected to mention the high degree of selectivity and the fact that nonemployed persons can also belong to the party. See *With Fidel* (Chicago: Playboy Press, 1975), p. 87.

5. *Estatutos del partido*, pp. 11–13, 55. An example of an application for party membership in the late 1960s can be found in *Cuba* 8 (January 1969): 76–77. In addition to name, age, marital status, residence, and number of dependents, this form requested information on past military service (including participation in mass mobilizations during national emergencies and in military operations), education, including skills-training courses, social class, prerevolutionary activities and membership in mass organizations, volunteer labor, work plans, and criminal record, if any. It ended by asking the applicant to state an opinion of the Communist party, of religion, and of himself.

While some types of misbehavior—such as adultery—prior to membership were not bars to membership, they were apparently grounds for expulsion if committed by a party member. No religious person could become a party member. For more on party membership and religion, see Aldo V. Büntig, "The Chuch in Cuba: Toward a New Frontier," in *Religion in Cuba Today*, ed. Alice Hageman and Philip Wheaton (New York: Association Press, 1971), pp. 112–113; Jose Yglesias, *In the Fist of the Revolution: Life in a Cuban Country Town* (New York: Vintage Books, 1969), pp. 79–80. For evidence that party members in rural Matanzas in the late 1960s still hung religious pictures on their walls, see Michael A. Pettit, "Social and Economic Change in the Community around a Sugar Mill in Cuba" (Ph.D. diss., University of California–Berkeley, 1973), p. 350.

6. Mario Rodríguez, "Experiencias del trabajo de educación del PURSC en Matanzas," *Cuba socialista* no. 41 (January 1965): 133; *Granma Weekly Review*, July 20, 1969, p. 10.

7. "Primer activo nacional de educación interna del partido," *Ediciones COR* no. 16 (1971): 5.

8. Ibid., pp. 8–10; Osvaldo Dorticós, "La teoría: instrumento indispensable de la práctica revolucionaria," *Economía y desarrollo* no. 11 (May–June 1972): 65.

9. "Primer activo," pp. 30, 33.

10. *Granma Weekly Review*, January 4, 1976, p. 9.

11. Petrenko, "Avangard Kubinskovo," p. 75; "Communist Party of Cuba," pp. 138–139; *Juventud rebelde*, July 24, 1975, p. 6; *Granma Weekly Review*, January 4, 1976, p. 9.

12. Nelson P. Valdés, *Cuba: ¿socialismo democrático o burocratismo colectivista?* (Bogotá: Ediciones Tercer Mundo, 1973), p. 19; *Granma Weekly Review*, October 8, 1967, p. 3; ibid., August 4, 1974, p. 3.

13. Computed from "Balance de la construcción del PURS," *Cuba socialista* no. 32 (April 1964): 133; Gil Green, *Revolution, Cuban Style* (New York: International Publishers, 1970), p. 76; Howard I. Blutstein et al., *Area Handbook for Cuba* (Washington, D.C.: Government Printing Office, 1971), p. 220; "Primer activo," p. 10; Petrenko, "Avangard Kubinskovo," p. 75; "Communist Party of Cuba," p. 138; G. Zafesov, "Cuba: Signs of Momentous Changes," *International Affairs* (Moscow) 9 (September 1974): 116; "Thirty Years of Socialist Progress," *World Marxist Review* 18, no. 1 (January 1975): 77; *Granma Weekly Review*, January 4, 1976, p. 9; *Anuario 1972*, p. 18; *Anuario 1973*, p. 22; *Anuario 1974*. p. 22. Population for 1975 is based on a compound annual rate of population growth at 2 percent.

14. *Granma Weekly Review*, April 16, 1967, p. 3; ibid., April 23, 1967, p. 3; ibid., April 30, 1967, p. 4; ibid., May 28, 1967, p. 2; ibid., September 28, 1969, p. 3.

15. Alternative estimates for March–April 1962 give 75,000 and 72,000. In addition to members, there were 3,518 candidates for membership in 1963, 4,795 in 1964, and 16,772 in 1967. Carlos Quintela, "La juventud cubana y la revolución," *Cuba socialista* no. 8 (April 1962): 37; Adolfo Rivero, "La Unión de Jóvenes Comunistas de Cuba," ibid., no. 12 (August 1962): 48; "Breve reseña del reciente Congreso Nacional de la Asociación de Jóvenes Rebeldes," ibid., no. 9 (May 1962): 136; *Aclaraciones: Periódico Hoy* (Havana: Editora Política, 1966), 3: 63; Miguel Martín, "Nueva etapa de la Unión de Jóvenes Comunistas cubanos," *Cuba socialista* no. 36 (August 1964): 50;

Granma Weekly Review, January 15, 1967, p. 4; Luis López, "Séptima conferencia nacional UJC," *Verde olivo* 16, no. 14 (April 7, 1974): 5; *Granma*, April 5, 1975, p. 3; ibid., January 8, 1976, p. 2; ibid., April 2, 1977, p. 1.

16. López, "Séptima conferencia," p. 5; *Granma Weekly Review*, April 14, 1974, p. 3.

17. *Granma Weekly Review*, July 25, 1971, p. 2; ibid., August 12, 1973, pp. 1, 2.

18. Ibid., April 23, 1972, p. 8; ibid., April 14, 1974, p. 2; ibid., April 17, 1977, p. 6; *Granma*, March 26, 1977, p. 1; ibid., April 2, 1977, pp. 2, 4.

19. Martín, "Nueva etapa," p. 68.

20. *Granma Weekly Review*, April 14, 1974, p. 2.

21. Ibid., p. 2; *Gramma*, April 2, 1977, p. 1.

22. "El núcleo de revolucionarios activos y algunos aspectos de su funcionamiento," *Cuba socialista* no. 7 (March 1962): 123–125; *Revolución*, February 23, 1963.

23. Fidel Castro, "El PURS, espina dorsal de la revolución," *Cuba socialista* no. 19 (March 1963): 18; Eduardo Yasells, "El Partido en el Turquino," *Verde olivo* 4, no. 40 (October 6, 1963): 14.

24. Isidoro Malmierca, "El fortalecimiento de las organizaciones de masas en la región de Mayabeque," *Cuba socialista* no. 23 (July 1963): 131–132.

25. Miguel Martín, "Informe al Congreso," *Cuba socialista* no. 62 (October 1966): 108; Hernán Barrera, "Building the United Party of the Socialist Revolution in Cuba," *World Marxist Review* 6, no. 12 (December 1963): 56–58; *Granma Weekly Review*, August 28, 1966, p. 3; ibid., February 17, 1974, p. 3; ibid., September 3, 1967, p. 4; ibid., December 8, 1974, p. 2; ibid., January 4, 1976, p. 9; Petrenko, "Avangard Kubinskovo," p. 76; "Communist Party of Cuba," p. 139.

26. *Revolución*, August 24, 1964, p. 5; José Matar, "Debemos promover los mejores cuadros a los organismos superiores de dirección," *Guía para la acción* no. 15 (March 1965): 31.

27. "Intervención del compañero Armando Hart sobre organización," *Cuba socialista* no. 51 (November 1965): 51.

28. *Granma*, February 6, 1976, p. 2; ibid., February 17, 1976, p. 4.

29. Ibid., April 10, 1975, p. 3.

30. *Granma Weekly Review*, October 5, 1969, p. 4; ibid., May 14, 1967, p. 11.

31. Joel Domenech, "Aplicación del plan de eficiencia industrial," *Cuba socialista* no. 63 (November 1966): 48–51.

32. Pedro Margolles, "Building up a System of Representative Bodies," *World Marxist Review* 18, no. 2 (February 1975): 61; *La constitución de los órganos de poder popular* (Havana: Imprenta Federico Engels, 1974), pp. 17–18.

33. *Granma Weekly Review*, September 8, 1974, p. 5.

34. Ibid., July 11, 1971, p. 4.

35. Ramiro Valdés, "Discurso pronunciado en la clausura de la II reunión nacional de las secretarías de construcción del partido," *Ediciones COR* no. 14 (1971): 9–11, 15.

36. "Resolución sobre la política de formación, selección, ubicación, promoción y superación de los cuadros," *Economía y desarrollo* no. 36 (July–August 1976): 169–171; *Granma Weekly Review*, September 12, 1976, p. 12.

37. Asteria Perdomo, "La lucha del regional de San José de las Lajas por dominar las tareas de la producción," *Cuba socialista* no. 32 (April 1964): 128–129, 131; Isidoro

Malmierca, "El método de las tres vías y los tres principios para el crecimiento normal del partido," *Cuba socialista* no. 35 (July 1964): p. 134.

38. *Granma Weekly Review,* February 1, 1970, p. 4.

39. "Discurso del compañero Osvaldo Dorticós," *Cuba socialista* no. 51 (November 1965): 57.

40. *Granma,* February 7, 1973, p. 1; *Granma Weekly Review,* January 11, 1976, pp. 2–3.

41. *Granma,* March 16, 1974, p. 2; ibid., April 16, 1975, p. 1; ibid., July 31, 1975, p. 1; *Granma Weekly Review,* March 2, 1975, p. 3; ibid., August 10, 1975, p. 7; ibid., September 28, 1975, p. 5; ibid., October 12, 1975, p. 5; ibid., October 19, 1975, p. 1; ibid., October 26, 1975, p. 1; ibid., November 2, 1975, p. 1; ibid., November 16, 1975, p. 1.

42. In many instances *family* can be taken literally. In addition to the brothers Fidel and Raúl Castro and Raúl's wife, Vilma Espín, the leaders of the revolution include Armando Hart, minister of culture, and his wife Haydée Santamaría, president of the main international cultural center in Cuba, Casa de las Américas. Both have been associated with the Castro brothers since the early days of the struggle against Batista. Aldo Santamaría, longtime chief of the navy, is Haydée's brother. The late Juan Marinello, the prerevolutionary Communist party's presidential candidate and a member of Batista's cabinet in the 1940s, was ambassador to UNESCO since 1963; his nephew, Zoilo, is president of the Academy of Sciences. One of Cuba's most respected military officers, José Ramón Fernández, has since become minister of education; his wife, Asela de los Santos, is director of teacher training at the ministry. All are members of the Central Committee (Juan Marinello until 1977). Nor is this an exhaustive list; it suggests that the long-standing Cuban tradition of trusting the affairs of state to relatives has not been interrupted.

43. *Granma,* December 21, 1975, p. 1; *Granma Weekly Review,* January 11, 1976, p. 3.

44. *Granma Weekly Review,* January 11, 1976, p. 2.

45. "Vida de la organización revolucionaria," *Cuba socialista* no. 8 (April 1962): 136–137; *Verde olivo* 16, no. 42 (October 20, 1974): 52; Oneida Álvarez, "Revolutionary Cuba's Economic Development," *World Marxist Review* 17, no. 11 (November 1974): 99; George Volsky, "Cuba Fifteen Years Later," *Current History* 66, no. 389 (January 1974): 11.

46. "Discurso del Comandante Fidel Castro el 23 de agosto de 1970: X aniversario de la Federación de Mujeres Cubanas," *Pensamiento crítico* no. 45 (October 1970): 61; *Verde olivo* 14, no. 31 (July 30, 1972): 3–4; *Granma Weekly Review,* January 6, 1974, p. 3; ibid., May 1, 1977, p. 1; *Educación* 2, no 6 (July–September 1972): 36, 39.

47. *Granma,* April 5, 1976, p. 2; ibid., July 16, 1976, p. 1; ibid., November 30, 1976, p. 1; *Granma Weekly Review,* January 4, 1976, p. 2; ibid., June 19, 1977, p. 1.

48. Petrenko, "Avangard Kubinskovo," p. 76; "Communist Party of Cuba," p. 138.

49. "Acuerdos sobre la construcción del PURS," *Cuba socialista* no. 20 (April 1963): 118–120; "Vida de la organización revolucionaria," *Cuba socialista* no. 14 (October 1962): 121–122; *Granma,* July 3, 1975, p. 2.

50. *Granma,* March 4, 1974, p. 1; ibid., March 5, 1974, p. 1; ibid., March 7, 1974, p. 2; ibid., March 8, 1974, p. 2; ibid., March 11, 1974, pp. 1–2; ibid., March 16,

1974, p. 2; *Granma Weekly Review*, January 13, 1974, p. 3; ibid., March 24, 1974, p. 7; ibid., March 31, 1974, p. 12.

51. *Granma Weekly Review*, January 4, 1976, p. 9.

52. *Estatutos del partido*, pp. 33–35.

53. Secundino Guerra, "Los seccionales del Partido en La Habana," *Cuba socialista* no. 18 (February 1963): 126–127; Luis Méndez, "El avance del Partido en Matanzas," ibid., no. 30 (February 1964): 144–147; José Fuertes Jiménez, "Problemas de organización del Partido en las unidades agropecuarias de Camagüey," ibid., no. 39 (November 1964): 124–128.

54. *Estatutos del partido*, pp. 15, 27; "Resolución sobre la política de formación," p. 170.

55. F. Castro, "El PURS, espina dorsal," p. 18.

56. See Lionel Soto's articles in *Cuba socialista*, especially "Don años de instrucción revolucionaria," no. 18 (February 1963): 37–38, and "Las escuelas de instrucción revolucionaria en el ciclo político-técnico," no. 41 (January 1965): 77.

57. Richard Fagen, *The Transformation of Political Cutlure in Cuba* (Stanford: Stanford University Press, 1969), pp. 107, 136–137; see also Lionel Soto's articles in *Cuba socialista:* "Las escuelas de instrucción revolucionaria y la formación de cuadros," no. 3 (November 1961): 28–41; "Nuevo desarrollo de la instrucción revolucionaria," no. 12 (August 1962): 32–45; "Las escuelas de instrucción revolucionaria en una nueva fase," no. 30 (February 1964): 62–77; "El quinto aniversario de las escuelas de instrucción revolucionaria," no. 53 (January 1966): 72–91.

58. *Granma Weekly Review*, March 17, 1974, p. 9; ibid., January 4, 1976, p. 9; *Granma*, December 2, 1975, p. 5; ibid., July 16, 1976, p. 3.

59. *Granma Weekly Review*, December 22, 1974, p. 4.

60. *Granma Weekly Review*, January 4, 1976, pp. 8–9; ibid., January 11, 1976, p. 2. The same themes are developed, less eloquently, in the 1975 party statutes. See *Estatutos del partido*, pp. 14–17.

9. THE CIVIC SOLDIER

1. Samuel P. Huntington, *The Soldier and the State* (Cambridge, Mass.: Harvard University Press, 1957), pp. 80–85.

2. The terms are taken from Amos Perlmutter, "The Praetorian State and the Praetorian Army: Toward a Taxonomy of Civil-Military Relations in Developing Politics," in *Political Development and Social Change*, ed. J. L. Finkle and R. W. Gable (New York: Wiley, 1971), pp. 314–324.

3. See, for instance, Gino Germani and Kalman Silvert, "Politics, Social Structure and Military Intervention in Latin America," *European Journal of Sociology* 2 (1961):62–81; Morris Janowitz, *The Military in the Political Development of New Nations* (Chicago: University of Chicago Press, 1964); Samuel P. Huntington, *Political Order in Changing Societies* (New Haven: Yale University Press, 1968), chap. 4.

4. The role theory described here is based on that of Robert L. Kahn, Donald M. Wolfe, Robert P. Quinn, and J. Diedrick Snoek, *Organizational Stress: Studies in Role Conflict and Ambiguity* (New York: Wiley, 1964), pp. 11–35.

5. H. A. Simon, *Administrative Behavior* (New York: MacMillan, 1961), p. 118. P. M. Blau has argued that the attainment of organizational objectives (such as military

security) generates a stress on finding new objectives (such as those in the areas of politics or economics). I think it is likely that organizational growth has been a specific goal of the military organizations or, at the very least, that the prevention of organizational decline has been such a goal. The concept of the civic soldier has legitimized shifts in objectives or missions of the military organization as perceived by the entire elite. In turn, the ability to shift objectives, as Samuel Huntington has argued, adds to the organizational age of the military organization, so that it becomes more fully institutionalized. See P. M. Blau, *The Dynamics of Bureaucracy* (Chicago: University of Chicago Press, 1955), p. 195; Huntington, *Political Order*, pp. 13–17; W. H. Starbuck, "Organizational Growth and Development," in *Handbook of Organizations*, ed. J. G. March (Chicago: Rand McNally, 1965), pp. 451–533.

6. Ricardo Adam y Silva, *La gran mentira* (Havana: Editorial Lex, 1947); Louis A. Pérez, *Army Politics in Cuba, 1898–1958* (Pittsburgh: University of Pittsburgh Press, 1976), chaps. 2–5.

7. Fulgencio Batista, *Revolución social o política reformista* (Havana: Prensa Indoamericana, 1944), pp. 58–59, 62, 82–85, 123–124, 127; *Cuba's Three Year Plan* (Havana: Cultural S.A., 1937); Consejo Corporativo de Educación, Sanidad y Beneficencia, *Militarismo, anti-militarismo, pseudomilitarismo* (Ceiba del Agua, Cuba: Talleres del Instituto Cívico-Militar, 1939), pp. 5–6, 8, 82, 106; Edmund Chester, *A Sergeant Named Batista* (New York: Holt, 1954); Pérez, *Army Politics in Cuba*, chaps. 6–11.

8. José Suárez Amador, "Octavo aniversario de L.C.B.," *Verde olivo* 11, no. 28 (July 12, 1970): 4–5; ibid., 4, no. 47 (November 24, 1963): 5, 10–11; *Granma*, March 5, 1966, p. 8; ibid., March 13, 1966, p. 8; *Granma Weekly Review*, January 4, 1976, p. 8.

9. For a discussion of the various estimates of the numbers of people killed in the 1950s and 1960s, see Jorge I. Domínguez, "The Civic Soldier in Cuba," in *Political-Military Systems: Comparative Perspectives*, ed. Catherine M. Kelleher (Beverly Hills, Calif.: Sage Publications, 1974), pp. 216–218; see also Hugh Thomas, *Cuba: The Pursuit of Freedom* (New York: Harper & Row, 1971), pp. 1024–1025, 1042, 1044; Raúl Castro, "Graduación del III curso de la escuela básica superior 'General Máximo Gómez,' " *Ediciones al orientador revolucionario* no. 17 (1967): 11; *Granma Weekly Review*, June 13, 1971, pp. 2–3; ibid., December 12, 1971, p. 6; ibid., January 4, 1976, p. 7; Julio C. Fernández, "¿Qué fue el bandidismo?" *Bohemia* 68, no. 23 (June 4, 1976):44–49. See Carlos Rivero Collado's *Los sobrinos del tío Sam* (Havana: Instituto Cubano del Libro, 1976) for a fascinating, though obviously partisan, history of Cuban-exile counterrevolutionary activities written by the son of Batista's former prime minister, who became a revolutionary double agent operating in the United States until 1974.

10. *Granma Weekly Review*, January 4, 1976, p. 7.

11. Alfredo Reyes, "Ejército de la tiranía," *Verde olivo* 7, no. 45 (November 12, 1966): 23, 27–28.

12. For Prime Minister Castro's estimates, see *Granma Weekly Review*, December 12, 1971, p. 6; ibid., December 1, 1974, p. 7. See also Osvaldo Dorticós, "El error que no cometeremos jamás es el de no estar alerta," *Cuba socialista* no. 59 (July 1966): 1, 10–12; *Granma*, April 16, 1973, p. 1; ibid., August 9, 1975, p. 2; ibid., June 8, 1976, p. 4; ibid., April 20, 1976, p. 2; *Granma Weekly Review*, September 28, 1975, p. 7; *Verde olivo* 16, no. 43 (October 27, 1974): 17–18; International Institute for Strategic

Studies, *The Military Balance 1966–67* (London, 1966), p. 11 (hereafter cited as *IISS*); *IISS, 1970–71*, p. 76; *IISS, 1974–75*, p. 65; *IISS, 1975–76*, p. 64; Gabriel García Márquez, "Colombian Author Writes on Cuba's Angola Intervention," *Washington Post*, January 10, 1977, p. A14; T. N. Dupuy and Wendell Blanchard, *Almanac of World Military Power*, 2d ed. (Dunn Loring, Va.: Dupuy, 1972), p. 24; Howard I. Blutstein, Lynne Cox Anderson, Elinor C. Betters, Deborah Lane, Jonathan A. Leonard, and Charles Townsend, *Area Handbook for Cuba* (Washington, D.C.: Government Printing Office, 1971), p. 439. For a history of the Frontier Corps and its auxiliary units, see Eliseo Alberto, "De pie en la frontera," *Cuba internacional* 6, no. 61 (September 1974): 20, 23, 25.

13. *IISS, 1975–76*, p. 64; *IISS, 1974–75*, p. 65; *IISS, 1970–71*, p. 76; *IISS, 1968–69*, p. 12; IISS, *1966–67*, p. 11; Stockholm International Peace Research Institute, *World Armaments and Disarmament Yearbook, 1973* (Stockholm: Almqvist and Wiksell, 1973), pp. 248–249, 337 (hereafter cited as *World Armaments*); *World Armaments, 1972*, p. 141; Dupuy and Blanchard, *Almanac of World Power*, pp. 24–25 and glossary; John Stanley and Maurice Pearton, *International Trade in Arms* (New York: Praeger, 1972), p. 216; *Granma*, April 18, 1972, p. 2 (I am grateful to Carmelo Mesa-Lago for this reference); U.S., Congress, House, Committee on Foreign Affairs, Subcommittee on Inter-American Affairs, "Soviet Activities in Cuba," in *Hearings*, 93rd Cong. (Washington, D.C.: Government Printing Office, 1974), p. 56; *Granma Weekly Review*, December 12, 1976, p.11.

14. Raúl Castro, "Las FAR rinden profundo y sentido homenaje al vigésimo aniversario," *Bohemia* 65, no. 31 (August 3, 1973): 28; idem, "Graduación del III curso."

15. *Granma Weekly Review*, April 17, 1973, p. 2; *Granma*, April 16, 1973, p. 1; ibid., April 16, 1975, p. 2.

16. "Algunos aspectos relacionados con la ley del servicio militar general y su reglamento," *Verde olivo* 17, no. 4 (January 26, 1975): 54; *Granma*, March 18, 1975, p. 3; ibid., July 11, 1975, p. 2; *Granma Weekly Review*, December 1, 1974, p. 7; ibid., July 3, 1977, p. 3; Raúl Castro, "Sabemos que el imperialismo se debilita," *Verde olivo* 17, no. 29 (July 20, 1975): 4; "Sistema de registro militar," ibid., no. 12 (March 23, 1975): 61.

17. "Sobre el trabajo político en el aseguramiento a los ejercicios de tiro con armas de infantería," *Verde olivo* 16, no. 24 (June 16, 1974): 28–29, 31.

18. On army schools, see González Tosca, "Escuelas," ibid., 13, no. 49 (December 6, 1971): 51, 87–90; on navy schools, Agenar Martí, "A toda máquina," *Cuba internacional* 6, no. 60 (August 1974): 12–13; "Convocatoria," *Verde olivo* 18, no. 7 (February 15, 1976): 36–39; Lisanka, "Escuela de cadetes inter-armas 'General Antonio Maceo,' " ibid., 17, no. 21 (May 25, 1975): 37; "Primer encuentro de egresados del ITM," ibid., no. 27 (July 6, 1975): 52; Eloísa Ballester, "Por una mejor eficiencia económica," ibid., 18, no. 20 (May 16, 1976): 53. See also ibid., 9, no. 17 (April 28, 1968), pp. 5–7, 10; *Granma Weekly Review*, May 30, 1971, p. 6; ibid., January 20, 1974, p. 7; *Granma*, July 24, 1975, p. 3; Raúl Castro, "La emulación socialista," *Verde olivo* 17, no. 5 (February 2, 1975): 11. On military research, see Centro Nacional de Investigaciones Científicas, *Informe, 1969* (Havana: Universidad de La Habana, 1969), p. 12; Comisión Nacional Cubana de la UNESCO, "Los estudiantes investigan," *Boletín* 12, no. 48 (January–February 1973): 14; *Granma*, December 25, 1974, p. 1.

19. *Granma Weekly Review,* December 16, 1973; *Granma,* July 12, 1976, p. 4; ibid., July 15, 1976, p. 3; ibid., November 25, 1976, p. 1.

20. Sergio Canales and Leonel Gil, "La casa central de las FAR," *Verde olivo* 17, no. 30 (July 27, 1975): 14, 16–17; Héctor de Arturo and Jorge Blanco, "Primera conferencia del partido en el EJT," ibid., no. 46 (November 16, 1975): 17; Lisanka, "Brigada aérea de la guardia 'Playa Girón,' " ibid., 18, no. 17 (April 25, 1976): 43.

21. *Granma Weekly Review,* August 8, 1976, p. 3.

22. R. Castro, "Sabemos," p. 3; Mario Rodríguez, "El estado mayor," *Verde olivo* 17, no. 47 (November 23, 1975): 35; Raúl Castro, "Con la realización de la maniobra," ibid., no. 50 (December 14, 1975): 16–17, 54; Joaquín Quinta, "La maniobra," ibid., p. 55; "Maniobra 'Primer Congreso,' " ibid., 18, no. 1 (January 4, 1976): 38; *Granma,* December 5, 1975, p. 1.

23. García Márquez, "Colombian Author," p. A14; idem, "Cuba en Angola: Operación Carlota," *Proceso* (January 1977): 14; *New York Times,* February 17, 1977, p. 1; *Granma,* June 8, 1976, p. 4. For a mistaken estimate by the United States government, see Drew Middleton, "The Cuban Soldier in Angola," *New York Times,* March 3, 1976, p. 4.

24. For a study of the racial composition of the Cuban armed forces, see Jorge I. Domínguez, "Racial and Ethnic Relations in the Cuban Armed Forces: A Non-Topic," *Armed Forces and Society* 2, no. 2 (February 1976): 273–290; the method described in that article has been applied to January 1976 data for Cuba's three armies drawn from *Verde olivo,* 18, no. 4 (January 25, 1976): 15–16, and ibid., no. 5 (February 1, 1976): 56–57. See also Georgie Anne Geyer, "Cuba in Angola: A New Look," *Boston Globe,* June 20, 1976, p. 56.

25. To establish the dates, compare *Verde olivo* 17, no 34 (August 24, 1975): 12; ibid., no. 35 (August 31, 1975): 60; and ibid., no. 37 (September 14, 1975): 55. President Marien Ngouabi of the Congo, one of Cuba's key allies during the Angolan war, arrived in Cuba on September 13, 1975; he was the only one of eight heads of state visiting Cuba in that year to spend all his public time in military-related activities. Cuban military personnel had been in the Congo as early as mid-August; see E. G. Viamonte, "Impresiones de una visita," in *Verde olivo* 17, no. 38 (September 21, 1975): 10. For other changes in top commands, see ibid., no. 39 (September 28, 1975): 54; ibid., no. 40 (October 5, 1975); ibid., no. 42 (October 19, 1975); ibid., 18, no. 32 (August 8, 1976): 16, 61; *Granma,* July 24, 1976, p. 1; ibid., July 28, 1976, p. 4. For Fidel Castro's acknowledgment of the presence of Cuban forces in Angola in October 1975, see *Granma,* April 20, 1976, p. 2; for an acknowledgement of an even earlier arrival, see Barry A. Sklar, "Cuba: Normalization of Relations," Issue Brief no. IB75030, Congressional Research Service, Library of Congress (March 3, 1976), p. 23.

26. *Granma Weekly Review,* January 4, 1976, p. 7.

27. For a detailed discussion of these costs, see Jorge I. Domínguez, "The Cuban Operation in Angola: Costs and Benefits for the Cuban Armed Forces," *Cuban Studies* 8, no. 1 (January 1978). See also Fiscalía Militar de las FAR, "Los estímulos y las correcciones disciplinarias," *Verde olivo* 17, no. 47 (November 23, 1975): 22–24; idem, "Las reclamaciones en las FAR," ibid., 18, no. 31 (August 1, 1976): 40; "Las resoluciones y acuerdos del primer congreso del partido comunista de Cuba," ibid., no. 18 (May 2, 1976): 30; Sklar, "Cuba: Normalization of Relations," p. 12.

28. For an extended discussion of these activities, see Jorge I. Domínguez, "The Armed Forces and Foreign Relations," in *Cuba in the World*, ed. Cole Blasier and Carmelo Mesa-Lago (Pittsburgh: University of Pittsburgh Press, 1978); see also William J. Durch, "The Cuban Military in Africa and the Middle East: From Algeria to Angola," Center for Naval Analyses, professional paper no. 201 (Arlington, Va., 1977).

29. *Verde olivo* 4, no. 47 (November 24, 1963): 19. For a discussion of the early development of the civic soldier (although the author does not use that term) in the Cuban armed forces in the late 1950s, during the rebellion, and in the early 1960s, see Louis A. Pérez, Jr., "Army Politics in Socialist Cuba," *Journal of Latin American Studies* 8, no. 2 (November 1976): 251–264.

30. *Verde olivo* 4, no. 47 (November 24, 1963): 19–20, 52; "El proyecto de ley del servicio militar obligatorio," *Cuba socialista* no. 28 (December 1963): 85–87.

31. *Granma*, April 14, 1966, p. 8. I was mistaken in my "Civic Soldier in Cuba," pp. 219–220, 232; Casillas did not become chief of staff, and Castilla was not head of UMAP.

32. *Granma*, April 14, 1966, p. 8; ibid., March 16, 1966, p. 4; *Verde olivo* 7, no. 43 (October 30, 1966): 14–15, supplement; ibid., 8, no. 11 (March 19, 1967): 34–38; ibid., no. 12 (March 26, 1967): 27–30; ibid., no. 18 (May 7, 1967): 19–21; ibid., no. 19 (May 14, 1967): 36–39; see also Jose Yglesias, *In the Fist of the Revolution: Life in a Cuban Country Town* (New York: Vintage Books, 1968), pp. 274–302; Lourdes Casal, "Literature and Society," in *Revolutionary Change in Cuba*, ed. Carmelo Mesa-Lago (Pittsburgh: University of Pittsburgh Press, 1971), p. 459.

33. *Verde olivo* 4, no. 47 (November 24, 1963): 10–11; ibid., no. 4 (January 27, 1963): 52–53; ibid., 11, no. 28 (July 12, 1970): 5; *Granma*, March 5, 1966, p. 8.

34. The percentages assume that the size of the military remained stationary in this period at about 110,000 for the regular forces and 250,000 for all forces. The numbers were taken from *Granma Weekly Review*, July 18, 1971, p. 9. This modifies substantially information in my "Civic Soldier in Cuba," p. 221.

35. Fidel Castro, "Brigada invasora Che Guevara," *Verde olivo* 8, no. 44 (November 5, 1967): 6–7; Fidel Vascos, "Brigada invasora Che Guevara: año 1," ibid., 9, no. 45 (November 10, 1968): 6–7; ibid., 10, no. 45 (November 9, 1969): 7–9, 62; ibid., 11, no. 4 (January 25, 1970): 32; "Algunas tareas cumplidas por las FAR en 1970," ibid., no. 52 (December 27, 1970): 14; René Dumont, "The Militarization of Fidelismo," *Dissent* (September–October 1970): 417–420; K. S. Karol, *Guerrillas in Power* (New York: Hill and Wang, 1970), pp. 444–450, 534–544.

36. *Política internacional* 4, no. 16 (1966): 214–215.

37. R. Castro, "Gaduación del III curso," p. 22; *Granma Weekly Review*, January 7, 1968, p. 3.

38. *Granma Weekly Review*, August 12, 1973, p. 2; *Granma*, April 3, 1975, p. 5; *Juventud rebelde*, January 5, 1975, p. 1.

39. *Granma*, August 5, 1975, p. 3; ibid., April 2, 1977, p. 2.

40. de Arturo and Blanco, "Primera conferencia del partido," p. 18.

41. "Acto de fin de zafra del EJT en Matanzas," *Verde olivo* 18, no. 21 (May 23, 1976): 52.

42. "A paso de victoria se llama Matanzas," *Bohemia* 65, no. 20 (May 18, 1973): 26; *Granma*, January 5, 1976, p. 5; ibid., January 6, 1976, p. 3; ibid., March 24, 1976, p. 1; ibid., July 13, 1976, p. 3; *Bohemia* 68, no. 16 (April 16, 1976): 60.

43. *Granma Weekly Review*, April 3, 1977, p. 1; García Márquez, "Cuba en Angola," pp. 7, 14; Georgie Ann Geyer, "Cuba in Angola," p. 56. For a general discussion, see Domínguez, "Armed Forces and Foreign Relations."

44. *Granma Weekly Review*, January 4, 1976, p. 7.

45. One possibility is that military officers who favored nonmilitary tasks were appointed to civilian posts in the 1970s, while more professional officers who resisted the idea were not. The theory is difficult to prove, though there is some evidence to back it up. Some professional officers have remained within the armed forces, among them Division General Senén Casas Regueiro, chairman of the Joint Chiefs of Staff, first deputy minister of the armed forces, and a veteran of the Angolan war. Other professional officers, however, have been appointed to major civilian posts. José Ramón Fernández, a leading officer in the 1950s, educated a generation of officers to recognize the need for military competence, but even he favored the civic-soldier role and was himself appointed minister of education in 1973; Diocles Torralba, former chief of the air force and antiaircraft defense, preceded Casas Regueiro as chairman of the Joint Chiefs of Staff and joined the executive committee of the cabinet in 1972. Finally, some officers in charge of some professional military activities in the armed forces are hardly typical of professional officers; such is the case of Division General Rogelio Acevedo, deputy minister of the armed forces for technical training and weapons in the mid-1970s, who had led the militia and served in civic-soldier positions in the 1960s.

46. *Granma Weekly Review*, March 23, 1975, p. 4; "Los estudiantes universitarios ven materializado un viejo deseo," *Verde olivo* 17, no. 49 (December 7, 1975); *Granma*, January 30, 1976; ibid., February 22, 1976, p. 1.

47. *Granma Weekly Review*, p. 3; see also "El proyecto de ley del servicio militar obligatorio," *Verde olivo* 4, no. 47 (November 24, 1963): 53–54; ibid., 13, no. 32 (August 8, 1971): 9; *Granma Weekly Review*, July 30, 1967, p. 11; ibid., April 16, 1972, p. 7.

48. *Granma Weekly Review*, December 1, 1974, p. 7; *Granma*, July 11, 1975, p. 2.

49. *Granma Weekly Review*, August 12, 1973, p. 2; Fiscalía Militar, "Los estímulos," pp. 22, 24.

50. *Granma Weekly Review*, January 4, 1976, p. 7.

51. Hugh Hanning, *The Peaceful Uses of Military Forces* (New York: Praeger, 1967).

52. Roman Kolkowicz, *The Soviet Military and the Communist Party* (Princeton: Princeton University Press, 1967), pp. 36–79, 309–321.

53. John Gittings, *The Role of the Chinese Army* (New York: Oxford University Press, 1967), pp. 29–32, 176–201; Ellis Joffe, *Party and Army: Professionalism and Political Control in the Chinese Officer Corps, 1949–1964* (Cambridge, Mass.: Harvard University, East Asian Research Center, 1965), pp. 80–87 (hereafter cited as *Party and Army in China*).

54. Karol, *Guerrillas in Power;* Dumont, "Militarization of Fidelismo"; Andrés Suárez, "How the Cuban Regime Works" (unpublished, 1972).

55. *Verde olivo* 4, no. 7 (February 17, 1963): 6–7.

56. José Causse Pérez, "La construcción del partido en las Fuerzas Armadas Revolucionarias de Cuba," *Cuba socialista* no. 47 (July 1965): 51–66; Raúl Castro, "Problemas del funcionamiento del partido en las FAR" *Cuba socialista* no. 55 (March

1966): 45–58; *Verde olivo* 4, no. 44 (November 2, 1963): 35–41; ibid., 4, no. 50 (December 15, 1963): 3, 12; ibid., no. 51 (December 22, 1963): 3–10, 58–59, 66.

57. E. Yasells, "Reseña de una asamblea,' *Verde olivo* 8, no. 51 (December 24, 1967): 11.

58. Ibid., 7, no. 52 (December 13, 1966): 4; ibid., 8, no. 51 (December 24, 1967): 12; ibid., 11, no. 40 (October 4, 1970): 8, 10; *Granma*, March 1, 1966, p. 4; ibid., August 4, 1975, p. 3; ibid., June 8, 1976, p. 4; *Granma Weekly Review*, January 4, 1976, p. 7; ibid., December 12, 1976, p. 12; *Bohemia*, Vol. 65, no. 31 (August 3, 1973), p. 28.

59. Raymond Garthoff, "The Military in Russia, 1861–1965," in *The Armed Forces and Society*, ed. Jacques Van Doorn (The Hague: Mouton, 1968), pp. 247, 253.

60. Kolkowicz, *Soviet Military and Communist Party*.

61. For a fascinating discussion of this behavior, see Timothy Colton, "Army, Party and Development in Soviet Politics" (Ph.D. diss., Harvard University, 1974).

62. Quoted in Rosendo Gutiérrez, "Segunda asamblea de balance," *Verde olivo* 9, no. 9 (March 3, 1968): 11.

63. "Indicaciones sobre el proceso asambleario," ibid., 14, no. 42 (October 15, 1972): 55–59.

64. "Reunión nacional de instructores para el trabajo de la UJC en las FAR," ibid., 18, no. 9 (February 29, 1976): 96; "Tercer activo del Partido en la DAAFAR," ibid., no. 28 (July 11, 1976): 53.

65. "Indicaciones,": 55–59.

66. "Trabajo político partidista para elevar la conciencia técnica," *Verde olivo* 16, no. 22 (June 2, 1974): 31; D. Kindelán, "Décimo aniversario de la U.J.C.-F.A.R.," ibid., no. 25 (June 23, 1974): 54.

67. Kolkowicz, *Soviet Military and Communist Party*, p. 74.

68. Luis Aguilar, *Cuba 1933* (Ithaca: Cornell University Press, 1972), pp. 187–188.

69. José Suárez Núñez, *El gran culpable* (Caracas, 1963), pp. 64, 91–92.

70. Computed from *Política internacional* 6, nos. 22–24 (1968): 93.

71. *Granma Weekly Review*, March 16, 1969, p. 7; ibid., August 31, 1969, p. 1; *Verde olivo* 11, no. 34 (August 23, 1970): 8; *Bohemia* 65, no. 31 (August 3, 1973): 27; Abelardo Colomé, "Continuamos luchando," *Verde olivo* 17, no. 31 (August 3, 1975): 18.

72. *Política internacional* 6, nos. 22–24 (1968): 93; *Granma Weekly Review*, March 16, 1969, p. 7; *Granma* April 17, 1975, p. 2; Juan Escalona, "Las FAR y los reservistas," *Verde olivo* 18, no. 17 (April 25, 1976): 17–18.

73. *Verde olivo* 9, no. 17 (April 28, 1968): 5–6; ibid., 8, no. 19 (May 14, 1967): 7; ibid., no. 20 (May 21, 1967): 18; *Granma Weekly Review*, July 20, 1969, p. 10.

74. *Granma*, December 3, 1975, p. 2.

75. "Entrenamiento de tiro antiaéreo," *Verde olivo* 17, no. 13 (March 30, 1975): 21.

76. Causse Pérez, "La construcción del partido," pp. 54–55; *Granma Weekly Review*, January 10, 1971, pp. 10–11; ibid., January 24, 1971, pp. 10–11; ibid., March 5, 1966, p. 8.

77. R. Castro, "Problemas del funcionamiento del partido," pp. 56–57; *Verde olivo* 10, no. 2 (January 12, 1969): 29; ibid., 11, no. 40 (October 4, 1970): 8–9; "El

trabajo de las organizaciones políticas y las organizaciones del partido y la U.J.C. en aseguramiento de preparación política de oficiales, clases y soldados," ibid., 16, no. 23 (June 9, 1974): 30–31; "Informe central del Vice Ministro Jefe de la Dirección Política," ibid., no. 17 (April 28, 1974): 55; "Sobre el trabajo político en el aseguramineto a los ejercicios de tiro con armas de infantería," ibid., no. 24 (June 16, 1974): 28–29, 31.

78. Venancio Rivas Pérez, "Evaluación de los oficiales de las FAR," *Verde olivo* 17, no. 9 (March 2, 1975): 19, 21, 23.

79. *Granma Weekly Review,* May 14, 1967, p. 11.

80. *Granma,* May 20, 1966, p. 5; Yasells, "Reseña de una asamblea," pp. 11–12; "Primera asamblea de balance del partido," *Verde olivo* 8, no. 51 (December 24, 1967): 61; "Sección política de la marina de guerra revolucionaria," ibid., 9, no. 2 (January 14, 1968): 38; "Primera asamblea de balance del partido comunista de Cuba en el cuerpo blindado," in ibid., no. 7 (February 18, 1968): 13–15; Gutiérrez, "Segunda asamblea de balance," pp. 8–12; "Asamblea de balance del partido en el ejército de Oriente," ibid., 10, no. 5 (February 2, 1969): 52–53; "Balance del partido en el cuerpo ejército de Camagüey," ibid., no. 42 (October 19, 1969): 25; "Segunda asamblea de balance del partido comunista de Cuba en una unidad en Matanzas," ibid., no. 43 (October 26, 1969): 28; "Segunda asamblea de balance del partido en el ejército del centro," ibid., no. 44 (November 2, 1969): 58; "Segunda asamblea de balance del partido comunista de Cuba en el estado mayor general," in ibid., no. 49 (December 7, 1969): 32–33; "Segunda reunión del partido en las Fuerzas Armadas Revolucionarias," ibid., 11, no. 40 (October 4, 1970): 7–8.

81. Luis Méndez, "La asamblea provincial del PURS en Matanzas," *Cuba socialista* no. 31 (March 1964): 134–135.

82. *Granma,* October 4, 1974, p. 3.

83. Colton, "Army, Party and Development in Soviet Politics."

84. The following comments on China are based mainly on Joffe, *Party and Army in China,* pp. 57–72; Gittings, *Role of the Chinese Army,* chaps. 5, 8, 11, 12; Jürgen Domes, "The Cultural Revolution and the Army," *Asian Survey* 8, no. 5 (May 1968): 349–363; Harvey Nelsen, "Military Forces in the Cultural Revolution," *China Quarterly* no. 51 (July–September 1972): 444–474; Philip Bridgham, "The Fall of Lin Piao," ibid., no. 55 (July–September 1973): 427–449; Jonathan D. Pollack, "The Study of Chinese Military Politics: A Framework for Analysis," in *Political-Military Systems,* ed. Catherine M. Kelleher, pp. 239–270.

85. For further elaboration of this point of view, see two thoughtful pieces by William M. LeoGrande: "The Politics of Revolutionary Development: Civil-Military Relations in Cuba, 1959–1976" (Paper presented at annual meeting, Midwest Political Science Association, Chicago, April 21–23, 1977), pp. 26–32, 41–43; "Party Control and Political Socialization in Communist Civil Military Relations: The Case of Cuba" (Paper presented at ninth national convention, the American Association for the Advancement of Slavic Studies, Washington, D.C., October 13–16, 1977), pp. 27–29.

10. SETTING PUBLIC POLICY

1. For comparative perspectives, see Zbigniew Brzezinski and Samuel P. Huntington, *Political Power: USA/USSR* (New York: Viking Press, 1967), pp. 129–232; Frederick C. Barghoorn, *Politics in the USSR* (Boston, Little, Brown, 1966), pp.

213–257; Merle Fainsod, "Bureaucracy and Modernization: The Russian and Soviet Case," in *Bureaucracy and Political Development,* ed. Joseph LaPalombara (Princeton: Princeton University Press, 1963), pp. 233–267; Carl Beck, "Bureaucracy and Political Development in Eastern Europe," in ibid., pp. 268–300.

2. Ernesto Guevara, *Economic Planning in Cuba* (New York, 1961), p. 4; quoted in *Revolución,* March 3, 1960, p. 12.

3. Cuban Economic Research Project, *A Study on Cuba* (Coral Gables, Fla.: University of Miami Press, 1965), p. 766; Francisco García and Juan Noyola, "Principales objectivos de nuestro plan económico hasta 1965," *Cuba Socialista* no. 13 (1962): 11–16.

4. For a discussion of incrementalism and planning, see Robert A. Dahl and Charles E. Lindblom, *Politics, Economics and Welfare* (New York: Harper & Row, 1963), pp. 82–85; see also Karl W. Deutsch, *The Nerves of Government* (New York: Free Press, 1967). For a discussion of mobilization, see David Apter, *The Politics of Modernization* (Chicago: University of Chicago Press, 1965), pp. 359–360.

5. Edward Boorstein, *The Economic Transformation of Cuba* (New York: Monthly Review Press, 1968), pp. 184–204.

6. *Obra revolucionaria* no. 15 (1963): 33–38; ibid., no. 18 (1963): 7; ibid., no. 32 (1963): 12.

7. Speech of March 1964 in ibid., no. 10 (1964): 14; speech of February 1965 in George Lavan, ed., *Che Guevara Speaks* (New York: Merit Publishers, 1967), p. 115.

8. This discussion of policy parallels those in other socialist countries. In Cuba, reflections of it can be found in the following articles: for those favoring budgetary controls, see Ernesto Guevara, "Sobre la concepción del valor," *Nuestra industria: revista económica* no. 3 (1963): 3–9 (hereafter cited as *NI:RE*); Luis Álvarez Rom, "Las finanzas como un método de desarrollo político," ibid., no. 1 (1963): 13–21; Miguel Cossío, "Contribución al debate sobre la ley del valor," ibid., no. 4 (1963): 3–23; Ernesto Guevara, "El socialismo y el hombre," ibid., no. 14 (1965): 3–14. For arguments in favor of economic autonomy, see Alberto Mora, "En torno a la cuestión del funcionamiento de la ley del valor en la economía cubana en los actuales momentos," *Comercio exterior* 1, no. 3 (1963): 2–10; idem, "Sobre algunos problemas actuales de la construcción del socialismo," *NI:RE* no. 14 (1965): 15–27; Marcelo Fernández, "Desarrollo y funciones de la banca socialista en Cuba," *Cuba socialista* no. 30 (February 1964): 32–50; idem, "Planificación y control de la circulación monetaria," ibid., no. 33 (May 1964): 79–97; see also Salvador Vilaseca, "El Banco Nacional de Cuba y los sistemas de financiamiento," *NI:RE* no. 11 (1965): 3–19; Alban Lataste Hoffer, *Cuba: hacia una nueva economía política del socialismo* (Santiago: Editorial Universitaria, 1968), pp. 33–41. Several of these are translated in Bertram Silverman, ed., *Man and Socialism in Cuba: The Great Debate* (New York: Atheneum, 1971). For excellent, detailed discussions of these disputes, see Robert M. Bernardo, *The Theory of Moral Incentives in Cuba* (University, Ala.: University of Alabama Press, 1971); Archibald R. M. Ritter, *The Economic Development of Revolutionary Cuba* (New York: Praeger, 1974); Carmelo Mesa-Lago, ed., *Revolutionary Change in Cuba* (Pittsburgh: University of Pittsburgh Press, 1971), pt. 2.

9. Evidence of Guevara's strained personal relations with some of his political antagonists can be found in his *Reminiscences of the Cuban Revolutionary War,* trans. Victoria Ortiz (New York: Monthly Review Press, 1968), pp. 271, 280, 282.

10. Severo Aguirre, "El primer aniversario de las cooperativas cañeras," *Cuba socialista* no. 3 (1961): 24.

11. Dudley Seers, ed., *Cuba: The Economic and Social Revolution* (Chapel Hill: University of North Carolina Press, 1964), p. 133. The thirty-nine-pound figure applies only to Havana.

12. Ibid., p. 42.

13. On land reform, see Antonio Núñez Jiménez, "Revolución agraria en Cuba," *INRA* 2, no. 6 (1961): 7; Blas Roca, "Nueva etapa de la revolución cubana," *Cuba socialista* no. 5 (1962): 45; Carlos Rafael Rodríguez, "The Cuban Revolution and the Peasantry," *World Marxist Review* 8, no. 10 (October 1965): 62–71; Comisión Económica para América Latina, *El desarrollo industrial de Cuba*, ST/ECLA/Conf. 23/L. 63 (1966).

14. For further discussion of the problems leading to agricultural decay, see Seers, *Cuba: Economic and Social Revolution*, pp. 137–140.

15. Theodore Draper, *Castroism: Theory and Practice* (New York: Praeger, 1965), pp. 135–165.

16. Computed from Seers, *Cuba: Economic and Social Revolution*, p. 323.

17. Cuban cement statistics from *Panorama económico latinoamericano* 5 (1966): 283; Cuban electric-power statistics from *Granma Weekly Review*, January 7, 1968, p. 2; Economic Commission for Latin America, *Statistical Bulletin for Latin America* 3, no. 1 (1966): 69–83.

18. Carmelo Mesa-Lago, *The Labor Sector and Socialist Distribution in Cuba* (New York: Praeger, 1968), pp. 40–44, 69–73, 112–115, 145–150, 178–180.

19. The years 1964 and 1966 are selected for comparison because they are sufficiently removed both from the low ebb of 1962–1963 and from the push for the 1970 harvest to give a more nearly normal economic picture; sugar production for both years was about the same, so its impact on the rest of the economy is controlled. Both years also preceded the shift from material to moral incentives for labor, so that change need not be taken into account. For an earlier analysis, based on partial and inadequate data and consequently wrong, see Jorge I. Domínguez, "Sectoral Clashes in Cuban Politics and Development," *Latin American Research Review* 6, no. 3 (Fall 1971): 61–81.

20. Computed from *Boletín 1970*, p. 36; *Anuario 1973*, p. 41; *Anuario 1974*, p. 41.

21. *Granma Weekly Review*, October 8, 1967, p. 4.

22. Lataste, *Cuba: hacia una nueva economía*, pp. 36, 49; *Granma Weekly Review*, January 4, 1976, p. 2.

23. This short summary owes much to Lourdes Casal, "Literature and Society," in *Revolutionary Change in Cuba*, ed. Carmelo Mesa-Lago, pp. 447–469; Julio Matas, "Theater and Cinematography," in ibid., pp. 427–445; Mario Benedetti, "Present Status of Cuban Culture," in *Cuba in Revolution*, ed. Rolando Bonachea and Nelson P. Valdés (Garden City, N.Y.: Anchor Books, 1972), pp. 500–526; and Seymour Menton, *Prose Fiction of the Cuban Revolution* (Austin: University of Texas Press, 1975), pp. 123–156.

24. Fidel Castro, *Palabras a los intelectuales* (Havana: Ediciones del Consejo Nacional de Cultura, 1961), pp. 6–8, 11, 15–16, 18–19.

25. Alfredo Guevara, "Un cine de combate," *Pensamiento crítico* no. 42 (July 1970): 14, 26; José Antonio Portuondo, "Itinerario estético de la revolución cubana," *Unión* 14, no. 3 (September 1975): 12–13.

26. For the military point of view, see the following articles by Leopoldo Ávila (pseud.): "La vuelta a la manzana," *Verde olivo* 9, no. 42 (October 20, 1968): 18; "Las respuestas de Caín," ibid., no. 44 (November 3, 1968): 17–18; "Las provocaciones de Padilla," ibid., no. 45 (November 10, 1968): 17–18; "Antón se va a la guerra," ibid., no. 46 (November 17, 1968): 17–18; "Sobre algunas corrientes de la crítica y la literatura en Cuba," ibid., no. 47 (November 24, 1968): 15; "El pueblo es el forjador, defensor y sostén de la cultura," ibid., no. 48 (December 1, 1968): 17. See also idem, "Información política" ibid., no. 45 (November 10, 1968): 11, where literary work with revolutionary content is said to be praiseworthy even when its artistic quality is low.

27. Lourdes Casal, ed., *El caso Padilla: literatura y revolución en Cuba* (Miami: Ediciones Universal, 1971).

28. For the socialist-realist debate, see A. Guevara, "Un cine de combate," pp. 14, 26; Portuondo, "Itinerario estético," pp. 6–8, 12–13, 18; Roberto Fernández Retamar, "Hacia una intelectualidad revolucionaria en Cuba," *Cuadernos americanos* 15, no. 169 (November–December 1966): 46–47; Carlos Rafael Rodríguez, "Problemas del arte en la revolución," *Revolución y cultura* 1, no. 1 (October 1967): 19–20; for more recent issues, see Castilla, quoted in *Granma Weekly Review*, May 9, 1971, pp. 3, 5; and Pérez Herrero, quoted in ibid., September 29, 1974, p. 9. See also a major speech by Armando Hart, minister of culture, in ibid., April 24, 1977, pp. 4–6.

29. Rafael Escobar Linares, "Se hace camino al andar," *Bohemia* 67, no. 2 (January 10, 1975): 28; Evepe, "Sin proponer una polémica," ibid., no. 4 (January 24, 1975): 28; Jaime Sarusky, "Chabacanería, ¡no!" ibid., no. 14 (April 4, 1975): 28–29.

30. José Arcocha, "Dicotomías: Lezama Lima y Cabrera Infante," *Aportes* no. 11 (January 1969): 59–65; *Granma*, January 15, 1976, p. 5 (article 38*d*); ibid., April 24, 1975, p. 5; *Granma Weekly Review*, January 4, 1976, p. 3.

31. Raúl Castro, "El diversionismo ideológico: arma sutil que esgrimen los enemigos contra la revolución," *Verde olivo* 14, no. 30 (July 23, 1972): 4–15.

32. "La reforma de la enseñanza superior en Cuba," *Universidad de La Habana* no. 154 (January–February 1962): 55, 59, 67–68; Facultad de Humanidades, "Evaluación de los resultados generales del curso 1963–1964," ibid. no. 170 (November–December 1964): 73, 87, 90–91, 101, 112–113; Universidad de La Habana, *La Universidad de La Habana al Consejo Ejecutivo y a la Asamblea General de la Unión de Universidades de América Latina* (Havana, 1964), pp. 23, 41; computations from Luis Boza Domínguez, *La situación universitaria en Cuba* (Santiago: Editorial del Pacífico, 1962), pp. 119–124.

33. "Reforma de la enseñanza superior," pp. 55, 59, 67–68; computations from Universidad de La Habana, *La Universidad*, pp. 52–81.

34. Computed from Facultad de Humanidades, "Evaluación," p. 95.

35. J. B. Moré Benítez, "La revolución técnica y la Escuela de Ciencias Políticas," *Cuba socialista* no. 37 (September 1964): 68; *Granma*, November 23, 1970; ibid., April 25, 1974, p. 4; ibid., April 16, 1977, p. 2; ibid., June 3, 1977, p. 3; Emilio Fernández Conde, "La educación postgraduado," *Sobre educación superior* (January–June 1971): 83; Francisco Pividal Padrón, Gilberto García Espinosa, Margarita Otero, and Manuel Area, "La enseñanza universitaria por medio de encuentros o reuniones periódicas," ibid. (July–December 1971): 11–12; *Granma Weekly Review*, May 9, 1972, p. 5; ibid., September 15, 1974, p. 3.

36. *Granma Weekly Review*, March 5, 1972, pp. 4–5; *Cuban Economic News* 4,

no. 36 (1968): 12; Vicente Cubillas, "El instituto de oceanología de la Academia de Ciencias," *Mar y pesca* no. 17 (February 1967): 53; for a recognition of Fidel Castro's preeminent role in the formulation of science policy, see Osvaldo Dorticós, "Primer forum científico nacional de estudiantes universitarios," *Universidad de La Habana* nos. 198–199 (January–February 1973): 30. For a discussion of the organization of social science in Cuba, see Louis Wolf Goodman, "The Social Sciences in Cuba," *Items* 30, no. 4 (December 1976): 54–61; "Diez años de investigaciones en el Instituto de Economía," *Economía y desarrollo* no. 30 (July–August 1975). In general, the social sciences developed more slowly than the natural sciences; among the social sciences, economics developed much earlier and with greator vigor than other branches. Emphasis has always been placed on applied work.

37. Antonio Núñez Jiménez, "La reunión de las academias de ciencias socialistas," *Finlay: revista médico-histórica cubana* no. 8 (January–June 1967): 6–7.

38. Mose L. Harvey, Leon Goure, and Vladimir Prokofieff, *Science and Technology as an Instrument of Soviet Policy* (Coral Gables, Fla.: University of Miami, Center for Advanced International Studies, 1972), pp. 76–77, 79–81, 177–178, 182, 204, 207–208.

39. *Cuban Economic News* 1, no. 2 (August–September 1965): 9; ibid., no. 4 (October 1965): 10; ibid., 2, no. 18 (December 1966): 16; ibid., 4, no. 36 (1968): 12; ibid., 5, no. 39 (1969): 9–10; *Serie Actividades* no. 25 (1972): 3–4; "Inaugurado el Instituto Cubano de Física Nuclear," *Verde olivo* 10, no. 3 (January 19, 1969): 6; Cubillas, "Instituto de oceanología," p. 53.

40. Marcel Roche, "Notes on Science in Cuba," *Science* 169, no. 3943 (July 24, 1970): 349; *Granma Weekly Review*, March 5, 1972, pp. 4–5; ibid., March 2, 1975, p. 4; Zoilo Marinello, "La Academia de Ciencias de Cuba: presente y futuro" [in Russian], in *The Soviet Union and Cuba*, ed. Soviet Academy of Sciences, Institute of Ethnography (Moscow: Nauka, 1973), p. 178; "Science and Education in Cuba," *International Affairs* no. 1 (January 1976): 155.

41. Roche, "Notes on Science in Cuba," pp. 347–348; *Granma Weekly Review*, November 9, 1975, p. 6; Minerva Salado, "La ciencia cierta," *Cuba internacional* 6, no. 59 (July 1974): 21–25; "Los científicos hablan," *Boletín de la Comisión Nacional Cubana de la UNESCO* 11, no. 38 (March–April 1972): 19; "IV Seminario Científico," ibid., 13, no. 49 (January–February 1974): 2, 5, 6.

42. "Science and Education in Cuba," p. 155.

43. Departamento de Investigaciones Azucareras, "El central experimental Pablo Noriega," *Cuba azúcar* (July–September 1969): 10 (this sugar mill was called Occidente before the revolution); West Indies Sugar Corporation, *Annual Report* (1954): 3; ibid. (1955): 5–6; ibid. (1956): 5. Advances in research and development before the revolution were not limited to the sugar sciences. Over a thousand scientific reports on Cuban geology were written before 1959, although a majority of them were not published. See Gustavo Furrazola-Bermúdez, Constantino M. Judoley, Marina S. Mijailovskaya, Yuri S. Miroliubov, Ivan P. Novojatsky, Antonio Núñez Jiménez, and Juan B. Solsona, *Geología de Cuba* (Havana: Editora Nacional de Cuba, 1964), p. xi (see also the bibliography on pp. 227–239). There had also been extensive research and publication on fishing in the waters of the Cuban archipelago; the record of published research in this field dates back to the 1930s; see Mario Sánchez Riog and Federico Gómez de la Maza, *La pesca en Cuba* (Havana: Ministerio de Agricultura, 1952).

44. *Cuba azúcar* (September–October 1967): 20–21; Rafael Pedrosa, "Apertura de la conferencia," ibid. (November–December 1968): 10.

45. Computed from *Cuba azúcar* (September–October 1967): 20–21, 34; ibid. (November–December 1968): 26; Pedrosa, "Apertura de la conferencia," p. 10; idem, "Informe del Presidente de la ATAC," ibid. (October–December 1970): 53; ibid., (October–December 1972): 6, 13.

46. "Antes del ICIDCA no hubo ningún ICIDCA," *Bohemia* 65, no. 24 (June 15, 1973): 21 (the text of the article disproves its title); Pedrosa, "Apertura de la conferencia," p. 11; Leovigildo Fernández, "Palabras del director del centro de investigaciones de la caña de azúcar," *Cuba azúcar* (October–December 1970): 14.

47. "X años del ICIDCA," *Cuba azúcar* (April–June 1973): 41–42; Manuel Pereira, "Exploración y explotación del azúcar," *Cuba internacional* 7, no. 69 (May 1975): 27–28.

48. "Perspectivas de la industria cañera cubana: su integración y principales problemas a resolver a mediano y largo plazo," *Cuba azúcar* (April–June 1976): 5–9, 11. The academy's Institute for Sugar-Cane Research will specialize in developing high-yield sugar-cane varieties that lend themselves to mechanized farming and are easily cleaned, resistant to blight and disease, and usable in producing sugar-cane derivatives. It will also study fertilization and other plant-cultivation methods. The research center of the Iron and Steel and Machine Ministry will develop machinery and equipment to till the soil; sow, cultivate, and harvest the cane; store and preserve it; and transport it. The Ministry of the Sugar Industry's Sugar Research Institute, already installed at the Pablo Noriega Center, will concentrate on developing new ways to eliminate sugar-cane impurities and on new milling techniques. The research activities of the Ministry of Agriculture at the Pablo Noriega Center will emphasize cost-feasibility studies, especially ways of financing and auditing the performance of the new technologies and cane varieties on a commercial scale. The Institute for Research on Sugar-Cane Derivatives will build one experimental plant to produce paper from cane bagasse and another to produce molasses for animal feed.

49. Of the 114 papers presented in the 1970 sugar conference, the sugar-cane derivatives institute led with 32.4 percent; the rest of the Ministry of the Sugar Industry—including the Sugar Research Institute—accounted for an additional 8.8 percent. The University of Havana ranked second with 18.4 percent, while the Universities of Las Villas and Oriente presented 12.3 percent and 1.8 percent, respectively. The academy's Institute for Sugar-Cane Research placed third, with 17.5 percent. The academy's cybernetics department presented 4.4 percent of the papers, and the sugar enterprises accounted for an identical 4.4 percent. Computed from Pedrosa, "Informe del Presidente de la ATAC," pp. 54–55.

50. Computed from "X aniversario de la Academia de Ciencias," *Boletín de la Comisión Nacional Cubana de la UNESCO* 11, no. 38 (March–April 1972): 31.

51. *Granma Weekly Review*, January 7, 1973, p. 2.

52. Centro Nacional de Investigaciones Científicas, *Informe, 1969* (Havana: Universidad de La Habana, 1969), pp. 7–8 (hereafter cited as CNIC, *Informe*); Györy Rozsa, "La organización de la ciencia y la cultura en Cuba," *Revista mexicana de sociología* 31, no. 3 (July–September 1969): 636–638; Roche, "Notes on Science in Cuba," pp. 348–349.

53. *Granma Weekly Review*, January 7, 1973, pp. 2–3; *Serie actividades* no. 25

(1972): 20, 22; G. Yayo Morejón, "Ante el V seminario científico del CENIC," *Bohemia* 67, no. 25 (June 20, 1975): 84. See also Osvaldo Dorticós, "Crear un espíritu técnico, una voluntad técnica," *Economía y desarrollo* no. 28 (March–April 1975): 20–21.

54. "Los estudiantes investigan," *Boletín de la Comisión Nacional Cubana de la UNESCO* 12, no. 48 (January–February 1973): 18; Luis O. Gálvez, "Estrategia de dirección en la actividad de investigación y desarrollo," *Economía y desarrollo* no. 25 (September–October 1974): 12–13; United Nations, *Statistical Yearbook, 1974* (New York, 1975), p. 850; *Granma Weekly Review,* January 4, 1976, p. 3.

55. Harvey et al., *Science and Technology in Soviet Policy,* pp. 41–45, 189; Graham Jones, *The Role of Science and Technology in Developing Countries* (London: Oxford University Press, 1971), pp. 11, 43, 46, 49.

56. *Granma,* February 24, 1975, p. 3; ibid., March 27, 1975, p. 4; ibid., May 29, 1975, p. 4; ibid., July 4, 1975, p. 2; *Granma Weekly Review,* June 8, 1975, p. 5; ibid., October 12, 1975, p. 8; ibid., February 6, 1977, p. 8; ibid., February 20, 1977, p. 2; Gálvez, "Estrategia," p. 20; Pedro Luis Sotolongo, "Planeamiento a mediano plazo de las investigaciones científicas," *Economía y desarrollo* no. 26 (November–December 1974): 49–50, 52, 55–57, 61–62; Tirso W. Sáenz and Emilio García Capote, "Algunos conceptos básicos sobre política científica," *Economía y desarrollo* no. 27 (January–February 1975): 64.

57. *Granma,* August 9, 1976, pp. 1, 4.

58. Harvey Brooks, *The Government of Science* (Cambridge, Mass.: M.I.T. Press, 1968), pp. 35, 44, 79, 138–148; Jones, *Role of Science in Developing Countries,* p. 48.

59. *Serie actividades* no. 25 (1972): 16; CNIC, *Informe, 1969,* p. 12; Pedrosa, "Informe del Presidente de la ATAC," pp. 54–55; *Granma Weekly Review,* February 20, 1972, p. 3; ibid., March 2, 1975, p. 4; *Bohemia* 67, no. 10 (March 7, 1975): 59; *Granma,* May 22, 1975, p. 1; ibid., July 1, 1975, p. 2.

60. *Granma Weekly Review,* March 5, 1972, pp. 4–5; *Serie actividades* no. 25 (1972): 22; *Bohemia* 67, no. 10 (March 7, 1975), p. 59.

61. Universidad de La Habana, *La Universidad de La Habana* (Havana, 1970), p. 20; Roche, "Notes on Science in Cuba," p. 347.

62. *Granma Weekly Review,* May 18, 1969, pp. 2–5; Barry Reckford, *Does Fidel Eat More than Your Father?* (London: Andre Deutsch, 1971), pp. 143–161.

63. He helped write 56 of the 101 articles published by the institute between his arrival in 1965 and 1970, or an average of nine articles a year. See Instituto de Ciencia Animal, *Instituto de Ciencia Animal* (Havana: Universidad de La Habana, 1970), pp. 5, 16–17, 25; "Los científicos hablan," *Boletín de la Comisión Nacional Cubana de la UNESCO* 11, no. 38 (April–May 1972): 20.

64. Jones, *Role of Science in Developing Countries,* pp. 124–125.

65. The term is from Don K. Price, *The Scientific Estate* (Cambridge, Mass.: Harvard University Press, 1967), p. 83.

66. *Bohemia* 67, no. 24 (June 13, 1975): 82; *Granma,* May 12, 1975, p. 3; ibid., July 11, 1975, p. 4; ibid., December 15, 1975, p. 5; ibid., January 23, 1976, p. 3; ibid., February 20, 1976, p. 5; ibid., April 23, 1976, p. 5; ibid., August 8, 1975, p. 3; ibid., March 15, 1976, p. 5.

67. *Granma,* July 5, 1976, p. 4; ibid., February 13, 1976, p. 6; ibid., July 7, 1975, p. 4; ibid., July 7, 1976, p. 4.

68. *Granma*, May 12, 1975, p. 2; ibid., May 16, 1975, p. 5; "Guerra sin tregua a la chapucería," *Bohemia* 67, no. 19 (May 9, 1975): 82–83; ibid., no. 22 (May 30, 1975): 82–83.

69. *Bohemia* 67, no. 16 (April 18, 1975): 83; ibid., no. 20 (May 16, 1975): 82; ibid., no. 21 (May 23, 1975): 82; ibid., no. 25 (June 20, 1975): 83; ibid., no. 26 (June 27, 1975): 98; *Granma*, May 16, 1975, p. 5; ibid., June 13, 1975, p. 4.

70. *Aclaraciones: Periódico Hoy* (Havana: Editora Política, 1966), 3: 202; *Verde olivo* 9, no. 12 (March 24, 1968): 5.

71. Marvin Leiner with Robert Ubell, *Children Are the Revolution: Day Care in Cuba* (New York: Viking Press, 1974), pp. 103–106, 109–110, 112, 125–126, 151, 153–155, 173–174, 176–177.

72. Aldo J. Büntig, "The Church in Cuba: Toward a New Frontier," in *Religion in Cuba Today*, ed. Alice Hageman and Philip Wheaton (New York: Association Press, 1971): pp. 95–128; Leslie Dewart, *Christianity and Revolution: The Lesson of Cuba* (New York: Herder and Herder, 1963); Jorge I. Domínguez, "Cuban Catholics and Castro," *Worldview* 15, no. 2 (February 1972): 24–29.

73. James Wilkie, "Statistical Indicators of the Impact of National Revolution on the Catholic Church in Mexico, 1910–1967," *Journal of Church and State* 12, no. 1 (Winter 1970): 97; computed from *Anuario 1974*, p. 22; Alfred L. Padula, Jr., "The Fall of the Bourgeoisie: Cuba, 1959–1961" (Ph.D. diss., University of New Mexico, 1974), p. 425; Hageman and Wheaton, *Religion in Cuba*, p. 30; Manuel Fernández, "La crisis actual del catolicismo en Cuba," *Reunión* nos. 93–94 (January–February 1977): 2.

74. For these texts, see Hageman and Wheaton, *Religion in Cuba*, pp. 288–294, 301, "Image of Catholic Church Improving," *Cuba Review* 5, no. 2 (June 1975): 33; *Granma*, November 16, 1976, p. 3.

75. Fernández, "La crisis actual," pp. 2–3; "Entrevista con Uxmal Livio Díaz," *Areíto* 3, nos. 2–3 (1976): 33.

76. Sergio Arce Martínez, "The Mission of the Church in a Socialist Society," in *Religion in Cuba*, ed. Hageman and Wheaton, pp. 216–243; Jacinto Ordóñez, "Seminaries in the Seventies," *Cuba Review* 5, no. 3 (September 1975): 30–31.

77. "Entrevista con Uxmal Livio Díaz," pp. 30–35.

78. Fidel Castro, "A combatir al enemigo en todos los frentes," *Cuba socialista* no. 20 (April 1963): 5, 7–10; Blas Roca, "La lucha ideológica contra las sectas religiosas," ibid., no. 22 (June 1963): 34–39, 41; *Verde olivo* 11, no. 51 (December 20, 1970): 42–43; *Granma Weekly Review*, May 9, 1971, p. 4.

79. *Granma*, January 15, 1976, p. 5; *Reunión*, nos. 83–84 (March–April 1976): 2–3.

80. *Granma Weekly Review*, February 1, 1976, p. 8; Margaret Crahan, "Religious Freedom in Cuba," *Cuba Review* 5, no. 3 (September 1975): 24.

81. José Armas, "Timbiriches y timbiricheo," *Verde olivo* 9, no. 41 (October 13, 1968): 8–9.

82. *Granma Weekly Review*, March 24, 1968, p. 9; ibid., November 25, 1973, p. 10.

83. Lisandro Otero with Francisco Martínez Hinojosa, *Cultural Policy in Cuba* (Paris: UNESCO, 1972), pp. 29–36.

84. *Boletín 1971*, p. 291; *Anuario 1972*, p. 252.

85. Enrique Valdés Pérez, "Así soy yo," *Bohemia* 67, no. 20 (May 16, 1975): 28; Evepe, "Sin proponer," p. 28.

86. Jorge Hernández, Angel Eng, María Bermúdez, and Mariela Columbié, "Estudio sobre el divorcio," *Humanidades* ser. 1 (Ciencias Sociales), no. 3 (January 1973): 42; Eugenio Rodríguez Balari, "Trabajo y desarrollo del Instituto de la Demanda Interna," *Economía y desarrollo* no. 21 (January–February 1974): 153–155, 158, 161–162.

87. *Granma Weekly Review*, October 20, 1974, pp. 4–5; Pedro Martínez Pérez, "Nuevo sistema judicial," *Cuba internacional* 3, no. 28 (December 1971): 74; Pedro Margolles, "Building up a System of Representative Bodies," *World Marxist Review* 18, no. 2 (February 1975): 63.

88. *Granma*, March 3, 1975, p. 3.

89. *Granma Weekly Review*, March 16, 1975, p. 6.

90. Computed from *Granma*, November 29, 1974, p. 2.

91. Ibid., April 10, 1975, pp. 1, 7; ibid., May 30, 1975, p. 2; *Bohemia* 67, no. 9 (February 28, 1975): 50; ibid., no. 16 (April 18, 1975): 42. For a brief discussion of the effect of popular discussion on the text of the law against loafing, see Ian McColl Kennedy, "Cuba's *Ley Contra la Vagancia*—The Law on Loafing," *UCLA Law Review* 20, no. 6 (August 1973): 1188.

92. *Granma*, May 16, 1975, p. 4; ibid., May 17, 1975, p. 5; ibid., May 24, 1975, p. 1; ibid., May 27, 1975, p. 1; ibid., January 15, 1976, p. 3; *Granma Weekly Review*, May 25, 1975, p. 3.

93. *Granma*, May 28, 1975, p. 1; ibid., January 15, 1976, p. 3.

94. Economists have already described the process of planning in Cuba, including its achievements and failures, very well, and their work need not be duplicated here. See, for example, Carmelo Mesa-Lago and Luc Zephirin, "Central Planning," in *Revolutionary Change in Cuba*, ed. Carmelo Mesa-Lago, pp. 145–184; James O'Connor, *The Origins of Socialism in Cuba* (Ithaca: Cornell University Press, 1970), chaps. 8, 9; Bernardo, *Theory of Moral Incentives;* Ritter, *Economic Development of Cuba;* Lataste, *Cuba: hacia una nueva economía;* René Dumont, *Cuba: ¿es socialista?* trans. Mariela Álvarez (Caracas: Editorial Tiempo Nuevo, 1970).

95. *Granma Weekly Review*, January 4, 1976, p. 2.

96. Ritter, *Economic Development of Cuba*, p. 291.

97. Ibid., pp. 291–292; see also, for example, Ministerio de Industrias, Dirección Económica, "Proposición de un sistema de precios utilizando los costos planificados como precios de entrega dentro del sector estatal," *NI:RE* nos. 22–23 (June 1967): 91–92; Michael Pettitt, "Social and Economic Change in the Community around a Sugar Mill in Cuba" (Ph.D., diss., University of California–Berkeley, 1973), pp. 346–347, 349–350; *Granma Weekly Review*, April 17, 1977, p. 5.

98. Bernardo, *Theory of Moral Incentives*, p. 66; *Granma Weekly Review*, December 17, 1972, p. 9.

99. "Discurso del Presidente de la República, Dr. Osvaldo Dorticós, en la escuela de cuadros de mando del Ministerio de la Industria Ligera," *Pensamiento crítico* no. 45 (October 1970): 141–142.

100. Boris Gorbachev, "Cuba: la revolución y la economía," *Panorama latinoamericano* no. 185 (April 15, 1974): 4–6; "XV aniversario de la creación de la Junta Central de Planificación," *Economía y desarrollo* no. 30 (July–August 1975): 238.

101. Armando López Coll and Armando Santiago, "Notas sobre el proceso de planificación en Cuba," *Economía y desarrollo* no. 29 (May–June 1975): 17, 21–22.

102. *Granma Weekly Review*, January 4, 1976, p. 2; ibid., March 14, 1976, p. 2; *Granma*, December 6, 1975, p. 4; ibid., December 30, 1975, p. 2; ibid., November 29, 1976, pp. 3–6; ibid., January 12, 1977, pp. 2, 4; ibid., January 13, 1977, p. 2.

11. AGRARIAN CONFLICT AND PEASANT POLITICS

1. On agrarian politics in prerevolutionary Cuba, see Lowry Nelson, *Rural Cuba* (1950; reprint ed., New York: Octagon Books, 1970); Alberto Arredondo, *Cuba: tierra indefensa* (Havana: Editorial Lex, 1945); Cuban Economic Research Project, *Cuba: Agriculture and Planning* (Coral Gables, Fla.: University of Miami Press, 1965). See also Michel Gutelman, *L'agriculture socialisée à Cuba* (Paris: Maspero, 1967); Sergio Aranda, *La revolución agraria en Cuba* (Mexico: Siglo XXI, 1968); René Dumont, *Cuba: ¿es socialista?* trans. Mariela Álvarez (Caracas: Editorial Tiempo Nuevo, 1970); David Barkin, "Cuban Agriculture: A Strategy of Economic Development," *Studies in Comparative International Development* 7, no. 1 (Spring 1972): 19–38.

2. Juan and Verena Martínez Alier, *Cuba: economía y sociedad* (Paris: Ruedo Ibérico, 1972), pp. 80–81; Alfred L. Padula, Jr., "The Fall of the Bourgeoisie: Cuba, 1959–1961" (Ph.D. diss., University of New Mexico, 1974), Chaps. 3–4.

3. Oscar Seiglie y Llata, *El contrato de arrendamiento de finca rústica, el latifundio, y legislación azucarera* (Havana: Editorial Lex, 1953), pp. 219–221, 137–138.

4. Cuban-American Sugar Corporation, *Annual Report* (1936): 3, 6; ibid (1937): 2, 6; ibid (1938): 3, 8.

5. United Fruit Company, *Some Facts Regarding the Development and Operation of the United Fruit Company Sugar Properties in the Republic of Cuba* (Preston, Cuba, 1944), pp. 6, 15, 17–18, 43–44, 63–64, 94.

6. Cuban-American Sugar Corporation, *Annual Report* (1938): 4.

7. West Indies Sugar Corporation, *Annual Report* (1937); ibid. (1944); ibid. (1945); ibid. (1948); ibid. (1949): 1; ibid. (1951): 1; ibid. (1954): 1–4.

8. Martínez Alier, *Cuba*, p. 86; Cuban Economic Research Project, *A Study on Cuba* (Coral Gables, Fla.: University of Miami Press, 1965), p. 518 (hereafter cited as CERP, *Study*); West Indies Sugar Corporation, *Annual Report* (1947).

9. Eduardo Varona Martínez and Rafael González Labrada, *El colono* (Havana: Impresores Ucar, García, 1958), pp. 70, 77–78; CERP, *Study*, pp. 518–519, 522–523; Seiglie, *Contrato de arrendamiento*, p. 210; Alberto Arredondo, *Reforma agraria: la experiencia cubana* (Río Piedras: Editorial San Juan, 1969), p. 95; Martínez Alier, *Cuba*, p. 85.

10. West Indies Sugar Corporation, *Annual Report* (1954): 3.

11. Carlos Márquez Sterling, *Historia de Cuba* (New York: Las Americas, 1969), pp. 543–544; Ruby Hart Phillips, *Cuba: Island of Paradox* (New York: McDowell, Obolensky, 1959), p. 232.

12. Martínez Alier, *Cuba*, pp. 91–92.

13. "Cuestión de jornales," *Tierra libre* 9, no. 6 (June 1945): 3, 5; ibid., no. 7 (July 1945): 24–26; ibid., 10, no. 9 (October 1946): 3, 10, 16–17; Blas Roca, Carlos Rafael

Rodríguez, and Manuel Luzardo, *En defensa del pueblo* (Havana: Arrow Press, 1945), pp. 33, 39, 59.

14. Francisco Pérez de la Riva, *El café: historia de su cultivo y explotación en Cuba* (Havana: Jesús Montero, 1944), pp. 220, 324–326; *Tierra libre* 4, no. 5 (May 1940): 5, 21–22.

15. Carlos Rafael Rodríguez, "El abastecimiento nacional," in Roca, Rodríguez, Luzardo, *En defensa del pueblo*, pp. 77, 80–81; see also Martínez Alier, *Cuba*, pp. 81–83.

16. The pattern of Supreme Court decisions in rural land-eviction cases in selected years from 1940 through 1959 was as follows:

	Cases won by landowner	Cases won by peasant
1940	2	0
1945	14	4
1948	25	6
1950	27	8
1952	24	8
1955	12	5
1956	17	5
1957	18	6
1958 (5 months)	9	2
1959	9	6

Provincial and national totals for the years listed above were these:

	Cases won by landowner	Cases won by peasant	Cases won by landowner: cases won by peasant
Pinar del Río	29	10	2.9
Havana	31	9	3.4
Matanzas	10	5	2.0
Las Villas	29	8	3.6
Camagüey	17	7	2.4
Oriente	41	11	3.7
Cuba	157	50	3.1

Computed from *La jurisprudencia al día: civil* (1940); ibid. (1945); ibid. (1948); ibid. (1950); ibid. (1952); ibid. (1953); ibid. (1955); ibid. (1956); ibid. (1957); ibid. (1958); ibid. (1959); ibid. (1960). No land-eviction cases reached the Supreme Court in 1960. These statistics include only farm evictions and exclude both the very few cases where the state was evicted by private individuals and those involving *fincas urbanas*, that is, houses, other buildings, and empty lots in urban areas. In addition, cases are included in this count only if the winner can be clearly identified. Because case records rarely reveal exactly how many people were affected, it has not been possible to calculate the number of individuals or families evicted.

17. The most famous eviction disputes in the prerevolutionary years were those in two areas of the province of Oriente, Realengo 18 and Ventas de Casanova, during the

1930s and 1940s. Because the evictions were not enforced, they also became examples of successful peasant resistance and led to what few instances there were of prerevolutionary agrarian reform. Another occurred at Hato del Estero in Camagüey in 1942, but the most famous dispute, tied to an insurrection against Batista, occurred at Las Maboas in 1958. Francisco Simón, "La tragedia del arrendatario rural," *Tierra libre* 4, no. 8 (August 1940): 17; Aníbal Echezarreta, "El Ing. López y el desalojo a los campesinos," ibid., 6, no. 5 (May 1942): 5; Ciro Espinosa, "Desalojo campesino de sus tierras," ibid., 8, no. 9 (September 1944): 5; Antero Regalado, "Esa alianza empezó cuando los campesinos del Realengo 18 se unieron para enfrentarse a los latifundistas y tuvieron a su lado a los obreros," *ANAP* nos. 9–10 (September–October 1964): 36–39, 41; *Granma*, September 6, 1966, p. 4; ibid., August 29, 1970, p. 2; Raúl Castro, "El congreso campesino en armas," *ANAP* (October 1973): 9.

18. Leonel Antonio de la Cuesta, ed., *Constituciones cubanas* (New York: Ediciones Exilio, 1974), p. 320; Manuel Martínez Escobar, *El desahucio y su jurisprudencia*, 2nd ed. (Havana: Cultural, 1942), pp. 504–505; *La jurisprudencia al día: sección de legislación* (1945): 371–372, 878; *La jurisprudencia al día: materia inconstitucional* (1946): 80, 196; ibid (1947): 8, 101.

19. *La jurisprudencia al día: sección de legislación* (1948): 1047–56; ibid. (1949): 20–21.

20. Ibid. (1950): 434–435, 1299–1300; ibid. (1951): 645–646, 1308; Agustín Ravelo Nariño, *El contrato de arrendamiento de finca rústica en la legislación cubana* (Santiago: Tipografía San Román, 1956), p. 362.

21. *La jurisprudencia al día: sección de legislación* (1952): 432–433, 797–802.

22. Ibid. (1953): 107ff.; Martínez Alier, *Cuba*, pp. 144–146; Ravelo Nariño, *Contrato de finca rústica*, pp. 225–226, 316–323, 421–423, 457–459.

23. Francisco López Goicochea, *El desahucio: doctrina del Tribunal Supremo de Cuba, 1947–1952* (Havana: Empresa Editora de Publicaciones, 1954), pp. 213–249. See also Alberto Blanco, "El movimiento jurídico en los primeros cincuenta años de independencia" in *Historia de la nación Cubana*, ed. Ramiro Guerra y Sánchez, José M. Pérez Cabrera, Juan J. Remos, and Emeterio S. Santovenia (Havana: Editorial Historia de la Nación Cubana, 1952), 8: 375–381.

24. Computed from *1946 Census*, p. 1018; Arredondo, *Reforma agraria*, p. 95.

25. Arredondo, *Reforma agraria*, p. 199.

26. Phillips, *Cuba: Island of Paradox* p. 186; *Tierra libre* 4, no. 8 (August 1940): 5; ibid., 5, no. 10 (October 1941): 25–26; ibid., no. 11 (November 1941): 10–12; ibid., 6, no. 6 (June 1942): 3; ibid., no. 8 (August 1942): 8; ibid., no. 10 (October 1942): 8; ibid., 8, no. 10 (October 1944): 15; ibid., 10, no. 8 (August 1946): 6.

27. Eduardo Suárez Rivas, *Un pueblo crucificado* (Miami: Service Offset Printers, 1964), pp. 246–247, 296; Arredondo, *Reforma agraria*, p. 199; International Bank for Reconstruction and Development, *Report on Cuba* (Washington, D.C., 1951), p. 93; Fulgencio Batista, *Respuesta* (Mexico: Imprenta Manuel León Sánchez, 1960), p. 473.

28. Rolando Bonachea and Nelson P. Valdés, *Revolutionary Struggle, 1947–1958: The Selected Works of Fidel Castro* (Cambridge, Mass.: M.I.T. Press, 1972), 1: 185; Grupos de Propaganda Doctrinal Ortodoxa, *Doctrina del Partido Ortodoxo* (Havana: Fernández, 1951), pp. 11, 58–60; Loree Wilkerson, *Fidel Castro's Political Programs from Reformism to Marxism-Leninism* (Gainesville: University of Florida Press, 1965),

pp. 30–31; "Los colonos en palacio," *Tierra libre* 17, nos. 4–5 (April–May 1953): 1; Martínez Alier, *Cuba*, p. 96.

29. Pearson product-moment correlations were computed for the variables in table 11.3 across the six provinces. The proportion of sugar farmers was statistically independent of all other variables (correlations under .3), although it was slightly inversely related, predictably enough, to the proportions of squatters and of court-ordered evictions. Thus the impact of sugar farming on tenure patterns can only be observed at the subprovincial level, for which no appropriate data are available. Other relationships, however, can be observed at the provincial level. The correlations between the proportions of squatters and of very small farms and between the proportions of squatters and of court-ordered land evictions are strong: .93 and .66, respectively. Thus areas with a large number of squatters were also more likely to have very small farms and a higher-than-average frequency of land evictions. The importance of Oriente province is also evident in the legal documents from 1959 and 1960 examined by Juan and Verena Martínez Alier; see *Cuba*, p. 152.

30. In the 1960s, the Cuban Academy of Sciences identified seventeen cases of "major peasant struggle" between the 1902 and 1958, ten of which occurred in Oriente province. The "thesis" on the agrarian question for the First Party Congress—that is, the main document detailing the party's agrarian policies—identified forty-five, twenty of which occurred in Oriente; the rest were divided about equally among the five westernmost provinces. Both numbers, however, clearly understate the amount of rural conflict at the time; they represent only incidents that reached a scale sufficient to intrude into national politics. Academia de Ciencias de Cuba and Academia de Ciencias de la URSS, *Atlas nacional de Cuba* (Havana: 1970), p. 129 (hereafter cited as Academia, *Atlas*); Comité Central del Partido Comunista de Cuba, Departamento de Orientación Revolucionaria, *Sobre la cuestión agraria y las relaciones con el campesinado* (Havana: Instituto Cubano del Libro, 1976), pp. 15–16.

31. Computations from *1946 Census*, pp. 400, 465, 998.

32. For detailed evidence, see Hugh Thomas, *Cuba: The Pursuit of Freedom* (New York: Harper & Row, 1971), pp. 900–908, 914–916, 924, 935–938, 1010–11, 1043; Ramón Bonachea and Marta San Martín, *The Cuban Insurrection, 1952–1959* (New Brunswick, N.J.: Transaction Books, 1974), pp. 90–91, 100–105, 182–184; Ernesto Guevara, *Reminiscences of the Cuban Revolutionary War*, trans. Victoria Ortiz (New York: Monthly Review Press, 1968), pp. 51–53, 178–184, 192–195, 197; Ramón Barquín, *Las luchas guerrilleras en Cuba: de la colonia a la Sierra Maestra* (Madrid: Editorial Playor, 1975), pp. 267–271, 327–332. See also E. J. Hobsbawm, *Primitive Rebels* (New York: Norton, 1959), chap. 2.

33. Theodore Draper, *Castroism: Theory and Practice* (New York: Praeger, 1965), p. 74.

34. Barrington Moore, Jr., *Social Origins of Dictatorship and Democracy* (Boston: Beacon Press, 1966), chap. 9; Eric Wolf, *Peasant Wars of the Twentieth Century* (New York: Harper & Row, 1969), pp. 276–302.

35. The text is in Ovidio García Regueiro, *Cuba: raíces y frutos de una revolución* (Madrid: IEPAL, 1970), pp. 299–302.

36. Jorge García Montes and Antonio Alonso Ávila, *Historia del partido comunista de Cuba* (Miami: Rema Press, 1970), pp. 553–554; José Suárez Núñez, *El gran culpa-*

ble (Caracas, 1963), pp. 80, 85, 88–90; Márquez Sterling, *Historia de Cuba,* p. 610; Barquín, *Luchas guerrilleras,* p. 394.

37. Barquín, *Luchas guerrilleras,* pp. 363–364, 487–488, 512; and Padula, "Fall of the Bourgeoisie," p. 75.

38. R. Castro, "Congreso campesino," p. 6; Bonachea and San Martín, *Cuban Insurrection,* pp. 189–190, 195–197; Barquín, *Luchas guerrilleras,* pp. 650–651.

39. Text in García Regueiro, *Cuba: raíces y frutos,* pp. 319–336.

40. Sidney W. Mintz, "The Rural Proletariat and the Problem of Rural Proletarian Consciousness," *Journal of Peasant Studies* 1, no. 3 (April 1974): 299–300.

41. Severo Aguirre, "El primer año de las cooperativas cañeras," *Cuba socialista* no. 3 (November 1961): 19–20; Martínez Alier, *Cuba,* chap. 5.

42. Computed from Brian H. Pollitt, "Employment Plans, Performance and Future Prospects in Cuba," in *Third World Employment,* ed. Richard Jolly et al. (London: Penguin Books, 1973), p. 255. In an earlier publication I did not sufficiently appreciate these distinctions among beneficiaries of revolutionary policies in rural Cuba. See Jorge I. Domínguez, "Sectoral Clashes in Cuban Politics and Development," *Latin American Research Review* 6, no. 3 (Fall 1971): 61–81.

43. Text in García Regueiro, *Cuba: raíces y frutos,* pp. 308–309. See also *Revolución,* February 20, 1959, p. 15; ibid., February 21, 1959, p. 1; ibid., February 25, 1959, pp. 1, 14; ibid., May 22, 1959, p. 8; ibid., July 2, 1959, p. 1; ibid., July 11, 1959, pp. 1, 17; Martínez Alier, *Cuba,* pp. 176–178.

44. Martínez Alier, *Cuba,* pp. 125–131.

45. Ibid., pp. 100–105; Arredondo, *Reforma agraria,* pp. 96–97.

46. Academia, *Atlas,* p. 74, shows that southern Matanzas was the most intensively cultivated sugar-growing area on the island in 1965; between 50 and 80 percent of its arable soil was given over to cane.

47. Computed from *1946 Census,* pp. 397–398, 462, 465, 996.

48. Eric Wolf has suggested that the social bases of rural revolution are to be found first among what he calls "middle" peasants, who were among neither the richest nor the poorest peasants, and among poor but free peasants, who were neither slaves nor serfs, whose settlements are only under marginal control from the outside. Wolf's comments on the second group fit the case of the Cuban squatters well. The southern Matanzas peasants parallel Wolf's middle peasants quite closely; they were the bulwarks of counterrevolution. Wolf has argued that "it is the very attempt of the middle and free peasant to remain traditional which makes him revolutionary." In Cuba, middle peasants were not revolutionary while the revolution was going on and became counterrevolutionary when it came into power. Cuba's poor but free squatters were revolutionary when Wolf expected them to be but not later, when the revolutionary government made more vigorous effort than any previous government to break with tradition. See Wolf, *Peasant Wars,* pp. 289–292 and the remainder of his concluding chapter. On the subject of peasant revolutions, see also Moore, *Social Origins,* chap. 9. Cuba's peasant counterrevolution resembles most closely the German peasant rebellion of 1524–1525 as described by Moore. This Bauernkrieg, or Peasants' War, was begun by relatively well-to-do peasants, with moderate demands that were subsequently radicalized. The peasants were defeated in part because they failed successfully to establish a link with nonpeasant groups in the society. Important differences between the two cases are the lesser importance of religion and the wider variety of

nonmilitary instruments available to the government in Cuba. The revolutionary situation among Cuban squatters, however, does not have a clear parallel in Moore's work. See also Charles Tilly, "Revolutions and Collective Violence," in *Handbook of Political Science*, ed. Fred Greenstein and Nelson Polsby (Reading, Mass.: Addison-Wesley, 1975), vol. 3.

49. Carlos Rafael Rodríguez, "Cuatro años de reforma agraria," *Cuba socialista* no. 21 (May 1963): 14–15. For the legal documents, see Martínez Alier, *Cuba*—the most radical on pp. 114, 127, 131, 144, 183, 184, 185, 189, 190; the least radical on pp. 145, 178; see also pp. 125, 128, 135, 151, 156, 162, 169, 188, 198.

50. Fidel Castro, "Discurso del Primer Ministro en el Comité Provincial de Matanzas," *Cuba socialista* no. 9 (May 1962): 19–23; Raúl García Pelaez, "La construcción del Partido en la provincia de Matanzas," ibid., no. 16 (December 1962): 118–123; Hernán Barrera, "Building the United Party of the Socialist Revolution in Cuba," *World Marxist Review* 6, no. 12 (December 1963): 56–58.

51. The account that follows is based on Rodríguez, "Cuatro años de reforma," pp. 1–15; F. Castro, "Discurso en Matanzas," pp. 19–25; Nivaldo Herrera, "La ofensiva política en las zonas campesinas de Matanzas," *Cuba socialista* no. 39 (November 1964): 79–90; Darío Carmona, "Justicia en la tierra," *Cuba* 1, no. 5 (September 1962): 40–42; idem, *Prohibida la sombra* (Havana: Ediciones Unión, 1965): 41–46, 72–85.

52. Michael A. Pettitt, "Social and Economic Change in the Community around a Sugar Mill in Cuba" (Ph.D. diss., University of California–Berkeley, 1973), p. 72.

53. Text in García Regueiro, *Cuba: raíces y frutos*, pp. 339–340; see also Arredondo, *Reforma agraria*, pp. 223–224.

54. Michael F. Jimenez, "Revolutionary Agrarian Policy and the Cuban Peasantry" (seminar paper, Harvard University, 1972).

55. Oscar Duyos, "Los problemas actuales del acopio y los precios de compra de los productos agrícolas," *Cuba socialista* no. 33 (May 1964): 75. I am grateful to Michael F. Jimenez for calling this article to my attention.

56. Computed from José Acosta, "Las leyes de reforma agraria en Cuba y el sector privado campesino," *Economía y desarrollo* no. 12 (July–August 1972): 114–115.

57. "Notas económicas: nueva luz sobre la agricultura privada," *Cuba socialista* no. 60 (August 1966): 129–131; see also "Hacia la sistematización de los precios de acopio de productos agrícolas," ibid., no. 48 (August 1965): 122–124. Computations from *Boletín 1971*, pp. 120, 122; *Anuario 1972*, pp. 128, 130.

58. Duyos, "Problemas actuales del acopio," p. 76; Rodríguez, "Cuatro años de reforma," pp. 12–14; idem, "La revolución cubana y el campesinado," *Cuba socialista* no. 53 (January 1966): 42; idem, "The Cuban Revolution and the Peasantry," *World Marxist Review* 8, no. 10 (October 1965): 66–67. For a useful discussion of peasant support for counterrevolution in the Morón region of Camagüey, see Víctor González, "El trabajo de la Unión de Jóvenes Comunistas en el campo," *Cuba socialista* no. 44 (April 1965): 47–60.

59. "Plan de fortalecimiento de los organismos de la ANAP," *ANAP* 5, no. 4 (April 1965): 4–5; "Acuerdos de la plenaria de la ANAP," ibid., no. 10 (October 1965): 5; "Lucha abierta contra la especulación," ibid., 6, no. 10 (October 1966): 4–5.

60. Alfredo Menéndez Cruz, "La transformación de las cooperatives cañeras en granjas cañeras," *Cuba socialista* no. 14 (October 1962): 31, 37–40; Antonio Núñez Jiménez, "Revolución agraria en Cuba," *INRA* 2, no. 6 (June 1961): 7; Blas Roca,

"Nueva etapa de la revolución cubana," *Cuba socialista* no. 5 (January 1962): 45; Carlos Rafael Rodríguez, "El nuevo camino de la agricultura cubana," ibid., no. 27 (November 1963): 83–84.

61. Antero Regalado, "El camino de la cooperación agraria en Cuba," *Cuba socialista* no. 22 (June 1963): 48–52; *Granma*, May 6, 1975, p. 4; ibid., May 16, 1977, p. 6; José Acosta, "La revolución agraria en Cuba y el desarrollo económico," *Economía y desarrollo* no. 17 (May–June 1973): 155–156.

62. Regalado, "Camino de la cooperación agraria," pp. 49, 51–52; Lise Rochon, "La sociedad agropecuaria 'Jesús Feliú': un caso de cambio en el medio rural bajo un régimen socialista de transición," *Etnología y folklore* no. 4 (July–December 1967): 23–36.

63. Antero Regalado, "El crédito a los pequeños agricultores en Cuba," *ANAP* 6, no. 10 (October 1966): 18.

64. Idem, "Credits for Small Farmers in Cuba," *World Marxist Review* 8, no. 3 (March 1965): 31.

65. Arnaldo Milián, "Las cooperativas campesinas de créditos y servicios en Las Villas," *Cuba socialista* no. 21 (May 1963): 54–55.

66. "El II congreso nacional de la ANAP," ibid., no. 25 (September 1963): 117–118.

67. "Plan de fortalecimiento de la ANAP," pp. 6, 8.

68. Regalado, "Camino de la cooperación agraria," p. 50.

69. "El crédito global a los agricultores," *ANAP* 7, no. 8 (August 1967): 15, 17; *Granma Weekly Review*, July 18, 1967.

70. *Granma Weekly Review*, May 28, 1967, p. 3; ibid., June 18, 1967, pp. 4, 12.

71. "Acuerdos de la comisión de producción," *ANAP* 7, nos. 5–6 (May–June 1967): 15; Jorge Michelena, "En la base campesina 'Porfirio Cabrera' se producen ventas de arroz por la libre," ibid., no. 10 (October 1967): 12–13; idem, "El plátano por la libre en el municipal Alvaro Reynoso," ibid., no. 11 (November 1967): 19–20; "Sobre las ventas por la libre," ibid., no. 12 (December 1967): 6–7. For a list of items available on the black market in 1968–1969 and price comparisons with the legal market given to a United States anthropologist by a black-market merchant, see Pettitt, "Social and Economic Change," pp. 299–301.

72. "Sobre las siembras a partido," *ANAP* 8, no. 2 (February 1968): 12.

73. "Reglamento general de la ANAP," ibid., 7, nos. 5–6 (May–June 1967): 22.

74. "Notas económicas," pp. 127–128.

75. Computed from *1967 Census*, pp. 100–107. An additional 223,497 head of cattle, which the census could not attribute to any particular farm, are excluded from these statistics.

76. "La resolución 120 del INRA constituye una nueva medida de justicia revolucionaria," *ANAP* 6, no. 7 (July 1966): 20–21; *Granma Weekly Review*, January 29, 1967.

77. Boris Gorbachev and Arnold Kalinin, "Algunos aspectos socio-económicos y políticos de la experiencia de la revolución cubana," *Panorama latinoamericano* no. 96 (May 4, 1970): 11–12; "Dictamen de la comisión de producción al IV Congreso nacional campesino," *ANAP* (December 1971–January 1972): 20. The statistical coverage for organized peasant participation is poor and, at times, contradictory. Tables 11.9 and 11.10 represent a best effort, though they should be used with caution.

78. "Dictamen de la comisión de producción," p. 20; Fidel Castro, "La alianza obrero-campesina," *Economía y desarrollo* no. 9 (January–February 1972): 23; *Granma*, December 27, 1971, p. 5; "Notas económicas," p. 128; *Granma Weekly Review*, January 4, 1976, p. 6; ibid., May 29, 1977, pp. 2–3. For a general discussion, see Vladimir Bondarchuk, "La economía cubana en vísperas del I Congreso del Partido Comunista de Cuba," *América Latina* no. 4 (1975): 9–11.

79. *Verde olivo* 9, no. 14 (April 7, 1968): 26; "Dictamen de la comisión de producción," p. 25.

80. "Dictamen de la comisión de producción," pp. 20–21.

81. "Dictamen de la comisión de organización al IV Congreso nacional campesino," *ANAP* (December 1971–January 1972): 33–35; Juan Changó Leyva, "La avanzada campesina en Matanzas," *ANAP* no. 8 (August 1974): 17.

82. "Dictamen de la comisión de organización," p. 32; *Granma*, December 31, 1971, p. 2.

83. Juan Changó Leyva, "Un compromiso entre las lomas," *ANAP* (April 1973): 8–9.

84. "Acuerdos de la comisión de producción," p. 17; "II Congreso de la ANAP," p. 118; "Reglamento de la ANAP," p. 22; Carmelo Mesa-Lago, "Farm Payment Systems in Socialist Cuba," *Studies in Comparative Communism* 9, no. 3 (Autumn 1976): 281–282.

85. *Granma Weekly Review*, January 9, 1972, p. 2; "Dictamen de la comisión de organización," p. 32.

86. *Granma Weekly Review*, November 18, 1973, p. 3.

87. "Síntesis de las conclusiones," *ANAP* 8, no. 2 (February 1968): 10; *Granma*, January 3, 1972, p. 5; "Dictamen de la comisión ideológica al IV Congreso nacional campesino," *ANAP* (December 1971–January 1972): 43; Pedro Rojas, "Iniciado el curso de orientación política, 1973–1974," *ANAP* (November 1973): 17.

88. Computed from *Granma*, December 10, 1975, p. 4; *Granma Weekly Review*, November 30, 1975, p. 1; ibid., January 4, 1976, p. 6.

89. Computed from "Elección del comité ejecutivo nacional," *ANAP* 7, nos. 5–6 (May–June 1967): 11; "Comité nacional de la ANAP," *ANAP* (December 1971–January 1972): 17; see also "Dictamen de la comisión de organización," p. 37; Pedro Rojas, "En su lugar la educación," *ANAP* (November 1973): 11.

90. José Acosta, "La revolución," p. 155; "Transformación de la familia campesina," *ANAP* (December 1973): 17; Alfredo Reyes Trejo, "El campesino cubano marcha con su revolución," *Verde olivo* 16, no. 20 (May 19, 1974): 37; *Granma*, June 4, 1975, p. 3.

91. *Granma Weekly Review*, February 15, 1976, p. 9; *ANAP* (May 1975): 27.

92. Departamento de Orientación Revolucionaria, *Sobre la cuestión agraria*, pp. 51–52, 61–64.

93. *Granma Weekly Review*, May 29, 1977, pp. 2–3.

94. Ibid., p. 4; *Granma*, October 1, 1976, p. 6; ibid., May 16, 1977, p. 5.

95. *Granma Weekly Review*, May 29, 1977, p. 3; *Granma*, May 16, 1977, p. 5.

96. *Granma*, October 21, 1976, p. 3; ibid., May 16, 1977, p. 4; ibid., May 17, 1977, pp. 1, 3; ibid., May 18, 1977, pp. 1, 3; *Granma Weekly Review*, May 22, 1977, p. 5.

12. POLITICAL CULTURE

1. See Gabriel Almond and Sidney Verba, *The Civic Culture* (Boston: Little, Brown, 1965), pp. 11–13; Lucian Pye and Sidney Verba, eds., *Political Culture and Political Development* (Princeton: Princeton University Press, 1965), pp. 7–10, 513; Samuel P. Huntington and Jorge I. Domínguez, "Political Development," in *Handbook of Political Science*, ed. Fred I. Greenstein and Nelson W. Polsby (Reading, Mass.: Addison-Wesley, 1975), 3:15–32.

2. Frederick C. Barghoorn, *Politics in the USSR* (Boston: Little, Brown, 1966); Richard H. Solomon, *Mao's Revolution and the Chinese Political Culture* (Berkeley and Los Angeles: University of California Press, 1971).

3. Richard R. Fagen, *The Transformation of Political Culture in Cuba* (Stanford: Stanford University Press, 1969), pp. 14, 16. Comité Central del Partido Comunista de Cuba, Departamento de Orientación Revolucionaria, *Sobre la lucha ideológica* (Havana: Instituto Cubano del Libro, 1976), pp. 28–33.

4. Enrique A. Baloyra, "Political Leadership in the Cuban Republic, 1944–1958" (Ph.D. diss., University of Florida–Gainesville, 1971), pp. 125–127, 152. Little is known about the methodology of these surveys, but, given conventional practice at the time, they are likely to cover the urban areas only and to oversample nonpoor residents of Havana.

5. Universidad Central Marta Abreu de Las Villas, *La educación rural en Las Villas* (Havana: Impresores Ucar, García, 1959), pp. viii, 10–12, 111–112, 123, 136, 152. Only 55.4 percent of the rural schoolteachers in Las Villas actually cooperated with the university's survey. Within each rural school district, a 5-percent sample was selected at random. According to Brian Pollitt, it probably underrepresented the poorest people, since the reliance on schoolteachers excluded areas without schools. A comparison of the survey results with the 1953 census shows that agricultural workers were underrepresented. Because the survey universe was established in March through May 1958, when migratory workers from Las Villas were harvesting in Camagüey, they were excluded when the survey sample was actually drawn in May and June. Areas with inadequate postal service were also excluded. Las Villas province is not representative of the rest of rural Cuba; its agriculture was highly diversified and the value of its production high. Consequently the survey oversampled the nonpoor rural population, people who had contact with government through schools and were generally peasants rather than agricultural workers. For the present purpose this bias is helpful. Agricultural workers are more apt to be joiners because of their participation in unions than peasants are. Peasants are at times both stubborn and parochial, a tendency that makes their enthusiasm for cooperative effort all the more striking. See Brian Pollitt, "Estudios acerca del nivel de vida rural en la Cuba prerevolucionaria: un análisis crítico," *Teoría y práctica* nos. 42–43 (November–December 1967):38–44. Age differences reported in the text were statistically significant at the .05 level in a chi-square test.

6. Oscar Echevarría Salvat, *La agricultura cubana, 1934–1966* (Miami: Ediciones Universal, 1971), pp. 5–9, 12, 24. Demographic findings are, in general, compatible with the pertinent data from the 1953 census. In the province of Oriente, however, blacks and the totally destitute were still underrepresented. For the purposes of the survey, agricultural workers were defined as those 400,000 people who lived in

areas with populations under 150 persons that lacked medical and legal services, electricity, and recreational facilities, and whose chief source of income came from laboring for a third person who either owned or represented the owner of land and capital; Pollitt, "Estudios de vida rural," pp. 45–49.

7. Lydia Cabrera, *La sociedad secreta Abakuá* (Havana: Ediciones C.R., 1958), pp. 9, 13–14, 19–22, 59–60; Rafael López Valdés and Pedro Deschamps, "La sociedad secreta Abakuá en un grupo de obreros portuarios," *Etnología y folklore* no. 2 (July–December 1966): 5, 12, 15, 23–25; Rafael López Valdés, "La sociedad secreta Abakuá y los procesos de cambio en los obreros manuales del puerto de La Habana," in *VII Congrès International des Sciences Anthropologiques et Ethnologiques* (Moscow: Nauka, 1971), vol. 11.

8. John DuMoulin, "The Participative Art of the Afro-Cuban Religions," *Abhandlungen und Berichte des Staatlichen Museums für Völkerkunde Dresden* (Berlin) 21 (1962): 63–65; "Diez refranes lucumíes," *Cuba* 3, no. 31 (November 1964): 43. For a bibliography of anthropological research in Cuba before and since the revolution, see Roberto Nodal, "Current Trends of Anthropological Research in Cuba," Caribbean Series (University of Wisconsin–Milwaukee, Department of Afro-American Studies, August 1976).

9. Michael Kenny, "Twentieth-Century Spanish Expatriates in Cuba: A Subculture," *Anthropological Quarterly* 34, no. 2 (April 1961): 86–88, 90–91.

10. Ross Danielson, "Cuban Health Care in Process: Models and Morality in the Early Revolution," in *Topias and Utopias in Health*, ed. Stanley Ingman and Anthony Thomas (The Hague: Mouton, 1975), p. 325.

11. George M. Stabler, "Bejucal: Social Values and Changes in Agricultural Practices" (Ph.D. diss., Michigan State University, 1958), pp. 63–64, 66–67, 73–74.

12. Ibid., pp. 76–77, 78–83, 85–88, 94–96, 131.

13. Ibid., pp. 50–51, 123, 129, 130, 135, 162, 166.

14. Jorge Mañach, *Indagación del choteo*, 2nd ed. (Havana: La Verónica, 1940), pp. 19–20, 31, 33, 40–41, 54–57, 62–63, 65, 71, 74.

15. Leon Rozitchner, *Moral burguesa y revolución*, 3rd ed. (Buenos Aires: Editorial Tiempo Contemporáneo, 1969), pp. 9–10, 19–26, 34–35, 57, 61, 116–117, 130–131, 179.

16. John DuMoulin et al., "Monocultivo y proletarización: dos ejemplos de Las Villas," *Ciencias sociales contemporáneas* 1, no. 1 (August 1965): 119, 127–128. For the same effect, see James Petras, *Politics and Social Forces in Chilean Development* (Berkeley and Los Angeles: University of California Press, 1970), pp. 275–283.

17. Mateo Jover Marimón, "The Church," in *Revolutionary Change in Cuba*, ed. Carmelo Mesa-Lago (Pittsburgh: University of Pittsburgh Press, 1971), pp. 400–401.

18. Universidad de Las Villas, *Educación rural*, pp. 30, 32, 215; Echevarría Salvat, *Agricultura cubana*, pp. 14–17; Stabler, "Bejucal: Values and Changes," pp. 77–78. For a comparative assessment, J. Lloyd Mecham, *Church and State in Latin America*, rev. ed. (Chapel Hill: University of North Carolina Press, 1966), pp. 423–424.

19. René de la Huerta Aguiar, "Espiritismo y otras supersticiones en la población cubana," *Revista del hospital psiquiátrico de La Habana* 2, no. 1 (January–March 1960): 45–47.

20. Gerardo Nogueira Rivero, "El sincretismo religioso como una causa desencadenante y/o determinante de síndromes neuróticos y pseudopsicóticos en el niño

cubano," *Revista del hospital psiquiátrico de La Habana* 3, no. 1 (January–March 1962): 42.

21. For a discussion of the political difficulties of gathering reliable anthropological data in Cuba by a scholar supportive of revolutionary rule, see Michael Pettitt, "Social and Economic Change in the Community around a Sugar Mill in Cuba" (Ph.D. diss., University of California–Berkeley, 1973), pp. 10, 343–344. See also Oscar Lewis, Ruth M. Lewis, and Susan M. Rigdon, *Four Men: Living the Revolution* (Urbana: University of Illinois Press, 1977), pp. vii–xxx.

22. Louis Jones, Lenna Jones, and Edith Falcón, "Actitudes vocacionales de estudiantes de 1960 y 1965," *Psicología y educación* 2, no. 5 (January–March 1965): 41–42, 44, 47, 50, 52. The first survey included seventh graders only; the second survey included students from the three years of junior high school. Both surveys drew random samples, but the second was also stratified by academic year and gross school socioeconomic level.

23. Computed from Gustavo Torroella, *Estudio de la juventud cubana* (Havana: Comisión Nacional Cubana de la UNESCO, 1963), pp. 8, 9, 11 (the UNESCO study covered Cuba, Canada, France, India, Japan, and Malaya); André Berge, "Young People in the Orient and Occident: General Report on the Survey," *International Journal of Adult and Youth Education* 16, no. 2 (1964): 58 (I am grateful to Lourdes Casal for calling these studies to my attention). Torroella conducted a systematic and stratified sample among senior-high-school and university students, aged sixteen through twenty-three, in the cities of Havana, Santa Clara, and Santiago. Unfortunately, the only available cross-tabulations simply distinguish the students as being at, under, or over age eighteen. Schoolteachers and university professors took the survey.

24. Computed from Torroella, *Estudio de la juventud*, pp. 95–97, 109, 119; Berge, "Young People in Orient and Occident," pp. 72–73.

25. Computed from Torroella, *Estudio de la juventud*, p. 118.

26. Computed from ibid., pp. 97, 114, 115, 116, 117; Berge, "Young People in Orient and Occident," pp. 66–68, 71, 79.

27. Computed from Torroella, *Estudio de la juventud*, pp. 130–131, 90, 82, 74, 86–89; Berge, "Young People in Orient and Occident," pp. 78–79, 65, 63.

28. Huntington and Domínguez, "Political Development," pp. 66–90; Karl W. Deutsch, *Nationalism and Social Communications*, 2nd ed. (Cambridge, Mass.: M.I.T. Press, 1966); idem, "International Communication: The Media and Flows," *Public Opinion Quarterly* 20, no. 1 (Spring 1956).

29. Universidad Central de las Villas, *Educación rural*, pp. 78, 80, 115–116, 119.

30. Stabler, "Bejucal: Values and Changes," pp. 131, 129, 126.

31. Computed from Torroella, *Estudio de la juventud*, p. 105.

32. *Aclaraciones: Periódico Hoy* (Havana: Editora Política, 1966), pp. 331, 457.

33. Computed from Torroella, *Estudio de la juventud*, pp. 112–113, 129, 130–131.

34. "La lucha contra el oscurantismo es una lucha ideológica," *Con la guardia en alto* 8, no. 6 (June 1969): 11; Jorge Calderón González, *Amparo: millo y azucena* (Havana: Casa de las Américas, 1970), pp. 222, 225–226.

35. Manuel Fernández, "La crisis actual del catolicismo en Cuba," *Reunión*, nos. 93–94 (January–February, 1977): 2–3; Jover Marimón, "Church," p. 401; computed from Universidad Central de la Villas, *Educación rural*, p. 32; Echevarría Salvat, *Agri-*

cultura cubana, pp. 15–16; Torroella, *Estudio de la juventud*, foldout between pp. 130–131; Margaret E. Crahan, "Salvation through Christ or Marx: Attitudes of Cuban Churchpeople before and after the Revolution" (Paper presented at meeting of the Latin American Studies Association, Atlanta, March 1976), p. 7.

36. Computed from Torroella, *Estudio de la juventud*, pp. 105–106.

37. Fernando Ortiz, "Por la integración de blancos y negros," *Estudios afrocubanos* 5 (1945–1946): 221–233.

38. Verena Martínez-Alier, *Marriage, Class and Colour in Nineteenth-Century Cuba: A Study of Racial Attitudes and Sexual Values in a Slave Society* (London: Cambridge University Press, 1974), especially pp. 91–99.

39. Geoffrey E. Fox, "Cuban Workers in Exile," *Transaction* 8, no. 11 (September 1971): 21–30.

40. Roberto Fraga Arroyo, "Estudio estadístico de 200 primeros casos, haciendo énfasis en la sintomatologia, psicodinamia y resultados terapéuticos obtenidos en pacientes tratados," *Revista cubana de pediatría* 30, no. 2 (February 1958): 98.

41. Lourdes Casal, *"Images of Cuban Society among Pre- and Post-Revolutionary Novelists"* (Ph.D. diss., New School for Social Research, 1975), chaps. 4, 6. Casal used fifteen novels for the prerevolutionary and fifteen for the postrevolutionary periods, excluding novels published by Cubans outside of Cuba, novels that could not be located through the United States Library of Congress, science-fiction novels, and others that were not realistic in style, that did not deal with a discernible Cuban setting, or that dealt with pre-1930 topics; unfortunately she also eliminated detective stories.

42. Ernesto Guevara, "Man and Socialism in Cuba," in *Man and Socialism in Cuba: The Great Debate* ed. Bertram Silverman (New York: Atheneum, 1971).

43. Coded and computed from "Y tu, y tu, y tu . . . ¿ por qué vas a Camagüey?" *Cuba* 7 (June 1968): 27–35. A "revolutionary" response had to include references to at least one of the following: the good of the country or of the revolution, obedience to leadership, revolutionary consciousness, the duties of the good Communist, the need for cooperation and participation, gratitude to the country or the revolution, or comments about national economic development.

44. Tests of statistical significance have been performed on attitudinal and background variables, even though technically they are not pertinent to a nonrandom sample; they are meant only to reveal the more important relationships. Two-tailed t-tests for differences of means were used to test for differences in age, in number of school years completed, and in work experience (mean age of those gainfully employed). Chi-square tests were used to test for differences in sex, work (whether or not the subject had been gainfully employed prior to volunteering), and membership in revolutionary organizations. Chi-square tests were also used to test for relationships between motivations. Statistical significance is reported at the .05 level; the word *strongly* in the text indicates significance at least at the .01 level.

45. Norman H. Nie, G. Bingham Powell, Jr., and Kenneth Prewitt, "Social Structure and Developmental Relationships," pts. 1 and 2, *American Political Science Review* 63 (1969): 361–378, 808–832; Alex Inkeles, "Participant Citizenship in Six Developing Countries," ibid., pp. 1120–41; Sidney Verba and Norman H. Nie, *Participation in America* (New York: Harper & Row, 1972); Almond and Verba, *Civic Culture*, pp. 315–321.

46. All at .01 for a chi-square test with one degree of freedom, and two two-tailed

t-tests for 7 and 16 degrees of freedom respectively. Work experience could not be tested in relation to draft evasion.

47. Chi-square tests were significant at .02 for revolutionary beliefs and at .01 for organizational membership, both for one degree of freedom; a two-tailed t-test was significant at .02 for age, for 26 degrees of freedom. Work experience could not be tested.

48. Maurice Zeitlin, *Revolutionary Politics and the Cuban Working Class* (New York: Harper Torchbooks, 1970), pp. 13–28, 197–199; the text reanalyzes his data.

49. Eutimio Pérez, "Asamblea de la alimentación," *Verde olivo* 13, no. 5 (January 31, 1971): 4.

50. *Granma Weekly Review*, November 25, 1973, p. 7.

51. Zeitlin, *Revolutionary Politics*, pp. 247, 250, 254–260, 264–265.

52. Torroella, *Estudio de la juventud*, pp. 133–134; Berge, "Young People in Orient and Occident," pp. 70–71.

53. Casal took twenty random samples of one page from each of the thirty novels studied; positive and negative references to twelve values were recorded; within each page the sentence became the unit of analysis. The final score for each value is the sum of all positive references minus the sum of all negative references.

54. Pearson product-moment correlation based on the natural-scale scores, not the ranks, is 0.78.

55. Casal, "Images" pp. 270–278; Casal took random samples of twenty different pages from each novel; each page became the unit of analysis and was treated as a separate story, and scored them for imagery on need for achievement.

56. Alberto P. Díaz, "Guanamaca: una comunidad haitiana," *Etnología y folklore* no. 1 (1966): 28.

57. Rosalía García Herrera, "Observaciones etnológicas de dos sectas religiosas afrocubanas en una comunidad Lajera, La Guinea," *Islas* no. 43 (September–December 1972): 145, 147–150, 155, 157, 179–180.

58. Rafael González and Rubén Medina, "Trabajo investigación-desarrollo Escambray, 1971–1972," *Universidad de La Habana*, nos. 198–199 (1973): 97, 99, 102–105.

59. Lise Rochon, "La sociedad agropecuaria 'Jesús Feliú': un caso de cambio en el medio rural bajo un régimen socialista de transición," *Etnología y folklore* no. 4 (July–December 1967): 23–28, 32–36.

60. Douglas Butterworth, "Grass Roots Political Organization in Cuba: A Case of the Committees for the Defense of the Revolution," in *Latin American Urban Research*, ed. Wayne Cornelius and Felicity Trueblood (Beverly Hills, Calif.: Sage publications, 1974), 4:183–202.

61. Mónica Sorín and Luis Gavilando, "Acerca del rendimiento académico en una escuela universitaria," *Etnologia y folklore* no. 2 (July–December 1966): 75–76, 79, 83–84.

62. Martha Morales, Gilberto Valdés, Beatriz Díaz, and Elva Díaz, "Estudio preliminar sobre algunos factores que inciden en las realizaciones docentes de los alumnos de primer año," *Sobre educación superior* (July–December 1970): 43, 45–48. They used a nine-variable multiple regression, statistically significant at the .05 level in both samples for the two variables noted.

63. Marifeli Pérez-Stable, "Cuba's Workers 1975: A Preliminary Analysis" (Paper

presented at meeting of the Latin American Studies Association Atlanta, March 1976), pp. 13–16.

64. Sorín and Gavilando, "Acerca del rendimento académico," pp. 75–76, 79, 83–84.

65. Ernesto Guevara, "Notes on Man and Socialism in Cuba," in *Che Guevara Speaks,* ed. George Lavan (New York: Merit, 1967), p. 136.

66. See Susan Kaufman Purcell, "Modernizing Women for a Modern Society: The Cuban Case," in *Female and Male in Latin America,* ed. Ann Pescatello (Pittsburgh: University of Pittsburgh Press, 1973).

67. Jones et al., "Actitudes vocacionales," pp. 44, 47, 50, 52.

68. Torroella, *Estudio de la juventud,* pp. 101–102.

69. John DuMoulin, "Santa Fe: ideología y opinión sobre problemas locales," *Etnología y folklore* no. 6 (July–December 1968): 5, 10–11.

70. Ibid., p. 14.

71. Ibid.

72. Ibid., p. 19.

73. Computed from ibid., p. 16.

74. Computed from *Granma Weekly Review,* July 23, 1967, p. 6. See also Valery Volkov, "Isle of Pines: The Past and the Present," *New Times* no. 30 (July 1975): 30. For evidence on the politicization of marriage among party officials in rural Matanzas, see Pettitt, "Social and Economic Change," p. 329.

75. Mongo P., "Brochazos: la minifalda," *Bohemia* 67, no. 11 (March 14, 1975): 95. Comité Central del Partido Comunista de Cuba, Departamento de Orientación Revolucionaria, *Sobre el pleno ejercicio de la igualdad de la mujer* (Havana: Imprenta Federico Engels, 1976), pp. 48–49 (hereafter cited as *Igualdad de la mujer*). Another indication that sexism continues to impinge upon relations between men and women is the persistence of the *piropo*—a kind of courteous or flirtatious remark expressed frequently by men to women in public. A study of piropos published in Cuba argued that this "art form" was disappearing, as men became more conscious of the role of women in society, but the same article showed that piropos still flourished in the 1960s and 1970s, though some of them had become "politicized." Some examples of the new versions are: "Take me along to voluntary work, beautiful"; "You put an end to underdevelopment"; "Give me a scholarship in your heart"; "Honey, how many ration cards do you have?"; "Gorgeous, you are overfulfilling the norm"; "You are like the history of Cuba, old but interesting." These were taken from the following articles in *Signos* 5, no. 1 (September–December 1973): Remberto de Oráa, "El piropo en La Habana," p. 43; Gualberto Báez, "Piropos en Camajuaní," p. 46; Rolando González, "Piropos en Santa Clara," p. 47; Julio Jiménez, "Piropos en Cienfuegos," p. 48; and S. F., "Piropos con respuesta," p. 50.

76. Jorge Hernández, Angel Eng, María Bermúdez, and Mariela Columbié, "Estudio sobre el divorcio," *Humanidades* ser. 1 (Ciencias Sociales), no. 3 (January 1973): 32–34, 50, 55, 66, 67, 75–85.

77. Pérez-Stable, "Cuba's Workers 1975," pp. 16–17.

78. *Granma,* April 26, 1975, p. 4.

79. *Verde olivo* 9, no. 40 (October 6, 1968): 61; *Granma Weekly Review,* May 16, 1971, p. 5; ibid., June 13, 1971, p. 4.

80. "Bodas de compromiso," *Con la guardia en alto* 12, no. 6 (June 1973): 22–23.

81. Rafael Prohías and Lourdes Casal, *The Cuban Minority in the United States: Preliminary Report on Need Identification and Program Evaluation* (Washington, D.C.: Cuban National Planning Council, 1974), p. 63; Gustavo Gutiérrez, *El empleo, el subempleo y el desempleo en Cuba* (Havana: Consejo Nacional de Economía, 1958), tables 2, 5; *Anuario 1972*, pp. 21, 34.

82. Computed from Ana Ramos, "La mujer y la revolución en Cuba," *Casa de las Américas* 11, nos. 65–66 (March–June 1971):68; *Granma Weekly Review*, August 31, 1969, p. 4; *Igualdad de la mujer*, pp. 16–17; *Anuario 1973*, p. 22. There is further evidence that citizens held to their own views even against the wishes of the public authorities: the case of a father successfully preventing his son's going away to school in the face not only of clear ideological favor for schooling but of the actual intervention of a school official to persuade the father to change his mind is reported in rural Matanzas in the late 1960s. See Pettitt, "Social and Economic Change," p. 329. For further data on the various views of individual women concerning paid work, see ibid., pp. 331–332.

83. Ramiro Pavón, "El empleo femenino en Cuba," *Santiago* no. 20 (December 1975): 107.

84. Ibid., pp. 114, 121.

85. Marvin Leiner, with Robert Ubell, *Children Are the Revolution: Day Care in Cuba* (New York: Viking Press, 1974), pp. 35–36; computed from *Anuario 1974*, p. 41.

86. Pavón "Empleo femenino," pp. 127–128; *Granma*, June 1, 1976, p. 2.

87. *Anuario 1972*, p. 22; *Anuario 1973*, p. 26.

88. *Granma*, October 12, 1976, p. 1; ibid., October 19, 1976, p. 1.

89. *Igualdad de la mujer*, pp. 28–30.

90. Ibid., pp. 32–33.

91. See Jose Yglesias, *In the Fist of the Revolution: Life in a Cuban Country Town* (New York: Vintage Books, 1968), chaps. 6, 9; Elizabeth Sutherland, *The Youngest Revolution: A Personal Report on Cuba* (New York: Dial Press, 1969), pp. 169–190. For a discussion of social issues in the role of women in Cuba before the revolution, see Nelson P. Valdés, "Women and Sexual Relations in Cuba: Family, Consensual Unions, Divorce and Prostitution before 1959" (Paper presented at Conference on Women and Change, Boston University, May 6–7, 1977). For a critical discussion of the role of women in Cuba since the revolution from a Marxist perspective, see Marifeli Pérez-Stable's paper, "The Emancipation of Cuban Women," presented at the same conference.

92. Pearson product-moment correlation between rate of psychiatric admissions and gross social product per capita was 0.80; between psychiatric consultations and admissions, 0.14; between psychiatric consultations and gross social product per capita, 0.00. All were for eleven observations from 1964 through 1974. GSP statistics, in constant prices for 1964 and 1966 in table 5.15, were assumed to be in current prices for this calculation.

93. José Bustamante, Antonio Roselló, Alelí Jordán, Elsa Pradera, Míriam Vila, Astrid González, and Alvaro Insúa, "Las drogas: su efecto en el aprendizaje," *Vida universitaria* nos. 216–217 (July–December 1969): 26.

94. *Anuario 1973*, p. 263; *Anuario 1974*, p. 267; *Revolución*, December 9, 1964, p. 1.

95. Pinar del Río, with 6.3 percent of the population, had only 3.3 percent of the businesses, while Las Villas had 23.5 percent of the businesses but only 15.9 percent of the population.

96. Computed from *Verde olivo* 9, no. 14 (April 7, 1968): 26; *Granma Weekly Review*, April 7, 1968, p. 3; *1970 Census*, pp. 12, 15. All data, except the number of items sold, can be calculated simply. The government gave detailed data on one Havana business with gross daily income of 66.40 pesos selling over 200 items a day. Assuming that each item represents one contact with a consumer, that all those with daily gross income of 50 pesos or more (including the 20 percent of businesses with gross daily income over 100 pesos) sold exactly 200 items a day, and that those with gross daily income of 49 pesos or less sold nothing, the number of items sold or consumer contacts every day is 5,296,000. Assuming that sales of 200 items a day are typical of those with gross daily income between 50 pesos and 99 pesos, that sales of 300 items a day are typical of those with higher gross daily sales, and that sales of 100 items a day are typical of those with lower gross daily sales, then the number of items sold or consumer contacts per day rises to 8,373,100, a somewhat higher number than the estimated 1968 population.

97. Fernández, "La crisis actual del catolicismo," p. 3; computed from *Granma Weekly Review*, October 8, 1967, p. 3; *Granma*, October 19, 1976, p. 1.

98. *Sobre la lucha ideológica*, pp. 7–8, 28–33.

99. For a comparison with Rumania, see Kenneth Jowitt, "An Organizational Approach to the Study of Political Culture in Marxist-Leninist Systems," *American Political Science Review* 68, no. 3 (September 1974): 1184.

APPENDIX A. THE IMPACT OF INTERNATIONAL ECONOMIC FACTORS ON INTERNAL AFFAIRS: THREE PERSPECTIVES

1. Part of this material summarizes a few pages of my essay, "Consensus and Divergence: The State of the Literature on Inter-American Relations in the 1970s," *Latin American Research Review* 13, no. 1 (1978): 87–126. For the dependency perspectives, see Hélio Jaguaribe, *Political Development: A General Theory and a Latin American Case Study* (New York: Harper & Row, 1973); Fernando Henrique Cardoso, "Associated-Dependent Development: Theoretical and Practical Implications," in *Authoritarian Brazil*, ed. Alfred Stepan (New Haven: Yale University Press, 1973); André Gunder Frank, *Capitalism and Underdevelopment in Latin America*, rev. ed. (New York: Monthly Review Press, 1969), especially p. 3; Susanne J. Bodenheimer, "The Ideology of Developmentalism," *Sage Professional Papers in Comparative Politics* 1, no. 15 (1971), especially pp. 36–40; idem, "Dependency and Imperialism," in *Readings in U.S. Imperialism*, ed. K. T. Fann and Donald Hodges (Boston: Porter Sargent, 1971), pp. 155–182; Theotonio Dos Santos, *Dependencia económica y cambio revolucionario en América Latina* (Caracas: Editorial Nueva Izquierda, 1970); Osvaldo Sunkel, "Integration capitaliste et desintegration nationale en Amérique Latine," *Politique Étrangère* 35, no. 6 (1970): 641–699; see also the special issue on dependency, *Journal of Interamerican Studies and World Affairs* 15, no. 1 (February 1973). For Cuban studies relying on this approach, see Francisco López Segrera, *Cuba: capitalismo dependiente y subdesarrollo, 1510–1959* (Havana: Casa de las Américas, 1972), pp. 207–247; Oscar Pino Santos, *El asalto a Cuba por la oligarquía financiera yanqui* (Havana: Casa

de las Américas, 1973). For the transnational perspective, see Samuel P. Huntington, "Transnational Organizations in World Politics" *World Politics* 25, no. 3 (April 1973), especially pp. 333–337, 355–368; Huntington, of course, has paid considerable attention to internal politics elsewhere, but not in the context of his discussion of external agents as they impinge on host countries.

APPENDIX B. CHANGES IN THE HEIGHT OF CUBANS

1. Dudley A. Sargent, "The Height and Weight of the Cuban Teachers," *Popular Science Monthly* 58, no. 5 (March 1901): 480, 483–484, 488.

2. Israel Castellanos, "La talla de los delincuentes en Cuba," *Revista técnica policial y penitenciaria* 6, nos. 1–6 (January–June 1937): 68, 86, 92, 95, 100, 116–118, 120. For the body weight of the same population, see idem, *El peso corporal en los delincuentes en Cuba* (Havana: Imprenta El Siglo XX, 1935), especially pp. 40, 49, 53–54, 58, 61, 67.

3. Frederick S. Hulse, "The Comparative Anthropometry of Cubans and Andalusians" (Ph.D. diss., Harvard University, 1933), pp. 1–2, 28, 150, 174, table XII (pp. 48–49).

4. Georges Rouma, "Le développement physique de l'écolier cubain: blanc, nègre et mulâtre," *Bulletin de la Société d'Anthropologie de Bruxelles* 35 (1920); pertinent methodological data on pp. 256, 258–259, 263; see also p. 399 for data on women.

5. Teresa Laska-Mierzejewska, "Morphological and Developmental Difference between Negro and White Cuban Youths," *Human Biology* 42, no. 4 (December 1970): 581–582, 590–591, 593, 595. Methodological data on the difficult problem of race determination are reported in idem, "Menarche in Cuban Girls," *Przeglad Antropologiczny* 32, no. 1 (1966): 31–35.

6. I have reached these conclusions from an independent examination of Laska-Mierzejewska's data; they are the same as those she reached on the basis of the same data. Although the data from the joint East European-Cuban project were written up in a slightly different way by M. F. Pospisil, who used only the earlier portions of the survey, he also reached the two principal conclusions. See his "El peso y la talla de los escolares de la ciudad de La Habana," *Serie ciencias biológicas* no. 3 (May 1969): 64, 68, 71–72, 74–75.

7. For a discussion of this point, in relation to anthropometrical data, see Teresa Laska-Mierzejewska, "Desarrollo y maduración de los niños y jóvenes habaneros," *Materialy I Prace Antropologiczne* 74 (1967): 42, 50–51.

8. Foreign Policy Association, Commission on Cuban Affairs, *Problems of the New Cuba* (New York: Little and Ives, 1935), pp. 215–216; Julián Alienes Urosa, *Características fundamentales de la economía cubana* (Havana: Banco Nacional, 1950), p. 41; computations from *1953 Census*, p. 75.

9. Emilio Unanue, *Siclemia pasiva en Cuba,* quoted in José F. Corral and Emilio Unanue, "Survey sobre hemoglobinas en la raza negra en Cuba: reporte preliminar," *Revista cubana de laboratorio clínico* 14, no. 2 (April–June 1960): 57–59; Heriberto Vidal et al., "Pesquisaje de hemoglobinas anormales en un hospital pediátrico," *Revista cubana de pediatría* 46, no. 2 (March–April 1974): 150; Luis Heredero et al., "Screening electrofonético de hemoglobinas: análisis de 15,000 muestras en La Habana," ibid., p. 154.

10. Castellanos, "La talla," pp. 122–123, 126. Statistical tests to investigate whether there were differences among provinces were never significant.

APPENDIX C. RACIAL INEQUALITY IN PUBLIC HEALTH

1. *1953 Census*, pp. 49–50.
2. Silvio Ruiz Miranda et al., "Frecuencia de las quemaduras en niños," *Revista cubana de pediatría* 46, no. 6 (November–December 1974): 546, 547, 552, 553; Guillermo Hernández Amador et al., "Nuestros resultados en 3301 quemaduras infantiles tratadas en el hospital 'William Soler' durante un período de 10 años (1962–1972), ibid., 45, nos. 4–6 (July–December 1973): 394.
3. Rafael Calvó Fonseca, "Estudio del parasitismo en nuestro medio, visto principalmente como causa de mortalidad," *Revista Kuba de medicina tropical y parasitología* 11, nos. 7–12 (1955): 59; Antonio Martínez Cárdenas and Zaida Betancourt Rodríguez, "Estudio médico-social de 1000 niños," *Revista cubana de pediatría* 33, nos. 4–6 (April–June 1961): 115, 116, 118, 120; Pedro Domingo, "La vacunación BCG y su aplicación en Cuba," *Revista cubana de tuberculosis* 17, no. 3 (July–September 1953): 175; Rafael Meneses Mañas et al., "Aspectos anatomopatológicos de la tuberculosis en Cuba," ibid., no. 4 (October–December 1953): 385; T. Valledor et al., "Tuberculosis primaria de la piel en la infancia," *Revista cubana de pediatría* 26, no. 3 (March 1954): 147, 153; José Mir del Junco et al., "Análisis de 245 casos egresados del servicio de tuberculosis del hospital infantil docente 'Dr. Angel Aballí' desde el primero de enero de 1965 hasta el 30 de junio de 1971," ibid., 45, no. 2 (March–April 1973): 184; Guillermo Fernández Baquero et al., "Revisión clínico-patológica de 200 pacientes del hospital antileproso del Rincón," *Revista cubana de medicina tropical* 26, nos. 1–2 (January–August 1974): 59.
4. Federico Fusté Amieba et al., "Causas de muerte en el prematuro," *Revista cubana de pediatría* 26, no. 6 (June 1954): 367; Emilio Soto Pradera et al., "Cifras estadísticas de un año de trabajo en la unidad de prematuros de la Clínica de Maternidad Obrera de La Habana," ibid., 27, no. 5 (May 1955): 286; Ubaldo Farnot and Olimpo Moreno, "Prematuridad," *Archivos del Hospital Universitario General Calixto García* 8, no. 2 (March–April 1956): 117–119; Emilio Soto Pradera and Juan Silverio Latour, "Dosificación de calcio en la sangre de 395 prematuros aparentemente normales," ibid., 30, no. 6 (June 1958): 315, 317.
5. Rafael Calvó Fonseca, "La última epidemia de poliomielitis, 1952–1953: aspectos epidemiológicos," *Anales de la Academia de Ciencias Médicas, Físicas y Naturales de La Habana* 92, no. 2 (1953–1954): 262–264; José Ramón Crespo, "La epidemia de poliomielitis de 1952 a 1953," ibid., p. 273; René Montero de la Pedraja et al., "La sepsis en el niño prematuro," *Revista cubana de pediatría* 29, no. 5 (May 1957); idem, "Brote epidémico de diarreas a escherichia coli Oiii-B4 observado en el centro de prematuros de La Habana," ibid., 29, no. 4 (April 1957): 201–202; José Jordán Rodríguez et al., "Etiología de la diarrea aguda del lactante," ibid., 30, no. 11 (November 1958): 574–575; R. Martín Jiménez, "Epidemia de meningitis aséptica en La Habana," ibid., 32, no. 10 (October 1960): 498.
6. Rafael Estrada, "Cáncer del pulmón," *Archivos del Hospital Universitario General Calixto García* 3, no. 1 (January–February 1951): 45–46; Calixto Cardevilla Azoy et al., "Cáncer de colon y recto: revisión estadística," *Revista cubana de*

cirugía 12, no. 2 (March–April 1973): 139–140; Carlos Alberto Chacón et al., "Cáncer de la mama: resultados del tratamiento quirúrgico," ibid., nos. 4–6 (July–December 1973): 368; Orlando Carreras Ruiz, "Revisión de 63 casos de cáncer labial," *Revista cubana de medicina* 13, no. 6 (November–December 1974): 732; idem, "Tratamiento quirúrgico de las metástasis carcinomatosas cervicales," *Revista cubana de cirugía* 13, no. 6 (November–December 1974): 599, 602.

7. Horacio de la Torre et al., "Comunicación interventricular," *Revista cubana de cardiología* 20, nos. 3–4 (July–December 1959): 223–224; Manuel Lima Fernández, "Nuestra experiencia en los primeros 100 casos atendidos en una unidad de cuidados coronarios," *Revista cubana de medicina* 13, no. 6 (November–December 1974): 661; Hatuey Alvarez Guilián et al., "Doscientos casos de infarto cardíaco," ibid. 13, no. 5 (September–October 1974): 443–445; Alberto Hatim Ricardo et al., "Hipertensión arterial: revisión de 200 casos," ibid., 11, nos. 5–6 (September–December 1972): 591, 593; Ignacio Macías Castro, "Modelo experimental de un programa de salud nacional para la atención integral de paciente con hipertensión arterial," ibid., 14, no. 1 (January–February 1975): 19–21; Manuel Alea Goenaga, "Estudio estadístico de 75 pacientes del sexo femenino operados de várices en el hospital provincial de Pinar del Río en los años 1969–1970," *Revista cubana de cirugía* 11 (1972), suppl. pp. 167–168; Nelson Taylor Hill, "Várices quirúrgicas: revisión de los casos ingresados en el hospital docente 'General Calixto García' durante los dos ultimos años," ibid., 11 (1972), suppl. p. 178.

8. J. M. Portuondo de Castro et al., "Observaciones sobre 50 comas diabéticas estudiadas en el Hospital Universitario Gral. Calixto García," *Archivos del Hospital Universitario General Calixto García* 7, no. 6 (November–December 1955): 427–428; Oscar Mateo de Acosta, "Registro nacional de consumidores de productos antidiabéticos," *Revista cubana de medicina* 12, no. 2 (March–April 1973): 164, 168, 171, 173; Carlos Durán Llobera and José Bidart Labourdette, "Gangrena diabética: análisis estadístico en 30 casos," *Revista cubana de cirugía* 11, nos. 5–6 (September–December 1972): 495.

9. Gonzalo Aróstegui, "Tratamiento quirúrgico: estudio de 645 casos tratados de 1947 a 1953. Resultados. Conclusiones," *Anales de la Academia de Ciencias Médicas, Físicas y Naturales de la Habana* 93, no. 1 (1954–1955): 65; Enrique Zayas Portela and Fidel Larraondo Núñez, "Estudios sobre la enfermedad reumática," *Revista cubana de cardiología* 14, no. 1 (January–March 1953): 25; Alejandro García Gutierrez et al., "Resultados de anastomosis portasistémicas en las hipertensiones portales de causa intrahepática," *Revista cubana de cirugía* 13, no. 3 (May–June 1974): 291, 293; Jorge P. Alfonso, "Anuria obstructiva," ibid., 12, no. 2 (March–April 1973): 185, 188–189; Jorge P. Alfonso et al., "La arteriografía en el trasplante renal," ibid., nos. 4–6 (July–December 1973): 125, 132–133; Hiram Castro-López Ginard, "Incidencia de las enfermedades psiquiátricas en un área del regional Centro-Habana," *Revista cubana de medicina* 13, no. 4 (July–August 1974); José Triana García, "Complicaciones de la cirugía del tiroides," *Revista cubana de cirugía* 14, no. 1 (January–February 1975): 36.

10. Henry Ronda Marisy, "Cuerpo extraño en el esófago," *Revista cubana de cirugía* 13, no. 6 (November–December 1974): 625, 632.

APPENDIX D. TEXTUAL CHANGES IN THE DRAFT CONSTITUTION OF 1976 AND THE DRAFT FAMILY CODE

1. The texts used for comparison were published in *Granma*, April 10, 1975, pp. 3–6; ibid., January 15, 1976, pp. 4–7.

2. The texts of the draft law and the final law are taken from Comité Central del Partido, Departamento de Orientación Revolucionaria, *A discusión: proyecto de código de familia* (Havana, 1974); *Granma*, March 3, 1975, pp. 3–5.

APPENDIX E. MEMBERS OF THE PEOPLE'S SOCIALIST PARTY IN THE COMMUNIST PARTY'S CENTRAL COMMITTEE

1. My own effort over the years to identify members of the Central Committee has been aided by Professor Andrés Suárez of the University of Florida–Gainesville and by the Central Intelligence Agency's *Directory of Personalities of the Cuban Government, Official Organizations, and Mass Organizations* (Washington, D.C., 1974).

APPENDIX F. COOPERATION AMONG CUBAN SCIENTISTS

1. Coded and computed from *Revista cubana de laboratorio clínico* 2–15 (1948–1961); *Revista cubana de cardiología* 12–21 (1951–1960); *Archivos del Hospital Universitario General Calixto García* 3–12 (1951–1960); *Revista cubana de pediatría* 26–35 (1954–1963); ibid., 44–47 (1972–1975); *Revista Kuba de medicina tropical y parasitología* 4–16 (1948–1960); *Revista cubana de medicina tropical* 1–2 (1962–1963); ibid., 11–14 (1972–1975); *Revista cubana de cirugía* 1–2 (1962–1963); ibid., 12–14 (1972–1975).

2. Cubans tend to cooperate with foreigners more than they do with each other. The proportion of multiple authorship is systematically higher in columns 4 and 5 of table F.1, which include Cubans working with foreigners, with fellow Cubans, or alone, than it is in columns 6 and 7, which exclude foreigners altogether. Cooperation with foreigners may reflect the desire to acquire scientific knowledge from abroad, scientific traditions where senior foreign scientists work with younger Cuban scientists, or possibly even a political decision. Cooperation with foreigners, however, is not essential for every field of Cuban science; medical science continues to be conducted primarily by Cubans only.

3. The Pearson product-moment correlation between these two variables is 0.45 for seven paired observations in table F.1.

4. The Pearson product-moment correlation between these two variables is 0.95 for seven paired observations in table F.1.

BIBLIOGRAPHY

The bibliography lists only cited publications that relate directly to Cuba; works mentioned to call attention to comparative or theoretical issues have been excluded here. Census and other general statistical publications of the Cuban government are listed separately.

STATISTICAL PUBLICATIONS OF THE CUBAN GOVERNMENT

Census Publications

Census of Cuba, Office of the Director. *Report on the Census of Cuba, 1899.* Washington, D.C.: Government Printing Office, 1900.

Oficina del Censo de los Estados Unidos. *Censo de la República de Cuba, 1907.* Washington, D.C.: U.S., Bureau of the Census, 1908.

República de Cuba. *Censo de la República de Cuba, 1919.* Havana: Maza, Arroyo y Caso, 1920.

―――― *Informe general del censo de 1943.* Havana: Fernández, 1945.

Ministerio de Agricultura. *Memoria del censo agrícola nacional, 1946.* Havana: Fernández, 1951.

Oficina Nacional de los Censos Demográfico y Electoral. *Censos de población, vivienda y electoral: informe general (enero 28 de 1953).* Havana: Fernández, 1955.

Dirección Central de Estadística. *Memoria del censo ganadero (31 de agosto de 1967).* Havana: Junta Central de Planificación, 1969.

―――― *Censo de población y viviendas, 6 de septiembre de 1970: datos preliminares.* Havana: Junta Central de Planificación, 1971.

Statistical Yearbooks

Dirección General de Estadística. *Anuario estadístico de Cuba, 1957.* Havana: Fernández, 1958.

Dirección Central de Estadística. *Boletín estadístico, 1964.* Havana: Junta Central de Planificación, 1966.

——— *Compendio estadístico de Cuba, 1966.* Havana: Junta Central de Planificación, 1966.

——— *Boletín estadístico de Cuba, 1968.* Havana: Junta Central de Planificación, 1970.

——— *Boletín estadístico de Cuba, 1970.* Havana: Junta Central de Planificación, 1972.

——— *Boletín estadístico de Cuba, 1971.* Havana: Junta Central de Planificación, 1973.

——— *Anuario estadístico de Cuba, 1972.* Havana: Junta Central de Planificación, 1974.

——— *Anuario estadístico de Cuba, 1973.* Havana: Junta Central de Planificación, 1973.

——— *Anuario estadístico de Cuba, 1974.* Havana: Junta Central de Planificación, 1974.

BOOKS AND ARTICLES

"A paso de victoria se llama Matanzas." *Bohemia* 65, no. 20 (May 18, 1973).

Aaron, Harold R. "Why Batista Lost." *Army* 15, no. 14 (September 1965).

Aballí, Arturo J. "Distrofias infantiles en nuestro medio." *Revista cubana de pediatría* 30, no. 9 (September 1958).

Abrantes, José. "La unidad monolítica en torno al partido y a Fidel." *Bohemia* 67, no. 25 (June 20, 1975).

Academia de Ciencias de Cuba and Academia de Ciencias de la URSS. *Atlas nacional de Cuba.* Havana, 1970.

Aclaraciones: Periódico Hoy. Havana: Editora Política, 1966.

Acosta, José. "Las leyes de reforma agraria en Cuba y el sector privado campesino." *Economía y desarrollo,* no. 12 (July–August 1972).

——— "La revolución agraria en Cuba y el desarrollo económico." *Economía y desarrollo,* no. 17 (May–June 1973).

Acosta, Maruja, and Hardoy, Jorge. *Urban Reform in Revolutionary Cuba.* New Haven: Yale University, Antilles Research Program, 1973.

"Acto de fin de zafra del EJT en Matanzas." *Verde olivo* 18, no. 21 (May 23, 1976).

"Acuerdos de la comisión de producción." *ANAP* 7, nos. 5–6 (May–June 1967).

"Acuerdos de la plenaria de la ANAP." *ANAP* 5, no. 10 (October 1965).

"Acuerdos sobre la construcción del PURS." *Cuba socialista,* no. 20 (April 1963).

Adam y Silva, Ricardo. *La gran mentira.* Havana: Editorial Lex, 1947.

Agüero, Frank. "Nuevo sistema judicial." *Verde olivo* 13, no. 14 (April 14, 1971).

Aguilar, Luis E. *Cuba 1933: Prologue to Revolution.* Ithaca: Cornell University Press, 1972.

Aguirre, Benigno. "Differential Migration of Cuban Social Races." *Latin American Research Review* 11, no. 1 (1976).

Aguirre, Severo. "El primer aniversario de las cooperativas cañeras." *Cuba socialista,* no. 3 (1961).

Alberto, Eliseo. "De pie en la frontera." *Cuba internacional* 6, no. 61 (September 1974).

Alea Goenaga, Manuel. "Estudio estadístico de 75 pacientes del sexo femenino operados de várices en el hospital provincial de Pinar del Río en los años 1969–1970." *Revista cubana de cirugía* 11 (1972), supplement.

Alfonso, Jorge P. "Anuria obstructiva." *Revista cubana de cirugía* 12, no. 2 (March–April 1973).

Alfonso, Jorge P., et al. "La arteriografía en el transplante renal." *Revista cubana de cirugía* 12, nos. 4–6 (July–December 1973).

"Algunas tareas cumplidas por las FAR en 1970." *Verde olivo* 11, no. 52 (December 27, 1970).

"Algunos aspectos relacionados con la ley del servicio militar general y su reglamento." *Verde olivo* 17, no. 4 (January 26, 1975).

Alienes Urosa, Julián. *Características fundamentales de la economía cubana*. Havana: Banco Nacional, 1950.

Alvarez, Oneida. "Revolutionary Cuba's Economic Development." *World Marxist Review* 17, no. 11 (November 1974).

Álvarez Guilián, Hatuey, et al. "Doscientos casos de infarto cardíaco." *Revista cubana de medicina* 13, no. 5 (September–October 1974).

Álvarez Rom, Luis. "Las finanzas como un método de desarrollo político." *Nuestra industria: revista económica*, no. 1 (1963).

Amaro, Nelson. *La revolución cubana . . . ¿por qué?* Guatemala City: Talleres Gráficos Rosales, 1967.

Amigó, Gustavo. "La iglesia católica en Cuba." *Revista javeriana* 28, no. 138 (September 1947).

―――― "La iglesia católica en Cuba." *Revista javeriana* 28, no. 140 (November 1947).

Amnesty International. *Report on Torture*. London: Gerald Duckworth, 1973.

"Antes del ICIDCA no hubo ningún ICIDCA." *Bohemia* 65, no. 24 (June 15, 1973).

Arañaburu, José. "El trabajo de los CDR a la luz de la creación de los poderes populares se fortalece, se profundiza, se hace mucho más necesario." *Con la guardia en alto* 14, no. 5 (May 1975).

Aranda, Sergio. *La revolución agraria en Cuba*. Mexico: Siglo XXI, 1965.

Arce Martínez, Sergio. "The Mission of the Church in a Socialist Society." In *Religion in Cuba Today*, edited by Alice Hageman and Philip Wheaton. New York: Association Press, 1971.

Arcocha, José. "Dicotomías: Lezama Lima y Cabrera Infante." *Aportes*, no. 11 (January 1969).

Armas, José. "Timbiriches y timbiricheo." *Verde olivo* 9, no. 41 (October 13, 1968).

Arnes, David. "Negro Family Types in a Cuban *Solar*." *Phylon* 11, no. 2 (1950).

Aróstegui, Gonzalo. "Tratamiento quirúrgico: estudio de 645 casos tratados de 1947 a 1953. Resultados. Conclusiones." *Anales de la Academia de Ciencias Médicas, Físicas y Naturales de La Habana* 93, no. 1 (1954–1955).

Arredondo, Alberto. *Cuba: tierra indefensa*. Havana: Editorial Lex, 1945.

―――― *Reforma agraria: la experiencia cubana*. Río Piedras: Editorial San Juan, 1969.

"Asamblea de balance del partido en el ejército de Oriente." *Verde olivo* 10, no. 5 (February 2, 1969).

"Las asambleas de selección de obreros ejemplares en la provincia de Las Villas." *Cuba socialista,* no. 13 (September 1962).

Ávila, Leopoldo [pseud.]. "Antón se va a la guerra." *Verde olivo* 9, no. 46 (November 17, 1968).

———— "Las provocaciones de Padilla." *Verde olivo* 9, no. 45 (November 10, 1968).

———— "El pueblo es el forjador, defensor y sostén de la cultura." *Verde olivo* 9, no. 48 (December 1, 1968).

———— "Las respuestas de Caín." *Verde olivo* 9, no. 44 (November 3, 1968).

———— "Sobre algunas corrientes de la crítica y la literatura en Cuba." *Verde olivo* 9, no. 47 (November 24, 1968).

———— "La vuelta a la manzana." *Verde olivo* 9, no. 42 (October 20, 1968).

Aymerich, Ramón. "De la base al Congreso." *ANAP,* November 1971.

Ayón, María de los Angeles. "El movimiento obrero en el monopolio eléctrico." In *Monopolios norteamericanos en Cuba: contribución al estudio de la penetración imperialista.* Havana: Instituto Cubano del Libro, 1973.

Azicri, Max. "The Governing Strategies of Mass Mobilization: The Foundations of Cuban Revolutionary Politics." *Latin American Monograph Series,* no. 2. Erie, Pa.: Northwestern Pennsylvania Institute for Latin American Studies, 1977.

———— "A Study of the Structure of Exercising Power in Cuba: Mobilization and Governing Strategies (1959–1968)." Ph.D. dissertation, University of Southern California, 1975.

———— "Women's Development through Revolutionary Mobilization: A Study of the Federation of Cuban Women." Paper presented at annual meeting, International Studies Association, March 16–20, 1977, in St. Louis, Mo. Mimeographed.

Báez, Gualberto. "Piropos en Camajuaní." *Signos* 5, no. 1 (September–December 1973).

Báez, Luis. "Hacia una mayor calidad, organización y conciencia." *Bohemia* 67, no. 8 (February 21, 1975).

Baklanoff, Eric N. "International Economic Relations." In *Revolutionary Change in Cuba,* edited by Carmelo Mesa-Lago. Pittsburgh: University of Pittsburgh Press, 1971.

"Balance de la construcción del PURS." *Cuba socialista,* no. 32 (April 1964).

"Balance del partido en el cuerpo ejército de Camagüey." *Verde olivo* 10, no. 42 (October 19, 1969).

"Balance del 72." *ANAP,* February 1973.

Ballester, Eloísa. "Por una mejor eficiencia económica." *Verde olivo* 18, no. 20 (May 16, 1976).

Baloyra, Enrique. "Political Leadership in the Cuban Republic, 1944–1958." Ph.D. dissertation, University of Florida–Gainesville, 1971.

Banco Nacional de Cuba. *La economía cubana en 1956–1957.* Havana: Editorial Lex, 1958.

———— *Economic Development Program, Progress Report,* no. 1 (1956).

Barkin, David. "Cuban Agriculture: A Strategy of Economic Development." *Studies in Comparative International Development* 7, no. 1 (Spring 1972).

Barquín, Ramón. *Las luchas guerrilleras en Cuba: de la colonia a la Sierra Maestra.* Madrid: Editorial Playor, 1975.

Barrera, Hernán. "Building the United Party of the Socialist Revolution in Cuba." *World Marxist Review* 6, no. 12 (December 1963).

Batista, Fulgencio. *Piedras y leyes.* Mexico: Ediciones Botas, 1961.

—— *Respuesta.* Mexico: Imprenta Manuel León Sánchez, 1960.

—— *Revolución social o política reformista.* Havana: Prensa Indoamericana, 1944.

Beals, Carleton. *The Crime of Cuba.* Philadelphia: Lippincott, 1933.

Bekarevich, Anatolii. *Cuba.* Moscow: Nauka, 1970.

—— "Principios de colaboración entre Cuba y la URSS." *Panorama latinoamericano* (Novosti), no. 98 (May 25, 1970).

Bekarevich, Anatolii; Bondarchuk, Vladimir N.; and Kukharev, N.M. *Cuba in Statistics.* Moscow: Academy of Sciences of the USSR, Institute of Latin America, 1972.

Bekarevich, Anatolii, and Kukharev, N. M. *The Soviet Union and Cuba.* Moscow: Nauka, 1973.

Bender, Lynn Darrell. "U.S. Claims against the Cuban Government: An Obstacle to Rapprochement." *Inter-American Economic Affairs* 27, no. 1 (Summer 1973).

Benedetti, Mario. "Present Status of Cuban Culture." In *Cuba in Revolution,* edited by Rolando Bonachea and Nelson P. Valdés. Garden City, N.Y.: Anchor Books, 1972.

Benjamin, Jules R. "The Machadato and Cuban Nationalism." *Hispanic American Historical Review* 55 (February 1975).

Berge, André. "Young People in the Orient and Occident: General Report on the Survey." *International Journal of Adult and Youth Education* 16, no. 2 (1964).

Berman, Jesse. "The Cuban Popular Tribunals." *Columbia Law Review* 69, no. 8 (December 1969).

Bernardo, Robert M. *The Theory of Moral Incentives in Cuba.* University, Ala.: University of Alabama Press, 1971.

Blackburn, Robin. "Prologue to the Cuban Revolution." *New Left Review* (London), October 1963.

Blanco, Alberto. "El movimiento jurídico en los primeros cincuenta años de independencia." In *Historia de la nación cubana,* edited by Ramiro Guerra y Sánchez et al. Vol. 8. Havana: Editorial Historia de la Nación Cubana, 1952.

Blasier, Cole. "The Elimination of United States Influence." In *Revolutionary Change in Cuba,* edited by Carmelo Mesa-Lago. Pittsburgh: University of Pittsburgh Press, 1971.

Blutstein, Howard I.; Anderson, Lynne Cox; Betters, Elinor C.; Lane, Deborah; Leonard, Jonathan A.; and Townsend, Charles. *Area Handbook for Cuba.* Washington, D.C.: Government Printing Office, 1971.

"Bodas de compromiso." *Con la guardia en alto* 12, no. 6 (June 1973).

Bonachea, Ramón, and San Martín, Marta. *The Cuban Insurrection, 1952–1959.* New Brunswick, N.J.: Transaction Books, 1974.

—— "The Military Dimension of the Cuban Revolution. In *Cuban Communism,* edited by Irving L. Horowitz. 2nd ed. New Brunswick, N.J.: Transaction Books, 1972.

Bonachea, Rolando. "A Briefly Annotated Bibliography of Fidel Castro's Works: 1959–1970." *Cuban Studies Newsletter* 3, no. 2 (June 1973).

Bonachea, Rolando, and Valdés, Nelson P., eds. *Cuba in Revolution.* Garden City, N.Y.: Anchor Books, 1972.

—— *Revolutionary Struggle, 1947–1958: The Selected Works of Fidel Castro.* Cambridge, Mass.: M.I.T. Press, 1972.

Bondarchuk, Vladimir N. "La economía cubana en vísperas del I Congreso del Partido Comunista de Cuba." *América Latina,* no. 4 (1975).

Bonsal, Philip W. *Cuba, Castro and the United States.* Pittsburgh: University of Pittsburgh Press, 1971.

Boorstein, Edward. *The Economic Transformation of Cuba.* New York: Monthly Review Press, 1968.

Booth, David. "Cuba, Color and the Revolution." *Science and Society* 40, no. 2 (Summer 1976).

Borges, Milo A. *Compilación ordenada y completa de la legislación cubana de 1899 a 1950.* Vols. 1–3. 2nd ed. Havana: Editorial Lex, 1952.

Borodatov, V. A.; Ramís Ramos, H.; Salnikov, N. E. "Las investigaciones soviético-cubanas de la economía pesquera." In *Investigaciones pesqueras soviético-cubanas,* edited by Instituto de Investigaciones Científicas de la Economía Pesquera Marina y de la Oceanografía de Toda la Unión and Centro de Investigaciones Pesqueras de Cuba. Vol. 1. Moscow: Editorial Pischevaja Promyshlennost, 1965.

Boti, Regino, and Pazos, Felipe. "Algunos aspectos del desarrollo económico de Cuba." *Revista bimestre cubana* 75 (July–December 1958).

Boughton, George J. "Soviet-Cuban Relations, 1956–1960." *Journal of Inter-American Studies and World Affairs* 16, no. 4 (November 1974).

Bowe, William J. "Cuba Notes: Wednesday, October 6–Monday, October 11, 1976." Mimeographed. Chicago, n.d.

Bowles, Samuel. "Cuban Education and the Revolutionary Ideology." *Harvard Educational Review* 41, no. 4 (November 1971).

Boynton, Maryanna Craig. "Effects of Embargo and Boycott: The Cuban Case." Ph.D. dissertation, University of California–Riverside, 1972.

Boza Domínguez, Luis. *La situación universitaria en Cuba.* Santiago: Editorial del Pacífico, 1962.

Bravo, Flavio. "Recabamos una vez más la ayuda de esta poderosa organización de masas." *Con la guardia en alto* 12, nos. 3–4 (March–April 1973).

"Breve reseña del reciente Congreso Nacional de la Asociación de Jóvenes Rebeldes." *Cuba socialista,* no. 9 (May 1962).

Büntig, Aldo V. "The Church in Cuba: Toward a New Frontier." In *Religion in Cuba Today,* edited by Alice Hageman and Philip Wheaton. New York: Association Press, 1971.

Bustamante, José A.; Roselló, Antonio; Jordan, Alelí; Pradera, Elsa; Vila, Mariana; González, Astrid; and Insúa, Álvaro. "Las drogas: su efecto en el aprendizaje." *Vida universitaria,* nos. 216–217 (July–December 1969).

Butterworth, Douglas. "Grass Roots Political Organization in Cuba: A Case of the Committees for the Defense of the Revolution." In *Latin American Urban Research,* edited by Wayne Cornelius and Felicity Trueblood. Vol. 4. Beverly Hills, Calif.: Sage Publications, 1974.

Cabrera, Lydia. *La sociedad secreta Abakuá.* Havana: Ediciones C.R., 1958.

Calderón González, Jorge. *Amparo: millo y azucena.* Havana: Casa de las Américas, 1970.

Calvó Fonseca, Rafael. "Estudio del parasitismo en nuestro medio, visto principalmente como causa de mortalidad." *Revista Kuba de medicina tropical y parasitología* 11, nos. 7–12 (1955).

——— "La incidencia del parasitismo intestinal en niños menores de un año." *Revista
cubana de pediatría* 30, no. 9 (September 1958).

——— "La última epidemia de poliomielitis, 1952–1953: aspectos epidemiológicos."
Anales de la Academia de Ciencias Médicas, Físicas y Naturales de La Habana 92,
no. 2 (1953–1954).

Canales, Sergio, and Gil, Leonel. "La casa central de las FAR." *Verde olivo* 17, no. 30
(July 27, 1975).

"Las candidaturas senatoriales de la Coalición Socialista Democrática y la Unión Revolucionaria Comunista." *Fundamentos* 4, no. 29 (January 1944).

Carbonell, Miguel Angel. "Las generaciones libertadoras: veinticinco años de independencia." In *Historia de la nación cubana*, edited by Ramiro Guerra y Sánchez et
al. Vol. 8. Havana: Editorial Historia de la Nación Cubana, 1952.

Cárdenas, Aída. "La sangre ya no es mercancía." *Bohemia* 65, no. 18 (May 14,
1973).

Cardevilla Azoy, Calixto, et al. "Cáncer de colon y recto: revisión estadística." *Revista
cubana de cirugía* 12, no. 2 (March–April 1973).

Carmona, Darío. "Justicia en la tierra." *Cuba* 1, no. 5 (September 1962).

——— *Prohibida la sombra.* Havana: Ediciones Unión, 1965.

Carneado, José Felipe. "La discriminación racial en Cuba no volverá jamás." *Cuba
socialista*, no. 5 (January 1962).

Carreras Ruiz, Orlando. "Revisión de 63 casos de cáncer labial." *Revista cubana de
medicina* 13, no. 6 (November–December 1974).

——— "Tratamiento quirúrgico de las metástasis carcinomatosas cervicales." *Revista
cubana de cirugía* 13, no. 6 (November–December 1974).

"Carta a los afiliados del Partido Socialista Popular." *Fundamentos* 4, no. 31 (March
1944).

"Una carta del Partido Socialista Popular a Batista." *Fundamentos* 4, no. 38 (October
1944).

"Carta del Partido Socialista Popular al Dr. Grau San Martín." *Fundamentos* 4, no. 38
(October 1944).

Carvajal, Juan F. "Observaciones sobre la clase media en Cuba." In *Materiales para el
estudio de la clase media en América Latina: la clase media en México y Cuba*,
edited by Theo R. Crevenna. Vol. 2. Washington, D.C.: Unión Panamericana,
1950.

Casal, Lourdes. "Images of Cuban Society Among Pre- and Post-Revolutionary Novelists." Ph.D. dissertation, New School for Social Research, 1975.

——— "Literature and Society." In *Revolutionary Change in Cuba*, edited by Carmelo Mesa-Lago. Pittsburgh: University of Pittsburgh Press, 1971.

Casal, Lourdes, ed. *El caso Padilla: literatura y revolución en Cuba.* Miami: Ediciones
Universal, 1971.

Castellanos, Israel. *El peso corporal en los delincuentes en Cuba.* Havana: Imprenta El
Siglo XX, 1935.

——— "La talla de los delincuentes en Cuba." *Revista técnica policial y penitenciaria*
6, nos. 1–6 (January–June 1937).

Castiñeiras, Juan M. "La industria ligera en la etapa actual." *Cuba socialista,* no. 34 (June 1964).

Castro, Fidel. "A combatir al enemigo en todos los frentes." *Cuba socialista,* no. 20 (April 1963).

———— "La alianza obrero-campesina." *Economía y desarrollo,* no. 9 (January–February 1972).

———— "Brigada invasora Che Guevara." *Verde olivo* 8, no. 44 (November 5, 1967).

———— "Discurso del Primer Ministro en el Comité Provincial de Matanzas." *Cuba socialista,* no. 9 (May 1962).

———— *Discursos para la historia.* Havana: Imp. Emilio Gall, 1959.

———— *Palabras a los intelectuales.* Havana: Ediciones del Consejo Nacional de Cultura, 1961.

———— *El partido marxista-leninista.* Buenos Aires: Ediciones La Rosa Blindada, 1965.

———— "¡Un pueblo así es un pueblo invencible!" *Cuba socialista,* no. 16 (December 1962).

———— "El PURS, espina dorsal de la revolución." *Cuba socialista,* no. 19 (March 1963).

Castro, Raúl. "Con la realización de la maniobra." *Verde olivo* 17, no. 50 (December 14, 1975).

———— "El congreso campesino en armas." *ANAP,* October 1973, pp. 6–9.

———— "El diversionismo ideológico: arma sutil que esgrimen los enemigos contra la revolución." *Verde olivo* 14, no. 30 (July 23, 1972).

———— "La emulación socialista." *Verde olivo* 17, no. 5 (February 2, 1975).

———— "Las FAR rinden profundo y sentido homenaje al vigésimo aniversario." *Bohemia* 65, no. 31 (August 3, 1973).

———— "Graduación del III curso de la escuela básica superior 'General Máximo Gómez,'" *Ediciones al orientador revolucionario,* no. 17 (1967).

———— "Problemas del funcionamiento del partido en las FAR." *Cuba socialista,* no. 55 (March 1966).

———— "Sabemos que el imperialismo se debilita." *Verde olivo* 17, no. 29 (July 20, 1975).

Castro-López Ginard, Hiram. "Incidencia de las enfermedades psiquiátricas en un área del regional Centro-Habana." *Revista cubana de medicina* 13, no. 4 (July–August 1974).

Causse Pérez, José. "La construcción del partido en las Fuerzas Armadas Revolucionarias de Cuba." *Cuba socialista,* no. 47 (July 1965).

Central Intelligence Agency. *Cuba: Foreign Trade.* Washington, D.C., 1975.

———— *The Cuban Economy: A Statistical Review, 1968–1976.* Washington, D.C.: Library of Congress, 1976.

———— *Directory of Personalities of the Cuban Government, Official Organizations, and Mass Organizations.* Washington, D.C., 1974.

Centro Nacional de Investigaciones Científicas. *Informe, 1969.* Havana: Universidad de La Habana, 1969.

Cepero Bonilla, Raúl. "El canje de billetes: un golpe a la contrarrevolución." *Cuba socialista,* no. 2 (October 1961).

———— "Política azucarera, 1952–1958." In *Obras históricas,* by Raúl Cepero Bonilla. Havana: Instituto de Historia, 1963.

Chacón, Carlos Alberto, et al. "Cáncer de la mama: resultados del tratamiento quirúrgico." *Revista cubana de cirugía* 12, nos. 4–6 (July–December 1973).

Chacón y Reyes, Julio. "Antecedentes del azúcar a granel en Cuba." *Cuba azúcar*, July–August 1966, pp. 16–23.

"Changes in the Work of Party Branches in Cuba." *World Marxist Review* 5, no. 8 (August 1962).

Changó Leyva, Juan. "La avanzada campesina en Matanzas." *ANAP*, no. 8 (August 1974).

———— "Un compromiso entre las lomas." *ANAP*, April 1973, pp. 8–9.

Chapman, Charles E. *A History of the Cuban Republic.* 1927. Reprint. New York: Octagon Books, 1969.

Chester, Edmund. *A Sergeant Named Batista.* New York: Holt, 1954.

Chía, Jesús. "El monopolio en la industria del jabón y del perfume." In *Monopolios norteamericanos en Cuba: contribución al estudio de la penetración imperialista.* Havana: Instituto Cubano del Libro, 1973.

"Los científicos hablan." *Boletín de la Comisión Nacional Cubana de la UNESCO* 11, no. 38 (April–May 1972).

Clytus, John, with Rieker, Jane. *Black Man in Red Cuba.* Coral Gables, Fla.: University of Miami Press, 1970.

"CMEA and Raw Materials Prices." *World Marxist Review* 18, no. 5 (May 1975).

Colomé, Abelardo. "Continuamos luchando." *Verde olivo* 17, no. 31 (August 3, 1975).

"Los colonos en palacio." *Tierra libre* 17, nos. 4–5 (April–May 1953).

Comisión de Orientación Revolucionaria. *Mil fotos: Cuba.* Havana: Ediciones COR, 1966.

Comisión Económica para América Latina. *El desarrollo industrial de Cuba.* ST/ECLA/Conf. 23/L. 63, 1966.

Comisión Nacional Cubana de la UNESCO. "Los estudiantes investigan." *Boletín* 12, no. 48 (January–February 1973).

Comité Central del Partido Comunista de Cuba, Comisión de Estudios Jurídicos. *Órganos del sistema judicial.* Havana: Empresa de Medios de Propaganda, 1975.

Comité Central del Partido Comunista de Cuba, Departamento de Orientación Revolucionaria. *A discusión: proyecto de código de familia.* Havana, 1974.

———— *Estatutos del partido comunista de Cuba.* Havana: Imprenta Federico Engels, 1976.

———— *Política educacional.* Havana: Instituto Cubano del Libro, 1976.

———— *Sobre el pleno ejercicio de la igualdad de la mujer.* Havana: Imprenta Federico Engels, 1976.

———— *Sobre la cuestión agraria y las relaciones con el campesinado.* Havana: Instituto Cubano del Libro, 1976.

———— *Sobre la lucha ideológica.* Havana: Instituto Cubano del Libro, 1976.

———— *Sobre los órganos del poder popular.* Havana: Imprenta Federico Engels, 1976.

"Comité nacional de la ANAP." *ANAP*, December 1971–January 1972, p. 17.

"Communist Party of Cuba." *World Marxist Review* 17, no. 3 (March 1974).

"Como aprecian los socialistas el IV Congreso de la CTC." *Fundamentos* 5, no. 41 (January 1945).

"Comunicado conjunto en la lucha contra la delincuencia." *Con la guardia en alto* 6, no. 2 (March 1967).

"Comunicado de la CTC." *Pensamiento crítico,* no. 48 (October 1970).

"Los comunistas en Nuevitas." *Cuba internacional* 4, no. 36 (August 1972).

"Conclusiones del IV chequeo de la emulación nacional y planes en los frentes de los CDR para 1964." *Guía para la acción,* no. 5 (December 1963).

Confederación de Trabajadores de Cuba, Secretaría de Finanzas. *Balance general, 1943–1944.* Havana: Editorial Cenit, [1944?].

Consejo Corporativo de Educación, Sanidad y Beneficencia. *Militarismo, anti-militarismo y seudo-militarismo.* Ceiba del Agua: Talleres del Instituto Cívico-Militar, [1939?].

La constitución de los órganos de poder popular. Havana: Imprenta Federico Engels, 1974.

Conte, Rafael, and Capmany, José. *Guerra de razas: negros contra blancos en Cuba.* Havana: Imprenta Militar de Antonio Pérez, 1912.

"Convoca la ANAP al cuarto Congreso campesino." *ANAP,* September 1971, p. 29.

"Convocatoria." *Verde olivo* 18, no. 7 (February 15, 1976).

Córdova Cordobés, Efrén. "Problemas actuales de la intervención del Estado en la economía laboral cubana." *Anuario de la Facultad de Ciencias Sociales y Derecho Público,* 1955–1956.

Corral, José F., and Unanue, Emilio. "Survey sobre hemoglobinas en la raza negra en Cuba: reporte preliminar." *Revista cubana de laboratorio clínico* 14, no. 2 (April–June 1960).

Cossío, Miguel. "Contribución al debate sobre la ley del valor." *Nuestra industria: revista económica,* no. 4 (1963).

Cotayo, Nicolás León. "Un recorrido por el sistema penal cubano." *Cuba internacional* 5 (May 1973).

Cotera O'Bourke, Margarita de la. ¿*Quién es quién en Cuba?* Havana: Julián Martín, 1925.

Crahan, Margaret. "Religious Freedom in Cuba." *Cuba Review* 5, no. 3 (September 1975).

——— "Salvation through Christ or Marx: Attitudes of Cuban Churchpeople before and after the Revolution." Paper presented at meeting, Latin American Studies Association, March 1976, in Atlanta. Mimeographed.

"El crédito global a los agricultores." *ANAP* 7, no. 8 (August 1967).

Crespo, Ramón. "La epidemia de poliomielitis de 1952 a 1953." *Anales de la Academia de Ciencias Médicas, Físicas y Naturales de La Habana* 92, no. 2 (1953–1954).

Crozier, Brian. "Soviet Pressures in the Caribbean: The Satellisation of Cuba." *Conflict Studies,* no. 35 (May 1973).

Cruz, Agustín. "It Took Only Three Years: The Destruction of a Law Firm." *American Bar Association Journal* 50, no. 1 (January 1964).

"IV Seminario Científico." *Boletín de la Comisión Nacional Cubana de la UNESCO* 13, no. 49 (January–February 1974).

Cuba, Santiago. "Acerca de los Tribunales Populares." *Cuba socialista,* no. 24 (August 1963).

——— "La lucha contra la criminalidad." *Revista cubana de jurisprudencia* 2, no. 8 (September–October 1963).

——— "Los Tribunales Populares." *Verde olivo* 7, no. 41 (October 16, 1966).

"Cuba económica." *Economía y desarrollo,* no. 10 (March–April 1972).

"Cuba económica." *Economía y desarrollo*, no. 22 (March–April 1974).

"Cuba económica." *Economía y desarrollo*, no. 25 (September–October 1974).

"Cuba económica." *Economía y desarrollo*, no. 34 (March–April 1976).

Cuban Economic Research Project. *Cuba: Agriculture and Planning.* Coral Gables, Fla.: University of Miami Press, 1965.

———*Labor Conditions in Communist Cuba.* Coral Gables, Fla.: University of Miami Press, 1963.

———*A Study on Cuba.* Coral Gables, Fla.: University of Miami Press, 1965.

Cuba's Three Year Plan. Havana: Cultural, 1937.

Cubillas, Vicente. "El instituto de oceanología de la Academia de Ciencias." *Mar y pesca*, no. 17 (February 1967).

Cuesta, Leonel Antonio de la, ed. *Constituciones cubanas.* New York: Ediciones Exilio, 1974.

"Cuestión de jornales." *Tierra libre* 9, no. 6 (June 1945).

Danielson, Ross. "Cuban Health Care in Process: Models and Morality in the Early Revolution." In *Topias and Utopias in Health*, edited by Stanley Ingman and Anthony Thomas. The Hague: Mouton, 1975.

Darusenkov, O. "Cuba Builds Socialism." *International Affairs*, no. 11 (November 1975).

de Arturo, Héctor, and Blanco, Jorge. "Primera conferencia del partido en el EJT." *Verde olivo* 17, no. 46 (November 16, 1975).

"X aniversario de la Academia de Ciencias." *Boletín de la Comisión Nacional Cubana de la UNESCO* 11, no. 38 (March–April 1972).

"XV aniversario de la creación de la Junta Central de Planificación." *Economía y desarrollo*, no. 30 (July–August 1975).

Departamento de Investigaciones Azucareras. "El central experimental Pablo Noriega." *Cuba azúcar* (July–September 1969).

Depestre, René. "Letter from Cuba." *Présence africaine* (English ed.), no. 28 (1965).

Dewart, Leslie. *Christianity and Revolution: The Lesson of Cuba.* New York: Herder and Herder, 1963.

Díaz, Alberto P. "Guanamaca: una comunidad haitiana." *Etnología y folklore*, no. 1 (January–June 1966).

——— "La semana santa haitiano-cubana." *Etnología y folklore*, no. 4 (July–December 1967).

Díaz, Wilfredo. "Un país que no sea ahorrativo no avanza." *Con la guardia en alto* 10, no. 9 (September 1971).

"Dictamen de la comisión de organización al IV Congreso nacional campesino." *ANAP*, December 1971–January 1972, pp. 32–37.

"Dictamen de la comisión de producción al IV Congreso nacional campesino." *ANAP*, December 1971–January 1972, pp. 20–29.

"Dictamen de la comisión ideológica al IV Congreso nacional campesino." *ANAP*, December 1971–January 1972.

"Diez años de investigaciones en el Instituto de Economía." *Economía y desarrollo*, no. 30 (July–August 1975).

"Diez años de trabajo." *ANAP*, April 1971, pp. 41–43.

"X años del ICIDCA." *Cuba azúcar* (April–June 1973).

"Diez refranes lucumíes." *Cuba* 3, no. 31 (November 1964).

Dinerstein, Herbert. *The Making of a Missile Crisis: October 1962*. Baltimore: Johns Hopkins University Press, 1976.

Dirección Nacional de los Tribunales Populares. *Manual de los Tribunales Populares*. Havana: Ministerio de Justicia, 1966.

"Discurso del Comandante Fidel Castro el 23 de agosto de 1970: X aniversario de la Federación de Mujeres Cubanas." *Pensamiento crítico*, no. 45 (October 1970).

"Discurso del Comandante Fidel Castro en la plenaria provincial de la CTC." *Pensamiento crítico*, no. 45 (October 1970).

"Discurso del compañero Osvaldo Dorticós." *Cuba socialista*, no. 51 (November 1965).

"Discurso del Presidente de la República, Dr. Osvaldo Dorticós, en la escuela de cuadros de mando del Ministerio de la Industria Ligera." *Pensamiento crítico*, no. 45 (October 1970).

Dolz, Ricardo. *El proceso electoral de 1916*. Havana: Imprenta y Papelería La Universal, 1917.

Domenech, Joel. "Aplicación del plan de eficiencia industrial." *Cuba socialista*, no. 63 (November 1966).

———— "Experiencias del trabajo de reestructuración y depuración de las ORI en La Habana." *Cuba socialista*, no. 10 (June 1962).

Domingo, Pedro. "La vacunación BCG y su aplicación en Cuba." *Revista cubana de tuberculosis* 17, no. 3 (July–September 1953).

Domínguez, Jorge I. "Armed Forces and Foreign Relations." In *Cuba in the World*, edited by Cole Blasier and Carmelo Mesa-Lago. Pittsburgh: University of Pittsburgh Press, 1978.

———— "An Assessment of Human Rights Conditions." In *Human Rights and International Relations*, by Jorge I. Domínguez, Richard Falk, Nigel Rodley, and Ben Whitaker. New York: McGraw-Hill, 1978.

———— "The Civic Soldier in Cuba." In *Political-Military Systems: Comparative Perspectives*, edited by Catherine M. Kelleher. Beverly Hills, Calif.: Sage Publications, 1974.

———— "Cuban Catholics and Castro." *Worldview* 15, no. 2 (February 1972).

———— "Institutionalization and Civil-Military Relations in Cuba." *Cuban Studies* 6, no. 1 (January 1976).

———— "Racial and Ethnic Relations in the Cuban Armed Forces: A Non-Topic." *Armed Forces and Society* 2, no. 2 (Winter 1976).

———— "Revolutionary Values and Development Performance: China, Cuba and the Soviet Union." In *Values in Development*, edited by Harold Lasswell, Daniel Lerner, and John Montgomery. Cambridge: M.I.T. Press, 1977.

———— "Sectoral Clashes in Cuban Politics and Development." *Latin American Research Review* 6, no. 3 (Fall 1971).

———— "Taming the Cuban Shrew." *Foreign Policy*, no. 10 (Spring 1973).

Domínguez, Jorge I., and Mitchell, Christopher. "The Roads Not Taken: Institutionalization and Political Parties in Cuba and Bolivia." *Comparative Politics* 9, no. 2 (January 1977).

Dorta Duque, Francisco. *Justificando una reforma agraria*. Madrid: Raycar, 1960.

Dorticós, Osvaldo. "Análisis y perspectivas del desarrollo de la economía cubana." *Economía y desarrollo*, no. 12 (July–August 1972).

———— "Los cambios institucionales y políticos de la revolución socialista cubana." *Cuba socialista*, no. 1 (September 1961).

———— "Crear un espíritu técnico, una voluntad técnica." *Economía y desarrollo*, no. 28 (March–April 1975).

———— "El error que no cometeremos jamás es el de no estar alerta." *Cuba socialista*, no. 59 (July 1966).

———— "Primer forum científico nacional de estudiantes universitarios." *Universidad de La Habana*, nos. 198–199 (January–February 1973).

———— "La revolución cubana en su cuarto aniversario." *Cuba socialista*, no. 17 (January 1963).

———— "La teoría: instrumento indispensable de la práctica revolucionaria." *Economía y desarrollo*, no. 11 (May–June 1972).

Dorticós Mauri, Eduardo. "Problemas de la estadística en el sector agropecuario." *Cuba socialista*, no. 35 (July 1964).

"Dos experiencias de la reestructuración de los Núcleos Revolucionarios Activos en Marianao." *Cuba socialista*, no. 12 (August 1962).

Drake Galinena, Teodoro, with Tenorio, Guillermina, and Martínez Cobiella, Olga. "Consideraciones bacteriológicas de exámenes de agua de consumo: estudio de mil casos." *Revista cubana de laboratorio clínico* 5, no. 5 (January–March 1951).

Draper, Theodore. *Castroism: Theory and Practice*. New York: Praeger, 1965.

———— *Castro's Revolution: Myths and Realities*. New York: Praeger, 1962.

Dumont, René. *Cuba: ¿es socialista?*. Translated by Mariela Álvarez. Caracas: Editorial Tiempo Nuevo, 1970.

———— "The Militarization of Fidelismo." *Dissent*, September–October 1970, pp. 418–428.

DuMoulin, John. "The Participative Art of the Afro-Cuban Religions." *Abhandlungen und Berichte des Staatlichen Museums für Völkerkunde Dresden* (Berlin) 21 (1962).

———— "Santa Fe: ideología y opinión sobre problemas locales." *Etnología y folklore*, no. 6 (July–December 1968).

DuMoulin, John; Zimmerman, Margarita; and Tirado, Hernán. "Monocultivo y proletarización: dos ejemplos de Las Villas." *Ciencias sociales contemporáneas* 1, no. 1 (August 1965).

Dupuy, T. N., and Blanchard, Wendell. *The Almanac of World Military Power*. 2nd ed. Dunn Loring, Va.: Dupuy, 1972.

Durán Llobera, Carlos, and Bidart Labourdette, José. "Gangrena diabética: análisis estadístico en 30 casos." *Revista cubana de cirugía* 11, nos. 5–6 (September–December 1972).

Durch, William J. "The Cuban Military in Africa and the Middle East: From Algeria to Angola." Professional paper no. 201. Arlington, Va.: Center for Naval Analyses, 1977.

Duyos, Oscar. "Los problemas actuales del acopio y los precios de compra de los productos agrícolas." *Cuba socialista*, no. 33 (May 1964).

Dyer, Donald R. "Urbanism in Cuba." *Geographical Review* 57, no. 2 (April 1957).

Echevarría Salvat, Oscar. *La agricultura cubana, 1934–1966*. Miami: Ediciones Universal, 1971.

Echezarreta, Aníbal. "El Ing. López y el desalojo a los campesinos." *Tierra libre* 6, no. 5 (May 1942).

"Editorial: ante las elecciones." *Fundamentos* 4, no. 33 (May 1944).

Eisenhower, Dwight D. *Waging Peace*. Garden City, N.Y.: Doubleday, 1965.

"Elección del comité ejecutivo nacional." *ANAP* 7, nos. 5–6 (May–June 1967).

"Emulación: tareas y metas de los CDR." *Con la guardia en alto* 6, no. 6 (June 1967).

"Entrenamiento de tiro antiaéreo." *Verde olivo* 17, no. 13 (March 30, 1975).

"Entrevista con Uxmal Livio Diaz." *Areíto* 3, nos. 2–3 (1976).

Escalante, Aníbal, and Marinello, Juan. "El trabajo de los socialistas en la última legislatura." *Fundamentos* 5, no. 41 (January 1945).

Escalante, César. "Los Comités de Defensa de la Revolución." *Cuba socialista*, no. 1 (September 1961).

Escalona, Juan. "Las FAR y los reservistas." *Verde olivo* 18, no. 17 (April 25, 1976).

Escobar Linares, Rafael. "Se hace camino al andar." *Bohemia* 67, no. 2 (January 10, 1975).

Espinosa, Ciro. "Desalojo campesino de sus tierras." *Tierra libre* 8, no. 9 (September 1944).

"Estos siete años han sido años de lucha, de sacrificios y victorias." *Con la guardia en alto* 6, no. 10 (October 1967).

Estrada, Rafael. "Cáncer del pulmón." *Archivos del Hospital Universitario General Calixto García* 3, no. 1 (January–February 1951).

"Los estudiantes investigan." *Boletín de la Comisión Nacional Cubana de la UNESCO* 12, no. 48 (January–February 1973).

"Los estudiantes universitarios ven materializado un viejo deseo." *Verde olivo* 17, no. 49 (December 7, 1975).

Evans, Bette. "The Moral versus Material Incentives Controversy in Cuba." Ph.D. dissertation, University of Pittsburgh, 1972.

Evepe. "Sin proponer una polémica." *Bohemia* 67, no. 4 (January 24, 1975).

"Evolución del producto social global." *Economía y desarrollo*, no. 32 (November–December 1975).

F., S. "Piropos con respuesta." *Signos* 5, no. 1 (September–December 1973).

Facultad de Ciencias Médicas, Universidad de La Habana. *Docencia de las ciencias médicas en Cuba*. Havana: Ministerio de Salud Pública, 1966.

Facultad de Humanidades. "Evaluación de los resultados generales del curso 1963–1964." *Universidad de La Habana*, no. 170 (November–December 1964).

Fagen, Richard R. "Charismatic Authority and the Leadership of Fidel Castro." *Western Political Quarterly* 18, no. 2, pt. 1 (June 1965).

——— *The Transformation of Political Culture in Cuba*. Stanford: Stanford University Press, 1969.

Fagen, Richard R.; Brody, Richard A.; and O'Leary, Thomas J. *Cubans in Exile: Disaffection and the Revolution*. Stanford: Stanford University Press, 1968.

Farber, Samuel. "Revolution and Social Structure in Cuba, 1933–1959." Ph.D. dissertation, University of California–Berkeley, 1969.

Farnot, Ubaldo, and Moreno, Olimpo. "Prematuridad." *Archivos del Hospital Universitario General Calixto García* 8, no. 2 (March–April 1956).

Farnsworth, Clyde H. "The Communists' Soaring Debt." *New York Times*, (June 6, 1976), sec. 3, pp. 1, 5.

Fermoselle, Rafael. *Política y color en Cuba: la guerrita de 1912.* Montevido: Ediciones Geminis, 1974.

Fernández, Carlos. "El XI congreso nacional de la CTC-R." *Cuba socialista,* no. 6 (February 1962).

Fernández, Julio Carlos. "¿Qué fue el bandidismo?" *Bohemia* 68, no. 23 (June 4, 1976).

Fernández, Leovigildo. "Palabras del director del centro de investigaciones de la caña de azúcar." *Cuba azúcar,* October–December 1970.

Fernández, Manuel. "La crisis actual del catolicismo en Cuba." *Reunión,* nos. 93–94 (January–February 1977).

Fernández, Marcelo. "Desarrollo y funciones de la banca socialista en Cuba." *Cuba socialista,* no. 30 (February 1964).

———— "Planificación y control de la circulación monetaria." *Cuba socialista,* no. 33 (May 1964).

Fernández Baquero, Guillermo, et al. "Revisión clínico patológica de 200 pacientes del hospital antileproso del Rincón." *Revista cubana de medicina tropical* 26, nos. 1–2 (January–August 1974).

Fernández Conde, Emilio. "La educación postgraduado." *Sobre educación superior,* January–June 1971.

Fernández Retamar, Roberto. "Hacia una intelectualidad revolucionaria en Cuba." *Cuadernos americanos* 15, no. 169 (November–December 1966).

Fiscalía Militar de las FAR. "Los estímulos y las correcciones disciplinarias." *Verde olivo* 17, no. 47 (November 23, 1975).

———— "Las reclamaciones en las FAR." *Verde olivo* 18, no. 31 (August 1, 1976).

FitzGerald, Frances. "A Reporter at Large: Slightly Exaggerated Enthusiasms." In *The New Cuba: Paradoxes and Potentials,* edited by Ronald Radosh. New York: Morrow, 1976.

Fitzgibbon, Russell H. *Cuba and the United States, 1900–1935.* Menasha, Wis.: Banta, 1935.

Fitzgibbon, Russell H., and Healey, H. Max. "The Cuban Elections of 1936." *American Political Science Review* 30, no. 4 (August 1936).

Foreign Policy Association, Commission on Cuban Affairs. *Problems of the New Cuba.* New York: Little and Ives, 1935.

Fox, Geoffrey E. "Cuban Workers in Exile." *Transaction* 8, no. 11 (September 1971).

———— "Honor, Shame and Women's Liberation in Cuba: Views of Working Class Emigré Men." In *Female and Male in Latin America,* edited by Ann Pescatello. Pittsburgh: University of Pittsburgh Press, 1973.

Fraga Arroyo, Roberto. "Estudio estadístico de 200 primeros casos haciendo énfasis en la sintomatología, psicodinamia y resultados terapéuticos obtenidos en pacientes tratados." *Revista cubana de pediatría* 30, no. 2 (February 1958).

Free, Lloyd A. *Attitudes of the Cuban People toward the Castro Regime.* Princeton: Institute for International Social Research, 1960.

Freidberg, Sidney. "The Measure of Damages in Claims Against Cuba." *Inter-American Economic Affairs* 23, no. 1 (Summer 1969).

Fuertes Jiménez, José. "Hacia un partido más vigoroso en Camagüey." *Cuba socialista,* no. 34 (June 1964).

———— "Problemas de organización del Partido en las unidades agropecuarias de Camagüey." *Cuba socialista,* no. 39 (November 1964).

———— "El trabajo organizativo en Camagüey." *Cuba socialista*, no. 15 (November 1962).

Furrazola-Bermúdez, Gustavo; Judoley, Constantino M.; Mijailovskaya, Marina S.; Miroliubov, Yuri S.; Novojatsky, Ivan P.; Núñez Jiménez, Antonio; and Solsona, Juan B. *Geología de Cuba*. Havana: Editora Nacional de Cuba, 1964.

Fusté Amieba, Federico, et al. "Causas de muerte en el prematuro." *Revista cubana de pediatría* 26, no. 6 (June 1954).

Gallagher, Mary B. "The Public Address of Fidel Castro Ruz: Charismatic Leader of a Modern Revolution." Ph.D. dissertation, University of Pittsburgh, 1970.

Gálvez, Luis O. "Estrategia de dirección en la actividad de investigación y desarrollo." *Economía y desarrollo*, no. 25 (September–October 1974).

García, Francisco, and Noyola, Juan. "Principales objetivos de nuestro plan económico hasta 1965." *Cuba socialista*, no. 13 (1962).

García Díaz, Salustiano. "Las industrias de subproductos y derivados de la caña y del azúcar." *Anuario azucarero de Cuba* 22 (1958).

García Gutiérrez, Alejandro, et al. "Resultados de anastomosis portasistémicas en las hipertensiones portales de causa intrahepática." *Revista cubana de cirugía* 13, no. 3 (May–June 1974).

García Herrera, Rosalía. "Observaciones etnológicas de dos sectas religiosas afrocubanas en una comunidad Lajera, La Guinea." *Islas*, no. 43 (September–December 1972).

García Márquez, Gabriel. "Castro in the War Room: Tactical Advice to Angola." *Washington Post*, January 11, 1977, p. A11.

———— "Colombian Author Writes on Cuba's Angola Intervention." *Washington Post*, January 10, 1977, p. A14.

———— "Cuba en Angola: Operación Carlota." *Proceso*, January 1977, pp. 6–15.

———— "Cuba in Africa: Seed Che Planted." *Washington Post*, January 12, 1977, p. A12.

García Montes, Jorge, and Alonso Ávila, Antonio. *Historia del partido comunista de Cuba*. Miami: Rema Press, 1970.

García Mouri, Eduardo. "Proceso de institucionalización en el sindicalismo cubano: papel de los sindicatos según el XIII Congreso CTC." Paper presented at Seminar on Institutionalization in Cuba, Institute of Cuban Studies, March 24–29, 1975, in Caracas. Mimeographed.

García Peláez, Raúl. "La construcción del Partido en la provincia de Matanzas." *Cuba socialista*, no. 16 (December 1962).

García Regueiro, Ovidio. *Cuba: raíces y frutos de una revolución*. Madrid: IEPAL, 1970.

García Tudurí, Mercedes. "La enseñanza en Cuba en los primeros cincuenta años de independencia." In *Historia de la nación cubana*, edited by Ramiro Guerra y Sánchez et al. Vol. 10. Havana: Editorial Historia de la Nación Cubana, 1952.

———— "Resumen de la historia de la educación en Cuba." *Exilio* 3, nos. 3–4, and 4, no. 1 (Winter 1969–Spring 1970).

Garner, Jean-Pierre. *Une ville, une révolution: La Havane*. Paris: Editions Anthropos, 1973.

Gavrikov, Yuri. "América Latina y los países del CAME: algunos problemas de la colaboración." *Panorama latinoamericano* (Novosti), no. 150 (July 1, 1972).

—— "URSS-Cuba: colaboración y solidaridad." *Panorama latinoamericano* (Novosti), no. 163 (February 15, 1973).

Gellman, Irwin F. *Roosevelt and Batista: Good Neighbor Diplomacy in Cuba, 1933–1945.* Albuquerque: University of New Mexico Press, 1973.

Geyer, Georgie Anne. "Cuba in Angola: A New Look." *Boston Globe,* June 20, 1976, pp. 55–56.

Gil, Roberto. "Cada día más: ojos y oídos de la revolución." *Con la guardia en alto* 10, no. 8 (August 1971).

Gilly, Adolfo. *Inside the Cuban Revolution.* Translated by Félix Gutiérrez. New York: Monthly Review Press, 1964.

Goldenberg, Boris. *The Cuban Revolution and Latin America.* New York: Praeger, 1965.

—— "The Rise and Fall of a Party: The Cuban Communist Party (1925–1959)." *Problems of Communism* 19, no. 4 (July–August 1970).

Gonzalez, Edward. "Castro's Revolution, Cuban Communist Appeals and the Soviet Response." *World Politics* 21, no. 1 (October 1968).

—— *Cuba under Castro: The Limits of Charisma.* Boston: Houghton Mifflin, 1974.

—— "Political Succession in Cuba." *Studies in Comparative Communism* 9, nos. 1–2 (Spring–Summer 1976).

González, Fernando. "Población y desarrollo: consideraciones generales." *Economía y desarrollo,* no. 27 (January–February 1975).

González, Rafael, and Medina, Rubén. "Trabajo investigación-desarrollo Escambray, 1971–1972." *Universidad de La Habana,* nos. 198–199 (1973).

González, Rolando. "Piropos en Santa Clara." *Signos* 5, no. 1 (September–December 1973).

González, Sara, and Gómez, Carmen. "La FMC y la educación: diez años de trabajo." *Mujeres* 10, no. 8 (1970).

González, Víctor. "El trabajo de la Unión de Jóvenes Comunistas en el campo." *Cuba socialista,* no. 44 (April 1965).

González Tosca. "Escuelas." *Verde olivo* 13, no. 49 (December 6, 1971).

Goodman, Louis Wolf. "The Social Sciences in Cuba." *Items* 30, no. 4 (December 1976).

Gorbachev, Boris. "Cuba: algunas cuestiones de su integración económica con los países del socialismo." *Panorama latinoamericano* (Novosti), no. 171 (August 1, 1973).

—— "Cuba: la revolución y la economía." *Panorama latinoamericano* (Novosti), no. 185 (April 15, 1974).

Gorbachev, Boris, and Kalinin, Arnold. "Algunos aspectos socio-económicos y políticos de la experiencia de la revolución cubana." *Panorama latinoamericano* (Novosti), no. 96 (May 4, 1970).

Goure, Leon, and Weinkle, Julian. "Soviet-Cuban Relations: The Growing Integration." In *Castro, Cuba and Revolution,* edited by Jaime Suchlicki. Coral Gables, Fla.: University of Miami Press, 1972.

Grau San Martín, Ramón. *La revolución cubana ante América.* Mexico: Imprenta Manuel León Sánchez, 1936.

Green, Gil. *Revolution, Cuban Style.* New York: International Publishers, 1970.

Greve, Frank, and Perez, Miguel. " 'Boniato Massacre': What Really Happened?" *Miami Herald,* May 24, 1976, p. 15-A.

———— "Castro's Jails: Still Bulging 17 Years Later." *Miami Herald,* May 23, 1976, pp. 1, 16-A.

———— "Heavy Political Tones Dominate Style of Justice under Castro." *Miami Herald,* May 24, 1976, pp. 1, 14-A.

Grobart, Fabio. "Como se cumplen las resoluciones de la II Asamblea Nacional." *Fundamentos* 4, no. 40 (December 1944).

———— "Una emulación de tipo especial." *Fundamentos* 2, no. 16 (November 1942).

———— "El movimiento obrero cubano de 1925 a 1933." *Cuba socialista* 6, no. 60 (August 1966).

———— "La II Asamblea Nacional del Partido Socialista Popular." *Fundamentos* 4, no. 38 (October 1944).

Grupos de Propaganda Doctrinal Ortodoxa. *Doctrina del Partido Ortodoxo.* Havana: Fernández, 1951.

Guerra, Secundino. "Los seccionales del partido en La Habana." *Cuba socialista,* no. 18 (February 1963).

"Guerra sin tregua a la chapucería." *Bohemia* 67, no. 19 (May 9, 1975).

Guerra y Sánchez, Ramiro; Pérez Cabrera, José M.; Remos, Juan J.; and Santovenia, Emeterio S., eds. *Historia de la nación cubana.* 10 vols. Havana: Editorial Historia de la Nación Cubana, 1952.

Guevara, Alfredo. "Un cine de combate." *Pensamiento crítico,* no. 42 (July 1970).

Guevara, Ernesto. *Economic Planning in Cuba.* New York, 1961.

———— "Man and Socialism in Cuba." In *Man and Socialism in Cuba,* edited by Bertram Silverman. New York: Atheneum, 1971.

———— *Reminiscenes of the Cuban Revolutionary War.* Translated by Victoria Ortiz. New York: Monthly Review Press, 1968.

———— "Sobre la concepción del valor." *Nuestra industria: revista económica,* no. 3 (1963).

———— "El socialismo y el hombre." *Nuestra industria: revista económica,* no. 14 (1965).

Guillén, Ramón. "Plan de automatización de la industria azucarera de Cuba." *Cuba azúcar,* April–June 1969, pp. 2–12.

Gutelman, Michel. *L'agriculture socialisée à Cuba.* Paris: Maspero, 1967.

Gutiérrez, Gustavo. "La convención constituyente y la Constitución de 1940." In *Historia de la nación cubana,* edited by Ramiro Guerra y Sánchez et al. Vol. 8. Havana: Editorial Historia de la Nación Cubana, 1952.

———— *El empleo, el subempleo y el desempleo en Cuba.* Havana: Consejo Nacional de Economía, 1958.

Gutiérrez, Rosendo. "Segunda asamblea de balance." *Verde olivo* 9, no. 9 (March 3, 1968).

Gutiérrez Muñiz, José. "Conferencia mundial de población: opiniones de Cuba." *Economía y desarrollo,* no. 29 (May–June 1975).

Guttmacher, Sally, and García, Lourdes. "Social Science and Health in Cuba: Ideology, Planning and Health." In *Topias and Utopias in Health,* edited by Stanley Ingman and Anthony Thomas. The Hague: Mouton, 1975.

Gvozdariov, Boris. "URSS-Cuba: unidad de criterios y posiciones." *Panorama latinoamericano* (Novosti), no. 184 (April 1, 1974).

"Hacia la sistematización de los precios de acopio de productos agrícolas." *Cuba socialista*, no. 48 (August 1965).

Hagelberg, Gerald B. *The Caribbean Sugar Industries: Constraints and Opportunities.* New Haven: Yale University, Antilles Research Program, 1974.

Hageman, Alice, and Wheaton, Philip, eds. *Religion in Cuba Today.* New York: Association Press, 1971.

Halperin, Maurice. *The Rise and Decline of Fidel Castro.* Berkeley and Los Angeles: University of California Press, 1972.

Handke, Horst, and Mohrmann, Elli. "Relaciones públicas de un monopolio estadounidense en América Latina." In *Monopolios norteamericanos en Cuba: contribución al estudio de la penetración imperialista.* Havana: Instituto Cubano del Libro, 1973.

Harnecker, Marta. *Cuba: ¿dictadura o democracia?* Mexico: Siglo XXI, 1975.

Hart, Enrique. "Discurso de apertura ante los tribunales." *Revista cubana de jurisprudencia* 2, no. 8 (September–October 1963).

Hass, Henry, "El año: en la defensa e investigación del azúcar." *Anuario azucarero de Cuba* 22 (1958).

Hatim Ricardo, Alberto, et al. "Hipertensión arterial: revisión de 200 casos." *Revista cubana de medicina* 11, nos. 5–6 (September–December 1972).

Heredero, Luis, et al. "Screening electrofonético de hemoglobinas: análisis de 15,000 muestras en La Habana." *Revista cubana de pediatría* 46, no. 2 (March–April 1974).

Hernández, Jorge; Eng, Angel; Bermúdez, María; and Columbié, Mariela. "Estudio sobre el divorcio." *Humanidades*, ser. 1 (Ciencias Sociales), no. 3 (January 1973).

Hernández, Roberto. "La atención médica en Cuba hasta 1958." *Journal of Inter-American Studies and World Affairs* 11, no. 4 (October 1969).

Hernández, Roberto, and Mesa-Lago, Carmelo. "Labor Organization and Wages." In *Revolutionary Change in Cuba*, edited by Carmelo Mesa-Lago. Pittsburgh: University of Pittsburgh Press, 1971.

Hernández Amador, Guillermo, et al. "Nuestros resultados en 3301 quemaduras infantiles tratadas en el hospital 'William Soler' durante un período de 10 años (1962–1972)." *Revista cubana de pediatría* 45, nos. 4–6 (July–December 1973).

Herrera, Nivaldo. "La ofensiva política en las zonas campesinas de Matanzas." *Cuba socialista*, no. 39 (November 1964).

Hill, Nelson Taylor. "Várices quirúrgicas: revisión de los casos ingresados en el hospital docente 'General Calixto García' durante los dos últimos años." *Revista cubana de cirugía* 11 (1972), supplement.

Horrego Estuch, Leopoldo. *Legislación social de Cuba.* Havana: Editorial Librería Selecta, 1948–1949.

——— *Martín Morúa Delgado: vida y mensaje.* Havana: Editorial Sánchez, 1957.

Huerta Aguiar, René de la. "Espiritismo y otras supersticiones en la población cubana." *Revista del hospital psiquiátrico de La Habana* 2, no. 1 (January–March 1960).

Hulse, Frederick S. "The Comparative Anthropometry of Cubans and Andalusians." Ph.D. dissertation, Harvard University, 1933.

Huteau, Michel, and Lautrey, Jacques. *L'éducation à Cuba*. Paris: Maspero, 1973.

Ibarra, Jorge. "Agosto de 1906: una intervención amañada." *Revista de la Biblioteca Nacional José Martí*, third period, vol. 15, no. 1 (January–April 1973).

Ichaso, Francisco. "Ideas y aspiraciones de la primera generación republicana." In *Historia de la nación cubana*, edited by Ramiro Guerra y Sánchez, et al. Vol. 8. Havana: Editorial Historia de la Nación Cubana, 1952.

"Image of Catholic Church Improving." *Cuba Review* 5, no. 2 (June 1975).

"Inaugurado el Instituto Cubano de Física Nuclear." *Verde olivo* 10, no. 3 (January 19, 1969).

"Indicaciones sobre el proceso asambleario." *Verde olivo* 14, no. 42 (October 15, 1972).

"Información política." *Verde olivo* 9, no. 45 (November 10, 1968).

"Informe central del Vice Ministro Jefe de la Dirección Política." *Verde olivo* 16, no. 17 (April 28, 1974).

"Informe del comandante Raúl Castro al Comité Central del Partido Comunista de Cuba." *Verde olivo* 9, no. 5 (February 4, 1968), and *Verde olivo* 9, no. 6 (February 11, 1968).

"Informe del Fiscal en el juicio seguido a Aníbal Escalante y 36 acusados más." *Verde olivo* 9, no. 6 (February 11, 1968).

Instituto de Ciencia Animal. *Instituto de Ciencia Animal*. Havana: Universidad de La Habana, 1970.

Instituto de Investigaciones Científicas de la Economía Pesquera Marina y de la Oceanografía de Toda la Unión and Centro de Investigaciones Pesqueras de Cuba, *Investigaciones pesqueras soviético-cubanas*. Moscow: Editorial Pischevaja Promyshlennost, 1965–1971.

"Integración del Secretariado y de Comisiones de la Dirección Nacional de las ORI." *Cuba socialista*, no. 7 (March 1962).

International Bank for Reconstruction and Development. *Report on Cuba*. Washington, D.C., 1951.

International Commission of Jurists. *Cuba and the Rule of Law*. Geneva: H. Studer, 1962.

"Intervención del compañero Armando Hart sobre organización." *Cuba socialista*, no. 51 (November 1965).

"Intervención del compañero Carlos Rafael Rodríguez en la reunión del Comité Central." *Verde olivo* 9, no. 6 (February 11, 1968).

Jackson, D. Bruce. *Castro, the Kremlin, and Communism in Latin America*. Baltimore: Johns Hopkins University Press, 1969.

Jacquenay, Theodore. "The Yellow Uniforms of Cuba." *Worldview* 20, nos. 1–2 (January–February 1977).

Jenks, Leland H. *Our Cuban Colony*. New York: Vanguard Press, 1928.

Jiménez, Julio. "Piropos en Cienfuegos." *Signos* 5, no. 1 (September–December 1973).

Jimenez, Michael F. "Revolutionary Agrarian Policy and the Cuban Peasantry." Seminar paper, Harvard University, 1972. Mimeographed.

Jolly, Richard. "Education: The Pre-Revolutionary Background." In *Cuba: The Economic and Social Revolution*, edited by Dudley Seers. Chapel Hill: University of North Carolina Press, 1964.

Jones, Louis. "Investigación del aprovechamiento escolar en la educación primaria en el curso de 1961–1962." *Psicología y educación* 1, no. 1 (January–May 1964).

Jones, Louis; Jones, Lenna; and Falcón, Edith. "Actitudes vocacionales de estudiantes de 1960 y 1965." *Psicología y educación* 2, no. 5 (January–March 1965).

Jordán Rodríguez, José, et al. "Etiología de la diarrea aguda del lactante." *Revista cubana de pediatría* 30, no. 11 (November 1958).

Jover Marimón, Mateo. "The Church." In *Revolutionary Change in Cuba*, edited by Carmelo Mesa-Lago. Pittsburgh: University of Pittsburgh Press, 1971.

Jústiz, Cándido, and Martínez, Lucas. "Los CDR en las zonas campesinas." *Guía para la acción*, no. 4 (October 1963).

Kahl, Joseph. "The Moral Economy of a Revolutionary Society." In *Cuban Communism*, edited by Irving L. Horowitz. New Brunswick, N.J.: Transaction Books, 1970.

Karol, K. S. *Guerrillas in Power.* New York: Hill and Wang, 1970.

Kennedy, Ian McColl. "Cuba's *Ley Contra la Vagancia*—The Law on Loafing." *UCLA Law Review* 20, no. 6 (August 1973).

Kenny, Michael. "Twentieth-Century Spanish Expatriates in Cuba: A Subculture." *Anthropological Quarterly* 34, no. 2 (April 1961).

Kindelán, D. "Décimo aniversario de la U.J.C.–F.A.R." *Verde olivo* 16, no. 25 (June 23, 1974).

Klein, Herbert S. *Slavery in the Americas.* Chicago: Quadrangle Books, 1967.

Krishna Iyer, V. R. *Cuban Panorama.* Trivandrum: Prabatham, 1967.

Lamar Schweyer, Alberto. *Cómo cayó el presidente Machado.* 2nd ed. Havana: M. Cárdenas, 1938.

Lancís y Sánchez, Antonio. "Elecciones y administración en la República." *Anuario de la Facultad de Ciencias Sociales y Derecho Público*, 1952.

Laska-Mierzejewska, Teresa. "Desarrollo y maduración de los niños y jóvenes habaneros." *Materialy I Prace Antropologiczne* 74 (1967).

—— "Menarche in Cuban Girls." *Przeglad Antropologiczny* 32, no. 1 (1966).

—— "Morphological and Developmental Difference between Negro and White Cuban Youths." *Human Biology* 42, no. 4 (December 1970).

Lataste Hoffer, Albán. *Cuba: hacia una nueva economía política del socialismo.* Santiago: Editorial Universitaria, 1968.

Lavan, George, ed. *Che Guevara Speaks.* New York: Merit Publishers, 1967.

Lazo, Raúl. "El centro de investigaciones pesqueras." *Bohemia* 67, no. 4 (October 3, 1975).

Leiner, Marvin, with Ubell, Robert. *Children Are the Revolution: Day Care in Cuba.* New York: Viking Press, 1974.

LeoGrande, William M. "Party Control and Political Socialization in Communist Civil Military Relations: The Case of Cuba." Paper presented at 9th national convention, American Association for the Advancement of Slavic Studies, October 13–16, 1977, in Washington, D.C. Mimeographed.

—— "The Politics of Revolutionary Development: Civil-Military Relations in Cuba, 1959–1976." Paper presented at annual meeting, Midwest Political Science Association, April 21–23, 1977, in Chicago. Mimeographed.

Leon, Charles P. "The National Bank of Cuba: A Study in Institutional Change." Ph.D. dissertation, New York University, 1964.

León, Raúl. "La planificación del comercio exterior." *Cuba socialista*, no. 28 (December 1963).

Le Riverend, Julio. *La república: dependencia y revolución.* Havana: Instituto del Libro, 1969.

Lewis, Oscar; Lewis, Ruth M.; and Rigdon, Susan M. *Four Men: Living the Revolution.* Urbana: University of Illinois Press, 1977.

———— *Four Women: Living the Revolution.* Urbana: University of Illinois Press, 1977.

———— *Neighbors: Living the Revolution.* Urbana: University of Illinois Press, 1978.

Ley de organización del sistema judicial. Havana: Ministerio de Justicia, 1973.

Leyva, Ricardo. "Health and Revolution in Cuba." In *Cuba in Revolution,* edited by Rolando Bonachea and Nelson P. Valdés. Garden City, N.Y.: Anchor Books, 1972.

Lezcano, Jorge. "Informe central presentado al pleno." *Con la guardia en alto,* 14, no. 4 (April 1975).

Liebowitz, Michael. "The Cuban Health Care System: A Study in the Evaluation of Health Care Systems." M.D. dissertation, Yale University, 1969.

Lima Fernández, Manuel. "Nuestra experiencia en los primeros 100 casos atendidos en una unidad de cuidados coronarios." *Revista cubana de medicina* 13, no. 6 (November–December 1974).

Lisanka. "Brigada aérea de la guardia 'Playa Girón.' " *Verde olivo* 18, no. 17 (April 25, 1976).

———— "Escuela de cadetes inter-armas 'General Antonio Maceo.' " *Verde olivo* 17, no. 21 (May 25, 1975).

Lobo, Julio. "Necesaria la modernización agrícola e industrial." *Anuario azucarero de Cuba* 22 (1958).

Lockwood, Lee. *Castro's Cuba, Cuba's Fidel.* New York: Vintage Books, 1969.

"Lograr una base organizativa sólida." *Mujeres* 10, no. 8 (1970).

López, Jorge, and Díaz, Wilfredo. "¿Qué es un distrito?" *Con la guardia en alto* 10, no. 2 (February 1971).

López, Jorge, and Gill, Roberto. "¿Cumple Ud. con el deber de educar y formar a sus hijos?" *Con la guardia en alto* 11, nos. 1–2 (January–February 1972).

López, Luis. "Séptima conferencia nacional UJC." *Verde olivo* 16, no. 14 (April 7, 1974).

López Coll, Armando, and Santiago, Armando. "Notas sobre el proceso de planificación en Cuba." *Economía y desarrollo,* no. 29 (May–June 1975).

López Goicochea, Francisco. *El desahucio: doctrina del Tribunal Supremo de Cuba, 1947–1952.* Havana: Empresa Editora de Publicaciones, 1954.

López Segrera, Francisco. *Cuba: capitalismo dependiente y subdesarrollo 1510–1959.* Havana: Casa de las Américas. 1972.

López Valdés, Rafael. "La sociedad secreta Abakuá y los procesos de cambio en los obreros manuales del puerto de La Habana." In *VII Congrès International des Sciences Anthropologiques et Ethnologiques.* Vol. 11, Moscow: Nauka, 1971.

López Valdés, Rafael, and Deschamps, Pedro. "La sociedad secreta Abakuá en un grupo de obreros portuarios." *Etnología y folklore,* no. 2 (July–December 1966).

Lozano Casado, F. *La personalidad del General José Miguel Gómez.* Havana: Imprenta y Papelería de Rambla, Bouza, 1913.

"Lucha abierta contra la especulación." *ANAP* 6, no. 10 (October 1966).

"La lucha contra el oscurantismo es una lucha ideológica." *Con la guardia en alto* 8, no. 6 (June 1969).

McCook Martínez, Jorge. "Angiología social: experiencia en Cuba." *Revista cubana de cirugía* 11, nos. 5–6 (September–December 1972).

MacGaffey, Wyatt, and Barnett, Clifford. *Twentieth-Century Cuba.* Garden City, N.Y.: Anchor Books, 1965.

Macías Castro, Ignacio. "Modelo experimental de un programa de salud nacional para la atención integral del paciente con hipertensión arterial." *Revista cubana de medicina* 14, no. 1 (January–February 1975).

Maidanik, Kiva, and Poliakov, Mijail. "El triunfo del pueblo cubano y el proceso revolucionario mundial." *América Latina*, no. 1 (1974).

Malmierca, Isidoro. "El fortalecimiento de las organizaciones de masas en la región de Mayabeque." *Cuba socialista*, no. 23 (July 1963).

―――― "La lucha por la fuerza de las filas del Partido en La Habana." *Cuba socialista*, no. 26 (October, 1963).

―――― "La marcha de la construcción del Partido en La Habana." *Cuba socialista*, no. 14 (October 1962).

―――― "El método de las tres vías y los tres principios para el crecimiento normal del partido." *Cuba socialista*, no. 35 (July 1964).

Mañach, Jorge. *Indagación del choteo.* 2nd ed. Havana: Verónica, 1940.

"Maniobra 'Primer Congreso.'" *Verde olivo* 18, no. 1 (January 4, 1976).

Mankiewicz, Frank, and Jones, Kirby. *With Fidel.* Chicago: Playboy Press, 1975.

Margolles, Pedro. "Building up a System of Representative Bodies." *World Marxist Review* 18, no. 2 (February 1975).

Marieu, Jean. "Quelques données récentes sur la population cubaine." *Les cahiers d'outre-mer* 27, no. 106 (April–June 1974).

Marinello, Zoilo. "La Academia de Ciencias de Cuba: presente y futuro" [in Russian]. In *The Soviet Union and Cuba*, edited by the Soviet Academy of Sciences, Institute of Ethnography. Moscow: Nauka, 1973.

Márquez Sterling, Carlos. *Historia de Cuba.* New York: Las Americas, 1969.

Martí, Agenar. "A toda máquina." *Cuba internacional* 6, no. 60 (August 1974).

Martí, Jorge. "Class Attitudes in Cuban Society on the Eve of the Revolution." *Specialia Interamericana*, no. 3 (August 1971).

Martín, Miguel. "Informe al Congreso." *Cuba socialista*, no. 62 (October 1966).

―――― "Nueva etapa de la Unión de Jóvenes Comunistas cubanos." *Cuba socialista*, no. 36 (August 1964).

Martín Jiménez, R. "Epidemia de meningitis aséptica en La Habana." *Revista cubana de pediatría* 32, no. 10 (October 1960).

Martínez Alier, Juan and Verena. *Cuba: economía y sociedad.* Paris: Ruedo Ibérico, 1972.

Martínez Alier, Verena. *Marriage, Class and Color in Nineteenth-Century Cuba: A Study of Racial Attitudes and Sexual Values in a Slave Society.* London: Cambridge University Press, 1974.

Martínez Cárdenas, Antonio, and Betancourt Rodríguez, Zaida. "Estudio médico-social de 1000 niños." *Revista cubana de pediatría* 33, nos. 4–6 (April–June 1961).

Martínez Escobar, Manuel. *El desahucio y su jurisprudencia.* 2nd ed. Havana: Cultural, 1942.

Martínez Pérez, Pedro. "Nuevo sistema judicial." *Cuba internacional* 3, no. 28 (December 1971).

Masó, Alberto. "Tareas fundamentales." *Con la guardia en alto* 6, no. 5 (May 1967).

Matar, José. "Debemos promover los mejores cuadros a los organismos superiores de dirección." *Guía para la acción*, no. 15 (March 1965).

———— "Sigue impetuoso el desarrollo de los CDR." *Con la guardia en alto* 3, no. 1 (September 1964).

———— "Tres años de lucha y experiencia." *Guía para la acción*, no. 4 (October 1963).

Matas, Julio. "Theater and Cinematography." In *Revolutionary Change in Cuba*, edited by Carmelo Mesa-Lago. Pittsburgh: University of Pittsburgh Press, 1971.

Mateo de Acosta, Oscar. "Registro nacional de consumidores de productos antidiabéticos." *Revista cubana de medicina* 12, no. 2 (March–April 1973).

Mazorra, Oscar, and Montero, Mario. "Estudio demográfico de 'Valle del Perú.'" *Economía y desarrollo*, no. 6 (April–June 1971).

Méndez, Luis. "La asamblea provincial del PURS en Matanzas." *Cuba socialista*, no. 31 (March 1964).

———— "El avance del Partido en Matanzas." *Cuba socialista*, no. 30 (February 1964).

Méndez, Mario. "Crecimiento." *Con la guardia en alto* 11, no. 9 (September 1972).

Menéndez Cruz, Alfredo. "La transformación de las cooperatives cañeras en granjas cañeras." *Cuba socialista*, no. 14 (October 1962).

Meneses Mañas, Rafael, et al. "Aspectos anatomopatológicos de la tuberculosis en Cuba." *Revista cubana de tuberculosis* 17, no. 4 (October–December 1953).

Menton, Seymour. *Prose Fiction of the Cuban Revolution*. Austin: University of Texas Press, 1975.

Mesa-Lago, Carmelo. "Availability and Reliability of Statistics in Socialist Cuba." *Latin American Research Review* 4, no. 2 (Spring 1969).

———— *Cuba in the 1970s*. Albuquerque: University of New Mexico Press, 1974.

———— *Cuba: teoría y práctica de los incentivos*. Latin American Studies Series, occasional paper no. 7. Pittsburgh: University of Pittsburgh, 1971.

———— "Economic Policies and Growth." In *Revolutionary Change in Cuba*, edited by Carmelo Mesa-Lago. Pittsburgh: University of Pittsburgh Press, 1971.

———— "Economic Significance of Unpaid Labor in Socialist Cuba." *Industrial and Labor Relations Review* 22, no. 3 (April 1969).

———— "Farm Payment Systems in Socialist Cuba." *Studies in Comparative Communism* 9, no. 3 (Autumn 1976).

———— "The Labor Force, Employment, Unemployment and Underemployment in Cuba: 1899–1970." *Sage Professional Papers in International Studies* 1, no. 9 (1972).

———— *The Labor Sector and Socialist Distribution in Cuba*. New York: Praeger, 1968.

Mesa-Lago, Carmelo, ed. *Revolutionary Change in Cuba*. Pittsburgh: University of Pittsburgh Press, 1971.

Mesa-Lago, Carmelo, and Zephirin, Luc. "Central Planning." In *Revolutionary Change in Cuba*, edited by Carmelo Mesa-Lago. Pittsburgh: University of Pittsburgh Press, 1971.

Michelena, Jorge. "En la base campesina 'Porfirio Cabrera' se producen ventas de arroz por la libre." *ANAP* 7, no. 10 (October 1967).

——— "El plátano por la libre en el municipal Álvaro Reynoso." *ANAP* 7, no. 11 (November 1967).

"La microemulación oriental del deber y el honor." *Bohemia* 65, no. 26 (June 29, 1973).

Middleton, Drew. "The Cuban Soldier in Angola." *New York Times*, March 3, 1976, p. 4.

Milián, Arnaldo. "Las cooperativas campesinas de créditos y servicios en Las Villas." *Cuba socialista*, no. 21 (May 1963).

——— "Experiencias de las JUCEI en Las Villas." *Cuba socialista*, no. 3 (November 1961).

Miller, Allan Reed. *The Politics of Intervention: The Military Occupation of Cuba, 1906–1909.* Columbus: Ohio State University Press, 1968.

Ministerio de Industrias, Dirección Económica. "Proposición de un sistema de precios utilizando los costos planificados como precios de entrega dentro del sector estatal." *Nuestra industria: revista económica*, nos. 22–23 (June 1967).

Mir del Junco, José, et al. "Análisis de 245 casos egresados del servicio de tuberculosis del hospital infantil docente 'Dr. Angel Aballí' desde el primero de enero de 1965 hasta el 30 de junio de 1971." *Revista cubana de pediatría* 45, no. 2 (March–April 1973).

Miranda, Raúl. *Siluetas de candidatos.* Matanzas: Imprenta y Librería La Pluma de Oro, 1910.

Monopolios norteamericanos en Cuba: contribución al estudio de la penetración imperialista. Havana: Instituto Cubano del Libro, 1973.

Mont'Alegre, Omer. "Das alternativas de 1974 as perspectivas de 1975." *Brasil açucareiro* 85, no. 3 (March 1975).

Montero de la Pedraja, René, et al. "Brote epidémico de diarreas a escherichia coli Oiii-B4 observado en el centro de prematuros de La Habana." *Revista cubana de pediatría* 29, no. 4 (April 1957).

——— "La sepsis en el niño prematuro." *Revista cubana de pediatría* 29, no. 5 (May 1957).

Moore, Carlos. "Cuba: The Untold Story." *Présence africaine* (English ed.), no. 24 (1964).

Mora, Alberto. "En torno a la cuestión del funcionamiento de la ley del valor en la economía cubana en los actuales momentos." *Comercio exterior* 1, no. 3 (1963).

——— "Sobre algunos problemas actuales de la construcción del socialismo." *Nuestra industria: revista económica*, no. 14 (1965).

Morales, Martha; Valdés, Gilberto; Díaz, Beatriz; and Díaz, Elva. "Estudio preliminar sobre algunos factores que inciden en las realizaciones docentes de los alumnos de primer año." *Sobre educación superior*, July–December 1970.

Moré Benítez, J. B. "La revolución técnica y la Escuela de Ciencias Políticas." *Cuba socialista*, no. 37 (September 1964).

Moreno, José A. "From Traditional to Modern Values." In *Revolutionary Change in Cuba*, edited by Carmelo Mesa-Lago. Pittsburgh: University of Pittsburgh Press, 1971.

——— "Justice and Law in Latin America: A Cuban Example." *Journal of Inter-American Studies and World Affairs* 12, no. 3 (July 1970).

Morgan, Ted. "Cuba." *New York Times Magazine*, December 1, 1974, pp. 27–29, 100–113, 116–117, 122, 126.

Moses, Carl. "Judicial Control of the Constitutionality of Legislation in Cuba." Ph.D. dissertation, University of North Carolina, 1958.

Munro, Dana G. *Intervention and Dollar Diplomacy in the Caribbean, 1900–1921.* Princeton: Princeton University Press, 1964.

——— *The United States and the Caribbean Republics, 1921–1933.* Princeton: Princeton University Press, 1974.

Mustelier, Gustavo. *La extinción del negro.* Havana: Imprenta de Rambla, Bouza, 1912.

Nash, Dennison, and Schaw, Louis C. "Achievement and Acculturation: A Japanese Example." In *Context and Meaning in Cultural Anthropology,* edited by Melford E. Spiro. New York: Free Press, 1965.

——— "Personality and Adaptation in an Overseas Enclave." *Human Organization* 21, no. 4 (Winter 1962–1963).

Navarro, Vicente. "Health Services in Cuba." *New England Journal of Medicine* 287, no. 10 (November 9, 1972).

Nelson, Lowry. *Cuba: The Measure of a Revolution.* Minneapolis: University of Minnesota Press, 1972.

——— *Rural Cuba.* 1950. Reprint. New York: Octagon Books, 1970.

——— "The Social Class Structure in Cuba." In *Materiales para el estudio de la clase media en América Latina: la clase media en México y Cuba,* edited by Theo R. Crevenna. Vol. 2. Washington, D.C.: Unión Panamericana, 1950.

Newman, Philip C. *Cuba before Castro: An Economic Appraisal.* New Delhi: Prentice-Hall of India, 1965.

"1969." *Con la guardia en alto* 8, no. 9 (September 1969).

Nodal, Roberto. "Current Trends of Anthropological Research in Cuba." Caribbean Series, special research report. Milwaukee: University of Wisconsin, Department of Afro-American Studies, August 1976.

Nogueira Rivero, Gerardo. "El sincretismo religioso como una causa desencadenante y/o determinante de síndromes neuróticos y pseudopsicóticos en el niño cubano." *Revista del hospital psiquiátrico de La Habana* 3, no. 1 (January–March 1962).

"Notas económicas: nueva luz sobre la agricultura privada." *Cuba socialista,* no. 60 (August 1966).

"El núcleo de revolucionarios activos y algunos aspectos de su funcionamiento." *Cuba socialista,* no. 7 (March 1962).

Núñez Jiménez, Antonio. "La reunión de las academias de ciencias socialistas." *Finlay: revista médico-histórica cubana,* no. 8 (January–June 1967).

——— "Revolución agraria en Cuba." *INRA* 2, no. 6 (June 1961).

O'Connor, James. *The Origins of Socialism in Cuba.* Ithaca: Cornell University Press, 1970.

Oráa, Remberto de. "El piropo en La Habana." *Signos* 5, no. 1 (September–December 1973).

Ordóñez, Jacinto. "Seminaries in the Seventies." *Cuba Review* 5, no. 3 (September 1975).

"Organización y funcionamiento de un núcleo por departamentos." *Cuba socialista,* no. 8 (April 1962).

Organization of American States, Inter-American Commission on Human Rights. *Fifth Report on the Status of Human Rights in Cuba.* OEA/Ser. G/CP/INF. 872/76, June 1, 1976.

———— Report Regarding the Situation of Human Rights in Cuba. OEA/Ser. L/V/II.17, Doc. 4 rev., June 13, 1967.

———— Second Report on the Situation of Political Prisoners in Cuba OEA/Ser. L/V/II.23, Doc. 6, rev. 1, November 17, 1970.

Orris, Peter. "The Role of the Consumer in the Cuban National Health System." M.P.H. thesis, Yale University, 1970.

Ortega, Luis. "Las raíces del Castrismo." In Diez años de revolución cubana. Río Piedras: Editorial San Juan, 1970.

Ortiz, Fernando. La crisis política cubana. Havana: Imprenta y Papelería La Universal, 1919.

———— La decadencia cubana. Havana: Imprenta y Papelería La Universal, 1924.

———— "Defensa cubana contra el racismo antisemita." Revista bimestre cubana 70 (1955).

———— "Por la integración de blancos y negros." Estudios afrocubanos 5 (1945–1946).

Otero, José M., and Castaño, Gladys. "La mujer en la producción." Mujeres 10, no. 8 (1970).

Otero, Lisandro, with Martínez Hinojosa, Francisco. Cultural Policy in Cuba. Paris: UNESCO, 1972.

P., Mongo. "Brochazos: la minifalda." Bohemia 67, no. 11 (March 14, 1975).

Padula, Alfred L., Jr. "The Fall of the Bourgeoisie: Cuba, 1959–1961." Ph.D. dissertation, University of New Mexico, 1974.

Partido Conservador Nacional. Programa. Havana: Imprenta La Prueba, 1919.

Pavón, Ramiro. "El empleo femenino en Cuba." Santiago, no. 20 (December 1975).

Pazos, Felipe. "Comentarios a dos artículos sobre la revolución cubana." El trimestre económico 29, no. 113 (January–March 1962).

Pedrosa, Rafael. "Apertura de la conferencia." Cuba azúcar, November–December 1968, pp. 9–11.

———— "Informe del Presidente de la ATAC." Cuba azúcar, October–December 1970, pp. 52–55.

Peraza, Fermín. Diccionario biográfico cubano. Havana: Ediciones Anuario Bibliográfico Cubano, 1951.

Perdomo, Asteria. "La lucha del regional de San José de las Lajas por dominar las tareas de la producción." Cuba socialista, no. 32 (April 1964).

Pereira, Manuel. "Exploración y explotación del azúcar." Cuba internacional 7, no. 69 (May 1975).

Pérez, Eutimio. "Asamblea de la alimentación." Verde olivo 13, no. 5 (January 31, 1971).

Pérez, Lisandro. "The Demographic Dimensions of the Educational Problem in Socialist Cuba." Cuban Studies 7, no. 1 (January 1977).

Pérez, Louis A., Jr. Army Politics in Cuba, 1898–1958. Pittsburgh: University of Pittsburgh Press, 1976.

———— "Army Politics in Socialist Cuba." Journal of Latin American Studies 8, no. 2 (November 1976).

———— "Capital, Bureaucrats and Policy: The Economic Contours of United States–Cuban Relations, 1916–1921." Inter-American Economic Affairs 29, no. 1 (Summer 1975).

———— "Perspectives on the Rebel Army." Mimeographed.

Pérez Cubillas, José. "El impuesto sobre la renta personal y el cincuentenario de la República." *Anuario de la Facultad de Ciencias Sociales y Derecho Público,* 1952.

Pérez de la Riva, Francisco. *El café: historia de su cultivo y explotación en Cuba.* Havana: Jesús Montero, 1944.

Pérez-López, Jorge. "An Index of Cuban Industrial Output, 1930–1958." Ph.D. dissertation, State University of New York–Albany, 1974.

Pérez-Stable, Marifeli. "Cuba's Workers, 1975: A Preliminary Analysis." Paper presented at meeting, Latin American Studies Association, March 1976, in Atlanta. Mimeographed.

———— "The Emancipation of Cuban Women." Paper presented at Conference on Women and Change, Institute of Cuban Studies and Boston University, May 6–7, 1977, in Boston. Mimeographed.

———— "Los sindicatos en perspectiva." Paper presented at Seminar on Institutionalization in Cuba, Institute of Cuban Studies, March 24–29, 1975, in Caracas. Mimeographed.

"Perfeccionamiento del sistema nacional de educación." *Bohemia* 67, no. 5 (January 31, 1975).

Periú, María de los Angeles. "Experiencias de la educación obrera y campesina en Cuba." *Cuba socialista,* no. 42 (February 1965).

"Perspectivas de la industria cañera cubana: su integración y principales problemas a resolver a mediano y largo plazo." *Cuba azúcar,* April–June 1976, pp. 5–11.

Petrenko, F. "Avangard Kubinskovo Naroda." *Partinaia Zhizn,* no. 8 (April 1973).

Pettitt, Michael A. "Social and Economic Change in the Community around a Sugar Mill in Cuba." Ph.D. dissertation, University of California–Berkeley, 1973.

Petushko, Ivan. "Desarrollo integral de la industria azucarera de Cuba." *América Latina,* no. 1 (1975).

Phillips, Ruby Hart. *Cuba: Island of Paradox.* New York: McDowell, Obolensky, 1959.

Piedra, Carlos M. *La inamovilidad de los trabajadores.* Havana: Cultural, 1945.

Pino, Mario del. "La donación de sangre en Cuba." *Cuadernos de historia de la salud pública,* no. 43 (1969).

Pino Santos, Oscar. *El asalto a Cuba por la oligarquía financiera yanqui.* Havana: Casa de las Américas, 1973.

Pividal Padrón, Francisco; García Espinosa, Gilberto; Otero, Margarita; and Area, Manuel. "La enseñanza universitaria por medio de encuentros o reuniones periódicas." *Sobre educación superior,* July–December 1971.

"Plan de fortalecimiento de los organismos de la ANAP." *ANAP* 5, no. 4 (April 1965).

Plasencia, Azucena. "Cuadros administrativos." *Bohemia* 67, no. 26 (June 27, 1975).

———— "Montaña adentro: la batalla del sexto grado." *Bohemia* 67, no. 10 (March 7, 1975).

Playa Girón: derrota del imperialismo. Havana: Ediciones R, 1962.

Pollitt, Brian H. "Employment Plans, Performance and Future Prospects in Cuba." In *Third World Employment,* edited by Richard Jolly et al. London: Penguin Books, 1973.

———— "Estudios acerca del nivel de vida rural en la Cuba prerevolucionaria: un análisis crítico." *Teoría y práctica,* nos. 42–43 (November–December 1967).

Portocarrero, J. R. *El problema político-financiero-social de Cuba.* Havana, 1921.

Portuondo, José Antonio. "Itinerario estético de la revolución cubana." *Unión* 14, no. 3 (September 1975).

Portuondo de Castro, J. M., et al. "Observaciones sobre 50 comas diabéticas estudiadas en el hospital universitario General Calixto García." *Archivos del Hospital Universitario General Calixto García* 7, no. 6 (November–December 1955).

Pospisil, M. F. "El peso y la talla de los escolares de la ciudad de La Habana." *Serie ciencias biológicas*, no. 3 (May 1969).

"Primer activo nacional de educación interna del partido." *Ediciones COR*, no. 16 (1971).

"Primer encuentro de egresados del ITM." *Verde olivo* 17, no. 27 (July 6, 1975).

"Primera asamblea de balance del partido." *Verde olivo* 8, no. 51 (December 24, 1967).

"Primera asamblea de balance del partido comunista de Cuba en el cuerpo blindado." *Verde olivo* 9, no. 7 (February 18, 1968).

Proclamas y leyes del gobierno provisional de la revolución, 1959. Havana: Editorial Lex, 1959.

Prohías, Rafael, and Casal, Lourdes. *The Cuban Minority in the United States: Preliminary Report on Need Identification and Program Evaluation.* Washington, D.C.: Cuban National Planning Council, 1974.

"El proyecto de ley del servicio militar obligatorio." *Cuba socialista*, no. 28 (December 1963).

"El proyecto de ley del servicio militar obligatorio." *Verde olivo* 4, no. 47 (November 24, 1963).

Purcell, Susan Kaufman. "Modernizing Women for a Modern Society: The Cuban Case." In *Female and Male in Latin America*, edited by Ann Pescatello. Pittsburgh: University of Pittsburgh Press, 1973.

"El PURS en las montañas de Oriente." *Cuba socialista*, no. 24 (August 1963).

"¿Qué es el Poder Local?" *Bohemia* 59, no. 36 (September 8, 1967).

Quinta, Joaquín. "La maniobra." *Verde olivo* 17, no. 50 (December 14, 1975).

Quintela, Carlos. "La juventud cubana y la revolución." *Cuba socialista*, no. 8 (April 1962).

Raggi, Carlos M. "Contribución al estudio de las clases medias en Cuba." In *Materiales para el estudio de la clase media en América Latina: la clase media en México y Cuba*, edited by Theo R. Crevenna. Vol. 2. Washington, D.C.: Unión Panamericana, 1950.

Ramos, Ana. "La mujer y la revolución en Cuba." *Casa de las Américas* 11, nos. 65–66 (March–June 1971).

Randall, Margaret. "La mujer cubana en 1974." *Casa de las Américas* 15, no. 89 (March–April 1975).

Ravelo Nariño, Agustín. *El contrato de arrendamiento de finca rústica en la legislación cubana.* Santiago: Tipografía San Román, 1956.

Reckford, Barry. *Does Fidel Eat More than Your Father?* London: André Deutsch, 1971.

"La reforma de la enseñanza superior en Cuba." *Universidad de La Habana*, no. 154 (January–February 1962).

Regalado, Antero. "El camino de la cooperación agraria en Cuba." *Cuba socialista*, no. 22 (June 1963).

———— "Cinco años de la vida de la ANAP." *Cuba socialista*, no. 57 (May 1966).

———— "El crédito a los pequeños agricultores en Cuba." *ANAP* 6, no. 10 (October 1966).

———— "Credits for Small Farmers in Cuba." *World Marxist Review* 8, no. 3 (March 1965).

———— "Esa alianza empezó cuando los campesinos del Realengo 18 se unieron para enfrentarse a los latifundistas y tuvieron a su lado a los obreros." *ANAP*, nos. 9–10 (September–October 1964).

———— "Las funciones de la ANAP." *Cuba socialista*, no. 35 (July 1964).

———— "Proclamamos que a ocho años de revolución nuestra clase obrera tiene un magnífico aliado en nuestro campesinado." *ANAP* 7, nos 5–6 (May–June 1967).

"Reglamento general de la ANAP." *ANAP* 7, nos 5–6 (May–June 1967).

"Rendición de cuentas." *Bohemia* 67, no. 3 (March 28, 1975).

"La resolución 120 del INRA constituye una nueva medida de justicia revolucionaria." *ANAP* 6, no. 7 (July 1966).

"Resolución sobre la política de formación, selección, ubicación, promoción, y superación de los cuadros." *Economía y desarrollo*, no. 36 (July–August 1976).

"Las resoluciones y acuerdos del primer congreso del partido comunista de Cuba." *Verde olivo* 18, no. 18 (May 2, 1976).

"Respuesta del comandante Fidel Castro, primer secretario del Partido Comunista de Cuba y primer ministro del Gobierno Revolucionario, a las declaraciones del Gobierno chino." *Política internacional* 4, no. 13 (First Quarter 1966).

"Reunión nacional de chequeo de la emulación." *Con la guardia en alto* 6, no. 2 (February 1967).

"Reunión nacional de instructores para el trabajo de la UJC en las FAR." *Verde olivo* 18, no. 9 (February 29, 1976).

"Reunión nacional de septiembre." *Con la guardia en alto* 8, no. 10 (October 1969).

Reyes Trejo, Alfredo. "El campesino cubano marcha con su revolución." *Verde olivo* 16, no. 20 (May 19, 1974).

———— "Ejército de la tiranía." *Verde olivo* 7, no. 45 (November 12, 1966).

Riera Hernández, Mario. *Cuba libre, 1875–1958*. Miami: Colonial Press, 1968.

———— *Cuba política, 1899–1955*. Havana: Impresora Modelo, 1955.

———— *Historial obrero cubano*. Miami: Rema Press, 1965.

———— *Un presidente constructivo*. Miami, 1966.

Risquet, Jorge. "La construcción del Partido en la provincia de Oriente." *Cuba socialista*, no. 15 (November 1962).

Ritter, Archibald R. M. *The Economic Development of Revolutionary Cuba: Strategy and Performance*. New York: Praeger, 1974.

Rivas Pérez, Venancio. "Evaluación de los oficiales de las FAR." *Verde olivo* 17, no. 9 (March 2, 1975).

Rivero, Adolfo. "La Unión de Jóvenes Comunistas de Cuba." *Cuba socialista*, no. 12 (August 1962).

Rivero Collado, Carlos. *Los sobrinos del tío Sam*. Havana: Instituto Cubano del Libro, 1976.

Rivero Muñiz, José. *El primer partido socialista cubano*. Havana: Imprenta Nacional, 1962.

Roberts, C. Paul, and Hamour, Mukhtar, eds. *Cuba, 1968: Supplement to the Statistical Abstract of Latin America.* Los Angeles: University of California, Latin American Center, 1970.

Roca, Blas. "Algunos problemas de las relaciones cubano-americanas en la postguerra." *Fundamentos* 5, no. 44 (April 1945).

———— "Algunos problemas de nuestro trabajo electoral." *Fundamentos* 3, nos. 27–28 (November–December 1943).

———— "El camino hacia la unidad nacional." *Fundamentos* 5, no. 43 (March 1945).

———— "Dos cartas." *Fundamentos* 5, no. 44 (April 1945).

———— "Fortalezcamos la vigilancia revolucionaria en nuestras filas." *Fundamentos* 3, no. 19 (March 1943).

———— "La lucha ideológica contra las sectas religiosas." *Cuba socialista*, no. 22 (June 1963).

———— "Nueva etapa de la revolución cubana." *Cuba socialista*, no. 5 (January 1962).

———— "Significación y alcance de la entrevista Grau-CTC." *Fundamentos* 4, no. 37 (September 1944).

———— "Specific Features of Socialist Democracy in Cuba." *World Marxist Review* 20, no. 2 (February 1977).

———— *El triunfo popular en las elecciones.* Havana, 1946.

Roca, Blas; Rodríguez, Carlos Rafael; and Luzardo, Manuel. *En defensa del pueblo.* Havana: Arrow Press, 1945.

Roca, Sergio. "Cuban Economic Policy and Ideology: The Ten Million Ton Sugar Harvest." *Sage Professional Papers in International Studies* 4, no. 02-044, 1976.

———— "Distributional Effects of the Cuban Revolution: Urban versus Rural Allocations." Paper presented at 88th annual meeting, American Economic Association, December 1975, in Dallas, Tex. Mimeographed.

Roche, Marcel. "Notes on Science in Cuba." *Science* 169, no. 3943 (July 24, 1970).

Rochon, Lise. "La sociedad agropecuaria 'Jesús Feliú': un caso de cambio en el medio rural bajo un régimen socialista de transición." *Etnología y folklore*, no. 4 (July–December 1967).

Rodríguez, Andrés. "Alta conciencia, alta productividad." *Bohemia* 67, no. 4 (January 24, 1975).

Rodríguez, Carlos Rafael. "El abastecimiento nacional." In *En defensa del pueblo*, by Blas Roca, Carlos Rafael Rodríguez, and Manuel Luzardo. Havana: Arrow Press, 1945.

———— "The Advantages of Socialism Are the Basis of Our Achievements." *New Times*, no. 1 (January 1974).

———— "Cuatro años de reforma agraria." *Cuba socialista*, no. 21 (May 1963).

———— "The Cuban Revolution and the Peasantry." *World Marxist Review* 8, no. 10 (October 1965).

———— "Las elecciones del primero de junio." *Fundamentos* 4, nos. 34–35 (June–July 1944).

———— "Los logros de la economía cubana." *Economía y desarrollo*, no. 25 (September–October 1974).

———— "El nuevo camino de la agricultura cubana." *Cuba socialista*, no. 27 (November 1963).

———— "Problemas del arte en la revolución." *Revolución y cultura* 1, no. 1 (October 1967).

———— "La revolución cubana y el campesinado." *Cuba socialista*, no. 53 (January 1966).

Rodríguez, Delfín, et al. "Latifundismo y especulación: notas para la historia agraria de la Isla de Pinos, 1900–1958." *Serie Isla de Pinos*, no. 23.

Rodríguez, Mario. "El estado mayor." *Verde olivo* 17, no. 47 (November 23, 1975).

———— "Experiencias del trabajo de educación del PURSC en Matanzas." *Cuba socialista*, no. 41 (January 1965).

Rodríguez Balari, Eugenio. "Trabajo y desarrollo del Instituto de la Demanda Interna." *Economía y desarrollo*, no. 21 (January–February 1974).

Rodríguez Beruff, Jorge. "La reforma agraria cubana (1959–1964): el cambio institucional." *Revista de ciencias sociales* 14, no. 2 (June 1970).

Roig de Leuchsenring, Emilio. *La colonia superviva*. Havana: Imprenta El Siglo XX, 1925.

———— *Males y vicios de Cuba republicana*. Havana: Oficina del Historiador de la Ciudad de La Habana, 1959.

Rojas, Pedro. "En su lugar la educación." *ANAP*, November 1973.

———— "Iniciado el curso de orientación política, 1973–1974." *ANAP*, November 1973.

Ronda Marisy, Henry. "Cuerpo extraño en el esófago." *Revista cubana de cirugía* 13, no. 6 (November–December 1974).

Rosell, Mirta. *Luchas obreras contra Machado*. Havana: Instituto Cubano del Libro, 1973.

Rouma, Georges. "Le développement physique de l'écolier cubain: blanc, nègre et mulâtre." *Bulletin de la Société d'Anthropologie de Bruxelles* 35 (1920).

Rozitchner, Leon. *Moral burguesa y revolución*. 3rd ed. Buenos Aires: Editorial Tiempo Contemporáneo, 1969.

Rozsa, Györy. "La organización de la ciencia y la cultura en Cuba." *Revista mexicana de sociología* 31, no. 3 (July–September 1969).

Ruiz Miranda, Silvio, et al. "Frecuencia de las quemaduras en niños." *Revista cubana de pediatría* 46, no. 6 (November–December 1974).

Sáenz, Tirso W., and García Capote, Emilio. "Algunos conceptos básicos sobre política científica." *Economía y desarrollo*, no. 27 (January–February 1975).

Salado, Minerva. "La ciencia cierta." *Cuba internacional* 6, no. 59 (July 1974).

Saladrigas, René. "Criterios para una reestructuración político-administrativa de Cuba." *Cuba socialista*, no. 17 (January 1963).

Sánchez Roca, Mariano. *Compilación ordenada y completa de la legislación cubana de 1951 a 1958*. Vol. 4. Havana: Editorial Lex, 1960.

Sánchez, Roig, Mario, and Gómez de la Maza, Federico. *La pesca en Cuba*. Havana: Ministerio de Agricultura, 1952.

Sandoval, José Enrique. "Ordenamiento social." In *Historia de la nación cubana*, edited by Ramiro Guerra y Sánchez et al. Vol. 9. Havana: Editorial Historia de la Nación Cubana, 1952.

Sanguily, Manuel. *Defensa de Cuba*. Edited by Emilio Roig de Leuchsenring. Havana: Oficina del Historiador de la Ciudad de La Habana, 1948.

San Martín, Marta, and Bonachea, Ramón. "The Military Dimension of the Cuban

Revolution." In *The Cuban Revolution,* edited by Irving L. Horowitz. 2nd ed. New Brunswick, N.J.: Transaction Books, 1972.

Santovenia, Emeterio S., and Shelton, Raúl M. *Cuba y su historia.* 2nd ed. Miami: Rema Press, 1966.

Sargent, Dudley. "The Height and Weight of the Cuban Teachers." *Popular Science Monthly* 58, no. 5 (March 1901).

Sarusky, Jaime. "Chabacanería, ¡no!" *Bohemia* 67, no. 14 (April 4, 1975).

"Science and Education in Cuba." *International Affairs,* no. 1 (January 1976).

"Sección política de la marina de guerra revolucionaria." *Verde olivo* 9, no. 2 (January 14, 1968).

Seers, Dudley, ed. *Cuba: The Economic and Social Revolution.* Chapel Hill: University of North Carolina Press, 1964.

"Segunda asamblea de balance del partido comunista de Cuba en el estado mayor general." *Verde olivo* 10, no. 49 (December 7, 1969).

"Segunda asamblea de balance del partido communista de Cuba en una unidad en Matanzas." *Verde olivo* 10, no. 43 (October 26, 1969).

"Segunda asamblea de balance del partido en el ejército del centro." *Verde olivo* 10, no. 44 (November 2, 1969).

"Segunda reunión del partido en las Fuerzas Armadas Revolucionarias." *Verde olivo* 11, no. 40 (October 4, 1970).

"El II congreso nacional de la ANAP." *Cuba socialista,* no. 25 (September 1963).

Seiglie y Llata, Oscar. *El contrato de arrendamiento de finca rústica, el latifundio, y la legislación azucarera.* Havana: Editorial Lex, 1953.

"La selección del trabajador ejemplar." *Cuba socialista,* no. 9 (May 1962).

Silverman, Bertram, ed. *Man and Socialism in Cuba: The Great Debate.* New York: Atheneum, 1971.

Simón, Francisco. "La tragedia del arrendatario rural." *Tierra libre* 4, no. 8 (August 1940).

"Síntesis de acuerdos tomados por la Dirección Nacional de los CDR en su última reunión." *Con la guardia en alto* 7, no. 11 (November 1968).

"Síntesis de las conclusiones." *ANAP* 8, no. 2 (February 1968).

"Sistema de registro militar." *Verde olivo* 17, no. 12 (March 23, 1975).

Sklar, Barry A. "Cuba: Normalization of Relations." Issue Brief no. IB75030. Library of Congress, Congressional Research Service, March 3, 1976.

Smith, Earl E. T. *The Fourth Floor.* New York: Random House, 1962.

Smith, Robert F. *The United States and Cuba: Business and Diplomacy, 1917–1960.* New Haven: College and University Press, 1960.

"Sobre el trabajo político en el aseguramiento a los ejercicios de tiro con armas de infantería." *Verde olivo* 16, no. 24 (June 16, 1974).

"Sobre las siembras a partido." *ANAP* 8, no. 2 (February 1968).

"Sobre las ventas por la libre." *ANAP* 7, no. 12 (December 1967).

Solaún, Mauricio. "El fracaso de la democracia en Cuba." *Aportes,* no. 13 (July 1969).

Sorín, Mónica, and Gavilando, Luis. "Acerca del rendimiento académico en una escuela universitaria." *Etnología y folklore,* no. 2 (July–December 1966).

Soto, Lionel. "Dos años de instrucción revolucionaria." *Cuba socialista,* no. 18 (February 1963).

———— "Las escuelas de instrucción revolucionaria en el ciclo político-técnico." *Cuba socialista*, no. 41 (January 1965).

———— "Las escuelas de instrucción revolucionaria en una nueva fase." *Cuba socialista*, no. 30 (February 1964).

———— "Las escuelas de instrucción revolucionaria y la formación de cuadros." *Cuba socialista*, no. 3 (November 1961).

———— "Nuevo desarrollo de la instrucción revolucionaria." *Cuba socialista*, no. 12 (August 1962).

———— "El quinto aniversario de las escuelas de instrucción revolucionaria." *Cuba socialista*, no. 53 (January 1966).

Soto Pradera, Emilio, et al. "Cifras estadísticas de un año de trabajo en la unidad de prematuros de la Clínica de Maternidad Obrera de La Habana." *Revista cubana de pediatría* 27, no. 5 (May 1955).

Soto Pradera, Emilio, and Silverio Latour, Juan. "Dosificación de calcio en la sangre de 395 prematuros aparentemente normales." *Revista cubana de pediatría* 30, no. 6 (June 1958).

Sotolongo, Pedro Luis. "Planeamiento a mediano plazo de las investigaciones científicas." *Economía y desarrollo*, no. 26 (November–December 1974).

Stabler, George M. "Bejucal: Social Values and Changes in Agricultural Practices." Ph.D. dissertation, Michigan State University, 1958.

Stanley, John, and Pearton, Maurice. *The International Trade in Arms*. New York: Praeger, 1972.

Steffens, Heidi. "Notes from Abroad: Cuba—The Day Women Took Over Havana." *Ms.* 3, no. 10 (April 1975).

Stokes, William. "The Cuban Parliamentary System in Action, 1940–1947." *Journal of Politics* 11, no. 2 (May 1949).

———— "The 'Cuban Revolution' and the Presidential Elections of 1948." *Hispanic American Historical Review* 32, no. 1 (February 1951).

———— "National and Local Violence in Cuban Politics." *Southwestern Social Science Quarterly* 34, no. 2 (September 1953).

Suárez, Andrés. "La construcción del socialismo en Cuba: el papel del partido." Paper presented at Seminar on Institutionalization in Cuba, Institute of Cuban Studies, March 24–29, 1975, in Caracas. Mimeographed.

———— *Cuba: Castroism and Communism, 1959–1960*. Cambridge, Mass.: M.I.T. Press, 1967.

———— "How the Cuban Regime Works." Paper presented at meeting, South East Conference on Latin American Studies, April 1972, in Chapel Hill, N.C. Mimeographed.

———— "The Politics of Cuba under Castro: How Socialist is Cuba?" Paper presented at annual meeting, American Political Science Association, September 1973, in New Orleans, La. Mimeographed.

———— "Soviet Influence and Cuban Factions." In *Soviet and Chinese Influence in the Third World*, edited by Alvin Z. Rubinstein. New York: Praeger, 1975.

Suárez Amador, José. "Octavo aniversario de L.C.B." *Verde olivo* 11, no. 28 (July 12, 1970).

Suárez Moreno, José. "El código de familia." *Verde olivo* 16, no. 24 (June 16, 1974).

Suárez Núñez, José. *El gran culpable*. Caracas, 1963.

Suárez Rivas, Eduardo. *Un pueblo crucificado*. Miami: Service Offset Printers, 1964.

Suchlicki, Jaime. *University Students and Revolution in Cuba, 1920–1968*. Coral Gables, Fla.: University of Miami Press, 1969.

Sutherland, Elizabeth. *The Youngest Revolution: A Personal Report on Cuba*. New York: Dial Press, 1969.

Tang, Peter S. H., and Maloney, Joan. *The Chinese Communist Impact on Cuba*. Chestnut Hill, Mass.: Research Institute on the Sino-Soviet Bloc, 1962.

"Tarea no. 1 de los CDR: vigilancia revolucionaria." *Con la guardia en alto* 7, no. 12 (December 1968).

"Tercer activo del Partido en la DAAFAR." *Verde olivo* 18, no. 28 (July 11, 1976).

"III congreso de la FEEM." *Verde olivo* 16, no. 1 (January 6, 1974).

Testé, Ismael. *Historia eclesiástica de Cuba*. Burgos: Tipografia de la Editorial El Monte Carmelo, 1969.

"Thirty Years of Socialist Progress." *World Marxist Review* 18, no. 1 (January 1975).

Thomas, Hugh. *Cuba: The Pursuit of Freedom*. New York: Harper & Row, 1971.

Torre, Horacio de la, et al. "Comunicación interventricular." *Revista cubana de cardiología* 20, nos. 3–4 (July–December 1959).

Torre Mulhare, Mirta de la. "Sexual Ideology in Pre-Castro Cuba: A Cultural Analysis." Ph.D. dissertation, University of Pittsburgh, 1969.

Torroella, Gustavo. *Estudio de la juventud cubana*. Havana: Comisión Nacional Cubana de la UNESCO, 1963.

"El trabajo de las organizaciones políticas y las organizaciones del partido y la U.J.C. en aseguramiento de preparación política de oficiales, clases, y soldados." *Verde olivo* 16, no. 23 (June 9, 1974).

"Trabajo político partidista para elevar la conciencia técnica." *Verde olivo* 16, no. 22 (June 2, 1974).

"Transformación de la familia campesina." *ANAP*, December 1973.

Trelles, Carlos M. *El progreso (1902 a 1905) y el retroceso (1906 a 1922) de la República de Cuba*. Havana: Imprenta El Score, 1923.

Triana García, José. "Complicaciones de la cirugía del tiroides." *Revista cubana de cirugía* 14, no. 1 (January–February 1975).

Tribunal de Cuentas. *Recopilación y análisis de los ingresos presupuestales de Cuba*. Havana, 1953.

Unanue, Emilio. *Siclemia pasiva en Cuba*. Havana, 1941.

United Fruit Company. *Some Facts Regarding the Development and Operation of the United Fruit Company Sugar Properties in the Republic of Cuba*. Preston, Cuba, 1944.

U.S., Arms Control and Disarmament Agency. *World Military Expenditures, 1971*. Washington, D.C.: Government Printing Office, 1972.

———— *World Military Expenditures and Arms Trade, 1963–1973*. Washington, D.C.: Government Printing Office, 1975.

U.S., Congress, House, Committee on Foreign Affairs, Subcommittee on Inter-American Affairs. "Soviet Activities in Cuba." In *Hearings*, 92nd Congress, 2nd session. Washington, D.C.: Government Printing Office, 1972.

———— "Soviet Activities in Cuba." In *Hearings*, 93rd Congress. Washington, D.C.: Government Printing Office, 1974.

U.S., Congress, Senate, Committee on the Judiciary, Subcommittee to Investigate the Administration of the Internal Security Act and Other Internal Security Laws. *Hearings,* 86th Congress, 2nd session, August–September 1960, and 87th Congress, 1st session, January–February 1961, February 1962. Washington, D.C.: Government Printing Office.

U.S., Congress, Senate, Select Committee to Study Governmental Operations with Respect to Intelligence Activities. *Alleged Assassination Plots Involving Foreign Leaders: An Interim Report.* 94th Congress, 1st session. Washington, D.C.: Government Printing Office, 1975.

U.S., Department of Commerce. "United States Commercial Relations with Cuba: A Survey." In U.S., Congress, House, Committee on International Relations, Subcommittees on International Trade and Commerce and on International Organizations, "U.S. Trade Embargo of Cuba," *Hearings,* 94th Congress, 2nd session. Washington, D.C.: Government Printing Office, 1976.

U.S., Department of Commerce, Bureau of Foreign Commerce. *Investment in Cuba.* Washington, D.C.: Government Printing Office, 1956.

Universidad Central Marta Abreu de Las Villas. *La educación rural en Las Villas.* Havana: Impresores Ucar, García, 1959.

Universidad de La Habana. *La Universidad de La Habana.* Havana, 1970.

——— *La Universidad de La Habana al Consejo Ejecutivo y a la Asamblea General de la Unión de Universidades de América Latina.* Havana, 1964.

Valdés, Nelson P. *Cuba: ¿socialismo democrático o burocratismo colectivista?* Bogotá: Ediciones Tercer Mundo, 1973.

——— "La diplomacia del azúcar." *Aportes,* no. 18 (October 1970).

——— "Health and Revolution in Cuba." *Science and Society* 35, no. 3 (Fall 1971).

——— "Women and Sexual Relations in Cuba: Family, Consensual Unions, Divorce and Prostitution before 1959." Paper presented at Conference on Women and Change, Institute of Cuban Studies and Boston University, May 6–7, 1977, in Boston. Mimeographed.

Valdés, Nelson P., and Bonachea, Rolando. "Fidel Castro y la política estudiantil de 1947 a 1952." *Aportes,* no. 22 (October 1971).

Valdés, Ramiro. "Discurso pronunciado en la clausura de la II reunión nacional de las secretarías de construcción del partido." *Ediciones COR,* no. 14 (1971).

Valdés Pérez, Enrique. "Así soy yo." *Bohemia* 67, no. 20 (May 16, 1975).

Valledor, T., et al. "Tuberculosis primaria de la piel en la infancia." *Revista cubana de pediatría* 26, no. 3 (March 1954).

Varona Martínez, Eduardo, and Gonzalez Labrada, Rafael. *El colono.* Havana: Impresores Ucar, García, 1958.

Vascos, Fidel. "Brigada invasora Che Guevara: año 1." *Verde olivo* 9, no. 45 (November 10, 1968).

Viamonte, E. G. "Impresiones de una visita." *Verde olivo* 17, no. 38 (September 21, 1975).

"Vida de la organización revolucionaria." *Cuba socialista,* no. 8 (April 1962).

"Vida de la organización revolucionaria." *Cuba socialista,* no. 10 (June 1962).

"Vida de la organización revolucionaria." *Cuba socialista,* no. 14 (October 1962).

Vidal, Heriberto, et al. "Pesquisaje de hemoglobinas anormales en un hospital pediátrico." *Revista cubana de pediatría* 46, no. 2 (March–April 1974).

Vignier, Marta. "Una entrevista de Prensa Latina." *Con la guardia en alto* 6, no. 2 (February 1967).

Vilaseca, Salvador. "El Banco Nacional de Cuba y los sistemas de financiamiento." *Nuestra industria: revista económica*, no. 11 (1965).

Vilches González, Isidro A. *Derecho cubano del trabajo*. Havana: Jesús Montero, 1948.

Volkov, Valery. "Isle of Pines: The Past and the Present." *New Times*, no. 30 (July 1975).

Volsky, George. "Cuba Fifteen Years Later." *Current History* 66, no. 389 (January 1974).

Wallich, Henry C. *Monetary Problems of an Export Economy*. Cambridge, Mass.: Harvard University Press, 1950.

Wilkerson, Loree. *Fidel Castro's Political Programs from Reformism to Marxism-Leninism*. Gainesville: University of Florida Press, 1965.

Williams, William Appleman. *The United States, Cuba and Castro*. New York: Monthly Review Press, 1962.

Wolter del Río, Germán. "La hacienda de la república independiente." In *Historia de la nación cubana*, edited by Ramiro Guerra y Sánchez et al. Vol. 9. Havana: Editorial Historia de la Nación Cubana, 1952.

Wood, Bryce. *The Making of the Good Neighbor Policy*. New York: Columbia University Press, 1961.

Wood, Dennis. "The Long Revolution: Class Relations and Political Conflict in Cuba, 1868–1968." *Science and Society* 34, no. 1 (Spring 1970).

Woodward, Ralph Lee. "Urban Labor and Communism in Cuba." *Caribbean Studies* 3, no. 3 (October 1963).

"Y tu, y tu, y tu . . . ¿por qué vas a Camagüey?" *Cuba* 7 (June 1968).

Yasells, Eduardo. "El partido en el Turquino." *Verde olivo* 4, no. 40 (October 6, 1963).

———— "Reseña de una asamblea." *Verde olivo* 8, no. 51 (December 24, 1967).

Yayo Morejón, G. "Ante el V seminario científico del CENIC." *Bohemia* 67, no. 25 (June 20, 1975).

Yglesias, Jose. *In the Fist of the Revolution: Life in a Cuban Country Town*. New York: Vintage Books, 1969.

Zafesov, G. "Cuba: Signs of Momentous Changes." *International Affairs* (Moscow), no. 9 (September 1974).

Zayas Portela, Enrique, and Larraondo Núñez, Fidel. "Estudios sobre la enfermedad reumática." *Revista cubana de cardiología* 14, no. 1 (January–March 1953).

Zeitlin, Maurice. *Revolutionary Politics and the Cuban Working Class*. New York: Harper Torchbooks, 1970.

INDEX

Abakuá, 49, 466–467

ABC party, 59, 77, 99–100, 102

Academy of Science, 396–398, 400, 403–407, 422; centralization in, 397; and Institute for Sugar-Cane Research, 396, 400

Acción Republicana party (–1944), 59, 99–101; (1944–), 102–104, 107

Acevedo, Rogelio, 373

Acosta, Armando, 311, 313, 533

Advanced Peasants' Movement, 296–297, 456–457, 459. See also Exemplary

Advanced Workers' Movement, 275, 278–279, 318–319. See also Exemplary

Agency for Agricultural Development (DAP), 160

Agramonte, Roberto, 103, 113–114, 132

Agrarian reform: (–1959), 78, 129–130, 430–431, 433–435, 437–438, 462; (1959–), 113, 145, 173–174, 423–424, 440–441; act (1959), 143, 146, 195, 209, 234, 438, 443, 447–448, 462; act (1963), 182, 201, 209, 445–447, 451–452; economic effects of, 387–389; policies, 424, 452–453, 459, 463

Agricultural workers, 22, 23, 92, 143, 174, 182, 202, 275, 293, 296–297, 320, 423–424, 428, 431, 436–438, 440, 442–445, 447–448, 453, 457, 459, 462–463, 491; standard of living of, 73–74, 186, 228, 390, 428, 441, 457; and Sugar Workers' Union, 86, 88; attitudes of, 466, 470–471, 476. See also wages; workers and peasants

Agriculture: legislation regulating, 34, 423, 425–427, 429–431, 433–434, 436, 462; production in, 174–180, 387–390, 446–448, 452, 456; dispute over, 383–391. See also Agrarian reform; Sugar

Agriculture, Ministry of, 62, 234, 309, 389, 400, 460–461, 469

Air Force, 126, 249, 309, 348, 349, 351–352. See also Armed forces

Alcoholic beverages, 413–414

Almeida, Juan, 307–308, 332

Alonso Pujol, Guillermo, 104

Álvarez, Aurelio, 428

Álvarez Rom, Luis, 385, 390

Ameijeiras, Efigenio, 230–231

Amnesty, 37, 38, 78. See also Prisoners

Angolan war, 2, 8, 162, 333, 344–345, 348–351, 353–356, 361, 363, 367, 374, 378

Aragonés, Emilio, 211

Arango, Miguel, 40, 45, 51

Arce Martínez, Sergio, 412

Armed forces, 77, 79, 123, 191, 193–195, 225–226, 344–345, 467; (1959–), 137, 161, 230, 374, 525, 528, 530; and August (1933) coup, 58, 76; and coup attempt (1941), 65; in the 1950s, 64, 120, 123, 126–127, 129, 131; and military mobilization for production, 274, 348, 356–362, 374, 377, 453; and order of battle, 346–350; reserves, 346–348, 350, 355, 360, 370, 376, 378; and force structure, 349–350, 353; doctrine of, 349–350,

Armed forces (continued)
353–354, 362–363, 378; schools of, 351–352, 365, 369–371, 378; ranks and hierarchy of, 352–353, 365–366, 369–373; professionalism in, 341–342, 348–353, 355–356, 358, 361, 364–365, 369–371, 374, 378; reorganization of (1973), 343, 359, 362, 375, 377; and war games, 350, 354, 360; and antibandit forces (LCB), 345–346, 357; and overseas combat, 345, 353–354; insubordination and resistance in, 355, 360, 363–364, 378; and courts-martial, 254, 256, 371; and public relations, 279; in comparison with other countries, 363–365, 367–368, 374–377. See also Angolan war; Army of Working Youth; Civic soldier

Armed Forces, Ministry of, 343

Arms supplies, 358; from the United States, 64, 117, 131; from the United Kingdom, 142; from Belgium, 146; from Czechoslovakia, 151; from the Soviet Union, 151, 154–155, 346

Army, 348, 352, 354; Western, 308, 350–351; Central, 308, 314; Eastern, 350, 358, 355; and Joint Chiefs of Staff, 126, 308–309, 354, 366

Army of Working Youth, 322, 343–344, 347–348, 353, 359–361, 364, 377–378. See also Armed Forces; Military mobilization for production

Arrufat, Antón, 393

Arts, 204, 225, 382, 393–394, 407, 414. See also Intellectuals; Literature and political conflict

Asbert, Ernesto, 37, 39

Assemblies: party, 211–212, 315, 320, 331, 334; mass, 281, 286, 299, 303; labor, 229, 274–276, 292–293, 299–301, 414, 488; local- and provincial-government, 247, 255, 282–284, 288–291, 529–530; to discuss legislation, 265, 270–271, 299, 301, 415–417, 528, 531–532; in armed forces, 365, 367, 371–372; in rural areas, 443–444, 456, 460. See also Political mobilization; Political participation

Association of Rebel Youth (AJR), 209, 279, 321. See also Communist Youth Union

Auténtico party, 100–104, 107–108, 112, 127, 194

Authoritarianism, 6, 340

Autonomy, 6, 191, 237, 305, 338–340, 513–514; Cuban, from the United States, 11, 19, 44, 51, 54–55; Cuban, from the Soviet Union, 163, 349–350; of incumbents from interest groups, 12, 41, 98, 128; of parties from interest groups, 40; of government from interest groups, 36, 41, 44, 51, 56, 98, 109; of government agencies from presidency, 96; from Fidel Castro, 206, 210, 260; of revolutionary elite, 139, 143, 146–147, 528–531; of revolutionary government and party from society, 163, 288, 315, 327, 462; of organizations, 207, 210, 259, 280–281, 324, 414; of party elite, 316, 330; of party schools, 331; of Communist Youth Union from party, 322–323; of local government, 281–285, 291, 508; of labor from government, 97, 195, 205, 272, 278, 292; of Committees for the Defense of the Revolution, 263–264, 266–267; of peasants and the National Association of Small Peasants, 424, 444–445, 451, 453, 457–459, 461, 463; of state enterprises, 385–387, 391; and armed forces, 353, 368; of churches, 413, 421; of intellectuals and scientists, 392, 403, 406–407, 421, 537, 539; of individuals, 408, 421, 465, 470–471, 474, 509; in comparison with other countries, 542n11

Banks, 5, 33, 68, 95, 129, 147, 195, 434; (1959–), 229, 234, 417, 420; foreign, 33, 55, 67, 69, 95–96, 146; National Bank, 92, 95–96, 117, 144, 156–157, 186, 235–236, 242, 279, 313, 386–387, 390–391, 446–447, 451, 459–460. See also Monetary policy

Barnet, Ramón, 106

Barquín, Ramón, 120, 126–127

Basic Industries, Ministry of, 159, 235, 309, 390

Batista, Fulgencio, 2, 8, 57, 59, 60, 79, 82, 84, 96, 99–104, 109, 119, 124, 173, 344, 357–358, 424, 469–470; coup led by (1933), 58, 77, 78, 369; coup led by (1952), 6, 56, 95, 97, 103–104, 110–111, 113, 123, 132, 193, 253, 346, 427; presidency of (1940–1944), 65, 88–89, 106, 308, 430; presidency of (1952–1958), 62, 67, 69, 72–73, 80, 87, 90, 92, 94, 106, 182, 205, 387, 429, 431, 434, 436; overthrow of, 64–65, 96, 106, 111, 116–117, 120–122, 125–133, 192, 194, 196–197, 199, 206, 211, 249, 271, 345, 423, 435, 437

Bay of Pigs: invasion, 1, 140, 148, 209, 253, 331, 345, 445, 469–470, 485

Bayamo, 472, 483, 491

Bejucal, 468–471, 482

Beliefs and values, 464–465, 470, 477–478, 491, 493, 498, 508–511; continuity of, 465, 472–473, 476, 478, 487–488, 489, 491, 494, 508–511; patterns of change in, 465, 472–474, 476, 508, 511; resistance to change in, 465, 490–491; fusion of old and new, 491, 494, 498, 510–511; of subcultures, 465, 487, 507–508, 540; and discipline, 362, 464, 469, 488, 492, 510; and hedonism, 477–478, 489, 510; about civic liberties, 488–490, 510; in comparison with other countries, 489
Belknap, Reginald, 16–17
Black market, 232, 418, 444, 455–456, 461, 492, 507
Boitel, Pedro, 207
Boti, Regino, 117, 144, 383, 386, 390
Bourgeoisie, 66, 69, 71, 194–195, 469, 507, 510; rural, 388–389
Bravo, Flavio, 303, 307, 309, 533
Budget, 94, 387–388, 398, 406–407, 417, 419–420; approval of, 29–30, 81, 92; military, 344, 346–347, 350, 353, 358–359, 364
Buena Ventura, 492
Bureaucracy, 7, 56, 97–98, 109, 137–138, 147, 149, 159–161, 165, 189, 192–193, 202, 206, 230, 232–243, 261, 273, 282–285, 301, 304, 320, 340, 389, 402–403, 408–410, 415, 417–419, 445, 450, 457, 461, 463, 477, 510, 529–530; disputes within, 382–387, 391, 394, 406–407, 421; relations of, with Communist party, 306, 311, 321, 323–329, 338; and reorganization of ministries, 233–236, 390; promotions within, 210–211, 220, 232, 324, 326–327, 329, 372, 419; and bureaucrats dismissed, 234, 240, 284, 390. *See also* Stability; State enterprises
Business, 66, 69, 89–90, 93, 128–129, 137, 141, 147, 174, 195–196, 198, 202, 231–232, 413, 428–429, 455, 466, 506–507. *See also* Industrialization; Nationalism; Sugar growers; Sugar mills
Buttari, Edgardo, 106

Cabaiguán, 447
Cabrera Infante, Guillermo, 393
Caffrey, Jefferson, 59, 63, 79, 99, 114
Calcines, Ramón, 533
Calderío, Francisco, *see* Roca, Blas
Calderío, Leónides, 443
Camacho, Julio, 314
Camagüey: province of, 23, 93, 126, 184, 212, 216, 244, 272, 301, 314, 317, 322, 373, 453, 483, 490, 508, 521, 523–525; University of, 404–405. *See also* Regions and provinces
Campos Marquetti, Generoso, 49
Cantillo, Eulogio, 126
Capitalism, 5, 51, 60, 70, 148, 188, 431, 507, 513–514. *See also* Hegemony
Capitalist countries, 154, 156
Cárdenas, 284–285, 288, 303, 467
Cárdenas, Raúl de, 106
Carpentier, Alejo, 394
Cartelization, 87
Casanova, José Manuel, 95
Castellanos, Nicolás, 104
Castilla, Belarmino, 307, 309, 393, 402
Castro, Fidel, 1, 64, 104, 132, 307, 310, 345, 482; as rebel leader, 65, 112, 121–125, 127–128, 196–197, 345, 373, 423, 435–437, 462; as party leader, 192, 207, 210–211, 216–218, 324, 330–336, 338, 364, 444; as government leader, 151, 153, 159, 161, 165, 171, 183–184, 187, 193, 198, 200–201, 204, 207–209, 229–233, 235–236, 243–244, 247–249, 254, 259, 264–265, 269–270, 273, 275, 281, 347, 352–353, 355, 359, 361, 363, 410, 413, 418, 440, 451, 455, 459–461, 494; as decision maker, 143, 145, 248, 357, 364, 381–385, 391–394, 405–407, 416, 418, 420–422; as source of power, 7, 142, 191, 206, 212, 217, 381, 396, 406–408, 410, 420–422, 490; ideology of, 116–118, 120, 124, 129–130, 434–435, 458. *See also* Charisma
Castro, Ramón, 383
Castro, Raúl, 270, 307, 310, 533; as rebel leader, 64, 437–438; as party leader, 311, 322–323, 327, 331; as government leader, 180, 235–236, 263, 276, 283; as armed forces minister, 149, 193, 347, 352, 356, 366, 371, 395
Cebreco, Agustín, 49
Cement, 68, 389
Centennial Youth Column, 322, 359, 485–487, 493, 498
Central Committee, 162, 197, 226, 243, 306–316, 324–326, 330–335, 372–375, 378, 416, 458, 502–503, 533–534; control by, 267; expulsion from, 230, 262, 312, 533–534. *See also* National Directorate
Central Intelligence Agency, 64–65, 146; and assassination plots, 148, 231

Central Planning Board (JUCEPLAN), 154, 160, 234–236, 303, 386, 417–419
Centralization: of politics, 6, 66, 137–139, 147–149, 151, 160, 165, 189–193, 197, 207, 244, 252, 260, 281–285, 290, 338–340, 382–383, 394–395, 418–422, 460–461, 508, 528–531; disputes over, 385–387, 390–391, 406–407, 410, 421
Céspedes, Carlos Manuel de, 58, 76–77, 99, 106
Charisma, 4, 12, 28, 55–56, 206, 237; of Fidel Castro, 197–199, 201, 259; routinization of, 197, 212, 217–218, 233, 244, 249, 261, 298, 330, 337–340. See also Legitimacy
Chibás, Eduardo, 103, 112–114, 193, 466
Chibás, Raúl, 129
China, 151, 161–162, 165
Chomón, Faure, 330, 590nl
Choteo, 469–470
Ciego de Ávila, 508
Cienfuegos, 15, 120, 126–127, 244, 433
Cienfuegos, Camilo, 127
Cienfuegos, Osmany, 307–308, 533
Civic dialogue, 125
Civic soldier, 342, 353, 356–357, 361–362, 364–365, 376–378; and paths to power, 308–313, 330, 336, 373. See also Armed forces; Role
Civil aviation, 228, 293–294, 411, 478, 480–481
Civilian-military relations, 341–342, 344–345, 355–356, 358–359, 361, 365, 367, 376–378. See also Civic soldier
Cleavages, 2, 5, 12, 29, 38, 40, 44, 46, 49, 51–52, 56–57, 95, 97–99, 101–104, 109, 123, 131, 194; (1959–), 192, 196, 219, 364, 369, 491
Coffee: farmers, 428–429; Stabilization Institute, 429
Cofiño, Ángel, 96
Colgate-Palmolive-Peet, 35, 66
Committees for the Defense of the Revolution (CDR), 162, 208–209, 253, 255–256, 261–267, 280, 282, 303, 350, 409, 415, 492, 498, 530; leadership of, 262–263, 265–267, 324; and Communist party, 324–325; and labor, 262–264. See also Mass organizations; Political mobilization; Political Participation
Communications, 478–481, 509
Communist parties in Latin America, 199, 533
Communist party (–1958), 50–51, 57, 63, 77, 78, 115–116, 118, 489; and elections, 99–104,

107–109; and labor, 96–97, 102; and People's Socialist party (PSP), 102, 206, 209, 533–534; and rural areas, 428, 434; and anti-Communism, 60, 111, 124
Communist party (1959–), 7, 194, 209, 261, 337–340, 493; statutes of, 315–316, 331, 334, 336; growth of, 211–214, 259, 320–321, 336; social composition of, 214–216, 306, 318–321, 339, 405, 443, 502–503; schools, 215–217, 336–337, 339; education in, 316–317, 320; membership procedures of and expulsion from, 7, 162, 192, 211–214, 217, 306, 315–316, 329, 365, 413, 590n5; reorganization of (1960s), 211, 214, 217–218, 329; reorganization of (1970s), 160, 327, 332, 336; and First Party Congress, 8, 149, 172, 202, 204, 243–244, 270, 277, 280, 291, 306, 310–313, 315–316, 318, 321, 324, 328, 330–332, 336, 394, 413, 416, 419–420, 458–459, 497, 510, 527, 533–534; and rural areas, 443–444, 453; and prerevolutionary Communists, 210–212, 262, 306, 308–311, 313, 330, 364, 382, 420, 440, 533–534; anti-Communism, 142, 206; centralization within, 315–316, 329–331, 333, 335–336, 338; and corruption, 230–233; influence of, 247, 282, 286, 297, 396; control by, 204–205, 210, 255, 257, 266–267, 272, 281, 287–292, 299–300, 302, 304–305, 323–329, 335, 407–410, 416, 458, 463, 501, 503; and admission of mistakes, 275, 443–444
Communist party, United States, 116
Communist Youth Union, 272, 279–280, 321–323, 339, 355, 393, 493, 527; growth of, 321–322; social composition of, 318–320, 322; influence of, 247, 255, 282, 287, 290, 315, 396; and Communist party, 315, 320, 329, 337. See also Association of Rebel Youth (AJR)
Congress, 56, 59, 110–112, 133, 191, 193, 427; internal structure of, 42–43, 102–106; legislation passed by, 29, 30, 31, 34, 36, 37, 38, 46, 80–81, 87, 92, 430–431; relations of, with executive branch, 6, 32, 41, 79, 81–82
Consciousness, revolutionary, 170, 210–211, 229–230, 232–233, 270–271, 273–274, 298–299, 352, 361–362, 452–453, 456, 476–477, 485–487, 497. See also Beliefs and values; Ideology; New socialist citizen
Conservative party, 15, 29, 38–41, 45–46, 48–49, 51, 107; and Partido Moderado, 14.

See also Democratic party; National Democratic Union party

Constitution, 4, 56, 261; (1901), 13, 29, 30, 41, 100; (1940), 80–82, 88–89, 101, 110, 120, 123, 130, 133, 204–205, 243, 416, 430–431; and fundamental law, 250–251; draft, 416–417, 526–531; (1976), 8, 193, 203–205, 236, 243–244, 251, 256–257, 283, 285, 288–289, 291, 325, 338, 394, 412–413, 526–531

Consumers: goods and services for, 174, 180, 182, 185, 278–279, 388, 410, 414, 453, 456; demands by, 203, 303, 382, 413–415, 446, 495

Cooperation, 461, 464–465, 467, 469–471, 490–492, 494, 508; among groups, 57, 132–133, 194–195, 411; and mutual aid, 225, 296–297, 456–457, 467–468, 490–491, 508; among scientists, 392, 395, 487, 494, 535–540; and individualism, 464, 467–471, 473, 489, 508, 537; attitudes about, 466–468, 470, 474, 477–478, 489–490.

Cooperatives, rural, 387–388, 446–452, 454, 457–461, 463, 468; credit-and-service, 448–451; agrarian societies, 448–450, 454, 491. *See also* National Association of Small Peasants

Corinthia expedition, 120, 127

Corruption, 4, 5, 36, 40–41, 45–46, 56, 81, 84, 93–95, 101, 103–104, 108–110, 112–114, 116, 119–120, 123, 128–129, 131–133, 344, 433, 464, 469–470; (1959–), 192, 211, 217, 229–233, 368, 418, 443–445, 510

Cortina, José Manuel, 106

Council for Mutual Economic Assistance (CMEA), 152, 156, 158, 160, 419

Council of Ministers: (1902–1958), 31, 80, 87, 99, 104, 106, 111, 125, 129; (1959–), 7, 146, 192, 194, 203, 243–244, 250–251, 256–257, 313, 381–382, 415, 529–531; turnover in, 240–243, 386; executive committee of, 235–236, 307–310, 313, 325, 419, 503, 529–530

Council of State, 236, 243–244, 257, 307–310, 314–315, 394, 503–504, 528–531

Counterrevolution, 141, 174, 199, 209, 220, 251, 253, 255–256, 261, 265, 346, 350, 393–394, 418, 424, 441–445, 447, 462. *See also* Escambray; Insurrections; Matanzas

Courts, 4, 6, 61, 90, 191–193, 244, 248–253, 259, 261, 278, 427, 430, 501, 529–532; Supreme Court, 85, 88–89, 99, 110–111,

133, 249–253, 256–257, 428–432, 435–436, 441, 552n58, 611n16; popular tribunals, 254–258; in comparison with other countries, 556n2. *See also* Law; Legitimacy

Crime, 6, 193, 217, 231–232, 251–253, 255–256, 258, 265, 456, 469, 489, 492, 506–507

Criticism, 204–205, 211, 219–220, 271, 273–274, 276–277, 279, 300, 303–305, 335, 338, 377, 384, 391, 411–413, 414, 421, 473, 489; in armed forces, 358, 365–366, 371–372

Crowder, Enoch, 18–19, 36, 45, 46

Cuba Cane Corporation, 45, 51

Cuban American Sugar Company, 45, 51, 425

Cuban Labor Confederation (CTC): (–1959), 90, 96–97, 102, 128; (1959–), 207–208, 296, 415, 501, 530; leadership of, 271, 294–295; congress (1959), 207, 271; congress (1961), 271–273; congress (1966), 271; congress (1973), 183–184, 229, 272, 275–278, 280, 293–295, 457, 488; and Communist party, 325

Cuban National Labor Confederation (CNOC), 50–51

Cuban Pioneers' Union (UPC), 279, 322, 456

Cuban-Soviet Commission for Economic, Scientific and Technical Collaboration, 159–160, 235

Cuban Women's Federation (FMC), 208, 267–271, 275, 280, 287–288, 297–298, 410, 422, 444, 456, 483, 494, 496–497, 500–501, 530; and Communist party, 324–325; and labor unions, 269–270

Cubelas, Rolando, 207, 231

Cuervo Rubio, Gustavo, 60, 101–104, 106

Curbelo, Raúl, 314

Czechoslovakia, 151, 153, 162–163, 211

Davis, Norman H., 45

Day care centers, 179, 184, 228, 267–270, 410, 490, 496–497, 500–501, 504

Democracy, 82–83, 100, 205, 293–295, 298, 302, 305, 332, 416; and democratic centralism, 335, 339, 367–369

Democratic party, 100–104, 107–108, 193. *See also* Conservative party; National Democratic Union party

Díaz Astaraín, Rolando, 373

Distribution: economic, 4, 56–57, 90–91, 98, 128–130, 132–133, 139, 173, 180, 182, 185–186, 188–192, 196, 199–201, 221,

Distribution (*continued*)
227–229, 233, 259, 344, 424, 434; of housing, 186–188; of health care, 221–224; of day care centers, 268–269; of population, among racial categories, 224–227
Divorce, *see* Marriage
Domenech, Joel, 307, 309, 326, 533
Domingo y Morales del Castillo, Andrés, 106
Dorticós, Osvaldo, 161, 179, 184, 230, 233–234, 236, 243, 274, 307, 310, 316, 401, 418, 533
Drugs, 231, 492, 506, 524–526

Echevarría, José Antonio, 127
Economy: growth of, and living standard, 4, 11, 12, 52, 55, 57, 139, 144, 186, 188–190, 192, 221, 229, 254, 340, 492, 506, 513–520, 542n12; (1902–1933), 26, 38, 41, 49, 70, 84; (1934–1958), 72–74, 90, 92–94, 98, 130–132, 429; (1959–), 139, 148, 173–180, 182, 259, 358, 383, 390, 463, 477, 499; decline of, 174–180, 185, 188–189, 199, 235, 239, 377, 383–384, 387–389, 413, 475, 485. *See also* Rationing; Wages
Education, 4, 11, 24, 25, 45, 71, 139, 184, 200, 202, 204, 218–219, 267, 344, 441, 456, 461, 521, 530; and literacy, 4, 24, 25, 47, 71–72, 139, 165, 167, 169–170, 172, 224, 267, 436, 442, 490; (1934–1958), 71–72, 79, 466; (1959–), 166–172, 261, 265, 370, 392, 396, 409, 416, 444, 463; and private and religious schools, 71, 109, 166, 195, 411, 413, 425, 519–520; of adults, 165–167, 171, 265, 408, 458; military, 361–362, 378; and attitudes, 472, 474–475, 477, 483, 485–486, 489, 491, 493–496, 500, 510
Education, Ministry of, 94, 106, 112, 242, 282–283, 309, 408, 466
Eisenhower, Dwight D., 146
Elections, 4, 12, 18, 19, 37–44, 52, 56, 80, 84, 98, 109, 123, 132, 204, 298, 465–466, 468–470; (1905), 15; (1908), 26; (1920), 45, 49; (1922), 38; (1924), 45; (1936), 99, 104; (1939), 100, 107; (1940), 59, 102, 107; (1944), 96, 101–102, 104, 107, 465; (1948), 96, 103, 107, 124, 465; (1952), 103, 107, 113, 132; (1954), 124, 466; (1958), 124, 211; (1967), 286–288, 501, 508; (1974), 286–288, 302, 501, 504; (1976), 289–291, 302, 501, 508; called off, 144–145, 201, 217, 302; procedures for, 244, 247, 273, 275, 286–289, 292–297, 501, 503, 528–530; and lack of autonomy, 260–261, 286,
288–289, 291–293, 295, 298, 305; in local government, 282, 286–291; of judges, 255, 257; in Communist party, 331–332, 334–335; in armed forces, 368; in Committees for the Defense of the Revolution, 266; in labor unions, 272, 275, 291–296, 302; in National Association of Small Peasants, 296–297, 460–461; of women, 501–504, 508
Elite, 6, 124, 132, 340; opposition, exported, 139–141; revolutionary, 137, 192, 199, 208, 214, 226, 230, 233, 248, 263–264, 298, 307–317, 320, 333, 335–337, 345, 367, 376, 378, 415–416, 420, 422, 464–465, 472, 476, 510, 533, 535; circulation of, 7, 12, 106, 114, 141; control by, 212, 276, 281, 302, 330, 382–383, 392, 417, 419; admission of mistakes by, 275, 281; in comparison with other countries, 558n32
Equality, 184–186, 188–189, 192, 227–229, 270–271, 273, 288, 461, 464, 489, 490, 492, 497; and inequality, 74–75, 133, 139, 171, 224–227, 294, 353, 366–367, 423–424, 427, 452–453, 495, 515, 519, 521, 525–526. *See also* Distribution
Escalante, Aníbal, 162, 210–212, 214, 217, 231, 262, 310–311, 313, 323, 378, 534. *See also* Microfaction
Escalante, César, 209
Escambray: Second National Front, 127; rebellion in (1960s), 345, 357; region of, 457, 490–491. *See also* Regions and provinces
Escape clauses, 205, 251–252, 283, 530–531
Espín, Vilma, 268, 270
Estrada Palma, Tomás, 13–15, 17, 29, 30–32, 36, 38, 44, 49, 51, 76, 106, 203
Exemplary: worker, 211–214, 306, 315–316; peasant, 296–297; soldier, 365; youth, 322; parenthood, 261; socialist, 473, 475. *See also* Advanced Peasants' Movement; Advanced Workers' Movement
Exiles, 120, 124, 137, 139–141, 146, 148, 165, 174, 184, 186–189, 200, 220–222, 225, 234, 254, 257, 345, 348–349, 396, 411, 474, 480, 484, 489, 493, 499–500, 504–505, 536

Factions, 138, 160–163, 165, 189, 193, 335–336, 420–421, 533–421, 533–534
Family, 217, 230, 268, 410, 444, 453, 456, 460, 485, 488, 490–492, 494–495, 498, 504, 509–510, 531–532; and mothering, 285, 409, 456, 498, 504; attitudes about, 474–477, 484,

496–497; and armed forces, 356, 371; relations among revolutionary elite, 331, 593n42; in comparison with other countries, 476

Family Code, 258, 270–271, 301, 415–417, 498, 501, 531–532

Federation of Secondary-School Students, 279, 322

Feedback: in government, 300, 304; between belief and behavior, 473

Fernández, Marcelo, 385, 387, 391

Fernández, Rigoberto, 17

Figueroa, Agapito, 272, 295

Film, 282–283, 392–394, 414, 420, 530

Fishing Institute, 160, 537–539

Foreign-born immigrants, 143, 467–468, 490; impact of, on population, 515, 517; and fifty-percent law, 78, 114, 517; deportation of, 50–51, 114–115, 517

Foreign investment, private 20–21, 22, 55, 61, 66, 69–70, 90, 98, 115–118, 130–131, 138, 149, 159, 164–165, 189; and ownership of sugar mills, 22, 55; and divestment, 66–67, 70, 73, 76, 133; socialization of, 141, 145. *See also* Hegemony

Foreign policy, 205, 311–312, 333–334, 382, 528–529, 530; and Cuban foreign aid, 356, 361

Foreign Trade, Ministry of, 159, 232–234, 384, 386, 389, 530

Formalization: of the state, 204–205, 243–244, 247–249, 258–259, 527–531. *See also* Constitution; Institutionalization

Freedom of association, 124, 204, 410–413, 465

Fullam, William F., 15

García, Calixto, 28

García, Guillermo, 307–308, 332

García Buchaca, Edith, 393

Generations, 119–120, 331, 394, 466, 469, 485–486, 493, 495–496; and generationalism, 114, 119–120

German Democratic Republic, 151, 162

Gómez, José Miguel, 14, 17, 30, 36–40, 45, 48–50, 106

Gómez, Juan Gualberto, 49

Gómez, Máximo, 29, 45

Gómez, Miguel Mariano, 59, 79, 99–100, 104, 106, 111

Gonzales, William, 16, 17

González Marturelos, Luis, 263, 266

Good Neighbor policy, 59, 61, 66

Government, 527–531; regulation by, 4, 5, 36, 41, 56, 84, 90, 96–98, 128–130, 133, 204, 220, 424; expenditures by, 32, 33, 56, 83, 201; weight of, on society and economy, 5, 12, 41, 52–53, 56, 80, 83–84, 94, 203–204, 259, 465, 514; scope and domain of, 33, 201, 205, 408, 535, 537, 540; access to, 56, 86, 95–98, 101, 106–107, 109, 194, 230–231, 408, 424, 451, 462; control by, 191, 204–205, 395, 409–410, 414, 415–417, 421, 449, 452–454, 457, 459–463, 501, 528–531. *See also* Local government

Granma, landing of, 196, 199, 230, 373, 435

Grau, Ramón, 99, 124, 194; presidency of (1933–1934), 58–59, 65, 66, 77–79, 100–104, 119, 203; presidency of (1944–1948), 60–63, 80, 82, 87, 89, 93, 96, 106, 108, 110, 112–115, 428–430, 434

Gross material product, 174, 176, 182. *See also* Economy

Gross national product, 179–180, 359, 401. *See also* Economy

Gross social product, 174, 176, 179, 182, 505–506. *See also* Economy

Guanamaca, 490–491, 508

Guantánamo, 17, 47–48, 244, 290, 437; U.S. naval base at, 16, 48

Guas Inclán, Rafael, 106–107

Güell, Gonzalo, 65

Guerra Bermejo, Raúl, 358

Guerrillas abroad, 309, 331, 353, 533. *See also* Angolan war

Guevara, Alfredo, 392

Guevara, Ernesto "Che", 1, 127, 145–146, 230, 235, 309, 333, 353, 485, 494; as decision maker, 383, 385–387, 389–391, 400

Guiteras, Antonio, 77–79

Hart, Armando, 307, 310, 314, 326, 329, 337, 359–360, 372

Havana: city of, 15, 23, 46, 48, 99, 104, 112–114, 121–123, 126–127, 186, 218, 220, 223–224, 228, 243, 253, 256, 285, 290, 311, 317, 409, 414–415, 447, 467, 472, 481–482, 492, 497–498, 506, 508, 519–525; province of, 39, 107–108, 113, 184, 206, 211–214, 217, 222–223, 244, 268–269, 301, 314–315, 329, 335, 453–454, 458, 474, 506, 516, 520–521, 524. *See also* Regions and provinces

Havana Labor Federation, 50–51

Hawley, R. B., 51

Health, 79, 139, 184–185, 188, 200, 221–224, 226–227, 261–263, 265, 267, 284, 344, 408, 413, 425, 441, 461, 463, 467–468, 488, 501, 530; mental, 223, 230, 472, 484, 505–506, 510, 525; and race, 521–526; research organization, 402–403

Hegemony, 513–514, 541n1; United States, 54–55, 59–60, 63–64, 65–66, 99–100, 133, 163, 189; and dependence on United States, 60, 66, 115; Soviet, 138, 149, 163, 165, 189, 206, 259; and dependence on Soviet Union, 147, 340, 414

Height of Cubans, 75, 515–520

Hernández, Eusebio, 39–40

Hernández Cartaya, Enrique, 46

Herrera, Alberto, 44, 58, 76

Hershey Corporation, 21–22

Hevia, Carlos, 59, 78, 106, 113, 132

History Will Absolve Me, 116, 129, 197, 434

Holguín, 405, 429, 446, 491. *See also* Regions and provinces

Homosexuality, 256, 356–357, 371, 392–393

House of Representatives, 15, 36, 38, 42–43, 49, 79, 102, 104–107, 226, 501, 503; in comparison with other countries, 545n45

Housing, 139, 186–188, 225, 247, 363, 408, 414, 495–496, 521; and Urban Reform Act, 147, 186. *See also* Distribution; Equality

Ideology, 100, 102, 104, 108, 110, 112–120, 264–265, 280, 299, 304–305, 340, 344, 407, 410, 413–414, 473, 475, 478, 482, 491, 493–494, 499, 505–507, 510, 527–528; and ideological diversionism, 270, 394–395, 420, 510; and Marxism-Leninism, 336–337, 392, 396, 405, 510; and Communist party theses, 331, 457–458, 497; of Communist party, 211, 277, 327, 332, 339, 394; of revolutionary government, 143, 204, 258, 272–273; and contradictions, 276; and religion, 411–413; and armed forces, 352–353, 367–368, 371; about rural areas, 424, 437, 452, 454, 458; in comparison with other countries, 341

Imperialism, 11–13, 45, 54–55, 58–60, 65, 73, 117, 163, 165, 189, 513–514, 541n1; and dependence, 53–54; anti-imperialism, 111, 115, 424; in Venezuela, 542n11. *See also* Platt amendment

Incentives, 227–229, 235, 273–274, 277, 352–353, 363, 386, 390, 411, 452, 456, 485, 500, 509; and economic motivations, 110, 121–123, 132, 464, 473, 475, 477–478, 485–486, 488, 495

Industrialization, 69, 93, 129–130, 144–145, 147–148, 173–180, 195–196, 201, 228, 239, 389–390, 463; dispute over, 383–391; and pollution, 247–248, 285, 398, 408; and infant industries, 35; and foreign-owned industries, 55, 67; and Ministry of Industries, 234–235, 383, 386–387, 389–391, 399, 446, 488. *See also* Basic Industries, Ministry of; Light Industry, Ministry of; Mining and Metallurgy, Ministry of

Information gathering: by government, party, and mass organizations, 205, 303–305, 325, 334, 371–372, 414, 458, 488, 504, 506–507; problems of validity and reliability in, 474, 476, 485, 487, 497; and rejecting information, 382–384, 417. *See also* Public opinion

Institute for Research on Animal Husbandry, 405–407, 422

Institute for the Study of Internal Demand, 303

Institutionalization, 5, 6, 12, 26, 82, 92, 94–95, 97, 104–106, 109, 192, 194–195, 206, 217, 234, 237, 242–244, 258–260, 280–281, 296, 298, 307, 340, 444, 471–472, 510, 541n1; loss of, 41–42, 132, 263–264, 320, 336; of Communist party, 330–334, 339; of Committees for the Defense of the Revolution, 263, 266–267; of Cuban Women's Federation, 271; of armed forces, 353, 359, 361, 367, 371, 374; of National Association of Small Peasants, 458, 463; in science, 397; in comparison with other countries, 545n45. *See also* Autonomy; Formalization

Insurrections, 11, 14, 15, 16, 29, 44, 46, 48–49, 78, 344; "revolution of 1933," 58, 77, 107, 424; (1957–1958), 125–133, 345, 435–438; (1959–), 208, 342, 345–346, 424, 441–445, 447; economic effects of, 173. *See also* Counterrevolution; Escambray; Matanzas; Oriente

Integrated Revolutionary Organization (ORI), 209–214, 534

Intellectuals, 46, 112, 117, 130, 225, 317, 395, 401, 420, 490, 528; and policy disputes; 391–394, 407, 421–422; censorship of, 392–394, 396; and Cuban National Union of Writers and Artists, 357, 392–394, 412, 422; and Ministry of Culture, 310, 394. *See also* Arts; Literature and political conflict

Interest Groups, 2, 5, 12, 13, 56, 57, 86, 90, 95,

98, 101, 106, 109, 127–130, 191, 194–196, 381, 385, 409, 421–422, 427, 429

Internal Trade, Ministry of, 234, 239, 282, 389, 413, 455

International Monetary Fund, 144

Isle of Pines, 244, 253, 404–405, 495–497, 508, 530

Jesús Feliú: agrarian society, 491, 508

Jones-Costigan Sugar Act, 60, 62, 85. *See also* United States

Khrushchev, Nikita, 149

La Guinea, 490–491, 508

Labor: unions, 5, 44, 50–51, 56–57, 84, 86–87, 89, 92, 94, 96–97, 121, 182, 225, 229, 255, 273–275, 298, 466–467, 470, 491, 493; leaders, 96–97, 229, 275, 278, 318–319, 492–493; reorganization of (1970s), 276–277, 280; -related legislation, 34, 50, 62, 77–79, 87–90, 273, 277, 413, 418, 425, 501; and antiloafing law, 184, 251, 268, 299, 456; councils, 257, 274–275, 278; general conditions of, 272–273, 275, 296, 391; and employment, underemployment, and unemployment, 57, 61, 91–92, 94, 98, 121, 131, 133, 139, 147, 174, 181–184, 188, 201–202; and job security, 89–90, 90, 111, 250, 477, 551n57, 552n58; and rebellion, 119, 121–123, 127, 130; and support for revolutionary government, 192, 218–219; voluntary, 182–183, 265, 267, 274, 276, 324, 359–360, 453, 459, 468, 474, 485–487, 493, 530; shortage, 182–184, 270, 274, 322, 447, 494, 499; and Communist party, 324–325; attitudes toward, 487–489; demands of, 142–143, 273; and opposition to revolutionary government, 140, 220, 259, 273, 390; in comparison with other countries, 554n80. *See also* Agricultural workers; Wages

Labor, Ministry of, 61, 77, 97, 242, 272, 409

Land tenure, 85, 423, 429, 431–434, 436, 438, 441–443, 462–463; conflicts over, 433–434, 443–444; state and private (1959–), 447–448, 451–455, 457–459; nonsugar rural legislation on, 423, 425, 430, 432–433, 438, 462

Landowners, 423–424, 429–430, 433–434, 436–437, 441–442, 444–445, 461; small and large, 448–450, 452–455, 463. *See also* Agrarian reform

Lansing, Robert, 16

Laredo Brú, Federico, 46, 80, 87, 99, 106

Las Villas, 23, 46, 93, 101, 120, 128, 184, 224, 244, 272, 314, 409, 430, 433, 447, 466, 470, 471, 481–482, 490, 516, 520–521; University of, 404. *See also* Regions and provinces

Latifundia, 130, 436–438, 442

Latin American countries, 59, 61–62, 66, 97, 162; Cuba in comparison with other, 115, 124–125, 145, 165, 195, 223, 243, 254, 257; 554n80

Law, 193, 201, 203–204, 259, 415, 417, 431; socialist legality, 249, 257; firms, 252–253, 257–258, 415

Legitimacy, 2, 4, 11–12, 16, 28, 40–41, 48, 52, 54, 55–57, 64, 98–100, 110, 119–122, 145, 191–192, 197–198, 200–201, 216, 298, 302, 305, 437, 461, 469–470, 508; legal-rational, 30, 56, 77, 79–80, 82, 234, 240, 257–259, 298, 300, 339–340, 417, 531; and performance, 77–78, 80, 109, 123, 128, 131–132, 137, 199, 229, 286, 337; revolution as source of, 145–146, 193, 196, 199, 201, 258, 261, 298, 305, 337; international 159, 162; of citizen contacts with representatives, 284–285; of armed forces' activities, 344–345; loss of, 112, 114, 116–117, 123–126, 131–133, 382. *See also* Charisma; Constitution; Elections; Institutionalization

Lezama Lima, José, 393–394

Lezcano, Jorge, 266–267

Light industry, 196

Light Industry, Ministry of, 235, 390

Liberal party: (1902–1933), 14–18, 29, 38–41, 44–46, 49–51, 78; (1934–1958), 99–104, 106–108, 193

Literature and political conflict, 382, 392–394, 407, 414, 484, 489–490, 494, 530

Lobo, Julio, 93

Local government, 243, 248–249, 263, 265, 298, 320, 444, 447, 501–504, 508, 528–530; impact of, on decisions, 281, 284–285, 304, 408, 418, 421, 459; and Juntas de Coordinación, Ejecución e Inspección (JUCEI), 281–282; Matanzas experiment in, 282–291, 453

Lottery, 36–38, 94

Luzardo, Manuel, 533–534

Maceo, Antonio, 29

Machado, Gerardo, 2, 25, 30–33, 35, 37,

Machado, Gerardo (*continued*)
   41–44, 50–53, 58, 66, 76, 78, 80, 83–84, 104,
   106–107, 119, 120, 344
Machado, José R., 307, 310, 314, 330
Mail, 204, 408, 478–481
Malmierca, Isidoro, 533
Malmierca, María Teresa, 267, 289
Manzanillo, 17, 50
Márquez Sterling, Manuel, 59, 78
Marshall, George C., 62
Marriage, 45, 230, 270, 301, 415–416, 471, 482,
   484, 497–498, 501, 528, 531–532; and di-
   vorce, 187, 258, 414–415, 497–498, 501, 504,
   531–532
Martí, José, 28
Martín, Miguel, 272, 332–333, 533–534
Martínez Sáenz, Joaquín, 95–96
Martínez Sánchez, Augusto, 230
Masó, Bartolomé, 29, 38
Mass media, 197, 199, 204–205, 206, 210,
   318–319, 381–382, 412, 421, 481–482, 496;
   press, 94, 113–114, 124–125, 167–168, 195,
   284, 304, 317, 355, 416, 490; letters to the
   editor, 408–410; *Revolución*, 206–207; *Hoy*,
   206, 308, 410; *Granma*, 248, 409, 414, 495,
   497, 527; *Bohemia*, 124, 409, 482; *Verde
   olivo*, 357, 393; radio, 196, 482, 495, 497;
   television, 209, 229, 394, 414, 469; and
   disputes, 386–387, 392–394
Mass organizations, 6, 192, 207–209, 220, 234,
   257, 260–261, 280–282, 286, 289, 303–305,
   408, 415–416, 424, 444–445, 467, 491, 493,
   508, 510, 530; and Communist party, 306,
   320, 323–325, 329, 337–339; and belief
   change, 464, 473, 485–487, 490, 496–497
Matanzas: city of, 127, 409, 412, 467; province
   of, 108, 184, 202, 233, 244, 282–291, 314,
   316, 325, 360, 405, 409, 501–504, 521, 523;
   peasant revolt in, 441–445, 447, 451,
   453–454, 461–463. *See also* Regions and
   provinces
Matar, José, 262–263, 266, 533
Matthews, Herbert, 124
Méndez, Luis, 313
Mendieta, Carlos, 39–40, 44, 46, 99, 120;
   presidency of (1934–1935), 59, 65, 78–79,
   87, 106
Menocal, Mario García, 16–18, 36–40, 44–45,
   49–51, 60, 78, 99–100, 106, 120
Merchant Marine and Ports, Ministry of, 159,
   235, 318–319, 348, 351, 373

Messersmith, George S. 60, 65
Microfaction, 162, 217, 262, 311, 334–335, 391,
   533. *See also* Escalante, Aníbal
Mikoyan, Anastas, 146
Milián, Arnaldo, 307, 309–310, 313–314, 330,
   533
Military mobilization for production, 274, 348,
   356–362, 374, 377, 453. *See also* Army of
   Working Youth
Military officers: in politics, 306, 311, 313, 332,
   342, 355, 364–378; and Communist party,
   318, 334–335, 353, 364–372, 378; and
   Communist Youth Union, 365–371, 375,
   378; and party conference, 331, 368; as
   political instructors, 365–368; indoctrination
   of, 364, 370–371, 378; and cleavages within
   armed forces, 364; and models exported to
   civilian life, 364, 372–376, 378. *See also* Civic
   soldier; Role
Military service, 343, 350, 360–362, 395, 413,
   485–486; and selective service, 226,
   355–357, 362, 378; alternatives to, 322, 362,
   485–486; training for, 211, 355, 370
Military styles and militarization, 280, 342, 358,
   367, 374, 376–378; in high schools, 361–362
Military Units to Aid Production (UMAP), 357,
   392, 412
Militia, 208–209, 253, 275, 324, 350–351, 373,
   395, 456
Minifundia, 435, 441
Mining and Metallurgy, Ministry of, 159, 163,
   235, 242, 309, 390
Miret, Pedro, 307, 309, 330
Miró Cardona, José, 125
Missile crisis, 1, 138, 149
Mobility, 205, 225, 277, 482; attitudes about,
   475–476, 484, 494–495
Modernization, 3–4, 11, 12, 80, 133, 172, 223,
   270, 304, 394, 427, 465, 472–474, 476, 478,
   487, 498–500, 505–506, 509, 511, 541nl; of
   armed forces, 349–350; of peasants, 424, 440,
   446–447, 463, 491. *See also* Education; Polit-
   ical participation; Social mobilization;
   Women
Moncada barracks, attack on, 116, 124,
   196–197, 199
Monetary policy, 33, 92, 179, 182, 228–229,
   277, 279, 385, 509
Montalvo, Rafael, 45, 106
Montané, Jesús, 267, 279, 327
Mora, Alberto, 385, 390

Mortality, 76, 184–185; infant, 76, 139, 184–185, 188, 200
Morúa, Martín, 46, 49–50
Mujal, Eusebio, 90, 96–97, 128, 292

Naranjo, José, 313
National Assembly, 8, 243–244, 247–249, 257, 290, 314–315, 417, 502–504, 528–530
National Association of Small Peasants (ANAP), 209, 267, 280, 298, 303, 388, 415, 424, 445–460; congress (1963), 458; congress (1967), 448–449, 451–453, 457–458; congress (1971), 296–297, 303, 453, 455–458, 460; congress (1977), 459–460; statutes of, 452, 457; procedures of, 296–297; local chapters of, 296, 444–445, 451–452, 456–458, 463; leadership of, 451, 457–458, 460, 463; membership growth of, and expulsions from, 456, 458; social composition of, 296, 444–445, 451, 454, 457, 463; lobbying by, 424, 445–447, 452, 456–457, 459, 461, 463; control of, over peasants, 447, 459–460, 463
National Council on Science and Technology, 402–403
National Cuban party, 104, 107
National Democratic Union party, 99–100. *See also* Conservative party
National Directorate, 210, 311, 323, 330, 332, 502–503, 534
National income, 23, 26, 27, 32, 70, 72–73, 83, 92, 115, 163, 174, 177, 201, 204, 346
National Institute for Agrarian Reform (INRA), 143, 239, 250, 303, 308, 314, 373, 383, 385, 387, 389–391, 396–400, 431, 438, 440, 443, 447–448, 451, 459–460
National Rifle Association, 409, 422
Nationalism, 4, 45, 58, 114–119, 121, 130–131, 133, 142–143, 191, 196, 200–201, 416, 510, 514; and national integration, 478–485, 509; and nationalization, 67, 115, 147; and denationalization, 22–23, 117; and antisemitism, 115. *See also* Product-cycle model
Nationalist Union party, 44, 78, 99–101
Navy, 126–127, 348, 351, 366, 373, 396
Neopatrimonial politics, 35, 41, 52. *See also* Corruption
Net material product, 201. *See also* Economy
New socialist citizen, 206, 240, 273, 298, 304, 357, 362, 464, 485–494, 500, 505, 540; as

source of change, 473–476, 478, 509–511; in rural areas, 446–447, 458, 461
Norweb, R. Henry, 61, 63
Núñez, Emilio, 40
Núñez Jiménez, Antonio, 389
Núñez Portuondo, Ricardo, 103–104, 108

Oligarchy, 305, 316, 334, 338, 460
Organizations: and organizational loyalties and stakes, 342, 344, 353, 376–378, 384–387, 390–391, 396, 400, 407, 411, 417, 421–422, 446. *See also* Factions; Mass organizations; Political organizations
Oriente, 16, 23, 46–47, 49–50, 108, 113, 120–122, 184, 212, 214, 222, 244, 275–276, 301, 308, 310, 311, 314–315, 331–332, 334, 365, 433, 440–441, 446, 451, 453, 472, 521, 523–524, 526; University of, 404; rebellion in (1950s), 121–122, 126–129, 249, 423, 429, 435–437
Ortiz, Fernando, 34
Ortodoxo party, 101, 103, 107–108, 112–115, 127, 130, 193–194, 434, 470
Otero, Lisandro, 393, 414

Pablo Noriega sugar mill, 400
Padilla, Heberto, 393
País, Frank, 127
Particularism, 89, 94–95, 102, 210, 247–248, 284–285. *See also* Patron-client relations; Political participation
Party cells, 210–211, 315–316, 323, 326–327, 329, 331, 334–335, 365, 368, 371. *See also* Communist party (1959–)
Party commissions, 211–212, 217–218, 365–366
Patriotic Coalition, 39
Patron-client relations, 38, 113, 196, 211, 230, 286, 444–445, 451, 468, 513–514; and patronage, 141, 231
Pazos, Felipe, 117, 129, 144
Peasants, 192, 357, 389, 391, 417, 423–424, 429, 432–433, 438, 440, 443–445, 447, 451, 457, 462, 490–491, 528; and support for government policies, 458, 461; and Communist party, 320; revolts by, 435–438, 441, 444–445; and opposition to government policies, 424, 448, 450, 454, 460–461, 490; sales of land by, 453, 455; private sales by, 202–204, 296, 444, 447, 451–452, 455–456, 459–461, 506; in comparison with other

Peasants (continued)
countries, 614n48. See also Agricultural
workers; Agriculture; Land tenure; National
Association of Small Peasants; Squatters
Peña, Lázaro, 96, 272, 276–277, 457, 533
People's Socialist party (PSP), see Communist
party (–1958)
Pérez Herrero, Antonio, 270, 335, 394, 405
Perico, 409, 444
Peso: exchange rate for, 61, 228
Petroleum, 67, 118, 142, 146, 152, 157–158,
162–163
Pinar del Río, 108, 127, 244, 314, 325, 404–405,
429, 521, 524. See also Regions and provinces
Planning, 147, 160, 237, 417–420, 421–422,
452–453; and plans (1960s), 383, 417–418;
and five-year plan (1976–1980), 148, 235,
419; and specialized and integrated plans,
453–456, 458–459, 461, 463, 490; in science,
402–404, 407; participation in, 300. See also
Central Planning Board; State enterprises
Platt amendment, 13, 19, 28–30, 38–41,
44–45, 53, 59, 61, 65, 77–79; and Plattism,
59–60
Pluralization: of politics, 11, 13, 19, 38, 50, 52,
59, 70–71, 76, 84, 131, 141, 147, 149, 151,
159, 165, 411
Police, 112, 208–209, 252, 267; and Ministry of
the Interior, 252, 263, 309, 318–319, 348,
351, 354, 366, 370, 373
Policymaking, 82, 98; (1959–), 281, 381, 383,
391, 408, 415–417, 420–422, 457, 460,
527–532; patterns of change in, 383–384,
391; sources of power for, 382, 396, 400, 446;
hierarchical process of, 381–382, 384, 391,
417, 421–422; in Communist party, 330–334;
in science, 402–403, 405–407; and armed
forces, 342, 357, 393–394, 396, 403, 422; and
prerevolutionary Communists, 386, 391
Political Bureau, 197, 230, 243, 248, 272,
307–310, 314, 316, 325–326, 330–335, 416,
419, 503–504
Political competition, 6, 7, 41, 53, 98, 109,
204–205, 233, 255, 286–290, 292–293, 295,
298, 305, 334, 340, 437, 465, 470, 501; and
policymaking, 382
Political mobilization, 72, 139, 173, 192, 196,
206–208, 210, 218, 221, 266, 274, 298–302,
304–305, 323–327, 410, 437–438, 447, 456,
458, 460, 463, 514; and mobilizational system, 264, 267, 281, 381, 384, 391, 394, 406,
408, 421; and demobilization, 280, 323
Political organizations, 57, 97–98, 133, 159, 192,
201, 206–207, 210, 220, 234–235, 259,
280–281, 284, 411, 594n5; lobbying by
(1959–), 382, 409–410, 412, 414–415, 417,
421–422, 446–447, 527–532; as sources of
power in disputes, 382, 386–387, 391–394,
396, 406–408, 420, 422; in rural areas,
423–424, 436–438, 440, 444, 462–463, 466,
491
Political participation, 4, 24–26, 55, 71, 109,
125, 193, 201, 304–305, 465–466, 508;
(1959–), 169, 212, 218, 260, 276, 280–281,
298–299, 304–305, 463, 464, 470, 473,
503–504, 510; attitudes about, 467, 486–487,
493; impact of, on policymaking, 7, 247,
263–264, 281, 302, 304–305, 333, 382,
408–410, 415–417, 419–422, 527–532; and
complaints, 284–285, 303–304, 382,
408–410, 412–413, 420–457; government
control over, and autonomy of, 139, 172–173,
189, 260, 281, 296, 304, 416–417; in comparison with other countries, 586n65. See also
Political mobilization; Structural change
Political parties, 6, 29, 38–43, 44–46, 49, 52,
56, 57, 95, 97–98, 109, 191, 194–196,
468–470, 508; programs of, 57, 98, 108,
112–113; and party switching, 12, 38–43, 52,
99–102; and cooperative party system,
41–44; in comparison with other countries,
545n43
Political violence, 18, 57, 110, 131, 133, 199,
436–438; gangs, 111–112, 127
Politicization: of issues, 171, 174, 264, 328–329,
485, 508; of people, 367, 371, 508; of science,
universities, and schools, 395–396, 401,
405–407
Popular party: (–1933), 39, 41, 49; (1934–),
100–101
Presidency, 6, 19, 30, 31, 32, 38, 65, 66, 94, 96,
428, 431; brokerage role of, 56, 86, 89–90, 97,
109; (1976–), 236, 243–244, 528, 530
Presno, José, 106
Pressures from below, 142–143, 174, 275–277,
301–302, 462
Preston, Thomas, 405–406
Prices and inflation, 139, 148, 174, 179–180,
184–185, 227–228, 419–420, 446–447, 451,
459–460. See also Incentives; Rationing

Prío, Antonio, 104

Prío, Carlos, 120, 127, 194; presidency of (1948–1952), 67, 69, 73, 80, 81–82, 87, 89, 92, 95–96, 103–104, 108, 132, 427, 429–430, 433–434

Prisoners: and torture, 78, 116, 253–254, 357; and imprisonment, 162, 193, 225, 232, 249, 335, 363, 393, 456, 469–470, 509; height of, 515–520

Procter and Gamble, 35, 66

Product-cycle model, 66–67, 115

Professional associations, 125, 128, 196, 257

Profit sharing, 277, 420, 459

Prostitution, 253, 256, 492, 498

Public Health, Ministry of, 106, 283, 403, 498

Public opinion, 113, 118–119, 142, 182, 198, 204, 218–220, 303–305, 381, 415–416, 421, 474, 504, 510; and information about government, 465–466, 469–470, 508

Public works, 37, 38, 41. *See also* Corruption

Purposes of politics, 5–6, 33, 38, 41, 52, 220–221, 233. *See also* Corruption; Neopatrimonial politics

Race, 7–8, 46–49, 57, 75, 133, 218, 220, 224–227, 229, 308, 412, 466–467, 478, 489, 509; and Independent Party of Color, 46–49, 519; and armed forces, 354; and health, 521–526; and height differences, 515–519; and racism, 114–115, 225, 468, 483–485; in comparison with other countries, 545n51. *See also* Abakuá

Radicalism: in politics, 7, 77, 162, 188, 240, 259, 273, 280, 297, 306, 308, 320, 339–340, 362, 391, 410, 435, 440, 443, 453, 462, 476, 485, 494, 498, 500, 505–506, 509. *See also* Revolutionary offensive

Railroads, 20, 56, 62

Ramírez, José, 457–459, 533

Rationing, 182, 185–186, 205, 220, 228–229, 231, 274, 278–279, 410, 413

Realist party, 100–101

Rebel army, 306, 308, 310, 331, 342, 365, 370, 377, 436–438. *See also* Armed forces; Civic soldier

Recall of elected officials, 278, 288–289, 291, 493

Reciprocity Treaty, 21, 35, 60–61, 65, 115

Recruitment, 210–214, 261, 264–265, 267–268, 322, 325, 337, 352–353, 365, 368, 443. *See*

also Communist party (1959–); Elite; Mass organizations

Regions and provinces, 57, 85, 88–89, 108–109, 131, 133, 171, 218, 222, 224, 228–229, 244–246, 256–257, 289, 354, 409, 428, 433, 436, 442, 444, 446, 454–455, 460, 467–468, 472, 483, 490–492, 506, 508, 519–526; and Communist party, 217–218, 313–314, 316–317, 323, 329, 334, 366; and scientific work, 404

Religion, 7, 45, 57, 109, 204, 217, 226, 332, 356, 371, 382, 410–413, 421, 464, 471–472, 478, 482–483, 489, 509; Protestantism, 226, 411–412, 471; Jehovah's Witnesses, 226, 356, 412, 491; Judaism, 226, 411; Afro-Cuban, 466–467, 471–472, 483, 490–492; and secularism, 467, 471–472, 483, 490, 508; in comparison with other countries, 411, 471. *See also* Education; Roman Catholic church

Remos, Juan, 106

Representation, 205, 217, 261, 325, 340, 460–461, 463, 484; of individuals, 284–285; in elections for government office, 287–291; in mass-organization elections, 291–298, 460; in Communist party, 316, 318, 320, 331–332, 337, 339

Repression, 6, 78, 79, 116, 123, 125, 128, 131, 199, 208, 252, 261, 304, 345, 357, 410, 444–445, 447, 456, 466–467, 489, 511; and Committees for the Defense of the Revolution, 263–265; in comparison with other countries, 558n33. *See also* Police; Prisoners

Revolución del callo, 195

Revolutionary Directorate, 210, 311; and University of Havana Student Directorate, 78, 127, 209–210

Revolutionary offensive, 182, 410, 455, 485, 505–507

Reyes García, Jesús, 373

Rice, 161–162

Risk taking, 217, 329, 477

Risquet, Jorge, 268, 276

Rivero Agüero, Andrés, 64, 106

Rizo, Julián, 288, 314

Roca, Blas, 115, 247–248, 307–308, 392, 415–416, 443, 533

Rodríguez, Carlos Rafael, 104, 179, 235, 241na, 307–308, 385, 391, 443, 447, 533

Role, 194, 456, 482, 497, 504, 509; sent, 342; intrasender, conflict, 328, 343, 362, 377;

Role (continued)
  intersender, conflict, 328, 343, 344, 362, 377;
  expansion of civic-soldier, 342–344, 353, 359,
  367, 374–378; civilian-military, shifts in, 313,
  356; of party and bureaucracy, 326–329, 338;
  of unions, 276–278
Roman Catholic church, 7, 45, 94, 109, 125,
  129–130, 195–196, 226, 411, 471–472, 483;
  and beliefs, 469, 471, 482–483, 508. See also
  Religion
Roosevelt, Franklin D., 44, 58
Roosevelt, Theodore, 14
Root, Elihu, 14
Rule making, 44, 80–81, 84, 87–88, 147, 203,
  528–531; and legislation, 29, 32, 77, 89, 102,
  247–248, 282–283, 415–417, 421; and decrees, 31–32; in comparison with other countries, 551n47
Rumania, 151, 153, 163
Rural areas: standard of living in, 423, 461–463;
  profits in, 424–425, 459, 463; credit in, 433,
  446, 448, 450–451, 453, 459–460, 463,
  468–469; commodity-producers' associations
  in, 428–429, 451; evictions in, 423, 429–438,
  441, 455–456, 462. See also Agricultural
  workers; Agriculture; National Association of
  Small Peasants; Peasants; Squatters

Sáenz, Tirso, 401, 405
Saladrigas, Carlos, 106
Sánchez Arango, Aureliano, 120
Santa Clara, 409, 519–521
Santa Isabel de las Lajas, 470, 490, 546n53
Santiago, 47, 116, 316, 523
Santos Jiménez, Rafael, 106
Science, 336, 395, 509, 535–540; applied and
  basic, 401, 403–404, 406; variations in, by
  discipline, 487, 508, 535–540; and scientific
  journals and papers, 399, 401, 536–539; as
  applied to sugar products, 91, 93, 385,
  399–400; and scientists, 198, 318–319, 391,
  395, 401, 494; and foreigners, 399, 405–406,
  420, 487, 535, 537–540; competition in,
  397–398, 401–403; and political conflict, 382,
  392, 396, 400, 405–407, 421–422; ministries
  for, 235–236; centralization in, 395–397,
  400–404; government control of, 401–403,
  405–407; in comparison with other countries,
  396, 398, 401–402, 407
Seasons, 57, 91–92, 181, 184, 274, 359, 442,
  517. See also Labor

Secretariat, 197, 211, 307–310, 314–316, 330,
  332–335, 416, 503
Senate, 15, 36, 38, 42–43, 46, 49, 79, 100, 102,
  104–105, 226
Serra, Clementina, 533–534
Sierra Cristal, 437
Sierra Maestra, 129, 433, 435–437, 442–443,
  447, 461–462
Smith, Earl E. T., 64–65, 117
Social bandits, 436–437
Social bases of politics, 192, 218–220, 259, 298,
  302, 443
Social classes, 5, 23, 28, 56–57, 76, 84,
  102–104, 114, 125, 133, 194–195, 224–225,
  516, 518–519; (1959–), 169, 187–188,
  191–192, 200, 214–220, 222, 226–229, 232,
  258, 264, 269, 332, 362, 478–479; upper
  class, 78, 113–114, 122, 489; middle class,
  113, 122, 186, 470; lower class, 113–114;
  working class, 200, 275–276, 278, 286, 360,
  528; in rural areas, 424, 429, 442–443, 445,
  451, 491; and health, 521–526; and attitudes,
  467, 472, 484, 492–493, 496, 510
Social mobilization, 19, 55, 132, 137, 304–305,
  443, 463, 542n11; (1902–1933), 24–26, 27,
  44, 47, 48, 52, 71; (1934–1958), 71–73, 76, 84,
  98; (1959–), 139, 169, 172–173, 189, 392
Social scientists in Cuba, 303, 391, 414
Social services, 139, 179, 184–185, 188, 199,
  201, 210, 240, 274, 303, 408, 496–497. See
  also Day care centers; Education; Health;
  Housing
Socialism, 40, 143, 147, 149, 173, 179, 182, 189,
  191, 204, 229, 234, 273, 416, 465, 473, 477,
  486, 492, 536; and socialist values, 464–465,
  471, 473, 476–478, 489–490, 495, 507; and
  socialist realism and populism, 393–394, 407,
  420; and economic organization, 382,
  385–387, 458–459; and socialist parties, 50;
  in comparison with other countries, 477. See
  also New socialist citizen
Socialist countries, 149–153, 163, 165, 236, 394;
  and science in Cuba, 396, 407; comparisons
  with, 203, 247, 311–312, 462, 464
Socialization: of means of production, 55–56,
  62, 84, 132, 137, 141–143, 146–147,
  173–174, 182, 186, 195, 201–204, 208, 234,
  250, 265, 382, 388–389, 413, 443, 448,
  450–451, 455, 458–459, 462, 487–488,
  506–507
Soviet Union: and support for Cuba, 1, 345;

military aid from, 149, 151, 158–159, 165, 349, 352, 354; economic aid from, 146, 150–155, 158–160, 165, 180; and trade with Cuba, 149–150, 155–157, 414; and sanctions against Cuba, 162–163, 165, 533; as source of power in Cuba, 7, 382, 384, 391, 407–408, 420, 422; and centralization of Cuban politics, 3, 418; and Cuban bureaucracies, 159, 236, 242, 259, 382; and Cuban Communist party, 162–163, 306, 308, 320, 334, 336

Spain, 12, 29, 45, 467, 517; and Spanish societies in Cuba, 467–468; and ownership of sugar mills, 22. *See also* Foreign-born immigrants

Squatters, 98, 110–111, 127, 131–133, 423–424, 428, 431–438, 441–442, 462; land invasions by, 440–441. *See also* Agrarian reform; Land tenure

Stability: of system, 54, 56–57, 63–65, 106, 109, 133; of organizations, 206, 236–240, 242–243, 259; of personnel in office, 42–43, 57, 106, 192, 206, 240–243, 259, 265–266; of political parties, 57, 104–105, 107–108; of Communist party (1959–), 217, 334–335, 338; of armed forces, 349, 353; of unions, 272, 281; in rural areas, 424, 451, 460

State enterprises, 192, 232, 234, 237–240, 242, 385–387, 404, 408, 413, 418–420, 447, 451; managers of, 141, 147–148, 174, 235, 273–274, 278, 285, 301, 320, 355, 384, 389, 418–420, 422, 476, 529–530; managers of, and Communist party, 323, 329. *See also* Planning

Steinhart, Frank, 14–15

Strikes, 44, 50–51, 84, 428; and grievance procedures, 274–276, 278; (1902), 49; (1933), 119; (1934–1935), 78; (1952), 96; (1957–1958), 121–123, 127; (1959), 142–143, 195; absenteeism (1970), 275–276, 377

Structural change, 192, 203, 206, 208, 210, 231, 234, 243, 252, 260, 281, 299, 304–305, 465, 470, 491–492, 494, 504–505, 508–509, 511; and structural explanations of change, 465, 473, 475, 478, 488, 491

Students, 198, 207, 528; attitudes and values of, 474–478, 482–485, 489, 494–495

Suárez Fernández, Miguel, 103

Suárez Rivas, Eduardo, 104

Sugar: investments in, 20, 67, 425; production of, and industry structure, 20–22, 25, 45, 50, 55, 69, 84, 145, 174, 470; production of, 23,

48, 52, 65, 147–148, 176–177, 180, 383–384, 389–390, 425; price of, 50, 66, 84–87, 148, 151, 156–158, 180, 499; regulation of, 63, 84–87, 90–91, 95, 194, 423–424, 427, 429; international trade in, 65–66, 86, 148, 161; and Sugar Coordination Act, 85–87, 91, 111, 129–130, 423, 425, 427–431, 433–435, 462; and Sugar Stabilization Institute, 86–87, 95, 97, 128, 427; and blackstrap molasses, 426–428; and Cuban Sugar Technicians' Association (ATAC), 399; and Cuban Institute for Research on Sugar-Cane Derivatives, 399–400, 402; and Sugar Research Institute, 400; harvest, mobilization for, 265, 267, 274, 357–361, 364, 377; harvest (1970), 174, 199, 239, 274, 282, 333, 364, 377, 418, 452, 505

Sugar growers, 5, 62–64, 84–87, 90, 95, 128–130, 194–196, 423–429, 431, 438, 441, 445, 451–452, 462; and National Association of Sugar Growers, 129, 424, 428–429, 431, 433–434, 441; and conflicts with mill owners, 424–427, 461; and cooperation with mill owners, 427–428; and conflict with agricultural workers, 428, 441, 461

Sugar Industry, Ministry of, 235, 242, 390, 399

Sugar mills, 119, 131, 152, 235, 399, 425, 451; owners of, 5, 64, 67–68, 84–87, 90, 95, 128–130, 194–196, 424, 427–428, 445; and administration cane, 23, 425, 427, 432, 438; and United States, 62–63, 67–68, 86, 424; and National Association of Sugar-Mill Owners, 93, 95, 424

Symbolism, 210, 249, 259, 352, 413, 416–417, 438, 441, 464, 471, 531

Tabernilla Dolz, Francisco, 65, 126

Taft, William H., 15, 19

Tariffs: United States, 20–22, 35, 60; Cuban, 35, 41, 60, 68, 92–93, 428. *See also* Jones-Costigan Sugar Act; Reciprocity Treaty; Trade

Tarrau, Julio, 533–534

Taxes, 61, 79, 91–92, 111, 128–129, 131, 151, 202, 417, 420, 428, 430, 451, 459, 463; and tax exemptions, 67, 117

Tenants, agricultural, 22, 85, 424–425, 429–431, 433–434, 438, 441; and sharecroppers, 22, 85, 424, 429–431, 433–434, 438, 441, 447, 452

Terrorism, 44, 59, 78, 112, 127, 199, 411. *See also* ABC party; Insurrections

Textiles, 68, 94, 195, 216

Torralba, Diocles, 307, 309

Torres, Felipe, 311, 313, 533

Torriente, Cosme de la, 59, 125

Totalitarianism, 276, 298, 304, 465, 472, 474, 476, 500, 509, 511

Trade: foreign, 23, 24, 69–70, 73, 76, 115, 149–151, 153–156, 161–165, 387, 391; and imports, 61, 150, 173, 388, 390, 406; terms of, 148, 155–158, 180; and effects on internal policy, 384; internal, 147, 201, 387, 506–507

Transportation, 201, 242, 308, 495–496

Tribunal de Cuentas, 92

Trotskyites, 96

Truman, Harry S., 62

Twenty-sixth of July Movement, 533; (–1958), 117, 121, 129–130; (1959–), 144, 206–207, 209–211, 308, 311, 335, 440

Two-track political system, 5, 12, 56, 97, 109, 128, 131, 191, 194–195, 338

United Fruit Company, 425

United Party of the Socialist Revolution (PURS), 209, 323, 330, 332. *See also* Communist party (1959–)

United States: Army, 14, 65; Marines, 15, 17; Navy, 16–19, 58–59; business in Cuba, 15–17, 21, 22, 55, 62–63, 66–67, 130, 141, 173, 196, 425, 437–438; claims against Cuba, 61, 549n28; Department of State, 18, 59, 61–64; Embassy in Havana, 58–59, 62–63; Congress, 22, 62; policy toward Cuba, fragmentation of, 13–15; occupations of Cuba, 1, 13, 15, 17, 18, 20, 29, 36, 45, 46, 50, 54; intervention, 16–18, 40, 44–45, 48, 57, 58, 59, 66, 99, 130, 196; interference, 11, 12, 17, 18, 40, 55, 58, 66, 77, 98; and pluralization of Cuban politics, 3, 11, 13, 16, 52–53, 55, 65–66, 138; as viewed by Cubans, 118, 142; and revolutionary rule, 3; aid to Cuba (1959), 144–145; relations with Cuba (1959–1961), 137–148, 158, 163, 195, 200, relations with Cuba (1961–), 349, 445; and sanctions against Cuba, 146–148, 164–165, 174, 221, 383, 411, 480–481, 509

Universities, 169, 317, 396, 403–405; reform of (1962), 395, 405; academic freedom in, 395–396, 405; research in, 395, 402; students in, 401, 416–418; and schools of law, 257, 395–396; and Ministry of Higher Education, 403, 406

University of Havana, 46, 77, 321, 326, 392, 402, 404, 406–407, 417; rector of, 405–406; and National Center for Scientific Research (CNIC), 351, 397–398, 400, 403–404; research in, 395, 397–398, 402; reform of (1962), 395; political control of, 396, 405, 413; students at, 58, 77, 119, 196, 492–493, 506, 516; and University Students' Federation (FEU), 46, 112, 207–208, 279–280, 322, 493

Urbanization, 72, 186–187, 390, 409, 431, 436, 453, 462, 467, 479–481; and urban attitudes, 92, 113–114, 118, 198, 218–219, 492; and urban rebellion, 120, 127, 131

Urrutia, Manuel, 146

Utilities, 20–21, 184–185, 195, 389, 409, 488; Cuban Electric Company, 78, 90, 114, 118; General Electric Company, 51; Electric Power Enterprise, 160, 228; socialization of, 55, 115–118, 130, 145

Valdés, Ramiro, 307–308, 328

Valle, Sergio del, 307, 309

Vanguard: party, 212, 298, 328, 338; workers, 229, 301, 492–493; military, 352; revolutionary, 199, 487, 494. *See also* Advanced Peasants' Movement; Advanced Workers' Movement; Exemplary

Varona, Enrique José, 16, 40, 46

Veiga, Roberto, 272, 300

Wages: and legislation, 34, 87–88, 91, 277, 282, 418, 420, 428, 441; (1902–1933), 26–27; (1934–1958), 57, 72, 75, 85, 90, 92, 111, 121–122, 445; (1959–), 139, 180–183, 227–229, 243, 273–274, 390, 501

Water supply, 284–285, 408, 488, 495

Weber, Max, 35, 36

Welles, Sumner, 44, 58–60, 63, 78, 114, 119

West Indies Sugar Corporation, 93, 128, 425–427

Willis, Malcolm, 405–406

Wilson, Woodrow, 16, 17

Wood, Leonard, 14

Women, 75, 256, 265, 362, 509–510, 528; and men, 268, 270, 484, 489, 494–495, 497–498, 501, 504, 623n75; attitudes, of and toward, 485–486, 494–497; and feminism, 485, 498, 501, 509; modernization of, 270; and religion, 471, 483; height of, 515–517, 518–520; health of, 522, 524; in politics, 26, 79, 209, 287–288, 296–298, 302, 316, 324, 501–504,

508–509; in work force, 267, 270, 297, 456, 493–501, 504, 509. *See also* Cuban Women's Federation

Workers and peasants: alliance between, 200, 454, 457, 462, 528; conflict, between 423, 440, 442–444, 457, 460–462

Yoruba, 466–467. *See also* Abakuá, Race

Zayas, Alfredo, 15, 18, 31, 32, 36, 37, 39, 45–46, 49–50, 106

Zaydín, Ramón, 59, 104